Constitutional Law Today

Constitutional Law Today

Foundations for Criminal Justice

SAN DIEGO

Frank Schmalleger, John M. Scheb and Hemant Sharma

Bassim Hamadeh, CEO and Publisher
Carolyn Meier, Publisher
Danielle Gradisher, Project Editor
Alia Bales, Associate Production Manager
Jess Estrella, Senior Graphic Designer
Alexa Lucido, Licensing Manager
Ursina Kilburn, Interior Designer
Stephanie Adams, Senior Marketing Program Manager
Natalie Piccotti, Director of Marketing
Kassie Graves, Senior Vice President, Editorial
Jamie Giganti, Director of Academic Publishing

Cover Images:
Copyright © 2015 iStockphoto LP/Gilmanshin.
Copyright © 2022 iStockphoto LP/Willard.
Copyright © 2019 iStockphoto LP/Adonis page.

Interior images:
Copyright © 2011 Depositphotos/Joeblack.
Copyright © 2017 Depositphotos/zolnierek.
Copyright © 2017 Depositphotos/rfphoto.

Printed in the United States of America.

3970 Sorrento Valley Blvd., Ste. 500, San Diego, CA 92121

"For Christine Niedermeyer"
—Frank Schmalleger

"To my late father: soldier, lawyer, judge, scholar, and mentor"
—John M. Scheb

"To the late Sharda Sharma: physician, mother, and friend"
—Hemant K. Sharma

Brief Contents

Preface   xxxi

CHAPTER 1   Constitutional Law and Criminal Justice 1

CHAPTER 2   The Constitutional System 31

CHAPTER 3   Constitutional Sources of Rights 85

CHAPTER 4   The First Amendment: Freedoms of Speech, Press, and Assembly 141

CHAPTER 5   The First Amendment: Protections for Religious Freedom 201

CHAPTER 6   The Second Amendment: The Right to Keep and Bear Arms 239

CHAPTER 7   The Fourth Amendment: Freedom from Unreasonable
Searches and Seizures 275

CHAPTER 8   The Fourth Amendment: Warrantless Searches 321

CHAPTER 9   The Fourth Amendment: Electronic Surveillance and Detection 385

CHAPTER 10   The Fourth Amendment: Arrest, Detention, and Use of Force 439

CHAPTER 11   The Fifth Amendment: Rights of the Accused 489

CHAPTER 12   The Sixth Amendment: Rights Essential to a Fair Trial 545

CHAPTER 13   The Eighth Amendment: Prohibition of Excessive Bail,
Excessive Fines, and Cruel and Unusual Punishments 603

CHAPTER 14   The Eighth Amendment: The Death Penalty and Prisoners' Rights . . . 659

Appendix A: The Constitution of The United States of America   711
Appendix B: Glossary of Key Terms   729
Table of Cases   753
Index   763

Detailed Contents

Preface. xxxi

CHAPTER 1   **Constitutional Law and Criminal Justice**. 1

Learning Objectives   1

Key Cases   1

Introduction   2

Why Constitutional Law is Important to Criminal Justice   2

  The Role of Courts in Developing Constitutional Law   3

The Idea of Constitutionalism   4

  Constitutional Supremacy   5

  Judicial Review   5

Adoption and Ratification of the U.S. Constitution   6

  The Articles of Confederation   6

  Crafting a New Constitution   7

    Representation in Congress   8

    The Presidency   8

    Creation of a Supreme Court   9

    Slavery and the Constitution   10

  Ratification of the Constitution   12

  Adoption and Ratification of the Bill of Rights   12

  Subsequent Amendments   14

    The Fourteenth Amendment   14

Constitutional Interpretation   15

  Originalism   16

  A Living Constitution?   17

Constitutional Development   20

  Constitutional Democracy   20

  The Administrative/Regulatory State   21

  The Proliferation of Federal Criminal Law   21

Expansion of Civil Rights and Liberties   *23*

Constitutional Issues in Criminal Cases   *23*

Remedies for Constitutional Violations   *24*

Conclusion   26

Discussion Questions   26

Endnotes   26

CHAPTER 2   **The Constitutional System** **31**

Learning Objectives   31

Key Cases   32

Introduction   32

Structural Features of the Constitutional System   32

Separation of Powers   *32*

Checks and Balances   33

Delegation of Legislative Power   34

Federalism   *35*

Legalization of Marijuana: A Case Study in Federalism   36

The Legislative Branch of Government   37

State Legislative Powers   *37*

Ballot Initiatives and Referenda   38

Legislative Powers of Local Governments   *39*

Legislative Authority of Congress   *39*

The Power of Congress to Enact Federal Criminal Laws   41

The Executive Branch   44

Law Enforcement Agencies   *44*

Prosecutorial Agencies   *44*

Prosecutorial Discretion   46

Regulatory Agencies   *47*

Criminal Referrals   47

Jails and Prisons   *48*

The Military Justice System   *49*

The Role of the Chief Executive   *49*

Appointment and Removal Powers   49

Executive Orders, Memoranda, and Directives   51

The DACA Controversy   52

Emergency Powers   53

Martial Law and Suspension of Habeas Corpus   54

Using the Military in Law Enforcement   55

Executive Clemency   56

Is a President Immune from Criminal Investigation?   56

The Judiciary   58

State Court Systems   58

The Federal Court System   59

U.S. District Courts   60

U.S. Courts of Appeals   61

Article I Courts   62

The United States Supreme Court   63

Immigration Courts   65

The Tribal Court System   66

The Exercise of Judicial Review   67

Constitutional Interpretation   67

The Doctrine of "Saving Construction"   68

Access to Judicial Review   69

Pretrial Motions   69

Appeals from Criminal Convictions   70

Petitions for Habeas Corpus   70

Injunctions   70

Lawsuits Against Officials to Vindicate Constitutional Rights   71

Immunity from Civil Liability   72

Qualified Immunity   73

Conclusion   74

Discussion Questions   75

Endnotes   75

CHAPTER 3   Constitutional Sources of Rights 85

Learning Objectives   85

Key Cases   86

Introduction   86

Rights Protected by the Unamended Constitution   86

Limitation of Treason   87

Prohibition of Bills of Attainder and Ex Post Facto Laws   88

Habeas Corpus   89

> Federal Habeas Corpus Review of State Prisoners' Cases   89

> Compensation for the Wrongfully Convicted   91

The Bill of Rights   91

The Importance of the Bill of Rights in the Administration of Justice   92

The Ninth and Tenth Amendments   92

The Original Inapplicability of the Bill of Rights to State and Local Governments   92

The Civil War Amendments   93

The Thirteenth Amendment   93

The Fourteenth Amendment   94

The Fifteenth Amendment   94

Reconstruction-Era Civil Rights Legislation   95

Due Process of Law: The Fifth and Fourteenth Amendments   97

Procedural Due Process   98

Due Process Rights in a Police Disciplinary Hearing   99

Due Process and the Rights of the Accused   101

> The Vagueness Doctrine   102

Substantive Due Process   103

Incorporation of the Bill of Rights   104

The Theory of Incorporation   104

Initial Resistance to Incorporation   105

The Process of Incorporation Begins   105

Incorporation of the First Amendment Freedoms   106

Incorporation of Rights Essential to Criminal Justice   107

> The Warren Court   108

The Status of Incorporation Today   110

The Constitutional Right of Privacy   111

Reproductive Freedom   112

> The Abortion Decisions   112

Sexual Freedom   114

The Right to Die   115

Compulsory Vaccination   116

Equal Protection of the Laws: The Fourteenth Amendment   117

Brown v. Board of Education and Modern Civil Rights Law   118

The Suspect Classification Doctrine   118

Expanding Prohibitions of Discrimination   119

Sex Discrimination   119

Sexual Harassment in the Workplace   121

Equal Pay Considerations   121

Other Claims of Discrimination   122

Age Discrimination   122

Sexual Orientation and Gender Identity Discrimination   123

Disability Discrimination   124

Affirmative Action   125

The *Paradise* Decision and Race Discrimination in Officer Hiring   126

The Frank Ricci Case: "Reverse Discrimination" in Promotion Exams   127

Equal Protection and Criminal Justice   128

Selective Enforcement and Prosecution   128

Jury Selection   128

Racial Profiling   128

Disparate Impact of Criminal Laws   130

Conclusion   132

Discussion Questions   133

Endnotes   133

CHAPTER 4   **The First Amendment: Freedoms of Speech, Press, and Assembly** **141**

Learning Objectives   141

Key Cases   142

Introduction   142

First Amendment Rights and Criminal Justice   143

Key Elements of First Amendment Jurisprudence   144

Modern First Amendment Jurisprudence   145

Strict Judicial Scrutiny   145

The Overbreadth Doctrine   145

Advocacy of Unlawful Conduct   147
   The Clear and Present Danger Doctrine   147
      Clear and Probable Danger   148
   Imminent Lawless Action   148
   Speech Integral to Criminal Conduct   149
Fighting Words, True Threats, and Hate Speech   150
   Fighting Words   150
      Confrontations Between Citizens and Police Officers   151
   True Threats   152
   Hate Speech and Offensive Speech   153
Symbolic Speech and Expressive Conduct   155
   Burning One's Draft Card   155
   Burning the American Flag   156
   Cross Burning   157
Obscenity, Indecency, and Profanity   158
   Defining Obscenity   158
   Pornography on the Internet   159
   Child Pornography   159
   Regulation of Adult-Oriented Businesses   161
   Profanity   162
Freedom of the Press   163
   The Prohibition of Prior Restraint   164
      The *Pentagon Papers* Case   165
      Can Government Prevent the Press from Publishing Secrets about Nuclear Weapons?   165
   Defamation   166
   Access to Government Information   168
   Protection of Confidential Sources   168
   The Free Press/Fair Trial Problem   169
   Regulation of Electronic Media   170
   Profanity and Indecency in the Media   171
   The Internet and Social Media: Section 230 and FOSTA-SESTA   171
      Can Government Prevent "Big Tech" from Censoring Social Media?   172
Commercial Speech   173

Expression and Assembly in the Public Forum   174

   Public, Nonpublic, and Private Forums   *174*

      Designated and Limited Public Forums   176

      Private Forums   177

      Critical Infrastructure Trespass Bills: A New Private Forum?   177

      Graffiti, Street Art, and the Government Speech Doctrine   179

   Time, Place, and Manner Regulations   *180*

      Noise Ordinances   182

      Curfews   182

      Buffer Zones   182

Freedom of Association   184

First Amendment Rights of Public Employees   185

   Rights of Police Officers and Other Law Enforcement Personnel   *186*

      Other Speech-Related Considerations   187

First Amendment Rights of Students   187

   First Amendment Rights on College Campuses   *189*

Conclusion   190

Discussion Questions   191

Endnotes   192

CHAPTER 5   The First Amendment: Protections for Religious Freedom 201

Learning Objectives   201

Key Cases   202

Introduction   202

Separation of Church and State   203

   Sunday Closing Laws and Liquor Sales   *204*

   Religion and Public Education   *204*

      The School Prayer Cases   204

      Creationism v. Evolution   205

      Government Assistance to Religious Schools   205

   Official Acknowledgements of Religion   *206*

      Official Prayers   206

      Nativity Scenes and Other Holiday Displays   207

      Displays of the Ten Commandments   207

A Cross Display and the Potential Demise of the Lemon *Test*   *208*

Tax Exemptions and Subsidies   *209*

Free Exercise of Religion: Interpretive Foundations   210

Incorporation of the Free Exercise Clause   211

Protection of Religious Beliefs   *212*

The Warren Court Takes a Strong View on Religiously Motivated Action   *212*

The Rehnquist Court Repudiates the Sherbert *Test*   *213*

The Religious Freedom Restoration Act   *215*

Religious Assembly and Expression   216

The COVID-19 Cases   216

The Right to Proselytize and Solicit Funds   *218*

Patriotic Rituals and Civic Duties   219

Conscientious Objection to Military Service   *219*

Religious Freedom in the Military   *219*

Unconventional Religious Practices   220

Polygamy   *221*

The *Sister Wives* Case   221

Use of Illegal Drugs   *222*

Animal Sacrifice   *225*

Snake Handling   *225*

Sacramental Sex?   *226*

Religion and the Welfare of Children   226

Compulsory School Attendance   *227*

Compliance with Civil Rights Laws   227

The Landmark Hobby Lobby *Case*   *228*

Freedom of Religion Versus LGBTQ Rights   *229*

Religion in the Public Sector Workplace   230

Religious Expression in the Workplace   *230*

Dress Codes and Grooming Requirements   *231*

Exemption from Policies and Work Assignments   *231*

Employee Prayer in the Public School Setting   232

Religious Rights of Prisoners   232

Conclusion   233

Discussion Questions   234

Endnotes   235

CHAPTER 6   **The Second Amendment: The Right to Keep and Bear Arms** **239**

Learning Objectives   239

Key Cases   239

Introduction   240

The Meaning of the Second Amendment   240

    Early Second Amendment Jurisprudence   *241*

    The Landmark Heller *Decision*   *242*

       Justice Scalia's Assessment of the Militia Clause   242

       Justice Scalia's Interpretation of "Right of the People"   243

       Justice Scalia's Interpretation of "Arms"   243

       Justice Scalia's Construction of "Keep and Bear"   243

       The *Heller* Dissents   244

    Incorporation of the Second Amendment   *245*

       The Importance of Incorporation   246

    *Post-*Heller/McDonald *Supreme Court Decisions*   *247*

Federal Regulation of Firearms and Other Weapons   250

    The National Firearms Act   *250*

       Constitutional Basis of the National Firearms Act   250

       Suppressors   251

    The Gun Control Act of 1968   *251*

       A Closer Look at Federal Restrictions on Gun Purchases   252

    Firearm Owners' Protection Act of 1986   *252*

    The Brady Handgun Violence Prevention Act   *253*

       Supreme Court Decisions Related to Background Checks   255

    Restricting Felons from Possessing Firearms   *256*

    Restoration of Gun Rights for Felons   *256*

    The Short-Lived Federal Assault Weapons Ban   *257*

    Regulating Undetectable Firearms and "Ghost Guns"   *259*

    Federal Prohibition of Bump Stocks *via Rulemaking*   *260*

    The Bipartisan Safer Communities Act of 2022   *260*

State and Local Gun Laws   261

    State Assault Weapon Bans   *261*

    Magazine Capacity Limits   *262*

    The Right to Bear Arms: Open and Concealed Carry   *263*

    Weapons on College Campuses   *263*

    Gun-Free Zones   *263*

    Red Flag Laws   *264*

    Privacy Rights of Gun Owners   *265*

    State Age Restrictions on Gun Purchases   *266*

    Gun Rights for Law Enforcement Personnel   *267*

Conclusion   268

Discussion Questions   269

Endnotes   269

CHAPTER 7   The Fourth Amendment: Freedom from Unreasonable Searches and Seizures 275

Learning Objectives   275

Key Cases   276

Introduction   276

Adoption and Extension of the Fourth Amendment   276

    Incorporation of the Fourth Amendment   *277*

What Constitutes a Search or Seizure?   277

    Reasonable Expectations of Privacy   *278*

    The Trespass Doctrine Redux   *281*

    An Arrest is a Seizure *Under the Fourth Amendment*   *284*

To Whom Does the Fourth Amendment Apply?   284

    Searches and Seizures by Nongovernmental Actors   *285*

The Warrant Requirement   286

    The Process for Obtaining a Warrant   *287*

        Anticipatory Search Warrants   288

    The Particularity Requirement   *289*

    Execution of Search Warrants   *289*

    No-Knock Warrants and Police Raids   *290*

The Scope of a Search Pursuant to a Warrant   292

Detention of Persons on the Premises During a Search   293

Use of Force in the Execution of a Warrant   293

Testing the Basis of the Warrant Ex Post Facto   294

Probable Cause   294

Defining Probable Cause   294

Use of Informants' Tips in Seeking Search Warrants   295

The *Aguilar-Spinelli* Test   296

The Totality of Circumstances Test   296

The Exclusionary Rule   297

Establishment of the Exclusionary Rule   297

Initial Refusal to Extend the Exclusionary Rule to the State Courts   298

The Silver Platter *Doctrine*   298

Mapp v. Ohio (1961)   298

Limiting the Exclusionary Rule   299

Standing to Invoke the Exclusionary Rule   300

The Good Faith Exception   301

The Fruit of the Poisonous Tree Doctrine   302

The Inevitable Discovery Exception   303

Suing the Police: An Alternative to the Exclusionary Rule?   304

Immunity of Police Officers   307

The Doctrine of *Consent Once Removed* and *the Pearson* Approach   309

Recent Pro-Law Enforcement Developments in Qualified Immunity   310

Federal Criminal Charges for a Violation of Constitutional Rights   312

Conclusion   312

Discussion Questions   313

Endnotes   314

CHAPTER 8   **The Fourth Amendment: Warrantless Searches 321**

Learning Objectives   321

Key Cases   322

Introduction   322

Consent Searches   322

What Constitutes Consent? 323

The Scope of a Search Based on Consent 324

Third-Party Consent 324

The Plain View Doctrine 326

Searches of Crime Scenes 329

Searches Incident to Arrest 331

Cell Phone Searches Incident to Arrest 334

Searches Based on Exigent Circumstances 335

Hot Pursuit 337

Imminent Destruction of Evidence 339

Evanescent Evidence 341

Sneak and Peek Searches 343

Sneak and Peak Search Warrants 344

Inventory Searches 345

Traffic Stops and Roadside Searches of Automobiles 348

Traffic Stops: Getting Pulled Over 348

Requests to Exit a Vehicle During a Traffic Stop 350

Anonymous Tips Leading to Traffic Stops 351

Automobile Searches at Roadside 353

Warrantless Searches of Motor Homes and Rental Cars 355

Canine Searches at Roadside 356

The Court Addresses the Reliability of Police Dogs 357

Limits on Canine Searches 359

DUI-Related Searches 361

Implied Consent Laws 362

Routine and Special Needs Searches 362

Border Searches 363

Routine Versus Nonroutine Border Searches 364

Searches of Electronic Devices at the Border 365

Prison and Jail Searches 365

Searches of Probationers and Parolees 366

Searches in Public Schools 367

Administrative Searches 369

Airport Searches   *371*

Fourth Amendment Workplace Rights of Government Employees, Including Police Officers   *373*

Conclusion   374

Discussion Questions   375

Endnotes   377

CHAPTER 9   **The Fourth Amendment: Electronic Surveillance and Detection**. **385**

Learning Objectives   385

Key Cases   386

Introduction   386

Concealed Microphones   386

Wiretaps   390

The Nixon Administration's Program of Warrantless Wiretapping   *391*

Pen Registers and Trap and Trace Devices   393

The Electronic Communications Privacy Act (ECPA) of 1986   *394*

Information Stored "in the Cloud"   *395*

Remote Camera and Video Surveillance   396

Cameras Directed at Particular Persons or Places   *397*

Red Light and Speed Detection Cameras   *398*

Facial Recognition Technology   400

Thermal Imagers   403

Drone Searches   405

Metal Detectors and Body Scanners   406

Tracking Devices   408

GPS Trackers   *409*

Searches of Cell Phones and Other Electronic Devices   411

Faraday Bags and the Imminent Destruction of Evidence   *412*

Beyond Cell Phones: Justice Alito's Concerns in Riley v. California   *413*

Does Plain View *Apply to the Contents of Electronic Devices?*   *413*

Cell Phone Location Tracking   415

Mass Electronic Surveillance   417

The USA PATRIOT Act   *418*

The National Security Agency's Mass Surveillance Programs   *418*

    Bulk Telephone Metadata Collection   419

    The PRISM Program   419

    Litigation over NSA Mass Surveillance   419

The USA FREEDOM Act   *421*

Social Media and Other Internet Activity   422

  The IP Address: A Unique Identifier?   *423*

Interception of Electronic Messages   428

Conclusion   429

Discussion Questions   430

Endnotes   431

CHAPTER 10   The Fourth Amendment: Arrest, Detention, and Use of Force. **439**

Learning Objectives   439

Key Cases   440

Introduction   440

Arrest Pursuant to a Warrant   441

Warrantless Arrests   442

  Warrantless Arrests for Minor Misdemeanors   *443*

  Warrantless Arrests in the Home   *443*

  Prompt Appearance Before a Magistrate   *444*

Citizen's Arrest   445

Use of Force in Making Arrests   447

  What Constitutes Excessive Force?   *447*

  Use of Force Against Fleeing Suspects   *450*

  Tasers and Stun Guns   *453*

  Pepper Spray   *456*

  Use of Dogs in Making Arrests   *457*

  Chokeholds   *459*

  Use of Flash-Bang Grenades   *461*

  Duty to Intervene   *463*

  Misconduct Reporting and Decertification   *463*

Investigatory Detention and Pat-Down Searches   466

    What Constitutes Reasonable Suspicion?   *467*

        Racial Profiling   468

        The High Crime Neighborhood and Running from Police   468

        Drug Courier Profiles   469

        Law Enforcement Intuition and Detective Work   470

    How Long May Police Detain Suspicious Persons?   *471*

    What if Other Incriminating Evidence Is Revealed by a Pat-Down Search?   *472*

    Investigatory Detention of Automobiles   *473*

Identification Checks   474

Roadblocks and Checkpoints   475

Immunity from Arrest   476

    Diplomatic Immunity   *477*

Conclusion   479

Questions for Thought and Discussion   480

Endnotes   481

CHAPTER 11   **The Fifth Amendment: Rights of the Accused** **489**

Learning Objectives   489

Key Cases   490

Introduction   490

The Foundational Importance of Due Process   490

    The Reasonable Doubt Standard   *491*

    The Vagueness Doctrine   *493*

    Recusal   *495*

The Grand Jury   495

    Grand Jury Secrecy   *496*

    Exclusion of Grand Jurors Based on Race   *496*

    Evidence in Grand Jury Proceedings   *496*

    Grand Jury Powers   *497*

    Rights of Witnesses Appearing Before Grand Juries   *498*

Double Jeopardy   499

   Multiple Charges for the Same Offense   *500*

   Prosecutions in State and Federal Court for the Same Offense   *501*

Compulsory Self-Incrimination   502

   Incorporation of the Self-Incrimination Clause   *503*

   Laws Requiring People to Incriminate Themselves   *503*

Police Interrogations and Incriminating Statements   504

   Prompt Presentment   *504*

   Early Approaches to Confessions and Due Process   *504*

   The Warren Court's Approach to Police Interrogation   *507*

   The Landmark Miranda *Decision*   *509*

   How Does a Suspect Invoke the Right to Remain Silent?   *512*

   When Can Police Reinitiate an Interrogation?   *513*

   What Constitutes Custodial Interrogation?   *515*

   What Is Interrogation? Offhand Remarks   *516*

   Routine Booking Questions and Physical Evidence Exceptions   *517*

   Exceptions to Miranda   *518*

      Impeachment of the Defendant's Testimony   518

      The Public Safety Exception   519

      The Inevitable Discovery Exception   520

      Other Fruit of the Poisonous Tree Confession Cases   523

   Factors Affecting Admissibility of Confessions   *523*

      Police Deception   524

      Does Admission of an Improper Confession Automatically Require Reversal of a Conviction?   525

      The Problem of False Confessions   527

      The Use of Recorded Confessions   528

   An International Miranda *Right?*   *529*

Identification Procedures and Physical Evidence Obtained from the Accused   531

   Bodily Intrusions   *532*

      Blood and Breath Testing of Impaired Drivers   533

      DNA Testing   533

Conclusion   534

Discussion Questions   535

Endnotes   536

**CHAPTER 12   The Sixth Amendment: Rights Essential
to a Fair Trial** **545**

Learning Objectives   545

Key Cases   546

Introduction   546

The Fundamental Nature of the Right to Counsel   546

Counsel at Public Expense for Indigent Defendants   547

Appointed Counsel in Misdemeanor Cases   549

The Public Defender System   550

The Right to Counsel during Interrogation   552

Invoking the Right to Counsel   552

Further-Questioning Decisions   554

Ineffective Assistance of Counsel   555

Self-Representation   556

The Right to Trial by Jury   557

Do Petty Offenses Merit Jury Trials?   557

Juvenile Justice   558

Plea Bargaining   559

The Right to a Speedy Trial   562

The Speedy Trial Act of 1974   563

Investigative Delay   564

Delays Due to Dropped Charges   564

Delays Due to Incarceration in Another Jurisdiction   565

The Right to a Public Trial   566

The Free Press/Fair Trial Problem   567

Change of Venue   568

Voir Dire   569

Gag Orders   569

Restrictions Imposed on Juries   569

Cameras in the Courtroom   570

Evidence in Criminal Trials   570

The Right of Confrontation   571

Eyewitness Testimony   573

Recorded Testimony of Witnesses Who Do Not Appear at Trial   575

Types of Privilege   576

Child Witnesses   576

Lower Court Rulings on Video Testimony   577

Compulsory Process   578

Disclosure of Exculpatory Evidence   580

Admissibility of Scientific Evidence and Expert Testimony   581

Constitutional Issues Associated with Trial Juries   583

Jury Size   583

Qualifications to Serve on a Jury   584

Jury Selection Procedures   585

Death Qualification of Jurors   587

Jury Instructions   587

The Unanimity Requirement   587

The Deadlocked Jury   589

Jury Nullification   589

The Jury's Role in Sentencing   590

Sentencing Enhancements   590

The Federal Sentencing Guidelines   590

Mandatory Minimum Sentences   591

Conclusion   592

Discussion Questions   593

Endnotes   593

CHAPTER 13   **The Eighth Amendment: Prohibition of Excessive Bail, Excessive Fines, and Cruel and Unusual Punishments** 603

Learning Objectives   603

Key Cases   603

Introduction   604

Bail and Pretrial Detention   604

The Prohibition of Excessive Bail   605

Bounty Hunters   605

Pretrial Detention   *608*

  The Scope of Pretrial Detention in the United States   689

  State-Level Bail Reforms   609

  Where Does Bail Money Go?   611

  Pretrial Detention of Juveniles   613

  Pretrial Detention in Domestic Assault Cases   613

  Use of Force in Pretrial Detention   613

  Other Claims by Pretrial Detainees   614

  Pretrial Confinement in a Mental Institution   615

Excessive Fines   615

Civil Asset Forfeiture   *616*

  How Does Civil Asset Forfeiture Work?   617

  Where Does Civil Forfeiture Money Go?   617

  The Equitable Sharing Program   618

  How Prevalent is Civil Forfeiture?   619

  Civil Forfeiture and the Right to Counsel   620

  Other Interesting Civil Forfeiture Cases   623

Cruel and Unusual Punishments   627

Evolving Standards of Decency   *627*

Status Offenses   *627*

Revocation of Probation for Failure to Pay Fines or Make Restitution   *628*

  The Supreme Court Limits, but Does Not Prohibit, Incarceration for Failure to Pay   629

  Reform Efforts in the Wake of *Bearden v. Georgia*   630

Corporal Punishment   *632*

Mandatory Sentences and Mass Incarceration   632

Mandatory Minimum Sentences   *634*

  The Crack Cocaine Discrepancy   635

  Other Mandatory Minimum Reforms   636

  Mandatory Minimums in Gun Crime Cases   638

  Three Strikes Laws   639

  Mandatory Punishments for Sex Offenders   641

  Civil Commitment of Dangerous Offenders Who Have Completed Their Prison Terms   642

Hate Crimes Enhancements   *642*

Consecutive and Concurrent Sentencing   *643*

100% Service and Parole   *644*

Life Sentences for Juvenile Offenders   *645*

Conclusion   647

Discussion Questions   648

Endnotes   649

CHAPTER 14   **The Eighth Amendment: The Death Penalty and Prisoners' Rights** **659**

Learning Objectives   659

Key Cases   660

Introduction   660

Capital Punishment: The Background   661

The Willie Francis Case and Botched Executions   661

Furman v. Georgia: The Supreme Court Strikes Down the Death Penalty   *662*

Gregg v. Georgia: The Court Reinstates Capital Punishment   *663*

Understanding the Sentencing Phase in a Capital Case   664

Judge or Jury?   666

Jury Unanimity   667

Ineffective Counsel in the Sentencing Phase   667

Death-Eligible Offenses   *668*

Death Penalty for Felony Murder   668

Federal Crimes That Are Death Eligible   669

Methods of Execution   670

The Firing Squad   *670*

The Electric Chair   *672*

The Gas Chamber   *673*

Lethal Injection   *673*

The Death Penalty and the Offender's Mental State   677

Intellectual Disability and the Death Penalty   *678*

Equity Considerations in Capital Punishment   681

Race and the Death Penalty   *682*

Prisoners' Rights   684

The Right to Medical Treatment   *685*

Use of Force in Prison Settings   *687*

Protection from Harm   *689*

Prison Conditions   *690*

Prison Overcrowding   *693*

Solitary Confinement   *695*

Conclusion   698

Discussion Questions   699

Endnotes   700

Appendix A: The Constitution of The United States of America 711

Appendix B: Glossary of Key Terms 729

Table of Cases 753

Index 763

Preface

This book is designed as an introduction to constitutional law for students of criminal justice, especially for those who are contemplating careers as law enforcement or corrections officers, prosecutors, defense attorneys, judges, or other criminal justice professionals. Accordingly, we focus on those aspects of constitutional law that most impact the day-to-day operations of the criminal justice system. These aspects include the power of Congress and the state legislatures to enact criminal prohibitions as well as the numerous constitutional provisions that provide substantive and/or procedural protection against the enforcement of the criminal law. Thus, we examine the constitutional rights that affect criminal procedure, such as the right to counsel, the freedom from unreasonable searches and seizures, the protection against compulsory self-incrimination, and the right to trial by jury. But we also explore the substantive rights that limit the enactment and enforcement of criminal statutes, including the freedoms of religion, speech, press, and assembly as well as the right to keep and bear arms and the right to privacy and personal autonomy. Throughout the book we stress the importance of the principles of due process and equal protection of the laws. We also devote considerable attention to the prohibition of cruel and unusual punishment as it relates to sentencing policies, the rights of prisoners, and the death penalty.

Any treatment of constitutional law must give primary attention to the decisions of the Supreme Court of the United States, and we certainly do that. However, because the Supreme Court decides only a small number of cases each term, we also point out a number of important decisions by lower federal courts and, in a few instances, state courts. We also devote considerable attention to nonjudicial actors, including presidents, attorneys general, governors, prosecutors, and, of course, law enforcement officers. This is because we believe a full understanding of constitutional law must consider the social, political, and economic contexts from which constitutional questions arise.

Pedagogical Features

To enliven the text and provide additional context, we include several recurring shadow boxes. To illuminate the relevance of case precedent in practical circumstances, each chapter contains shadow boxes, entitled The Constitution in Action. These boxes provide real-world examples that highlight the application of constitutional principles or illustrate the workings of the constitutional system. Moreover, because it is the Supreme Court that serves as the final arbiter of how to interpret key words and phrases in the Constitution, we include boxes, entitled Jurisprudence, that highlight major decisions of the high Court. We also use *Obiter Dicta* boxes to feature key quotations from Supreme Court decisions.

One of the most important concerns of contemporary constitutional law and scholarship today is social justice, or the lack thereof. Given the obvious connection between constitutional law and social justice, primarily through the principle of equal protection of the law, we also include a recurring feature that highlights their connection, entitled The Constitution and Social Justice. These boxes examine important events, both historic and modern, such as the infamous Scottsboro Case from the early 1930s and the murder of George Floyd in the spring of 2020. These boxes also address some very contemporary issues, including the reliability of facial recognition software, the use of algorithms to set cash bail, and the rights of transgender prisoners. Through assessment of these issues, this question emerges: Is our Constitution—which emerged from the eighteenth century Enlightenment but has evolved through formal amendment as well as judicial interpretation—compatible with present-day notions of equality and social justice?

Finally, to offer perspectives that speak to the rights and responsibilities of those individuals who are charged with enforcing the criminal law, each chapter includes a recurring feature we call Focus on Law Enforcement. It is undeniable that law enforcement officials have arduous jobs that entail taxing physical and mental demands, while carrying inherent risks that arise on a daily basis. Ultimately, officers' need to conform their conduct to the myriad constitutional parameters outlined in this book while simultaneously attempting to preserve not only public safety but also their own presents an enormous challenge for those who devote their lives to careers in law enforcement. In these boxes, we examine how the constitutional issues discussed in this book not only serve to protect the interests of accused criminals but also can protect officers in the workplace.

Constitutional law can be extremely technical. Our goal is to make what can be an abstruse subject accessible to undergraduates who study criminal justice. We have, therefore, tried to minimize the use of legal jargon, although it is necessary to educate students on the essential vocabulary of the law. To assist readers in assimilating this vocabulary, we have included definitions of key terms in the margins.

* * *

We wish to extend our gratitude to Carolyn Henderson Meier, our editor at Cognella, for her confidence in us and her ongoing support for this project. We also need to thank the editorial staff at Cognella, including Danielle Gradisher, Project Editor, Alia Bales, Associate Production Manager, and Christian Berk, Copy Editor, for their excellent assistance.

We trust that instructors and students will find the book useful and engaging. Of course, we assume responsibility for any errors or omissions.

Frank Schmalleger, PhD
Distinguished Professor Emeritus
The University of North Carolina, Pembroke

John M. Scheb, PhD
Professor
University of Tennessee, Knoxville

Hemant K. Sharma, PhD
Senior Lecturer
University of Tennessee, Knoxville

November 10, 2022

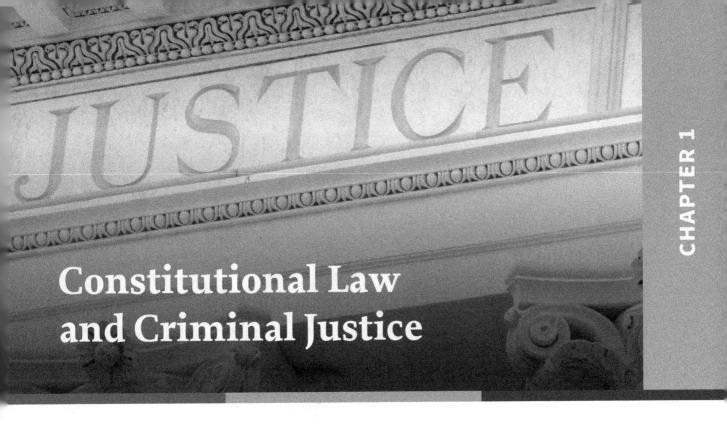

CHAPTER 1

Constitutional Law and Criminal Justice

"If men were angels, no government would be necessary. If angels were to govern men, neither internal nor external controls on government would be necessary. In framing a government which is to be administered by men over men, the great difficulty lies in this: You must first enable the government to control the governed; and in the next place, oblige it to control itself."

—James Madison, Federalist No. 51

Learning Objectives

After reading this chapter, you should understand the following:

1. Why constitutional law is important to criminal justice
2. How and why the Constitution was adopted, ratified, and amended
3. The nature of judicial review and its relationship to constitutional supremacy
4. The different schools of thought on how the Constitution should be interpreted
5. How the constitutional system has evolved since its founding

Key Cases

Marbury v. Madison, 5 U.S. 137 (1803)
Scott v. Sandford, 60 U.S. 393 (1857)

Powell v. Alabama, 287 U.S. 45 (1932)
Bond v. United States, 572 U.S. 844 (2014)
Roe v. Wade, 410 U.S. 113 (1973)

Introduction

A constitution is a nation's fundamental law. It defines the structure of government as well as the relationship between government and the persons under that government's authority. In the United States, we actually have fifty-one constitutions: the Constitution of the United States and fifty state constitutions. Because constitutions necessarily employ broad terminology, they require interpretation. In our country, the primary responsibility of constitutional interpretation falls on the courts of law. The national government and each of the fifty state governments has its own system of courts. In the course of deciding civil and criminal cases, federal and state courts are called upon to interpret relevant constitutional provisions. The body of cases in which courts render these interpretations is known as constitutional law. Thus, constitutional law is case law—courts interpret constitutional provisions as needed to resolve particular cases.

> **CONSTITUTIONAL LAW:** The body of judicial decisions interpreting provisions of the Constitution.
>
> **CASE LAW:** The law as enunciated by courts in deciding cases.

The Constitution of the United States is the "supreme law of the land," and the interpretations of the supreme law by the highest Court in the United States represent the most important component of constitutional law. Therefore, in this book, we focus primarily (but not exclusively) on decisions by the U.S. Supreme Court. And because this book is designed for students of criminal justice, we focus on the interpretation of those provisions of the U.S. Constitution that most profoundly affect the criminal justice system.

Why Constitutional Law is Important to Criminal Justice

If people were angels, to paraphrase James Madison, there would be no need for a criminal justice system. Because that clearly is not the case, every society must develop mechanisms for controlling conduct that inflicts harm on people or the society at large. An essential consideration for any civilized society is how to balance the rights of people accused of crimes and the overall objective of maintaining safety across society at large.

In the United States and other developed nations, the law defines what activity constitutes a crime and the appropriate procedures for enforcing criminal prohibitions. The substantive criminal law defines offenses as well as legal defenses available to those accused of crimes, whereas procedural criminal law defines the processes through which the criminal law is applied—including investigation, arrest, collection of evidence, pretrial court procedures, trials, sentencing, appeals, and administration of punishment.

As we shall see, the U.S. Constitution contains numerous provisions affecting criminal justice. These provisions limit the kinds of behavior that can be criminalized, the methods available to law enforcement, and the sanctions that can be imposed on those found guilty of a crime. These provisions also affect the procedures courts employ in adjudicating criminal cases and sentencing offenders. The interpretation of these provisions by the courts determines, to a great extent, the operation of the criminal justice system, and when these concepts are implemented in a fashion that consistently treats all people equally and fairly—whether they be perpetrators of crimes or victims of crimes—the term justice is applied.

SUBSTANTIVE CRIMINAL LAW: The branch of the law that defines crimes and punishments.

PROCEDURAL CRIMINAL LAW: The branch of the law that sets forth the procedures to be followed in law enforcement and the prosecution and adjudication of criminal cases.

JUSTICE: The condition in which people are treated fairly and receive what they deserve.

The Role of Courts in Developing Constitutional Law

Most of the court decisions affecting the criminal justice system involve persons accused or convicted of crimes. Trial courts, following rules of evidence as well as rules of criminal procedure, determine whether accused persons are guilty of crimes. In reviewing criminal convictions, appellate courts often consider the constitutionality of the laws under which persons are charged; the procedures employed by police, prosecutors, and trial judges; and the sentences imposed upon those convicted of crimes.

While all appellate courts, both state and federal, contribute to the development of constitutional law, the United States Supreme Court is the preeminent source of constitutional interpretation. Although the Supreme Court renders a relatively small number of decisions each year, its decisions are the most authoritative and impactful. Lower courts look to the decisions of the Supreme Court for guidance in deciding the cases that come before them.

In general, American courts follow the principle of stare decisis, which calls for adherence to that which has been decided before, with the objective of treating like cases in similar fashion. Yet from time to time, landmark judicial decisions alter the way in which

TRIAL COURTS: Tribunals that make findings of fact and apply laws in determining which side should prevail in a civil or criminal case.

APPELLATE COURTS: Higher courts that review the decisions of trial courts.

STARE DECISIS: The common-law doctrine that holds that courts should follow precedent.

the criminal justice system functions. Accordingly, in the last fifty years, major decisions by the Supreme Court concerning search and seizure, arrest, and interrogation, among other topics, have changed the way that law enforcement officials do their jobs in contemporary American society.

Current events have a direct impact on how constitutional law manifests, in terms of real-world practice—something that will represent an important consideration throughout the course of this text. For example, recent high-profile police use-of-force cases have shone a spotlight on questionable police practices, even as most police interactions with citizens remain amicable. Protest movements have brought First Amendment rights to the forefront of academic discussion, as some protests have turned violent, even as the vast majority have remained peaceful. Moreover, notions of social justice continue to pervade the dialogue surrounding law enforcement and criminal prosecution—particularly in regard to mass incarceration, a term that is used to reflect the dramatic rise in the nation's prison population over the past five decades—with concerns that application of certain laws, such as drug-related statutes, might disproportionately impact lower-income communities around the country. Hence, the interpretation of the Constitution and the application of constitutional principles to real-world problems are intrinsically related to issues of social justice in America.

MASS INCARCERATION: The condition in which an unusually large proportion of the population is imprisoned.

The Idea of Constitutionalism

As we noted previously, the purpose of a constitution is to structure, empower, and limit government. Again, paraphrasing Madison, a constitution obliges the government to control itself. Of course, there must be a mechanism to enforce the constitution; otherwise, it is merely suggestive or aspirational. Most governments have constitutions; not all take them seriously.

The absence of meaningful constitutional limitations is a hallmark of authoritarian government. In a democracy, meaningful constitutional limitations on the power of government are essential. It is now widely accepted that democracy means more than majority rule; it requires that citizens (indeed, all persons) have rights that protect them from deleterious government action.

Constitutional limitations on government are extremely important with respect to criminal justice, as criminal prosecution involves a contest between a powerful government and a much less powerful private party. Through criminal prosecution, government can take one's property, liberty, and, in extreme cases, one's life. Constitutional limitations take two forms: (1) governments can be limited in their ability to define conduct as criminal, and (2) private parties have rights that must be respected by the government throughout the investigatory, prosecutorial, and judicial process.

Generally, we think of a constitution as being one written document—a nation's charter. But sometimes, as in the case of ancient Athens and modern Britain, a constitution includes a set of legal texts as well as general understandings of how the government should operate. Thus, Magna Carta (1215), the English Bill of Rights (1689), and other basic laws enacted by Parliament are key components of the United Kingdom's constitution. So too are the fundamental principles of the English common law. Equally important, however, are the customs, or *conventions*, of governance that have evolved over many centuries.

After the Glorious Revolution of 1688, the English Parliament asserted its supremacy over the Crown. Parliament considered, but rejected, the idea of drafting a written constitution. In the wake of the American Revolution, the founders of the United States took a different course. They believed it was important for this nation's constitutions (both state and federal) to be written down for all to see. They hoped this would promote constitutional clarity and determinacy. As we shall demonstrate throughout this book, the existence of a written constitution does not altogether eliminate uncertainty about the meaning of its provisions. In the United States, the courts (both state and federal) have taken on the role of operationalizing constitutional provisions—that is, saying what these provisions actually mean in the context of specific disputes. Collectively, these decisions define constitutional law.

Constitutional Supremacy

Magna Carta was adopted in 1215 to limit the powers of the English Crown. The essential idea was that even the king had to respect the law and the rights of his subjects. Although it was frequently ignored by subsequent monarchs, Magna Carta represented an important step in the emergence of constitutional government in England. So too was the emergence of Parliament. By the late seventeenth century, Parliament had become the principal policymaking institution of English government. But what would limit Parliament's authority?

In *Dr. Bonham's Case* (1610), Sir Edward Coke, Chief Justice of the Court of Common Pleas, declared that "in many cases, the common law will control Acts of Parliament."[1] Yet this idea of a higher law to which acts of Parliament are subordinated never took hold. Instead, the English Constitution came to embrace the idea of parliamentary supremacy. Even today, there is no mechanism by which an act of Parliament can be declared unconstitutional.

Judicial Review

The American constitutional system is different. The United States Constitution, in Article VI, describes itself as "the supreme law of the land." Thus, it stands above ordinary legislation. In *Marbury v. Madison* (1803),[2] the single most important judicial decision in American constitutional law, Chief Justice John Marshall observed that "an act of the Legislature repugnant to the Constitution is void." In the wake of *Marbury*, federal and state

JUDICIAL REVIEW:
The power of courts to strike down laws and other actions of government that violate constitutional principles.

CONSTITUTIONAL SUPREMACY: The idea that a constitution is superior to ordinary legislation.

courts assumed the power to strike down governmental actions and policies deemed unconstitutional. This power, known as judicial review, is widely considered to be essential to the maintenance of constitutional supremacy in the United States. Judicial review is the mechanism by which our Constitution is rendered more than a set of suggestions or aspirations. A formidable power wielded by the judiciary, judicial review has been employed to decide a presidential election,[3] force the resignation of a president,[4] and strike down numerous federal, state, and local laws.

Adoption and Ratification of the U.S. Constitution

After independence from Britain was declared in July 1776, the thirteen former colonies began work on their own written constitutions. By the time the British surrendered to General Washington at Yorktown, all thirteen states had their own constitutions, laws, and institutions of government in place. As former British colonies, the new states were accustomed to operating under the English common law and more or less adopted the common law as their own.[5] One wishing to study criminal law in late-eighteenth-century America would read Blackstone's *Commentaries on the Laws of England* (specifically, volume 4, *Public Wrongs*). It was at the state and local level where criminal justice was administered. There was no federal criminal justice system at that time.

The Articles of Confederation

ARTICLES OF CONFEDERATION: The first constitution for the United States, adopted in 1777 and ratified in 1781.

In 1781, America's first national constitution, the Articles of Confederation, went into effect. The Articles had been drafted by the Second Continental Congress in 1777 but were formally ratified four years later when Maryland became the last state to ratify them. Under the Articles, a weak national government sought to maintain "a firm league of friendship" among thirteen autonomous states. Congress was the only institution of national government, and it had no power to tax or regulate commerce. There was no independent executive branch to provide national leadership and no system of national courts to referee disputes between states or administer justice in civil cases in which the parties resided in different states. Amendments to the document required the consent of all states. Moreover, during this critical period for the new American republic, states enacted tariffs and other barriers to interstate commerce, thus preventing the emergence of a national economy.

Beginning in 1786 and lasting into early 1787, a series of armed uprisings in the United States, largely in the Northeast, helped highlight the inability of state governments to adequately respond to unrest. These uprisings—which could be considered early incarnations of protest movements that have colored many eras of U.S. history up to the present day—were particularly centered around high taxes and rising interest rates, which had left a number of farmers in debt and at risk of losing their land. Daniel Shays, a veteran of the Revolutionary War and a Massachusetts farmer, became a leader within this movement. In a series of events known collectively as Shays's Rebellion, his followers attacked courthouses and other government buildings, largely to challenge the judicial decisions that were used to collect debts (whether owed to private lenders or to the government). Shays and his followers even attempted to capture a federal supply of weapons housed in Springfield, Massachusetts, but that effort was thwarted by the state's militia. Nevertheless, politicians took notice of the number of people rallying to support Shays's cause. The "perpetual union" contemplated by the Articles seemed destined to fall apart.

Crafting a New Constitution

Realizing this arrangement was unsustainable, in February 1787, Congress authorized a national convention for the express purpose of revising the Articles of Confederation. That convention, which met in Philadelphia during the summer of 1787, opted to scrap the Articles of Confederation and draft a new constitution for the fledgling nation. In so doing, the fifty delegates from twelve of the thirteen states (Rhode Island chose not to participate) had to grapple with some very difficult issues.

How could the national government be made functional while, at the same time, preserving the sovereignty of the states? There was no serious consideration of abolishing the state governments and creating a unitary system of government. Yet the national government had to be empowered to act on the nation's behalf, create an environment in which interstate and international commerce could flourish, and settle disputes among the states. The arrangement they settled upon, which came to be known as federalism, called for the national government to have exclusive power to declare war, coin money, and regulate immigration. States were free to maintain their own laws and institutions as long as they did not conflict with the federal Constitution or the laws adopted pursuant to it. Congress would be empowered to "lay and collect taxes," "provide for the common defence and general welfare," regulate interstate and foreign commerce, and "make all laws which shall be necessary and proper for carrying into

FEDERALISM: The constitutional division of sovereignty between a central government and a set of regional governments.

execution the foregoing powers. …"[6] James Madison, the chief architect of the Constitution, observed that "[t]he powers delegated by the proposed Constitution to the federal government are few and defined. Those which are to remain in the State governments are numerous and indefinite."[7]

Representation in Congress

One of the most difficult issues facing the Constitutional Convention was how to structure representation in Congress. Under the Articles of Confederation, Congress was a unicameral (i.e., one-house) body in which each state was equally represented. Under a plan proposed by the New Jersey delegation, this arrangement would be maintained. In contrast, the Virginia Plan called for the creation of a bicameral Congress in which representation in both chambers would be based on states' populations. Ultimately, after a compromise fostered by the Connecticut delegation, both principles of representation would be incorporated into a bicameral Congress. In the Senate, every state would be equally represented by two senators. In the House of Representatives, representation would be based on state population. Both chambers would have to agree to proposed legislation, making it more difficult for Congress to enact new laws.

TABLE 1.1 An Overview of the Articles in the U.S. Constitution

ARTICLE I	The legislative branch
ARTICLE II	The executive branch
ARTICLE III	The judicial branch
ARTICLE IV	Relations among the states
ARTICLE V	How the Constitution is to be amended
ARTICLE VI	The supremacy of the constitution and federal law and treaties
ARTICLE VII	How the Constitution is to be ratified

The Presidency

One of the principal weaknesses of the Articles of Confederation was that there was no provision for executive leadership in the national government. Nevertheless, there remained widespread antipathy toward centralized power and certainly no support for the creation of a new monarchy in America. The delegates to the Constitutional Convention perceived the need for a chief executive, but they feared the concentration of executive power in one person. After much debate, they, of course, did decide to create a single president who would preside over a separate executive branch of government. Rather than follow the British example and create a parliamentary system in which the chief executive (i.e., prime minister) is the head of the party controlling the legislature, the framers of the Constitution embraced the principle of separation of powers under which the legislative, executive, and judicial functions are vested in separate branches of the government.

The president would be elected by an elite body, known as the Electoral College, the members of which would be chosen in a manner determined

SEPARATION OF POWERS: The principle of constitutional design by which legislative, executive, and judicial powers are vested in separate branches of the government.

by the state legislatures. The president would be subject to reelection for an unspecified number of four-year terms.[8] The powers of the presidency would be quite limited, however, and the president would be required to "take Care that the Laws be faithfully executed."[9]

The framers of the Constitution surely did not expect the American presidency to evolve into the behemoth it is today. With the notable exception of Alexander Hamilton, who believed "[e]nergy in the executive is the leading character in the definition of good government,"[10] the framers had no desire for the presidency to become the preeminent institution of American government. Rather, they agreed with James Madison that "[i]n republican government, the legislative authority necessarily predominates."[11] Even so, the inclusion in Article II of the Vesting Clause—which states, "The executive power shall be vested in a President of the United States"—has ensured that the president retains control over much of the federal bureaucracy; this includes control over the numerous law enforcement personnel who prioritize and enforce federal laws—as we will discuss in the next chapter.

Creation of a Supreme Court

Another striking deficiency of the Articles of Confederation was the absence of a national judiciary. There was no court that could settle disputes between states or parties residing in different states. While some of the delegates to the Constitutional Convention favored the creation of a system of federal courts, the framers opted to create "one supreme Court, and in such inferior Courts as the Congress may from time to time ordain and establish."[12] Of course, after the Constitution went into effect, Congress would act to create a federal court system, which we will examine later in this chapter. The framers said little about the powers of the Supreme Court and certainly did not explicitly provide for the power to strike down unconstitutional legislation. But as we noted previously, the Supreme Court asserted that power in *Marbury v. Madison* (1803), and it has come to be an integral feature of the American constitutional system.

JURISPRUDENCE

The Supreme Court Establishes the Power of Judicial Review
Marbury v. Madison, 5 U.S. 1 (1803)

In 1801, William Marbury was appointed to become a federal district court judge by outgoing President John Adams, who represented the Federalist Party. Adams had lost the November 1800 election to political rival Thomas Jefferson, of the Democratic-Republican Party. However, John Marshall, who was the Secretary of State under President Adams, failed to deliver Marbury his required paperwork (a "judicial commission") before Jefferson was inaugurated—perhaps, because Marshall had been named Chief Justice of the Supreme Court in the waning days of the Adams's presidency. The new administration under President Jefferson, including Secretary of State James Madison, refused to honor Marbury's judicial commission—with some scholars suggesting

the document itself might have been destroyed, perhaps marking the first federal crime committed within the White House!

Marbury sued Madison in an effort to be instated as a federal judge. The case was brought directly to the Supreme Court, with Marbury's lawyers suggesting the high Court was capable of hearing the case before any lower court because of the Judiciary Act of 1789. But Justice Marshall rejected that contention in his majority opinion for this 4–0 decision. Marshall said the Supreme Court lacked the ability to hear the matter on "original jurisdiction" because Article III, Section 2 of the U.S. Constitution only permitted that in "[c]ases affecting Ambassadors, other public Ministers and Consuls, and those in

(continued)

which a State shall be Party." Since none of those criteria applied, Marshall's opinion left the matter for lower courts to hear first, with the Supreme Court having the possibility of hearing it later on "appellate jurisdiction."

This narrow focus on jurisdiction extricated Justice Marshall from the tricky task of having to rule on the validity of a judicial commission he had originally been charged with delivering as a part of his previous job. Marshall also avoided the possibility of having an order from the Supreme Court ignored by Jefferson's White House, which seemed averse to offering a judgeship to a political rival. As a result, instead of risking a situation in which the Court as an institution might look weak, Justice Marshall elevated it to a place of strength by striking down a portion of the Judiciary Act of 1789 that permitted the case to be brought to the Supreme Court on original jurisdiction. In so doing, Marshall established a precedent that the Court holds the power to evaluate and overturn actions from the other branches of government. In the end, Marbury opted not to bring

the case to the lower courts, and the principle of judicial review retains its vitality in the American political system today.

Finally, it is important to recognize that Marshall's opinion buttressed not only the power of the Supreme Court but also the sanctity of the U.S. Constitution. Marshall's majority opinion made this abundantly clear when he said: "Between these alternatives there is no middle ground. The Constitution is either a superior, paramount law, unchangeable by ordinary means, or it is on a level with ordinary legislative acts, and, like other acts, is alterable when the legislature shall please to alter it." In offering clear support for the first of these "alternatives," Marshall concluded his opinion by declaring: "Thus, the particular phraseology of the Constitution of the United States confirms and strengthens the principle, supposed to be essential to all written Constitutions, that a law repugnant to the Constitution is void, and that courts, as well as other departments, are bound by that instrument."

The most controversial aspect of the framers' provision for a Supreme Court would be the selection and tenure of the justices—they would be appointed to life terms by the president with the consent of the Senate. Given the tremendous authority vested in a court armed with the power of judicial review, this arrangement might seem undemocratic. But to the framers, life tenure was essential to the maintenance of judicial independence and, beyond that, constitutional supremacy. In commenting on the provision for a life-tenured, unelected Court, Alexander Hamilton assured his fellow citizens that the judiciary would be the "least dangerous" branch of the new government:

> The judiciary ... has no influence over either the sword or the purse; no direction either of the strength or of the wealth of the society; and can take no active resolution whatever. It may truly be said to have neither FORCE nor WILL, but merely judgment; and must ultimately depend upon the aid of the executive arm even for the efficacy of its judgments.[13]

In the next chapter, we will assess the applicability of this statement to the modern structure of federal and state courts as well as to the military and tribal courts that comprise the American legal system today.

Slavery and the Constitution

In 1776, the Declaration of Independence proclaimed that "all men are created equal, that they are endowed by their Creator with certain unalienable Rights, that among these are Life, Liberty and the pursuit of Happiness. ..." Yet at the time the new Constitution was being drafted, nearly one in five Americans was held in bondage. The great majority of slaves lived in the Southern states, which had economies that were primarily agricultural. For the owners of great plantations, slavery was a source of tremendous wealth (and political influence). Southern delegates to the Constitutional Convention did not want the new national government to have the power to abolish the institution of slavery or interfere with the slave trade. While slaves had no legal rights, Southern delegates wanted them to be counted for the purpose of allocating seats in the House of Representatives. Many of the delegates from the North wanted slavery abolished altogether, but to force the issue might well have derailed the constitutional convention.

Ultimately, as they did on the issue of representation, the delegates compromised. Congress would be empowered to ban the importation of slaves but not until 1808. Slaves would be counted as 3/5 of a person for the purpose of determining representation in Congress. These two compromises allowed the Convention to move forward in crafting a new constitution, but they also had the effect of perpetuating the institution of slavery. It would take a civil war and a constitutional amendment to abolish slavery, but its legacy remains a source of conflict and injustice today.

Ratified in 1865 following the conclusion of the Civil War, the Thirteenth Amendment abolished slavery and involuntary servitude throughout the United States. However, that amendment included an exception that read as follows: "except as a punishment for crime." Thus, for more than 150 years, many states have sought to profit off the labor of their prison populations, with the phrase "working on a chain gang" used to illustrate the concept of forced labor performed by inmates. In some cases, states have been known to contract with private companies to put prisoners to work at low wages—such as a formerly-used California program that was called the "convict lease" system.[14] In certain situations, prisoners might voluntarily choose to work, but there are examples of prisoners being punished for a refusal to take part in low-wage labor. For example, in April 2018, a lawsuit was filed against a privately-run detention facility in Georgia, where detained illegal immigrants were forced to work for 50 cents an hour, and one was subjected to solitary confinement for a refusal to work.[15]

Even so, recent years have seen the rise of movements to prohibit involuntary servitude from being used as a punishment. In 2018, Colorado became the first state to remove language that permitted this type of involuntary servitude from its state constitution, with more than 66 percent of the state's voters approving this change. Voters in Utah and Nebraska would do the same two years later, and in 2022, California's legislature passed a bill ending the practice there. (We further discuss the rights of prisoners in chapter 14.)

JURISPRUDENCE

The Infamous *Dred Scott* Decision
Scott v. Sandford, 60 U.S. 393 (1857)

In 1833, a slave by the name of Dred Scott was taken by his owner from Missouri, where slavery was legal, to Illinois, and then to the Wisconsin territory, where slavery was prohibited by the Missouri Compromise of 1820. Upon his return to Missouri several years later, Dred Scott filed a lawsuit, asserting that his residency on free soil nullified his status as a slave. After the Missouri Supreme Court ruled against him, Scott turned to the federal judiciary. In 1857, the U.S. Supreme Court ruled against him as well. Writing for a Court divided 7–2, Chief Justice Roger B. Taney (himself a slave owner) averred that persons of African descent, whether slave or free, were not and could never become citizens of the United States. Indeed, said Taney, they "had no rights or privileges except such as those who held the power and the Government might choose to grant them." The opinion went on to hold that the Missouri Compromise, which prohibited slavery in Northern states and territories, was an arbitrary deprivation of the property rights of slaveholders in violation of Due Process Clause of the Fifth Amendment.

Hailed in parts of the South and reviled in the North, the *Dred Scott* decision amplified the sectional conflict that resulted in the Civil War. After the Union victory

(continued)

in 1865, Congress amended the Constitution to nullify the Dred Scott decision. The Thirteenth Amendment (1865) abolished slavery, and the Fourteenth Amendment (1868) recognized the citizenship of the newly freed former slaves. However, the struggle to achieve civil rights and social justice for African Americans for would continue for the next 150 years, and many people believe that struggle is far from over.

It is worthwhile to note that the *Dred Scott* decision was only the second time in its history the Court struck down an act of Congress (the first being *Marbury v. Madison*). Not surprisingly, the ruling rekindled debate about the legitimacy of judicial review. It also resulted in a serious loss of prestige to the Court. Today, most constitutional scholars consider the Dred Scott case to be the worst decision in the history of the Supreme Court.

Ratification of the Constitution

On September 17, 1787, thirty-nine delegates placed their signatures on the new Constitution. But before it could take effect, the Constitution would have to be ratified by at least nine states. Ratification was by no means a foregone conclusion. Opponents of ratification, who were termed the Antifederalists, believed the proposed Constitution vested too much power in the national government, which they saw as a threat to individual liberty and the rights of the states. The Antifederalist position was stated eloquently in a series of anonymous essays entitled *Letters of the Federal Farmer*, published between October 1787 and January 1788.[16] In support of the Constitution, James Madison, Alexander Hamilton, and John Jay penned a series of newspaper essays, known collectively as *The Federalist Papers*. These essays proved to be extremely influential, especially in New York, where they were published in two popular newspapers. Notable among these is Federalist No. 51, which extolled the virtues of a system of government emphasizing separation of powers, with James Madison supporting this concept by saying, "Ambition must be made to counteract ambition." Equally noteworthy was Madison's Federalist No. 10, which supported the idea of elected officials making policy through a representative democracy—by warning against the possibility of a "tyranny of the majority" emerging from "direct democracy," where citizens vote on policy decisions themselves. Today, *The Federalist Papers* continue to be read by students, scholars, lawyers, and judges seeking to understand the intentions of the framers with regard to particular provisions of the Constitution.

By June 1788, the necessary nine states had ratified the Constitution. But the two largest and most influential states, Virginia and New York, had yet to do so. In Virginia, after a contentious debate at the ratifying convention, an agreement was worked out whereby the state would ratify on the understanding that the first order of business for the new Congress would be the creation of a Bill of Rights. Still, the vote was close— 89 in favor and 79 opposed. In late July, New York followed suit, and by May 1790, all thirteen states had ratified.

Adoption and Ratification of the Bill of Rights

As previously noted, one of the principal objections to the Constitution as it emerged from the Philadelphia Convention was that it lacked sufficient protection for the rights of individuals and states. This was in sharp contrast to the existing state constitutions, all of which enumerated the rights and liberties of citizens. To rectify this shortcoming, in 1789, the First Congress considered twelve constitutional amendments proposed by James Madison. The rights enumerated in Madison's proposal were framed as limitations on the federal government as well as the states. States' rights advocates in Congress prevailed in limiting these restrictions to the federal government. After all, states had their own constitutions to protect rights from infringement by state governments. Ten of the twelve amendments passed by Congress were ratified by the requisite nine states in 1791. Collectively, these first ten amendments to the Constitution became known as the **Bill of Rights**. (We will discuss the contents of these amendments, as well as the two that were not ratified, extensively in subsequent chapters.)

A quick perusal of the Bill of Rights makes clear that the framers were concerned about the potential abuse of the criminal justice system. Many of the rights listed in the first eight amendments deal specifically with criminal justice. Yet the precise meaning of these provisions is far from clear. For example, what constitutes an unreasonable search or seizure? What exactly is double jeopardy? What does it mean to confront one's accusers? What punishments are considered cruel and unusual? In our legal system, these are questions for the courts and, in particular, the Supreme Court to answer. The answers have profound importance for the administration of justice.

STATES' RIGHTS: The rights reserved for the states by the Tenth Amendment.

BILL OF RIGHTS: The first ten amendments to the Constitution.

TABLE 1.2   An Overview of the Bill Of Rights

Amendment	Rights Protected
FIRST	Freedom of religion Freedom of speech Freedom of the press Freedom of assembly Right to petition government for redress of grievances
SECOND	Right to keep and bear arms
THIRD	Freedom from quartering troops in private homes
FOURTH	Freedom from unreasonable searches and seizures
FIFTH	Right to a grand jury indictment before trial Freedom from double jeopardy Right to just compensation when property is taken for public use Freedom from compulsory self-incrimination Right to due process of law
SIXTH	Right to counsel Right to a speedy and public trial Right to trial by an impartial jury Right to be informed of criminal charges Right to confront one's accusers Right to compulsory process to obtain witnesses in one's defense
SEVENTH	Right to trial by jury in civil cases
EIGHTH	Freedom from excessive bail Freedom from excessive fines Freedom from cruel and unusual punishments
NINTH	Unenumerated rights are retained by the people
TENTH	Right of states to retain powers not surrendered to the federal government

As originally conceived, the Bill of Rights protected rights from infringement by the federal government but not from the states.[17] For the better part of our Nation's history, people had to look to their respective state constitution and state courts for relief when state or local governments infringed their rights. A person prosecuted in a state court had no meaningful protection under the federal Constitution. This would eventually change, of course, but only after the Supreme Court interpreted another landmark constitutional amendment.

Subsequent Amendments

The framers of the Constitution believed the nation's fundamental law should not be easily changed. Therefore, they made it extremely difficult to amend the Constitution. An amendment requires a 2/3 affirmative vote in both houses of Congress; then, at least 3/4 of the states must approve the proposed amendment before it can become part of the Constitution. This is why the Constitution has been amended only seventeen times since the ratification of the Bill of Rights. A number of significant proposals to amend the Constitution have failed, either because they did not receive sufficient support in Congress, or they failed to garner sufficient support from the states.

Many of the amendments that were adopted have had a profound effect on American society. For instance, the Thirteenth Amendment (1865) abolished the institution of slavery. The Fifteenth Amendment (1870) prohibited racial discrimination with respect to voting rights. The Nineteenth Amendment (1920) granted women the right to vote. The Twenty-Sixth Amendment (1971) lowered the voting age to eighteen. One amendment, the Eighteenth (1919), brought about the national prohibition of alcohol, but a subsequent amendment, the Twenty-First (1933), ended Prohibition.

The Fourteenth Amendment

Without question, the most significant constitutional amendment since the Bill of Rights was the Fourteenth Amendment (1868). Adopted in the wake of the Civil War, this landmark amendment prohibited states from depriving persons of life, liberty, or property without due process of law and denying persons within their jurisdictions the equal protection of the laws. It also granted Congress legislative authority in the field of civil rights. Congress used this authority by enacting a series of civil rights measures during the Reconstruction Era. The Supreme Court, while initially resistant, eventually used the Due Process and Equal Protection Clauses to end segregation and greatly expand the rights of people accused of crimes.[18] Moreover, in a series of decisions beginning

DUE PROCESS OF LAW: The requirement that government follow the law and treat people fairly when taking actions that affect their lives, liberties, or property.

EQUAL PROTECTION OF THE LAWS: The constitutional principle that requires similarly situated persons to be treated equally under law.

in the late nineteenth century, the Court interpreted the Fourteenth Amendment (specifically, the Due Process Clause) as making nearly all of the provisions of the Bill of Rights enforceable against the states.[19] The Fourteenth Amendment thus paved the way for modern legislative and judicial policies in the field of civil rights and liberties. It also profoundly changed the relationship between the national government and the states. As the result of this amendment, and all the judicial decisions and legislation that flowed from it, states must conform to national standards of rights and liberties. We discuss this amendment in greater detail in chapter 3.

THE CONSTITUTION IN ACTION
How a Bad Grade Led to Ratification of the Twenty-Seventh Amendment

Most students of American government are well aware that the phrase "Bill of Rights" refers to the first ten amendments to the U.S. Constitution. These ten were part of a batch of more than twenty prospective amendments that James Madison presented to Congress in 1789. Of that original grouping, two-thirds of the House of Representatives passed seventeen, and then the Senate pared the list by approving twelve via a two-thirds majority in that chamber. The twelve proposed amendments were then sent to the states for ratification. By 1791, ten had been ratified by the requisite three-fourths of the states. These ten amendments became what we know of as the Bill of Rights.

One of the two proposals that was not ratified would have added a new member to the U.S. House of Representatives with every 50,000-person increase in the nation's overall population. Although we know the House of Representatives currently has 435 members, if that amendment had been ratified, it could be composed of more than 6,500 people today.

The second proposal sent to the states from Madison's original batch actually would be ratified more than two centuries later. This proposal said that if members of Congress voted to give themselves an increase in their yearly pay, such an increase would not go into effect until after the next election. This was sent to the states for ratification in 1789, with Maryland becoming the first to ratify it, doing so in December 1789. There was no time limit by which ratification had to occur, but nearly two centuries later, in 1977, only eight more states had ratified the proposal—29 short of the required three-fourths threshold.

Ultimately, it was a college paper—and a student disgruntled with his grade—that would help generate the momentum that drove more states toward ratification of this amendment. In 1982, Gregory Watson, who was enrolled in an introductory class on American government at the University of Texas, wrote a paper in which he suggested that the "pay raise amendment" could still be ratified. The teaching assistant who graded this paper responded that Watson's theory was incorrect, and he was given a C for his work. Watson appealed to the head professor for the class, but the request for a grade change was denied. So in response, Watson began writing letters to state legislators around the country in an effort to Promote ratification. A legislator in Maine named William Cohen spurred a movement in his state senate, and in 1983, Maine ratified the amendment. The campaign gained momentum across multiple states throughout the 1980s, and by 1992, 35 states had ratified it. Three more would do so in 1992, with Alabama and Missouri ratifying on May 5th, and, finally, Michigan on May 7th of that year. At long last, an amazing 202 years and seven months after being passed by Congress, the Twenty-Seventh Amendment was etched onto the text of the U.S. Constitution (and Watson would indeed have his grade changed to an A thirty-five years after submitting that paper).

Constitutional Interpretation

In *Marbury v. Madison* (1803), Chief Justice John Marshall asserted that "[i]t is, emphatically, the province and duty of the judicial department, to say what the law is."[20] Marshall was referring not only to the interpretation of legislation but to the role of the courts in determining the meaning of the Constitution itself. But how, more

Obiter Dicta

"Time works changes, brings into existence new conditions and purposes. Therefore a principle, to be vital, must be capable of wider application than the mischief which gave it birth. This is peculiarly true of constitutions. They are not ephemeral enactments, designed to meet passing occasions. They are, to use the words of Chief Justice Marshall, 'designed to approach immortality as nearly as human institutions can approach it.' The future is their care, and provision for events of good and bad tendencies of which no prophecy can be made. In the application of a constitution, therefore, our contemplation cannot be only of what has been, but of what may be."

—*Justice Joseph McKenna, writing for the Supreme Court in* Weems v. United States, *217 U.S. 349 (1910).*

ORIGINALISM: The idea that a constitutional provision must be interpreted according to its accepted meaning at the time it was adopted.

than two centuries after the Constitution was adopted, is it to be understood and applied to issues of the current day? What, for example, does the right to keep and bear arms include in an age of sophisticated and extremely lethal firearms? How does the Fourth Amendment prohibition of unreasonable searches and seizures apply to high-tech surveillance? What does freedom of speech mean in an age of social media? And so on ...

Originalism

One approach, originalism, holds that that the Constitution should be interpreted according to the generally accepted meaning of its words and phrases at the time the document was created. This approach entails a more "static" examination of the document and is averse to the creation of "new rights" through the judicial branch. Supreme Court Justice Hugo Black, who served on the high Court from 1937 to 1971, was a noted advocate of originalism, having once declared that: "Our Constitution was not written in the sands to be washed away by each wave of new judges blown in by each successive political wind."[21] He offered that sentiment in a dissenting opinion written in support of a man who had been convicted of trafficking cocaine and heroin in violation of federal law—with Black's opinion putting forth a list of eight different violations of Fifth and Sixth Amendment protections that he claimed the majority had neglected, including perceived neglect of the right to remain silent, the right to a trial by jury, the right to counsel, and the right to confront witnesses (topics we will address in chapters 11 and 12).

Supreme Court Justice Antonin Scalia, the best-known contemporary exponent of this approach, carried on Black's adherence to originalism while serving from 1986 until 2016, often insisting in speeches that the Constitution "means today not what current society, much less the court, thinks it ought to mean, but what it meant when it was adopted."[22] Thus, for Justice Scalia, the Eighth Amendment has nothing to do with the constitutionality of the death penalty, simply because the phrase "cruel and unusual punishments" was not understood to include the death penalty at the time the Bill of Rights was adopted.[23]

In *D.C. v. Heller* (2008)—which struck down a D.C. ban on handgun possession in the home—Justice Scalia's 64-page majority opinion made more than two dozen references to the word "founding," including in his assessment of what phrases like "keep arms" and "bear arms" should mean in contemporary society, as guided by a telescope of the past.[24] For example, he observed that, "By the time of the founding, the right to have arms had become fundamental for English subjects," with a subsequent citation offered to the noted common-law era writings of

William Blackstone, whose Commentaries are described as constituting "the preeminent authority on English law for the founding generation."[25] Interestingly, though, even the noted originalist Scalia offered the observation that "the Second Amendment extends, prima facie, to all instruments that constitute bearable arms, even those that were not in existence at the time of the founding"—perhaps a recognition of the fact that a centuries-old document must inevitably be reconciled with certain considerations that its initial craftsmen could not have fathomed.

A Living Constitution?

In contrast to originalism, Justice Oliver Wendell Holmes, writing for the Supreme Court in *Missouri v. Holland* (1920),[26] offered a very different perspective on constitutional interpretation:

> [W]hen we are dealing with words that also are a constituent act, like the Constitution of the United States, we must realize that they have called into life a being the development of which could not have been foreseen completely by the most gifted of its begetters. It was enough for them to realize or to hope that they had created an organism; it has taken a century and has cost their successors much sweat and blood to prove that they created a nation. The case before us must be considered in the light of our whole experience and not merely in that of what was said a hundred years ago.

Justice Holmes was suggesting that we have a living Constitution, one that evolves as the nation moves forward through history. Eighty-seven years after Justice Holmes' observation, Justice Thurgood Marshall, the first African American to serve on the Supreme Court, struck a similar note:

LIVING CONSTITUTION: The notion that the meaning of the Constitution evolves over time through changing judicial interpretation.

> I do not believe that the meaning of the Constitution was forever "fixed" at the Philadelphia Convention. Nor do I find the wisdom, foresight, and sense of justice exhibited by the Framers particularly profound. To the contrary, the government they devised was defective from the start, requiring several amendments, a civil war, and momentous social transformation to attain the system of constitutional government, and its respect for the individual

freedoms and human rights, we hold as fundamental today. When contemporary Americans cite "The Constitution," they invoke a concept that is vastly different from what the Framers barely began to construct two centuries ago.[27]

The phrase "living Constitution" suggests that the document—and its key words and phrases—should evolve to meet the needs and challenges of a changing world. Such a framework inherently allows for the definitions of key terms in the Constitution to shift over time—a fact that critics like Justice Scalia point to as yielding inconsistent interpretation.[28]

Without question, the Constitution has evolved markedly over the centuries. The changes have come not only by way of significant amendments but also through changing judicial interpretations. As one prominent example, consider the Supreme Court's decision in *Roe v. Wade* (1973),[29] which effectively legalized abortion in this country. *Roe* was based on a "right of privacy" that appears nowhere in the text of the Constitution. It represented a dramatic change in public policy brought about not through constitutional amendment but via judicial interpretation. *Roe v. Wade* proved to be enormously controversial. Beginning with Ronald Reagan in the 1980s, Republican presidents expressed their opposition to *Roe* and attempted to place justices on the Supreme Court who would reconsider that decision. In June 2022, in what turned out to be a bombshell decision, the Court overturned *Roe*, thus returning the decision as to whether to criminalize abortion to the states. But recriminalizing abortion may not be a foregone conclusion, even in conservative states. In Kansas, for example, voters in August 2022 opted to preserve their state's constitutional protection of reproductive freedom. Without question, the issue of abortion will be high on the agendas of state legislatures and state courts in the coming years. (For further discussion of reproductive rights, see chapter 4.)

The idea that it is the role of courts to foster constitutional change has always been a controversial one. In 1803, President Thomas Jefferson wrote, "Our peculiar security is in the possession of a written Constitution. Let us not make it a blank paper by construction."[30] One hundred and sixty-two years later, Justice Hugo Black objected to the concept of a living Constitution:

> I realize that many good and able men have eloquently spoken and written, sometimes in rhapsodical strains, about the duty of this Court to keep the Constitution in tune with the times. The idea is that the Constitution must be changed from time to time and that this Court is charged with a duty to make those changes. For myself, I must with all deference reject that philosophy. The Constitution makers knew the need for change and provided for it. Amendments suggested by the people's elected representatives can be submitted to the people or their selected agents for ratification. That method of change was good enough for our Fathers, and being somewhat old-fashioned I must add it is good enough for me.[31]

At this point, it is important to recognize that *originalism* and *living constitutionalism* are broad terms, and there are many variations within each approach. Ultimately, the approach one chooses to adopt in evaluating key words or phrases in the Constitution—such as the meaning of "interstate commerce" or "unreasonable search and seizure"—can play a crucial role in shaping the document's application to specific cases and controversies. In the end, the interpretations that matter most are the ones emanating from the U.S. Supreme Court.[32]

As readers proceed through this textbook, they should evaluate the strengths and weaknesses of each of these broad approaches to constitutional interpretation and, perhaps, consider if there is a middle ground between these two general ideas—as well as if certain amendments are more compatible with one approach or the other. Of course, constitutional interpretation is not limited to the amendments. Matters of congressional, presidential, and judicial power require interpretation of the main corpus of the Constitution. Two hundred and thirty some years after the Constitution was written, federal courts still grapple with the problem of applying eighteenth-century language to twenty-first-century issues.

THE CONSTITUTION IN ACTION
Prohibition, Its Repeal, and the Regulation of Alcohol

Although constitutional amendments have typically sought to protect civil rights and liberties, the Eighteenth Amendment was altogether different. Ratified on January 16, 1919, this amendment banned the "manufacture, sale, or transportation of intoxicating liquors" throughout the country. In October of that year, Congress passed the Volstead Act,[33] also known as the National Prohibition Act, to facilitate enforcement of the Eighteenth Amendment. The amendment would take effect one year after its ratification, with the era known as *Prohibition* beginning on January 17, 1920.

Yet neither the Volstead Act nor the Eighteenth Amendment made it illegal to consume alcohol—and doctors and pharmacies actually could prescribe alcohol for medical purposes. Thus, demand for spirits still existed on the part of individual consumers, and illegal 'bootlegging' operations—often driven by organized crime syndicates—arose in the 1920s. The Volstead Act did provide for a federal bureaucracy that was tasked with enforcing the restrictions of Prohibition. Originally, the Department of Treasury's Bureau of Internal Revenue (in 1953, renamed Internal Revenue Service) would serve as the primary agency for enforcing bans on the manufacture, sale, and transportation of alcohol. Within that Bureau, a Prohibition Unit was created in 1920, and by 1927, that unit had become its own entity, called the Bureau of Prohibition. In 1930, the Bureau was renamed the Alcohol Beverage Unit and moved into the Department of Justice, where it was housed inside the Bureau of Investigations (later to be called the FBI).

Not surprisingly, the U.S. prison population increased dramatically during this era. Prior to 1914, less than 3,000 people were incarcerated in federal prisons, but by 1932, that figure ballooned by more than 300 percent, with the number of people convicted of federal crimes increasing by over 500 percent across this time frame.[34] (We discuss historical trends in the U.S. prison population in greater detail in chapter 13.)

On December 5, 1933, with public opinion on alcohol consumption and the temperance movement having shifted markedly, the Twenty-First Amendment was ratified to repeal the Eighteenth Amendment. Federal prohibitions on alcohol production, sale, and transportation officially ended that day. In the aftermath of Prohibition's repeal, the Bureau of Prohibition was moved back into the Department of Treasury and renamed the Alcohol Tax Unit. In 1968, it would become the Bureau of Alcohol, Tobacco, and Firearms, known popularly as the ATF. (We discuss that agency in greater detail in chapter 6, which addresses the Second Amendment and gun rights.)

A key feature of the Twenty-First Amendment is that it leaves it up to individual states to determine if they wish to maintain a ban on alcohol, with Section 2 of the amendment stating, "The transportation or importation into any State, Territory, or possession of the United States for delivery or use therein of intoxicating liquors, in violation of the laws thereof, is hereby prohibited." Mississippi, for example, retained its ban on the manufacture and sale of liquor until 1966, when it became the last state to fully repeal such prohibitions.

To this day, federal law allows for home brewing of 200 gallons of beer and wine per year, within any home where two or more adults reside.[35] Some states also permit individual counties to set alcohol policies, which could impact matters such as whether to allow alcohol sales at all, to place limits on sales in grocery stores, to ban sales on Sundays, or to allow open containers of alcohol in public places or even in cars. In some locations, policies related to beer are set by city or county "beer boards," whereas policies for distilled spirits like vodka, whiskey, and gin tend to be governed by a state alcoholic beverage commission.

Prior to 1984, states also retained the ability to set their own drinking ages, with Oklahoma adopting different drinking ages for men and women—until the Supreme Court declared that approach to be a violation of the Equal Protection Clause of the Fourteenth Amendment.[36] The National Minimum Drinking Age Act of 1984, however, required all states to increase their minimum drinking ages to 21 years or risk losing federal highway funding.

(continued)

The Supreme Court upheld this law in *South Dakota v. Dole* (1984),[37] which rejected contentions that the Act amounted to an impermissible form of coercive federalism that might have violated Article I's spending power limitations or even the Twenty-First Amendment.

The Court again offered an alcohol-related ruling in 2019, when it found that Section 2 of the Twenty-First Amendment did not permit Tennessee's Alcoholic Beverage Commission to impose a two-year residency requirement on the acquisition of a license to own and operate a retail liquor store.[38] The majority opinion by Justice Samuel Alito stated that the Twenty-First amendment was "not a license to impose all manner of protectionist restrictions on commerce in alcoholic beverages." The Court added that the Commerce Clause of Article I precludes a state "from discriminating against 'citizens and products of other States.'" Overall, the nation's alcohol regulations—which arise through a patchwork of federal statutes, constitutional amendments, state legislative acts, local ordinances, and even Supreme Court decisions—reflect the principles of federalism and separation of powers in practice.

Constitutional Development

The U.S. Constitution has evolved over the last twenty-three decades, both through formal amendment and judicial interpretation. Indeed, the country has changed in so many ways, but the Constitution remains relevant. Every day, lawyers and judges wrestle with the meaning of the Constitution, quite often in criminal cases where the interpretation of the document can mean incarceration or freedom, or even life or death, for defendants.

Constitutional Democracy

The men who drafted the Constitution were drawn from the nation's elite, and the document they produced contained a number of undemocratic features. Most notably, their inability or unwillingness to abolish slavery ran counter to the Declaration of Independence, which proclaimed that "all men are created equal." The Electoral College was created to choose the president because the founders did not trust the masses to make this choice. Likewise, the Senate was originally chosen by the state legislatures and not by the electorate. In the early days of the Republic, all of the institutions of government, at both the national and state levels, were controlled by White men of property. Women were essentially second-class citizens and had no right to vote. Most persons of African descent were held in bondage and, accordingly, had no legal rights.[39]

The abolition of slavery, the elimination of property qualifications for voting, the expansion of the suffrage to include African Americans and women, and the direct election of the U.S. Senate have made the political system more democratic—that is, more open to participation by those who were once excluded. Of course, the system is far from a perfect democracy, and judges, lawyers, and politicians still argue over voting rights and broader issues of social justice. But through constitutional amendments and changing interpretations of existing constitutional language, as well as legislative changes at the state and federal level, the constitutional republic designed by the framers has moved far along the path toward a constitutional democracy. Generally, the United States is known as having a representative democracy, in which individuals elect officials who, in turn, create policy through the legislative process—bound by the parameters of the Constitution. Nevertheless, vestiges of *direct democracy* remain in more than half the states, where voters retain the ability to vote directly on amendments to state constitutions or, perhaps, on pieces of legislation. We discuss these types of direct democracy, including some examples that deal with the criminal justice system, in chapter 2.

The Administrative/Regulatory State

Another megatrend of American constitutional development is the emergence of bureaucracy at all levels of government—not only for the purpose of service delivery but for regulation of various activities. The term administrative state is often used to denote this phenomenon, but the term regulatory state is equally apt in conveying the imposition of regulation upon the populace. Today, virtually every business, industry, and profession is regulated by government at some level. So too are recreational activities such as boating, hunting, and fishing. These regulations come about by way of delegated power from Congress and the state legislatures, which can permit bureaucratic agencies staffed with unelected officials to craft regulations through the *rulemaking* process. For example, in 2018, the Bureau of Alcohol, Tobacco, Firearms and Explosives issued a rule that interpreted a 1934 gun law as banning gun attachments known as "bump stocks";[40] with that declaration, the items became illegal under federal law. In the end, agencies are empowered to adopt and enforce regulations and even adjudicate cases. Agencies can issue fines, and in some instances, agencies refer violations of regulations for criminal prosecution through the Department of Justice. We discuss cases of administrative referral for criminal prosecution in greater detail in chapter 2; further, the concept of administrative searches will be addressed in our chapters covering the Fourth Amendment.

The Proliferation of Federal Criminal Law

As for criminal justice, the most significant constitutional development has been the proliferation of federal criminal law (and, with it, law enforcement agencies and corrections facilities). While criminal justice was almost exclusively a state and local function in the early days of the Republic, in the twentieth century, Congress created a vast federal criminal code containing roughly 65,000 specific offenses. As we shall see in the next chapter, broad interpretation of Congress's Article I legislative powers by the courts has facilitated this transformation.

With certain criminal episodes, in fact, the location where the offense occurs could determine whether it is a state or federal charge. Speeding in a national park, for instance, would be a federal offense. An assault on a Native American reservation that involved an "intent to cause serious bodily injury" could be a federal crime under the Major Crimes Act of 1885.[41] An assault of a postal worker would be a federal crime under 18 U.S.C. § 1114, and assaulting a flight attendant on an airplane would be a federal crime under 49 U.S.C. § 46504 and §

SOCIAL JUSTICE: Equal rights under the law and fairness in the division of wealth, privilege, and opportunity in society.

CONSTITUTIONAL REPUBLIC: A state in which representatives are elected and the rules of government are set forth in a constitution.

CONSTITUTIONAL DEMOCRACY: A constitutional republic in which rights, especially the right to vote, are guaranteed to all citizens.

ADMINISTRATIVE STATE: A government characterized by a high level of bureaucracy.

REGULATORY STATE: A government characterized by numerous regulations promulgated by bureaucratic agencies.

46506. Other assaults, as noted in our following discussion of *Bond v. United States* (2014),[42] might be left for state authorities to address, pursuant to powers reserved to the states via the Tenth Amendment, which we address in the next chapter.

JURISPRUDENCE

Can Attempting to Poison Someone Be a Federal Chemical Weapons Offense?
Bond v. United States, 572 U.S. 844 (2014)

Under the U.S. system of federalism, certain types of conduct can result in either a state criminal charge or a federal criminal charge—or even both. A key issue, though, is whether the federal government has the authority to criminalize the conduct in question—since the scope of federal law is supposed to be restricted to the enumerated powers and implied powers under Article I of the U.S. Constitution, with remaining powers reserved to the states under the Tenth Amendment.

A case that tested the application of these principles was decided by the Supreme Court in 2014. In *Bond v. United States* (2014), a woman named Carol Anne Bond believed that another woman, Ms. Haynes, was having an affair with her husband. In an attempt at retaliation, Bond, who had experience working with chemical substances through her job as a microbiologist, repeatedly placed two chemical irritants she purchased on Amazon.com on Ms. Haynes's doorknob, car, and mailbox. Ms. Haynes suffered a rash on her hand as a result of Bond's actions and reported the matter to local police in Philadelphia, Pennsylvania, seeking an assault charge. However, local police were not interested in pursuing an investigation into the matter—perhaps, because of the relatively minor nature of the victim's injuries and the voluminous criminal caseload one would expect in a major city.

In turn, with state criminal charges no longer a viable option, Ms. Haynes asked the local office of the U.S. Postal Service to initiate an investigation for potential federal offenses—since tampering with a mailbox could be a federal crime.[43] A postal inspector then set up hidden cameras, which revealed Bond in the act of placing chemical irritants on the mailbox. The case was then referred to federal prosecutors for criminal charges, and the U.S. Attorney for the Eastern District of Pennsylvania took a unique approach by bringing charges against Bond for violation of a federal law called the Chemical Weapons Convention Implementation Act of 1998.

At trial in federal district court, Bond was found guilty of violating that law, and the U.S. Court of Appeals for the Third Circuit affirmed. But on appeal, the Supreme Court would reverse her conviction.

Chief Justice John Roberts wrote the opinion of the Court in *Bond v. United States* (2014), which represented the second time the high Court produced a ruling in this case.[44] Roberts indicated that Bond's conduct did not comport with the congressional intent underlying the passage of the Chemical Weapons Convention Implementation Act, which he suggested was designed to stop acts of chemical warfare, whereas the criminal activity in question here was better addressed through the application of state law. In this regard, Roberts wrote the following:

> Bond's conduct is serious and unacceptable—and against the laws of Pennsylvania. But the background principle that Congress does not normally intrude upon the police power of the States is critically important. In light of that principle, we are reluctant to conclude that Congress meant to punish Bond's crime with a federal prosecution for a chemical weapons attack. … It is also clear that the laws of the Commonwealth of Pennsylvania (and every other State) are sufficient to prosecute Bond. Pennsylvania has several statutes that would likely cover her assault. … In sum, the global need to prevent chemical warfare does not require the Federal Government to reach into the kitchen cupboard, or to treat a local assault with a chemical irritant as the deployment of a chemical weapon. There is no reason to suppose that Congress—in implementing the Convention on Chemical Weapons—thought otherwise.

Expansion of Civil Rights and Liberties

The final megatrend in American constitutional development is the expansion of civil rights and liberties through constitutional amendment, legislation and judicial interpretation of statutes and constitutional provisions. Although this process began during the Reconstruction Period after the Civil War, it stalled until the latter half of the twentieth century. By far the most significant developments occurred in the 1960s, as Congress passed a series of landmark civil rights statutes, and the Supreme Court under Chief Justice Earl Warren rendered numerous decisions expanding rights and liberties. We will examine many of these decisions in the chapters that follow.

Constitutional Issues in Criminal Cases

As we will discuss in the remainder of this textbook, criminal cases can pose a variety of constitutional questions for the courts. These could involve situations where a law itself (*on its face*) might violate an amendment, or where the law *as applied* by law enforcement in an individual instance represents a constitutional violation. The following are some examples to consider as a starting point for our inquiry:

- If the case involves the enforcement of a federal law, the question of whether Congress had the authority to enact the law might arise. Or does the law deal with a matter reserved to the states under the Tenth Amendment? (If the case involves enforcement of a state or local law, it is up to the courts of that state to decide whether the legislative body had the authority to enact it.)
- Does the law, on its face or as applied, abridge the rights enshrined in the First Amendment (i.e., the freedoms of speech, press, assembly, and the free exercise of religion)? Does the law constitute an unconstitutional establishment of religion in violation of the First Amendment?
- Does the law on its face, or as applied, infringe the right to keep and bear arms recognized by the Second Amendment?
- Does the law, on its face or as applied, constitute a denial of procedural or substantive due process in violation of the Fifth or Fourteenth Amendment?
- Does the law, on its face or as applied, deprive persons of the equal protection of laws as guaranteed by the Fourteenth Amendment?
- Was physical evidence in the case obtained in violation of the Fourth Amendment prohibition against unreasonable searches and seizures?
- Did police violate the defendant's Fourth Amendment rights by making an improper arrest or using excessive force?
- Were incriminating statements by the defendant admitted into evidence in violation of the Fifth Amendment protection against compulsory self-incrimination?
- Was the defendant subjected to double jeopardy as prohibited by the Fifth Amendment?
- Was the defendant denied the right to counsel as guaranteed by the Sixth Amendment?
- Was the defendant given a fair trial by an impartial jury as also provided by the Sixth Amendment?
- Was the defendant required to post excessive bail or subjected to an excessive fine in violation of the Eighth Amendment?
- Was the defendant subjected to cruel and unusual punishment in violation of the Eighth Amendment, either by the penalty imposed or the conditions of confinement?

A large body of case law is associated with each of these issues, and we will examine a good bit of that case law as we move through the succeeding chapters.

THE CONSTITUTION AND SOCIAL JUSTICE

The Infamous *Scottsboro* Case

A foundational principle of the American criminal justice system is the presumption of innocence. Accordingly, some of the biggest failures of this system involve instances in which innocent individuals are convicted and punished for crimes they did not commit. That was certainly true in the *Scottsboro* case, one of the most infamous miscarriages of justice in U.S. history.

This case originated with a fight that occurred in a railway car on a Southern Railroad freight train in March 1931. Police responded to this incident and arrested nine Black teenagers, who ranged in age from 13 to 19. At first, the charges were minor ones related to the fight. However, two women who had also been on the train accused the teenagers of rape.

The young men were taken to a jail in Scottsboro, Alabama, and the Alabama National Guard was deployed to prevent an angry mob from storming the jail. A trial was held in April 1931, and an all-White jury found the boys guilty of rape; eight of them were sentenced to death. By contemporary standards of criminal procedure, the trial was an abomination. The defendants were not represented by counsel and, though innocent of the charges, were unable to mount any sort of effective defense.

The U.S. Supreme Court reviewed the case, and in *Powell v. Alabama* (1932),[45] the convictions of the Scottsboro boys were vacated, declaring they had been deprived of their right to counsel under the Fourteenth Amendment's Due Process Clause. Subsequent trials—and guilty verdicts—would ensue, and in January 1935, after the Alabama Supreme Court refused to provide relief to the defendants, the Supreme Court of the United States once again set aside the guilty verdicts. In *Norris v. Alabama* (1935),[46] the high Court specifically took issue with the exclusion of Black people from juries in Alabama, noting that, "For this long-continued, unvarying, and wholesale exclusion … from jury service we find no justification with the constitutional mandate." That mandate, it follows, was connected to notions of due process and equal protection under the Fourteenth Amendment.

Despite this second victory at the nation's highest Court, four of the Scottsboro defendants would be convicted again of rape in subsequent trials that took place later, in the 1930s. After several decades, though, pardons would be issued to each of those four—one by Alabama Governor George Wallace in 1976 and three more by the Alabama Board of Pardons and Paroles in 2013. To this day, the Scottsboro case remains an exemplar of criminal procedures that were applied in a manner inconsistent with basic constitutional protections designed to ensure equal justice under law.

Remedies for Constitutional Violations

A primary consequence of a constitutional violation in a criminal case is that a conviction or punishment may be overturned by an appellate court, a process that we discuss in greater detail in chapter 2. Additionally, in subsequent chapters, we will address how law enforcement officials might be sued for conduct that violates constitutional rights. Under a law codified at 42 U.S.C. § 1983 (referring to Title 42, Section 1983 of the U.S. Code), state and local officials can be held personally liable through lawsuits over violations of constitutional rights. Thus, it remains imperative for law enforcement officials to have a thorough understanding of these constitutional protections.

However, there is no law that specifically allows for lawsuits against federal law enforcement officials who might violate constitutional rights. There is a 1971 Supreme Court decision that allows for lawsuits against federal officials in limited situations,[47] as we will discuss in chapter 8, but use of this so-called *Bivens* doctrine has become a "disfavored judicial activity," according to a 2020 Supreme Court ruling that prevented a lawsuit against a U.S. Border Patrol agent who was involved in a cross-border shooting that killed a teenager from Mexico.[48] This principle was reiterated in a 2022 Supreme Court decision that prevented a lawsuit against a Border Patrol agent who was accused of excessive use of force.[49]

Additionally, as we will discuss in later chapters, many officers are given qualified immunity when they face lawsuits for conduct in the line of duty. Under this doctrine, law enforcement personnel cannot be held liable for their actions in the course of their job duties, unless the actions violate "clearly established" precedents that have established a constitutional violation in a particular fact pattern.[50] Even so, in situations when a lawsuit against an individual officer cannot be sustained, Supreme Court precedent might allow for a suit to be brought against a department for improper training—as demonstrated through "policies" or "customs" (or a lack thereof).[51] And beyond these civil remedies, there is federal law that allows for criminal charges against those who violate constitutional rights "under color of law."[52] Therefore, a variety of corrective measures exist for violations of constitutional rights, heightening the importance of understanding the various constitutional parameters we will examine in subsequent chapters.

FOCUS ON LAW ENFORCEMENT
The Need for Constitutional Policing

Even a glance at the news over the last several years reveals deep problems in law enforcement. We the People expect law officers to obey the law themselves and to respect the constitutional rights of those they encounter. Unfortunately, in some situations, this is not the case. Unlawful searches and seizures, the excessive use of force, and racial profiling are not consistent with the requirements of the federal and state constitutions, nor are they indicative of professionalism. Today, some suggest there is a crisis of legitimacy in the criminal justice system. Some Americans, particularly those in minority communities, have experienced a loss of trust in police and prosecutors. Some reformers demand the "demilitarization" of law enforcement,[53] and others even call for the "defunding" of the police (although exactly what that means in practical terms might range from lowering budgets to supplementing police activity with the assistance of social workers and mental health professionals).[54] Nonetheless, with violent crime rates rising in many major cities in 2022[55] and many departments finding it difficult to recruit new officers,[56] the need for policing and robust law enforcement resources remains crucial in the United States. It is, therefore, imperative that current and future law enforcement officers are well educated in the requirements of constitutional policing and are given the support they need to effectively carry out their duties.

Of course, it is undeniable that law enforcement officials have arduous jobs that entail taxing physical and mental demands, while carrying inherent risks that arise on a daily basis. According to data from the National Law Enforcement Officers Memorial Fund, across federal, state, tribal, and local law enforcement agencies, there were 458 officers who died in the line of duty in 2021—a figure that included COVID-deaths, deaths resulting from assaults and shootings, and traffic-related fatalities.[57] The FBI also maintains a dataset known as the Law Enforcement Officers Killed and Assaulted Data Collection (LEOKA), which showed that intentional killings of officers were at a twenty-year high in 2021.[58] Because the suicide rate among police is very high, a newly established FBI database tracks suicides by those working in law enforcement.[59] Risks faced by officers, it follows, are numerous and extremely serious.

Overall, the need to conform their conduct to the myriad constitutional boundaries outlined in this book, while simultaneously attempting to preserve not only public safety but also their own, presents an enormous challenge for the people who devote their lives to careers in law enforcement. Our objective in this text, then, is to offer guidance on how to confront, within the parameters of the Constitution, the many challenges inherent to policing in contemporary American society. Ultimately, as the director of the U.S. Department of Justice's Bureau of Justice Assistance noted in April 2022, "Constitutional policing is foundational to a just and equitable society, and it remains the bedrock of effective public safety."[60]

Conclusion

Throughout this textbook, we will assess how key words and phrases within the U.S. Constitution continue to impact the enactment and enforcement of criminal laws today. That assessment will entail an examination of Supreme Court decisions that have determined the constitutionality of criminal statutes and the methods used by federal, state, and local authorities who are charged with enforcing those laws.

We strive to convey examples that will prove instructive for practitioners who work in criminal justice fields—including police officers, detectives, prosecutors, defense attorneys, paralegals, judges, magistrates, and others. In a world where the actions of criminal justice professionals are dissected under mass media and social media microscopes on a daily basis—and where individual members of society may find themselves interacting with members of law enforcement in a variety of contexts—it is imperative that students and practitioners possess a thorough understanding of constitutional law.

Toward this objective, in this opening chapter, we have examined the adoption and ratification of the Constitution, its interpretation by the courts, and its relevance to criminal justice. In chapter 2, we delineate the elements of the constitutional system, with an emphasis on how each of the three branches of government plays a role in creating and implementing the criminal law. Subsequent chapters will provide a detailed explanation of how the judicial interpretation of key constitutional amendments impacts the criminal justice system and the lives of those who interact with it or work within it. Finally, throughout this text, we will connect our discussion of the Constitution to the process of appealing criminal cases and, more generally, to the notion of remedying violations of rights—whether those rights adhere to accused criminals, victims of crimes, or the individuals whose vocations require them to enforce criminal laws in a just fashion.

Discussion Questions

1. In what specific ways can the U.S. Constitution affect the creation and enforcement of criminal laws?
2. How did the institution of slavery affect the drafting of the Constitution? How and when was the Constitution amended to abolish slavery?
3. Why do courts of law have the power to strike down legislation they determine to be unconstitutional? Is this power contrary to the idea of democracy?
4. Beyond the text of the Constitution, what factors do judges consider when they apply constitutional principles to contemporary issues?
5. Why is the national government more involved in the administration of justice today than the Framers of the Constitution intended or expected?

Endnotes

1   *Bonham v. College of Physicians*, 77 Eng. Rep. 638 (1610).
2   *Marbury v. Madison*, 5 U.S. 137 (1803).
3   *Bush v. Gore*, 531 U.S. 98 (2000).
4   *United States v. Nixon*, 418 U.S. 683 (1974).

5   *See* Ford W. Hall, *The Common Law: An Account of its Reception in the United States*, 4 Vand. L. Rev. 791 (1951).

6   U.S. Const. art. I, § 8.

7   James Madison, *Federalist No. 45: The Alleged Danger From the Powers of the Union to the State Governments Considered*, *in* The Federalist Papers (Clinton Rossiter ed., 1961).

8   The ability of presidents to serve an unlimited number of terms was altered by Twenty-Second Amendment (1951), which provides: "No person shall be elected to the office of the President more than twice. ..."

9   U.S. Const. art. II, § 3.

10 James Madison, *Federalist No. 70: The Executive Department Further Considered*, *in* The Federalist Papers (Clinton Rossiter ed., 1961).

11 James Madison, *Federalist No. 51: The Structure of the Government Must Furnish the Proper Checks and Balances Between the Different Departments*, *in* The Federalist Papers (Clinton Rossiter ed., 1961).

12 U.S. Const. art. III, § 1.

13 James Madison, *Federalist No. 78: The Structure of the Government Must Furnish the Proper Checks and Balances Between the Different Departments*, *in* The Federalist Papers (Clinton Rossiter ed., 1961).

14 Adam Beam, *California Assembly Advances Involuntary Servitude Amendment*, L.A. Times, Mar. 22, 2022, https://www.latimes.com/california/story/2022-03-22/california-assembly-advances-involuntary-servitude-amendment.

15 Azadeh Shahshahani, *Why Are For-Profit US Prisons Subjecting Detainees to Forced Labor?* The Guardian, May 17, 2018, https://www.theguardian.com/commentisfree/2018/may/17/us-private-prisons-forced-labour-detainees-modern-slavery.

16 The author has generally been thought to be Richard Henry Lee, one of the principal architects of the Articles of Confederation, but this remains in doubt.

17 *Barron v. Baltimore*, 32 U.S. 243 (1833).

18 *See, e.g.*, *Brown v. Board of Education*, 347 U.S. 483 (1954).

19 *See, e.g.*, *Gitlow v. New York*, 268 U.S. 652 (1925).

20 *Marbury v. Madison*, 5 U.S. (1 Cranch) 137 (1803).

21 *Turner v. United States*, 396 U.S. 398 (1970).

22 This was a phrase Scalia recited in numerous speeches and interviews given around the United States over the course of his judicial career. For a transcript and audio recording of one interview in which the phrase was uttered, *see* Nina Totenberg, *Supreme Court Justice Antonin Scalia Was Known For His Dissents*, NPR, https://www.npr.org/2016/02/15/466783882/supreme-court-justice-antonin-scalia-was-know-for-his-acerbic-dissidents.

23 *See, e.g.*, *Atkins v. Virginia*, 536 U.S. 304 (2002) (for Justice Scalia's dissent); *Roper v. Simmons*, 543 U.S. 551 (2005).

24 *District of Columbia v. Heller*, 554 U.S. 570 (2008).

25 In making that assertion, Scalia cited to Justice Kennedy's majority opinion in *Alden v. Maine*, 527 U.S. 706 (1999).

26 *Missouri v. Holland*, 252 U.S. 416 (1920).

27 Justice Thurgood Marshall, Speech at Annual Seminar of the San Francisco Patent and Trademark Law Association in Maui, Hawaii (May 6, 1987).

28 *See* Antonin Scalia & Bryan Garner, Reading Law: The Interpretation of Legal Texts (2012).

29 *Roe v. Wade*, 410 U.S. 113 (1973).

30 Letter from Thomas Jefferson, to Wilson Nicholas (1803).

31 *Griswold v. Connecticut*, 381 U.S. 479 (1965) (Black, J. dissenting).

32 *See* Bruce Ackerman, *The Living Constitution*, 120 Harv. L. Rev. 1737 (2007); David Strauss, *Do We Have a Living Constitution?* 59 Drake L. Rev. 973 (2011); Andrew Conan, *Living Constitutional Theory*, 66 Duke L.J. 99 (2017).

33   The Volstead Act (National Prohibition Act), Pub. L. 66–66, 41 Stat. 305 (1919).

34   Carroll H.Wooddy, *The Growth of the Federal Government, 1915–1932, in* Mark Thornton, Alcohol Prohibition Was a Failure, 157 Cato Institute Policy Analysis (1991), https://www.cato.org/policy-analysis/alcohol-prohibition-was-failure.

35   The federal limit allows for 200 gallons of beer and an additional 200 gallons of wine or cider, as per the federal regulation codified in 27 C.F.R. 24.75. The quantity limit is lowered to 100 gallons for a one-adult home. For more information, see Pub. L. 95–458, 92 Stat. 1255, which amended the IRS code. A full discussion of this topic appears on the National Conference for State Legislatures website. See Heather Morton, Home manufacture of Alcohol State Statutes, NCSL, https://www.ncsl.org/research/financial-services-and-commerce/home-manufacture-of-alcohol-state-statutes.aspx

36   *Craig v. Boren*, 429 U.S. 190 (1976).

37   *South Dakota v. Dole*, 483 U.S. 203 (1987).

38   *Tennessee Wine and Spirits Retailers Association v. Thomas, Exec. Director of the Tennessee Alcoholic Beverage Commission*, 588 U.S. ___ (2019).

39   *Scott v. Sandford*, 60 U.S. 393 (1857).

40   27 C.F.R. Parts 446, 478, and 479 (The 1934 law at issue is the National Firearms Act of 1934, Pub. L. 73–474, 48 Stat. 1236, 26 U.S.C.: Internal Revenue Code.).

41   *See Keeble v. United States*, 412 U.S. 205 (1973) (Without a showing of that intent to cause serious bodily injury, the matter would be heard in Tribal court.). *See* Major Crimes Act of 1885, 23 Stat. 385. We discuss Tribal courts in greater detail in chapter 2.

42   *Bond v. United States*, 572 U.S. 844 (2014).

43   18 U.S.C § 1705.

44   The first Supreme Court decision in this matter, *Bond v. United States*, 564 U.S. 211 (2011), addressed the issue of whether Bond had standing to raise a Tenth Amendment claim, with the Court finding that she did and remanding the matter to the Third Circuit.

45   *Powell v. Alabama*, 287 U.S. 45 (1932).

46   *Norris v. Alabama*, 294 U.S. 587 (1935).

47   *Bivens v. Six Unknown Named Agents of the Federal Bureau of Narcotics*, 403 U.S. 388 (1971) (This case applied to lawsuits for Fourth Amendment violations only, and subsequent cases would expand the *Bivens* doctrine to permit lawsuits for violations of the Fifth Amendment, *Davis v. Passman*, 442 U.S. 228 (1979), and the Eighth Amendment, *Carlson v. Green*, 446 U.S. 14 (1980). We discuss this matter in greater detail in chapter 7.).

48   *Hernandez v. Mesa*, 589 U.S. ___ (2020) (quoting *Aschroft v. Iqbal*, 556 U.S. 662 (2009)).

49   *Egbert v. Boule*, 596 U.S. ___ (2022).

50   *See, e.g., District of Columbia v. Wesby*, 583 U.S. ___ (2018).

51   *Monell v. Departmet of Social Services of the City of New York*, 436 U.S. 658 (1978).

52   18 U.S.C. § 242.

53   *See* Charlotte Lawrence & Cyrus J. O'Brien, *Federal Militarization of Law Enforcement Must End*, ACLU, May 12, 2021, https://www.aclu.org/news/criminal-law-reform/federal-militarization-of-law-enforcement-must-end (We discuss this topic in greater detail in chapter 7, where we address the federal government's "1033 program," which allows for the transfer of federal military equipment to state and local police agencies.).

54   *See* Christine Fernando, *Collaboration with Police Divides Social Workers Across US*, ABC News, Mar. 17, 2021, https://abcnews.go.com/Lifestyle/wireStory/collaboration-police-divides-social-workers-us-76507263.

55   Thomas Abt, Eddie Bocanegra, & Emada Tingirides, *Violent Crime in the U.S. Is Surging. But We Know What to Do About It*, Time, Jan. 12, 2022, https://time.com/6138650/violent-crime-us-surging-what-to-do/.

56   Greg Mellen, Why Law Enforcement Is Facing Unprecedented Challenges in Hiring and Keeping Recruits, police1.com, Nov. 22, 2021, https://www.police1.com/police-recruiting/articles/why-law-enforcement-is-facing-unprecedented-challenges-in-hiring-and-keeping-recruits-pFiTKCXrne6ccNfB/.

57   Of those deaths, 301 were related to COVID-19, which generally has been classified as a line-of-duty death, given that exposure to other people inheres in the act of policing; eighty-four deaths were listed as being the result of felonious assaults with 61 of those 84 connected to shootings; more than 70 deaths occurred in traffic-related incidents; and two deaths were tied to the long-term impacts of dust particles that impacted the health of first responders who were at scene of the World Trade Center collapse on September 11, 2001. *See* National Law Enforcement Memorial and Museum, 2021 End-Of-Year Preliminary Law Enforcement Officers Fatalities Report, https://nleomf.org/wp-content/uploads/2022/01/2021-EOY-Fatality-Report-Final-web.pdf.

58   Federal Bureau of Investigation, Law Enforcement Officers Killed and Assaulted (LEOKA) Program, https://www.fbi.gov/services/cjis/ucr/leoka; *see also* Emma Tucker & Priya Krishnakumar, *Intentional Killings of Law Enforcement Officers Reach 20-Year High, FBI Says*, CNN, Jan. 13, 2022, https://www.cnn.com/2022/01/13/us/police-officers-line-of-duty-deaths/index.html.

59   Federal Bureau of Investigation, Law Enforcement Suicide Data Collection (LESDC), https://www.fbi.gov/services/cjis/ucr/law-enforcement-suicide-data-collection (More than 150 law enforcement suicides were reported in the U.S. in 2021; we discuss this topic in chapter 3.).

60   U.S. Department of Justice, Office of Public Affairs, Department of Justice Launches Law Enforcement Knowledge Lab, April 27, 2022, https://www.justice.gov/opa/pr/department-justice-launches-law-enforcement-knowledge-lab.

Credit

CHAPTER 2

The Constitutional System

"... *The Constitution sought to divide the delegated powers of the new federal government into three defined categories, legislative, executive and judicial, to assure, as nearly as possible, that each Branch of government would confine itself to its assigned responsibility. The hydraulic pressure inherent within each of the separate Branches to exceed the outer limits of its power, even to accomplish desirable objectives, must be resisted.*"

—Chief Justice Warren E. Burger, Writing for the Supreme Court in *Immigration and Naturalization Service v. Chadha*, 462 U.S. 919 (1983)

Learning Objectives

After reading this chapter, you should understand the following:

1. How separation of powers and federalism define the structure of the constitutional system
2. The sources of Congress's power to enact legislation
3. The role of the executive branch of government in enforcing and influencing constitutional law
4. The structure and jurisdiction of the various federal and state courts
5. The central role of the judicial branch in developing constitutional law
6. The mechanisms by which courts address constitutional questions and redress violations of constitutional rights

Key Cases

McCulloch v. Maryland, 17 U.S. 316 (1819)
Ex parte Milligan (1866), 71 U.S. 2 (1866)
Youngstown Sheet and Tube v. Sawyer, 343 U.S. 579 (1952)
United States v. Nixon, 418 U.S. 683 (1974)
Gonzales v. Raich, 545 U.S. 1 (2005)
Trump v. Hawaii, 585 U.S. ___ (2018)

Introduction

In this chapter, we examine the principles, institutions, and agencies that define the constitutional system. Each branch and every level of government contributes to the development of constitutional law, even though "[i]t is emphatically the province and duty of the judicial department to say what the law is."[1] We begin by delineating the principal structural principles that undergird the system. We then examine the legislative branch, focusing primarily on the legislative authority of the U.S. Congress. Next, we explore the executive branch, with emphasis on the powers of the presidency. Finally, we survey the judiciary, focusing on the United States Supreme Court.

Structural Features of the Constitutional System

SEPARATION OF POWERS: Constitutional principle by which the legislative, executive, and judicial powers are located in different branches of government.

FEDERALISM: The division of sovereignty between the national government and the state and local governments.

The principal structural features of the American constitutional system are separation of powers and federalism. While federalism refers to the relationship *between* the national government and the states (and their subordinate governmental entities: counties, cities, and towns), separation of powers applies *within* the federal government, each of the fifty state governments, and, to a lesser extent, local governments.

Separation of Powers

As we previously noted, separation of powers refers to a governmental structure in which the legislative, executive, and judicial functions are located in separate branches of government. The legislative branch, which includes Congress and the fifty state legislatures, enacts laws and approves budgets for the operation of government. The executive branch, headed by the president at the national level and governors in the fifty states, enforces and implements the laws. Law enforcement agencies and prosecutors fall within the executive branch of government. The judicial branch, which includes the federal courts and fifty state court systems, interprets the laws and applies them to specific cases. It is, of course, the courts that adjudicate criminal cases—a process that involves pretrial procedures, trials, and appeals.

The concept of separation of powers can be traced to the Enlightenment-era French philosopher Montesquieu. Like other political philosophers of the Enlightenment, Montesquieu's principal concern was preventing government from infringing the liberties of the citizen. Madison and the other framers of the U.S. Constitution readily embraced Montesquieu's idea.

Above all, the framers feared the concentration of power, whether in a monarch or a parliament. In Federalist No. 47, James Madison expressed this view succinctly: "The accumulation of all powers, legislative, executive, and judiciary, in the same hands, whether of one, a few, or many ... may justly be pronounced the very definition of tyranny."

Checks and Balances

Montesquieu also asserted, and the framers of the U.S. Constitution accepted, the need for a system of checks and balances, so each branch of government would have the means to check the actions of the others. For example, the president can veto bills passed by Congress, while Congress can override a presidential veto by a two-thirds vote of both houses. The president can nominate federal judges, ambassadors, and high executive officials, but these nominations must be approved by the Senate. Congress has the power to declare war, but the president is commander-in-chief of the armed forces. Should the president abuse the powers of the office, Congress can remove them through the impeachment process. Likewise, federal judges are subject to impeachment. The idea is that assertions of power are counterbalanced by other assertions of power. Or as James Madison put it in Federalist No. 51, "Ambition must be made to counteract ambition."

Perhaps, the most important check on Congress and the executive branch is the power of judicial review. This power is not explicitly provided for in the Constitution; it was assumed by the Supreme Court in *Marbury v. Madison*. Using this power, the Supreme Court has effectively forced the resignation of one president (Richard Nixon)[2] and facilitated the inauguration of another (George W. Bush).[3] It has had major impacts on public policy, especially with respect to civil rights and liberties.

CHECKS AND BALANCES: Mechanisms built into a constitution to prevent one branch from exerting authority without influence from the other branches.

For instance, racial segregation required by law would not have ended when it did were it not for *Brown v. Board of Education of Topeka* (1954)[4] and a host of subsequent judicial decisions. Moreover, homosexual activity would remain a crime in many states but for the Court's landmark decision in *Lawrence v. Texas* (2003).[5]

Delegation of Legislative Power

The separation of powers is not absolute. In the modern era, with the growth of the administrative state, Congress has delegated the power to enact rules and regulations to executive agencies. Consider, for instance, the copious rules adopted by the Environmental Protection Agency, the Consumer Product Safety Commission, the Federal Communications Commission, and the myriad other federal agencies. The same phenomenon occurs at the state level and, to a lesser extent, in local government. In some instances, executive agencies actually define criminal conduct. For example, under the federal Endangered Species Act,[6] the U.S. Fish and Wildlife Service and the National Marine Fisheries Service determine which species are listed as endangered. To knowingly kill an animal listed as endangered without securing the necessary permit is a crime and can expose the offender to a substantial fine and even imprisonment.

Some argue that the delegation of legislative power to agencies within the executive branch is a violation of the separation of powers principle. The Supreme Court has embraced this argument in principle, but only rarely has it struck down an act of Congress on this basis. The most notable example of this occurred in 1935, when the Court struck down the National Industrial Recovery Act (NIRA),[7] the cornerstone of President Roosevelt's New Deal. Under the NIRA, Congress authorized the president to establish an agency to create "codes of fair competition" for major industries. The Schechter Poultry Corporation, a Long Island-based chicken wholesaler, was criminally prosecuted for eighteen violations of the Live Poultry Code promulgated under the NIRA. Ultimately, the company avoided criminal liability when the Supreme Court unanimously declared the NIRA unconstitutional. Writing for the Court in *Schechter Poultry Corp. v. United States* (1935),[8] Chief Justice Charles Evans Hughes noted that under the NIRA, "the discretion of the President in approving or prescribing codes, and thus enacting laws for the government of trade and industry throughout the country, is virtually unfettered." In a concurring opinion, Justice Benjamin Cardozo said of the statute, "This is delegation running riot."

Clearly, the contemporary Supreme Court would not permit Congress to delegate its lawmaking power wholesale to an executive agency. But minimal and moderate delegations have routinely passed muster. Indeed, not since the *Schechter* decision has the Court struck down an act of Congress for violating the nondelegation doctrine. *Mistretta v. United States* (1989)[9] nicely illustrates the tendency of the modern Court in this area. Under the Sentencing Reform Act of 1984,[10] Congress created the United States Sentencing Commission and delegated to it the power to create sentencing guidelines for the federal courts. The idea was to reduce disparities that plagued criminal sentencing. The Sentencing Commission was located in the judicial branch; indeed, three of its seven members were selected from the ranks of federal judges. John Mistretta, who had been convicted of selling cocaine, challenged his sentence on the grounds that the sentencing guidelines represented an unconstitutional delegation of legislative power. By an 8–1 vote, the Supreme Court rejected Mistretta's challenge. In upholding Congress' decision to allow an agency of the judicial branch to set policy governing criminal sentencing, Justice Harry Blackmun wrote that "our jurisprudence has been driven by a practical understanding that, in our increasingly complex society, replete with ever-changing and more technical problems, Congress simply cannot do its job absent an ability to delegate power under broad general directives."

In one of his most memorable dissenting opinions, Justice Antonin Scalia accused the Congress of creating "a sort of junior varsity Congress."

Federalism

The one feature that most defines the American constitutional system is federalism—the division of sovereignty between the national government and the fifty state governments. This means the national government and each of the fifty states has its own governmental machinery—its own legislature, its own executive branch, and its own courts. In terms of criminal justice, each has its own criminal laws, law enforcement agencies, prosecutors, and prisons. The original idea was that the national government and the states would have different spheres of activity, thus minimizing the opportunity for conflict. Of course, as time has passed and the nation has evolved, the national government has come to be much more involved in matters historically left to the states, including criminal justice. The growth of federal activity in the domestic sphere has markedly changed the nature of the federal system. The term cooperative federalism is often used to characterize the modern relationship between the national government and the states. To be sure, there is considerable cooperation between the two levels of government in areas such as transportation, education, health care, environmental protection, and criminal justice. At the same time, the potential for conflict between levels of government has increased.

Under the Supremacy Clause of Article VI of the Constitution, federal laws trump countervailing state laws as long as the former are constitutional. In *McCulloch v. Maryland* (1819),[11] the Supreme Court struck down a Maryland law imposing a tax on notes issued by a bank chartered by the federal government. Writing for the Court, Chief Justice John Marshall asserted that "the power to tax involves the power to destroy" and that "the power to destroy may defeat and render useless the power to create. ..." In Marshall's view, the state of Maryland could not be permitted to destroy, or even inhibit, an institution legitimately created by the national government. The *McCulloch* decision, one of the bedrocks of American constitutional law, established firmly the doctrine of national supremacy.

In the modern era, the Supreme Court has gone so far as to say that state laws are unconstitutional if they intrude into areas of federal control, even in the absence of an overt conflict of laws. This is known as the doctrine of preemption. For example, in *Arizona v. United States* (2012),[12] the Court struck down several provisions of an Arizona law that addressed the issue of illegal immigration. In a 5–4 decision, the Court

COOPERATIVE FEDERALISM: The modern notion of federalism, stressing cooperation between the national and the state and local governments.

NATIONAL SUPREMACY: The doctrine holding that when federal and state powers collide, the federal government prevails, assuming the federal government's action is constitutional.

PREEMPTION: The doctrine that federal law supersedes state law, either expressly or by implication; can also apply to state law superseding local law.

held that these provisions were preempted by federal law. Justice Anthony Kennedy wrote the Court's majority opinion, observing, "Federal law makes a single sovereign responsible for maintaining a comprehensive and unified system to keep track of aliens within the Nation's borders."[13] (We discuss this matter in greater detail in chapter 10, which addresses arrest and investigatory detention.)

Legalization of Marijuana: A Case Study in Federalism

One of the most fascinating case studies in modern federalism involves the issue of marijuana legalization. The sale and possession of marijuana has been illegal under federal and state laws for many decades. But in recent years, a number of states have legalized marijuana for medical and even recreational use. Does this place them in conflict with federal law? Arguably not, as states are not obligated to criminalize something the federal government has chosen to make a crime. At the same time, the fact that a state has chosen to legalize marijuana does not immunize persons in that state from federal prosecution, as persons are subject to the jurisdiction of both sovereigns.

THE CONSTITUTION IN ACTION
The Ongoing Evolution of U.S. Marijuana Policies

In light of the elaborate regime of federal drug laws in effect in the United States today, it may seem difficult to fathom the laws of 1600s colonial America, where Maryland, Pennsylvania, and Virginia allowed hemp, which is of the same species as the cannabis plant,[14] to be used as currency—with Connecticut, Massachusetts, and Virginia actually requiring farmers to grow hemp. Even through the 1800s, drug use remained largely unregulated throughout the United States.

That would change at the turn of the twentieth century. Labeling requirements for medicinal products that contained marijuana were required by the Pure Food and Drug Act of 1906. But the movement to create laws impacting drug possession would not be initiated through federal action, arising instead through the states. In 1913, California, Indiana, Maine, and Wyoming would become the first states to prohibit marijuana. The first major federal drug law would arrive the following year with passage of the Harrison Act,[15] which impacted opiates and coca products; this law did not ban possession but, instead, required the payment of a tax on the distribution, importation, or production of such substances.

During the Prohibition era, some of the criminal infrastructure that arose to distribute alcohol also turned to trafficking in drugs, and by 1931, twenty-nine states had banned possession of marijuana—with scholars today debating whether fears of use by immigrant populations might have driven such bans.[16] In turn, the Federal Bureau of Narcotics was created in 1930. (It became the Drug Enforcement Administration in 1973.) The Marihuana Tax Act,[17] passed by Congress in 1937, required the payment of a tax on the transfer of cannabis products. As we will discuss in chapter 11, this law was struck down by the Supreme Court in 1969 for violating the self-incrimination protections of the Fifth Amendment.[18]

It would not take Congress long to respond to that decision, though, with passage of a new comprehensive federal drug law. The Controlled Substances Act of 1970 placed drugs into "Schedules," with Schedule I drugs being the most tightly regulated, due to what Congress deemed to be a lack of accepted medical uses and a high potential for addiction; criminal penalties were attached to the production, distribution, or possession of Schedule I drugs like marijuana and Schedule II drugs like cocaine.[19]

By the 1990s, however, federalism would essentially drive this process in reverse, as states initiated the process of legalizing marijuana. In 1996, California became the first to legalize marijuana for medicinal purposes, and four more states would do so through ballot initiatives, before Hawaii became the first to legalize it through its state legislature in 2000. Today, more than thirty states allow for some form of medicinal usage.

Recreational possession of marijuana, meaning possession for any reason and not just medicinal purposes—usually with quantity limitations, cultivation licensing requirements, and even some public place limitations—was first brought about through ballot initiatives in the states of Colorado and Washington in 2012. Today, legalization of marijuana for "recreational purposes" has passed in more than 20 states, largely through statewide votes but with some state legislatures recently leading the way.[20]

Even as states continue to legalize marijuana possession, it still remains illegal under the federal Controlled Substances Act, whether for medical or recreational reasons. Yet no presidential administration since 2005 has attempted to use the Department of Justice to aggressively enforce federal marijuana laws in the states. In this regard, a 2013 memorandum from the Office of the Attorney General to all federal prosecutors essentially called for not enforcing federal drug laws in states that chose to legalize marijuana, with limited exceptions to this idea crafted for matters like gang-related trafficking and usage by minors.[21] The federal government *could* use its superior fiscal resources to induce the states that have legalized marijuana to reverse course, but that appears unlikely to occur. If anything, the coming years will likely see the relaxation of the federal prohibition of cannabis.[22]

In December 2020, a majority in the U.S. House of Representatives voted to remove federal penalties for marijuana possession; no action was taken in the U.S. Senate. In June 2021, Justice Clarence Thomas, one of the most conservative members of the Supreme Court, went so far as to suggest that the federal law criminalizing marijuana "may no longer be necessary."[23]

The Legislative Branch of Government

Congress and the fifty state legislatures exist primarily to make laws, including the statutes that define crimes and punishments. It is axiomatic in our legal system that one cannot be prosecuted for a crime in the absence of a law making one's action a crime. What are the sources and limits of legislative power in the American constitutional system?

> **STATUTES:** Generally applicable laws enacted by legislatures.

State Legislative Powers

State legislatures were in operation under new state constitutions for more than a decade before the First Congress convened under the U.S. Constitution in March of 1789. One of the first orders of business for the new state legislatures was the reception of the English common law. Rather than enact statutes to address the many issues of civil and criminal law, it made sense to simply embrace the common law. The common law had been in effect during the colonial period and was well-known to lawyers, judges, and legislators. Of course, over time, the common law would be codified, so today, all states have a criminal code based on statutes enacted by the legislature.[24] Even though these codes stemmed from English common law, many antiquated common-law principles have been abolished. For example, rape is now a gender-neutral offense, and one can be guilty of raping one's spouse. And new offenses, such as cybercrimes and environmental crimes, have been introduced into to state criminal codes.

POLICE POWER: The power of a state legislature to enact laws to protect public order, health, safety, welfare, and decency.

The state legislatures are vested with police power (i.e., the authority to enact laws governing the public health, safety, order, morality, and welfare). In forging legislation, state legislatures are not dependent on positive grants of legislative power in their respective state constitutions. In other words, the police power is an inherent power of the state legislatures. It is also a plenary power, subject only to specific constitutional limitations and to a general requirement of "reasonableness."[25] In a concurring opinion in *The License Cases* (1847),[26] Justice John McLean elaborated on the scope of these police powers by noting the following:

> In all matters of government, and especially of police, a wide discretion is necessary. It is not susceptible of an exact limitation, but must be exercised under the changing exigencies of society. In the progress of population, of wealth, and of civilization, new and vicious indulgencies spring up, which require restraints that can only be imposed by the legislative power. When this power shall be exerted, how far it shall be carried, and where it shall cease, must mainly depend upon the evil to be remedied. [27]

Ballot Initiatives and Referenda

BALLOT INITIATIVE: A process through which a requisite number of voters can petition a state legislature to hold a statewide referendum on an issue of public policy.

REFERENDUM: An election in which the voters decide a question of policy, typically regarding the passage or repeal of a state statute or constitutional provision.

VICTIMS' RIGHTS: Refers to the various rights possessed by victims of crimes.

While most criminal justice policy is, in fact, established by state legislatures, in about half of the states, individual residents are permitted to impact the legislative process via ballot initiatives and referenda. Typically, a ballot initiative (or ballot measure) involves circulating a petition with the text of a proposed law or state constitutional amendment. If a requisite number of signatures is met,[28] then the petition is placed before the voters in a referendum. A majority of voters choosing the "Yes" option generally results in the petition becoming a law, although some states may require a supermajority of 55 or 60 percent, and even initiatives that do pass can be subject to judicial review and funding from state legislative budgets. As previously noted, marijuana legalization has primarily occurred via this process.[29]

An important issue affecting criminal justice that has been addressed recently via initiative and referendum is that of victims' rights. Since 2008, more than a dozen states have passed versions of something called "Marsy's Law."[30] These laws are named after Marsy Nicholas, who was murdered in California in 1983, and although versions vary from state to state, all of them require some form of notification to crime victims and their families when court hearings are held in their respective cases.

Along the same lines, a referendum can be held simply to abolish an existing law. Recently, this process was employed in an attempt to abolish the death penalty in some states. However, in 2016, a majority of voters in California, Nebraska, and Oklahoma rejected abolition attempts and retained capital punishment in their respective states.

It is important to note that the United States Constitution makes no provision for initiative and referendum. To the Founding Fathers, this form of direct democracy was unthinkable. Indeed, for them, even representative democracy was dangerous if left unchecked by constitutional limitations.

Legislative Powers of Local Governments

Local governments have their own lawmaking bodies, usually denominated as county commissions, city and town councils, boards of supervisors, and so on. These bodies do not possess inherent legislative powers but, rather, depend on grants of power from their respective state legislatures. Indeed, local governments are not sovereign entities; they owe their very existence to their respective state constitutions and statutes.

Local governing bodies possess limited legislative powers. They may enact ordinances dealing with local matters and effective only within their geographical jurisdictions. Even so, local ordinances are subject to preemption by state legislation. And of course, they are bound to respect constitutional limitations. Local ordinances can define crimes but only misdemeanors punishable by relatively small monetary fines and/or short terms of incarceration in city or county jails. Examples include traffic violations, public intoxication, disorderly conduct, criminal trespass, unlawful assembly, setting off fireworks, making excessive noise after midnight, having open containers of alcoholic beverages on public streets, and so on. Major crimes, known as felonies, (as well as more serious misdemeanors) are defined in the state criminal codes.

Legislative Authority of Congress

Unlike the state legislatures, Congress's legislative power is limited to positive grants of power in the federal Constitution. One finds these grants of power in Article I, Section 8 of the Constitution as well as in several constitutional amendments. The enumerated powers of Congress—to tax, spend, declare war, coin money, and so on—are extremely important. Equally important are its implied powers under the Necessary and Proper Clause, which authorizes Congress "[t]o make all Laws which shall be necessary and proper for carrying into Execution

DIRECT DEMOCRACY: A government by the people directly, whereby the people vote directly on policy making rather than electing representatives who craft policy on behalf of society.

REPRESENTATIVE DEMOCRACY: A system in which voters elect representatives to make decisions on their behalf.

ORDINANCES: Laws enacted by local governing bodies.

MISDEMEANORS: Less serious crimes for which the maximum penalty is a fine or a term of incarceration of less than one year.

FELONIES: More serious crimes that carry prison sentences usually greater than one year.

ENUMERATED POWERS: Legislative powers explicitly stated in a constitution.

IMPLIED POWERS: Legislative powers implied by constitutional language.

the [enumerated] Powers, and all other Powers vested by this Constitution in the Government of the United States, or in any Department or Officer thereof."

In *McCulloch v. Maryland* (1819), the Supreme Court upheld the establishment of a national bank, even though Congress was not explicitly authorized to do so. In one of his most noteworthy opinions, Chief Justice John Marshall reasoned that the creation of a national bank was "necessary and proper" to the execution of Congress's enumerated fiscal powers. Marshall stated the doctrine of implied powers as follows: "Let the end be legitimate, let it be within the scope of the constitution, and all means which are appropriate, which are plainly adapted to that end, which are not prohibited, but consist with the letter and spirit of the constitution, are constitutional." Using its implied powers, Congress has enacted many measures that might be constitutionally questionable otherwise. The military draft is related to the enumerated power to raise and support and army. The creation of the Internal Revenue Service is in furtherance of Congress' power to tax. Are these measures, strictly speaking, both "necessary" and "proper"? Ever since *McCulloch v. Maryland*, the federal courts have been quite deferential to Congress regarding the scope of its implied powers.

FOCUS ON LAW ENFORCEMENT

Congress Takes Action to Assist 9/11 First Responders

Some of the most significant acts of bravery on the part of law enforcement officers and fire fighters occurred on September 11, 2001, when those who have come to be known as "first responders" provided rescue and recovery efforts at the primary sites of the terrorist attacks, including the World Trade Center, the Pentagon, and the crash site of United Airlines Flight 93 in Shanksville, Pennsylvania. Sadly, exposure to dust and other particles that were thrust into the air as a result of the attacks, particularly from the collapse of the World Trade Center's Twin Towers, left many first responders and other nearby survivors with life-altering medical conditions.

A 2021 article in *Scientific American* summarized these issues as follows: "Nearly 3,000 people died during the deadliest terrorist attack in world history. But in the two decades since then, the number of deaths among survivors and responders—who spent months inhaling the noxious dust, chemicals, fumes and fibers from the debris—has continued creeping up. Researchers have identified more than 60 types of cancer and about two dozen other conditions that are linked to Ground Zero exposures. As of today, at least 4,627 responders and survivors enrolled in the World Trade Center (WTC) Health Program have died."[31]

The World Trade Center Health Program was created when Congress passed the James Zadroga 9/11 Health and Compensation Act.[32] According to the Centers for Disease Control (CDC), which oversees the program, it "offers high-quality, compassionate healthcare to those directly affected by the September 11th terrorist attacks," by offering "medical monitoring and treatment for emergency responders, recovery and cleanup workers, and volunteers who helped at the World Trade Center, the Pentagon, and the crash site near Shanksville, Pennsylvania."[33] More than 80,000 responders and 30,000 survivors have been enrolled in the program since its inception.[34]

The same 2010 law also created the 9/11 Victim Compensation Fund, which provides financial assistance to families of the deceased and survivors. That law expired on October 1, 2015, but following testimony in front of Congress from comedian Jon Stewart and a group of first responders, the World Trade Center Health Program was reauthorized in December 2015 with a directive for it to remain in place until 2090; the 9/11 Victim Compensation Fund was, at that time, reauthorized for five years. However, by September 2018, the special master tasked with overseeing it revealed issues with funding for the 9/11 Victim Compensation Fund, claiming that some 18,000 pending claims would be cut by 50% and future payouts would be reduced by 70%.

In 2019, though, Congress passed the Never Forget the Heroes: James Zadroga, Ray Pfeifer, and Luis Alvarez Permanent Authorization of the September 11th Victim

Compensation Fund Act.[35] This law provided financial backing of the fund through 2090, it allowed payment of past claims that were underpaid, and it permitted the program to make adjustments for inflation.

As of 2021, data indicated that "[a]bout 74 percent of responders in the WTC Health Program have been diagnosed with at least one physical or mental health condition directly linked to 9/11 exposure, including 20 percent with cancer and 28 percent with a mental health condition."[36] All of this, of course, connects to these individuals bravely accepting the challenges of their jobs on September 11, 2001.

The Power of Congress to Enact Federal Criminal Laws

In the early days of the Republic, criminal justice was not considered a priority for the national government. The states were responsible for administering the criminal law, which was based largely on the English common law. The vast majority of crimes were offenses against state laws, and states would remain free to prosecute and punish these crimes as they saw fit. Today, the situation is very different.

Title 18 of the U.S. Code, "Crimes and Criminal Procedure," where most federal crimes are codified, contains more than 1,000 specific offenses. Other offenses are scattered throughout the U.S. Code. In fiscal year 2020, the federal courts imposed sentences in 64,659 criminal cases. These cases were most likely to involve immigration offenses (41%), followed by drug offenses (26%) and weapons offenses (12%). The remaining cases involved various and sundry crimes, including fraud, theft, embezzlement, robbery, child pornography, money laundering, and sexual abuse.[37]

What is the source of Congress's power to enact criminal statutes? In Article I, Section 8, Congress is granted the power "[t]o provide for the punishment of counterfeiting the securities and current coin of the United States" and "define and punish piracies and felonies committed on the high seas. ..." These provisions, while important, do not provide a constitutional basis for the creation of a criminal code. However, other enumerated powers, which may not, at first glance, seem to have much to do with the criminal law, provide foundations for the enactment of federal criminal statutes. Chief among these is the Commerce Clause of Article I, Section 8, which gives Congress the power "[t]o regulate Commerce with foreign Nations, and among the several States, and with the Indian Tribes." This has long been interpreted to allow Congress to federalize criminal activity that crosses state lines. For example, the Federal Kidnapping Act,[38] better known as the Lindbergh Law, makes kidnapping a federal crime if the victim is taken across state lines. Likewise, while theft is ordinarily a state offense, taking stolen property across state lines is a federal crime.[39] Similarly, it is a federal offense to take a person across state lines for purposes of prostitution.[40]

Obiter Dicta

"The Federal Government undertakes activities today that would have been unimaginable to the Framers in two senses; first, because the Framers would not have conceived that any government would conduct such activities; and second, because the Framers would not have believed that the Federal Government, rather than the States, would assume such responsibilities. Yet the powers conferred upon the Federal Government by the Constitution were phrased in language broad enough to allow for the expansion of the Federal Government's role."

—*Justice Sandra Day O'Connor, writing for the Court in* New York v. United States, *505 U.S. 144 (1992).*

In the modern era, the Supreme Court has interpreted the Commerce Clause to allow Congress to regulate even those intrastate activities that have a substantial effect on interstate commerce. In turn, under this interpretation, the Commerce Clause provides Congress with something approaching a federal police power. Numerous federal criminal prohibitions, including those aimed at white collar and organized crime, environmental crime, weapons offenses, and even drug offenses are grounded in the Commerce Clause.

As an example of the breadth of this interpretation, consider *Gonzales v. Raich* (2005),[41] where the Court upheld the federal prohibition of simple possession of home-grown marijuana for personal use. Speaking for the Court, Justice John Paul Stevens found that activity to have a substantial relation to interstate commerce and, therefore, deemed it to be well within federal jurisdiction. Specifically, Stevens offered the following observation: "Our case law firmly establishes Congress' power to regulate purely local activities that are part of an economic 'class of activities' that have a substantial effect on interstate commerce." In buttressing this assertion, he cited *Perez v. United States* (1971), which we summarize in the Jurisprudence box below.[42] Stevens also said that "Congress had a rational basis for believing that failure to regulate the intrastate manufacture and possession of marijuana would leave a gaping hole in the [Controlled Substances Act]."

JURISPRUDENCE

Can Loansharking Be a Federal Crime?
Perez v. United States, 402 U.S. 146 (1971)

Perez was convicted of "loansharking" in violation of 18 U.S.C. § 894, which prohibits the collection of debts by extortionate means. On appeal, Perez challenged the constitutionality of the statute, arguing that Congress had no power under the Commerce Clause to criminalize a local activity. In an 8–1 decision, the Supreme Court rejected Perez's argument and upheld the statute. Writing for the Court, Justice William O. Douglas connected "the loanshark racket" to organized crime, which has an adverse impact on interstate commerce. Douglas observed that "loansharking in its national setting is one way organized interstate crime holds its guns to the heads of the poor and the rich alike and syphons funds from numerous localities to finance its national operations." In dissent, Justice Potter Stewart asserted that "the Framers of the Constitution never intended that the National Government might define as a crime and prosecute such wholly local activity through the enactment of federal criminal laws."

In 2021, Justice Clarence Thomas, who dissented from the 2005 *Raich* decision, railed against the continued viability of that case in light of the federal government's refusal to actually enforce federal marijuana laws in states where it has been legalized. Thomas offered the following declaration as a dissenting opinion in *Akimbo LLC v. United States* (2021),[43] a case in which the high Court refused to grant cert., leaving in place a Tenth Circuit decision that effectively denied IRS tax deductions for business expenses related to a marijuana dispensary that was legally operated under Colorado state law. In a widely publicized opinion, Justice Thomas wrote:

> Whatever the merits of *Raich* when it was decided, federal policies of the past 16 years have greatly undermined its reasoning. Once comprehensive, the Federal Government's current approach is a half-in, half-out regime that simultaneously tolerates and forbids local use of marijuana. This contradictory and unstable state of affairs strains basic principles of federalism and conceals traps for the unwary.

The doctrine of implied powers is also extremely important in providing constitutional justification for the enactment of criminal prohibitions. The following are a few examples:

- If Congress has the authority to establish the Social Security program, which the Supreme Court held that it did in 1937,[44] then it has the implied power to criminalize Social Security fraud.[45]
- If Congress can authorize the construction of federal buildings, which no one doubts that it can, then surely, it can make vandalism of those buildings a federal crime.[46]
- If Congress can create the military draft, itself an exercise of implied powers, then it can criminalize draft evasion as a second-order implied power.[47]

The broad interpretation of the Commerce Clause and the other enumerated powers, along with the doctrine of implied powers, provides Congress a basis to enact criminal laws with respect to nearly any activity. Thus, it is important for students of criminal justice to recognize that some illegal acts could yield either a state or federal prosecution—or even both. Drug trafficking is a classic example, since both state and federal laws criminalize trafficking of controlled substances. As a result, under the principle of dual sovereignty, which indicates that state and federal courts exist as separate entities, it is possible for charges to be brought in both state and federal court for such an offense.[48] In these situations, prosecutors at the state and federal level likely would communicate with one another to determine an appropriate course of action in regard to which charges would be brought into court first. For example, former Minnesota Police Officer Derek Chauvin was found guilty of second-degree murder in the death of George Floyd; the trial judge sentenced Chauvin to 22.5 years in state prison. Subsequently, the Department of Justice brought federal charges against Chauvin for violating Floyd's civil rights; a plea deal was reached in that matter under which Chauvin would plead guilty but serve his 252-month federal sentence concurrent with—or at the same time as—his state sentence; his incarceration for both sentences would occur in federal prison. (In chapter 11, we will discuss the Supreme Court's refusal to apply the concept of Double Jeopardy in contexts like this.)

THE CONSTITUTION IN ACTION
The Supremacy Clause and Federal Legalization of Hemp

Because the Supremacy Clause of Article VI of the U.S. Constitution indicates that federal law trumps state law in those situations in which the two are in conflict, the passage of a federal law not only impacts the activities of federal law enforcement personnel but also the day-to-day activities of state and local law enforcement. A key example can be in seen in federal policy regarding hemp—a plant that is similar to marijuana but with no more than 0.3% THC (tetrahydrocannabinol), which is the active ingredient in marijuana that creates a "high." Hemp plants are used for many purposes, such as making beer, clothing, rope, soap, shampoo, and even building materials.

An act of Congress legalized hemp throughout the United States on January 1, 2019, removing it from the purview of the Controlled Substances Act. This shift was not a part of some broad-ranging drug reform bill but, rather, arose through a provision inserted in the Agriculture Improvement Act of 2018, also known as the Farm Bill of 2018.[49]

Some states have responded to the federal legalization of hemp by banning the smoking of hemp, and some allow possession of hemp but ban its distribution or require a license to grow it.[50] For law enforcement officials at the local level, an issue arises from the fact that hemp and marijuana plants look so similar and have similar odors. As a result, obtaining a criminal conviction for marijuana possession could require a lab test that demonstrates a particular plant contains more than 0.3% THC. That, in turn, can be a costly proposition in an area where numerous marijuana possession cases are prosecuted.

(continued)

A specific derivative of hemp that has gained visibility recently is CBD, which is an acronym for cannabidiol. Myriad stores selling CDB products, including edibles, lotions, and even non-THC flowers, have spread throughout the United States since hemp was legalized. Here, too, enforcing state laws that might ban the use of certain gummy or candy products could require extensive lab testing. Ultimately, the federal legalization of hemp products has tangible consequences for officers who investigate drug possession matters, lab technicians tasked with testing evidence, and prosecutors who must prove criminal cases to juries beyond a reasonable doubt.

The Executive Branch

The executive branch of government participates in the criminal justice system in a variety of ways, including law enforcement, prosecution, and the operation of jails and prisons. Chief executives—presidents, governors, and mayors—set the tone for criminal justice policy and exercise powers that affect law enforcement and prosecution.

Law Enforcement Agencies

At the federal level, with the explosive growth of the federal criminal law, there are myriad law enforcement agencies. The oldest is the U.S. Marshall's Service, which dates back to 1789. It is located within the U.S. Department of Justice (DOJ), along with the Federal Bureau of Investigation (FBI), the Drug Enforcement Administration (DEA), and the Bureau of Alcohol, Tobacco, Firearms, and Explosives (ATF). While the DOJ houses the most prominent law enforcement agencies, there are more than sixty federal agencies that have criminal enforcement authority. These include the Department of Homeland Security, the Internal Revenue Service, the U.S. Postal Service, the Environmental Protection Agency, the National Park Service, the U.S. Forest Service, and the U.S. Fish and Wildlife Service, just to name a few. The armed forces also have their own police agencies, including the well-known Naval Criminal Investigative Service (NCIS) and the U.S. Army's Military Police Corps (MPs).

At the local level, law enforcement is performed by county sheriffs and their deputies, municipal police departments, and, in some jurisdictions, constables. At the state level, there are police agencies, often referred to as state troopers or the highway patrol. Every state has some sort of investigatory agency, such as the Florida Department of Law Enforcement and the Kentucky Department of Criminal Investigation. States also have wildlife officers and park rangers with criminal law enforcement responsibilities.

Prosecutorial Agencies

Prosecutors are lawyers who represent the government in criminal cases. At the federal level, the chief prosecutors are the U.S. attorneys, who are part of the Department of Justice, headed by the attorney general. There is one U.S. attorney for each of the ninety-four federal judicial districts. U.S. Attorneys are appointed by the president with the consent of the Senate and serve four-year terms (but can be fired by the president before their terms are complete).[51]

Every state has its own office of attorney general, but most state prosecutions are brought by state attorneys or district attorneys. City and county attorneys sometimes prosecute violations of local ordinances in city or county courts. State and local prosecutors are typically elected but are sometimes appointed. State laws vary considerably in this regard.

THE CONSTITUTION IN ACTION
The U.S. Department of Justice

The evolution of constitutional law is not entirely the product of the federal courts. The U.S. Department of Justice (DOJ) plays a key role in interpreting and applying—and, in some situations, bringing cases that spur the creation of—Supreme Court precedent. Established in 1789 as an entity called the Office of the Attorney General, the DOJ can be thought of as the federal government's "legal office." The head of the DOJ is the attorney general, who is appointed by the president with approval of a majority vote in the U.S. Senate. The AG serves as a member of the U.S. Cabinet and can be fired by the president. In June 2021, Attorney General Merrick Garland showed how powerful his office can be when he ordered a halt to all federal executions. Previously, we have noted that the AG plays an important role in determining which federal crimes should be targeted by federal law enforcement resources.

Another important figure within the DOJ is the solicitor general (SG), who is the fourth-highest official in the department. Any time the United States is a party to a case at the Supreme Court—such as when an executive order or act of Congress is being evaluated, the SG advocates for the position of the federal government. The Office of the Solicitor General also determines whether to appeal cases from the Circuit Courts when the United States is the losing party.

The DOJ is comprised of a number of "divisions." For example, the Civil Division represents the position of the government in civil cases, which can include monetary suits against the United States. This division also brings lawsuits to recover money lost through criminal activity, such as fraud related to federal programs or federally insured loans. There is an Antitrust Division that implements antitrust laws through both civil and criminal enforcement actions—often after referral from the Securities and Exchange Commission. There is also a Civil Rights Division, which can play a crucial role in applying federal discrimination laws by bringing forth criminal prosecutions and civil lawsuits. The Criminal Division, as the name aptly indicates, plays a role in investigations and prosecutions related to violations of federal criminal law.

Along these lines, it is important to note that, when it comes to enforcement of criminal statutes, administrative agencies of the federal government do not have prosecutorial authority. When they uncover evidence of criminal wrongdoing, they must refer the case to the DOJ for criminal prosecution.

The DOJ also houses five agencies that have critical roles in the criminal justice system. First, the U.S. Marshals Service (USMS) is the oldest of all federal law enforcement agencies, having been created by Congress in 1789. Today, it plays a lead role in the following law enforcement contexts: tracking fugitives who cross state lines, executing arrest warrants issued by federal judges, and moving federal prisoners who might be transferred from one correctional facility to another. The USMS also oversees and operates the Witness Protection Program, which provides new identities to key witnesses in cases when the safety of those individuals might have been compromised as a result of providing testimony against an accused criminal.

Next, there is the Federal Bureau of Investigation (FBI), which was established as the Bureau of Investigation in 1908. The FBI is largely an investigatory arm of the DOJ, and agents are tasked with investigating violations of federal criminal laws, including those that deal with the following: civil rights offenses, organized crime, terrorism, cybercrimes, espionage, and white-collar crimes like fraud. As noted earlier, the DOJ also contains the Bureau of Alcohol, Tobacco, Firearms, and Explosives (ATF); this agency is charged with investigating violations of federal laws and regulations that address alcoholic beverages, tobacco, guns, and explosives. The ATF can also issue permits and licenses for the possession of certain weapons, as we will discuss in chapter 6.[52]

Additionally, the DOJ contains the Drug Enforcement Administration (DEA), which plays an important role in enforcing federal drug laws. And finally, the DOJ also houses the Bureau of Prisons (BOP), which was created in 1930 for the purpose of overseeing and administering the federal prison system. Overall, the DOJ plays a crucial role in terms of applying criminal justice principles at the federal level.

Prosecutorial Discretion

Typically, prosecutors have enormous discretion in deciding whether to bring criminal charges and, if so, which particular charges to file. They also determine the course of a prosecution, including whether to offer a plea deal, what strategy to follow at trial, and what penalties to seek upon conviction. Justice Potter Stewart, speaking for the Supreme Court in *Bordenkircher v. Hayes* (1978),[53] noted that "so long as the prosecutor has probable cause to believe that the accused committed an offense defined by statute, the decision whether or not to prosecute, and what charge to file or bring before a grand jury, generally rests entirely in his discretion." Justice Stewart also recognized that "the breadth of discretion that our country's legal system vests in prosecuting attorneys carries with it the potential for both individual and institutional abuse." Previously, in *Oyler v. Boles* (1962),[54] the Court had said that the decision to prosecute must not be based on "an unjustifiable standard such as race, religion, or other arbitrary classification." Even so, the Court has signaled its unwillingness to scrutinize the exercise of **prosecutorial discretion**. Justice Lewis Powell, writing for the Court in *Wayte v. United States* (1985),[55] observed:

> Examining the basis of a prosecution delays the criminal proceeding, threatens to chill law enforcement by subjecting the prosecutor's motives and decision making to outside inquiry, and may undermine prosecutorial effectiveness by revealing the Government's enforcement policy. All these are substantial concerns that make the courts properly hesitant to examine the decision whether to prosecute.

One of the more interesting recent developments with respect to prosecutorial discretion has been the election of progressive prosecutors who refuse to prosecute people under laws of which they disapprove.[56] These tend to be laws enacted by Republican-controlled state legislatures and deal with matters such as abortion, voting, and protest activity. Is this lawlessness or just another example of necessary checks and balances?

PROSECUTORIAL DISCRETION: The authority of prosecutors to decide whether to file criminal charges and, if so, which charges to bring.

JURISPRUDENCE

A Fisherman Faces Federal Charges for Oversized Red Grouper
Yates v. United States, 574 U.S. 528 (2015)

There are several facets to prosecutorial discretion. The first key aspect involves whether to charge. Another involves whether to plea bargain—perhaps, through seeking a reduced sentence in exchange for a guilty plea. Determining which specific crime to charge also falls within the purview of prosecutorial discretion.

An apt example comes from the Supreme Court decision in *Yates v. United States* (2015).

In this case, a fisherman named John Yates was arrested for an alleged violation of a federal law called the Sarbanes–Oxley Act. This law was passed by Congress in response to the ENRON scandal of the early 2000s, which involved a company that created false accounting documents for the purposes of artificially inflating stock prices. As the investigation in that case ramped up, ENRON employees shredded documents to eliminate evidence of wrongdoing. Accordingly, a key component of the Sarbanes-Oxley Act makes it a federal crime to destroy "records" and "tangible objects" germane to a criminal investigation.

However, in the case at hand, Mr. Yates was not some kind of corporate executive. Rather, he was captaining a fishing boat off the coast of Florida. The criminal case began not through an investigation of the FBI but, rather, when an official from the Florida Fish and Wildlife Conservation Commission boarded the boat. That official also was deputized to work for a federal agency called the National Marine Fisheries Service, which is housed within the Department of Commerce. The agent boarded Yates's boat to conduct a routine inspection of the sizes of fish that had been caught by Yates and his crew. Federal regulations at the time required that red grouper be at least twenty inches in length to be caught and harvested.[57]

Following his inspection of all fish on the vessel, the agent announced that he had found seventy-two fish that were under twenty inches. These "illegal" fish were placed into their own wooden crates, and the agent gave orders for these crates to be turned over to him when the boat returned to shore. A citation was the expected consequence.

After four days passed, the boat returned to shore, and the same agent opened the crates. But many of the undersized fish were gone. During questioning by the agent, one crew member admitted that these fish had been thrown overboard at Yates's direction. The matter was then referred to a U.S. attorney's office in Florida.

After thirty-two months had passed, a criminal case was brought against Yates for violating the Sarbanes–Oxley Act, on the theory that he had destroyed evidence germane to a criminal investigation. Following a trial, he was convicted and sentenced to thirty days in prison. Following a lengthy appeals process that spanned nearly a decade, Yates's conviction was reversed by the Supreme Court, with the majority finding that the legislative intent underlying Sarbanes–Oxley was incompatible with the assertion that a fish was covered by the meaning of terms like "document," "record," or "tangible object." Because the items that the law specifically banned a person from destroying were not at hand here, Yates's conviction was overturned. In the end, the Supreme Court's majority found that the prosecutor's attempt to apply this law to the conduct at hand did not comport with the legislative intent evinced by key words in the statute.

Regulatory Agencies

As we noted in chapter 1, one of the hallmarks of modern American government is the proliferation of regulatory agencies at the federal, state, and even local level. These agencies are endowed with authority to make and enforce regulations within specific jurisdictional areas. For instance, the Federal Aviation Administration makes and enforces regulations dealing with civilian aviation. Enforcement of agency regulations usually involves a monetary fine or other civil penalty, as regulatory agencies lack the authority to bring a criminal case on their own. However, when they uncover evidence of criminal wrongdoing, they can refer matters to the appropriate prosecutorial agencies.

Criminal Referrals

At the federal level, regulatory agencies can refer matters to the Department of Justice for criminal prosecution. Agencies that are more likely to do so include the Environmental Protection Agency (EPA), which investigates environmental offenses, and the Securities and Exchange Commission, which reviews abnormal stock transactions. A recent example from another agency appeared in the midst of the COVID-19 pandemic. In May 2020, the Small Business Administration (SBA) referred a matter to the Department of Justice seeking criminal charges against two Rhode Island businessmen who submitted false documents to fraudulently obtain

Paycheck Protection Program loans from the SBA. These were the first (of many) criminal charges brought against parties who attempted to take advantage of federal loans provided by an act of Congress to assist struggling businesses.[58] The actual criminal charges filed by the Department of Justice included conspiracy to commit bank fraud and conspiracy to make false statements.[59]

Another instructive example comes from a matter that stemmed from a Food and Drug Administration (FDA) investigation into a salmonella outbreak emanating from tainted peanut butter products. Nine people died as a result of illnesses stemming from this outbreak, and hundreds more became ill. As we will note in later chapters, a "responsible corporate officer" can be brought into court for crimes allegedly connected to a company's actions. Accordingly, in 2015, a man named Stewart Parnell, who was the CEO of Peanut Corp. of America, was charged with more than 70 federal crimes related to this salmonella outbreak; these offenses included wire fraud, conspiracy, knowingly shipping tainted food across state lines, and obstruction of justice. Evidence against him included copies of company emails indicating he authorized the shipped of food products that he knew contained a risk of spreading salmonella. His sentence of 28 years in federal prison is thought to be the most severe punishment levied against a company executive in a case that addressed tainted food products.

In some situations, the DOJ may be slow to bring criminal cases, even as agencies—or impacted businesses—request action. For example, in 2021, the Federal Aviation Administration indicated that more than 3,000 incidents of unruly passengers had been reported on U.S. flights, a massive increase over the usual number of 100 to 150 such incidents that occur in a typical year.[60] The increase was attributed in part to noncompliance with mask regulations. The FAA holds the power to issue monetary fines but lacks the ability to bring a criminal case. Thus, in June 2021, a coalition of U.S.-based air carriers sent a letter to Attorney General Merrick Garland requesting that the Department of Justice strongly consider bringing federal criminal prosecutions for assaults committed on airplanes.[61]

Jails and Prisons

County jails usually are under the control of the sheriff. City jails are often run by municipal police departments. Every state has its own agency for the administration of prisons, often called the Department of Corrections. At the federal level, the Bureau of Prisons, located within DOJ, operates the federal government's prison system. In recent decades, the federal government and many states have contracted with private companies to operate prisons for profit. As of 2022, about 8% of the nation's prisoners are housed in private prisons.[62]

For most of the nation's history, courts paid little attention to the rights of prisoners. Conditions of confinement were often unsafe and unsanitary, with inmates being provided very poor nutrition and little in the way of education or health care. That began to change in the 1970s, as the Supreme Court issued a series of decisions on prisoners' rights. (We will discuss these decisions in some detail in chapter 14.)

Today, there are nearly two million people incarcerated in the nation's prisons and jails, an incarceration rate higher than any of the world's other democracies. To a large extent, mass incarceration—also known to some as the "carceral state"—reflects public policy decisions made decades ago during a time of rising crime rates.[63] Prisons and jails today tend to be overcrowded. Moreover, there is little evidence that incarceration results in rehabilitation of offenders. Increasingly, courts and legislators are looking toward alternatives to institutional incarceration, such as house arrest and electronic monitoring.

The Military Justice System

The military is under the control of the president and is, therefore, considered part of the executive branch of government. The set of criminal laws that apply to members of the military is known as the Uniform Code of Military Justice (UCMJ). This Code is established by Congress, pursuant to power authorized under Article I, Section 8 of the U.S. Constitution. Overall, the UCMJ addresses offenses that are typically covered in general laws that address all civilians, but it also includes offenses that are specific to the military, such as desertion.

Violations of the UCMJ are not tried in civilian courts but, rather, are tried in military proceedings, known as courts-martial. According to the Supreme Court's decision in *Solorio v. United States* (1987),[64] a court-martial can be convened to try any active-duty military personnel, regardless of whether the offense in question is "service-connected." The key is simply that a person is an active member of the military.

A court-martial proceeding differs from trials in civilian courts in that military personnel known as judge advocates, who are personnel that serve in the Judge Advocate General's Corps, play key roles. More specifically, a JAG officer can serve as a judge, prosecutor, or defense counsel in a particular case. Executive orders from the president of the United States set rules of evidence in military proceedings, and these rules are written in the *Manual for Courts-Martial.*

In regard to appeals, individual branches of the U.S. Armed Forces can have their own panels for reviewing decisions of courts-martial. Additionally, there is a U.S. Court of Appeals for the Armed Forces, which is comprised of judges who serve for fifteen-year terms after being nominated by the president and confirmed by the Senate; cases from the individual branches of the military can funnel into this appellate court. All military death penalty cases are reviewed by the U.S. Court of Appeals for the Armed Forces, which also has the discretion to hear other matters on appeal—perhaps, at the behest of a judge advocate.

The Role of the Chief Executive

Chief executives often initiate legislative policies that affect criminal justice. For example, the 1994 Crime Bill fostered by the Clinton Administration dramatically increased federal funding for police departments and prisons. It also banned assault weapons for ten years, expanded the scope of the federal death penalty, and required states to establish sex offender registries.[65] The veto power possessed by presidents and governors, and to a lesser extent by local mayors, can also be employed to affect criminal justice policy by blocking legislation.

Appointment and Removal Powers

Through their appointment and removal powers, chief executives can set the tone for the administration of justice. The president appoints federal judges, including Supreme Court justices, subject to the consent of the Senate. However, federal judges serve "during good behavior" and cannot be removed from office except through impeachment. In some states, judges are appointed by governors, although many are elected. In some cities, mayors appoint judges of the local courts. The choices that chief executives make in appointing judges tend to be based, at least to some extent, on considerations of partisanship and ideology. In this way, chief executives have an indirect influence on the development of the law.

Chief executives have varying degrees of control over prosecutors and law enforcement officials. Shortly after taking office in 2017, President Donald Trump requested the resignation of forty-seven U.S. attorneys. The move was politically controversial but certainly not unprecedented. A year and a half later, President Trump obtained the resignation of Attorney General Jeff Sessions, with whom he had a long-running dispute. In perhaps his

IMPEACHMENT: The constitutional mechanism for removing officials from office, usually through a vote taken by members of a legislative body.

UNITARY EXECUTIVE: The theory that the executive branch should be completely under the control of the chief executive.

most controversial exercise of the removal power, President Trump, in 2017, fired FBI director James Comey. Were these firings constitutional?

In *Myers v. United States* (1926),[66] the Supreme Court held that executive branch officials may be removed at will by the president, unchecked by the Congress. A decade later, in *Humphrey's Executor v. United States* (1935),[67] the Court modified this holding somewhat, ruling that Congress can insulate officials of "quasi-legislative" independent agencies (in this case, the Federal Trade Commission) from presidential removal. The Court reaffirmed and amplified this position in *Wiener v. United States* (1958),[68] when it held that the unique nature of independent agencies requires that removal must be for legitimate cause, whether or not Congress has so stipulated. Nevertheless, the attorney general, U.S. attorneys, and the director of the FBI are not part of an independent agency; hence, they remain under direct control of the president.

A key principle underlying a president's ability to remove the head of an executive branch agency is the notion of the unitary executive, which holds that the president controls all of the executive branch bureaucracy. This idea connects to language of the Vesting Clause of the U.S. Constitution's Article II, which says: "The executive Power shall be vested in a President of the United States of America."[69] The Supreme Court has applied this concept in two recent decisions. First, in *Seila Law v. Consumer Financial Protection Bureau* (2020),[70] the Court addressed an act of Congress that provided that the head of a new federal agency called the Consumer Financial Protection Bureau could only be fired for "inefficiency, neglect of duty, or malfeasance." The majority opinion by Chief Justice Roberts ruled that this qualification violated the principle of separation of powers because it precluded the president from a firing an agency head for any reason.[71] The Court reiterated this position a year later in *Collins v. Yellin* (2021),[72] which dealt with an act of Congress that limited the president's ability to remove the head of the Federal Housing Finance Agency; the law in question placed a "for cause" caveat on any firing. The Court again said that such a restriction violated the principle of separation of powers, since Congress was preventing the president from controlling the head of an executive branch agency.

At the state level, governors tend to have less control over prosecutors. In most states, attorneys general, as well as district attorneys, are elected. In such instances, removal from office is left to the voters. At the local level, city and county attorneys tend to be appointed by mayors and serve at their pleasure. As for law enforcement, the heads of state police agencies are often appointed by governors, but state laws usually provide that such officials can only be removed for cause. County sheriffs are elected officials and are not subject to removal by mayors or county executives. City police chiefs, on the other hand, can be removed by mayors or city managers but, generally, only for cause.

Executive Orders, Memoranda, and Directives

Presidents, governors, and mayors all have the authority to issue executive orders to agencies and officials under their control. A **presidential memorandum** (in the past, referred to as a presidential letter) is similar to an **executive order**, but unlike the latter, the former are not numbered and do not have to be published in the *Federal Register*. A **presidential directive** is less formal still and can take the form of an oral communication to a subordinate. Ostensibly, all of these presidential actions could involve orders to actors within the executive branch of government to implement—or, conversely, to not enforce at all—specific federal laws.

Executive orders, memoranda, and directives can have a profound effect on the administration of justice. In the final days of his term, President Trump issued an executive order to enhance the protection of federal law enforcement officers, prosecutors, and judges, principally by allowing them to carry concealed firearms.[73] That same day, he issued an order aimed at reducing criminal liability for violations of agency regulations.[74] However, the latter order was rescinded by President Joe Biden several months later.[75] Reflecting a very different philosophy from that of his predecessor, President Biden issued an executive order instructing the attorney general not to renew contracts with private companies operating criminal detention facilities.[76]

Although there is no specific language in the Constitution authorizing presidents to issue executive orders, the Supreme Court has upheld the practice as an inherent power of the presidency. In the case of *In re Neagle* (1890),[77] the Court upheld an executive order appointing a deputy U.S. Marshall to provide security for a Supreme Court justice. In upholding the order, the Court cited "the general obligation imposed upon the President of the United States by the Constitution to see that the laws be faithfully executed, and the means placed in his hands, both by the Constitution and the laws of the United States, to enable him to do this. ..."[78]

Of course, executive orders must be consistent with statutory and constitutional provisions. In *Korematsu v. United States* (1944),[79] citing the need to protect national security, the Supreme Court upheld President Franklin Roosevelt's infamous executive order authorizing the "relocation" of Japanese Americans during World War II. But eight years later, in *Youngstown Sheet and Tube Co. v. Sawyer* (1952),[80] the Court held that

PRESIDENTIAL MEMORANDUM: An official written directive by the president similar to an executive order but without the requirement that it be published in the *Federal Register*.

EXECUTIVE ORDER: An official written directive issued by the president based on statutory or constitutional authority and published in the *Federal Register*.

PRESIDENTIAL DIRECTIVE: A broad term that includes executive orders, presidential memoranda, and presidential proclamations.

President Truman had transgressed statutory and constitutional limitations when he ordered a temporary federal takeover of the nation's steel mills. Students of constitutional law have long debated whether those two decisions could be reconciled.

The DACA Controversy

President Barack Obama made extensive use of executive orders and memoranda, but perhaps his most significant order came in the form of a directive issued to the Department of Homeland Security. In 2012, President Obama announced the creation of the Deferred Action for Childhood Arrivals (DACA) program and directed the Secretary of Homeland Security to issue a memorandum outlining the policy.[81] The Administration's approach allowed persons who were brought to the United States illegally by their parents to avoid deportation if they met certain criteria.[82] Because Congress had considered and failed to enact a law to accomplish the same thing, critics argued that the president had transcended his constitutional authority and usurped the role of Congress. In 2017, the Trump administration attempted to rescind the DACA program,[83] but in a 5–4 decision in 2020, the Supreme Court blocked that effort, holding that the Administration had acted "arbitrarily and capriciously" in trying to do so.[84] Then, on the very day he was inaugurated as president, Joe Biden issued a memo to the Secretary of Homeland Security, directing him to "take all actions he deems appropriate, consistent with applicable law, to preserve and fortify DACA."[85] These developments illustrate the potential impact of unilateral presidential action on public policy but also how policies can shift dramatically from one administration to the next.

THE CONSTITUTION AND SOCIAL JUSTICE
The System Responds to the Death of George Floyd

In basic terms, social justice can be thought of as an attempt to effectuate fairness and equality in society. Government, and in particular courts of law, have an important role to play in fostering social justice. The Fourteenth Amendment's guarantee of equal protection of the laws figures prominently in this effort.

Our readers have no doubt heard of the events that took the life of George Floyd in Minneapolis, Minnesota on May 25, 2020. Floyd died after a Minneapolis police officer, Derek Chauvin, pressed his knee onto Floyd's neck for more than eight minutes. Weeks of protests ensued around the country, with expressions of outrage and demands for justice and reform.

In the context of this incident, the movement toward "justice" can take many forms. It begins, in some sense, with the criminal case against the officer whose conduct led to Floyd's death. As we have noted in this chapter, Chauvin was found guilty of second-degree murder in state court and also pled guilty to federal civil rights charges brought by the Department of Justice. Floyd's family also sued the police officers involved in Floyd's death as well as the City of Minneapolis, under 42 U.S.C. § 1983. That suit resulted in a $27 million out-of-court settlement.

But a movement toward social justice necessitates efforts at effectuating broad-based changes that can transcend a given moment in time—with the overarching objective of ensuring that present-day inequities are rectified in the future. In an effort to move toward that objective, on June 16, 2020, President Trump signed a seven-page executive order entitled "Safe Policing for Safe Communities."[86]

The E.O. opened by stressing the overall need for law enforcement in this country, stating: "Law enforcement officers provide the essential protection that all Americans require to raise their families and lead productive lives." It then declared that the U.S. Attorney General would invoke the assistance of "independent credentialing bodies" that were to assist local law enforcement agencies "assess and improve their practices and policies." To provide an incentive for law enforcement agencies, the E.O. granted the attorney general authority power to withhold discretionary funds from police departments that failed to acquire "appropriate credentials from a reputable independent credentialing body certified by the Attorney General."

The E.O. also said that these "independent credentialing bodies" would evaluate police departments based on use-of-force education, de-escalation techniques, assistance provided for officers who were identified as being in need of additional training, and efforts at community engagement. The order sought assurances from police departments that "use-of-force policies prohibit the use of chokeholds … except in those situations where the use of deadly force is allowed by law."

The E.O. also directed the Attorney General and the Secretary of Health and Human Services to "identify and develop" frameworks for helping police interact with the following groups: the homeless, those with mental health issues, and those suffering from addiction disorders. The Order even advocated for "co-responder programs," which would be directed at making social workers and mental health professionals available to assist with police interactions.

Finally, the E.O. requested that the attorney general, the assistant to the president for domestic policy, and the director of the office of management and budget make suggestions for proposed legislation to Congress "to enhance the tools and resources available to improve law enforcement practices and build community engagement."

Ultimately, progress toward the goals expressed in the E.O. will require funding from the Congress. That is because, in keeping with constitutional principles of separation of powers, an executive order confined to directing the actions of officials in the federal executive branch. Therefore, tangible outcomes benefitting individual police departments and their communities will need to be advanced through the passage of federal and state legislation. That, of course, is to be expected as one seeks social justice within a system of government built upon the principles of federalism and separation of powers.

Emergency Powers

In February and March of 2022, President Joe Biden (as well as leaders of European countries) announced tough economic sanctions to penalize Russia for its unprovoked invasion of Ukraine. These sanctions were not developed and enacted by Congress but, rather, imposed via executive orders. In issuing these orders, President Biden relied heavily on the International Emergency Economic Powers Act (IEEPA) of 1977,[87] which authorizes the president to freeze foreign assets and block economic transactions in response to an "unusual and extraordinary threat … to the national security, foreign policy, or economy of the United States." By enacting such broad legislation, Congress gave the president the authority to deal quickly and decisively with international emergencies, but in so doing, Congress accelerated a long-term trend of ceding power to the Executive Branch.

Two years before Russia's attack on Ukraine, the COVID-19 pandemic focused national attention on the emergency powers of chief executives. Governors, mayors, and even the president of the United States issued a variety of emergency orders in response to a public health crisis the likes of which had not been seen for more than a century. On March 13, 2020, the White House issued a proclamation declaring COVID-19 as a public health emergency and triggering a host of measures by various federal agencies, including the Centers for Disease Control and Prevention (CDC), the Federal Emergency Management Agency (FEMA), and Department of Health and Human Services (HHS).[88] President Trump's action was authorized by the National Emergencies Act passed by Congress in 1976.[89] But as presidents routinely do, President Trump also invoked his inherent powers as president.

The Supreme Court has never definitively embraced the concept of inherent emergency powers, but its decisions in *Korematsu v. United States* and *In re Neagle* are suggestive in this regard. Nevertheless, Congress has enacted a number of laws granting emergency powers to the president.[90] As Justice Robert Jackson recognized in his oft-cited concurrence in *Youngstown v. Sawyer* (1952), "[w]hen the President acts pursuant to an express or implied authorization of Congress, his authority is at its maximum, for it includes all that he possesses in his own right plus all that Congress can delegate."

As a means of reducing the spread of COVID-19, governors and mayors issued stay-at-home orders, curfews, travel restrictions, closures of businesses, and bans on public gatherings. Needless to say, many of these orders were extremely controversial and several were challenged in court. In *South Bay United Pentecostal Church v. Newsom* (2020),[91] the Supreme Court observed that the "Constitution principally entrusts '[t]he health and safety of the people' to the politically accountable officials of the States" and that "[w]hen those officials 'undertake to act in areas fraught with medical and scientific uncertainties,' their latitude 'must be especially broad.'" It is worth noting that courts tend to be highly deferential to government during times of emergency, regardless of whether assertions of governmental power are based on statutory or constitutional provisions.

Martial Law and Suspension of Habeas Corpus

Throughout American history, state governors have activated the National Guard to assist in responding to emergencies. National Guard troops have assisted local authorities in responding to fires, floods, hurricanes, and other natural disasters. On occasion, they have been called on to assist in riot control. In June 2020, after the death of George Floyd at the hands of Minneapolis police, protests swept the nation. Violent confrontations between police and protesters, as well as incidents of looting and arson, led governors in more than twenty states to activate the Guard to support the police and help restore order.

Martial law entails much more than this. It means civilian authority has been displaced by the military. It means the military has the authority to arrest civilians and try them before military tribunals. It means the writ of habeas corpus, by which civilians who have been arrested assert their right to due process of law, is suspended.

There is no explicit provision in the U.S. Constitution for the imposition of martial law. However, Article I, Section 9 does allow the suspension of habeas corpus "when in Cases of Rebellion or Invasion the public Safety may require it." During the Civil War, President Lincoln suspended habeas corpus and authorized the military to arrest and try civilians who were deemed a threat to the Union war effort. In 1866, the year after the war ended and President Lincoln was assassinated, the Supreme Court ruled that the president's order was unconstitutional. Writing for the Court in *Ex parte Milligan*,[92] Justice David Davis opined

MARTIAL LAW: A condition in which the military temporarily assumes control of law enforcement in a particular area.

WRIT OF HABEAS CORPUS: A court order requiring an official holding a person in custody to appear in court, so the legality of that custody can be determined.

that "[m]artial rule can never exist where the courts are open, and in proper and unobstructed exercise of their jurisdiction." Davis observed that "civil liberty and this kind of martial law cannot endure together; the antagonism is irreconcilable, and, in the conflict, one or the other must perish." Moreover, only Congress had the power to suspend the writ of habeas corpus. Congress did act to suspend the writ in 1863,[93] but that came two years after Lincoln's order.

On December 7, 1941, immediately after the Japanese attack on Pearl Harbor, the territorial governor of Hawai'i proclaimed martial law, suspended the writ of habeas corpus, and surrendered his executive powers to the military. The asserted legal authority for this action was the Organic Act passed by Congress in 1900, establishing the government for the territory of Hawai'i.[94] The day after Congress declared war on Japan, President Roosevelt telegrammed the territorial governor approving the declaration of martial law. The civilian courts were closed, and civilians accused of crimes were tried by military tribunals. In a manner reminiscent of *Ex parte Milligan*, the Supreme Court ruled against the imposition of martial law but not until the year after the World War II ended and President Roosevelt was dead. Speaking for the Court in *Duncan v. Kahanamoku* (1946),[95] Justice Hugo L. Black observed, "Our system of government clearly is the antithesis of total military rule and the founders of this country are not likely to have contemplated complete military dominance within the limits of a Territory made part of this country and not recently taken from an enemy."

As part of President George W. Bush's response to the terrorist attacks of September 11, 2001, alleged enemy combatants captured during the "war on terror" were incarcerated at the U.S. Naval Base at Guantanamo Bay, Cuba. In a series of decisions, the Supreme Court ruled that these inmates were entitled to habeas corpus relief and due process of law.[96] Yet the Court did not say they were entitled to trial in civilian courts, and the government established military tribunals at Guantanamo to conduct their trials. Adjudication of these cases has been extremely slow, and the five men accused of plotting the 9/11 attacks remain incarcerated while awaiting trial.

Using the Military in Law Enforcement

One of the tenets of American constitutionalism is the subordination of military to civilian authority. In 1878, Congress passed the Posse Comitatus Act[97] to prohibit the military from being directly involved in civilian law enforcement. The Act does not apply to the National Guard when it is mobilized by a state governor, nor does it apply to the Coast Guard during peacetime. The Insurrection Act of 1807 does allow the military to be employed in federal law enforcement in cases of civil disorder or rebellion.[98] The Act has been invoked more than twenty times, most recently in 1992 when President George H.W. Bush dispatched troops to Los Angeles to quell a riot.

In perhaps the most famous incident in which the military was employed to quell public disorder, President Eisenhower ordered troops from the 101st Airborne Division to Little Rock, Arkansas in 1957 to enforce the desegregation of Central High School. Presidents Kennedy and Johnson also employed federal troops to enforce civil rights compliance against recalcitrant Southern states. These circumventions of the Posse Comitatus Act were authorized not only by the Insurrection Act but also by the Enforcement Acts,[99] passed after the Civil War to enforce the equal protection of the laws.

In 2020, President Trump threatened to invoke the Insurrection Act to respond to the violent protests that erupted in the wake of the police killing of George Floyd, but that threat never materialized. In January 2021, when rioters stormed the Capitol after attending a pro-Trump rally, the Insurrection Act could have been invoked, but the White House declined to do so. Rather, upon request of the mayor of D.C., the Army deployed National Guard units around the Capitol to support the U.S. Capitol Police in their response.

Executive Clemency

Clemency refers to the power of a chief executive to pardon a person for commission of a crime or commute the sentence of one convicted of a crime. The power is rooted in Anglo-Saxon law and was referred to historically as the "royal prerogative of mercy."[100] The fifty state constitutions vest the clemency power in governors, although in some states, there are procedural limitations on the exercise of this power. Article II, § 2, cl. 1 of the U.S. Constitution grants the president the power to "grant Reprieves and Pardons ... except in Cases of Impeachment." Writing for the Supreme Court in *Schick v. Reed* (1974),[101] Chief Justice Warren E. Burger explained that "[t]he plain purpose of the broad power conferred by § 2, cl. 1, was to allow plenary authority in the President to 'forgive' the convicted person in part or entirely, to reduce a penalty in terms of a specified number of years, or to alter it with conditions which are in themselves constitutionally unobjectionable."

Is a President Immune from Criminal Investigation?

EXECUTIVE PRIVILEGE: The power of a chief executive to withhold certain information from disclosure to the public or to other governmental actors.

In *United States v. Nixon* (1974), the Supreme Court recognized executive privilege, whereby some executive branch documents and communications can be withheld from scrutiny by other government officials. However, the majority opinion in this landmark case also found that this privilege cannot be used to hinder a criminal investigation.[102] Speaking for a unanimous Court, Chief Justice Warren E. Burger offered the following important declaration about criminal justice principles:

> ... [Executive] privilege must be considered in light of our historic commitment to the rule of law. ... We have elected to employ an adversary system of criminal justice in which the parties contest all issues before a court of law. The need to develop all relevant facts in the adversary system is both fundamental and comprehensive. The ends of criminal justice would be defeated if judgments were to be founded on a partial or speculative presentation of the facts. The very integrity of the judicial system and public confidence in the system depend on full disclosure of all the facts, within the framework of the rules of evidence. To ensure that justice is done, it is imperative to the function of courts that compulsory process be available for the production of evidence needed either by the prosecution or by the defense.

Chief Justice Burger concluded that "when the ground for asserting privilege as to subpoenaed materials sought for use in a criminal trial is based only on the generalized interest in confidentiality, it cannot prevail over the fundamental demands of due process of law in the fair administration of criminal justice." Burger's opinion also harkened back to *Marbury v. Madison* in saying that, "Many decisions of this Court ... have unequivocally reaffirmed the holding of *Marbury v. Madison* ... that '[i]t is emphatically the province and duty of the judicial department to say what the law is.'" In the end, *United States v. Nixon* forced President Nixon to turn over audio recordings that implicated him in the cover-up of a break-in at the Watergate Hotel, eventually leading to his resignation as president.

More recently, in *Trump v. Vance* (2020),[103] the Court articulated the idea that presidents do not have absolute immunity to ignore a subpoena that is issued by a state grand jury. Writing for the Court in this matter, Chief Justice John Roberts reiterated the principles outlined in *United States v. Nixon*, by saying that "no citizen, not even the President, is categorically above the common duty to produce evidence when called upon in a criminal proceeding."

JURISPRUDENCE

SCOTUS Evaluates the Trump "Travel Ban"
Trump v. Hawaii, 585 U.S. ____ (2018)

In some instances, the Supreme Court of the United States (SCOTUS) has the opportunity to address the substance of both a statutory question and a constitutional question within the context of one dispute. The case of *Trump v. Hawaii* (2018) provided that opportunity. On September 24, 2017, President Trump signed Presidential Proclamation 9645. This offered a revised, third version of a so-called "travel ban" after two earlier versions, issued via executive orders, had been struck down by federal courts.[104] The third version placed a variety of limitations on entry to the United States for people travelling from the following countries: Iran, Libya, North Korea, Somalia, Syria, Venezuela, and Yemen. The exact restrictions associated with this third version varied from country to country.[105] Once again, though, lower federal courts halted the travel ban from remaining in effect.[106]

On June 26, 2018, the Supreme Court overturned the lower court decisions with a 5–4 ruling, which upheld the third version of the travel ban. Even though the lower courts had struck down the ban as a violation of the First Amendment's Establishment Clause, based on the theory that it adversely impacted Muslim-majority countries, Chief Justice Roberts' majority opinion stated that the "travel ban" was "facially neutral toward religion."

In addition to finding that the Establishment Clause had not been violated, the majority opinion also noted that "the Proclamation is squarely within the scope of Presidential authority under the INA," with Roberts referring to the law as providing a "comprehensive delegation to restrict entry into the United States"—a point that would later support presidentially imposed limits on entry to the United States during the COVID-19 pandemic.[107]

Finally, it is important to note that Chief Justice Roberts' majority opinion did make a point to address another controversial executive action, as Roberts repudiated the Supreme Court's 1944 *Korematsu* decision[108]—which upheld the exclusionary order following FDR's Executive Order 9066—by saying, "*Korematsu* was gravely wrong the day it was decided, has been overruled in the court of history, and—to be clear—'has no place in law under the Constitution.'"[109] The final phrase in that quote paid homage to Justice Robert Jackson's dissent in the *Korematsu* case. We discuss that case, and its implications for equal treatment under the Constitution, in subsequent chapters.

ORIGINAL JURISDICTION: The authority of a court of law to adjudicate a case for the first time.

APPELLATE JURISDICTION: The authority of a court to review the decisions of lower courts.

REASONABLE DOUBT: The standard of proof in a criminal case: the government must prove all the elements of a crime beyond a reasonable doubt.

PREPONDERANCE OF EVIDENCE: Evidentiary standard under which a proposition is deemed to be true if there is more evidence for it than against it.

The Judiciary

Under our federal system, each of the fifty states maintains its own courts, as does the federal government. There are significant variations in nomenclature and procedures across these fifty-one court systems, but there are certain features they all have in common. Every court system includes courts of original jurisdiction, which is where criminal and civil cases begin. And all have courts of appellate jurisdiction to hear appeals from the lower courts.

Courts can hear civil cases, which typically involve claims for monetary damages or injunctions, as well as criminal cases. Although the latter represent the primary focus of this textbook, we take note of the fact that standards of proof differ in civil cases and criminal cases. As most observers of criminal justice understand, a guilty verdict (or conviction) in a criminal cases requires meeting the high threshold of proof beyond a reasonable doubt, whereas a civil verdict can be based on the lesser standard of proof by a preponderance of evidence, which can be thought of as one side having slightly more evidence than the other, as if the scales of justice tipped slightly in one direction. As we move through this textbook, we will see contexts in which even less-demanding standards are applied to matters, such as the issuance of search warrants (chapters 7–9), pat-down searches (chapter 10), arrest warrants (chapter 10), and even as justification for bringing a case to trial (chapter 12). For now, we simply discuss the basic framework and functions of the American court system.

State Court Systems

Every state has a set of trial courts and one or more appellate courts. Trial courts are organized by county, "district," or "circuit." Major trial courts are often called circuit, district, or superior courts. Most states have courts of limited jurisdiction to adjudicate misdemeanors and conduct pretrial proceedings in felony cases. Some states have specialized courts for juvenile cases. At the appellate level, every state has a court of last resort, usually called the "supreme court." Most states have an intermediate level of appellate courts to hear routine appeals and allow the court of last resort to focus on the most important cases or ones over which the intermediate appellate courts are in conflict. Figure 2.1 shows a model state court system. In reality, most state court systems are more complicated.

The overwhelming majority of criminal prosecutions take place in state courts, as most crimes are offenses against state laws. State courts

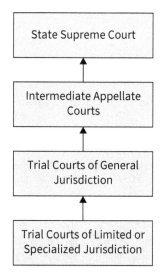

FIGURE 2.1 A Model State Court System.

must follow the statutes and constitutions of their respective states and, often, must interpret those laws. The state court of last resort is final with respect to interpretation of state law. Of course, state law must not conflict with federal law or the U.S. Constitution. And state courts must follow federal law to the extent that it applies to the states. To the extent that a state judicial decision rests squarely on state law, and assuming that state law does not violate the federal Constitution, it is unreviewable in federal court.

State court judges are selected in a variety of ways: partisan election, nonpartisan election, gubernatorial appointment, legislative appointment, or merit selection. Some states employ elections for trial judges and appointment or some version of merit selection for the appellate judges. The question of how judges should be selected and retained in office turns on a debate over judicial independence versus accountability. Those who favor judicial elections believe judges, like other government officials, should be accountable to the voters. Advocates of judicial appointment tend to stress the need for judicial independence.[110]

The Federal Court System

As we noted earlier in this chapter, Article III of the Constitution provides for "one supreme Court, and ... such inferior Courts as the Congress may from time to time ordain and establish." The first Congress set about the task of creating the federal court system when it passed the Judiciary Act of 1789,[111] and Congress has enacted many laws since then to create the federal judiciary we have today. In addition to the Supreme Court, the principal components of the federal judiciary are the United States District Courts and the U.S. Courts of Appeals (see figure 2.2). As directed by Article II of the U.S. Constitution, judges on all of these courts are appointed by the president with the "advice and consent" of the Senate.[112] Filibusters are not allowed in the Senate during any court confirmation hearings. As provided in Article III, Section 1, these judges "hold their Offices during good Behaviour," which means that they serve life terms as long as they are not removed through the impeachment process. This is designed to promote their independence from Congress and the executive branch.

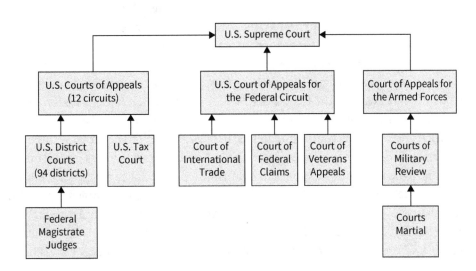

FIGURE 2.2   The Federal Court System.

Note: Includes "Article I" as well as "Article III" courts.

U.S. District Courts

The U.S. District Court is the principal trial court in the federal system, having jurisdiction over both criminal and civil cases. The country is divided into 94 federal judicial districts, which are built along, and within, state lines. Every state has at least one district, as does Puerto Rico, the District of Columbia, Guam, the North Marianna Islands, and the Virgin Islands. Each district has its own federal prosecutor's office, and most have a federal public defender's office, as we will discuss in chapter 12.

In most cases, one judge presides over a trial in the District Court, although a three-judge panel is required "when an action is filed challenging the constitutionality of the apportionment of congressional districts or the apportionment of any statewide legislative body."[113] In *Shapiro v. McManus* (2015),[114] the Supreme Court held that a three-judge panel must be convened in cases involving the constitutionality of legislative redistricting. In chapter 14, we will discuss three-judge panels in conjunction with cases that involve the release of incarcerated prisoners based on conditions that are deemed "cruel and unusual" in violation of the Eighth Amendment.

The district judges appoint magistrate judges to assist them. Magistrate judges serve 8-year terms. They conduct pretrial proceedings in criminal cases and, with the consent of both parties, can try civil cases; they also can issue federal search warrants.

Federal district courts hold jurisdiction over cases involving violations of federal law, which can include offenses that take place on federal property, such as in national parks, post offices, or other federal buildings—though in some areas, local law enforcement might have concurrent jurisdiction in such cases. Federal courts also hold jurisdiction over cases involving bankruptcies, treaties, disputes between two or more states, and requests for writs of habeas corpus.

Additionally, Article III, Section 2 of the U.S. Constitution indicates that federal district courts can hear all of cases of "admiralty and maritime jurisdiction", which federal law has been interpreted to include crimes committed on "high seas, [or on] any other waters within the admiralty and maritime jurisdiction of the United States and out of the jurisdiction of any particular State."[115] More specifically, through other laws and presidential proclamations, states retain jurisdiction over offenses committed on waterways and islands within three nautical miles of their shorelines, whereas federal jurisdiction over the "high seas" pertains to activity that occurs between three and twelve nautical miles from shore.[116] Federal courts also have jurisdiction over any offenses committed on U.S.-registered ships—even if those offenses occur when the ship is outside the waterways of the United States.[117] But an attack on foreign vessels by a U.S. ship in foreign waters would not be subject to prosecution under U.S. federal law.[118] All actions of Naval or other military personnel in any waterway could be addressed in federal court.[119] The Clean Water Act of 1972 also created federal jurisdiction for environmental offenses in "navigable waterways of the United States."[120]

Enemy combatants who engage in terrorist acts against the United States around the world can also be brought to federal district courts for trial. This was the case for two suspects charged in the 2012 attack on the U.S. Special Mission in Benghazi, Libya. Four Americans, including a U.S. ambassador, were killed in the attack. After being captured in Libya, the suspects were brought to trial in the U.S. District Court for the District of Columbia, where both were convicted.[121] We discuss the topic of "enemy combatants" in greater detail in chapter 12.

U.S. Courts of Appeals

The U.S. Courts of Appeals, also known as Circuit Courts, hear appeals from the District Courts. The country is divided into twelve regional circuits, each of which subsumes a number of judicial districts (see figure 2.3). For example, the Sixth Circuit encompasses all of the district courts located in Michigan, Ohio, Kentucky, and Tennessee. One of the twelve geographically-drawn Circuit Courts is the U.S. Court of Appeals for the District of Columbia Circuit; there also is a "thirteenth circuit," called the U.S. Court of Appeals for the Federal Circuit, which was created in 1982 and hears appeals of decisions of the U.S. Patent and Trademark Office, the U.S. Court of International Trade, and the Court of Federal Claims.[122] Congress creates the boundaries of the federal district and circuit courts. The most-recently created geographic circuit is the Eleventh, which was formed in 1982 by partitioning off Alabama, Georgia, and Florida from the Fifth Circuit, of which they were formerly aligned.

The Circuit Courts are collegial courts; cases are decided by panels of three judges, who hear oral arguments and issue written opinions. As appellate courts, the Circuit Courts are not fact-finding bodies; their role is simply to decide whether the District Court correctly applied the law to the case on appeal. Circuit courts hear oral arguments and issue written opinions. In rare circumstances, appeals of a three-judge panel's decision can be heard by all judges of the court, known as an en banc rehearing. Generally, a split among circuit courts on a key question of law can help to precipitate Supreme Court review of a legal issue. This was the case in 2015,

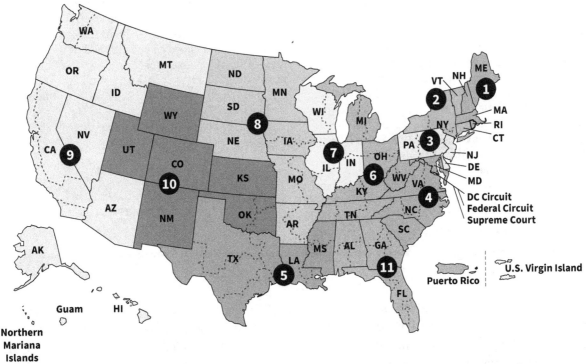

Geographic Boundaries
of United States Courts of Appeals and United States District Courts

FIGURE 2.3   Map of the Federal Circuits.

when the high Court resolved a split among the federal circuit courts with its decision in *Obergefell v. Hodges*, which legalized same-sex marriage.[123]

JURISPRUDENCE

The Importance of Meeting Deadlines for Appeals
Houston v. Lack, 487 U.S. 266 (1988)

Timeliness in filing appeals is essential. If a deadline is missed, even by one day, an appeal is generally forfeited. In *Houston v. Lack* (1988), a deadline became the core issue in the case of Prentiss Houston, who was incarcerated in a Tennessee prison for the crime of murder. In 1986, the U.S. District Court for the Western District of Tennessee rejected his request for a writ of habeas corpus—a request revolving around an ineffective counsel claim.[124] Serving as his own attorney, from prison, Houston wrote an appeal of that denial. The deadline for the District Court to receive that notice of appeal was 30 days after its ruling. (The appeal would ultimately be filed with the U.S. Court of Appeals for the Sixth Circuit, but the process was to begin with timely notification to the District Court, which would then prepare an official record of the case.) Houston placed his written appeal to the District Court into an envelope addressed to that court and handed it to prison officials 27 days after the original judgment. Those officials refused his request to certify the letter, claiming costs were an issue. By the time the letter arrived at the District Court, on the morning of the 31st day following the judgment, the deadline had passed by one day. As a result, Houston's appeal was turned away for being filed late.

With the assistance of counsel named Penny White, Houston appealed to the Supreme Court, which granted certiorari. Ultimately, by a 5–4 decision, the Court ruled in Houston's favor, indicating that for inmates who are acting *pro se*, an appeal is considered to be "delivered," for the purposes of deadlines, on the day it is handed to prison officials for mailing. Justice Brennan's majority opinion for a 5–4 Court noted that, "The situation of prisoners seeking to appeal without the aid of counsel is unique." He then highlighted the limited options available to an incarcerated *pro se* appellant by saying, "Unlike other litigants, *pro se* prisoners cannot personally travel to the courthouse to see that the notice is stamped 'filed'." Brennan next pointed out that prison officials might have limited motivation to assist an inmate in filing an appeal, noting, "Worse, the *pro se* prisoner has no choice but to entrust the forwarding of his notice of appeal to prison authorities whom he cannot control or supervise, and who may have every incentive to delay." In summarizing concerns related to incarcerated *pro se* defendants, Justice Brennan concluded: "Unskilled in law, unaided by counsel, and unable to leave the prison, his control over the processing of his notice necessarily ceases as soon as he hands it over to the only public officials to whom he has access—the prison authorities. ..."

Overall, two lessons emerge from this case:

1. Deadlines in law are essential to meet, as an appeal in a criminal case can be forfeited simply for being one day late.
2. Even so, when protocols are broken, a lawyer can always attempt to forge an argument that seeks an exception to the rules.

Article I Courts

In addition to the courts created by Congress under Article III, Congress has used its authority under Article I to create a number of specialized tribunals sometimes called "legislative courts" (again, see figure 2.2). These include the Court of Federal Claims, the Tax Court, the Court of Appeals for the Armed Forces, the Court of Appeals for Veterans' Claims, and the Bankruptcy Courts. With the exception of the Bankruptcy Court judges, who are appointed by federal district courts and serve 14-year terms, Article I judges are appointed by the president to 15-year terms.

The United States Supreme Court

The existence of a Supreme Court is guaranteed by Article III of the U.S. Constitution. Since 1869, the number of justices has been set by Congress at nine—despite occasional political banter concerning the notion of "packing the Court" with more justices, with Franklin Delano Roosevelt and Joe Biden among the presidents to broach that subject in public statements.[125]

The Supreme Court has limited original jurisdiction; nearly all of its cases come to it on appeal from lower federal courts or the state courts of last resort. While the Court's original jurisdiction is fixed by Article III, Section 2 of the Constitution, its appellate jurisdiction is determined by Congress.[126] With the exception of having to review cases decided by three-judge panels in the District Courts, the Court's appellate jurisdiction is almost entirely discretionary.[127]

The Court exercises its discretionary appellate jurisdiction through the writ of **certiorari**. As long as there is a question of federal law involved, the Court may "grant cert." to review any decision of a lower federal court or a state court of last resort. The Court is highly selective, though. While it receives more than 8,000 petitions for certiorari each year, the Court tends to grant less than 100 of them. The decision to grant cert. is made by a vote of the justices. Under the Court's "rule of four," at least four justices must cast an affirmative vote in order for certiorari to be granted. The cases in which the Court grants cert. tend to be the most important and difficult ones. Where the lower courts are in conflict on a point of federal law, or when the Justice Department asks the Court to review a case, it is more likely to grant cert.

When the Court grants cert., lawyers for parties to the case submit written briefs; as can outside groups, known as *amicus curiae*, meaning "friend of the court." Oral arguments at the high Court involve each side being allotted thirty minutes to present the case, with the justices frequently interrupting with questions. Written opinions from the Court tend to be released within months of the oral argument. The Court's term generally runs from October to June, with opinions in the more high-profile cases generally released in the term's final days.

Even outside of its normal term, the Court also has the power to issue injunctions that "stay" the implementation of lower court rulings, federal laws, state laws, and executive orders. Known to some as the Court's *shadow docket* because such decisions generally are made without oral argument and sometimes without benefit of a written opinion, these decisions can have powerful ramifications even before a case is decided *on the merits.* For example, in October 2021, the Court opted not to issue

CERTIORARI: The mechanism by which an appellate court exercises its discretion in deciding to review a lower court decision.

such an injunction in regard to a Texas law that allowed civil suits against abortion providers, letting the law take effect.[128] In a September 2021 speech at Notre Dame University, Justice Alito responded to critics of the so-called shadow docket by saying he preferred to have it referred to as the *emergency docket*, noting that these rulings are generally temporary and not to be used as precedent, with a full oral argument and written opinion likely to arrive after a decision on injunctive relief is released.[129]

THE CONSTITUTION IN ACTION

Historic Confirmation Sends Ketanji Brown Jackson to Supreme Court

In April 2022, Judge Ketanji Brown Jackson was confirmed to serve on the Supreme Court of the United States by a 53–47 vote of the U.S. Senate, making her the first Black female to ascend to a position on the nation's highest Court. In addition to that distinction, Jackson also became the first person with experience as a public defender to serve on the Supreme Court.[130]

Justice Jackson was born and raised in Washington, D.C., and she attended Harvard University for her undergraduate degree, majoring in government—subsequently adding a law degree from Harvard Law School. Her professional experience following her legal education included serving as a clerk for Supreme Court Justice Stephen Breyer, the justice whom she eventually would replace following his retirement from the high Court. Jackson also worked in private practice law firms, held the position of Vice Chair of the U.S. Sentencing Commission, and spent two years as a federal public defender in the District of Columbia.

She began her tenure as a federal judge in 2013 after President Obama nominated her to serve on the U.S. District Court for the District of Columbia. She later was appointed to the U.S. Court of Appeals for the D.C. Circuit in June 2021, following a nomination to that post by President Biden. Among Jackson's notable rulings as a federal judge was a written opinion that ordered President Trump's White House counsel, Don McGahn, to meet the demands of a legislative subpoena that called for his testimony in front of a House Committee; in that opinion, she cited to *The Federalist Papers* in declaring that, "Stated simply, the primary takeaway from the past 250 years of recorded American history is that Presidents are not kings," adding that "no one is above the law."[131] Elsewhere, in a prisoner's-rights decision, *Pierce v. District of Columbia* (2015),[132] she ruled that the D.C. Department of Corrections had violated the Americans with Disabilities Act when prison officials failed to provide a deaf inmate with reasonable accommodations to facilitate communication with prison staff. And in 2019, Judge Jackson issued a ruling that halted, temporarily, the Trump administration's efforts to expand the concept of expedited removal so that anyone deemed to be in the United States illegally for a period of two years or less could be deported without a formal Immigration Court proceeding.[133] Jackson's decision in that case, though, was later overturned by the D.C. Circuit.[134]

After being nominated to serve on the Supreme Court by President Biden in February 2022, Jackson endured a multi-day questioning by members of the Senate Judiciary Committee, which included criticism of her prior decisions that had been overturned by higher courts as well as some odd queries that likely have never been asked in the history of Supreme Court confirmation hearings. In one exchange, for instance, a senator spoke of children's books that were in the library for a private school attended by one of Jackson's children—discussion that culminated in the following question: "Are babies racist?" Another senator asked Jackson to "provide a definition for the word woman." Additionally, Jackson was asked: "Is it your hidden personal agenda to incorporate critical race theory into our legal system?" In speaking of CRT, Jackson replied, "It doesn't come up in my work as a judge. It's never something I've studied or relied on, and it wouldn't be something that I would rely on if I were on the Supreme Court." Other questions revolved around Jackson's prior sentencing record as a judge as well as hot-button issues, such as gun rights and abortion.[135]

Jackson's confirmation was temporarily stalled by an 11–11 vote in the Senate Judiciary Committee, with a full vote of the Senate membership needed to advance the nomination out of committee, so that yet another full vote of the Senate could take place in regard to her actual confirmation to the Court. Both votes resulted in the same margin in Jackson's favor, with all 50 Democrats and three Republicans providing approval for her to make history in joining the nation's highest Court. In a sign of the ideological polarization that has become prevalent in the United States, Jackson's confirmation marked the fourth straight time that the Senate failed to provide more than 55 votes in favor of a Supreme Court nominee, with such a streak of close votes being unprecedented in U.S. history.

Immigration Courts

It is important for scholars of criminal justice to be aware of a federal court framework that actually resides wholly within the executive branch. More specifically, Immigration Courts are a part of the broader Executive Office for Immigration Review, itself an agency within the Department of Justice. These courts can hear a wide array of matters, perhaps involving some of the following: situations involving illegal entry into the U.S.; deportation proceedings for immigrants who have committed crimes in the U.S. while in the country lawfully (e.g., on a student or work visa); reviews of requests for asylum, which can be made by persons who are fleeing persecution in their home countries. Midway through fiscal year 2022, 24,689 deportation orders were given by immigration judges (comprising 22.7% of all deportation cases heard).[136] In fiscal year 2019, immigration courts granted 18,851 approvals in asylum cases (comprising 20.62% of all requests heard).[137]

There are substantive differences between immigration court proceedings and trials that occur in federal district courts. Decisions are made exclusively by an immigration judge.[138] And because these courts are a part of the executive branch's Department of Justice, many of the judges are "administrative law judges" who have been selected by the attorney general. The attorney general could, in theory, request that immigration judges enforce immigration laws in a specific way, and it is possible for the attorney general to remove a judge from a case.

In addition, certain constitutional protections that apply in federal district courts are not applicable in immigration courts. Notably, a lawyer is not provided for a litigant in immigration court if they cannot afford one. They could hire their own counsel, but in a federal district court, a person accused of criminal charges can have a lawyer appointed by the court, pursuant to Sixth Amendment rights, which we will discuss in chapter 12. Overall, according to the American Immigration Council, fewer than 40% of those who appear in immigration courts are represented by counsel.[139]

As of 2022, there are approximately 60 immigration courts around the United States, and there are 330 immigration judges nationwide. These courts tend to be overloaded with cases, and as of May 2021, there was a backlog of more than one million immigration cases across the country, which represented more than double the caseload of all U.S. district courts combined.[140]

Finally, a litigant in an immigration court proceeding does have outlets for appealing an immigration judge's decision. The first avenue of appellate review resides with the Board of Immigration Appeals, which is based in Virginia and staffed by approximately 20 judges, who are hired

ASYLUM: Protection granted persons who have fled their home countries because they fear persecution; those granted asylum are eligible for permanent residency in the United States.

by the Department of Justice; in FY 2019, this court completed 19,448 of 55,971 cases that were filed.[141] Beyond that, appeals of immigration rulings can be brought to the U.S. Circuit Courts or to the Supreme Court of the United States, if those courts exercise their discretion to review such matters.

The Tribal Court System

Reflecting the principle of Native sovereignty, the Indian Reorganization Act of 1934[142] permitted Native American tribes to create their own laws that govern criminal activity on reservations as well as tribal courts to enforce those laws. According to the U.S. Bureau of Indian Affairs, there are roughly 400 tribal courts around the country.[143] These courts have criminal jurisdiction over Native Americans who commit offenses on Native land as well as civil jurisdiction over any persons who commit **torts** on Native land. Additionally, under the Violence Against Women Reauthorization Act of 2013,[144] Tribal courts have been given jurisdiction to address cases involving domestic violence and violations of protection orders, regardless of whether defendants were Native or non-Native; approximately thirty tribes have implemented such courts, which are the only tribal proceedings that must respect the right to counsel.

Under federal law,[145] a person's third domestic violence offense on Native land can be prosecuted in federal court. In *United States v. Bryant* (2016),[146] the Supreme Court ruled that two tribal convictions qualify as prior convictions, regardless of whether the defendant was represented by counsel in the prior cases.

If a tribe lacks funding for its own tribal court system or chooses not to operate one, there is the option of a Court of Indian Offences—often known as a "CFR court" because its existence is permitted by 25 CRF Part 11 of the Code of Federal Regulations. There are five of these courts around the country, some of which cover more than one tribe. Federal magistrate judges hear these cases, and appeals can be made to the Court of Indian Offences.[147]

Under the Major Crimes Act of 1885,[148] certain felony offenses that occur on tribal land, if they are committed by a Native American, can become a federal crime prosecuted in a U.S. district court. With subsequent amendments to the Major Crimes Act taken into account, those offenses now number more than a dozen.[149] Furthermore, the Supreme Court has allowed for federal courts to consider some "lesser-included offenses," as defined under applicable state law in the location where one of these "major" crimes occurs.[150] Some tribal courts also continue to prosecute offenses listed under the Major Crimes Act, and that practice has been upheld by the Ninth Circuit.[151]

TORTS: Non-criminal wrongs done intentionally or through negligence, the remedy for which is a civil suit for damages.

In a recent landmark decision, *McGirt v. Oklahoma* (2020),[152] the Court indicated that a state could not exercise jurisdiction over a Native American who commits, on Tribal land, a crime listed in the Major Crimes Act; notably, this case also indicated that almost half of the state of Oklahoma was still Native land, belonging to the Creek Nation—meaning any crimes committed in that area by a Native would need to be prosecuted in tribal court or a federal district court. In analyzing this opinion, an article by David Weiden in *The New York Times* focused on the fact that, "Although the percentages vary from year to year, federal officials frequently refuse to prosecute murders, assaults and sex crimes referred from tribal or state police departments. In 2018, 39 percent of all referred crimes were declined, and over a quarter of those cases were sexual assaults against children and adults."[153] The author noted that these denials often can result in offenders going free because of a corresponding lack of state authority.

In 2022, the Court modified the *McGirt* decision in holding that state courts have concurrent jurisdiction over criminal offenses committed against Native Americans by non-Natives on Native land.[154] The decision observed that Native land is to be considered part of the state in which it is located. In dissent, Justice Stephen Breyer observed that the Court's decision "allows Oklahoma to intrude on a feature of tribal sovereignty recognized since the founding."

The Exercise of Judicial Review

Today, the power of judicial review is exercised not only by the Supreme Court but also by other Article III federal courts and state courts. What began as a controversial assertion of power has become widely accepted as an essential feature of the system of checks and balances. In criminal matters, judicial review generally entails a court interpreting aspects of the Constitution or a law. The latter, known as statutory interpretation, simply involves determining what the law means in the context of a particular case. For example, in 2022, the Supreme Court overturned the guilty verdicts against two doctors accused of improperly prescribing opioids in violation of the Controlled Substances Act—but the federal law itself was left intact, with the majority reasoning that the government had not met the standard of proof required by the statute.[155] It is also important to note that when the Supreme Court renders a statutory decision, a legislature can override that interpretation by amending the statute. An example arose from *United States v. Stevens* (2010), where the majority struck down a federal law criminalizing depictions of animal cruelty by noting the "alarming breadth" of the statute.[156] Congress responded by amending the law to include the words "is obscene," and in 2015 the Fifth Circuit upheld the revised version against a First Amendment challenge.[157]

Constitutional Interpretation

The interpretation of the U.S. Constitution is the most important function of the Supreme Court. In matters of constitutional interpretation, Congress cannot override a judicial decision merely through legislation. When it comes to the interpretation of key words and phrases in the Constitution and its amendments, the Court is said to have "the last word." Accordingly, there are only two ways the Supreme Court's interpretation of the Constitution can be undone. One way is for the Court to overturn its own precedents. For instance, in

RACIAL PROFILING: The illegitimate use of race as an indicator of criminal suspicion.

Brown v. Board of Education (1954),[158] the Court rejected the "separate but equal" doctrine that had served as the constitutional justification for laws requiring racial segregation.[159] More recently, in *Lawrence v. Texas* (2003), the Court struck down a state ban on certain types of private sexual activity, overturning the precedent from *Bowers v. Hardwick* (1986).[160]

The other way that judicial interpretation of the Constitution can be reversed is through constitutional amendment. This has happened on four occasions in U.S. history. First, the Eleventh Amendment, which was ratified in 1798, overturned the Supreme Court's ruling for *Chisholm v. Georgia*, which had permitted federal courts to hear suits brought against a state by individuals from other states.[161] Next, the Fourteenth Amendment (ratified in 1868) overruled the Supreme Court's decision in *Dred Scott v. Sandford*,[162] which held that ancestors of slaves could never be considered U.S. citizens. Subsequently, the Sixteenth Amendment (ratified in 1913) overturned 1895 decisions that found a federal income tax to violate the Constitution.[163] Finally, the most recent example is the Twenty-Sixth Amendment (ratified in 1971). That Amendment lowered the voting age to eighteen for all elections in this country. A year earlier, in *Oregon v. Mitchell* (1970),[164] the Court had held that Congress did not have the power to lower the voting age in state and local elections.

The Doctrine of Saving Construction

In certain situations, a case might arise that could involve the possibility of both statutory and constitutional interpretation. Under the doctrine of *saving construction*, courts will typically look for ways to avoid constitutional questions—perhaps, by interpreting a statute in a fashion so as to do so. For example, in chapter 4, we will discuss a case in which a child pornography statute was *saved* from being struck down on constitutional grounds due a limiting interpretation of the statute itself. More specifically, in *Osborne v. Ohio* (1990),[165] Justice Byron White's majority opinion upheld an Ohio law that made it a crime to "possess or view any material or performance that shows a minor who is not the person's child or ward in a state of nudity." The majority opinion made it clear that the Court was interpreting the law in a limited fashion, such that it would only apply to "lewd exhibition" or "graphic focus on the genitals." Therefore, any "innocuous" images of nude children would not be addressed by applications of the law; as a result, there was no need to address constitutional questions related to that possibility.

In 2021, the Supreme Court offered a statutory interpretation that impacted the conduct of a police sergeant in Georgia. Sgt. Nathan Van Buren had used the computer in his patrol car to conduct an inquiry on a specific license plate in exchange for money. An undercover FBI operation revealed that he agreed to accept $5,000 from a man who claimed to need information on the license plate of a woman's car. Van Buren was charged with a federal crime for allegedly violating the Computer Fraud and Abuse Act,[166] which was passed by Congress in 1986 and makes it illegal "to access a computer with authorization and to use such access to obtain or alter information in the computer that the accesser is not entitled so to obtain or alter." He was found guilty of violating this law in federal district court, and the Eleventh Circuit affirmed. However, on review, the Supreme Court found that the intent underlying this law was not applicable to Van Buren's conduct. Justice Barrett's majority opinion said, "This provision covers those who obtain information from particular areas in the computer—such as files, folders, or databases—to which their computer access does not extend. It does not cover those who, like Van Buren, have improper motives for obtaining information that is otherwise available to them."

She went on to envision a world in which an alternative result emanated from the Court, positing that: "If the 'exceeds authorized access' clause criminalizes every violation of a computer-use policy, then millions of otherwise law-abiding citizens are criminals. Take the workplace. Employers commonly state that computers and electronic devices can be used only for business purposes. So on the Government's reading of the statute, an employee who sends a personal e-mail or reads the news using her work computer has violated the CFAA." Additionally, the Court recognized that under this interpretation, the statute would "criminalize everything from embellishing an online-dating profile to using a pseudonym on Facebook." Ultimately, although the conduct in question might have been a violation of police department policy, the Supreme Court found that it did not rise to the level of a federal crime.

Access to Judicial Review

Courts do not sit as Platonic guardians or councils of revision that supervise and modify enactments of legislatures. Rather, they address constitutional issues as needed to resolve real controversies between adverse parties, including citizens, corporations, and governmental entities. Those controversies begin either as criminal prosecutions or civil lawsuits. While most of these controversies are settled before going to trial, some involve trials and subsequent appeals, and a select few make their way to the U.S. Supreme Court. In this section, we discuss various mechanisms through which constitutional questions come before the courts.

Pretrial Motions

In a criminal prosecution or a civil suit involving a governmental entity, constitutional issues often arise by way of pretrial motions. For example, a criminal defendant can move for the dismissal of charges on the

PRETRIAL MOTIONS: Requests by either party to a case seeking a ruling or an order prior to the commencement of a trial.

ground that the statute upon which the prosecution is based is unconstitutional. Additionally, defendants in criminal cases often move for the suppression of evidence, claiming it was obtained in violation of their constitutional rights. Trial judges must rule on such motions, and their rulings are subject to appeal. An appeal that occurs before a trial takes place is often called an *interlocutory appeal.*

Appeals from Criminal Convictions

Under federal and state laws, parties convicted of crimes have the right to appeal to a higher court. In most instances, such appeals are heard by intermediate appellate courts. Generally, further appellate review is granted at the discretion of courts of last resort, although states often their supreme courts to hear appeals in death penalty cases. Quite often such appeals involve constitutional questions—most commonly, issues arising under the Fourth, Fifth, Sixth, and Eighth Amendments. But these appeals can also raise questions about the constitutionality of criminal prohibitions.

Petitions for Habeas Corpus

Habeas corpus, the ancient common-law device recognized in Article I, Section 9 of the U.S. Constitution, allows prisoners to challenge the legality of their confinement. Historically, habeas corpus was often used to insure that people arrested would have their "day in court." In the modern American practice, habeas corpus provides a means for federal courts to review the constitutionality of state criminal convictions. Within certain limits, prisoners who have exhausted their remedies in state courts can petition federal courts for habeas corpus relief. Some of the most common issues raised by petitioners seeking post-conviction habeas corpus relief are the following: ineffective assistance of counsel, errors by the trial judge, prosecutorial misconduct, bias during jury selection, and cruel and unusual punishments. Congress placed some limits on the use of habeas corpus petitions with passage of the Antiterrorism and Effective Death Penalty Act of 1996,[167] which placed restrictions on second habeas corpus petitions brought by state prisoners who already have filed such petitions in federal court. (This topic is discussed in greater detail in the following chapter).

Injunctions

INJUNCTION: A court order requiring a party to do or cease doing something.

A person facing a serious threat of prosecution under a statute they believe to be unconstitutional can seek an injunction to restrain a prosecutor from enforcing the law. Although there is no explicit statutory authorization for federal courts to issue injunctions to restrain the enforcement of unconstitutional statutes, the Supreme Court has long recognized injunctive relief to fall within the equitable powers of federal district judges.[168] In *Bell v. Hood* (1946),[169] the Court observed that "it is established practice for this Court to sustain the jurisdiction of federal courts to issue injunctions to protect rights safeguarded by the Constitution and to restrain individual state officers from doing what the 14th Amendment forbids the State to do." While this quotation refers to injunctions against enforcement of state laws, federal courts can also enjoin federal officials from enforcing acts of Congress. For example, in *Reno v. American Civil Liberties Union* (1996),[170] the Supreme Court upheld an injunction issued against Attorney General Janet Reno to prohibit enforcement of provisions of the Communications Decency Act that were found to violate the First Amendment. A **permanent injunction** is issued only after notice and hearing—the essential elements of due process. Prior to holding a hearing, a judge may issue a **preliminary injunction** but only after providing notice to the defendant and determining that the plaintiff is likely to succeed on the merits and will suffer irreparable harm without immediate relief.[171]

Lawsuits Against Officials to Vindicate Constitutional Rights

A number of federal laws allow aggrieved parties to sue officials for violating their constitutional rights. Notably, 42 U.S.C. § 1983 allows persons to sue state officers and others acting "under color of any law, statute, ordinance, regulation, custom, or usage of any State" to recover monetary damages for the violation of their rights. This provision stems from the Civil Rights Act of 1871,[172] one of a series of landmark civil rights measures Congress enacted shortly after the Civil War. The term "under color of ... law" means the person being sued, if not a state or local official, must have been operating with authority stemming from state law or policy. Police officers are often named as defendants in such matters, usually in cases involving the use of force. For example, in July 2020, George Floyd's family filed a Section 1983 suit against the four police officers whose use of excessive force led to Floyd's death as well as the City of Minneapolis.[173]

What about federal law enforcement officers who violate people's constitutional rights? Can they be sued for damages as well? In *Bivens v. Six Unknown Federal Narcotics Agents* (1971),[174] the Supreme Court recognized that "[h]istorically, damages have been regarded as the ordinary remedy for an invasion of personal interests in liberty."

PERMANENT INJUNCTION: A court order permanently enjoining the defendant with respect to some unlawful action; issued only after notice to the defendant and a hearing.

PRELIMINARY INJUNCTION: An injunction issued without a hearing but only after the judge has determined the plaintiff is likely to succeed on the merits and will suffer irreparable harm without immediate relief.

With that declaration, the Court created a cause of action similar to Section 1983 but limited to suits against federal officers. As with Section 1983 cases, these so-called *Bivens* actions often involve claims that federal law enforcement agents caused injuries by engaging in unconstitutional searches, seizures, or arrests, which are prohibited by the Fourth Amendment.

Immunity from Civil Liability

ABSOLUTE IMMUNITY:
Doctrine under which judges, prosecutors, legislators, and certain other officials are completely immunized against civil liability for their official actions.

There are some individuals who are entitled to absolute immunity from civil lawsuits, as long as the actions giving rise to a suit are considered to be within the course of normal job duties. For example, the Supreme Court has long held that Section 1983 did not remove "the immunity of legislators for acts with the legislative role."[175] Additionally, the Court has provided absolute immunity from civil damages to a president in regard to actions stemming from their official duties;[176] even so, in a 1997 case involving President Bill Clinton, the Court refused to extend immunity to a civil suit over matters unrelated to Clinton's duties as president.[177]

More germane to the criminal justice context, the Supreme Court has indicated that judges cannot be subjected to a Section 1983 lawsuit for "acts within the judicial role," with Chief Justice Warren's majority opinion for a 1967 case observing that a judge's "errors may be corrected on appeal, but he should not have to fear that unsatisfied litigants may hound him with litigation charging malice or corruption. Imposing such a burden on judges would contribute not to principled and fearless decisionmaking, but to intimidation."[178] Warren's opinion went on to say: "We do not believe that this settled principle of law was abolished by § 1983, which makes liable 'every person' who under color of law deprives another person of his civil rights."[179]

The Supreme Court also has held that prosecutors have absolute immunity connected to performance of their job duties. In a seminal case on this topic, *Imbler v. Pachtman* (1976),[180] a California man convicted of a 1961 murder and sentenced to death was ultimately released in 1970 after new evidence was uncovered and raised in a habeas corpus proceeding in federal district court. After the Ninth Circuit upheld the decision to release the man, he filed a Section 1983 action against multiple parties, including the prosecutor in his case, Los Angeles Deputy District Attorney Richard Pachtman.[181] On review, the Supreme Court rejected the possibility of a Section 1983 lawsuit against the prosecutor, with Justice Powell's majority opinion saying that "a prosecutor enjoys absolute immunity from § 1983 suits for damages when he acts within the scope of his prosecutorial duties." Justice Powell drew a parallel to the immunity afforded to judges in declaring the following:

> The common law immunity of a prosecutor is based upon the same considerations that underlie the common law immunities of judges and grand jurors acting within the scope of their duties. These include concern that harassment by unfounded litigation would cause a deflection of the prosecutor's energies from his public duties, and the possibility that he would shade his decisions instead of exercising the independence of judgment required by his public trust.

In 1981, the Supreme Court extended the principle of absolute immunity to the work of public defenders. In this case, the Court indicated that a man who had been found guilty of robbery could not sue his public defender from the Polk County (Iowa) Offender Advocate's Office.[182] The public defender had asked a court to let her withdraw from this man's appeal because she found that his claims were "wholly frivolous." The Iowa Supreme Court allowed the attorney to withdraw and dismissed the appeal. The U.S. Supreme Court then quashed the man's claims for Section 1983 lawsuit, with Justice Powell's majority opinion saying that "a public defender does not act under color of state law when performing a lawyer's traditional functions as counsel to a defendant in a criminal proceeding."

Of course, absolute immunity in all of these cases is based upon the principle of a person "acting within the scope of job duties," which could afford some leeway for lawsuits when lawyers or judges deviate from those parameters. Moreover, this immunity from a civil lawsuit under Section 1983 does not preclude the possibility that an attorney or judge could be sanctioned by a state bar association or even face criminal charges for something like intentionally tampering with evidence.

Beyond those employed within the criminal justice system, the Supreme Court also has made it clear that witnesses and grand jurors are immune from Section 1983 liability for the content of the testimony they provide.[183]

Qualified Immunity

Government officials not cloaked with absolute immunity performing discretionary functions enjoy **qualified immunity** from civil liability, which means a plaintiff must show that the defendant violated "clearly

QUALIFIED IMMUNITY: Immunity from civil liability that protects public officials for their actions, unless they violate clearly established statutory or constitutional rights that a reasonable person should have known about.

established statutory or constitutional rights of which a reasonable person would have known."[184] In *Malley v. Briggs* (1986),[185] the Supreme Court observed that qualified immunity "provides ample protection to all but the plainly incompetent or those who knowingly violate the law." This controversial doctrine makes it much more difficult to recover damages by suing the police. In recent years, especially in the wake of highly publicized instances of questionable actions by the police, there have been increasing demands for Congress to act to abolish or limit qualified immunity. In March 2021, Congresswoman Ayanna Pressley (D-Mass.) introduced a bill in the House of Representatives to eliminate qualified immunity, but Congress has thus far not acted on the measure. (For more information on qualified immunity and lawsuits against the police generally, see chapter 7.)

Conclusion

In this chapter, we have outlined some of the basic principles of the U.S. Constitution, such as separation of powers, checks and balances, and federalism. We have attempted to illustrate how these principles apply in the context of key criminal justice issues like marijuana policy, alcohol regulations, and immigration, among other topics. We also have addressed numerous Supreme Court decisions that applied these constitutional principles to real-world controversies over the fairness of key words and phrases within criminal laws as well as techniques used in enforcing them.

Ultimately, the nexus between constitutional law and criminal justice is the idea that a constitution is capable of providing a consistent framework for ensuring that laws are created and enforced in a manner that treats all people equally and fairly. Of course, it would be naïve to suggest that the mere existence of a constitution guarantees just outcomes in the application of criminal law. In the end, the search for justice and fairness in criminal contexts will continually evolve through an amalgam of government actors, including the federal, state, and local legislators, who write (and sometimes rewrite) criminal statutes; the chief executives, who issue executive orders that can impact how (or even if) criminal laws are implemented—and who also might choose the heads of key executive branch law enforcement agencies that are tasked with enforcing criminal proscriptions; the prosecutors, who utilize their discretion to decide when to bring specific charges in criminal cases; and, of course, the state and federal trial judges and appellate judges, who evaluate the constitutionality of actions stemming from the other branches of government.

In many ways, all of these actors are constrained, to some extent, by constitutional directives—whether that be Article I limitations on the powers of Congress, Article II limitations on federal executive authority, Article III limitations on the breadth and scope of judicial power, or even limits on the ability of state actors to put forth certain directives that might actually fall within the purview of federal power. Yet the reality is that government officials in all branches of government, at all levels of government, are constantly attempting to stretch the boundaries of their authority. In these moments, courts play a critical function in the pursuit of justice. As we have seen in this chapter, the critical concept of judicial review, as established in the 1803 *Marbury v. Madison decision*,[186] can be applied to the interpretation of key words and phrases in both constitutional provisions and criminal statutes themselves. Overall, then, the courts can play an integral role in bringing uniformity to the actions of government officials by presenting (hopefully) consistent interpretations of guiding principles that underlie American government.

Of course, Supreme Court justices, and even lower court judges, are prone to disagree over the meaning of key constitutional precepts—as are individual members of society. Indeed, one person's vision of a just outcome might be different than another's—and perceptions could certainly vary when one is the victim of crime, as opposed to the person accused of committing a crime, or even the person tasked with enforcing the criminal law. Across all of these perspectives, constitutional law aims to provide a consistent set of principles to guide the pursuit of criminal justice. In the ensuing chapters, we will frame this pursuit around an assessment of how key words and phrases in constitutional amendments, as interpreted by the courts, impact the creation and application of criminal law in the United States.

Discussion Questions

1. Is it a violation of separation of powers for an agency within the executive branch to adopt regulations, enforce those regulations, and also adjudicate cases involving violations of such regulations?
2. Why is the Commerce Clause of the Constitution significant in the development of federal criminal law?
3. Beyond enforcing judicial decisions, what means do presidents have to shape criminal justice policy?
4. What is the extent of the U.S. Supreme Court's appellate jurisdiction? What is the primary mechanism by which this jurisdiction is exercised?
5. What is the difference between statutory interpretation and constitutional interpretation? What are some examples of each?
6. Under what circumstances can someone sue a state official for violating their constitutional rights? What barriers stand in the way of such a remedy?

Endnotes

1   *Marbury v. Madison*, 5 U.S. 137 (1803).
2   *United States v. Nixon*, 418 U.S. 683 (1974).
3   *Bush v. Gore*, 531 U.S. 98 (2000).
4   *Brown v. Board of Education*, 347 U.S. 483 (1954).
5   *Lawrence v. Texas*, 539 U.S. 558 (2003).
6   Endangered Species Act of 1973, Pub. L. No. 93–205, 87 Stat. 884.
7   National Industrial Recovery Act of 1933, Pub. L. No. 73–67, 48 Stat. 195.
8   *A.L.A. Schechter Poultry Corp. v. United States*, 295 U.S. 495 (1935).
9   *Mistretta v. United States*, 488 U.S. 361 (1989).
10 Sentencing Reform Act of 1984, Pub. L. No. 98–473, 98 Stat 1837.
11 *McCulloch v. Maryland*, 17 U.S. 316 (1819).
12 *Arizona v. United States*, 567 U.S. 387 (2012).
13 *Id.*
14 Unlike marijuana, hemp has no more than 0.3% THC (tetrahydrocannabinol).
15 The Harrison Narcotics Tax Act of 1914, Pub. L. 63–223, 38 Stat. 785.

16   *See* Isaac Campos, *Mexicans and the Origins of Marijuana Prohibition in the United States: A Reassessment*, 32 Soc. Hist. of Alc. and Drugs 6–37 (2018) (a survey of competing arguments in literature).

17   Marihuana Tax Act of 1937, Pub. L. 75–238, 50 Stat. 551.

18   *Leary v. United States*, 395 U.S. 6 (1969).

19   The Controlled Substances Act was Title II of the Comprehensive Drug Abuse Prevention and Control Act, Pub L. 91–513, 84 Stat. 1236. Drugs were placed into categories from Schedule I to Schedule V. Schedule I drugs include heroin, LSD, and ecstasy. Schedule II drugs, which are said to have "some accepted medical uses," include cocaine, oxycodone, and methamphetamines.

20   Florida rejected legalization with such a vote of the people in 2014 as did voters in North Dakota in 2018. State legislatures that legalized include Connecticut, Illinois, New York, Rhode Island, and Vermont.

21   *See* James M. Cole, *Memorandum for all United States Attorneys* (2013) (covers the subject of "guidance regarding marijuana enforcement"), https://www.justice.gov/iso/opa/resources/3052013829132756857467.pdf.

22   We also should note that some states have chosen to *decriminalize* marijuana. This means marijuana remains illegal, but offenders are issued citations rather than being arrested, and punishment takes the form of a monetary fine instead of jail time. In Oregon, a ballot initiative passed in 2020 required that all recreational drugs, including heroin and cocaine, be decriminalized—with an emphasis on providing avenues for rehabilitation services as an alternative to even paying fines.

23   Statement of Thomas, J., *Standing Akimbo v. United States*, 594 U.S. ___ (2021).

24   Louisiana is exceptional in this regard; its civil and criminal codes stem from French and Spanish legal sources rather than from English common law.

25   Samuel M. Soref, *The Doctrine of Reasonableness in the Police Power*, 15 Marq. L. Rev. 3 (1930).

26   *The License Cases*, 46 U.S. 592 (1847).

27   *Id.*

28   The number of required signatures can be set by state legislatures or even by ballot initiatives. In California, the figure for a proposed law is 5 percent of all votes cast for the governor in the previous election and 8 percent for a state constitutional amendment. In Florida, a certain number of signatures must come from each of the state's congressional districts.

29   Prior to 2016, all marijuana legalization came about through initiatives and referenda.

30   Among the thirteen states to pass a *Marsy's Law* are California (the first, in 2008), Florida, Georgia, Nevada, North Carolina, North Dakota, Ohio, and South Dakota. Such laws were passed but overturned by courts in Montana and Kentucky.

31   Tara Haelle, *Health Effects of 9/11 Still Plague Responders and Survivors*. Sci. Am., Sept. 10, 2021, https://www.scientificamerican.com/article/health-effects-of-9-11-still-plague-responders-and-survivors/.

32   James Zadroga, *9/11 Health and Compensation Act of 2010*, Pub. L. 111–347, 124 Stat. 3623.

33   The CDC also notes: "The Program also provides initial screenings and treatment to those who were present on the day of the attacks or who worked, lived, or went to school in the New York City disaster area on September 11th or the months that followed. This group is known as Survivors." *See* Centers for Disease Control, *9.11 World Trade Center Health Program*, https://www.cdc.gov/wtc/ataglance.html.

34   *Id.*

35   Never Forget the Heroes: James Zadroga, Ray Pfeifer, and Luis Alvarez Permanent Authorization of the September 11th Victim Compensation Fund Act, Pub. L 116-34, 133 Stat. 1040.

36 Haelle, *supra* note 31.

37 U.S. Sentencing Commission, *Overview of Federal Criminal Cases*, Fiscal Year 2020 (2021), https://www.ussc.gov/research/data-reports/overview-federal-criminal-cases-fiscal-year-2020.

38 Federal Kidnapping Act of 1932 (Lindbergh Law), Pub. L. 72-189, 47 Stat. 326 (codified at 18 U.S.C. § 1201 (1932)).

39 18 U.S.C. § 2314.

40 18 U.S.C. § 2421.

41 *Gonzales v. Raich*, 545 U.S. 1 (2005).

42 The Court also cited *Wickard v. Filburn*, 317 U.S. 111 (1942), in which the majority upheld production quotas imposed by Congress upon wheat farmers via the Agricultural Adjustment Act of 1938.

43 *Standing Akimbo v. United States*, 594 U.S. ____ (2021) (statement of Justice Clarence Thomas).

44 *See Steward Machine Co. v. Davis*, 301 U.S. 548 (1937); *Helvering v. Davis*, 301 U.S. 619 (1937).

45 42 U.S.C. § 408.

46 18 U.S.C. § 1361.

47 50 U.S.C. § 3811.

48 *See, e.g., Gamble v. United States*, 587 U.S. ____ (2019).

49 Agriculture Improvement Act of 2018, Pub. L. 115–334, 132 Stat. 4490.

50 *See* National Conference of State Legislatures, *State Industrial Hemp Statutes* (2020), https://www.ncsl.org/research/agriculture-and-rural-development/state-industrial-hemp-statutes.aspx.

51 28 U.S.C. § 541(c). *See United States v. Solomon*, 216 F. Supp. 835 (S.D.N.Y. 1963); *United States v. Hilario*, 218 F. 3d 19 (1st Cir. 2000) (See for relevant precedent. Under federal law, an Attorney General could fill an opening for a U.S. attorney position for 120 days and under some circumstances, if that replacement is not confirmed by the Senate within 120 days, federal law permits the judges of that federal district court to appoint a temporary replacement. *See* 28 U.S.C. § 546.).

52 The ATF possesses regulatory authority over certain classes of weapons pursuant to the National Firearms Act of 1934. We discuss this matter in chapter 6.

53 *Bordenkircher v. Hayes*, 434 U.S. 357 (1978).

54 *Oyler v. Boles*, 368 U.S. 448 (1962).

55 *Wayte v. United States*, 470 U.S. 598 (1985).

56 Andrea Cipriano, *Progressive Prosecutors Refuse to Prosecute GOP Laws*, The Crime Report, Oct. 19, 2021, https://thecrimereport.org/2021/10/19/progressive-prosecutors-refuse-to-prosecute-gop-laws/.

57 50 CFR §622.37(d)(2)(ii) (effective April 2, 2007) (This standard would be changed to 18 inches); *see* 50 C.F.R. § 622.37(d)(2)(iv) (eff. May 18, 2009).

58 The program was created pursuant to funding provided by Families First Coronavirus Response Act of 2020, Pub. L. 116–127, 134 Stat. 178.

59 *See* Department of Justice, *Two Charged in Rhode Island with Stimulus Fraud*, https://www.justice.gov/opa/pr/two-charged-rhode-island-stimulus-fraud/.

60 FAA, *Unruly Passenger Data*, https://www.faa.gov/data_research/passengers_cargo/unruly_passengers/.

61 Letter from coalition of U.S.-based air carriers to Attorney General Merrick B. Garland, https://www.airlines.org/wp-content/uploads/2021/06/Aviation-Coalition-Letter-to-AG-Garland.pdf.

62 The Sentencing Project, *Private Prisons in the United States*, Mar. 3, 2021, https://www.sentencingproject.org/publications/private-prisons-united-states/.

63   *See, e.g.,* Anti-Drug Abuse Act of 1986, Pub. L. 99–570, 100 Stat. 3207.

64   *Solorio v. United States*, 483 U.S. 435 (1987).

65   Violent Crime Control and Law Enforcement Act of 1994, Pub. L. 103–322, 108 Stat. 1796.

66   *Myers v. United States*, 272 U.S. 52 (1926).

67   *Humphrey's Executor v. United States*, 295 U.S. 602 (1935).

68   *Wiener v. United States*, 357 U.S. 349 (1958).

69   U.S. Const. art. II, § 1, cl. 1. (Gouverneur Morris is credited as the clause's author).

70   *Seila Law v. Consumer Financial Protection Bureau*, 591 U.S. ____ (2020).

71   The case arose when a law firm sought to evade the Bureau's request for documents by challenging the constitution-ality of the Bureau's existence. Although Justice Roberts took issue with the parameters for firing the Bureau's head, Roberts found the issue "severable" from the question of whether the Bureau should exist, leaving it intact—provided that new parameters for the headship were enacted.

72   *Collins v. Yellin*, 594 U.S. ____ (2021).

73   Exec. Order. No 13977 (2021).

74   Exec. Order. No 13980 (2021).

75   Exec. Order. No 14029 (2021).

76   Exec. Order. No 14006 (2021).

77   *In re Neagle*, 135 U.S. 1 (1890).

78   *Id.*

79   *Korematsu v. United States*, 323 U.S. 214 (1944).

80   *Youngstown Sheet & Tube Co. v. Sawyer*, 343 U.S. 579 (1952).

81   Memorandum from U.S. Department of Homeland Security Secretary Janet Napolitano, *Exercising Prosecutorial Discretion with Respect to Individuals Who Came to the United States as Children* (June 15, 2012).

82   DACA allows individuals who are under the age of 31 and who arrived in the U.S. when they were younger than 16 years old to receive two-year "deferments" from deportation—meaning they will not be deported; they also become eligible for work permits and Social Security and Medicare benefits. Those with felony criminal convictions are ineligible, but most misdemeanor convictions do not make a person ineligible, although "significant misdemeanors" could. These two-year deferrals are renewable upon re-application. In 2014, DACA was expanded by executive action to include deportation deferrals for parents of children who were in the United States legally—a program called "DAPA" (Deferred Action for Parents of Americans and Lawful Permanent Residents). Texas and other states sued the federal government, suggesting that DAPA was incompatible with federal immigration laws and unconstitutional under separation of powers principles. *See United States v. Texas*, 579 U.S. 547 (2016) (In this ruling, a 4–4 tie from the Supreme Court, which had only eight justices due to the February 2016 death of Justice Scalia, left in place a Fifth Circuit ruling that had found the DAPA program to be unconstitutional. An attempt by the Obama Administration to apply DACA to people of any age also was struck down. The citation for the Fifth Circuit case is *Texas v. United States*, 787 F.3d 733 (5th Cir. 2015). The original DACA program was not impacted by these decisions.).

83   Memorandum from U.S. Department of Homeland Security Acting Secretary Elaine C. Duke, *Memorandum on Rescission of Deferred Action For Childhood Arrivals (DACA)* (Sept. 5, 2017).

84   *Department of Homeland Security v. Regents of The University of California*, 591 U.S. ____ (2020).

85   Memorandum from President Joseph R. Biden, Jr., *Preserving and Fortifying Deferred Action for Childhood Arrivals (DACA)* (Jan. 20, 2021).

86   Exec. Order No. 13929 (2020).

87   International Emergency Economic Powers Act of 1977, Pub. L. 95–223, 91 Stat. 1626.

88   Pres. Proc. No. 994 (2020).

89   National Emergencies Act of 1976, Pub. L. 94–412, 90 Stat. 1255 (codified at 50 U.S.C. §§ 1601–51 (1976)).

90   Brennan Center for Justice, *A Guide to Emergency Powers and Their Use*, https://www.brennancenter.org/sites/default/files/2019-10/AGuideToEmergencyPowersAndTheirUse_2.13.19.pdf.

91   *South Bay United Pentecostal Church v. Newsom*, 590 U.S. ___ (2020).

92   *Ex parte Milligan*, 71 U.S. 2 (1866).

93   An Act Relating to Habeas Corpus, 12 Stat. 755 (1863).

94   Hawaiian Organic Act, Pub. L. 56–339, 31 Stat. 141 (1900).

95   *Duncan v. Kahanamoku*, 327 U.S. 304 (1946).

96   *Rasul v. Bush*, 542 U.S. 466 (2004); *Hamdi v. Rumsfeld*, 542 U.S. 507 (2004); *Hamdan v. Rumsfeld*, 548 U.S. 557 (2006); *Boumediene v. Bush*, 553 U.S. 723 (2008).

97   Posse Comitatus Act of 1878, Pub. L. 45–263, 20 Stat. 145 (codified at 18 U.S.C. § 1385 (1878)).

98   Insurrection Act of 1807, Pub. L. 9–39, 2 Stat. 443 (codified at 10 U.S.C. §§ 251–55 (1807)).

99   Enforcement Act of 1870, 16 Stat. 140 (1870); Enforcement Act of 1871, 16 Stat. 433 (1871); Second Enforcement Act of 1871 (Ku Klux Klan Act), 17 Stat. 13 (1871).

100 William F. Duker, *The President's Power to Pardon: A Constitutional History*, 18 Wm. & Mary L. Rev. 475 (1977), https://scholarship.law.wm.edu/wmlr/vol18/iss3/3.

101 *Schick v. Reed*, 419 U.S. 256 (1974).

102 *United States v. Nixon*, 418 U.S. 683 (1974) (For further explication of executive privilege's applicability when Congress requests documents from the president, *see Trump v. Mazars*, 591 U.S. ___ (2020), where Justice Roberts created a four-factor test for such matters; that test includes an assessment of "a valid legislative purpose" balanced against "burdens imposed on the presidency.").

103 *Trump v. Vance*, 591 U.S. ___ (2020).

104 *See* Exec. Order No. 13769 (2017) (from which the first "travel ban" arose); *Washington v. Trump*, 847 F. 3d 1151 (9th Cir. 2017) (which halted implementation of this executive order); Exec. Order No. 13780 (2017) (which enacted the second version of the "travel ban"); *International Refugee Assistance Proj. (IRAP) v. Trump*, 857 F. 3d 554 (4th Cir. 2017) and *Hawaii v. Trump*, 859 F. 3d 741 (9th Cir. 2017) (the two circuit court decisions that blocked this order).

105 For example, regarding Syria, both immigrants with lawful entry paperwork and nonimmigrants (e.g., tourists) were banned from entering the United States. For Somalia, only immigrants were barred from entry but not those people who had valid travel or business visas for entry to the United States. In April 2018, Chad was removed from this list per the following order: Pres. Proc. No. 9723 (2018); that came after Chad increased security measures surrounding passport issuance. After the Supreme Court's decision in *Trump v. Hawaii* (2018), more countries were added to the original list, including Eritrea, Kyrgyzstan, Myanmar, Nigeria, Sudan, and Tanzania via this order: Pres. Proc. No. 9983 (2020).

106 *Hawaii v. Trump*, 265 F. Supp. 3d 1140 (Haw. 2017); *Trump v. Hawaii*, 878 F. 3d 662 (9th Cir. 2017).

107 *See, e.g.*, Pres. Proc. No. 9984 (2020); Pres. Proc. No. 9993 (2020); Pres. Proc. No. 10315 (2021).

108 *Korematsu v. United States*, 322 U.S. 214 (1944) (Jackson, J., dissenting).

109 *Trump v. Hawaii*, 585 U.S. ___ (2018).

110 Under a system known as *merit selection*, a state's governor chooses a judicial nominee from a list of potential candidates created by an independent panel. In *merit retention* systems, voters select *yes* or *no* as to whether a state judge gets another term in office. Whereas federal judges have life tenure, most state judges serve defined terms, usually with an opportunity for reappointment. For further reading on state methods for judicial selection, *see* Martin H. Redish & Aronoff, Jennifer, *The Real Constitutional Problem with State Judicial Selection: Due Process, Judicial Retention, and the Dangers of Popular Constitutionalism*, 56 Wm. & Mary L. Rev. 1 (2014).

111 Judiciary Act of 1789, 1 Stat. 73.

112 U.S. Const. art. II, § 2. In 2013, a Democrat-controlled Senate eliminated filibusters during confirmation hearings for district court, circuit court, and executive branch positions. In 2017, a Republican-controlled Senate eliminated filibusters during Supreme Court confirmation hearings in the lead-up to Neil Gorsuch's 54–45 confirmation vote on April 17, 2017; sixty votes would have been needed to stop a filibuster under Senate "cloture" procedures.

113 28 U.S.C. § 2284(a).

114 *Shapiro v. McManus*, 577 U.S. 39 (2015).

115 18 U.S.C. § 7.

116 *See* Submerged Lands Act of 1953, 43 U.S.C. §§ 1301-1303. (This allows states to retain jurisdiction over offenses committed on waterways, islands, or submerged land within three nautical miles of a shoreline.); Pres. Proc. 5928, (1988) (This proclamation set the outer boundaries of federal jurisdiction at twelve nautical miles from a shoreline); U.S. Department of Justice, *Maritime Jurisdiction* (2020) (a nautical mile is equivalent to 1.151 miles on land), https://www.justice.gov/archives/jm/criminal-resource-manual-670-maritime-jurisdiction.

117 18 U.S.C. § 7(1) (This law defines an American ship as "any vessel belonging in whole or in part to the United States or any citizen thereof"); *United States v. Flores*, 289 U.S. 137 (1933).

118 *See United States v. Holmes*, 18 U.S. 412 (1890); *United States v. Palmer* 16 U.S. 610 (1818).

119 *United States v. Bevans*, 16 U.S. 336 (1818).

120 Clean Water Act of 1972, Pub. L. 92–500, 86 Stat. 816, 33 U.S.C. §§ 1251-1276. In *Rapanoa v. United States*, 547 U.S. 715 (2006), Justice Scalia's plurality opinion referenced *Webster's Second* in saying that "... on its only plausible interpretation, the phrase 'the waters of the United States' includes only those relatively permanent, standing or continuously flowing bodies of water 'forming geographic features' that are described in ordinary parlance as 'streams[,] ... oceans, rivers, [and] lakes.'" He added, "The phrase does not include channels through which water flows intermittently or ephemerally, or channels that periodically provide drainage for rainfall." A prior decision, *Solid Waste Agency of Northern Cook County v. U.S. Army Corps of Engineers*, 531 U.S. 159 (2001), had previously refused to allow federal jurisdiction over "non-navigable, isolated, intrastate ponds that lack a sufficient connection to traditional navigable waters." *See United States v. Riverside Bayview Homes, Inc.* 474 U.S. 121 (1985); *County of Maui, Hawaii v. Hawaii Wildlife Fund*, 590 U.S. ___ (2020) (for discussion of adjacent waterways or discharges that travel into navigable waterways or through groundwater).

121 U.S. Dept. of Justice, Office of Public Affairs, *Ahmed Abu Khatallah Sentenced to 22 Years in Prison for September 2012 Attack in Benghazi, Libya*, June 27, 2018, https://www.justice.gov/opa/pr/ahmed-abu-khatallah-sentenced-22-years-prison-september-2012-attack-benghazi-libya; U.S. Dept. of Justice, Office of Public Affairs, *Mustafa Al-Imam Sentenced to More than 19 years in Prison for September 2012 Terrorist Attack in Benghazi, Libya*, Jan. 23, 2020, https://www.justice.gov/opa/pr/mustafa-al-imam-sentenced-more-19-years-prison-september-2012-terrorist-attack-benghazi-libya.

122 *See* United States Court of Appeals for the Federal Circuit, *About the Court* (this court primarily hears civil cases), https://cafc.uscourts.gov/home/the-court/about-the-court/.

123   *Obergefell v. Hodges*, 576 U.S. 664 (2015) (The Sixth Circuit was the lone circuit to suggest that states could continue to ban same-sex marriage.); *see DeBoer v. Snyder*, 772 F.3d 388 (6th Cir. 2014); Other circuits had legalized same-sex marriage: *Bostic v. Schaefer*, 760 F.3d 352 (4th Cir. 2014); *Perry v. Brown*, 671 F.3d 1052 (9th Cir. 2012); *Baskin v. Bogan*, 766 F.3d 648 (7th Cir. 2014); *Kitchen v. Herbert*, 755 F.3d 1193 (10th Cir. 2014).

124   *Houston v. Lack*, 625 F. Supp. 786 (W.D. Tenn. 1986).

125   Evan Osnos, *Biden Inherits FDR's Supreme Court Problem*, The New Yorker, Apr. 18, 2021.

126   According to Article III, Sect. 2, of the U.S. Constitution, the Supreme Court can hear cases on original jurisdiction under the following limited circumstances: "all cases affecting ambassadors, other public ministers and consuls, and those in which a state shall be party."

127   28 U.S.C. § 1253.

128   *Whole Woman's Health et al. v. Austin Reeve Jackson, Judge, et al., On Application For Injunctive Relief*, 594 U.S. ___ (2021). *See* Louis Jacobson, *The Supreme Court's "Shadow Docket": What You Need to Know*, PolitiFact, The Poynter Institute, Oct. 18, 2021, https://www.politifact.com/article/2021/oct/18/supreme-courts-shadow-docket-what-you-need-know/.

129   Adam Liptak, *Alito Responds to Critics of the Supreme Court's "Shadow Docket."* N.Y. Times, Sept. 30, 2021.

130   Justice Thurgood Marshall did have experience serving as counsel for indigent defendants through his role with the NAACP Legal Defense Fund.

131   *Comm. on Judiciary v. McGahn*, 415 F. Supp. 3d 148 (D.D.C. 2019); *See* Bobby Allyn, *In Blow to White House, Federal Judge Rules That Don McGahn Must Testify*, NPR, Nov. 25, 2019, https://www.npr.org/2019/11/25/782705643/federal-judge-rules-that-mcgahn-must-testify-delivering-blow-to-white-house.

132   *Pierce v. Dist. of Columbia*, 146 F. Supp. 3d 197 (D.D.C. 2015).

133   *Make the Road New York v. McAleenan*, 405 F. Supp. 3d 1 (D.D.C. 2019) (Prior to a July 2019 policy change from the Trump administration, Immigration and Customs Enforcement officials could apply expedited removal to those illegal immigrants caught within 100 air miles of a U.S. border within 14 days of entering the country; the policy shift lengthened the 14-day period to two years, and it also eliminated the 100-mile limit by allowing expedited removal to apply anywhere in the United States.).

134   *Make the Road New York v. Wolf*, 962 F.3d 612 (D.C. Cir. 2020).

135   Marguerite Ward, *GOP Leaders Used Judge Ketanji Brown Jackson's Hearing to Rebuke Critical Race Theory. Scholars Say It's A Disgraceful Attempt To Disqualify Her*, Business Insider, March 25, 2022, https://www.businessinsider.com/gop-leaders-using-ketanji-brown-jacksons-hearing-to-rebuke-critical-race-theory-2022-3; Myah Ward, *Blackburn to Jackson: Can You Define 'the Word Woman'?* Politico, March 22, 2022, https://www.politico.com/news/2022/03/22/blackburn-jackson-define-the-word-woman-00019543.

136   *See* TRAC Immigration, *Outcomes of Deportation Proceedings in Immigration Court by Nationality, State, Court, Hearing Location, and Type of Charge Scholars at Syracuse University* (2022), https://trac.syr.edu/phptools/immigration/court_backlog/deport_outcome_charge.php.

137   *See* Department of Justice, *Executive Office for Immigration Review Adjudication Statistics; Asylum Decision Rates*, Apr. 18, 2022 (for asylum decision statistics), https://www.justice.gov/eoir/page/file/1248491/download.

138   Federal law explicitly prevents a federal district court judge from handling these immigration cases. *See* 8 U.S.C. § 1357.

139   Ingrid Eagly & Steven Shafer, *Access to Counsel in Immigration Court*, American Immigration Council, Sept. 28, 2016, https://www.americanimmigrationcouncil.org/research/access-counsel-immigration-court.

140   *See* TRAC Immigration, *Immigration Court Backlog Tool: Pending Cases and Length of Wait by Nationality, State, Court, and Hearing Location* (2022), https://trac.syr.edu/phptools/immigration/court_backlog/.

141   *See* Department of Justice, *Executive Office for Immigration Review Adjudication Statistics; Case Appeals Filed, Completed, and Pending*, Apr. 18, 2022, https://www.justice.gov/eoir/page/file/1248501/download.

142   Indian Reorganization Act of 1934, Pub. L. 73–383, 48 Stat. 984.

143   U.S. Department of Interior, Indian Affairs, Tribal Court Systems, https://www.bia.gov/CFRCourts/tribal-justice-support-directorate.

144   Violence against Women Reauthorization Act of 2013, Pub. L. 113–4; 127 Stat. 55; *see* 25 U.S.C. § 1304 (the specific provision related to Native American domestic violence cases).

145   18 U.S.C §177(a).

146   *United States v. Bryant*, 579 U.S. 140 (2016).

147   There are five Courts of Indian Offences around the country: the Albuquerque CFR Court; the Southern Plains CFR Court; the Western Region CFR Court; the Eastern Oklahoma Region CFR Court; and the Southwest Region CFR Court. These courts are established through agreements between the U.S. Bureau of Indian Affairs and individual tribes.

148   Major Crimes Act of 1885, 23 Stat. 385 (codified at 18 U.S.C. § 1153 (1885)) (The Major Crimes Act was passed in response to the Supreme Court's decision in *Ex parte Crow Dog*, 109 U.S. 556 (1883), where the Court ruled that federal courts lacked the jurisdiction to address a case in which one Native person had killed another Native person on Native land—because Congress had not explicitly afforded for a murder charge in that situation. The murder in question involved the killing of Chief Spotted Tail by Crow Dog, both of the Rosebud Sioux Tribe, on Tribal land. After this murder occurred, Tribal elders determined that the concept of "restorative justice" should yield a punishment of restitution, in which the family of Crow Dog would give Spotted Tail's family money, horses, and other goods. State police, however, arrested Crow Dog; he was then charged with murder in federal court and sentenced to death by hanging. The Supreme Court ruled that this trial was improper without a congressional grant of jurisdiction for federal courts. The Major Crimes Act was, in turn, passed in 1885 and upheld by the Supreme Court in *United States v. Kagama*, 118 U.S. 375 (1886).).

149   Offenses include: murder; manslaughter; kidnapping; maiming; rape; arson; burglary; robbery; larceny; felony child abuse or neglect; assault with intent to commit rape, assault with a dangerous weapon, and assault resulting in serious bodily injury. A separate law, 18 U.S.C § 177(a), makes it a federal crime for a Native American be a three-time offender of domestic violence laws. In *United States v. Bryant*, 579 U.S. 140 (2016), the Supreme Court found that tribal convictions, even when no right to counsel was applied, can, in fact, count as offenses that make a person a habitual offender under this statute.

150   *Keeble v. United States*, 412 U.S. 205 (1973) (In this case, the Supreme Court found it acceptable that a Native American defendant was charged in federal court with "assault with intent to commit serious bodily injury"—despite the fact that the Major Crimes Act only allotted for "assault *resulting* in serious bodily injury" [emphasis added] to be a federal crime. The high Court relied upon a caveat in federal law that allows for "assault resulting in serious bodily injury" to be "defined and punished in accordance with the laws of the State in which such offense was committed." Because this crime occurred in South Dakota, where "assault with intent to commit serious bodily injury" was in fact a legislatively defined offense, the Court permitted that charge in federal court. In addition, the Supreme Court also indicated that a jury should have been given an instruction to consider a lesser-included-offense of "simple assault." In this regard, Justice Brennan's majority opinion relied upon Federal Rule of Criminal Procedure 31(c),

which says that "The defendant may be found guilty of an offense necessarily included in the offense charged. ..." The majority opinion framed this interpretation as providing a benefit to the accused, saying that: "... our decision today neither expands the reach of the Major Crimes Act nor permits the Government to infringe the residual jurisdiction of a tribe by bringing prosecutions in federal court that are not authorized by statute. We hold only that, where an Indian is prosecuted in federal court under the provisions of the Act, the Act does not require that he be deprived of the protection afforded by an instruction on a lesser included offense, assuming of course that the evidence warrants such an instruction.").

151 *Wetsit v. Stafne*, 44 F.3d 823 (9th Cir. 1995).

152 *McGirt v. Oklahoma*, 591 U.S. ___ (2020) (The state of Oklahoma had prosecuted McGirt for sex offenses against a child under the age of 18, but the Court found that only federal courts held jurisdiction over this offense because he was a member of the Creek Nation, and the offenses took place on land that belonged to the Creek Nation. In relying upon analysis of treaties and statutes from the 1800s, the majority opinion from Justice Gorsuch concluded that approximately 19 million acres in the eastern part of Oklahoma still belonged to the Creek Nation.).

153 David Heska Wanbli Weiden, *This 19th-Century Law Helps Shape Criminal Justice in Indian Country*, N.Y. Times, June 19, 2020 (citing U.S. Department of Justice: *Indian Country Investigations and Prosecutions*, https://www.justice.gov/otj/page/file/1231431/download).

154 *Oklahoma v. Castro-Huerta*, 597 U.S. ___ (2022).

155 *Xiulu Ruan v. United States*, 597 U.S. ___ (2022). The Court said that "the Government must prove beyond a reasonable doubt that the defendant knowingly or intentionally acted in an unauthorized manner," resulting in an enhanced burden for a prosecutor seeking a guilty verdict.

156 *United States v. Stevens*, 559 U.S. 460 (2010) (evaluating 18 U.S.C. § 48).

157 *United States v. Richards*, 755 F.3d 269 (5th Cir. 2014); the amended law is: Animal Crush Video Prohibition Act of 2010, Pub. L. 111–294, 124 Stat. 3177.

158 *Brown v. Board of Education*, 347 U.S. 483 (1954).

159 The "separate but equal" doctrine was established in *Plessy v. Ferguson*, 163 U.S. 537 (1896) and remained the "law of the land" until it was repudiated in a series of decisions beginning with *Brown v. Board of Education* in 1954. The doctrine was finally abolished in *Loving v. Virginia*, 388 U.S. 1 (1967), which found a state ban on interracial marriage to violate the Equal Protection Clause of the Fourteenth Amendment.

160 *Lawrence v. Texas*, 539 U.S. 558 (2003); *Bowers v. Hardwick*, 478 U.S. 186 (1986).

161 *Chisholm v. Georgia*, 2 U.S. 419 (1793).

162 *Dred Scott v. Sandford*, 60 U.S. 393 (1857).

163 See, e.g., *Pollock v. Loan and Trust Company*, 157 U.S. 429 (1895).

164 *Oregon v. Mitchell*, 400 U.S. 112 (1970).

165 *Osborne v. Ohio*, 495 U.S. 103 (1990).

166 Computer Fraud and Abuse Act of 1986 (CFAA), Pub. L. 99–474, 100 Stat. 1213, 18 U.S.C. § 1030.

167 Antiterrorism and Effective Death Penalty Act of 1996, Pub. L. 104–132, 110 Stat. 1214.

168 *Ex parte Young*, 209 U.S. 123 (1908).

169 *Bell v. Hood*, 327 U.S. 678 (1946).

170 *Reno v. ACLU*, 521 U.S. 844 (1997).

171 *Winter v. Natural Resources Defense Council, Inc.*, 555 U.S. 7 (2008).

172 Civil Rights Act of 1871, 17 Stat. 13.

173   *See Monell v. Dept. of Social Services*, 436 U.S. 658 (1978) (The Supreme Court held that municipalities can be sued under Section 1983.).

174   *Bivens v. Six Unknown Federal Narcotics Agents*, 403 U.S. 388 (1971).

175   *Pierson v. Ray*, 386 U.S. 547 (1967) (citing *Tenney v. Brandhove*, 341 U.S. 367 (1951)); *see Eastland v. United States Servicemen's Fund*, 421 U.S. 491 (1975).

176   *See, e.g., Nixon v. Fitzgerald*, 457 U.S. 731 (1982).

177   *Clinton v. Jones*, 520 U.S. 681 (1997).

178   *Pierson v. Ray*, 386 U.S. 547 (1967) (Chief Justice Warren's majority opinion in *Pierson v. Ray* discussed the common-law origins of absolute immunity for judges by quoting from an 1872 case precedent, saying, "Few doctrines were more solidly established at common law than the immunity of judges from liability for damages for acts committed within their judicial jurisdiction, as this Court recognized when it adopted the doctrine in *Bradley v. Fisher* (1872). This immunity applies even when the judge is accused of acting maliciously and corruptly, and it 'is not for the protection or benefit of a malicious or corrupt judge, but for the benefit of the public, whose interest it is that the judges should be at liberty to exercise their functions with independence and without fear of consequences.'" Later, in *Stump v. Sparkman*, 435 U.S. 349 (1978), the Court offered absolute immunity to a Judge Stump from Dekalb County, Indiana, who had signed an order mandating a tubal ligation procedure for a mentally disabled 15-year-old girl. The request for the procedure was made by the girl's mother pursuant to an Indiana law in place at the time. The Court found that Judge Stump was entitled to the protection of absolute immunity because he "performed the type of act normally performed only by judges and … he did so in his capacity as a Circuit Court Judge." Justice White's majority opinion suggested that: "The Indiana law vested in Judge Stump the power to entertain and act upon the petition for sterilization. He is, therefore, under the controlling cases, immune from damages liability even if his approval of the petition was in error." In dissent, Justice Stewart, declared that: "[W]hat Judge Stump did … was in no way an act 'normally performed by a judge.' Indeed, there is no reason to believe that such an act has ever been performed by *any* other Indiana judge, either before or since." Furthermore, the dissent declared that: "A judge is not free, like a loose cannon, to inflict indiscriminate damage whenever he announces that he is acting in his judicial capacity."

179   *Id.*

180   *Imbler v. Pachtman*, 424 U.S. 409 (1976).

181   Perhaps surprisingly, it was Pachtman who had brought the new, exonerating evidence to light. According to the majority opinion for this case, Pachtman wrote a letter to California's governor explaining that "newly discovered corroborating witnesses for [the defendant's] alibi, as well as new revelations about [the] prime witness['s] background which indicated that he was less trustworthy." The defense attorney lauded this post-conviction "detective work" from the prosecutor as being "'[i]n the highest tradition of law enforcement and justice', and as a premier example of 'devotion to duty.'" Yet the defendant still filed a Section 1983 lawsuit against this prosecutor based on an accusation that the prosecutor had "knowingly used false testimony and suppressed material evidence."

182   *Polk County v. Dodson*, 454 U.S. 312 (1981).

183   *Briscoe v. LaHue*, 460 U.S. 325 (1983); *see Imbler, supra* note 180 (for discussion of grand jurors).

184   *Harlow v. Fitzgerald*, 457 U.S. 800 (1982).

185   *Malley v. Briggs*, 475 U.S. 335 (1986).

186   *Marbury v. Madison*, 5 U.S. 137 (1803).

CHAPTER 3

Constitutional Sources of Rights

"We could, of course, facilitate the process of administering justice to those who violate criminal laws by ignoring ... the entire Bill of Rights—but it is the very purpose of the Bill of Rights to identify values that may not be sacrificed to expediency. In a just society those who govern, as well as those who are governed, must obey the law."

—Justice John Paul Stevens,
Dissenting in *United States v. Leon*, 468 U.S. 897 (1984)

Learning Objectives

After reading this chapter, you should understand the following:

1. The individual rights protected by the Constitution prior to the adoption of the Bill of Rights
2. Why the Bill of Rights is critically important to the administration of criminal justice
3. The significance of the post-Civil War amendments to the Constitution
4. The profound importance of due process of law in the administration of justice and protection of individual liberty
5. How and why the protections of Bill of Rights were extended to cover actions and policies of state and local governments
6. The origin of the right of privacy and its impact on criminal law
7. Why the Equal Protection Clause of the Fourteenth Amendment is fundamentally important in the law of civil rights

Key Cases

The Civil Rights Cases, 109 U.S. 3 (1883)
Tharpe v. Sellers, 583 U.S. ___ (2018)
Timbs v. Indiana, 586 U.S. ___ (2019)
Jacobson v. Massachusetts, 197 U.S. 11 (1905)
Brown v. Board of Education, 347 U.S. 483 (1954)
Griswold v. Connecticut, 381 U.S. 479 (1965)
Dobbs v. Jackson Women's Health Organization, 595 U.S. ___ (2022)
Lawrence v. Texas, 539 U.S. 558 (2003)

Introduction

Any time Congress, a state legislature, or a local governing body enacts a law defining a crime and providing a penalty, there is a potential conflict with the U.S. Constitution. A criminal law can be challenged either because the legislative body lacked the authority to enact it or because its enforcement trenches upon constitutionally protected liberties. (In the next three chapters, we examine how rights enshrined within the First and Second Amendments limit the enactment and enforcement of criminal prohibitions affecting the freedoms of speech, press, and assembly and the right to keep and bear arms, respectively.) And of course, the enforcement of unquestionably constitutional laws still carries the potential to violate constitutional rights. From arrest to punishment (and everything that happens in between), the administration of justice necessarily implicates a number of constitutional provisions.

In this chapter, we provide an overview of the constitutional rights that affect the criminal justice system. These include rights found in the Constitution as it was drafted in Philadelphia in 1787, the Bill of Rights that was added in 1791 shortly after ratification, and subsequent constitutional amendments. Of particular importance is the Fourteenth Amendment, with its guarantees of due process of law and equal protection of the laws.

DUE PROCESS OF LAW: The right to be treated fairly by the state and to have an opportunity to contest adverse state action.

EQUAL PROTECTION OF THE LAWS: Equal justice under the law for all persons; the right to be free from official discrimination based on race, ethnicity, religion, gender, sexual orientation, and other characteristics.

Rights Protected by the Unamended Constitution

As we saw in Chapter 1, the Antifederalists objected to the Constitution because it lacked a Bill of Rights. However, as Alexander Hamilton stressed in Federalist No. 84, the document drafted in Philadelphia was not totally devoid of important protections of liberty. These included a limitation on prosecutions for treason, prohibitions of bills of attainder and ex post facto laws, and a provision safeguarding the writ of habeas corpus. The common denominator of these provisions was, and remains today, a desire to limit the government's powers of arrest and prosecution.

Limitation of Treason

Treason is the crime of betraying one's country to a foreign enemy. The English common law viewed treason as singularly heinous, far worse than a felony, and punishments for those convicted of treason were especially brutal. Moreover, the Crown abused the crime of treason, using it as a means of punishing political opponents. To ensure that such abuse would not take place in the United States, Article III, Section 3 of the Constitution provides: "Treason against the United States, shall consist only in levying War against them, or in adhering to their Enemies, giving them Aid and Comfort." And to make it more difficult for the government to prosecute people for treason, the same section provides: "No Person shall be convicted of Treason unless on the Testimony of two Witnesses to the same overt Act, or on Confession in open Court." In *Ex parte Bollman* (1807),[1] Chief Justice John Marshall opined "that the crime of treason should not be extended by construction to doubtful cases," and the federal courts have followed this dictum. Consequently, convictions for treason have been rare in this country. And throughout this nation's history, the U.S. government has executed only one person for treason. William Bruce Mumford was hanged in 1862 for the offense of destroying a U.S. flag in the midst of the Civil War.

The most recent Supreme Court decisions on treason arose in the aftermath of World War II. In *Haupt v. United States* (1947),[2] the Supreme Court upheld the conviction of a man who sheltered Nazi saboteurs during the War, saying that "[t]he law of treason makes and properly makes conviction difficult but not impossible." In *Kawakita v. United States* (1952),[3] the Court upheld the treason conviction of a Japanese American who had tortured American prisoners of war held in Japan during World War II. Tomoya Kawakita had been sentenced to death in 1948, but President Eisenhower commuted the sentence to life in prison. In 1963, President John F. Kennedy ordered Kawakita deported to Japan.

Julius and Ethel Rosenberg, a married couple, were put to death in 1953 after being convicted of providing the Soviet Union with classified information about U.S. capabilities related to radar, sonar, and nuclear weapons. But the Rosenbergs were convicted of espionage and not, as many believe, treason. Today, federal prosecutors are more likely to

TREASON: The crime of giving *aid and comfort* to the enemies of one's own country or levying war against one's own country.

prosecute accused traitors for espionage or some other national security offense, rather than the offense of treason, which is constitutionally difficult to prosecute.

Prohibition of Bills of Attainder and Ex Post Facto Laws

BILL OF ATTAINDER: A legislative act declaring a party guilty of a crime without use of judicial trial.

EX POST FACTO LAW: A law that criminalizes an act theretofore noncriminal and allows for retroactive prosecution of that act. Also, any law that retroactively increases punishments or changes evidentiary rules to facilitate a conviction.

A bill of attainder is a legislative act that imposes punishment for a crime without a trial in a court of law. An ex post facto law is a statute that criminalizes an act after the fact and allows for the prosecution of a person for that act, even though it was legal at the time it was done. As with treason, English monarchs abused bills of attainder and ex post facto laws by getting Parliament to enact them against the supposed enemies of the Crown. To prevent such abuse from occurring in this country, Article I, Section 9 of the Constitution provides: "No Bill of Attainder or ex post facto Law shall be passed." Article I, Section 10 extends these injunctions to the state legislatures.

Given these explicit constitutional prohibitions, American courts have had little to say about bills of attainder. Historically, the most noteworthy case involved a post-Civil War statute that required attorneys to swear they had not participated in the rebellion as a condition of practicing before federal courts. In *Ex parte Garland* (1866),[4] the Court struck down the law, saying: "All enactments of this kind partake of the nature of bills of pains and penalties, and are subject to the constitutional inhibition against the passage of bills of attainder, under which general designation they are included." Similarly, in *United States v. Brown* (1965),[5] the Supreme Court held that a federal law banning members of the Communist Party from serving as officers of labor unions was, in effect, a bill of attainder.

A decade after the Constitution was ratified, the Supreme Court expounded on the prohibition of ex post facto laws. In *Calder v. Bull* (1798),[6] Justice Samuel Chase identified four types of laws that fall within the prohibition:

> 1st. Every law that makes an action done before the passing of the law, and which was innocent when done, criminal, and punishes such action. 2d. Every law that aggravates a crime, or makes it greater than it was when committed. 3d. Every law that changes the punishment, and inflicts a greater punishment, than the law annexed to the crime when committed. 4th. Every law that alters the legal rules of evidence

and receives less or different testimony than the law
required at the time of the commission of the offense
in order to convict the offender.

Justice Chase's delineation remains relevant in the modern era. For
instance, in *Miller v. Florida* (1987), the Supreme Court said that sentencing guidelines not in effect when a crime was committed could not be
used to increase punishment for that crime.[7] Similarly, in *Carmell v. Texas*
(2000),[8] the Supreme Court reversed a conviction for sexual assault of
a minor in a case where a law that removed a requirement for a child
victim's testimony to be corroborated was applied retroactively.

Habeas Corpus

Habeas corpus is a common-law mechanism dating back to at least the
twelfth century.[9] As we noted in Chapter 1, Article I, Section 9 of the Constitution states, "The privilege of the Writ of Habeas Corpus shall not
be suspended, unless when in Cases of Rebellion or Invasion the public
Safety may require it." We also observed how the Supreme Court in 1866
refused to allow President Lincoln to suspend habeas corpus unilaterally
during the Civil War[10] and how after World War II the Court invalidated
the suspension of the writ in the Hawai'i territory.[11] The writ of habeas
corpus continues to play an important role in the judicial protection of
civil rights and liberties.

> **HABEAS CORPUS:** A court order requiring a person in custody to be brought before a court to determine the legality of that custody.

Some of the most dramatic habeas corpus cases in recent decades
were filed on behalf of inmates at the terrorist detention facility at the
American naval base at Guantanamo Bay, Cuba. The George W. Bush
Administration took the position that foreign nationals held outside the
United States proper did not have the right to seek habeas corpus relief
in the federal courts. The Supreme Court disagreed, saying in *Rasul v.
Bush* (2004)[12] that "[a]liens held at the base, no less than American citizens, are entitled to invoke the federal courts' authority." This prompted
Congress to enact a law stripping the federal courts of jurisdiction over
habeas corpus petitions from "enemy combatants" housed outside the
United States.[13] In *Boumediene v. Bush* (2008),[14] the Court struck down this
provision as an unconstitutional suspension of habeas corpus. One can
infer from the decisions cited that habeas corpus, both as an individual
right and as a judicial power, is closely guarded by the courts.

Federal Habeas Corpus Review of State Prisoners' Cases

Pursuant to federal law passed in 1867, state prisoners can use a habeas
corpus petition to ask federal courts—generally, starting with a district

court—to examine whether their incarceration violates the Constitution, federal laws, or treaties.[15] A 1948 amendment to federal law requires that a state prisoner has "exhausted the remedies available in the courts of the State" before seeking federal habeas relief.[16] A number of the Supreme Court's most impactful decisions with respect to the administration of justice, in fact, have come in cases that originated as petitions for habeas corpus.[17] In the 1960s, the Supreme Court under Chief Justice Earl Warren issued a series of rulings that broadened a state prisoner's access to habeas corpus review in federal courts.[18] Since the 1960s, however, more conservative rulings from Supreme Court have established limits on the use of federal habeas corpus petitions. In 1976, for example, the Court said that a habeas petition would not be permitted for Fourth Amendment search and seizure appeals when that issue "has previously been afforded an opportunity for full and fair litigation ... in the state courts."[19] In the 1990s, in an effort to halt "abuses" of the writ, the Court also put limits on the use of multiple habeas petitions by one inmate.[20]

In 1996, Congress moved to further limit the use of federal habeas corpus petitions with the passage of the Antiterrorism and Effective Death Penalty Act of 1996 (AEDPA).[21] This law indicates that any subsequent habeas petition after the first one must pass through a "gatekeeping" function of the U.S. Courts of Appeals; therefore, a circuit court would have to issue a motion allowing the prisoner to file successive habeas petitions in the federal district courts.[22] In 1996, the Supreme Court upheld the statute after a challenge from a Georgia death row inmate,[23] but in 2020, the Court noted that a "motion to alter or amend" a habeas ruling, which must occur within 28 days of judgment, "does not count as a second or successive habeas application."[24]

The AEDPA also says that a petition for habeas relief requires "a substantial showing of the denial of a constitutional right."[25] In its decision in *Miller-El v. Cockrell* (2003),[26] the Supreme Court found that lower courts had erred in failing to use this standard; the lower courts, instead, had sought "clear and convincing evidence" of a constitutional violation related to a prosecutor's consideration of race in jury selection (amounting to a constitutional violation, as we will discuss in Chapter 12). However, the Supreme Court said the focus should have revolved around the lower standard of a "substantial showing" of a constitutional violation.

Interestingly, in *Herrera v. Collins* (1993),[27] the Supreme Court held that actual innocence is not, on its own, a valid reason for federal courts to grant habeas corpus relief. Yet in *Schlup v. Delo* (1995),[28] the Court found that a claim of innocence that *also* raises a constitutional violation can move forward as a habeas petition. This type of issue can become particularly relevant when new DNA evidence comes to light in exonerating a long-incarcerated inmate. Along these lines, in *House v. Bell* (2006),[29] the Supreme Court granted a Tennessee inmate a hearing in federal district court to address an ineffective counsel claim that revolved around newly discovered DNA evidence. The majority opinion from Justice Kennedy said this was "... the rare case where—had the jury heard all the conflicting testimony—it is more likely than not that no reasonable juror viewing the record as a whole would lack reasonable doubt."

JURISPRUDENCE

Juror's Racist Comments Spur Habeas Corpus Petition
Tharpe v. Sellers, 583 U.S. ___ (2018)

In *Tharpe v. Sellers* (2018), the Supreme Court addressed the matter of Keith Tharpe, who was sentenced to death in 1990 for the murder and kidnapping of his sister-in-law.

Seven years after Tharpe was found guilty, one of the jurors in his case made racist statements, provided in an affidavit, indicating that racial prejudice may have played a role in the jury's deliberations regarding Tharpe, a Black man. The juror used the N-word in saying "there are two types of black people" before indicating that Tharpe, "who wasn't in the 'good' black folks category in my book, should get the electric chair for what he did"; this juror even said that "[s]ome of the jurors voted for death because they felt Tharpe should be an example to other blacks who kill blacks." Other comments invoked the Bible in a misguided attempt to justify prejudice.

Based on this evidence of juror prejudice, Tharpe raised a habeas corpus claim in federal district court, but that court denied the motion and the Eleventh Circuit agreed with the lower court's decision. Success in a habeas claim typically requires a showing that the defendant has been "prejudiced" by an error, as opposed to the error being "harmless."[30] Moreover, federal courts tend to defer to the findings of state courts on factual matters, with the Supreme Court's majority opinion in this case summarizing the Eleventh Circuit's denial of habeas

relief as being tied to the defendant having "failed to produce any clear and convincing evidence contradicting the state court's determination that [the racist juror's] presence on the jury did not prejudice [Tharpe]."

However, the Supreme Court's per curiam opinion declared that: "Our review of the record compels a different conclusion." Based on what it called the "remarkable affidavit" of this juror, the opinion found that, "[a]t the very least, jurists of reason could debate whether Tharpe has shown by clear and convincing evidence that the state court's factual determination was wrong." The opinion found there was "compelling evidence" that racial prejudice had imbued the jury's deliberations in the sentencing phase of this death penalty case. The Court did observe that the factual findings of state courts were "binding" upon federal courts—including the Supreme Court—unless there was "clear and convincing evidence" to override those findings. Here the juror's statements were found to meet that threshold.

Compensation for the Wrongfully Convicted

It is worth noting that thirty-seven states allow for some type of monetary compensation for those who have erroneously served prison time, although such laws do not create a cause of action against judges, prosecutors, or individual officers. In this regard, The Innocence Project has found that the average amount of time served by a person exonerated by DNA evidence is fourteen years. States that allow for compensation to the wrongfully incarcerate vary in terms of mechanisms, with some requiring the passage of a legislative act to authorize such a claim in an individual case and others allowing civil suits against municipalities. These state laws also can vary in regard to things like maximum payouts, which often set a fixed dollar amount per year served in prison.[31]

The Bill of Rights

To address the criticism that the Constitution lacked sufficient protection for liberty, the First Congress in 1789 adopted a series of amendments that, when ratified in 1791, became the Bill of Rights. Reflected in these amendments are the concerns of Americans stemming from their colonial and Revolutionary War experience, such as the First Amendment's protection of the freedoms of speech, press, and assembly, the Second Amendment's right to keep and bear arms, the Third Amendment's prohibition against soldiers being quartered in citizens' homes, and the Seventh Amendment's guarantee of a jury trial in civil cases. Reflecting a desire to avoid the religious conflict that plagued England for centuries, the First Amendment prohibited Congress from making laws "respecting an establishment of religion, or prohibiting the free exercise thereof."

The Importance of the Bill of Rights in the Administration of Justice

Underlying the Bill of Rights is the belief that citizens must be protected from the government's power to arrest, prosecute, and punish. Criminal justice was very much on the minds of Americans in the late-eighteenth century, as they were well aware of a long history of abuse of the criminal law. Accordingly, the Fourth Amendment forbids unreasonable searches and seizures. The Fifth Amendment prohibits double jeopardy and compulsory self-incrimination and guarantees due process of law. The Sixth Amendment recognizes the right to counsel, the right to confront one's accusers, trial by jury, and several other important rights. The Eighth Amendment prohibits excessive bail, excessive fines, and cruel and unusual punishments. (Subsequent chapters will examine these amendments and their provisions affecting criminal justice.)

The Ninth and Tenth Amendments

To address the concern that an enumeration of rights might lead courts to infer that the Bill of Rights was a complete catalog of liberties, the Ninth Amendment states, "The enumeration in the Constitution, of certain rights, shall not be construed to deny or disparage others retained by the people." Finally, to allay fears that the new national government would run roughshod over the states, the Tenth Amendment provides: "The powers not delegated to the United States by the Constitution, nor prohibited by it to the States, are reserved to the States respectively, or to the people." Both the Ninth and Tenth Amendments raise difficult interpretive problems: Exactly what rights are reserved to the people? Precisely what powers are reserved to the states? Of course, we have courts to answer difficult interpretive questions.

As we shall see, the Supreme Court has, from time to time, accepted the Ninth Amendment's invitation to recognize other rights retained by the people. But the Court has based these unenumerated rights on broad interpretations of other constitutional language. For example, in *NAACP v. Alabama* (1958),[32] the Court recognized the freedom of association, which is nowhere mentioned in the Constitution, as an implicit right linked to the First Amendment freedoms of speech and assembly. Similarly, in *Kent v. Dulles* (1958),[33] the Court recognized the right to travel abroad as an essential element of liberty protected by the Fifth Amendment.

Despite the obvious fact that the powers of the national government have grown dramatically since its founding, the Tenth Amendment remains important in the jurisprudence of federalism. Writing for the Supreme Court in *Printz v. United States* (1997),[34] the Supreme Court summarized the import of the Tenth Amendment:

> Congress cannot compel the States to enact or enforce a federal regulatory program. ... Congress cannot circumvent that prohibition by conscripting the States' officers directly. The Federal Government may neither issue directives requiring the States to address particular problems, nor command the States' officers, or those of their political subdivisions, to administer or enforce a federal regulatory program.

The Original Inapplicability of the Bill of Rights to State and Local Governments

It was widely understood at the time the Bill of Rights was ratified that its provisions were intended to apply to the federal government and not to the states. After all, the states had their own constitutions, all of which contained enumerations of rights. In *Barron v. Baltimore* (1833),[35] the Supreme Court embraced this interpretation. At issue was whether one whose property had been effectively taken by the City of Baltimore could invoke the

Just Compensation Clause of the Fifth Amendment. Writing for the Court, Chief Justice John Marshall held that "the provision in the Fifth Amendment to the Constitution, declaring that private property shall not be taken for public use without just compensation, is intended solely as a limitation on the power of the United States, and is not applicable to the legislation of the states." Thus, one whose rights were infringed by a state or local government had to look to the state courts for relief. Persons accused or convicted of crimes under state law had no recourse to the federal courts. That would change, of course, but only after a bloody civil war, a landmark amendment to the Constitution, and a series of judicial decisions interpreting key language in that amendment.

The Civil War Amendments

In the infamous Dred Scott Case (1857),[36] the Supreme Court embraced the institution of slavery and held that it could not be regulated by Congress. Chief Justice Roger Taney's opinion for the Court went so far as to assert that persons of African descent, whether in bondage or free, were not and could never become citizens of the United States. This decision, which was celebrated by slave owners and met with outrage by abolitionists, hastened the outbreak of the Civil War. In the midst of that war, President Lincoln issued the Emancipation Proclamation (1863), declaring that "... all persons held as slaves within any State or designated part of a State, the people whereof shall then be in rebellion against the United States, shall be then, thenceforward, and forever free ..." Within five years after the war ending, the Constitution had been amended three times, all in an effort to protect the rights of the newly freed former slaves.

The Thirteenth Amendment

The Thirteenth Amendment (1865) provides, "Neither slavery nor involuntary servitude, except as a punishment for crime whereof the party shall have been duly convicted, shall exist within the United States, or any place subject to their jurisdiction." In *Bailey v. Alabama* (1911),[37] the Supreme Court, speaking through Justice Charles Evans Hughes, opined that "[t]he plain intention [of the Thirteenth Amendment] was to abolish slavery of whatever name and form and all its badges and incidents; to render impossible any state of bondage; to make labor free, by prohibiting that control by which the personal service of one man is disposed of or coerced for another's benefit, which is the essence of involuntary servitude." However, despite the Court's noble language in *Bailey*, it would take a century for the "badges and incidents" of slavery to be abolished, and some would argue that the task remains incomplete.

JURISPRUDENCE

Is the Military Draft a Violation of the Thirteenth Amendment?
Arver v. United States, 245 U.S. 366 (1918)

To raise an army to fight in World War I, Congress enacted the Selective Service Act of 1917, which established a military draft and provided that "any person who shall willfully fail or refuse to present himself for registration or to submit thereto as herein provided, shall be guilty of a misdemeanor. ..." Opponents of the draft, including

(*continued*)

libertarians and socialists, argued that compulsory military service was a form of "involuntary servitude" and, therefore, a violation of the Thirteenth Amendment. In upholding Congress's power to establish a draft, the Court brushed aside the Thirteenth Amendment argument. Speaking for a unanimous Supreme Court, Chief Justice Edward White said that "... we are unable to conceive upon what theory the exaction by government from the citizen of the performance of his supreme and noble duty of contributing to the defense of the rights and honor of the nation, as the result of a war declared by the great representative body of the people, can be said to be the imposition of involuntary servitude in violation of the prohibitions of the Thirteenth Amendment. ..."

The Fourteenth Amendment

Ratified in 1868, the Fourteenth Amendment recognized the constitutional rights of the newly freed former slaves and gave Congress the authority to enact legislation to protect those rights. Overturning the Supreme Court's Dred Scott decision, Section 1 begins by stating, "All persons born or naturalized in the United States, and subject to the jurisdiction thereof, are citizens of the United States and of the State wherein they reside." Section 1 goes on to prohibit states from enforcing laws "which shall abridge the privileges or immunities of citizens of the United States" and says that no state shall "deprive any person of life, liberty, or property, without due process of law; nor deny to any person within its jurisdiction the equal protection of the laws."

. In the twentieth century, these guarantees of due process and equal protection would provide foundations for numerous judicial decisions protecting civil rights and liberties, including many expanding the rights of persons accused or convicted of crimes. For example, the Supreme Court's best known criminal justice decision, *Miranda v. Arizona* (1966),[38] was based on the Due Process Clause, while its landmark desegregation decision in *Brown v. Board of Education* (1954)[39] was based squarely on the Equal Protection Clause.

The Fifteenth Amendment

Ratified in 1870, the Fifteenth Amendment declares that "[t]he right of citizens of the United States to vote shall not be denied or abridged by the United States or by any state on account of race, color, or previous condition of servitude." It also gives Congress legislative authority to enforce the right to vote. But it would take nearly a century (replete with federal court decisions and Congressional enactments) for this prohibition to take full effect, as Southern states utilized a variety of means, including poll taxes and literacy tests, to prevent African Americans from voting.

One not-so-subtle form of disenfranchisement was the "grandfather clause," by which citizens descended from those registered to vote prior to Reconstruction were permanently enfranchised, while others were subjected to literacy tests to register. In *Guinn & Beal v. United States* (1915),[40] the Supreme Court invalidated Oklahoma's version of the grandfather clause, finding "no discernible reason other than the purpose to disregard the prohibitions of the [Fifteenth] Amendment by creating a standard of voting which on its face was, in substance, but a revitalization of conditions which, when they prevailed in the past, had been destroyed by the self-operative force of the Amendment."

Of course, *Guinn & Beal* and similar judicial decisions were not enough to overcome racial disenfranchisement. The landmark Voting Rights Act of 1965[41] suspended literacy tests and waived accumulated poll taxes in states where less than 50% of eligible voters were registered. It also prohibited the covered states from implementing changes to their elections laws without "preclearance" from the Attorney General or a federal district court. In upholding the statute in *South Carolina v. Katzenbach* (1966),[42] the Supreme Court concluded its opinion by expressing the hope that "millions of non-white Americans will now be able to participate for the first time on an equal basis in the government under which they live." But today, as Congress considers legislation to combat voter suppression, some would say that the promise of the Fifteenth Amendment has yet to be fulfilled.[43]

VOTER SUPPRESSION: A term applied to a variety of policies and practices designed to discourage voting by minorities.

Reconstruction-Era Civil Rights Legislation

All three of the Civil War Amendments contain language granting Congress the power to enforce their prohibitions through "appropriate legislation." Between 1866 and 1871, Congress enacted a series of landmark civil rights statutes, and provisions of these statutes remain important components of federal civil rights law today.

The Civil Rights Act of 1866 provided that citizens of all races have the same rights to make and enforce contracts; to sue and give evidence in the courts; and to own, purchase, sell, rent, and inherit property.[44] The Supreme Court has held that the law "bars all racial discrimination, private as well as public, in the sale or rental of property," and that the statute, thus construed, is a valid exercise of the power of Congress to enforce the Thirteenth Amendment."[45]

The 1866 statute also made it a crime for any person acting "under color of any law, statute, ordinance, regulation, or custom" to "subject, or cause to be subjected, any inhabitant of any State or Territory to the deprivation of any right secured or protected by this act." Police officers have been prosecuted under the modern form of this provision[46] for the excessive use of force, which is considered a deprivation of the Fourth Amendment right to be free from unreasonable searches and seizures. The most notorious prosecution of this kind stemmed from the horrendous beating of Rodney King by Los Angeles police officers in 1991. Although four officers charged in the incident were acquitted in state court, two were prosecuted in federal court and sentenced to thirty months in prison.[47]

The Civil Rights Act of 1870, also known as the Enforcement Act, was adopted to enforce the Fifteenth Amendment's prohibition of racial discrimination with respect to voting rights. The statute made it a misdemeanor for a state or local official to deny a person's right to vote "on account of race, color, or previous condition of servitude." It also made it a misdemeanor to use force, bribery, or intimidation to prevent, delay or obstruct the right to vote in any election or to engage in a conspiracy to do so. In a provision aimed at the Ku Klux Klan, the law made it a felony for two or more persons to "band or conspire together, or go in disguise upon the public highway, or upon the premises of another," with the intent to deprive a person of their constitutional rights."[48]

In 1871, Congress enacted another statute that would become an important part of modern civil rights law. Under the Civil Rights Act of 1871,[49] persons acting under color of state law were made personally liable for violating the constitutional rights of others. As discussed in chapter 1, lawsuits under this statute are commonly referred to as "Section 1983 actions" because the Act is codified in Title 42 of the United States Code at Section 1983. The 1871 Act also allowed civil suits against those conspiring to violate civil rights of others.[50] These provisions did not create new substantive rights; rather, they provided a remedy for those whose civil rights were violated by persons acting under the aegis of state or local authority. Even cities can be found liable under Section 1983, as long as the plaintiff can demonstrate that the civil rights violation resulted from a city law or policy.[51]

The final civil rights law passed by Congress during Reconstruction was the Civil Rights Act of 1875,[52] which stated that "all persons within the jurisdiction of the United States shall be entitled to the full and equal enjoyment of the accommodations, advantages, facilities, and privileges of inns, public conveyances on land or water, theaters, and other places of public amusement." However, in *The Civil Rights Cases* (1883),[53] the Supreme Court declared the Act unconstitutional, as it applied to private establishments. The principle underlying the decision, known as the state action doctrine, remains an important part of civil rights law today. The idea is that the Fourteenth Amendment was aimed at actions of the states depriving persons of equal protection of the laws but not at private discrimination. Therefore, Congress's legislative power under Section 5 of the Fourteenth Amendment is limited to laws aimed at state and local governments or persons acting under their auspices. In a lone dissent in *The Civil Rights Cases*, Justice John M. Harlan criticized the Court for basing its decision "upon grounds entirely too narrow and artificial." In Harlan's view, "the substance and spirit of the recent amendments of the Constitution have been sacrificed by a subtle and ingenious verbal criticism."

The Civil Rights Act of 1875 was the last statute of its kind for more than eighty years. During that time, states enacted the Jim Crow laws, making racial segregation official, and did so with the blessing of the Supreme Court.[54] For its part, Congress did nothing to address what had become a prevalent regime of segregation in the South. That would

STATE ACTION DOCTRINE: The judicial doctrine under which the Fourteenth Amendment's due process and equal protection clauses apply only to governmental policies and actions, as opposed to private party actions.

eventually change, of course, and in the modern era, both Congress and the Supreme Court would take action to protect civil rights. We will discuss those actions in the Equal Protection of the Laws section below.

JURISPRUDENCE

State Judge Convicted Under Federal Civil Rights Law
United States v. Lanier, 520 U.S. 259 (1997)

David Lanier was a Chancery Court judge for two counties in West Tennessee. He was found guilty in federal court of violating 18 U.S.C. § 242 after a jury heard testimony that he had sexually assaulted at least five women, some on multiple occasions, in his chambers at the courthouse. Normally, a case like this would be tried in state court under a state criminal law dealing with sexual assault. In this case, though, a state prosecution was extremely unlikely, as the local district attorney was Judge Lanier's brother!

The federal case against Judge Lanier proceeded on a novel theory, namely that his conduct violated his victims' right to bodily integrity, an implicit element of the liberty protected by the Fourteenth Amendment. The U.S. Court of Appeals for the Sixth Circuit reversed Lanier's conviction, holding that there needed to be a precedent showing a clearly established constitutional right that was "fundamentally similar" to the case at hand. Speaking for the Sixth Circuit sitting en banc, Chief Judge Gilbert S. Merritt observed that federal courts should not "create or extend criminal law by using a common-law process of interpretation. If Congress has

not been clear about the type of conduct that it wishes to criminalize, courts should not hold a defendant criminally liable by creating a new federal crime."

In a unanimous decision, the Supreme Court reversed the Sixth Circuit, finding this standard for a § 242 violation to be "unnecessarily high." Instead, the Court said that § 242 could apply as long as it was "reasonably clear at the relevant time that the defendant's conduct was criminal." One is tempted to conclude that the Court was willing to stretch § 242 so that Judge Lanier's egregious misconduct would not go unpunished. However, it should be noted that this decision set an important precedent under which federal authorities can prosecute state and local officials for a wide range of conduct that interferes with a person's "liberty."

After the high Court's decision, Lanier, who was out on bail while his appeal was being resolved, fled to Mexico. He was captured by Mexican authorities and extradited to the United States, where he served a twenty-five year sentence. Lanier passed away in February 2022. His obituary made no mention of the landmark Supreme Court decision to which he was a party.

Due Process of Law: The Fifth and Fourteenth Amendments

The term "due process of law" appears twice in the Constitution—once in the Fifth Amendment (aimed at the federal government) and again in the Fourteenth Amendment (applicable to the states). The concept is an ancient one, going as far back as Magna Carta (1215), which stated, "No free man shall be seized or imprisoned, or stripped of his rights or possessions, or outlawed or exiled, or deprived of his standing in any other way, nor will we proceed with force against him, or send others to do so, except by the lawful judgment of his equals or by the law of the land." A 1354 act of Parliament restated the principle as follows: "No man of what state or condition he be, shall be put out of his lands or tenements nor taken, nor disinherited, nor put to death, without he be brought to answer by due process of law."[55]

Interestingly, the Tennessee Constitution still uses the language of Magna Carta in providing that "no man shall be taken or imprisoned, or disseized of his freehold, liberties or privileges, or outlawed, or exiled, or in any manner destroyed or deprived of his life, liberty or property, but by the judgment of his peers, or the law of the land."[56] James Madison's formulation of the principle, which appears in the Fifth Amendment and is echoed in the Fourteenth Amendment, is more succinct: "No person shall be ... deprived of life, liberty or property without due process of law."

Procedural Due Process

In its classic sense, due process entails procedural protections against governmental action that deprive a person of life, liberty, or property. The fundamental elements of procedural due process are adequate notice and a fair hearing. One has the right to know that the government intends to take life, liberty, or property. In a criminal prosecution, notice is provided through the formal charging process. If one is stopped for speeding or running a red light, the citation issued by the officer constitutes notice of prosecution. Additionally, a person charged with a criminal offense, no matter how minor, has the right to a trial in a court of law. This constitutes the hearing element of due process.

The requirements of notice and hearing apply not only to criminal prosecutions but also to civil and administrative actions brought by the government. If, for instance, a local government seeks to take private property for public use (the power of eminent domain), it must notify the owner and provide an opportunity to contest the action in court. If a state agency imposes a fine for the violation of its regulations, it too must provide notice of the charge and an opportunity to contest the charge in an administrative hearing. Even the termination of welfare benefits has been held to require fair notice and a fair hearing.[57]

The degree of procedural protection depends on the nature of the deprivation. As the Supreme Court observed in *Ex parte Wall* (1883),[58] due process requires "that kind of procedure ... which is suitable and proper to the nature of the case, and sanctioned by the established customs and usages of the courts." When the government seeks to take life, as it does in a death penalty case, procedural due process is at its maximum. (In chapter 14 we will examine the elaborate procedures that characterize a death penalty prosecution.) At the opposite end of the spectrum, when one receives a parking ticket, which in many jurisdictions is not

PROCEDURAL DUE PROCESS: The requirement that government provide fair notice and a fair hearing before depriving a person of life, liberty, or property.

EMINENT DOMAIN: The power of government to take private property for public use.

a criminal offense but a minor regulatory infraction, due process requires no more than the opportunity to meet with a hearing officer to contest the ticket.[59]

Due Process Rights in a Police Disciplinary Hearing

The Supreme Court has long held that if public employees can assert a "property interest" in their employment, typically by showing a contract for employment, then any disciplinary action requires procedural due process—which usually takes the form of written notice and a fair hearing, as we discussed earlier in this chapter. For police officers, a deprivation hearing that triggers due process concerns could connect to things like decertification, firing, or suspension. Even a loss of benefits could trigger a required hearing under Supreme Court precedent.[60] These types of hearings are generally overseen by an arbitrator or an administrative law judge.

In 1985, the Supreme Court ruled in favor of a security guard who was fired by the Cleveland (Ohio) Board of Education after a background check conducted almost a year after he began work revealed a prior felony conviction for grand larceny. He claimed to be under the impression that the conviction was a misdemeanor and, thus, did not report it on his application. Justice White delivered the opinion of the Court, which found that, "An essential principle of due process is that a deprivation of life, liberty, or property 'be preceded by notice and opportunity for hearing appropriate to the nature of the case.'"[61]

Even so, there have been situations in which the Supreme Court has upheld the use of written notice of firing, as long as a hearing then occurs post-firing.[62] Moreover, in *Mathews v. Eldridge* (1976),[63] the Court outlined a balancing test that allows for an administrative action (e.g., a department suspension) to occur prior to a hearing, as long as there is some protection afforded via a post-action hearing. Among the factors to be balanced are the employee's right to employment, the government's interest in some adverse action taken against the employee, and the risk of an "erroneous deprivation."

These factors were applied in *Gilbert v. Homar* (1997),[64] a case in which the Supreme Court reviewed the suspension of a university police officer. Richard J. Homar was employed as an officer at East Stroudsburg University of Pennsylvania, but he was suspended without pay when the university was notified that he had been arrested on drug-related charges. Homar claimed that this suspension prior to a hearing amounted to a violation of the Due Process Clause of the Fourteenth Amendment. Although the Third Circuit found in Homar's favor, the Supreme Court reversed, finding that application of the *Eldridge* decision meant only that Homar was "entitled to a very limited hearing prior to his termination, to be followed by a more comprehensive post-termination hearing."

More specifically, in applying *Eldridge* factors, Justice Scalia's opinion for a unanimous Court indicated that a prehearing suspension, which was temporary both in terms of "length" and "finality," was acceptable when balanced against the government interests at stake when an officer "of great public trust and high public visibility" is arrested for a drug-related offense. The Court's opinion highlighted the fact that "due process is flexible," and as a result, there can be instances in which a presuspension hearing is not needed. Justice Scalia expounded on this point, saying: "The purpose of any pre-suspension hearing would be to assure that there are reasonable grounds to support the suspension without pay. ... But here that has already been assured by the arrest and filing of charges." An important point, however, lies in the need for a hearing to occur prior to full termination of employment; the key is that this hearing can come after the employee has been suspended.

FOCUS ON LAW ENFORCEMENT

D.C. Officer's Suicide Ruled a "Line-of-Duty" Death Following a Second Hearing

Officer Jeffrey Smith, a 12-year patrolman for the D.C. Metropolitan Police, was summoned to help defend the U.S. Capitol during the riots of January 6th, 2021. Video evidence showed he was assaulted by a mob and hit in the head with a metal pole. He was treated for his injuries at the D.C. Fire and Police Clinic, where he was given ibuprofen and sent home. He was ordered to return to duty nine days later, but on the drive in to work, he took his own life on the George Washington Parkway by shooting himself with his service weapon. The day before, he had returned to the medical clinic that treated him but was pronounced fit to return to service.

In March 2022, the District of Columbia's Police and Firefighters' Retirement and Relief Board ruled that Officer Smith's death would be classified as a "line-of-duty" death, paving the way for his family to receive benefits, including health benefits and pension benefits. A prior decision of the Board in August of 2021 had denied this request, but in keeping with principles of due process, a more thorough hearing, in which evidence of the impact the attack had on the officer, was conducted seven months later.

In speaking of the March 2022 hearing, an attorney for his family said, "We took the evidence from the autopsy to prove that Jeff suffered a traumatic brain injury on January 6"; the attorney added that "... the chain of events was set in motion January 6th and the chain was not broken." Officer Smith's widow said, "When my husband left for work that day, he was the Jeff that I knew. When he returned after experiencing the event, being hit in the head, he was a completely different person. I do believe if he did not go to work that day, he would be here and we would not be having this conversation."[65]

The March 2022 ruling from the Board marked the first time that the suicide of a D.C. metropolitan police officer had ever been declared a line-of-duty death. Whereas the U.S. military almost always treats a suicide as a line-of-duty death,[66] state and local police departments generally do not. The Public Safety Officer's Benefits Program, run by the Bureau of Justice Assistance in the U.S. Department of Justice, provides a death benefit of $370,000 to be paid to the family of any federal, state, local, or tribal police officers and firefighters who dies in the line of duty; however, there is no payment if the death is "caused by the officer's intention."[67] States vary in terms of how line-of-duty deaths are defined. For example, in Florida, a heart attack is treated as a line-of-duty death, but a suicide is not. Furthermore, in some states, the matter of defining a line-of-duty death is left to local departments.

The D.C. Metropolitan Police Department offers spouses of officers who die in the line-of-duty continued payment of 100 percent of the officer's salary and a one-time payment of $50,000; deaths that are not considered to be in the line-of-duty result in 33% of salary continuing to be paid. Health and pension benefits also can accompany line-of-duty deaths. Officer Smith was not the only D.C. officer to commit suicide in the aftermath of the January 6th riot. Officer Howard S. Liebengood worked long shifts the three days after the riot and killed himself after returning home on January 9th, 2021. And by August of 2021, two more officers who worked during the Capitol riots (Kyle DeFreytag and Gunther Hashida) had also taken their lives. Officer Liebengood's wife wrote a letter to a member of Congress imploring action by the government, saying, "The mental and emotional well-being of these officers can no longer be overlooked or taken for granted."[68]

Sadly, according to the FBI's Law Enforcement Suicide Data Collection (LESDC), there were more than 150 law enforcement suicides in 2021.[69] In 2022, President Biden signed the Public Safety Officers Support Act,[70] which defines suicide as a line of duty death for all federal officers, thereby making their survivors eligible for benefits.

Due Process and the Rights of the Accused

As we have seen, the Bill of Rights contains a number of important procedural protections for persons accused of crimes: the right to counsel, the right to confront the government's witnesses, the right to trial by jury, and several others. In the modern era, the Supreme Court has held that most of these rights are essential elements of due process in the criminal justice context.[71] The Court also has recognized that the presumption of innocence and the reasonable doubt standard are essential elements of due process in criminal cases. In *Coffin v. United States* (1895),[72] the Court said that "the presumption of innocence in favor of the accused is the undoubted law, axiomatic and elementary, and its enforcement lies at the foundation of the administration of our criminal law." Similarly, in *In re Winship* (1970),[73] the Court held that "the Due Process Clause protects the accused against conviction except upon proof beyond a reasonable doubt of every fact necessary to constitute the crime with which he is charged."

PRESUMPTION OF INNOCENCE: The rule whereby a defendant in a criminal trial is presumed innocent and the prosecution must prove the defendant's guilt.

REASONABLE DOUBT STANDARD: The requirement in a criminal case for the prosecution to prove the defendant's guilt beyond a reasonable doubt.

MENS REA: The mental element of a crime; criminal intent.

JURISPRUDENCE

Does Due Process Require States to Recognize the Insanity Defense?
Kahler v. Kansas, 589 U.S. ___ (2020)

The insanity defense, which has roots in English law, is well established under federal and state laws. The essential idea is that severe mental illness can negate the criminal intent element (*mens rea*) of a crime. However, several states have abolished or modified the defense. Does the Due Process Clause permit a state to do this? Do defendants, in effect, have a constitutional right to plead insanity? Consider the following excerpts from the majority and dissenting opinions. In your opinion, which side has the better argument?

- Justice Kagan Delivered the Opinion of the Court, saying the following in part:

In Kansas, a defendant can invoke mental illness to show that he lacked the requisite *mens rea* (intent) for a crime. He can also raise mental illness after conviction to justify either a reduced term of imprisonment or commitment to a mental health facility. But Kansas, unlike many States, will not wholly exonerate a defendant on the ground that his illness prevented him from recognizing his criminal act as morally wrong. The issue here is whether the Constitution's Due Process Clause forces Kansas to do so—otherwise said, whether that Clause compels the acquittal of any defendant who, because of mental illness, could not tell right from wrong when committing his crime.

Contrary to Kahler's view, Kansas takes account of mental health at both trial and sentencing. It has just not adopted the particular insanity defense Kahler would like. That choice is for Kansas to make—and, if it wishes, to remake and remake again as the future unfolds. No insanity rule in this country's heritage or history was ever so settled as to tie a State's hands centuries later. For that reason, we affirm the judgment below.

- Justice Breyer, with whom Justice Ginsburg and Justice Sotomayor join, dissenting:

Kansas has not simply redefined the insanity defense. Rather, it has eliminated the core of a defense that has existed for centuries: that the defendant, *due to mental illness,* lacked the mental capacity necessary for his conduct to be considered morally blameworthy." He then spoke to the

(continued)

scope the origins of the insanity defense, observing that, "Seven hundred years of Anglo-American legal history, together with basic principles long inherent in the nature of the

criminal law itself, convince me that Kansas' law 'offends … principle[s] of justice so rooted in the traditions and conscience of our people as to be ranked as fundamental.'"

The Vagueness Doctrine

VOID-FOR-VAGUENESS DOCTRINE: The doctrine, derived from due process, which holds that excessively vague criminal laws are invalid because they fail to provide adequate notice of what is permissible and what is prohibited.

The Supreme Court has said repeatedly that a vague criminal statute violates due process because it fails to provide adequate notice about what conduct is permissible and what is prohibited. The void-for-vagueness doctrine "is a well-recognized requirement, consonant alike with ordinary notions of fair play and the settled rules of law" because a vague criminal prohibition "violates the first essential of due process."[74] Writing for the Court in *Grayned v. City of Rockford* (1972),[75] Justice Thurgood Marshall noted, "A vague law impermissibly delegates basic policy matters to policemen, judges, and juries for resolution on an ad hoc and subjective basis, with the attendant dangers of arbitrary and discriminatory applications." To avoid the vice of vagueness, the Court has said that a law must "define the criminal offense with sufficient definiteness that ordinary people can understand what conduct is prohibited and in a manner that does not encourage arbitrary and discriminatory treatment."[76]

In *Johnson v. United States* (2015),[77] the Supreme Court invoked the vagueness doctrine to strike down a provision of the Armed Career Criminal Act of 1984. That provision increased punishments for possession of a firearm by a convicted felon in the case that the defendant had three or more previous convictions for a "violent felony," which included any felony "that presents a serious potential risk of physical injury to another." Speaking for the Court, Justice Antonin Scalia observed, "Invoking so shapeless a provision to condemn someone to prison for 15 years to life does not comport with the Constitution's guarantee of due process."

JURISPRUDENCE

The Supreme Court Strikes Down Chicago's Gang Congregation Ordinance
City of Chicago v. Morales, 527 U.S. 41 (1999)

Enacted in 1992, the Chicago "Gang Ordinance" provided that a person congregating with one or more "known criminal street gang members" was not allowed "to remain in any one place with no apparent purpose." If a police officer determined that such a person was in a public place with "no apparent purpose," then a command to "disperse" could be given and a refusal to disperse could result in arrest. The punishment for this crime was a fine of up to $500, incarceration of up to 6 months, and up to 120 hours of community service.

More than 89,000 dispersal orders were given, and 42,000 arrests were made under this ordinance during the three years it was in effect.

Typically, restrictions like these that place limits on a person's ability to remain in a public place are known as "loitering" offenses, a topic we cover in greater detail in chapter 4. The Supreme Court's review of *City of Chicago v. Morales*, though, focused upon the Due Process Clause of the Fourteenth Amendment. Justice Stevens' majority opinion used this amendment to declare found that it was to be voided for "vagueness," in violation of due process principles. The majority opinion from Justice Stevens suggested that vague laws are problematic for two reasons, as evident when he said: "... in this instance the city has enacted an ordinance that affords too much discretion to the police and too little notice to citizens who wish to use the public streets." In other words, the ordinance itself failed to clearly describe what conduct that will constitute a crime and, thus, could result in ordinary people finding it difficult to conform conduct to the parameters of the ordinance. Beyond that, police are granted too much discretion in enforcement, which the Court feared could result in arbitrary or unequal enforcement.

Thinking about this case in simple terms, students might consider why a person could be standing on a public sidewalk without evincing a clear sign of an "apparent purpose," as required by this law. In this regard, Justice Stevens's majority opinion hypothesized if "enjoying a cool breeze on a warm evening" could be an example of why someone might be outside—a "purpose" that might not be "apparent" to an approaching officer. Moreover, in an odd twist, if members of a criminal gang actually met on a public sidewalk to plan illegal activity, they might be evincing the "apparent purpose" required by the ordinance, and therefore, the ordinance might even be said to be flawed from the standpoint of curtailing criminal street gang violence.

Substantive Due Process

The Supreme Court has long held that due process entails more than procedural rights. Under the doctrine of substantive due process, government may not enforce laws that are irrational, unfair, unreasonable, or unjust, even if those laws do not run afoul of specific constitutional prohibitions. The doctrine is controversial in that critics say it invites judges to second guess the wisdom of the people's elected representatives.

Beginning in the late nineteenth century, a pro-business Supreme Court used this doctrine to strike down laws regulating business. In the leading case of the era, *Lochner v. New York* (1905),[78] the Court struck down a state law limiting the hours that employees could work in bakeries. Ostensibly a measure to protect workers' health, the measure was defended as an expression of the state's police power. The Supreme Court rejected this justification, saying that "the real object and purpose were simply to regulate the hours of labor ... in a private business, not dangerous in any degree to morals or in any real and substantial degree to the health of the employees." The Court concluded that "[u]nder such circumstances, the freedom of master and employee to contract with each other in relation to their employment, and in defining the same, cannot be prohibited or interfered with without violating the Federal Constitution." In one of his more celebrated dissenting opinions, Justice Oliver Wendell Holmes, Jr. castigated the majority for imposing the doctrine of laissez-faire on the Fourteenth Amendment,

SUBSTANTIVE DUE PROCESS: The doctrine that due process requires laws to be fair, reasonable, and just and not unreasonably intrusive on a person's liberty.

POLICE POWER: The authority of state legislatures to make laws to promote public health, safety, order, welfare, and decency.

saying that "a constitution is not intended to embody a particular economic theory." In Holmes's view, "the word 'liberty' in the Fourteenth Amendment is perverted when it is held to prevent the natural outcome of a dominant opinion, unless it can be said that a rational and fair man necessarily would admit that the statute proposed would infringe fundamental principles as they have been understood by the traditions of our people and our law."

Ultimately, Justice Holmes's view prevailed when *Lochner v. New York* was overturned by the Supreme Court in 1937.[79] But the doctrine of substantive due process remains viable. It has been utilized by the Court to recognize the right to pursue a lawful occupation,[80] the right to travel freely across state lines,[81] the right to marry,[82] the right to procreate,[83] and the right to direct the upbringing and education of one's children.[84]

By far the most impactful, and controversial, application of the doctrine is in the recognition of a constitutional right of privacy. This development is so significant, especially with respect to the criminal law, that we devote a major section to it (to follow). But first, we examine another major application of due process: the extension of the Bill of Rights to actions of state and local governments.

Incorporation of the Bill of Rights

As we saw earlier in the chapter, it was well established early on that the Bill of Rights imposed limitations on the national government but not the state and local governments. The Fourteenth Amendment would fundamentally alter this arrangement but not by explicit text in the Amendment. Rather, in a series of decisions beginning in 1897, the Supreme Court would interpret the Due Process Clause of the Fourteenth Amendment as "incorporating" nearly all of the provisions of the Bill of Rights (see figure 3.1).

The Theory of Incorporation

Scholars and judges have long debated whether the drafters of the Fourteenth Amendment intended for it to incorporate the Bill of Rights. In his dissenting opinion in *Adamson v. California* (1947),[85] Justice Hugo L. Black argued that the Privileges or Immunities Clause of Section 1 of the Fourteenth Amendment (which says: "No State shall make or enforce any law which shall abridge the privileges or immunities of citizens of the United States") embraced the rights enumerated in the first ten amendments to the Constitution. Neither Justice Black's predecessors nor his successors on the Court accepted this argument. An early decision restricting the meaning of "privileges or immunities" remains good law today.[86] Rather, the justices focused on the words "liberty" and "due process," also found in Section 1 of the Fourteenth Amendment. The theory they adopted is that these terms subsume, or "incorporate," the substantive and procedural protections of the Bill of Rights. But the Court never held that the Fourteenth Amendment incorporates the Bill of Rights in toto. Rather, the justices moved incrementally, as they are prone to do, considering each of the provisions of the Bill of Rights in a separate case. In the end, through a laborious process

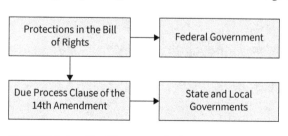

FIGURE 3.1 The Theory Underlying Incorporation of the Bill of Rights

of **selective incorporation**, the Court arrived at a result very close to what Justice Black had long advocated, even though it achieved this result by a different interpretive route.

Initial Resistance to Incorporation

At first, the Supreme Court was reluctant to go down this road. In *United States v. Cruikshank* (1876),[87] the Court held that neither the First Amendment freedom of assembly nor the Second Amendment right to keep and bear arms applied to the states under the Fourteenth Amendment. The Court continued to resist the theory of incorporation for several decades.

In *Hurtado v. California* (1884),[88] the Court refused to require states to follow the grand jury clause of the Fifth Amendment. In federal prosecutions for felonies, the Fifth Amendment requires an **indictment** by a **grand jury** before the case can be brought to trial. Under the California law at issue in *Hurtado*, the formal charging process entailed the filing of a charging document called an **information** followed by a hearing in open court. At the hearing, the accused had the right to be represented by counsel and could cross-examine witnesses for the state. The judge, rather than a grand jury, would then make a determination on whether the state had established probable cause to warrant a criminal prosecution. The Supreme Court held that this procedure satisfied the interests of due process.

More dramatically, in *Maxwell v. Dow* (1900),[89] the Court refused to apply the Sixth Amendment right to trial by jury to the state courts. In a passage that is shocking to contemporary sensibilities, the Court asserted that "[t]rial by jury has never been affirmed to be a necessary requisite of due process of law." Assuming a posture of extreme deference, the Court insisted that "there can be no just fear that the liberties of the citizen will not be carefully protected by the States respectively." In a similar vein, the Court, in *Twining v. New Jersey* (1908),[90] held that "due process does not require that [a defendant] be exempted from compulsory self-incrimination in the courts of a State that has not adopted the policy of such exemption." It would take many decades, but as we shall see, these two decisions would eventually be overturned by the modern Supreme Court.

The Process of Incorporation Begins

The first case in which the Supreme Court embraced the theory of incorporation had nothing to do with criminal justice or the civil liberties of individuals. Rather, it involved the property rights of corporations. In *Chicago, B&Q RR v. Chicago* (1897),[91] the Court reviewed a case in which

SELECTIVE INCORPORATION: The judicial doctrine under which specific provisions of the Bill of Rights deemed essential to a scheme of ordered liberty are applied to state action via the Due Process Clause of the Fourteenth Amendment.

INDICTMENT: A formal criminal charge handed down by a grand jury.

GRAND JURY: A group of citizens convened either to conduct an investigation or determine whether there is sufficient evidence to warrant an indictment.

INFORMATION: A formal criminal charge filed by a prosecutor.

the city of Chicago, exercising its power of eminent domain, took a strip of land owned by the railroad in order to widen a street. A jury awarded the railroad only token compensation for its loss, which the company claimed was a violation of due process. The City of Chicago argued that judicial review under the Due Process Clause should be limited to procedural issues. The Supreme Court disagreed, saying: "In determining what is due process of law, regard must be had to substance, not to form"—an obvious reference to the doctrine of substantive due process. On the merits, the Court sided with the railroad company, holding that "a judgment of a state court, even if it be authorized by statute, whereby private property is taken for the state or under its direction for public use, without compensation made or secured to the owner, is, upon principle and authority, wanting in the due process of law required by the fourteenth amendment. ..." By ruling that the Due Process Clause embraced the principle of just compensation, a right made explicit in the Fifth Amendment, the Court created the precedential foundation for the incorporation of the Bill of Rights.

Incorporation of the First Amendment Freedoms

Three decades passed before the Court would incorporate another provision of the Bill of Rights. In the two decades between 1927 and 1947, the Court moved to incorporate the First Amendment freedoms of speech, press, assembly, and religion. These decisions were important not only because they involved freedoms considered to be fundamental in a democratic society but also because they imposed limits on state legislatures and courts regarding criminal law.

In *Fiske v. Kansas* (1927),[92] the Court reviewed a conviction under a Kansas statute that prohibited "criminal syndicalism," which the law defined as "the doctrine which advocates crime, physical violence, arson, destruction of property, sabotage, or other unlawful acts or methods, as a means of accomplishing or effecting industrial or political ends, or as a means of effecting industrial or political revolution. ..." According to the statute, anyone who advocated "the duty, necessity, propriety or expediency of crime, criminal syndicalism, or sabotage" was guilty of a felony. In reversing the conviction of a labor activist, the Supreme Court said that:

> ... the Syndicalism Act has been applied in this case to sustain the conviction of the defendant without any charge or evidence that the organization in which he secured members advocated any crime, violence or other unlawful acts or methods as a means of effecting industrial or political changes or revolution. Thus applied, the Act is an arbitrary and unreasonable exercise of the police power of the State, unwarrantably infringing the liberty of the defendant in violation of the due process clause of the Fourteenth Amendment.

Although the *Fiske* Court did not explicitly incorporate the freedom of speech into the Due Process Clause, later courts viewed this case as establishing that precedent. Indeed, *Fiske v. Kansas* was the first time in its history that the Supreme Court reversed a conviction based on the principle of free speech, though not explicitly invoking the First Amendment.

In *Near v. Minnesota* (1931),[93] the Court struck down a state law authorizing censorship of "malicious" and "scandalous" publications. In his majority opinion, Chief Justice Charles Evans Hughes concluded that by allowing prior restraint of publications, the statute was "an infringement of the liberty of the press guaranteed by the Fourteenth Amendment." The First Amendment freedom of the press was simply assumed to apply to the states via the Due Process Clause.

Reversing another conviction for criminal syndicalism, the Supreme Court, in *DeJonge v. Oregon* (1937),[94] incorporated freedom of assembly into the Fourteenth Amendment. Chief Justice Hughes wrote: "If the persons assembling have committed crimes elsewhere, if they have formed or are engaged in a conspiracy against the public peace and order, they may be prosecuted for their conspiracy or other violation of valid laws." However, he added that "... peaceable assembly for lawful discussion cannot be made a crime."

Three years later, in *Cantwell v. Connecticut* (1940),[95] the Court incorporated the free exercise of religion. The defendants were Jehovah's Witnesses who were arrested for a breach of the peace after they distributed literature, solicited funds, and engaged in controversial religious speech on a public street. The Court reversed the convictions and struck down the statute on which they were based. Speaking through Justice Owen Roberts, the Court held "that the statute, as construed and applied to the appellants, deprives them of their liberty without due process of law in contravention of the Fourteenth Amendment." This time, the Court was explicit with respect to incorporation, saying, "The fundamental concept of liberty embodied in that Amendment embraces the liberties guaranteed by the First Amendment."

Then, in 1947, the Court completed its incorporation of the First Amendment, when it held that the prohibition against the establishment of religion applies not only to Congress but to the state and local governments as well. Writing for the Court in *Everson v. Board of Education*,[96] Justice Hugo Black focused on the interpretation of the Establishment Clause and simply noted precedents in which "the Fourteenth Amendment was interpreted to make the prohibitions of the First [Amendment] applicable to state action abridging religious freedom."

Incorporation of Rights Essential to Criminal Justice

In *Palko v. Connecticut* (1937),[97] the Supreme Court held that, to merit incorporation into the Fourteenth Amendment, a provision of the Bill of Rights must be "implicit in the concept of ordered liberty." On the basis of that rather vague test, the *Palko* Court refused to apply the Fifth Amendment's Double Jeopardy Clause to the states. Likewise, in *Betts v. Brady* (1942),[98] the Court refused to recognize the Sixth Amendment right to counsel as fundamental. Speaking through Justice Owen Roberts, the Court concluded that "we cannot say that the [Fourteenth] Amendment embodies an inexorable command that no trial for any offense, or in any court, can be fairly conducted and justice accorded a defendant who is not represented by counsel."

PRIOR RESTRAINT: Official censorship prior to publication.

The tide began to turn in 1948 when the Supreme Court decided *In re Oliver*,[99] where the issue was whether due process requires state courts to observe the right to a public trial, as the Sixth Amendment requires the federal courts to do. Justice Hugo Black, a staunch advocate of total incorporation of the Bill of Rights, wrote the opinion of the Court: "It is 'the law of the land' that no man's life, liberty or property be forfeited as a punishment until there has been a charge fairly made and fairly tried in a public tribunal."

The Court took another significant step the following year when, in *Wolf v. Colorado* (1949),[100] it incorporated the Fourth Amendment protection against unreasonable searches and seizures. Justice Felix Frankfurter's majority opinion noted that "[t]he security of one's privacy against arbitrary intrusion by the police—which is at the core of the Fourth Amendment—is basic to a free society." However, the Court stopped short of requiring state courts to follow the exclusionary rule, which prohibits the use in court of illegally obtained evidence.[101] Justice Frankfurter admitted that "the exclusion of evidence may be an effective way of deterring unreasonable searches" but concluded that it was not the Supreme Court's place to tell state courts how to enforce the Fourth Amendment's prohibition.

EXCLUSIONARY RULE:
A judicial rule holding that evidence obtained in violation of the Fourth Amendment is generally not admissible in a criminal prosecution of the person whose rights were violated.

The Warren Court

The incorporation of the Bill of Rights took a quantum leap in the 1960s. Under Chief Justice Earl Warren, who was appointed in 1953, the Court launched a veritable revolution in criminal justice. An important component of that revolution was the nationalization of standards of criminal procedure, and the incorporation of the Bill of Rights was crucial in that process.

In *Mapp v. Ohio* (1961), the Warren Court picked up where Justice Frankfurter had left off in 1949 and applied the Fourth Amendment exclusionary rule to the states. Justice Tom Clark's majority opinion insisted that, without the exclusionary rule, "the assurance against unreasonable federal searches and seizures would be 'a form of words,' valueless and undeserving of mention in a perpetual charter of inestimable human liberties." In Justice Clark's view, allowing a state court to ignore the exclusionary rule "serves to encourage disobedience to the Federal Constitution which it is bound to uphold."

A year after *Mapp v. Ohio*, the Court incorporated the Cruel and Unusual Punishments Clause of the Eighth Amendment. In *Robinson v. California* (1962),[102] the Court also established the principle that one cannot be criminally prosecuted merely for one's status—in this case, the condition of being addicted to narcotics. Justice Potter Stewart's opinion for the Court noted that under the California law at issue in the case, "a person can be continuously guilty of this offense, whether or not he has ever used or possessed any narcotics within the State, and whether or not he has been guilty of any antisocial behavior there." This, said Justice Stewart, "inflicts a cruel and unusual punishment in violation of the Fourteenth Amendment." The use of the Cruel and Unusual Punishments Clause in this context was quite novel, but the Warren Court was well known (and much criticized) for its unconventional interpretations of the Constitution. The real importance of *Robinson v. California* was that it set the stage for later judicial decisions on state death penalty laws and the conditions of confinement in state prisons.

Among the most important Warren Court decisions affecting criminal justice was *Gideon v. Wainwright* (1963),[103] where the Court overturned *Betts v. Brady*. Speaking for the Court, Justice Hugo Black asserted that "[t]he right of one charged with crime to counsel may not be deemed fundamental and essential to fair trials in some countries, but it is in ours." It is important to understand that in *Gideon*, the Court did not merely hold that people accused of crimes in state courts have the right to hire an attorney; that proposition was never in doubt. Rather, it held that indigent defendants accused of felonies must be furnished counsel at public expense because, as Justice Black noted, "[a]ny person haled into court, who is too poor to hire a lawyer, cannot be assured a fair trial unless counsel is provided for him."

A year after the *Gideon* decision, in *Malloy v. Hogan* (1964),[104] the Court overturned *Twining v. New Jersey* and held that state courts must respect the privilege against compulsory self-incrimination. In his opinion for the Court, Justice William Brennan argued that "[i]t would be incongruous to have different standards determine the validity of a claim of privilege ... depending on whether the claim was asserted in a state or federal court." This paved the way for the Court's landmark decision in *Miranda v. Arizona* (1966),[105] which protected the freedom from compulsory self-incrimination by requiring police to inform suspects in custody of their rights prior to interrogation.

Likewise, in *Duncan v. Louisiana* (1968),[106] which overturned *Maxwell v. Dow* and applied the right to trial by jury to the states, the Court noted "the deep commitment of the Nation to the right of jury trial in serious criminal cases as a defense against arbitrary law enforcement." Therefore, said Justice Byron White, "the Fourteenth Amendment guarantees a right of jury trial in all criminal cases which—were they to be tried in a federal court—would come within the Sixth Amendment's guarantee."

Palko v. Connecticut (1937), where the Court refused to require the states to respect the Fifth Amendment's prohibition of double jeopardy, was overturned by the Warren Court in 1969. Writing for the majority in *Benton v. Maryland* (1969),[107] Justice Thurgood Marshall observed that "*Palko* represented an approach to basic constitutional rights which this Court's recent decisions have rejected." In Justice Marshall's view, "[t]he fundamental nature of the guarantee against double jeopardy can hardly be doubted."

As a consequence of the Supreme Court's decisions incorporating provisions of the Bill of Rights, state legislatures could no longer pass laws impinging on First Amendment rights without these laws being subjected, at least potentially, to federal judicial review. Moreover, persons who had been convicted in state courts on the basis of illegally obtained evidence or coerced confessions could challenge their convictions in federal court. So could those who were denied a jury trial, subjected to double jeopardy, deprived of legal representation, or subjected to excessive punishments or inhumane conditions of confinement.

Of course, the Supreme Court could not by itself review the numerous convictions in which these issues were being raised. Instead, the Court expanded the role of the federal district courts in reviewing state convictions via the writ of habeas corpus.[108] Prisoners who had exhausted their appellate remedies in the state courts were able to seek relief in federal district court. Indeed, the expansion of federal habeas corpus review was a crucial component of the Warren Court's criminal justice revolution.

The Status of Incorporation Today

In 1971 (two years after Chief Justice Earl Warren retired), the Court recognized that "the Eighth Amendment's proscription of excessive bail has been assumed to have application to the States through the Fourteenth Amendment."[109] After that decision, it would be nearly four decades before the Court moved to incorporate another provision of the Bill of Rights. That decision, *McDonald v. City of Chicago* (2010),[110] would prove to be intensely controversial, as it had the effect of subjecting state and local gun control laws to federal judicial review. Nine years later, in *Timbs v. Indiana* (2019),[111] the Court incorporated the Excessive Fines Clause of the Eighth Amendment.

JURISPRUDENCE

The Supreme Court's Most Recent Incorporation Case
Timbs v. Indiana, 586 U.S. ___ (2019)

Tyson Timbs was convicted in an Indiana court of distributing heroin and was sentenced to pay a fine of approximately $1,200. Additionally, though, the state attempted to invoke the concept of civil asset forfeiture, which allows law enforcement agents to seize property when there is probable cause of a connection to illegal activity. Accordingly, Timbs's vehicle, a Land Rover purchased for $42,000 using money acquired from the crime, was seized. Indiana's Supreme Court indicated that this seizure did not violate the Eighth Amendment's Excessive Fines Clause—even though the maximum punishment for his offense was $10,000—because

the Eighth Amendment's Excessive Fines Clause had not been incorporated into the Fourteenth Amendment. On review, the U.S. Supreme Court reversed the decision. Justice Ruth Bader Ginsburg wrote for a unanimous Court and quoted from the last case to incorporate an amendment: *McDonald v. Chicago* (2010). Ginsburg used that Second Amendment decision to indicate that incorporation is appropriate when a constitutional provision is "fundamental to our scheme of ordered liberty" or "deeply rooted in this Nation's history and tradition." In applying this standard, the *Timbs* decision marked only the third case of incorporation since 1969.

After *McDonald* and *Timbs*, only three provisions of the Bill of Rights were left unincorporated: the Third Amendment's prohibition against quartering troops in citizens' homes, the Fifth Amendment's grand jury clause, and the Seventh Amendment's guarantee of the right to a jury trial in civil lawsuits "at common law" (see table 3.1).

Neither the Third nor the Seventh Amendment is apt to generate the kind of litigation that would lead to a Supreme Court decision. And there is little chance the Court would overturn *Hurtado v. California* and impose the grand jury requirement on the states, given that the information/preliminary hearing model better serves the interests of defendants. Thus, for all intents and purposes, the incorporation of the Bill of Rights is now complete. Consequently, state and local governments are held to the same standards as the national government with respect to laws, policies, and actions that impinge on the rights enshrined in the Bill of Rights.

TABLE 3.1   Chronology of Supreme Court Decisions "Incorporating" the Bill of Rights

Year	Provision (Amendment)	Decision
1897	Right to just compensation when property is taken for public use (V)	*Chicago, B. & Q. R. Co. v. Chicago*
1927	Freedom of speech (I)	*Fiske v. Kansas*
1931	Freedom of the press (I)	*Near v. Minnesota*
1937	Freedoms of assembly and petition (I)	*De Jonge v. Oregon*
1940	Free exercise of religion (I)	*Cantwell v. Connecticut*
1947	Prohibition of establishment of religion (I)	*Everson v. Board of Education*
1948	Right to a public trial (VI)	*In re Oliver*
1949	Prohibition of unreasonable searches and seizures (IV)	*Wolf v. Colorado*
1962	Cruel and unusual punishment (VIII)	*Robinson v. California*
1963	Right to counsel (VI)	*Gideon v. Wainwright*
1964	Compulsory self-incrimination (V)	*Malloy v. Hogan*
1965	Confrontation of hostile witnesses (VI)	*Pointer v. Texas*
1966	Right to an impartial jury (VI)	*Parker v. Gladden*
1967	Right to compulsory process to obtain favorable witnesses (VI)	*Washington v. Texas*
1967	Right to a speedy trial (VI)	*Klopfer v. North Carolina*
1968	Right to trial by jury (VI)	*Duncan v. Louisiana*
1969	Prohibition of double jeopardy (V)	*Benton v. Maryland*
1971	Prohibition of excessive bail (VIII)	*Schilb v. Kuebel*
2010	Right to keep and bear arms (II)	*McDonald v. Chicago*
2019	Prohibition of excessive fines (VIII)	*Timbs v. Indiana*

The Constitutional Right of Privacy

Some of the most controversial decisions of the modern Supreme Court have been those involving reproductive rights and sexual freedom. Without question, the most intensely disputed decision in the last fifty years was *Roe v. Wade* (1973),[112] in which the Court effectively legalized abortion throughout the United States. As any casual observer of American politics is surely aware, in 2022 that landmark decision was overturned

RIGHT OF PRIVACY: The unenumerated constitutional right shielding certain intimate personal decisions from governmental interference.

by a more conservative Court, thus returning control over abortion law to the states. *Roe* and other decisions involving reproductive freedom were based on the constitutional right of privacy, a right not explicitly mentioned in the Constitution, which partially accounts for the controversy surrounding the decision. The term "privacy" is something of a misnomer in this context, as the right has more to do with personal autonomy. It is, as Justice Louis Brandeis once observed, "the right to be let alone—the most comprehensive of rights, and the right most valued by civilized men."[113]

Reproductive Freedom

The constitutional right of privacy was first articulated by the Supreme Court in *Griswold v. Connecticut* (1965),[114] in which the Court struck down a state law criminalizing the use of contraceptives as applied to married couples. The vote was 7–2. Justice William O. Douglas's majority opinion attempted to anchor this newly articulated right in the Bill of Rights, observing that "specific guarantees in the Bill of Rights have penumbras, formed by emanations from those guarantees that help give them life and substance." Yet he also insisted, "We deal with a right of privacy older than the Bill of Rights." Striking an indignant tone, Justice Douglas asked, "Would we allow the police to search the sacred precincts of marital bedrooms for telltale signs of the use of contraceptives? The very idea is repulsive to the notions of privacy surrounding the marriage relationship."

In a concurring opinion, Justice Arthur Goldberg focused on the Ninth Amendment, arguing that "the right of privacy in the marital relation is fundamental and basic—a personal right 'retained by the people' within the meaning of the Ninth Amendment." In separate opinions concurring in the judgment, Justices Byron White and John M. Harlan stressed the "liberty" protected from state action by the Fourteenth Amendment.

Justices Hugo Black and Potter Stewart dissented from what they believed was an unwarranted interpretation of the Constitution. Justice Black wrote: "The Court talks about a constitutional 'right of privacy' as though there is some constitutional provision or provisions forbidding any law ever to be passed which might abridge the 'privacy' of individuals. But there is not." Justice Stewart agreed, saying, "I can find no such general right of privacy in the Bill of Rights, in any other part of the Constitution, or in any case ever before decided by this Court." Stewart characterized the Connecticut law as "uncommonly silly" but noted that it is not the role of the Court "to say whether we think this law is unwise, or even asinine."

In *Griswold*, the Court invalidated the Connecticut anticontraception statute only insofar as it infringed the rights of married couples. Seven years later, in *Eisenstadt v. Baird* (1972),[115] the Court struck down a similar law with respect to unmarried persons. Speaking for the Court in *Eisenstadt*, Justice William Brennan noted: "If the right of privacy means anything, it is the right of the individual, married or single, to be free from unwarranted governmental intrusion into matters so fundamentally affecting a person as the decision whether to bear or beget a child." *Eisenstadt* thus paved the way for *Roe v. Wade*, the landmark decision on abortion that would come down less than a year later.

The Abortion Decisions

Roe v. Wade was the first in a series of decisions over a fifty-year time span in which the Court would wrestle with the most divisive sociomoral issue since slavery. In a 7–2 decision, the Court struck down a Texas statute that made it a crime to "procure" or "attempt" an abortion, with the exception of one "procured or attempted by medical advice for the purpose of saving the life of the mother." While the decision was hailed by many as a great leap forward for women's rights, it is fair to say that no other decision in the modern era has generated more criticism than has *Roe*. Opponents of the decision often point to the fact that in deciding the case, the Court held that an unborn child is not a "person" within the meaning of the Constitution and, therefore, has no constitutional right to life. Rather, the Court recognized the government's interest in protecting the unborn child but held that this interest does not become "compelling" until that point in pregnancy where the fetus is "viable." Up to that point, roughly the end of the second trimester, the state's interest must give way to the mother's right to privacy. As for the source and scope of that right, Justice Harry Blackmun's majority opinion asserted that the "right of privacy, whether it be founded in the Fourteenth Amendment's concept of personal liberty and restrictions upon state action, as we feel it is, or ... in the Ninth Amendment's reservation of rights to the people, is broad enough to encompass a woman's decision whether or not to terminate her pregnancy."

As the Supreme Court became more conservative in the 1980s, supporters of *Roe v. Wade* feared that the decision might be overturned. That did not happen, at least not right away, but the Court did grant states more leeway in regulating abortion. In *Planned Parenthood v. Casey* (1992),[116] the Court said it would uphold regulations as long as they did not constitute an "undue burden" on a woman's right to choose abortion. Regulations that have been upheld include waiting periods, informed consent requirements, and parental notification in the case of minors seeking abortions. However, requirements that doctors performing abortions in clinics have admitting privileges in nearby hospitals and that clinics have hospital-grade facilities were struck down as undue burdens in 2016 and 2020 decisions from the high Court.[117]

In *Dobbs v. Jackson* Women's Health (2022),[118] the Supreme Court overturned *Roe v. Wade* and *Planned Parenthood v. Casey*, which had safeguarded a woman's right to choose an abortion for nearly 50 years. As a result, the Court paved the way for individual states to criminalize the provision of an abortion, which more than a dozen states did almost immediately via "trigger laws" that were designed to take effect upon the overturn of *Roe*. Generally, such laws created criminal penalties for abortion providers, but not for women who sought an abortion.

The *Dobbs* case addressed a Mississippi law that attempted to ban abortion after 15 weeks into a pregnancy. The Fifth Circuit, relying on *Roe*, had halted the ban as unconstitutional—yet the Supreme Court granted certiorari. Justice Amy Coney Barrett's arrival at the Court in 2020 signaled a potential shift in the Court's abortion jurisprudence, as the Court had for more than a decade refused to review lower court decisions that struck down abortion bans at less than 20 weeks into a pregnancy. Ultimately, as presaged by a leaked draft of Justice Alito's majority opinion, which was revealed by website Politico in May 2022, a five-vote majority on the high Court not only upheld the Mississippi law but also explicitly overturned *Roe v. Wade* and *Planned Parenthood v. Casey*, thereby allowing states to set their own policies on abortion.

Justice Samuel Alito's majority opinion in *Dobbs* declared that "... *Roe* and *Casey* must be overruled. The Constitution makes no reference to abortion, and no such right is implicitly protected by any constitutional provision. ..." Alito insisted that the rights conferred by the term "liberty" in the Due Process Clauses of the Fifth and Fourteenth Amendments must be "deeply rooted in the Nation's history and tradition" and "implicit in the concept of ordered liberty," phrases that had appeared in several prior decisions. In applying this standard to the matter at hand, Alito called the right to abortion "entirely unknown in American law" prior to the "latter part of the 20th century." He stressed the fact that three-fourths of U.S. states made abortion a crime at the time that the Fourteenth Amendment was ratified in 1868.

The dissenting opinion by Justices Breyer, Kagan, and Sotomayor expressed concern for the Supreme Court's legitimacy in light of the reversal of decades of precedent as a result of new justices having joined the Court in the past five years. Specifically, they observed:

> Now a new and bare majority of this Court—acting at practically the first moment possible—overrules *Roe* and *Casey*. ... It eliminates a 50-year-old constitutional right that safeguards women's freedom and equal station. It breaches a core rule-of-law principle, designed to promote constancy in the law. In doing all of that, it places in jeopardy other rights, from contraception to same-sex intimacy and marriage. And finally, it undermines the Court's legitimacy.

Beyond that, the dissent criticized the majority's reliance on original understanding of the Constitution, saying:

> Those responsible for the original Constitution, including the Fourteenth Amendment, did not perceive women as equals, and did not recognize women's rights. When the majority says that we must read our foundational charter as viewed at the time of ratification (except that we may also check it against the Dark Ages), it consigns women to second-class citizenship.

Subsequent to *Dobbs*, some states banned abortion even in cases of incest and rape, with exceptions permitted only in cases impacting the mother's health. Some states even considered criminalizing the act of traveling across state lines to obtain an abortion, counseling others to get an abortion, or acquiring a so-called "abortion pill." On the other hand, some states took actions to protect a woman's right to choose. For example, in Kansas, where the matter was put to a statewide referendum, a 59% to 41% majority voted to protect abortion rights. It remains to be seen how other states will address this controversial issue.

Sexual Freedom

Historically, the laws of many states included a number of sexual prohibitions, including adultery, fornication, incest, and sodomy. In *Bowers v. Hardwick* (1985),[119] the Supreme Court rejected a challenge to Georgia's sodomy statute as applied to homosexual conduct, saying the claim "that any kind of private sexual conduct between consenting adults is constitutionally insulated from state proscription is unsupportable." In dissent, four justices chided the Court for refusing to recognize "the fundamental interest all individuals have in controlling the nature of their intimate associations with others." The decision was a controversial one and certainly provided impetus to a growing LGBT rights movement.

As societal attitudes toward sex and, in particular, homosexuality became more liberal in the decades that followed, it was not surprising that in 2003 the Court overturned *Bowers v. Hardwick*. Speaking for a majority of six justices in *Lawrence v. Texas* (2003),[120] Anthony Kennedy began his opinion by noting, "Liberty presumes an autonomy of self that includes freedom of thought, belief, expression, and certain intimate conduct." Referring to the two gay men who were prosecuted by the state of Texas, Kennedy insisted that "[t]he State cannot demean their existence or control their destiny by making their private sexual conduct a crime." He concluded his opinion for the Court by observing that "[a]s the Constitution endures, persons in every generation can invoke its principles in their own search for greater freedom." In one of his more caustic dissents, Justice Antonin Scalia asserted that "[w]hat Texas has chosen to do is well within the range of traditional democratic action, and its hand should not be stayed through the invention of a brand-new 'constitutional right' by a Court that is impatient of democratic change."

What are the implications of *Lawrence v. Texas* for other laws prohibiting sexual conduct outside marriage? To the extent that sexual conduct involves minors or takes place in public, *Lawrence* offers no protection. Nor does it shield any form of nonconsensual sex from prosecution. But as Justice Scalia noted in his *Lawrence* dissent, laws prohibiting bigamy, incest, adultery, and fornication by consenting adults are open to attack. It should be noted, though, that the laws against fornication and adultery largely have been repealed, and those that remain on the books are seldom enforced. Bigamy and incest remain offenses in nearly all states, and there appears to be little sentiment for doing away with such prohibitions, either among the courts or the public at large.

The Right to Die

Beginning in the mid-1970s, state courts began to hold that the constitutional right of privacy extended to decisions by competent adults facing terminal conditions to refuse medical treatment and thereby hasten death. In the leading case of the era, *In re Quinlan* (1976),[121] the New Jersey Supreme Court allowed parents to exercise this right on behalf of their daughter, who was in a vegetative state and could not communicate. Some proponents of the so called "right to die" went so far as to suggest that the right of privacy extended to the right to commit suicide. After all, if one's life belongs to oneself, why should the state interfere with decisions regarding life and death?

The Supreme Court has said little about the right to die. In *Cruzan v. Missouri Health Department* (1990),[122] the Court recognized the right to refuse medical treatment but held it must be balanced against the state's legitimate interest in preserving life. Similarly, in *Washington v. Glucksberg* (1997),[123] the Court recognized the right to die in some situations but, nevertheless, upheld a state law criminalizing physician-assisted suicide. Noting that "Americans are engaged in an earnest and profound debate about the morality, legality, and practicality of physician-assisted suicide," the Court said that its "holding permits this debate to continue, as it should in a democratic society." Today, ten states permit doctor-assisted suicide in cases of terminally ill but mentally competent patients. These include the state of Washington, which enacted the Death with Dignity Act[124] a decade after its law banning physician-assisted suicide was upheld by the Supreme Court. Legalization of such practices has come about in different ways, including ballot initiatives (Colorado, Oregon, and Washington), votes of state legislatures (California, Maine, New Jersey, and Vermont), and state supreme court decisions (Montana).

THE CONSTITUTION IN ACTION
"Dr. Death" Sentenced for Murder in Assisted Suicide Case

Jack Kevorkian was a Michigan-based doctor who claimed to have helped more than 130 people end their lives via physician-assisted suicide. He was first charged with murder in 1990, when he helped an Alzheimer's patient end her life, but the charges were dropped. He was charged again in 1994 but was found not guilty by a jury. Even so, authorities would bring another prosecution against him in 1998, when he was arrested by police in Michigan for his role in ending the life of a terminally ill patient named Thomas Youk, who suffered from ALS (Lou Gehrig's Disease). In this case, Kevorkian was found guilty of second-degree murder and sentenced to a term of imprisonment of 10 to 25 years. He served 8 years of that sentence before being granted parole in 2007. A condition of his parole was that he forego involvement in assisting or promoting the idea of physician-aided suicided. Nonetheless, "Dr. Death," as Kevorkian came to be known, would remain an advocate for assisted suicide until his own death in 2011.

Obiter Dicta

"There is, of course, a sphere within which the individual may assert the supremacy of his own will and rightfully dispute the authority of any human government, especially of any free government existing under a written constitution, to interfere with the exercise of that will. But it is equally true that, in every well-ordered society charged with the duty of conserving the safety of its members the rights of the individual in respect of his liberty may at times, under the pressure of great dangers, be subjected to such restraint, to be enforced by reasonable regulations, as the safety of the general public may demand."

—*Justice John M. Harlan (the elder), writing for the Supreme Court in* Jacobson v. Massachusetts, *197 U.S. 11 (1905).*

Compulsory Vaccination

The year 2021 saw a nationwide campaign to vaccinate the public against the virus that produced the COVID-19 pandemic of 2020. Achieving "herd immunity" requires that most people get the vaccine, although the precise proportion required in the case of the novel coronavirus is unknown. As of August 2022, about two-thirds of Americans had been fully vaccinated against the novel coronavirus. Yet millions of Americans had refused to take the vaccine for various reasons. As new and more contagious variants of the coronavirus began to spread within the unvaccinated population, policymakers contemplated measures to promote vaccination.

In July 2021, the Biden Administration announced rules requiring federal employees and contractors to get vaccinated to avoid frequent mandatory testing for COVID-19. State and local officials contemplated similar policies, while some resorted to financial incentives to promote vaccination. But there was very little discussion of the enactment of outright mandates.

Several constitutional questions are implicit in this discussion. Would the president have the authority to issue a nationwide vaccine mandate by way of executive order? Would Congress have that authority? What about a state statute or local ordinance requiring people to get vaccinated? Could such a law be challenged as a violation of the right of privacy? Of course, when dealing with a communicable disease, such as COVID-19, an individual's decision to take or not take the vaccine affects other members of the community, not just oneself.

The issue of compulsory vaccination has arisen before. In *Jacobson v. Massachusetts* (1905),[125] the Supreme Court upheld a law requiring people to get vaccinated against smallpox. Recognizing the collective action problem inherent in combatting an epidemic, the Court was "... unwilling to hold it to be an element in the liberty secured by the Constitution of the United States that one person, or a minority of persons, residing in any community and enjoying the benefits of its local government, should have the power thus to dominate the majority when supported in their action by the authority of the State." The majority opinion also added that, "According to settled principles, the police power of a State must be held to embrace, at least, such reasonable regulations established directly by legislative enactment as will protect the public health and the public safety."

In August 2021, the Supreme Court demonstrated its continued adherence to the *Jacobson* precedent when it refused to overturn a lower court order that upheld vaccine requirements for students at Indiana

University. Students at IU had challenged the mandate but were rebuffed by a federal district court and the Seventh Circuit.[126]

On January 13, 2022, the Supreme Court issued two decisions on federal vaccine mandates. Unlike *Jacobson*, these cases involved the powers of federal agencies delegated by Congress. In *National Federation of Independent Business v. Department of Labor, OSHA*,[127] the high Court struck down the Department of Labor's vaccine mandate for businesses with more than 100 employees. In a 6–3 opinion, the Supreme Court stated:

> Administrative agencies are creatures of statute. They accordingly possess only the authority that Congress has provided. The Secretary [of Labor] has ordered 84 million Americans to either obtain a COVID-19 vaccine or undergo weekly medical testing at their own expense. This is no everyday exercise of federal power.

The Court's opinion culminated with the declaration that OSHA can set "*workplace* safety standards, not broad public health measures" [emphasis in original].

The Court's second vaccine case in January 2022, *Biden v. Missouri*,[128] produced a 5–4 decision, upholding a federal vaccine mandate affecting all health care workers in medical facilities that accepted Medicare and Medicaid. In evaluating the rule put forth by the Secretary of Health and Human Services to create this directive, the Court's per curiam opinion found that the mandate "falls within the authorities that Congress has conferred upon him." Extrapolating this idea to a wider perspective, the opinion concluded by saying the following:

> The challenges posed by a global pandemic do not allow a federal agency to exercise power that Congress has not conferred upon it. At the same time, such unprecedented circumstances provide no grounds for limiting the exercise of authorities the agency has long been recognized to have.

Equal Protection of the Laws: The Fourteenth Amendment

The principal intention of the drafters of the Fourteenth Amendment was to protect the rights of African Americans, most of whom had just been emancipated from slavery. Early on, though, the Supreme Court showed little sympathy for persons suffering from racial discrimination. Earlier in the chapter, we saw how, in *The Civil Rights Cases* (1883), the Court circumscribed the legislative power of Congress under Section 5 of the Fourteenth Amendment. Similarly, in *Plessy v. Ferguson* (1896),[129] the Court upheld a Louisiana law mandating racial segregation on passenger trains. It did so by invoking the separate but equal doctrine, under which mandatory separation was not seen as a denial of equal protection. Justice Henry Billings Brown, speaking for eight of the nine justices, observed that "[i]f one race be inferior to the other socially, the Constitution of the United States cannot put them upon the same plane."

In one of the most famous dissenting opinions in the history of the Supreme Court, Justice John M. Harlan insisted that "[t]he arbitrary separation of citizens on the basis of race ... is a badge of servitude wholly inconsistent with the civil freedom and the equality before the law established by the Constitution." In an oft-quoted statement, Justice Harlan declared: "Our Constitution is color-blind, and neither knows nor tolerates classes among citizens. In respect of civil rights, all citizens are equal before the law."

SEPARATE BUT EQUAL DOCTRINE: The discredited doctrine that held segregation of the races was not a denial of equal protection of the law.

Brown v. Board of Education and Modern Civil Rights Law

Justice Harlan's dissent in *Plessy* would be largely vindicated by the Court in *Brown v. Board of Education* (1954), when it declared that "in the field of public education, the doctrine of 'separate but equal' has no place." Chief Justice Earl Warren's majority opinion for a unanimous Court also spoke of minority children being sent to segregated schools by saying, "To separate them from others of similar age and qualifications solely because of their race generates a feeling of inferiority as to their status in the community that may affect their hearts and minds in a way unlikely ever to be undone." The *Brown* decision provided the impetus for a civil rights movement that would successfully attack overt racial discrimination, both in court and in Congress. Concerted congressional and judicial action in the years to come would establish the framework of modern civil rights law.

During the 1960s, Congress exercised its powers under the Fourteenth and Fifteenth Amendments, as well as its authority under the Commerce Clause, to enact sweeping protections of civil rights. The Civil Rights Act of 1964 prohibited racial discrimination in public accommodations, employment, and by educational institutions that receive federal funds.[130] Specifically, Title VII of the Civil Rights Act of 1964[131] bars employment discrimination on the basis of race, color, religion, sex, or national origin. This Act also established the Equal Employment Opportunity Commission (EEOC), which, along with the U.S. Department of Justice, can enforce fines against those who violate civil rights laws. Subsequently, Congress also passed the Voting Rights Act of 1965, which eliminated barriers to minority participation in elections, such as literacy tests.[132] And the Civil Rights Act of 1968, also known as the Fair Housing Act, prohibited discrimination in the sale and rental of housing.[133] For its part, the Supreme Court of the 1960s readily upheld Congress's legislative actions in the civil rights field against a number of constitutional challenges.[134]

STRICT SCRUTINY: An approach to judging official discrimination based on race, religion, or national origin in which that discrimination is presumed to be unconstitutional; to overcome this presumption, government must demonstrate that its actions are narrowly tailored to furthering a compelling interest.

Thirteen years after *Brown*, the Court struck down the last vestige of the Jim Crow laws when it invalidated a state law making interracial marriage a crime. In *Loving v. Virginia* (1967),[135] the Court could find "no legitimate overriding purpose independent of invidious racial discrimination" to justify the prohibition and concluded that "restricting the freedom to marry solely because of racial classifications violates the central meaning of the Equal Protection Clause."

SUSPECT CLASSIFICATION DOCTRINE: The judicial doctrine under which official discrimination based on race, religion, or national origin is considered to be inherently suspect and, therefore, subjected to strict scrutiny.

The Suspect Classification Doctrine

The Supreme Court has held repeatedly that racial classifications are inherently suspect and must be subjected to strict scrutiny by the courts.[136] According to the suspect classification doctrine, the burden of persuasion in such cases rests on the government, which must be able to articulate a **compelling interest** to support the discrimination. Moreover, a racially discriminatory policy must be **narrowly tailored**, which is to say that it must inflict no more harm than is necessary to achievement of that compelling interest.

Not since the infamous Japanese relocation case of 1944 has the Court upheld an invidious racial discrimination,[137] and it is difficult to imagine a case in which a law that imposes a disability on a racial minority would pass constitutional muster. Discrimination based on national origin and religion also has been recognized as inherently suspect and, hence, is subject to strict scrutiny as well.

Expanding Prohibitions of Discrimination

The Fourteenth Amendment says that a state may not "deny to any person within its jurisdiction the equal protection of the laws." This broad phrasing has allowed both Congress and the courts to recognize the civil rights not only of racial and ethnic minorities but of women, disabled persons, immigrants, religious groups, and LGBTQ persons. Although the Fourteenth Amendment permits Congress to address discrimination by states, the Supreme Court has held repeatedly that Congress may rely on the Commerce Clause to prohibit discrimination in the private sector as well. Accordingly, Congress has enacted laws to prohibit discrimination on the basis of gender, age, disability, and religion.[138] Thus, there is a wide array of federal laws prohibiting various types of discrimination in housing, employment, and access to public accommodations. Beyond that, by passing the Civil Rights Act of 1991,[139] Congress allowed for discrimination to take two forms: (a) intentional (known as "disparate treatment" discrimination") and (b) unintentional (known as "disparate impact" discrimination), whereby employment practices that may not intentionally discriminate could be in violation of Title VII if there is a disproportionately adverse effect on minorities.

Ultimately, discrimination protections could impact the creation of laws as well as the enforcement of laws—and they also hold relevance for employees working in criminal justice settings, as those individuals are protected against discrimination in the workplace. Understanding how to approach all of these situations, from constitutional and statutory standpoints, is crucial to notions of equal protection under the law. We consider various forms of potential discrimination in the sections below.

Sex Discrimination

The Supreme Court has rendered a number of impactful decisions interpreting the Equal Protection Clause as it relates to sex-based

COMPELLING INTEREST: A government interest so strong it justifies infringement of fundamental rights.

NARROWLY TAILORED: The requirement for a policy that impinges on constitutional rights to be constructed in such a way as to limit the extent to which it curtails those rights.

discrimination. In *Reed v. Reed* (1971),[140] the Court opened the courthouse door to constitutional challenges to laws treating men and women differently. Writing for a unanimous bench, Chief Justice Warren E. Burger said, "To give a mandatory preference to members of either sex over members of the other ... is to make the very kind of arbitrary legislative choice forbidden by the Equal Protection Clause of the Fourteenth Amendment.

In *Frontiero v. Richardson* (1973),[141] the Supreme Court invalidated an Air Force policy that discriminated against female servicepersons with respect to spousal benefits. However, the Court stopped short of holding that sex discrimination must be viewed through the same judicial lens as discrimination based on race. In future cases, the Court would articulate a different test for judging sex discrimination claims—one that employs "heightened" or "intermediate" scrutiny.

In *Craig v. Boren* (1976),[142] the Supreme Court held that "... to withstand constitutional challenge, ... classifications by gender must serve important governmental objectives and must be substantially related to achievement of those objectives." In this case, the Court struck down an Oklahoma law that discriminated between men and women in terms of the minimum age to buy beer with 3.2% alcohol content. Under the statute, women could buy 3.2% beer at age 18; men had to be 21. The state had proffered evidence that young men were more likely to drink and drive and more likely to get into traffic accidents. But in the Court's view, the statute failed the test of intermediate scrutiny, as Oklahoma's evidence was not sufficiently persuasive.

In the 1980s and 90s, the Supreme Court addressed admissions processes involving single-sex educational institutions. In *Mississippi University for Women v. Hogan* (1982),[143] the Court ruled in favor of a man who wanted to attend what was an all-female nursing school. The Court found that the school lacked a "significant interest" in preventing men from applying to the university. Then, in *United States v. Virginia* (1996),[144] the Court invalidated the male-only admissions policy at the Virginia Military Institute. Justice Ruth Bader Ginsburg's opinion for the Court concluded that state had failed to establish an "exceedingly persuasive justification" for excluding women from VMI. Noting that VMI "offers an educational opportunity no other Virginia institution provides," Justice Ginsburg concluded: "Women seeking and fit for a VMI-quality education cannot be offered anything less, under the Commonwealth's obligation to afford them genuinely equal protection."

Although sex discrimination is not subject to strict judicial scrutiny (but, rather, heightened scrutiny), it is very difficult for government to

HEIGHTENED SCRUTINY (OR INTERMEDIATE SCRUTINY): A judicial approach to judging gender-based discrimination as well as time, place, and manner regulations of the exercise of First Amendment rights. Under heightened scrutiny, government carries the burden of providing an exceedingly persuasive justification for its policies.

articulate an "exceedingly persuasive justification" for treating men and women differently. Some would argue that the "exceedingly persuasive justification" test is very similar to the "compelling interest" test required by strict scrutiny. This test applies to sex discrimination in law enforcement.

From the time the first female police officer was sworn into duty in 1908 in Portland, Oregon, the number of female officers steadily rose until the year 2000, when it began to level off. As of 2021, female officers accounted for just under 13% of all officers serving in the United States—but only 7% of state troopers nationwide were women, and only 3% of leadership positions in law enforcement were held by females.[145]

Sexual Harassment in the Workplace

Beyond the protections afforded by the Fourteenth Amendment, as noted above, Title VII of the Civil Rights Act precludes discrimination based on sex. In *Meritor Savings Bank v. Vinson* (1986),[146] the Court found that sexual harassment in the workplace, when it is "severe or pervasive" as to "alter the conditions of employment and create an abusive working environment," can amount to a violation of Title VII as a form of sex discrimination. In the majority opinion for that case, Justice Rehnquist declared that sexual harassment that "creates a hostile or offensive environment for members of one sex is every bit the arbitrary barrier to sexual equality at the workplace that racial harassment is to racial equality." The Court defined "hostile workplace" more specifically in future cases.[147]

A study from attorney Terrence P. Dwyer collated media-reported incidents of sexual harassment of female officers in law enforcement settings from 2000–2019. He found that 55% of cases ended up in federal court as civil suits, 36% were brought into state courts, and the rest were handled through internal or state-run administrative procedures. Dwyer observed that the average monetary award after a trial was more than $1.16 million, and the average settlement was nearly $390,000. More than 31% of cases arose in cities with a population greater than 250,000 people.[148]

Equal Pay Considerations

The Equal Pay Act (EPA) of 1963[149] precludes discrimination on the basis of sex when it comes to pay for "substantially similar work" that is performed "under similar working conditions" in the same work setting; four exceptions allow for pay differences that do not violate this law[150]:

- pay differences based on seniority
- pay differences based on merit
- pay differences based on quality or quantity of production
- pay differences based on any factor other than sex

Circuit courts have split on whether pay at a prior job can be a relevant consideration in regard to the fourth factor.[151] In 2012, a group called the Institute for Women's Policy Research built upon data from a Bureau of Labor Statistics study released two years prior to indicate that average median salaries for male and female police and sheriff's officers were very close, coming in at $948 a week for men and $938 for women.[152] For female officers, sex discrimination also could apply to any adverse action taken against someone who is pregnant, as the Family Leave and Medical Act requires employers to offer employees unpaid leave for a period of up to 12 weeks for certain medical or family care reasons.[153]

THE CONSTITUTION IN ACTION
Do Women Have a Constitutional Right to Go Topless?

Most state and local laws consider it to be "public nudity" for a woman to expose her breasts in public. Obviously, the same prohibition does not apply to men. Is this an unconstitutional form of sex discrimination? In early 2019, the Tenth Circuit Court of Appeals struck down an ordinance of this kind, observing that a law premised on "generalizations about 'the way women are' … will fail constitutional scrutiny because it serves no important governmental objective."[154] A few months later, the Eighth Circuit ruled the opposite way in a similar case from Missouri.[155] Elsewhere, in 2019, the New Hampshire Supreme Court upheld a woman's conviction for violating a local ordinance that makes it a misdemeanor for a woman to expose her breasts in public "with less than a fully opaque covering of any part of the nipple."[156] In January 2020, the Supreme Court declined to review the case.

RATIONAL BASIS TEST:
The requirement that a law or policy must be rationally related to a legitimate governmental interest.

MINIMAL SCRUTINY: A judicial approach to judging laws that infringe on liberty generally or discriminate on the basis of characteristics not subject to strict or heightened scrutiny.

Other Claims of Discrimination

Other discrimination claims—beyond those involving race, religion, national origin, or gender—are reviewed at a "lesser" standard through something called the rational basis test. Under this test, which is also known as minimal scrutiny, discrimination is presumed lawful. It is up to the party challenging the discrimination to show that it lacks a rational basis—that is, the discrimination is not a reasonable means of achieving a legitimate governmental interest. To take an easy example, consider the laws that require doctors to be licensed to practice medicine. By definition, such laws discriminate against those who do not have medical licenses, but few would argue that such laws lack a rational basis.

Age Discrimination

One type of discrimination that is typically subjected to the rational basis test is discrimination based on age. Again, to take an easy example, consider the laws that restrict driver's licenses to persons over sixteen. One might quibble with the particular age requirement, but few would argue that the state lacks a rational basis for prohibiting the very young from operating automobiles.

In *Massachusetts Board of Retirement v. Murgia* (1976),[157] the Supreme Court considered the case of Robert Murgia, who was a police officer in the Uniformed Branch of the Massachusetts State Police. Although he claimed to be in excellent physical and mental health, Murgia was forced to retire on his fiftieth birthday, pursuant to a state law that established this as the mandatory retirement age for uniformed state police officers. He filed a lawsuit seeking to retain his job, claiming a violation of the Equal Protection Clause of the Fourteenth Amendment. In reviewing the case, the Supreme Court noted that because there was no "suspect class" in this case—meaning no racial discrimination—strict scrutiny would not apply. The Court also noted that public employment did not constitute a "fundamental right," which is another way that strict scrutiny could have been applied. Instead, the Court used the rational basis test, which only requires the state's lawyers to demonstrate a "legitimate interest" and a "rational relationship" between that interest and the retirement age. When discussing the application of this test, the Court's syllabus for this per curiam opinion noted that the mandatory retirement age was "rationally related to the State's announced legitimate objective of protecting the public by assuring the physical preparedness of its uniformed police."

More specifically, the per curiam opinion observed that "... through mandatory retirement at age 50, the legislature seeks to protect the public by assuring physical preparedness of its uniformed police." The opinion also said, "Since physical ability generally declines with age, mandatory retirement at 50 serves to remove from police service those whose fitness for uniformed work presumptively has diminished with age. This clearly is rationally related to the State's objective."

In dissent, Justice Marshall took umbrage with the lesser rational basis test employed for age discrimination cases, stating, "There is simply no reason why a statute that tells able-bodied police officers, ready and willing to work, that they no longer have the right to earn a living in their chosen profession merely because they are 50 years old should be judged by the same minimal standards of rationality that we use to test economic legislation that discriminates against business interests."

The Supreme Court also considered age discrimination cases on two other occasions. In *Vance v. Bradley* (1979),[158] the Court upheld a retirement age of 60 years old for those working in the U.S. Foreign Service. Later, in *Gregory v. Ashcroft* (1991),[159] the justices upheld the state of Missouri's imposition of mandatory retirement for state judges at age 70. Across all of these cases, the rational basis approach—and not strict scrutiny or intermediate scrutiny—was applied.

All states continue to use some type of retirement age for uniformed officers, although a 2019 report from the U.S. Government Accountability Office highlighted potential benefits of raising such ages. In particular, the report studied the value of raising the minimum retirement age for U.S. Capitol Police Officers from 57 to 60; the report noted that benefits to officers from continued employment could be achieved with "only a modest increase in costs" for the government.[160]

Notably, beyond the protections of the Fourteenth Amendment, a federal law, called the Age Discrimination in Employment Act (ADEA) of 1967, places limitations on employment discrimination against persons 40 years of age and older.[161] Given the low standard of rational basis review used in the Supreme Court's Fourteenth Amendment age discrimination cases, some might choose to bring such lawsuits via this federal law.

Sexual Orientation and Gender Identity Discrimination

In 1996, the same year it decided the VMI case, the Court held for the first time that gay and lesbian Americans are deserving of judicial solicitude under the Equal Protection Clause. In *Romer v. Evans* (1996),[162] the Court struck down an amendment to the Colorado constitution that prohibited the enactment of civil rights protections on the basis of sexual orientation. Justice Anthony Kennedy's opinion for the Court asserted that "[a] law declaring that in general it shall be more difficult for one group of citizens than for all others to seek aid from the government is itself a denial of equal protection of the laws in the most literal sense." Justice Kennedy applied the rational basis test in declaring that the amendment "is a status-based enactment divorced from any factual context from which we could discern a relationship to legitimate state interest."

He also quoted a 1973 precedent in stating that a "desire to harm a politically unpopular group cannot constitute a *legitimate* governmental interest."[163]

Nearly two decades later, Justice Kennedy would write an even more impactful opinion for the Court dealing with the rights of gay and lesbian Americans. In a 5–4 decision in *Obergefell v. Hodges* (2015),[164] the Court struck down state laws prohibiting same sex marriage. According to Justice Kennedy, "the right to marry is a fundamental right inherent in the liberty of the person, and under the Due Process and Equal Protection Clauses of the Fourteenth Amendment couples of the same-sex may not be deprived of that right and that liberty." Interestingly, though, Justice Kennedy did not invoke a specific level of judicial scrutiny. From a different perspective, reflecting his originalist view of constitutional interpretation, Justice Scalia's dissent chided the majority for having "discovered in the Fourteenth Amendment a 'fundamental right' overlooked by every person alive at the time of ratification, and almost everyone else in the time since."

The Supreme Court's decisions recognizing the rights of LGBT persons have not been confined to constitutional interpretation. In a 7–2 decision in *Bostock v. Clayton County* (2020),[165] the Court construed Title VII of the 1964 Civil Rights Act as prohibiting workplace discrimination on the basis of sexual orientation or gender identity. Referring to Title VII's ban on sex discrimination, Justice Neil Gorsuch's majority opinion concluded that "discrimination based on homosexuality or transgender status necessarily entails discrimination based on sex; the first cannot happen without the second." He went on to say that "It doesn't matter if other factors besides the plaintiff's sex contributed to the decision. ... If the employer intentionally relies in part on an individual employee's sex when deciding to discharge the employee ... a statutory violation has occurred." Justice Brett Kavanaugh dissented, accusing the Court of judicial activism: "In judicially rewriting Title VII, the Court today cashiers an ongoing legislative process, at a time when a new law to prohibit sexual orientation discrimination was probably close at hand."

One year later, in June 2021, the high Court refused to grant certiorari in a case that addressed bathroom access for transgender students in public school. The Court's refusal left in place a Fourth Circuit decision that struck down a Virginia school district's ban on use of a bathroom that did not correspond to a student's sex at birth. The Fourth Circuit opinion used intermediate scrutiny and declared that the school's policy was not "substantially related to a sufficiently important government interest" and, thus, amounted to a violation of the Fourteenth Amendment.[166]

Disability Discrimination

As previously noted, if a public employer or government official is involved—as would be the case within a police department—a discrimination lawsuit brought by an employee could revolve around either the Fourteenth Amendment or applicable federal law (whereas a suit against a private employer could only rely upon federal law and not the Constitution). In those situations where a choice exists, using federal law, instead of the Equal Protection Clause, as the basis for a lawsuit might be preferred for a plaintiff *if* a federal law creates a higher burden for an employer to meet.

For example, in disability cases, the Supreme Court's approach to applying the Fourteenth Amendment has revolved around the lesser standard of rational basis review.[167] Alternatively, a person who feels a disability has led to employment discrimination might consider a lawsuit brought under Title II of the Americans with Disabilities Act (ADA) of 1990, which prohibits disability discrimination by state or local public entities.[168] In 2008, Congress amended that law, broadening definitions of the word *disability* to encompass "a physical or mental impairment that substantially limits one or more major life activities of such individual."[169] Do keep in mind, however, that the ADA allows for employers to make "reasonable accommodations" for those with disabilities and also requires that an employee is "otherwise qualified" for a job. In addition to the ADA, Section 501 and 505 of the Rehabilitation Act of 1973,[170] as amended, prohibits discrimination against federal employees who have disabilities.

In 2001, the Supreme Court interpreted federal law to require that the PGA Tour permit golfer Casey Martin to use a golf cart during official tour events, with the Court noting that this amounted to a "reasonable accommodation" for Martin's disability, which was a circulatory system disorder that impacted his ability to walk.[171] More recently, the federal Genetic Information Nondiscrimination Act of 2008[172] banned discriminatory employment actions taken against a person based on their genetic information, such as family history of disease or other information revealed through genetic testing or DNA analysis.

The Americans with Disabilities Act can also impact how police officers interact with individual members of society, since the law requires police services to be made available to those with disabilities. A common application of this idea is the provision of an accommodation for those individuals who have difficulty hearing or speaking. The government's official ADA website, www.ada.gov, contains a special page called "Americans with Disabilities Act Information for Law Enforcement." On this site, links can be found to documents that are designed to assist officers in communicating with those who are deaf or hard of hearing.[173] We discuss this topic in further detail in chapters 11 and 12, in which we consider *Miranda* rights.

Affirmative Action

One of the most controversial aspects of civil rights law over the last half century is affirmative action, a policy designed to benefit members of historically marginalized groups by giving them preferences in college admissions, hiring, and government contracting. Although advocates of affirmative action consider it to be a benign form of discrimination, it is discrimination by definition and, therefore, implicates the Equal Protection Clause. Indeed, the Supreme Court has held, irrespective of their good intentions, race-conscious affirmative action programs must be subjected to strict scrutiny, and several programs have been invalidated by the Court, including the use of quotas in higher education admissions.[174] On the other hand, the Court has upheld affirmative action programs in higher education on the ground that promoting student

AFFIRMATIVE ACTION:
Policies and programs that provide preferential treatment based on race, ethnicity, gender, or other characteristics.

diversity is a compelling governmental interest.[175] Nevertheless, the Court has said that such programs must be "narrowly tailored"—that is, they must achieve their stated diversity goals with minimal harm to other groups of students; to this end, the Court has found that race can only be considered as "one of many factors" in defining diversity in the college admissions process.[176]

The Paradise Decision and Race Discrimination in Officer Hiring

Other federal court cases have addressed race discrimination in the context of public sector hiring practices. For example, in *United States v. Paradise* (1987),[177] the Court applied the Equal Protection Clause to a race discrimination case involving the Alabama Department of Public Safety, which handled the hiring and firing of state troopers. This case had its origins all the way back in 1972, when a federal district court in Alabama found that for almost four decades, the Alabama Department of Public Safety "had excluded blacks from all positions, including jobs in the upper ranks," with the district court describing this discriminatory conduct as "unquestionably a violation of the Fourteenth Amendment."[178] As a corrective measure, the district court ordered the implementation of a quota system, wherein 25% of the state trooper force should comprise black officers, in keeping with the demographics of the state's overall labor force. Decades later, in the plurality opinion in *Paradise*, the Supreme Court addressed this 1972 district court order by saying that "the pervasive, systematic, and obstinate discriminatory conduct of the Department created a profound need and a firm justification for the race-conscious relief ordered by the District Court."

The district court revisited this issue in 1979, noting that although progress had been made in entry-level hiring of Alabama state troopers, other issues still remained—in light of the fact that of 223 troopers who had attained the rank of corporal or higher in the state, the court noted that "there is still not one black."[179] In response, the district court put forth a "consent decree," whereby the department would take steps to improve that figure.

By 1983, four Black officers had been promoted to the upper ranks, but still unsatisfied with the lack of further progress, the district court issued a new order—this time implementing a specific "one-for-one promotion" system for upper ranks in the Alabama Department of Public Safety, including for positions of corporal, lieutenant, and captain. This order required that for each White officer who was promoted, a corresponding promotion for a Black officer would be made, until the overall percentage within a specific rank amounted to 25% Black officers—with an exception made for situations in which no qualified Black candidate was available (e.g., if none had yet served the appropriate tenure needed for a specific rank).[180] In 1985, the Eleventh Circuit upheld this "one-for-one" promotion order against a Fourteenth Amendment challenge.[181]

Two years later, the Supreme Court weighed in. Upholding that promotion order, Justice Brennan's plurality opinion in *Paradise* applied the legal test of strict scrutiny (which controls race-based discrimination claims) and found that "... the race-conscious relief at issue here is justified by a compelling interest in remedying the discrimination that permeated entry-level hiring practices and the promotional process alike." He went on to add the following:

> In determining whether race-conscious remedies are appropriate, we look to several factors, including the necessity for the relief and the efficacy of alternative remedies; the flexibility and duration of the relief, including the availability of waiver provisions; the relationship of the numerical goals to the relevant labor market; and the impact of the relief on the rights of

third parties. ... When considered in light of these factors, it was amply established, and we find that the one-for-one promotion requirement was narrowly tailored to serve its several purposes, both as applied to the initial set of promotions to the rank of corporal and as a continuing contingent order with respect to the upper ranks.

With that set of declarations, the culmination of fifteen years of litigation had arrived. Today, according to 2018 data from the U.S. Census Bureau, the demographics of the nationwide police officers are as follows: 61.5% White, 15.5% Black, and 14.5% Latino.[182]

The Frank Ricci Case: "Reverse Discrimination" in Promotion Exams

More than twenty years after the *United States v. Paradise* decision, the Court took a different approach to first-responder promotions in *Ricci v. DeStefano* (2009).[183] In this case, 118 firefighters in New Haven, Connecticut, took promotion exams (made up of written and oral components) seeking to attain ranks of lieutenant or captain, for which there were eight and seven openings, respectively. The City Charter mandated that each open position be filled from among the candidates with the top three exam scores; in effect, this resulted in those with the top ten scores on the lieutenant exams being eligible for the eight open lieutenant positions and the top nine scorers being eligible for the seven captain positions. There had been twenty-seven exams completed by Black candidates, but of those firefighters who were eligible for the two positions based on the test scores, seventeen were White, two were Hispanic, and none were Black. As a result, local officials on the New Haven Civil Service Board—some, perhaps, fearing a lawsuit over a "significant statistical disparity" (in the words of Justice Kennedy)—deadlocked 2–2 on a vote over whether the test scores should be kept; that led to the scores being discarded.

A group of 20 New Haven firefighters, including nineteen White firefighters and one Hispanic firefighter, filed suit against the mayor to challenge the decision to discard the scores. The lead plaintiff in the lawsuit was Frank Ricci, who had been a firefighter for eleven years. He quit a second job to study for the exam, and because he was dyslexic, he paid a voice actor $1,000 to record the textbooks as audiotapes; he also created flashcards and put himself through a mock oral exam.[184] Ultimately, he finished sixth out of seventy-seven candidates on the lieutenant exam, making him eligible for one of the open positions.

After a federal district court and the Second Circuit ruled against Ricci and the other firefighters, the Supreme Court found in their favor, declaring that the decision to discard the test scores unfairly impacted the candidates who had performed well on the exams. Rather than approaching this case through a Fourteenth Amendment paradigm, the suit revolved around interpretation of Title VII of the Civil Rights Act. In this regard, Justice Kennedy's majority opinion indicated that, "Fear of litigation alone cannot justify an employer's reliance on race to the detriment of individuals who passed the examinations and qualified for promotions. The city discarding the test results was impermissible under Title VII." The majority opinion also observed the following:

> The City's actions would violate the disparate-treatment prohibition of Title VII absent some valid defense. All the evidence demonstrates that the City chose not to certify the examination results because of the statistical disparity based on race—*i.e.*, how minority candidates had performed when compared to white candidates. As the District Court put it, the City rejected the test results because "too many whites and not enough minorities would be promoted were the lists to be certified." ... Without some other justification, this

express, race-based decision making violates Title VII's command that employers cannot take adverse employment actions because of an individual's race.

Two years after the high Court's decision in this case, the city of New Haven settled the lawsuit by agreeing to pay the 20 firefighters a total of $2 million in back pay as well as interest and added pension benefits; the settlement also included approximately $3 million in lawyers' fees.[185]

Equal Protection and Criminal Justice

The killing of George Floyd by Minneapolis police officers in May 2020 stimulated a national conversation, not only about the use of force by police but also the treatment of African Americans and other racial minorities in the criminal justice system. For its part, the Supreme Court began to recognize this issue as early as 1932. In two decisions stemming from the infamous Scottsboro Case,[186] the Court held that a group of young African American men was denied due process and equal protection of the law when they were summarily tried and sentenced for the crime of rape—a crime it turned out they did not commit.

Nine decades after the Scottsboro Case, and a more than a century and a half after the abolition of slavery, challenges related to race and the criminal justice system remain. What the Supreme Court has said and done about some of the most critical of these challenges is detailed in the following sections.

Selective Enforcement and Prosecution

The Supreme Court has held that selective application of the criminal law on the basis of race is a violation of equal protection.[187] To prevail in a claim of selective prosecution, one must demonstrate that persons of a different race were not prosecuted for the same offense. Speaking for the Court in *United States v. Armstrong* (1996),[188] Chief Justice Rehnquist observed that "a credible showing of different treatment of similarly situated persons-adequately balances the Government's interest in vigorous prosecution and the defendant's interest in avoiding selective prosecution."

Jury Selection

The Supreme Court has held repeatedly that exclusion of jurors on the basis of race is unconstitutional.[189] One way this exclusion can take place is through the peremptory challenge of prospective jurors. Historically, peremptory challenges were absolute. Unlike a challenge for cause, an attorney was not required to state a reason for objecting to a juror. Prosecutors would often use peremptory challenges to exclude Black candidates from juries, especially in cases where defendants were also Black. In *Batson v. Kentucky* (1986),[190] the Supreme Court modified peremptory challenges based ostensibly on race. If, for example, a Black defendant objects to a peremptory challenge to a Black juror, the burden is on the prosecution to state a race-neutral reason for challenging that juror. The judge must then decide whether to allow the challenge. Writing for the Court, Justice Byron White said, "By requiring trial courts to be sensitive to the racially discriminatory use of peremptory challenges, our decision enforces the mandate of equal protection and furthers the ends of justice." (We discuss the matter of jury selection in greater detail in chapter 12.)

Racial Profiling

In reality, profiling is an essential part of police work. Police officers and detectives need to channel limited resources toward the investigation and apprehension of alleged criminals. This inevitably requires discerning characteristics that apply generally to certain types of criminal behavior. However, when racial demographics figure into this process, the term racial profiling comes into play—as does the Equal Protection Clause.

Typically, assertions of racial profiling arise in two primary contexts: auto stops and pat-downs (stop-and-frisks). As we will learn in subsequent chapters dealing with the Fourth Amendment, both of these interactions must be based on "reasonable suspicion" of criminal activity. Supreme Court precedent has made it clear that race cannot be used in the process of assessing reasonable suspicion. For example, in *United States v. Brignoni-Ponce* (1975),[191] which dealt with a traffic stop effectuated by border patrol agents near the U.S.–Mexico border, the Court ruled that law enforcement officials cannot initiate a traffic stop based solely on the rationale that the occupants of the car appear to be of Mexican descent. This idea was reiterated in the Court's 2012 decision in *Arizona v. United States* (2012),[192] in which the majority noted that the Constitution prohibits the use of "race, color or national origin" as a factor in initiating an interaction designed to assess immigration status. Additionally, in *Florida v. J.L.* (2000),[193] the Court held that an anonymous tip that reported a "Black man wearing a plaid shirt and holding a gun" did not provide sufficient "indicia of reliability" to justify a pat down of one of three Black men in the area. Ultimately, searches and seizures can implicate both the Fourth Amendment and the Fourteenth Amendment's Equal Protection Clause, depending on the reasons that underlie a specific search or seizure.

Although it has evinced a clear aversion to racial profiling, the Supreme Court has upheld general profiles of criminal activity—such as the "drug courier profile." For example, in *United States v. Sokolow* (1983),[194] the Court addressed the matter of James Sokolow, who was stopped by DEA agents inside the Honolulu, Hawaii, airport. The reason for the initial interaction was based on reasonable suspicion that Sokolow had exhibited several traits of being a drug courier. Specifically, he paid more than $2,000 in cash for his airline ticket; he flew round-trip to and from Miami, staying there for only 48 hours; he did not have any checked luggage; he was traveling under a different name than his own; and agents said he appeared to be nervous. The Supreme Court ruled in favor of the agents, finding that the "totality of circumstances" in this matter provided a justification for the police action. The majority opinion quoted from *United States v. Cortez* (1981),[195] saying that, "In evaluating the validity of a stop such as this, we must consider 'the totality of the circumstances—the whole picture.'" The Court added the following quote from the *Cortez* case to crystallize the generalized nature, and need,

RACIAL PROFILING: The impermissible practice in which law enforcement authorities target people based on race.

CRITICAL RACE THEORY: An academic perspective that stresses the foundational nature of slavery in the creation of the United States and the idea that the nation's laws and institutions are inherently racist and, therefore, unjust.

for forming some types of "profiles" to guide police action in determining reasonable suspicion for traffic stops and pat-downs:

> The process does not deal with hard certainties, but with probabilities. Long before the law of probabilities was articulated as such, practical people formulated certain common-sense conclusions about human behavior; jurors as factfinders are permitted to do the same—and so are law enforcement officers.

In the end, the Supreme Court has made it clear that many factors can play a role in this process—but race should never be the sole factor. Whether it can be a factor at all is a question that remains unresolved. (We discuss this issue in greater detail in chapter 10.)

THE CONSTITUTION AND SOCIAL JUSTICE
Are Constitutional Rights Enough? The Challenge of Critical Race Theory

Despite the marked progress in protecting the constitutional rights of minorities, racial discrimination remains a reality in modern America. Moreover, the economic divide between Black and White Americans remains as large today as it was at the height of the Civil Rights Movement. Adding to this divide is the fact that African Americans are five times more likely than Whites to be incarcerated in state prisons.[196]

Some on the political left have questioned whether constitutional rights, at least as currently conceived, are sufficient to overcome the legacy of slavery. Those who subscribe to **critical race theory** (CRT) believe White supremacy is woven into the very fabric of the constitutional system. As an academic school of thought, CRT is rooted in Neo-Marxism, which challenges conventional liberal democratic notions of rights. In their book, *Critical Race Theory: An Introduction*, Richard Delgado and Jean Stefancic write: "Unlike traditional civil rights discourse, which stresses incrementalism and step-by-step progress, critical race theory questions the very foundations of the liberal order, including equality theory, legal reasoning, Enlightenment rationalism, and neutral principles of constitutional law."[197]

Some more radical proponents of CRT believe the American constitutional system should be radically transformed. One might wonder what sort of constitutional system, if any, would be a better guarantor of social justice than the one that emerged from the liberalism of the Enlightenment. But is the current constitutional system up to the challenge posed by the persistence of racial inequality?

In 2021, CRT became the focus of a national controversy after conservative media outlets published stories about parents protesting the teaching of CRT in the public schools. By July 2021, eight states had enacted laws restricting the teaching of CRT in grades K–12. Critics of the legislation expressed concern that these laws would stifle any teaching about slavery and the ongoing problem of racism in American society.

Disparate Impact of Criminal Laws

In 1976, the Supreme Court held that only intentional discrimination qualifies as a violation of the Equal Protection Clause.[198] Yet there are situations in which a law is written in a fashion that does not overtly or intentionally discriminate against any people, but ultimately, the law's enforcement produces a **disparate impact** on certain groups. In such instances, it is up to Congress to provide a remedy, using its broad legislative powers.

DISPARATE IMPACT:
Facially neutral policies that have unequal effects on different groups.

Mandatory minimum drug sentences, which were commonly doled out in the 1980s and 1990s, provide a good example of disparate impact. These are sentences given for drug offenses that correlate exclusively to the amount or weight of the drug possessed—with a judge having little or no discretion to deviate from the mandatory minimum. Often, these types of laws can have a disproportionate impact on low-income populations, as we will discuss in chapter 13, which addresses the Eighth Amendment and punishment. As with our discussion of racial profiling, which will overlap the Fourth and Fourteenth Amendments, matters of punishment can raise questions of equality as well.

Throughout the 1980s and 1990s, the use of "crack cocaine," a solid substance made by mixing powdered cocaine with water and baking soda, was more likely within lower-income communities. Under the federal Anti-Drug Abuse Act of 1986,[199] a person caught in possession of 50 grams of crack cocaine would be given a mandatory ten-year prison sentence. Conversely, the same ten-year sentence for possessing pure, powdered cocaine would require being caught with 5,000 grams of cocaine. For comparison purposes, 50 grams would be the size of a typical candy bar, whereas 5,000 grams would fill a typical suitcase.

In 2010, Congress took steps to remedy this disparate impact with passage of the Fair Sentencing Act.[200] This law did away with federal "mandatory minimums" for any person who faced charges of possessing crack cocaine for the first time. This law also reduced the weight thresholds, so the disparity between crack cocaine and pure cocaine sentences was no longer a 100 to 1 ratio but closer to 18 to 1.

Another significant reform was achieved when bipartisan efforts in both the House and Senate led to the passage of the First Step Act of 2018,[201] which President Trump signed into law on December 21, 2018. This statute further limited the use of mandatory minimums and provided judges with the ability to use *safety valves*, which enabled them to deviate from mandatory drug sentences. This law also permitted resentencing of those who had previously been sentenced to mandatory minimums. However, in *Terry v. United States* (2021),[202] the Supreme Court said that resentencing under the First Step Act would only be available to those who were given a mandatory minimum—as opposed to lengthy sentence for drug possession that was given by a judge who had discretion in choosing a sentence because the quantities possessed fell below mandatory minimum thresholds.

(In subsequent chapters, we will outline ramifications of this law for other sentencing considerations as well as for prison conditions.)

Presidents also have the ability to help rectify sentencing disparities via their pardoning and commutation powers, as discussed in chapter 2. A pardon clears a criminal record, while a commutation reduces a sentence (usually to release a person immediately) but leaves in place a criminal record. During his two terms, President Obama commuted 1,715 sentences, more than any prior president in U.S. history—a total that included 560 life sentences. President Trump continued the trend of commuting the sentences of drug offenders, offering more than 200 acts of commutation or pardon.

President Biden issued his first pardons in April 2022, clearing the records of three felons, including a former Secret Service agent accused of a crime in 1964; Biden also offered clemency to 75 others—a group that had served an average of ten years in prison, with approximately one-third of them likely to have received a lesser sentence had they been convicted following the passage of the First Step Act of 2018. In announcing these acts of clemency during what he called "Second Chance Month,"[203] President Biden also indicated that $145 million in federal funds would be made available to provide job training for incarcerated individuals and that the U.S. Small Business Administration would no longer take criminal history into account when making decisions on grant applications. Said President Biden of these criminal justice efforts: "America is a nation of laws and second chances, redemption, and rehabilitation."[204] Later, in October 2022, President Biden announced an intention to pardon people convicted of marijuana possession under federal law.

Conclusion

In this chapter, we examined the rights protected by the Constitution prior to the addition of the Bill of Rights, including limitations on prosecutions for treason, recognition of the writ of habeas corpus, and protections against ex post facto laws and bills of attainder. We also provided an overview of the Bill of Rights, taking into account its importance in the administration of justice. We discussed the constitutional amendments that followed the Civil War as well as the civil rights legislation enacted by Congress pursuant to these amendments, legislation that continues to have relevance in the contemporary struggle for equal rights. We delved into the judicial interpretation of the Fourteenth Amendment, giving considerable attention to the concept of due process (both procedural and substantive), the incorporation of the Bill of Rights, the recognition of the right of privacy, and the application of the Equal Protection Clause to discriminatory governmental actions and policies. Overall, the constitutional and statutory protections of civil rights and liberties are important both for those accused or convicted of crimes as well as those responsible for the everyday enforcement of the criminal law. In the chapters that follow, we will examine the provisions of the Bill of Rights that have particular relevance to the administration of criminal justice.

Discussion Questions

1. Why is treason a rarely prosecuted offense?
2. Which provision of the Bill of Rights is most important in the administration of justice?

3. How did the Fourteenth Amendment affect the legislative power of Congress?
4. What is the difference between procedural and substantive due process?
5. On what basis did the Supreme Court extend the protections of the Bill of Rights to cover actions and policies of state and local governments?
6. How has the constitutional right of privacy affected criminal laws affecting sexual behavior?
7. Should gender-based discrimination be subject to strict scrutiny by the courts?

Endnotes

1   *Ex parte Bollman*, 8 U.S. 75 (1807).
2   *Haupt v. United States*, 330 U.S. 631 (1947).
3   *Kawakita v. United States*, 343 U.S. 717 (1952).
4   *Ex parte Garland*, 71 U.S. 333 (1866).
5   *United States v. Brown*, 381 U.S. 437 (1965).
6   *Calder v. Bull*, 3 U.S. 386 (1798).
7   *Miller v. Florida*, 482 U.S. 423 (1987).
8   *Carmell v. Texas*, 529 U.S. 513 (2000).
9   *See* Neil Douglas McFeeley, *The Historical Development of Habeas Corpus*, 30 S.M.U.L. Rev. 585 (2016) (a detailed history of the writ's origins).
10 *Ex parte Milligan*, 71 U.S. 2 (1866).
11 *Duncan v. Kahanamoku*, 327 U.S. 304 (1946).
12 *Rasul v. Bush*, 542 U.S. 466 (2004).
13 Military Commissions Act of 2006, Pub. L. 109–366, 120 Stat. 2600, 10 U.S.C. §§ 948–949.
14 *Boumediene v. Bush*, 553 U.S. 723 (2008).
15 Habeas Corpus Act of 1867, 14 Stat. 385 (1867).
16 28 U.S.C. § 2254 (Exceptions to the exhaustion requirement exist under this law if "there is an absence of available State corrective process; or circumstances exist that render such process ineffective to protect the rights of the applicant.").
17 *See, e.g., Gideon v. Wainwright*, 372 U.S. 335 (1963); *Sheppard v. Maxwell*, 384 U.S. 333 (1966); *In re Gault*, 387 U.S. 1 (1967).
18 *See, e.g., Irvin v. Dowd*, 359 U.S. 394 (1959) (finding that "the doctrine of exhaustion of state remedies ... does not bar resort to federal habeas corpus if the petitioner has obtained a decision on his constitutional claims from the highest court of the State, even though, as here, that court could have based its decision on another ground"); *Fay v. Noia*, 372 U.S. 391 (1963) (finding that the "exhaustion" requirement could be met even without the filing of a request for discretionary appeal to a state supreme court, provided that this avenue for appeal to a state court was not available at the time of filing a federal habeas claim; in the same year, the Warren Court indicated that a defendant also could raise a claim with federal courts even if counsel had deliberately failed to raise an earlier appeal in state court on the same point); *see Townsend v. Sain*, 372 U.S. 293 (1963).
19 *Stone v. Powell*, 428 U.S. 465 (1976).

20 *McCleskey v. Zant*, 499 U.S. 467 (1991). One year later, the Court held that an inmate's failure to raise a claim in state court meant that claim could not be raised in federal court, unless there would be a "fundamental miscarriage of justice"; *see Keeney v. Tamayo-Reyes*, 504 U.S. 1 (1992). In a correlated ruling, the Court found that an inmate, prior to raising a habeas claim in federal court, must first raise that issue with a state court by at least seeking a petition for discretionary review, if that would be a part of their state's "ordinary appellate review procedure"; *see O'Sullivan v. Boerckel*, 526 U.S. 838 (1999).

21 Anti-Terrorism and Effective Death Penalty Act, Pub. L. 104–132, 110 Stat. 1214, 28 U.S.C. §§ 2241–2255. .

22 28 U.S.C. § 2244(b)(3)(A). Although a motion for reconsideration can be filed within 28 days of a habeas judgment, a new petition on a matter already decided by a federal court is not permitted; however, there is an exception to this rule that can apply if new Supreme Court precedent impacts the claim.

23 *Felker v. Turpin*, 518 U.S. 1047 (1996).

24 *Bannister v. Davis*, 590 U.S. ___ (2020).

25 28 U.S.C. § 2253(c)(2).

26 *Miller-El v. Cockrell*, 537 U.S. 322 (2003) (The majority opinion said the following about the "substantial showing" standard: "A petitioner satisfies this standard by demonstrating that jurists of reason could disagree with the district court's resolution of his constitutional claims or that jurists could conclude the issues presented are adequate to deserve encouragement to proceed further.")

27 *Hererra v. Collins*, 506 U.S. 390 (1993).

28 *Schlup v. Delo*, 513 U.S. 298 (1995).

29 *House v. Bell*, 547 U.S. 518 (2006).

30 *See, e.g., Brecht v. Abrahamson*, 507 U.S. 619 (1993).

31 The Innocence Project, *Compensating the Wrongly Convicted*, https://innocenceproject.org/compensating-wrongly-convicted/.

32 *NAACP v. Alabama ex rel Patterson*, 357 U.S. 449 (1958).

33 *Kent v. Dulles*, 357 U.S. 116 (1958).

34 *Printz v. United States*, 521 U.S. 898 (1997).

35 *Barron v. Baltimore*, 32 U.S. 243 (1833).

36 *Scott v. Sandford*, 60 U.S. 393 (1857).

37 *Bailey v. Alabama*, 219 U.S. 219 (1911).

38 *Miranda v. Arizona*, 384 U.S. 436 (1966).

39 *Brown v. Board of Education*, 347 U.S. 483 (1954).

40 *Guinn & Beal v. United States*, 238 U.S. 347 (1915).

41 Voting Rights Act of 1965, Pub. L. No. 89–110, 79 Stat. 437 (codified at 52 U.S.C. § 10101, §§ 10301–10314, §§ 10501–10508, §§ 10701–10702 (1965)).

42 *South Carolina v. Katzenbach*, 383 U.S. 301 (1966).

43 *See, e.g.*, Will Wilder & Stuart Baum. *5 Egregious Voter Suppression Laws from 2021*. Brennan Center for Justice (Jan. 31, 2022), https://www.brennancenter.org/our-work/analysis-opinion/5-egregious-voter-suppression-laws-2021

44 Civil Rights Act of 1866, 14 Stat. 27–30. *See* 42 U.S.C. §§ 1981, 1982 (modern counterparts).

45 *Jones v. Alfred H. Mayer Co.*, 392 U.S. 409 (1968).

46 *See* 18 U.S.C. § 242.

47 *See Koon v. United States*, 518 U.S. 81 (1996).

48   18 U.S.C. § 241 (an amended form of this prohibition).

49   Civil Rights Act of 1871, 17 Stat. 13 (codified at 42 U.S.C. § 1983 (1871)).

50   *See* 42 U.S.C. § 1985.

51   *Monell v. Department of Social Services*, 436 U.S. 658 (1978).

52   Civil Rights Act of 1875, 18 Stat. 335–337.

53   *The Civil Rights Cases*, 109 U.S. 3 (1883).

54   *Plessy v. Ferguson*, 163 U.S. 537 (1896).

55   Faith Thompson, *Magna Carta: Its Role in the Making of the English Constitution, 1300–1629* (1948).

56   Tenn. Const., Art. I, Sec. 8.

57   *Goldberg v. Kelly*, 397 U.S. 254 (1970).

58   *Ex parte Wall*, 107 U.S. 265 (1883).

59   *See, e.g., Van Harken v. Chicago*, 103 F.3d 1346 (7th Cir 1997).

60   *See., e.g., Goldberg v. Kelly*, 397 U.S. 254 (1970) (found the need for a hearing before the government can revoke a person's government benefits—in this case, welfare benefits); *Goss v. Lopez*, 419 U.S. 565 (1975) (involved the suspension of a student at a public school, with the Court finding that a hearing should have been afforded).

61   *Cleveland Board of Education v. Loudermill*, 470 U.S. 532 (1985) (citing *Mullane v. Central Hanover Bank & Trust Co.*, 339 U.S. 306 (1950)) (The *Loudermill* decision also quoted to a 1972 case in observing that "some kind of a hearing" should precede "the discharge of an employee who has a constitutionally protected property interest in his employment," although that need not apply to a situation where a contract is expiring [e.g., with a one-year contract that is not renewed]). *See Board of Regents v. Roth*, 408 U.S. 564 (1972).

62   *See, e.g., Arnett v. Kennedy*, 416 U.S. 134 (1974).

63   *Mathews v. Eldridge*, 424 U.S. 319 (1976).

64   *Gilbert v. Homar*, 520 U.S. 924 (1997).

65   Jessica Schneider, *First on CNN: DC Police Officer's Suicide Days After Capitol Attack Declared Line-Of-Duty Death After Months-Long Fight by Widow*, CNN, Mar. 9, 2022, https://www.cnn.com/2022/03/09/politics/smith-police-officer-line-of-duty-death-january-6/index.html.

66   A study shows that between October 1, 2009, and November 29, 2016, of 1,080 suicides, 95% were treated as occurring in the line of duty. The standard used by the military is to define a suicide as such based upon a finding that the solider was "mentally unsound." Major Aaron L. Lancaster, *Line of Duty Investigations: Battered, Broken and in Need of Reform*, 225 Military L. Rev. 597 (2017).

67   *See* Bureau of Justice Assistance, *Public Safety Officers' Benefits Program*, U.S. Dept. of Justice (One-time payments for those who suffer a catastrophic disability are also available, as are $1,200 continuing education benefits payments for children.), https://bja.ojp.gov/program/psob.

68   Shaila Dewan, *He Killed Himself after the Jan. 6th Riot. Did He Die in the Line of Duty?* N.Y. Times, July 29, 2021; updated Aug. 5, 2021, https://www.nytimes.com/2021/07/29/us/police-suicides-capitol-riot.html.

69   FBI, *Law Enforcement Suicide Data Collection*, https://www.fbi.gov/services/cjis/ucr/law-enforcement-suicide-data-collection.

70   Public Safety Officers Support Act of 2022, Pub. L. 117–172, 136 Stat. 2098, 34 U.S.C. § 10281.

71   *See, e.g., Duncan v. Louisiana*, 391 U.S. 145 (1968).

72   *Coffin v. United States*, 156 U.S. 432 (1895).

73   *In re Winship*, 397 U.S. 358 (1970).

74 *Connally v. General Construction Co.*, 269 U. S. 385, 391 (1926).

75 *Grayned v. City of Rockford*, 408 U.S. 104 (1972).

76 *Kolender v. Lawson*, 461 U.S. 352 (1983).

77 *Johnson v. United States*, 576 U.S. 591 (2015).

78 *Lochner v. New York*, 198 U.S. 45 (1905).

79 *West Coast Hotel Co. v. Parrish*, 300 U.S. 379 (1937).

80 *Meyer v. Nebraska*, 262 U.S. 390 (1923).

81 *Shapiro v. Thompson*, 394 U.S. 618 (1969). Similarly, the right to travel outside the country was recognized in *Kent v. Dulles*, 357 U.S. 116 (1958).

82 *Zablocki v. Redhail*, 434 U.S. 374 (1978).

83 *Skinner v. Oklahoma*, 316 U.S. 535 (1942).

84 *Pierce v. Society of Sisters*, 268 U.S. 510 (1925).

85 *Adamson v. California*, 332 U.S. 46 (1947).

86 *The Slaughter-House Cases*, 83 U.S. 36 (1873).

87 *United States v. Cruikshank*, 92 U.S. 542 (1876).

88 *Hurtado v. California*, 110 U.S. 516 (1884).

89 *Maxwell v. Dow*, 176 U.S. 581 (1900).

90 *Twining v. New Jersey*, 211 U.S. 78 (1908).

91 *Chicago, Burlington & Quincy Railroad Co. v. City of Chicago*, 166 U.S. 226 (1897).

92 *Fiske v. Kansas*, 274 U.S. 380 (1927).

93 *Near v. Minnesota*, 283 U.S. 697 (1931).

94 *DeJonge v. Oregon*, 299 U.S. 353 (1937).

95 *Cantwell v. Connecticut*, 310 U.S. 296 (1940).

96 *Everson v. Board of Education*, 330 U.S. 1 (1947).

97 *Palko v. Connecticut*, 302 U.S. 319 (1937).

98 *Betts v. Brady*, 316 U.S. 455 (1942).

99 *In re Oliver*, 333 U.S. 257 (1948).

100 *Wolf v. Colorado*, 338 U.S. 25 (1949).

101 The exclusionary rule had been required in federal courts since *Weeks v. United States*, 232 U.S. 383 (1914).

102 *Robinson v. California*, 370 U.S. 660 (1962). It is a fundamental principle of criminal law that for there to be a crime, there must be a wrongful act, or actus reus. One cannot be prosecuted merely for one's status. For example, drug dealing is a crime, but the status of being a drug dealer is not.

103 *Gideon v. Wainwright*, 372 U.S. 335 (1963).

104 *Malloy v. Hogan*, 378 U.S. 1 (1964).

105 *Miranda v. Arizona*, 384 U.S. 436 (1966).

106 *Duncan v. Louisiana*, 391 U.S. 145 (1968).

107 *Benton v. Maryland*, 395 U.S. 784 (1969).

108 *See Sanders v. United States*, 373 U.S. 1 (1963); *Fay v. Noia*, 372 U.S. 391 (1963); *Townsend v. Sain*, 372 U.S. 293 (1963).

109 *Schilb v. Kuebel*, 404 U.S. 357 (1971).

110 *McDonald v. City of Chicago*, 561 U.S. 742 (2010).

111 *Timbs v. Indiana*, 586 U.S. ___ (2019).

112   *Roe v. Wade*, 410 U.S. 113 (1973).

113   *Olmstead v. United States*, 277 U.S. 438 (1928) (Brandeis, J., dissenting).

114   *Griswold v. Connecticut*, 381 U.S. 479 (1965).

115   *Eisenstadt v. Baird*, 405 U.S. 438 (1972).

116   *Planned Parenthood of Southeastern Pennsylvania v. Casey*, 505 U.S. 833 (1992).

117   *Whole Woman's Health v. Hellerstedt*, 579 U.S. 582 (2016); *June Medical Services L.L.C. v. Russo*, 591 U.S. ___ (2020).

118   *Dobbs v. Jackson Women's Health*, 597 U.S. ___ (2022).

119   *Bowers v. Hardwick*, 478 U.S. 186 (1985).

120   *Lawrence v. Texas*, 539 U.S. 558 (2003).

121   *See, e.g., In re Quinlan*, 355 A.2d 647 (NJ 1976).

122   *Cruzan v. Missouri Department of Health*, 497 U.S. 261 (1990).

123   *Washington v. Glucksberg*, 521 U.S. 702 (1997).

124   Death with Dignity Act, RCW 70.245.

125   *Jacobson v. Massachusetts*, 197 U.S. 11 (1905).

126   An appeal from the ruling of the Seventh Circuit was denied by Justice Amy Coney Barrett on August 12, 2021: *Klaassen v. Trustees of Indiana University*; Case No. 21A15; *Ryan Klaassen v. Trustees of Indiana University*, No. 21–2326 (7th Cir. 2021); *Klaassen v. Trustees of Indiana University*, No. 1:21-cv-238 DRL-SLC (N.D. In. 2021). The district court judge suggested that students had alternatives at their disposal, including the following: taking online courses, taking a semester off, or attending a different school.

127   *National Federation of Independent Business v. Department of Labor* (combined with *Ohio et al. v. Department of Labor*), 595 U.S. ___ (2022) (rule codified at 86 Fed. Reg. 61402).

128   *Biden v. Missouri et al.* (combined with *Becerra, Secretary of Health and Human Services, et al. v. Louisiana, et al.*), 595 U.S. ___ (2022) (rule codified at 86 Fed. Reg. 61561–61627).

129   *Plessy v. Ferguson*, 163 U.S. 537 (1896).

130   Civil Rights Act of 1964, Pub. L. 88-352, 78 Stat. 241.

131   42 U. S. C. § 2000e

132   Voting Rights Act of 1965, Pub. L. 89-110, 79 Stat. 437.

133   Civil Rights Act of 1968, Pub. L. 90-284, 82 Stat. 73.

134   *See, e.g., Heart of Atlanta Motel v. United States*, 379 U.S. 241 (1964); *Katzenbach v. McClung*, 379 U.S. 294 (1964); *South Carolina v. Katzenbach*, 383 U.S. 301 (1966); *Jones v. Alfred H. Mayer Co.*, 392 U.S. 409 (1968).

135   *Loving v. Virginia*, 388 U.S. 1 (1967).

136   *United States v. Carolene Products Co.*, 304 U.S. 144, 153 n.4 (1938) (Justice Harlan Fiske Stone observed that "... prejudice against discrete and insular minorities may be a special condition, which tends seriously to curtail the operation of those political processes ordinarily to be relied upon to protect minorities, and which may call for a correspondingly more searching judicial inquiry.").

137   *See Korematsu v. United States*, 323 U.S. 214 (1944). One year prior, the Court also had upheld curfew orders directed at specifically at Japanese Americans; *see Yasui v. United States*, 320 U.S. 115 (1943); *Hirabayashi v. United States*, 320 U.S. 81 (1943); these decisions were overturned by lower federal court rulings in the 1980s; *Yasui v. United States*, 772 F. 2d 1496 (9th Cir. 1985); *Hirabayashi v. United States*, 828 F. 2d 591 (9th Cir. 1987). We discuss curfews in greater detail in chapter 4.

138 *See, e.g.*, Age Discrimination in Employment Act of 1967, Pub. L. 90–202, 81 Stat. 602; Title IX of the Education Amendments of 1972, Pub. L. 92318, 86 Stat. 373; Americans with Disabilities Act of 1990, Pub. L. 101-336, 104 Stat. 327.

139 Civil Rights Act of 1991, Pub. L. No. 102-166, 105 Stat. 1071 (codified at 42 U.S.C. § 1981 (1991)); *see Ricci v. DeStefano*, 557 U.S. 557 (2009) (Supreme Court interpretation of this law).

140 *Reed v. Reed*, 404 U.S. 71 (1971).

141 *Frontiero v. Richardson*, 411 U.S. 677 (1973).

142 *Craig v. Boren*, 429 U.S. 190 (1976).

143 *Mississippi University for Women v. Hogan*, 458 U.S. 718 (1982).

144 *United States v. Virginia*, 518 U.S. 515 (1996).

145 Lindsey Van Ness, *Percentage of Women in State Policing Has Stalled Since 2000*, USA Today, Oct. 24, 2021, https://www.usatoday.com/story/news/nation/2021/10/24/percentage-women-state-policing-has-stalled-over-two-decades/6107115001/.

146 *Meritor Savings Bank v. Vinson*, 477 U.S. 57 (1986).

147 In *Harris v. Forklift Systems*, 510 U.S. 17 (1993), the Court found that "whether an environment is 'hostile' or 'abusive' can be determined only by looking at all the circumstances. These may include the frequency of the discriminatory conduct; its severity; whether it is physically threatening or humiliating, or a mere offensive utterance; and whether it unreasonably interferes with an employee's work performance. The effect on the employee's psychological well-being is, of course, relevant to determining whether the plaintiff actually found the environment abusive. But while psychological harm, like any other relevant factor, may be taken into account, no single factor is required." The *Harris* Court observed that a workplace must be "objectively" hostile, taking into account the perspective of a reasonable person, and also "subjectively" hostile, meaning hostile to the person raising a claim. Later, in *Oncale v. Sundowner Offshore Services*, 523 U.S. 75 (1998), the Court found that a man is permitted to raise a Title VII claim related to sexual harassment. Additionally, in *Faragher v. City of Boca Raton*, 524 U.S. 775 (1998), the Court ruled that an employer (even a government agency) can be held liable for the conduct of employees who engage in sexually harassing behavior.

148 Terrence P. Dwyer, *The High Cost and Toll of Sexual Harassment and Gender Discrimination in Law Enforcement: Part 1*, police1.com, Apr. 8, 2021, https://www.police1.com/officer-misconduct-internal-affairs/articles/the-high-cost-and-toll-of-sexual-harassment-and-gender-discrimination-in-law-enforcement-part-1-Unl4lBmsX3UPlGGO/.

149 Equal Pay Act of 1963, Pub. L. No. 88-38, 77 Stat. 56 (codified at 29 U.S.C. § 206 (1963)).

150 29 U.S.C. § 206(d)(1).

151 *Aldrich v. Randolph Cent. Sch. Dist.*, 963 F.2d 520 (2nd Cir. 1992); *Price v. Lockheed Space Ops. Co.*, 856 F.2d 1503 (11th Cir. 1988); *EEOC v. J.C. Penney Co.*, 843 F.2d 249 (6th Cir. 1992); *Wernsing v. Department of Human Services*, 427 F.3d 466 (7th Cir. 2005); *Taylor v. White*, 321 F.3d 710 (8th Cir. 2003); *Rizo v. Yovino*, 950 F.3d 1217 (9th Cir. 2020).

152 Steven McDonnell, *Salary Differences Between Male Police Officers and Female Police Officers*, CHRON (The study reported that median weekly wage for male officers was $948 and $938 for female officers.), https://work.chron.com/salary-differences-between-male-police-officers-female-police-officers-29671.html.

153 Family and Medical Leave Act of 1993, Pub. L. 103-3, 107 Stat. 6, 29 U.S.C. § 2601.

154 *Free the Nipple v. City of Fort Collins*, 916 F.3d 792 (10th Cir. 2019).

155 *Free the Nipple v. Springfield, Missouri*, 923 F.3d 508 (8th Cir. 2019).

156 *State of New Hampshire v. Lilley*, 204 A.3d 198 (N.H. 2019).

157 *Massachusetts Board of Retirement v. Murgia*, 427 U.S. 307 (1975).

158   *Vance v. Bradley*, 440 U.S. 93 (1979).

159   *Gregory v. Ashcroft*, 501 U.S. 452 (1991).

160   U.S. Government Accountability Office, *Capitol Police: Potential Effects of Raising the Mandatory Retirement Age*, Dec. 18, 2019, https://www.gao.gov/products/gao-20-137r.

161   Age Discrimination in Employment Act (ADEA) of 1967, Pub. L. No. 90-202, 81 Stat. 602 (codified at 29 U.S.C. §§ 621–634 (1967)). For Supreme Court interpretation of this law involving an employee at the U.S. Department of Veterans Affairs, *see Babb v. Wilkie*, 589 U.S. ____ (2020).

162   *Romer v. Evans*, 517 U.S. 620 (1996).

163   *United States Dept. of Agriculture v. Moreno*, 413 U.S. 528 (1973).

164   *Obergefell v. Hodges*, 576 U.S. 644 (2015).

165   *Bostock v. Clayton County*, 590 U.S. ____ (2020).

166   *Gavin Grimm v. Gloucester County School Board*, No. 19–1952 (4th Cir. 2020), cert. denied by the Supreme Court on June 28, 2021.

167   *See Sutton v. United Air Lines, Inc.*, 527 U.S. 471 (1999); *Toyota Motor Mfg., Kentucky, Inc. v. Williams*, 534 U.S. 184 (2002); also note that *City of Cleburne v. Cleburne Living Center* (473 U.S. 432 91985) involved use of the lesser standard of rational basis review for a case involving mental disabilities—even though the group representing the interests of disabled persons won the case.

168   Americans with Disabilities Act of 1990, Pub. L. No. 101–336, 104 Stat. 327 (codified at 42 U.S.C. § 12101 (1990)); *see PGA Tour, Inc. v. Casey Martin*, 532 U.S. 661 (2001) (for Supreme Court interpretation of this law).

169   Americans with Disabilities Amendments Act of 2008, Pub. L. 110–325, Stat. (codified at 42 U.S.C. § 12101 (2008)) (The amendment says that "major life activities include, but are not limited to, caring for oneself, performing manual tasks, seeing, hearing, eating, sleeping, walking, standing, lifting, bending, speaking, breathing, learning, reading, concentrating, thinking, communicating, and working.")

170   Rehabilitation Act of 1973, Pub. L. No. 93–112, 87 Stat. 355 (codified at 29 U.S.C. § 701 (1973)).

171   *PGA Tour, Inc. v. Casey Martin*, 532 U.S. 661 (2001).

172   Genetic Information Nondiscrimination Act of 2008, Pub L. 110–233, 122 Stat. 881 (codified at 29 U.S.C. § 216(e) (2008)).

173   Americans with Disabilities Act, *Americans with Disabilities Act Information for Law Enforcement*, Dec. 1, 2008, https://www.ada.gov/policeinfo.htm.

174   *See, e.g., Regents of the University of California v. Bakke*, 438 U.S. 265 (1978); *City of Richmond v. J.A. Croson Co.*, 488 U.S. 469 (1989); *Gratz v. Bollinger*, 539 U.S. 244 (2003); *Adarand Constructors, Inc. v. Peña*, 515 U.S. 200 (1995).

175   *Grutter v. Bollinger*, 539 U.S. 306 (2003); *Fisher v. University of Texas*, 579 U.S. 365 (2016).

176   *Grutter v. Bollinger, id.; Gratz v. Bollinger, supra* note 174.

177   *United States v. Paradise*, 480 U.S. 149 (1987).

178   *Id.* (quoting *NAACP v. Allen*, 340 F. Supp. 703 (M.D. Ala. 1972)).

179   *Id.* (quoting *Paradise v. Shoemaker*, 470 F. Supp. 439 (M.D. Ala. 1979)).

180   *Paradise v. Prescott*, 580 F. Supp. 171 (M.D. Ala. 1983).

181   *Paradise v. Prescott*, 767 F.2d 1514 (11th Cir. 1985).

182   Courtney Brown & Stef W. Knight, *More Black Police Officers, Yet the Killings Persist*, Axios, June 8, 2020, https://www.axios.com/police-diversity-george-floyd-5a712a37-9e43-4b24-985b-829abd76e56b.html. *See* U.S. Census Bureau, *American Community Survey* (2018) (Data in the previous article are derived from this survey.), https://www.census.

140 | Constitutional Law Today: Foundations for Criminal Justice

gov/programs-surveys/acs; *see* Lauren Leatherby & Richard A. Oppel, Jr., *Which Police Departments are as Diverse as Their Communities*, N.Y. Times (Sept. 23, 2020) (additional demographics derived from other data of the Bureau of Justice Statistics from 2016), https://www.nytimes.com/interactive/2020/09/23/us/bureau-justice-statistics-race.html; NACJD, *Law Enforcement Management and Administrative Statistics (LEMAS)*, (ICPSR 37323) (2016) (for Bureau of Justice Statistics data) https://www.icpsr.umich.edu/web/NACJD/studies/37323.

183 *Ricci v. DeStefano*, 557 U.S. 557 (2009).

184 Adam Liptak, *Justices to Hear White Firefighters' Bias Claims*, N.Y. Times (April 9, 2009), https://www.nytimes.com/2009/04/10/us/10scotus.html.

185 Bryan Wright, *Connecticut Firefighters Settle Reverse Discrimination Suit For $2 Million*, NPR, July 28, 2011, https://www.npr.org/sections/thetwo-way/2011/07/28/138792038/connecticut-firefighters-settle-reverse-discrimination-suit-for-2-millions.

186 *Powell v. Alabama*, 287 U.S. 45 (1932); *Norris v. Alabama*, 294 U.S. 587 (1935).

187 *Oyler v. Boles*, 368 U.S. 448 (1962).

188 *United States v. Armstrong*, 517 U.S. 456 (1996).

189 *See, e.g.*, *Strauder v. West Virginia*, 100 U.S. 303 (1880); *Glasser v. United States*, 315 U.S. 60 (1942); *Carter v. Jury Commission*, 396 U.S. 320 (1970).

190 *Batson v. Kentucky*, 476 U.S. 79 (1986).

191 *United States v. Brignoni-Ponce*, 422 U.S. 873 (1975).

192 *Arizona v. United States*, 567 U.S. 387 (2012).

193 *Florida v. J. L.*, 529 U.S. 266 (2000).

194 *United States v. Sokolow*, 490 U.S. 1 (1989).

195 *United States v. Cortez*, 449 U.S. 411 (1981).

196 Ashley Nellis, *Color of Justice: Racial and Ethnic Disparity in State Prisons*, The Sentencing Project (October 13, 2021), https://www.sentencingproject.org/publications/color-of-justice-racial-and-ethnic-disparity-in-state-prisons/.

197 Richard Delgado & Jean Stefancic, Critical Race Theory: An Introduction 3 (3rd ed. 2017).

198 *Washington v. Davis*, 426 U.S. 229 (1976).

199 Anti-Drug Abuse Act of 1986, Pub. L. 99–570, 100 Stat. 3207 (codified at 21 U.S.C. Ch. 13 (1986)).

200 Fair Sentencing Act of 2010, Pub. L. 111–220, 124 Stat. 2372, 21 U.S.C. § 801.

201 First Step Act of 2018, Pub. L. 115–391, 132 Stat. 5194.

202 *Terry v. United States*, 593 U.S. ____ (2021).

203 Pres. Proc. 10362 (2022).

204 Joey Garrison, *Biden Pardons Three Felons, Commutes Sentences of 75 Others, in First Use Of Clemency Powers*, USA Today, Apr. 26, 2022, https://www.usatoday.com/story/news/politics/2022/04/26/biden-pardon-3-commute-sentences-75-first-use-clemency-power/7446588001/.

Credit

IMG 3.1: Copyright © 2021 Depositphotos/Wirestock.

CHAPTER 4

The First Amendment
Freedoms of Speech, Press, and Assembly

"Give me the liberty to know, to utter, and to argue freely according to conscience, above all liberties."

—John Milton, *Areopagitica* (1644)

Learning Objectives

After reading this chapter, you should understand the following:

1. Why freedom of expression is considered a "foundational" freedom
2. The point at which advocacy of illegal conduct is not constitutionally protected
3. Whether fighting words, true threats, and hate speech are protected by the First Amendment
4. The limits of expressive conduct as an exercise of free speech
5. How the law regarding obscenity, indecency, and profanity has changed in the modern era
6. How the freedom of the press limits government efforts to censor and regulate mass media
7. Why commercial speech merits First Amendment status
8. The degree to which expression and assembly in the public forum are protected by the First Amendment
9. How courts view freedom of association as an implicit First Amendment right
10. The free speech rights of police officers and other public employees
11. The First Amendment rights of students

Key Cases

Schenck v. United States, 249 U.S. 47 (1919)
Brandenburg v. Ohio, 395 U.S. 444 (1969)
United States v. O'Brien, 391 U.S. 367 (1968)
Texas v. Johnson, 491 U.S. 397 (1989)
Cohen v. California, 403 U.S. 15 (1971)
New York Times Co. v. United States, 403 U.S. 713 (1971)
New York Times Co. v. Sullivan, 376 U.S. 254 (1964)
Garcetti v. Ceballos, 547 U.S. 410 (2006)

Introduction

To flourish, a democratic society must embrace the value of free expression, which includes the freedom of speech and the freedom of the press. Citizens must be free to engage in discourse about their government, politics, and the issues of the day. And the mass media must be free not only to inform the public but also to criticize the powers that be. Public opinion must be formed freely—not shaped solely by government propaganda.

A country that celebrates personal freedom must value freedom of expression above all else, for as Supreme Court Justice Benjamin Cardozo said in 1937, it is "the matrix, the indispensable condition, of nearly every other form of freedom."[1] An essential aspect of free expression is the freedom of the press. The press must be able to report the news and express opinions without interference from the state. Likewise, people must be free to assemble in the public square to communicate their demands and concerns to the government. The First Amendment encapsulates all of these rights: "Congress shall make no law ... abridging the freedom of speech, or of the press; or the right of the people peaceably to assemble, and to petition the Government for a redress of grievances." As indicated by its text, the First Amendment protects these fundamental rights against infringement by the federal government. As discussed in the previous chapter, First Amendment freedoms are also shielded from state and local government action by the Fourteenth Amendment via the doctrine of incorporation. Still, it is up to the courts (and, ultimately, the people) to guard against encroachments on these fundamental freedoms.

Today, one only has to glance at social media to know that most expression is trivial, trite, and ephemeral. And much of it (again, see social media) is biased, ignorant, or just plain stupid. And some expression, easily accessible these days via the internet, is hateful, pornographic, or otherwise deeply offensive. Some expression is patently false and can damage reputations or lead people to act in ways they otherwise would not. And then there is expression that many perceive as a danger to public safety, order, or even national security. And finally, what about expression that challenges the very ideas of democracy, constitutionalism, and freedom? Questions immediately arise: Must society tolerate all expression to protect that which is truly valuable? And who is to be the arbiter of what is worth protecting? We must keep these in mind as we examine the contours of the First Amendment.

First Amendment Rights and Criminal Justice

In chapter 1, we discussed the importance of constitutional policing, which requires that law enforcement officers understand and abide by the law and respect the constitutional rights of those they encounter. These include the First Amendment freedoms of speech and assembly, both of which require officers to demonstrate enormous restraint as well as a robust understanding of relevant constitutional law. At what point does a citizen cross the line when speaking provocatively to an officer, threatening people, or advocating violence? When can a demonstration be halted and a raucous crowd dispersed? Is incitement of lawless action ever protected by the First Amendment?

Prosecutors and defense lawyers have to stay abreast of changes in the criminal law wrought by constitutional interpretation. Some offenses, such as "criminal syndicalism," have been invalidated altogether via judicial review. Other crimes, such as obscenity and unlawful assembly, have been interpreted narrowly, so as to avoid outright invalidation. Profanity laws today are presumptively unconstitutional and seldom enforced. Even panhandling laws are constitutionally suspect. As courts continue to address such matters, it is crucial that law enforcement officers stay abreast of constitutional developments that affect the criminal law.

THE CONSTITUTION IN ACTION
Criminal Laws That Could Impact First Amendment Rights

Some criminal statutes are especially likely to result in an accused person invoking the First Amendment's freedom of speech protection as a defense. The following are some examples:

New York, S 240.08, Inciting to riot: "A person is guilty of inciting to riot when he urges ten or more persons to engage in tumultuous and violent conduct of a kind likely to create public alarm."

Florida, 877.03, Breach of the peace; disorderly conduct: "Whoever commits such acts as are of a nature to corrupt the public morals, or outrage the sense of public decency, or affect the peace and quiet of person who may witness them, or engages in brawling or fighting, or engages in such conduct as to constitute a breach of peace or disorderly conduct, shall be guilty of a misdemeanor of the second degree."

Georgia, 16-11-39.1, Harassing communications: "(a) A person commits the offense of harassing communications if such person: (1) Contacts another person repeatedly via telecommunication, e-mail, text messaging, or any other form of electronic communication for the purpose of harassing, molesting, threatening, or intimidating such person or the family of such person; (2) Threatens bodily harm via telecommunication, e-mail, text messaging, or any other form of electronic communication."

Nebraska, 28-311.01, Terroristic threats: "(1) A person commits terroristic threats if he or she threatens to commit any crime of violence: (a) With the intent to terrorize another; (b) With the intent of causing the evacuation of a building, place of assembly, or facility of public transportation; or (c) In reckless disregard of the risk of causing such terror or evacuation."

Tennessee, 39-17-313, Aggressive panhandling: "A person commits aggressive panhandling who solicits a donation of money or goods in the following manner: (1) By intentionally touching the person being solicited without the person's consent; (2) By intentionally obstructing the path of the person, or of the vehicle of the person, being solicited; (3) By following a person who is walking away from the person soliciting the donation. ..."

18 U.S. Code § 794, Espionage and Censorship; Gathering or delivering defense information to aid foreign government: "Whoever, with intent or reason to believe that it is to be used to the injury of the United States or to the advantage of a foreign nation, communicates, delivers, or transmits ... to any foreign government ... any document,

(continued)

writing, code book, signal book, sketch, photograph, photographic negative blueprint, plan, map, model, note, instrument, appliance, or information relating to national defense, shall be punished by death or by imprisonment for any term of years or for life ..."

18 U.S. Code § 875, Extortion and threats; interstate communications: "... (c) Whoever transmits in interstate or foreign commerce any communication containing any threat to kidnap any person or any threat to injure the person of another, shall be fined under this title or imprisoned not more than five years, or both."

Key Elements of First Amendment Jurisprudence

The First Amendment begins with the phrase, "Congress shall make *no* law ..." [emphasis added]. Some interpret this as meaning no restriction on expression is permissible. Justice Hugo Black was famous for believing that the "First Amendment was a bold effort to ... to establish a country with no legal restriction of any kind upon the subjects people could investigate, discuss, and deny."[2] Expressing the same sentiment, Justice William O. Douglas wrote, "The First Amendment, its prohibition in terms absolute, was designed to preclude courts as well as legislatures from weighing the values of speech against silence."[3]

The courts have never embraced an absolutist view of the First Amendment. As Justice Oliver Wendell Holmes observed in *Schenck v. United States* (1919),[4] "The most stringent protection of free speech would not protect a man in falsely shouting fire in a theatre and causing a panic." In the *Schenck* case, Holmes went on to articulate the clear and present danger doctrine, under which expression that creates a clear and present danger to national security or the public welfare can be suppressed.

In *Chaplinsky v. New Hampshire* (1942),[5] the Court said there are classes of speech that are categorically excluded from First Amendment protection:

> There are certain well defined and narrowly limited classes of speech, the prevention and punishment of which have never been thought to raise any constitutional problem. These include the lewd and obscene, the profane, the libelous, and the insulting or "fighting" words—those which by their very utterance inflict injury or tend to incite an immediate breach of the peace. It has been well observed that such utterances are no essential part of any exposition

CLEAR AND PRESENT DANGER DOCTRINE: The doctrine under which the First Amendment does not protect speech that constitutes a clear and present danger of accomplishing something the government has a right to prohibit.

of ideas, and are of such slight social value as a step to truth that any benefit that may be derived from them is clearly outweighed by the social interest in order and morality.

Modern First Amendment Jurisprudence

In the modern (i.e., post-WWII) era the Supreme Court dramatically increased constitutional protection for expressive freedom. Although certain categories of expression are still considered beyond the pale, they tend to be strictly defined so as to leave maximum room for "uninhibited, robust, and wide-open" discussion of public issues.[6] The Court also has expanded the definition of "speech," so all means of expression, regardless of medium, fall within the scope of the First Amendment. This has made it easier for persons accused of violating criminal laws to mount First Amendment challenges to those laws. Beyond that, the Court has narrowed the scope of the clear and present danger doctrine and has tended to side with media on questions of press freedom. Moreover, the Court has held that statutes and regulations that curtail First Amendment rights must be subjected to **strict scrutiny** by the courts.

Strict Judicial Scrutiny

Under modern **fundamental rights doctrine**, most First Amendment freedoms can be limited only on the basis of a governmental interest that is "compelling."[7] Protecting the national security from imminent harm is most certainly a **compelling governmental interest**. So too is the protection of children. Of course, individual justices differ as to what constitutes a compelling governmental interest, but there is a general reluctance to allow infringements on First Amendment rights without a very strong justification. When a law is challenged on First Amendment grounds, the burden of persuasion usually rests with the government. And it is a heavy burden indeed.

The Overbreadth Doctrine

Under the **overbreadth doctrine**, a statute can be declared unconstitutional if "a substantial number of its applications are unconstitutional, judged in relation to the statute's plainly legitimate sweep."[8] Even one whose speech is not entitled to constitutional protection can challenge a law that might be applied to limit the protected speech of others. In 1987, the Supreme Court stated, "Criminal statutes must be scrutinized

STRICT SCRUTINY: The most rigorous legal framework through which courts evaluate fundamental rights and liberties, by requiring government to justify restrictions with a narrowly tailored policy in furtherance of a compelling governmental interest; also used by courts to analyze claims of racial discrimination under the Fourteenth Amendment.

FUNDAMENTAL RIGHTS DOCTRINE: A reference to those individual rights and liberties that are deemed most essential within an ordered society and which are protected rigorously by courts.

COMPELLING GOVERNMENTAL INTEREST: A key component of the legal test of strict scrutiny, this refers to a government interest that is crucial enough to justify a restriction on a person's fundamental rights or liberties.

OVERBREADTH DOCTRINE: A legal standard indicating that a government restriction, often on expression, burdens more conduct than is necessary to further a government objective, indicating the individual conduct in question should remain protected.

with particular care ...; those that make unlawful a substantial amount of constitutionally protected conduct may be held facially invalid even if they also have legitimate application."[9]

As a result of the Court's modern First Amendment jurisprudence, there have been tremendous changes in the law (and, ultimately, public policy) dealing with such matters as libel, obscenity, profanity, and the advocacy of unlawful conduct. Suffice it to say that, under modern constitutional interpretation, Americans today enjoy much broader First Amendment protection than was true historically.

THE CONSTITUTION IN ACTION
Is There a First Amendment Right to Video Record the Police?

Over the past two decades, police–citizen interactions have been fundamentally altered by the advent of cell phones that have video cameras, as well as the ease with which citizen-created videos can be posted to social media websites. Although the Supreme Court of the United States has not directly addressed the question of whether filming police interactions with individuals is protected under the First Amendment, several lower court decisions have indicated an emerging consensus toward safeguarding such activity.

For example, in *Gilk v. Cunniffee* (2011),[10] the U.S. Court of Appeals for the First Circuit ruled in favor of a man who was arrested for filming a police–citizen interaction on the Boston Common in Massachusetts. The majority opinion for this case said, "Gathering information about government officials in a form that can readily be disseminated to others serves a cardinal First Amendment interest in protecting and promoting the free discussion of governmental affairs." Public access to information, it follows, can be a First Amendment consideration.

The Seventh Circuit offered a similar ruling in *ACLU v. Alvarez* (2012),[11] which barred the state of Illinois from enforcing a state law that criminalized the act of filming police in the exercise of their duties. Here the majority opinion stated, "Criminalizing all nonconsensual audio recording necessarily limits the information that might later be published or broadcast—whether to the general public or to a single family member or friend—and thus burdens First Amendment rights." Six years later, the Third Circuit's decision in *Fields v. City of Philadelphia* (2018)[12] took note of a burgeoning trend among courts nationwide, saying, "Today we join this growing consensus. Simply put, the First Amendment protects the act of photographing, filming, or otherwise recording police officers conducting their official duties in public."

More recently, in *Martin v. Rollins* (2021),[13] the First Circuit revisited this issue to indicate that the right to record police activity encompasses a right to do so in secret. This court indicated that a right to record in secret is connected to an "interest in promoting public awareness of the conduct of law enforcement," adding that this could include "documenting their heroism, dispelling claims of their misconduct, or facilitating the public's ability to hold them to account for their wrongdoing." At least within the states covered by the jurisdiction of the First Circuit, clandestine recordings of police activity are subject to First Amendment protection.

However, this principle could come into conflict with recent efforts by some states to pass laws that protect the privacy rights of police officers. For instance, an Oklahoma law that took effect in 2021 makes it a crime to publicly reveal the identity of a police officer.[14] This has left some wondering if a video of police activity that shows an officer's nametag would run afoul of this law if the video were posted on the internet. How courts untangle such situations—in terms of balancing officer privacy and the public's right to view government action—remains to be seen.

Moreover, an interesting police response to being videotaped by the public was on display in April 2022 in Santa Ana, California, when officers played loud Disney music from their police vehicle while interaction with a suspected car thief was videotaped by an onlooker. Officers indicated that the inclusion of the music would preclude any videos from being uploaded to YouTube, which automatically filters out material that could infringe upon copyrights—such as a song. The Chief of Police in Santa Ana, however, expressed displeasure with this tactic.[15]

Advocacy of Unlawful Conduct

Does the First Amendment protect one's right to advocate something the law prohibits? During much of the twentieth century, this question was often posed to the courts in the context of government efforts to suppress radical speech, mainly from the left but sometimes from the right. Anarchists and communists ran afoul of the law for advocating revolution. Socialists were prosecuted for advocating resistance to the military draft. Right-wing extremists were prosecuted for advocating violence against those who promoted civil rights for minorities. One who takes an absolutist view of the First Amendment believes that all speech, no matter how offensive or threatening, must be tolerated. As previously noted, the courts have never adopted this view, but in the latter half of the twentieth century, the Supreme Court assumed a much more protective posture with respect to advocacy of unlawful conduct.

The Clear and Present Danger Doctrine

Schenck v. United States (1919), the Supreme Court's first major free speech decision, emerged from the context of World War I. Charles Schenck, the General Secretary of the Socialist Party of America, was convicted of violating the Espionage Act of 1917 for distributing fliers urging young men to resist the military draft. In reviewing the conviction, the Supreme Court considered whether the mere advocacy of unlawful conduct was protected under the First Amendment. In a unanimous decision, the Court rejected Schenck's constitutional claim. Speaking for the Court, Justice Oliver Wendell Holmes observed that "[w]hen a nation is at war, many things that might be said in time of peace are such a hindrance to its effort that their utterance will not be endured so long as men fight, and that no Court could regard them as protected by any constitutional right." One key sentence from Holmes's opinion in *Schenck* formed the basis of a doctrine that persists today, albeit in a modified form: "The question in every case is whether the words used are used in such circumstances and are of such a nature as to create a clear and present danger that they will bring about the substantive evils that Congress has a right to prevent." The Court evidently believed that Schenck's activities posed a clear and present danger to military recruitment and, thus, to the American effort in the Great War.

In retrospect, the clear and present danger doctrine seems fairly reactionary. But in *Herndon v. Lowry* (1937),[16] the doctrine was employed in *defense* of free speech. In attempting to justify a man's conviction for incitement to insurrection, the state of Georgia argued that speech with a "dangerous tendency" should not merit constitutional protection. Justice Owen Roberts' opinion for the Supreme Court disagreed, noting that the statute under which the defendant was convicted "amounts merely to a dragnet which may enmesh anyone who agitates for a change of government if a jury can be persuaded that he ought to have foreseen his words would have some effect in the future conduct of others."

Similarly, in *Thornhill v. Alabama* (1940),[17] the Court invoked the clear and present danger doctrine as a means of defending the rights of a man convicted for "picketing" outside a company during a strike. Writing for eight members of the Court, Justice Frank Murphy averred that "no clear and present danger of destruction of life or property, or invasion of the right of privacy, or breach of the peace can be thought to be inherent in the activities of every person who approaches the premises of an employer and publicizes the facts of a labor dispute involving the latter."

Clear and Probable Danger

The Smith Act, enacted in 1940, made it a federal crime to "knowingly or willfully advocate, abet, advise, or teach the duty, necessity, desirability, or propriety of overthrowing or destroying any government in the United States by force or violence."[18] After World War II, as the United States and Soviet Union entered the Cold War, federal authorities became increasingly concerned about "the communist menace" here at home. In 1948, the government charged Eugene Dennis, General Secretary of the Communist Party USA, and ten of his comrades with violating the Smith Act. After what was at that time the longest trial in American history, all eleven defendants were found guilty and sentenced to five years in prison.

In *Dennis v. United States* (1951),[19] the Supreme Court upheld the convictions against a challenge based on the First Amendment. The Court produced no majority opinion, but Chief Justice Fred Vinson's plurality opinion adopted a less stringent version of the clear and present danger doctrine. According to what became known as the clear and probable danger test, the question was "whether the gravity of the 'evil,' discounted by its improbability, justifies such invasion of free speech as is necessary to avoid the danger." Applying this test, Vinson concluded that the actions of the defendants "created a 'clear and present danger' of an attempt to overthrow the Government by force and violence." In dissent, Justice Douglas suggested that the Court had succumbed to the anticommunist hysteria then gripping the nation. He concluded that there was "no evidence whatsoever showing that the acts charged, *viz.*, the teaching of the Soviet theory of revolution with the hope that it will be realized, have created any clear and present danger to the Nation." Similarly, Justice Black expressed the hope that "in calmer times, when present pressures, passions and fears subside, this or some later Court will restore the First Amendment liberties to the high preferred place where they belong in a free society."

Justice Black's hopes were realized to some extent in 1957 when the Warren Court reversed convictions of fourteen communists. In *Yates v. United States*,[20] the Court reinterpreted the Smith Act to prohibit only the "advocacy and teaching of concrete action for the forcible overthrow of the Government," as distinct from the "advocacy and teaching of forcible overthrow as an abstract principle." And in *Scales v. United States* (1961),[21] the Court construed the Smith Act to prohibit only "active" membership, as distinct from "nominal" membership in an organization advocating overthrow of the government. Without overturning the *Dennis* decision, the Court enhanced the protection of First Amendment freedoms by narrowing the scope of criminal liability under the Smith Act.

Imminent Lawless Action

The leading free speech case of the modern era is *Brandenburg v. Ohio* (1969),[22] where the Court adopted a stronger version of the clear and present danger doctrine. The case involved members of the Ku Klux Klan, which held a rally on private property during which they burned a cross, displayed weapons, and made threats against the federal government. No actual violence took place; nevertheless, the state of Ohio prosecuted Brandenburg, a Klan leader, under a "criminal syndicalism" statute that made it a crime to advocate "crime, sabotage, violence, or unlawful methods of terrorism as a means of accomplishing industrial or political reform." Brandenburg was convicted, fined $1,000, and sentenced to one to ten years in prison. The Supreme Court reversed the conviction and struck down the statute, holding that "the constitutional guarantees of free speech and free press do not permit a State to forbid or proscribe advocacy of the use of force or of law violation except where such advocacy is directed to inciting or producing imminent lawless action and is likely to incite or produce such action." In other words, advocacy of crime or violence is by itself not enough to warrant criminal prosecution. Intervention by the authorities can take place only where there is *imminent lawless action.*

Speech Integral to Criminal Conduct

In *Fox v. Washington* (1915),[23] the Supreme Court upheld a state law that made the mere advocacy of criminal conduct a misdemeanor as long as it was "confined to encouraging an actual breach of law." Of course, under *Brandenburg v. Ohio* (1969), mere advocacy can never be a crime unless accompanied by "imminent lawless action." But what about criminal conspiracies and solicitation of crimes? In *Giboney v. Empire Storage & Ice Co.* (1949),[24] Justice Black said that "it has never been deemed an abridgment of freedom of speech or press to make a course of conduct illegal merely because the conduct was in part initiated, evidenced, or carried out by means of language, either spoken, written, or printed." This principle was followed in *United States v. Williams* (2008),[25] which was a case involving a man who used an internet chat room to offer to exchange pornographic photos of children.

Michael Williams was convicted in federal court of "pandering" and possessing child pornography and was sentenced to five years in prison. In reversing Williams's conviction for pandering, the Eleventh Circuit held that "non-commercial, non-inciteful promotion of illegal child pornography" is protected speech under the First Amendment.[26] The Supreme Court, per Justice Antonin Scalia, disagreed. Noting that "[o]ffers to engage in illegal transactions are categorically excluded from First Amendment protection," the Court held that "offers to provide or requests to obtain child pornography are categorically excluded from the First Amendment."

> **IMMINENT LAWLESS ACTION:** The doctrine established by the Supreme Court holding that speech advocating illegal action, which has a likelihood of quickly producing such action, does not merit First Amendment protection.

THE CONSTITUTION IN ACTION
Can Flashing One's High-Beam Headlights Be a First Amendment Issue?

Many of our readers are no doubt familiar with a common practice employed by drivers who see a "speed trap" set up near the side of a road. In an attempt to warn oncoming traffic of that police presence, drivers will often flash their car's high-beam headlights. In some areas of the country, though, a citation could be issued for improper use of those lights. Yet in recent years, some courts have recognized First Amendment protection for this type of activity.

Among the courts that have ruled in favor of drivers who flash high-beam lights at oncoming drivers to warn of a nearby "speed trap" are two federal district courts: one in Missouri in 2014[27] and one in Wisconsin in 2019.[28] State courts also have provided such protections, including a New Jersey court in 1999,[29] a Florida court in 2012,[30] and an Oregon court in 2014.[31] It remains to be seen if more jurisdictions will embrace this broadened interpretation for freedom of expression, but oncoming drivers in places where this conduct is protected will likely be thankful for the indication to slow down and avoid a speeding ticket!

Fighting Words, True Threats, and Hate Speech

The old adage about "sticks and stones" notwithstanding, words can hurt. They can instill fear, anxiety, and pain. Sometimes they can provoke a violent response. At what point does a speaker cross the line beyond that which the First Amendment protects? The Supreme Court has addressed this question in numerous cases.

Fighting Words

In April 1940, Walter Chaplinsky drew a crowd on a public sidewalk as he verbally attacked organized religion. A town marshal approached Chaplinsky and asked him to "keep it down." Chaplinsky persisted in his loud harangue, and the marshal returned, whereupon Chaplinsky called him a "God-damned racketeer" and a "damned fascist." Chaplinsky was arrested and charged with a breach of the peace. Were Chaplinsky's insults directed at the marshal constitutionally protected free speech? In unanimous decision, the Supreme Court held they were not. In the Court's opinion, Chaplinsky's insults amounted to fighting words, which the Court defined as those which "by their very utterance, inflict injury or tend to incite an immediate breach of the peace."

Seven years later, in *Terminiello v. Chicago* (1949),[32] the Court narrowed the definition of fighting words to include only those utterances that "produce a clear and present danger of a serious intolerable evil that rises above mere inconvenience or annoyance." Arthur Terminiello, a suspended Catholic priest, was convicted of a breach of the peace after he gave an inflammatory speech inside a Chicago auditorium. Outside the building, a large crowd gathered to protest Terminiello's speech. The Supreme Court described the crowd as "angry and turbulent." At Terminiello's trial, the judge instructed the jury that "misbehavior may constitute a breach of the peace if it stirs the public to anger, invites dispute, brings about a condition of unrest, or creates a disturbance, or if it molests the inhabitants in the enjoyment of peace and quiet by arousing alarm." Terminiello was convicted and fined $100. The Supreme Court reversed the conviction and held that the law, as interpreted by the trial judge, violated the First Amendment. Speaking through Justice William O. Douglas, the Court said freedom of speech "may indeed best serve its high purpose when it induces a condition of unrest, creates dissatisfaction with conditions as they are, or even stirs people to anger."

In *Gooding v. Wilson* (1972),[33] the Court struck down a Georgia law that provided that "[a]ny person who shall, without provocation, use

FIGHTING WORDS: Speech inherently likely to provoke a violent reaction from an ordinary person and, therefore, not deserving of protection under the First Amendment.

to or of another, and in his presence ... opprobrious words or abusive language, tending to cause a breach of the peace ... shall be guilty of a misdemeanor. ..." Justice William Brennan's opinion for the Court found the prohibition to be overbroad, noting that "dictionary definitions of 'opprobrious' and 'abusive' give them greater reach than 'fighting' words." Had the statute been narrowly construed by the Georgia courts as proscribing only fighting words, it likely would have survived judicial review. But the Court defined fighting words as those which "have a direct tendency to cause acts of violence by the person to whom, individually, the remark is addressed."

Confrontations Between Citizens and Police Officers

Certainly, encounters between police and citizens often involve hostile and profane language. Yet in *Lewis v. City of New Orleans* (1974),[34] the Supreme Court reversed a conviction under a local ordinance that made it "a breach of the peace for any person wantonly to curse or revile or to use obscene or opprobrious language toward or with reference to any member of the city police while in the actual performance of his duty." The record in the case showed that the defendant used profanity toward an officer, and the officer responded in kind. The Court found that "the proscription of the use of 'opprobrious language,' embraces words that do not, 'by their very utterance, inflict injury or tend to incite an immediate breach of the peace.'" Therefore, in light of *Gooding v. Wilson*, the Court held the ordinance to be fatally overbroad.

JURISPRUDENCE

Is Flipping Off a Police Officer Protected Speech?
Cruze-Gulyas v. Minard, 918 F.3d 494 (6th Cir. 2019)

Our readers are likely familiar with the manner in which some drivers who experience frustration on the roadways convey their feelings to other drivers through a simple hand gesture—specifically by raising one hand with four fingers held down and one particular finger pointing upward. Of course, some might wonder if such an expressive act is worthy of First Amendment protection.

In 2019, the U.S. Court of Appeals for the Sixth Circuit offered what is believed to be the first appellate court opinion in U.S. history to address this question. Specifically, the Sixth Circuit afforded protection to a person who displayed a middle finger towards a police officer. The case involved a Michigan woman named Debra Cruze-Gulyas, who was pulled over for speeding. The police officer gave her a ticket for a nonmoving violation, ostensibly as a means of being lenient. As Cruze-Gulyas was driving away, though, she extended one hand out the window toward the officer and showed her middle finger. In response, the officer immediately pulled her over for a second time and issued another citation—this time a speeding ticket.

Cruze-Gulyas challenged her second citation in federal court, and the Sixth Circuit ruled the second traffic stop—and subsequent citation for speeding—to be a violation of the First Amendment right to freedom of expression. The majority opinion from Judge Jeffrey Sutton began by declaring, "Fits of rudeness or lack of gratitude may violate the Golden Rule. But that doesn't make them illegal or for that matter punishable. ..." He went on to state that, "Any reasonable officer would know that a citizen who raises her middle finger engages in speech protected by the First Amendment." However, it remains to be seen if other jurisdictions outside of the Sixth Circuit embrace this perspective, and until that occurs, it might be wise for drivers to carefully consider the use of hand gestures when communicating with law enforcement officials!

True Threats

Under federal law, threatening terrorism is a felony punishable by up to 10 years in prison.[35] A number of states have similar laws. Federal law also makes it a crime to transmit in interstate commerce "any communication containing any threat ... to injure the person of another."[36] States also have laws criminalizing threats of violence. Of course, threats involve speech, so the courts must interpret these prohibitions in light of the First Amendment.

The leading case in this area is *Watts v. United States* (1969),[37] in which a young man drafted to fight in Vietnam addressed a crowd of protesters, saying, "If they ever make me carry a rifle the first man I want to get in my sights is L.B.J." In a unanimous decision, the Supreme Court reversed Watts's conviction for threatening the life of the president. The Court's per curiam opinion readily acknowledged that "the statute under which petitioner was convicted is constitutional on its face" but insisted that the law "must be interpreted with the commands of the First Amendment clearly in mind." Thus, the Court held that the statute must be construed to prohibit only true threats and not "political hyperbole."

Reflecting on the *Watts* decision, Justice O'Connor's plurality opinion in *Virginia v. Black* (2003) noted that true threats "encompass those statements where the speaker means to communicate a serious expression of an intent to commit an act of unlawful violence to a particular individual or group of individuals." Justice O'Connor observed that "... a prohibition on true threats protects individuals from the fear of violence and the disruption that fear engenders, as well as from the possibility that the threatened violence will occur."

However, the Supreme Court's 2015 decision in *Elonis v. United States*[38] evinced a lack of consensus among the justices as to what level of criminal intent is required to prove a true threat in a criminal trial. In this case, a man named Anthony Elonis had posted Facebook multiple messages threatening harm to coworkers, his wife, a local sheriff's office, state police, the FBI, and even elementary schools (although he did not specify which one). Elonis claimed to be an aspiring rap artist, posting these messages under his "stage name" of Tone Elonis, and he said the threats were merely music lyrics intended to be a "therapeutic" release of emotion. Although he was found guilty of violating a federal law (18 U.S.C. § 875) that criminalized the transmission of threats through channels of interstate commerce, the Supreme Court vacated his conviction. Chief Justice Roberts wrote the majority opinion, which indicated that the district court had erred in

TRUE THREATS: Credible communications calling for violence against other persons.

not asking the jury to locate an appropriate level of criminal intent in Elonis' postings. But the justices could not agree on what specific level of criminal intent needed to be shown, leaving that matter for lower courts to untangle.[39]

Hate Speech and Offensive Speech

Most advanced democratic countries have laws prohibiting "advocacy of national, racial or religious hatred that constitutes incitement to discrimination, hostility or violence."[40] In the wake of recent clashes between White supremacists and civil rights protesters, many have called for the restriction of hate speech in the United States. The Supreme Court has never recognized a hate speech exception to the First Amendment, and any legislation along these lines would be strictly scrutinized by the courts.

The most relevant Supreme Court decision in this area is *R.A.V. v. St. Paul* (1992),[41] where the Court struck down a city ordinance that provided:

> Whoever places on public or private property a symbol, object, appellation, characterization or graffiti, including, but not limited to, a burning cross or Nazi swastika, which one knows or has reasonable grounds to know arouses anger, alarm or resentment in others on the basis of race, color, creed, religion or gender commits disorderly conduct and shall be guilty of a misdemeanor.

Justice Scalia's opinion for the Court held that "the ordinance goes even beyond mere content discrimination, to actual viewpoint discrimination." The Court did not overturn its previous decisions on fighting words but held that the law cannot single out certain messages in prohibiting fighting words.

More recently, in *Matal v. Tam* (2017),[42] the Court struck down a provision of federal law called the Lanham Act,[43] which prohibited registration of trademarks that "disparage ... or bring ... into contemp[t] or disrepute" any "persons, living or dead." Simon Tam, leader of the rock group The Slants, brought the lawsuit to challenge the U.S. Patent and Trademark Office's refusal to trademark the name of his band. In announcing the judgment of the Court, Justice Samuel Alito observed, "Speech that demeans on the basis of race, ethnicity, gender, religion, age, disability, or any other similar ground is hateful; but the proudest boast of our free speech jurisprudence is that we protect the freedom to express 'the thought that we hate.'"[44]

HATE SPEECH: A category of speech that discriminates against or denigrates individuals based on demographic characteristics but which the Supreme Court has, nonetheless, protected under the First Amendment.

Two years later, in *Iancu v. Brunetti* (2019),[45] the Court overturned another decision of the U.S. Patent and Trademark Office (USPTO). This time, protection was offered to a clothing company that desired to trademark the name of its company, Friends You Can't Trust, which was abbreviated in a manner that carried a potentially profane reference: F.U.C.T. In overturning the USPTO's refusal to grant a trademark for F.U.C.T., Justice Kagan's majority opinion struck down part of the Lanham Act that prohibited trademarks for material deemed "immoral" or "scandalous." Kagan found the USPTO decision to be "viewpoint discrimination," and she also noted that Justice Alito's opinion in *Matal* said a "bedrock First Amendment principle" was that the "government cannot discriminate against 'ideas that offend.'"[46]

JURISPRUDENCE

The Westboro Baptist Church and the First Amendment
Snyder v. Phelps, 562 U.S. 443 (2011)

Westboro Baptist Church (WBC) is an organization based in Kansas, founded by a man named Fred Phelps and members of his family. Although the church has named itself the Westboro Baptist Church, we should note that it is not affiliated with any mainstream or traditional Baptist churches, and it should not be construed to represent any aspect of the Baptist faith. Members of the WBC have gained notoriety for more than two decades by traveling the country to gather on sidewalks with signs that convey homophobic and anti-Semitic messages as well as derogatory statements about the U.S. military. In particular, a common practice for members of the WBC has been to conduct picketing activity near the funerals of individuals who have died in the course of military service. More than forty states have responded by passing laws that limit how close a protest can occur in proximity to a military funeral, with 300 to 500 feet away being a typical time–place–manner restriction.[47]

On March 10, 2006, members of the WBC picketed at the funeral of Lance Cpl. Matthew Snyder, who had died one week earlier while serving in Iraq. Snyder's family responded by filing a lawsuit against the WBC in Maryland state court. The lawsuit included claims for damages related to intentional infliction of emotional distress and defamation of character. After a trial, the jury ruled in favor of the Snyder family, ordering the WBC to pay approximately $5 million in damages. Church members appealed, and the U.S. Court of Appeals for the Fourth Circuit overturned the jury award, citing a First Amendment violation. The case then went to the Supreme Court.

In an 8–1 decision, the high Court declared the WBC's activity was protected by the First Amendment, and thus, no damages could be awarded to the Phelps family. In his majority opinion, Justice Roberts took note of the fact that the picketing took place 1,000 feet away from the funeral service and "did not itself disrupt the funeral." Roberts also stated that "... Westboro addressed matters of public import on public property, in a peaceful manner, in full compliance with the guidance of local officials." The majority opinion concluded with this important declaration regarding freedom of expression in the United States:

> Speech is powerful. It can stir people to action, move them to tears of both joy and sorrow and— as it did here—inflict great pain. On the facts before us, we cannot react to that pain by punishing the speaker. As a nation, we have chosen a different course—to protect even hurtful speech on public issues to ensure that we do not stifle public debate.

As the lone dissenting justice, Samuel Alito declared: "Our profound national commitment to free and open debate is not a license for the vicious verbal assault that occurred in this case. ... [The Church may not] intentionally inflict severe emotional injury on a private person at a time of intense emotional sensitivity by launching vicious verbal attacks that make no contribution to public debate."

Symbolic Speech and Expressive Conduct

The First Amendment explicitly protects freedom of speech. Early on, courts drew a distinction between speech and conduct and held that only the former was entitled to constitutional protection. In the modern era, the speech–conduct distinction has given way to a broader perspective that recognizes that *symbolic speech* and *expressive conduct* are also protected by the First Amendment. Examples of symbolic speech include wearing a campaign button, placing a bumper sticker on a car, wearing a black armband, holding up a sign at a rally or demonstration, or wearing a T-shirt with any sort of message on it. Expressive conduct is more active—such as publicly burning one's draft card, burning one's bra, or even burning the American flag. But constitutionally, symbolic speech and expressive conduct are both aspects of expression protected by the First Amendment.

Jurisprudentially, the recognition of symbolic speech began with *Stromberg v. California* (1931),[48] where a member of the Young Communist League was convicted of violating a statute that made it a crime to display a red flag (long associated with communism) at a public meeting. The Supreme Court reversed the conviction and declared the statute unconstitutional on vagueness grounds. Chief Justice Hughes's opinion for the Court did not specifically state that the display of a flag was constitutionally protected expression, but that was the implication of the decision.

In *Tinker v. Des Moines Independent Community School District* (1969),[49] three students were suspended from a public school for wearing black armbands to protest the Vietnam War. They brought suit against the school district, claiming that their First Amendment rights had been violated. The federal district judge who heard the case "recognized that the wearing of an armband for the purpose of expressing certain views is the type of symbolic act that is within the Free Speech Clause of the First Amendment."[50] Yet he dismissed the suit on the ground that the school authorities' action "was reasonable in order to prevent disturbance of school discipline," even though the students had caused no disruption. The Eighth Circuit upheld the district court's decision without issuing an opinion. But in a landmark ruling, the Supreme Court reversed, saying that for "the State in the person of school officials to justify prohibition of a particular expression of opinion, it must be able to show that its action was caused by something more than a mere desire to avoid the discomfort and unpleasantness that always accompany an unpopular viewpoint."

Burning One's Draft Card

In 1966, David Paul O'Brien burned his draft card on the courthouse steps in Boston in protest of the Vietnam War. He was promptly arrested and charged with violating a federal statute that makes it a crime to knowingly destroy or mutilate that document. After a jury trial in federal district court, O'Brien was convicted and sentenced to six years in prison. In *United States v. O'Brien* (1968),[51] the Supreme Court upheld the conviction and the statute on which it was based. The Court recognized the "communicative element in O'Brien's conduct" but refused to hold that it was "constitutionally protected activity." Chief Justice Earl Warren delivered the opinion of the Court, holding that the law was not aimed at suppressing speech but, rather, at furthering "the Government's substantial interest in assuring the continuing availability of issued Selective Service certificates. ..."

The *O'Brien* decision established a test that courts continue to follow with regard to laws and regulations that impose an "incidental restriction" on expressive conduct. The restriction must further an important governmental interest unrelated to the suppression of expression, and any restriction on expressive freedom must be no greater than what is essential to further that interest. By applying these components to the matter hand, the Court recognized the following:

1. Congress has been granted a constitutional power to "raise and support armies" in Article I.
2. The "important interest" lies in protecting the "administrative function" of the draft system by maintaining a supply of "draft cards."
3. Maintaining a federal method of registering for the Selective Service and raising an army are objectives unrelated to speech.
4. No other "less-restrictive" method for protecting the supply of draft cards exists aside from halting this activity.

Burning the American Flag

Nothing gets patriotic Americans more incensed than the public burning of the American flag. Can this symbol of our nation be protected from desecration, or does the First Amendment protect this form of expressive conduct? That was the question before the Supreme Court in *Texas v. Johnson* (1989),[52] when Gregory Johnson was prosecuted "for desecration of a venerated object" by the state of Texas after he burned an American flag outside the 1984 Republican National Convention in Dallas. Justice Brennan's opinion for a sharply divided Supreme Court rejected Texas's argument that its "interest in preserving the flag as a symbol of nationhood and national unity justify [Johnson's] criminal conviction for engaging in political expression." Brennan also opined that "[t]he State's interest in preventing breaches of the peace does not support his conviction, because Johnson's conduct did not threaten to disturb the peace." One of the four dissenters in the case, Justice John Paul Stevens said, "The value of the flag as a symbol cannot be measured." In Stevens's view, "... sanctioning the public desecration of the flag will tarnish its value—both for those who cherish the ideas for which it waves and for those who desire to don the robes of martyrdom by burning it."

The Court's decision set off a firestorm of controversy and criticism. For its part, Congress enacted the Flag Protection Act of 1989,[53] which provided, "Whoever knowingly mutilates, defaces, physically defiles, burns, maintains on the floor or ground, or tramples upon any flag of the United States shall be fined under this title or imprisoned for not more than one year, or both." The following year, in *United States v. Eichman*,[54] the Supreme Court invalidated this statute. Again, Justice Brennan wrote for a divided Court, reaffirming what the Court had declared in *Texas v. Johnson*. In the years to follow, critics of the decision in Congress tried several times, always unsuccessfully, to amend the Constitution to protect the flag. Had they been successful, it would have been the first time in history the Constitution was amended to limit civil liberties.

Texas v. Johnson was not the first Supreme Court case to address protections surrounding the American flag. In *Spence v. State of Washington* (1974),[55] the Court analyzed a state law that made it illegal to display an American flag "to which is attached or superimposed figures, symbols, or other extraneous material." Harold Spence was arrested for violating this law after he attached removable masking tape in the shape of a peace symbol to an American flag displayed outside of his home in Seattle. In overturning Spence's conviction, the Court said, "An intent to convey a particularized message was present, and in the surrounding circumstances the likelihood was great that the message would be understood by those who viewed it. We are confronted then with a case of prosecution for the expression of an idea through activity."[56]

Cross Burning

One of the most notorious and offensive examples of symbolic speech is the burning of a cross, which has long been associated with the virulent racism of the Ku Klux Klan. In *Virginia v. Black* (2003),[57] the Supreme Court held that a state can criminalize cross burning if it is done with the intent to intimidate. Virginia law made it a felony "for any person or persons, with the intent of intimidating any person or group of persons, to burn, or cause to be burned, a cross on the property of another, a highway or other public place." Speaking for the Court, Justice O'Connor concluded, "The First Amendment permits Virginia to outlaw cross burnings done with the intent to intimidate because burning a cross is a particularly virulent form of intimidation." However, when prosecuting persons under the statute, the government must prove the intent to intimidate; intent cannot be inferred from the mere act of burning the cross. Therefore, burning a cross on one's own property might be protected expression, especially if there are no threats made against particular persons or groups. But burning a cross in someone else's front yard with the intent to intimidate them clearly would not be protected by the First Amendment.

Obiter Dicta

"If there is a bedrock principle underlying the First Amendment, it is that the government may not prohibit the expression of an idea simply because society finds the idea itself offensive or disagreeable."

—*Justice William J. Brennan, Writing for the Supreme Court in* Texas v. Johnson, *491 U.S. 397 (1989)*

THE CONSTITUTION IN ACTION
Federal Courts Review Constitutionality of Mask Mandates

In April 2020, Maryland Governor Larry Hogan issued an executive order requiring masks to be worn inside all of the state's retail businesses and while on any public transportation.[58] Violations of this order could be punished as a misdemeanor criminal offense. A group called Antietam Battlefield KOA filed suit in federal district court claiming that, among other things, the mask mandate was a violation of the First Amendment's protection for freedom of speech.

In rejecting this group's First Amendment claims, Judge Catherine Blake of the U.S. District Court for the District of Maryland extensively cited the Supreme Court's decision in *Texas v. Johnson* (1989). Specifically, the judge said: "In deciding whether particular conduct possesses sufficient communicative elements to bring the First Amendment into play [the Supreme Court has] asked whether '[a]n intent to convey a particularized message was present and [whether] the likelihood was great that the message would be understood by those who viewed it."[59]

Although the plaintiff's written argument suggested that obeying a mask mandate would compel them to display a "sign of capture on the battlefield," the judge refuted this argument by saying that such a message was not "overwhelmingly apparent" (quoting *Texas v. Johnson*, (1989)) and then adding "... especially in the context of COVID-19, wearing a face covering would be viewed as a means of preventing the spread of COVID-19, not as expressing any message." The judge also referenced another Supreme Court decision, suggesting it would be "possible to find some kernel of expression in almost every activity ... but such a kernel is not sufficient to bring ... activity within the protection of the First Amendment."[60] The judge went on to say that even if the court were to accept that a refusal to wear a mask is an expressive act, strict scrutiny would still favor the government because "[s]lowing the spread of COVID-19 is a compelling government interest."

(continued)

A similar conclusion was reached by the U.S. District Court for the District of Minnesota in one of its 2020 decisions. In this case, Judge Patrick Schiltz said that "[e]ven if wearing or not wearing a face covering was inherently expressive," a mask mandate would be constitutional under *United States v. O'Brien* (1968), which requires an important or substantial government interest to justify a restriction on expression—and also under the smallpox vaccine decision in *Jacobson v. Massachusetts* (1905), which requires the government to show a "real or substantial relationship" to a public health crisis; under both precedents, stopping the spread of COVID-19 would be sufficient to turn away a First Amendment challenge.[61]

Obscenity, Indecency, and Profanity

Historically, American courts recognized no constitutional protection for expression of a sexual nature. And they were highly deferential toward federal and state criminal prosecutions for obscenity. When determining what was obscene, American courts generally followed a test articulated by the Court of Queen's Bench in 1868, to wit: "whether the tendency of the matter charged as obscenity is to deprave and corrupt those whose minds are open to such influences, and into whose hands a publication of this sort may fall."[62] This "bad tendency" test was adopted by the Supreme Court in *Rosen v. United States* (1896),[63] in which the Court's opinion did not even mention the First Amendment.

Defining Obscenity

OBSCENITY: Extreme pornography not protected under the First Amendment and incompatible with contemporary community standards.

In *Roth v. United States* (1957),[64] the Supreme Court ruled that obscenity is beyond the pale of First Amendment protection. Writing for the Court, Justice Brennan observed that "implicit in the history of the First Amendment is the rejection of obscenity as utterly without redeeming social importance." But it rejected the bad tendency test in favor of a test more protective of sexually oriented expression. "Obscene material is material which deals with sex in a manner appealing to prurient interest," wrote Justice Brennan. In other words, obscenity is sexually oriented material that arouses lascivious thoughts. Clearly, this definition was inadequate.

In the years to come, the justices would struggle with the definition of obscenity—in some cases, saying that to be obscene, a particular work, taken as a whole, must be "patently offensive" and "utterly without redeeming social value."[65] In *Bantam Books v. Sullivan* (1963),[66] Justice Brennan's Opinion of the Court acknowledged the "dim and uncertain line" that separated obscenity from protected expression. In a concurring opinion the following year, Justice Potter Stewart conceded the difficulty of articulating a definition of obscenity but, nevertheless, insisted, "I know it when I see it."[67]

Eventually, in *Miller v. California* (1973),[68] the Court announced a three-part test for determining obscenity, and this definition remains good law today. To qualify as obscene, a publication or performance would have to meet all three of these criteria:

> (a) whether "the average person, applying contemporary community standards" would find that the work, taken as a whole, appeals to the prurient interest, ... (b) whether the work depicts or describes, in a patently offensive way, sexual conduct specifically defined by the applicable state law, and (c) whether the work, taken as a whole, lacks serious literary, artistic, political, or scientific value.

A year later, in *Jenkins v. Georgia*,[69] the Court made clear that only "hard-core" pornography would qualify as obscenity. The case involved a theater owner from Albany, Georgia, who had been prosecuted for showing *Carnal Knowledge*, a Hollywood film that dealt with sex but was anything but hard-core porn. The *Jenkins* decision rendered some clarity but did not solve what Justice Harlan called "the intractable obscenity problem."[70] Prosecutors, judges, juries, and appellate courts continued to struggle with the operational definition of obscenity.

Pornography on the Internet

The advent of the internet created a new medium in which pornography could flourish. By the mid-1990s, there were thousands of websites featuring hardcore porn. In 1996, Congress passed the Communications Decency Act (CDA),[71] which made it a federal crime to knowingly transmit "obscene or indecent" content to minors. It also prohibited the "knowing" display of "patently offensive" content in a way that it would be available to someone under 18.

In *Reno v. American Civil Liberties Union* (1997),[72] the Supreme Court struck down the statute as overbroad. Justice Stevens's majority opinion acknowledged that the Court has "repeatedly recognized the governmental interest in protecting children from harmful materials." However, Stevens said "that interest does not justify an unnecessarily broad suppression of speech addressed to adults." The Court's principal concern was that the term "indecency," being much broader than "obscenity," extends a criminal prohibition to expression protected by the First Amendment. In 2003, Congress amended the CDA to remove the indecency provisions. Today, the prohibition is limited to obscenity and child pornography.[73]

Prosecutions for obscenity have become increasingly rare. When cases are brought, they are hard to win, as trial judges and appellate courts must grapple with the First Amendment issues that are invariably raised by defense lawyers. Prosecutors, especially at the state and local levels, often respond to public pressure. Public attitudes about pornography have softened, and prosecutors today rarely face public criticism for being lenient on pornography. Today, pornography is readily available on the internet and through cable television and, indeed, is a thriving commercial activity. There is little prospect for this to change. Child pornography is a different matter entirely. Federal and state authorities aggressively investigate and prosecute those who produce or even possess pornographic materials depicting minors.

Child Pornography

In *New York v. Ferber* (1982),[74] the Court held that government's compelling interest in protecting children allows it to criminalize pornography involving minors, even if that material is not legally obscene. Justice

Byron White, writing for the Court, noted that child pornography is "intrinsically related to the sexual abuse of children" and concluded that it is categorically excluded from First Amendment protection. Similarly, in *Osborne v. Ohio* (1990),[75] the Court upheld an Ohio statute that made it a crime to "possess or view any material or performance that shows a minor who is not the person's child or ward in a state of nudity." In upholding the law, the Court (again, via Justice White) stressed that the Ohio Supreme Court had construed the law to apply only to "lewd exhibition" or "graphic focus on the genitals." Thus, "innocuous" images of nude children would not be subject to the prohibition.

In 1996, Congress enacted a law that criminalized any type of virtual or simulated child pornography, even if real children were not involved in the production of the material. In *Ashcroft v. Free Speech Coalition* (2002),[76] the Supreme Court ruled that Congress had gone too far. Justice Anthony Kennedy's majority opinion concluded that the law "proscribes a significant universe of speech that is neither obscene under *Miller* nor child pornography under *Ferber*." In Kennedy's opinion, child pornography as defined in *Ferber* is limited to that which depicts real human beings. As Justice Kennedy noted, "Virtual child pornography is not 'intrinsically related' to the sexual abuse of children, as were the materials in *Ferber*." In dissent, Chief Justice Rehnquist lamented the Court's decision, saying that "Congress has a compelling interest in ensuring the ability to enforce prohibitions of actual child pornography, and we should defer to its findings that rapidly advancing technology soon will make it all but impossible to do so."

JURISPRUDENCE

Can Congress Criminalize the Depiction of Animal Cruelty?
United States v. Stevens, 559 U.S. 460 (2010)

In a decision that addressed a disturbing subject, the Supreme Court's ruling in *United States v. Stevens* (2010) examined so-called "animal crush videos." These videos were outlawed by Congress in 1999 under 18 U.S.C. § 48, which made it a federal crime if a person "creates, sells, or possesses a depiction of animal cruelty," provided that this act is done "for commercial gain" and through channels of interstate or foreign commerce; "animal cruelty" was defined by the statute to encompass a situation "in which a living animal is intentionally maimed, mutilated, tortured, wounded, or killed"—if that conduct was against federal or state law in the place where "the creation, sale, or possession" of the video had occurred. Although the specific acts of animal cruelty shown in these videos might have already been illegal under relevant state or federal animal cruelty laws, this federal statute targeted the videos themselves.

The majority opinion in this case defined such videos by observing that, "According to the House Committee Report on the bill, such videos feature the intentional torture and killing of helpless animals," with the Court adding, "Crush videos often depict [a person] slowly crushing animals to death 'with their bare feet or while wearing high heeled shoes,' sometimes while 'talking to the animals in a kind of dominatrix pattern.'" The Court also said, "Apparently these depictions 'appeal to persons with a very specific sexual fetish who find them sexually arousing or otherwise exciting.'"

In an 8–1 decision, though, the Supreme Court struck down the federal statute criminalizing the depiction of animal cruelty on the ground that the prohibition was substantially overbroad. Chief Justice Roberts delivered the opinion of the Court, saying in part: "We read §48 to create a criminal prohibition of alarming breadth. To begin with, the text of the statute's ban on a 'depiction of animal cruelty' nowhere requires that the depicted conduct be cruel. That text applies to 'any ... depiction' in which 'a living animal is intentionally maimed, mutilated, tortured, wounded, or killed.'" Roberts's opinion noted that a video of hunting activity that might have been legal in the state where the video was created could have become an illegal item in a state where such conduct was prohibited.

Nevertheless, Roberts also added, "We therefore need not and do not decide whether a statute limited to ... depictions of extreme animal cruelty would be constitutional. We hold only that §48 is not so limited but is instead substantially overbroad, and therefore invalid under the First Amendment." Accordingly, Congress would amend the 1999 statute, with President Obama signing a revised version known as the Animal Crush Video Prohibition Act of 2010;[77] among the substantive changes, the revised version required that the video in question be deemed obscene, and exceptions were allotted for "normal veterinary or agricultural husbandry practices; the slaughter of animals for food; or hunting, trapping, or fishing."

The first appellate review of the new law arrived with the Fifth Circuit's 2014 decision in *United States v. Richards*,[78] which involved a case brought against a man and woman in Texas. The man, Mr. Justice, had filmed the woman, Ms. Richards, in a video of her "binding animals (a kitten, a puppy, and a rooster), sticking the heels of her shoes into them, chopping off their limbs with a cleaver, removing their innards, ripping off their heads, and urinating on them." The court noted that in the video "Richards is scantily clad and talks to both the animals and the camera, making panting noises. ..." Richards and Justice were convicted of state animal cruelty charges in Texas, for which she received 10 years in prison, and he received 50 years. Additionally, each of them was charged under the Animal Crush Video Prohibition Act. However, a federal district court initially dismissed that indictment by declaring the law to be a violation of the First Amendment. On review, the Fifth Circuit reversed, upholding the law by declaring that it "is narrow and tailored to target unprotected speech that requires the wanton torture and killing of animals." Ms. Richards subsequently pled guilty to the federal charge and was sentenced to three years and nine months for that offense, and Mr. Justice was found guilty in federal district court, receiving a sentence of 57 months in federal prison.[79]

Regulation of Adult-Oriented Businesses

In cities across America there are clubs that feature nude or seminude dancing. Is this constitutionally protected expression? Do laws that prohibit public nudity apply to such establishments? How far can local governments go in regulating this kind of entertainment? The Supreme Court has dealt with this issue in two cases, but in neither case did the Court produce a majority opinion. In *Barnes v. Glen Theater* (1991),[80] the Court upheld a requirement that dancers in such establishments wear "pasties" and a "G-string" to comply with the Indiana's public nudity law. Chief Justice Rehnquist's plurality opinion recognized that erotic dancing is entitled to some degree of First Amendment protection, but "the requirement that the dancers don pasties and a G-string does not deprive the dance of whatever erotic message it conveys; it simply makes the message slightly less graphic."

Likewise, in *Erie v. Pap's AM* (2000),[81] the Court upheld a local ordinance requiring erotic dancers to wear pasties and a G-string. Again there was no majority opinion. Writing for a plurality, Justice O'Connor recognized that "nude dancing of the type at issue here is expressive conduct, although we think that it falls only within the outer ambit of the First Amendment's protection." She concluded, "The requirement that dancers wear pasties and G-strings is a minimal restriction ... and the restriction leaves ample capacity to convey the dancer's erotic message."

One way many communities regulate adult-oriented businesses is through zoning. In *Renton v. Playtime Theatres, Inc.* (1986),[82] the Supreme Court upheld this approach. The city of Renton, Washington adopted an ordinance prohibiting adult movie theaters from being located within 1,000 feet of any school, church, park, or residential zone. The Court sustained the ordinance as a legitimate time, place, and manner regulation.

Writing for a majority of seven justices, Chief Justice Rehnquist concluded that "the Renton ordinance represents a valid governmental response to the 'admittedly serious problems' created by adult theaters." In dissent, Justice Brennan, joined by Justice Marshall, argued that "Renton's zoning ordinance selectively imposes limitations on the location of a movie theater based exclusively on the content of the films shown there." In their view, the ordinance was "plainly unconstitutional under the standards established by the decisions of this Court."

Profanity

PROFANITY: A term typically used to describe curse words and other language that might offend some members of society.

Historically, profanity, like obscenity, warranted no constitutional protection from the courts. Recall that in *Chaplinsky v. New Hampshire* (1942), the Supreme Court mentioned profanity in its enumeration of types of expression categorically beyond the scope of the First Amendment. That view changed dramatically with the Court's decision in *Cohen v. California* (1971),[83] where a young man was convicted of "offensive conduct" for walking into a courthouse wearing a jacket that bore the slogan, "Fuck the draft." In reversing Cohen's conviction, the Supreme Court observed that "while the particular four-letter word being litigated here is perhaps more distasteful than others of its genre, it is nevertheless often true that one man's vulgarity is another's lyric." When providing expressive protections to Cohen's act of wearing a jacket, Justice Harlan's majority opinion went on to say that "it is largely because government officials cannot make principled distinctions in this area that the Constitution leaves matters of taste and style so largely to the individual." Harlan also noted that the "presence of unwitting listeners or viewers does not serve automatically to justify curtailing all speech capable of giving offense," adding that a person who disliked the image could "avoid further bombardment of their sensibilities simply by averting their eyes."

Although many states and local communities still have profanity laws on the books, prosecutions are uncommon, and convictions are often overturned on appeal. A well-known case is *People v. Boomer* (2002),[84] when a Michigan appellate court struck down a state statute that prohibited "indecent, immoral, obscene, vulgar or insulting language in the presence or hearing of any woman or child. ..." The court found it "... unquestionable that [the statute under which Boomer was convicted], as drafted, reaches constitutionally protected speech, and it operates to inhibit the exercise of First Amendment rights." In this matter, Boomer had uttered profanities after falling out of a canoe and into Michigan's Rifle River.

THE CONSTITUTION IN ACTION

Profane T-Shirt Leads to Arrest, Section 1983 Lawsuit

Wood v. Eubanks, No. 20-3599 (6th Cir. 2022)

In this case, a man named Michael Wood entered a county fair in Clark County, Ohio, wearing a T-shirt with the words "Fuck the Police" imprinted on the front of it. Police officers working at the fair ordered him to leave and escorted him from the fairgrounds—based solely on the shirt, which he had covered up by the point he was being escorted out. Mr. Wood verbally insulted the officers as he was being led out of the fair, and he was arrested for disorderly conduct. While being taking into custody, Mr. Wood told the officers he was engaging in "a constitutionally protected activity," to which a sheriff's deputy replied, "Not in my home." The criminal charge against Wood was dismissed by a prosecutor, who said the state lacked any lay witnesses for demonstrating that Wood's "words and conduct amounted to 'fighting words' under the First Amendment."

Wood then filed a Section 1983 lawsuit claiming retaliation for protected speech. On this cause of action, the court said, "To prevail, Wood must demonstrate three elements: (1) 'that he engaged in constitutionally protected speech,' (2) 'that he suffered an adverse action likely to chill a person of ordinary firmness from continuing to engage in protected speech,' and (3) 'that the protected speech was a substantial or motivating factor in the decision to take the adverse action.'"[85] The majority ruled in Wood's favor, finding that his speech was "clearly established" as protected. More specifically, the majority opinion observed that the "fighting words doctrine has become very limited," adding that "profanity alone is insufficient to establish criminal behavior."[86] The opinion stated: "We have routinely protected the use of profanity when unaccompanied by other conduct that could be construed as disorderly," with a reference offered to a case where an officer was called an "asshole" and an "idiot";[87] the court also cited to another case where an officer was called "son of a bitch" and "fat slob," with that opinion observing that "[e]ven crass language used to insult police officers does not fall within the 'very limited' unprotected category of 'fighting words.'"[88] Whereas such language is clearly disrespectful to those working in law enforcement, there seems to be a First Amendment protection established in case law.

Yet the Sixth Circuit's opinion in *Wood v. Eubanks* did point out that threatening language could result in a valid disorderly conduct charge, noting one case in which a man said to DEA agents, "I don't appreciate you and your monkeys following me and if you keep it up I'll rip your head off."[89] The Sixth Circuit also observed that "we have repeatedly held that the state can punish an 'individual whose act of speaking, by virtue of its time and manner, plainly obstructed ongoing police activity involving a third party.'"[90]

In the end, the Sixth Circuit ruled that, "[w]hile Wood's speech was profane, the circumstances did not create a situation where violence was likely to result." Therefore, his speech was protected under the First Amendment, and the officers in question, though understandably upset by the content of Wood's message, were not entitled to qualified immunity.

Freedom of the Press

In 1798, Congress enacted a law that made it a crime to publish "any false, scandalous and malicious writing or writings against the government of the United States, or either house of the Congress of the United States, or the President of the United States. ..." The Sedition Act[91] was used to punish critics of President John Adams, including nearly twenty Republican newspaper editors and even a member of Congress. Invoking the First Amendment, the Virginia General Assembly adopted a resolution asserting that the Sedition Act was based on "a power not delegated by the Constitution, but, on the contrary, expressly and positively forbidden by one of the amendments thereto. ..."[92]

In retrospect, the Sedition Act seems blatantly unconstitutional. However, the Act expired at the end of President Adams's term in March 1801, so the Supreme Court never had the chance to review the statute. Had the Court been given that opportunity, it is not at all clear the Court would have invalidated the law. After all, the power of judicial review was not established prior to *Marbury v. Madison* in 1803.[93] Moreover, seditious libel was a crime under English common law, and despite the Virginia Resolution quoted above, not everyone in the new republic believed that the First Amendment was intended to abolish this offense. Thomas Jefferson, President Adams's successor, pardoned everyone who had been convicted under the Sedition Act (all of whom were his supporters), and in 1840, Congress enacted a measure repaying fines exacted from those convicted under the Act.[94]

SEDITIOUS LIBEL:
A term derived from English law to indicate that speech criticizing the government or advocating the overthrow of government could be punished.

The Prohibition of Prior Restraint

William Blackstone, whose *Commentaries on the Laws of England* (1765–1770) were the definitive statement of the common law, said this about the freedom of the press:

> The liberty of the press is indeed essential to the nature of a free state; but this consists in laying no *previous* restraints upon publications, and not in freedom from censure for criminal matter when published. Every freeman has an undoubted right to lay what sentiments he pleases before the public; to forbid this is to destroy the freedom of the press; but if he publishes what is improper, mischievous or illegal, he must take the consequence of his own temerity.[95]

PRIOR RESTRAINT:
Commonly known as censorship, this term describes an attempt by the government to prevent the public release of information—perhaps, by censoring the publication of a newspaper article or book; an act that will be closely scrutinized by courts.

In other words, one might be prosecuted or sued for what one publishes (or says, for that matter), but one should not be prevented from publishing it (or saying it). Despite the common-law prohibition of prior restraint, it was common well into the twentieth century for local authorities to censor books, magazines, plays, and films, mainly on grounds of obscenity or indecency.

In 1931, the Supreme Court decided a landmark case in which a local newspaper was shut down by court order. In *Near v. Minnesota*,[96] the Court struck down a state law that authorized injunctions against "a malicious, scandalous and defamatory newspaper, magazine or other periodical." Chief Justice Charles Evans Hughes's opinion embraced Blackstone's statement about "*previous* restraints upon publications" but denied that it was an absolute prohibition. Hughes suggested that protection of the national security might, in some circumstances, require an injunction against the press. He also mentioned obscenity as a justification for prior restraint. However, he stressed the role of the press in exposing malfeasance in government and concluded that allowing an injunction in this case would be contrary to a central purpose of the First Amendment.

The Pentagon Papers Case

The question of prior restraint arose again in *New York Times v. United States* (1971),[97] which is the famous *Pentagon Papers* case. The Nixon administration obtained an injunction against the *Times* to prevent it from publishing a series of documents detailing the history of Vietnam War policymaking that were secreted out of the Pentagon by a disaffected analyst. In a 6–3 decision, the Supreme Court rebuffed the Administration. The decision was unusual in that there was no opinion of the Court, only a brief per curiam opinion citing *Near v. Minnesota*, which noted the "heavy presumption against" prior restraint and stated the government had not carried its burden of persuasion. That brief statement was followed by nine individual opinions—six concurring and three dissenting. Justice Black's concurrence insisted that "every moment's continuance of the injunctions against these newspapers amounts to a flagrant, indefensible, and continuing violation of the First Amendment." He bemoaned the fact that "some of my Brethren are apparently willing to hold that the publication of news may sometimes be enjoined." In Black's view, "Such a holding would make a shambles of the First Amendment." In dissent, Chief Justice Warren E. Burger, who was appointed to the Court by President Nixon two years earlier, suggested that "a complex modern government" requires "the effective exercise of certain constitutional powers of the Executive." In a similar vein, Justice Harry Blackmun (also a Nixon appointee) stressed the primacy of the Executive Branch in the field of foreign affairs as well as its "responsibility for the Nation's safety." Ultimately, the Nixon Administration lost the case because it was unable to persuade at least five members of the Court that national security would suffer imminent and irreparable harm if the *Pentagon Papers* saw the light of day.

It is interesting to note that Daniel Ellsberg, the analyst who turned over the *Pentagon Papers* to the press, was prosecuted for espionage, theft of government property, and conspiracy. The case was dismissed, however, after the trial judge learned of unlawful surveillance of the defendant.

Can Government Prevent the Press from Publishing Secrets about Nuclear Weapons?

In 1979, a federal judge in Wisconsin, citing "grave, direct, immediate and irreparable harm to the United States," issued an injunction to prevent *The Progressive* magazine from publishing an article entitled "The H-Bomb Secret: How We Got It, Why We're Telling It."[98] The injunction was lifted after six months, when it was determined the information contained in the article had already made its way into publication elsewhere. *The Progressive* then published its article. The *Pentagon Papers* case and *United States v. The Progressive* make clear than an injunction against the press can only be issued under the most extreme threats to national security. Not since 1979 has any federal court issued an injunction to prevent publication of anything.

Defamation

DEFAMATION: A false public statement that causes damage to the reputation of a person or business.

SLANDER: Defamation of character through spoken word.

LIBEL: Defamation of character through written word or electronic media.

ACTUAL MALICE: Judicial standard that requires "public figures" to demonstrate intentional falsehood or reckless disregard of the truth to prevail on a defamation claim.

PUBLIC FIGURE: A person who has, by virtue of their choice in occupation or by voluntarily making public statements about political issues, achieved a level of notoriety or fame in society, such as a politician or person running for office; if such a person brings a defamation lawsuit, proof of actual malice—or reckless disregard for the truth—is required.

Defamation is a wrongful injury to someone's reputation by dissemination of a falsehood. The spoken form is called slander; the written form is known as libel. Defamation is not a crime; it is a tort, and the remedy for which is a civil suit for damages. In *New York Times v. Sullivan* (1964),[99] the Supreme Court held that when a public official sues the press for libel, the plaintiff must show that the defendant acted with actual malice, defined as knowledge that the story was false or at least "reckless disregard" of the truth. Justice Brennan's opinion for the Court indicated that this requirement was necessary, given the "profound national commitment to the principle that debate on public issues should be uninhibited, robust, and wide-open. ..." In his view, such debate "may well include vehement, caustic, and sometimes unpleasantly sharp attacks on government and public officials." In this case, the public official was a police commissioner in Alabama.

The actual malice standard articulated in *New York Times v. Sullivan* was soon extended beyond public officials to public figures.[100] As the Court explained in 1974, "public officials and public figures usually enjoy significantly greater access to the channels of effective communication and hence have a more realistic opportunity to counteract false statements than private individuals normally enjoy."[101]

Critics of *New York Times v. Sullivan* and the decisions that followed from it argue it is too difficult for victims of libel to obtain redress in the courts. President Donald Trump, who frequently chided the press for "fake news," once said, "Our current libel laws are a sham and a disgrace and do not represent American values or American fairness."[102] Yet in a 1789 speech given by James Madison to the U.S. House of Representatives in support of proposed amendments for the Bill of Rights—a document that patently seems to represent "American values"—Madison made it clear that the overarching intent of a proposal that would later become the First Amendment was as follows: "The people shall not be deprived or abridged of their right to speak, to write, or to publish their sentiments; and the freedom of the press, as one of the great bulwarks of liberty, shall be inviolable." Madison's underlying point, it seems, was that a key to the functioning of a democratic republic is the ability of people to criticize government officials.[103]

The key to applying Madison's core principles to defamation of character may rest in how courts differentiate public figures from private persons—particularly in an era in which ordinary people can voluntarily create widely-viewed social media profiles that essentially establish public personas. Older Supreme Court case precedent offers

JURISPRUDENCE

The Supreme Court Reviews a Magazine Ad Mocking a Minister
Hustler Magazine v. Falwell, 485 U.S. 46 (1988)

In November 1983, the inside of the front cover of *Hustler Magazine* featured an advertisement for Campari Liqueur that was created as a parody aimed at the Reverend Jerry Falwell, a prominent figure on the religious right. The parody included a reference to Falwell having sex with his mother in an outhouse with correlated discussion of a goat. While no reasonable person would have believed that the statements contained in the parody were true, Reverend Falwell sued *Hustler* and publisher Larry Flynt for libel and intentional infliction of emotional distress. After a jury ruled in Falwell's favor on the latter claim, awarding him $200,000, Flynt appealed to the Supreme Court. In a unanimous decision, the high Court overturned the jury verdict, applying the rule announced in *New York Times v. Sullivan* to claims of infliction of emotional distress brought by public figures.

Chief Justice Rehnquist delivered the opinion of the Court, saying in part: "We conclude that public figures and public officials may not recover for the tort of intentional infliction of emotional distress by reason of publications such as the one here at issue without showing, in addition, that the publication contains a false statement of fact which was made with 'actual malice,' *i.e.,* with knowledge that the statement was false or with reckless disregard as to whether or not it was true." In extrapolating an underlying justification for this ruling, which had notable ramifications for comedians and others who poke fun at public figures, the opinion said, "This … reflects our considered judgment that such a standard is necessary to give adequate 'breathing space' to the freedoms protected by the First Amendment." Justice Rehnquist also stated, "The Court of Appeals interpreted the jury's finding [on the libel claim] to be that the ad parody 'was not reasonably believable,' … and, in accordance with our custom, we accept this finding." The fact that a reasonable person would not have taken this ad seriously, then, was crucial to the analysis. Additionally, in regard to the intentional infliction of emotional distress claim, Rehnquist observed, "… [F]or reasons heretofore stated, this claim cannot, consistently with the First Amendment, form a basis for the award of damages when the conduct in question is the publication of a caricature such as the ad parody involved here."

some instructive advice. For example, in providing contours for distinguishing "public officials" from "private figures," Justice Lewis Powell's majority opinion in *Gertz v. Welch* (1974)[104] said the following:

> That designation may rest on either of two alternative bases. In some instances an individual may achieve such pervasive fame or notoriety that he becomes a public figure for all purposes and in all contexts. More commonly, an individual voluntarily injects himself or is drawn into a particular public controversy, and thereby becomes a public figure for a limited range of issues. In either case, such persons assume special prominence in the resolution of public questions.

Further clarifying this standard, Powell went on to indicate that, "[a]bsent clear evidence of general fame or notoriety in the community, and pervasive involvement in the affairs of society, an individual should not be deemed a public personality for all aspects of his life." In the case at hand, Gertz was a private attorney representing a family in a lawsuit against a police department, and ultimately, the Court found he should not be treated as a public figure for the purpose of applying defamation standards.

In a noteworthy November 2021 decision, a judge in Connecticut found Alex Jones, host of the political show InfoWars, liable for defamation. The case stemmed from comments Jones made about the Sandy Hook Elementary School shooting of 2012. Jones had falsely claimed that the shooting was a hoax, and family members of the victims claimed viewers of Jones's show had targeted them with harassing comments.[105] Moreover, in August 2022, a Texas jury found Jones liable for defamation and infliction of emotional distress in another case stemming from Jones's comments about the Sandy Hook shooting.[106]

Access to Government Information

The Supreme Court has on many occasions spoken of the solemn duty of the press to act as a watchdog over government. But is there a constitutional right of access to government information? In *Zemel v. Rusk* (1965),[107] in upholding a ban on travel to Cuba, the Supreme Court suggested otherwise. The Court noted that "the prohibition of unauthorized entry into the White House diminishes the citizen's opportunities to gather information he might find relevant to his opinion of the way the country is being run, but that does not make entry into the White House a First Amendment right." It concluded that "[t]he right to speak and publish does not carry with it the unrestrained right to gather information."

This means not only that the government is not constitutionally required to share information with the press, but it may also sequester certain information through a classification system. The Supreme Court has consistently recognized the President's "authority to classify and control access to information bearing on national security."[108] And of course, the disclosure or publication of classified information is a felony.[109] It should be noted, though, that the Freedom of Information Act[110] creates a statutory right of access to government information, although it does not apply to classified documents, ongoing investigations, and other sensitive information, nor does it apply to "rough drafts" of government reports,[111] or confidential business documents submitted to the government.[112]

Protection of Confidential Sources

Reporters often rely on unnamed sources and argue that the protection of these sources is essential to the journalistic enterprise. The argument is that, without a guarantee of anonymity, many sources would refuse to come forward. Does the First Amendment confer on journalists a privilege to refuse to identify their sources? That question came before the Supreme Court in *Branzburg v. Hayes* (1972).[113] Paul Branzburg, a reporter at the *Louisville Courier-Journal*, wrote a story about illegal drugs for which he interviewed drug users and observed people manufacturing hashish. Branzburg was subsequently subpoenaed by a grand jury and asked to reveal the names of his sources. Branzburg refused and was held in contempt. In a 6–3 decision, the Supreme Court refused to recognize a "reporter's privilege" in the First Amendment. Writing for the Court, Justice Byron White could "perceive no basis for holding that the public interest in law enforcement and in ensuring effective grand jury proceedings is insufficient to override the consequential, but uncertain, burden on news gathering that is said to result from insisting that reporters, like other citizens, respond to relevant questions put to them in the course of a valid grand jury investigation or criminal trial." In dissent, Justice Stewart (joined by Justices Brennan and Marshall) complained that "[t]he Court's crabbed view of the First Amendment reflects a disturbing insensitivity to the critical role of an independent press in our society."

The decision in *Branzburg v. Hayes* remains good law today. However, most states now have some sort of **shield law** to protect reporters with respect to testimony before state and local courts and grand juries. On several occasions, Congress has attempted, but failed, to pass a law creating a reporter's privilege at the federal level.

Moreover, protections for sources themselves can vary based on what information is revealed. For instance, in *Haig v. Agee* (1981), the Supreme Court found that a former CIA agent was not protected by the First Amendment because his attempts to reveal the identities of undercover agents and confidential sources carried a "substantial likelihood of 'serious damage' to national security or foreign policy."[114] This precedent could be relevant to dialogue over Edward Snowden, the former National Security Agency contractor who leaked information to the media about government practices that included "spying" on "metadata" derived from email and phone records of American citizens. Snowden fled the United States after these revelations and currently is residing in Russia, which will not extradite him to the United States to face criminal charges. If he were to return to the United States, charges under the Espionage Act of 1917 could be brought. We discuss this matter in greater detail in chapter 9, which addresses the topic of electronic surveillance.

SHIELD LAW: A law enacted to protect reporters from being required to provide testimony in a criminal proceeding when doing so might force a reporter to reveal the identity of confidential informants.

The Free Press/Fair Trial Problem

A person accused of a crime has a right to a fair trial by an unbiased jury, yet the press has a right to cover trials. In chapter 12, we will examine a number of measures trial judges routinely take to protect this right in the face of potentially prejudicial publicity. But here we are concerned specifically with the right of the press to cover criminal proceedings. Can a judge, on the unopposed motion of the defendant, conduct a trial in secret? What about pretrial hearings on motions to suppress evidence? Can such hearings be closed to the press and public? Can a judge enjoin the press from reporting certain facts about a case?

In *Richmond Newspapers v. Virginia* (1980),[115] the Supreme Court reversed a Virginia Supreme Court ruling that allowed a trial judge to close a trial to the press and the public. Chief Justice Burger's plurality opinion observed that "the right to attend criminal trials is implicit in the guarantees of the First Amendment; without the freedom to attend such trials, which people have exercised for centuries, important aspects of freedom of speech and 'of the press could be eviscerated.'" Concurring in the judgment, Justice Brennan concluded that "our ingrained tradition of public trials and the importance of public access to the broader purposes of the trial process, tip the balance strongly toward the rule that trials be open."

The Court has said that the open trial rule applies to jury selection as well as the trial proper. In *Press-Enterprise Co. v. Superior Court of California* (1984),[116] while not ruling out closure of pretrial proceedings altogether, the Court held that "[t]he presumption of openness may be overcome only by an overriding interest based on findings that closure is essential to preserve higher values, and is narrowly tailored to serve that interest." In extreme circumstances, a trial judge may order a portion of a pretrial proceeding to be conducted secretly, but any such order will be strictly scrutinized by the appellate courts.

In 2010, the Court reiterated this idea in a case in which a lone observer was asked to vacate a courtroom in Georgia just prior to jury selection. That observer turned out to be the defendant's uncle, and the Court ruled that even excluding one person from viewing jury selection amounted to a violation of constitutional rights. Although the per curiam opinion for this case focused on the Sixth Amendment, the opinion bluntly stated a core First Amendment concept related to public access to information: "Trial courts are obligated to take every reasonable measure to accommodate public attendance at criminal trials." The opinion went on to cite to the *Press-Enterprise Co.* case, offering this caveat: "There are no doubt circumstances where a judge could conclude that threats of improper communications with jurors or safety concerns are concrete enough to warrant closing *voir dire*. But in those cases, the particular interest, and threat to that interest, must 'be articulated along with findings specific enough that a reviewing court can determine whether the closure order was properly entered.'"[117]

An example of such unique circumstances arose in 2018 when the U.S. District Court for the Southern District of New York held multiple pretrial proceedings in secret during preparation for the drug trafficking trial of Joaquín Guzmán Loera, known to many as "El Chapo." The rationale for holding these hearings in clandestine fashion was connected to security concerns surrounding this high-profile defendant.

Regulation of Electronic Media

The federal government has regulated the broadcasting industry since the enactment of the Radio Act of 1927.[118] The Communications Act of 1934[119] created the Federal Communications Commission and gave it the authority to allocate frequencies and regulate transmission power. The FCC is an independent agency of the federal executive branch, and the Communications Act indicates that its primary goal is "regulating interstate and foreign commerce in communication by wire and radio so as to make available … a rapid, efficient, Nationwide, and world-wide wire and radio communication service with adequate facilities at reasonable charges."[120] The FCC exerts authority over television, radio, internet, and satellites, among other communication sources. It has approximately 1,500 employees and an annual budget of around $350 million. The FCC is divided into seven bureaus and eleven offices.

Typical activities for FCC officials include creating rules and licensing standards for what kind of content can be transmitted in public broadcasts. For example, viewers of broadcast television could see different types of programs or advertisements during the daytime as opposed to late at night. There could, for instance, be types of nudity that cannot appear on broadcast television, and the FCC has even established "seven words" that cannot be said on broadcast airwaves, whether TV or radio. At one point in its history, the FCC even enforced a Fairness Doctrine, introduced in 1949, to ensure equal treatment was given to controversial issues of public importance that were covered on broadcast media. Although this doctrine was upheld by the Supreme Court in *Red Lion Broadcasting Co. v. FCC* (1969), the FCC removed it in 1987, and President Reagan vetoed congressional efforts to revive the doctrine.[121]

Profanity and Indecency in the Media

Under federal law, the FCC has the power to regulate "obscene, indecent, or profane" content on the airwaves.[122] In *Federal Communications Commission v. Pacifica Foundation* (1978),[123] the Supreme Court upheld the FCC's authority to prohibit indecent speech on radio and TV, upholding a fine issued to a broadcast company after comedian George Carlin uttered the "Seven Words You Can Never Say on Television" during an afternoon radio show; that decision remains good law today. However, the proliferation of cable and satellite TV as well as the internet has allowed audio and video programming to reach mass audiences without regard to FCC regulations, as the FCC has no jurisdiction over these media. When *The Howard Stern Show* was on broadcast radio, the FCC frequently fined radio stations that carried the program for airing material the FCC deemed to be indecent. In 2006, the program moved to satellite radio, placing it beyond the reach of the FCC. It is also true that public attitudes about profanity have changed dramatically since the *Pacifica* case was decided in 1978. Today, it is common to hear profane language on broadcast TV and radio, and the FCC rarely takes action against such programs.

The Internet and Social Media: Section 230 and FOSTA-SESTA

The advent of the Internet and, in particular, social media accessible by smartphones has dramatically shifted the national conversation about First Amendment freedoms. Republicans and conservatives complain of censorship by the giant internet companies and social media platforms. According to conventional constitutional interpretation, they are private forums and, thus, able to set the rules of discourse without running afoul of the First Amendment.[124] In June 2021, former President Donald Trump announced he was suing Facebook, Twitter, and Google for censoring his speech by banning him from their platforms. The former president claimed these bans amounted a violation of the First Amendment. Precedent would suggest this suit might well be dismissed for failure to state a cause of action. After all, the First Amendment limits government, not private companies like Twitter, Facebook, and Google.

As of 2022, Section 230 of the federal Communications Decency Act provides broad protections from civil suits. Section 230 specifically states that: "No provider or user of an interactive computer service shall be treated as the publisher or speaker of any information provided by another information content provider."[125] Accordingly, Section 230 has essentially allowed "big tech" companies to regulate their own content—which might involve deciding whether or not to block certain postings or users—without fear of civil or criminal liability. During his time in office, President Trump, expressing concern over censorship, lobbied unsuccessfully for Congress to repeal Section 230. Additionally, some Democrats have called for reforming Section 230 as a means of motivating tech companies to take steps to halt speech that incites hatred or violence.

There is one key limitation on the scope of Section 230, which results from a 2018 law passed by Congress. This law is known as FOSTA-SESTA.[126] The acronym represents an amalgam of a House bill known as the Fight Online Sex Trafficking Act (FOSTA) and a Senate bill known as the Stop Enabling Sex Traffickers Act (SESTA). A combined versions of these bills passed by a 388–25 vote in the House and a 97–2 vote in the Senate in 2018 before being signed into law by President Trump. This law amended Section 230 of the Communications Decency

Act and a 1910 federal prostitution law called the Mann Act. According to one scholar, these amendments "abrogate[ed] previous interpretations that construed § 230 as an impervious shield for internet providers, even those who aided sex traffickers."[127] FOSTA-SESTA subjects all websites to criminal and civil penalties if they are found to be "knowingly assisting, facilitating, or supporting sex trafficking" and creates the possibility of criminal charges against internet providers under the Mann Act if they are found to "promote or facilitate prostitution" or demonstrate "reckless disregard of the fact that such conduct contributed to sex trafficking."

Following the passage of FOSTA-SESTA, some websites, including the well-known Craigslist, removed their "personals" listings—out of fear that such content could subject the website's owners to criminal or civil liability related to prostitution or human-trafficking offenses. Yet a 2021 report from the Government Accountability Office (GAO) indicated that only one criminal prosecution had been brought by the Department of Justice under FOSTA-SESTA in the three years immediately following its passage. Part of the reason for that low number could be that existing laws related to racketeering and money laundering have been employed to address human trafficking.[128]

Clearly, human trafficking is a serious issue for society to confront, as noted in a report from the U.S. State Department, which indicated the number of worldwide victims of sex trafficking had more than doubled from 2011 to 2017, with the specific number of victims exceeding 100,000.[129] However, critics of FOSTA-SESTA suggest the law has done little to curtail sex trafficking and has instead shifted communications surrounding such activity to other channels—perhaps including dangerous face-to-face encounters—thereby making it more difficult for law enforcement to launch investigations.[130]

It is worth considering whether Congress, using its legislative power under Section 5 of the Fourteenth Amendment, can and should enact other laws setting the ground rules for online discourse—or if such activity amounts to a form of censorship that is subject to attack on First Amendment grounds. In particular, some scholars have raised concerns about potential First Amendment violations related to government censorship of internet content under FOSTA-SESTA, but owing to the lack of federal prosecutions under the statute, court review has not occurred.[131]

Beyond this federal legislation, nearly all states have created the crime of cyberstalking to address harassment in online forms. In 2021, Florida went a step further, making it a crime to publish someone's personal information—such as name, phone number, and home address—on the internet, an act commonly known as "doxing." State laws such as this are also likely to be reviewed by courts in the coming years.

Can Government Prevent "Big Tech" from Censoring Social Media?

In 2022, legislators in Texas passed a law aimed at limiting the ability of social media companies to censor the posts created by users of their websites. Although the Fifth Circuit allowed the law to take effect, the Supreme Court stayed the lower court's ruling.[132] The high Court's majority was comprised of a unique coalition that included Chief Justice Roberts, joined by fellow conservative justices Kavanaugh and Barrett as well liberal justices Breyer and Sotomayor. In dissent, Justice Alito spoke of "the power of dominant social media corporations to shape public discussion on the important issues of the day." Legal briefs filed with the Court by the group opposing the law spoke of "an unprecedented assault on the editorial discretion of private websites," adding that the law "would compel platforms to disseminate all sorts of objectionable viewpoints—such as Russia's propaganda claiming that its invasion of Ukraine is justified, ISIS propaganda claiming that extremism is warranted, neo-Nazi or KKK screeds denying or supporting the Holocaust, and encouraging children to engage in risky or unhealthy behavior. ..." A similar law in Florida would have banned social media companies from blocking content emanating from political candidates or media outlets—but that law's implementation was halted by the Eleventh Circuit in 2022.[133] Judge Kevin Newsom's opinion for that 3-0 majority said, "Put simply, with minor exceptions, the government can't tell a private person or entity what to say or how to say it." He also observed that "... it is substantially likely that social media companies—even the biggest ones—are private actors whose rights the First Amendment protects."

Commercial Speech

Commercial speech has been defined by the Supreme Court as "expression related solely to the economic interests of the speaker and its audience."[134] In 1976, the Court noted it had not "denied protection on the ground that the speech in issue was 'commercial speech'" and, moreover, indicated there is a First Amendment right for consumers to "receive information and ideas."[135] However, subsequent cases have made it clear the right to express a commercial message is protected at a lesser level than other forms of speech, such as political speech. As Justice Scalia once noted, commercial speech holds a "subordinate position in the scale of First Amendment values."[136]

In 1980, in a case that clarified the scope of commercial speech safeguards, the Supreme Court created a four-part test for addressing the constitutionality of commercial speech. The first prong establishes a threshold for First Amendment protection; it indicates that commercial speech should "concern lawful activity and not be misleading." Next, there needs to be a showing that "the asserted government interest is substantial." Finally, the Court will assess "whether the regulation directly advances the governmental interest asserted" and then "whether [the regulation] is not more extensive than is necessary to serve that interest."[137]

Using this test, the Supreme Court has struck down a Rhode Island law that banned the advertising of liquor prices,[138] and in a separate case, it ruled in favor of Coors Inc., which challenged a federal law that prevented beer labels from displaying a beer's alcohol content.[139] In terms of its applicability to criminal justice contexts, the commercial-speech doctrine could impact how a protestor is treated if their message relates

COMMERCIAL SPEECH: Speech that relates to the economic interests of the speaker and which is often protected by the Supreme Court at a lower level than other types of speech, such as political speech.

to commercial, as opposed to political, activity. Beyond that, enforcement of zoning regulations in regard to signs posted by businesses could invoke the commercial speech doctrine as well.

THE CONSTITUTION IN ACTION
The Stolen Valor Act: Is False Speech Worthy of Protection?

Originally passed by Congress in 2005, the Stolen Valor Act made it a federal crime for a person to make false claims about receiving a military medal. One prosecution under this law involved a man named Xavier Alvarez, who served on the Water District Board of Claremont, California. He publicly made false claims about earning a Congressional Medal of Honor, and prosecutors brought his case to trial in federal district court. After Alvarez was found guilty of violating the Stolen Valor Act, his conviction was overturned by the Supreme Court of the United States—in a ruling that seemed to provide protection for "false speech." Although there was no majority opinion for this 6–3 decision, Justice Kennedy's plurality opinion offered an important advisory statement: "The remedy for speech that is false is speech that is true. … This is the ordinary response in a free society."[140] In essence, Kennedy's point was that instead of government taking steps to punish false speech, maintaining the free exchange of ideas—regardless of veracity—was essential.

Following this decision, the Stolen Valor Act was amended in 2013 to make it a crime to lie about military service with the intent to profit from the lie. Overall, the *Alvarez* decision could have implications for false statements made by political candidates, since the case indicates such statements are likely to merit First Amendment protection.

Expression and Assembly in the Public Forum

One of the most difficult problems for law enforcement agencies is maintaining public order and safety without trampling the rights of those who assemble and express themselves in public. The First Amendment guarantees "the right of the people peaceably to assemble." Obviously, public assemblies can become disorderly, and even violent, and speakers addressing crowds sometimes provoke such disorder. A speaker can be arrested for incitement to riot but only when there is actual violence or imminent lawless action. The same standard applies to assemblies; there must be actual violence or imminent lawless action before a public gathering can be declared an unlawful assembly. To protect First Amendment rights, courts must closely scrutinize convictions for unlawful assembly, disorderly conduct, and incitement to riot stemming from demonstrations in the public forum.

PUBLIC FORUM: Open areas of land that are maintained by government, such as public parks, sidewalks, and town squares, which courts have traditionally protected for public gatherings and open displays of expression.

Public, Nonpublic, and Private Forums

A public forum is a space historically associated with public assemblies or designated by government as a venue for assembly and expression.

Public streets, parks, and the grounds outside public buildings, such as courthouses, state capitols, executive offices, and so on, are generally considered to be public forums. Speech in such areas—particularly political speech—is likely to be protected through the lens of strict scrutiny. Writing in *Hague v. Committee for Industrial Organization* (1939),[141] Justice Owen J. Roberts observed the following:

> Wherever the title of streets and parks may rest, they have immemorially been held in trust for the use of the public and, time out of mind, have been used for purposes of assembly, communicating thoughts between citizens, and discussing public questions. Such use of the streets and public places has, from ancient times, been a part of the privileges, immunities, rights, and liberties of citizens.

Not all public properties qualify as a public forum, however. As the Supreme Court recognized in 1981,[142] "... the First Amendment does not guarantee access to property simply because it is owned or controlled by the government." Military bases, courtrooms, prisons, airport terminals, and law enforcement offices are obvious examples of government facilities that are considered by the courts to be **nonpublic forums**. In *International Society for Krishna Consciousness, Inc. (ISKCON) v. Lee* (1992),[143] the Supreme Court held that an airport terminal is a nonpublic forum; thus, a ban on solicitation of money therein was to be judged by a general reasonableness standard—not by traditional First Amendment standards connected to strict scrutiny. More specifically, the **rational basis test** was used; this is a test that tends to favor the government by requiring the government to show two things: a "legitimate interest" (which is a lesser standard than the compelling interest required under strict scrutiny) and a "rational relationship" between the legitimate interest and the government action. Narrow tailoring, a key component of strict scrutiny, is not required. With its decision in the *ISKCON* case, the Supreme Court upheld a ban on the repetitive solicitation of funds in the three major airports in New York City and New Jersey—ostensibly because of a rational relationship between that action and a legitimate government interest in promoting efficient travel. It seems unlikely that the promotion of efficient travel would have amounted to a compelling interest if strict scrutiny had been used. As a result, the choice of test—as determined by the nature of the forum in which expression occurs—can play a crucial role in shaping the contours of free speech protections.

NONPUBLIC FORUM: A government-controlled area also designated for a specific purposes and to which access can be restricted, such as an airport; speech and assembly rights in such places may be protected by courts at lesser levels than in traditional open spaces like public forums.

RATIONAL BASIS TEST: A deferential test through which courts evaluate the constitutionality of government action impinging on individual rights and liberties by determining if it is rationally related to a legitimate government interest.

At first glance, the distinction between a public and private forum seems straightforward, but it can be problematic. Consider the following example. During the 1960s, college campuses were commonly the setting for antiwar and civil rights demonstrations. Most campuses have a quadrangle or some other central green space that is frequently used for various kinds of gatherings. That space is easily identifiable as a public forum. It is also obvious that the dean's office, a classroom, or a dormitory would be considered a nonpublic forum. But what about the exterior spaces around university buildings where loud demonstrations might be disruptive to students and faculty? In *Grayned v. City of Rockford* (1972),[144] the Supreme Court upheld a local ordinance that prohibited making noise near a school that disturbs the operations of the school. "The crucial question," the Court said, "is whether the manner of expression is basically compatible with the normal activity of a particular place at a particular time."

THE CONSTITUTION IN ACTION
The January 6th Capitol Riot

On January 6, 2021, as members of the U.S. Congress were in the process of certifying the Electoral College victory of President-Elect Joe Biden, a mob consisting of hundreds of people forced its way past U.S. Capitol Police and into the halls of the U.S. Capitol building—marking the first widespread breach of the structure since the War of 1812. Members of Congress were forced into a lockdown, and five deaths were reportedly linked to this insurrection. In July and August of 2021, testimony by members of the U.S. Capitol Police in front of the House Select Committee on the January 6 Attack would reveal the brutality of the assaults they faced that day—which included being Tased and beaten with nearby objects—as the officers attempted to protect members of Congress and property housed within the Capitol building.

The mob consisted primarily of pro-Trump supporters, many of whom were inspired by false claims of election fraud. Some of these individuals had been in attendance when President Trump and other politicians spoke nearby in Washington, D.C., earlier in the day. Those who had gathered to demonstrate on the grounds outside of the U.S. Capitol and in other nearby outdoor spaces were likely in a public forum, and thus, their presence and protesting probably would be protected by the First Amendment. Because the Capitol building is a nonpublic forum, those who forcibly entered the building will find it difficult to raise a claim of freedom of assembly or expression.

Accordingly, in the months following the January 6th attack, more than 600 arrests were made by federal officials, with many individuals located by law enforcement as a result of social media posted that boasted about being present inside the Capitol. Some of the most common federal criminal charges levied included the following: civil disorder; obstruction of an official proceeding; entering and remaining in a restricted building or grounds; disorderly and disruptive conduct in a restricted building or grounds; disorderly conduct in a Capitol building; parading, demonstrating or picketing in a Capitol building; assaulting, resisting or impeding certain officers; obstruction of law enforcement; and acts of physical violence on the Capitol grounds.

Designated and Limited Public Forums

Meeting rooms, auditoriums, gymnasiums, amphitheaters, and other such facilities, if they are made available to the public for meetings or performances, are considered designated public forums. The First Amendment applies to such forums in the same way it applies to traditional public forums. The limited public forum is a subcategory of the designated public forum. A classroom on a state university campus is normally a nonpublic forum. However, if the university invites a certain group (e.g., K–12 teachers) to come to that classroom for a meeting, the room becomes a limited public forum. As the Supreme Court recognized in 1995, "confining a forum to the limited and legitimate purposes for which it was created may justify the State in reserving it for certain groups or for the discussion of certain topics."[145] But having created a limited public forum, the government cannot discriminate against participants based on their viewpoint. For example, in *Good News Club v. Milford Central School*,[146] the Supreme Court held that a public school that allowed student clubs to use its facilities after-hours could not deny access to a religious club. Writing for the Court, Justice Thomas concluded that "the exclusion of the Good News Club's activities ... constitutes unconstitutional viewpoint discrimination."

Private Forums

Buildings, facilities, and outdoor spaces owned by private entities are not subject to the First Amendment; therefore, there is no federal constitutional right to assemble or engage in expressive conduct in such **private forums**. A shopping mall is typically considered to be a private forum; the owners of the mall have every right to control expressive activities therein. In *Lloyd Corporation v. Tanner* (1972),[147] the Supreme Court observed that a privately owned shopping center does not "lose its private character merely because the public is generally invited to use it for designated purposes." Nevertheless, a state may interpret its own constitution more broadly in this respect and may designate the common areas of malls and shopping centers as public forums.[148] If so, state courts must also rely on their respective state constitutions when adjudicating cases involving assembly or expression in such areas.

Critical Infrastructure Trespass Bills: A New Private Forum?

As we have seen, the ability to exercise First Amendment assembly and speech rights in a given place can depend on whether that particular location is classified as a public or private forum. Recently, some state legislatures have taken steps to limit access to areas known as "critical infrastructure sites" by passing laws that, in effect, delineate these areas as private forums subject to trespassing laws.

The Department of Homeland Security defines "critical infrastructure" by saying it "includes the vast network of highways, connecting bridges and tunnels, railways, utilities, and buildings necessary to maintain normalcy in daily life. Transportation, commerce, clean water and

DESIGNATED PUBLIC FORUM: A government-controlled facility that has been made available to the public for certain uses, such as for meeting or performances; these often include meeting rooms, auditoriums, gymnasiums, and amphitheaters that might otherwise be closed to the public.

LIMITED PUBLIC FORUM: A subcategory of the *designated public forum*; a facility made available for use by a specific group but to which other groups must be allowed access in an effort to accommodate expression of different viewpoints; an example would be a classroom on a public university campus that has been opened for use by an outside group.

PRIVATE FORUM: A building, facility, or outdoor space owned by a private entity, such as a shopping mall; constitutional protections do not confer assembly or speech rights in such settings.

JURISPRUDENCE

The Supreme Court Limits the Rights of Protestors
Adderley v. Florida, 385 U.S. 39 (1966)

In 1966, the Supreme Court considered a case that originated when Harriet Adderley and thirty-one other students from Florida A&M University were arrested and convicted for trespassing after they held a demonstration on the grounds of the jail in Leon County, Florida. Their purpose was to protest the arrest of some of their fellow students who had participated in a civil rights protest the previous day. The demonstration was confined to the grounds outside the jail. At no time did the students attempt to enter the jail or impede vehicular traffic in and out of the jailhouse grounds. Were they exercising their constitutional rights or trespassing on government property? The answer depended upon whether the space they occupied qualified as a public or nonpublic forum.

Justice Hugo Black delivered the opinion of the Court, which ruled against the students by suggesting, "Nothing in the Constitution of the United States prevents Florida from even-handed enforcement of its general trespass statute against those refusing to obey the sheriff's order to remove themselves from what amounted to the curtilage of the jailhouse." Douglas also deferred to the state's interpretation of how to control its own land, noting, "The State, no less than a private owner of property, has power to preserve the property under its control for the use to which it is lawfully dedicated. For this reason, there is no merit to the petitioners'

argument that they had a constitutional right to stay on the property, over the jail custodian's objections. ..." He went on to say, "Such an argument has as its major unarticulated premise the assumption that people who want to propagandize protests or views have a constitutional right to do so whenever and however and wherever they please. ... The United States Constitution does not forbid a State to control the use of its own property for its own lawful nondiscriminatory purpose."

In dissent, Justice William O. Douglas hypothesized about the long-term ramifications of this decision by stating, "Today, a trespass law is used to penalize people for exercising a constitutional right. Tomorrow, a disorderly conduct statute, a breach of the peace statute, a vagrancy statute will be put to the same end." Justice Douglas also recognized that the content of the speakers' message likely influenced the police response; to this point, he observed: "It is said that the sheriff did not make the arrests because of the views which petitioners espoused. That excuse is usually given, as we know from the many cases involving arrests of minority groups for breaches of the peace, unlawful assemblies, and parading without a permit. ... [B]y allowing these orderly and civilized protests against injustice to be suppressed, we only increase the forces of frustration which the conditions of second-class citizenship are generating amongst us."

electricity all rely on these vital systems."[149] In practical terms, these locations can include energy or utility companies, wastewater plants, telecommunications sites, railroad switchyards, oil or gas refineries, and more.

Overall, state laws vary in terms of what specific facilities are covered under the rubric of "critical infrastructure," but according to a 2020 article from the *National Conference of State Legislatures*, "Since 2018, at least 13 states—Indiana, Iowa, Kentucky, Louisiana, Mississippi, Missouri, North Dakota, Oklahoma, South Dakota, Tennessee, Texas, Virginia and West Virginia—have passed laws that either criminalize unlawful entry to critical infrastructure facilities or enhance the penalties associated with those offenses."[150] West Virginia's Critical Infrastructure Protection Act[151] makes it a misdemeanor to trespass "with the intent to interrupt lawful operations or to damage a critical infrastructure facility." The crime escalates to a felony if there is "an intent to vandalize, tamper with, or damage any equipment." Elsewhere, Ohio's SB33 makes is felony to trespass with intent to "tamper" with a critical infrastructure site,[152] and Indiana law makes the act of trespassing a on a critical infrastructure site a felony in and of itself.[153] Of course, terms like *damage* and *tamper* could be described as vague; as one scholar has noted, knocking over cones or setting fire to an oil pipeline could be treated as the same under such terminology.[154]

Certainly, preventing acts of vandalism at these locations is a matter of national security, given the crucial importance of energy and water, in particular, for the nation's overall infrastructure. Additionally, though, many of these state measures are specifically targeted at limiting protest activity at oil pipeline construction sites—which have been popular locations for protests by environmental groups and Native Americans, who fear adverse impacts related to pipeline construction near Indigenous lands. In fact, some scholars have hypothesized that Indigenous persons might be unfairly targeted by such laws.[155] Ultimately, these "critical infrastructure" laws can blur the lines between public forum and private forum—and courts will eventually untangle specific applications of First Amendment doctrines in these settings.

Graffiti, Street Art, and the Government Speech Doctrine

The term *graffiti* has historically been used to reference an unauthorized painting on public or private property—perhaps on the side of a building or on a public street or sidewalk. More recently, the terms *street art* or *street murals* have been applied to this activity as a means of showing broader acceptance for messages connected to this genre.

In the past, a city might have tried to curtail such activity. For example, in the early 2000s, New York City attempted to ban the sale of aerosol paint cans and broad-tipped markers and paint brushes to anyone under the age of 21—only to have the U.S. Court of Appeals for the Second Circuit deem this ban a violation of the First Amendment because it was not narrowly tailored to meet the state's compelling interest of stopping graffiti by juveniles.[156]

Recently, some cities have become more accommodating of street art. However, it is important for those who partake in such activity to understand the distinction between a private and public forum. For instance, painting the letters "BLM" on private property (that the painter does not own) would likely yield a vandalism charge. Even so, doing the same thing on a public sidewalk might not—although states and cities can vary dramatically in terms of how they treat this topic, with differences potentially connecting to details as specific as whether chalk or paint was used.[157]

New York City and Washington, D.C. are among the jurisdictions that require an individual or group to request a permit before painting on any public spaces—such as buildings or even roadways. Lawsuits arose in the summer of 2020 when New York City officials authorized the painting of a yellow "Black Lives Matter" mural on the street outside of Trump Tower on Fifth Avenue. Subsequently, a conservative women's group called Women for America First was denied a permit to paint its own mural on city streets and brought suit, claiming a violation of the First Amendment. In 2021, a federal district court judge ruled against the women's group and in favor of the city, noting that the government retained the right to control messages displayed directly on government property.[158]

The **government speech doctrine**, which is rooted in Supreme Court precedent, allows government entities to control messages placed on government property or emanating through channels of government. In 2015, the Supreme Court used the government speech doctrine to reject the First Amendment claims of

GOVERNMENT SPEECH DOCTRINE: The doctrine under which governmental entities can take positions on issues without facing First Amendment challenges for viewpoint discrimination.

TIME, PLACE, AND MANNER REGULATIONS: Restrictions on assembly or expression that are content-neutral and do not completely ban activity but, rather, place limitations regarding how or when assembly or speech can occur; such restrictions are usually evaluated by courts with the legal test of intermediate scrutiny.

INTERMEDIATE SCRUTINY: A legal doctrine through which courts evaluate time, place, and manner restrictions as well as sex discrimination cases; requires restrictions to be justified by a narrowly tailored significant (or substantial) government interest and the provision of ample alternatives for people to exercise their rights.

CONTENT NEUTRALITY: A government restriction on speech that does not discriminate based on viewpoint but, rather, applies equally to all expression, regardless of content.

a group called Sons of Confederate Veterans. The group claimed a free speech violation because the Texas Department of Motor Vehicles (DMV) had rejected a request for specialty-issue license plates with preprinted Confederate flag images on them. Even though the DMV had authorized other groups to create preprinted license plate images, the Supreme Court found there was no requirement to do the same for the Sons of Confederate Veterans. Specifically, Justice Breyer's majority opinion said, "When the government speaks, it is not barred by the Free Speech Clause of the First Amendment from determining the content of what it says," later adding, "it is entitled to promote a program, to espouse a policy, or to take a position."[159]

In a unanimous 2022 decision,[160] though, the Court held that the City of Boston violated the First Amendment when it rejected a group's request to temporarily fly a "Christian flag" on one of three flag poles outside of City Hall—even though over the past decade other groups had been permitted to fly their own banners. Rejecting application of the government speech doctrine, the majority opinion said that "we look at the extent to which Boston actively controlled these flag raisings and shaped the messages the flags sent," which the Court asserted was the "most salient feature of this case." The Court also considered "whether the public would tend to view the speech at issue as the government's," finding that it would not.

Time, Place, and Manner Regulations

The Supreme Court has long recognized that government may impose reasonable time, place, and manner regulations on assemblies and expression in the public forum. Such regulations typically are evaluated through the lens of a test called intermediate scrutiny, which means government action (1) must be content neutral, (2) must be narrowly tailored to further a substantial or significant government interest, and (3) must not "unreasonably limit alternative avenues of communication.[161] Using this test, in 2020, a federal district court upheld a Maryland executive order limiting gatherings of people to ten or fewer. This was said to be a valid time, place, and manner restriction. The judge said the order was justified by the substantial interest of stopping the spread of COVID-19 and that it left open ample alternatives for people to communicate through "the Internet, newspapers, or signs."[162]

Local governments often use a permitting process to regulate assemblies in public spaces. These permits are designed to allow police departments to make necessary accommodations with respect to traffic control and ensure that opposing groups will not occupy the same space at the same time. Recent history shows what can happen when ideologically opposed groups confront one another in public.

THE CONSTITUTION AND SOCIAL JUSTICE
From Charlottesville to George Floyd: Government Response to Protests

Over the past five years, several examples of protests involving competing groups have arisen. For example, tragic events unfolded in Charlottesville, Virginia in August 2017, when hundreds of people gathered over the course of two days to protest the decision of city leaders to remove a statue of Confederate General Robert E. Lee from a public park. In the build-up to this protest, statutes of Confederate veterans—and displays of Confederate flags—had become hotly-debated topics in many areas of the country. In some locations, laws or ordinances have been created to protect monuments from defacement, and Charlottesville would become a flashpoint for this topic, with members of White Nationalist and Neo-Nazi groups descending on the city to express discontent over the statue's removal.

On the night of Friday, August 11th, 2017, protestors carried tiki torches and Nazi flags, uttering racist chants as they marched through the city. Clashes between protestors and counter-protestors from Civil Rights groups would turn violent a day later. Governor Terry McAuliffe declared a state of emergency around noon on Saturday, and President Trump issued a Tweet just after 1 p.m. in an effort to halt violence. It read as follows: "We condemn in the strongest possible terms this egregious display of hatred, bigotry, and violence on many sides, on many sides. It's been going on for a long time in our country. … It has no place in America."[163]

Shortly thereafter, a car traveling backward at high speeds hit a crowd of counter-protestors in downtown Charlottesville, injuring 19 people and killing one, a woman named Heather Heyer. The driver, James Alex Fields, was found guilty of state charges for first-degree murder, hit and run, and malicious wounding; he also pled guilty to twenty-nine federal hate crime charges. He received multiple life sentences.

Three years later, widespread protests would ensue around the country, following the death of George Floyd on May 25, 2020. Although the majority of these gatherings were peaceful, some protests included instances of looting, arson, violence, property damage, and physical altercations among protestors and police or counter-protestors; in some cases, people were seriously injured or killed and businesses were destroyed. Some states called in the National Guard in an attempt to maintain order. Additionally, curfews were used in more than fifty cities, including Atlanta, Chicago, Denver, Minneapolis, Nashville, Memphis, Philadelphia, Los Angeles, Louisville, Salt Lake City, and Seattle.

Ultimately, many arrests occurred at protests over George Floyd's death, but analysis conducted months later indicated that the majority of lower-level charges were dropped—either by police departments or by prosecutors' offices, with some additional cases dismissed by courts. Cities with high rates of dropped cases following arrests related to George Floyd protests included the following: Dallas (95%), Detroit (93%), Houston (93%), Los Angeles (93%), Minneapolis (90%), New York (83% in Brooklyn and 64% in Manhattan), Philadelphia (95%), Portland (82%), and San Francisco (100%); these figures have led some to wonder if "mass arrest" had been used as a form of crowd control.[164]

In the aftermath of recent protest activity, some states have created laws designed to curtail violent demonstrations. Florida is among the states that passed laws addressed at protestors, and its 61-page "Combatting Public Disorder" law makes it a misdemeanor to engage in "mob intimidation" and a felony to damage any historical property (e.g., a Confederate monument) or engage in a "riot" (which is defined as three or more people engaging in violent or disorderly conduct).[165] Meanwhile, Tennessee has made it a felony to camp overnight on the grounds of its state capitol building. Elsewhere, laws passed in Arkansas, Iowa, and Oklahoma create penalties for blocking traffic during a protest, and the Oklahoma statute specifically absolves drivers of liability if they hit (and even injure) a protestor.[166] Judicial review of these laws—which could be targeting activity worthy of First Amendment protections in some cases—will likely ensue. Overall, though, the manner in which police treat protestors—in attempting to forge the delicate balance preventing violence and respecting First Amendment freedoms—will remain a salient issue for years to come.

Noise Ordinances

Police frequently receive complaints about loud parties late at night. Excessive noise that creates a nuisance to one's neighbors is considered a misdemeanor breach of the peace. Historically, the enforcement of such ordinances has been highly discretionary at the officer level. These ordinances have been attacked on vagueness grounds, but in principle, they are justified as time, place, and manner regulations.[167] To address the vagueness problem, some cities have enacted ordinances that proscribe noise at particular decibel (db) levels for different times of day. Often, outdoor rock concerts have to end by 11 PM or midnight to satisfy such ordinances.

In *Ward v. Rock Against Racism* (1989),[168] the Supreme Court upheld a New York City regulation limiting sound amplification of concerts in Central Park. Justice Kennedy, writing for the Court, found that the regulation was "narrowly tailored to serve the substantial and content-neutral governmental interests of avoiding excessive sound volume and providing sufficient amplification." Moreover, the regulation left open "ample channels of communication." Thus, it was determined to be a reasonable time, place, and manner regulation.

Curfews

Another type of government regulation that can raise claims related to freedom of speech, freedom of association, and freedom of assembly is a curfew. This is an order—usually given at the local level by a mayor—for people in a specified location to remain off the streets and in their homes after a certain hour. The power for local officials to issue such orders generally derives from state law that allows curfews in emergency situations, such as following hurricanes, floods, fires, riots, protests, or, more recently, in the face of an ongoing pandemic.

An infamous example arose in the City of Long Beach, California in April 1992. There, a curfew was imposed subsequent to a jury verdict acquitting four police officers in the beating of a man named Rodney King—an incident that was caught on videotape. In response to the not guilty verdicts, there was widespread rioting, looting, and setting of fires in Los Angeles County. That led the City of Long Beach to institute a curfew that mandated people to refrain from being present in public places between the hours of 7:00 p.m. and 6:00 a.m. On review, a California appellate court rejected First Amendment challenges and upheld this curfew. Key factors in favor of the ruling included the following: the curfew exempted police officers and firefighters; it only permitted the arrest of persons who refused direct requests from law enforcement officials to obey the curfew; the curfew was not aimed at any single group of individuals and, instead, applied equally to everyone throughout the City; finally, the curfew was considered a restriction on conduct, as opposed to the content of speech.[169]

Overall, neither federal circuit courts nor the Supreme Court have demonstrated an inclination to overturn curfew orders. For example, in 1994, the Supreme Court refused to hear the appeal of a Fifth Circuit decision that upheld a curfew placed on juveniles in Dallas, Texas. In 1999, the Court also denied certiorari in a curfew case from Virginia. In other 1990s cases, the Eleventh Circuit upheld use of curfews after a hurricane, and the D.C. Circuit upheld a curfew placed on juveniles within the District of Columbia.[170] No developments in recent years have altered this trend of allowing local governments to enact reasonable curfews in times of emergency.

Buffer Zones

Clinics that offer abortion services have been common targets of protest. Opponents of abortion often gather on the sidewalks leading to clinics. Sometimes, protesters have confronted women seeking the services of such clinics and have even tried to block their access. Obviously, freedom of speech and assembly do not give one the right to prevent another from exercising her constitutional rights. In *Madsen v. Women's Health*

Center (1994),[171] the Supreme Court upheld a Florida state court injunction that imposed a 36-foot buffer zone around the entrance to a clinic that performed abortions. However, the Court struck down other elements of the injunction, including a ban on the display of images observable by patients inside the clinic, because, in the words of Chief Justice Rehnquist, "these provisions sweep more broadly than necessary to accomplish the permissible goals of the injunction." This case stands for the proposition that injunctions against protesters must be strictly scrutinized by the appellate courts.

More recently, in *McCullen v. Coakely* (2014),[172] the Supreme Court struck down a Massachusetts law that banned picketers from being within thirty-five feet of the entrance of any abortion clinic. Using intermediate scrutiny, the Court found that the significant interest of protecting public safety and order near an abortion clinic was not narrowly tailored because it "burden[ed] too much speech" that had nothing to do with public safety (e.g., personal conversations, counseling, and peaceful distribution of literature). Chief Justice Roberts's majority opinion noted that political speech on public sidewalks is deserving of a high level of protection:

> It is no accident that public streets and sidewalks have developed as venues for the exchange of ideas. Even today, they remain one of the few places where a speaker can be confident that he is not simply preaching to the choir. With respect to other means of communication, an individual confronted with an uncomfortable message can always turn the page, change the channel, or leave the Web site. Not so on public streets and sidewalks. There, a listener often encounters speech he might otherwise tune out. In light of the First Amendment's purpose 'to preserve an uninhibited marketplace of ideas in which truth will ultimately prevail,' this aspect of traditional public fora is a virtue, not a vice.

Roberts made it clear that law enforcement retained the ability to enforce existing statutes that addressed "harassment" or "obstruction of entrances"; additionally, he indicated that the state legislature could pass a more narrowly tailored law, such as the eight-foot "buffer zone" upheld in *Hill v. Colorado*.[173]

Intermediate scrutiny was likewise used in an earlier case, *Frisby v. Schultz* (1988),[174] in which the Court upheld an ordinance that prohibited picketing in front of a residential home in the town of Brookfield, Wisconsin. The ordinance came in response to picketing that occurred directly outside the private home of an abortion doctor. The Supreme Court found a significant interest in protecting residential privacy with ample alternatives available to the protesters, who were free to picket in the town center, picket in front of the doctor's office, or distribute flyers.

A recent Supreme Court case on this topic is *Reed v. Town of Gilbert* (2015),[175] in which zoning regulations that impacted the size, number, and location of signs placed on properties in Gilbert, Arizona were found to violate the First Amendment. Although lawyers for the town officials claimed intermediate scrutiny should apply to this case, the Supreme Court found the restrictions to be "content-based" (as opposed to content neutral) because they applied differently based on the information contained in specific signs. Under the elevated standard of strict scrutiny, restrictions on the posting of signs in this town were deemed invalid.

The Court previously applied this concept in *Boos v. Barry*,[176] when it employed strict scrutiny in striking down a Washington, D.C. ban on picketers holding up signs within 500 feet of an embassy if a sign would bring the embassy's government into "public odium" or "public disrepute." Even though this appeared to be a time–place–manner restriction at first glance, because the Court found it to be a content-based restriction that turned on the nature of the message invoked, the analysis was escalated to include application of strict scrutiny. The Court ultimately ruled that the petitioners' First Amendment rights had been violated when they were denied a permit to hold signs outside the Soviet Union's embassy.

THE CONSTITUTION IN ACTION
Panhandling and the First Amendment

A classic example of time–place–manner restrictions comes in the form of regulations state and local governments have placed on panhandling. In and of itself, the act of asking another person for money—whether for a political campaign or for a cheeseburger—seems to derive First Amendment protection. For example, in *Village of Schaumburg v. Citizens for a Better Environment* (1980),[177] the Supreme Court's majority opinion said, "Solicitation for money is closely intertwined with speech" and that "solicitation to pay or contribute money is protected under the First Amendment." That idea was echoed in a political context in *Citizens United v. Federal Election Commission* (2010),[178] which recognized the free speech rights of corporations in the context of electioneering communications.

Yet in *International Society for Krishna Consciousness v. Lee* (1992),[179] the Court upheld restrictions on solicitation of money inside an airport. And in 1990, the Court refused to review a Second Circuit decision that upheld a ban on panhandling in New York City subways.[180] More recently, in *Cutting v. City of Portland* (2015),[181] the First Circuit struck down a Maine law that banned panhandling while on a median in a roadway. In the end, although an outright ban on asking for money seems unlikely to pass constitutional muster, reasonable time–place–manner restrictions on that activity are likely to be upheld by courts.

Freedom of Association

FREEDOM OF ASSOCIATION: A liberty that the Supreme Court has recognized as a correlate to the First Amendment rights to freedom of speech and assembly to protect the ability of individuals to gather with other like-minded individuals, often to form political alliances.

Nowhere in the First Amendment, or anywhere in the Constitution, is there mention of freedom of association. Yet it has long been recognized by the Supreme Court as an implied First Amendment right.[182] In *Roberts v. United States Jaycees* (1984),[183] the Supreme Court said that the "right to associate with others in pursuit of a wide variety of political, social, economic, educational, religious, and cultural ends" is implicit in the First Amendment. Nevertheless, in *Roberts*, the Court upheld a Minnesota law that required a civic group to accept women as members, finding the state had a compelling interest in eradicating sex discrimination and that this interest was unrelated to the suppression of speech. In later cases, the Court reaffirmed this precedent, leading to civic groups and social clubs across the country opening membership to women.[184] However, in *Hurley v. Irish American Gay, Lesbian, and Bisexual Group of Boston* (1995),[185] the Court held that the State of Massachusetts could not force the private organization that runs Boston's annual St.

Patrick's Day parade to accept an LGBT group as a participant in the parade. Given the sponsor's disapproval of homosexuality, the majority held that forcing them to accept LGBT participants would violate their First Amendment rights.

A key contemporary debate surrounding freedom of association connects to the efforts of some states to punish even peaceful protestors if other people around them turn violent—a form of "guilt by association." In its 1982 decision in *NAACP v. Claiborne Hardware Co.*,[186] the Supreme Court noted there should be no liability for damages placed upon nonviolent peaceful activity, even if there are indirect links to adverse impacts. The majority opinion from Justice Stevens declared that "the Court has consistently disapproved governmental action imposing criminal sanctions or denying rights and privileges solely because of a citizen's association with an unpopular organization." Justice Stevens also directly addressed the idea of protection for political association by saying, "We have not been slow to recognize that the protection of the First Amendment bars subtle, as well as obvious, devices by which political association might be stifled. Thus, we have held that forced disclosure of one's political associations is ... inconsistent with the First Amendment's guaranty of associational privacy"; he added that "guilt by association is a philosophy alien to the traditions of a free society and the First Amendment itself."

First Amendment Rights of Public Employees

Unlike private companies, which can limit their employees' expressive activities, government agencies at all levels are subject to the strictures of the First Amendment. But can the First Amendment rights of public employees such as police officers, firefighters, and teachers be limited as a condition of employment? Historically, the answer to this question was a profound "yes." The classic judicial opinion in this regard comes from the Massachusetts Supreme Judicial Court, which, in 1892, upheld the firing of a police officer who violated a regulation that absolutely barred officers from soliciting contributions for political causes. Writing for the court (before he was a justice on the U.S. Supreme Court), Oliver Wendell Holmes, Jr. said the following:

> The petitioner may have a constitutional right to talk politics, but he has no constitutional right to be a policeman. There are few employments for hire in which the servant does not agree to suspend his constitutional rights of free speech as well as of idleness by the implied terms of his contract. The servant cannot complain, as he takes the employment on the terms which are offered him. On the same principle the city may impose any reasonable condition upon holding offices within its control.[187]

As a federal constitutional matter, that view eventually was discarded in favor of one in which the rights of public employees to express themselves on matters of public concern are balanced against the governmental interest in organizational efficiency and employee morale. The seminal case in this regard is *Pickering v. Board of Education* (1968),[188] in which the Supreme Court sided with a teacher who was fired for publishing a letter criticizing his employer—the local board of education. Justice Marshall's opinion for the Court concluded that, "absent proof of false statements knowingly or recklessly made by him, a teacher's exercise of his right to speak on issues of public importance may not furnish the basis for his dismissal from public employment."

The Court's analysis proceeded through two phases: (1) determining if the employee "spoke as a citizen on a matter of public concern"; and (2) assessing if the employer had "an adequate justification for treating the employee differently from any other member of the general public," such as to avoid disruptions in the workplace. These factors have become a litmus test for evaluating the constitutionality of job-related speech.

Rights of Police Officers and Other Law Enforcement Personnel

Not all speech is protected in the context of public employment, though. An instructive Supreme Court case is *Connick v. Myers* (1983).[189] In this case, an assistant district attorney in New Orleans was fired from her job based on the content of a questionnaire she created and distributed among coworkers. The questionnaire criticized transfer policies within the D.A.'s office. The Supreme Court ruled against her First Amendment claims, suggesting public employee speech is only worthy of protection when it involves a matter of "public concern." To this point, Justice White's majority opinion reiterated the core holding from the *Pickering* case by saying that "a public employee does not relinquish First Amendment rights to comment on matters of public interest by virtue of government employment."

More than two decades later, the Court revisited the issue of workplace speech in *Garcetti v. Ceballos*.[190] Ceballos worked as a prosecutor in the Los Angeles County District Attorney's Office, where he served under Gil Garcetti, who was the District Attorney. Ceballos relayed comments to a defense attorney that criticized how the D.A.'s office was approaching one particular case. As a result, Ceballos was later denied a promotion. He filed a lawsuit, claiming his First Amendment rights had been violated. However, the Supreme Court ruled against him, finding that "job-related speech" can result in disciplinary action—and since criticism of how a case was being handled by another prosecutor in his office was patently a job-related action, he was not protected from an adverse employment action.

Specifically, Justice Kennedy's majority opinion said that the speech at issue was made "pursuant to Ceballos' official duties." Therefore, Ceballos could not satisfy the first prong of the *Pickering* test. The opinion indicated the Court should be reluctant to take on a role that entails "judicial oversight of communication between and among government employees and their superiors in the course of official business." Justice Kennedy did, however, indicate other pathways besides the First Amendment for an employee in a similar situation, including state or federal whistleblower protection laws, state labor laws, or regulations related to improper termination.

In dissent, Justice David Souter pointed to precedent in which the Court ruled in favor of a government employee who was fired after raising complaints to a superior about the racial composition of a school's staff[191] and another case in which the Court found that a school board had violated the First Amendment by failing to allow nonunion members to speak at board meetings.[192]

FOCUS ON LAW ENFORCEMENT
The Supreme Court Protects an Intemperate Remark by a Police Officer

Ardith McPherson was fired from her job as a Deputy Constable in Harris County, Texas. The reason for termination stemmed from comments she made about the attempted assassination of Ronald Reagan in 1981.

Specifically, after President Reagan was shot, McPherson told a coworker, "Shoot, if they go for him again, I hope they get him." That comment was relayed to superiors, and she was fired. In *Rankin v. McPherson* (1987),[193] the

Supreme Court ruled that McPherson should be reinstated to her job because even though the speech could easily be perceived as distasteful, this firing amounted to a violation of her First Amendment rights. Justice Thurgood Marshall's majority opinion made use of the two-part test from the *Pickering* decision. Applying this framework, the Court found that (1) the speech was about a topic of "public concern" and (2) there was no concern related to this speech causing a disruption in the workplace. Beyond that, there was no evidence that imminent lawless action would result from the threat. Thus, McPherson prevailed and retained her position.

Other Speech-Related Considerations

The Supreme Court's First Amendment analysis in *United States v. National Treasury Employees Union* (1995)[194] is important for those officers who wish to accept money in exchange for making speeches or writing articles, even covering subject matter related to their job duties. In this case, the Court struck down part of a federal law called the Ethics in Government Act, which had banned federal employees from receiving any honoraria for speeches and articles. Justice Stevens's majority opinion found "serious doubt [regarding] the Government's submission that Congress perceived honoraria as so threatening to the efficiency of the entire federal service as to render the ban a reasonable response to the threat." Writing for the dissent, Chief Justice Rehnquist declared that the majority's "application of the First Amendment understates the weight which should be accorded to the governmental justifications for the honoraria ban and overstates the amount of speech which actually will be deterred."

More recently, in 2018, the Supreme Court held that a public employee cannot be forced to pay union fees if they choose not to do so, finding it to be the "compelled subsidization of private speech."[195] That case precludes the possibility of union fees being automatically deducted from a public employee's paycheck.

Overall, police officers and other law enforcement personnel would seem to retain the highest level of First Amendment protection when they speak on matters of public importance, as opposed to job-related speech. But the evaluation of situations in which these two categories collide, perhaps within the context of a Facebook post about a police shooting, could be a matter for future court cases to untangle. Finally, we should note that officers are subject to the same categories of prohibited speech that have been carved out through Supreme Court precedent, including defamation, obscenity, advocating imminent lawless action, and fighting words.

First Amendment Rights of Students

Although nothing in the Constitution distinguishes the rights of school children as distinct from the rights of other persons, Supreme Court case precedent has carved out specific principles to use as guidance in cases when students assert First Amendment rights in the face of school discipline.

The first "school speech" case in the Court's history addressed a common activity in most elementary school classrooms: the recitation of the pledge of allegiance. In *West Virginia State Board of Education v. Barnette* (1943),[196] the Supreme Court stated that the First Amendment guarantee for freedom of speech protected students who wanted to refrain from either saluting the American flag or saying the pledge of allegiance. As a result, suspensions for failing to take part in these activities were ruled to be unconstitutional.

As discussed earlier in this chapter, another major Supreme Court case that addressed speech in a school setting was *Tinker v. Des Moines* (1969). In this case, three students were suspended from school for wearing black armbands in protest of the Vietnam War. In reversing those suspensions, the Supreme Court noted that students do not "shed their constitutional rights at the schoolhouse gates" and, ultimately, found there was no likelihood of these armbands causing a disruption in the learning environment; in fact, other students at the school had actually worn Nazi armbands—without causing disruptions and without receiving suspension. However, a caveat for future cases appeared with the Supreme Court's declaration that rights of minors in a school setting may not be "coextensive" with rights in other public settings, with the key being whether a substantial disruption to the school environment is involved.[197]

Two subsequent cases from the 1980s, in fact, would see the Supreme Court rule against student speech in school settings. In *Bethel v. Fraser* (1986),[198] the Supreme Court upheld the suspension of a student who was disciplined for using vulgar language while speaking on stage at a school assembly. Later, in *Hazelwood v. Kuhlmeier* (1988),[199] the Supreme Court ruled that a school principal had the authority censor stories about teen pregnancy and divorce that students had written for a school newspaper. In deciding this case, the Court found that a school newspaper carried the "imprint" of the school and was akin to a "private forum"; furthermore, using the rational basis test, the Court said the school had a "legitimate interest" for the censorship: protecting the privacy of those mentioned in the articles.

Next, in *Morse v. Frederick* (2007),[200] the Court upheld disciplinary action taken against a student by the principal of a Juneau, Alaska, high school. The student, Frederick, had displayed a sign that said "Bong Hits 4 Jesus," during a school event and was suspended for ten days. Ultimately, the Supreme Court ruled against the student, with Chief Justice Roberts's majority opinion noting that the school had an "important, indeed, perhaps compelling interest" in preventing the promotion of drug use.

The use of that phrase—which had previously been written by Justice Scalia in a 19995 decision that upheld drug testing of high school football players—seemed to indicate use of a *hybrid level* of scrutiny that lies somewhere between strict and intermediate, as if a high school represents a unique entity somewhere between public and nonpublic forums.[201] In simple terms, Roberts's majority opinion indicated that speech in a school environment is deserving of less protection than, say, speech on a public sidewalk—particularly when taking into account the doctrine of in loco parentis, a Latin term that means "in place of the parents." Two years later, the Court applied similar logic when it denied cert in *Barr v. Lafon*,[202] a case in which the U.S. Court of Appeals for the Sixth Circuit upheld the decision of school officials who banned Confederate flag displays on the campus of William Blount High School in Maryville, Tennessee.

The high Court would revisit the matter of a high school student's speech with its 2021 decision in *Mahanoy Area School District v. B.L.*,[203] which addressed the scope of "off-campus speech." In this case, a high school cheerleader in Pennsylvania was disciplined by her school after she posted a curse word on the social media app Snapchat. Specifically, after being cut from her varsity cheerleading team, she posted, "Fuck Cheer." The post was made outside of school hours and while she was off of school property. Even so, she was suspended from the junior varsity cheerleading team for one school year. Her parents filed a lawsuit that alleged a First Amendment violation, and both the district court and the Third Circuit agreed, with the latter suggesting schools could never suspend students for off-campus speech based on the "substantial disruption" doctrine articulated in *Tinker v. Des Moines*.

The Supreme Court granted certiorari and the majority opinion affirmed that the student's suspension should be overturned. Justice Breyer's majority opinion made it clear that the doctrine of in loco parentis was inapplicable when speech occurs in an off-campus setting. However, the Court overturned the Third Circuit's rigid reliance on the "substantial disruption" approach, with Breyer leaving open the possibility of schools invoking suspensions for some kinds of off-campus speech. In particular, the majority opinion said that a school would need to illustrate a "special interest" to suspend a student for off-campus speech. Thus, even though that standard did not apply in the cheerleader case, disciplinary action taken against a student who posts some type of imminent threat against a school on social media could be deemed constitutional.

First Amendment Rights on College Campuses

College campuses certainly present different environments than high schools, and free speech controversies in college and university settings have long carried contentious connotations. An infamous incident related to the speech rights of college students occurred on May 4, 1970, when four unarmed students at Kent State University in Kent, Ohio were shot and killed—on their college campus—when members of the Ohio National Guard opened fire on a crowd that had gathered to protest U.S. military action in Vietnam. This tragic event marked the first time in U.S. history that any college student had ever been killed during an anti-war protest, and none of those who shot at the students were ever convicted of a crime connected to the incident.

Two subsequent Supreme Court cases would directly address speech protections on college campuses. In *Healy v. James* (1972),[204] the Court ruled in favor of students who were denied a permit to hold an anti-war protest at Central Connecticut State University. One year later, in *Papish v. University of Missouri* (1973),[205] the Court ruled in favor of a student who was expelled from the University of Missouri for distributing a so-called "underground newspaper" that contained controversial stories. In this per curiam opinion, the Court referenced its earlier ruling from *Healy v. James*, saying the following: "We think *Healy* makes it clear that the mere dissemination of ideas—no matter how offensive to good taste—on a state university campus may not be shut off in the name alone of 'conventions of decency.'"

However, two decades later, the Court indicated the commercial speech doctrine still applies in college settings. In *State University of New York v. Fox* (1989),[206] the Court ruled against a group of students who claimed their First Amendment rights were violated by a state law that prohibited them from holding parties for commercial product demonstrations in their dorm rooms. (State law specifically banned private commercial activity in all university facilities.) The Court referred to the student activity in question under the rubric of *Tupperware parties*, in reference to the plastic food storage containers that were often sold to college students, along with plates and glasses, in the 1980s—often occurring as a part of social gatherings. Using the commercial speech test discussed earlier in this chapter, the Supreme Court found the university had a substantial interest in "promoting an educational, rather than commercial, atmosphere on SUNY's campuses, promoting safety and security, preventing commercial exploitation of students, and preserving residential tranquility."

Subsequently, the Court's decision in *Rosenberger v. Rectors and Visitors of the University of Virginia* (1995)[207] made it clear that First Amendment protections dictate that if colleges and universities choose to offer funding to student groups, then access to such funding must not be restricted based on a group's particular message or point of view. Ruling in favor of a religious student group, Justice Kennedy's majority opinion spoke of a "danger … to speech from the chilling of individual thought and expression." Kennedy invoked the classical concept of liberal education:

> The quality and creative power of student intellectual life to this day remains a vital measure of a school's influence and attainment. For the University, by regulation, to cast disapproval on particular viewpoints of its students risks the suppression of free speech and creative inquiry in one of the vital centers for the nation's intellectual life, its colleges and university campuses.

Once again, language in the high Court's opinion offered a high level of protection for speech on college campuses.

Moreover, such safeguards seem to apply equally to university faculty, who were protected by the Supreme Court's 1968 decision in *Keyishian v. Board of Regents*.[208] In that case, New York's state legislature passed so-called "teacher loyalty" laws that required faculty members at public universities to sign statements declaring that they had not been previously—and were not currently—affiliated with any "subversive groups" that advocated "overturning" or "overthrowing" the United States government—with the Communist Party being an example of such a group. Striking down this requirement, Justice William Brennan's majority opinion noted, "Our Nation is deeply committed to safeguarding academic freedom, which is of transcendent value to all of us, and not merely to the teachers concerned. That freedom is therefore a special concern of the First Amendment, which does not tolerate laws that cast a pall of orthodoxy over the classroom."

In 2021, the Court's decision in *Uzuegbunam v. Preczewski*[209] went so far as to allow a former student at Georgia Gwinnett College to sue for "nominal damages" (generally meaning small dollar amounts) after campus police prevented him from speaking and distributing literature about his religious beliefs in a designated "free-speech zone" on campus. Even though campus officials had already reversed a policy that prevented this activity, the Court's decision allowed a lawsuit for monetary damages to move forward in regard to a violation of First Amendment rights. Overall, this decision continued a decades-long trend of Supreme Court cases providing rigorous shields for speech on college campuses.

Conclusion

Robust protections for freedom of expression, assembly, and press are essential for the survival of a democratic regime. After all, the free exchange of ideas—and the ability to speak openly and critically about government—is essential for individuals to participate effectively in the policy-making processes of a representative system.

Accordingly, since the earliest moments of the United States, such guarantees have been inscribed in the Bill of Rights, and over time, they have been rigorously protected by the Supreme Court. Repeatedly, the high Court has made it clear that even speech that offends is worthy of protection—as is symbolic speech (like wearing an armband), and conduct-imbued speech (like burning a flag), assembling in groups to protest actions of government, or reporting on controversial government activity through the press.

However, freedom of speech safeguards have never been considered absolute in the United States. The Supreme Court has carved out specific categories that are not deserving of First Amendment protection, including defamation of character, speech advocating imminent lawless action, fighting words, and obscenity.

Even beyond those prohibited categories of speech, there can be government regulations placed upon other types of expression and assembly—provided that courts accept the existence of an appropriately tailored government interest. Overall, context can dictate the level of protection afforded to a speaker. Two key factors typically play a role in the analysis: (1) the nature of a speaker's message and (2) the location in which they are speaking. For example, political speech in a public forum is likely to be protected at a high level, usually under the legal test of strict scrutiny. Yet other types of speech, such as commercial speech or conduct with expressive components, could be protected at lower levels—as could speech in nonpublic or private forums or speech in school settings.

The nature of a particular government restriction can also factor into First Amendment analysis. For instance, a typical time, place, and manner restriction only needs to meet the threshold of a significant government interest and provide a speaker with ample alternatives to relay a message; on the other hand, an outright ban on—or criminal charges for—expressive activity or assembly will likely be examined more strictly by courts. Overall, the appropriate legal test can vary from case to case, highlighting the complexity of First Amendment jurisprudence.

Contemporary issues connected to the First Amendment and social justice include how protestors are treated while exercising their rights—and how to appropriately punish protest activity that turns violent against people or property. Additionally, the ability of reporters to shield the identities of confidential sources remains the source of ongoing legal battles regarding the scope of free press protections.

In the end, crucial First Amendment provisions related to expression and assembly remain the "matrix" Justice Benjamin Cardozo described them to be 80 years ago in *Palko v. Connecticut* (1937), for these concepts provide a bedrock foundation undergirding the other constitutional protections we will discuss in later chapters.

Discussion Questions

1. The First Amendment says, "Congress shall *make no law* … abridging the freedom of speech, or of the press; or the right of the people peaceably to assemble …" (emphasis added). Does that language imply that those freedoms are to be regarded as absolutes?

2. Pennsylvania, like many other states, criminalizes *terroristic threats*. According to Pennsylvania Consolidated Statutes, Title 18, § 2706(a), "A person commits the crime of terroristic threats if the person communicates, either directly or indirectly, a threat to: (1) commit any crime of violence with intent to terrorize another; (2) cause evacuation of a building, place of assembly or facility of public transportation; or (3) otherwise cause serious public inconvenience, or cause terror or serious public inconvenience with reckless disregard of the risk of causing such terror or inconvenience." Is this statute subject to constitutional attack? If so, on what grounds?

3. Institutions of higher learning have an obligation to foster a safe environment where students can learn and grow. State colleges and universities are subject to the limitations found in the First Amendment; they are not permitted to abridge the freedom of speech. Would the following policy, enacted by a hypothetical state university, survive judicial review? What arguments can be made for and against the following policy? "A student who engages in expression of any form that threatens, harasses, stigmatizes, marginalizes, or otherwise victimizes another person on the basis of race, ethnicity, national origin, immigration status,

sex, sexual orientation, or gender identity, irrespective of whether the expression occurs on or off campus, is subject to reprimand, suspension, or expulsion, depending on the nature and severity of the offense."

4. Is flipping off a police officer a form of constitutionally protected symbolic speech? Or is it fighting words?

5. The hypothetical state of Arcadia enacted a law making it a felony for anyone to "publish or post online any photograph of a person under the age of 18 in a state of nudity or engaged in any sexual conduct." Joel Draco was convicted of violating the statute after he posted a series of explicit nude photos of children to a site on the dark web. Can he invoke the First Amendment doctrine of overbreadth in his defense?

6. Do regulations restricting advertising of tobacco products violate the First Amendment?

7. Does Congress have the legislative authority to regulate speech on social media and the internet? If so, what sort of regulation would be likely to survive judicial review under the First Amendment?

8. Consider a hypothetical local ordinance that provides the following: "When three or more persons gather and conduct themselves in a manner that threatens a disturbance of the peace, police may declare that gathering an unlawful assembly. If after an unlawful assembly has been declared by the police, members of that assembly refuse to comply with a police order to disperse, they are guilty of a misdemeanor punishable by thirty days in jail or a $500 fine or both." Would this ordinance be subject to a facial attack? On what grounds? Is it likely that the ordinance would survive a constitutional challenge?

9. Can you find examples of ways states attempt to punish nonviolent protestors in a manner that might be inconsistent with Supreme Court precedent regarding freedom of association?

10. If a police officer is disciplined by their department for the content of their speech, what factors will determine if that speech is protected under the First Amendment?

11. What legal standards have the Supreme Court crafted for speech in school settings? How do these standards differ from those used outside of school settings? How do college campuses differ from high schools in regard to protections for speech and assembly?

Endnotes

1 *Palko v. Connecticut*, 302 U.S. 319 (1937).

2 Hugo L. Black, *The Bill of Rights*, 35 N.Y.U. L.REV. 865, 880-81 (1960).

3 *Roth v. United States*, 354 U.S. 476 (1957) (Douglas, J., dissenting).

4 *Schenck v. United States*, 249 U.S. 47 (1919).

5 *Chaplinsky v. New Hampshire*, 315 U.S. 568 (1942).

6 *New York Times v. Sullivan*, 376 U.S. 254 (1964).

7 "The Government may ... regulate the content of constitutionally protected speech in order to promote a compelling interest if it chooses the least restrictive means to further the articulated interest." *Sable Communications v. FCC*, 492 U.S. 115 (1989).

8 *Washington State Grange v. Washington State Republican Party*, 552 U. S. 442, 449, n. 6 (2008).

9 *City of Houston v. Hill*, 482 U.S. 451 (1987).

10 *Gilk v. Cunniffee*, 655 F. 3d 78 (1st Cir. 2011).

11 *ACLU v. Alvarez*, 679 F. 3d 583 (7th Cir. 2012).

12 *Fields v. City of Philadelphia*, 862 F.3d 353 (3d Cir. 2017).

13 *Martin v. Rollins*, No. 19–1586 (1st Cir. 2020) (This decision indicated that a Massachusetts law that banned recordings of a conversation unless both parties to the conversation had given consent to be recorded could not be applied in the context of police–citizen interactions.).

14 Oklahoma HB 1643 (2021).

15 Helena Wegner, *Police blast Disney music to stop YouTuber from filming them in California, video shows*, Sac. Bee, Apr. 21, 2022.

16 *Herndon v. Lowry*, 301 U.S. 242 (1937).

17 *Thornhill v. Alabama*, 310 U.S. 88 (1940).

18 Alien Registration Act of 1940, popularly known as the Smith Act, Pub. L. 76-670, 54 Stat. 670, 18 U.S.C. § 2385.

19 *Dennis v. United States*, 341 U.S. 494 (1951).

20 *Yates v. United States*, 354 U.S. 298 (1957).

21 *Scales v. United States*, 367 U.S. 203 (1961).

22 *Brandenburg v. Ohio*, 395 U.S. 444 (1969).

23 *Fox v. Washington*, 236 U.S. 273 (1915).

24 *Giboney v. Empire Storage & Ice Co.*, 336 U. S. 490 (1949).

25 *United States v. Williams*, 553 U.S. 285 (2008).

26 *Williams v. United States*, 444 F. 3d 1286 (11th Cir. 2006).

27 *Elli v. City of Ellisville*, 997 F. Supp. 2d 980 (E.D. Mo. 2014).

28 *Obriecht v. Splinter*, 18-cv-877-slc (W.D. Wis. Apr. 23, 2019).

29 *State v. Luptak*, A-6074-97T1 (Superior Court of New Jersey Appellate Division, 29 July 1999).

30 *See* Meghan Neal, *Flashing headlights to warn of speed trap protected by the First Amendment: Judge*, New York Daily News, May 23, 2012.

31 *State of Oregon v. Hill*, Citation No. 034117 (Jackson Cty. (Ore.) Justice Ct. Apr. 9, 2014).

32 *Terminiello v. City of Chicago*, 337 U.S. 1 (1949).

33 *Gooding v. Wilson*, 405 U.S. 518 (1972). A year earlier, in *Cohen v. California*, 403 U.S. 15 (1971), the Court defined fighting words as "personally abusive epithets which, when addressed to the ordinary citizen, are, as a matter of common knowledge, inherently likely to provoke violent reaction."

34 *Lewis v. City of New Orleans*, 415 U.S. 130 (1974).

35 18 U.S.C. § 2332b(c)(1)(g).

36 18 U. S. C. § 875(c).

37 *Watts v. United States*, 394 U.S. 705 (1969).

38 *Elonis v. United States*, 575 U.S. 723 (2015).

39 The Court indicated the jury's reliance on a showing of negligence, the lowest level of mens rea (or "criminal intent"), was not sufficient to justify a conviction for a true threat. Therefore, the lower court's use of this standard, through asking the jurors to act as reasonable observers in discerning the "objective intent" of Elonis's Facebook postings, was flawed. The phrase "objective intent" is often used in criminal law to allow a "reasonable person" to view a situation from their perspective and discern if criminal intent can be ascribed to behavior in question. The Court indicated that use of this standard meant that jurors had not adequately assessed if Elonis was even aware that his "lyrics" could be construed as a "true threat," and thus, appropriate consideration of his "subjective intent"—which requires looking into the mind of the speaker—was lacking because only a "negligence" perspective was used. However,

there was disagreement among the justices as to whether a "reckless" or a "knowing" level of criminal intent would be acceptable for justifying a conviction in such a case; as a result, no set standard was offered for future cases.

40 International Covenant on Civil and Political Rights (ICCPR).

41 *R.A.V. v. City of St. Paul*, 505 U.S. 377 (1992).

42 *Matal v. Tam*, 582 U.S. ___ (2017).

43 Trademark Act of 1946, better known as the Lanham Act, Pub. L. 79-489, 60 Stat. 427, 15 U.S.C. §§ 1051-1072.

44 Quoting *United States v. Schwimmer*, 279 U.S. 644, 655 (1929) (Holmes, J., dissenting).

45 *Iancu v. Brunetti*, 588 U.S. ___ (2018).

46 *Matal v. Tam, supra* note 42 (The references to the "bedrock First Amendment principle" and "ideas that offend" were drawn by Kagan directly from this case.).

47 Examples of buffer zones include Illinois (200 feet), Iowa (1,000 feet), Missouri (300 feet), Nebraska (500 feet), Oklahoma (300 feet), and Texas (1,000 feet). The Respect for America's Fallen Heroes Act, Pub. L. 109-228, 120 Stat. 387, 38 U.S.C. § 101 requires protestors to be 300 feet from a federally controlled cemetery.

48 *Stromberg v. California*, 283 U.S. 359 (1931).

49 *Tinker v. Des Moines Independent Community School District*, 393 U.S. 503 (1969).

50 *Tinker v. Des Moines Independent Community School District*, 258 F. Supp. 971 (S.D. Iowa 1966).

51 *United States v. O'Brien*, 391 U.S. 367 (1968).

52 *Texas v. Johnson*, 491 U.S. 397 (1989).

53 Flag Protection Act of 1989, Pub. L. 90-381, 103 Stat. 777.

54 *United States v. Eichman*, 496 U.S. 310 (1990).

55 *Spence v. State of Washington*, 418 U.S. 405 (1974).

56 Earlier, the Court's decision in *Street v. New York*, 394 U.S. 576 (1969) set aside a conviction for malicious mischief under New York law stemming from Street's burning an American flag and simultaneously saying, "We don't need an American flag." This decision did not focus upon the act of the flag being burned but, rather, the use of Street's "constitutionally-protected" statement in the trial against him.

57 *Virginia v. Black*, 538 U.S. 343 (2003).

58 E.O. 20-04-15-01, April 15, 2020, Lawrence Hogan, Governor of Maryland.

59 *Antietam Battlefield KOA v. Lawrence J. Hogan*, Governor of Maryland, 461 F. Supp. 3d 214 (D. Md. 2020) (citing *Texas v. Johnson*, 491 U.S. 397 (1989)).

60 *Id.* (citing *City of Dallas v. Stanglin*, 490 U.S. 19 (1989)) (ruled that gathering for dancing was not an expressive act, and thus, a city ordinance limiting dance hall admission to those 14 and older was constitutional.).

61 *Minnesota Voters Alliance v. Walz*, Governor of Minnesota, 492 F. Supp. 3d 822 (D. Minn. 2020) (citing *United States v. O'Brien*, 391 U.S. 367 (1968) and *Jacobson v. Massachusetts*, 197 U.S. 11 (1905)).

62 *Regina v. Hicklin*, L.R. 3 Q.B. 360 (1868).

63 *Rosen v. United States*, 161 U.S. 29 (1896).

64 *Roth v. United States*, 354 U.S. 476 (1957).

65 *See, e.g., Memoirs v. Massachusetts*, 383 U.S. 413 (1966) (Brennan, J., plurality opinion).

66 *Bantam Books, Inc. v. Sullivan*, 372 U.S. 58 (1963).

67 *Jacobellis v. Ohio*, 378 U.S. 184 (1964) (Stewart, J., concurring).

68 *Miller v. California*, 413 U.S. 15 (1973).

69 *Jenkins v. Georgia*, 418 U.S. 153 (1974).

70   *Interstate Circuit, Inc. v. Dallas*, 390 U.S. 676 (1968) (Harlan, J., concurring and dissenting opinion).

71   Communications Decency Act of 1996, Pub. L. No. 104–104, 110 Stat. 133.

72   *Reno v. American Civil Liberties Union*, 521 U.S. 844 (1997).

73   *See* 47 U.S.C. § 223(d).

74   *New York v. Ferber*, 458 U.S. 747 (1982).

75   *Osborne v. Ohio*, 495 U.S. 103 (1990).

76   *Ashcroft v. Free Speech Coalition*, 535 U.S. 234 (2002).

77   Animal Crush Video Prohibition Act of 2010, Pub. L. 111-294, 124 Stat. 3177, 18 U.S.C. § 48.

78   *United States v. Richards*, 755 F.3d 269 (5th Cir. 2014).

79   U.S. Department of Justice, *Houston Man Sent to Federal Prison for Producing and Distributing Animal Crush Videos* (Aug. 19, 2016), https://www.justice.gov/usao-sdtx/pr/houston-man-sent-federal-prison-producing-and-distributing-animal-crush-videos.

80   *Barnes v. Glen Theatre*, Inc., 501 U.S. 560 (1991).

81   *Erie v. Pap's A. M.*, 529 U.S. 277 (2000).

82   *Renton v. Playtime Theatres, Inc.*, 475 U.S. 41 (1986).

83   *Cohen v. California*, 403 U.S. 15 (1971).

84   *People v. Boomer*, 655 N.W.2d 255 (M.I. 2002).

85   *Westmoreland v. Sutherland*, 662 F.3d 714, 718 (6th Cir. 2011).

86   *Wood v. Eubanks*, No. 3:18-cv-00168 (6th Cir., Feb. 8, 2022) (citing *Wilson v. Martin*, 549 F. App'x 309, 311 (6th Cir. 2013)).

87   *Hagedorn v. Cattani*, 715 F. App'x 499, 506 (6th Cir. 2017).

88   *Kennedy v. City of Villa Hills*, 635 F.3d 210 (6th Cir. 2011) (citing *Greene v. Barber*, 310 F.3d 889 (6th Cir. 2002).

89   *Harris v. United States*, 422 F.3d 222 (2005).

90   *King v. Ambs*, 519 F.3d 607 (6th Cir. 2008); *Schliewe v. Toro*, 138 F. App'x 715 (6th Cir. 2005).

91   An Act for the Punishment of Certain Crimes Against the United States, 1 Stat. 596 (1798).

92   The Debates in the Several State Conventions of the Adoption of the Federal Constitution, 553–554 (Jonathan Elliot ed., vol. 4 1876).

93   *Marbury v. Madison*, 5 U.S. 137 (1803).

94   Act of July 4, 1840, 6 Stat. 802 (1840).

95   Sir William Blackstone, Commentaries on the Laws of England 151–152 (vol. 4 1769).

96   *Near v. Minnesota*, 283 U.S. 697 (1931).

97   *New York Times Co. v. United States*, 403 U.S. 713 (1971).

98   *United States v. The Progressive*, 476 F. Supp. 990 (W.D. Wis. 1979).

99   *New York Times Co. v. Sullivan*, 376 U.S. 254 (1964).

100 *Curtis Publishing Co. v. Butts*, 388 U.S. 130 (1967).

101 *Gertz v. Robert Welch, Inc.*, 418 U.S. 323 (1974).

102 President Donald J. Trump, Comments Made During Media Coverage of Cabinet Meeting (Jan. 10, 2018).

103 James Madison, Madison Speech in the House of Representatives, Library of Congress, https://www.loc.gov/exhibits/creating-the-united-states/interactives/bill-of-rights/speech/enlarge3-transcribe.html.

104 *Gertz v. Robert Welch, Inc.*, 418 U.S. 323 (1974).

105 Dave Mistich, *Conspiracy Theorist Alex Jones Ruled Liable in Sandy Hook Defamation Case*, NPR (Nov. 15, 2021), https://www.npr.org/2021/11/15/1055864452/alex-jones-found-liable-for-defamation-in-sandy-hook-hoax-case.

106 Jury grants $45 million in punitive damages in Alex Jones defamation case, Texas Tribune, August 5, 2022, https://www.texastribune.org/2022/08/05/alex-jones-sandy-hook-punitive/

107 *Zemel v. Rusk*, 381 U.S. 1 (1965).

108 *Department of the Navy v. Egan*, 484 U.S. 518 (1988).

109 18 U.S.C. § 798.

110 Freedom of Information Act, Pub. L. 89–487, 80 Stat. 250 (codified at 5 U.S.C. § 552).

111 *U.S. Fish and Wildlife Services v. Sierra Club*, 592 U.S. ___ (2021) (Sierra Club sought access to rough drafts of a report created by the Fish and Wildlife Service about the impact that underwater cooling machinery had on marine life.).

112 *Food Marketing Institute v. Argus Leader Media*, 588 U.S. ___ (2019) (A media outlet sought disclosure of the names of businesses that accepted food stamps.).

113 *Branzburg v. Hayes*, 408 U.S. 665 (1972).

114 *Haig v. Agee*, 453 U.S. 280 (1981).

115 *Richmond Newspapers v. Virginia*, 448 U.S. 555 (1980).

116 *Press-Enterprise Co. v. Superior Court of California*, 464 U.S. 501 (1984).

117 *Presley v. Georgia*, 558 U.S. 209 (2010) (citing *id.*).

118 Radio Act of 1927, Pub. L. 69–632, 44 Stat. 1162.

119 Communications Act of 1934, Pub. L. 73–416, 48 Stat. 1064 (codified at 47 U.S.C. § 151).

120 47 U.S.C. § 151.

121 *Red Lion Broadcasting Co. v. FCC*, 395 U.S. 367 (1969).

122 18 U.S.C. § 1464.

123 *Federal Communications Commission v. Pacifica Foundation*, 438 U.S. 726 (1978).

124 *See, e.g., Manhattan Community Access Corp. v. Halleck*, 587 U.S ___ (2019) (The Court ruled that a private, nonprofit corporation that operated a public-access TV station is not to be considered a government actor, and thus, the First Amendment was not applicable to claims against the station by its employees.).

125 Communications Decency Act, 47 U.S.C. § 230.

126 Fight Online Sex Trafficking Act-Stop Enabling Sex Traffickers Act of 2018, Pub. L. 155-164, 132 Stat. 1253.

127 Emily Morgan, *On FOSTA and the Failures of Punitive Speech Restrictions*, 115 Nw. U. L. Rev. 503–548 (2020).

128 U.S. Government Accountability Office, Sex Trafficking, Online Platforms and Federal Prosecutions, Report to Congressional Committees (June 2021), GAO 21–385.

129 U.S. Department of State, Trafficking in Persons Report, 2016.

130 *The pitfalls of anti-sex-trafficking law give Congress a warning.* The Washington Post (Editorial Board). June 26, 2021, https://www.washingtonpost.com/opinions/2021/06/26/pitfalls-an-anti-sex-trafficking-law-give-congress-warning/

131 *See* Morgan, *supra* note 127 (a summary of criticisms of FOSTA-SESTA).

132 *Netchoice LLC v. Paxton*, 596 U.S. ___ (2022).

133 *Netchoice LLC v. Attorney General, State of Florida*, No. 21-12355 (11th Cir. 2022).

134 *Central Hudson Gas & Electric Corporation v. Public Service Commission of New York*, 447 U.S. 557 (1980).

135 *Virginia Pharmacy Board v. Virginia Consumer Council*, 425 U.S. 748 (1976).

136 *State University of New York v. Fox*, 492 U.S. 469 (1989).

137   *Central Hudson Gas & Electric Corporation v. Public Service Commission of New York, supra* note 134 (Using this test in this case, the Court halted an attempt by the Public Service Commission of New York to prevent utility companies from encouraging the use of electricity. This attempt by the state agency was said to violate the First Amendment.).

138   *44 Liquormart, Inc. v. Rhode Island*, 517 U.S. 484 (1996).

139   *Rubin v. Coors Brewing Co.*, 514 U.S. 476 (1995) (The law in question was the Federal Alcohol Administration Act of 1935, 49 Stat. 977.).

140   *United States v. Alvarez*, 567 U.S. 709 (2012).

141   *Hague v. Committee for Industrial Organization*, 307 U.S. 496 (1939).

142   *United States Postal Service v. Council of Greenburgh Civic Associations*, 453 U.S. 114 (1981).

143   *International Society for Krishna Consciousness, Inc. v. Lee*, 505 U.S. 830 (1992).

144   *Grayned v. City of Rockford*, 408 U.S. 104 (1972).

145   *Rosenberger v. Rector and Visitors of University of Virginia*, 515 U.S. 819 (1995).

146   *Good News Club v. Milford Central School*, 533 U.S. 98 (2001).

147   *Lloyd Corp., Ltd. v. Tanner*, 407 U.S. 551 (1972).

148   *Pruneyard Shopping Ctr. v. Robins*, 447 U.S. 74 (1980).

149   Department of Homeland Security, *Critical Infrastructure*, https://www.dhs.gov/science-and-technology/critical-infrastructure

150   Dan Shea, *Balancing Act: Protecting Critical Infrastructure and People's Right to Protest*, State Legislatures Magazine, July 21, 2020, https://www.ncsl.org/research/energy/state-policy-trend-protecting-critical-infrastructure-and-peoples-right-to-protest-magazine2020.aspx.

151   W. Va. Code §61-10-34

152   Ohio Senate Bill 33 (2021).

153   Indiana Senate Bill 471 (2019).

154   Kaylana Mueller-Hsia, *Anti-Protest Laws Threaten Indigenous and Climate Movements*, Brennan Center for Justice, Mar. 17, 2021, https://www.brennancenter.org/our-work/analysis-opinion/anti-protest-laws-threaten-indigenous-and-climate-movements.

155   *Id. See, e.g.*, South Dakota's SB 151 (2020) (The bill criminalizes trespassing at "construction areas," which could include pipelines. SB 151 makes it a misdemeanor to trespass onto critical infrastructure facilities and a felony if the trespass results in "a substantial interruption to infrastructure operations or other public services").

156   *Vincent v. Bloomberg*, 476 F. 3d 74 (2nd Cir. 2007).

157   *See* American Bar Association, *Understanding the First Amendment Limitations on Government Regulation of Artwork American Bar Association*, Jan. 2, 2017 (For further reading on restrictions related to public art displays, including relevance of commercial speech doctrines), https://www.americanbar.org/groups/state_local_government/publications/state_local_law_news/2016-17/winter/understanding_first_amendment_limitations_government_regulation_artwork/.

158   *Women for America First v. De Blasio et al.*, No. 1:2020cv05746 (S.D.N.Y. 2021).

159   *Walker, Chairman Texas Department of Motor Vehicles Board v. Texas Division*, 576 U.S. 200 (2015) (citing *Pleasant Grove City v. Summum*, 555 U.S. 460 (2009) (in the first portion of this quote)).

160   *Shurtleff v. City of Boston*, 596 U.S. ____ (2022).

161   *Clark v. Community for Creative Non-Violence*, 468 U.S. 288 (1984).

162   *Antietam Battlefield KOA v. Lawrence J. Hogan, Governor of Maryland*, 461 F. Supp. 3d 214 (D. Md. 2020).

163 @DonaldTrump, TWITTER August 13, 2021 (1:05PM)

164 *See* Tom Perkins, *Most Charges Against George Floyd Protestors Dropped, Analysis Shows*, The Guardian, Apr. 17, 2021 (Figures for New York City do not include more than 5,000 cases dropped by courts.), https://www.theguardian.com/us-news/2021/apr/17/george-floyd-protesters-charges-citations-analysis.

165 Florida HB1, Combatting Public Disorder (2021).

166 *See* PEW, *Eight States Enact Anti-Protest Laws*, June 21, 2021 (an overview of recently passed laws of this ilk), https://www.pewtrusts.org/en/research-and-analysis/blogs/stateline/2021/06/21/eight-states-enact-anti-protest-laws.

167 *See, e.g.,* *Grayned v. City of Rockford*, 408 U.S. 104 (1972) (struck down the city's anti-picketing ordinance as overly broad but upheld the city's anti-noise ordinance as narrowly-tailored to furthering the compelling interest of reducing disruptions to educational environments).

168 *Ward v. Rock Against Racism*, 491 U.S. 781 (1989).

169 *In re Juan C.*, 33 Cal.Rptr.2d 919 (Cal. Ct. App. 1994).

170 *See Qutb v. Strauss*, 11 F.3d 488 (5th Cir. 1993) (cert denied in *Qutb v. Bartlett*, 511 U.S. 1127 (1994)); *Schleifer v. City of Charlottesville*, 159 F.3d 843 (4th Cir. 1998) (cert denied in 526 U.S. 1018 (1999)); *Smith v. Avino*, 91 F.3d 105 (11th Cir. 1996); *Hutchins v. D.C.*, 188 F.3d 531 (D.C. Cir. 1999).

171 *Madsen v. Women's Health Center, Inc.*, 512 U.S. 753 (1994).

172 *McCullen v. Coakley*, 573 U.S. 464 (2014).

173 *Hill v. Colorado*, 530 U.S. 703 (2000).

174 *Frisby v. Schultz*, 487 U.S. 474 (1988).

175 *Reed v. Town of Gilbert,* 576 U.S. 155 (2015).

176 *Boos v. Barry*, 485 U.S. 312 (1988) (In this case, the Court upheld a separate ban on three or more persons congregating together within 500 feet of an embassy if law enforcement deemed the group to be "a threat to the security or peace of the embassy.").

177 *Village of Schaumburg v. Citizens for a Better Environment*, 444 U.S. 620 (1980).

178 *Citizens United v. Federal Election Commission*, 558 U.S. 310 (2010).

179 *International Society for Krishna Consciousness v. Lee*, 505 U.S. 672 (1992).

180 *Young v. New York City Transit Authority*, 903 F.2d 146 (2nd Cir. 1990).

181 *Cutting v. City of Portland*, Maine, 802 F. 3d 79 (1st Cir. 2015).

182 *NAACP v. Alabama ex rel Patterson*, 357 U.S. 449 (1958).

183 *Roberts v. United States Jaycees*, 468 U. S. 609 (1984).

184 *See Rotary International v. Rotary Club of Duarte*, 482 U.S. 537 (1987); *New York State Club Association v. City of New York*, 487 U.S. 1 (1988).

185 *Hurley v. Irish American Gay, Lesbian, and Bisexual Group of Boston*, 515 U.S. 557 (1995).

186 *NAACP v. Claiborne Hardware Co.*, 485 U.S. 886 (1982) (citing *Healy v. James*, 408 U.S. 169 (1972)).

187 *McAuliffe v. Mayor of New Bedford*, 29 N.E. 517 (Mass., 1892).

188 *Pickering v. Board of Education*, 391 U.S. 563 (1968).

189 *Connick v. Myers*, 461 U.S. (1983).

190 *Garcetti v. Ceballos*, 547 U.S. 410 (2006).

191 *Givhan v. Western Line Consolidated School District*, 439 U.S. 410 (1979).

192 *Madison Joint School District Number 8 v. Wisconsin Employment Relations Commission*, 429 U.S. 167 (1976).

193 *Rankin v. McPherson*, 483 U.S. 378 (1987).

194   *United States v. National Treasury Employees Union*, 513 U.S. 454 (1995).

195   *Janus v. American Federation of State, County, and Municipal Employees*, 585 U.S. ____ (2018).

196   *West Virginia State Board of Education v. Barnette*, 319 U.S. 624 (1943).

197   *Tinker v. Des Moines*, 393 U.S. 503 (1969).

198   *Bethel School District No. 403 v. Fraser*, 478 U.S. 675 (1986).

199   *Hazelwood v. Kuhlmeier*, 484 U.S. 260 (1988).

200   *Morse v. Frederick*, 551 U.S. 393 (2007).

201   *See Vernonia v. Acton*, 515 U.S. 646 (1995).

202   *Barr v. Lafon*, 538 F. 3d 554 (6th Cir. 2008).

203   *Mahanoy Area School District v. B.L.*, 594 U.S. ____ (2021).

204   *Healy v. James*, 408 U.S. 169 (1972).

205   *Papish v. University of Missouri*, 410 U.S. 667 (1973).

206   *Board of Trustees of State University of New York v. Fox*, 492 U.S. 469 (1989).

207   *Rosenberger v. Rectors and Visitors of the University of Virginia*, 515 U.S. 819 (1995).

208   *Keyishian v. Board of Regents*, 385 U.S. 589 (1967).

209   *Uzuegbunam v. Preczewski*, 592 U.S. ____ (2021).

Credit

CHAPTER 5

The First Amendment
Protections for Religious Freedom

"The Religion ... of every man must be left to the conviction and conscience of every man; and it is the right of every man to exercise it as these may dictate."

—James Madison, "A Memorial and Remonstrance" (1785)

Learning Objectives

After reading this chapter, you should understand the Supreme Court's jurisprudence as it relates to the Religion Clauses of the First Amendment, specifically the following:

1. Separation of church and state
2. The interpretation of the Free Exercise Clause
3. Religious assembly and expression
4. Religious objections to patriotic rituals and civic duties
5. Unconventional religious practices
6. Religion and the welfare of children
7. Religious objections to compliance with civil rights laws
8. Religion in the public workplace
9. The religious rights of prisoners

Key Cases

Everson v. Board of Education, 330 U.S. 1 (1947)

Abington School District v. Schempp, 374 U.S. 203 (1963)

Sherbert v. Verner, 374 U.S. 398 (1963)

Employment Division v. Smith, 494 U.S. 872 (1990)

Church of the Lukumi Babalu Aye v. City of Hialeah, 508 U.S. 520 (1993)

Gonzales v. O Centro Espírita Beneficente União do Vegetal, 546 U.S. 418 (2006)

Burwell v. Hobby Lobby Stores, 573 U.S. 682 (2014)

Introduction

ESTABLISHMENT CLAUSE: The first clause of the First Amendment, which prohibits government from establishing religion.

FREE EXERCISE CLAUSE: The second clause of the First Amendment, which protects an individual's right to exercise religious beliefs.

Prior the establishment of the United States in the late 1700s, for centuries, much of Europe was torn apart by religious persecution and warfare. To prevent that from happening in the newly-formed United States—and, in particular, to protect the rights of those who had fled to North America as a means of escaping religious persecution at the hands of the British— the framers of the First Amendment to the U.S. Constitution provided two distinct protections for religious freedom. Specifically, the text of the amendment states that "Congress shall make no law respecting an establishment of religion, or prohibiting the free exercise thereof. ..." The former clause is known as the Establishment Clause, often described as providing "freedom from" government imposition of religion upon the populace; the latter clause is termed the Free Exercise Clause and is said to preserve "freedom of" religion by preserving an individual right to religious exercise. In the modern era, both clauses have generated a sizable body of case law as courts have grappled with their application. In this chapter, we will explore the Supreme Court's Establishment Clause and Free Exercise Clause jurisprudence. We will devote more attention to the Free Exercise Clause because cases arising under that provision are much more likely to involve criminal prosecution. However, we also cover the Establishment Clause, as judicial precedent on this topic could be relevant if government officials attempt to foist religious principles upon society in the context of criminal statutes.

Beyond these provisions, we also should note that Article VI of the U.S. Constitution makes it clear that "no religious Test shall ever be required as a Qualification to any Office or public Trust under the United States." Thus, no local, state, or federal entity can require a religious statement or qualification as a condition of running for or holding elected office in this country. By the same token, no one can be disqualified from public office because they hold a ministerial position in a religion.[1] Overall, creating—and maintaining—a society in which people of different religious faiths could peacefully coexist was a paramount objective for the founders of this nation.

Separation of Church and State

Although the phrase "separation of church and state" does not appear in the text of the First Amendment, in 1802, President Thomas Jefferson expressed the view that the Establishment Clause was intended to build "a wall of separation between church and State."[2] Other scholars of that era echoed this principle, and in the 1830s, Alexis de Tocqueville observed that organized religion held "quiet sway" over the United States "because of the complete separation of church and state."[3] It would take more than a century, but in *Everson v. Board of Education* (1947),[4] the Supreme Court adopted President Jefferson's metaphor, and since then, separation of church and state has become part of the national lexicon. Writing for the Court in *Everson*, Justice Hugo summarized the import of the Establishment Clause as follows:

> ... [N]either a state nor the Federal Government can set up a church. Neither can pass laws which aid one religion, aid all religions, or prefer one religion over another. Neither can force nor influence a person to go to or to remain away from church against his will or force him to profess a belief or disbelief in any religion. No person can be punished for entertaining or professing religious beliefs or disbeliefs, for church attendance or non-attendance. No tax in any amount, large or small, can be levied to support any religious activities or institutions, whatever they may be called, or whatever form they may adopt to teach or practice religion. Neither a state nor the Federal Government can, openly or secretly, participate in the affairs of any religious organizations or groups, and vice versa.

SEPARATION OF CHURCH AND STATE: A principle that courts have found implicit in the Establishment Clause of the First Amendment, which indicates a bifurcation between government and religion.

Of course, Justice Black's litany did not cover all possible ways government practices might run afoul of the Establishment Clause, and in the modern era, the Supreme Court has decided numerous cases of this kind.

Sunday Closing Laws and Liquor Sales

Historically, many states prohibited businesses from operating on Sundays. In *McGowan v. Maryland* (1961),[5] seven store employees were prosecuted for violating a state law prohibiting most commercial activities on Sundays. The Supreme Court upheld the law against a challenge based in part on the Establishment Clause. Chief Justice Earl Warren wrote the Court's opinion, observing the following:

> The present purpose and effect of most of them is to provide a uniform day of rest for all citizens; the fact that this day is Sunday, a day of particular significance for the dominant Christian sects, does not bar the State from achieving its secular goals. To say that the States cannot prescribe Sunday as a day of rest for these purposes solely because centuries ago such laws had their genesis in religion would give a constitutional interpretation of hostility to the public welfare, rather than one of mere separation of church and State.

That same year, the Court upheld a similar law from Pennsylvania.[6] In both cases, the Court was unmoved by the fact that Jewish people and others who recognize Saturday as the Sabbath were placed at an economic disadvantage by the laws. Today, the issue is largely moot, as most of the Sunday closing laws have been repealed. However, some states, counties, and cities continue to restrict the sale or service of alcoholic beverages on Sundays—through statutes often known as "blue laws." Critics of such restrictions continue to argue that they violate the religion clauses of the First Amendment.

Religion and Public Education

Some of the most controversial decisions of the modern Supreme Court have involved religiously oriented practices in public schools. Of course, public schools are under the primary control of state and local governments, but in the *Everson* case, the Court held that the Establishment Clause applies to state and local governments, even local school boards, by way of the Fourteenth Amendment and the principle of incorporation.

The School Prayer Cases

In the 1960s, the Supreme Court under Chief Justice Earl Warren created a firestorm of controversy when it struck down the practices of prayer and Bible reading in the public schools. In *Engel v. Vitale* (1962),[7] the Court invalidated a New York Board of Regents policy that established the voluntary recitation of a brief generic prayer by children in the public schools at the start of each school day. Then, in *Abington School District v. Schempp* (1963),[8] the Court struck down the practice of teacher-led Bible readings and the daily recitation of the Lord's Prayer.

In the wake of *Abington School District v. Schempp*, federal judges across the country issued injunctions against prayer and Bible reading in the public schools. Given the popularity of these practices, it was not surprising that a torrent of criticism ensued.[9] Despite the blowback, the Supreme Court continued to reaffirm, and even expand, these decisions. For example, in *Wallace v. Jaffree* (1985),[10] the Court struck down an Alabama law that required public school students to observe a moment of silence "for the purpose of meditation or voluntary prayer" at the start of each school day. Seven years later, in *Lee v. Weisman* (1992),[11] the Court held unconstitutional the practice of inviting a member of the clergy to deliver a nonsectarian prayer at a public-school graduation ceremony. And in *Santa Fe School District v. Doe* (2000),[12] the Court struck down a public high school's policy of allowing students to elect a chaplain to deliver invocations before football games. Writing for the majority in the *Santa Fe* case, Justice John P. Stevens stated, "Even if we regard every high school student's decision to attend a home football game as purely voluntary, we are nevertheless persuaded that the delivery of a pregame prayer has the improper effect of coercing those present to participate in an act of religious worship."

Creationism v. Evolution

In 1925, John Scopes, a high school biology teacher in Tennessee, was convicted of teaching evolution in violation of state law. Forty-three years later, the Supreme Court struck down a similar statute of a neighboring state. In *Epperson v. Arkansas* (1968),[13] the Court ruled a state cannot "prevent its teachers from discussing the theory of evolution because it is contrary to the belief of some that the Book of Genesis must be the exclusive source of doctrine as to the origins of man." In response to this decision, Louisiana enacted a law prohibiting the teaching of evolution in public schools, unless it was accompanied by instruction in "creation science." In *Edwards v. Aguillard* (1987),[14] the Supreme Court declared the law unconstitutional. Writing for the Court, Justice Brennan concluded "the primary purpose" of the statute was "to endorse a particular religious doctrine," rather than further the legitimate interests of the state in fostering different points of view in the classroom.

Government Assistance to Religious Schools

In *Everson v. Board of Education* (1947), the Supreme Court upheld a policy allowing for reimbursement to parents who used public transportation to get their children to and from school—even private religious schools. The Court concluded that the policy "... does no more than provide a general program to help parents get their children, regardless of their religion, safely and expeditiously to and from accredited schools." In other words, the policy was valid because it was neutral regarding religion. Similarly, in *Board of Education v. Allen* (1968),[15] the Court upheld a New York law requiring public schools to lend textbooks free of charge to students in private schools, including religious schools. Justice Byron White's opinion for the Court relied heavily on the *Everson* precedent: "Perhaps free books make it more likely that some children choose to attend a sectarian school, but that was true of the state-paid bus fares in *Everson*, and does not alone demonstrate an unconstitutional degree of support for a religious institution." However, in *Lemon v. Kurtzman* (1971),[16] the Court struck down a Rhode Island law providing for state-paid salary supplements for teachers in private schools, most of whom taught in Catholic schools. The Court found that the arrangement fostered "excessive entanglement" between the state and religious institutions. The Court articulated a test to determine whether a public policy violates the Establishment Clause. According to what came to be known as the *Lemon* test, a challenged policy (1) must have a "secular purpose,"

LEMON TEST: A legal framework evolving from the Supreme Court's 1963 decision in *Lemon v. Kurtzman* and used by courts to examine laws or government action implicating the Establishment Clause of the First Amendment; it requires the government to justify a policy by demonstrating a secular purpose, showing that religion is neither advanced nor inhibited, and establishing religion and government are not excessively entangled.

SECULAR PURPOSE: A nonreligious justification for a law or government policy; a key component of *Lemon* test analysis pursuant to the Establishment Clause.

(2) must not have the principal or primary effect of "inhibiting or advancing religion," and (3) must avoid an "excessive government entanglement with religion."

Official Acknowledgements of Religion

Since the beginning of the Republic, government at all levels has acknowledged religion in various ways. The first Congress authorized the appointment of chaplains for the Senate and House of Representatives and, to this day, the Senate and House open their sessions with a prayer. In 1954, Congress added the words "under God" to the Pledge of Allegiance and, two years later, made "In God We Trust" the official motto of the United States. Thus far, activists dedicated to the separation of church and state have been unsuccessful at challenging these policies. In 2004, the Supreme Court unanimously rejected a challenge to the inclusion of "under God" in the Pledge of Allegiance, holding that the plaintiff lacked standing to bring the suit.[17] More recently, a federal appeals court rejected a challenge to the government's practice of including the motto "In God We Trust" on the nation's currency, saying that the practice "comports with the original understanding of the Establishment Clause."[18]

Official Prayers

In *Marsh v. Chambers* (1983),[19] the Supreme Court refused to strike down Nebraska's policy of beginning legislative sessions with prayers offered by a Protestant chaplain retained at the taxpayers' expense. Writing for the Court, Chief Justice Warren E. Burger made no pretense of applying the *Lemon* test. Rather, he relied heavily on history and the need for accommodation of popular religious beliefs. In dissent, Justice William Brennan observed that "if any group of law students were asked to apply the principles of *Lemon* to the question of legislative prayer, they would nearly unanimously find the practice to be unconstitutional."

More recently, in *Town of Greece v. Galloway* (2014),[20] the Court upheld a local board's practice of opening its monthly meetings with a prayer offered by a member of the local clergy. Citing *Marsh v. Chambers* and stressing that "the Establishment Clause must be interpreted 'by reference to historical practices and understandings,'" Justice Kennedy's majority opinion found no violation of the Establishment Clause. In particular, Kennedy spoke of a tradition of prayer before legislative sessions dating back to the Founding era. *Lemon v. Kurtzman* was not mentioned in the opinion, and it appeared the Court had moved away from this test, at least with respect to government acknowledgements of religion in legislative contexts. Instead, Kennedy's opinion focused on the fact that there was no "denigration" of any religious views, nor any "coercion" to adopt any specific religious faith. Moreover, he denoted a secular purpose in "building a spirit of cooperation" before legislative debate. In dissent, Justice Elena Kagan took umbrage with the majority's position by declaring:

> When the citizens of this country approach their government, they do so only as Americans, not as members of one faith or another. And that means that even in a partly legislative body, they should not confront government-sponsored worship that divides them along religious lines. I believe, for all the reasons I have given, that the Town of Greece betrayed that promise. I therefore respectfully dissent from the Court's decision.

In Boston, Massachusetts, as in many cities, the city council opens its sessions with prayers offered by members of the local clergy. In January 2021, a group known as the Satanic Temple filed suit against the City of Boston, saying it was denied the opportunity to offer such a prayer. In its complaint, the group said, "We just want an equal opportunity—one guaranteed by the Constitution—to invoke Satan." In July 2021, a federal judge denied the City's motion to dismiss, thus allowing the case to move forward.[21]

Nativity Scenes and Other Holiday Displays

Historically, many cities and counties have included nativity scenes in Christmas displays located on public property. In *Lynch v. Donnelly* (1984),[22] the Supreme Court upheld the inclusion of a nativity scene in an outdoor Christmas display sponsored by the city of Pawtucket, Rhode Island. The display also included Santa Claus, a Christmas tree, and a banner reading, "Seasons Greetings." Speaking for a sharply divided Court, Chief Justice Burger barely mentioned the *Lemon* test. Burger relied on history and the fact that the nativity scene had become, for many, a "neutral harbinger of the holiday season," rather than a symbol of Christianity. In dissent, Justice Harry Blackmun observed that the Court had relegated the nativity scene "... to the role of a neutral harbinger of the holiday season, useful for commercial purposes but devoid of any inherent meaning and incapable of enhancing the religious tenor of a display of which it is an integral part."

Five years later, in County of *Allegheny v. ACLU* (1989),[23] the Court held that a nativity scene located inside a county courthouse with the accompanying words "Gloria in Excelsis Deo" conveyed a religious message in violation of the Establishment Clause. Justice Blackmun's plurality opinion noted "that the crèche bears a sign disclosing its ownership by a Roman Catholic organization," and this "demonstrates that the government is endorsing the religious message of that organization, rather than communicating a message of its own." Clearly, setting and context had much to do with the Court's decision in this particular matter. In the same decision, though, the Court found no violation associated with the display of a Christmas tree and a menorah outside of the courthouse building. Both of those items were said to be secular symbols that connoted celebration of the holiday season.

Overall, when it comes to holiday displays on government property, it is not unusual for areas of some state capitol buildings around the country to be designated as *free speech zones*, which allow permits to be granted for displays that are not government funded. For example, in Illinois, individuals or groups can apply to temporarily post holiday decorations in the rotunda of the State Capitol Building—provided that no taxpayer funds are involved. In 2018, after a nativity scene and menorah went on display there, the Satanic Temple was granted a permit to display a statue of a snake-wrapped arm holding an apple. Similar efforts have led to a display from the Church of the Flying Spaghetti Monster being placed in the Virginia State Capitol, which also allows various holiday displays to be temporarily posted every winter. Elsewhere, in 2013, after a private group was given a permit to place a nativity scene in the rotunda of the Florida State Capitol, a man named Chaz Stevens was granted a permit to display a *Festivus Pole* made of Pabst Blue Ribbon beer cans. Festivus is a fictitious holiday created on the television sitcom *Seinfeld*. Mr. Stevens indicated that his display was motivated by a desire to challenge the presence of the Nativity scene, saying: "This is about separation of church and state. The government shouldn't be in the business of allowing a mixture of church and state."[24] Often, it seems, when the government does allow religious displays on public property, groups will put forth additional items as a form of protest.

Displays of the Ten Commandments

When it comes to displays of the Ten Commandments, the Supreme Court has offered conflicting opinions. In *Stone v. Graham* (1980),[25] the Supreme Court invalidated a Kentucky law requiring the Ten Commandments to be posted in all public-school classrooms. In a brief per curiam opinion, the Court observed that "[t]he preeminent purpose for posting the Ten Commandments on schoolroom walls is plainly religious in nature." Likewise, in *McCreary County v. ACLU* (2005),[26] the Court's 5–4 majority struck down such displays inside of two Kentucky courthouses, noting their "predominantly religious purpose." Although court officials attempted to advance a secular purpose connected to honoring foundations of the American legal system, the Court's majority was not persuaded. Concerns over preserving justice and fairness in the legal process—and not allowing religious principles to pervade it—were paramount.

Nonetheless, in *Van Orden v. Perry*,[27] decided the same day as the *McCreary* case, the Court upheld the display of a monument bearing the inscription of the Ten Commandments on the grounds of the Texas statehouse. A key distinction in this 5–4 decision (with Justice Kennedy serving as the swing vote) was that the display was outdoors and could be avoided by individuals who chose not to see it. Chief Justice Rehnquist's majority opinion differentiated the display on the ground of the Texas Capitol from the displays struck down in prior cases by saying the following:

> Texas has treated her Capitol grounds monuments as representing the several strands in the State's political and legal history. The inclusion of the Ten Commandments monument in this group has a dual significance, partaking of both religion and government.

The majority opinion also noted there was no "captive audience" being forced to view the Ten Commandments, with the display referred to as a "passive monument." In a lengthy dissent, Justice Stevens opined that the Court's decision "makes a mockery of the constitutional ideal that government must remain neutral between religion and irreligion."

In response to this decision, some states have placed Ten Commandments displays on the grounds of their state capitols. In turn, the Satanic Temple has unsuccessfully petitioned to display a bronze statue of Baphomet, which is a winged goat-like creature, next to a Ten Commandments display on the grounds of the Arkansas State Capitol—although litigation is pending. A similar attempt launched by the Satanic Temple in Oklahoma led to the state's supreme court requiring the removal of a privately-funded Ten Commandments display there in 2015—but the state legislature has launched attempts to override this decision.[28] Overall, when it comes to displays of the Ten Commandments, context is crucial; outdoor displays seem less likely to run afoul of the Establishment Clause than indoor displays, but state constitutional provisions can also prove crucial to such analysis.

A Cross Display and the Potential Demise of the *Lemon* Test

In *American Legion v. American Humanist Association* (2019),[29] the Supreme Court addressed the constitutionality of a 40-foot concrete cross that had stood in the center of a Maryland town for more than 90 years. The cross was built in Prince George's County, Maryland to honor the sacrifices of World War I veterans, and in its 7–2 decision on this matter, the Court ruled that the placement of the cross on public land did not violate the Establishment Clause of the First Amendment. Justice Samuel Alito's majority opinion found that the cross furthered the secular purpose of honoring military veterans. Alito also pointed out that other images of crosses are displayed for secular reasons across America, such as in military cemeteries or even in the logos for companies like Blue Cross and Blue Shield, the American Red Cross, the Bayer Group, and Johnson & Johnson. To the surprise of some observers, Justice Kagan penned a concurring opinion in which she suggested that an order to remove the cross would have been inconsistent with the "values of neutrality and inclusion that the First Amendment demands."

An important aspect of this decision was the plurality opinion by Justice Alito, who suggested that the *Lemon* test should not guide the analysis. Alito adumbrated that even though the *Lemon* decision sought to provide a "grand unified theory of the Establishment Clause," the Court should adopt "a more modest approach that focuses on the particular issue at hand and looks to history for guidance." He turned to history, stating, "The practice begun by the First Congress stands out as an example of respect and tolerance for differing views, an honest endeavor to achieve inclusivity and nondiscrimination, and a recognition of the important role that religion plays in the lives of many Americans. Where categories of monuments, symbols, and practices with a longstanding history follow in that tradition, they are likewise constitutional." Although future cases will reveal if the *Lemon* test survives, Alito's statement could serve as a harbinger of a shift in how the Supreme Court addresses cases implicating the First Amendment and religious rights.

Tax Exemptions and Subsidies

Religious institutions, along with other charitable or nonprofit organizations, have traditionally been given federal, state, and local tax exemptions. In some ways, these types of cases carry implications for both the Establishment Clause and the Free Exercise Clause. For example, in *Walz v. Tax Commission* (1970),[30] the Supreme Court upheld a local property tax exemption for churches. Justice William O. Douglas dissented, writing, "If believers are entitled to public financial support, so are nonbelievers. A believer and nonbeliever under the present law are treated differently because of the articles of their faith." More recently, in 2007, the Supreme Court refused to halt the prospect of government funds going to faith-based organizations—an idea initiated under the George W. Bush administration.[31]

The use of public funds for individual tuition payments at religious schools has also been approved by the Supreme Court. In 2002, for instance, the Court allowed for "vouchers," which are typically government-funded credits, to be applied to tuition at religious schools.[32] Later, the Court made a similar ruling in *Espinoza v. Montana Department of Revenue* (2020),[33] which struck down a provision in Montana's state constitution barring taxpayer-funded tuition assistance from being used at religious schools, even though such aid could have been used at nonreligious private schools; the Court's 5–4 majority found that practice to be a violation of the Free Exercise Clause. Chief Justice Roberts's opinion for the *Espinoza* case cited case precedent from the Court's decision in *Trinity Lutheran Church of Columbia v. Comer* (2017),[34] where a 7–2 majority found in favor of a church that had sought state grant money for refurbishing a playground, only to be told that the state constitution forbade the provision of aid to a religious organization. Justice Roberts's majority opinion in that case found the need for playground renovations to be "secular" and "neutral"; accordingly, violations of both the Establishment Clause and the Free Exercise Clause were said to overlap.

A similar 2022 decision from the Supreme Court, *Carson v. Makin*,[35] also indicated that the state of Maine could not prevent state-funded tuition assistance for attendance at private schools from being used at religious schools. In dissent, Justice Sotomayor said, "This Court continues to dismantle the wall of separation between church and state that the Framers fought to build."

In concluding this section, it is important to note that the Establishment Clause of the First Amendment has yielded a tremendous body of jurisprudence. Table 5.1 lists some of the more prominent Supreme Court

TABLE 5.1   Key Establishment Clause Decisions

Actions That Are Not Permitted
Ten Commandments displayed inside government buildings (*McCreary County, KY v. ACLU*)
Nativity scenes displayed inside government buildings (*Allegheny County, PA v. ACLU*)
Teacher-led prayer in public schools (*Engel v. Vitale; Abington v. Schempp*)
Prayer at public high school graduation ceremonies (*Lee v. Weisman*)
Prayer at public high school football games (*Santa Fe v. Doe*)
Teaching of creationism in public schools (*Edwards v. Aguillard*)
Mandatory moment of silence at the start of school day (*Wallace v. Jaffrey*)
Taxpayer funding of private school teacher salaries (*Lemon v. Kurtzman*)
Actions That Are Permitted
Ten Commandments displayed outside government buildings (*Van Orden v. Perry*)
Nativity scenes displayed outdoors on government property (*Lynch v. Donnelly*)
Christmas tree display or menorah display on government property (*Allegheny County, PA v. ACLU*)
Prayer before legislative session (*Marsh v. Chambers*)
Religious groups using school property after hours (*Lamb's Chapel v. Center Moriches School Dist.*)
Use of taxpayer funded scholarship at religious school (*Espinoza v. Montana Dept. of Revenue*)
Use of taxpayer funded vouchers for tuition at religious schools (*Zelman v. Simmons-Harris*)
Tax exemptions for churches (*Walz v. Tax Commission*)
Government funds for faith-based organizations (*Hein v. Freedom from Religion Foundation*)

decisions in this area. There is every reason to believe that this important provision of the Bill of Rights will continue to be contested in the courts for years to come.

Free Exercise of Religion: Interpretive Foundations

The Supreme Court first interpreted the Free Exercise Clause in *Reynolds v. United States* (1878),[36] which upheld a ban on plural marriage. Members of the Church of Jesus Christ of Latter Day Saints who resided in what was at that time was the Utah territory were prosecuted under federal law for engaging in polygamy. Writing for a unanimous bench, Chief Justice Morrison Waite opined that under the Free Exercise Clause, "Congress was deprived of all legislative power over mere opinion, but was left free to reach actions which were in violation of social duties or subversive of good order." In Waite's view, to grant an exemption to the criminal law based on religious beliefs "would be to make the professed doctrines of religious belief superior to the law of the land, and, in effect, to permit every citizen to become a law unto himself."

Reynolds v. United States greatly restricted the scope of religious freedom. After all, the phrase "free exercise of religion" implies constitutional protection for religious conduct as well. But what sort of conduct should be protected? Religiously motivated conduct includes assembling for worship, proselytizing, soliciting funds, running educational programs, and doing charitable work. But it can also involve refusal to participate in patriotic ceremonies, refusal to send one's children to school, refusal of medical treatment, refusal to serve in the military, and even refusal to abide by civil rights laws. And some unconventional religious practices, such as polygamy, run afoul of the criminal law. Are such actions, when reflective of sincere religious belief, unprotected by the First Amendment because they are, in the words of Chief Justice Waite, a "violation of social duties or subversive of good order"? As we shall see, the modern Supreme Court has devoted considerable attention to this problem.

Incorporation of the Free Exercise Clause

Prior to 1940, state and local governments were unbound by the Free Exercise Clause and, hence, were free to impose whatever burdens on religious belief and expression were permissible under their own constitutions. In some states, religious persecution was tolerated; in others, it was a matter of policy. Jewish people, Roman Catholics, Baptists, Mormons, Jehovah's Witnesses, and other religious sects felt the sting of discrimination and outright persecution. And of course, Native Americans were often subjected to forcible conversion to Christianity.

In *Cantwell v. Connecticut* (1940),[37] the Supreme Court incorporated the Free Exercise Clause into the Due Process Clause of the Fourteenth Amendment, thus making it applicable to state action. The *Cantwell* case involved members of the Jehovah's Witnesses who went door-to-door in a predominantly Roman Catholic community, proselytizing and soliciting funds. They were convicted of violating a state law that required prior approval of such activities, which the Supreme Court found to be an unconstitutional prior restraint on their exercise of First Amendment rights. With this decision, the Court opened up a great number of state and local policies and practices to federal judicial review.

Obiter Dicta

"The free exercise of religion means, first and foremost, the right to believe and profess whatever religious doctrine one desires. ... The government may not compel affirmation of religious belief, ... punish the expression of religious doctrines it believes to be false, ... impose special disabilities on the basis of religious views or religious status, ... or lend its power to one or the other side in controversies over religious authority or dogma. ..."

—*Justice Antonin Scalia, writing for the Supreme Court in* Employment Division v. Smith, *494 U.S. 872 (1990).*

SHERBERT TEST: A judicial framework created by the Supreme Court to evaluate cases involving First Amendment free exercise of religion claims; it requires the government to justify an undue burden upon the exercise of a sincere religious belief by demonstrating a compelling interest that is implemented in the least restrictive means for religious exercise.

SINCERE RELIGIOUS BELIEF: A religious belief deemed to be authentic enough, based on long-standing practices and regular meetings of participants, to justify the assertion of a free exercise claim.

UNDUE BURDEN: A governmental restriction upon religious exercise deemed to be sufficient enough to require justification, under the *Sherbert* test, via an assessment of a compelling interest and least restrictive means of implementation.

COMPELLING INTEREST: A justification strong enough to support limits placed on the fundamental rights of individuals who are impacted by laws, actions, or other government policies.

Protection of Religious Beliefs

According to the doctrine articulated in *Cantwell v. Connecticut*, religious belief is absolutely protected by the First Amendment. The Supreme Court has held fast to this principle. Three years after the incorporation of the Free Exercise Clause, the Supreme Court overturned precedent and upheld the right of schoolchildren who were Jehovah's Witnesses to refuse to recite the Pledge of Allegiance or salute the American flag. Speaking for the Court in *West Virginia State Board of Education v. Barnette* (1943),[38] Justice Robert Jackson proclaimed that "no official, high or petty, can prescribe what shall be orthodox in politics, nationalism, religion, or other matters of opinion, or force citizens to confess by word or act their faith therein." Similarly, in *Torcaso v. Watkins* (1961),[39] the Supreme Court unanimously struck down a provision of the Maryland Constitution requiring public officials to declare their belief in the existence of God. Speaking for a unanimous bench, Justice Black declared that "neither a State nor the Federal Government can constitutionally force a person 'to profess a belief or disbelief in any religion.'" Of course, cases in which public policy impinges directly on religious beliefs are few and far between. The more difficult problem, constitutionally speaking, is what degree of protection is to be afforded for religiously motivated conduct.

The Warren Court Takes a Strong View on Religiously Motivated Action

Consistent with its philosophy of enhancing constitutional protection for disfavored minorities, the Supreme Court under Chief Justice Earl Warren adopted a strong position on the constitutional protection to be afforded for religiously motivated conduct. In *Sherbert v. Verner* (1963),[40] the Court held that laws burdening religiously motivated conduct should be subjected to strict judicial scrutiny. As we saw in previous chapters, strict judicial scrutiny entails a presumption of unconstitutionality. To overcome that presumption, government must be able to articulate a compelling interest. It must also demonstrate that its policy is narrowly tailored to minimize its impact on religiously motivated conduct.

In specific terms, for modern courts, analysis under the *Sherbert test* proceeds through two phases. First, the individual asserting a free exercise of religion violation must show (1) a "sincere religious belief" and (2) that government is placing an "undue burden" on that belief. If the individual fails to demonstrate both, the case will be resolved in favor of the government. Conversely, if the individual

JURISPRUDENCE

The Supreme Court Establishes a Key Test for Free Exercise Cases
Sherbert v. Verner, 374 U.S. 398 (1963)

Adele Sherbert, a Seventh-day Adventist, sought unemployment benefits after she was fired from her job in a textile mill for refusing to work on Saturdays. The South Carolina Employment Security Commission ruled she could not receive unemployment benefits because her refusal to work on Saturday constituted a failure without good cause to accept available work. That ruling was upheld by a trial judge and the state supreme court. The U.S. Supreme Court reversed. Speaking for the Court, Justice Brennan said that "to condition the availability of benefits upon this appellant's willingness to violate a cardinal principle of her religious faith effectively penalizes the free exercise of her constitutional liberties."

Justice Brennan went on to "consider whether some compelling state interest enforced in the eligibility provisions of the South Carolina statute justifies the substantial infringement of appellant's First Amendment right." The state suggested that "the filing of fraudulent claims by unscrupulous claimants feigning religious objections to Saturday work might not only dilute the unemployment compensation fund, but also hinder the scheduling by employers of necessary Saturday work." In response, Brennan wrote that "even if the possibility of spurious claims did threaten to dilute the fund and disrupt the scheduling of work, it would plainly be incumbent upon the appellees to demonstrate that no alternative forms of regulation would combat such abuses without infringing First Amendment rights." Because the state made no such showing, its justification for denying benefits to Ms. Sherbert was rejected. Brennan concluded his opinion by clearly stating the holding of the Court: "South Carolina may not constitutionally apply the eligibility provisions so as to constrain a worker to abandon his religious convictions respecting the day of rest." This decision established a strong presumption in favor of the free exercise of religion.

is successful in these two prongs, the burden shifts to the government to illustrate the following (1) a compelling interest to justify the undue burden and (2) that the government action taken represents the "least restrictive means" of furthering the compelling interest without infringing upon religious liberty—or, in other words, that no "less restrictive" alternative policy could be created.

The Rehnquist Court Repudiates the *Sherbert* Test

In *Employment Division v. Smith* (1990),[41] the Supreme Court rejected a claim by members of the Native American Church that their ritualistic use of peyote constituted the free exercise of religion. Justice Antonin Scalia held for the majority that "if prohibiting the exercise of religion is merely the incidental effect of a generally applicable and otherwise valid law, the First Amendment has not been offended." The Court thus overturned *Sherbert v. Verner* and reverted to the approach taken in *Reynolds v. United States* by focusing on whether a law was "general" and "neutral" in application. In dissent, Justice Harry Blackmun argued

LEAST RESTRICTIVE MEANS: A component of the *Sherbert* test, which is used by courts to evaluate free exercise of religion claims; this component requires a compelling interest advanced by the government to justify infringement upon religious exercise to be examined closely to determine if another policy could also advance the compelling interest but with a more limited intrusion upon religious liberty.

that the compelling interest test should apply and that the ban was not narrowly tailored to achieve a compelling state interest.

JURISPRUDENCE

Peyote Use in Native American Religious Rituals
Employment Division v. Smith, 494 U.S. 872 (1990)

Alfred Smith and Galen Black, members of the Native American Church, were dismissed from their jobs as drug rehabilitation counselors because they ingested the hallucinogenic drug peyote as part of a religious ceremony. Subsequently, the Oregon Employment Division determined they had been fired for misconduct and denied their applications for unemployment compensation. The Oregon Supreme Court held that their conduct was protected by the Free Exercise Clause, which is precisely the question that came before the U.S. Supreme Court. Splitting 6–3, the high Court reversed the Oregon Supreme Court and held that the First Amendment did not protect the sacramental use of an illegal drug. Writing for the Court, Justice Antonin Scalia held that "if prohibiting the exercise of religion is merely the incidental effect of a generally applicable and otherwise valid law, the First Amendment has not been offended."

Justice Scalia's opinion thus repudiated the compelling interest test articulated in *Sherbert v. Verner* (1963). In language reminiscent of *Reynolds v. United States* (1879), he wrote: "The government's ability to enforce generally applicable prohibitions of socially harmful conduct, like its ability to carry out other aspects of public policy, 'cannot depend on measuring the effects of a governmental action on a religious objector's spiritual development.'" Noting the increasing religious diversity of the country, Justice Scalia insisted that "we cannot

afford the luxury of deeming *presumptively invalid*, as applied to the religious objector, every regulation of conduct that does not protect an interest of the highest order." He also lamented the possibility of a "system in which each conscience is a law unto itself or in which judges weigh the social importance of all laws against the centrality of all religious beliefs."

In dissent, Justice Blackmun (joined by Justices Brennan and Marshall) argued for the maintenance of the *Sherbert* test. Applying that standard, Blackmun concluded that "Oregon's interest in enforcing its drug laws against religious use of peyote is not sufficiently compelling to outweigh respondents' right to the free exercise of their religion." In reaching that conclusion, he noted that "[t]he carefully circumscribed ritual context in which respondents used peyote is far removed from the irresponsible and unrestricted recreational use of unlawful drugs." Justice Blackmun dismissed the state's assertion of "an interest in protecting the health and safety of its citizens from the dangers of unlawful drugs," noting that the State offered "no evidence that the religious use of peyote has ever harmed anyone."

In response to this decision more than twenty states have passed laws legalizing the use of peyote in religious services—as has the federal government, which did so via passage of the American Indian Religious Freedom Act Amendments of 1994, as applied to "bona fide religious ceremonies."[42]

In 2021, Justice Samuel Alito delivered a strong critique of the *Smith* decision, harkening back to the Prohibition era. Concurring in the judgment in *Fulton v. Philadelphia* (2021),[43] Alito wrote the following:

> Suppose that the Volstead Act, which implemented the Prohibition Amendment, had not contained an exception for sacramental wine. … The Act would have been consistent with *Smith* even though it would have prevented the celebration of a Catholic Mass anywhere in the United States. Or suppose that a State, following the example of several European

countries, made it unlawful to slaughter an animal that had not first been rendered unconscious. That law would be fine under *Smith* even though it would outlaw kosher and halal slaughter. Or suppose that a jurisdiction in this country, following the recommendations of medical associations in Europe, banned the circumcision of infants. A San Francisco ballot initiative in 2010 proposed just that. A categorical ban would be allowed by *Smith* even though it would prohibit an ancient and important Jewish and Muslim practice. Or suppose that this Court or some other court enforced a rigid rule prohibiting attorneys from wearing any form of head covering in court. The rule would satisfy *Smith* even though it would prevent Orthodox Jewish men, Sikh men, and many Muslim women from appearing. Many other examples could be added.

Finally, it is important to note that the holding in *Employment Division v. Smith* applied only to laws of general applicability. Even under the *Smith* approach, laws that target particular religious groups or discriminate on the basis of religion are still subject to strict judicial scrutiny.[44]

The Religious Freedom Restoration Act

The Supreme Court's decision in *Employment Division v. Smith* brought on a wave of criticism, even from the religious right. Within four years, Congress enacted the **Religious Freedom Restoration Act (RFRA)**,[45] which attempted to restore the *Sherbert* test by providing the following:

a. Government shall not substantially burden a person's exercise of religion even if the burden results from a rule of general applicability ...
b. Government may substantially burden a person's exercise of religion only if it demonstrates that application of the burden to the person—
    1. is in furtherance of a compelling governmental interest; and
    2. is the least restrictive means of furthering that compelling governmental interest.

But in *City of Boerne v. Flores* (1997),[46] the Court declared RFRA unconstitutional as applied to state and local actions. In a 6–3 decision, the Court held that Congress did not have the power under Section 5 of the Fourteenth Amendment to contradict the Court's interpretation of the Free Exercise Clause. Justice Anthony Kennedy, speaking for the

RELIGIOUS FREEDOM RESTORATION ACT (RFRA): A 1993 federal law, passed in response to the Supreme Court's decision in *Employment Decision v. Smith*, requiring courts to evaluate free exercise of religion cases according to the *Sherbert* test. Based on case precedent and a congressional amendment, it applies only to the actions of federal officials.

majority, stressed the primacy of the Court as interpreter of the Constitution, saying, "RFRA contradicts vital principles necessary to maintain separation of powers and the federal balance." However, the *Boerne* decision did allow RFRA to be applied to federal law enforcement, as Congress is free to recognize exceptions to federal criminal prohibitions. In fact, the law was amended by Congress to reflect this point in 2003.

It should also be noted that state courts are free to interpret their own constitutions so as to provide greater (never lesser) protection to rights than is provided by the Supreme Court's interpretation of the Federal Constitution. In this context, state courts can adopt their own version of the *Sherbert* test. Moreover, nearly half the states have adopted their own versions of RFRA, which more or less codify the *Sherbert* test. With the foregoing considerations in mind, we now turn to some of the major areas of controversy under the Free Exercise Clause.

Religious Assembly and Expression

The right to assemble for worship is at the very heart of the Free Exercise Clause. Yet this right, like other First Amendment freedoms, is not absolute. It may be restricted on the basis of a compelling governmental interest, as long as the restriction is narrowly tailored to produce the least possible harm to the right of free exercise.

Religious assemblies in the public forum are judged by the same standards as political assemblies. Time, place, and manner regulations are permissible, as long as they are not applied in a discriminatory manner. In *Fowler v. Rhode Island* (1953),[47] for example, the Supreme Court held that a local ordinance was unconstitutional as applied to prohibiting Jehovah's Witnesses from preaching in a public park while allowing Catholic masses and Protestant church services there. Refer back to chapter 4 for more discussion on time, place, and manner restrictions.

The COVID-19 Cases

In 2020 and 2021, the Supreme Court dealt with a series of cases involving restrictions on the right to assemble for worship. These cases stemmed from orders issued by governors in several states designed to impede the transmission of the novel coronavirus. In principle, the need to protect the public health from a pandemic is quite clearly a compelling governmental interest—but specific application of COVID-related protections must not treat religious gatherings differently than others.

The high Court's first look at this issued arrived with the May 2020 decision in *South Bay United Pentecostal Church v. Newsom*,[48] in which the majority refused to halt an order from California Governor Gavin Newsom; that order had limited attendance at church services to 25% of building capacity and set a maximum of 100 total occupants. The majority indicated there was no likelihood of a Free Exercise Clause violation because secular businesses were also subject to similar restrictions on occupancy.

Later, with a July 2020 ruling in *Calvary Chapel Dayton Valley v. Sisolak*,[49] the Supreme Court left in place an order from Nevada's governor, Steven Sisolak, which capped attendance at churches to 50 total people, despite the fact that casinos and other businesses in the state were permitted to allow crowds of up to 50% of their total capacity with no limits in place on total occupancy. In dissent, Justice Alito invoked the Constitution in drawing parallels across different businesses, saying the following:

A church, synagogue, or mosque, regardless of its size, may not admit more than 50 persons, but casinos and certain other favored facilities may admit 50% of their maximum occupancy—and in the case of gigantic Las Vegas casinos, this means that thousands of patrons are allowed. That Nevada would discriminate in favor of the powerful gaming industry and its employees may not come as a surprise, but this Court's willingness to allow such discrimination is disappointing. We have a duty to defend the Constitution, and even a public health emergency does not absolve us of that responsibility.

Justice Gorsuch also wrote a dissent for this Nevada decision, chiding the majority's lack of concern for First Amendment protections by declaring, "The world we inhabit today, with a pandemic upon us, poses unusual challenges. But there is no world in which the Constitution permits Nevada to favor Caesars Palace over Calvary Chapel."

In subsequent months, though, after Justice Amy Coney Barrett was appointed to the Court by President Trump, a shift occurred, and the Court seemed to more inclined to embrace these dissenting voices. For instance, in November 2020, the Court evaluated an order from then-New York Governor Andrew Cuomo, who attempted to limit attendance at religious services to either 10 or 25 attendees. In *Roman Catholic Diocese of Brooklyn v. Cuomo* (2020),[50] the Supreme Court enjoined enforcement of the order, saying the following:

> Members of this Court are not public health experts, and we should respect the judgment of those with special expertise and responsibility in this area. But even in a pandemic, the Constitution cannot be put away and forgotten. The restrictions at issue here, by effectively barring many from attending religious services, strike at the very heart of the First Amendment's guarantee of religious liberty.

Later, in January 2021, the Supreme Court had a chance to revisit the aforementioned Nevada restrictions but refused to grant cert to review a Ninth Circuit decision that found the Nevada capacity limits on religious services to be a violation of the First Amendment. This amounted to a reversal of the Court's July 2020 position on policies in that state and, ultimately, enabled church services in Nevada to offer the same capacity limits given to other businesses.

One month later, in February 2021, the Court reexamined restrictions on religious services in California, and this time, a majority of justices prevented an attempt by California's governor to ban in-person church services altogether. Even so, the Court left 25% capacity limits intact and also refused to overturn a ban on "singing and chanting" inside of churches.[51]

Other decisions from lower federal courts addressed nuanced issues related to the pandemic. For example, an opinion from the Sixth Circuit halted efforts by Kentucky's governor to ban *drive-up* church services.[52] And an August 2021 decision from a federal district court in Michigan ruled in favor of student–athletes at Western Michigan University, where university officials had mandated all members of varsity sports teams to be vaccinated against COVID-19. The district court found the university had erred in not offering the students religious exemptions to this requirement.[53] Generally, the trend across judicial decisions during the COVID-19 pandemic involved guaranteeing churches would not be treated differently than other businesses—honoring First Amendment protections connected to both the Free Exercise Clause and the Establishment Clause of the First Amendment.

FOCUS ON LAW ENFORCEMENT

NYPD Sees More Than 5,000 Requests for Vaccine Exemptions

In November 2021, New York City Police Commissioner Dermot Shea said that 34 police officers and 40 civilian members of the New York Police Department (NYPD) had not complied with the mayor's requirement for all city employees to acquire vaccines for COVID-19. Those numbers amounted to less than 0.15% of all NYPD employees.[54]

However, those figures did not take into account the individuals who had applied for religious or medical exemptions, which news reports indicated to be in excess of 5,000 employees of the NYPD.[55] The City allowed those individuals to continue working, even past deadlines that led to other unvaccinated workers being placed on unpaid leave, while their requests were being evaluated. In February 2022, Mayor Eric Adams announced that more than 1,400 city employees had been fired for failing to get vaccinated against COVID-19, but that number only included 36 employees of the NYPD.[56]

Different states treat the application of religious exceptions to vaccine requirements in different ways. As of August 2022, only six states will not allow parents to use any religious exemptions to vaccine requirements for children attending schools, which could involve school mandates for things like measles, mumps, or rubella vaccines, among others. Those states are California, Connecticut, Maine, Mississippi, New York, and West Virginia.[57] All other states allow for some kind of religious or personal belief exception. Certainly, the states listed here could be said to vary dramatically in terms of their political cultures, so the fact that each has arrived at the decision to bar religious exceptions to vaccines highlights the complexity of applying religious protections in society. Even in those states allowing religious exceptions, variation exists regarding what a parent needs to demonstrate, with some states, such as Tennessee, requiring a signed statement from parents. Overall, as COVID-19 vaccine mandates arise in some academic and employment settings, the manner in which state legislatures and courts respond to this issue will be critical to observe.

The Right to Proselytize and Solicit Funds

As noted earlier, the Supreme Court's seminal decision in *Cantwell v. Connecticut* (1940) recognized that the right to proselytize and solicit funds on behalf of one's faith is an essential component of the free exercise of religion. Thus, in *Watchtower Bible & Tract Society v. Village of Stratton* (2002),[58] the Supreme Court struck down a local law requiring all door-to-door solicitors to obtain a permit from the mayor before going door to door. Justice Stevens's majority opinion noted that "[e]ven if the issuance of permits by the mayor's office is a ministerial task that is performed promptly and at no cost to the applicant, a law requiring a permit to engage in such speech constitutes a dramatic departure from our national heritage and constitutional tradition." Like *Cantwell v. Connecticut*, this case is one of a long line in which the Jehovah's Witnesses have successfully challenged restrictions on canvassing and solicitation.

We must recognize, though, that the right to proselytize and solicit has limits. In its decision for *International Society for Krishna Consciousness v. Lee* (1992),[59] the Court upheld a ban on solicitation in a publicly operated airport terminal. The Court held that airport terminals are nonpublic forums, and as a result, a prohibition against solicitation need only satisfy a reasonableness standard. Speaking for the Court, Chief Justice Rehnquist said, "We have no doubt that under this standard the prohibition on solicitation passes muster." (For more discussion of this case, see the analysis of freedom of speech in chapter 4.)

Patriotic Rituals and Civic Duties

In general, it is not uncommon for some religious expression matters to overlap with free speech protections. A perfect illustration can be seen in a pair of Supreme Court decisions from the early 1940s. In 1935, Billy and Lillian Gobitis, members of the Jehovah's Witnesses, were expelled from a Pennsylvania public school for refusing to salute the American flag. In *Minersville School District v. Gobitis* (1940),[60] the Supreme Court upheld the expulsion, saying "conscientious scruples have not, in the course of the long struggle for religious toleration, relieved the individual from obedience to a general law not aimed at the promotion or restriction of religious beliefs." But three years later, in *West Virginia Board of Education v. Barnette* (1943), the Court sided with members of the Jehovah's Witnesses who refused to allow their children to participate in a public-school flag salute and Pledge of Allegiance. In a much-quoted majority opinion, Justice Robert Jackson wrote, "To believe that patriotism will not flourish if patriotic ceremonies are voluntary and spontaneous, instead of a compulsory routine, is to make an unflattering estimate of the appeal of our institutions to free minds." Jackson concluded "the action of the local authorities in compelling the flag salute and pledge transcends constitutional limitations on their power, and invades the sphere of intellect and spirit which it is the purpose of the First Amendment to our Constitution to reserve from all official control."

Conscientious Objection to Military Service

The Supreme Court has never held that the Free Exercise Clause requires the government to allow conscientious objection to military service. This is because since the Civil War, there has been a statutory right of conscientious objection. Enacted after World War II, the Universal Military Training and Service Act[61] exempts persons who are conscientiously opposed to participation in war in any form by reason of their religious training and belief from military service. In *United States v. Seeger* (1965),[62] the Supreme Court interpreted this provision broadly, holding that conscientious objector status was not limited to those professing the conventional belief in God. Accordingly, an atheist can claim conscientious objector status as long as there is a "sincere and meaningful belief which occupies in the life of its possessor a place parallel to that filled by the God." Of course, in the absence of a military draft, the issue is academic.

Religious Freedom in the Military

In *Goldman v. Weinberger* (1986),[63] the Supreme Court upheld an Air Force regulation that prohibited the wearing of visible religious clothing or accessories. The case involved an Orthodox Jew who wished to wear his yarmulke while on duty. Chief Justice Rehnquist's majority opinion was highly deferential to the military and its asserted need for uniformity in dress, concluding "the First Amendment does not require the military to accommodate such practices in the face of its view that they would detract from the uniformity sought by the dress regulations." In dissent, Justice William Brennan chided the Court for "eliminating, in all but name only, judicial review of military regulations that interfere with the fundamental constitutional rights of service personnel."

THE CONSTITUTION IN ACTION

How to Start Your Own Church under IRS Rules

Those interested in starting a new church—whether for some illicit purpose, as in the case of a *marijuana church*, or for a more traditional religious reason—might find it useful to know that the primary government agency for conferring *official* status upon a church is the federal government's Internal Revenue Service (IRS). The primary benefit to acquiring this status through the IRS's 501(c)(3) application process is that an officially recognized church is entitled to unique tax deductions and could, thus, take in donations without having to pay taxes on that money. Church officials could even use such money for lavish properties, cars, airplanes, and more—provided that a legitimate church function is connected to the use of those items, but a failure to show such a link could result in violations of federal tax laws. Moreover, churches can become eligible for government-funded grant money that might be available to *faith-based* organizations, which are generally defined as groups that have a religious mission and attempt to assist the needy. Beyond that, showing a "sincere religious belief" under the *Sherbert* test might be easier to demonstrate it the context of a formal religious organization, such as a church.

Nevertheless, the IRS has never provided mandatory terminology for defining what constitutes a church. But the agency's website does indicate there are "attributes of a church that have been developed by the IRS and by court decisions."[64] The following list appears on the IRS website to help guide fledgling churches through the process of the agency evaluating requests for a group to be formally recognized as a church. Although no single factor controls the analysis more than others, collective use of these criteria could play a role in IRS decisions on applications for churches and religious organizations to be considered nonprofit entities:

- Distinct legal existence
- Recognized creed and form of worship
- Formal code of doctrine and discipline
- Distinct religious history
- Organization of ordained ministers
- Ordained ministers selected after completing prescribed courses of study
- Literature of its own
- Established places of worship
- Regular congregations
- Regular religious services
- Schools for religious instruction

Source: https://www.irs.gov/charities-non-profits/churches-religious-organizations/churches-defined.

Unconventional Religious Practices

Earlier in the chapter, we discussed the Supreme Court's first Free Exercise case, *Reynolds v. United States* (1878), wherein the Court rejected the claim that religious freedom includes the right to practice polygamy. Twelve years later, the Court unanimously reaffirmed this position. Speaking for the Court in *Davis v. Beason* (1890),[65] Justice Stephen J. Field observed, "However free the exercise of religion may be, it must be subordinate to the criminal laws of the country, passed with reference to actions regarded by general consent as properly the subjects of punitive legislation." Justice Field also commented that "never before in the history of this country has it been seriously contended that the whole punitive power of the government for acts, recognized by the general consent of the Christian world in modern times as proper matters for prohibitory legislation, must be suspended in order that the tenets of a religious sect encouraging crime may be carried out without hindrance."

Justice Field's comment foreshadowed the numerous cases that have come to the courts in the last half century challenging the application of criminal laws to unconventional religious practices. As the country has become more religiously diverse, litigation involving unconventional religious practices has become more common. The Supreme Court's decision in *Sherbert v. Verner* opened the door to claims that such practices are protected by the First Amendment, unless the government can articulate compelling reasons for outlawing them. Rejecting that approach, Justice Scalia's opinion for the Court in *Employment Division v. Smith* sought to prevent litigation over which of these practices are protected by the First Amendment. According to that opinion, one's religious beliefs do not excuse compliance with facially neutral criminal prohibitions. In Scalia's view, allowing exemptions to criminal laws based on religious beliefs "would open the prospect of constitutionally required exemptions from civic obligations of almost every conceivable kind."

The Religious Freedom Restoration Act, passed in response to *Employment Division v. Smith*, attempted to restore the *Sherbert* test. Although the Court invalidated RFRA as applied to state laws, it was amended by Congress and remains in effect with respect to federal prohibitions. As noted earlier, many states have enacted their own versions of RFRA; thus, state courts often apply some form of the *Sherbert* test in cases arising under the religious freedom protections of their respective state constitutions. With this rather complicated framework in mind, let's consider some of the most salient disputes over unconventional religious practices.

Polygamy

We begin with the classic example of an unconventional practice: polygamy. Despite the Supreme Court's seemingly definitive pronouncements on the subject, the issue of polygamy is still being litigated in state and federal courts. Polygamy is illegal in all fifty states; the offense is known as bigamy—the crime of having more than one spouse. In many cases, bigamy involves fraud and deception, but occasionally, courts will address cases in which bigamy is consensual. The Church of Jesus Christ of Latter Day Saints (aka Mormonism) has long since disavowed the practice, but some *fundamentalist* Mormons still practice polygamy without the blessing of the Church. Some prosecutors ignore the practice as long as no one files a complaint. In Utah, state and local officials have adopted a policy whereby people are not prosecuted for bigamy as long as there is no related offense, such as fraud, abuse, or child sexual assault.

The Sister Wives *Case*

In 2013, a federal district court struck down a Utah statute that made it a crime for a person who, "knowing he has a husband or wife or knowing the other person has a husband or wife, ... cohabits with another person."[66] The decision came in a case involving a polygamous family featured on the TV show *Sister Wives*. Kody Brown and his wives Meri Brown, Janelle Brown, Christine Brown, and Robyn Sullivan brought suit to challenge the constitutionality of the law. In its opinion, the district court strongly criticized the Supreme Court's decision in *Reynolds v. United States*. Conceding that the law was *facially* neutral, the court concluded that it was not *operationally* neutral and, therefore, refused to apply the principle enunciated in *Employment Division v. Smith*. Using strict scrutiny, the court invalidated the statute on multiple grounds, including free exercise of religion and the right of privacy.[67] However, on appeal, the Tenth Circuit vacated the decision, holding that the case was moot in light of state officials' policy of not prosecuting religious polygamists.[68] The Supreme Court denied certiorari, thereby ending the legal battle involving the "Sister Wives."[69] Jonathan Turley, the lawyer who represented the plaintiffs, vowed to continue the fight, saying, "Plural and unconventional families will continue to strive for equal status and treatment under the law."[70]

THE CONSTITUTION IN ACTION
Satanic Temple Challenges Texas Abortion Law

The Satanic Temple is an organization based in Salem, Massachusetts. It advocates for what some might call alternative forms of religious rights—generally, in an effort to highlight issues related to separation of church and state. The group received 501(c)3 status as a recognized church in 2019. In 2021, when the state of Texas passed a law that restricted abortions after six weeks into a pregnancy (allowing for civil suits against providers who violated the law), the Satanic Temple appealed to the FDA, suggesting a religious exception to the law should be permitted to pursuant to the Religious Freedom Restoration Act. In particular, the Satanic Temple indicated that certain abortion pills were a part of their religious rituals and should be protected accordingly. A spokesperson for the temple issued a statement that read: "I am sure Texas Attorney General Ken Paxton—who famously spends a good deal of his time composing press releases about Religious Liberty issues in other states—will be proud to see that Texas' robust Religious Liberty laws, which he vociferously champions, will prevent future Abortion Rituals from being interrupted by superfluous government restrictions meant only to shame and harass those seeking an abortion."[71] In reality, there was no evidence of any *abortion rituals* taking place, but the Satanic Temple was attempting to make a point about the scope of religious exceptions to existing laws.

Use of Illegal Drugs

A year after the U.S. Supreme Court decided *Sherbert v. Verner*, the California Supreme Court reviewed a case in which members of the Navajo tribe were convicted of possessing peyote, after they consumed the hallucinogenic drug as part of an ancient ritual. In *People v. Woody* (1964),[72] the California court held that "since the defendants used the peyote in a bona fide pursuit of a religious faith, and since the practice does not frustrate a compelling interest of the state, the application of the statute improperly defeated the immunity of the First Amendment. ..." Appellate courts in several other states have followed the lead of the California Supreme Court.[73]

In 1973, the Tennessee Supreme Court heard a drug possession case involving Stephen Gaskin, a self-styled spiritual leader who established a commune known as "The Farm" near Summertown, Tennessee. Defending himself against a charge of marijuana possession, Gaskin asserted at trial that he and members of his group used marijuana for spiritual reasons:

> Well we found that it's a way to meditation that helps us to pray and to understand our Creator and also it helps us to see the truth in our personal problems and in our interactions with each other and that when we have prayer we try to get as high as we can so that we all can have the best vision we can so we can see what's going on; it's a meditation thing, it's well substantiated by people in religion that the experience that you can have with marihuana is identical to the religious experience that you can have spontaneously without it.[74]

The Tennessee Supreme Court was not impressed and unanimously upheld Gaskin's conviction and three-year prison sentence. The court relied primarily on *Reynolds v. United States* and failed to mention *Sherbert v. Verner*.

In 1979, the Florida Supreme Court did apply the *Sherbert* test in reviewing a marijuana possession case involving members of the Ethiopian Zion Coptic Church. Members of the church had smuggled sizable quantities of marijuana from Jamaica to Miami, and criminal convictions followed in state court. On appeal, the Florida Supreme Court recognized that the church represented a sincere religious belief and made use of cannabis as a sacrament in its services. But the court also found that the state's compelling interest in protecting the public health and safety from a "dangerous drug" outweighed any free exercise interests at stake.[75]

As we have noted, in 1990 the Supreme Court refused to adopt the position taken by the California Supreme Court in *People v. Woody*. Under *Employment Division v. Smith* (1990), the First Amendment requires no exemptions from generally applicable laws. This decision prompted Congress not only to enact the Religious Freedom Restoration Act but to adopt a law aimed specifically at protecting the peyote ritual of the Native American Church. The American Indian Religious Freedom Act Amendments of 1994[76] provide that "the use, possession, or transportation of peyote by an Indian for bona fide traditional ceremonial purposes in connection with the practice of a traditional Indian religion is lawful, and shall not be prohibited by the United States or any State."

As discussed earlier in this chapter, after the Court's decision in *City of Boerne v. Flores*, which declared RFRA unconstitutional as applied to state and local laws, Congress amended RFRA to apply only to the federal government. Consequently, unconventional religious practices that run afoul of federal law must be subjected to the *Sherbert* test. A leading case in this regard is *Gonzales v. O Centro Espírita Beneficente União do Vegetal* (2006).[77] In that case, a religious organization in New Mexico filed suit in federal court to prevent the government from interfering with its ritualistic use of hoasca, a tea that contains a psychedelic drug known as DMT. This substance is illegal under the federal Controlled Substances Act, as a Schedule I controlled substance. As a result, U.S. customs agents seized bottles of tea that church members attempted to import from Brazil.

In reviewing this action, a unanimous Court adhered to RFRA and used the *Sherbert* test to rule in favor of the church. Applying the first part of the test, the Court found the church held a sincere religious belief, as evidenced by its regular meetings and centuries-long existence as a religion in Brazil, which included use of hoasca tea in its religious services. Next, the Court said the seizure of the tea bottles pursuant to the Controlled Substances Act amounted to an undue burden upon religious exercise. In response, the government advanced three compelling interests in an attempt to justify the seizure: (1) protecting the health and safety of church members who ingest the tea; (2) lessening the risk of any recreational use or distribution of the drug; (3) adhering to international treaties the United States had joined to halt drug trafficking. The Court ruled that all three compelling interests failed when it came to analysis under the final component of the *Sherbert* test: consideration of "least restrictive means." In particular, the Court said there was no evidence that the health of users would be adversely impacted by the limited quantities of DMT in the tea; in addition, Chief Justice Roberts's majority opinion indicated there was no evidence of recreational transfer or international trafficking in hoasca tea. Therefore, the government could not justify banning the use of hoasca for religious purposes.

Of course, this decision was limited to the narrow uses of the particular substance in question and was not directly germane to other forms of drug use. For example, a man in Arizona named Danny Ray Hardesty unsuccessfully attempted to use the *Gonzales v. O Centro Espirita* case precedent to appeal his conviction for marijuana possession. He claimed the drugs seized from his car during a traffic stop were connected to sacramental use in an organization called the Church of Cognizance. Arizona's Supreme Court used the *Sherbert* test (pursuant to the state's Free Exercise of Religion Act) in rejecting his claim. Notably, the court observed that because Hardesty was driving with a bag of marijuana on his passenger seat while smoking a joint, the state had a compelling interest in maintaining the safety of drivers on the roadways. With that assertion, Hardesty's case was distinguished from the *O Centro* precedent.[78]

JURISPRUDENCE

Indiana Court Addresses "Weed Church"
First Church of Cannabis v. Marion County
Case No. 49C01-1507-Mi-022522 (Marion Co. Cir. Ct., July 6, 2018)

In March 2015, shortly after Indiana Governor Mike Pence signed a Religious Freedom Restoration Act that was set to take effect statewide on July 1, Bill Levin opened the First Church of Cannabis in Indianapolis. Levin had received IRS recognition for his church and hoped to provide parishioners with the ability to use cannabis during religious services as well as to purchase marijuana in the church's gift shop. Because marijuana was a controlled substance in that state, though, the church held off on providing its preferred sacrament and, instead, filed suit in an Indiana court, seeking a declaration that marijuana use should be protected under the state's RFRA. A reviewing court in Marion County rejected this claim, using components of the *Sherbert* test in doing so.

In her opinion in this case, Judge Sheryl Lynch expressed concerns over how sincere a religious belief could be when the founder admitted he came up with the idea for the church while watching the cartoon TV show *The Flintstones* and was charging $4.20 in monthly dues from each member. Beyond that, Judge Lynch addressed other components of the *Sherbert* test, noting the following:

> Several courts have already concluded that, when it comes to claims of sacramental marijuana use, regardless of whether a party can show a substantial burden on a sincerely held religious belief, the government nevertheless has a compelling interest in protecting public health and safety and enforcing marijuana prohibitions—without exception for religious sacrament—is the least restrictive means of advancing that interest.

Judge Lynch buttressed her ruling by saying, "The undisputed evidence demonstrates that permitting a religious exemption to laws that prohibit the use and possession of marijuana would hinder drug enforcement efforts statewide and negatively impact public health and safety." She added that "law enforcement would be faced with many new challenges," including retraining or replacement of drug-sniffing dogs, if such an exception to state drug law were granted. She also spoke of a "lack of clarity on how individuals permitted to use marijuana for religious purposes would obtain or grow marijuana."

Among the other courts cited by Judge Lynch in her opinion were the U.S. Court of Appeals for the Seventh Circuit, which in 2003, rejected a Rastafarianism defense to conditions of parole that banned the use of marijuana.[79] Additionally, she pointed to a 2017 decision from the Eighth Circuit, which rejected a religious defense to heroin possession charges by recognizing a "compelling government interest in mitigating the risk that heroin will be diverted to recreational users."[80] Finally, Judge Lynch also pointed to the Ninth Circuit's 2016 decision refuting a religious exemption claim from a Hawaii group that called itself Cannabis Ministry. The majority opinion for that Ninth Circuit ruling said: "We have little trouble concluding that the government has a compelling interest in preventing drugs set aside for sacramental use from being diverted to non-religious users ... insofar as diverted cannabis could foreseeably fall into the hands of minors, or otherwise expose them to the hazards associated with illegal, recreational drug use," with the Ninth Circuit also noting a "compelling interest in protecting the physical and psychological well-being of minors."[81]

In the end, despite attempts by attorneys to link marijuana use to the hoasca exception provided in *Gonzales v. O Centro*, appellate courts have resisted ascribing free exercise of religion protections to marijuana usage. Whether this approach will shift as more and more states begin to legalize marijuana remains to be seen.

Animal Sacrifice

Another controversial aspect of religious exercise is animal sacrifice. In 1987, the City of Hialeah, Florida enacted an ordinance making it a crime to "unnecessarily kill, torment, torture, or mutilate an animal in a ... ritual or ceremony not for the primary purpose of food consumption." Adoption of the ordinance came in response to the establishment of a Santeria church that practiced ritualistic animal sacrifice in the area. In *Church of the Lukumi Babalu Aye v. City of Hialeah* (1993),[82] the Supreme Court invalidated the ordinance under the Free Exercise Clause. In his opinion for a unanimous Court, Justice Kennedy noted that the law was not a generally applicable criminal prohibition but, rather, singled out practitioners of Santeria by forbidding animal slaughter only within the context of religious rituals. Thus, the case was not controlled by *Employment Division v. Smith*. Instead, applying the *Sherbert* test, the Court could discern no compelling interest that would justify the ban on ritualistic animal slaughter. The City cited the need to protect public health and prevent animal cruelty but did not explain "why commercial operations that slaughter 'small numbers' of hogs and cattle do not implicate its professed desire to prevent cruelty to animals and preserve the public health." Rather, said Justice Kennedy, the disputed ordinance "pursues the city's governmental interests only against conduct motivated by religious belief."

Snake Handling

There are several churches in which ministers and members of the congregation handle poisonous snakes during worship services. Most of these churches are located in Southern Appalachia, and parishioners tend to believe God will protect them from being harmed by serpents—with the act of handling serving as a test of faith. From time to time, one hears of someone being transported to the hospital, or even dying, after being bitten by a rattlesnake at one of these services.

Most states have laws that make it a crime to possess certain dangerous animals. Tennessee law, for example, makes it an offense "to display, exhibit, handle, or use a poisonous or dangerous snake or reptile in a manner that endangers the life or health of any person."[83] In 1975, the Tennessee Supreme Court upheld this statute, noting "a substantial and compelling state interest in the face of a clear and present danger so grave as to endanger paramount public interests."[84] Despite the court's decision, the practice continues in rural Tennessee. It also continues in Kentucky, where in 2014, a pastor named Jamie Coots, who had appeared on the National Geographic TV program "Snake Salvation," died from a snakebite inflicted during a worship service.

THE CONSTITUTION IN ACTION
Snake Handling Preacher in Tennessee Avoids Indictment

In 2013, Andrew Hamblin, pastor of Tabernacle Church of God in LaFollette, Tennessee, was arrested for violating state law that made it is a misdemeanor to "display, exhibit, handle, or use a poisonous or dangerous snake in a manner or reptile that endangers the life or health of any person."[85] Although it would seem Hamblin's decision to hold a live rattlesnake during his religious services in front of in-person audiences amounted to a breach of this statute, a grand jury in his county opted not to indict him. Thus, the charges were dismissed without a trial. Some might suggest this amounts to an example of jury nullification, whereby a jury of one's peers—typically made up of like-minded individuals from the same geographic area—chooses not to apply existing law to specific conduct. In this case, it was almost as if the grand jury played the role of an appellate court in applying free exercise of religion protections early on in the legal process, eliminating any chance of a prosecutor seeking a guilty verdict at trial.

Sacramental Sex?

To merit judicial consideration for protection under the Free Exercise Clause, a practice must be based on sincere religious beliefs.[86] In 1991, the U.S. Court of Appeals for the Ninth Circuit heard a case involving a couple that professed to be the high priest and priestess of The Church of the Most High Goddess. The practice in question involved sex between members of the congregation and the "priestess"—but only after a "donation" was made. The court noted that the couple had previously been charged with keeping a house of ill fame. Their newly created "religion" was, in the court's view, merely a cover for illegal prostitution. The Court rejected their First Amendment claim, holding that their beliefs were not sincere.[87]

Religion and the Welfare of Children

One of the functions of state government is safeguarding the interests of those who cannot take care of themselves, including children and those with severe mental illness or intellectual disabilities. The law refers to this role as parens patriae, which means *parent of the country*. This doctrine permits the state to intervene to protect the interests of children from parents who are abusive or neglectful. It also comes into play when parents refuse to allow medical treatment for their children. Courts will generally allow state intervention in such cases if there is clear and convincing evidence that refusal of medical treatment is life-threatening.[88]

In *Prince v. Massachusetts* (1944),[89] the Supreme Court discussed the parens patriae doctrine as it relates to compulsory vaccination of children:

> Acting to guard the general interest in youth's well being, the state as *parens patriae* may restrict the parent's control by requiring school attendance, regulating or prohibiting the child's labor, and in many other ways. Its authority is not nullified merely because the parent grounds his claim to control the child's course of conduct on religion or conscience. Thus, he cannot claim freedom from compulsory vaccination for the child more than for himself on religious grounds. The right to practice religion freely does not include liberty to expose the community or the child to communicable disease or the latter to ill health or death.

PARENS PATRIAE:
A theory suggesting government holds the responsibility for caring for individuals who are not capable of caring for themselves; this could apply to government officials acting in place of parents who are not serving the best interests of a child.

Moreover, courts have uniformly held that parents may not refuse to allow medical professionals to administer blood transfusions in emergency cases when it is necessary to save the life of their child—a matter that has been critical in cases involving certain faiths that oppose such transfusions.[90]

Compulsory School Attendance

Although in *Prince v. Massachusetts* the Court recognized the constitutionality of compulsory school attendance laws, in *Wisconsin v. Yoder* (1972),[91] the Court made an exception for members of the Old Order Amish religion. Amish parents who refused to allow their children to attend high school had been fined $5 for violating the state's compulsory school attendance law. Applying the test delineated in *Sherbert v. Verner*, the Supreme Court held that Wisconsin's compulsory attendance law could not be constitutionally applied to the Old Order Amish.

Writing for the majority, Chief Justice Burger stressed the fact that the education of the Amish teenager continued in the home, with emphasis on practical skills and moral values. In dissent, Justice William O. Douglas criticized the Court's decision for failing to consider the best interests of the young people involved. Had the case been litigated after the *Employment Division v. Smith* decision, the outcome might well have been different.

Compliance with Civil Rights Laws

It is well established law that churches have the right to select their own ministers without interference from the government.[92] Adopting what is termed the **ministerial exception**, the Supreme Court said in 2012 that religious organizations are exempt from discrimination suits brought by employees who serve as clergy.[93] The rationale underlying this opinion—which vacated a lawsuit brought by an employee claiming discrimination under the Americans with Disabilities Act—was that government dictates regarding whom a religious organization could hire or fire for "ministerial positions" would violate both the Establishment and Free Exercise Clauses of the First Amendment.

In 2020, the Supreme Court expanded this exception to include teachers in religious schools—even those teachers without specified religious duties. In the majority opinion for this case, Justice Alito said, "Under this [ministerial exception], courts are bound to stay out of employment disputes involving those holding certain important positions with

MINISTERIAL EXCEPTION: An idea created by the Supreme Court to suggest religious organizations, like churches and religious schools, can make employment decisions regarding certain important positions without consideration of potential violations of existing employment discrimination laws.

churches and other religious institutions." His invocation of the phrase "certain important positions" leaves ample room for debate in future cases—but certainly suggests that the exception applies beyond clergy, as long as some connection to what Alito calls the "core of the mission" for an organization applies to the job in question.[94] Despite this broadening, the ministerial exception remains fairly narrow in the sense that the two key Supreme Court precedents on this topic have entailed analysis of the Americans with Disabilities Act; thus, the ministerial exception might not provide a license for religious organizations to ignore other civil rights laws at this time, although future litigation certainly could alter that idea.

JURISPRUDENCE

Does Free Exercise of Religion Include the Right to Discriminate?
Bob Jones University v. United States, 461 U.S. 574 (1983)

In 1976, the Internal Revenue Service revoked Bob Jones University's tax-exempt status because its racially discriminatory admissions policies were deemed to be contrary to public policy. These policies prohibited the admission of any individuals involved in an interracial marriage or who advocated interracial marriage or dating. Bob Jones University claimed, among other things, this action violated the Free Exercise Clause of the First Amendment. Yet on appeal, the Supreme Court ruled against the school.

Chief Justice Burger delivered the opinion of the Court, saying the following in part: "This Court has long held the Free Exercise Clause of the First Amendment to be an absolute prohibition against governmental regulation of religious beliefs. ... As interpreted by this Court, moreover, the Free Exercise Clause provides substantial protection for lawful conduct grounded in religious belief. ... However, '[n]ot all burdens on religion are unconstitutional. ... The state may justify a limitation on religious liberty by showing that it is essential to accomplish an overriding governmental interest.'"

Applying the prongs of the *Sherbert* test, Burger also spoke to the substantive public policy considerations at stake in the university policy by saying, "The governmental interest at stake here is compelling. ... [T]he Government has a fundamental, overriding interest in eradicating racial discrimination in education—discrimination that prevailed, with official approval, for the first 165 years of this Nation's constitutional history." He then weighed that compelling interest against the alleged burdens on religious exercise by saying: "That governmental interest substantially outweighs whatever burden denial of tax benefits places on petitioners' exercise of their religious beliefs. The interests asserted by petitioners cannot be accommodated with that compelling governmental interest, ... and no 'less restrictive means,' ... are available to achieve the governmental interest."

The Landmark *Hobby Lobby* Case

Recent years have seen a number of business owners refuse to comply with laws they find morally objectionable. For example, the owners of Hobby Lobby brought suit to challenge the Affordable Care Act's mandate for businesses to provide employees with access to health care plans that covered certain types of contraceptives. In *Burwell v. Hobby Lobby Stores, Inc.* (2014)[95] the Supreme Court ruled that closely held for-profit corporations are exempt from a federal law its owners religiously object to if there is a less restrictive means of furthering the law's interest. The decision was based on RFRA, not the First Amendment, and the Court went through the four components of the *Sherbert* test.

First, the Court assessed whether a sincere religious belief was apparent. On this point, the majority found that a corporation is capable of holding a sincere religious belief. In this case, that notion was limited to a "closely held" corporation—defined by the IRS as one for which 50% or more of the stock is owned by five or fewer people—but a 2020 Supreme Court decision would expand this idea to all for-profit and nonprofit companies.[96] Moreover, the religious belief in question was the idea that life begins at conception. The Court then determined there was an "undue burden" connected to the Affordable Care Act's requirement to provide contraception coverage that allegedly conflicted with the company owners' belief in this idea.

The government responded by suggesting there was a compelling interest in "ensuring cost-free contraception access for women," and the Court's majority did in fact accept that proposition. Nevertheless, the Court found that Hobby Lobby prevailed on the final component of the *Sherbert* test because the Affordable Care Act was not offering the "least restrictive means" for furthering women's access to contraception without burdening religious exercise; along these lines, the conservative majority actually suggested tax dollars could be used to pay for contraception access, instead of Hobby Lobby's business funds. Thus, based on the fourth prong of the *Sherbert* test, Hobby Lobby won its case.

Freedom of Religion Versus LGBTQ Rights

Since the Supreme Court effectively legalized same-sex marriage, some business owners have refused to do business with same-sex couples. In *Masterpiece Cakeshop v. Colorado Civil Rights Commission* (2018),[97] a bakery owner refused to bake a wedding cake for a same-sex marriage and was cited and fined for discrimination by the state's Civil Rights Commission. In reviewing the case, the Supreme Court held that the bakery owner had been denied the free exercise of religion because members of the Commission made statements, in a formal hearing, showing hostility to his religious beliefs. Justice Kennedy wrote for the Court, saying, "The official expressions of hostility to religion in some of the commissioners' comments—comments that were not disavowed at the Commission or by the State at any point in the proceedings that led to affirmance of the order—were inconsistent with what the Free Exercise Clause requires." However, the opinion's reliance on the specific process involved in this particular case limited the scope of the precedent because the Court failed to squarely face the core issue at hand: does the Free Exercise Clause protect a business owner's refusal to deal with customers whose conduct the owner finds morally objectionable?

Three years later, in *Fulton v. Philadelphia* (2021),[98] the Court again dealt with the issue of free exercise of religion and discrimination against LGBTQ persons but in a very different context. The City of Philadelphia had terminated its contract with Catholic Social Services when it learned CSS would not certify same-sex couples as foster parents. CSS brought suit and ultimately prevailed in the Supreme Court. Writing for the Court, Chief Justice Roberts said the law that allowed the City to terminate the contract with CSS was neither neutral nor generally applicable. Therefore, Roberts held that *Employment Division v. Smith* was inapplicable to the case and applied strict scrutiny instead. He concluded the following:

> CSS seeks only an accommodation that will allow it to continue serving the children of Philadelphia in a manner consistent with its religious beliefs; it does not seek to impose those beliefs on anyone else. The refusal of Philadelphia to contract with CSS for the provision of foster care services unless it agrees to certify same-sex couples as foster parents cannot survive strict scrutiny, and violates the First Amendment.

THE CONSTITUTION AND SOCIAL JUSTICE
Freedom of Religion and Cultural Diversity

A fundamental aspect of social justice is the idea that all persons, irrespective of race, ethnicity, gender, sexual orientation, or religion, stand equal before the law. So many of the religion cases that have reached the Supreme Court have involved the rights of religious minorities: Mormons, Jews, Jehovah's Witnesses, Seventh-Day Adventists, Amish, Muslims, and others. To the extent that members of religious minorities are free to practice their faith undisturbed by law or policy, the cause of social justice has been served. As Justice Robert Jackson observed in *West Virginia Board of Education v. Barnette* eight decades ago, "[w]e can have intellectual individualism and the rich cultural diversities that we owe to exceptional minds only at the price of occasional eccentricity and abnormal attitudes." The right to be different in religion or anything else "is not limited to things that do not matter much." In Jackson's view, Americans have "the right to differ as to things that touch the heart of the existing order." Indeed, the right to be different is key to the attainment of social justice.

Religion in the Public Sector Workplace

The Free Exercise Clause applies to the public sector workplace at all levels of government. Furthermore, Title VII of the Civil Rights Act of 1964 prohibits religious discrimination in the workplace, whether public or private. Discrimination in hiring, firing, or promoting employees on the basis of religion obviously runs afoul of this prohibition. An employer must accommodate an employee's sincerely held religious beliefs and practices, unless doing so would produce an undue hardship.[99] Such accommodations include allowing employees to take breaks to pray during the workday and take days off for religious holidays.

Religious Expression in the Workplace

There is not a right of religious expression in the workplace per se, but managers must take care to have clear policies that do not discriminate against religious expression. In 1996, the Ninth Circuit sided with a state worker who was suspended and reprimanded for posting religious messages on materials that he circulated in the workplace. The court determined the employee had been discriminated against on the basis of religious expression.[100]

Whether religious expression in the workplace warrants discipline or removal also depends on the nature of the expression and whether it interferes with the functions of the office. In 1995, the Eighth Circuit held that a public employee was improperly dismissed for holding voluntary prayers in his office and referring to scripture during office meetings.[101] The Florida county for which he worked did not produce evidence that allowing such activities would produce an undue hardship. On the other hand, the Second Circuit held that two state health workers were properly disciplined after they proselytized to clients.[102] The two employees told a gay patient that God disapproved of his homosexual lifestyle. In upholding their suspension, the court noted that one of the two employees had been permitted to lead a prayer at a staff meeting. The agency evinced no hostility to religion; it only insisted on professionalism in dealing with clients.

Future cases will assess the scope of the Supreme Court's decision in *Bostock v. Clayton County* (2020),[103] which held that employment discrimination based on sexual orientation or gender identity is a violation of

Title VII of the Civil Rights Act of 1964. Whether any religious exceptions, perhaps in the form of a ministerial exception, would be tolerated in regard to applying this precedent remains to be seen.

Dress Codes and Grooming Requirements

Dress codes and grooming requirements enacted by employers can run afoul of constitutional or statutory protections for religion. For instance, in 2005, two Muslim firefighters in Washington, D.C. successfully used the Religious Freedom Restoration Act to challenge a department policy that prohibited them from growing beards.[104] Similarly, in a 2015 private-sector case that has ramifications for public agencies as well, the Supreme Court held an employer cannot refuse to hire a woman because her Muslim faith requires her to wear a hijab at work. This matter stemmed from a suit brought against Abercrombie & Fitch by a woman who said she was denied employment because the company's dress code did not make allowances for her religious attire. She filed a complaint with the Equal Employment Opportunity Commission, which brought suit in federal district court on her behalf; she won and was awarded $20,000. However, the Tenth Circuit would reverse this decision, finding instead for Abercrombie & Fitch.

The Supreme Court granted review, and in its decision in *EEOC v. Abercrombie & Fitch* (2015),[105] the majority reinstated the original $20,000 award. Specifically, the Court applied Title VII of the Civil Rights Act of 1964, and Justice Scalia's majority opinion stated, "[T]he rule for disparate-treatment claims based on a failure to accommodate a religious practice is straightforward: An employer may not make an applicant's religious practice, confirmed or otherwise, a factor in employment decisions." Use of the words "a factor" indicates that *any* consideration of religious practices would be prohibited in an employment decision.

In an earlier matter, the U.S. Department of Justice helped negotiate a settlement between a sixth-grade student and an Oklahoma public school after she was suspended from school for eight days for refusing to remove her hijab while in class, in violation of the school's *no hats* policy. A lawsuit filed in federal district court alleged the student's rights under the Equal Protection Clause of the Fourteenth Amendment had been violated, and a settlement (known as a *consent order*) required the school to allow the student to wear her hijab and also mandated the school to make similar religious accommodations for other students who held a "bona fide" religious objection to the school's dress code.[106]

Exemption from Policies and Work Assignments

Although the Supreme Court has not provided specific guidance regarding whether public employees can be exempted from particular job assignments or employment policies, circuit courts have confronted this matter. For example, in 1988, the Eighth Circuit held that the Free Exercise Clause did not require the operators of a nuclear power plant to exempt employees with religious objections from participating in a drug testing program. In rejecting the Free Exercise Claim, the court noted the compelling public safety interest at stake and held that the drug testing program was the least restrictive means of furthering that interest.[107]

Elsewhere, in 2003, an Indiana court rejected a Free Exercise claim brought by a police officer who objected to being assigned to protect a casino due to his religious scruples against gambling. The court held that the officer's assignment "did not materially burden his right of religious freedom."[108] To hold otherwise would set a precedent whereby Roman Catholic officers who object to abortion could refuse an assignment to protect the entrance to a women's health clinic, Baptist officers who object to alcohol could refuse to arrest those who vandalize a liquor store, and so on.

Employee Prayer in the Public School Setting

As noted above in our discussion of the Establishment Clause, the Supreme Court has been fairly staunch in limiting teacher-led prayer and other devotional exercises in public schools. However, those decisions do not prohibit students and teachers from praying on their own. But what is the appropriate time and place for such personal devotion? This question came before the Supreme Court in 2022 in *Kennedy v. Bremerton School District*.[109] There, the Court ruled in favor of a public high school football coach who sought to pray on the 50-yard line of the football field—silently and on his own (although in view of students and fans)—at the conclusion of each of his team's games. He was placed on leave and his contract was not renewed after he refused to heed the school board's directive to cease the prayer. He sued claiming a violation of both free exercise and Establishment Clause principles. Writing for a majority of six justices, Justice Neil Gorsuch opined: "Respect for religious expressions is indispensable to life in a free and diverse Republic—whether those expressions take place in a sanctuary or on a field, and whether they manifest through the spoken word or a bowed head." In a strongly worded dissent, Justice Sotomayor asserted that the majority "elevates one individual's interest in personal religious exercise, in the exact time and place of that individual's choosing, over society's interest in protecting the separation between church and state, eroding the protections for religious liberty for all."

Religious Rights of Prisoners

Obviously, imprisonment prevents the exercise of many constitutional rights, but it does not negate constitutional rights altogether. As Justice Sandra Day O'Connor observed in *Turner v. Safley* (1987),[110] "Prison walls do not form a barrier separating prison inmates from the protections of the Constitution." Accordingly, the Supreme Court has held that prisoners have the right to practice their religion.[111] Congress reinforced this position by enacting the Religious Land Use and Institutionalized Persons Act (RLUIPA) in 2000.[112] Much like RFRA, the RLUIPA prohibits prison officials from enforcing a policy that substantially burdens the free exercise of religion, unless they can demonstrate they have a compelling interest that cannot be achieved through less restrictive means for doing so.

In *Holt v. Hobbs* (2015),[113] the Supreme Court relied on RLUIPA to strike down an Arkansas prison policy that prohibited a Muslim inmate from growing a half-inch beard. The Court's majority rejected the argument that prison officials would not be able to tell prisoners apart if facial hair were allowed. Another argument citing a need to prevent prisoners from hiding contraband in facial hair failed because prison guards could search a small beard with a comb, just as they do when searching the hair on a prisoner's head.

JURISPRUDENCE

Supreme Court Protects Religious Exercise During an Execution
Ramirez v. Collier, 595 U.S. ___ (2022)

In March 2022, the Supreme Court of the United States ruled in favor of a Texas death row inmate named John Ramirez, who wanted to have a Baptist minister be permitted pray out loud and touch him at the moment of his execution. Although these practices had long been permitted in Texas, in 2019, the state banned both the touching of an inmate and the use of oral prayer during all executions.

Writing for an 8–1 majority, Chief Justice Roberts applied the Religious Land Use and Institutionalized Persons Act to the Ramirez case. This law requires the government to demonstrate a compelling interest, applied in the least restrictive manner, to justify an infringement upon religious exercise in correctional settings. In the case at hand, two interests were put forth by the state. First, it was suggested that "absolute silence" was necessary to "monitor the inmate's condition" during an execution. Rejecting this claim, Justice Roberts noted "there is a rich history of clerical prayer at the time of a prisoner's execution, dating back well before the founding or our Nation." With that in mind, Roberts suggested there was no evidence of clergy's presence having created a risk to an inmate during a prior execution. Second, the government suggested audible prayer "could be exploited to make a statement to the witnesses or officials, rather than the inmate." The majority opinion also dismissed this concern, suggesting it amounted to "conjecture regarding what a hypothetical spiritual advisor might do in some future case." Overall, in granting an injunction to allow the religious exercise sought in this case, Justice Roberts said Ramirez was "likely to suffer irreparable harm in the absence of injunctive relief because he will be unable to engage in protected religious exercise in the final moments of his life."

The lone dissenter in this case, Clarence Thomas, suggested the RLUIPA was being exploited, declaring that "Ramirez has manufactured more than a decade of delay to evade the capital sentence lawfully imposed by the State of Texas." Thomas paid homage to the crime's victim, noting that in 2004, Ramirez stabbed a man named Pablo Castro 29 times during a robbery that resulted in the taking of a mere $1.25. Justice Thomas also referred to the RLUIPA by saying, "Congress created a potent tool with which prisoners can protect their sincerely held religious beliefs. But, like any tool, it can be wielded abusively. And few have a greater incentive to do so than death-row inmates." He went on to say that "federal courts ... have a duty to dismiss piecemeal, later-breaking, dilatory, specious, speculative or manipulative litigation." In this matter, the state of Texas announced in February of 2021 that the execution date for Ramirez would be September 8, 2021—and it was upon learning of this date that Ramirez initiated a grievance proceeding with the prison and, subsequently, the federal lawsuit that led to this Supreme Court decision.

A key point in the majority opinion was that a death row inmate need not exhaust all avenues of administrative review within a prison system before bringing a claim such as this before a federal court. A footnote from Chief Justice Roberts' opinion observed that such administrative review might not "permit complete exhaustion of execution-related claims in a timely manner before a scheduled execution," which Roberts addressed in tangential fashion by noting, "Compensation paid to his estate would not remedy this harm, which is spiritual rather than pecuniary."

Conclusion

In this chapter, we examined the two key religion clauses of the First Amendment: the Establishment Clause and the Free Exercise Clause. For the founders of this country, both clauses were essential for preserving religious freedom in the United States, particularly in light of the persecution that had plagued Britain and much of Europe for centuries.

Over time, the Supreme Court has established tests, or legal doctrines, for analyzing the religion clauses. For the Establishment Clause, which was intended to prohibit government imposition of religion upon the people, the Court crafted the *Lemon* test. Its three components involve assessment of whether government action has a secular purpose, whether it advances or inhibits religion, and whether it entangles government and religion. This test has been applied to school prayer, legislative prayer, displays of holiday items, displays of the Ten Commandments, taxpayer-funded educational scholarships, and more. Ultimately, the context of each specific case—such as whether a religious display is indoors or outdoors or in a school or a courthouse—can result in varied decisions from appellate courts. Notably, recent Supreme Court cases indicate the *Lemon* test might be evolving into a disfavored framework, with the Court trending in the direction of being more tolerant of religious expression in government forums, provided that no coercion or denigration of faith is apparent. An exception to this trend is prayer in public schools, which has repeatedly been found to violate the Establishment Clause.

For the Free Exercise Clause, the Supreme Court has made use of the *Sherbert* test for the majority of recent cases—in keeping with a directive advanced by Congress with passage of the Religious Freedom Restoration Act, which is a law that seemed to urge courts to be more sensitive to granting exceptions to laws or government policies in the name of religious freedom. Generally speaking, the *Sherbert* test creates a sizable obstacle for the government when it seeks to place an undue burden upon the exercise of a sincere religious belief, since such a burden must be justified by a compelling interest that is advanced in a manner that represents the least restrictive means of limiting religious exercise. Of course, it is possible that a court could construe a law that is deemed *neutral* and *generally applicable* as being outside the scope of *Sherbert* test analysis, in light of the *Employment Division v. Smith* decision. Even so, it seems as if the Supreme Court has recently trended toward using the *Sherbert* test in cases that involve federal officials or policies—while many states have passed their own versions of religious freedom laws to mandate use of that test as well.

Overall, a general theme of this chapter is whether and when the courts should invoke the Free Exercise Clause to afford exceptions to existing laws in the name of religious exercise—whether such laws address employment discrimination, drug use, snake handling, polygamy, or a host of other issues. Ostensibly, case precedent has made it clear that, on some occasions, religious exercise can prove to be a viable defense against criminal charges or even grounds for appealing a criminal conviction.

Finally, we also have examined the religious rights of public employees, which include police officers, parents who seek the authority to make difficult medical decisions for their children, and even prisoners who find themselves incarcerated after being convicted of crimes. Generally, these issues make it clear that forging a balance between the protection of individual liberty and the well-being of society lies at the core of any analysis of the two Religion Clauses of the First Amendment.

Discussion Questions

1. Suppose a professor at a public university puts up a holiday display in their classroom that includes the following: a nativity scene, a Christmas tree, parchment with the Ten Commandments typed on it, and a menorah. In addition, at the beginning of each class, the professor asks students to look at the display, bow their heads, and join in a silent prayer to "give thanks to God for all he has given us." How would a court evaluate everything that is going on here? What precedents and legal tests would control the analysis? What would be considered a violation of the Establishment Clause, and what would not?

2. Find an example of a situation in which a person sought an exception from an existing law or government policy based on a purported exercise of religious freedom. What legal test should be used to evaluate that claim, and how would the analysis proceed on each component of the test?

3. In what ways do speech and assembly rights overlap with religious freedoms when it comes to religious exercise in public places? How are the legal tests used for speech cases and religion cases similar? How are they different, if at all? What case precedents speak to both concepts?

4. What are some patriotic duties to which a person might object on religious grounds? What parts of the First Amendment—and what related case precedents—are most germane to analysis of these situations? What legal test would be appropriate if a school suspended a student who refused to take part in a school activity because of a religious belief? What if the school requirement in question were a vaccination mandate?

5. From snake handling to drug use to polygamy, there are many activities in society that implicate requests from individuals seeking exceptions to existing laws or government policies. What potential issues face a legal system that grants such exceptions? What potential issues face a system that does not? Are there any compelling interests that seem to apply across a variety of such claims? Additionally, consider how the evaluation of a *marijuana church* might evolve as more and more states legalize the drug; how might that analysis differ from the evaluation of a *heroin church*?

6. Under what circumstances is it appropriate for parents to make medical decisions for children? When is it problematic for the religious beliefs of parents to impact medical decisions made for their children? What legal tests would be most appropriate if courts had to evaluate such situations? How would a court analyze a situation in which a parent seeks to use religious exceptions to avoid vaccination mandates for children imposed by a local school board?

7. Is there anything problematic about the Supreme Court's creation of a "ministerial exception" to employment discrimination laws? Are there any positives associated with this exception? How does this exception carry implications for both the Establishment Clause and the Free Exercise Clause? To what laws has this exception been applied already—and to what laws might it be applied in the future?

8. Are the rights of workers in government jobs coextensive with the rights of employees in other contexts? What legal tests are applicable when a public employee claims a violation of religious freedoms connected to compliance with workplace policies? How would a court evaluate a request from a public employee who wishes to avoid a mandatory vaccine requirement?

9. What are some specific ways prisoners might attempt to claim violations of religious liberty while incarcerated? Why was a specific federal law created to address this topic? Was the First Amendment insufficient in any way when applied in such contexts? What are common compelling interests the government might advance in prison settings? What legal tests should control religious freedom cases stemming from prisons?

Endnotes

1   *McDaniel v. Paty*, 435 U.S. 618 (1978).

2   Letter from Thomas Jefferson to the Danbury Baptist Association (1802).

3   Alexis de Tocqueville, *Democracy in America*, ed. J. P. Mayers and Max Lerner, trans. George Lawrence (New York: Harper & Row, 1969), 271–72.

4   *Everson v. Board of Education*, 330 U.S. 1 (1947).

5   *McGowan v. Maryland*, 366 U.S. 420 (1961).

6   *Braunfeld v. Brown*, 366 U.S. 599 (1961).

7   *Engel v. Vitale*, 370 U.S. 421 (1962).

8   *Abington School District v. Schempp*, 374 U.S. 203 (1963).

9   Paul G. Kauper, *The Warren Court: Religious Liberty and Church–State Relations*, 67 Mich. L. Rev. 269–288 (1968).

10 *Wallace v. Jaffree*, 472 U.S. 38 (1985).

11 *Lee v. Weisman*, 505 U.S. 577 (1992).

12 *Santa Fe Independent School Dist. v. Doe*, 530 U.S. 290 (2000).

13 *Epperson v. Arkansas*, 393 U.S. 97 (1968).

14 *Edwards v. Aguillard*, 482 U.S. 578 (1987).

15 *Board of Education v. Allen*, 392 U.S. 236 (1968).

16 *Lemon v. Kurtzman*, 403 U.S. 602 (1971).

17 *Elk Grove Unified School District v. Newdow*, 542 U.S. 1 (2004).

18 *New Doe Child #1 v. United States*, 901 F.3d 1015 (8th Cir. 2018).

19 *Marsh v. Chambers*, 463 U.S. 783 (1983).

20 *Town of Greece v. Galloway*, 572 U.S. 565 (2014).

21 *Satanic Temple, Inc. v. City of Boston*, Civil Action No. 21-cv-10102-ADB (D. Mass. Jul. 21, 2021).

22 *Lynch v. Donnelly*, 465 U.S. 668 (1984).

23 *County of Allegheny v. American Civil Liberties Union*, 492 U.S. 573 (1989).

24 Jessica Palombo, *Florida Man Airs Grievances With Festivus Pole in Capitol*, NPR, Dec. 11, 2013, https://www.npr.org/2013/12/11/250200281/florida-man-airs-grievances-with-festivus-pole-in-capitol.

25 *Stone v. Graham*, 449 U.S. 39 (1980).

26 *McCreary County v. ACLU*, 545 U.S. 844 (2005).

27 *Van Orden v. Perry*, 545 U.S. 677 (2005).

28 Janelle Stecklein, *Legislature Tries to Display Ten Commandments Again*, The Norman Transcript, May 16, 2018, https://www.normantranscript.com/news/oklahoma/legislature-tries-to-display-ten-commandments-again/article_a0a9efd4-ab7f-59b9-82d9-2d6aed10001f.html .

29 *American Legion et al. v. American Humanist Association*, 588 U.S. ___ (2019).

30 *Walz v. Tax Commission of the City of New York*, 397 U.S. 664 (1970).

31 *Hein v. Freedom from Religion Foundation*, 551 U.S. 587 (2007).

32 *Zelman v. Simmons-Harris*, 536 U.S. 639 (2002).

33 *Espinoza v. Montana Dept. of Revenue*, 591 U.S. ___ (2020).

34 *Trinity Lutheran Church of Columbia v. Comer*, 582 U.S. ___ (2017).

35 *Carson v. Makin*, 596 U.S. ___ (2022) .

36 *Reynolds v. United States*, 98 U.S. 145 (1878).

37 *Cantwell v. Connecticut*, 310 U.S. 296 (1940).

38 *West Virginia State Board of Education v. Barnette*, 319 U.S. 624 (1943).

39 *Torcaso v. Watkins*, 367 U.S. 488 (1961).

40 *Sherbert v. Verner*, 374 U.S. 398 (1963).

41 *Employment Division v. Smith*, 494 U.S. 872 (1990).

42 American Indian Religious Freedom Act Amendments of 1994, Pub. L. No. 103-344, 108 Stat. 3125, 42 U.S.C. § 1996a.

43 *Fulton v. Philadelphia*, 593 U.S. ___ (2021) (Alito, J. concurring).

44 *Trinity Lutheran Church of Columbia, Inc. v. Comer*, 582 U.S. ___ (2017).

45 Religious Freedom Restoration Act of 1993, Pub. L. No. 103-141, 107 Stat. 1488, 42 U.S.C. § 2000bb-2000bb-4.

46 *City of Boerne v. Flores*, 521 U.S. 507 (1997).

47 *Fowler v. Rhode Island*, 345 U.S. 67 (1953).

48   *South Bay United Pentecostal Church v. Newsom*, 590 U.S. ____ (2020).

49   *Calvary Chapel Dayton Valley v. Sisolak*, 591 U.S. ____ (2020).

50   *Roman Catholic Diocese of Brooklyn v. Cuomo*, 592 U.S. ____ (2020).

51   *Calvary Chapel Dayton Valley v. Sisolak*, 982 F.3d 1228 (9th Cir. 2020).

52   *Maryville Baptist Church, Inc. v. Beshear*, 455 F. Supp. 3d 342 (W.D. Ky. 2020).

53   *Emily Dahl v. The Board of Trustees of Western Michigan University, et al.*, No. 1:21-cv-757 (W.D. Mi. 2021).

54   Craig McCarthy & Tina Moore, *Here's How Many NYPD Cops Are on Unpaid Leave over Vax Mandate*, N.Y. Post, Nov. 1, 2021, https://nypost.com/2021/11/01/heres-how-many-nypd-cops-are-on-unpaid-leave-over-vaccine-mandate/.

55   Tina Moore, Larry Celona, & Kenneth Garger, *Unvaccinated Cops Given New February Deadline for COVID Jab*, N.Y. Post, Jan. 30, 2022, https://nypost.com/2022/01/30/unvaxxed-cops-given-new-february-deadline-for-covid-jab/.

56   Carl Campanile & Nolan Hicks, *Mayor Adams Fires 1,430 NYC Workers for Refusing to Get COVID Vaccine*, N.Y. Post, Feb. 14, 2022, https://nypost.com/2022/02/14/over-1400-nyc-workers-fired-for-refusing-covid-vaccine/.

57   National Conference of State Legislatures, *States with Religious and Philosophical Exemptions from School Immunization Requirements*, https://www.ncsl.org/research/health/school-immunization-exemption-state-laws.aspx.

58   *Watchtower Bible & Tract Society v. Village of Stratton*, 536 U.S. 150 (2002).

59   *International Society for Krishna Consciousness v. Lee*, 505 U.S. 672 (1992).

60   *Minersville School District v. Gobitis*, 310 U.S. 586 (1940).

61   The current law is codified at 50 U.S.C. § 456(j).

62   *United States v. Seeger*, 380 U.S. 163 (1965).

63   *Goldman v. Weinberger*, 475 U.S. 503 (1986).

64   Internal Revenue Service, *Churches Defined*, https://www.irs.gov/charities-non-profits/churches-religious-organizations/churches-defined.

65   *Davis v. Beason*, 133 U.S. 333 (1890).

66   Utah Code § 76-7-101.

67   *Brown v. Buhman*, 947 F.Supp.2d 1170, 1176 (D.Utah 2013).

68   *Brown v. Buhman*, 822 F.3d 1151 (10th Cir. 2016).

69   *Brown v. Buhman*, 581 U.S. ____ (2017).

70   Brady McCombs & Sam Hananel, *US Supreme Court Won't Hear 'Sister Wives' Bigamy Law Appeal*, AP News, https://apnews.com/article/7b09c5f1fd904b678eaa63e4cce77d47.

71   Brett Bachman, *Why Satanists May Be The Last, Best Hope to Save Abortion Rights in Texas*, Salon, Sept. 4, 2021, https://www.salon.com/2021/09/04/why-satanists-may-be-the-last-best-hope-to-save-abortion-rights-in-texas/.

72   *People v. Woody*, 61 Cal.2d 716 (Cal. 1964).

73   *See, e.g.*, *State v. Whittingham*, 504 P.2d 950 (Ct. App. 1973); *Whitehorn v. State*, 561 P.2d 539 (Okla. Ct. Crim. App. 1976).

74   *Gaskin v. State*, 490 S.W.2d 521 (Tenn. 1973).

75   *Town v. State ex rel. Reno*, 377 So. 2d 648 (1979).

76   American Indian Religious Freedom Act Amendments of 1994, Pub. L. 103-344, 108 Stat. 3124, 42 U.S.C. § 1996.

77   *Gonzales v. O Centro Espírita Beneficente União do Vegetal*, 546 U.S. 418 (2006).

78   *State of Arizona v. Danny Ray Hardesty*, 222 Ariz. 363, 214 P.3d 1004 (Ariz. 2009).

79   *United States v. Israel*, 317 F.3d 768 (7th Cir. 2003).

80   *United States v. Anderson*, 854 F.3d 1033 (8th Cir. 2017).

81 *United States v. Christie*, 825 F.3d 1048 (9th Cir. 2016).

82 *Church of the Lukumi Babalu Aye v. City of Hialeah*, 508 U.S. 520 (1993).

83 Tenn. Code. Ann. § 39-17-101(a).

84 *State ex rel. Swann v. Pack*, 527 S.W.2d 99 (Tenn. 1975).

85 Tenn. Code Ann. § 39-17-101.

86 *United States v. Ballard*, 322 U.S. 78 (1944).

87 *Tracy v. Hahn*, 940 F.2d 1536 (9th Cir. 1991).

88 *See, e.g., Matter of Hamilton*, 657 S.W.2d 425 (Ct. App. 1983).

89 *Prince v. Massachusetts*, 321 U.S. 158 (1944).

90 *See* Stephan R. Paul, *Child Welfare vs. Parental Religious Views: What Do Pediatricians Do When Parents Refuse Life-Saving Care for Their Child?* 32 *AAP News: The Official Magazine of the American Pediatric Association* 20 (2011) (further reading on court cases related to blood transfusions and other child medical issues), https://publications.aap.org/aapnews/article-abstract/32/5/20/9433/Child-welfare-vs-parental-religious-viewsWhat-do?redirectedFrom=fulltext.

91 *Wisconsin v. Yoder*, 406 U.S. 205 (1972).

92 *Serbian Eastern Orthodox Diocese for United States and Canada v. Milivojevich*, 426 U. S. 696 (1976).

93 *Hosanna Tabor Evangelical Lutheran Church and School v. EEOC*, 565 U. S. 171 (2012).

94 *Our Lady of Guadalupe School v. Morrissey-Berru*, 591 U.S. ___ (2020).

95 *Burwell v. Hobby Lobby Stores, Inc.*, 573 U.S. 682 (2014).

96 *Little Sisters of the Poor v. Pennsylvania*, 591 U.S. ___ (2020).

97 *Masterpiece Cakeshop v. Colorado Civil Rights Commission*, 584 U.S. ___ (2018).

98 *Fulton v. Philadelphia*, 593 U.S. ___ (2021).

99 *Ansonia Board of Education v. Philbrook*, 479 U.S. 60 (1986).

100 *Tucker v. State of California Dept. of Education*, 97 F.3d 1204, 1215 (9th Cir. 1996).

101 *Brown v. Polk County*, 61 E.3d 650 (8th Cir. 1995).

102 *Knight v. Connecticut Department of Public Health*, 275 F.3d 156 (2nd Cir. 2001).

103 *Bostock v. Clayton County*, 590 U.S. ___ (2020).

104 *Potter v. District of Columbia*, 558 F.3d 542 (D.C. Cir. 2009).

105 *Equal Employment Opportunity Commission v. Abercrombie & Fitch Stores*, 575 U.S. ___ (2015).

106 The court case was filed in 2003 as *Hearn & United States v. Muskogee Public School District*; details of the settlement negotiated by the Department of Justice can be found on the DOJ website: Department of Justice, *Justice Department Reaches Settlement Agreement with Oklahoma School District in Muslim Student Headscarf Case*, May 19, 2004, https://www.justice.gov/archive/opa/pr/2004/May/04_crt_343.htm.

107 *Rushton v. Nebraska Public Power Dist.* 844 F.2d 562 (8th Cir. 1988).

108 *Enders v. Indiana State Police*, 794 N.E.2d 1089 (Ind. Ct. App. 2003).

109 *Kennedy v. Bremerton School District*, 597 U.S. ___ (2022).

110 *Turner v. Safley*, 482 U.S. 78 (1987).

111 *Cruz v. Beto*, 405 U.S. 319 (1972).

112 Religious Land Use and Institutionalized Persons Act, Pub. L. 106–274, 114 Stat. 803, 42 U.S.C. § 2000cc-2000cc-5.

113 *Holt v. Hobbs*, 574 U.S. 352 (2015).

Credit

CHAPTER 6

The Second Amendment
The Right to Keep and Bear Arms

"Like most rights, the right secured by the Second Amendment is not unlimited. From Blackstone through the 19th-century cases, commentators and courts routinely explained that the right was not a right to keep and carry any weapon whatsoever in any manner whatsoever and for whatever purpose."

—Justice Antonin Scalia, writing for the Supreme Court
in *District of Columbia v. Heller*, 554 U.S. 570 (2008).

Learning Objectives

After reading this chapter, you should understand the following:

1. The debate over the meaning of the Second Amendment
2. The scope of federal regulation of firearms and other weapons
3. Current constitutional issues in state and local gun regulation

Key Cases

United States v. Miller, 307 U.S. 174 (1939)
District of Columbia v. Heller, 554 U.S. 570 (2008)
McDonald v. City of Chicago, 561 U.S. 742 (2010)

Caetano v. Massachusetts, 577 U.S. 411 (2016)

New York Rifle and Pistol Association v. Bruen 597 U.S. ____ (2022)

Introduction

The Second Amendment to the U.S. Constitution states, "A well regulated Militia, being necessary to the security of a free state, the right of the people to keep and bear Arms, shall not be infringed." In recent years, the Second Amendment has been the subject of intense debate. The interpretation of this language is key to determining the constitutionality of federal, state, and local laws regulating the manufacture, sale, possession, and use of firearms. Those who argue for a restrictive interpretation of the Second Amendment typically favor stronger gun control measures, while those who view the right to keep and bear arms as a personal right typically oppose such measures. The backdrop to this debate is the epidemic of gun violence that plagues the United States, as seen in the fact that in 2019, more than 37,000 gun-related deaths occurred in the country—second worldwide only to Brazil.[1] Moreover, among "high income nations and territories" with populations over 10 million, the United States had the highest level of firearm-related homicides per 100,000 people, with more than twice as many as the country with the next-highest number.[2]

Even so, calls for "gun control"—which is a general term capable of manifesting in myriad ways—must take context into account. For example, as we will see in this chapter, handguns tend to be treated differently under the law than rifles and shotguns, Likewise, semi-automatic pistols and rifles are treated differently than fully automatic firearms. Similarly, possession of weapons inside the home has been addressed differently by government officials—and by the courts—than possession outside the home. In the end, untangling how the words and phrases of the Second Amendment apply to these (and other) situations lies at the heart of assessing the constitutionality of government attempts at controlling an individual's capacity to possess arms.

In this chapter, we begin with a discussion of major Supreme Court decisions concerning interpretation of the Second Amendment. With that foundation in place, we proceed to an assessment of the existing body of federal gun laws and regulations and then conclude with a look at state and local restrictions on the possession of different types of weapons. Ultimately, the Supreme Court's construction of this key amendment offers a framework for what the federal government, state governments, and local governments can and cannot do when it comes to restricting an individual's ability to access a weapon.

The Meaning of the Second Amendment

Although media pundits and politicians are prone to offering opinions on how to properly construe the Second Amendment, students of criminal justice are well aware that the Supreme Court serves as the final arbiter of key words and phrases in any constitutional amendment. Yet throughout the history of this nation, justices of the high Court have offered a limited number of opinions that directly address the Second Amendment—with the most significant of these decisions arriving in the past fifteen years (with, perhaps, more on the horizon in the next decade). In this section, we provide an overview of major Supreme Court rulings on the Second Amendment.

At the outset, it is important to recognize that, although some politicians might be prone to declaring themselves *pro-Second Amendment* in speeches given on the campaign trail, key words in the amendment's text are open to different interpretations. For instance, some scholars suggest the reference to a "well-regulated militia" in the amendment's opening clause implies a limitation on an individual right to bear arms when disconnected from military service. Other words in the amendment could be left open to debate as well. For example, "people" might exclude certain individuals who have their gun rights revoked, such as convicted felons; "keep and bear" can be applied differently to possession inside the home than possession outside the home; and "arms" could be read to encompass an array of weapons, ranging from machine guns to knives to stun guns to martial arts nunchaku. Let us now consider how the Supreme Court has addressed some of the interpretive issues.

Early Second Amendment Jurisprudence

The first major Supreme Court decision that addressed key provisions of the Second Amendment arose in 1875. In *United States v. Cruikshank* (1875),[3] Chief Justice Morrison Waite said the right to keep and bear arms "is not a right granted by the Constitution. Neither is it in any manner dependent upon that instrument for its existence." This dictum was consistent with the widely held view that the Second Amendment was adopted to preserve states' rights to maintain "well regulated" militias and not to confer a personal right to keep and bear arms outside that context.

Decades later, in *United States v. Miller* (1939),[4] the Court again focused upon the Militia Clause of the Second Amendment, upholding a federal law that banned the interstate transportation of certain firearms. In this case, a man named Jack Miller was prosecuted in the U.S. District Court for the Western District of Arkansas under the National Firearms Act of 1934 (which we will discuss in greater detail later in this chapter). The specific charge was connected to Miller's transporting of a double-barreled sawed-off shotgun—a weapon banned under the Act—across state lines from Oklahoma to Arkansas. Although Miller claimed the protection of the Second Amendment, the Court rejected his argument and offered an assessment of what the word *militia* meant at the time of the nation's founding. Specifically, Justice James C. McReynolds observed that: "The sentiment of the time strongly disfavored standing armies; the common view was that adequate defense of country and laws could be secured through the Militia—civilians primarily, soldiers on occasion." With this assessment providing a framework for Second Amendment interpretation, Justice McReynolds concluded the following:

> In the absence of any evidence tending to show that possession or use of a "shotgun having
> a barrel of less than eighteen inches in length" at this time has some reasonable relationship
> to the preservation or efficiency of a well regulated militia, we cannot say that the Second
> Amendment guarantees the right to keep and bear such an instrument.

This language is somewhat ambiguous, however. It can be read as consistent with the notion that there is no personal right to keep and bear arms under the Second Amendment. But it can also be read to mean only Congress has the authority to regulate the types of arms individuals wish to keep and bear—particularly since this case involved an act of Congress.

More than half a century would go by before the Supreme Court built upon the *Miller* decision, and even then, a 1980 case offered a mere footnote regarding the Second Amendment's Militia Clause. In *Lewis v. United States* (1980),[5] which dealt with the loss of gun rights by a convicted felon, the Supreme Court commented in a footnote on the meaning of the Second Amendment by quoting the *Miller* case, saying it "guarantees no right to keep and bear a firearm that does not have 'some reasonable relationship to the preservation or efficiency of a well regulated militia.'" The Court's dictum in *Lewis*, though, did not end the debate over the Second Amendment. Rather, the debate intensified as the National Rifle Association and various conservative groups urged that the Second Amendment should be viewed as protecting an individual right to possess guns, irrespective of any service in a militia. The Supreme Court would encounter this matter directly in 2008.

The Landmark *Heller* Decision

In *District of Columbia v. Heller* (2008),[6] the Supreme Court addressed a challenge brought forth by Dick Heller, a police officer who sought to overturn the district's ban on handgun possession in the home. Although the district did, on rare occasions, issue permits for in-home possession of firearms, even if such a permit was granted, the gun had to be kept with a trigger lock or disassembled. In a 5–4 decision, the Court overturned the district's ban and trigger-lock requirement, declaring the Second Amendment protects a personal right to possess a firearm for "traditionally lawful purposes," irrespective of one's service in any militia. Writing for a sharply divided Court, Justice Scalia observed:

> Undoubtedly some think that the Second Amendment is outmoded in a society where our standing army is the pride of our Nation, where well-trained police forces provide personal security, and where gun violence is a serious problem. That is perhaps debatable, but what is not debatable is that it is not the role of this Court to pronounce the Second Amendment extinct.

Interpreting the language of the Second Amendment, Justice Scalia's lengthy opinion provided ample citations to literature derived from the time period spanning the Founding era through the post-Civil War period, ostensibly to build upon his assertion that: "In interpreting this text, we are guided by the principle that '[t]he Constitution was written to be understood by the voters; its words and phrases ... used in their normal and ordinary ... meaning.'"[7] He clarified his application of "normal meaning" by declaring that "it excludes secret or technical meanings that would not have been known to ordinary citizens in the founding generation." With that starting point offered on the third page of his opinion, Scalia proceeded to provide the Court's first-ever in-depth examination of individual words and phrases in Second Amendment.

Justice Scalia's Assessment of the Militia Clause

In a critical part of his *Heller* opinion, Justice Scalia rejected the interpretation of the Militia Clause that had prevailed since the *Cruikshank* decision, with Scalia professing to restore the original meaning of the Second Amendment. He did so by declaring that the phrase "[a] well-regulated militia being necessary to the security of a free state ..." amounted to a "prefatory clause." Accordingly, since the word *preface* connotes something that could be deemed introductory or background material, the invocation of that label seems to minimize the importance of the militia reference. Beyond that, Scalia went on to describe the subsequent clause of the Second Amendment—which speaks of a right to keep and bear arms—as the "operative clause." Clearly, in his view, the latter was meant to be construed as more important than the former. In summary, we can bifurcate the clauses as follows:

- **prefatory clause:** "A well-regulated Militia being necessary to the security of a free State"
- **operative clause:** "[T]he right of the people to keep and bear Arms shall not be infringed"

Through this distinction, the majority opinion for *D.C. v. Heller* conferred, for the first time in the Court's history, a right for Americans to possess a gun even if they are not associated with any military—or militia—organizations.

Justice Scalia's Interpretation of "Right of the People"

Scalia's opinion next turned to a close interpretation of key terms and phrases in the operative clause, beginning with the word *people*. Based on the federal Gun Control Act of 1968 (which we will discuss later in this chapter), there are ways an individual can be deemed a "prohibited possessor" and, thus, lose the right to possess a firearm. Among the categories of people under this umbrella are the following: convicted felons, illegal immigrants, dishonorably-discharged members of the military, those who are adjudicated to be mentally ill, individuals charged with misdemeanor domestic violence crimes under applicable state laws, and those under the age of 21.[8] Scalia's opinion left this framework for "prohibited possessors" intact, as evidenced when he said that "nothing in our opinion should be taken to cast doubt on longstanding prohibitions on the possession of firearms by felons and the mentally ill, or laws forbidding the carrying of firearms in sensitive places such as schools and government buildings, or laws imposing conditions and qualifications on the commercial sale of arms." But he also made it clear that Second Amendment protections apply to those who do not fall into this category—regardless of any service in an organization resembling a Founding-era militia.

Justice Scalia's Interpretation of "Arms"

Scalia's opinion also confronted the meaning of the word *arms*. Of course, his assessment of this crucial term is somewhat limited by the nature of the case before the Court. After all, the matter dealt with a D.C. ban on handgun possession in the home. But rather than provide a holding for this opinion that was exclusively limited to handguns, Scalia offered a somewhat broader protection for individual weapons possession, saying that "arms" in the Second Amendment should refer to "weapons typically possessed by a law-abiding citizen." That phrasing certainly left ample room for interpretation, but handguns were offered as exemplars of this category. Nevertheless, Scalia also discussed an opposing category by indicating that the federal government retains the ability to regulate so-called "dangerous and unusual weapons." Therefore, Scalia's opinion ultimately supports the viability of the National Firearms Act of 1934 and, in so doing, leaves the core holding of *United States v. Miller* (1939) in place—since that case dealt with a sawed-off shotgun.

Justice Scalia's Construction of "Keep and Bear"

As noted previously, Scalia's opinion was limited by the facts of the D.C. case, and thus, his interpretation of the words *keep and bear* conferred a right to home ownership of a firearms and, directly speaking, nothing more. However, there is an ancillary rationale underlying the *Heller* case that deserves mention in this context. The opinion suggested that a critical reason for protecting handgun ownership in the home is the correlated "right" of self-defense, which Scalia called the "central component" of the Second Amendment and discussed in two forms: (1) protection from intruders (whether they be domestic or foreign) who might wish to harm a person or their property and (2) protection against an oppressive government, as was the case during the American Revolution. Scalia noted that "law-abiding citizens" are capable of safely possessing handguns and using them in conjunction with this concept of self-defense. In particular, he said that handguns are the "most preferred firearm in the nation to 'keep' and use for protection of one's home and family."

The Heller *Dissents*

As noted, the *Heller* decision was 5–4. Two of the Court's most liberal justices, John Paul Stevens and Stephen Breyer, wrote lengthy dissenting opinions challenging Justice Scalia's methodology and conclusions. For his part, Justice Stevens took issue with the Court's interpretation of the original understanding of the Second Amendment:

> The Court would have us believe that over 200 years ago, the Framers made a choice to limit the tools available to elected officials wishing to regulate civilian uses of weapons, and to authorize this Court to use the common-law process of case-by-case judicial lawmaking to define the contours of acceptable gun control policy. Absent compelling evidence that is nowhere to be found in the Court's opinion, I could not possibly conclude that the Framers made such a choice.

While agreeing with Justice Stevens, Justice Breyer argued the D.C. ban should be upheld even under Justice Scalia's "individual right" interpretation of the Second Amendment. In his view:

> ... the District's law is consistent with the Second Amendment even if that Amendment is interpreted as protecting a wholly separate interest in individual self-defense. That is so because the District's regulation, which focuses upon the presence of handguns in high-crime urban areas, represents a permissible legislative response to a serious, indeed life-threatening, problem.

Despite relentless criticism from advocates of heightened gun control, the *Heller* decision remains the law of the land. Indeed, it has been extended and reinforced by the Court's later decisions, including another landmark decision involving the application of the Second Amendment to state and local gun laws. It is to that decision we now turn our attention.

JURISPRUDENCE

Homeowner Invokes Self-Defense in Protecting His Cow
Beard v. United States, 158 U.S. 550 (1895)

The concept of self-defense plays a key role in Justice Scalia's *D.C. v. Heller* opinion, but that is not the first Supreme Court decision to focus on this concept. In *Beard v. United States* (1895), the Court addressed a case involving a man who was at his home in Arkansas when an intruder armed with a gun tried to steal a cow. The homeowner then used his own gun to kill the would-be thief—not by shooting the man but by striking him over the head with the weapon. After a trial in a federal court that held jurisdiction because the incident took place on Native American land, the homeowner was convicted of manslaughter.

However, on appeal, the Supreme Court overturned the conviction, noting a common law principle that there is "no duty to retreat to the wall" on one's own property. Writing for the Court, Justice John Marshall Harlan observed, "The defendant was where he had the right to be, when the deceased advanced upon him in a threatening manner and with a deadly weapon, and if the accused did not provoke the assault, and had at the time reasonable grounds to believe, and in good faith believed, that the deceased intended to take his life, or do him great bodily harm, he was not obliged to retreat nor to consider whether he could safely retreat, but was entitled to stand his ground and meet any attack made upon him with a deadly weapon in such way and with such force as, under all the circumstances, he at the moment honestly believed, and had reasonable grounds to believe, were necessary to save his own life or to protect himself from great bodily injury."

Even though this decision dates from the nineteenth century, it has never been overturned and is still a valid precedent. Today, in fact, many state laws regarding justifiable homicide (i.e., self-defense) mirror language from this opinion. Tennessee law, for example, is typical in allowing for the use of lethal force in self-defense whenever there is "a reasonable fear of imminent, serious bodily injury or death,"[9] with statutes there also noting there is "no duty to retreat" when faced with such a threat—a concept that other states, such as Florida, have codified, using the phrase "stand your ground."[10] Ultimately, it would be wise for any gun owner to become familiar with the self-defense laws of their state, as such statutes can vary across jurisdictions. We discuss this concept in greater detail in the context of police use-of-force cases in chapter 10.

Incorporation of the Second Amendment

In previous chapters, we have discussed the importance of selective incorporation, whereby the Supreme Court uses the Fourteenth Amendment to make a right enshrined in the Bill of Rights applicable to the actions of state and local government. Along these lines, one might wonder why the Supreme Court did not incorporate the Second Amendment in its opinion in *D.C. v. Heller*. The simple reason is the District of Columbia is not a state, and therefore, incorporation was not an option for the Court in this particular case. But an opportunity for incorporation would arise from a challenge against a similar gun restriction in the City of Chicago, where handgun possession inside the home was also banned prior to the high Court's 2010 ruling in *McDonald v. Chicago*.[11]

Because the same justices who heard the *Heller* case were still on the Court two years later, the outcome of the *McDonald* case was never in doubt. By the same 5–4 margin as in *Heller*, the Court struck down Chicago's ban on handgun possession in the home, relying on similar rationales related to self-defense in the home as employed in *Heller*.

Justice Samuel Alito's majority opinion in *McDonald v. Chicago* spent time justifying the Supreme Court's ability to engage in selective incorporation of the Bill of Rights. Specifically, Alito insisted that the Due Process Clause of the Fourteenth Amendment provides a theoretical foundation for incorporation of the Bill of Rights. Notably, the Due Process Clause uses the word "state," as it says the following: "nor shall any *state* deprive any person of life, liberty, or property, without due process of law" (emphasis added); that reference to "state" is important, since it serves as an indicator that amendments can be made to apply to the actions of state government officials. Citing a long line of precedent, Alito noted that an amendment rises to the level of incorporation when it is "fundamental to our nation's ordered scheme of liberty." He argued that the Second Amendment fits this criteria, as it is relevant to the liberty discussed by Justice Scalia in the *Heller* opinion—that of self-defense in the home:

> In *Heller*, we held that the Second Amendment protects the right to possess a handgun in the home for the purpose of self-defense. Unless considerations of stare decisis counsel otherwise, a provision of the Bill of Rights that protects a right that is fundamental from an American perspective applies equally to the Federal Government and the States.

With this foundation in place, Justice Alito announced that Chicago's ban on handguns in the home should be struck down. With that, all existing bans on handgun possession in the home anywhere in the United States were deemed incompatible with the Second Amendment, as were rigid trigger-lock requirements that limited

FUNDAMENTAL RIGHT:
A right requiring a high level of judicial protection. Fundamental rights include those enumerated in the Bill of Rights as well as other implicit constitutional rights, such as the right of privacy.

STRICT SCRUTINY:
The highest level of judicial scrutiny of a challenged law or policy. Under strict scrutiny, a law is deemed unconstitutional, and the government carries the burden of proving otherwise.

COMPELLING INTEREST:
A governmental interest of the highest order, such as the protection of national security.

NARROW TAILORING:
A close fit between the end government seeks and the means it chooses to pursue that end, entailing a minimum of harm to constitutionally protected rights.

RATIONAL BASIS TEST:
The most lenient form of judicial scrutiny, this test merely requires a challenged law or policy to be rationally related to a legitimate governmental interest.

quick usage of a firearm for self-defense purposes. Furthermore, any possibility of a government entity passing a ban on handgun ownership in the home in the future, whether at the federal, state, or local level, was abrogated with the incorporation of the Second Amendment in this case.

The Importance of Incorporation

The *McDonald v. Chicago* decision raises an important query: why do legal scholars place such emphasis on incorporation? The answer connects to the importance of incorporation regarding future court cases on similar topics connected to an amendment. An incorporated right is often referred to as a fundamental right; accordingly, when cases involving such rights wind up in court, judges normally employ the strict scrutiny test, which favors the individual—not the government.

Through strict scrutiny, to justify a law or action that limits a fundamental right, the government must demonstrate two things: (1) a compelling interest, which can be thought of as an extremely strong reason for justifying the government action, and (2) narrow tailoring, which can be thought of as a close fit between the compelling interest and the action that government is taking—as if the government action must further the compelling interest directly, without any ancillary burden on individual conduct that should remain protected.

Because Second Amendment jurisprudence from the Supreme Court is still in a relative state of infancy—from the standpoint that there is a paucity of case precedent—it remains to be seen what legal frameworks will apply in a post-*Heller/McDonald* legal world. Needless to say, though, incorporation of the Second Amendment is a significant development. To highlight this point, we can turn to an assessment of the alternative test to strict scrutiny.

Without incorporation, if an amendment addressing a *non-fundamental* right is considered in a case, a court would likely use the rational basis test, which favors the government from the outset. Under this framework, the government must show the following: (1) a legitimate interest, which is a low standard to meet in that it is significantly easier to demonstrate than a *compelling* interest and might be thought of as a *decent reason* or a *pretty good reason*, and (2) a rational relationship, which can be thought of as a reasonable connection between the government action and the legitimate interest, without mandating the close fit inherent in a narrow tailoring assessment under strict scrutiny—since there is merely a need to show what can be called a *loose connection* between the government action and the *legitimate interest*.

Generally speaking, then, the rational basis test represents a lesser standard for the government to meet—one that is much easier for the government to pass than strict scrutiny. Prior to *McDonald v. Chicago*, it follows, weapons cases would only necessitate use of the rational basis test because the Second Amendment was not yet incorporated. With incorporation, strict scrutiny is likely to be used—although there is one other possibility.

Between these two tests lies the standard of intermediate scrutiny, which, as we have noted in previous chapters, originated in case precedents stemming from gender discrimination cases but has also been used for freedom of speech cases involving time, place, and manner restrictions. Under intermediate scrutiny, a government entity must demonstrate the following: (1) a significant interest, (2) narrow tailoring, and (3) an ample alternative for the individual to exercise a right. Since the Supreme Court has discerned some situations in which freedom of speech is protected via strict scrutiny and other situations in which it is protected by *lesser* tests, it remains to be seen if a similar categorical approach will be employed regarding Second Amendment assessments of different types of weapons and different contexts for possession.

Post-*Heller/McDonald* Supreme Court Decisions

In March 2016, the Supreme Court of the United States offered its first-ever opinion regarding stun guns. In *Caetano v. Massachusetts*,[12] the Court issued a brief per curiam opinion in response to a Massachusetts ban on stun guns. The Supreme Court suggested that Massachusetts's highest court had used flawed logic in upholding this ban. In particular, the Court said the Massachusetts court had placed improper emphasis on stun guns not being in use at the time of the Founding era and not being adaptable to military use; both criteria were deemed incompatible with the ruling in *D.C. v. Heller*. Specifically, the opinion said the lower court erred in saying stun guns were "unusual because they are 'a thoroughly modern invention,'" adding, "By equating unusual with 'in common use at the time of the Second Amendment's enactment,' the [lower] court's ... explanation is ... inconsistent with *Heller*." However, the Supreme Court stopped short of declaring such a ban unconstitutional—instead, opting to remand the case with a directive for reconsideration that was "consistent" with *D.C. v. Heller* and *McDonald v. Chicago*; those cases, as you know, had specifically extolled the virtue of self-defense.

Generally, the Supreme Court's ruling in *Caetano v. Massachusetts* indicated a reluctance on the part of the high Court to uphold bans on items like stun guns—but the justices did provide Massachusetts's

LEGITIMATE INTEREST:
A permissible goal—something government clearly is empowered to pursue.

RATIONAL RELATIONSHIP:
A reasonable connection between ends and means.

Obiter Dicta

"... [I]ncorporation of the Second Amendment right will to some extent limit the legislative freedom of the States, but this is always true when a Bill of Rights provision is incorporated. Incorporation always restricts experimentation and local variations, but that has not stopped the Court from incorporating virtually every other provision of the Bill of Rights.

—*Justice Samuel Alito, writing for the Supreme Court in* McDonald v. City of Chicago, *561 U.S. 742 (2010)*

officials with another chance to settle this matter on its own. On remand, in April 2018, the Supreme Judicial Court of Massachusetts struck down the state's ban as incompatible with the Second Amendment.[13] Consider how this case might impact restrictions on other personal self-defense devices—such as knives (which can be limited in blade length), Tasers (which can shoot an electric charge over distance through wires and prongs), and pepper spray—in the states or cities that proscribe or limit possession of those items. As of fall 2022, there were no longer any state-level bans on stun guns or Tasers, but some jurisdictions required carry permits to possess these devices outside the home.[14]

In 2021, the Supreme Court granted certiorari in *New York Pistol and Rifle Association v. Bruen* (2022),[15] which concerned New York's stringent restrictions on concealed carry of firearms. Such carrying requires a concealed-carry permit to be issued by the government, but a 108-year-old state law indicated that such a permit should only be granted upon a showing of "proper cause" by the individual seeking to carry. In the oral argument held in early November 2021, it was apparent that most of the justices were highly skeptical of the law. A key aspect of the argument was the degree to which administrative officials were given discretion to deny or approve permits. On the other hand, the justices seemed sympathetic to the argument that restrictions on carrying weapons into crowded venues, such as football stadiums, would fall under the reasonable regulations permitted under the *Heller* decision.

In June 2022, a 6-3 majority on the Supreme Court struck down the New York law. Justice Thomas's majority opinion built upon the self-defense considerations of *D.C. v. Heller* and *McDonald v. Chicago*, quoting to the former in observing that "confining the right to 'bear' arms to the home would make little sense given that self-defense is 'the *central component* of the [Second Amendment] right itself'" (bracket and italics his). Thomas's opinion did leave open the possibility for states to ban gun possession in "sensitive places," which likely would include locations like courthouses, schools, and legislative buildings. The opinion also allowed for the government to ban possession by "prohibited" persons (such as felons) and to regulate the acquisition of "dangerous and unusual" weapons like fully-automatic firearms.

Justice Breyer dissented, noting that: "In 2020, 45,222 Americans were killed by firearms. Since the start of this year (2022), there have been 277 reported mass shootings—an average of more than one per day. Gun violence has now surpassed motor vehicle crashes as the leading cause of death among children and adolescents." He went on to criticize the majority by saying that, "Many States have tried to address some of the dangers of gun violence just described by passing laws that limit, in various ways, who may purchase, carry, or use firearms of different kinds. The Court today severely burdens States' efforts to do so."

Justice Alito's concurring opinion responded directly to Justice Breyer, saying, "Much of the dissent seems designed to obscure the specific question that the Court has decided." Alito added that, "... it is hard to see what legitimate purpose can possibly be served by most of the dissent's lengthy introductory section. Why, for example, does the dissent think it is relevant to recount the mass shootings that have occurred in recent years? Does the dissent think that laws like New York's prevent or deter such atrocities?"

Besides New York, other states with similar "proper cause" or "good cause" requirements impacted by this decision included California, Hawaii, Maryland, Massachusetts, and New Jersey, as well as the District of Columbia. It is important to note that the Court's decision does not prevent states from enacting a basic permitting process for carrying firearms, but instead eliminates the need for an individual to demonstrate a specific need to carry a gun outside the home.

The state of New York responded to the *Bruen* decision by passing a law that banned gun possession in an expanded number of "safety sensitive" locations, including government buildings, public transportation (such as subways and buses), protests and rallies, libraries, and even Times Square. Of course, many commentators expected the state's new law to be challenged in court.

THE CONSTITUTION IN ACTION
The Nunchaku Cases: Law Professor Challenges New York Ban on Martial Arts Weapon

In 2008, the case of *Maloney v. Cuomo* was heard at the U.S. Court of Appeals for the Second Circuit.[16] This case revolved around a New York law that made it illegal to own nunchaku, the martial arts weapon consisting of two sticks tied together with a small rope or chain. (Arizona, California, and Massachusetts also had similar bans at the time.[17]) James Maloney, who is a law professor at the State University of New York-Maritime, invoked his "right to bear arms" in challenging this law, and the case went to the Second Circuit after a district court ruled against him. Judge Sonia Sotomayor wrote the opinion for the Second Circuit, before she was elevated to the Supreme Court in 2009.

As a baseline for evaluating Sotomayor's opinion, we must reiterate that the Second Amendment was not incorporated until 2010. Therefore, the "right to bear arms" was not considered a "fundamental right" at the time of *Maloney v. Cuomo* (2008); hence, Sotomayor found that the rational basis test was the appropriate framework for guiding the analysis. She made this point by quoting a prior Supreme Court opinion in saying, "Legislative acts that do not interfere with fundamental rights or single out suspect classifications carry with them a strong presumption of constitutionality and must be upheld if 'rationally related to a legitimate state interest.'"[18]

With that in place, Sotomayor evaluated the matter in terms of the rational basis test's two components by doing the following: First, regarding the existence of a legitimate government interest, Sotomayor found a legitimate interest in protecting public safety. Next, regarding the question of whether there is a rational relationship between a ban on nunchakus and protecting public safety, Sotomayor found no "valid recreational use" for what she called an "easily concealed … dangerous weapon" that could play a role in street crime like muggings. Thus, the ban passed both components of the rational basis test, and the government action was upheld.

However, incorporation of the Second Amendment means future cases likely will use a more demanding test when it comes to restrictions on weapons possession—instead of this rational basis test—and we can see why that is so important for this matter. In the aftermath of the *McDonald v. Chicago* ruling, in fact, Maloney would refile his case. Representing himself, he asked a federal district court to strike down New York's ban on nunchaku as a violation of the Second Amendment. After several years of legal wrangling, in December 2018, a judge on the U.S. District Court for the Eastern District of New York issued a ruling in *Maloney v. Singas*, declaring the state's ban on nunchakus to be unconstitutional.[19] The opinion stated that either strict or intermediate scrutiny could be appropriate in such a case—based on the logic that something more than the rational basis test is required. Specifically, the judge observed, "The test for determining the proper level of constitutional scrutiny with respect to a Second Amendment challenge has two factors: '(1) how close the law comes to the core of the Second Amendment right and (2) the severity of the law's burden on the right.'"[20] In the end, the judge held there is no significant government interest to justify a restriction on possession of nunchaku, saying: "Because the blanket ban imposed by Section 265.01(1) as applied to nunchaku easily fails constitutional muster under intermediate scrutiny, the Court need not decide whether intermediate or strict scrutiny should apply." With that, it is left to the Supreme Court to determine, through future cases, which types of weapons cases will be subject to strict scrutiny and which will be subject to intermediate scrutiny. However, one thing is clear: with incorporation, the rational basis test is no longer appropriate—which is why the New York ban on nunchaku was treated differently in the sequel to Maloney's lawsuit.

Federal Regulation of Firearms and Other Weapons

The enactment of the first major federal gun law stems from an incident that occurred on Valentine's Day in 1929, when seven people were gunned down in a garage on the north side of Chicago. The shooting involved members of rival bootlegging gangs, including associates of the infamous gangster Al Capone. Machine guns were used in this shooting, and media coverage seized upon the incident to draw attention to mob violence and the proliferation of automatic weapons. Much in the same way that contemporary mass shootings often lead to calls for new gun laws, this *focusing event* had a role in driving Congress to enact its first major firearms statute.

The National Firearms Act

The National Firearms Act of 1934[21] is the cornerstone of federal gun control legislation. Generally speaking, the law creates requirements related to so-called dangerous and unusual weapons.[22] Classes of weapons that are specifically defined in the law include machine guns (those firearms that can expel multiple rounds of ammunition with a single pull of a trigger), sawed-off shotguns (barrels under eighteen inches), and suppressors (better known as silencers). In 1968, the Act was amended by the Omnibus Crime Control and Safe Streets Act[23] to encompass "destructive devices," which includes grenades, bombs, missiles, and other explosive devices. The Act does not completely ban the weapons listed therein, but it does establish a federal regulatory scheme that can serve as a substantial barrier to ownership. Guns manufactured before 1898 are exempted from this process because they are considered to be antiques.

The Act also granted enforcement authority to the Bureau of Alcohol, Tobacco, Firearms and Explosives (ATF). The National Firearms Act requires the ATF to perform two functions regarding these weapons. First, there is a permitting process to acquire such items, and that can take several months to complete, with a prospective buyer needing to submit paperwork, a photograph, and fingerprints to the ATF, which can reject or accept applications. Second, if a permit is granted for someone to own a *dangerous and unusual weapon*, they must also pay a $200 tax. That amount has not changed since the National Firearms Act was passed in 1934. At that time, it would have been the equivalent of approximately $3,500 in today's currency. Currently, $200 is almost certain to be less than the cost of most weapons that fall under the purview of the National Firearms Act of 1934.

Constitutional Basis of the National Firearms Act

As discussed in chapter 2, federal law must be connected to one of the enumerated or implied powers granted to Congress in Article I, Section 8 of the U.S. Constitution. One specific enumerated power that can be used to justify the National Firearms Act is the power to regulate commerce among the states, based on the theory that guns travel through channels of interstate commerce, as discussed in *United States v. Miller* (1939). This theory was tested by a group of individuals in Montana who produced fully automatic weapons and grenades that were stamped *Made in Montana*. The idea was that if these weapons were made in the state for exclusive use within the state, then the federal government would be barred from regulating them through the National Firearms Act. Courts have not found this line of reasoning persuasive, ostensibly because the likelihood of such weapons impacting an interstate market seems high, and the Ninth Circuit, which has Montana within its jurisdiction, has previously upheld laws that address in-state conduct that is likely to affect interstate conduct.[24] Moreover, along these lines, in *United States v. Stewart* (2003),[25] the Supreme Court refused to review a Ninth Circuit decision that denied relief to a California man who claimed his "homemade machine gun" was outside the scope of federal regulation under the Commerce Clause.

There are some states and counties that have passed laws claiming to be exempt from federal gun laws. Many towns and counties have done so as well, with one report suggesting more than 60% of counties in the United States had made such a declaration as of 2021. This often involves a claim of being a *Second Amendment sanctuary*. However, such declarations are symbolic, as people in these states must still adhere to federal gun laws.[26]

Suppressors

A suppressor, also known as a *silencer*, is a firearm attachment that can help muffle the sound of a gunshot. Under the National Firearms Act of 1934, these items are to be regulated by the ATF. Practically speaking, for those who wish to legally purchase a suppressor, this means they would start out with the typical background check for buying a handgun from a dealer. Next, the following additional steps come into play; note that eight states specifically ban suppressors, so this process would not be available in those places:

- Complete a background check at a gun dealer that sells suppressors.
- Apply and obtain federal approval from the Bureau of Alcohol, Tobacco, and Firearms (ATF) to own a suppressor.
- The ATF will collect fingerprints and a photograph as a part of this process. The fingerprint requirement can be avoided by forming a company or legal trust to purchase the suppressor in lieu of an individual purchase.
- Pay a $200 federal tax known as a *transfer fee*.
- Finally, register the suppressor's serial number with ATF (something that is not needed for handgun purchases).

In June 2019, the Supreme Court refused to hear a challenge to the National Firearms Act classification for suppressors.[27] Even so, Congress has debated a bill called the Hearing Protection Act, which would remove suppressors from National Firearms Act requirements, but this bill has not passed in either the House or the Senate. Currently, individuals who are authorized to purchase a suppressor are not permitted to allow others to use it without immediate supervision.

The Gun Control Act of 1968

The Gun Control Act of 1968[28] was the second major federal gun law to be passed in U.S. history, and its primary objective was to establish the notion of "prohibited possessors," who are not allowed to purchase firearms. This group includes minors (defined as those under the age of eighteen for rifle purchases and under the age of twenty-one for handgun purchases), the mentally ill, convicted felons, fugitives from justice, illegal immigrants, other non-U.S. citizens (including those in the United States legally on visas), people who have renounced U.S. citizenship, individuals dishonorably discharged from the military, and those with domestic violence convictions or restraining orders against them. In 1996, this law was amended to apply even to misdemeanor domestic violence offenses that involved "physical force."[29]

This law also required newly manufactured guns to be inscribed with serial numbers. It even placed restrictions on mail-order sales of guns and ammunition and provided for government tracking of ammunition purchases (but these proscriptions were repealed with a 1986 law we will discuss). In keeping with the notion that *focusing events* can precipitate the passage of new laws, it is worth noting that limitations on mail-order purchases were initially proposed as a result of the assassination of President John F. Kennedy;

the man accused of killing him, Lee Harvey Oswald, is believed to have purchased a high-powered rifle through the mail. Today, mail-order purchases are permitted, provided they are from a federally licensed dealer incorporating a background check.

Along those lines, the Gun Control Act created specific regulations for those who sell firearms as a "regular course of trade or business with the principal objective of livelihood and profit through the repetitive purchase and resale of firearms."[30] Such individuals or companies register as federally licensed firearms dealers by acquiring a Federal Firearms License (FFL). Only these licensed dealers are permitted to participate in interstate firearm sales, and the Gun Control Act also subjects such sellers to federal inspections.

A Closer Look at Federal Restrictions on Gun Purchases

The Gun Control Act of 1968 prohibits gun purchases by anyone who is defined as an *unlawful user* of drugs. This phrase has interesting contemporary application in light of the recent legalization of marijuana by numerous states. Because marijuana possession is still illegal under federal law, even a person who holds a legal medical marijuana card to justify cannabis possession in a particular state could be banned from purchasing a gun. In fact, in 2016, the U.S. Court of Appeals for the Ninth Circuit ruled that a ban on gun purchases by those who hold a medical marijuana card is constitutional.[31]

Elsewhere, in its 2015 decision in *United States v. Meza-Rodriguez*, the Seventh Circuit upheld the Gun Control Act's prohibition against an illegal immigrant being in possession of a firearm. Meza-Rodriguez, a Mexican national who had unlawfully entered the United States, claimed his Second Amendment rights were violated when he was arrested for being in possession of a .22 caliber cartridge. The majority opinion noted, "Congress's interest in prohibiting persons who are difficult to track and who have an interest in eluding law enforcement is strong enough to support the conclusion that [the challenged provision] does not impermissibly restrict Meza–Rodriguez's Second Amendment right to bear arms."[32]

More recently, in 2021, the Fourth Circuit determined the Gun Control Act's ban on gun purchases by those between the ages of 18 to 21 years old amounted to a violation of the Second Amendment. The court's opinion said the prohibition does "not even pass intermediate scrutiny" because there was no indication of a significant government interest to prevent people of that age from buying firearms. But in an unusual turn of events, the petitioner in the case turned 21 years old before this decision became effective. Accordingly, the Fourth Circuit vacated the ruling as being moot.[33]

Firearm Owners' Protection Act of 1986

The Firearm Owners Protection Act of 1986[34] is generally referred to as the *Hughes Amendment*, in reference to the member of the House of Representatives who proposed it: William Hughes, a Democrat from New Jersey. It amended the Gun Control Act of 1968 by removing the ban on shipments of guns and ammunition through the mail, and it also did away with government tracking of ammunition sales. The Act created a concept known as *safe passage*, or *passing through protection*; this means if a person crosses state lines with a gun that is legally possessed in the originating state, that person can pass through another state, even without a specific carry permit for that state, as long as ammunition and the gun are kept in separate compartments of the car. In this regard, some states will also honor carry permits issued in other states, through an idea known as reciprocity.[35]

Another key provision in the Firearm Owners' Protection Act established a limit of only one inspection per year of federally licensed firearms dealers, unless multiple violations are assessed. In addition, the law prohibits the federal government from maintaining a computer registry that links gun owners to specific weapons, except for those weapons covered by the National Firearms Act. This law did include some limitations on firearms, particularly directed at machine guns. It banned the importation and new manufacturing of such fully automatic weapons after May 19, 1986. Exceptions were allotted for specified law enforcement and military purposes. Overall, this law manifested a number of compromises between those on both sides of the gun control debate.

The Brady Handgun Violence Prevention Act

The Brady Handgun Violence Prevention Act of 1994,[36] also referred to as the Brady Bill, created the United States' national background check system for gun purchases. The law is named after President Ronald Reagan's former press secretary, James Brady, who was permanently disabled after being shot by John Hinckley, who attempted to assassinate Reagan in 1981. Brady stepped in front of Hinckley in an attempt to protect President Reagan, and when Brady died in 2012, his cause of death was listed as resulting from the bullet that had remained lodged in his brain from the 1981 shooting. Because Hinckley was mentally ill and claimed that a famous actress had instructed him to shoot the president, calls for tighter enforcement of prohibitions on who can purchase a gun were widespread. Twelve years later, legislation was passed to address this issue.

The Brady Bill requires a background check before all firearms purchases made through federally licensed firearms dealers. Thus, this law has the effect of enforcing the *prohibited persons* concept crafted by the Gun Control Act of 1968 in mandating an assessment of whether a prospective purchaser is barred from buying a firearm. At first, background checks were to be conducted by local law enforcement officials, such as a sheriff's office. However, following lawsuits brought on behalf of local officials, the Supreme Court's decision in *Printz v. United States* (1997)[37] found it was unconstitutional, under the Tenth Amendment, for Congress to require local officials to take on this burden—which came with no financial backing and, hence, was viewed as an unfunded mandate. Subsequently, a computerized method known as the National Instant Criminal Background Check System was instituted, and it remains in effect today. Under most circumstances, it allows background checks to be completed in ten to fifteen minutes. Nonetheless, some states have created waiting periods beyond the time taken for the instant background check to conduct a more thorough assessment of potential firearms buyers. Interestingly, those individuals with common names might find themselves waiting a longer time for background checks to be completed.

BRADY BILL: A commonly employed moniker for the nation's federal law that requires background checks to be performed by federally licensed firearms dealers before they can sell firearms to prospective buyers.

UNFUNDED MANDATE: A federal legislative act that places a burden upon state and local officials without providing appropriate funding for enforcement of the act.

NATIONAL INSTANT CRIMINAL BACKGROUND CHECK SYSTEM: A national computerized database that contains information that can be used to quickly assess whether a specific person seeking to purchase a weapon falls into the category of a *prohibited possessor*—perhaps, for having a felony conviction or for having been institutionalized as mentally ill.

One particularly vexing area of the federal background check system is how to define mental illness. The federal standard is that a person who has been "involuntarily committed" to a mental health facility shall lose the ability to purchase a gun. Yet it is up to the states to report the names of these individuals to ensure placement in the background check database. Reporting can vary dramatically from state to state. For example, since the federal database took effect, Florida has entered more than 140,000 health records, but Wyoming has entered only 4. Forty-three states currently require reporting into the database, and the total number of mental illness reports to the federal database is now more than 5 million, which is up from roughly 230,000 in 2005.[38]

An interesting side note to this discussion is that, in 2016, the Obama Administration proposed a federal regulation to prevent gun purchases by those who had been deemed mentally incapable of managing their own disability benefits from the Social Security Administration. In 2017, though, after President Trump took office, the House and Senate used the Congressional Review Act[39] to revoke this rule by a majority vote in each chamber.

Another noteworthy area for discussion is that, as of 2022, although even internet and mail-order sales by federally licensed dealers require a background check, there are no required background checks for gun sales between private parties who are not federally licensed firearms dealers (defined as those who do not sell guns as a regular course of business). This leaves many sales from gun shows and websites outside the scope of the national background check system. Even so, more than ten states have enacted background check requirements (known as universal background checks) that impact all sales, including those between private parties at guns shows or online.[40] If a party that is required to conduct a background check before transferring a weapon fails to do so, they could face both criminal and civil liability.

A federal law called the Protection of Lawful Commerce in Arms Act of 2005[41] does protect manufacturers of guns from lawsuits based on how those products were used; consequently, victims and families of a mass shooting cannot sue the manufacturer of a gun or ammunition used in the shooting. Lawsuits for defective products are still permitted, and the law also mandates the presence of safety locks on newly-constructed weapons.

In February 2022, gun manufacturer Remington agreed to pay $73 million to families of victims of the Sandy Hook Elementary School shooting of 2012, which claimed the lives of six adults and twenty children aged six to seven years old. The shooter in this case used a semi-automatic weapon manufactured by Remington. Despite the existence of the 2005 federal law offering protection to gun manufacturers, the families filed suit under a novel approach, claiming Remington had violated state laws related to unfair trade practices because the company "knowingly marketed and promoted the Bushmaster XM15-E2S rifle for use in assaults against human beings."[42] Remington sought to have the case dismissed under the 2005 law, but the Supreme Court denied cert in *Remington Arms Co. v. Soto* (2019), effectively thwarting that attempt and allowing Connecticut courts to consider the suit.[43]

THE CONSTITUTION IN ACTION
Air Force Ordered to Pay Damages over Mass Shooting

In February 2022, a federal judge for the U.S. District Court for the Western District of Texas ruled that the U.S. Air Force must pay $230 million to survivors and families of the deceased from a 2017 mass shooting at a church in Sutherland Springs, Texas, which claimed the lives of 26 people between the ages of 5 and 72. The shooter was a member of the Air Force in 2012 when he was convicted, in a court-martial proceeding, of domestic assault for attacking his young stepson and wife; his wife suffered a fractured skull as a result of the assault. He was later given a bad conduct discharge from the Air Force in 2014.

However, the Air Force failed to report the criminal conviction, or the military discharge, to the federal database used to restrict gun sales to prohibited possessors. Thus, prior to the 2017 mass shooting, he was able to successfully pass a background check and purchase three firearms, one of which was used in the mass shooting. Either the domestic assault conviction or the bad conduct discharge would have disqualified him from purchasing weapons if it had been entered into the database. The Air Force should have reported each of those incidents to the National Instant Criminal Background Check System within 15 days.

In a 185-page ruling for this case, the district court judge said, "The Court concludes that the Government failed to exercise reasonable care in its undertaking to submit criminal history to the FBI," adding, "The Government's failure to exercise reasonable care increased the risk of physical harm to the general public, including Plaintiffs. And its failure … caused the deaths and injuries … at the Sutherland Springs First Baptist Church on November 5, 2017."[44]

Supreme Court Decisions Related to Background Checks

Three recent Supreme Court cases have addressed the federal background check system for gun purchases. First, in *Abramski v. United States* (2014),[45] the high Court examined charges brought against a man named Bruce Abramski, who had purchased a handgun on behalf of his uncle in the state of Virginia. Abramski was a former police officer who received a discount on gun purchases from certain dealers, which is why he made the purchase for his uncle, even though the uncle was in fact eligible to purchase a weapon on his own. Firearms purchases made on behalf of other people are known as *straw purchases* and are illegal under federal law. In the *Abramski* decision, the Supreme Court upheld his conviction for lying about a material fact on a federal document—that document being the firearm background check form. In particular, Justice Kagan's majority opinion noted, "Had Abramski admitted that he was not that purchaser, but merely a straw—that he was asking the dealer to verify the identity of, and run a background check on, the wrong individual—the sale here could not have gone forward."

Another decision, *United States v. Castleman* (2014),[46] addressed the case of a man convicted of misdemeanor domestic assault in Tennessee. This conviction, in turn, prohibited him from possessing a gun—but nevertheless, federal agents caught him selling guns and charged him as a prohibited possessor under federal law. Castleman argued that because his offense was a misdemeanor assault charge in a state where assault laws allowed for a conviction based merely on *offensive touching*, his gun rights should not be limited. The crux of this argument was the idea that federal law only bars gun ownership if "physical force" accompanies a misdemeanor act of domestic violence. The Supreme Court ruled against Castleman, authorizing states to apply a broad range of definitions for *domestic violence* and *physical force*, allowing for "offensive touching" to connote physical force. Justice Sotomayor's opinion indicated that this interpretation would further the legislative intent underlying the congressional efforts to reduce gun ownership by those with links to domestic violence issues.

Later, in *Voisine v. United States* (2016),[47] the Supreme Court reinforced this strict approach to limiting gun possession by those found guilty of domestic violence offenses. Voisine was convicted of domestic assault in Maine, which allowed for such a conviction based not only on intentional acts but also on reckless acts. Federal authorities learned that Voisine was in possession of firearms after investigating him for allegedly killing a bald eagle, and a conviction for being a prohibited possessor—based on the prior domestic violence offense—would follow. Voisine appealed, but the First Circuit ruled against him, as did the Supreme Court of the United States on review. Justice Kagan's majority opinion for the Court made it clear that even a misdemeanor domestic violence conviction stemming from a "reckless" action, defined in the opinion as one evincing "conscious disregard of a known risk" (a lower standard than an intentional act), could indeed serve as the basis for prohibiting gun possession by the offender. The majority again furthered the objective of protecting victims of domestic violence and also said that federal law can be reasonably interpreted to support this idea; that is because the 1996 amendment to the Gun Control Act of 1968, which addresses any domestic violence incident involving physical force, can be construed to encompass reckless acts—not just intentional or knowing acts.

Justice Clarence Thomas, who ended his ten years of silence in oral arguments during the argument for this case, wrote a dissent; as did Justice Sotomayor. This unlikely pairing raised concerns with the assumption that reckless acts will always meet the threshold of physical force. Some examples raised by the dissents to highlight limitations of the majority opinion included the following: a texting and driving accident that results in injury to a family member or dropping a plate on a spouse's foot; each of these scenarios could denote *reckless* acts that, in turn, prohibit gun possession under the majority's interpretation of federal law.

More recently, in *Rehaif v. United States* (2019),[48] the Supreme Court determined that for the government to convict a person for improperly possessing a gun, prosecutors must prove an individual knew that they were a prohibited possessor under federal law, but still went ahead with possessing a firearm anyway. This 5–4 ruling benefited an immigrant who had overstayed a student visa authorizing his presence in the United States (after he was dismissed from college for poor grades). Authorities learned he was in possession of a gun he used for target practice and charged him as a prohibited possessor under federal law. Justice Neil Gorsuch joined the four Democrat-appointed justices in a 5–4 majority, with Justice Breyer's majority opinion declaring that federal law governing this situation was unconstitutionally vague regarding the level of criminal intent required for a conviction. Specifically, Breyer said, "We conclude that in a prosecution under 18 U.S.C. § 922(g) and § 924(a)(2), the Government must prove both that the defendant knew he possessed a firearm and that he knew he belonged to the relevant category of persons barred from possessing a firearm."

Restricting Felons from Possessing Firearms

Under 18 U.S.C. § 922(g)(1), it is "unlawful for any person ... who has been convicted in any court of a crime punishable by imprisonment for a term exceeding one year ... to receive any firearm or ammunition which has been shipped or transported in interstate or foreign commerce." In FY 2018, there were more than 6,700 convictions under this statute.[49] The phrase "any court" includes not only federal courts but state and tribal courts as well. Most states have similar laws, but they vary considerably in terms of the qualifying felonies (e.g., all felonies versus violent felonies), the scope of their restrictions on gun rights (e.g., handguns versus other firearms), and the duration of such restrictions. It is possible, though not common, for someone to be prosecuted successively under 18 U.S.C. § 922(g)(1) and a counterpart state law. In *Gamble v. United States* (2019),[50] the Supreme Court held that such dual prosecutions did not constitute double jeopardy (see chapter 11).

Restoration of Gun Rights for Felons

Even though federal law indicates that a person who is convicted of a federal crime can petition the ATF for reinstatement of gun rights,[51] in practice, that has proven impossible since 1992, when Congress attached a stipulation to the ATF's budget appropriations that banned the ATF from expending any resources on the review of gun rights reinstatement requests from convicted felons. So those requests simply go answered. The Supreme Court reviewed this practice in *United States v. Bean* (2002),[52] which dealt with a man who had a felony conviction for attempting to take 200 rounds of ammunition across the U.S. border into Mexico. The Supreme Court found that "the absence of an actual denial of respondent's petition by ATF precludes judicial review."

In simple terms, because no action was taken by the agency, the man was not entitled to relief from the courts. Thus, the only viable avenue for a person seeking reinstatement of gun rights following a federal felony conviction is to attain a pardon from the president of the United States.

Some states do allow for the reinstatement of gun rights after a felony conviction, but procedures vary widely in terms of how this process is governed. In more than ten states, nonviolent felons have automatic restoration upon completing their punishment; in other states, restoration could be automatic after a set period of time without being convicted of another offense. A pardon from a governor could also restore gun possession rights.

The Short-Lived Federal Assault Weapons Ban

The National Firearms Act applies to fully automatic weapons, which are those that can fire more than one bullet with a single pull of a trigger; however, the law does not apply to so-called *semi-automatic* weapons, like the AR-15 rifle, which do not propel more than one bullet from a single pull of a trigger but automatically reload. One category of semiautomatic rifles (with specific types of grips) has been termed assault weapons by some in the media, and these were actually banned for a ten-year period of time by a federal law that carried the somewhat ironic name of Public Safety and Recreational Firearm Use Protection Act. The Act was part of the Violent Crime Control and Law Enforcement Act of 1994.[53] While much of this Act is still in effect today, the portion that banned *assault weapons* was only in effect between the years 1994 and 2004. Although it is unusual for a statute to have this sort of time limitation, or expiration date, it was likely needed to acquire enough votes among legislators to ensure passage. Of course, Democrats controlled Congress when the law was passed in 1994, but they had lost their majority in both the House and Senate by 2004; hence, it is no surprise the law was not renewed. Accordingly, after the law expired, states became free to regulate semi-automatic weapons as they wished, and we will discuss that matter in greater detail in the next section.

ASSAULT WEAPONS:
Military-style semiautomatic rifles and pistols containing detachable magazines capable of holding large numbers of rounds.

There also is relevant case precedent regarding application of the National Firearms Act in situations where a semi-automatic weapon has been modified. In *Staples v. United States* (1994),[54] a man purchased what he believed to be a semi-automatic weapon, which, at the time, was not banned under federal law. But the weapon had been modified from its original design, so it actually functioned as a fully automatic weapon. As a result, after he was caught in possession of this weapon, he was convicted of violating the National Firearms Act. On review, the Supreme Court overturned his conviction, with Justice Thomas's majority opinion declaring, "[T]o convict him under the Act, the Government should have been required to prove beyond a reasonable doubt that he knew the weapon he possessed had the characteristics that brought it within the statutory definition of a machinegun." In essence, Staples was able to successfully claim a *mistake of fact* because prosecutors failed to prove to a jury that he knew the weapon was actually an illegal one under federal law. Nevertheless, the outcome in similar cases to *Staples* could turn on how reasonable the mistake is.

In *United States v. Freed* (1971),[55] for example, the high Court upheld the conviction of man who had possessed grenades without filing for a permit with the ATF. He was charged with violating the National Firearms Act, and the majority opinion from Justice Douglas indicated a reasonable person would understand that possession of grenades requires a special federal permit. Justice Douglas also observed that the registration requirements of the National Firearms Act do not amount to a violation of the Fifth Amendment's Self-Incrimination Clause; specifically, Justice Douglas explained how the process of transferring such a weapon should proceed to comply with federal law:

> As noted, a lawful transfer of a firearm may be accomplished only if it is already registered. The transferor—not the transferee—does the registering. The transferor pays the transfer tax and receives a stamp denoting payment which he affixes to the application submitted to the Internal Revenue Service. The transferor must identify himself, describe the firearm to be transferred, and the name and address of the transferee. In addition, the application must be supported by the photograph and fingerprints of the transferee and by a certificate of a local or federal law enforcement official that he is satisfied that the photograph and fingerprints are those of the transferee and that the weapon is intended for lawful uses. Only after receipt of the approved application form is it lawful for the transferor to hand the firearm over to the transferee. At that time, he is to give the approved application to the transferee.

In essence, Justice Douglas highlighted the fact that registration should precede taking possession of such a weapon, and therefore, the registration requirement does not implicate a violation of the Fifth Amendment—since a person would need to disclose an intent to acquire such an item before actually taking possession of it. We will consider this issue in greater detail in chapter 11, where we address the high Court's decision in *Haynes v. United States* (1968).[56] That case resulted in some changes to how weapons are registered under the National Firearms Act—changes designed to ensure that the process described by Justice Douglas comports with the Self-Incrimination Clause of the Fifth Amendment.

THE CONSTITUTION IN ACTION
The Bureau of Alcohol, Tobacco, Firearms, and Explosives

Known generally as the ATF, the Bureau of Alcohol, Tobacco, Firearms and Explosives originated in 1886, when it was known as the Revenue Laboratory within the Department of the Treasury's Bureau of Internal Revenue. Following ratification of the Eighteenth Amendment in 1919, which banned alcohol sales nationwide, the Revenue Laboratory became the Bureau of Prohibition. By 1933, with the Twenty-First Amendment's repeal of Prohibition, it took on the name Alcohol Tax Unit. It was this agency that enforced the National Firearms Act after its passage in 1934. Subsequently, enactment of the Gun Control Act of 1968 changed the ATU into the Bureau of Alcohol, Tobacco, and Firearms Division of the Internal Revenue Service. ATF would later become its own Bureau within the Department of the Treasury in 1972. In 2002, the Homeland Security Act transferred the ATF from the Department of the Treasury to the Department of Justice; that act also added the word "Explosives" to the end of ATF's name—although that familiar three-letter moniker was retained for official purposes.

Today, weapons covered by the National Firearms Act need to be registered with the Bureau of Alcohol, Tobacco, Firearms, and Explosives. This process begins with a lengthy application process that must be completed before a person takes possession of any NFA weapons. The vetting process usually includes fingerprints and photographs, although registration through a corporate entity or trust may offer loopholes. If approval is granted, the ATF will require the owner's name and the item's serial number to be registered with the bureau. If a person is able to surmount these obstacles and obtain an NFA weapon, it is important to recognize that some weapons require notification to the ATF before being transported across state lines or being sold to another party. Violations of the law can be punishable by up to ten years in prison and a fine up to $500,000.

Beyond these statutorily defined regulatory and enforcement powers, the Bureau of Alcohol, Tobacco, Firearms, and Explosives derives authority from the NFA to classify weapons as falling under the purview of the act. The broad authority is conferred where the act specifically notes that "any other weapons" besides pistols or revolvers with rifled bores can be added at the discretion of the ATF's rulemaking process as long as said weapons are capable of being concealed.[57]

Regulating Undetectable Firearms and "Ghost Guns"

In 1988, Congress enacted the Undetectable Firearms Act,[58] which requires every firearm to have at least one metal part, ensuring anything that can fire a bullet can be discerned by a metal detector. A key area where this comes into play is the recent advent of guns created by 3D printers. Along these lines, in 2018, a Texas-based company called Defense Distributed began circulating online schematics that demonstrated how a person could make different types of guns (including handguns, rifles, and AR-15s) using a 3D printer. The U.S. State Department had attempted to block release of such schematics for several years, citing a U.S. government regulatory policy known as the International Traffic in Arms Regulations (ITAR). ITAR was crafted in 1976 as a set of bureaucratic rules (not congressional law); this regulatory scheme was meant to prevent the export of weapons technology from the United States and has been enforced by the State Department for decades.

In 2015, Defense Distributed filed a lawsuit against the State Department hoping to receive permission to post, on their Defense Distributed website, downloadable instructions for making 3D printed guns. Attorneys for Defense Distributed argued that a ban on posting this material would amount to a violation of the First Amendment right to freedom of expression. In late June 2018, a negotiated settlement between the Trump Administration's State Department and Defense Distributed brought a temporary conclusion to legal action and allowed for downloads to begin on August 1. Defense Distributed actually posted some documents only a few days earlier than that, with more than 1,000 downloads of such material occurring on the weekend of July 27–29, 2018.[59] However, nine states filed lawsuits in an attempt to block the posting of documents related to 3D printed guns. On July 31, 2018, a federal District Court judge in Washington issued an injunction that barred Defense Distributed from releasing their downloadable blueprints for 3D guns.[60] Litigation on this matter has continued in federal district and circuit courts since then, but to date, posting of these plans is still barred by the federal government.

In 2022, the ATF promulgated a new rule to regulate so-called "ghost guns," which is a term used to describe guns assembled through the creation or compilation of untraceable gun parts, such as frames and receivers. According to a White House press release, the rule "bans the business of manufacturing the most accessible ghost guns, such as unserialized 'buy build shoot' kits that individuals can buy online or at a store without a background check and can readily assemble into a working firearm in as little as thirty minutes with equipment they have at home."[61] The rule also requires "federally licensed dealers and gunsmiths taking any unserialized firearm into inventory to serialize that weapon." The purpose of the rule is to allow law enforcement to more easily trace weapons used in the commission of crimes.

Federal Prohibition of *Bump Stocks* via Rulemaking

A *bump stock* is an attachment that some suggest can enable a semi-automatic rifle to function as a fully automatic weapon. Prior to 2018, this device was legal under federal law, even though fully automatic guns were not. In the aftermath of the deadliest mass shooting in U.S. history, which claimed 58 lives in Las Vegas in 2017 and involved a shooter who reportedly used a bump stock, there were calls to have Congress ban bump stocks, but no such action was taken.

Some states, such as Connecticut, Rhode Island, and Florida, took the step of banning bump stocks on their own, as did some cities, like Cincinnati, Ohio, and Columbia, South Carolina. The Florida ban arose from grassroots movements led by high school students who staged protests, called *walk outs*, after a 2018 mass shooting resulted in seventeen deaths at Marjory Stoneman Douglas High School in Parkland, Florida. Later, the federal government would address this matter via a somewhat unusual pathway.

In December 2018, the Trump Administration indicated that, effective March 2019, bump stocks would be considered banned items under a new interpretation of the National Firearms Act of 1934. This occurred when the Department of Justice, which houses the Bureau of Alcohol, Tobacco, Firearms, and Explosives (ATF), promulgated a 2018 bureaucratic rule declaring the National Firearms Act of 1934 would be interpreted to encompass bump stocks, which would then be banned nationwide the following year.[62] In February 2019, a federal judge on the U.S. District Court for the District of Columbia upheld that rule, and in March 2019, the Supreme Court refused to grant cert in cases seeking to challenge this rule, allowing the lower court ruling to stand.[63] In turn, the new federal ban on bump stocks went into effect in March 2019. This was done without a single vote in Congress and pursuant only to the federal agency rulemaking process.

The Bipartisan Safer Communities Act of 2022

As noted above, the Gun Control Act of 1968 established baseline nationwide age limits for certain firearms purchases. Under that law, shotguns and rifles may only be sold to those who have reached the age of 18, a limitation that also applies to ammunition sales for those items. All other guns, including handguns, can only be sold to those 21 years of age or older. This issue came to the forefront of firearms dialogue in the aftermath of two mass shootings in May 2022, both perpetuated by 18-year-olds—one of which claimed ten lives at a supermarket in Buffalo, New York and the other resulting in the deaths of nineteen children and two teachers at an elementary school in Uvalde, Texas.

In the aftermath of these shootings, Congress passed a law called the Bipartisan Safer Communities Act of 2022,[64] which was signed into law by President Biden in June 2022. The law provided for enhanced background checks for persons under 21, requiring an examination of records dating back to age 16 in order to assess prior criminal activity and mental health issues. The law also provided millions of dollars to states that implement "red flag" laws and called for enhanced penalties for straw purchases. Additionally, the law closed a loophole in domestic violence cases. Under prior federal law, persons convicted of domestic violence or subject to a restraining order were barred from purchasing a gun if they had been married to or lived with the victim, or had a child with them. This so-called "boyfriend loophole" was closed by changing the wording of the law to apply to "recent or current" dating partners.

Selections from "The State of California's Penal Code Section 30515," 2020.

State and Local Gun Laws

State and local governments have numerous laws affecting the sale, possession, and use of firearms and other weapons. Under *McDonald v. Chicago*, all of these laws are potentially subject to judicial review in federal courts. They are also subject to attack under the state constitutions, most of which contain language supporting the right to keep and bear arms.

State Assault Weapon Bans

As of August 2022, only seven states (and the District of Columbia) had bans on assault weapons: California, Connecticut, Hawaii, Maryland, Massachusetts, New York, and New Jersey. One legal as well as practical problem implicit in these bans is how to differentiate assault weapons from other (presumably less lethal) semi-automatic rifles and pistols. In addition to listing particular prohibited models, the California law defines the generic characteristics of an assault weapon:

1. A semiautomatic, centerfire rifle that does not have a fixed magazine but has any one of the following:

    a. A pistol grip that protrudes conspicuously beneath the action of the weapon.
    b. A thumbhole stock.
    c. A folding or telescoping stock.
    d. A grenade launcher or flare launcher.
    e. A flash suppressor.
    f. A forward pistol grip.

2. A semiautomatic, centerfire rifle that has a fixed magazine with the capacity to accept more than 10 rounds.
3. A semiautomatic, centerfire rifle that has an overall length of less than 30 inches.
4. A semiautomatic pistol that does not have a fixed magazine but has any one of the following:

    a. A threaded barrel, capable of accepting a flash suppressor, forward handgrip, or silencer.
    b. A second handgrip.
    c. A shroud that is attached to, or partially or completely encircles, the barrel that allows the bearer to fire the weapon without burning the bearer's hand, except a slide that encloses the barrel.
    d. The capacity to accept a detachable magazine at some location outside of the pistol grip.

5. A semiautomatic pistol with a fixed magazine that has the capacity to accept more than 10 rounds.
6. A semiautomatic shotgun that has both of the following:

    a. A folding or telescoping stock.
    b. A pistol grip that protrudes conspicuously beneath the action of the weapon, thumbhole stock, or vertical handgrip.

7. A semiautomatic shotgun that does not have a fixed magazine.
8. Any shotgun with a revolving cylinder.
9. A semiautomatic centerfire firearm that is not a rifle, pistol, or shotgun, that does not have a fixed magazine, but that has any one of the following:

    a. A pistol grip that protrudes conspicuously beneath the action of the weapon.
    b. A thumbhold stock.

c. A folding or telescoping stock.
d. A grenade launcher or flare launcher.
e. A flash suppressor.
f. A forward pistol grip.
g. A threaded barrel, capable of accepting a flash suppressor, forward handgrip, or silencer.
h. A second handgrip.
i. A shroud that is attached to, or partially or completely encircles, the barrel that allows the bearer to fire the weapon without burning the bearer's hand, except a slide that encloses the barrel.
j. The capacity to accept a detachable magazine at some location outside of the pistol grip.

10. A semiautomatic centerfire firearm that is not a rifle, pistol, or shotgun, that has a fixed magazine with the capacity to accept more than 10 rounds.
11. A semiautomatic centerfire firearm that is not a rifle, pistol, or shotgun, that has an overall length of less than 30 inches. ...[65]

Although the Supreme Court has yet to consider the issue of assault weapons, several federal appeals courts have addressed state assault weapons bans. In 2017, the U.S. Court of Appeals for the Fourth Circuit upheld Maryland's ban.[66] Other circuit courts have also ruled to uphold bans on assault weapons.[67] The Supreme Court has yet to review the constitutionality of such bans, leaving the issue to state and lower federal courts to untangle.

In June 2021, a federal district judge in San Diego ruled that the California's definition of assault weapons violated the Second Amendment. In his opinion, Judge Roger Benitez noted that "the firearms deemed 'assault weapons' are fairly ordinary, popular, modern."[68] Later that month, the U.S. Court of Appeals for the Ninth Circuit stayed Judge Benitez's order, thus leaving California's assault weapons ban intact.[69] More recently, in August 2022, the Ninth Circuit ordered the case to be reconsidered by the district court in light of the Supreme Court's 2022 decision in *New York State Rifle & Pistol Association v. Bruen*, which, as discussed above, reflected a rigorous protection for Second Amendment rights.

Magazine Capacity Limits

Approximately ten states (and even some cities) have prohibitions related to a firearm's magazine capacity, with exact limitations ranging from ten to twenty rounds.[70] Federal courts have recently grappled with these divergent restrictions on large-capacity magazines. In 2017, the U.S.

LARGE-CAPACITY MAGAZINES: A term typically applied to a weapon capable of holding an amount of ammunition that is deemed illegal under state law.

Court of Appeals for the Fourth Circuit upheld magazine capacity limits emanating from the state of Maryland.[71] Previously, in 2013, a federal district court judge in New York struck down the state's ban on guns holding more than seven rounds, and the U.S. Court of Appeals for the Second Circuit agreed that this ban amounted to a violation of the Second Amendment.[72] New York responded with the passage of a ten-round ban, which remains in effect. California's ban on high-capacity magazines (set at ten rounds) has been reviewed more than once by the Ninth Circuit, which, in November 2021, upheld the law after an *en banc* rehearing reversed an earlier decision by a three-judge panel. But in December 2021, the Ninth Circuit announced that it would stay that decision for 150 days, preventing it from taking effect and temporarily allowing Californians to continue to possess such weapons.[73] Then, in June 2022, the Supreme Court vacated the Ninth Circuit's decision and remanded the case for reconsideration in light of *New York State Rifle & Pistol Association v. Bruen*.[74]

The Right to Bear Arms: Open and Concealed Carry

Historically, carrying a concealed weapon outside one's home or property was a criminal offense. Today, twenty-one states have passed laws that allow the carrying of a weapon outside the home without a permit—a concept known as permitless carry. These states can vary regarding whether such carrying must occur in a concealed fashion (such that the weapon is not visible to others) or *open carry* is permitted. All other states have laws allowing citizens to carry concealed weapons as long as they obtain a permit, and in those places, carrying a concealed weapon without a permit remains an offense. Most states permit citizens with a valid carry permit to openly carry a holstered handgun, although some require a special permit for open carry. Four states (California, Florida, Illinois, and South Carolina) and the District of Columbia require weapons carried outside the home to be concealed. Another issue is whether states will honor permits issued in other states. Again, there is tremendous variance here. States with stricter gun laws, such as Illinois, New York, and California, tend not to honor concealed carry permits issued by other states. Many states will honor out-of-state permits but with restrictions.

As noted above, in *New York State Rifle & Pistol Association v. Bruen* (2022), the Supreme Court struck down New York's law requiring applicants to show "proper cause" in order to get a carry permit. This decision is likely to have repercussions for gun carry laws across the country.

Weapons on College Campuses

Sixteen states ban gun possession on all college campuses, but approximately twenty other states leave the decision up to individual schools—which can vary on whether faculty or students are allowed to carry, whether certain buildings or stadiums are off limits for weapons possession, and whether certain weapons are prohibited (e.g., guns, knives, Tasers, etc.). Utah is the only state with a law that explicitly prevents colleges from banning guns on campus, while a 2012 ruling from the Colorado Supreme Court requires campuses in that state to allow gun possession by those over the age of 21 who have a valid carry permit.[75]

Gun-Free Zones

Beyond college and university settings, states also vary in terms of how they define other areas as *gun-free zones*, a term that is certain to include elementary and high schools but might also include places such as the following: daycare centers, churches, hospitals, state or local parks, and stadiums. Michigan, for example, has legalized guns in all of these places, as long as someone possesses a concealed-carry permit. Variation also exists regarding whether people can possess guns in bars, with Arizona, Georgia, and Ohio among the states allowing it. In Tennessee, bar and restaurant owners can decide for themselves if they wish to allow patrons to possess guns, and posting a sign serves as notice of a legally enforceable ban; that state also makes it a crime to be intoxicated while in possession of a firearm. In Missouri, it is not illegal to be in possession of a gun while intoxicated if the gun is used for self-defense purposes. Along with Tennessee, Louisiana, Maine, and Virginia allow guns in state parks and historic sites. The federal government allows guns in national parks, with the exception of certain buildings identified as gun-free.

Red Flag Laws

RED FLAG LAWS: State laws allowing judges to issue risk protection orders authorizing the temporary seizure of firearms from persons believed to be a threat to themselves or others.

RISK PROTECTION ORDER: An order issued by a judge authorizing the temporary seizure of firearms from a person believed to be a threat to themself or others.

In an effort to prevent gun violence by mentally ill persons, nineteen states have enacted red flag laws, which allow courts to order the temporary removal of firearms from persons who may present a danger to themselves or others. The process can be initiated on petition of the police or family members. Police officers who go to a residence to conduct a welfare check may seize weapons temporarily, while a petition for a risk protection order (RPO) is adjudicated. Typically, the standard of proof needed to obtain a temporary RPO is preponderance of the evidence, which means the judge determines it is more likely than not that the individual is dangerous. A final RPO, which may last up to one year, requires a higher standard of proof: the judge must find clear and convincing evidence of such danger. Of course, refusal to comply with an RPO is a criminal offense. When the RPO has expired, the weapons are returned to the person from whom they were taken. Of course, the court may decide, based on clear and convincing evidence, that the RPO should be extended.

Do such laws violate the right to keep and bear arms or the right to due process of law? In 2013, an Indiana appellate court upheld the state's red flag law against a challenge based in part on the Second Amendment.[76] Similarly, in 2016, the Connecticut Appellate Court upheld the state's red flag law against a Second Amendment challenge, saying "it does not restrict the right of law-abiding, responsible citizens to use arms in defense of their homes."[77] More recently, in 2019, the Florida First District Court of Appeal upheld the state's red flag law against a challenge based on due process claims.[78] In its opinion, the appellate court commented on the approach trial judges should take in determining whether to issue a risk protection order:

> Considering the array of factors and other provisions within the statute, we hold that although trial courts should carefully consider, *inter alia*, evidence

of serious or recurring mental illness, ... a lack thereof is not dispositive and does not preclude an RPO. The RPO statute contemplates "red flag" situations where a volatile individual demonstrates mental/emotional instability through threatening and erratic behavior. Such a person need not necessarily have been formally diagnosed with a serious or recurring psychosis.

In 2021, the Supreme Court's decision in *Caniglia v. Strom*[79] added an interesting caveat to these situations. In that case, the Court ruled that a Fourth Amendment violation occurred when police seized a California man's guns during the course of a welfare check requested by his wife, who claimed he had asked for her to "shoot him now." The Court found that this seizure of the man's weapons from his home could not be justified through the *community caretaker exception* to the warrant requirement. We will discuss this matter in greater detail in chapter 8, but for now, we note that this decision could provide an obstacle to warrantless gun seizures pursuant to state red flag laws. Even before this decision, though, red flag laws were used sparingly by authorities. In September 2022, the Associated Press issued a report indicating that "such laws in 19 states and the District of Columbia were used to remove firearms from people 15,049 times since 2020, fewer than 10 per 100,000 adult residents."[80]

Privacy Rights of Gun Owners

In 2011, Florida passed a law called the Firearm Owners' Privacy Act, which banned health care professionals in the state from asking a patient if they or family members owned guns or ammunition. However, in 2017, this law was struck down by the U.S. Court of Appeals for the Eleventh Circuit for violating the free speech rights of medical professionals.[81] Yet similar laws remain in place in Minnesota, Missouri, and Montana—as well as in Indiana, where employers cannot ask an employee if they own a gun.

In January 2022, the city of San Jose, California took an interesting step when its City Council passed an ordinance requiring all gun owners to carry liability insurance that would cover incidents involving accidental gun discharges.[82] The ordinance also required gun owners to pay a yearly fee of approximately $25 to $30 to fund a program geared toward suicide prevention and gun safety. Lawsuits challenging these measures, which were the first of their kind in the United States, ensued over the course of 2022.

THE CONSTITUTION IN ACTION
The *Vitter Amendment* and Gun Rights during a Natural Disaster

Federal law exists to specifically protect individuals against government seizures of weapons during a natural disaster. In the aftermath of Hurricane Katrina, the Disaster Recovery Personal Protection Act was proposed in Congress 2006 by a pair of legislators from Louisiana: Bobby Jindal of the U.S. House of Representatives and David Vitter of the U.S. Senate. The legislation was a response to the actions of New Orleans law enforcement officials during the response to Hurricane Katrina.

On September 8, 2005, the New Orleans Police Superintendent announced that firearms within the city limits would be confiscated by law enforcement officials—some of which were taken from abandoned homes, some of which were taken from gun owners lawfully in possession, some of which were taken from gun owners who were not permitted to possess, and some of which were stolen guns.[83] An exact number of how many guns were seized is unknown, but it is believed to be more than 1,000. On September 23, 2005, a federal district court ruled that the New Orleans Police Department was prohibited from effectuating warrantless seizures of firearms.[84] Despite that court

(continued)

ruling, the city took more than three years to return some weapons to their rightful owners, with the delay tied to a need to demonstrate "documented proof of ownership." In October 2008, an agreement to return the remaining weapons in police custody, believed to number more than 500, was forged as a part of the settlement in a lawsuit brought by the NRA.[85]

Today, the Disaster Recovery Personal Protection Act bans the seizure of lawfully-possessed guns during a federal disaster or emergency declaration (as those terms are defined by the federal Stafford Act).[86] The law does indicate that during a rescue or evacuation, a *temporary surrender* of a firearm can be mandated before a person is allowed to enter a rescue mode of transportation. The bill was passed as an amendment to the Department of Homeland Security Appropriations Act of 2007 and is commonly known as the *Vitter Amendment*.[87]

State Age Restrictions on Gun Purchases

Although federal law requires a person to be 21 to buy a handgun, states have differing policies regarding long guns, with some, including Alaska, Maine, Minnesota, and New York, allowing purchases or possession by those as young as 16 years old. Montana has no specific age limit for possession of any gun, but parents are prohibited from allowing anyone under the age of 14 from carrying a gun there.

The modern Supreme Court has recognized minors are entitled to constitutional rights—although in attenuated forms. These include First Amendment freedoms, privacy rights, freedom from unreasonable searches and seizures, and the rights to due process and equal protection of the laws.[88] Even so, there is little likelihood that the Supreme Court, or any court, would strike down laws restricting gun access to people who have not reached the voting age of 18.

In May 2022, the Ninth Circuit struck down a California law that banned sales of "long guns" and semi-automatic weapons to those between the ages of 18 and 21.[89] The majority opinion indicated that "the historical record showed that the Second Amendment protects the right of young adults to keep and bear arms, which includes the right to purchase." The opinion added, "America would not exist without the heroism of the young adults who fought and died in our revolutionary army." This decision left in place a requirement for those between the ages of 18 and 21 to acquire a hunting license before purchasing a long gun.

THE CONSTITUTION AND SOCIAL JUSTICE
An Author Posits Discrimination in Second Amendment Protections

In her 2021 book, *The Second: Race and Guns in a Fatally Unequal America*, Professor Carol Anderson argues that the primary motivation behind the adoption of the Second Amendment was to make sure the federal government could not disarm the state militias, which were needed to deter and put down slave uprisings. The book argues that the Second Amendment "came into being … steeped in anti-Blackness, swaddled in the desire to keep African-descended people rightless and powerless, and as yet another bone tossed to keep the South mollified and willing to stay aligned with the grand experiment of the United States of America." It also contends that the individual right to keep and bear arms interpretation of the Second Amendment has been applied in a way that discriminates against Black Americans. Professor Anderson writes, "The second a Black person exercises that right, the second they pick up a gun to protect themselves (or not), their life—as surely as Philando Castile's, as surely as Alton Sterling's, as surely as twelve-year-old Tamir Rice's—could be snatched away in that same fatal second." In Professor Anderson's view, "the Second Amendment is so inherently, structurally flawed, so based on Black exclusion and debasement, that, unlike the other amendments, it can never be a pathway to civil and human rights for 47.5 million African Americans."

This perspective on the Second Amendment is an example of Critical Race Theory (CRT), a school of thought that views the Constitution, and its classical liberal foundations, as inherently racist and, therefore, in need of fundamental revision—if not replacement. Of course, Professor Anderson's thesis is highly controversial. Critics point out that the Second Amendment was the descendant of the English Bill of Rights (1689), which demanded that, "… the subjects which are Protestants may have arms for their defence suitable to their conditions and as allowed by law. …" This language calls to mind the religious persecution and outright warfare that plagued England from the time of the Reformation. The inclusion of that language in the English Bill of Rights had nothing to do with the maintenance of slavery. The point is that history is complex, as were the motives of those who framed the U.S. Constitution and Bill of Rights. Still, there is no question that slavery and racism played a role in the foundation of this country's laws and institutions. The question is whether those laws and institutions are fatally flawed, as the subtitle of Professor Anderson's book suggests.

Gun Rights for Law Enforcement Personnel

Even prior to the Supreme Court's crucial decisions in *D.C. v. Heller* (2008) and *New York State Rifle & Pistol Association Inc. v. Bruen* (2022), Congress passed the Law Enforcement Officers Safety Act of 2004 (LEOSA),[90] which created a right for many active and retired police officers to carry a weapon in public in all fifty states, regardless of state gun laws in the place they might be carrying. There were exceptions. The law did not apply in places where federal law prohibited gun possession, such as in federal courthouses, many government buildings, and some national parks nor did it apply in the District of Columbia (hence an officer filing a Second Amendment lawsuit in *D.C. v. Heller*). Beyond that, it did not offer protection for gun possession when a person was under the influence of alcohol or drugs or was the subject of disciplinary action that could lead to suspension from their law enforcement role. LEOSA also did not supersede any state law that allowed private businesses to restrict firearm possession on their premises (as with bars and private clubs in most states) or where state law prohibited gun possession in state buildings or on state property (e.g., parks or school zones).

A 2010 amendment to LEOSA expanded its application to Amtrak Police and Federal Reserve Police; that amendment also made the law applicable to retired officers who had served a minimum of ten years in law enforcement (a lower threshold than the previous standard of fifteen years). Finally, the 2010 amendment applied the law to any state-level ammunition restrictions, such as where hollow-point rounds were banned (New Jersey) or magazine capacity limits existed (California); thus, officers could avoid those restrictions. In 2013, the law was amended again—this time to apply to military police officers and civilian officers of the federal government. The law does not apply to machine guns, suppressors, or "destructive devices," as defined by the National Firearms Act of 1934; but it is worth noting that a 1986 law that banned purchases of new machine guns created an exception for "a transfer to or by, or possession by or under the authority of, the United States or any department or agency thereof or a State, or a department, agency, or political subdivision thereof."[91] This would, presumably, allow possession of such a weapon under the color of a law enforcement agency, for law enforcement purposes.

Case precedent has offered further interpretations of the Law Enforcement Officers Safety Act of 2004. In *People v. Rodriguez*,[92] a New York court applied the protections of this law to a man who was a full-time construction worker but also an elected Constable for a police department in Pennsylvania; that interpretation allowed the man to evade a punishment for carrying a loaded weapon in his car in New York City, a crime that could have carried up to three years in prison. Another New York court found that the protections of LEOSA should apply to officers of the Coast Guard.[93] Additionally, a 2016 decision from the D.C. Circuit afforded protections of the law to retired officers of the D.C. Department of Corrections.[94] However, a 2012 decision from the D.C. Circuit refused to extend LEOSA to private security guards.[95] Overall, it is possible that a state-issued carry permit could allow any person the ability to carry a gun in a place LEOSA does not explicitly authorize.[96]

We also note that the First Step Act of 2018, which we discuss in chapter 14, allows employees working in federal correctional facilities to bring their guns to work, which is something that had been prohibited in most facilities prior to passage of that law.[97] The law also requires the Bureau of Prisons to ensure each federal correctional facility contained secure storage areas where a personal firearm could be stored, as possession within a secure perimeter remained illegal; another alternative offered by the First Step Act is for an employee to keep the weapon in their car inside of a locked box.

FOCUS ON LAW ENFORCEMENT

New Mexico Town Sells Badges, Creates *Officers* with Gun Rights

With a population of merely 432 people, according to the 2010 census, the small town of Lake Arthur, New Mexico, which sits 33 miles south of Roswell, seemed like an odd locale to employ a police force of more than 100 individuals. But that is precisely what arose as part of a program created in 2005 called the Lake Arthur Reserve Police Program. For a $400 annual fee, any individual could have joined this force and received a police badge and identification card. By 2018, there were at least 109 names listed as police officers connected to the town—more than 80% of whom did not even reside in the state of New Mexico.

New Mexico's State Police Chief, Pete Kassetas, derided this arrangement—which had made *officers* of several actors and businessmen—by denoting the differences between actual police officers in the state and the Lake Arthur Reserves as follows: "Twenty-two weeks of on-site closely evaluated training. The difference is the 14 step process to even get to the academy. The difference is that my officers aren't able to walk in, write a check and then leave with a badge and credentials and a gun." New Mexico State Representative Bill Rehm was even more blunt, saying, "It's kind of like going back to the Wild West."

An important point in this arrangement was that members of the Lake Arthur Reserves received a badge that could make them eligible to carry a loaded gun anywhere in the United States, regardless of local gun laws, under the Law Enforcement Officers Safety Act of 2004. In April 2018, the town's mayor announced the police chief had resigned, and the Lake Arthur Reserve Police Program would be terminated, with badges previously issued to reserve officers rescinded.[98]

Conclusion

The right to keep and bear arms is one of the most hotly contested constitutional rights. With key decisions in *D.C. v. Heller* (2008) and *McDonald v. Chicago* (2010), the Supreme Court offered protection for home ownership of handguns, and through the doctrine of incorporation in the latter, the Court likely has established a more stringent burden for government officials at all levels to meet if they wish to limit an individual's right to possess a weapon. Whether the weapon in question is a stun gun, Taser, nunchaku, or knife, federal, state, or local officials would likely face strict judicial scrutiny attempting to justify bans on such items. Moreover, in

New York State Rifle & Pistol Association Inc. v. Bruen (2022), the Court extended the *Heller* and *McDonald* rulings to recognize the right to carry weapons outside the home for the purpose of self-defense.

Those who favor stricter gun control measures, though, tend to believe that the Supreme Court got it wrong in *Heller*, *McDonald*, and *Bruen*. They argue the right to keep and bear arms should be limited to those in military service, in keeping with the militia clause of the Second Amendment and the Supreme Court's 1939 *United States v. Miller* decision, which upheld the federal National Firearms Act and its regulation scheme for so-called "dangerous and unusual weapons," like a sawed-off shotgun.

At this point, there seems to be little chance the Court will overturn the *Heller*, *McDonald*, and *Bruen* decisions in the foreseeable future. Given that reality, former Supreme Court Justice John P. Stevens once went so far as to call for the repeal of the Second Amendment. That, of course, is highly improbable. However, it is important to recognize that, under *Heller*, *McDonald*, and *Bruen*, there is room for reasonable local, state, and federal regulations on the sale, possession, and use of certain firearms and other types of weapons—particularly in regard to possession in certain places outside the home (e.g., schools, sports stadiums, or parks). Of course, reasonable people can and will disagree about what is *reasonable* in this context. Ultimately, application of the Second Amendment to such disagreements over specific gun control policies will likely result in additional litigation in the coming decades—given that Supreme Court jurisprudence related to gun policy has been scant; yet even that limited body of case precedent that does exist in regard to the Second Amendment has proved noteworthy when the high Court and lower courts choose to delve into this important issue that impacts virtually all aspects of American society.

Discussion Questions

1. What prompted the Supreme Court to abandon the "well regulated militia" interpretation of the Second Amendment in favor of an interpretation that stresses the individual right to keep and bear arms when it comes to handguns? Has the Court explicitly disavowed application of the militia clause to weapons such as grenades and machine guns? What other words and phrases in the Second Amendment have been addressed by Supreme Court decisions, and what key definitions of those words and phrases emerge?
2. Why was the federal government's ban on assault weapons so short-lived? Do you favor the revival of such a ban, or should this matter be left to the states? What have lower courts had to say on this issue? What other types of weapons vary in terms of how different states address their legality?
3. What standard of review should courts employ in reviewing the constitutionality of state and local gun control laws? Consider how the answer to that question might vary depending on the type of weapon or location of possession? What weapons are likely to be protected by a high standard, and what weapons are likely to be protected at a lower level—or will such distinctions become irrelevant?

Endnotes

1   World Population Review, *Gun Deaths by Country*, 2021, https://worldpopulationreview.com/country-rankings/gun-deaths-by-country.

2   Chile is second with a firearm homicide rate of 1.82 per 100,000 people. Institute for Health Metrics and Evaluation, *On Gun Violence, the United States Is an outlier*, http://www.healthdata.org/acting-data/gun-violence-united-states-outlier.

3   *United States v. Cruikshank*, 92 U.S. 542 (1875).

4   *United States v. Miller*, 307 U.S. 174 (1939).

5   *Lewis v. United States*, 445 U.S. 55 (1980).

6   *District of Columbia v. Heller*, 554 U.S. 570 (2008).

7   *Id.* (citing *United States v. Sprague*, 282 U.S. 716 (1931)).

8   Individual states are tasked with defining whom to identify as mentally ill. Federal law prohibits gun purchases by those under the age of 21, but possession of a firearm (independent of a purchase) may be permitted under applicable state laws. Moreover, the federal limitation is specific to handguns, as opposed to "long guns."

9   2010 Tennessee Code Title 39. Criminal Offenses § 39-11-611.

10 Florida Statutes, § 776.013.

11 *McDonald v. City of Chicago*, 561 U.S. 742 (2010).

12 *Caetano v. Massachusetts*, 577 U.S. 411 (2016).

13 *Ramirez v. Commonwealth*, 94 N.E. 3d 809 (Mass. 2018).

14 The last two remaining bans on these items were removed in 2022; by legislation in Hawaii and by federal court order in Rhode Island. States that require a carry permit to possess a Taser or stun gun outside the home include Connecticut, Delaware, Illinois, and New Mexico.

15 *New York State Rifle & Pistol Assn., Inc. v. Bruen*, 597 U. S. ____ (2022).

16 *Maloney v. Cuomo*, 554 F. 3d 56 (2nd Cir. 2009).

17 The Arizona and New York bans in place at that time have been struck down; the other two remain in effect.

18 *Maloney v. Cuomo, supra* note 16 (citing *Beatie v. City of New York*, 123 F.3d 707, 711 (2d Cir. 1997) (quoting *City of Cleburne v. Cleburne Living Ctr., Inc.*, 473 U.S. 432, 440 (1985))).

19 *Maloney v. Singas*, 351 F. Supp. 3d 222 (E.D.N.Y. 2018)

20 *Id.* (citing *N.Y. State Rifle & Pistol Association v. Cuomo*, 804 F.3d 242 (2d Cir. 2015)).

21 National Firearms Act of 1934, Pub. L. 73–474, 48 Stat. 1236.

22 This is the language Justice Scalia used for describing weapons covered under the National Firearms Act in his majority opinion for *D.C. v. Heller.*

23 Omnibus Crime Control and Safe Streets Act of 1968, Pub. L. 90-351, 82 Stat. 197, 28 U.S.C. §5845.

24 *See, e.g., Mont. Shooting Sports Ass'n v. Holder*, 727 F.3d 975 (9th Cir. 2013).

25 *United States v. Stewart*, 348 F. 3d 1132 (9th Cir. 2003) & 451 F.3d 1071 (9th Cir. 2006).

26 Among the states to make such declarations are Alaska, Arizona, Idaho, Montana, South Dakota, Tennessee, Utah, and Wyoming. *See* Bethany Blankley, *61% of U.S. counties now "Second Amendment sanctuaries"*, The Center Square, Jul. 4, 2021 (for data on the statistic regarding different counties), https://www.thecentersquare.com/national/61-of-u-s-counties-now-second-amendment-sanctuaries/article_12565326-d82b-11eb-8b83-8713ae288961.html.

27 *United States v. Cox*, No. 17–3034 (10th Cir. 2018).

28 Gun Control Act of 1968, Pub. L. 90-618, 82 Stat. 1213.

29 18 U.S.C. § 922(g)(9).

30 See 18 U.S. Code § 921.

31 *Wilson v. Lynch*, 835 F.3d 1083 (9th Cir. 2016).

32 *United States v. Meza-Rodriguez*, 798 F.3d 664 (7th Cir. 2015).

33   *Hirschfeld v. Bureau of Alcohol, Tobacco, Firearms, and Explosives*, 5 F. 4th 407 (4th Cir. 2021).

34   Firearm Owners Protection Act of 1986, Pub. L. 99–308, 100 Stat. 449.

35   *See* US Concealed Carry, *USCCA's Concealed Carry Reciprocity Map & Gun Laws by State* (for a map illustrating reciprocity of gun permits by state), https://www.usconcealedcarry.com/resources/ccw_reciprocity_map/.

36   Brady Handgun Violence Prevention Act of 1994, Pub. L. 103–159, 107 Stat. 1536, 18 U.S.C. §§ 921–922.

37   *Printz v. United States*, 521 U.S. 898 (1997).

38   Mental Health Reporting System, *Giffords Law Center*, https://giffords.org/lawcenter/gun-laws/policy-areas/background-checks/mental-health-reporting/.

39   Congressional Review Act of 1996, Pub. L. 104–121, 110 Stat. 847, 5 U.S.C. § 801-808.

40   These states include California, Colorado, Connecticut, Delaware, Illinois, New York, Oregon, Rhode Island, Maryland, Nevada, Pennsylvania, and Washington; in some places, background checks at gun shows are only required for handgun sales.

41   Protection of Lawful Commerce in Arms Act of 2005, Pub. L. 109–92, 119 Stat. 2095, 15 U.S.C. §§ 7901–7903.

42   *Br. of Resp'ts, Remington Arms Co. v. Soto*, October 4, 2019.

43   Bill Chappell, *Supreme Court Allows Sandy Hook Families' Case Against Remington Arms to Proceed*, NPR, Nov. 12, 2019, https://www.npr.org/2019/11/12/778487920/supreme-court-allows-sandy-hook-families-case-against-remington-to-proceed.

44   Allyson Waller, *Federal Judge Finds U.S. Government Inaction Mostly to Blame for Sutherland Springs Mass Shooting*, Texas Tribune, July 7, 2021, https://www.texastribune.org/2021/07/07/texas-sutherland-springs-shooting-court-ruling/; Alyssa Lukpat, *Air Force Ordered to Pay $230 Million to Victims of 2017 Church Shooting*, N.Y. Times, Feb. 7, 2022, https://www.nytimes.com/2022/02/07/us/air-force-sutherland-springs-shooting-settlement.html; *see Holcombe v. United States*, SA-18-CV-00555-XR (W.D. Tex., Feb. 7, 2022).

45   *Abramski v. United States*, 573 U.S. 169 (2014).

46   *United States v. Castleman*, 572 U.S. 157 (2014).

47   *Voisine v. United States*, 579 U.S. 686 (2016).

48   *Rehaif v. United States*, 588 U.S. ___ (2019).

49   U.S. Sentencing Commission, *Quick Facts-Felon in Possession of a Firearm, Fiscal Year 2018*, https://www.ussc.gov/sites/default/files/pdf/research-and-publications/quick-facts/Felon_In_Possession_FY18.pdf.

50   *Gamble v. United States*, 587 U.S. ___ (2019).

51   18 U.S.C. § 925(c).

52   *United States v. Bean*, 537 U.S. 71 (2002).

53   Violent Crime Control and Law Enforcement Act of 1994, Pub. L. 103–322, 108 Stat. 1796.

54   *Staples v. United States*, 511 U.S. 600 (1994).

55   *United States v. Freed*, 401 U.S. 601 (1971).

56   *Haynes v. United States*, 390 U.S. 85 (1968).

57   26 U.S.C. § 5845(e).

58   Undetectable Firearms Act of 1988, Pub. L. 100–649, 102 Stat. 3810.

59   Lisa Payne, *Texas Company Cleared to Put 3D-Printed Gun Designs Online*, Chicago Tribune, July 16, 2018, https://www.chicagotribune.com/nation-world/ct-texas-3d-printed-gun-20180726-story.html.

60   *Washington v. U.S. Department of State*, 315 F. Supp. 3d 1202 (W.D. Wash. 2018).

61   The White House, *FACT SHEET: The Biden Administration Cracks Down on Ghost Guns, Ensures That ATF Has the Leadership it Needs to Enforce Our Gun Laws*, April 11, 2022, https://www.whitehouse.gov/briefing-room/

statements-releases/2022/04/11/fact-sheet-the-biden-administration-cracks-down-on-ghost-guns-ensures-that-atf-has-the-leadership-it-needs-to-enforce-our-gun-laws/.

62   Bump-Stock-Type Devices, 27 C.F.R., Parts 447, 478, and 479 (Dec. 26, 2018).

63   *Guedes v. Bureau of Alcohol, Tobacco, Firearms, & Explosives*, 356 F. Supp. 3d 109 (D.D.C. 2019) (On March 28, 2019, the U.S. Supreme Court denied certiorari.).

64   Bipartisan Safer Communities Act of 2022, Pub. L. 117-159, 136 Stat. 1313.

65   Cal. Penal Code §30515.

66   *Kolbe v. Hogan*, 849 F.3d 114 (4th Cir. 2017).

67   *See, e.g., Friedman v. City of Highland Park, Illinois*, 784 F. 3d 406 (7th Cir. 2015); *Worman v. Healey*, 922 F.3d 26 (1st Cir. 2019).

68   *Miller v. Bonta*, Case No.: 19-cv-1537-BEN-JLB, (S.D. Cal. June 4, 2021).

69   *Miller v. Bonta*, Case No.: 3:19-cv-01537-BEN-JLB (9th Cir. June 21, 2021).

70   The states with magazine capacity limits include California, Colorado, Connecticut, Hawaii, Maryland, Massachusetts, New Jersey, New York, and Vermont. Virginia has a complex set of specifications related to guns holding over twenty rounds. Chicago, Denver, and New York are among the cities with magazine capacity limits.

71   *Kolbe v. Hogan*, 849 F. 3d 114 (4th Cir. 2017).

72   *New York State Rifle & Pistol Association v. Cuomo*, 804 F. 3d 242 (2nd Cir. 2015).

73   *Duncan v. Bonta*, No. 19-55376, D.C. No. 3:17-cv-01017-BEN-JLB (9th Cir. Nov. 30, 2021) (The en banc decision overturned the following case: *Duncan v. Becerra*, 970 F.3d 1133 (9th Cir. 2020).).

74   *Duncan v. Bonta*, Petition GRANTED. Judgment VACATED and case REMANDED for further consideration in light of *New York State Rifle & Pistol Assn., Inc. v. Bruen*, 597 U. S. ____ (2022), US Supreme Court, June 20, 2022.

75   *Regents of the University of Colorado v. Students for Concealed Carry on Campus*, 271 P.3d 496 (Colo. 2012).

76   *Redington v. State*, 121 N.E.3d 1053 (Ind. App. 2019).

77   *Hope v. State*, 133 A.3d 519 (Conn. App. Ct. 2016).

78   *Davis v. Gilchrist County Sheriff's Office*, 280 So.3d 524 (Fla. Dist. Ct. App. (2019).

79   *Caniglia v. Strom*, 593 U.S. __ (2021).

80   Bernard Condo, *Red Flag Laws Ge Little Use As Shootings, Gun Deaths Soar*. Associated Press, Sept. 2, 2022, https://apnews.com/article/buffalo-supermarket-shooting-highland-park-july-4-gun-violence-chicago-politics-5165bbcde8771eb-f09e7641674d0de9a

81   *Wollschlaeger v. Governor of Fla.*, 848 F.3d 1293 (11th Cir. 2017).

82   Martin Kaste, *San Jose Passes Law Requiring Gun Owners to Get Liability Insurance*, NPR, Jan. 27, 2022, https://www.npr.org/2022/01/27/1076049808/san-jose-passes-law-requiring-gun-owners-to-get-liability-insurance.

83   Alex Berenson & John Broder, *Police Begin Seizing Guns of Civilians*, N.Y. Times, Sept. 8, 2005, https://www.nytimes.com/2005/09/09/us/nationalspecial/police-begin-seizing-guns-of-civilians.html.

84   *Gettridge v. Gusman*, 2005 WL 3162040 (E.D. La. 2005). *See* Brandon L. Garrett & Tania Tetlow, *Criminal Justice Collapse: The Constitution after Hurricane Katrina*, 56 Duke L.J. 127 (2006) (for further reading).

85   NRA Institute for Legislative Action, *A Decade Later, Remember New Orleans ... Gun Confiscation Can (and Has) Happened in America*, Aug. 21, 2015, https://www.nraila.org/articles/20150821/a-decade-later-remember-new-orleans-gun-confiscation-can-and-has-happened-in-america; *see* Associated Press, *Louisiana: City Will Give Back Guns*, N.Y. Times, Oct. 8, 2008, https://www.nytimes.com/2008/10/09/us/09brfs-CITYWILLGIVE_BRF.html; Associated Press, *NRA to Settle Suit over Katrina gun seizures*, NBC News, Oct. 8, 2008, https://www.nbcnews.com/id/wbna27087738.

86   Robert T. Stafford Disaster Relief & Emergency Assistance Act, Pub. L. 100–707, 102 Stat. 4689,42 U.S.C. § 5121-5123.

87   Department of Homeland Security Appropriations Act of 2007, Pub. L. 109–295, 26 Stat. 653, 2 U.S.C. § 661(a)).

88   *See, e.g., In re Gault*, 387 U.S. 1 (1967); *Tinker v. Des Moines*, 393 U.S. 503 (1969); *New Jersey v. T.L.O.*, 469 U.S. 325 (1985).

89   *Jones et al. v. Bonta*, No. 20-56174 (9th Cir. 2022) (Intermediate scrutiny was used to evaluate the hunting license requirement. However, strict scrutiny was used to evaluate the ban on semi-automatic weapons, with the court choosing that test as suitable for a "total ban.").

90   Law Enforcement Officers Safety Act of 2004, Pub. L. 108–277; 118 Stat. 865; 18 U.S.C. § 926B and § 926C.

91   Firearms Owners' Protection Act of 1986, 18 U.S.C. § 922(o).

92   *People v. Rodriguez*, Supreme Court of the State of New York, County of New York (Part 41), Indictment Number 2917/06.

93   *People v. Booth*, 20 Misc. 3d 549 (County Court, Orange County, New York, 2008).

94   *DuBerry v. Dist. of Columbia*, 824 F.3d 1046 (D.C. Cir. 2016)

95   *Thorne v. United States*, 55 A.3d 873 (D.C. 2012).

96   Tennessee Code § 39-17-1350 (2019) ("[A]ny law enforcement officer may carry firearms at all times and in all places within Tennessee, on-duty or off-duty, regardless of the officer's regular duty hours or assignments, except as provided by subsection (c), federal law, lawful orders of court or the written directives of the executive supervisor of the employing agency." Subsection (c) says, "The authority conferred by this section shall not extend to a law enforcement officer: (1) Who is not engaged in the actual discharge of official duties as a law enforcement officer and carries a firearm onto school grounds or inside a school building during regular school hours unless the officer immediately informs the principal that the officer will be present on school grounds or inside the school building and in possession of a firearm. If the principal is unavailable, the notice may be given to an appropriate administrative staff person in the principal's office; (2) Who is consuming beer or an alcoholic beverage or who is under the influence of beer, an alcoholic beverage, or a controlled substance or controlled substance analogue; or (3) Who is not engaged in the actual discharge of official duties as a law enforcement officer while attending a judicial proceeding." Thus, if state law permitting guns in a park area that was off-limits for carrying a gun under federal law, the state permit could provide added protection. *See* James. M. Baranowski, *Law Enforcement Officer Safety Act: Off-Limit Areas?* NRA Explore (for further reading on this idea), https://le.nra.org/understanding-leosa/off-limit-areas/.

97   First Step Act of 2018, Pub. L. 115–391, 132 Stat. 5194, 18 U.S.C. § 1.

98   Zachary Mider & Zeke Faux, *NM Town Stops Badge Program*, Albuquerque Journal, April 18, 2018; *see* Larry Barker, *Playing Cop: The Lake Arthur Badge Scheme*, KRQE News 13—Breaking News, Albuquerque, Apr. 26, 2018, https://www.krqe.com/news/larry-barker/playing-cop-the-lake-arthur-badge-scheme/.

CHAPTER 7

The Fourth Amendment

Freedom from Unreasonable Searches and Seizures

"The right of the people to be secure in their persons, houses, papers and effects, against unreasonable searches and seizures, shall not be violated, and no Warrants shall issue but upon probable cause, supported by Oath or affirmation, and particularly describing the place to be searched and the persons or things to be seized."

—U.S. Constitution, Fourth Amendment

Learning Objectives

After reading this chapter, you should understand the following:

1. Why the Fourth Amendment was adopted
2. What constitutes a search or seizure
3. Where, when, and to whom the Fourth Amendment applies
4. The scope of the warrant requirement
5. The fundamental importance of probable cause
6. The functions and limitations of the exclusionary rule
7. How the doctrine of qualified immunity limits lawsuits against the police

Key Cases

Katz v. United States, 389 U.S. 347 (1967)
United States v. Jones, 565 U.S. 400 (2012)
Florida v. Jardines, 569 U.S. 1 (2013)
Weeks v. United States, 232 U.S. 383 (1914)
Mapp v. Ohio, 367 U.S. 643 (1961)
United States v. Leon, 468 U.S. 897 (1984)

Introduction

In the day-to-day enforcement of the law, no constitutional provision is more important than the Fourth Amendment. Because a violation of this amendment can result in the suppression of incriminating evidence, it is crucial for law enforcement officers to have a thorough understanding of what the amendment requires and what it prohibits. It is equally crucial for persons who have encounters with the police to understand their Fourth Amendment rights. As with the other constitutional provisions examined in this book, our focus is on how the courts have interpreted and applied this critically important amendment. Because Fourth Amendment jurisprudence is so rich and complex, we have divided our treatment of the amendment into four chapters. In this chapter, we look at the basic components of the Fourth Amendment. In subsequent chapters, we will examine the application of this amendment to warrantless searches, electronic surveillance, and even to situations involving arrest and investigatory detention.

Adoption and Extension of the Fourth Amendment

The idea that a person should be protected against official searches and seizures is rooted in the common law,[1] yet English kings (and later Parliament) frequently authorized unbridled searches by agents of the Crown.[2] In colonial Massachusetts, courts issued the infamous Writs of Assistance, which authorized customs officials to inspect ships, warehouses, and even private homes for contraband. The purpose of the writs was to ferret out smuggling and, thus, enhance tax revenue for the Crown. The writs were a form of general warrant, which gives officials blanket authority to search any person or premises suspected of harboring evidence of illegal activity.

GENERAL WARRANT: A warrant that is not particular regarding the place to be searched or the things to be seized.

In a 1761 lawsuit, attorney James Otis called the Writs of Assistance "the worst instrument of arbitrary power, the most destructive of English liberty and the fundamental principles of law, that ever was found in an English lawbook."[3] Otis railed particularly against the authority to search private homes, saying that under the common law, "A man's house is his castle; and while he is quiet, he is as well guarded as a prince in his castle."[4] The Writs of Assistance helped galvanize resistance to British rule and lingering outrage over the Writs motivated the inclusion of the Fourth Amendment in the Bill of Rights. The amendment's requirement that warrants must "particularly describ[e] the place to be searched and the persons or things to be seized" is directly traceable to early Americans' aversion to general warrants. Of course, even the Fourth Amendment does not provide that all searches and seizures be justified by a warrant, and it only offers a direct prohibition on those searches that are *unreasonable*. Therefore, it has been left to courts to untangle the breadth and scope of that important word.

Incorporation of the Fourth Amendment

Like the other amendments contained in the Bill of Rights, the Fourth Amendment originally applied only to searches and seizures by agents of the national government. It was not until 1949 that the Supreme Court held that the right to be free from an unreasonable search or seizure is incorporated within the Due Process Clause of the Fourteenth Amendment and, therefore, applicable to searches and seizures performed by state and local authorities. Writing for the Court in *Wolf v. Colorado*,[5] Justice Felix Frankfurter asserted, "The security of one's privacy against arbitrary intrusion by the police—which is at the core of the Fourth Amendment—is basic to a free society."

What Constitutes a Search or Seizure?

In *Olmstead v. United States* (1928),[6] the Supreme Court adopted a narrow conception of searches under the Fourth Amendment. The case involved a wiretap placed on a phone line in the basement of a building, where a suspected bootlegger kept an office. Because federal agents did not physically enter Olmstead's office, the Court determined that no search had taken place. Thus, it did not matter that the agents had failed to obtain a court order authorizing the wiretap. Chief Justice William Howard Taft, speaking for a sharply divided Court, opined that "one who installs in his house a telephone instrument with connecting wires intends to project his voice to those quite outside" and that "the wires beyond his house, and messages passing over them, are not within the protection of the Fourth Amendment." In an oft-quoted dissent, Justice Louis D. Brandeis observed the following:

> The progress of science in furnishing the government with means of espionage is not likely to stop with wiretapping. Ways may someday be developed by which the government, without removing papers from secret drawers, can reproduce them in court, and by which it will be enabled to expose to a jury the most intimate occurrences of the home. ... Can it be that the Constitution affords no protection against such invasions of individual security?

The *Olmstead* decision reflected what came to be known as the trespass doctrine. Under this doctrine, which originated from English Common Law, only a physical penetration of a protected space would

TRESPASS DOCTRINE:
The doctrine that to commit a Fourth Amendment violation, law enforcement agents must physically intrude on someone's property.

qualify as a search that triggers the requirements of the Fourth Amendment. This meant wiretaps and other forms of electronic eavesdropping did not implicate the Fourth Amendment. Police were free to use wiretaps and other types of listening devices without any prior judicial authorization.

Reasonable Expectations of Privacy

In 1967, a Supreme Court much more inclined toward the protection of civil liberties overturned the *Olmstead* precedent. In *Katz v. United States*,[7] the Court reversed a conviction in which government agents, acting without a warrant, attached a hidden microphone to the outside of a public telephone booth from which a suspected bookie often placed calls. The agents were able to record the suspect's voice and obtain evidence of illegal gambling transactions. Writing for the Court, Justice Potter Stewart observed that "electronically listening to and recording the petitioner's words violated the privacy upon which he justifiably relied while using the telephone booth, and thus constituted a 'search and seizure' within the meaning of the Fourth Amendment." After all, said Stewart, "the Fourth Amendment protects people—not places." As to precedent, Stewart noted that "the underpinnings of *Olmstead* ... have been so eroded by our subsequent decisions that the 'trespass' doctrine there enunciated can no longer be regarded as controlling."

The upshot of *Katz* is that the Fourth Amendment extends to any situation in which a person has a reasonable expectation of privacy. According to Justice John M. Harlan's concurrence in *Katz*, "there is a twofold requirement, first that a person have exhibited an actual (subjective) expectation of privacy and, second, that the expectation be one that society is prepared to recognize as 'reasonable.'" Justice Harlan elaborated, saying that "a man's home is, for most purposes, a place where he expects privacy, but objects, activities, or statements that he exposes to the 'plain view' of outsiders are not 'protected,' because no intention to keep them to himself has been exhibited." Unlike Mr. Katz's use of the phone booth to make private calls, "conversations in the open would not be protected against being overheard, for the expectation of privacy under the circumstances would be unreasonable."

REASONABLE EXPECTATION OF PRIVACY: An expectation that one's activities in a certain place are private. One must have exhibited a subjective expectation of privacy, and that expectation must be one that society is prepared to recognize as reasonable.

Much of the Supreme Court's modern Fourth Amendment jurisprudence has turned on the question of whether a person had a reasonable expectation of privacy in a given situation. The Court has said the "expectation of privacy must have a source outside of the Fourth Amendment either by reference to concepts of real or personal property law or to understandings that are recognized and permitted by society."[8] Of course, in the end it is the Court that determines what society recognizes and permits. Many of the cases we will discuss in this chapter, and the three that follow, involve precisely this issue: did the individual have a reasonable expectation of privacy in a given situation or with respect to particular communications? For now, let us consider some illustrative Supreme Court cases, including some in which the government prevailed and some in which the accused criminals won.

In *Winston v. Lee* (1985),[9] a man named Rudolph Lee entered a convenience store and attempted to perpetrate a robbery, shooting the shopkeeper in the process. The shopkeeper returned fire, striking Lee just below the collarbone; the bullet became lodged in Lee's upper chest. Police found Lee eight blocks away and took him to a hospital, where the shopkeeper positively identified him as the alleged robber.

Law enforcement sought to compel surgery to remove the bullet from Lee's collarbone, so it could be used as evidence, and a motion ordering such a surgery was given by a state court, over Lee's objection that subjecting him to a surgical procedure that required full anesthesia would amount to a violation of the Fourth Amendment. Lee appealed this order through the state and federal court systems, and the Supreme Court of the United States agreed to hear the case.

Justice William Brennan delivered the opinion of the Court, which utilized the reasonable expectation of privacy framework by balancing the individual level of intrusion against the government interest at stake. Applying these criteria, the opinion indicated the following:

> [T]he intrusion on respondent's privacy interests entailed by the operation can only be characterized as severe. On the other hand, although the bullet may turn out to be useful to the Commonwealth in prosecuting respondent, the Commonwealth has failed to demonstrate a compelling need for it.

Justice Brennan noted that the high intrusion connected with a forced surgery could not be justified when balanced against the government interest in the evidence, ostensibly because the government had other means—including an eyewitness identification—to prosecute the case against Lee.

Another case in which the expectation of privacy doctrine was used to overturn a conviction was *Bond v. United States* (2000).[10] In this case, a man was carrying methamphetamine in a duffle bag he brought onto a bus. As the bus traveled from California into Texas (on its way to Arkansas), a border patrol agent boarded the bus to check passengers' immigration status. While walking down the aisle of the bus, the agent squeezed a duffle bag that was above Mr. Bond's head. By touch, the officer felt that the bag contained a *brick-like* object he suspected to be drugs, so he asked Mr. Bond for permission to open the bag. Bond consented to the search, which revealed the presence of drugs. He was later convicted of violating federal drug laws and sentenced to 57 months in prison. In a 7–2 decision, the Supreme Court found Mr. Bond's Fourth Amendment rights had been violated. In speaking to the expectation of privacy in this situation, Chief Justice Rehnquist's majority opinion stated the following:

> Here, petitioner sought to preserve privacy by using an opaque bag and placing that bag directly above his seat. Second, we inquire whether the individual's expectation of privacy is "one that society is prepared to recognize as reasonable."[11] When a bus passenger places a bag in an overhead bin, he expects that other passengers or bus employees may move it for one reason or another. Thus, a bus passenger clearly expects that his bag may

be handled. He does not expect that other passengers or bus employees will, as a matter of course, feel the bag in an exploratory manner. But this is exactly what the agent did here. We therefore hold that the agent's physical manipulation of petitioner's bag violated the Fourth Amendment.

Chief Justice Rehnquist's opinion differentiated the agent's *exploratory* inquiry in squeezing the bag type from the type of manipulation that a person reasonably expects when other passengers might touch their luggage. The Chief Justice thereby afforded an expectation of privacy to the traveler who carries items in an opaque bag and keeps the bag close to their person. Moreover, since the agent's physical exploratory manipulation of the bag occurred before Bond gave consent to search, the consent could be negated through the fruit of the poisonous tree doctrine. But in dissent, Justice Stephen Breyer offered tangential advice for would-be drug traffickers, indicating that "the traveler who wants to place a bag in a shared overhead bin and yet safeguard its contents from public touch should plan to pack those contents in a suitcase with hard sides, irrespective of the Court's decision today."

A decade later, the Court made it clear that a person holds a heightened expectation of privacy inside their own home. In *Kyllo v. United States* (2001),[12] the Court held that a federal agent's use of a thermal imaging device pointed at a private home from a public vantage point to detect the heat signature of an indoor marijuana grow was a search and thereby triggered the Fourth Amendment. Writing for a closely divided Court, Justice Antonin Scalia concluded that when "the Government uses a device that is not in general public use, to explore details of the home that would previously have been unknowable without physical intrusion, the surveillance is a 'search' and is presumptively unreasonable without a warrant." To highlight the intrusive nature of "through-the-wall surveillance," Scalia noted that "The Agema Thermovision 210 might disclose, for example, at what hour each night the lady of the house takes her daily sauna and bath—a detail that many would consider 'intimate.'" Accordingly, Kyllo's criminal conviction was overturned.

Other decisions from the high Court have been friendlier to government interpretations of the Fourth Amendment. In *California v. Ciraolo* (1986),[13] for instance, the Court held that that aerial observation of a suspect's back yard, which ultimately resulted in a prosecution for growing marijuana, was not a search within the meaning of the Fourth Amendment. Chief Justice Burger's opinion for a sharply divided bench concluded that "[i]n an age where private and commercial flight in the public airways is routine, it is unreasonable for respondent to expect that his marijuana plants were constitutionally protected from being observed with the naked eye from an altitude of 1,000 feet."

More recently, in *Maryland v. King* (2013),[14] the Supreme Court evaluated a Maryland law that authorized police collection of DNA samples from any individual arrested for "serious offenses" (a phrase that legislators might have written in intentionally vague terms in order to provide added leeway for law enforcement). The DNA was to be gathered by taking a cotton swab of the cheek cells inside a person's mouth. The DNA would then be entered into a national database called the Combined DNA Index System (CODIS), which can match a DNA sample with previously cataloged DNA, perhaps connected to prior crime scenes.

In the instant case, Alonzo King was arrested for assault after pointing a gun at a group of people. After his arrest, his DNA was collected, and a match in CODIS linked him to a prior rape case; based on the DNA match, he was later convicted of that crime. A state appeals court found that the acquisition of King's DNA amounted to an unreasonable search in violation of the Fourth Amendment. The state appealed to the Supreme Court of the United States, which granted certiorari and reversed the lower court with a 5–4 decision.

Employing the *reasonable expectation of privacy* framework, Justice Anthony Kennedy's majority opinion deemed the intrusion to be minimal because it was painless and noninvasive. In juxtaposition, Kennedy found that the nature of the government interests at stake should be described as *substantial*. Specifically, the two primary interests were solving *cold cases* and protecting officer and guard safety by properly ascertaining the danger posed by an arrestee (based on their prior criminal history). Hence, an important government interest balanced against a *low* intrusion upon the individual resulted in the Maryland DNA collection procedure being upheld.

Even so, Justice Scalia penned a dissenting opinion joined by Justices Ginsburg, Sotomayor, and Kagan. Scalia's dissent suggested that fingerprints examined through the national Automated Fingerprint Identification System (AFIS) could provide a less-intrusive method for furthering the government interest in identifying the potential danger posed by an arrestee—a notion buttressed by the fact that fingerprint results tend to be isolated much more quickly than DNA results, with the latter taking almost four months to receive in this case. Additionally, Scalia took issue with the majority opinion's characterization of DNA collection as posing a low level of intrusion. For Scalia, the intrusion was less about a cheek swab and more about cataloging and storing DNA in a database for an unlimited time frame. Moreover, he took umbrage with the vague standards invoked by the phrase *serious offense*, saying the following:

> The Court disguises the vast (and scary) scope of its holding by promising a limitation it cannot deliver. The Court repeatedly says that DNA testing, and entry into a national DNA registry, will not befall thee and me, dear reader, but only those arrested for 'serious offense[s].' ... I cannot imagine what principle could possibly justify this limitation, and the Court does not attempt to suggest any. If one believes that DNA will 'identify' someone arrested for assault, he must believe that it will 'identify' someone arrested for a traffic offense. ... Make no mistake about it: As an entirely predictable consequence of today's decision, your DNA can be taken and entered into a national DNA database if you are ever arrested, rightly or wrongly, and for whatever reason.

We will discuss this case in greater detail under the rubric of searches incident to arrest in chapter 8.

The Trespass Doctrine Redux

Despite the overturning of *Olmstead v. United States*, the trespass doctrine is still alive and well. In *Soldal v. Cook County* (1992),[15] the Supreme Court ruled that a seizure had occurred when a mobile home was forcibly removed during the process of evicting the residents. The Fourth Amendment came into play even though there was no invasion of privacy. In his opinion for a unanimous Court, Justice Byron White noted that "our cases unmistakably hold that the Amendment protects property as well as privacy."

Similarly, in *United States v. Jones* (2012),[16] the Supreme Court held that the warrantless use of a GPS tracking device attached to a suspect's vehicle constituted a search under the Fourth Amendment. Justice Scalia's opinion for the Court explained that a search need not constitute an invasion of privacy; a trespass to real or personal property is enough to trigger the Fourth Amendment. According to Justice Scalia, "The text of the Fourth Amendment reflects its close connection to property, since otherwise it would have referred simply to 'the right of the people to be secure against unreasonable searches and seizures'; the phrase 'in their persons, houses, papers, and effects' would have been superfluous." Scalia's majority opinion also made it clear "the *Katz* reasonable-expectation-of-privacy test has been *added to*, not *substituted for*, the common-law trespassory test."

In the *Jones* case, police attached a GPS tracker to the undercarriage of an automobile that was parked in a public place. The device was then used to track Mr. Jones' movements for twenty-eight days and link him to suspected drug trafficking. The warrant authorizing the use of this device had expired (by one day) by the time the officers attached the tracker, and further, the warrant was valid in the District of Columbia, but the tracker was attached in Maryland.

In a unanimous decision, the Court found that Mr. Jones' Fourth Amendment rights had been violated. Scalia's majority opinion, which was joined by four other justices, focused upon the attachment of the GPS tracker as a trespass. A concurring opinion authored by Justice Alito, though, said that the tracking represented a violation of a reasonable expectation of privacy, largely because of the duration of the surveillance—as if a person being followed on public roads by a physical police car for twenty-eight days would have taken notice of such activity. Showing homage to both the trespass doctrine and the reasonable expectation of privacy approach, Justice Sonia Sotomayor wrote separately to embrace each perspective. We will discuss this case in greater detail in chapter 9, where we examine government surveillance methods. For now, we emphasize the fact that Justice Scalia used this opinion to highlight the relevance of the trespass doctrine for deeming a physical intrusion of private property to be a violation of the Fourth Amendment.

It is important to recognize that to merit Fourth Amendment protection against a search or seizure of property, one does not have to own that property. A possessory interest is all that is required. Even so, it is critical to note that a person has no Fourth Amendment rights with respect to property that has been abandoned.[17] For example, the Court has found that trash left by the curb of a home lacks an expectation of privacy, and thus, police can sift through roadside garbage without a warrant.[18] This issue often arises when cities attempt to clean up homeless encampments. The homeless residents will often flee the scene, temporarily leaving their tents, sleeping bags, and other personal effects behind. Have they abandoned their property, or are their effects protected by the Fourth Amendment? Courts continue to struggle with this question. In 1990, the Supreme Court did discern an expectation of privacy in a brown paper bag that a person placed on top of a car as police approached him, noting that the close proximity between the man and his bag indicated that it had not been abandoned.[19] The Court also has said that "a passenger who lets a package drop to the floor of the taxicab in which he is riding can hardly be said to have 'abandoned' it," adding that "[an] occupied taxi is not ... an open field."[20]

That declaration indicates that not all trespasses to property are searches under the Fourth Amendment. The Court has said repeatedly that when agents enter the open fields surrounding a home, even if they are on the homeowner's property, there is no Fourth Amendment protection.[21] In *Hester v. United States* (1924), in the midst of Prohibition, the Court upheld the seizure of a broken moonshine jug and a moonshine bottle dropped by men who fled after they detected the nearby presence of federal authorities. The men were on their private property but were more than 150 yards from their home. Justice Oliver Wendell Holmes, writing for the Court, said that "the special protection accorded by the Fourth Amendment to the people in their 'persons, houses, papers and effects' is not extended to the open fields. The distinction between the latter and the house is as old as the common law."

However, over time, the Court also has made it clear that when agents enter a home's curtilage looking for evidence, a search obviously has taken place. Defining the term curtilage, Justice Scalia's majority opinion in

Florida v. Jardines (2013),[22] which dealt with a police search on the front porch of a home, said the following:

> We therefore regard the area "immediately surrounding and associated with the home"—what our cases call the curtilage—as "part of the home itself for Fourth Amendment purposes." ... That principle has ancient and durable roots. ... This area around the home is "intimately linked to the home, both physically and psychologically" and is where "privacy expectations are most heightened." ... While the boundaries of the curtilage are generally "clearly marked," the "conception defining the curtilage" is at any rate familiar enough that it is "easily understood from our daily experience." Here there is no doubt that the officers entered it: The front porch is the classic exemplar of an area adjacent to the home and "to which the activity of home life extends."[23]

OPEN FIELDS: A person's real property lying beyond the curtilage.

CURTILAGE: Under common law, the enclosed space surrounding a dwelling house.

JURISPRUDENCE

Police Bring a K-9 Unit to the Front Porch of a Home
Florida v. Jardines, 569 U.S. 1 (2013)

This case originated when police received an unverified tip that a man named Joelis Jardines was selling marijuana out of his home. Without acquiring a search warrant or permission to search, officers—accompanied by a K-9 unit—walked into the front yard of Jardines's property. Upon reaching the porch, the officers led the dog around on a six-foot leash, allowing it to sniff around the entirety of the home's entrance. The dog alerted to the smell of marijuana. Police then used that information in the affidavit for a search warrant, which was granted by a judge. Jardines was arrested and charged with a violation of state drug laws. The trial court suppressed the evidence against Jardines, and after the Florida Third District Court of Appeals reversed that decision, the Florida Supreme Court opined that Jardines's Fourth Amendment rights had, indeed, been violated. On review, the Supreme Court of the United States agreed with this conclusion, with Justice Scalia's majority opinion once again focusing upon the idea of a *trespass* in finding a Fourth Amendment violation.

The specific trespass in this case was the officer's act of leading the dog around the curtilage of Jardines's property without first acquiring a warrant. Although Scalia noted that a "customary invitation" might inhere in regard to approaching the front door of some homes, no such invitation exists to conduct a warrantless search without permission of the homeowner. Accordingly, an officer could, in theory, approach the front door of a home and knock, in the hopes of speaking with the homeowner (as might a postal worker, for example); but in this case, the introduction of a trained narcotics-sniffing dog, which was led around the porch by an officer holding a lengthy leash—altered the nature of such a visit. As Scalia said, "A police officer not armed with a warrant may approach a home and knock, precisely because that is 'no more than any private citizen might do.' But introducing a trained police dog to explore the area around the home in hopes of discovering incriminating evidence is something else. There is no customary invitation to do *that.*"

A key for Justice Scalia in applying the trespass doctrine in both the *Jones* and *Jardines* cases was that, in his words, it helps to "keep easy cases easy." After all, had these cases been addressed through a *reasonable expectation of privacy* framework, that might have required an assessment of expectations connected to privacy on public roadways or to marijuana fumes that escape into the air above a home's porch. To the latter, Scalia said the following in the *Jardines* case:

> Thus, we need not decide whether the officers' investigation of Jardines' home violated his expectation of privacy under *Katz*. One virtue of the Fourth Amendment's property-rights baseline is that it keeps easy cases easy. That the officers learned what they learned only by physically intruding on Jardines' property to gather evidence is enough to establish that a search occurred.

The trespass doctrine has remained relevant for Supreme Court decision making even after Justice Scalia's death, with Justice Sotomayor continuing its usage in *Collins v. Virginia* (2018).[24] In this case, a police officer was led to believe Collins was in possession of a stolen motorcycle based on pictures Collins had posted on Facebook. Without a warrant, the officer walked onto Collins's property and approached an open-air carport that was adjacent to the home. Under the carport was a large item hidden beneath a tarp. The officer removed the tarp and located the stolen motorcycle.

In finding that Collins' Fourth Amendment rights had been violated, Justice Sotomayor observed that "[j]ust like the front porch, side garden, or area 'outside the front window', the driveway enclosure where Officer Rhodes searched the motorcycle constitutes 'an area adjacent to the home and to which the activity of home life extends,' and so is properly considered curtilage." She then went on to apply the trespass doctrine by saying, "So long as it is curtilage, a parking patio or carport into which an officer can see from the street is no less entitled to protection from trespass and a warrantless search than a fully enclosed garage." She added, "A plain-view seizure thus cannot be justified if it is effectuated 'by unlawful trespass.'"[25] We will revisit this case in chapter 8 to discuss why the Court felt that a so-called *automobile exception* also was not applicable here.

An Arrest is a *Seizure* Under the Fourth Amendment

Normally, we think of seizures in terms of physical items retrieved by the police to use as evidence. But an arrest of a person also is a form of seizure, which means that arrests are governed by the requirements of the Fourth Amendment and should be based upon a showing of probable cause. Even a relatively brief detention can qualify as a seizure, although a detention that is not an arrest could be governed by a lesser standard than probable cause.[26] Given the importance of constitutional restraints on the police, we devote an entire chapter to the Fourth Amendment as it relates to arrest and detention (see chapter 10).

To Whom Does the Fourth Amendment Apply?

Not all searches and seizures implicate the Fourth Amendment. For example, the Supreme Court has held that a search conducted by federal agents of a noncitizen's property located outside the United States does not trigger the Fourth Amendment.[27] On the other hand, the Supreme Court has held that the Fourth Amendment protects all persons inside the United States and its territories, including those who may be in the country illegally.[28]

Searches and Seizures by Nongovernmental Actors

The Supreme Court has long said that the Fourth Amendment does not apply to searches conducted by private individuals who are not acting at the behest of the government. In 1921, for instance, the Court opined that the Fourth Amendment "was intended as a restraint upon the activities of sovereign authority, and was not intended to be a limitation upon other than governmental agencies. ..."[29]

A modern illustration of this principle is seen in *United States v. Jacobsen* (1984),[30] when FedEx employees opened a damaged package and found bags of white powder inside. The employees contacted the Drug Enforcement Administration, which dispatched agents to test the powder. When the test revealed the substance to be cocaine, the agents obtained a search warrant for the residence to which the package was addressed. The question before the Supreme Court in this case was whether the initial search by FedEx employees and the subsequent warrantless testing by the DEA violated the Fourth Amendment. Upholding the use of the seized evidence, the Court concluded "the federal agents did not infringe any constitutionally protected privacy interest that had not already been frustrated as the result of private conduct."

In deciding whether a private citizen has acted as an agent of the government, a court must consider (1) whether the authorities knew about and acquiesced in the citizen's actions and (2) whether the citizen was motivated by a desire to assist law enforcement. Hence, the seizure of an illegal weapon by a privately employed security guard would ordinarily fall outside the prohibitions of the Fourth Amendment. However, if that security guard had an ongoing relationship with local police or had agreed to assist the police in a particular matter that determination might well be different.

An interesting example of a *private-party search* involved a computer hacker from Turkey who accessed the computer of a man who lived in Montgomery, Alabama. The hacker discovered evidence of child pornography on this computer and forwarded that to the Montgomery Police Department. In a 2003 case called *United States v. Steiger*,[31] the U.S. Court of Appeals for the Eleventh Circuit upheld the use of this evidence in court, finding police had not instructed the man in Turkey to conduct the search.

A correlated idea involves the *third-party doctrine*, which was articulated in *Couch v. United States* (1973).[32] In this case, the Court found that where information was voluntarily given to an accountant, a client's expectation of privacy was relinquished—and as such, the Fourth Amendment did not preclude those documents from being given to the Internal Revenue Service pursuant to a subpoena served on the accountant. This suggests that information voluntarily turned over to a third party might lose any connection to an "expectation of privacy." This also could include things that are given to a private mail courier like UPS (but not necessarily the U.S. Postal Service, since that would be considered a government agency). Nevertheless, the state of Texas has taken the step of banning the use of evidence derived from searches conducted by private parties. Moreover, in its 2018 decision in *Carpenter v. United States*,[33] the Supreme Court indicated that the third-party doctrine does not apply to cell phone location data cataloged by providers like Verizon or AT&T. Some of these companies had been granting police access to individual cell phone GPS history, but he Court's 5–4 majority, led by Chief Justice Roberts (joined by Justices Ginsburg, Breyer, Sotomayor, and Kagan), found that this practice amounted to a violation of the Fourth Amendment. We discuss this case again in chapter 9, which addresses electronic surveillance.

THE CONSTITUTION IN ACTION
Genealogy Websites Provide DNA for Solving Cold Cases

The use of DNA profiling in solving crimes became prevalent by the mid-1990s. The typical technique involved extracting a DNA profile from trace evidence left at a crime scene, with crime lab technicians able to derive a DNA profile from blood, saliva, semen, hair, skin cells, and other sources. That DNA profile could then be matched with samples taken from individual suspects. Even though a warrant typically would be needed to acquire such a sample for matching, some law enforcement officials will seek out items that a suspect has discarded, such as a cigarette butt or even a utensil or glass left behind at a restaurant. Because these items are considered abandoned, their acquisition is compatible with the Fourth Amendment.

More recently, companies that people voluntarily use to trace genealogy have played a role in solving crimes. DNA turned over to these companies by those looking to outline a "family tree" would fall under the third-party doctrine and therefore could be made accessible to law enforcement without a warrant. The key is that even though most perpetrators of crimes are unlikely to voluntarily relinquish their DNA to anyone else, DNA testing is capable of identifying familial matches. Thus, comparing a sample from a crime scene to all samples in a genealogy database could reveal matches to relatives of a potential criminal and, with added detective work involving searches of public records like birth and wedding certificates, authorities might be able to locate to the actual criminal.

This is how law enforcement officials in California were able apprehend a man known as the Golden State Killer in 2018, eventually charging him with offenses dating back to the 1970s. This was believed to be the first major cold case solved via ancestral DNA searches. The offender was arrested after evidence from crime scenes was matched against an open-source genealogy website called GEDmatch, leading police to relatives of the offender. Based on interviews with these relatives and physical descriptions of the offender provided by surviving victims, police zeroed in on a specific suspect. Detectives then sifted through garbage left by the side of the curb outside of this suspect's home and found a tissue; DNA from that tissue was matched to DNA from a prior crime scene, leading to the man's arrest.[34] In July 2020, the 74-year-old offender plead guilty to numerous charges, including murder, rape, kidnapping, and robbery. He was given fifteen life sentences in prison. Ultimately, because DNA evidence was acquired from websites where individuals voluntarily turned over samples—and through abandoned items left in the trash—no Fourth Amendment violations had occurred.

The Warrant Requirement

SEARCH WARRANT:
An order issued by a judge or magistrate authorizing officials to search a particular place and seize particular things.

PROBABLE CAUSE:
Knowledge of specific facts giving one reasonable grounds for believing that criminal activity is afoot.

A search warrant is an order issued by a judge or magistrate that authorizes a search for a particular thing at a particular place. In evaluating this process, the Supreme Court has said that a "neutral and detached magistrate" is crucial in maintaining the integrity of the Fourth Amendment.[35] To obtain a search warrant, a law enforcement officer must take an oath or sign an affidavit attesting to certain facts that, if true, constitute probable cause to support the issuance of a warrant. Although the Supreme Court has upheld warrantless searches under exigent circumstances, it has expressed a strong preference for warrants. The issuance of a warrant creates a presumption of a legal search. As the Court recognized in 1965, "in a doubtful or marginal case, a search under a warrant may be sustainable where without one it would fall."[36]

The Process for Obtaining a Warrant

To obtain a search warrant, a police officer must make an application to a judge or magistrate with appropriate jurisdiction. The application must state the basis for the search and describe with particularity the place to be searched and the thing or things to be seized if found. Historically, an officer had to appear physically before a judge or magistrate to obtain a search warrant. Today, the process is often done electronically, which is much more expeditious. In most jurisdictions, magistrates are available around the clock.

Because the Fourth Amendment states "no Warrants shall issue but upon probable cause," the officer must include an **affidavit** stating under oath facts that provide a reasonable basis to believe that a search of a particular person or place is likely to yield evidence of crime. An affidavit normally requires a showing of the officer's law enforcement credentials, as well. A judge or magistrate must then make an independent probable cause determination based on what is included in the affidavit. In *Coolidge v. New Hampshire*,[37] the Supreme Court rejected the idea that a search warrant could be issued by a state's Attorney General, as that would essentially vitiate principles of separation of power by allowing the executive branch to issue and execute search warrants.

How Closely Do Judges Read Search Warrant Requests?

In 2018, an article in *The Salt Lake Tribune* raised questions about whether magistrates and judges in the state of Utah were carefully reading and evaluating requests for search warrants. A public-records request by a libertarian think tank, Libertas Institute, revealed judges in the state had approved approximately 9,400 warrant requests in a one-year time frame beginning with April 2017. Of that sample, the *Tribune* noted, "The overall average time a judge spent reviewing the warrants was about eight minutes, but nearly 60 percent were given the green light in less than three, and 3 percent were approved in under 30 seconds."[38]

In response, a local judge on Utah's Third District Court, James Blanch said, "There's very little that we take more seriously than the constitutional underpinnings of search warrants. You don't want to be a rubber stamp. Nobody wants to be a rubber stamp." He added that "[t]he ones in the middle of the night are more urgent, like a blood draw for DUIs. So they need to be addressed promptly." Judge Blanch also observed that if a warrant had previously been rejected, a second submission could be reviewed quickly to see if necessary changes had been made. However, Libertas President Connor Boyack pointed to some troubling examples,

EXIGENT CIRCUMSTANCES: Extreme situations that demand immediate action.

AFFIDAVIT: A sworn declaration attesting to a set of facts.

such as a nine-page affidavit for the search of a massage parlor being approved in 26 seconds in October 2017, and a five-page affidavit for the placement of a GPS locator on car being approved in June 2017 after 34 seconds of review.[39] Ultimately, public records of the nature revealed in Utah are rarely available, and as a result, extrapolating findings from this article to other contexts is difficult, but the idea of added transparency regarding the process through which warrants are granted is worthy of discussion.

THE CONSTITUTION IN ACTION
An Unprecedented Search of an Ex-President's Home

No person is above the law when it comes to a search warrant. In August 2022, a federal magistrate judge in Florida issued a warrant for the FBI to search Mar-a-Lago, the home of former President Donald Trump. The warrant, which was executed three days later, stated that authorities were looking for classified documents believed to be stored improperly, in violation of federal law.[40]

The working definition of classified documents in the United States stems from a 2009 executive order that says the U.S. government has three categories for defining classified documents.[41] The first (or 'lowest') of these levels involves documents labeled as "confidential"; this means the material "reasonably could be expected to cause damage to the national security"; the second level is "secret," which refers to material that has potential to cause "serious damage to national security"; lastly, there is the classification of "top secret," which applies to a risk of "exceptionally grave damage" to national security if information is disclosed. In general, a particular "clearance level" is needed for a person to access a classified document. Although a variety of government agencies could possess the authority to define an item as classified, a president does have the authority to declassify materials—but in order to do so there are protocols that must be followed in conjunction with appropriate government agencies that may have a connection to the materials.

Following the search at Mar-a-Lago, the FBI determined that twenty boxes containing eleven sets of classified documents were seized. Four of these were in the category of "top secret," three were in the category of "secret," and three were said to be "confidential." Moreover, within the "top secret" category itself, a sub-category of "sensitive compartmented information" can apply to certain information gathered through intelligence sources; one set of documents seized from Mar-a-Lago fell into this category.[42]

The federal magistrate judge who signed the warrant would later release a redacted version of the affidavit submitted by federal officials. The redactions were designed to protect confidential sources and methods relied upon in the FBI's investigation. The release of the affidavit, with its myriad redactions, did little to quell public curiosity or partisan furor over what was a highly unusual search and seizure.

ANTICIPATORY SEARCH WARRANT: A warrant issued based on probable cause to believe that at a future time evidence of a crime will be found at a specific place.

Anticipatory Search Warrants

Typically, a search warrant is issued based on probable cause to believe that an immediate search will produce evidence of crime. However, in many instances, especially those involving illegal drug transactions, a magistrate will issue an anticipatory search warrant based on the expectation that evidence (often contraband) will be found at a particular place and time in the future. In *United States v. Grubbs* (2006),[43] the

Supreme Court explained that anticipatory search warrants "require the magistrate to determine (1) that it is now probable that (2) contraband, evidence of a crime, or a fugitive will be on the described premises (3) when the warrant is executed." Speaking through Justice Scalia, the Court held that:

> ... for a conditioned anticipatory warrant to comply with the Fourth Amendment's require-ment of probable cause, two prerequisites of probability must be satisfied. It must be true not only that if the triggering condition occurs 'there is a fair probability that contraband or evidence of a crime will be found in a particular place,' ... but also that there is prob-able cause to believe the triggering condition will occur. The supporting affidavit must provide the magistrate with sufficient information to evaluate both aspects of the proba-ble-cause determination.

The Particularity Requirement

The Fourth Amendment allows only those search warrants "particularly describing the place to be searched and the persons or things to be seized." The Supreme Court has said that "limiting the authorization to search to the specific areas and things for which there is probable cause to search ... ensures that the search will be carefully tailored to its justifications, and will not take on the character of the wide-ranging exploratory searches the Framers intended to prohibit."[44] The fact that an officer's application for a search warrant listed things to be seized with particularity does not matter; the warrant itself must contain this listing.[45]

In *Stanford v. Texas* (1965),[46] the Supreme Court invalidated a search for which the warrant authorized the seizure of "books, records, pamphlets, cards, receipts, lists, memoranda, pictures, recordings and other written instruments concerning the Communist Party of Texas." Officers seized fourteen boxes of material, including books by Karl Marx, Jean-Paul Sartre, Hugo Black, and Pope John XXIII. They also seized household bills, receipts, insurance policies, personal correspondence, and even Stanford's marriage certificate. No records associated with the Communist Party were found. The Court invalidated the search and held that the "indiscriminate sweep" of the warrant was "constitutionally intolerable." Justice Stewart's majority opinion noted that "the Fourth and Fourteenth Amendments guarantee to John Stanford that no official of the State shall ransack his home and seize his books and papers under the unbridled authority of a general warrant. ..." To hold otherwise, said Stewart, "would be false to the terms of the Fourth Amendment, false to its meaning, and false to its history."

Along the same lines, the Supreme Court's decision in *Ybarra v. Illinois* (1979)[47] made it clear that if police have a warrant to search a business (in that case, a bar), it does not offer a justification to "pat down" individ-uals inside the business who were not linked to activity described in the warrant. We will discuss pat-down searches in greater detail in chapter 10.

Execution of Search Warrants

Unlike arrest warrants, search warrants are time limited. A search based on an expired warrant is presump-tively invalid. In executing a warrant at a home, police generally must knock on the door and announce their presence. Justice Clarence Thomas's opinion for the Court in *Wilson v. Arkansas* (1995)[48] argued that the knock and announce requirement was deeply imbedded in English common law and understood to be part and parcel of the Fourth Amendment when the Bill of Rights was ratified. However, Thomas's opinion acknowledged that under exigent circumstances, the knock-and-announce requirement might not apply:

> The Fourth Amendment's flexible requirement of reasonableness should not be read to mandate a rigid rule of announcement that ignores countervailing law enforcement interests. As even petitioner concedes, the common-law principle of announcement was never stated as an inflexible rule requiring announcement under all circumstances.

Under the *Wilson* decision, the knock-and-announce requirement may be dispensed with "under circumstances presenting a threat of physical violence," or in situations "where police officers have reason to believe that evidence would likely be destroyed if advance notice were given."

JURISPRUDENCE

How Long Must Police Wait After Knocking and Announcing Their Presence?
United States v. Banks, 540 U.S. 31 (2003)

FBI agents obtained a warrant to search an apartment belonging to a suspected drug dealer. Upon arrival, police knocked on the door and announced their presence. They waited 15–20 seconds, then employed a battering ram to effect entry to the apartment. Inside, they found cocaine and weapons. In appealing his conviction on federal drug and weapons charges, Lashawn Banks argued officers failed to wait sufficient time before forcing their way into his apartment. In a unanimous decision, the Supreme Court rejected that argument and upheld Banks's conviction. Justice David Souter spoke for the Court, saying, "Though we agree ... that this call is a close one, we think that after 15 or 20 seconds without a response, police could fairly suspect that cocaine would be gone if they were reticent any longer."

No-Knock Warrants and Police Raids

In *Richards v. Wisconsin* (1997),[49] the Court ruled that states may not create a blanket "drug exception" to the knock and announce requirement. To make a no-knock entry, said the Court, "police must have a reasonable suspicion that knocking and announcing their presence, under the particular circumstances, would be dangerous or futile, or that it would inhibit the effective investigation of the crime by, for example, allowing the destruction of evidence." Additionally, one year later, the Supreme Court stated that, in executing a no-knock entry, police are not responsible for property damage that was necessary to achieve entry.[50]

Critically, in its decision in *Hudson v. Michigan* (2006),[51] the Supreme Court indicated that a failure to knock and announce would not automatically render evidence seized by police inadmissible in court. Therefore, this decision has the ultimate effect of shifting the knock-and-announce rule to an advisory concept. After all, if officers enter without knocking and announcing and then face no repercussions in regard to the admissibility of evidence that is subsequently seized, it ostensibly is left up to individual law enforcement agencies to police a knock-and-announce policy themselves.

As a result, because of the *Hudson* decision, the concept of a *police raid* involving entry to a home—without knocking or announcing the law enforcement presence—has become acceptable, under the Fourth Amendment, with or without the acquisition of a specific no-knock search warrant. There are still jurisdictions where state laws, regulations, or even department policies might require officers to seek out no-knock search warrants, and some areas have banned no-knock warrants altogether, as we discuss in the following box. In some sense, knocking and announcing could be a preferred police practice in order to avoid the possibility of a homeowner mistakenly thinking the police are actually criminals breaking into a home—and, even worse, a homeowner resorting to a perceived act of self-defense. Even so, as of 2022, Oregon, Virginia, and Tennessee are the only states with laws that explicitly ban no-knock warrants, and Florida banned them through a 1994 state supreme court decision.[52] Utah does not allow no-knock warrants for searches that are only seeking evidence of drugs. Maine and Kentucky restrict no-knock warrants to cases involving known violent offenders or where a risk to officer safety is posed by knocking and announcing their presence, with time limits prohibiting late-night raids in Kentucky.[53] Thirteen states have laws that explicitly allow no-knock warrants.[54]

Overall, it is difficult to extrapolate broader conclusions about police raids in general because widespread data on this practice is scant. Only Maryland and Utah require data to be kept on SWAT raids. Yet an ACLU study of 800 raids conducted by 20 different law enforcement agencies in 2011–2012 revealed that 80% involved execution of search warrants, with the report noting that these raids were "usually for drugs [60% of the time], and disproportionately in communities of color."[55] Moreover, *The New York Times* has noted that, from 2010 to 2016, police raids resulted in 94 deaths, including 13 officers.[56] One of the most prominent deaths was that of Breonna Taylor in Louisville, Kentucky, which is discussed in the following box.

NO-KNOCK ENTRY:
A situation in which law enforcement agents, perhaps pursuant to a no-knock warrant, execute entry without knocking or announcing their presence.

THE CONSTITUTION AND SOCIAL JUSTICE

The Killing of Breonna Taylor

Breonna Taylor, a 26-year-old African American woman, was shot and killed by police in Louisville, Kentucky on March 23, 2020, following a botched raid on her apartment. Police had a search warrant to enter Taylor's apartment, but the crux of their investigation centered around two men who lived at a different property. Those men were suspected of selling drugs, and in an affidavit for a search warrant for Taylor's apartment, a police officer claimed he had "verified through a U.S. Postal Inspector that [one of the men] has been receiving packages" at Taylor's home, adding that "it is not uncommon for drug traffickers to receive mail packages at different locations to avoid detection from law enforcement." A Jefferson County circuit judge approved the warrant. Subsequent to Taylor's death, a police sergeant indicated, "Investigators believe the wording on the affidavit is misleading." The detective who submitted the affidavit later admitted that he had not directly received information from a U.S. postal inspector.[57]

Just after midnight on the night of the raid, police used a battering ram to break down the door to Taylor's apartment. The warrant indicated that it required a knock and announce, and police claimed they did identify themselves. Taylor and her boyfriend, Kenneth Walker, were in bed and awakened by the noise of police entering, but the boyfriend would later claim that police did not identify themselves and that he feared Taylor's ex-boyfriend was breaking into the apartment. As the door was taken off its hinges by officers, Walker fired his weapon toward the door, striking a police officer in the leg. Officers responded by firing their weapons into the apartment, and Ms. Taylor was struck by at least eight bullets. No medical assistance was provided for more than twenty minutes, and an ambulance that been parked nearby had been told to leave earlier, in a departure from typical police raid practices.[58]

Ultimately, no drugs were found in Taylor's apartment, and no charges were filed against Mr. Walker. An officer who blindly fired ten shots into the apartment was terminated from his job, as was a detective who fired at Taylor. Additionally, the detective who sought the warrant also was fired. Taylor's ex-boyfriend, Jamarcus Glover, the man whom police claimed was receiving packages at Taylor's apartment, was arrested on drug charges in August of 2020. He told reporters that Taylor had nothing to do with his drug activity.[59]

Taylor's death spurred nationwide dialogue about no-knock warrants, particularly those executed late at night. Louisville would ban the practice in June 2020 (with an ordinance named after Taylor), and Kentucky's legislature would pass legislation limiting no-knock warrants in April 2021. Some cities, such as Memphis and Indianapolis, have done so as well. In August 2021, the Department of Justice announced that the FBI, DEA, and U.S. Marshals would limit use of no-knock warrants, unless needed to avoid death or serious injury. We will discuss the topic of police raids in greater detail in chapter 10.

The Scope of a Search Pursuant to a Warrant

The permissible scope of a search is defined by the object of the search as identified in the warrant. In *United States v. Ross* (1982),[60] the Supreme Court said the following:

> A lawful search of fixed premises generally extends to the entire area in which the object of the search may be found, and is not limited by the possibility that separate acts of entry or opening may be required to complete the search. Thus, a warrant that authorizes an officer to search a home for illegal weapons also provides authority to open closets, chests, drawers, and containers in which the weapon might be found. A warrant to open a foot-locker to search for marihuana would also authorize the opening of packages found inside.

On the other hand, a warrant to search for a fugitive believed to be hiding in a home would not allow police to rummage through drawers and boxes, as those are not places where a person could be sequestered.

Detention of Persons on the Premises During a Search

During a search based on a warrant, police may temporarily detain persons in the area that is being searched. In *Michigan v. Summers* (1981),[61] the Supreme Court recognized two primary justifications for detaining persons on the scene during a search: (1) "the legitimate law enforcement interest in preventing flight in the event that incriminating evidence is found"; and (2) "the interest in minimizing the risk of harm to the officers." However, in *Bailey v. United States* (2013),[62] where the individual being searched was in his car more than a mile away from the apartment for which police had a warrant, the Court limited the authority to detain persons to the immediate area being searched, saying that:

> Detentions incident to the execution of a search warrant are reasonable under the Fourth Amendment because the limited intrusion on personal liberty is outweighed by the special law enforcement interests at stake. Once an individual has left the immediate vicinity of a premises to be searched, however, detentions must be justified by some other rationale.

Use of Force in the Execution of a Warrant

The Supreme Court has recognized that the reasonable use of force is inherent in the right to detain individuals pursuant to a search warrant. Chief Justice Rehnquist, writing for a unanimous Court in *Muehler v. Mena* (2005),[63] stated that "*Summers* itself stressed that the risk of harm to officers and occupants is minimized 'if the officers routinely exercise unquestioned command of the situation.'"

We will address police use of force cases in greater detail in chapter 10, which deals with arrests and investigatory detention. For now, we note that the key Supreme Court case on this topic is *Graham v. Connor* (1989).[64] In that case, the Court indicated police use of force matters should be evaluated through an "objective reasonableness" standard, with the majority opinion from Chief Justice Rehnquist clarifying that standard as follows: "The 'reasonableness' of a particular use of force must be judged from the perspective of a reasonable officer on the scene, rather than with the 20/20 vision of hindsight." He also noted that: "The calculus of reasonableness must embody allowance for the fact that police officers are often forced to make split-second judgments—in circumstances that are tense, uncertain, and rapidly evolving—about the amount of force that is necessary in a particular situation." Therefore, the level of force used by a police officer can be analyzed by assessing whether that force was reasonable in relation to the circumstances when it was used.

JURISPRUDENCE

Can the Number of Officers Executing a Warrant Amount to Excessive Use of Force?
Estate of Redd v. Love, 848 F.3d 899 (10th Cir. 2017)

In 2018, the Tenth Circuit's decision in *Estate of Redd v. Love* addressed the conduct of officials from the FBI and the Bureau of Land Management (BLM). This case stemmed from a joint investigation in which the two agencies procured search and arrest warrants connected to the theft and trafficking of Native American artifacts in the western part of the United States, primarily in Utah. The warrants were executed by twelve teams of agents from the FBI and BLM. All agents wore body armor and carried a firearm. One of the warrants was for the arrest of a Mr. and Mrs. Redd, and twenty-two agents were involving in raiding that property, where the Redds were arrested and their home was searched, without incident. After posting bail, Mr. Redd committed suicide.

(continued)

His estate sued the government, citing excessive force on the theory that twenty-two armed agents should not have been needed to arrest two individuals accused of nonviolent crimes. The Tenth Circuit ruled there was no constitutional violation in this case, relying on *Graham v. Connor* and using a *totality of circumstances* approach. The majority opinion said, "We leave open the possibility that sending a large number of agents to execute a search warrant and arrest warrant for a nonviolent crime can amount to excessive force. But this isn't that case."

Among the details that the majority found to support the use of a large number of agents were the following: (1) distrust shown by residents of the area toward the federal government; (2) the agents' belief that two adult sons inside the house had hostility toward the government, buttressed by the fact that one made phone threats as the search was taking place; (3) the search of the residence entailed looking through more than 800 artifacts; (4) Redd had a previous arrest for desecrating a dead body while digging for artifacts.[65] In the future, if factors such as these are not present, it is feasible that an excessive number of officers could be an indication of excessive use of force, but to date, no federal court appears to have ruled that way in a specific case.

Testing the Basis of the Warrant *Ex Post Facto*

The Fourth Amendment makes clear that search warrants must be based on probable cause. That determination is made by the judge or magistrate who is asked to issue a warrant. But what if the officer seeking the warrant knowingly made false statements in the affidavit? In *Franks v. Delaware* (1978),[66] the Supreme Court held that a defendant who makes "a substantial preliminary showing that a false statement knowingly and intentionally, or with reckless disregard for the truth, was included by the affiant in the warrant affidavit, and if the allegedly false statement is necessary to the finding of probable cause" is entitled to a pretrial hearing to retroactively determine the sufficiency of the grounds for issuing the warrant. The majority opinion also noted, "In the event that, at that hearing, the allegation of perjury or reckless disregard is established by the defendant by a preponderance of the evidence, and, with the affidavit's false material set to one side, the affidavit's remaining content is insufficient to establish probable cause, the search warrant must be voided, and the fruits of the search excluded." Thus, if, in the absence of false statements, the affidavit would not have supported a probable cause determination, the defendant is entitled to have the case dismissed.

Probable Cause

Our attention turns now to the crucial concept of probable cause. Arguably, probable cause is a more fundamental constitutional value than is the warrant requirement. As we will see in the next chapter, the Supreme Court has recognized numerous exceptions to the warrant requirement but usually has insisted that warrantless searches must be based on probable cause. In some circumstances, as we will discuss next chapter, searches can be justified by the lesser standard of reasonable suspicion, which has been defined as "something more than a hunch."[67] Among the areas where such a standard could be employed are initiating an auto stop,[68] school searches,[69] border searches,[70] and pat-down searches.[71]

Defining Probable Cause

Probable cause is difficult to define with precision. In 1925, the Supreme Court said that probable cause exists when the facts known to the police "are sufficient in themselves to warrant a man of reasonable caution in the belief" that an offense has been committed.[72] In 1949, the Court endorsed this definition, adding the following:

> In dealing with probable cause, however, as the very name implies, we deal with probabilities. These are not technical; they are the factual and practical considerations of everyday life on which reasonable and prudent men, not legal technicians, act.[73]

With respect to search warrants, a magistrate has probable cause to issue a warrant when there is a reasonable likelihood that a search of a particular place or seizure of a particular thing will produce evidence of criminal wrongdoing. In *Illinois v. Gates* (1983),[74] the Supreme Court indicated that a "substantial chance" or "fair probability" of criminal activity could suffice for meeting the standard of probable cause. Of course, there is an inherent requirement for probable cause to be grounded in truthful evidence, as the Court noted in *Franks v. Delaware* (1978),[75] where the majority opinion said:

> [W]hen the Fourth Amendment demands a factual showing sufficient to comprise 'probable cause,' the obvious assumption is that there will be a '*truthful* showing'. ... This does not mean 'truthful' in the sense that every fact recited in the warrant affidavit is necessarily correct, for probable cause may be founded upon hearsay and upon information received from informants, as well as upon information within the affiant's own knowledge that sometimes must be garnered hastily. But surely it is to be 'truthful' in the sense that the information put forth is believed or appropriately accepted by the affiant as true.[76]

Use of Informants' Tips in Seeking Search Warrants

Police often receive anonymous tips which, if they seem credible, may warrant investigation. But an anonymous tip is usually inadequate as the basis for the issuance of a warrant. This is because, as the Supreme Court recognized in *Florida v. J.L.* (2000),[77] "an anonymous tip alone seldom demonstrates the informant's basis of knowledge or veracity." However, an anonymous tip that leads police to uncover corroborating information might well support a probable cause determination. On the other hand, a tip from a confidential informant can, by itself, support a probable

CONFIDENTIAL INFORMANT: An informant whose identity is known to the police but held in confidence.

cause determination by the magistrate. A confidential informant is a person whose identity is known to the police but held in confidence. Indeed, police often rely on confidential informants in their applications for search warrants. Often, these informants have criminal records and have provided useful information to police in the past.

The Aguilar-Spinelli Test

In *Aguilar v. Texas* (1964),[78] the Supreme Court held that, while an affidavit may rely on **hearsay**, it must contain information that support the credibility and reliability of the informant. In *Spinelli v. United States* (1969),[79] the Court reaffirmed this holding. Under the *Aguilar-Spinelli* test, police were required to inform magistrates of the reasons an informant should be deemed credible and reliable, including the informant's basis of knowledge in obtaining the information. It is fair to say that this requirement made it more difficult for police to obtain warrants based solely on tips from confidential informants and nearly impossible to get warrants based on anonymous tips alone. Like many of the decisions of the Warren Court in the criminal justice field, *Aguilar* and *Spinelli* seemed to be predicated on a suspicious attitude toward traditional police practices. A limited number of states retain use of this standard today, including Alaska, Massachusetts, New York, Tennessee, Vermont, and Washington.

The Totality of Circumstances Test

In *Illinois v. Gates* (1983),[80] which we discussed previously, a more conservative Supreme Court replaced the *Aguilar-Spinelli* test with a **totality of circumstances** approach, which has become the preferred framework in most jurisdictions. Justice Rehnquist's opinion for the Court asserted that the *Aguilar-Spinelli* test "encouraged an excessively technical dissection of informants' tips, with undue attention being focused on isolated issues that cannot sensibly be divorced from the other facts presented to the magistrate." Under the totality of circumstances test, "[t]he task of the issuing magistrate is simply to make a practical, common sense decision whether, given all the circumstances set forth in the affidavit before him, including the 'veracity' and 'basis of knowledge' of persons supplying hearsay information, there is a fair probability that contraband or evidence of a crime will be found in a particular place." The Court hastened to add that "magistrates remain perfectly free to exact such assurances as they deem necessary, as well as those required by this opinion, in making probable cause determinations." In *Massachusetts v. Upton* (1984),[81] the Court held that the totality

HEARSAY: Statements made by someone other than a witness offered in evidence at a trial or hearing.

TOTALITY OF CIRCUMSTANCES TEST: A test for determining probable cause based on the entire collection of relevant facts in a particular case.

of circumstances standard was to be given a broad interpretation by lower courts. Moreover, reviewing courts should show deference to the probable cause determinations of issuing magistrates. To second guess a magistrate's probable cause determinations is, according to the Court, "inconsistent both with the desire to encourage use of the warrant process by police officers and with the recognition that, once a warrant has been obtained, intrusion upon interests protected by the Fourth Amendment is less severe than otherwise may be the case."

We will address this topic of informants again in chapter 8, where we discuss traffic stops based on anonymous 911 calls of erratic driving, which the Supreme Court upheld in *Navarette v. California* (2014)[82] as compatible with the Fourth Amendment, by using the totality of circumstances approach. Additionally, in chapter 10, we will observe that the Court's decision in *Adams v. Williams* (1972)[83] upheld pat-down searches based on informant tips given, in-person, to police officers.

The Exclusionary Rule

How are the protections of the Fourth Amendment to be enforced? In a line of decisions going back to 1914, the Supreme Court has held that illegally obtained evidence is inadmissible in a criminal prosecution. Although there are several exceptions to the principle, this exclusionary rule is the primary mechanism by which the Fourth Amendment is enforced. In the pages that follow, we discuss the origin and development of the exclusionary rule, as well as the exceptions to it.

EXCLUSIONARY RULE: Procedural rule excluding from evidence obtained illegally by the police.

Establishment of the Exclusionary Rule

In *Weeks v. United States* (1914),[84] a federal marshal searched a man's home without a warrant and seized incriminating letters and other documents. Fremont Weeks petitioned the trial court to return the seized documents, so they could not be used in evidence against him. The federal judge presiding over the case denied the motion, and Weeks was convicted of using the U.S. Mail to send lottery tickets, an offense under federal law. On review, the Supreme Court reversed Weeks's conviction and held that the illegally obtained evidence was improperly admitted at trial. Speaking for a unanimous bench, Justice William R. Day opined:

> If letters and private documents can thus be seized
> and held and used in evidence against a citizen

accused of an offense, the protection of the Fourth Amendment, declaring his right to be secure against such searches and seizures, is of no value, and, so far as those thus placed are concerned, might as well be stricken from the Constitution.

Initial Refusal to Extend the Exclusionary Rule to the State Courts

Weeks was a federal criminal case, and the Court's holding applied only to federal criminal trials. Thirty-five years later, in *Wolf v. Colorado* (1949),[85] the Court held that states must abide by the Fourth Amendment. However, the Court refused to apply the exclusionary rule to the state courts. Writing for the Court, Justice Felix Frankfurter granted that "in practice the exclusion of evidence may be an effective way of deterring unreasonable searches" but concluded that "it is not for this Court to condemn as falling below the minimal standards assured by the Due Process Clause a State's reliance upon other methods which, if consistently enforced, would be equally effective." In a strongly worded dissent, Justice Frank Murphy took issue with Frankfurter's assertion that "other methods" of enforcing the Fourth Amendment might be "equally effective" as the exclusionary rule:

> The conclusion is inescapable that but one remedy exists to deter violations of the search and seizure clause. That is the rule which excludes illegally obtained evidence. Only by exclusion can we impress upon the zealous prosecutor that violation of the Constitution will do him no good. And only when that point is driven home can the prosecutor be expected to emphasize the importance of observing constitutional demands in his instructions to the police.

The *Silver Platter* Doctrine

In *Lustig v. United States* (1949),[86] the Court held that evidence gathered by state and local police who committed Fourth Amendment violations in the process was still admissible in federal court. Justice Frankfurter's plurality opinion stated that "the crux of that doctrine is that a search is a search by a federal official if he had a hand in it; it is not a search by a federal official if evidence secured by state authorities is turned over to the federal authorities on a silver platter." Eleven years later, in *Elkins v. United States* (1960),[87] the Court rejected this silver platter doctrine. Writing for a sharply divided bench, Justice Stewart declared:

> Free and open cooperation between state and federal law enforcement officers is to be commended and encouraged. Yet that kind of cooperation is hardly promoted by a rule that implicitly invites federal officers to withdraw from such association and at least tacitly to encourage state officers in the disregard of constitutionally protected freedom.

The *Elkins* decision foreshadowed a landmark ruling a year later that would fully embrace the exclusionary rule.

Mapp v. Ohio (1961)

Without question, *Mapp v. Ohio* (1961)[88] is one of the most important decisions rendered by the Supreme Court in the criminal justice field. In essence, the Court overturned part of *Wolf v. Colorado* and held that the exclusionary rule is required in state as well as federal courts. Justice Tom Clark's majority opinion in *Mapp* insisted that "… without the *Weeks* rule the assurance against unreasonable federal searches and seizures would be 'a form of words,' valueless and undeserving of mention in a perpetual charter of inestimable human liberties," before adding that, "so too, without that rule, the freedom from state invasions of privacy would be so ephemeral and so neatly severed from its conceptual nexus with the freedom from all brutish means of coercing evidence as not to merit this Court's high regard as a freedom 'implicit in the concept of ordered liberty.'" In dissent, Justice John M. Harlan (the younger) chided the majority for overturning precedent: "In overruling the *Wolf* case, the Court, in my opinion, has forgotten the sense of judicial restraint which, with due regard for *stare decisis*, is one element that should enter into deciding whether a past decision of this Court should be overruled."

SILVER PLATTER DOCTRINE: Antiquated doctrine under which federal and state authorities could share illegally obtained evidence before the exclusionary rule was made applicable to all jurisdictions.

JURISPRUDENCE

The Supreme Court Incorporates the Exclusionary Rule
Mapp v. Ohio, 367 U.S. 643 (1961)

Acting on a tip that a bombing suspect was hiding inside the home belonging to Dollree Mapp, Cleveland police arrived at Mapp's home and demanded that they be allowed to enter. Mapp requested that the police show her a search warrant. The police left but returned several hours later and forced their way into the home over Ms. Mapp's protest. There was no record of any warrant having been issued. The police failed to locate the bombing suspect, but they did find some pornographic materials in a trunk in the basement. Mapp was arrested, tried, and convicted under the Ohio obscenity statute.

Divided 7–2, the U.S. Supreme Court reversed Mapp's conviction, holding that the evidence had been improperly admitted against her, as it had been obtained in violation of the Fourth Amendment's warrant requirement. Writing for the Court, Justice Tom Clark observed that the decision to apply the exclusionary rule to the state courts "gives to the individual no more than that which the Constitution guarantees him, to the police officer no less than that to which honest law enforcement is entitled, and, to the courts, that judicial integrity so necessary in the true administration of justice."

The impact of *Mapp v. Ohio* is difficult to overstate. The decision forced prosecutors at the state and local levels (where most criminal cases occur) to take the Fourth Amendment seriously. In particular, there was an increased reliance on search warrants in the wake of Mapp. For example, in New York City, in the year prior to Mapp, no search warrants were issued, but in the year following Mapp, more than 1,000 warrants were obtained. Moreover, Mapp led to improved training of police officers. With the possibility that crucial evidence would be lost due to officer error, it became critical for police to be trained in the dos and don'ts of search and seizure.

Limiting the Exclusionary Rule
In the 1970s, a more conservative Court under Chief Justice Warren E. Burger moved to limit the application of the exclusionary rule. Rather

than viewing the rule as part and parcel of the Fourth Amendment, the Burger Court viewed it as merely a judicially created device designed to deter the police from violating people's Fourth Amendment rights. The Burger Court's approach was to balance the social cost of applying the rule against the deterrent value in a given context. Accordingly, in 1974, the Court refused to exclude illegally obtained evidence from grand jury proceedings.[89] Similarly, in 1976, the Court held the exclusionary rule does not apply to deportation hearings.[90]

Standing to Invoke the Exclusionary Rule

In *Rakas v. Illinois* (1978),[91] the Court held that one does not have standing to invoke the exclusionary rule unless that person's Fourth Amendment rights were violated by the police. Thus, one who sequesters incriminating evidence on someone else's person or property cannot invoke the exclusionary rule if that evidence is obtained through an illegal search. For example, in *Rawlings v. Kentucky* (1980),[92] a man was convicted of drug possession after he admitted the marijuana taken from his girlfriend's purse belonged to him. The search of the girlfriend's purse was judged to be unlawful; nevertheless, the evidence recovered from the purse could be used against Mr. Rawlings because the illegal search was directed at another person's property. Hence, he could not invoke the exclusionary rule. In another case decided that year, *United States v. Salvucci* (1980),[93] the Court refused to grant standing to raise a Fourth Amendment claim regarding evidence seized from the home of an accused criminal's mother, with the majority opinion saying that the accused lacked a "possessory interest" in mail kept at her home.

In addition, through decisions in *Minnesota v. Olson* (1990)[94] and *Minnesota v. Carter* (1998),[95] the Supreme Court has held that "overnight guests" in another person's home are to be granted standing to assert claims under the Fourth Amendment. However, people who might be described as "commercial visitors" (such as drug dealers) or "temporary guests" are likely to lack standing. In the *Carter* case, for example, two men who were visiting another person's house for the sole purpose of carrying out a drug deal were found to lack standing to challenge the constitutionality of a police officer *peeping* through slits in a closed blind by pressing his face against a window while standing outside the home. Ultimately, because the men lacked standing, the Supreme Court did not need to assess the substantive question of whether that viewing was a violation of the Fourth Amendment.

In spite of these high Court decisions, there are states that provide for *automatic standing* to raise a Fourth Amendment claim in any situation

STANDING: The right to challenge an action in court because one has suffered or is likely to suffer a real and substantial injury or deprivation of rights.

that evidence is admitted against a defendant in court; these states include Louisiana, Massachusetts, Pennsylvania, Michigan, New Hampshire, New Jersey, and Vermont. As noted earlier in this text, a state is allowed to provide additional protection to an individual, beyond what is offered through Supreme Court decisions, in the event that state chooses to do so (whether through legislation or state court precedent).

The Good Faith Exception

In *Michigan v. DeFillippo* (1979),[96] the Supreme Court ruled that an arrest based on an officer's "good faith reliance" on an ordinance that would later be ruled unconstitutional can still be deemed a valid arrest. Five years later, in *United States v. Leon* (1984),[97] the Court held that when a magistrate issues a search warrant based on an erroneous probable cause determination, the evidence need not be suppressed. If the error is the magistrate's and not the officer's, excluding the evidence would have no deterrent value.

This **good faith exception** is controversial, to say the least. Critics argue it does not matter who violated the Fourth Amendment; excluding evidence is to only way to remedy the violation. Dissenting in the *Leon* case, Justice William Brennan argued, "A proper understanding of the broad purposes sought to be served by the Fourth Amendment demonstrates that the principles embodied in the exclusionary rule rest upon a far firmer constitutional foundation than the shifting sands of the Court's deterrence rationale."

Despite such criticism, the Court under Chief Justice Roberts has maintained the good faith exception. For example, in *Davis v. United States* (2011),[98] the majority opinion observed that an officer's reliance on case precedent that is valid at the time of a search and seizure serves as a good faith exception to the exclusionary rule if that precedent is later overturned. Two years earlier, in *Herring v. United States* (2009),[99] the Court even applied the good faith exception to a case in which police made an arrest based on an outdated warrant. In this case, Bennie Herring went to a police impound lot in Coffee County, Alabama to retrieve items from his pickup truck after it had been towed there. When he arrived, police conducted a background check, and a clerk from a neighboring county mistakenly notified the police that there was an active warrant for Herring's arrest. Police then pursued Herring as he drove away from the impound lot in a different vehicle. He was pulled over and arrested. A search incident to that arrest revealed methamphetamines and a firearm. In turn, Herring faced federal charges for drug possession and for being a felon in possession of a firearm.

GOOD FAITH EXCEPTION: An exception to the exclusionary rule under which evidence need not be suppressed as long as officers were acting in good faith reliance on a search warrant that was later determined to be unsupported by probable cause.

However, officials from the neighboring county had failed to recognize that the warrant in question was an expired one because their computer system had not been updated in five months; a phone call explaining that fact was made, but this occurred after the search and arrest had taken place. Herring was convicted and sentenced to 27 months in federal prison. After the Eleventh Circuit affirmed Herring's conviction, the Supreme Court agreed to hear the case. The high Court affirmed the lower court, even though the drugs and gun would not have been found without the improper arrest. Writing for the Court, Chief Justice Roberts concluded that "when police mistakes are the result of negligence such as that described here, rather than systemic error or reckless disregard of constitutional requirements, any marginal deterrence does not 'pay its way.'"

This principle was applied by the Supreme Court three years later in *Heien v. North Carolina* (2014),[100] when a man was pulled over for having one broken brake light on the rear of his car. A subsequent search of the vehicle revealed cocaine, and Heien was charged with drug trafficking under state law. He appealed his conviction based on the fact that North Carolina law only requires one working brake light on a vehicle. On review from the North Carolina Supreme Court, which found no Fourth Amendment violation, the Supreme Court agreed that this was a valid traffic stop. In expanding the scope of good faith exceptions, Justice Roberts's majority opinion stated the officer had merely committed a "reasonable mistake of law." In dissent, Justice Sotomayor said, "the meaning of the law is not probabilistic in the same way that factual determinations are." She added that "an officer's mistake of law, no matter how reasonable, cannot support the individualized suspicion necessary to justify a seizure under the Fourth Amendment." She went on to say, "I have not seen any persuasive argument that law enforcement will be unduly hampered by a rule that precludes consideration of mistakes of law" and referenced the *Herring* decision in declaring: "[T]here is nothing in our case law requiring us to hold that a reasonable mistake of law can justify a seizure under the Fourth Amendment, and quite a bit suggesting just the opposite." States are, of course, free to reject this notion of "good faith mistakes," which occurred in a decision from Tennessee's Supreme Court that was released the same year as the *Heien* ruling.[101]

In 2016, the Supreme Court's decision in *Utah v. Strieff*[102] applied a so-called "attenuation doctrine," which appears to provide a framework for determining when a good faith mistake is, or is not, a valid one. In this case, the Court acknowledged that a pat-down search that yielded drug evidence had been conducted improperly, in violation of the Fourth Amendment—but also said that evidence derived from that pat-down could be admitted at trial because of the existence of an outstanding warrant against the suspect for a traffic violation. This was despite the fact that the arresting officer knew nothing of the warrant's existence at the time the pat-down occurred and only learned of it after effectuating an arrest. The majority opinion from Justice Thomas explained the attenuation doctrine by saying, "Evidence is admissible when the connection between unconstitutional police conduct and the evidence is remote or has been interrupted by some intervening circumstance, so that 'the interest protected by the constitutional guarantee that has been violated would not be served by suppression of the evidence obtained.'"[103] The *Strieff* opinion cited *Brown v. Illinois* (1975),[104] identifying three factors to consider when applying the attenuation doctrine: (1) the "temporal proximity" between the unconstitutional activity and the search or seizure, (2) the existence of "intervening circumstances," and (3) the "flagrancy and purpose" of the police misconduct. We will address this case in greater detail in chapter 10, where we address pat-down searches.

The Fruit of the Poisonous Tree Doctrine

In *Silverthorne Lumber Co. v. United States* (1920),[105] the Supreme Court extended the exclusionary rule to derivative evidence. As the metaphor goes, if the tree is poisonous, so is the fruit. Thus, evidence derived from inadmissible evidence is likewise inadmissible. The fruit of the poisonous tree doctrine was reaffirmed in *Nardone v. United States* (1939)[106] and *Wong Sun v. United States* (1963);[107] it remains good law today. However, as early as the *Silverthorne* case, the Supreme Court recognized that an independent source leading to the discovery of the disputed evidence negates the application of the fruit of the poisonous tree doctrine. In *Segura v. United States* (1984),[108] the Court reaffirmed the independent source doctrine, saying, "The exclusionary rule does not apply ... if the connection between the illegal police conduct and the discovery and seizure of the evidence is 'so attenuated as to dissipate the taint,' ... as, for example, where the police had an 'independent source' for discovery of the evidence."

The Inevitable Discovery Exception

In 1984, the Supreme Court created the inevitable discovery exception to the fruit of the poisonous tree doctrine. In this case, a suspect told police where he had disposed of a body, but the suspect's statements were later determined to be inadmissible because of a *Miranda* violation. Those statements had led one group of officers to the victim's body in the woods. In *Brewer v. Williams* (1977),[109] the Supreme Court disallowed the use of the body and associated forensic evidence, as it was all deemed to be the fruit of the poisonous tree. Reviewing the case for a second time seven years later, in *Nix v. Williams* (1984),[110] the Court took note of the fact that, at the time the suspect made the inadmissible statements, a separate search was underway in the area the body was found. The Court accepted the prosecution's argument that the body inevitably would have been found, regardless of the suspect's inadmissible statements. Writing for the majority, Chief Justice Burger observed, "Exclusion of physical evidence that would inevitably have been discovered adds nothing to either the integrity or fairness of a criminal trial." We discuss this case in greater detail in chapter 11, which addresses the right to remain silent.

DERIVATIVE EVIDENCE: Evidence derived from or obtained only as a result of other evidence.

FRUIT OF THE POISONOUS TREE DOCTRINE: The doctrine under which evidence is deemed to be inadmissible if it was derived from other inadmissible evidence.

INEVITABLE DISCOVERY EXCEPTION: An exception to the fruit of the poisonous tree doctrine that allows the admission of evidence derived from inadmissible evidence if it inevitably would have been discovered independently by lawful means.

THE CONSTITUTION IN ACTION
The 1033 Program and Police Militarization

The use of SWAT raids raises concerns related to the notion of *police militarization*. Along these lines, under a federal *1033 program*, which was established by Congress in a temporary fashion in 1989 and then made permanent in 1996, the Department of Defense is permitted to give military equipment to local police departments across the country. Typically, departments make a request, expressing a reason for needing some item, and that request is addressed on a first-come, first-served basis. Reasons offered in these requests often include objectives like countering drug operations or stopping active shooters.

(continued)

A 2021 report from the ACLU found that "[s]ince [1033's] inception in 1996, nearly 10,000 jurisdictions have received more than $7 billion of equipment. This includes combat vehicles, rifles, military helmets," as well as planes, rifles, scopes, grenades, bayonets, night vision gear. The report also said, "Today, state and local law enforcement possess more than 60,000 military grade rifles, 1,500 combat-ready trucks and tanks, 500 unmanned ground vehicles (functionally landed drones), and dozens of military aircraft, machine gun parts, bayonets, and even an inert rocket launcher." Additionally, the report found that "[e]ighty institutions of higher education currently possess seven less-lethal firing devices, six mine-resistant vehicles, an armored truck, another combat vehicle, 159 shotguns and pistols, and 622 assault rifles. Nine K–12 schools' police officers have 96 assault rifles, and one K–12 school—Spring Branch ISD—received a mine resistant vehicle in 2019." Finally, the ACLU report showed no significant fiscal savings for local police departments as a result of the 1033 program, with the report saying, "Manually constructing a dataset of these law enforcement budgets from 2011–2020, we found no evidence that 1033 transfers decrease police budgets."[111]

In 2015, an executive order from President Obama banned the transfer of several items under 1033, including grenade launchers, bayonets, camouflage uniforms, firearms over .50 caliber, and weaponized aircrafts.[112] But that was repealed by President Trump in August 2017 with an Executive Order, entitled Restoring State, Tribal, and Local Law Enforcement's Access to Life-Saving Equipment and Resources.[113]

President Trump's first attorney general, Jeff Sessions, defended the 2017 order and the 1033 program in general by saying, "Studies have shown this equipment reduces crime rates, reduces the number of assaults against police officers, and reduces the number of complaints against police officers."[114] A 2020 study called "Police Militarization and Violent Crime," though, showed no statistically significant evidence of a reduction in crime rates in jurisdictions that receive equipment under 1033.[115] Yet a 2017 study from researchers at the University of Tennessee also indicated that "acquisition of surplus military equipment through the US Department of Defense Law Enforcement Support Officers 1033 Program does not cause police to be more aggressive."[116] We will discuss the concept of police raids in greater detail in chapter 10.

Suing the Police: An Alternative to the Exclusionary Rule?

Enacted during the Reconstruction Era as part of the Civil Rights Act of 1871,[117] 42 U.S.C. § 1983 authorizes civil suits against persons acting "under color of any statute, ordinance, regulation, custom, or usage, of any State or Territory or the District of Columbia" who violate another person's rights under the Constitution or federal law. The concept "under color of law" refers to someone, not necessarily a public official, who is "clothed with the authority of state law."[118] Because such suits are brought against individuals, police officers who violate a person's constitutional rights do so at the risk of their own assets. This is especially the case when a court awards punitive damages because "the defendant's conduct is shown to be motivated by evil motive or intent, or when it involves reckless or callous indifference to the federally protected rights of others."[119] According to a 2022 Supreme Court decision, a Section 1983 lawsuit can be brought against police by a defendant in a criminal case even without a not guilty verdict being rendered in their case.[120] However, also in 2022, the Supreme Court ruled that an officer's alleged violation of Miranda Rights could not serve as the basis for a Section 1983 lawsuit.[121]

In a 1992 decision, the Supreme Court distilled the underlying rationale for allowing a Section 1983 suit, saying its purpose is "to deter state actors from using the badge of their authority to deprive individuals of their federally guaranteed rights and to provide related relief to victims if such deterrence fails."[122] In untangling the meaning of the word "deprive" in a prior case, *Daniels v. Williams* (1986),[123] the Court refused to permit a Section 1983 action when an inmate in a Richmond, Virginia prison allegedly suffered back and ankle injuries after slipping on a pillow a corrections deputy had negligently left on a staircase. Chief Justice Rehnquist said,

"Not only does the word 'deprive' in the Due Process Clause connote more than a negligent act, but we should not 'open the federal courts to lawsuits where there has been no affirmative abuse of power.'" That quote cited a 1981 decision in which the Supreme Court dismissed a Section 1983 lawsuit brought by a Nebraska prison inmate, who sought damages for the loss of mail-order hobby materials that were delivered to his prison but misplaced by officials who failed to follow appropriate package delivery protocols.[124] Therefore, although Section 1983 does not contain a specific intent requirement, precedent suggests some level of culpability beyond mere negligence should exist for a Section 1983 lawsuit to be successful.

In *Monell v. Department of Social Services* (1978),[125] the Supreme Court held that municipalities can be found liable under Section 1983. They cannot be held liable merely for the actions of their employees (e.g., police officers) but only when their policies and practices result in civil rights violations. According to Justice O'Connor's majority opinion in *Board of County Commissioners of Bryan County v. Brown* (1997),[126] to sue a municipality "a plaintiff must show that the municipal action was taken with the requisite degree of culpability and must demonstrate a direct causal link between the municipal action and the deprivation of federal rights." Moreover, cities cannot be held liable for punitive damages, with the Supreme Court holding in 1981 that "considerations of history and policy do not support exposing a municipality to punitive damages for the bad faith actions of its officials."[127]

Although there is no comparable federal law to Section 1983 to explicitly authorize such suits against federal officers, the Supreme Court in *Bivens v. Six Unknown Named Agents of the Federal Bureau of Narcotics* (1971)[128] recognized a similar cause of action against federal agents who violate a person's Fourth Amendment rights. The *Bivens* case originated in 1965, when federal narcotics agents raided the apartment of Webster Bivens and conducted a warrantless search for contraband. Even though the agents found nothing illegal, they still arrested Bivens. He was later released when a federal magistrate (then called a U.S. Commissioner) found no justification for detention. Subsequently, Bivens filed a lawsuit in federal court, seeking damages from the agents. Both the federal district court and the U.S. Court of Appeals for the Second Circuit dismissed his case for not properly stating a claim for relief, but the Supreme Court allowed the suit to move forward. This decision gave rise to what is known as a *Bivens* remedy.

While the *Bivens* remedy emerged in the Fourth Amendment context, subsequent cases applied the remedy to Fifth and Eighth Amendment

BIVENS **REMEDY:** A lawsuit filed against a federal official for an alleged violation of a constitutional right, as permitted under certain circumstances by the Supreme Court in *Bivens v. Six Unknown Named Agents* (1971).

violations.[129] In recent years, though, the Supreme Court has foreclosed its application to new contexts, such as in a line of cases in which Arab and Asian men brought suits against the Attorney General, the FBI Director, and other government and corrections officials to contest detention tactics used in the aftermath of the 9/11 attacks.[130] In a 2009 case of this ilk, the Court indicated "*Bivens* is not designed to hold officers responsible for acts of their subordinates."[131] Subsequently, in the majority opinion for a 2017 case, Justice Kennedy said, "*Bivens* will not be extended to a new context if there are 'special factors counseling hesitation in the absence of affirmative action by Congress.'"[132] He further noted that such special factors could include the fact that "[n]ational-security policy is the prerogative of the Congress and President." Regarding the *Bivens* doctrine generally, Justice Kennedy posed the following query: "The question is 'who should decide' whether to provide for a damages remedy, Congress or the courts?" He then declared: "The answer most often will be Congress."

More recently, in *Hernandez v. Mesa* (2020),[133] a majority opinion from Justice Alito refused to expand *Bivens* to a case where a U.S. Border Patrol Agent shot and killed an unarmed 15-year-old Mexican boy, who, along with teenage friends, was playing a game that involved running back and forth through a culvert that traversed the U.S. border between El Paso, Texas, and Ciudad Juarez, Mexico. The agent was standing on the U.S. side when he fired, with the bullet striking and killing the boy on the Mexico side. The boy's parents filed a *Bivens* action against the agent, but Justice Alito's majority opinion said that "expansion of *Bivens* is a 'disfavored judicial activity,'" noting that one "special factor" limiting applicability of *Bivens* to a cross-border shooting was the principle of separation of powers. More specifically, Alito observed that Congress, through passage of the Foreign Claims Act,[134] had given the executive branch the authority to make payments regarding "injuries suffered by aliens outside the United States."

In dissent, however, Justice Ginsburg noted the unlikely nature of such a payment, lamenting, "In short, it is all too apparent that to redress injuries like the one suffered here, it is *Bivens* or nothing." She also stated that "Hernandez's parents could have maintained a *Bivens* action had the bullet hit Hernandez while he was running up or down the United States side of the embankment."[135] Discussing the theory underlying a *Bivens* action, she suggested "[t]he purpose of *Bivens* is to deter the *officer*. ... And primary conduct constrained by the Fourth Amendment is an *officer's* unjustified resort to excessive force" (emphasis in original). Justice Thomas penned a concurring opinion, joined by Justice Neil Gorsuch, which challenged the very existence of the *Bivens* doctrine. Thomas called for the complete overturn of the concept by saying, "The analysis underlying *Bivens* cannot be defended. We have cabined the doctrine's scope, undermined its foundation, and limited its precedential value. It is time to correct this Court's error and abandon the doctrine altogether."

Two years later, Justice Thomas wrote the majority opinion for another *Bivens*-related case, *Egbert v. Boule* (2022),[136] and although that decision did not completely eradicate the doctrine, it went so far as to indicate that a *Bivens* remedy could not apply to the conduct of U.S. Border Patrol agents, thereby granting such agents virtual immunity against civil lawsuits. The suit in this case was brought forth by a man named Robert Boule, owner of a bed-and-breakfast called The Smugglers Inn—whose name was derived from the inn's location directly along the U.S.-Canada border in the state of Washington (and the fact that illegal border crossings allegedly have occurred by people crossing the border through the property). Boule claimed that a U.S. Border Patrol agent had walked onto his land and pushed Boule against a vehicle, with the agent then throwing him to the ground. Boule also said that after he complained about the incident, the same agent improperly reported him to the IRS and the Washington Department of Licensing.[137]

Boule filed a *Bivens* action that raised a Fourth Amendment excessive force claim and a First Amendment "retaliation" claim. In the majority opinion for the Supreme Court's review of this matter, Justice Thomas wrote: "We ask here whether a court is competent to authorize a damages action not just against Agent Egbert but against Border Patrol agents generally"—with Thomas concluding that "the answer, plainly, is no." In dissent, Justice Sotomayor observed that the facts of Boule's case closely matched those of the original *Bivens* decision from 1971; she specifically noted that: "Today's decision does not overrule *Bivens*. It nevertheless contravenes precedent and will strip many more individuals who suffer injuries at the hands of federal officers, and whose circumstances are materially indistinguishable from *Bivens*, of an important remedy." Thus, although *Bivens* technically remains a viable source for a lawsuit against federal law enforcement officials, the Supreme Court had significantly limited its practical applicability. In the end, because the *Bivens* remedy was judicially created, it is subject to limitation or elimination by the Supreme Court.

Immunity of Police Officers

Beyond these considerations, in recent years, the controversial doctrine of **qualified immunity** has made it difficult for an individual plaintiff to succeed on either a Section 1983 lawsuit or a *Bivens* claim. Qualified immunity suggests an officer cannot be sued for a violation of constitutional rights, unless there has been a violation of "clearly established" rights, a concept will we discuss below. Generally, for a right to be deemed "clearly established," a court will look to case precedent to see if any existing principles would have put an officer on notice that a particular type of conduct was unconstitutional or a violation of law.[138] Without a showing of such clearly established guidance, a suit against an officer cannot be sustained because qualified immunity would apply. In a 1986 decision, the Supreme Court expounded upon this protection by observing, "As the qualified immunity defense has evolved, it provides ample protection to all but the plainly incompetent or those who knowingly violate the law."[139] In a later case, the Court said qualified immunity should apply, unless an officer has committed "an error that 'just a simple glance' would have revealed";[140] in that case, officers executed a search warrant that was later deemed to be improperly granted, but the Court ruled that as long as an officer acted with "objective good faith" in executing a warrant, and provided that the warrant was not "so obviously defective that no reasonable officer could have believed it was valid," then an officer should not be subjected to personal liability in this type of situation.

QUALIFIED IMMUNITY: The doctrine under which government agents cannot be held liable for their actions in the course of their job duties, unless those actions violate clearly established constitutional rules.

Although most police actions giving rise to civil lawsuits will be evaluated through the lens of qualified immunity, Chief Justice Warren's opinion in *Pierson v. Ray* (1967)[141] identified a limited situation in which a police officer should be afforded absolute immunity from a Section 1983 lawsuit. That scenario was defined as follows: "[T]hey should not be liable if they acted in good faith and with probable cause in making an arrest under a statute that they believed to be valid." Warren went on to clarify this standard by saying, "Under the prevailing view in this country, a peace officer who arrests someone with probable cause is not liable for false arrest simply because the innocence of the suspect is later proved." The Chief Justice went so far as to declare, "A policeman's lot is not so unhappy that he must choose between being charged with dereliction of duty if he does not arrest when he has probable cause and being mulcted in damages if he does"—adding that "... the same consideration would seem to require excusing him from liability for acting under a statute that he reasonably believed to be valid, but that was later held unconstitutional, on its face or as applied."

Even in the absence of immunity, civil suits against police officers are not likely to be a viable option for the great majority of people whose Fourth Amendment rights are violated. Where there are no serious personal injuries or destruction of property, the damages plaintiffs can collect are quite limited. On the other hand, in cases when police use excessive force in conducting seizures or making arrests, civil suits can be a viable option. As noted previously, such suits also can be brought against a municipality for failing to provide adequate training of officers or policies governing their behavior.

FOCUS ON LAW ENFORCEMENT

Ride-Along Cases Alter the Nature of Television Show *Cops*

In early 1992, U.S. Attorney General William Barr announced the implementation of Operation Gunsmoke, which was a nationwide fugitive apprehension program that would involve U.S. marshals working with state and local police to take into custody thousands of dangerous fugitives for whom arrest warrants existed. During the course of the 10-week operation, more than 3,000 arrests were made in over 40 cities.

One of the targets of this operation was a Maryland man named Dominic Wilson, who had violated probation on felony charges of robbery, theft, and assault. Before 7 a.m. on April 16, 1992, a team consisting of deputy U.S. marshals and officers of the Montgomery County (MD) Police readied to enter a home at the address a police computer listed for Wilson. Three arrest warrants, one for each of his probation violations, had been issued by the Circuit Court for Montgomery County.

Although the warrants did not mention anything about members of media taking part in the search, the Operation Gunsmoke team was joined by a *Washington Post* reporter and photographer, who were invited in conjunction with the U.S. Marshals Service *ride-along*

program. This entire group made entry into the home, with the reporter observing and the photographer taking pictures. However, Dominic Wilson was not found to be in the home, which actually belonged to his parents, Charles and Geraldine, who were awakened by the team's entry. Armed officers detained Charles, who was in his underwear, by forcing him to the floor—as they mistakenly believed he was Dominic.

The parents filed lawsuits against the law enforcement officials involved, bringing a *Bivens* claim against the federal agents and a Section 1983 suit against the local police officers. In reviewing this matter in *Wilson v. Layne* (1999),[142] the Supreme Court reached something of a split decision. The Court ruled that "such a 'media ride along' does violate the Fourth Amendment," primarily because it "ignores the importance of the right of residential privacy at the core of the Fourth Amendment." Yet the majority opinion from Chief Justice Rehnquist also found that "because the state of the law was not clearly established at the time the search in this case took place, the officers are entitled to the defense of qualified immunity."

On the same day *Wilson v. Layne* was decided, the Court released a separate decision in *Hanlon v. Berger* (1999),[143] which also involved a ride-along. This case addressed a 1993 search in which U.S. Fish and Wildlife agents executed a warrant to inspect a 75,000-acre ranch in Montana, in pursuit of evidence concerning "illegal wildlife takings." The per curiam opinion for this case observed that the search party included a "multiple-vehicle caravan consisting of Government agents and a crew of photographers and reporters from Cable News Network, Inc. (CNN)." The Court cited the *Wilson* decision in reiterating that "police violate the Fourth Amendment rights of homeowners when they allow members of the media to accompany them during the execution of a warrant. ..." But once again, the Court noted that qualified immunity applied "because the law on this question before today's decision was not clearly established."

So even though a Fourth Amendment violation was said to connect to this practice of ride-alongs taking part in entry to private property, all officers involved in these matters were given qualified immunity from lawsuits. Nonetheless, a critical takeaway from these cases is that they firmly established a constitutional violation. Future cases of this type would therefore invoke an assessment of a clearly established right to be free from the presence of ride-along media during a police search of a home. Thus, officers who engage in such conduct in the future would not retain the benefit of qualified immunity.

For the reality television show *Cops*, which began in 1989 and routinely involved television cameras following police officers into homes, these decisions meant an immediate shift in how the show was produced; media and TV producers with cameras could no longer enter the home with immunity. As a result, *Cops* has persisted through its more than thirty years of television, largely by having camera crews film from public places—a necessity if officers involved in searches or home entries wish to retain qualified immunity.

The Doctrine of Consent Once Removed *and the* Pearson *Approach*

In 2009, the Supreme Court's ruling in *Pearson v. Callahan*[144] took umbrage with a two-part framework from a prior qualified immunity decision in *Saucier v. Katz* (2001).[145] The *Saucier* Court's unanimous opinion required courts to first consider whether a constitutional violation had occurred and to then determine whether a clearly established precedent had been violated. Justice Alito's majority opinion in *Pearson v. Callahan*, however, called this an "inflexible procedure" and said that "experience supports our present determination that a mandatory, two-step rule for resolving all qualified immunity claims should not be retained." Instead, the Court's decision in *Pearson* suggested the components of the two-part analysis could be addressed in any order; hence, if there were no *clearly established right* that had been violated, qualified immunity would automatically apply—and there would be no need for an assessment of whether a constitutional violation had occurred.

In the *Pearson* case, the Court found officers on the Central Utah Narcotics Task Force were entitled to qualified immunity in a suit alleging a Fourth Amendment violation. The search in question stemmed from an operation in which an undercover informant had been given consent to enter a trailer and purchase drugs. Officers waiting nearby would later enter the trailer after receiving a signal that the drug buy had been completed—but those officers did not have a warrant. Attorneys for the officers claimed that precedent in circuit courts (although not the specific circuit court covering Utah) had established the doctrine of *consent once removed*—which meant the undercover informant being granted consent to enter the trailer by its owner meant the officers could subsequently do so as well. Justice Alito agreed with the idea that some lower court precedents indicated that no "clearly established" right was violated. Specifically, Alito spoke of the case law by noting, "When the entry at issue here occurred in 2002, the 'consent-once-removed' doctrine had gained acceptance in the lower courts."[146] He then added an important declaration about the nature of lower court case precedent in framing what is—and what is not—a "clearly established" right:

> The officers here were entitled to rely on these cases, even though their own Federal Circuit had not yet ruled on "consent-once-removed" entries. The principles of qualified immunity shield an officer from personal liability when an officer reasonably believes that his or her conduct complies with the law. Police officers are entitled to rely on existing lower court cases without facing personal liability for their actions.

Some scholars have noted than an outgrowth of the *Pearson v. Callahan* approach is that courts often skip directly to an assessment of whether a *clearly established* precedent exists and thereby eschew the very analysis necessary to generate a *clearly established right* in the first place—which could limit the creation of precedents that emerge to protect constitutional liberties in the future.[147]

An illustrative example arises from the Supreme Court's ruling in *Mullenix v. Luna* (2015),[148] which addressed a Section 1983 lawsuit over police tactics used to terminate a high-speed automobile pursuit on an interstate highway in Texas. As a car eluded pursuit at speeds up to 110 mph, one team of officers placed spike strips in the roadway. However, just before the vehicle approached those spike strips, another officer standing on an overpass above the interstate fired six shots at the vehicle. The driver was struck and killed by four of the bullets, with his car continuing to travel and overturning after it made contact with the spike strips. The deceased's family brought a Section 1983 lawsuit against the officer who fired the shots, but the Supreme Court observed that no "clearly established" precedent spoke specifically to this scenario; therefore, the officer was entitled to qualified immunity because "the crux of the qualified immunity test is whether officers have 'fair notice' that they are acting unconstitutionally."[149] Notably, the Court also said, "We address only the qualified immunity question, not whether there was a Fourth Amendment violation in the first place...."

Recent Pro-Law Enforcement Developments in Qualified Immunity

In its more recent qualified immunity decisions, the Supreme Court has further clarified the scope of the all-important phrase *clearly established rights*, with these refinements generally tilting in favor of law enforcement officials. In a Fourth Amendment case called *District of Columbia v. Wesby* (2018),[150] the Court ruled in favor of D.C. Metropolitan Police Officers who faced a lawsuit for false arrest. The officers had entered an abandoned home where a party was occurring and, with no warrant, arrested partygoers for the crime of unlawful entry. Finding the officers were entitled to qualified immunity, the majority opinion from Justice Thomas said the crucial phrase "clearly established" should be taken to mean that, "at the time of the officer's conduct, the law was 'sufficiently clear that every reasonable official would understand that what he is doing' is unlawful."

In an especially critical statement, Justice Thomas invoked precedent in helping to define what is "clearly established," and observing that "[t]he precedent must be clear enough that every reasonable official would interpret it to establish the particular rule the plaintiff seeks to apply." He added, "It is not enough that the rule is suggested by then-existing precedent." Rather, he said it must be "beyond debate" and "settled law." In addition, Thomas indicated that the term "settled law" means "dictated by 'controlling authority' or 'a robust 'consensus of cases of persuasive authority.'"

Perhaps even more importantly than all of this information related to the definition of *clearly established*, Justice Thomas also held that qualified immunity would apply unless there was a clear connection between the facts of any *clearly established* precedent and the facts of the case at hand. To this point, he said the following:

> The "clearly established" standard also requires that the legal principle clearly prohibit the officer's conduct in the particular circumstances before him. The rule's contours must be so well defined that it is "clear to a reasonable officer that his conduct was unlawful in the situation he confronted." . . . This requires a high "degree of specificity."

The Supreme Court's qualified immunity jurisprudence did deviate—perhaps temporarily—from a rigid reliance on the facts of clearly established precedent with the ruling in *Taylor v. Riojas* (2020).[151] In this matter, Trent Taylor, an inmate in the Texas prison system, was confined in what the Court's per curiam opinion referred to as "shockingly unsanitary conditions." The opinion specifically observed that "[t]he first cell was covered, nearly floor to ceiling, in 'massive amounts' of feces': all over the floor, the ceiling, the window, the walls, and even 'packed inside the water faucet.'" Taylor was then moved to a "frigidly cold cell, which was equipped with only a clogged drain in the floor to dispose of bodily wastes," and when he urinated into the drain (after holding his bladder for approximately 24 hours), it overflowed and caused "raw sewage to spill across the floor." Because he had no clothing and this second cell had no bed, he had no choice but to sleep naked in the sewage.

Whereas the Fifth Circuit granted the prison officials involved in this case qualified immunity because of the dearth of applicable case precedent, the Supreme Court overturned, quoting *Brosseau v. Haugen* (2004)[152] (a police shooting case we will discuss in chapter 10) to declare the following:

> Qualified immunity shields an officer from suit when she makes a decision that, even if constitutionally deficient, reasonably misapprehends the law governing the circumstances she confronted. But no reasonable correctional officer could have concluded that, under the extreme circumstances of this case, it was constitutionally permissible to house Taylor in such deplorably unsanitary conditions for such an extended period of time.

Yet even though the *Taylor v. Riojas* case focused on an assessment of the "reasonable correctional officer," on October 18, 2021, the Supreme Court issued a pair of per curiam opinions that returned to a more rigid assessment of fact specificity in qualified immunity cases. In *Rivas-Villegas v. Cortseluna* (2021),[153] after the Ninth Circuit refused to grant qualified immunity in an excessive force case where an officer knelt on a suspect's neck, the Court reversed and provided the officer with that protection. The Ninth Circuit had found in favor of the suspect, Cortseluna, by saying there was clearly established precedent from the circuit's prior ruling in *LaLonde v. the County of Riverside* (2002),[154] which involved two police officers kneeling on a suspect who was face down and not resisting. Even so, the Court distinguished that precedent in three key ways: officers in the LaLonde matter were responding to a noise complaint, whereas a domestic violence incident occurred in Cortseluna's case; LaLonde was unarmed, but Cortseluna had a knife; and the so-called short duration of the kneeling (eight seconds) on Cortesluna.

In the second decision released that same day, *City Tahlequah, Oklahoma v. Bond*,[155] the Supreme Court found in favor of police officers who had responded to a domestic disturbance and, while inside the home's garage, shot a man who raised a hammer over his head as if he was preparing to throw the hammer or charge at officers. In the opinion for this case, the Court noted, "We have repeatedly told courts not to define clearly established precedent at too high a level of generality." The opinion added, "Not one of the decisions relied upon by the [Tenth Circuit] ... comes close to establishing that the officers' conduct was unlawful."

Practically speaking, then, it seems as though a plaintiff who brings a Section 1983 lawsuit or a *Bivens* lawsuit[156] must demonstrate that a Supreme Court precedent, or a federal circuit court precedent from the jurisdiction in which the case arises, has established that the government action in question is "clearly established" as unconstitutional. Moreover, the police conduct at hand needs to be essentially identical to the police conduct in the prior case in which government officials were said to have violated the Constitution. This can be a heavy burden to meet, and in turn, qualified immunity has evolved to provide officers of the law with a high degree of protection from personal liability in a civil suit. We discuss this topic in further detail in chapter 10, which addresses the police use-of-force cases that often form the basis of civil actions against law enforcement.

Federal Criminal Charges for a Violation of Constitutional Rights

It is important for all law enforcement personnel to realize that federal criminal charges also can attach—almost like a criminal version of Section 1983—to actions that deprive a person of constitutional rights. Under 18 U.S.C. § 242, entitled "Deprivation of Rights Under Color of Law," it is a crime if one "willfully subjects any person in any State, Territory, Commonwealth, Possession, or District to the deprivation of any rights, privileges, or immunities secured or protected by the Constitution or laws of the United States." A separate offense, under 18 U.S.C. § 241, can apply if two or more persons conspire to violate constitutional rights. The sentence for these offenses can be up to life in prison if a death results or up to ten years otherwise. Unlike civil suits, there is no qualified immunity to shield officers from criminal prosecution.

There are many examples of police being prosecuted under 18 U.S.C. § 242, often for the excessive use of force, which is considered a deprivation of the Fourth Amendment right to be free from unreasonable searches and seizures. One of the best known cases of this type involved two LAPD officers who were sentenced to thirty months in federal prison for their role in the brutal beating of motorist Rodney King in 1991.[157] That prosecution came after the officers, along with two of their colleagues, were acquitted of state charges by a California jury.

More recently, § 242 was the basis of the federal charge to which former Minneapolis police officer Derek Chauvin pleaded guilty in December 2021 in connection with the death of George Floyd. He had already been sentenced to state prison under Minnesota law for the crime of murder for his actions leading to Floyd's death. That did not prevent federal authorities from charging him under 18 U.S.C. § 242. As we will explain more fully in chapter 11, the doctrine of dual sovereignty permits successive federal and state prosecutions stemming from the same criminal episode.[158]

Conclusion

Probable cause and the warrant requirement are basic components of the Fourth Amendment, but the Supreme Court has said "the ultimate touchstone of the Fourth Amendment is 'reasonableness.'"[159] In this chapter, we have noted probable cause typically connects to showing a likelihood of criminal activity, and search warrants must be based on probable cause. Furthermore, a warrant must meet the elements of particularity, such as clearly defining the person or place to be searched and the item to be seized. Beyond that, we have addressed key aspects of how a warrant is executed, ranging from the knock-and-announce rule to searches of individuals on the premises.

We also discussed two primary approaches courts have taken when evaluating if government officials have violated the Fourth Amendment: the trespass doctrine, which is rooted in English Common Law, and the reasonable expectation of privacy test, which the Supreme Court established with its 1967 decision in *Katz v. United States*. The former focuses on whether a physical intrusion has occurred with private property, whereas the latter focuses on whether society would be willing to accept an expectation of privacy in a given situation as well as whether the nature of intrusion into an individual's expectation of privacy can be justified by an appropriate government interest.

This chapter also addressed the protection of qualified immunity, which can prevent a lawsuit against an individual officer who is accused of violating a person's constitutional rights. Qualified immunity tends to apply, unless an officer has violated a *clearly established* right—a term that generally means there is some existent case precedent that indicates a specific police action is incompatible with the Constitution. This doctrine can be especially salient—and potentially controversial—when applied to police use-of-force cases, which tend to address Fourth Amendment considerations.

Additionally, as we shall see in the next three chapters, the Supreme Court has historically upheld searches performed without a warrant as well as some searches based on reasonable suspicion rather than probable cause. Exigent circumstances and special needs can render searches reasonable, even in the absence of a search warrant or probable cause. Certainly, it would seem that a search would be more likely to yield evidence admissible in court when backed by a warrant, although even those can be challenged; but overall, a large body of warrantless searches have been sanctioned by appellate courts, as we will discuss next.

> ### Obiter Dicta
>
> "The test of reasonableness under the Fourth Amendment is not capable of precise definition or mechanical application. In each case, it requires a balancing of the need for the particular search against the invasion of personal rights that the search entails. Courts must consider the scope of the particular intrusion, the manner in which it is conducted, the justification for initiating it, and the place in which it is conducted."
>
> —*Chief Justice William Rehnquist, writing for the Supreme Court in* Bell v. Wolfish, *441 U.S. 520 (1979)*

Discussion Questions

1. Why did the framers of the Bill of Rights see the need to include a prohibition against unreasonable searches and seizures? Did they intend for this prohibition to apply to all law enforcement agents or only those of the federal government?

2. What are some examples of searches and seizures that could impact your life? What is the difference between a search and a seizure? Who are the agents of government most likely to effectuate such searches and seizures?

3. Does the Fourth Amendment restrict the actions of a private security guard working at a shopping mall? What about a postal worker or a UPS delivery driver? Along these lines, imagine someone who is not a government agent breaks into your home and steals a backpack, later dropping it along the side of a public street near your house. If a police officer came upon the bag and saw your name and address on the outside, then opened it, would an illegal item found inside could be admitted as evidence in a trial against you? What case precedents would be relevant to the discussion?

4. If an officer had a search warrant to examine a home to locate a six-foot-tall man, and once inside the home the officer opted to open a one-foot by two-foot backpack, finding cocaine inside of it, what factors would be discussed in determining if the evidence should be admissible in a criminal trial? How would the analysis shift if the warrant authorizing a search for rare coins and the same drug evidence were located in a backpack? What specific limits does the Fourth Amendment place on the specificity of a search pursuant to a warrant?

5. Can an anonymous tip, in and of itself, ever provide probable cause to obtain a search warrant? What are competing approaches different states might take to address this question? What case precedents are relevant to assessing the validity of a warrant based on information provided by an anonymous informant?

6. If the exclusionary rule is not an essential part of the Fourth Amendment, and is rather a judicially created device to deter police misconduct, what is the basis for the Supreme Court's decision in *Mapp v. Ohio*, requiring state courts to follow the rule? In the absence of the *Mapp* decision, what could have placed limitations on improper searches and seizures by state or local authorities?

7. What must a plaintiff in a civil suit alleging a Fourth Amendment violation by the police show to overcome the qualified immunity of the officers being sued? Should this immunity be maintained, abolished, or modified in some fashion?

Endnotes

1 *See Semayne v. Gresham*, 77 Eng. Rep. 194 (K.B. 1604); *Entick v. Carrington*, 95 Eng. 807 (C.P. 1765).

2 William Cuddihy & B. Carmon Hardy, *A Man's House Was Not His Castle: Origins of the Fourth Amendment to the United States Constitution*, 37 Wm. & Mary Q. 371–400 (1980).

3 John Adams's Reconstruction of Otis's Speech appears in *The Collected Political Writings of James Otis*, ed. Richard A. Samuelson (Indianapolis: Liberty Fund, 2015), 11–4. http://oll.libertyfund.org/titles/2703

4 *Id.* (quoting Thomas K. Clancy, *The Framer's Intent: John Adams, His Era, and the Fourth Amendment* 86 Ind. L.J. 979 (2011)).

5 *Wolf v. Colorado*, 338 U.S. 25 (1949).

6 *Olmstead v. United States*, 277 U.S. 438 (1928).

7 *Katz v. United States*, 389 U.S. 347 (1967).

8 *Rakas v. Illinois*, 439 U.S. 128 (1978).

9 *Winston v. Lee*, 470 U.S. 753 (1985).

10 *Bond v. United States*, 529 U.S. 334 (2000).

11   *Id.* (citing *Smith v. Maryland*, 442 U.S. 735 (1979)).

12   *Kyllo v. United States*, 533 U.S. 27 (2001).

13   *California v. Ciraolo*, 476 U.S. 207 (1986).

14   *Maryland v. King*, 569 U.S. 435 (2013).

15   *Soldal v. Cook County*, 506 U. S. 56 (1992).

16   *United States v. Jones*, 565 U.S. 400 (2012).

17   *Abel v. United States*, 362 U.S. 217 (1960).

18   *California v. Greenwood*, 486 U.S. 35 (1988).

19   *Smith v. Ohio*, 494 U.S. 541 (1990).

20   *Rios v. United States*, 364 U.S. 253 (1960).

21   *Hester v. United States*, 265 U.S. 57 (1924); *Oliver v. United States*, 466 U.S. 170 (1984).

22   *Florida v. Jardines*, 569 U.S. 1 (2013).

23   *Id.* (citing *Hester v. United States*, *supra* note 21; *California v. Ciraolo*, *supra* note 13; *Oliver v. United States*, 466 U.S. 170 (1984)).

24   *Collins v. Virginia*, 584 U.S. ___ (2018).

25   *Id.* (citing *Soldal v. Cook County*, 506 U.S. 56 (1992)).

26   *Davis v. Mississippi*, 394 U.S. 721 (1969).

27   *United States v. Verdugo-Urquidez*, 494 U.S. 259 (1990).

28   *INS v. Lopez-Mendoza*, 468 U. S. 1032 (1984).

29   *Burdeau v. McDowell*, 256 U.S. 465 (1921).

30   *United States v. Jacobsen*, 466 U.S. 109 (1984).

31   *United States v. Steiger*, 318 F.3d 1039 (11th Cir. 2003).

32   *Couch v. United States*, 409 U.S. 322 (1973).

33   *Carpenter v. United States*, 585 U.S. ___ (2018).

34   Sarah Zhange, *How a Genealogy Website Led to the Alleged Golden State Killer*, The Atlantic, Apr. 27, 2018, https://www.theatlantic.com/science/archive/2018/04/golden-state-killer-east-area-rapist-dna-genealogy/559070/; *see* Associated Press, Records *Show DNA from a Tissue Led to Golden State Killer Suspect Arrest*, nbcnews.com, June 1, 2018, https://www.nbcnews.com/news/us-news/records-show-dna-tissue-led-golden-state-killer-suspect-arrest-n879441.

35   *Coolidge v. New Hampshire*, 403 U.S. 443 (1971).

36   *United States v. Ventresca*, 380 U. S. 102 (1965).

37   *Coolidge v. New Hampshire*, *supra* note 35.

38   Jessica Miller, *New data show Utah judges are often spending less than three minutes viewing warrants before approval*, The Salt Lake Tribune, July 9, 2018, https://www.sltrib.com/news/2018/07/09/new-data-shows-utah/.

39   *Id.*

40   *See* 18 U.S.C. § 793(e), 18 U.S.C. § 1519; 18 U.S.C. § 2071.

41   Pres. Barack Obama, Exec. Order 13526, "Classified National Security Information" (Dec. 29, 2009).

42   Alex Leary, Aruna Viswanatha, and Sadie Gurman, *FBI Recovered 11 Sets of Classified Documents in Trump Search, Inventory Shows*, Wall Street Journal (Aug. 13, 2022), https://www.wsj.com/articles/fbi-recovered-eleven-sets-of-classified-documents-in-trump-search-inventory-shows-11660324501

43   *United States v. Grubbs*, 547 U.S. 90 (2006).

44   *Maryland v. Garrison*, 480 U.S. 79 (1987).

45   *Groh v. Ramirez*, 540 U.S. 551 (2004).

46   *Stanford v. Texas*, 379 U.S. 476 (1965).

47   *Ybarra v. Illinois*, 444 U.S. 85 (1979).

48   *Wilson v. Arkansas*, 514 U.S. 927 (1995).

49   *Richards v. Wisconsin*, 520 U.S. 385 (1997).

50   *United States v. Ramirez*, 523 U. S. 65 (1998).

51   *Hudson v. Michigan*, 547 U.S. 586 (2006).

52   *State v. Bamber*, 630 So. 2d 1048 (1994).

53   *See* KY SB 4.

54   *See* Michelle Mark & Rebecca Harrington, *33 States Still Regularly Allow the Kind of Police Raid That Killed Breonna Breonna Taylor*, The Insider, Sept. 24, 2020 (for further reading), https://www.insider.com/states-that-allow-no-knock-police-raids-breonna-taylor-2020-9.

55   ACLU, *War Comes Home: The Excessive Militarization of the American Policing*, June 2014, https://www.aclu.org/report/war-comes-home-excessive-militarization-american-police.

56   Kevin Sack, *Door Busting Drug Raids Leave a Trail of Blood*, N.Y. Times, Mar. 18, 2017, https://www.nytimes.com/interactive/2017/03/18/us/forced-entry-warrant-drug-raid.html.

57   Jason Riley, *Breonna Taylor Warrant Was 'Misleading,' Louisville Police Investigators Find*, WDRB.com, Oct. 7, 2020, https://www.wdrb.com/in-depth/breonna-taylor-warrant-was-misleading-louisville-police-investigators-find/article_5066abb4-08ee-11eb-983a-6f7458a23340.html.

58   Richard Oppel Jr., Derrick Bryson Taylor, & Nicholas Bogel-Burroughs, *What to Know About Breonna Taylor's Death*, N.Y. Times, Apr. 26, 2021, https://www.nytimes.com/article/breonna-taylor-police.html.

59   Phillip Bailey, Darcy Costello, & Tessa Duvall, *Exclusive: Breonna Taylor Had Nothing to Do With Illegal Drug Trade, Ex-Boyfriend Says*, Courier Journal, Aug. 27, 2020, https://www.courier-journal.com/story/news/local/breonna-taylor/2020/08/27/breonna-taylor-had-no-ties-drugs-ex-boyfriend-says/5641151002/.

60   *United States v. Ross*, 456 U.S. 798 (1982).

61   *Michigan v. Summers*, 452 U.S. 692 (1981).

62   *Bailey v. United States*, 568 U.S. 186 (2013).

63   *Muehler v. Mena*, 544 U.S. 93 (2005).

64   *Graham v. Connor*, 490 U.S. 386 (1989).

65   *See* Val Van Brocklin, *Can the Number of Police Officers Executing a Warrant Constitute an Excessive Use of Force?* police1.com, May 7, 2018 (for further reading), https://www.police1.com/legal/articles/can-the-number-of-police-officers-executing-a-warrant-constitute-excessive-force-dkvyMrzo5Npn7NFc/.

66   *Franks v. Delaware*, U.S. (1978).

67   *Terry v. Ohio*, 392 U.S. 1 (1968).

68   *Delaware v. Prouse*, 440 U.S. 648 (1979).

69   *New Jersey v. T.L.O.*, 469 U.S. 325 (1985).

70   Government officials do not even need reasonable suspicion for intrusive search of property at the border—for example, searching a car's gas tank (*U.S. v. Flores-Montano*, 541 U.S. 149 (2004)); however, agents must demonstrate reasonable suspicion for an "intrusive search" of people at the border—for example, a rectal exam/cavity search for drug smuggling (*U.S. v. Montoya de Hernandez*, 473 U.S. 531 (1985)).

71   *Terry v. Ohio*, 392 U.S. 1 (1968).

72 *Carroll v. United States*, 267 U. S. 132 (1925).

73 *Brinegar v. United States*, 338 U.S. 160 (1949).

74 *Illinois v. Gates*, 462 U.S. 213 (1983).

75 *Franks v. Delaware*, 438 U.S. 154 (1978).

76 Internal citations drawn from *States v. Halsey*, 257 F. Supp. 1002 1005 (SDNY 1966).

77 *Florida v. J.L.*, 529 U.S. 266 (2000).

78 *Aguilar v. Texas*, 378 U.S. 108 (1964).

79 *Spinelli v. United States*, 393 U.S. 410 (1969).

80 *Illinois v. Gates*, 462 U.S. 213 (1983).

81 *Massachusetts v. Upton*, 466 U.S. 727 (1984).

82 *Navarette v. California*, 572 U.S. 393 (2014).

83 *Adams v. Williams*, 407 U.S. 143 (1972).

84 *Weeks v. United States*, 232 U.S. 383 (1914).

85 *Wolf v. Colorado*, 338 U.S. 25 (1949).

86 *Lustig v. United States*, 338 U.S. 74 (1949).

87 *Elkins v. United States*, 364 U.S. 206 (1960).

88 *Mapp v. Ohio*, 367 U.S. 643 (1961).

89 *United States v. Calandra*, 414 U.S. 338 (1974).

90 *United States v. Janis*, 428 U. S. 433 (1976).

91 *Rakas v. Illinois*, 439 U.S. 128 (1978).

92 *Rawlings v. Kentucky*, 448 U.S. 98 (1980).

93 *United States v. Salvucci*, 448 U.S. 83 (1980).

94 *Minnesota v. Olson*, 495 U.S. 91 (1990).

95 *Minnesota v. Carter*, 525 U.S. 83 (1998).

96 *Michigan v. DeFillippo*, 443 U.S. 31 (1979).

97 *United States v. Leon*, 468 U.S. 897 (1984).

98 *Davis v. United States*, 564 U.S. 229 (2011).

99 *Herring v. United States*, 555 U.S. 135 (2009).

100 *Heien v. North Carolina*, 574 U.S. 54 (2014).

101 *State of Tennessee v. Jerry Phifer*, No. M2013-01401-CCA-R3-CD (Tenn. Crim. App. Sep. 23, 2014).

102 *Utah v. Strieff*, 579 U.S. 232 (2016).

103 *Id.* (citing *Hudson v. Michigan*, 547 U.S. 586 (2006)).

104 *Brown v. Illinois*, 422 U.S. 590 (1975).

105 *Silverthorne Lumber Co. v. United States*, 251 U.S. 385 (1920).

106 *Nardone v. United States*, 308 U.S. 338 (1939).

107 *Wong Sun v. United States*, 371 U.S. 471 (1963).

108 *Segura v. United States*, 468 U.S. 796 (1984).

109 *Brewer v. Williams*, 430 U.S. 387 (1977).

110 *Nix v. Williams*, 467 U.S. 431 (1984).

111 Charlotte Lawrence, *Federal Militarization of Law Enforcement Must End*, ACLU, May 12, 2021, https://www.aclu.org/news/criminal-law-reform/federal-militarization-of-law-enforcement-must-end/.

112 Exec. Order No. 13688 (2015).

113 Exec. Order No. 13809 (2017).

114 Jeff Sessions, Remarks at the 63rd Biennial Conference of the National Fraternal Order of Police, Aug. 28, 2017, https://www.justice.gov/opa/speech/attorney-general-sessions-delivers-remarks-63rd-biennial-conference-nation-al-fraternal; *see* Anna Gunderson, Elisha Cohen, Kayln Jackson Schiff, Tom S. Clark, Adam N. Glynn, & Michael Leo Owens, *Counterevidence of Crime-Reduction Effects from Federal Grants of Military Equipment to Local Police*, 5 Nature Human Behaviour 194–204 (2021), https://www.nature.com/articles/s41562-020-00995-5.

115 Kenneth Lowande, *Police Demilitarization and Violent Crime*, 5 Nature Human Behaviour 205–211 (2021), https://www.nature.com/articles/s41562-020-00986-6#citeas.

116 Matt Harris, *UT Study: Tactical Gear Does Not Cause Police to Be More Aggressive but More Oversight, Transparency Needed*, University of Tennessee Knoxville, Haslam College of Business (Aug. 29, 2017), https://haslam.utk.edu/news/ut-study-tactical-gear-does-not-cause-police-be-more-aggressive-more-oversight-transparency; *see* Matt Harris, Jinseong Park, Don Bruce, & Matt Murray, *Peacekeeping Force: Effects of Providing Tactical Equipment to Local Law Enforcement*, 9 American Economic Journal: Economic Policy 291–313 (2017).

117 Civil Rights Act of 1871, 17 Stat. 13.

118 *United States v. Classic*, 313 U. S. 299 (1941) (Later, the Supreme Court's decision in *West v. Atkins*, 487 U.S. 42 (1988), allowed for a Section 1983 lawsuit against a private-practice physician who had a contract to provide orthopedic services to prisoners at North Carolina's Central Prison Hospital. In that that case, the Court also observed, "It is firmly established that a defendant in a § 1983 suit acts under color of state law when he abuses the position given to him by the State.").

119 *Smith v. Wade*, 461 U.S. 30 (1983).

120 *Thompson v. Clark*, 596 U.S. ___ (2022). This decision interpreted Section 1983 to allow a tort claim for "malicious prosecution" to proceed so long as there is a "favorable termination" of the case for the defendant, which the Court interpreted as meaning there was any outcome except for a guilty verdict; thus, the prosecutor's decision to dismiss the case against Thompson was sufficient for his Section 1983 lawsuit to continue, even without a showing of inno-cence. Thompson had been arrested in Brooklyn, New York, after his sister-in-law called 911 to make an unfounded accusation that Thompson had abused his newborn daughter. After EMTs were denied entry to Thompson's apartment, four police officers entered, without a warrant, to effectuate an arrest. Thompson was charged with the crimes of obstructing governmental administration and resisting arrest, and he filed a Section 1983 alleging a Fourth Amend-ment violation, which can be raised via the tort of "malicious prosecution."

121 *Vega v. Tekoh*, 597 U.S. ___ (2022)

122 *Wyatt v. Cole*, 504 U.S. 158, 161 (1992).

123 *Daniels v. Williams*, 474 U.S. 327 (1986).

124 *Parratt v. Taylor*, 451 U.S. 527 (1981).

125 *Monell v. Department of Social Services of the City of New York*, 436 U.S. 658 (1978).

126 *Board of County Commissioners of Bryan City v. Brown*, 520 U.S. 397 (1997) (In this case, Justice O'Connor refused to allow the county to be held liable for knee injuries suffered by a woman who was forcibly removed from a car by an officer who used an *arm-bar* technique. O'Connor observed, "The plaintiff must ... demonstrate that, through its *deliberate* conduct, the municipality was the 'moving force' behind the injury alleged.").

127 *City of Newport v. Fact Concerts, Inc.*, 453 U.S. 247 (1981).

128 *Bivens v. Six Unknown Named Agents*, 403 U.S. 388 (1971).

129   *Davis v. Passman*, 442 U.S. 228 (1979) (applying *Bivens* to a violation of due process rights); *Carlson v. Green*, 446 U.S. 14 (1980) (applying *Bivens* to the Cruel and Unusual Punishment Clause).

130   In the aftermath of the 9/11 attacks, federal agents questioned more than 1,000 people whom the FBI alleged to be suspects in terrorist activity; approximately 200 of those individuals were labeled to be of "high interest" and incarcerated at the Administrative Maximum Special Housing Unit of the Metropolitan Detention Center in Brooklyn, New York. These individuals were kept in their jail cells for 23 hours per day and were not allowed to be released until "cleared" by the FBI. Lawsuits related to this detention included claims of improper physical abuse, strip searches, and body cavity searches, as well as alleged deprivations of food, religious freedoms, and the right to counsel. *Ashcroft v. Iqbal*, 556 U.S. 662 (2009); *Ashcroft v. Al-Kidd*, 563 U.S. 731 (2011); *Ziglar v. Abbasi*, 582 U.S. ___ (2017).

131   The case is *Ashcroft v. Iqbal*, 556 U.S. 662 (2009), but this quote is Justice Kennedy's interpretation of that 2009 ruling, as provided in his majority opinion in *Ziglar v. Abbasi*, 582 U.S. ___ (2017). Kennedy wrote the majority opinions for both cases.

132   *Ziglar v. Abbasi*, 582 U.S. ___ (2017).

133   *Hernandez v. Mesa*, 589 U.S. ___ (2020).

134   Foreign Claims Act of 1942 (Armed Forces Damages Settlement Act), Pub. L. 77–393, 55 Stat. 880 (codified at 10 U.S.C. § 2734).

135   In making that assertion, Justice Ginsburg cited *Tennessee v. Garner*, 471 U.S. 1 (1985).

136   *Egbert v. Boule*, 596 U.S. ___ (2022).

137   The report to the Washington Department of Licensing allegedly concerned a license plate on Boule's care that read "SMUGLER." The agent suggested that this violated state policies on license plates, but no action was taken by the state. The claims made to the IRS also resulted in no action against Boule.

138   *See, e.g., Wood v. Strickland*, 420 U.S. 308 (1975); *Anderson v. Creighton*, 483 U.S. 635 (1987); *Wilson v. Layne*, 526 U.S. 603 (1999); *Hanlon v. Berger*, 526 U.S. 808 (1999); *Saucier v. Katz*, 533 U.S. 194 (2001); *Brosseau v. Haugen*, 543 U.S. 194 (2004); *Messerschmidt v. Millender*, 565 U.S. 535 (2012); *Pearson v. Callahan*, 555 U.S. 223 (2009); *District of Columbia v. Wesby*, 583 U.S. ___ (2018); *Taylor v. Riojas*, 592 U.S. ___ (2020); *Hernandez v. Mesa*, 589 U.S. ___ (2020).

139   *Malley v. Briggs*, 475 U.S. 335 (1986).

140   *Messerschmidt v. Millender*, 565 U.S. 535 (2012) (quoting *Groh v. Ramirez*, 540 U.S. 551) (In *Messerschmidt*, the Court found that the Ninth Circuit had erred in suggesting that *Groh* offered a clearly established precedent to justify a denial of qualified immunity.).

141   *Pierson v. Ray*, 386 U.S 547 (1967).

142   *Wilson v. Layne*, 526 U.S. 603 (1999).

143   *Hanlon v. Berger*, 526 U.S. 808 (1999).

144   *Pearson v. Callahan, supra* note 138.

145   *Saucier v. Katz*, 533 U.S. 194 (2001).

146   Among the cases cited were *United States v. Diaz*, 814 F. 2d 454, 459 (7th Cir. 1987); *United States v. Bramble*, 103 F. 3d 1475 (9th Cir. 1996); *United States v. Pollard*, 215 F. 3d 643 (6th Cir. 2000); *State v. Henry*, 133 N. J. 104, 627 A. 2d 125 (1993); *State v. Johnston*, 184 Wis. 2d 794, 518 N. W. 2d 759 (1994); *United States v. Paul*, 808 F. 2d, 645, 648 (7th Cir. 1986); *United States v. Yoon*, 398 F. 3d 802 (6th Cir. 2005).

147   Aaron Nielson & Christopher Walker, *The New Qualified Immunity*, 89 So. Cal. L. Rev. 1 (2015).

148   *Mullenix v. Luna*, 577 U.S. 7 (2015).

149   *Id.* (citing *Hope v. Pelzer*, 536 U.S. 730 (2002)).

150 *District of Columbia v. Wesby*, 583 U.S. ___ (2018).

151 *Taylor v. Riojas*, 592 U.S. ___ (2020).

152 *Brosseau v. Haugen*, 543 U.S. 194 (2004).

153 *Rivas-Villegas v. Coresluna*, 595 U.S. ___ (2022)

154 *Lalonde v. County of Riverside*, 204 F.3d 947 (9th Cir. 2000).

155 *City Tahlequah, Oklahoma v. Bond*, 595 U.S. ___ (2022).

156 For examples of cases where the Court afforded qualified immunity in a *Bivens* claim, *see Reichle v. Howards*, 566 U.S. 658 (2012) (where two Secret Services agents assigned to protect Vice President Dick Cheney were afforded qualified immunity after being sued for removing a heckler who approached Cheney during a 2006 appearance at a mall in Beaver Creek, Colorado); *Saucier v. Katz*, 533 U.S. 194 (2001) (where the Court granted qualified immunity to a military policeman who removed a protestor from the audience at a 1994 speech given by Vice President Al Gore at Presidio Army Base in San Francisco. The notion of protecting the security of a government official played a role in each decision.).

157 *See Koon v. United States*, 518 U.S. 81 (1996).

158 *Gamble v. United States*, 587 U.S. ___ (2019).

159 *Brigham City v. Stuart*, 547 U. S. 398, 403 (2006).

Credit

IMG 7.1: Copyright © 2019 Depositphotos/zabelin.

CHAPTER 8

The Fourth Amendment

Warrantless Searches

"The Fourth Amendment has never been held to require that every valid search and seizure be effected under the authority of a search warrant."

—Chief Justice Fred Vinson, writing for the Supreme Court
in *Harris v. United States*, 331 U.S. 145 (1947).

Learning Objectives

After reading this chapter, you should understand why the Supreme Court has recognized the following types of warrantless searches and the rules governing them:

1. Consent searches
2. The plain view doctrine
3. Searches of crime scenes
4. Searches incident to arrest
5. Searches based on exigent circumstances
6. Sneak and peak searches
7. Inventory searches
8. Traffic stops and roadside searches of automobiles
9. Routine and *special needs* searches

Key Cases

Schneckloth v. Bustamonte, 412 U.S. 218 (1973)
Michigan v. Tyler, 436 U.S. 499 (1978)
Chimel v. California, 395 U.S. 752 (1969)
Warden v. Hayden, 387 U.S. 294 (1967)
Schmerber v. California, 384 U.S. 757 (1966)
Delaware v. Prouse, 395 U.S. 752 (1979)
Rodriguez v. United States, 575 U.S. 348 (2015)
New Jersey v. T.L.O., 469 U.S. 325 (1985)

Introduction

As noted in the conclusion of the previous chapter, the fundamental requirement of the Fourth Amendment is that searches and seizures be "reasonable."[1] Obtaining a warrant before performing a search or seizure creates a presumption of reasonableness. In this regard, the Supreme Court has gone so far as to declare: "Warrantless searches are presumptively unreasonable."[2] Even so, there are many situations in which it may not be reasonable to require police to obtain a warrant before initiating a search. Accordingly, the courts have recognized a number of exceptions to the warrant requirement. They have even held that, in certain situations, a limited search may proceed without probable cause, as long as there is reasonable suspicion criminal activity is afoot. Ultimately, neither term is explicitly well-defined in Supreme Court case precedent, although probable cause tends to connote a connection to the likelihood of criminal activity, whereas reasonable suspicion represents a "lower" standard that might be described merely as "something more than an officer's hunch."[3] Consequently, the jurisprudence dealing with warrantless searches is voluminous and complex. In this chapter, we examine the well-established exceptions to the warrant requirement as well as exceptions to the principle of probable cause.

REASONABLE SUSPICION: Suspicion based on specific and articulable facts that criminal activity is afoot.

Consent Searches

Regardless of their level of suspicion regarding possible criminal activity, police officers will often ask a person they encounter to consent to a search. This is especially common in automobile stops. Indeed, the great majority of warrantless searches are based on consent.[4]

Consent searches may be viewed as an exception to the Fourth Amendment altogether. To ask someone to consent to a search, police do not need probable cause or even reasonable suspicion. In this regard, the Supreme Court's majority opinion in *United States v. Drayton* (2002)[5] observed the following: "Even when law enforcement officers have no basis for suspecting a particular individual, they may pose questions, ask for identification, and request consent to search luggage—provided they do not induce cooperation by coercive means." However, the U.S. Court of Appeals for the Ninth Circuit has said that "refusal to consent to a stop or to a search does not give rise to reasonable suspicion or probable cause"—a sentiment accepted by courts across the United States.[6]

Essentially, when requesting consent to search, police are asking someone to waive their Fourth Amendment rights. As noted in the passage below, an individual who is asked to give consent for a police search typically retains the ability to refuse, but it is also axiomatic that persons may waive their constitutional rights, including those enshrined in the Fourth Amendment. Justice Samuel Alito, writing for the Supreme Court in *Kentucky v. King* (2011),[7] observed the following:

> When law enforcement officers who are not armed with a warrant knock on a door, they do no more than any private citizen might do. And whether the person who knocks on the door and requests the opportunity to speak is a police officer or a private citizen, the occupant has no obligation to open the door or to speak. And even if an occupant chooses to open the door and speak with the officers, the occupant need not allow the officers to enter the premises and may refuse to answer any questions at any time.

As we shall see, this exception to the warrant requirement based on consent is not at all simple.

What Constitutes Consent?

To be valid, consent must be freely and voluntarily given and not the result of police coercion. For officers to obtain consent merely by asserting their authority has long been recognized as impermissible, dating to a 1929 Supreme Court decision.[8] As the Supreme Court later declared in *Bumper v. North Carolina* (1968),[9] "Where there is coercion, there cannot be consent." Obviously, using force or intimidation to elicit consent would constitute coercion. In the *Bumper* case, though, police used deception—by claiming to possess a search warrant when they actually did

CONSENT SEARCHES:
Searches performed with the consent of the person whose person or property is being searched.

not have one. In reviewing this conduct, Justice Potter Stewart's majority opinion said that a grant of consent that followed the officers' false declaration of having warrant should be deemed involuntary, with Stewart specifically observing, "When a law enforcement officer claims authority to search a home under a warrant, he announces in effect that the occupant has no right to resist the search. The situation is instinct with coercion—albeit colorably lawful coercion."

Despite the limitations the Supreme Court has placed on the coercion of consent, under prevailing interpretation of the Fourth Amendment, officers are not required to inform suspects they have a right not to consent—per the high Court's decision in *Schneckloth v. Bustamonte* (1973).[10] Yet when determining whether to admit incriminating evidence obtained through a search allegedly based on the defendant's consent, the burden is on the prosecutor to show consent was freely and voluntarily given. Beyond that, when reviewing a search based on the alleged consent of the defendant, courts must consider the totality of circumstances, as noted in Justice Stewart's majority opinion in *Schneckloth*, which indicated, "Voluntariness is a question of fact to be determined from all the circumstances, and while the subject's knowledge of a right to refuse is a factor to be taken into account, the prosecution is not required to demonstrate such knowledge as a prerequisite to establishing a voluntary consent."

However, *Schneckloth v. Bustamonte* has been widely criticized. It is well known that many people are unaware they have a right not to consent or are conditioned to submit to the requests of those in positions of authority. Furthermore, one could argue that encounters with police are inherently coercive. Such criticisms have led some state courts to reject *Schneckloth v. Bustamonte* under the relevant provisions of their own state constitutions. In those states, officers are required to advise persons of their right to refuse consent.[11] Overall, regardless of the state, the best way to assert one's Fourth Amendment rights in such situations is to make use of the simple phrase, "I do not consent to a search."

The Scope of a Search Based on Consent

Consent searches are not unlimited in scope. In *Florida v. Jimeno* (1991),[12] the Supreme Court said that a "suspect may, of course, delimit as he chooses the scope of the search to which he consents." In his majority opinion, Chief Justice William Rehnquist observed, "It is very likely unreasonable to think that a suspect, by consenting to the search of his trunk, has agreed to the breaking open of a locked briefcase within the trunk, but it is otherwise with respect to a closed paper bag." Theoretically, one can terminate a consent search by clearly revoking one's consent, but as a practical matter, revocation of consent can become difficult if the search an officer has already started yields some reasonable suspicion or probable cause to invoke one of the valid categories of warrantless searches we will discuss in this chapter. We will thus address this concept at various points herein.

Third-Party Consent

A third party may consent to a search of real or personal property when there is common ownership or a sufficient relationship to that property. For example, in *Frazier v. Cupp* (1969),[13] the defendant's cousin consented to a search of the defendant's duffel bag. The Supreme Court held that this was valid consent because both men had used the bag and it had been left in the cousin's home. Two decades later, in *Illinois v. Rodriguez* (1990),[14] the Court indicated that a person who does not live in a particular dwelling could in fact grant consent for an officer to search that place as long as the officer has a "reasonable belief" that the person letting them in has authorization to do so. That might, for instance, allow the friend of a homeowner to consent to a search. In a 2006 decision, the Court even suggested that it would be "impractical to require the police to take affirmative steps to confirm the actual authority of a consenting individual whose authority was apparent";[15] that declaration provides broad latitude for an officer's reasonable belief that a person giving consent is authorized to do so.

This topic becomes particularly germane in the context of shared living spaces, something with which many college students are quite familiar. Generally speaking, a cohabitant may consent to a search of certain areas within a residence. Writing for the Court in *United States v. Matlock* (1974),[16] Justice Byron White observed that "when the prosecution seeks to justify a warrantless search by proof of voluntary consent, it is not limited to proof that consent was given by the defendant, but may show that permission to search was obtained from a third party who possessed common authority over or other sufficient relationship to the premises or effects sought to be inspected." A key phrase in that sentence is the reference to areas of "common authority." In a situation when a home is occupied by multiple persons who have their own bedrooms, consent to search is limited to the consenting person's bedroom—as well as the areas that the occupants might share in common, such as a kitchen, bathroom, or living room. Thus, a person could consent to a search of common areas but not to a search of the bedroom occupied solely by a roommate. Of course, if officers are lawfully present in a *common area*, things they might happen to observe from that vantage point could justify application of the plain view doctrine, which we discuss in the next section.

In *Georgia v. Randolph* (2006),[17] the Court confronted a situation in which cohabitants in a home disagreed about whether consent should be offered for a police search. Justice David Souter's majority opinion presented an exception to the standards articulated in *Matlock* by stating that "a warrantless search of a shared dwelling ... over the express refusal of consent by a physically present resident cannot be justified as reasonable." Therefore, if one person grants police consent to search a home, and then a cohabitant objects, the police must leave—even if the objection is raised after the consent-based search has begun. But Justice Souter made it clear that police who have been given consent to search are not required to then search the home for any potential objectors; specifically, Souter observed that, "it would needlessly limit the capacity of the police to respond to ostensibly legitimate opportunities in the field if we were to hold that reasonableness required the police to take affirmative steps to find a potentially objecting co-tenant before acting on the permission they had already received."

In a dissenting opinion, Chief Justice John Roberts raised concerns about "spousal abuse" in situations when cohabitants disagreed over granting consent to search. Eight years later, the Court would address this possibility with its decision in *Fernandez v. California* (2014).[18] In this case, a wife granted consent for police to search an apartment she shared with her husband—but the husband was present and objected. Upon noticing the wife had blood on her shirt and a bump on her nose, officers removed the husband from the apartment and arrested him. Police then returned one hour later and, with the wife's permission, conducted a search of the apartment; that search yielded evidence linking the husband to a robbery. On review, the Supreme Court upheld use of this evidence at trial. Justice Alito's majority opinion reaffirmed the core principle from *Georgia v. Randolph*, which he summarized as follows: "[T]he consent of one occupant is insufficient when another occupant is present and objects." However, in noting that the husband was not present to object to the search in *Fernandez* case, Alito went on to say, "We ... refuse to extend *Randolph* to the very different situation in this case, where consent was provided by an abused woman well after her male partner had been removed from the apartment they shared." Overall, the high Court has made it clear that an objector to a search of a shared residence must be physically present *when objecting* to nullify police authority to conduct a search.

Other aspects of consent to search a living quarters have come before the Supreme Court. For instance, the Court has made it clear that, absent an emergency, a landlord may not consent to a search of a tenant's apartment.[19] Along the same lines, a housekeeper may not consent to a search of the home in which they work, unless they are a resident of the home; and even then, consent would be limited to those areas they occupy (as well as the common areas of the home). Moreover, it is important that any third party who gives consent to a search is not acting as an agent of the police when doing so; we discuss this concept in greater detail in chapter 7.[20]

Elsewhere, the Court has found that a hotel clerk or manager generally may not consent to a police search of a patron's room. Along these lines, in *Stoner v. California* (1969),[21] the Supreme Court observed the following:

> No less than a tenant of a house, or the occupant of a room in a boarding house, ... a guest in a hotel room is entitled to constitutional protection against unreasonable searches and seizures. ... That protection would disappear if it were left to depend upon the unfettered discretion of an employee of the hotel.

More recently, a 2015 Supreme Court decision found that a City of Los Angeles ordinance that allowed police officers to search a hotel registry without a warrant amounted to a violation of the Fourth Amendment.[22] Writing for a 5-4 majority, Justice Sotomayor indicated that "the ordinance creates an intolerable risk that searches authorized by it will exceed statutory limits, or be used as a pretext to harass hotel operators and their guests."

The Plain View Doctrine

PLAIN VIEW DOCTRINE: The doctrine under which agents may make a warrantless seizure of evidence that comes into their plain view, as long as they have the right to be where they are when that evidence is discovered.

When evidence of a crime is in an officer's *plain view*, the officer does not need a warrant to seize that evidence—provided, of course, the officer makes the observation from a place they are permitted to be. In *Harris v. United States* (1968),[23] the Supreme Court held that "objects falling in the plain view of an officer who has a right to be in the position to have that view are subject to seizure and may be introduced in evidence." This plain view doctrine applies both to inadvertent discoveries and situations in which an officer is conducting a reasonable search for something else.[24] Hence, if an officer obtains a warrant to search a home for bomb-making materials and during the course of that search discovers an illegal automatic weapon, the latter is subject to seizure without a warrant. On the other hand, if an officer searching a home for a wanted fugitive opens drawers and boxes where no human being could hide and in so doing discovers illegal drugs, the plain view doctrine would not apply. The drugs could still be seized, as they are contraband, but they could not be used in evidence in a prosecution for drug possession.

CONTRABAND: Items that are illegal to possess.

The Supreme Court also has noted that a plain view search rests on the ability of an officer to demonstrate probable cause for discerning that an item is in fact contraband. Justice John P. Stevens's majority opinion in *Payton v. New York* (1980)[25] made this clear when he said, "The seizure of property in plain view involves no invasion of privacy, and is presumptively reasonable, assuming that there is probable cause to associate the property with criminal activity." Three years later, in *Texas v. Brown* (1983),[26] the Court confronted the conduct of an officer who effectuated a plain view seizure of balloons seen in the passenger seat of a man's car during a roadside stop; those balloons contained heroin, but defense attorneys argued that the heroin was only noticeable after the officer had improperly seized the balloons. The Texas Court of Criminal Appeals found that this seizure violated the Fourth Amendment because the presence of drugs was not "immediately apparent" to the officer upon seeing the balloons, and thus the plain view doctrine was inapplicable. However, the Supreme Court of the United States reversed, with Justice Lewis Powell's concurring opinion stating that probable cause could be inferred here "in light of the evidence that tied-off balloons are common containers for carrying illegal narcotics." Powell also added an important caveat for invocation of the plain view doctrine, stating that "a law enforcement officer may rely on his training and experience to draw inferences and make deductions that might well elude an untrained person."

The *Texas v. Brown* decision is important for another reason: it addresses the matter of an officer using an item to *enhance* their senses in the context of a plain view search. In this case, the officer used a flashlight to illuminate the presence of the balloons on the car's passenger seat, and Justice Rehnquist's majority opinion found no Fourth Amendment violation in the officer "changing positions" and shining the light. Previously, in a 1927 Prohibition-era case that predated articulation of the plain view doctrine, the Court similarly upheld the use of evidence observed by

Coast Guard officers who used searchlights to visually inspect a boat before boarding it; those officers uncovered illegally bootlegged grain alcohol, and the Court deemed this type of search acceptable within twelve miles of a U.S. shoreline.[27]

Later cases have authorized observations made by government agents from airplanes. In *Dow Chemical v. United States* (1986),[28] the Supreme Court upheld the EPA's use of a "standard ... aerial mapping camera" to photograph a business at altitudes of 12,000, 3,000, and 1,200 feet while "lawfully within navigable airspace." The majority opinion in that case did indicate that use of such photography in the context of a private home could be treated differently. Even so, in *California v. Ciraolo* (1986),[29] the Supreme Court upheld a warrantless search where police officers were flown in an airplane over the backyard of a person's house and then used binoculars to observe marijuana plants growing there, surrounded by high fences. Chief Justice Warren E. Burger's majority opinion stated, "[P]rotection of the home has never been extended to require law enforcement officers to shield their eyes when passing by a home on public thoroughfares. Nor does the mere fact that an individual has taken measures to restrict some views of his activities preclude an officer's observations from a public vantage point where he has a right to be and which renders the activities clearly visible." Three years later, this principle was applied to a case involving a helicopter search.[30]

But as discussed in chapter 7, in situations when police enhance their sensory perception to look inside the home with what might be called *unusual technology*, such as an infrared thermal imaging device,[31] then a search must be justified by a warrant—as opposed to the plain view doctrine. The nature of the technology utilized—and, perhaps, an individual's ability to *protect* against it (e.g., by closing one's blinds)—could play a role in evaluating the scope of plain view searches and seizures.

There are other limits to the plain view doctrine. In *Arizona v. Hicks* (1987),[32] police lawfully entered an apartment to search for weapons after receiving a report that a bullet had been fired from that apartment into an apartment below. During the search, they observed expensive audio equipment they suspected might be stolen. An officer then moved the equipment to take down the serial numbers. Upon receiving confirmation from police headquarters that the equipment was stolen, officers seized the items. On review, the Supreme Court disallowed the seizure because the serial numbers were not in plain view before the officers moved the equipment. The Court cited the seminal case on plain view, *Coolidge v. New Hampshire* (1971),[33] in saying, "The 'plain view' doctrine may not be used to extend a general exploratory search from one object to another until something incriminating at last emerges."

This concept of plain view also could apply to the notion of abandoned property, which was discussed in chapter 7. The Supreme Court has found that such items are not protected by the Fourth Amendment,[34] nor are things left in *open fields* outside of property boundaries,[35] including trash left on the curb outside of a person's home.[36] Nevertheless, there are some limits to the scope of what is deemed *abandoned*. For example, the Supreme Court has said that "a passenger who lets a package drop to the floor of the taxicab in which he is riding can hardly be said to have 'abandoned' it. An occupied taxi is not ... an open field."[37] Furthermore, in *Smith v. Ohio* (1990),[38] the Supreme Court said that a bag was not to be considered abandoned because it was placed on top of a car with the bag's owner nearby; thus, the bag was not subject to a warrantless seizure under the plain view doctrine.

Finally, it is important to recognize that the notion of a plain view doctrine encompasses all of an officer's senses, including smell, taste, hearing, and touch. In *Minnesota v. Dickerson* (1993),[39] for instance, the Supreme Court described a "plain feel exception," which could be used to justify a warrantless search in situations where an officer detects the presence of contraband item by touch. In this case, however, the Court found that the officer, who was conducting a pat-down search, could not have known—simply by touch—that the item he felt through outer clothing was in fact a bag filled with illegal drugs.

JURISPRUDENCE

Plain View Seizure of Clear Medical Vials Is Rejected by Federal Courts
United States v. Arredondo, 996 F.3d 903 (8th Cir. 2021)

In 2021, the Eighth Circuit confronted a case in which officers responded to a home following a call from a neighbor concerned about a disturbance that included sounds of doors slamming and a woman screaming. An officer rang the doorbell to this home, and an occupant partially opened the door. The officer's questioning about whether a woman was inside led the occupant to state that she was on the floor in a downstairs bedroom; at that point, the officer forced his way into the home pursuant to exigent circumstances. Further questioning of two male occupants and the woman ensued, indicating that the woman was drunk, but she said she was not hurt or facing any threats. An officer then asked one of the male occupants, Dane Arredondo, to retrieve identification, and when Arredondo went upstairs, the officer followed him. After approximately four minutes in that upstairs area, the officer noticed small clear vials, which led him to conduct research on his cell phone—and he ultimately determined that some of vials contained controlled substances. Arredondo explained he was a paramedic, but he could not produce prescriptions for the vials, which were seized. Federal drug charges were subsequently filed against him.

Pursuant to a pretrial motion, the district court judge concluded that, although the officer was permitted to be in the upstairs area because Arredondo had consented to the officer following him there, the vials should be suppressed because the "incriminating character" of the vials was not "immediately apparent." In reviewing an appeal from the prosecution, the Eighth Circuit agreed that the evidence should be suppressed. The Circuit Court's majority opinion avoided the question of whether the entry to the home itself or the officer walking upstairs were justified by exigent circumstances, noting that even if these were valid, the plain view doctrine did not authorize seizure of the vials.

Specifically, the majority said, "The plain view exception authorizes an officer to seize an object without a warrant if (1) the officer lawfully arrived at the location from which he or she views the object, (2) the object's 'incriminating character' is 'immediately apparent,' and (3) 'the officer has a lawful right of access to the object itself.'" In finding there was no probable cause, the court said of the officer: "When he came upon small glass containers that looked similar to containers that hold common household items, such as contact lenses, essential oils, or medications for insulin or fertility, there was no basis to immediately suspect contraband." The Court even offered the following important observation for plain view searches and seizures: "While [the officer] believed that the vials laying on the couch 'seem[ed] a little odd,' something seeming 'a little odd' is usually a hunch and not probable cause."

Searches of Crime Scenes

A correlated idea to the concept of plain view searches is the notion of searches that occur when police arrive at a crime scene. Imagine, for example, that police arrive at a house where a person appears to have been murdered. What can police do in terms of searching this home without first stopping to acquire a search warrant? Supreme Court case precedent has provided some guidance on this issue.

The decision in *Michigan v. Tyler* (1978)[40] involved a fire that occurred in a furniture store in Oakland County, Michigan just before midnight on January 21, 1970. Firefighters who had entered the store to extinguish the flames noticed evidence that pointed to arson. A fire chief and a police detective would later enter the scene around 2 a.m., before all the flames were doused, and they took pictures to use as evidence. Smoky conditions halted the investigation, but further evidence was gathered at 8 a.m. that day, after flames were completely extinguished. Weeks later, on February 16, a state arson investigator returned—with no search warrant—to gather additional evidence; subsequent visits and additional searches would follow. Ultimately, the furniture store owner was charged with arson, and at his trial, evidence garnered from the searches conducted the night of and the morning after the fire were admitted—as was evidence derived from the searches that occurred weeks later. On review, the Supreme Court upheld use of the evidence that was gathered on the night of and morning after the fire—but rejected use of evidence acquired without a search warrant in the weeks that followed. Justice Stewart's opinion for the Court declared that "once in the building [to fight a fire], officials may remain there for a reasonable time to investigate the cause of the blaze. Thereafter, additional entries to investigate the cause of the fire must be made pursuant to the warrant procedures governing administrative searches."

JURISPRUDENCE

Supreme Court Rejects Arizona's "Murder Scene Exception"
Mincey v. Arizona, 437 U.S. 385 (1978)

In *Mincey v. Arizona* (1978), the Supreme Court invalidated a "murder scene exception" recognized by the Arizona Supreme Court because it offered police an excessively broad ability to conduct warrantless searches of all parts of a location where a murder had allegedly occurred. In this case, an undercover police officer was shot in Mincey's apartment during a drug raid, and the officer later died. Homicide detectives arrived shortly after the shooting occurred, and without acquiring a warrant, they engaged in a four-day search that involved the following: photographing the entire apartment; opening drawers, closets, and cupboards; emptying clothing pockets; extracting bullet fragments from walls; pulling up sections of carpet; and seizing 200 to 300 objects.

In rejecting this expansive search, Justice Stewart's majority opinion stated that "a warrantless search must be 'strictly circumscribed by the exigencies which justify its initiation', and it simply cannot be contended that this search was justified by any emergency threatening life or limb." He went on to say that "a four-day search that included opening dresser drawers and ripping up carpets can hardly be rationalized in terms of the legitimate concerns that justify an emergency search." Justice Stewart rejected the state's purported justification of a "vital public interest in the prompt investigation of the extremely serious crime of murder." Stewart acknowledged, "No one can doubt the importance of this goal," but he added that "the public interest in the investigation of other serious crimes is comparable. If the warrantless search of a homicide scene is reasonable, why not the warrantless search of the scene of a rape, a robbery, or a burglary?" His concern, then, was that the murder scene exception in Arizona might lead to generalized exceptions for expansive searches of all locations where any crimes had occurred.

The *Mincey* decision would later feature prominently in the high Court's per curiam opinion in *Flippo v. West Virginia* (1999).[41] In this case, James Flippo made a 911 call, claiming he and his wife had been attacked while staying in a cabin in a West Virginia state park. Officers arrived on the scene and found Flippo's wife dead inside the cabin, with injuries to her head. Officers then spent sixteen hours searching the cabin; this included opening a briefcase and examining its contents, which included pictures and negatives that incriminated Flippo in his wife's death. The trial judge denied Flippo's motion to suppress the photographs and negatives that were taken from the briefcase, and the Supreme Court of West Virginia refused to review that decision. However, the U.S. Supreme Court unanimously reversed the trial court, finding that the lower court's "position squarely conflicts with *Mincey v. Arizona* ... where we rejected the contention that there is a 'murder scene exception' to the Warrant Clause of the Fourth Amendment." The Court's per curiam opinion indicated that police "may make prompt warrantless searches of a homicide scene for possible other victims or a killer on the premises" but added that "any general 'murder scene exception' [is] 'inconsistent with the Fourth and Fourteenth Amendments.'"

In terms of defining what constitutes a *prompt* search based on the **crime scene exception**, as suggested by the *Flippo* Court, it is valuable to reference the decision in *Thompson v. Louisiana* (1984),[42] where officers spent two hours searching a home after a dead body was found therein; that search yielded evidence that the deceased had been shot by his wife—evidence including a pistol found inside a closed drawer, a torn up note found in a waste basket, and a suicide note found inside an envelope that contained a Christmas card. These items were located by homicide investigators who arrived more than thirty minutes after other officers already had secured the scene and ensured that no other victims or suspects needed to be located. Even though the *Mincey* case involved a search that lasted sixteen days and the *Flippo* case involved a search that lasted 16 hours, the two-hour search in the *Thompson* matter fared no better from a constitutional standpoint, with the per curiam opinion in this case finding that "[a] two-hour general search remains a significant intrusion on petitioner's privacy and therefore may only be conducted subject to the constraints—including the warrant requirement—of the Fourth Amendment." For detailed searches of premises where a crime has occurred, officers who move beyond immediate observations of items in plain view are best served by taking the time to acquire a warrant—once the scene has been secured by a search for suspects or victims.

CRIME SCENE EXCEPTION: An exception to the warrant requirement under which police arriving promptly at a crime scene may conduct a brief search to secure the scene and locate evidence and suspects.

Searches Incident to Arrest

A different category of warrantless searches connects to police activity pursuant to an arrest. As we will discuss in chapter 11, the legal standard to justify an arrest is probable cause—the same threshold required of police when obtaining a search warrant. Of course, it may be difficult to obtain a search warrant in the immediate aftermath of an arrest. Beyond that, an officer's safety can depend upon evaluating the level of danger posed by an individual who is being taken into custody. To govern such situations, the Supreme Court has crafted specific parameters to guide warrantless searches that occur incident to an arrest.

The defining case on this topic is *Chimel v. California* (1969),[43] where the Court created a standard that legal scholars often refer to as the *arm's reach rule*—to indicate that an officer is permitted to conduct a warrantless search of an arrestee's person and any items within the arrestee's immediate reach. Justice Stewart's majority opinion offered the following justifications for this exception to the warrant requirement:

> [I]t is reasonable for the arresting officer to search the person arrested in order to remove any weapons that the latter might seek to use in order to resist arrest or effect his escape. Otherwise, the officer's safety might well be endangered, and the arrest itself frustrated. In addition, it is entirely reasonable for the arresting officer to search for and seize any evidence on the arrestee's person in order to prevent its concealment or destruction.

SEARCH INCIDENT TO ARREST: A warrantless search of a person being placed under arrest as well as the area within that person's immediate grasp and control.

Providing additional clarity regarding the area that can be searched, Stewart also indicated, "There is ample justification ... for a search of the arrestee's person and the area 'within his immediate control'— construing that phrase to mean the area from within which he might gain possession of a weapon or destructible evidence." The *Chimel* decision, though, placed clear limits on the scope of a warrantless search incident to arrest, which is discussed in the following Jurisprudence box.

JURISPRUDENCE

The Arm's Reach Rule for Searches Incident to Arrest
Chimel v. California, 395 U.S. 752 (1969)

On September 13, 1965, police officers went to the home of Ted Chimel in Santa Ana, California. The officers had a warrant to arrest Mr. Chimel for burglarizing a store that sold coins, but they did not have a warrant to search the home. Mr. Chimel was not at home when the officers arrived, but his wife allowed the officers to wait inside. After approximately fifteen minutes, Mr. Chimel returned home and was notified that he would be arrested. Officers then requested permission to "look around" the house, but Mr. Chimel refused. Undeterred, the officers announced their intention to search the entire house and ultimately did so, going through the three-bedroom home, including the attic and garage. The search, which lasted between forty-five minutes and one hour, involved officers opening drawers and moving around contents contained therein. Items including coins and tokens were seized and used against Chimel at trial. He was found guilty, and the conviction was upheld by both the California Court of Appeals and the California Supreme Court.

On review, though, the Supreme Court of the United States reversed. In an opinion that remains noteworthy for outlining the contours of the search incident to arrest exception to the warrant requirement, Justice Potter Stewart said that a search incident to arrest could involve officers searching the person being arrested as well as areas and items within that person's "immediate vicinity"—a standard that many have called the *arm's reach rule*. Key reasons for allowing this type of search involve protecting officer safety and preventing destruction of evidence. Stewart also defined the limits of these warrantless searches by declaring, "There is no comparable justification ... for routinely searching any room other than that in which an arrest occurs— or, for that matter, for searching through all the desk drawers or other closed or concealed areas in that room itself. Such searches, in the absence of well recognized exceptions, may be made only under the authority of a search warrant." In the end, application of this standard resulted in Chimel's conviction being overturned by the high Court—but the decision bearing his name continues to provide police with the ability to conduct warrantless searches of arrestees and their immediate surroundings.

In the two years after the *Chimel* decision, the Supreme Court twice confronted the matter of a person being arrested just outside of their home. First, *Shipley v. California* (1969)[44] involved a man being arrested while exiting his car fifteen to twenty feet from the entrance to his house. After the arrest, officers entered the home to conduct a search. Finding a violation of the Fourth Amendment, the Court's per curiam opinion quoted *Stoner v. California* (1969) in observing that a search "can be incident to an arrest only if it is substantially contemporaneous with the arrest and is confined to the *immediate* vicinity of the arrest."[45]

One year later, in *Vale v. Louisiana* (1970),[46] the Court in ruled in favor of a man whose home had been searched after police arrested him while he approached the front steps adjacent to the home's entrance. Justice Stewart wrote for the Court and said, "If a search of a house is to be upheld as incident to an arrest, that arrest must take place inside the house, not somewhere outside—whether two blocks away, ... twenty feet away, ... or on the sidewalk near the front steps." Later, in *Payton v. New York* (1980),[47] the Court clarified that "an arrest warrant founded on probable cause implicitly carries with it the limited authority to enter a dwelling in which the suspect lives when there is reason to believe the suspect is within." But the *Payton* decision also cited *Silverman v. United States* (1961),[48] where the Court observed that "[a]t the very core [of the Fourth Amendment] stands the right of a man to retreat into his own home and there be free from unreasonable governmental intrusion."

In *United States v. Robinson* (1973),[49] the *Chimel* decision was reexamined by the Supreme Court in the context of a minor offense. In this case, an officer searched Robinson after arresting him for operating a vehicle without a valid license. A cigarette package seized from Robinson's coat was found to contain packets of heroin, and he was later convicted of violating federal drug possession laws. On appeal, Robinson's attorneys suggested that the *Chimel* doctrine should not be applicable to this case because Robinson posed no clear threat to the officer's safety. An en banc panel of the D.C. Circuit did in fact overturn the conviction—but on review, the Supreme Court reversed the Circuit Court. Chief Justice Rehnquist delivered the majority opinion, which indicated that an officer's ability to conduct a warrantless search of an arrestee should not turn on any perceived danger that may or may not be posed by the person taken into custody. Rehnquist reinforced the core principles of *Chimel* as applied to a minor offense by stating, "The authority to search the person incident to a lawful custodial arrest, while based upon the need to disarm and to discover evidence, does not depend on what a court may later decide was the probability in a particular arrest situation that weapons or evidence would in fact be found upon the person of the suspect." Rehnquist also bluntly declared that a warrantless search incident to a valid arrest "requires no additional justification. It is the fact of the lawful arrest which establishes the authority to search. ..." This is provided, of course, that the search conforms to the boundaries set forth in *Chimel*.

Subsequently, the Supreme Court extended the *Chimel* rule to automobile searches connected to an arrest. In *New York v. Belton* (1981),[50] a state police officer in New York stopped a car for speeding, and after the officer detected the smell of marijuana and observed an envelope that contained marijuana, all four occupants were arrested. Pursuant to that arrest, the officer searched the vehicle and found cocaine in the jacket pocket of a passenger. The Supreme Court upheld use of the cocaine evidence at trial, with Justice Stewart's majority opinion finding that "police may ... examine the contents of any containers found within the passenger compartment, for if the passenger compartment is within reach of the arrestee, so also will containers in it be within his reach." Stewart added, "Such a container may, of course, be searched whether it is open or closed." Interestingly, more than six decades earlier—and of course prior to the existence of the *Chimel* doctrine—the Supreme Court's decision in *United States v. Lee* (1927)[51] indicated that a search of a boat could be accomplished "incident of a lawful arrest" of those individuals who were on the boat.

The apparently clear-cut rule for automobile searches incident to an arrest was tested decades later in *Arizona v. Gant* (2009).[52] Mr. Gant was arrested for driving a vehicle on a suspended license, and while he was handcuffed and locked in the back of the arresting officer's patrol car, Gant's vehicle was searched—with officers finding cocaine in the pocket of a jacket on the back seat. The Court of Appeals of Arizona and the Arizona Supreme Court both found the search in question to be unconstitutional, and on review, the Supreme Court agreed. The majority opinion by Justice Stevens stated that if a person is arrested outside their vehicle, the validity of a warrantless vehicle search of that vehicle could turn on whether the arrested person is close enough to the vehicle to access items within in—thereby overturning the *Belton* decision to make it compatible with baseline *Chimel* principles related to protecting officer safety.

Cell Phone Searches Incident to Arrest

Finally, we should recognize that all case precedents governing searches incident to an arrest are subject to the bright-line rule for cell phones established by the Supreme Court in *Riley v. California* (2014),[53] which we discuss in detail in chapter 9. This case makes it clear that searches of cell phones—even pursuant to an arrest where the phone is within the immediate control of the arrestee—should generally be supported by a search warrant (with limited exceptions). The majority opinion from Chief Justice Roberts specifically noted, "Cell phones differ in both a quantitative and a qualitative sense from other objects that might be kept on an arrestee's person." In essence, this quote spoke to both the amount of information that could be held on a cell phone as well as the personal nature of such information—with the confluence of these quantitative and qualitative considerations said to invoke a high expectation of privacy. Roberts's opinion juxtaposed that elevated privacy interest against the fact that data on a cell phone cannot be used as a "weapon to harm" to an officer's safety. Yet Roberts did allow for a warrantless physical inspection of a cell phone to ensure, for example, there is not a "razor blade hidden between the phone and its case."

Searches Based on Exigent Circumstances

The Supreme Court has used the term exigent circumstances to encompass situations in which some type of imminent emergency or threat of harm can be used to justify a warrantless search. Case precedent has specifically identified three subcategories of exigent circumstance exceptions to the warrant requirement: (1) emergency searches, (2) hot pursuit, and (3) imminent destruction of evidence.

The emergency search exception figures prominently in justifying warrantless entry into a home. Consider a situation in which a person is heard screaming for help from inside their house. Acquisition of a search warrant seems impractical in such a scenario, when immediate assistance might be needed and the time delay connected to procuring a warrant could imperil a person in distress. Along these lines, the Supreme Court's decision in *Mincey v. Arizona* (1978)[54] stated that "warrants are generally required to search a person's home or his person unless 'the exigencies of the situation' make the needs of law enforcement so compelling that the warrantless search is objectively reasonable under the Fourth Amendment."

As noted earlier, in a case decided less than one month after the *Mincey* ruling, *Michigan v. Tyler* (1978), the Court applied this principle to firefighters entering a home to extinguish a blaze, noting that "[a] burning building clearly presents an exigency of sufficient proportions to render a warrantless entry "reasonable."[55]

More recent cases have addressed the provision of *emergency aid* by police officers who conduct a warrantless entry into the home. In *Brigham City v. Stuart* (2006),[56] officers went to a home at 3 a.m. after receiving reports of a noise complaint. As they approached the house, the officers could hear screaming and shouting. Additionally, through windows and a screen door, they could see a physical altercation taking place in the kitchen, involving multiple individuals—including one who was spitting blood into a sink. Officers entered the home by opening a screen door and made arrests for disorderly conduct. Upholding this entry into the home as compatible with the Fourth Amendment, Chief Justice Roberts's majority opinion stated that "police may enter a home without a warrant when they have an objectively reasonable basis for believing that an occupant is seriously injured or imminently threatened with such injury." Roberts rejected contrary arguments suggesting that the injuries involved were not serious enough to justify an exigent circumstances entry:

> Nothing in the Fourth Amendment required [the officers] to wait until another blow rendered

EXIGENT CIRCUMSTANCES: Situations in which an emergency or imminent threat can be used to justify a warrantless search.

EMERGENCY SEARCHES: Warrantless searches conducted by police responding to emergencies, such as active shooters, fires, and bomb threats.

HOT PURSUIT: The close and avid pursuit of a fleeing suspect.

IMMINENT DESTRUCTION OF EVIDENCE: The situation in which police may conduct a warrantless search and seizure to prevent the immediate destruction of evidence.

someone 'unconscious' or 'semi-conscious' or worse before entering. The role of a peace officer includes preventing violence and restoring order, not simply rendering first aid to casualties; an officer is not like a boxing (or hockey) referee, poised to stop a bout only if it becomes too one-sided.

Roberts also addressed the manner in which officers entered the home in this case, noting, "The manner of the officers' entry was also reasonable. After witnessing the punch, one of the officers opened the screen door and [announced the police presence]. When nobody heard him, he stepped into the kitchen and announced himself again. Only then did the tumult subside. The officer's announcement of his presence was at least equivalent to a knock on the screen door. Indeed, it was probably the only option that had even a chance of rising above the din." For Roberts, the confluence of the emergency and the reasonable nature of entry into the home made this police action compatible with the Fourth Amendment.

Later, in *Michigan v. Fisher* (2009),[57] the Supreme Court confronted a case in which a homeowner indicated he did not want police officers to enter his home, but police officers made a judgment that emergency aid was needed. Specifically, as officers approached the house, they noticed three broken windows, with glass on the outside of the home. Looking through these window panes, officers saw blood coming from the homeowner's hands and witnessed him screaming and throwing things. An officer then pushed the front door open and entered the home. The homeowner pointed a rifle at the officer and was then arrested and charged with assault.

The Michigan Court of Appeals overturned the conviction in this case, suggesting the exigent circumstances exception to the warrant requirement did not apply because "the mere drops of blood did not signal a likely serious, life-threatening injury." However, on review, the U.S. Supreme Court reversed, with the per curiam opinion recognizing that, "Officers do not need ironclad proof of 'a likely serious, life-threatening' injury to invoke the emergency aid exception." The Court also rejected Fisher's argument that application of the emergency aid exception was undermined by the fact that officers never called for emergency medical personnel. The opinion addressed this concern and indicated that the test "is not what [an officer] believed, but whether there was 'an objectively reasonable basis for believing' that medical assistance was needed, or persons were in danger." In some ways, the *Fisher* decision leaves open the possibility for officers to utilize the exigent circumstances exception to the warrant requirement even when the report of an emergency turns out to be inaccurate—for example, if a neighbor reported screaming from an adjacent home, but the noise actually was emanating from a television set.

THE CONSTITUTION IN ACTION

Swatting Incident Leads to Fatal Police Shooting of Homeowner

On December 28, 2017, in Wichita, Kansas, an unarmed 28-year-old man named Andrew Finch was shot and killed by a police officer as Finch exited his home through the front door to see why police lights were flashing outside. Unbeknownst to Finch or the other family members who shared the home, including his mother and two children, Wichita Police had received a 911 call indicating a false report of a murder and hostage situation in their home. Such false reports are often known as *swatting*, and this call had been made from Los Angeles—apparently as a prank initiated by a dispute over an online video game. From a law enforcement perspective, even though the report turned out to be false, this type of call presents an exigent circumstance situation.

The origins of the tragic incident stemmed from two men from different parts of the country playing in an online *Call of Duty: WWII* video game tournament. The men argued about who was to blame for both of them losing a game and $1.50 each in wagers. The argument started in an online forum connected to the tournament host and then moved onto Twitter, where one of the men threatened to have the other *swatted*; the recipient of the threat responded by giving a fake address where he said he would be waiting, which turned out to be the address of Andrew Finch's home.

The man who made the threat followed through, enlisting the help of a 25-year-old homeless man named Tyler Barriss, who used a computer at a Los Angeles library to place a 911 call to Wichita authorities. In that call he claimed he had shot his father and was holding other family members hostage, which led officers from the Wichita Police Department to arrive at Finch's home. Within ten seconds after the unarmed Finch opened the door and stepped outside the house, he was shot once through the heart. He died seventeen minutes later at a local hospital.

Ultimately, for making the false 911 call, Barriss was charged with involuntary manslaughter under Kansas law, and he also pled guilty to forty-six federal charges—some related to telephone threats he had made in other contexts. He was sentenced to twenty years in federal prison. The video gamer who requested that Barriss make the call to Wichita authorities was sentenced to fifteen months in federal prison for conspiracy and obstruction of justice. The officer who shot Finch did not face any charges, and the Wichita Police Department classified the death as a "justifiable homicide."[58] In 2022, however, the Tenth Circuit ruled that qualified immunity did not apply to the officer's actions, allowing a civil suit brought by the Finch family to move forward.[59]

The Kansas legislature responded to this tragedy by passing a bill that makes it a felony to provide police with a false report that leads to injury; penalties can range from ten to forty-one years of incarceration. Additionally, in 2018, a member of the U.S. House of Representatives proposed the Andrew T. Finch Memorial Act, which would make it a federal crime to engage in false communications leading to an emergency response, with enhanced penalties if injury or death occurred; however, that bill never made it out of committee. Amendments to the Communications Act of 1934 also have been proposed to address this topic, but to date, nothing has reached the point of a vote in Congress.

Hot Pursuit

Another type of warrantless *exigent circumstance* search that has been authorized by the Supreme Court involves a concept that might sound like it came from a television show: *hot pursuit*. In simple terms, if a suspect is fleeing from the scene of a crime, and there is probable cause that a law has been broken, then police are permitted to enter a home in pursuit of that suspect—even without a search warrant or consent of the homeowner.

The initial Supreme Court case on this topic was *Warden v. Hayden* (1967).[60] In this case, an armed robber absconded from a cab company with more than $300 and then fled on foot, taking refuge in his nearby home. He was followed by two taxi drivers who reported the robbery and the location of the suspect to a police dispatcher. Officers were at the home within five minutes of the report, and they entered the dwelling without a warrant after the suspect's wife opened the door. The officers searched multiple rooms within the three-level house, ultimately finding the suspect in an upstairs bedroom. In addition, weapons were located in a nearby bathroom, and clothing that matched descriptions of what the suspect wore during the robbery was found in a washing machine. Reviewing this matter, the Supreme Court found no violation of the Fourth Amendment in either the entry to the home or the search for and seizure of evidence connected to the robbery. The latter was said to be justified in conjunction with the need to protect officer safety by securing any weapons that might be present, with Justice William Brennan's majority opinion noting the following:

> The Fourth Amendment does not require police officers to delay in the course of an investigation if to do so would gravely endanger their lives or the lives of others. Speed here

was essential, and only a thorough search of the house for persons and weapons could have insured that Hayden was the only man present and that the police had control of all weapons which could be used against them or to effect an escape.

Although the majority opinion in *Warden v. Hayden* did not explicitly use the term *hot pursuit*, a concurring opinion from Justice Abe Fortas employed the term when he stated that "[t]he use in evidence of weapons seized in a 'hot pursuit' search [is justifiable] because of the need to protect the arresting officers from weapons to which the suspect might resort."

Nearly a decade later, in *United States v. Santana* (1976),[61] the Supreme Court confronted a pursuit that began a matter of feet from the entrance of a house. In this case, officers had probable cause to believe that a woman named Dominga Santana was selling drugs from her home. Officers arrived at the home in a police van and saw Santana standing in the open doorway of the front entrance, some 15 feet away from the van. As officers exited the van and identified themselves, Santana retreated into the vestibule of the house. Officers pursued her through the open doorway and into the home, effectuating an arrest that led to a federal charge of possessing heroin with intent to distribute. Upholding the police action in this case, the Supreme Court's majority opinion said, "The fact that the pursuit here ended almost as soon as it began did not render it any the less a 'hot pursuit' sufficient to justify the warrantless entry into Santana's house."

There have been some limitations placed on hot pursuit searches. In *Payton v. New York* (1980),[62] the Supreme Court struck down a New York law that allowed officers to conduct a warrantless entry of a home to effectuate *any* felony arrest. The Court rejected this bright-line rule that applied to all situations, observing that the hot pursuit doctrine was not intended to be applicable to "routine arrests in which there was ample time to obtain a warrant." Following that decision, the Court's ruling in *Welsh v. Wisconsin* (1984)[63] indicated that "hot pursuit" entry into the home was not appropriate for "a nonjailable traffic offense that constituted only a civil violation under the applicable state law." Justice Brennan's majority opinion in this case also found the doctrine inapplicable "because there was no immediate or continuous pursuit of the petitioner from the scene of a crime ... [and] there was little remaining threat to the public safety."

Ultimately, the *Welsh v. Wisconsin* decision left some ambiguity regarding what types of misdemeanor offenses might, or might not, justify a warrantless hot pursuit entry into the home. The Supreme Court's recent decision in *Lange v. California* (2021)[64] attempted to provide clarity on this issue (although scholars might argue as to whether it actually did). In this case, an officer in a patrol car said he followed a vehicle traveling on public roadways because the driver was allegedly playing loud music with his windows down and honking his horn for no apparent reason. By the time the officer turned on his overhead lights, the driver (Lange) was approximately 100 feet from his home and, instead of stopping, Lange continued into his driveway, drove into his attached garage, and pressed a button to close the garage door. The pursuing officer parked his patrol car in Lange's driveway and walked up to the garage door just as it was closing, placing his foot under the garage to trigger a sensor that opened the garage door up all the way. The officer then walked into the garage and, upon seeing Lange, came to believe, for the first time, that he had been operating a vehicle while intoxicated. A sobriety test led to Lange's arrest and subsequent conviction on a misdemeanor charge of driving under the influence in violation of California state law. The California Court of Appeals upheld the conviction, suggesting any misdemeanor suspect who flees from an officer is subject to a warrantless hot pursuit entry into the home. On review, however, the Supreme Court of the United States unanimously reversed, finding that the police entry into Lange's garage was not justified by the hot pursuit doctrine and, thus, violated the Fourth Amendment. Justice Elena Kagan's opinion for the Court stated the following:

> The question presented here is whether the pursuit of a fleeing misdemeanor suspect always—or more legally put, categorically—qualifies as an exigent circumstance. We hold it does not. A great many misdemeanor pursuits involve exigencies allowing warrantless entry. But whether a given one does so turns on the particular facts of the case.

Justice Kagan also offered some guidance for that case-by-case approach:

> Our Fourth Amendment precedents thus point toward assessing case by case the exigencies arising from misdemeanants' flight. That approach will in many, if not most, cases allow a warrantless home entry. When the totality of circumstances shows an emergency—such as imminent harm to others, a threat to the officer himself, destruction of evidence, or escape from the home—the police may act without waiting.

Imminent Destruction of Evidence

We turn now to the third and final category of exigent circumstance searches the Supreme Court has authorized: warrantless police searches based on a need to prevent the **imminent destruction of evidence**. For casual observers of criminal justice issues, this category might seem inherently different than the other two categories—allowing warrantless police searches based on (1) providing emergency aid or (2) the pursuit of a fleeing felon; yet from a law enforcement perspective, the need to prevent evidence from being destroyed—particularly when such evidence can be easily consumed, disposed of, or perhaps flushed down a toilet—is paramount for holding criminals accountable. Thus, the Supreme Court has long indicated that officers can initiate a warrantless search, even of a home, to prevent the imminent destruction of evidence.[65]

Two 1963 cases resulted in majority opinions from the high Court speaking of "the imminent destruction of vital evidence," although in both decisions the majority said police had failed to demonstrate the applicability of this exception to the specific facts of their warrantless searches.[66] The seminal case in this area is *Schmerber v. California* (1966),[67] where the majority upheld the warrantless acquisition of a blood sample taken from a man named Schmerber, who was suspected of crashing his car while under the influence of alcohol. A doctor had procured the blood when Schmerber was taken to the hospital, despite his refusal to offer consent for the blood draw. Chemical analysis of the blood revealed Schmerber was intoxicated, and he was convicted in Los Angeles Municipal Court for "driving an automobile while under the influence of intoxicating liquor." On review, the Supreme Court upheld the use of this evidence at trial, with Justice Brennan's majority opinion observing, "The officer in the present case ... might reasonably have believed that he was confronted with an emergency, in which the delay necessary to obtain a warrant, under the circumstances, threatened 'the destruction of evidence'."

Later Supreme Court cases would apply the imminent destruction of evidence exception to searches at the home. For example, in *United States v. Santana* (1976), which focused heavily on the hot pursuit doctrine, the majority opinion's penultimate paragraph also observed, "Once Santana saw the police, there was likewise a realistic expectation that any delay would result in destruction of evidence."[68] Subsequently, in *Illinois v. McArthur* (2001),[69] police officers claimed to have probable cause that marijuana was being stored inside a home, and they used that as the basis for preventing McArthur from entering his home for approximately two hours as the officers waited for a search warrant to arrive. Upholding this police action, Justice Stephen Breyer's majority opinion found that officers "had good reason to fear that, unless restrained, [McArthur] would destroy the drugs before they could return with a warrant." Additionally, Breyer took note of the fact that officers "made reasonable efforts to reconcile their law enforcement needs with the demands of personal privacy by avoiding a warrantless entry or arrest and preventing McArthur only from entering his home unaccompanied." The combination of preventing destruction of evidence and the apparently limited intrusion on privacy—according to Justice Breyer—served as justification for the detention in question.

A decade later, an important guiding principle for police officers wishing to invoke the imminent destruction of evidence exception was offered in *Kentucky v. King* (2011). In this case, police officers set up a *controlled buy* of crack cocaine near an apartment complex in Lexington, Kentucky. An undercover officer witnessed the drug transaction and then radioed to other officers who were supposed to intercept the suspect. However, the suspect entered an apartment before officers could apprehend him—and to complicate matters, officers could not conclusively determine which of two apartments the suspect had entered; this eliminated use of the hot pursuit doctrine. Nevertheless, officers smelled marijuana coming from one apartment and banged loudly on the door, announcing their presence as police. Officers would later testify that what occurred next involved noises coming from the apartment that were consistent with evidence being destroyed—perhaps, people rushing about and sounds of a toilet flushing repeatedly. Officers then kicked in the door and saw marijuana and cocaine in plain view. A man named Hollis King, the original suspected drug dealer, was arrested and later convicted of violating state drug laws.

Justice Samuel Alito's opinion for the Supreme Court stated, "Under this doctrine, police may not rely on the need to prevent destruction of evidence when that exigency was 'created' or 'manufactured' by the conduct of the police." Even so, Justice Alito was careful to note, "In applying this exception ... courts require something more than mere proof that fear of detection by the police caused the destruction of evidence." Accordingly, the simple fact that officers announce their presence should not preclude a warrantless entry if the occupants of a home respond to the police presence by destroying evidence. In this regard, Alito recognized, "Destruction of evidence issues probably occur most frequently in drug cases because drugs may be easily destroyed by flushing them down a toilet or rinsing them down a drain." Then, in crystallizing a principle to take from this case, he added that, "Persons in possession of valuable drugs are unlikely to destroy them unless they fear discovery by the police. Consequently, a rule that precludes the police from making a warrantless entry to prevent the destruction of evidence whenever their conduct causes the exigency would unreasonably shrink the reach of this well-established exception to the warrant requirement." The opinion culminated with a rule to help guide the application of the imminent destruction of evidence exception to warrant requirements: "Where, as here, the police did not create the exigency by engaging or threatening to engage in conduct that violates the Fourth Amendment, warrantless entry to prevent the destruction of evidence is reasonable and thus allowed."

Despite firmly denoting that the officers in this case had not artificially created or manufactured an exigent circumstance, Justice Alito's opinion did not offer a final ruling regarding the constitutionality of the search; instead, the matter was remanded to the Supreme Court of Kentucky for a determination of whether the officers in this situation had probable cause to believe imminent destruction of evidence was occurring (based on hearing people rustling about and repeatedly flushing a toilet). On remand, the Kentucky Supreme

Court ruled in favor of King, reversing his conviction by noting, "Exigent circumstances do not deal with mere possibilities, and the Commonwealth must show something more than a possibility that evidence is being destroyed to defeat the presumption of an unreasonable search and seizure."[70]

Evanescent Evidence

Related to the imminent destruction of evidence is the notion of evanescent evidence, where the word *evanescent* refers to something that is fleeting or dissipating—perhaps, of its own accord, even without any human attempts to actively destroy it. The first Supreme Court decision to specifically use this term was *Cupp v. Murphy* (1973).[71] In this case, a man named Daniel Murphy was convicted of second-degree murder in the strangling death of his wife. Key evidence used against him at trial was a tissue sample from taken from underneath his fingernails. That evidence was acquired by police after Murphy voluntarily agreed to come to the police station to answer questions. While he was there, an officer noticed a dark spot that resembled dried blood under Murphy's fingernails and requested Murphy's permission to take a scraping from underneath the nails. Murphy refused, but despite his objections and without a search warrant, the police took the sample anyway. Tests revealed that skin and blood cells from the victim, as well as fragments of her nightgown, were underneath Mr. Murphy's fingernails.

> **EVANESCENT EVIDENCE:** Evidence that is likely to disappear if not seized immediately.

On appeal, the Supreme Court upheld the warrantless acquisition of this evidence. The majority opinion invoked the word *evanescent* in observing, "The rationale of *Chimel*, in these circumstances, justified the police in subjecting him to the very limited search necessary to preserve the highly evanescent evidence they found under his fingernails." Justice Stewart's majority opinion also observed that the imminent destruction of evidence concept was applicable here because "Murphy was sufficiently apprised of his suspected role in the crime to motivate him to attempt to destroy what evidence he could without attracting further attention." Specifically, in fact, Stewart said, "Testimony at trial indicated that, after he refused to consent to the taking of fingernail samples, he put his hands behind his back and appeared to rub them together." Thus, the confluence of evanescent evidence and the potential for imminent destruction seemed to play a role in this search being upheld by the high Court.

Later cases would ascribe the origins of the evanescent evidence concept to *Schmerber v. California* (1966), which, as previously noted, dealt with a warrantless blood draw in the search for evidence of impaired

PER SE RULE:
A generalized rule that does not take into account special circumstances.

driving. For example, *Missouri v. McNeely* (2013),[72] which also dealt with a warrantless blood test drawn from a driver thought be operating a vehicle while impaired, discussed the possibility of a "*per se* rule for blood testing in drunk-driving cases," where a per se rule means *applying in all cases* or, as noted earlier in this chapter, giving rise to a *categorical rule.* Specifically, the state of Missouri relied on the *Schmerber* case in seeking Supreme Court authorization for a standard whereby *all* situations in which an officer has probable cause to indicate a person is driving drunk would allow for a warrantless blood draw—based on the idea that blood-alcohol-content evidence is "inherently evanescent."

Evaluating this contention, Justice Sonia Sotomayor's majority opinion granted, "It is true that as a result of the human body's natural metabolic processes, the alcohol level in a person's blood begins to dissipate once the alcohol is fully absorbed and continues to decline until the alcohol is eliminated."[73] The opinion then cited *Schmerber* in suggesting "a significant delay in testing will negatively affect the probative value of the results," adding, "This fact was essential to our holding in *Schmerber*, as we recognized that, under the circumstances, further delay in order to secure a warrant ... would have threatened the destruction of evidence." However, despite the recognition that blood-alcohol evidence falls into the category of evanescent evidence, Justice Sotomayor refused to accept Missouri's argument for a *per se* rule, declaring instead that "... in drunk-driving investigations, the natural dissipation of alcohol in the bloodstream does not constitute an exigency in every case sufficient to justify conducting a blood test without a warrant." She concluded by saying that "where police officers can reasonably obtain a warrant before a blood sample can be drawn without significantly undermining the efficacy of the search, the Fourth Amendment mandates that they do so."

JURISPRUDENCE

Forced Vomiting and the *Shock the Conscience* Standard
Rochin v. California, 342 U.S. 165 (1952)

On July 1, 1949, three deputies representing the County of Los Angeles entered a residence that Richard Rochin shared with his mother, brothers, sisters, and common-law wife. Without a warrant, the officers entered the two-story home through an open front door and then forced their way into a second floor where Richard was sitting on a bed. When he saw the officers, he grabbed two capsules from a nearby nightstand and swallowed them. The officers then jumped on him and went about trying to extract those pills from his mouth. When those attempts were unsuccessful, officers handcuffed him and took him to a hospital. There, the officers directed a doctor to force a solution into Rochin's stomach, via an inserted tube, to induce vomiting. Ultimately, Rochin did vomit, and the two capsules were confiscated by police and found to contain morphine.

Rochin was charged with possessing a preparation of morphine, in violation of state law, and sentenced to sixty days in jail.

On review, the Supreme Court overturned his conviction. Although this case preceded the incorporation of the exclusionary rule in *Mapp v. Ohio* (1961),[74] the high Court unanimously found that the Due Process Clause had been violated by a search that "shocks the conscience." In his majority opinion, Justice Felix Frankfurter outlined the many flaws that undergirded police efforts to acquire evidence that might have been called *evanescent* some decades later. Frankfurter said, "[W]e are compelled to conclude that the proceedings by which this conviction was obtained do more than offend some fastidious squeamishness or private sentimentalism about combatting crime too energetically. This is conduct that shocks the conscience." After uttering that soon-to-be famous phrase, he offered comparisons to improper law enforcement tactics linked to medieval methods, saying, "Illegally breaking into the privacy of the petitioner, the struggle to open his mouth and remove what was there, the forcible extraction of his stomach's contents—this course of proceeding by agents of government to obtain evidence is bound to offend even hardened sensibilities. They are methods too close to the rack and the screw to permit of constitutional differentiation."

In a concurring opinion, Justice Hugo Black chastised the majority opinion for not defining more specific parameters for limiting police conduct of the sort displayed herein. Black lamented use of the "shock the conscience" approach as "nebulous," specifically saying, "I believe that faithful adherence to the specific guarantees in the Bill of Rights insures a more permanent protection of individual liberty than that which can be afforded by the nebulous standards stated by the majority." In some ways, Justice Black might take solace in the wide body of case precedent that has come to guide warrantless searches since this 1952 decision—but in another regard, the breadth of these exceptions could lead to accusations that modern opinions remain nebulous in protecting an individual's Fourth Amendment rights from government intrusion.

Sneak and Peek Searches

The sneak and peek search represents one of the most controversial categories of warrantless searches. It applies when an illegal search by law enforcement is followed by a subsequent valid search of the same property and, in essence, the latter search ends up serving as a means of excusing the first improper search. While it sounds odd for any police search that is patently unconstitutional to later be excused, this can happen as a result of the Supreme Court's precedent in *Murray v. United States* (1988).[75]

In *Murray*, the Court upheld the actions of police officers who essentially broke into a Boston, Massachusetts warehouse prior to acquiring a search warrant for that premises. The officers, acting based on tips provided by informants, had been conducting surveillance on two suspected drug dealers who drove large vehicles into and out of that warehouse. The vehicles were stopped by police after leaving the warehouse, and drug evidence was found inside the vehicles; the drivers were then arrested. Subsequently, officers decided to enter the warehouse without first obtaining a search warrant. Once inside, they observed bales of marijuana, but understanding that they did not have a search

SNEAK AND PEEK SEARCH: An illegal warrantless search that is later rectified by a warrant authorizing a more extensive search of the same premises.

warrant, the officers left the scene undisturbed and then applied for one. The request for the warrant did not mention the unauthorized entry into the warehouse, and that warrant was granted by a judge some eight hours after the officers had initially exited the warehouse.

On review, the Supreme Court upheld a trial court's use of the drug evidence seized inside this warehouse after procurement of the warrant. Justice Scalia's majority opinion in this case relied on the independent source doctrine. Applying that idea to the so-called "sneak and peek search" (which is a colloquial term not mentioned in the Court's opinion), Justice Scalia said the following:

INDEPENDENT SOURCE DOCTRINE: Doctrine under which improperly seized evidence can be admitted into evidence if police can demonstrate some other method by which the same evidence was lawfully acquired.

> As the Court today recognizes, the independent source exception to the exclusionary rule 'allows admission of evidence that has been discovered by means wholly independent of any constitutional violation.' ... The independent source exception, like the inevitable discovery exception, is primarily based on a practical view that, under certain circumstances, the beneficial deterrent effect that exclusion will have on future constitutional violations is too slight to justify the social cost of excluding probative evidence from a criminal trial. When the seizure of the evidence at issue is 'wholly independent of' the constitutional violation, then exclusion arguably will have no effect on a law enforcement officer's incentive to commit an unlawful search.

Linking these concepts to the case at hand, Justice Scalia found that the issuance of the search warrant—and, by extension, the officers' second entry into the warehouse—was "wholly independent" of the first, improper entry. Thus, the evidence seized pursuant to the search warrant was, according to the high Court's majority, properly admitted at trial—and, in turn, the sneak and peek exception was codified into precedent.

Sneak and Peak Search Warrants

Section 213 of the USA PATRIOT Act of 2001[76] authorized federal judges to issue warrants to allow sneak and peak searches. These searches are normally effected by covert entry and do not require notification to a property owner. However, sneak and peak warrants do not permit seizures; they are designed to allow officers to gain a quick view of what is taking place inside a particular premises. Issuance of such warrants requires a showing of probable cause. Generally speaking, under this law, sneak and peak warrants were designed to facilitate investigations of terrorism, but today they are used more commonly in drug investigations.

Inventory Searches

Typically, any law enforcement agency that impounds a car for reasons such as parking violations or abandonment, or even pursuant to the driver's arrest, will conduct an **inventory search** of that vehicle—often without a warrant or consent—and usually in the owner's absence. The primary justification for such a search is to provide an inventory of the vehicle's contents to ensure those items, particularly if they are valuable, are not damaged or lost while in police custody. Of course, such inventories carry the potential of revealing contraband or other evidence of crime.

> **INVENTORY SEARCH:**
> A search of a person being arrested or a vehicle being impounded to make an inventory of personal property found on that person or within that automobile.

The first Supreme Court case to address this topic was *Harris v. United States* (1968).[77] In this case, Harris was seen driving away from the scene of a robbery, and District of Columbia police later arrested him as he was entering that vehicle near his home. The car was impounded while police attempted to determine if Harris was the vehicle's rightful owner. Under D.C. Metropolitan Police Department policy for impounded vehicles at that time, an officer was tasked with searching the vehicle and removing any valuables. After an officer completed this search, he attempted to close the car's windows because it was beginning to rain. This required him to open each door and manually roll up the windows individually. Upon opening the passenger-side door, the officer saw the vehicle's registration card wedged onto the metal stripping over which the door would close. That registration card, which contained the name of the robbery victim, was used to demonstrate the car was stolen. Upholding the use of this card as evidence in Harris's robbery trial, the Supreme Court's per curiam opinion stated that "the discovery of the card was not the result of a search of the car, but of a measure taken to protect the car while it was in police custody. Nothing in the Fourth Amendment requires the police to obtain a warrant in these narrow circumstances."

Subsequently, in *Cady v. Dombrowski* (1973),[78] the Court addressed an inventory search conducted after a one-car accident led officers to have that damaged vehicle towed to a garage seven miles from their police station. The car was left there unattended overnight, and the driver was charged with the crime of operating a motor vehicle under the influence of alcohol. The following day, an officer went to conduct a search of the vehicle—without a warrant—in an attempt to locate a gun the driver, who was identified as a police officer named Dombrowski, was believed to possess. A gun was not found, but several bloody items were seized from the trunk, including police uniform trousers, a nightstick with the name *Dombrowski* on it, a raincoat, a car floor mat, and a towel. Police later learned that a dead body had been found on a farm owned by Officer Dombrowski's brother. Evidence seized from this vehicle was then used against Officer Dombrowski at trial, and he was found guilty of first-degree murder.

On review, the Supreme Court upheld two aspects of the police action in this case as consistent with the Fourth Amendment. First, the Court found that towing the car from the site of the accident in a rural Wisconsin town was acceptable, with Chief Justice Rehnquist's majority opinion observing that the vehicle "represented a nuisance, and there is no suggestion in the record that the officers' action in exercising control over it by having it towed away was unwarranted either in terms of state law or sound police procedure." Second, Rehnquist noted that "local police officers, unlike federal officers, frequently investigate vehicle accidents in which there is no claim of criminal liability and engage in what, for want of a better term, may be described as community caretaking functions, totally divorced from the detection, investigation, or acquisition of evidence relating to the violation of a criminal statute." He suggested one of those caretaking functions involved ensuring a possible weapon left in this unsecured vehicle did not fall into the wrong hands. On this point, Rehnquist said, "Where, as here, the trunk of an automobile, which the officer reasonably believed to contain a gun, was vulnerable to intrusion by vandals, we hold that the search was not 'unreasonable' within the meaning of the Fourth and Fourteenth Amendments." Under this portrayal, the officer was performing a service for the individual property owner and for the community in general—hence, Justice Rehnquist offered the genesis of a community caretaker exception to the warrant requirement. In dissent, Justice Brennan was less sanguine about the police motives in this case, suggesting, "The police knew what they were looking for, and had ample opportunity to obtain a warrant."

In 1976, the Supreme Court's *South Dakota v. Opperman*[79] decision addressed a more innocuous situation that led police to impound a car: too many unpaid parking tickets. Once that car arrived at the police impound lot, an officer searched the vehicle and cataloged its contents, which included marijuana found in the glove compartment. When the

COMMUNITY CARETAKER EXCEPTION: An exception to the warrant requirement that allows officers to seize evidence discovered during activities that are unrelated to criminal enforcement, such as providing assistance to people in distress.

owner arrived at the police station seeking to claim his vehicle, he was arrested and charged with possession of a controlled substance. Although the U.S. Supreme Court of South Dakota overturned his conviction, citing a violation of the Fourth Amendment, the Supreme Court disagreed, upholding this inventory search by suggesting it was a part of the police role in serving as a community caretaker—through ensuring that none of the individual's property was lost while the car was in law enforcement custody. Chief Justice Burger's majority opinion spoke of the "routine practice of securing and inventorying the automobiles' contents" and articulated three justifications for an inventory search of an impounded vehicle: (1) "the protection of the owner's property while it remains in police custody," (2) "the protection of the police against claims or disputes over lost or stolen property," and (3) "the protection of the police from potential danger." Burger also observed, "These caretaking procedures have almost uniformly been upheld by the state courts, which, by virtue of the localized nature of traffic regulation, have had considerable occasion to deal with the issue." That focus on deference to the judgment of local officials seems to be an important component of the "community caretaker" concept.

In *Illinois v. Lafayette* (1983),[80] the Supreme Court extended the inventory search doctrine to the contents of a shoulder bag a man had with him at the police station as he was being booked after an arrest on charges of disturbing the peace. In this case, the majority opinion cited *South Dakota v. Opperman* in recognizing that:

> ... it is reasonable for police to search the personal effects of a person under lawful arrest as part of the routine administrative procedure at a police station house incident to booking and jailing the suspect. The justification for such searches does not rest on probable cause, and hence the absence of a warrant is immaterial to the reasonableness of the search. Indeed, we have previously established that the inventory search constitutes a well-defined exception to the warrant requirement.

Less than a decade later, the high Court's decision in *Florida v. Wells* (1990)[81] placed some limits on the scope of an automobile inventory search. In this case, the officer conducting an inventory search opened a closed suitcase found inside the trunk of the vehicle, revealing the presence of marijuana. In determining that this evidence should have been inadmissible at trial, the majority opinion from Chief Justice Rehnquist suggested that because the Florida Highway Patrol lacked a uniform policy "with respect to the opening of closed containers encountered during an inventory search ... the instant search was not sufficiently regulated to satisfy the Fourth Amendment." He went on to say, "Our view that standardized criteria [and] established routine ... must regulate the opening of containers found during inventory searches is based on the principle that an inventory search must not be a ruse for a general rummaging in order to discover incriminating evidence" (internal citations omitted). But Rehnquist offered some leeway to law enforcing, noting that "[a] police officer may be allowed sufficient latitude to determine whether a particular container should or should not be opened in light of the nature of the search and characteristics of the container itself."

More recently, with its 2021 decision in *Caniglia v. Strom*,[82] the high Court refused to extend the community caretaker exception to searches of the home. In the *Caniglia* case, police had confiscated guns from a man after officers entered his home pursuant to a report of allegedly unstable mental behavior. Caniglia apparently had placed a gun on a table inside his home and asked his wife to end his life. She responded by leaving the house and spending the night in a hotel room, then calling police the next day when her husband did not reply to attempted contact. Police responded to the residence to conduct a welfare check and were able to convince Caniglia to be taken to a local hospital, via ambulance, for a psychiatric evaluation. Caniglia agreed to go only after officers promised not to seize his guns—but once he had left the premises, officers did, in fact, confiscate the weapons.

The Supreme Court's opinion in *Caniglia v. Strom*, written by Justice Clarence Thomas, harkened back to the first decision to speak of a community caretaking role in order to distinguish the present matter from that prior decision. More specifically, Thomas declared that *Cady v. Dombrowski* (1973) rested on the idea that "police officers who patrol the public highways are often called upon to discharge noncriminal community caretaking functions, such as responding to disabled vehicles or investigating accidents." He went on to say, "The question today is whether *Cady's* acknowledgment of these 'caretaking' duties creates a standalone doctrine that justifies warrantless searches and seizure in the home," with Thomas then declaring: "It does not." A key to this holding was the rationale that "[t]he 'very core' of the [Fourth Amendment's] guarantees is 'the right of a [person] to retreat into [their] own home and there be free from unreasonable government intrusion'"—a quote derived from Justice Scalia's majority opinion in *Florida v. Jardines* (2013).[83] In the end, the application of any exception to the warrant requirement seems to incur higher levels of scrutiny from reviewing courts when the search in question occurs in a person's home.

Traffic Stops and Roadside Searches of Automobiles

For the purposes of Fourth Amendment analysis, traffic stops can be dissected through a two-part process. According to the Supreme Court, there is one legal standard to pull a car over and another standard to search the car once it is stopped. For police to initiate a traffic stop, there must be reasonable suspicion of illegal activity; subsequently, to search a vehicle, an officer must demonstrate probable cause of illegal activity. We consider each phase of automobile stops separately in this section.

As a backdrop for this analysis, we recognize the Supreme Court has repeatedly indicated a lesser expectation of privacy adheres to an automobile than to a home. The majority opinion in *South Dakota v. Opperman* (1976),[84] for example, observed the following:

> Automobiles, unlike homes, are subjected to pervasive and continuing governmental regulation and controls, including periodic inspection and licensing requirements. As an everyday occurrence, police stop and examine vehicles when license plates or inspection stickers have expired, or if other violations, such as exhaust fumes or excessive noise, are noted, or if headlights or other safety equipment are not in proper working order. The expectation of privacy as to automobiles is further diminished by the obviously public nature of automobile travel.

Traffic Stops: Getting Pulled Over

The Supreme Court's seminal decision on this topic, *Delaware v. Prouse* (1979)[85] stated that police must have "reasonable suspicion" of a traffic violation or an arrestable offense to initiate a traffic stop. In this case, prior to initiating the traffic stop, the officer had observed "neither traffic or equipment violations nor any suspicious activity" (according to the majority opinion) and when the officer was asked about this stop during an evidence suppression hearing at the trial court, he bluntly declared, "I saw the car in the area and wasn't answering any complaints, so I decided to pull them off." The officer apparently just wanted to check the driver's license and registration. Once the car was stopped, the officer saw marijuana in plain view in the car, and the driver was arrested.

After the defense filed a pretrial motion to suppress the drug evidence, the trial judge ruled the traffic stop violated the Fourth Amendment, and thus, the seizure of the marijuana fell under the fruit of a poisonous tree doctrine. The Delaware Supreme Court agreed with the trial court's decision to suppress, as would the Supreme Court of the United States on review. Justice White's majority opinion noted that an automobile tends to carry a lesser expectation of privacy than a home, but he added the following caveat: "An individual operating or traveling in an automobile does not lose all reasonable expectation of privacy." To buttress this assertion, he expounded upon the fundamental importance of driving by saying, "Automobile travel is a basic, pervasive, and often necessary mode of transportation to and from one's home, workplace, and leisure activities." He also spoke to the level of intrusion at hand by observing that "random stops may entail 'a possibly unsettling show of authority,' and 'may create substantial anxiety.'" Justice White concluded that "except in those situations in which there is at least articulable and reasonable suspicion that a motorist is unlicensed or that an automobile is not registered, or that either the vehicle or an occupant is otherwise subject to seizure for violation of law, stopping an automobile and detaining the driver in order to check his driver's license and the registration of the automobile are unreasonable under the Fourth Amendment."

Ultimately, the standard of reasonable suspicion represents a low threshold—but it is a standard nonetheless, so police must have something specific to articulate as the source of a traffic stop. Of course, basic traffic violations like running a red light, speeding, or swerving out of a lane will suffice.[86] Even a minor violation like not wearing a seat belt is grounds to stop a vehicle in most places, although that can vary across jurisdictions (see below for the box discussing secondary offenses); and although a *pretextual stop*, meaning one in which the officer provides a false reason as a cover for stopping and searching a car, will not be upheld by the Supreme Court, if an actual traffic violation has occurred, that is sufficient for a stop.[87] Overall, reasonable suspicion must be something "more substantial than inarticulate hunches," per *Terry v. Ohio* (1968),[88] where the Court first used this standard by applying it to pat-down searches (see chapter 10).

A later auto stop case from the Supreme Court is *United States v. Arvizu* (2002),[89] which could be classified as a *win* for the police. In this case, the Court upheld a stop that occurred in Arizona near the U.S.–Mexico border. A U.S. border patrol agent was driving when he passed a vehicle on a remote road and then decided to turn around and follow it. The agent initiated a traffic stop based on a variety of factors that included the driver not waving at the officer as they passed each other, the driver having his hands in a 10 and 2 position on the steering wheel, the children in the back seat waving in an abnormal fashion and having their legs raised, and the driver suddenly taking a final exit before a border checkpoint. Once the vehicle was stopped, the officer detected bins containing marijuana under the legs of the children. More than 100 pounds of marijuana were seized, and the driver was charged with violating federal drug laws.

Evaluating this traffic stop, the Ninth Circuit noted that each individual factor used to justify the traffic stop, when taken in isolation, could be rationally explained as innocent activity; taking that approach, the Ninth Circuit said that the drug evidence should be inadmissible. However, on review, the Supreme Court disagreed. Instead of focusing upon each individual reasons on its own, Chief Justice Rehnquist employed the totality of circumstances approach and found that the officer's judgment in making the traffic stop comported with the Fourth Amendment; specifically, he said:

> When discussing how reviewing courts should make reasonable-suspicion determinations, we have said repeatedly that they must look at the 'totality of the circumstances' of each case to see whether the detaining officer has a 'particularized and objective basis' for suspecting legal wrongdoing. This process allows officers to draw on their own experience and specialized training to make inferences from and deductions about the cumulative information available to them that 'might well elude an untrained person.'[90]

This line of reasoning provides officers with the ability to take details that may seem innocuous on their own and collectively use them as grounds for a traffic stop.

JURISPRUDENCE

Are Police Checking Your License Plate as You Drive?
Kansas v. Glover, 589 U.S. ___ (2020)

A recent Supreme Court auto stop case addressed the police practice of following cars and checking license plate numbers in a computerized database *before* initiating a traffic stop. Charles Glover Jr. was pulled over after a police officer who was following him checked the vehicle's license plate and realized the car's registered owner had a suspended license. That became the sole justification for the traffic stop.

Upon initiating the stop, the officer realized Glover was driving his own car, which was registered in his name, and his license was indeed suspended. Glover was charged with the offense of driving without a license. On appeal, his lawyers challenged the validity of the auto stop by attacking the assumption that the owner of a vehicle is always the driver. His lawyers said this presumption equated to a violation of the Fourth Amendment because it failed to provide individualized reasonable suspicion for a traffic stop. The Supreme Court rejected this contention, saying the officer made a "commonsense inference" that the registered owner of a car is likely to be the person driving it. Therefore, the Court ruled that the traffic stop was a reasonable one, with Justice Thomas's majority opinion observing that "we have previously stated that officers, like jurors, may rely on probabilities in the reasonable suspicion context" (citing *United States v. Cortez*,[91] where officers used footprints in the desert to predict where a vehicle might stop to pick up illegal immigrants). Thomas also relied upon the totality of circumstances approach but noted that this could, in some cases, defeat the presumption that the registered owner is the one driving the vehicle—something that might be relevant for, say, a college student who drives a car registered in their parent's name. Whether situations like that lead to further refinement of this case precedent remains to be seen.

Requests to Exit a Vehicle During a Traffic Stop

When a vehicle has been stopped by police, it is plausible that an officer might ask for the driver to exit the vehicle. This could involve asking a driver to step onto the shoulder of the road, so an officer is not left attempting to converse while standing near the path of oncoming traffic. The key question, of course, is whether such a request is constitutional. According to precedent, it is.

In *Pennsylvania v. Mimms* (1977),[92] the Supreme Court found an officer's request for the driver to exit their vehicle during a traffic stop is a reasonable one—noting the protection of officer safety is a "legitimate and weighty" justification. In particular, the per curiam opinion said, "[W]e have specifically recognized the inordinate risk confronting an officer as he approaches a person seated in an automobile," with statistics related to police shootings at traffic stops offered to demonstrate "that a significant percentage of murders of police officers occurs when the officers are making traffic stops." The Court also spoke of "[t]he hazard of accidental injury from passing traffic to an officer standing on the driver's side of the vehicle. ..." These safety considerations were balanced against what the Court said were de minimis intrusions upon the driver's personal liberty associated with stepping out of the car—particularly in light of the fact that the driver's conduct had already evinced reasonable suspicion to support a traffic stop. Thus, no violation of the Fourth Amendment connects to such a request.

Later, in *Maryland v. Wilson* (1997),[93] the Court extended this concept to police requests for a *passenger* to exit a vehicle during a traffic stop. The majority opinion suggested that "danger to an officer from a traffic stop is likely to be greater when there are passengers in addition to the driver in the stopped car." And the Court did recognize that although "there is not the same basis for ordering the passengers out of the car as there is for ordering the driver out," perhaps since the passengers had not committed a traffic offense, the opinion concluded that "the additional intrusion on the passenger is minimal." Overall, once again, the safety interests at stake would trump any privacy considerations. As we will discuss in chapter 10, it is feasible for an officer to also conduct a pat-down search of a driver at a traffic stop, since the reasonable suspicion standard serves as justification for both a traffic stop and a pat down—and when it comes to a passenger, officer safety in the roadside setting likely justifies a cursory search for weapons being carried by all occupants of a vehicle.

Anonymous Tips Leading to Traffic Stops

Not every traffic stop is based on things an officer personally observes. In *Navarette v. California*,[94] the Supreme Court addressed a case in which a 911 caller reported their car had been run off the road by a passing driver. The caller described a silver Ford F-150 and gave the license plate number. Police were notified, and approximately twenty minutes later, officers observed a vehicle matching the description provided. However, as officers followed the car, they did not see anything to provide reasonable suspicion of a traffic violation. Nevertheless, police initiated a traffic stop based solely on the 911 call. Officers then smelled an odor of marijuana upon approaching the vehicle, and a subsequent search revealed thirty pounds of marijuana in the bed of the truck. The driver later pled guilty to a violation of state drug laws.

On review, the Supreme Court found there was no violation of the Fourth Amendment. Justice Thomas wrote the majority opinion, which said that the 911 call, on its own, provided police with the reasonable suspicion needed to stop Navarette's truck. Even though the call was anonymous—from the standpoint of the caller not giving their name—Justice Thomas suggested that the 911 system would provide a level of credibility for the tip because a false report to 911 might result in criminal charges against the caller, whose number could be traced. Beyond that, Thomas noted the caller provided specific information related to details about the vehicle and the time lapse between the call and the police stop was relatively brief. Taken together, these details presented enough information to meet the standard of reasonable suspicion.

During the oral argument for this case, an interesting moment arose when Chief Justice Roberts rejected a specific claim from Navarette's lawyer, who was arguing that police must witness illegal activity in person—instead of solely relying upon an anonymous tip. Roberts interrupted with the following question: "So if the tip—if the tip is, is this car is driving by and throwing bombs out the window, okay, every, you know, whatever, 500 yards, the police find the car, they have to wait until they see the person actually throw a bomb out the window themselves before pulling them over?"[95]

Justice Scalia's dissent had harsh words for those in the majority and what he said was a "new rule" that emanated from the Court's opinion: "So long as the caller identifies where the car is, anonymous claims of a single instance of possibly careless or reckless driving, called in to 911, will support a traffic stop." Scalia accused the majority of serving up "a freedom-destroying cocktail," consisting of two propositions he considered to be false: "(1) that anonymous 911 reports of traffic violations are reliable so long as they correctly identify a car and its location, and (2) that a single instance of careless or reckless driving necessarily supports a reasonable suspicion of drunkenness." Justice Scalia expressed concern about the "malevolent 911 caller," perhaps someone using a phone that is untraceable. Despite Scalia's concerns, the *Navarette* case has provided police with broad authority in effectuating traffic stops.

Previously, in *Alabama v. White* (1990),[96] the Supreme Court confronted a somewhat similar situation involving an anonymous caller to the Montgomery Police Department. Unlike the *Navarette* case, though, this caller did not offer an allegation of a traffic violation. Instead, the caller stated a woman named Vanessa White would be traveling from an apartment to a motel in a car, with cocaine kept in a briefcase in her possession. Details of White's vehicle were offered as well. Police followed White's vehicle from the apartment and initiated a traffic stop, based solely on the anonymous call, as she approached the motel. She then consented to a search of the vehicle, which revealed marijuana stored in the briefcase and cocaine in her pursue. On review, the Supreme Court upheld the search, offering a clarification on the lesser standard police need to meet for a traffic stop:

> Reasonable suspicion is a less demanding standard than probable cause not only in the sense that reasonable suspicion can be established with information that is different in quantity or content than that required to establish probable cause, but also in the sense that reasonable suspicion can arise from information that is less reliable than that required to show probable cause.

THE CONSTITUTION AND SOCIAL JUSTICE
Limitations on "Secondary Offenses" Strive to Bring Equity to Traffic Stops

In November 2021, Philadelphia became the first major U.S. city to prohibit police-initiated traffic stops for so-called *minor*—or *secondary*—offenses. This occurred via a vote of the city council, which passed the Driving Equity Act. According to this act, among the offenses that were deemed inappropriate for offering reasonable suspicion to enact a traffic stop were the following: driving with one headlight, driving with one brake light, having a license plate that is not clearly visible or fastened, driving without an inspection sticker or emissions sticker, having an item hanging from the rearview mirror, and driving with an expired vehicle registration (within 60 days of expiration). Ultimately, these violations are not to serve as the primary reason for a traffic stop. If an officer has a reason besides these for stopping a vehicle, such as speeding, then a citation for these other offenses could still be given. A companion bill also passed, which requires police to collect data concerning all traffic stops, including frequency of stops, reasons for stops, and demographics of those stopped.

The Philadelphia ordinance was drafted by city council member Isaiah Thomas, who said, "I've been driving in this city all my life, and so it starts with my foundational experiences as it relates to being pulled over for situations that didn't necessarily warrant a pull-over."[97] He added, "To many people who look like me, a traffic stop is a rite of passage—we pick out cars, we determine routes, we plan our social interactions around the fact that it is likely that we will be pulled over by police."[98]

The underlying concept behind the legislation is to limit what some have called *pretextual* traffic stops—stops for very minor offenses that are used as a precursor for more thorough investigation or to initiate a vehicle search. According to a study by the Defender Association of Philadelphia, 97% of police vehicle stops in that city are for low-level violations, and reducing those could result in approximately 300,000 fewer stops per year.[99] The Defender Association also has found that Black drivers accounted for 72% of approximately 310,000 traffic stops between October 2018 and September 2019, with data from 2021 showing Black drivers accounted for 67% of stops compared to just 12% of White drivers—despite the Black population of the city being 48%.[100]

The Philadelphia Police Department issued a statement regarding the new legislation, which said in part, "We believe this is a fair and balanced approach to addressing racial disparity without compromising public safety. ... This modified enforcement model for car stops furthers the Department's priority of addressing the issue of racial disparity in the Department's investigative stops and complements the Department's efforts to address these same issues in pedestrian stops."[101]

Elsewhere, the state of Virginia also has passed legislation that imposed a similar set of limitations on police traffic stops, including for improper window tint, the smell of marijuana, not having a light over a license plate, and loud exhaust. The city of Minneapolis has seen a policy change within the police department to reduce the number of traffic stops for minor violations, as well. It remains to be seen if this new approach will represent the start of a trend followed by other jurisdictions.

Automobile Searches at Roadside

Generally, under *Carroll v. United States* (1925),[102] probable cause is needed to justify a nonconsensual automobile search at roadside.[103] Normally, the reason for the traffic stop—if it is a routine violation like speeding—will not suffice for justifying a search of the vehicle. Evidence of probable cause typically arises in what an officer sees, hears, or smells while interacting with the driver. But it could also come from an external source, such as an informant who provides information that a specific car contains drugs.[104]

Of course, even without probable cause, an officer could request consent for a search, but as noted earlier in this chapter, a driver has the right to refuse to consent; without probable cause or consent, a search cannot be mandated.[105] However, a 1996 decision from the Supreme Court said police are not required to inform a driver they are free to go before asking for consent to search a car.[106] Moreover, a 2007 high Court decision indicated passengers in a car are in essence "seized" at the time of a traffic stop, as is the driver.[107] Accordingly, neither a driver nor a passenger should attempt to leave when an officer has stopped a car and is completing tasks related to the stop. If a constitutional violation is perceived during a traffic stop, it should be addressed later, in court.

Carroll v. United States (1925) also made clear that police do not need a warrant to conduct a roadside automobile search; an officer's judgment that probable cause exists can be sufficient, although that judgment is subject to judicial review. The lack of a warrant requirement in a roadside setting is known as the **automobile exception**. Certainly, this exception can be justified by practical safety considerations related to obtaining a search warrant while waiting on the side of a busy road. Additionally, as the Supreme Court stated in 1970, "the opportunity to search [at roadside] is fleeting, since a car is readily movable."[108] In a 1973 case, the Court's majority specifically spoke of a motivation for a driver to flee a traffic stop prematurely, noting, "This is strikingly true where the automobile's owner is alerted to police intentions and, as a consequence, the motivation to remove

AUTOMOBILE EXCEPTION: The doctrine under which police with probable cause may stop and search an automobile without a warrant.

Obiter Dicta

"One has a lesser expectation of privacy in a motor vehicle because its function is transportation and it seldom serves as one's residence or as the repository of personal effects. A car has little capacity for escaping public scrutiny. It travels public thoroughfares where both its occupants and its contents are in plain view. … This is not to say that no part of the interior of an automobile has Fourth Amendment protection; the exercise of a desire to be mobile does not, of course, waives one's right to be free of unreasonable government intrusion. But insofar as Fourth Amendment protection extends to a motor vehicle, it is the right to privacy that is the touchstone of our inquiry."

—*Justice Harry Blackmun, writing for the Supreme Court in* Cardwell v. Lewis, *417 U.S. 583 (1974)*

evidence from official grasp is heightened." Thus, the automobile exception is intended to allot for efficient completion of the search and seizure process at roadside, while minimizing risk of danger to the officer and also limiting the possibility of flight or destruction of evidence by the driver. It is important to note that states are free to provide additional protection to individuals beyond what the Supreme Court has offered. Along these lines, Pennsylvania's Supreme Court has ruled police in that state must obtain a warrant for all roadside searches, making it the only state in the country with such a mandate.[109] Given that warrants now can be obtained electronically in short order, this ruling does not impose unreasonable burdens on the police.

A 2018 decision from the Supreme Court established some limits on the scope of the automobile exception. In *Collins v. Virginia* (2018),[110] Justice Sotomayor wrote for an 8–1 majority, finding the automobile exception does not allow a police officer to walk onto a person's property, then look underneath a tarp covering an item. In this case, that action enabled the officer to locate a motorcycle that was parked beneath an open-air carport—and to determine the motorcycle was stolen. Finding this conduct violated the Fourth Amendment, Justice Sotomayor's opinion stated, "Contrary to Virginia's claim, the automobile exception is not a categorical one that permits the warrantless search of a vehicle anytime, anywhere, including in a home or curtilage."

When conceptualizing what types of police observations usually give rise to probable cause in roadside settings, previous Supreme Court cases have made it clear that probable cause could exist in situations such as these, depending on the full context, such as when an officer smells marijuana,[111] when an officer observes a visible syringe in the driver's pocket and the driver admits to using it for shooting heroin,[112] or when an officer sees a bullet on the front seat.[113] Of course, additional details, such as whether a state has legalized marijuana possession or allows for gun possession without a permit, could play a role in application of these precedents today. The high Court also has noted that if an officer has probable cause to search a car, then the ensuing search can include everything in the entirety of the vehicle, including the trunk[114] and even closed items like purses or backpacks.[115]

An interesting 1986 case addressed the nexus between the plain view doctrine and roadside searches. In *New York v. Class* (1986),[116] police officers pulled a man over for speeding and having a cracked windshield (each of which is a violation of New York state traffic laws). After initiating the traffic stop, an officer opened the driver's side door to look at the VIN, which is a unique number permanently inscribed on the vehicle for identification purposes. The number was covered by papers placed by the driver, and the officer bent down to move those; at that point, he spotted the presence of an illegal gun. Upholding the driver's arrest, the Supreme Court applied the plain view doctrine to the officer's reading of the VIN number, with Justice Sandra Day O'Connor's majority opinion saying:

> The VIN's mandated visibility makes it more similar to the exterior of the car than to the trunk or glove compartment. The exterior of a car, of course, is thrust into the public eye, and thus to examine it does not constitute a 'search.' ... In sum, because of the important role played by the VIN in the pervasive governmental regulation of the automobile and the efforts by the Federal Government to ensure that the VIN is placed in plain view, we hold that there was no reasonable expectation of privacy in the VIN.

In the end, the driver's alleged attempts to obscure the VIN—whether intentional or not—rendered the police search a valid inquiry.

Warrantless Searches of Motor Homes and Rental Cars

In the 1985 case of *California v. Carney*,[117] the Supreme Court confronted a warrantless search conducted by DEA agents who entered a motor home based on probable cause of drug activity taking place within it. Although the motor home was stationary and parked in a lot at the time of entry, the Supreme Court found no violation and said the automobile exception was still applicable. Chief Justice Burger wrote for a 6–3 majority, concluding, "While it is true that respondent's vehicle possessed some, if not many of the attributes of a home, it is equally clear that the vehicle falls clearly within the scope of the exception laid down in *Carroll* and applied in succeeding cases."

Of course, this opinion does seem to leave open the possibility for a motor home that has somehow been immobilized or anchored to the ground to be exempt from the automobile exception, owing to its reduced mobility. Yet the opinion also gives a less-than-flattering characterization of such vehicles by saying "a motor home lends itself easily to use as an instrument of illicit drug traffic and other illegal activity."

Subsequently, in *Soldal v. Cook County* (1992),[118] the Court ruled that when an officer of the law helps in the moving of a mobile home trailer in furtherance of an eviction order—in this case, an order mandating that the trailer be moved off a particular lot—that also carries ramifications for the Fourth Amendment. Specifically, the Court said that "the seizure and removal of the Soldals' trailer home implicated their Fourth Amendment rights . ..."

More than twenty-five years later, in *Byrd v. United States* (2018), the Court reviewed a search of a rental car.[119] In this case, a woman rented a car from Budget Car Rental and then allowed Mr. Byrd to drive it from New Jersey to Pittsburgh, even though Byrd's name was not on the rental agreement. Budget's rental agreement explicitly prohibited additional drivers. Byrd was stopped for an alleged traffic infraction on the Pennsylvania Turnpike,[120] and officers notified him that his car could be searched without his consent because his name was not on the rental agreement. In the trunk of his car, officers found heroin and body armor. Byrd faced federal charges for possession of heroin with intent to distribute, and for possession of body armor by an unauthorized person (because he had a prior felony conviction). After a federal District Court judge denied Byrd's motion to suppress the evidence, he entered a conditional guilty plea, which left him the right to appeal. However, his first appeal, which went to the Third Circuit, was unsuccessful.

On review, the Supreme Court of the United States reversed the lower courts and remanded the case for further consideration in light of two key principles. First, the high Court rejected the government's contention that drivers whose names do not appear on a rental agreement will always lack a reasonable expectation of privacy for the car's contents. Justice Anthony Kennedy's opinion for a unanimous court found that this "*per se* rule rests on too restrictive a view of the Fourth Amendment." (That finding, interestingly, also could benefit students who drive a car that is registered to a parent.) Second, Kennedy rejected Byrd's contention that the "occupant of a rental car always has an expectation of privacy in it based on mere possession and control," noting that this view "would include within its ambit thieves and others ... who would not have a reasonable expectation of privacy." Forging a middle ground between these positions, Kennedy's opinion indicated that Byrd did have an expectation of privacy in this case because police had no probable cause to believe that he had stolen the car. Hypothetically, a car that appeared to be broken into might give rise to a different conclusion—and thus, the rule that emerges from this case seems to be that the burden rests on police officers to demonstrate, by probable cause, that the person in possession of a vehicle is an unauthorized user.

JURISPRUDENCE

Follow-up on the Terrence Byrd Case Remand
United States v. Byrd, No. 19-2986 (3rd Cir. 2020)

Justice Kennedy's opinion in *Byrd v. United States* (2018) provided the accused a second chance at suppressing evidence that had been seized from the rental car he was driving. The opinion of the Court said that a person could indeed have an expectation of privacy in rental car, even when their name was not on the rental agreement—but the matter was remanded to lower courts for an assessment of two questions: (1) whether probable cause existed to justify the search and (2) whether there was evidence that Byrd had authored a scheme whereby he could facilitate commission of a crime (like drug trafficking) by fraudulently obtaining a rental car through a third party (when he might not be able to rent a car because of his criminal record). Kennedy noted that evidence to support of either of these two things could result in the forfeiture of an expectation of privacy and, thus, validate the search that occurred.

Unfortunately for Byrd, on remand, the district court confronted only the first question and determined the officers in this case did in fact have probable cause for the search—based on factors including the marijuana joint in his car, Byrd giving police an alias as his name, Byrd's prior drug arrests (which came up as officer's checked his identify in a computer), Byrd acting nervously, and Byrd admitting to officers he had used cocaine earlier in the day. On review, the Third Circuit affirmed these findings in 2020, agreeing that probable cause was present to justify a search of the rental car.

Canine Searches at Roadside

In *Illinois v. Caballes* (2005),[121] the Supreme Court said that if a drug-sniffing dog alerts at a vehicle, an officer has probable cause to search inside that vehicle—even without any other evidence to indicate probable cause of illegal activity. A dog alert on its own is sufficient for this purpose. Moreover, the Court also indicated police are permitted to lead a drug-sniffing dog around a car during a roadside stop on a public roadway without first demonstrating probable cause, or even reasonable suspicion, to justify doing so.

In this case, a man named Roy Caballes was pulled over for speeding after police radar indicated he was traveling 71 mph in a 65 mph zone. As one officer was writing a warning ticket, a different officer from a *drug interdiction team* arrived and led a canine around Caballes's car. The dog alerted at the trunk, which the officers opened, finding marijuana. The entire episode took less than ten minutes. Caballes was found guilty of violating state drug laws and received a twelve-year prison sentence. But the Illinois Supreme Court reversed his conviction for a Fourth Amendment violation connected to the dog search.

On review, however, the Supreme Court of the United States overturned the Illinois Supreme Court, ushering in a new era of drug dog searches. A key rationale in Justice Stevens's opinion for the high Court's 6–2 majority was that a dog search should be thought of as *sui generis*, meaning unique to itself. Stevens's opinion suggested that a trained drug-sniffing dog allegedly would alert only to illegal items, in which a person had no reasonable expectation of privacy—a presumption that placed great faith in the olfactory senses of dogs. Stevens did allow that if a driver were to be subjected to an unreasonable delay in waiting for a search dog to arrive, then that could adversely implicate Fourth Amendment rights, but absent such a finding, the dog sniff at roadside was not even to be considered a search for Fourth Amendment purposes.[122]

Justice Souter's dissent took umbrage with the idea that dogs can be trained to detect only contraband, offering the following declaration: "The infallible dog … is a creature of legal fiction." A separate dissent from Justice Ruth Bader Ginsburg went a step further, addressing intrusiveness and privacy considerations by saying that:

> A drug-detection dog is an intimidating animal. … Injecting such an animal into a routine traffic stop changes the character of the encounter between the police and the motorist. … Caballes—who, as far as Troopers Gillette and Graham knew, was guilty solely of driving six miles per hour over the speed limit—was exposed to the embarrassment and intimidation of being investigated, on a public thoroughfare, for drugs.

Addressing the majority's lack of concern for any privacy expectations in these situations, Ginsburg declared, "The Court has never removed police action from Fourth Amendment control on the ground that the action is well calculated to apprehend the guilty." She then lamented, "Under today's decision, every traffic stop could become an occasion to call in the dogs, to the distress and embarrassment of the law-abiding population"—something that she said "clears the way for suspicionless, dog-accompanied drug sweeps of parked cars along sidewalks and in parking lots."

In many ways, Justice Ginsburg recognized how widespread the canine search would become in the aftermath of the *Caballes* decision, which provided police with a powerful tool for conducting roadside vehicle searches. (Prior to this decision, some states required police to acquire a search warrant before even bringing a drug-sniffing dog around a car.) Today, the training of law enforcement animals is an industry of its own, and law enforcement canines have been taught to detect a variety of things, including drugs, bombs, human beings, and even devices that store data, such as a USB flash drive. In most jurisdictions, harming a police dog also can result in a charge of assault upon on an officer. In 2021, across the United States, twenty-one police dogs were killed in the line of duty.[123]

The Court Addresses the Reliability of Police Dogs

As discussed in the previous chapter, the Supreme Court's decision in *Florida v. Jardines* (2013) found a search warrant is required before police can use a drug-sniffing dog to search a person's home. Implicitly, this case recognized that a dog is capable of conducting a search and affecting a person's Fourth Amendment rights—but the *Jardines* holding left intact the core of Justice Stevens's *Illinois v. Caballes* opinion regarding warrantless roadside dog searches. However, because Jardines's case focused upon the dog being a part of a government *trespass* onto private property, legal scholars might be left to wonder if a dog jumping onto a car at roadside could amount to a Fourth Amendment violation—in the same way that police placing a GPS locator on a car was found to be a trespass in *United States v. Jones* (2012).[124] Perhaps a future case will address this matter.

Despite the *Jardines* decision potentially creating some doubt regarding the *sui generis* nature of dog searches, another 2013 decision engraved even more judicial faith for the canine sense of smell into the annals of Supreme Court case precedent. In *Florida v. Harris* (2013),[125] Justice Kagan delivered the opinion for a unanimous Court, which found that even apparent mistakes in real-world settings should not be taken to damage the credibility of a properly-trained drug-sniffing dog.

In this case, a man named Clayton Harris was pulled over for driving with an expired license plate, and during the traffic stop, the police officer led a drug-detection dog named Aldo around Harris's vehicle. Aldo, whose name featured prominently in Justice Kagan's opinion, alerted at the car, thereby giving the officer probable cause to search. That search revealed sizable quantities of the ingredients that are commonly used in manufacturing methamphetamine, including hydrochloric acid, matches, iodine crystals, and antifreeze. Yet Aldo was not trained to detect any of these items—and in fact, none of the drugs he was trained to locate were found in the car.

Moreover, weeks later, after Harris had been released from custody on bail, he was pulled over again by the same police officer—this time because Harris's car had a faulty brake light. Once again, Aldo was led around the car, and once again, Aldo alerted at the vehicle. The officer then searched the vehicle but found no evidence of drugs at all. After the trial court refused to suppress evidence against Harris that was derived from the first traffic stop, the Florida Supreme Court reversed the trial court, finding that Aldo's "hits and misses" in the field raised questions about the reliability of the dog's initial alert.[126]

On review, the Supreme Court of the United States reversed the ruling of Florida's highest court. Justice Kagan's majority opinion in *Florida v. Harris* suggested that a narrow focus on "hits and misses in the field" was the "antithesis of a totality of circumstances approach" that should be employed. Kagan instead suggested that information about the dog's training should serve as the key barometer in evaluating its credibility. Her opinion placed great faith in canines by saying that:

> ... if the dog alerts to a car in which the officer finds no narcotics, the dog may not have made a mistake at all. The dog may have detected substances that were too well hidden or present in quantities too small for the officer to locate. Or the dog may have smelled the residual odor of drugs previously in the vehicle or on the driver's person. Field data thus may markedly overstate a dog's real false positives. By contrast, those inaccuracies—in either direction—do not taint records of a dog's performance in standard training and certification settings.

Justice Kagan left open the possibility that an accused criminal could challenge the quality of a dog's training, but the burden of proof would rest on the accused to show flaws in that process—which can be challenging in light of the fact that many police departments now train their own canines. Kagan's opinion did provide yet another avenue for contesting the validity of a dog search: proving that the dog was *cued* to give an alert—or, in other words, was responding to a signal from an officer when alerting. Once again, though, the burden would rest on the accused criminal to provide proof this occurred. Overall, then, the *Florida v. Harris* opinion builds upon *Illinois v. Caballes* in offering robust support for law enforcement to use dogs in initiating roadside searches.

Limits on Canine Searches

A decade after *Caballes* was decided, Justice Ginsburg built upon her dissent in that case by writing a majority opinion that placed some limitations on dog searches during traffic stops. In *Rodriguez v. United States* (2015),[127] the Supreme Court addressed the time frame police have for utilizing a search dog in these contexts. Dennys Rodriguez was pulled over for swerving out of his lane and driving on the shoulder of a Nebraska highway. The officer completed the tasks of checking the driver's license and insurance and writing a warning ticket—and only afterward suggested he would walk his canine around the vehicle. The officer actually decided to detain Rodriguez until a second officer arrived and then utilized the canine, which alerted to the presence of methamphetamines in the car. A time period of seven to eight minutes spanned the gap between when the officer finished writing the warning ticket and when the dog alerted at the car. Ultimately, Rodriguez was sentenced to five years in prison for violating federal drug law.

Finding that Rodriguez's Fourth Amendment rights were violated, the Supreme Court's 6–3 majority—comprising Justices Scalia, Roberts, Ginsburg, Sotomayor, Kagan, and Breyer—stated police cannot prolong a traffic stop to wait for a canine unit to arrive or even to use a dog that is already on the scene. In other words, a police officer has only the amount of time it takes to address details related to the stop—typically, writing a ticket or checking driver's license, insurance, and vehicle registration before the officer must let the driver go on their way. As Justice Ginsburg noted in the majority opinion, a "routine traffic stop" should be a "relatively brief encounter," one which has a length that should be guided by the "mission" of the stop.[128]

The key principle that emanates from *Rodriguez v. United States* is that to delay a traffic stop beyond the time needed to complete tasks inherent in the stop's *mission*, law enforcement officials must demonstrate reasonable suspicion of drug activity or other criminal activity that can then justify prolonging the traffic stop for a dog search to occur. In most cases, that would involve some reasonable suspicion beyond what led to the traffic stop in the first place—unless, for instance, an odor of drug activity served as the basis for stopping the car originally. For an officer working alone, without such added suspicion, this decision might require simultaneously completing the tasks of the stop while also leading a dog around a vehicle.

In practice—even in the aftermath of the *Rodriguez* decision—what precisely constitutes an unreasonable delay in a roadside setting remains a matter for courts to untangle. As noted above, in *Illinois v. Caballes* (2005), ten minutes was deemed an acceptable time frame for writing a warning ticket for speeding. In *United States v. Sharpe* (1985),[129] the Supreme Court said it was reasonable for an officer to detain a driver for twenty minutes—in that case not to wait for a dog search but to wait for a DEA agent to arrive; that decision turned, in part, on the fact that the driver's own behavior in previously eluding the DEA agent's highway pursuit had contributed to the delay. Additionally, in *United States v. Place* (1983),[130] the Court's first decision to suggest "the canine sniff is *sui generis*," the majority opinion found that DEA agents had violated the Fourth Amendment rights of an airline passenger at New York's LaGuardia Airport by detaining him for ninety minutes while authorities sought out a drug dog to sniff his luggage. In the end, determining what exact time frame constitutes a reasonable delay when awaiting the arrival of a police K-9 unit can depend on a variety of context-specific parameters and, thus, requires a case-by-case approach—as guided by applicable case precedent.

FOCUS ON LAW ENFORCEMENT

Marijuana Legalization Leads to Police K-9 Retirements in Some States

Earlier in this text, we noted that state-by-state legalization of marijuana offers an apt exemplar of the principle of federalism in action. By 2022, more than eighteen states had legalized marijuana possession for recreational purposes (with quantity limits), and more than thirty states had legalized marijuana possession for medical purposes. This widespread legalization created unique practical consequences for police departments that utilized K-9 units. Drug-sniffing dogs that have been trained to detect marijuana, after all, become obsolete when the substance is legalized.

In June 2021, Sergeant Scott Amos, who is a canine training coordinator for the Virginia State Police, indicated that thirteen state police canines would be removed from their law enforcement roles, in anticipation of marijuana being legalized for recreational purposes on July 1 of that year. "With the new legislation," he said, "we've had to retire those K9s and start with brand new K9s that are not trained to smell marijuana." All of the retiring canines were adopted by their handlers, with Amos noting, "We get very attached to these dogs because we'll spend more time with the dogs throughout the week than we do with our own families." In speaking of the new dogs, Amos added, "They're going to be trained to search out methamphetamine, Ecstasy, heroin and cocaine and different derivatives of those narcotics." He described a practical consequence of training the new canines, which normally is a thirteen-week process, by saying, "There's a financial impact because the dogs cost money to bring in. Then, there's a time impact. All the handlers have to come back in and get retrained with their new K9 partners before they can be out on the road working again." Ultimately, noting the importance of this training process, he stated, "We don't want anyone to be subject to an illegal search because we didn't take the time to retrain handlers and train new dogs on something that's now legal."[131]

DUI-Related Searches

As noted in our discussion of evanescent evidence, the Supreme Court's *Missouri v. McNeely* (2013) ruling generally requires police to acquire a search warrant to mandate blood tests of motor vehicle operators who are suspected of driving under the influence of alcohol or intoxicating drugs. However, that case did leave exceptions for exigent circumstances, where law enforcement efforts must be focused on things besides seeking out a warrant, such as providing aid at an accident scene.[132]

In a subsequent decision, *Birchfield v. North Dakota* (2016),[133] the Court reiterated the idea that a warrant is needed for a blood draw, even incident to an arrest for DUI. However, Justice Alito's majority opinion also declared that the search incident to arrest exception does allow for a warrantless breath test in such a situation:

> The impact of breath tests on privacy is slight, and the need for BAC testing is great. We reach a different conclusion with respect to blood tests. Blood tests are significantly more intrusive, and their reasonableness must be judged in light of the availability of the less invasive alternative of a breath test.

Alito was not persuaded by the state's argument that a blood test was somehow less intrusive than a breath test because the breath test involved actual activity on the part of the person being investigated, whereas a blood draw merely requires someone to remain still. He also rejected the state's suggestion that an enhanced government interest supports warrantless blood draws because those can detect substances besides alcohol that might impair driving; Alito instead suggested that officers acquire a search warrant if they have probable cause of a driver being impaired by drugs (or, alternatively, that officers rely upon some exigent circumstances exception if time does not permit the acquisition of a warrant).

An odd exception to the warrant requirement for blood draws was articulated three years later in *Mitchell v. Wisconsin* (2019).[134] In this case, Gerald Mitchell was arrested for DUI when a roadside breath test revealed his blood alcohol content (BAC) to be three times the legal limit in Wisconsin. He was transported to a local police station for testing with a more sophisticated breath-analysis device but was unable to produce a sample because of his intoxicated state. Officers then had him transported to a hospital, where he became unconscious. Even so, a blood draw was taken in accord with a state law that says consent to any DUI test is implied unless a person expressly withdraws it—something that, of course, would be difficult for an unconscious person to do (unless, perhaps, something were written on their body to that effect). More than twenty states currently have laws similar to this one. In the end, Mitchell was convicted of DUI, and the Wisconsin Supreme Court upheld use of the blood draw as evidence against him.

On review, in a 5–4 decision for which Justice Alito penned a plurality opinion, the Court ruled if an individual is unconscious, police do not automatically need to acquire a warrant in order to mandate drawing that person's blood. A key rationale for Alito's opinion was that this type of situation could involve an exigent circumstance and, thus, provide an exception to the warrant requirement indicated in the Court's two prior blood-test decisions: *Birchfield v. North Dakota* (2016) and *Missouri v. McNeely* (2013). More specifically, Alito suggested that "[w]hen police have probable cause to believe a person has committed a drunk-driving offense and the driver's unconsciousness or stupor requires him to be taken to the hospital or similar facility before police have a reasonable opportunity to administer a standard evidentiary breath test, they may almost always order a warrantless blood test to measure the driver's BAC without offending the Fourth Amendment."

Of course, that is not what happened in Mitchell's case, as he was in fact given a breath test and even transported to a police station prior to be taken to the hospital. For that reason, it seems, the ultimate ruling for *Mitchell v. Wisconsin* was to remand the case for further proceedings—to determine if, in fact, an exigent circumstance actually did preclude police from having time to acquire a warrant. Specifically, Alito's opinion afforded Mitchell an opportunity to demonstrate one of two caveats that could eliminate the application of the exigent circumstances doctrine to his case: (1) a showing that his blood "would not have been drawn if police had not been seeking BAC information" and (2) "that police could not have reasonably judged that a warrant application would interfere with other pressing needs or duties" connected to Mitchell's care. In summary, as with many categories of warrantless searches, the constitutionality of a warrantless blood draw seems to depend upon minute factors specific to the context of an individual case.

Implied Consent Laws

Most states have laws requiring drivers to consent to a breath test when there is probable cause to believe they are intoxicated. The penalty for refusing to comply is the suspension of one's driver's license. The Supreme Court has upheld such laws as reasonable, in keeping with the government interest of preventing drunk driving. For instance, in *South Dakota v. Neville* (1983),[135] the Supreme Court upheld a South Dakota implied consent law that authorized not only revocation of a driver's license in situations when a motor vehicle operator refused a sobriety test but also allowed for that refusal to be used at a part of testimony in a criminal trial. The Court indicated the latter did not amount to a violation of the Fifth Amendment's Self-Incrimination Clause. We discuss that amendment in greater detail in chapter 11.

Routine and Special Needs Searches

The final broad category that we consider in this chapter encompasses a variety of warrantless searches that have been deemed acceptable through precedent, either because they address situations that have become routine, such as walking through a scanner at an airport, or because they fall into narrow categories for which, as the Supreme Court has said, *special needs* are apparent, such as searches of students in public schools or searches of individuals who are on probation. In situations when law enforcement need not meet any legal standard at all in order to conduct a search, we might say suspicionless searches are permitted.

In *Griffin v. Wisconsin* (1987),[136] Justice Scalia's majority opinion observed, "A State's operation of a probation system, like its operation of a school, government office or prison, or its supervision of a regulated industry, likewise presents 'special needs' beyond normal law enforcement that may justify departures from the usual warrant and probable cause requirements." As we address these categories, and others, it is interesting to note the variation in terms of certain warrantless searches that require absolutely no standards—meaning they do not even need to be based on low thresholds like reasonable suspicion—whereas other categories of warrantless searches might require a showing of probable cause or some lesser standard of proof. Overall, these subtle distinctions are crucial for criminal justice professionals to recognize to ensure warrantless searches comport with the Fourth Amendment.

Border Searches

Everyone who has traveled abroad is familiar with the power of customs and immigration officials to conduct searches of people and their effects upon entry into the United States. The Supreme Court recognized as early as 1925 that people entering the country may be subjected to routine searches. According to a dictum in the classic auto stop case of *Carroll v. United States*, "[t]ravelers may be so stopped in crossing an international boundary because of national self-protection reasonably requiring one entering the country to identify himself as entitled to come in, and his belongings as effects which may be lawfully brought in."[137] In 1977, the Court amplified this position, saying "searches made at the border, pursuant to the longstanding right of the sovereign to protect itself by stopping and examining persons and property crossing into this country, are reasonable simply by virtue of the fact that they occur at the border. ..."[138] In a following subsection, we discuss routine and nonroutine searches that occur at a border, but as a general rule, routine searches at a border do not require a warrant or even a showing of any probable cause or reasonable suspicion.

To qualify as a border search, though, the search must be conducted at the border or its functional equivalent. In terms of the latter, the border search doctrine would apply to passengers arriving on international flights at airports located in the interior of the country, since entry into the United States in, for example, Atlanta would amount to a stop at the functional equivalent of the border—since that is the first place in the United States that they are arriving. In other words, to be considered a valid border search, the search must be conducted at the point of entry into the country.

There are limits to the geographic scope of the border search doctrine. In *Almeida-Sanchez v. United States* (1973),[139] for example, the Supreme Court invalidated an automobile search by U.S. Border Patrol agents conducted more than twenty miles north of the border with Mexico; these patrols were known as *roving* patrols, wherein officers would stop any car, without any particularized suspicion—something Justice Stewart's majority opinion found to be "of a wholly different sort" than searches at the border itself or at the "functional equivalent" of a border. Similarly, in *United States v. Ortiz* (1975),[140] the Court disallowed the Border Patrol from conducting warrantless searches at checkpoints well inside the border, finding that a checkpoint established 66 road miles from the Mexican border was the equivalent of a roving traffic stop, and thus, a warrantless search of a car's trunk at that checkpoint was deemed unreasonable, even though it revealed the presence of three illegal immigrants hiding therein.

SUSPICIONLESS SEARCH: A search that is not based reasonable suspicion or probable cause.

BORDER SEARCH: A routine search of persons crossing the border into the United States.

Yet one year later, the Court's decision in *United States v. Martinez-Fuerte* (1976)[141] made it clear that checkpoints set up in the United States away from an international border can be compatible with the Fourth Amendment in terms of allowing Border Patrol agents to conduct "a routine and limited inquiry into residence status," such as when agents briefly stop cars to ask rudimentary questions or check basic paperwork related to a person's nationality or immigration status. The Court indicated these checkpoints must be permanent in nature (rather than temporarily assembled) and must present an "intrusion [that is] sufficiently minimal"; in the context of a balancing analysis, such a minimal intrusion will be outweighed by a government interest in curbing illegal immigration. Of course, automatically searching vehicles that arrive at this type of checkpoint would vitiate the *sufficiently minimal* threshold and, thus, violate the Fourth Amendment. A search could occur, nonetheless, if probable cause were discerned in the moment.

Another aspect of these stops is the idea of *selective referral*, which addresses how authorities determine which of those many cars going through a checkpoint are actually stopped for questioning of the occupants. In the *Martinez-Fuerte* decision, Justice Lewis Powell's majority opinion recognized this process may "involve some annoyance" but suggested that would be attenuated by the "public and relatively routine nature" of the questioning. Additionally, Powell offered a practical reality in observing that "selective referrals—rather than questioning the occupants of every car—tend to advance some Fourth Amendment interests by minimizing the intrusion on the general motoring public." However, the Supreme Court also has made it clear, in *United States v. Brignoni-Ponce* (1975),[142] that an officer driving a patrol car cannot simply pull a car over based on the occupants of the vehicle appearing to be of Mexican descent. That principle of not profiling based on physical characteristics can be extrapolated to "selective referrals" in checkpoint settings, in keeping with notions of equal protection under the Fourteenth Amendment.

Overall, a justification for these checkpoints originates from a 1951 Department of Justice policy that expands the jurisdiction of U.S. Border Patrol agents to encompass 100 miles from any U.S. international border. Over time, this has manifested in the form of traffic stop checkpoints on various roads that fall within 100 miles of a border; to reiterate, such checkpoints need to be of a permanent nature, which would involve established structures, as opposed to temporary barriers. Today, approximately two-thirds of all Americans live within 100 miles of a border,[143] and perhaps as a result, current Border Patrol policy indicates that such checkpoints should not be within 25 miles of a border, to minimize traffic congestion in those areas; but current policy also suggests that Border Patrol agents can search private property within 25 miles of a border without a warrant as long as that property is not a dwelling.[144]

Routine Versus Nonroutine Border Searches

Regarding searches that occur at a border or its functional equivalent, two categories emerge: routine and nonroutine searches. A routine border search is one that does not involve a serious invasion of privacy or an unreasonable delay to the traveler. As previously noted, no warrant, probable cause, or reasonable suspicion is needed for these. Simply being at a border or its functional equivalent is enough to subject a person to such searches. Routine searches include examination of passports and visas, inspections of luggage and personal items, removal of shoes and outer garments, and even the use of drug-sniffing dogs. Even the act of border agents taking a car apart to search its gas tank has been upheld as "routine" by the Supreme Court.[145]

Nonroutine border searches and seizures, including prolonged detentions, strip searches, and body cavity searches, do not fall under the border search doctrine. In these situations, according to the Supreme Court's decision in *United States v. Montoya de Hernandez* (1985),[146] agents must have reasonable suspicion that illegal activity is afoot before conducting such a nonroutine search. Even so, in some situations, reasonable suspicion might seem like a very low standard relative to the intrusion. In the *Montoya de Hernandez* case, for instance, a woman arrived at Los Angeles International Airport from Bogota, Columbia and was detained for 16 hours based on suspicion that she was smuggling drugs inside her body. Subsequently, a rectal exam led border agents to locate 88 balloons filled with cocaine. Although standards for search and seizure at the border may be lower than in other places, the Supreme Court has indicated that any intrusion into the body that "shocks the conscience" is presumptively invalid.[147]

Searches of Electronic Devices at the Border

Earlier in this chapter, we noted that the Supreme Court's decision in *Riley v. California* (2014) required police to obtain a search warrant before examining data kept on a cell phone. However, both U.S. Customs and Border Patrol (CBP) and Immigration and Customs Enforcement (ICE) have created policies instructing agents they can conduct warrantless searches of electronic devices at the border or at its functional equivalent.[148] These devices include smartphones, laptops, tablets, disks, drives, media players, and more—anything capable of holding data. In essence, these immigration agencies are operating on the presumption that the *Riley* decision did not address a border search and, therefore, is not applicable as precedent in such a context until a court says it is.

Both CBP and ICE have created two levels of searches for electronic devices. First, there is the *basic search*, in which an agent on the scene opens a device and scrolls through its data, which might include reading text messages, looking at phone numbers called, viewing photos, and so forth. If a password, thumbprint, or retina scan is needed to open a device, such cooperation can be demanded of the item's owner. Second, there is an *advanced search*, which involves connecting a person's electronic device to an external government device to copy information from the person's device or to conduct sophisticated analysis, such as a bulk assessment of website browsing history. The advanced search option requires approval from a superior officer and a showing of reasonable suspicion, according to CBP and ICE policies.

Federal circuit courts have split as to the constitutionality of these electronic device practices. In 2021, the First Circuit found no violation of the Fourth Amendment.[149] In 2019, the Fourth Circuit found a violation of the Fourth Amendment but held that the good faith exception deemed evidence acquired from these searches admissible in court.[150] Also in 2019, the Ninth Circuit ruled that the CBP and ICE policies were, indeed, a violation of the Fourth Amendment, overturning a federal district court in the process.[151] In 2021, the Supreme Court of the United States refused to grant cert in appeals stemming from all three of these cases (one of which was brought by the Department of Justice seeking to overturn the Ninth Circuit's ruling).[152] For now, this policy area remains ambiguous.

Prison and Jail Searches

Given the extremely low expectation of privacy that characterizes the jail or prison environment, guards have wide leeway to conduct warrantless searches of inmates. In *Bell v. Wolfish* (1979),[153] the Supreme Court upheld body cavity searches and room searches for pretrial detainees who were held while awaiting their cases being heard in court. These individuals were held at a short-term, federal facility in New York City known as the Metropolitan Correctional Center, and the Court approved of the facility's search and seizure policies as a reasonable balancing of interests, even if individuals in custody had not yet been convicted of crimes. Going a step further, a federal district court in Virginia has even noted that visitors to a prison are not permitted to withdraw the consent to search that is implicit in showing up at the prison; hence, if the search of a visitor commences there, consent cannot be revoked.[154]

A key aspect of prison searches, such as officers looking through a cell, is that they normally are unannounced, known as *random searches*. The Supreme Court upheld the use of these practices in *Hudson v. Palmer* (1984),[155] where Chief Justice Burger's majority opinion said, "A requirement that even random searches be conducted pursuant to an established plan would seriously undermine the effectiveness of this weapon. It is simply naive to believe that prisoners would not eventually decipher any plan officials might devise for 'planned random searches,' and thus be able routinely to anticipate searches." We address this case in greater detail in chapter 14, which discusses prison conditions.

In 2012, the Supreme Court ruled against a man charged with a minor traffic offense who claimed his two strip searches by prison officials violated the Fourth Amendment.[156] Justice Kennedy's majority opinion observed the strip searches "struck a reasonable balance between inmate privacy and the needs of the institutions," particularly in regard to preventing contraband like weapons, drugs, or alcohol from entering the prison environment. Along those lines, Kennedy noted that "seriousness of offense is a poor predictor of who has contraband," and beyond that, it would be difficult to apply a standard where different inmates were treated differently; thus, a uniform policy of searching all incoming detainees, regardless of offense, was deemed to be reasonable under the Fourth Amendment.

Searches of Probationers and Parolees

As we will discuss in chapter 13, a parolee is someone who has been sentenced to incarceration in a correctional facility but who has received an early release, typically through the decision of a parole board. Probation, by contrast, generally is imposed by a trial judge following a guilty verdict in a criminal case, as an alternative to incarceration. Probation often comes with conditions of behavior that, if not met, could result in incarceration.

In terms of the Fourth Amendment, individuals who are released from prison on parole are subject to searches without a warrant, even without probable cause or reasonable suspicion. An underlying rationale for this approach is that those individuals are still considered to be in the legal custody of the state but have just been given early release from prison, where they would be subjected to warrantless searches. In a 2006 case, in fact, the Supreme Court authorized an officer initiating a pat-down search of a parolee who was walking on a sidewalk and doing nothing to arouse reasonable suspicion. The officer found methamphetamines on the man, and he was arrested.[157] Upholding this search, the majority opinion by Justice Thomas drew an important distinction, noting "parole is more akin to imprisonment than probation is to imprisonment." With that in mind, it seems as though parolees are subject to warrantless searches of their homes, property, and even bodies—at any time, although a future case might be needed to examine the possibility of a more invasive search being deemed reasonable.

Regarding searches of those on probation, in a 1987 case, *Griffin v. Wisconsin* (discussed in the opening of this section), the Supreme Court upheld the warrantless search of the home of a man who was on probation—but did so with caveats that are unlikely to apply to the search of a parolee. In the case at hand, a police detective notified a probation officer that Joseph Griffin, who was on probation for disorderly conduct and resisting arrest, had a gun in his apartment—in violation of his terms of probation. Officers were then dispatched to search Griffin's residence, and after a gun was found, he was arrested.

Upholding this search, the Supreme Court noted that Wisconsin prison regulations specifically authorized a search of someone on probation, provided there was *reasonable grounds* to justify the search. That phrase *reasonable grounds* amounted to a lower threshold than probable cause but still required some effort on the part of law enforcement to assess the reliability of information concerning individual suspicion of a probation violation. In this case, a tip from a detective sufficed in meeting that standard, and Justice Scalia's majority opinion said it was "clear that the special needs of Wisconsin's probation system make the warrant requirement impracticable, and justify replacement of the standard of probable cause by 'reasonable grounds,' as defined by the Wisconsin Supreme Court."[158] He also observed that:

> A warrant requirement would interfere to an appreciable degree with the probation system, setting up a magistrate, rather than the probation officer, as the judge of how close a supervision the probationer requires. Moreover, the delay inherent in obtaining a warrant would make it more difficult for probation officials to respond quickly to evidence of misconduct.

Searches in Public Schools

Dialogue about special needs searches in the *Griffin v. Wisconsin* opinion heavily cited a school search opinion issued by the Supreme Court two years earlier: *New Jersey v. T.L.O.* (1985).[159] The *T.L.O.* decision remains the high Court's seminal decision on searches conducted by officials in public schools. In this matter, a teacher at a public high school in New Jersey caught a 14-year-old girl, identified as T.L.O. in court documents, and one of her classmates smoking cigarettes in a school bathroom. This was a violation of school policy, and the teacher escorted both students to meet with an assistant principal. When T.L.O. denied smoking cigarettes, the assistant principal opened her purse without her consent and began to search through its contents. He first noticed rolling papers and then proceeded to find marijuana, a pipe, plastic bags, a large quantity of $1 bills, an index card with the names of students who apparently owed her money, and two letters indicating she was dealing marijuana. This evidence was turned over to police, and T.L.O. faced delinquency charges in the Juvenile and Domestic Relations Court of Middlesex County. The Juvenile Court denied T.L.O.'s motion to suppress the evidence seized from her purse, and she was adjudicated delinquent and sentenced to

SPECIAL NEEDS SEARCH: A search performed in the absence of particularized suspicion, for the purpose of preventing or minimizing the risk of harm.

one year of probation. On appeal, the New Jersey Supreme Court reversed that decision, finding the assistant principal lacked reasonable grounds to link the purse to the smoking of cigarettes and had thus violated the Fourth Amendment.

However, the Supreme Court of the United States reversed the decision of New Jersey's highest court, with Justice White's majority opinion essentially agreeing with the lower court on a version of *reasonableness* being the correct standard to employ for evaluating school searches but also finding the lower court's analysis "reflects a somewhat crabbed notion of reasonableness." In short, Justice White found the assistant principal's action to be compatible with the Fourth Amendment. He began his analysis by addressing an important threshold matter, explaining why students retain some rights at school by harkening back to the Founding era:

> It may well be true that the evil toward which the Fourth Amendment was primarily directed was the resurrection of the pre-Revolutionary practice of using general warrants or 'writs of assistance' to authorize searches for contraband by officers of the Crown. ... But this Court has never limited the Amendment's prohibition on unreasonable searches and seizures to operations conducted by the police. Rather, the Court has long spoken of the Fourth Amendment's strictures as restraints imposed upon "governmental action"—that is, "upon the activities of sovereign authority."

Additionally, Justice White observed that whereas a prison cell might not carry expectations of privacy at all, the same could not be said of America's public schools, where students should retain, for example, the ability to bring some personal property on a daily basis (with keys and personal hygiene and grooming products given as examples). But the key is to balance "the child's interest in privacy" against "the substantial interest of teachers and administrators in maintaining discipline in the classroom and on school grounds"—with White suggesting that "drug use and violent crime in the schools [had] become major social problems."

Formulating a standard to guide future school search cases, Justice White observed that "[t]he warrant requirement ... is unsuited to the school environment" because it "would unduly interfere with the maintenance of the swift and informal disciplinary procedures needed in the schools." He further noted that a probable cause standard was itself too rigid, opting instead for "a standard of reasonableness that stops short of probable cause."[160] Perhaps idealistically, White concluded his opinion by saying "the reasonableness standard should ensure that the interests of students will be invaded no more than is necessary to achieve the legitimate end of preserving order in the schools." Formulating the outward boundaries of a reasonable school search, White offered some guidance by observing, "Such a search will be permissible in its scope when the measures adopted are ... not excessively intrusive in light of the age and sex of the student and the nature of the infraction."

More than two decades later, the Supreme Court issued an opinion that utilized Justice White's criteria as connected to a student's age and sex. In *Safford Unified School District v. Redding* (2009),[161] the Court found that the Fourth Amendment rights of a 13-year-old girl had been violated when an assistant principal ordered a school nurse to conduct a strip search based on suspicions the girl brought ibuprofen onto school property. Even under the low reasonableness standard of *New Jersey v. T.L.O.*, the girl's age rendered this search highly intrusive and could not be justified when balanced against a relatively low school interest in halting ibuprofen possession.

Although over-the-counter drugs might not implicate a weighty school interest, a 1995 decision from the Supreme Court in *Vernonia School District v. Acton*[162] involved a school district's concern about widespread recreational drug use among high-school students. As a result, all student–athletes at a New Jersey high school were subjected to drug testing for amphetamines, cocaine, and marijuana. A test was required at the start of their playing season, and 10% of each team was randomly tested at once-a-week intervals during the season. The manner of testing involved agents from a private company watching students from behind as they urinated into a cup. Upholding this drug testing program against Fourth Amendment challenges, Justice Scalia's majority opinion observed that being a part of a sports team carried lessened expectations of privacy. "School sports," he declared, "are not for the bashful. They require 'suiting up' before each practice or event, and showering and changing afterwards. Public school locker rooms, the usual sites for these activities, are not notable for the privacy they afford." He went on to say that "[s]omewhat like adults who choose to participate in a 'closely regulated industry,' students who voluntarily participate in school athletics have reason to expect intrusions upon normal rights and privileges, including privacy."

The lessened expectation of privacy, then, culled the level of intrusion, which itself was balanced against a school justification that Justice Scalia characterized as "an important—indeed, perhaps compelling— interest," one defined as "deterring drug use by our Nation's school children," which was particularly important in light of a preexisting drug problem at this particular school; a correlated interest in "protecting student-athletes from injury" also was discussed.

In 2002, the Supreme Court's decision in *Board of Education v. Earls*[163] would expand this principle to allow public schools to drug test all students who take part in any extracurricular activity—including choir, debate, and band; this opinion spoke of a "minimally intrusive" testing protocol and also noted limited punishments that only impacted participation in extracurricular activity. In the end, many variables can be brought forth when analyzing school searches—because that is precisely what a reasonableness framework permits.

Administrative Searches

The final category we consider in this chapter is that of warrantless administrative searches. These are searches conducted by government officials working for executive branch agencies. Although these agencies typically impose fines for violations of law or regulations, an administrative search could yield evidence of criminal activity; thus, referral to a prosecutor for criminal charges might ensue.

In *Griffin v. Wisconsin* (1987), the Supreme Court addressed the lesser standard that connects to administrative searches, saying, "We have also held ... that in certain circumstances government investigators conducting searches pursuant to a regulatory scheme need not adhere to the usual warrant or probable cause requirements as long as their searches meet 'reasonable legislative or administrative standards.'"[164] The key becomes determining what those circumstances are.

Two cases indicate that *closely-regulated industries* are subject to warrantless inspections. First, in *Colonnade Catering Corporation v. United States* (1970),[165] the Supreme Court upheld the actions of agents from the Bureau of Alcohol, Tobacco and Firearms (ATF), who conducted a warrantless inspection of a bar that they believed to be serving liquor from refilled bottles, in violation of federal law. Upholding the agents' actions, Justice William O. Douglas observed that purveyors of liquor belong to a class of businesses "long subject to close supervision and inspection." Subsequently, in *Biswell v. United States* (1972),[166] an ATF agent conducted a warrantless inspection of a pawn shop that had a federal license to sell firearms. The agent seized two sawed-off rifles for which the store owner lacked a proper license. The Supreme Court upheld this warrantless seizure, saying:

> Federal regulation of the interstate traffic in firearms is not as deeply rooted in history as is governmental control of the liquor industry, but close scrutiny of this traffic is undeniably of central importance to federal efforts to prevent violent crime. ... It is also apparent that if the law is to be properly enforced and inspection made effective, inspections without warrant must be deemed reasonable official conduct under the Fourth Amendment.

In sum, the *Colonnade* and *Biswell* decisions suggest that the Fourth Amendment only requires a demonstration of reasonableness for warrantless searches of closely regulated industries. A key rationale here is that businesses that make the choice to operate in these areas retain a lesser expectation of privacy because they are intentionally subjecting themselves to heightened government regulation. The next step lies in dissecting what constitutes a closely regulated industry.

In *Marshall v. Barlow's, Inc.* (1978),[167] the Supreme Court made it clear that this term should not apply uniformly to all businesses that take part in interstate commerce. In this decision, the Court invalidated a section of the Occupational Health and Safety Act of 1970 that allowed OSHA to conduct warrantless searches of all workplaces. Nevertheless, the Court indicated that, when attempting to obtain administrative search warrants, OSHA inspectors were not required to meet the standards of probable cause that guide the issuance of warrants in criminal contexts. More guidance would arrive in *New York v. Burger* (1987),[168] which upheld a warrantless inspection of a junkyard. In this case, the Court laid out a three-part framework for warrantless administrative searches, suggesting these searches should be upheld when the following criteria are met:

1. there is a substantial government interest buttressing the regulatory scheme;
2. the warrantless inspection is necessary for furthering the regulatory scheme; and
3. the inspection methods must provide a constitutional substitute for a warrant.

With those standards in place, government agencies certainly retain a significant amount of leeway in arguing for warrantless inspections of

CLOSELY REGULATED INDUSTRIES: Businesses subjected to long-standing and pervasive government regulation.

ADMINISTRATIVE SEARCH WARRANTS: Search warrants issued by judges or magistrates on the application of administrative personnel.

businesses under their purview. In simple terms, the **administrative search exception** and its focus on reasonableness turns the analysis into something of a balancing test among the previously articulated key factors.

ADMINISTRATIVE SEARCH EXCEPTION: Doctrine exempting searches by administrative agencies from normal Fourth Amendment requirements.

Airport Searches

A specific setting where people are likely to expect a search is at an airport. After the terrorist attacks of 9/11, Congress enacted legislation creating the Transportation Security Administration for the purpose of handling the screening of airline passengers and their luggage.[169] The TSA establishes policies for maintaining security in airports, and its budget for fiscal year 2020 was approximately $8 billion. Most travelers are quite familiar with the traditional measures we might call *routine* airport searches, such as showing an ID to a TSA agent before entering the boarding area; standing in the Advanced Imaging Technology (AIT) body scanner with arms above the head; placing carry-on luggage, laptops, and shoes on a conveyor belt for an imaging scan; limiting carry-on liquids to three ounces or less; not carrying guns into an airport; not speaking about weapons or bombs while in an airport; and even the *pat-frisk* that can occur if the body scan reveals an abnormality.

From a constitutional standpoint, it seems as though travelers who choose to enter an airport have consented to putting themselves in a position in which these routine measures are to be expected. One key question that federal circuit courts have confronted is whether a person can withdraw consent at airport. For example, the Eleventh Circuit addressed a case when a passenger placed his carry-on luggage onto the conveyor belt for an X-ray machine; when the bag entered the machine, the technician viewed an anomaly and pulled the bag for inspection—and at that point, the passenger to whom it belonged declared he no longer wanted to fly and tried to take the bag back. The bag was later found to contain cocaine. On review, the Eleventh Circuit said a passenger could not revoke consent in such a situation.[170] The Ninth Circuit dealt with a similar case involving a man who declared he no longer wished to fly after an X-ray technician announced a hand search of his luggage was forthcoming. The Ninth Circuit's opinion said, "[W]e hold that those passengers placing luggage on an x-ray machine's conveyor belt for airplane travel at a secured boarding area impliedly consent to a visual inspection and limited hand search of their luggage if the x-ray scan is inconclusive in determining whether the luggage contains weapons or other dangerous objects."[171]

Beyond consent-based justifications for airport searches, the administrative search exception for *special needs* situations—which, as previously discussed, removes the warrant and probable cause requirements by incurring a balancing test to examine *reasonableness*—also could provide an applicable justification for airport searches. After all, a government interest in preventing terrorism could be balanced against the low intrusion of most airport security measures to indicate compliance with the Fourth Amendment. Along these lines, Daniel Harawa's research indicated that "all of the federal appellate cases that have examined the constitutionality of airport screening measures after the advent of the TSA have followed the Ninth Circuit's lead in *United States v. Davis* and analyzed the airport security programs using the administrative search exception."[172] Elsewhere, R. Gregory Israelsen observes that "no court has ever struck down an airport security measure for failing the administrative search balancing test."[173] Although the Supreme Court has never specifically addressed airport search methods, Harawa says that the high Court has, "on three separate occasions, hinted that airport security checkpoints are justifiable under the administrative search exception to the Fourth Amendment"; in particular, he quotes to *Indianapolis v. Edmond*, which struck down roadway "drug checkpoints" but also indicated that its "holding does not affect the validity of border searches or searches at places like airports and government buildings."[174]

Although courts have deferred to the government's national security interests when it comes to airport searches, some scholars have noted that the TSA's AIT body scanners could implicate privacy concerns based on how much information the images reveal of a human body, with Alexander Reinert referring to the scans as a "virtual strip search."[175] As of 2022, no courts had objected to the use of AIT scanners in airports (for more information on this topic, see chapter 9).

Of course, all of the airport search measures we have discussed thus far deal with the routine protocols with which nearly all travelers are familiar. But what about nonroutine airport searches? Harawa outlines some types of *nontraditional* searches that have occurred in U.S. airports that the average person would not tend to expect, such as TSA agents forcing a mother to taste her own breast milk to prove it did not contain any illicit substances, a woman being asked to remove a nipple piercing at the AIT scanner line, and a woman being asked to remove her bra.[176] Case precedent on *nonroutine* airport searches is scant, but it is possible that a parallel could be drawn to border searches, for which nonroutine searches, such as cavity searches in a back room, must be justified by reasonable suspicion of illegal activity, according to the Supreme Court.[177] At least that standard requires some individualized suspicion, even though it does demonstrate deference to government agents.

Finally, most individuals who have traveled in airports have seen dogs being led around by TSA handlers. TSA operates its own Canine Training Center, and even administers a Canine Adoption Program for dogs that are retiring from service or who do not adequately complete their training.[178] The Supreme Court's decision in *Illinois v. Caballes* (2005), which, as previously noted, authorized roadside dog sniffs, seems applicable in airports as well, but the high Court has indicated that detaining an airline passenger for an unreasonable amount of time to wait for a dog to arrive is a violation of the Fourth Amendment.[179]

Looking toward emerging technologies that might implicate Fourth Amendment issues, in 2021, TSA began testing facial recognition software as a security measure as a part of a "pilot program" at certain airports.[180] In the next chapter, we will discuss potential reliability issues with such techniques and consider their implications for expectations of privacy.

Fourth Amendment Workplace Rights of Government Employees, Including Police Officers

A key aspect of understanding administrative searches lies in the recognition that the standards for these searches can impact the employees who work in government agencies. For example, in 1987, the Supreme Court found that government employers or supervisors are permitted to conduct warrantless searches of employees' desks and offices. The plurality opinion in *O'Connor v. Ortega*[181] indicated that such searches could be based on a reasonableness standard (with no warrant or probable cause)—as long the search connected to "noninvestigatory work-related reasons" and considered "operational realities of the workplace."

More recently, in *City of Ontario, California v. Quon* (2010),[182] which involved police officers in the town of Ontario, California, a unanimous Supreme Court observed there was no Fourth Amendment violation when a police chief read transcripts of text messages that employees had sent to one another on their work issued pagers. Those messages revealed that an affair was taking place in violation of department policy and led to suspensions of two officers. Reviewing this matter, the Court sided with the police chief, noting the search was "not excessively intrusive." A key factor was that the department paid for these pagers and the monthly billing, even though text message overage charges were the responsibility of employees. The individuals in question had exceeded their allotted messages in multiple consecutive months. Thus, the Court found that the chief attempting to assess whether those text message overages were the result of work-related communications or personal communications amounted to a valid work-related purpose. After all, if the overages were for work-related messages, then employees would be paying out of pocket for work functions, and the department should then look into a plan with a higher minimum number of messages; alternatively, if personal messages were driving the overages, then a work device was being used for personal conduct. Under either justification, according to the Court, the chief's search was a reasonable, work-related one, particularly since the punishment was not criminal in nature but instead was a form of workplace discipline.

Finally, we note that the Supreme Court has twice upheld drug testing of employees who work in *safety-sensitive* jobs. Both cases were decided in 1989 on the same day, March 21. In *National Treasury Employees Union v. Von Raab* (1989),[183] the Court upheld drug testing of those employees in the United States Customs Service who sought promotion to a drug interdiction unit or to any position that involved handling a firearm. The majority opinion from Justice Kennedy found that even without individualized suspicion or probable cause (and certainly without a search warrant), the drug testing program still met the standard of reasonableness based on a balancing of two factors: a low level of intrusion in a drug test run by an outside company—one that did not excessively intrude upon privacy when collecting urine samples—and a high government interest in ensuring the quality of employees who receive these key positions. Justice Kennedy concluded that "[t]he Government's compelling interests in preventing the promotion of drug users to positions where they might endanger the integrity of our Nation's borders or the life of the citizenry outweigh the privacy interests of those who seek promotion to these positions, who enjoy a diminished expectation of privacy by virtue of the special, and obvious, physical and ethical demands of those positions."

In the other case decided that same day, the Court upheld a Federal Railroad Administration rule that required any railroad employee to submit to blood and urine testing for drugs and alcohol following any major accident in which that employee was involved.[184] The majority opinion used a reasonableness standard and first addressed the potential intrusiveness of the search by saying, "[A]lthough urine tests require employees to perform an excretory function traditionally shielded by great privacy, the regulations reduce the intrusiveness of the collection process by requiring that samples be furnished in a medical environment, without direct observation." Next, that consideration was balanced against the government interest, with the Court stating, "In contrast, the governmental interest in testing without a showing of individualized suspicion is compelling. A substance-impaired railroad employee in a safety-sensitive job can cause great human loss. ..." Moreover, linking this case to past cases that used a reasonableness standard, the Court found the following:

> The Government's interest in regulating the conduct of railroad employees to ensure safety, like its supervision of probationers or regulated industries, or its operation of a government office, school, or prison, "likewise presents 'special needs' beyond normal law enforcement that may justify departures from the usual warrant and probable cause requirements."

This quotation offers an apt summary of the balancing test for evaluating the reasonableness of the myriad *special needs* searches discussed in this section. In the end, many such searches not only evade the warrant and probable cause requirements but could even avoid a need for showing individualized suspicion. Overall, reasonableness as a touchstone test tends to turn on balancing an intrusion upon the individual against some purported government interest, which is the hallmark of what has become known as the administrative search exception.

Conclusion

Nothing in the text of the Fourth Amendment requires government officials to acquire a warrant before conducting a search. While the procurement of a warrant certainly strengthens the case for a search to be considered reasonable, the Supreme Court has carved out numerous specific categories of acceptable warrantless searches.

Most notably, if a person gives consent for a search, no warrant is required—although that can become a complicated matter for courts to review if consent allegedly has been coerced or given by a third party, such as a roommate or landlord. Even without a warrant or consent, police can conduct a seizure of contraband items that are left in plain view, provided the officer is in a place they are lawfully allowed to be and there is probable cause to believe the item is connected to illegal activity. That principle also helps justify a limited crime scene exception, wherein police can conduct a rudimentary examination for evidence upon arriving at the scene of a crime—but that would not permit, for example, a more intricate search like opening closed drawers. More controversial invocations of plain view relate to the Supreme Court's authorization of *sneak and peek* searches, wherein an improper search is in essence excused by a later valid search.

Nuanced exceptions to the warrant requirement also apply to so-called *exigent circumstances*, of which three categories have been identified by the high Court: emergency aid, hot pursuit, and imminent destruction of evidence. These categories often relate to warrantless, nonconsensual entry into the home, and there are specific limits offered in case precedent for each of these—although those limits can be ambiguous at times, such as in the Court's recent allowance for hot pursuit entry of the home to apply to some misdemeanor crimes but not to others. In some situations, categories of warrantless searches can overlap, such as if an emergency aid entry leads to a plain view seizure of drugs that are left out in the open.

Roadside stops have been the source of much controversy—particularly, regarding accusations of *profiling*—and numerous Supreme Court cases have attempted to provide some level of standardization to these situations. As a baseline, the Court has noted vehicles implicate a lesser expectation of privacy when compared to the home. Accordingly, the lower standard of reasonable suspicion is all that officers must meet in order to initiate an automobile stop, and that itself can be shown through the deferential totality of circumstances approach. Although probable cause (or consent) is needed to conduct a subsequent search of the vehicle, no search warrant is needed at roadside under the *automobile exception*. Furthermore, for cars that are impounded, the concept of inventory searches by police acting as *community caretakers* becomes germane—but that notion, according to the high Court, is not applicable to searches and seizures within the home. Notably, dog searches of vehicles represent a unique category in that they can occur without a warrant, without probable cause, and without reasonable suspicion—and beyond that, a dog alert provides police with probable cause to justify a warrantless search ... thanks to the great faith multiple majority opinions have placed in canines' sense of smell.

A final category addressed in this chapter deals with *special needs* searches, which could involve airports, borders, prisons, homes of parolees or probationers, school settings, and closely regulated industries. Searches in these settings could even affect the rights of public employees working in such places, including police officers. Searches in these locations are particularly unique in that they can not only be conducted without a warrant but also might not implicate any need for probable cause or individualized reasonable suspicion; a mere showing of reasonableness could be sufficient, and in some situations, even that might not be required. To further complicate matters, in one particular location, such as a border crossing, different standards might apply to one act (e.g., removing the gas tank of a car—no probable cause or reasonable suspicion is needed), whereas another act invokes an altogether different standard (e.g., taking a person to a back room for a body cavity search—reasonable suspicion is needed). Understanding these subtle nuances that can separate one warrantless search category from another is crucial for students and practitioners of criminal justice as they attempt to discern how context-specific details implicate the real-world application of the Supreme Court's warrantless search exceptions.

Ultimately, as new government search and seizure measures develop through emerging technologies, it is important to recognize how appropriate categories of warrantless searches are relevant for evaluating compatibility with the Fourth Amendment. Some categories might even intertwine at times. In the end, when it comes to evaluating what amounts to an unreasonable search and seizure, context—and case precedent related to key terms like probable cause and reasonable suspicion—are paramount for untangling the juxtapositions inherent in the following objectives: protecting government interests like national security and public safety, while also preserving individual liberty.

Discussion Questions

1. A college student named Billy leases a room in a house along with four other people. Besides Billy, what individuals could plausibly consent to a search of this home, and what limits would come with that consent? If Billy were away when the consent was given, but arrived home to see police beginning a search, what recourse would Billy have for halting the search?

2. Consider how the plain view doctrine could apply to other senses besides what an officer sees. How might the nature of a *plain view* search differ if it is based on what an officer feels, hears, or touches? What is easier or harder about applying the plain view doctrine based on what one sees as opposed to use of the other senses?

3. Consider the following: police enter a home where a murder has just occurred, and firefighters also enter to douse a fire in the kitchen of the home. An open drawer in the kitchen contains lighter fluid and a spent match; in the living room, where a dead body is found, a bloody knife is on the floor. In a closed drawer nearby, there is a gun with ballistics that match a bullet taken from a crime scene one mile away. Out of all the evidence discussed herein, what can be used in court without acquisition of a search warrant?

4. What are the key justifications for allowing a warrantless search incident to an arrest, and what limitations has the Supreme Court placed on this exception to the warrant requirement? How has the Court handled automobile searches incident to an arrest, and how might this question link with other categories to permit a warrantless search in a way other than through the search incident to arrest exception?

5. What are three hypothetical pieces of evidence (or observations) police could have that would justify an emergency entry into a home? If the entry were valid based on information believed to be true in the moment officers had but, upon entering a home, officers realized there was no emergency, what other categories of warrantless searches might come into play in terms of permitting a seizure of evidence?

6. Explain the flaws in the Supreme Court's logic underlying the alleged constitutionality of *sneak and peek* searches. In what ways could this be abused? In what ways does society benefit from these searches? Is there any way to provide accountability for law enforcement officials who abuse this exception to the warrant requirement?

7. Explain when the community caretaker exception can apply and when it cannot, based on Supreme Court case precedent. Explain how this could be used to seize a gun from a mentally ill person without a warrant and a situation in which the community caretaker exception would not allow that.

8. Imagine an officer pulls someone over for having a bumper sticker. What could that sticker possibly say to justify the stop? Name three things that could offer police the probable cause to justify a roadside automobile search. Can you envision a scenario in which the information that gave reasonable suspicion for a traffic stop also yields probable cause for an auto search? Is there anything a police dog could do during a traffic stop to violate the Fourth Amendment? What avenues are available for challenging a dog search at roadside, and what avenues are not available? How does a dog search at roadside differ from one at the home, and why?

9. When thinking about "special needs" searches, consider a type of search that fits each of these categories: (1) requires individualized reasonable suspicion; (2) does not require any probable cause, reasonable suspicion, or a warrant; and (3) requires some other standard, perhaps one created at the state level. What differentiates *special needs* searches that span this continuum of differing standards of justification? What commonalities do they have? How has—and how will, in your opinion—technology change the nature of special needs analysis in schools and airports?

Endnotes

1 *Illinois v. Rodriguez*, 497 U. S. 177 (1990).

2 *United States v. Karo*, 468 U.S. 705 (1984).

3 *See, e.g., Terry v. Ohio*, 392 U.S. 1 (1968).

4 Ric Simmons, *Not "Voluntary" but Still Reasonable: A New Paradigm for Understanding the Consent Searches Doctrine*, 80 Ind. L.J. 773 (2005).

5 *United States v. Drayton*, 536 U.S. 194 (2002).

6 *United States v. Pulido-Baquerizo*, 800 F.2d 899 (9th Cir. 1986).

7 *Kentucky v. King*, 563 U.S. 452 (2011).

8 *Amos v. United States*, 255 U.S. 313 (1921).

9 *Bumper v. North Carolina*, 391 U.S. 543 (1968).

10 *Schneckloth v. Bustamonte*, 412 U.S. 218 (1973).

11 Colorado enacted a law in 2010 that requires police to inform individuals they have a right to refuse to consent to a search; that applies in the context of roadside stops and pedestrian stops. Some cities have adopted similar requirements, including New York City, New York; Columbia, Missouri; and three cities in North Carolina: Asheville, Durham, and Fayetteville.

12 *Florida v. Jimeno*, 500 U.S. 248 (1991).

13 *Frazier v. Cupp*, 394 U.S. 731 (1969).

14 *Illinois v. Rodriguez*, 497 U.S. 177 (1990).

15 *Georgia v. Randolph*, 547 U.S. 103 (2006).

16 *United States v. Matlock*, 415 U.S. 164 (1974).

17 *Georgia v. Randolph*, 547 U.S. 103 (2006).

18 *Fernandez v. California*, 571 U.S. 292 (2014).

19 *Chapman v. United States*, 365 U.S. 610 (1961).

20 *United States v. Jacobsen*, 466 U.S. 109 (1984); *see* Alameda County District Attorney's Office, *Searches by Civilians and Police Agents*, Point of View, https://le.alcoda.org/publications/files/NONPOLICESEARCHES.pdf.

21 *Stoner v. California*, 376 U.S. 483 (1969).

22 *City of Los Angeles v. Patel*, 576 U.S. 409 (2015).

23 *Harris v. United States*, 390 U.S. 234 (1968).

24 *Coolidge v. New Hampshire*, 403 U. S. 443 (1971).

25 *Payton v. New York*, 445 U.S. 573 (1980).

26 *Texas v. Brown*, 460 U.S. 730 (1983).

27 *United States v. Lee*, 274 U.S. 559 (1927).

28 *Dow Chemical v. United States*, 476 U.S. 227 (1986).

29 *California v. Ciraolo*, 476 U.S. 207 (1986).

30 *Florida v. Riley*, 488 U.S. 445 (1989).

31 *Kyllo v. United States*, 533 U.S. 27 (2001).

32 *Arizona v. Hicks*, 480 U.S. 321 (1987).

33 *Coolidge v. New Hampshire*, 403 U.S. 433, 466 (1971).

34 *Abel v. United States*, 362 U.S. 217 (1960).

35   *Hester v. United States*, 265 U.S. 57 (1924); *Oliver v. United States*, 466 U.S. 170 (1984).

36   *California v. Greenwood*, 486 U.S. 35 (1988).

37   *Rios v. United States*, 364 U.S. 253 (1960).

38   *Smith v. Ohio*, 494 U.S. 541 (1990).

39   *Minnesota v. Dickerson*, 508 U.S. 366 (1993).

40   *Michigan v. Tyler*, 436 U.S. 499 (1978).

41   *Flippo v. West Virginia*, 528 U.S. 11 (1999).

42   *Thompson v. Louisiana* 469 U.S. 17 (1984).

43   *Chimel v. California*, 395 U.S. 752 (1969).

44   *Shipley v. California*, 395 U.S. 818 (1969).

45   *Stoner v. California*, 376 U.S. 483 (1969).

46   *Vale v. Louisiana*, 399 U.S. 30 (1970).

47   *Payton v. New York*, 445 U.S. 573 (1980).

48   *Silverman v. United States*, 365 U.S. 505 (1961).

49   *United States v. Robinson*, 414 U.S. 218 (1973).

50   *New York v. Belton*, 453 U.S. 454 (1981).

51   *United States v. Lee*, 274 U.S. 559 (1927).

52   *Arizona v. Gant*, 556 U.S. 332 (2009) (overturned *New York v. Belton*, 453 U.S. 454 (1981), which had allowed a search of a vehicle pursuant to an arrest).

53   *Riley v. California*, 573 U.S. 373 (2014).

54   *Mincey v. Arizona*, 437 U.S. 385 (1978).

55   *Michigan v. Tyler, supra* note 40.

56   *Brigham City v. Stuart*, 547 U.S. 398 (2006).

57   *Michigan v. Fisher*, 558 U.S. 45 (2009).

58   *See* Roxanna Hegeman, *Government Resumes Prosecution in Deadly 'Swatting' Case*, AP News, Sept. 20, 2021, available at: https://apnews.com/article/health-police-trials-coronavirus-pandemic-conspiracy-f89c6e65a96c0fde918995d-8b488afc9.

59   *Finch v. Rapp and City of Wichita*, No. 20-3132 (10th Cir. Jul. 5, 2022). Although the Tenth Circuit allowed the suit to go forward against the officer who fired the shot, the court held that a suit against the city could not proceed.

60   *Warden v. Hayden*, 387 U.S. 294 (1967).

61   *United States v. Santana*, 427 U.S. 38 (1976).

62   *Payton v. New York*, 445 U.S. 573 (1980).

63   *Welsh v. Wisconsin*, 466 U.S. 470 (1984).

64   *Lange v. California*, 594 U.S. ___ (2021).

65   *See United States v. Rabinowitz*, 339 U.S. 56 (1950); *Miller v. United States*, 357 U.S. 301 (1958) (citing *People v. Maddox*, 46 Cal. 2d 301 (Calif. 1956)).

66   *Ker v. California*, 374 U.S. 23 (1963) (which found no evidence of "extraordinary circumstances" to justify the search in question); *Wong Sun v. United States*, 371 U.S. 471 (1963) (which found that an arrest was made without probable cause in violation of the Fourth Amendment—with the majority opinion noting that no sign of destruction of evidence was apparent and that a defendant's response to police entry with "flight down the hallway ... signified a guilty knowledge no more clearly than it did a natural desire to repel an apparently unauthorized intrusion").

67 *Schmerber v. California*, 384 U.S. 757 (1966).

68 Other cases to speak of imminent destruction of evidence providing a justification for warrantless home entry, even though neither of these cases were decided around that issue, include *Minnesota v. Olson*, 495 U.S. 91 (1990) and *Welsh v. Wisconsin*, 466 U.S. 740 (1984).

69 *Illinois v. McArthur*, 531 U.S. 326 (2001).

70 *King v. Commonwealth*, 386 S.W.3d 119 (Ky. 2012).

71 *Cupp v. Murphy*, 412 U.S. 291 (1973).

72 *Missouri v. McNeely*, 569 U.S. 141 (2013).

73 The testimony at the trial court in this matter suggested that the percentage of alcohol in a person's blood generally decreases by about 0.015% to 0.02% per hour after the alcohol has been fully absorbed into the blood. Factors like weight, gender, and method of consumption are also relevant to the analysis. Citation was offered to the following: Richard Stripp, *Forensic and Clinical Issues in Alcohol Analysis*, *in* Forensic Chemistry Handbook, 435–455 (Lawrence Kobilinsky, ed., 2012).

74 *Mapp v. Ohio*, 367 U.S. 643 (1961).

75 *Murray v. United States*, 487 U.S. 533 (1988).

76 USA PATRIOT Act of 2001, Pub. L. 107–56, 115 Stat. 272.

77 *Harris v. United States*, 390 U.S. 234 (1968).

78 *Cady v. Dombrowski*, 413 U.S. 433 (1973).

79 *South Dakota v. Opperman*, 428 U.S. 364 (1976).

80 *Illinois v. Lafayette*, 462 U.S. 640 (1983).

81 *Florida v. Wells*, 495 U.S. 1 (1990).

82 *Caniglia v. Strom*, 593 U.S. ___ (2021).

83 *Florida v. Jardines*, 569 U.S. 1 (2013).

84 *South Dakota v. Opperman*, *supra* note 79.

85 *Delaware v. Prouse*, 440 U.S. 648 (1979).

86 *State v. Smith*, 484 S.W.3d 393 (Tenn. 2016).

87 *Whren v. United States*, 517 U.S. 806 (1996).

88 *Terry v. Ohio*, 392 U.S. 1 (1968).

89 *United States v. Arvizu*, 534 U.S. 266 (2002)

90 *Id.* (citing *United States v. Cortes*, 449 U.S. 411; *Orleans v. United States*, 517 U.S. 690).

91 *United States v. Cortez*, 449 U.S. 411 (1981).

92 *Pennsylvania v. Mimms*, 434 U.S. 106 (1977).

93 *Maryland v. Wilson*, 519 U.S. 408 (1997).

94 *Navarette v. California*, 572 U.S. 393 (2014).

95 *See* Oyez, *Prado Navarette v. California* (for the oral argument), https://www.oyez.org/cases/2013/12-9490.

96 *Alabama v. White*, 496 U.S. 325 (1990).

97 Jonaki Mehta, *Why Philadelphia has banned low-level traffic stops*, NPR, Nov. 8, 2021, https://www.npr.org/2021/11/08/1052957246/why-philadelphia-has-banned-low-level-traffic-stops.

98 Maya Brown & Emma Tucker, *Philadelphia to Become First Major US City to Ban Police from Stopping Drivers for Low-Level Traffic Violations*, CNN, Oct. 30, 2021, https://www.cnn.com/2021/10/30/us/philadelphia-driving-equality-bill/index.html.

99 Sean Collins Walsh, *Philly Has Become the First Big City to Ban Traffic Stops Said to Criminalize 'Driving While Black,'* The Philadelphia Inquirer, Oct. 14, 2021, https://www.inquirer.com/news/philadelphia-city-council-isaiah-thomas-police-driving-while-black-20211014.html.

100 Adriana Diaz & James Gordon, *Philadelphia Becomes the First Major City to Ban Cops from Making Traffic Stops for Minor Violations After Data Showed 72% of Their Stops Were on Black Drivers,* DailyMail, Nov. 2, 2021, https://www.dailymail.co.uk/news/article-10155003/Philadelphia-major-city-ban-cops-making-traffic-stops-minor-violations.html.

101 Maya Brown & Emma Tucker, *Philadelphia to Become First Major US City to Ban Police From Stopping Drivers for Low-Level Traffic Violations,* CNN, Oct. 30, 2021, https://www.cnn.com/2021/10/30/us/philadelphia-driving-equality-bill/index.html.

102 *Carroll v. United States*, 267 U.S. 132 (1925).

103 *Id.; see United States v. Ross*, 456 U.S. 798 (1982) (a more recent reiteration of this standard).

104 *See Maryland v. Dyson*, 527 U.S. 465 (1999) (where a confidential informant notified police that a vehicle had illegal drugs in the trunk); *Pennsylvania v. Labron*, 518 U.S. 938 (1996) (where officers on foot—rather than police who had pulled over a car—noticed drug activity connected to the trunk of a vehicle); *United States v. Ross*, 456 U.S. 798 (1982) (where an informant notified police of drugs being kept in the trunk of a car and police then stopped the car and searched the trunk). In all of these cases, the Supreme Court upheld the searches based on the idea that enough probable cause to acquire a search warrant was present and the mobility of the vehicles rendered the automobile exception applicable.

105 *See, e.g., Knowles v. Iowa*, 525 U.S. 113 (1998) (where an officer stopped a man for speeding and then searched the car without probable cause or consent, finding marijuana in the process; the Supreme Court found that this search violated the Fourth Amendment).

106 *Ohio v. Robinette*, 519 U.S. 33 (1996).

107 *Brendlin v. California*, 551 U.S. 249 (2007).

108 *Chambers v. Maroney*, 399 U.S. 50 (1970).

109 *Commonwealth v. Alexander*, 243 A.3d 177 (Pa. 2020).

110 *Collins v. Virginia*, 584 U.S. ___ (2018).

111 *United States v. Johns*, 467 U.S. 478 (1985).

112 *Wyoming v. Houghton*, 526 U.S. 295 (1999).

113 *United States v. Ross*, 456 U.S. 798 (1982).

114 *Id.; Michigan v. Long*, 463 U.S. 1032 (1983).

115 *Wyoming v. Houghton*, 526 U.S. 295 (1999).

116 *New York v. Class*, 475 U.S. 106 (1986).

117 *California v. Carney*, 471 U.S. 386 (1985).

118 *Soldal v. Cook County*, 506 U.S. 56 (1992).

119 *Byrd v. United States*, 584 U.S. ___ (2018).

120 The exact nature of this infraction was only referenced as a "possible traffic infraction" in the Supreme Court opinion, which also noted that the officer felt suspicion because Byrd was driving a rental car (as evidenced by a bar code sticker) and had his hands in the *10 and 2* position while leaning back; the justification for the stop, though, was not the crux of the Supreme Court decision in this matter; neither did the Court consider if a marijuana cigarette in the car or Byrd using an alias amounted to probable cause for the search; these matters were left for consideration on remand.

121 *Illinois v. Caballes*, 543 U.S. 405 (2005).

122 *Id.* (citing *Indianapolis v. Edmond*, 531 U.S. 32, 40 (2000)); *United States v. Place*, 462 U.S. 696, 707 (1983).

123 Officer Down Memorial Page, Honoring Officers Killed in 2021, https://www.odmp.org/search/year/2021.

124 *United States v. Jones*, 565 U.S. 400 (2012).

125 *Florida v. Harris*, 568 U.S. 237 (2013).

126 *State v. Harris*, 71 So. 3d 757 (Fl. 2011).

127 *Rodriguez v. United States*, 575 U.S. 348 (2015).

128 *Id.* (citing *Knowles v. Iowa*, 525 U.S. 113 (1998)) (in suggesting that a traffic stop is more akin to the brief detention of a pat-down search under *Terry v. Ohio*, 392 U.S. 1 (1968) than it is to an arrest).

129 *United States v. Sharpe*, 470 U.S. 675 (1985).

130 *United States v. Place*, 462 U.S. 696 (1983).

131 Desiree Montilla, *Virginia State Police Retires 13 K9s After Marijuana Becomes Legal*, NBC12, June 1, 2021, https://www.nbc12.com/2021/06/01/virginia-state-police-retires-ks-after-marijuana-becomes-legal/.

132 This is idea that emerged in *Schmerber v. California*, 384 U.S. 757 (1966) and is reiterated in *Mitchell v. Wisconsin*, 588 U.S. ___ (2019); the latter spends time emphasizing the application of the exigent circumstances doctrine to warrantless blood draws.

133 *Birchfield v. North Dakota*, 579 U.S. ___ (2016).

134 *Mitchell v. Wisconsin*, 588 U.S. ___ (2019).

135 *South Dakota v. Neville*, 459 U.S. 553 (1983).

136 *Griffin v. Wisconsin*, 483 U.S. 868 (1987).

137 *Carroll v. United States*, 267 U.S. 132 (1925).

138 *United States v. Ramsey*, 431 U.S. 606 (1977).

139 *Almeida-Sanchez v. United States*, 413 U.S. 266 (1973).

140 *United States v. Ortiz*, 422 U.S. 891 (1975).

141 *United States v. Martinez-Fuerte*, 428 U.S. 543 (1976).

142 *United States v. Brignoni-Ponce*, 422 U.S. 873 (1975); *see United States v. Arizona*, 567 U.S. 387 (2012).

143 American Civil Liberties Union, *The Constitution in the 100-Mile Border Zone*, https://www.aclu.org/other/constitution-100-mile-border-zone.

144 American Civil Liberties Union, Washington Legislative Office, *Customs and Border Protection's (CBP's) 100-Mile Rule*, https://www.aclu.org/sites/default/files/field_document/14_9_15_cbp_100-mile_rule_final.pdf.

145 *United States v. Flores-Montano*, 541 U.S. 149 (2004).

146 *United States v. Montoya de Hernandez*, 473 U.S. 53 (1985).

147 *Rochin v. California*, 342 U.S. 165 (1952).

148 *See* CBP Directive No. 3340-049A, Border Search of Electronic Devices (2018) (the official Customs and Border Protection policy), https://www.cbp.gov/sites/default/files/assets/documents/2018-Jan/CBP-Directive-3340-049A-Border-Search-of-Electronic-Media-Compliant.pdf; ICE Directive No. 7-6.1, Border Searches of Electronic Devices (2009) (the official Immigration and Customs Enforcement policy), https://www.dhs.gov/xlibrary/assets/ice_border_search_electronic_devices.pdf.

149 *Alasaad v. Mayorkas*, 988 F.3d 8 (1st Cir. 2021).

150 *United States v. Aigbekaen*, 943 F.3d 713 (4th Cir. 2019).

151 *United States v. Cano*, 934 F.3d 1002 (9th Cir. 2019).

152 *United States v. Cano*, U.S. Supreme Court, No. 20-1043; *Merchant v. Mayorkas, Secretary of Homeland Security*, U.S. Supreme Court, No. 20-1505; *Raymond Idemudia Aigbekaen v. United States*, U.S. Supreme Court, No. 20-8057.

153 *Bell v. Wolfish*, 441 U.S. 520 (1979).

154 *United States v. Spriggs*, 827 F. Supp. 372 (E.D. Va. 1993).

155 *Hudson v. Palmer*, 468 U.S. 517 (1984).

156 *Florence v. Bd. of Chosen Freeholders of County of Burlington*, 556 U.S. 318 (2012).

157 *Samson v. California*, 547 U.S. 843 (2006).

158 *Griffin v. Wisconsin*, *supra* note 136.

159 *New Jersey v. T.L.O.*, 469 U.S. 325 (1985).

160 *Id.* In an attempt to define *reasonableness*, Justice White went on to say, "Determining the reasonableness of any search involves a twofold inquiry: first, one must consider 'whether the ... action was justified at its inception,' ...; second, one must determine whether the search as actually conducted 'was reasonably related in scope to the circumstances which justified the interference in the first place,' .... Under ordinary circumstances, a search of a student by a teacher or other school official will be 'justified at its inception' when there are reasonable grounds for suspecting that the search will turn up evidence that the student has violated or is violating either the law or the rules of the school. Such a search will be permissible in its scope when the measures adopted are reasonably related to the objectives of the search and not excessively intrusive in light of the age and sex of the student and the nature of the infraction."

161 *Safford Unified Sch. Dist. v. Redding*, 557 U.S. 364 (2009).

162 *Vernonia School District v. Acton*, 515 U.S. 646 (1995).

163 *Board of Education v. Earls.*, 536 U.S. 822 (2002).

164 *Griffin v. Wisconsin*, 483 U.S. 868 (1987) (citing *Camara v. Municipal* Court, 387 U.S. 523, 538 (1967); *New York v. Burger*, 482 U.S. 691, 702-703 (1987); *Donovan v. Dewey*, 452 U.S. 594, 602 (1981); *United States v. Biswell*, 406 U.S. 311, 316 (1972)).

165 *Colonnade Catering Corporation v. United States*, 392 U.S. 72 (1970).

166 *United States v. Biswell*, 406 U.S. 311 (1972).

167 *Marshall v. Barlow's, Inc.*, 436 U.S. 307 (1978).

168 *New York v. Burger*, 482 U.S. 691 (1987).

169 Aviation and Transportation Security Act, Pub. L. 107–71, 115 Stat. 597, 49 U.S.C. § 114(a) (The agency was reauthorized and given additional money with the TSA Modernization Act, which was a part of the following: FAA Reauthorization Act of 2018, Pub. L. 115-254, 132 Stat. 3186, 49 U.S.C. §§ 40101–40130.).

170 *United States v. Herzbrun*, 723 F.2d 773 (11th Cir. 1984).

171 *United States v. Pulido-Baquerizo*, 800 F.2d 899 (9th Cir. 1986); *see United States v. Aukai*, 497 F.3d 955 (9th Cir. 2007) (for a more recent Ninth Circuit case on this topic).

172 *United States v. Davis*, 482 F.2d 893 (9th Cir. 1973); *see* Daniel S. Harawa, *The Post-TSA Airport: A Constitution Free Zone?* 41 Pepp. L. Rev. 1 (2013).

173 R. Gregory Israelsen, *Applying the Fourth Amendment's National-Security Exception to Airport Security and the TSA*, 78 J. Air L. & Com. 501, 537 (2013).

174 Harawa, *supra* note 172, p. 34 (referencing *Indianapolis v. Edmond*, 531 U.S. 32, 47–48); the other two cases he mentions are: *Chandler v. Miller*, 520 U.S. 305, 323 (1997); *Nat'l Treasury Employees Union v. Von Raab*, 489 U.S. 656, 675 n.3 (1989).

175 *See, e.g.*, Harawa, *supra* note 172, Israelsen, *supra* note 173; Alexander A. Reinert, *'Special Needs' Theory via Airport Searches*, 106 NWU. L. Rev. Colloquy 207 (2012).

176 Harawa, *supra* note 172, p. 3.

177   *See, e.g., United States v. Montoya de Hernandez, supra* note 146.

178   Transportation Security Administration, *Canine Adoption Program*, https://www.tsa.gov/canine-adoption-program

179   *United States v. Place, supra* note 122.

180   Transportation Security Administration, *Evaluating Facial Identification Technology—Detroit Airport Pilot*, https://www.tsa.gov/biometrics-technology/evaluating-facial-identification-technology.

181   *O'Connor v. Ortega*, 480 U.S. 709 (1987).

182   *City of Ontario, California v. Quon*, 560 U.S. 746 (2010).

183   *National Treasury Employees Union v. Von Raab*, 489 U.S. 656 (1989).

184   *Skinner v. Railway Labor Executives' Association*, 489 U.S. 602 (1989).

Credit

CHAPTER 9

The Fourth Amendment

Electronic Surveillance and Detection

"The makers of our Constitution ... conferred, as against the Government, the right to be let alone— the most comprehensive of rights, and the right most valued by civilized men. To protect that right, every unjustifiable intrusion by the Government upon the privacy of the individual, whatever the means employed, must be deemed a violation of the Fourth Amendment."

—Justice Louis D. Brandeis, dissenting in *Olmstead v. United States*, 277 U.S. 438 (1928).

Learning Objectives

After reading this chapter, you should understand what the Fourth Amendment and related federal statutes require with respect to the following:

1. Concealed microphones
2. Wiretaps
3. Pen registers and trap and trace devices
4. Remote camera and video surveillance
5. Facial recognition software
6. Thermal imagers
7. Drone searches
8. Metal detectors and body imaging
9. Tracking devices
10. Computer and cell phone searches

11. Cell phone location tracking
12. Mass electronic surveillance
13. Social media and other internet activity
14. Interception of electronic messages

Key Cases

Silverman v. United States, 365 U.S. 505 (1961)
Katz v. United States, 389 U.S. 347 (1967)
United States v. United States District Court, 407 U.S. 297 (1972)
Smith v. Maryland, 442 U.S. 735 (1979)
Kyllo v. United States, 533 U.S. 27 (2001)
Riley v. California, 573 U.S. 373 (2014)
Carpenter v. United States, 585 U.S. ___ (2018)

Obiter Dicta

"Electronic surveillance is the greatest leveler of human privacy ever known. How most forms of it can be held 'reasonable' within the meaning of the Fourth Amendment is a mystery. To be sure, the Constitution and Bill of Rights are not to be read as covering only the technology known in the 18th century. ... At the same time, the concepts of privacy which the Founders enshrined in the Fourth Amendment vanish completely when we slavishly allow an all-powerful government, proclaiming law and order, efficiency, and other benign purposes, to penetrate all the walls and doors which men need to shield them from the pressures of a turbulent life around them and give them the health and strength to carry on."

—*Justice William O. Douglas, dissenting in* United States v. White, *401 U.S. 745 (1971).*

Introduction

As explained in chapter 7, the Supreme Court was initially reluctant to extend the protections of the Fourth Amendment beyond one's property.[1] That changed in 1967 when, in *Katz v. United States*,[2] the Court shifted the focus of the Fourth Amendment from property to privacy, saying "the Fourth Amendment protects people, not places." Coming out of *Katz*, courts employ a twofold test in determining whether one has a reasonable expectation of privacy in a given situation: (1) whether a person has exhibited a subjective expectation of privacy and (2) whether the expectation is one that society recognizes as *reasonable*. In this chapter, we will examine how the Fourth Amendment, as interpreted in *Katz* and many subsequent cases, limits the ability of government agencies to deploy electronic means of surveillance and detection. Herein, we will revisit some of the cases we have discussed from the previous two chapters, but we do so with the objective of explicating their relevance for the ways in which government surveillance implicates privacy rights under the Fourth Amendment.

Concealed Microphones

In the *Katz* case, agents placed a concealed microphone in a public telephone booth, so they could record what Mr. Katz was saying during his telephone conversations. Although similar government tactics using listening devices were upheld in the 1928 decision in *Olmstead v. United States* and a 1942 decision in *Goldman v. United States*—ostensibly because no *physical trespass* onto private property had occurred in those cases— the Supreme Court reversed course in *Katz v. United States*, holding that that this type of **eavesdropping** without prior judicial authorization violated the Fourth Amendment. In short, Katz was entitled to privacy in his telephone conversations, even in a public place, and the government had violated this privacy. As noted in chapter 7, this ruling enabled the Court to move beyond the *trespassory test* that guided prior Fourth Amendment jurisprudence. Under that approach, a physical intrusion into an individual's property interest had to occur in order for there to be a constitutional violation. But using the new "reasonable expectation of privacy" approach, as Justice Harlan famously called it in his concurring opinion in *Katz*, the Court began to focus upon broader privacy protections—a critical shift for search and seizure rights in a technologically changing world. Rejecting the government's emphasis on trespass-based arguments in *Katz*, the majority opinion written by Justice Potter Stewart said the following:

> The Government contends ... that the activities of its agents in this case should not be tested by Fourth Amendment requirements, for the surveillance technique they employed involved no physical penetration of the telephone booth from which the petitioner placed his calls. It is true that the absence of such penetration was at one time thought to foreclose further Fourth Amendment inquiry, ... for that Amendment was thought to limit only searches and seizures of tangible property. But '[t]he premise that property interests control the right of the Government to search and seize has been discredited.'"

Next, Justice Stewart examined the place where the government conducted its surveillance and rebutted an argument that the plain view doctrine should apply. He did so by observing, "The Government stresses the fact that the telephone booth from which the petitioner made his calls was constructed partly of glass, so that he was as visible after he entered it as he would have been if he had remained outside." To counter the government's argument, Stewart said this of Mr. Katz: "... [W]hat he sought to exclude when he entered the booth was not the

EAVESDROPPING: Refers to the tactic of listening in on a conversation without permission to do so.

intruding eye—it was the uninvited ear. He did not shed his right to do so simply because he made his calls from a place where he might be seen."

Justice Stewart went on to draw parallels to other contexts in which privacy rights could be protected, even outside the home, saying, "No less than an individual in a business office, in a friend's apartment, or in a taxicab, a person in a telephone booth may rely upon the protection of the Fourth Amendment. One who occupies it, shuts the door behind him, and pays the toll that permits him to place a call is surely entitled to assume that the words he utters into the mouthpiece will not be broadcast to the world." Then, in a statement that could be read today as harkening to a bygone era in how people once communicated, he opined, "To read the Constitution more narrowly is to ignore the vital role that the public telephone has come to play in private communication." With that, the general concept of *private communication* came under the purview of Fourth Amendment safeguards.

As noted previously, there was a time when the Court did, in fact, read the Constitution quite narrowly when it came to the use of concealed microphones. In *Goldman v. United States* (1942),[3] the Court upheld police use of a *detectaphone* that was placed against the wall of an adjacent room to listen in on telephone conversations. Nevertheless, the Court would change course nearly two decades later with its decision in *Silverman v. United States* (1961),[4] where police set up surveillance equipment inside a home that was directly adjacent to a dwelling where illegal gambling was suspected. Police established a base of operations in that adjacent home with the consent of the homeowner, and used an electronic listening device that was pushed under a base board and through a wall—such that the device touched a heating duct in the house occupied by those who would end up being arrested on gambling charges. That device was known as a *spike mic*, which the Court described as "a microphone with a spike about a foot long attached to, it together with an amplifier, a power pack, and earphones."

Evaluating this surveillance, the Court said that "the eavesdropping was accomplished by means of an unauthorized physical penetration into the premises occupied by the petitioners" and thus violated the Fourth Amendment. Explaining the importance of providing this protection within the home, Justice Stewart's majority opinion declared that "[t]he Fourth Amendment, and the personal rights which it secures, have a long history. At the very core stands the right of a man to retreat into his own home and there be free from unreasonable governmental intrusion." The majority then provided the following assessment as a parallel: "This Court has never held that a federal officer may, without warrant and without consent, physically entrench into a man's office or home, there secretly observe or listen, and relate at the man's subsequent criminal trial what was seen or heard." Of course, the rationales for this opinion focused on the notion of a *physical intrusion* (or *trespass*)—which left a need for the *Katz* decision to follow with more nuanced limitations on government action related to *expectations of privacy*, particularly in terms of surveillance outside of the home.

However, when it comes to hidden microphones worn by confidential informants, the situation is very different than what was discussed in *Katz*. In *Hoffa v. United States* (1966),[5] the Supreme Court upheld the use of testimony of an informant who spent considerable time with the defendant and regularly reported back details of conversations to the police. For an informant to wear a *wire* that records conversations is constitutionally similar. As Justice White recognized in his plurality opinion in *United States v. White* (1971),[6] "no different result is required if the agent, instead of immediately reporting and transcribing his conversations with defendant, either (1) simultaneously records them with electronic equipment which he is carrying on his person, ... (2)

or carries radio equipment which simultaneously transmits the conversations either to recording equipment located elsewhere or to other agents monitoring the transmitting frequency." As a result, the hidden microphone remains a valuable police tool to this day—although the sensitivity of those devices, and the ways they can be hidden, have certainly evolved over time.

JURISPRUDENCE

Police Hide a Microphone at a Grave Site
Kee v. City of Rowlett, 247 F.3d 206 (5th Cir. 2001)

As part of the investigation into the murder of two children, police in Rowlett, Texas placed a hidden microphone at the grave site where the burial service for the children took place. Police then recorded conversations and prayers by those who attended the burial service. Upon learning of the recording, the children's father and grandmother, Darlie Kee and Darin Routier, brought a federal lawsuit suit against the City of Rowlett under 42 U.S.C. § 1983, alleging a violation of their Fourth Amendment rights. The district court granted summary judgment in favor of the city and the Fifth Circuit affirmed, holding that the plaintiffs had failed to demonstrate a subjective expectation of privacy.

The majority opinion from the Fifth Circuit specifically said, "Perhaps most damaging to Kee and Routier's argument is that they failed to present evidence demonstrating any affirmative steps taken to preserve their privacy." In this regard, the court applied the *Katz* standard of what a person has done to evince a subjective expectation of privacy—observing that nothing in the record indicated the pair had attempted to modify the "tone, volume, or audibility" of their speaking to keep their discussion private while they were in a public location. The court went on to say, "While it is apparent from their affidavits that they did not expect government agents surreptitiously to be recording their prayers, they also were aware that the service was being conducted in an outdoor setting." In focusing more narrowly on what the speakers did not do, the court also declared, "Kee and Routier fail to allege that they took any steps to ensure that unwanted individuals were excluded or that they did anything to preserve the private nature of the service. They point to no reasonable safeguards or common-sense precautions taken to preserve their expectation of privacy."

Prior to the *Katz* decision, an early Supreme Court case on electronic eavesdropping arrived with the decision in *Rathbun v. United States* (1957).[7] Because at this point in U.S. history the high Court had not recognized the notion of an *expectation of privacy*, the Fourth Amendment was not applicable. Instead, the case revolved around interpretation of the Communications Act of 1934.[8] The portion of the law at issue was Section 605, which used a double negative in saying that "no person not being authorized by the sender shall intercept any communication and divulge or publish the existence, contents, substance, purport, effect, or meaning of such intercepted communication to any person. ..."

The Supreme Court was asked to decide if this law—and, really, the word *intercept*—should apply to the case of a man named Rathburn, who was in New York when he called a man named Sparkes. Unbeknownst to Rathburn, in advance of this conversation, Sparkes had actually requested that officers from the police department in his hometown of Pueblo, Colorado come over to his house and listen to what Rathburn was going to say. Thus, when Rathburn called Sparkes, there were two police officers in Sparkes's home eavesdropping on the conversation from a separate phone receiver in another room. Those officers would later testify in court that they overheard Rathburn threaten Sparkes's life.

Prior to the advent of cell phones, it was common for a household to have more than one phone receiver, all of which connected to the same number. With that in mind, the Supreme Court said there was no violation of federal law in what occurred here—ostensibly because police had not intercepted any communication or planted a new phone receiver; they were simply invited to listen in on a conversation. The majority opinion from Chief Justice Earl Warren even said that "one party may not force the other to secrecy merely by using a telephone." He then offered an analysis that might apply with equal force today if a court had to consider the Fourth Amendment ramifications when a person willingly allows law enforcement officials to listen in on a conversation:

> Common experience tells us that a call to a particular telephone number may cause the bell to ring in more than one ordinarily used instrument. Each party to a telephone conversation takes the risk that the other party may have an extension telephone and may allow another to overhear the conversation. When such takes place, there has been no violation of any privacy of which the parties may complain.

Before anyone starts creating recordings of conversations they have with other people, though, it is important to assess applicable state law. Today, thirty-five states allow for a recording to be made with just one party in a conversation offering consent, and that could, in fact, be the person who is doing the recording.[9] Federal law mirrors this approach and currently allows for a recording to be made with one-party consent.[10]

However, as of October 2021, thirteen states have passed laws that require *all* parties involved in a conversation to give consent to any recording of that conversation. Among these states, Oregon is unique in that it allows for one-party consent with a phone recording but requires all-party consent for in-person recordings. Additionally, the Nevada Supreme Court[11] and the Vermont Supreme Court[12] have imposed a requirement for all-party consent through case precedent. Ultimately, these types of laws or precedents establish key considerations for any assessments of expectations of privacy in those states—particularly, when it comes to evidence derived when people willingly allow police to listen in on conversations.[13]

Wiretaps

A **wiretap** allows a third party to listen to both sides of a telephone conversation. Whereas eavesdropping involves listening in on a conversation, perhaps with the assistance of a microphone, *wiretapping* (in its purest form) involves the attachment of some device—usually to a phone—to electronically intercept communication. Recall that in *Olmstead v. United States* (1928), the Supreme Court upheld wiretapping without a warrant as long as there was no physical penetration of the suspect's property. For decades after the *Olmstead* decision, law enforcement agencies routinely employed wiretapping without prior judicial authorization. Of course, the *Katz* decision overturned *Olmstead* and, therefore, made this practice presumptively unconstitutional. Moreover, Congress in 1968 enacted Title III of Omnibus Crime Control and Safe Streets Act,[14] which prohibits interception of electronic communications without a court order unless one party to the conversation consents. Under the statute, one party to the telephone conversation can consent to its being recorded by the authorities. In the absence of such consent, agents must obtain a wiretap order which, like an ordinary search warrant, must be issued by a judge or magistrate pursuant to a finding of probable cause.

Title III was passed two days after the Supreme Court issued a follow-up to the *Rathbun* decision and its interpretation of Section 605 of the Federal Communications Act. In *Lee v. Florida* (1968),[15] police in Orlando wanted to listen in on the phone conversations of a Mr. Lee. They ordered the local telephone company to install a new phone in the home of one of Mr. Lee's neighbors—and to connect that phone directly to the outside line that linked to Mr. Lee's house (the line that would essentially carry Mr. Lee's phone calls). A tape recorder and a set of earphones were attached to the new phone, along with a device called an automatic actuator, which could activate the recorder whenever the phone rang, thereby triggering a recording. Reviewing this conduct, the Supreme Court found that it violated the Federal Communications Act. Differentiating this case from *Rathbun*, Justice Stewart's majority opinion chastised the police by noting the following:

> What was done here was a far cry from the police activity in *Rathbun v. United States.* ... We viewed that situation as though one of the parties to the telephone conversation had simply "held out his handset so that another could hear out of it." ... In the present case, by contrast, there was neither "the consent of one party" nor a "regularly used" telephone "not ... installed ... just for [the] purpose" of surveillance. The conduct of the Orlando police, deliberately planned and carried out, clearly amounted to interception of the petitioners' communications within the meaning of § 605 of the Federal Communications Act.

Overall, as we will see throughout this chapter, when it comes to government attempts at electronic surveillance, federal law can be a powerful tool in supplementing the protections of the Fourth Amendment.

The Nixon Administration's Program of Warrantless Wiretapping

In *United States v. United States District Court* (1972),[16] the Supreme Court held that government officials are obligated to obtain judicial approval before undertaking electronic surveillance of persons inside the United States, even if national security issues are involved. The case stemmed from the warrantless wiretapping of phones belonging to members of a radical group that allegedly was conspiring to bomb a government building. But it was part of a larger program of warrantless surveillance directed at persons and groups deemed security threats.

WIRETAP: An electronic connection to a phone line that permits those conducting surveillance to listen to both sides of a conversation.

In its brief, the Nixon Administration urged the Court to adopt a national security exception to the Fourth Amendment and Title III, saying warrantless wiretaps were "necessary to protect the nation from attempts of domestic organizations to attack and subvert the existing structure of Government." Speaking for the Court, Justice Lewis Powell (a Nixon appointee), the Supreme Court soundly rejected this argument:

> Official surveillance, whether its purpose be criminal investigation or ongoing intelligence gathering, risks infringement of constitutionally protected privacy of speech. Security surveillances are especially sensitive because of the inherent vagueness of the domestic security concept, the necessarily broad and continuing nature of intelligence gathering, and the temptation to utilize such surveillances to oversee political dissent. We recognize, as we have before, the constitutional basis of the President's domestic security role, but we think it must be exercised in a manner compatible with the Fourth Amendment.

In an implicit rebuke to the Nixon Administration, Justice Powell also pointed out the danger to democracy in allowing government unrestricted powers of surveillance:

> History abundantly documents the tendency of Government—however benevolent and benign its motives—to view with suspicion those who most fervently dispute its policies. Fourth Amendment protections become the more necessary when the targets of official surveillance may be those suspected of unorthodoxy in their political beliefs. The danger to political dissent is acute where the Government attempts to act under so vague a concept as the power to protect "domestic security."

THE CONSTITUTION IN ACTION
The Church Committee Report on Government Surveillance

The Supreme Court has long upheld the authority of Congress to conduct investigations of executive branch agencies—investigations that can involve subpoenas for government officials to testify.[17] In 1975, the United States Senate formed the Senate Select Committee to Study Governmental Operations with Respect to Intelligence Activities. The purpose of this Committee was to examine whether executive branch intelligence-gathering agencies had engaged in unconstitutional activities. Known as the *Church Committee* because Senator Frank Church of Idaho was the Chair, the committee had nine members—five Democrats and four Republicans. Testimony was given to members of the committee—some provided in the form of closed-door hearings and some in the form of hearings that were open to the public. William Colby, head of the CIA, even testified. According to the U.S. Senate website's discussion of the Church Committee, there were 26 full committee meetings, 40 subcommittee hearings, and approximately 800 witnesses who testified either in public or closed sessions; committee members also examined 110,000 documents.[18]

The committee released a final report of its findings on April 29, 1976.[19] According to the Senate website's discussion of this report, "Investigators determined that, beginning with President Franklin Roosevelt's administration and continuing through the early 1970s, 'intelligence excesses, at home and abroad,' were not the 'product of any single party, administration, or man,' but had developed as America rose to a become a superpower during a global Cold War." The website observed that the report itself said, "Intelligence agencies have undermined the constitutional rights of citizens primarily because checks and balances designed by the framers of the Constitution to assure accountability have not been applied."

Some intelligence operations that were specifically revealed by the Church Committee included the following:

- Project MKUltra, under which U.S. citizens were given drugs like LSD, so experiments on mind control could be done;
- COINTELPRO, which dealt with undercover FBI agents joining (or, perhaps, infiltrating) civil rights and anti-war groups to conduct surveillance from within or to disrupt the groups' activities—this program even targeted individual people, including Martin Luther King, Jr. and elected officials;
- Operation Family Jewels, which was a CIA program designed to facilitate the assassination of certain foreign officials;
- Operation Mockingbird, which involved journalists working for the CIA and providing favorable coverage of the agency and its agents' actions;
- Projects Shamrock and Minaret, which were NSA programs that monitored communications among parties in the United States and abroad, with major telecommunications companies actually sharing information with the NSA—and the NSA also sharing such information with other government agencies.

The committee also uncovered that the NSA had a *watch list* that included the names of millions of Americans.

A permanent Senate Select Committee on Intelligence emerged from reforms suggested by the Church Committee. Additionally, the Hughes-Ryan Amendment to the Foreign Assistance Act of 1974 required the president to inform at least one congressional committee of clandestine CIA operations. Beyond those safeguards, though, secretive government surveillance activity has no doubt persisted since the Church Committee's final report was issued.

Pen Registers and Trap and Trace Devices

A **pen register** records the numbers dialed in outgoing phone calls from a particular phone number. A **trap and trace device** captures the phone numbers of calls coming into a specific phone number. Both devices have obvious utility to law enforcement. In *Smith v. Maryland* (1979),[20] the Supreme Court held that the use of a pen register is not a search within the meaning of the Fourth Amendment. The logic of the Court's decision meant it applied to trap and trace devices as well. In this case, a man had robbed a woman and then repeatedly made phone calls to her, including one in which he told her to stand outside on her porch just before he drove by her house.

Writing for a Court divided 6–3 in *Smith v. Maryland*, Justice Harry Blackmun observed that by using the phone, the defendant had "voluntarily conveyed numerical information to the telephone company and 'exposed' that information to its equipment in the ordinary course of business." In Blackmun's view, the defendant had no reasonable expectation of privacy with regard to the numbers he dialed. That information, which has come to be called **metadata**, was said to belong to the phone company. According to Blackmun, the defendant assumed the risk that the phone company would disclose the numbers he dialed to authorities.

PEN REGISTER: A device that records the numbers dialed from a particular phone line (outgoing calls).

TRAP AND TRACE DEVICE: A device that records phone numbers from which a particular number is dialed (incoming calls).

METADATA: Data associated with a phone call or other form of electronic communication, including the phone numbers or email addresses, date and time of the call, and duration of the call.

THIRD-PARTY DOCTRINE: The doctrine under which a person has no reasonable expectation of privacy with regard to information voluntarily given to a third party.

This position was based on the third-party doctrine, under which a person relinquishes an expectation of privacy over information voluntarily given to a third party. In a strongly worded dissent, Justice Stewart opined the following:

> I think that the numbers dialed from a private telephone—like the conversations that occur during a call—are within the constitutional protection recognized in *Katz*. It seems clear to me that information obtained by pen register surveillance of a private telephone is information in which the telephone subscriber has a legitimate expectation of privacy. The information captured by such surveillance emanates from private conduct within a person's home or office—locations that without question are entitled to Fourth and Fourteenth Amendment protection. Further, that information is an integral part of the telephonic communication that, under *Katz*, is entitled to constitutional protection, whether or not it is captured by a trespass into such an area.

Despite Justice Stewart's forceful dissent and considerable criticism in the years that followed, the Supreme Court has maintained the position taken in *Smith v. Maryland*. But not all state courts have followed this decision. In the wake of *Smith*, courts in several states have held that there is a reasonable expectation of privacy in one's phone records.[21] Relying on an enumerated right to privacy in its own state constitution, for instance, the Florida Supreme Court observed the following:

> The telephone numbers an individual dials or otherwise transmits represent personal information which, in most instances, the individual has no intention of communicating to a third party. This personal expectation is not defeated by the fact that the telephone company has that information.[22]

The Electronic Communications Privacy Act (ECPA) of 1986

In 1986, Congress adopted the Electronic Communications Privacy Act (ECPA).[23] Under Title III of the ECPA (the Pen Register Act[24]), which applies to federal, state, and local law enforcement, agents must obtain a court order before installing pen registers and trap and trace devices. To obtain an order, agents must certify that the information likely to be obtained is relevant to an ongoing criminal investigation. Orders allowing for the use of pen registers or trap and trace devices expire after sixty days, although courts are allowed to extend orders for an additional sixty days.[25] A key distinction here is that a court order does not need to be based on probable cause and is, thus, distinct from a search warrant.

The original definition of a pen register under the ECPA made reference to "a device which records or decodes electronic or other impulses which identify the numbers called or ... transmitted on the telephone line which [the] device is attached." Yet Section 216 of the PATRIOT Act would amend this definition to permit the application of a pen register to internet communications, such as in the case of capturing the websites a person had visited through their computer or cell phone or even the email addresses with which a person has communicated. Even so, the updated language also was clear to note that the contents of electronic activity (such as what was written in an email) should not be revealed by a pen register, with the new definition reading as follows: "a device or process which records or decodes dialing, routing, addressing, or signaling information transmitted by an instrument or facility from which a wire or electronic communication is transmitted, provided, however, that such information shall not include the contents of any communication."[26] We discuss this topic in greater detail in the social media section that follows, where we address cases in which law enforcement officials used a pen register to track specific computers tied to internet activity.

Widespread government use of pen registers was revealed by *The New York Times* in 2013. Scott Shane and Colin Moynihan wrote an article[27] indicating that, for a period of at least six years, DEA agents had relied upon telephone provider AT&T to offer access to a database of phone records. According to the article, under this arrangement, which was called the Hemisphere Project, "[t]he government pays AT&T to place its employees in drug-fighting units around the country. Those employees sit alongside Drug Enforcement Administration agents and local detectives and supply them with the phone data from as far back as 1987." The database was said to encompass all telephone calls that went through an AT&T *switch*, even if a call was not made by one of the company's customers, and four billion new calls could be added to the database each day as the program progressed. Moreover, the location from which a call was made could also be revealed.

In defense of this program, government officials indicated that it was especially helpful in tracking those criminals who constantly changed cell phones. Shane and Moynihan provided some examples, including a February 2013 investigation in which the database helped locate a woman in South Carolina who had made multiple bomb threats; a March 2013 investigation in which this database helped authorities uncover the new phone number and location of a criminal who pretended to be a Navy general and ran over a federal agent with a car; and a 2011 investigation in Seattle in which DEA agents "tracked drug dealers who were rotating prepaid phones, leading to the seizure of 136 kilos of cocaine and $2.2 million." Later in this chapter, we will discuss mass electronic surveillance of phone activity as conducted by the NSA—although in terms of sheer volume of calls assessed, the DEA's Hemisphere programs appears to have been more pervasive.

Information Stored "in the Cloud"

Under the Stored Communications Act of 1986[28] (which was Section II of the Electronic Communications Privacy Act), the federal government can compel a third party, such as a telephone provider or internet service provider, to turn over information stored by a private party in some types of internet settings—provided that government officials first obtain a search warrant. This can impact information stored on a *cloud*, a term many people use to describe storage servers that are accessed over the internet. For example, many users of an iPhone will upload pictures from their phone to Apple's iCloud service. Thus, government officials could compel Apple to reveal the contents of pictures and documents that a person has stored in their cloud, but that would need to be justified by a search warrant.

In 2018, Congress passed the CLOUD Act,[29] which indicted that an internet service provider could be compelled to give the government access to items held on a storage server, irrespective of whether that server was located in a foreign country or in the United States, though again, a search warrant would still be needed. This law was passed in response to a court case called *Microsoft Corp. v. United States*,[30] which arose when the FBI procured a search warrant (pursuant to the Stored Communications Act) requiring Microsoft to reveal a U.S. citizen's emails. Microsoft refused to do so—contending that the emails were stored on a Microsoft server that was physically located in Ireland (even though the person under investigation had no ties to Ireland). After the Second Circuit ruled in favor of Microsoft, the Supreme Court granted review, but when Congress passed the CLOUD Act, effectively updating the Stored Communications Act, the case was deemed moot and dismissed. The FBI was then issued a new search warrant pursuant to the CLOUD Act, and in regard to dismissal of the legal battle, Microsoft's lawyers issued a court filing that actually said, "Microsoft agrees with the government that there is no longer a live case or controversy between the parties with respect to the question presented."[31]

Remote Camera and Video Surveillance

Today, routine video surveillance has become commonplace. Highways, city streets, convenience stores, schools, parks, airports, and courthouses are just some of the myriad places where activities are recorded by video cameras. To the extent that people in public places are subjected to such surveillance, there is no invasion of privacy. And, of course, such surveillance is crucial to the maintenance of security. But it is not without controversy—particularly, when surveillance is targeted at particular groups. For example, reports have surfaced that in the aftermath of the 9/11 terrorist attacks, the New York Police Department trained cameras on mosques and also used automated license plate readers to acquire data about cars parked near mosques.[32]

Remote cameras also are used regularly in investigations concerning drug offenses. In *United States v. McIver and Eberle* (1999),[33] the Ninth Circuit reviewed the actions of U.S. Forest Service agents who installed motion-activated cameras to surveil an area of a national forest where marijuana plants were growing. Images captured by these cameras played a crucial role in an investigation that ultimately led to a conviction for conspiracy to produce marijuana. On appeal, the defendants claimed that the warrantless video surveillance by the Forest Service violated their reasonable expectations of privacy. The Ninth Circuit disagreed, saying that the defendants "failed to demonstrate that they had an objectively reasonable expectation of privacy in their cultivation of marijuana in an area open to the public." The court went on to laud the investigative techniques at hand, by saying: "We are ... persuaded that the use of photographic equipment to gather evidence that could be lawfully observed by a law enforcement officer does not violate the Fourth Amendment. The use of a motion activated camera under these circumstances appears to us to be a prudent and efficient use of modern technology."

Cameras Directed at Particular Persons or Places

In *California v. Ciraolo* (1986),[34] police received an anonymous tip that Dante Ciraolo was growing marijuana in his backyard. Because that tip alone was not enough to obtain a search warrant, police conducted a low-altitude plane flight—at an elevation of 1,000 feet—and photographed cannabis plants in Ciraolo's backyard. They then used the photos to obtain a warrant and seize the contraband. Splitting 5–4, the Supreme Court upheld the search, saying that Ciraolo's "expectation that his garden was protected from [aerial] observation is unreasonable and is not an expectation that society is prepared to honor." Chief Justice Burger and four of his colleagues essentially saw this case as an extension of the plain view doctrine, with the majority opinion declaring that:

> The Fourth Amendment protection of the home has never been extended to require law enforcement officers to shield their eyes when passing by a home on public thoroughfares. Nor does the mere fact that an individual has taken measures to restrict some views of his activities preclude an officer's observations from a public vantage point where he has a right to be and which renders the activities clearly visible.

In dissent, Justice Powell averred, "The indiscriminate nature of aerial surveillance, illustrated by [the] photograph of respondent's home and enclosed yard as well as those of his neighbors, poses 'far too serious a threat to privacy interests in the home to escape entirely some sort of Fourth Amendment oversight.'"[35]

The same day it decided the *Ciraolo* case, the Supreme Court held that higher-altitude photography of a chemical plant was not a search within the meaning of the Fourth Amendment. In *Dow Chemical Co. v. United States* (1986),[36] the Court concluded that this aerial surveillance (at altitudes of 12,000; 3,000; and 1,200 feet) was incapable of revealing intimate activities that would give rise to constitutional concerns. The fact that the photography was undertaken by the EPA pursuant to its regulatory mission also was a significant factor for the Court, with Chief Justice Burger's majority opinion stating that "[r]egulatory or enforcement authority generally carries with it all the modes of inquiry and investigation traditionally employed or useful to execute the authority granted."[37] Speaking for four dissenters, Justice Powell noted that the "EPA's aerial photography penetrated into a private commercial enclave, an area in which society has recognized that privacy interests legitimately may be claimed." In Powell's view, "the decision may signal a significant retreat from the rationale of prior Fourth Amendment decisions."

JURISPRUDENCE

Video Scanning of a Student's Room during an Online Exam
Ogletree v. Cleveland State University, No. 1:21-cv-00500-jpc (N.D. Ohio 2022)

During the COVID-19 pandemic, colleges and universities relied heavily on online instruction. Quite often, exams administered online require students to use software that prevents their web browsers from going to sites other than the exam site. It is also common to require students to activate their web cams so a remote proctor can view the room in which the student is taking the exam. A recording of the session can be made for later viewing by the instructor. Of course, all of this is designed to prevent cheating. But does requiring students to give access to their web cams violate their privacy rights? At a state college or university, this can become a constitutional question. In August 2022, a federal judge in Ohio held that requiring students to activate their

(*continued*)

web cams so that university personnel can scan their rooms is a violation of the Fourth Amendment.

Aaron Ogletree, a student at Cleveland State University, filed suit after he was required to submit to a remote room scan before beginning an online chemistry exam. In defending against the suit, the University argued that the room scan was not a search within the meaning of the Fourth Amendment. Judge J. Philip Calabrese concluded otherwise, writing that Ogletree "had an objectively reasonable expectation of privacy in his home—and one that society recognizes as reasonable." The University also argued that the use of the remote room scan was necessary to preserve the integrity of the online exam. Again, Judge Calabrese found otherwise: "Whatever the case, a record of sporadic and discretionary use of room scans does not permit a finding that room scans are truly, and uniquely, effective at preserving test integrity." Ultimately, the judge concluded that "... Mr. Ogletree's privacy interest outweighs Cleveland State's interests in scanning his room."

Red Light and Speed Detection Cameras

Many cities and counties across the country use cameras to identify traffic violations—in particular, speeding and running red lights. According to the National Conference of State Legislatures, as of 2022, local governments in twenty-two states made use of red light cameras, while sixteen states had local governments that were using speed detection cameras. Six states ban the use of both types of camera enforcement (MA, MS, NH, SC, TX, and WV), while Montana and South Dakota ban red light cameras and New Jersey and Wisconsin ban speed cameras. Nevada requires camera enforcement of traffic violations to be implemented in a law enforcement vehicle or facility, or through a camera operated directly by an officer.[38] As of 2021, 345 municipalities across the United States were using some type of camera enforcement for traffic violations, which was down from 533 in 2012.[39] Miami, Florida and Rochester, New York were among the cities to terminate the use of cameras in the past five years. At the federal level, the 2021 Infrastructure Investment and Jobs Act allows federal funds to be spent on traffic cameras.[40]

From a constitutional standpoint, it is difficult to argue that the use of such cameras violates the Fourth Amendment, given that driving on the public roads is a privilege and not a constitutional right. Beyond that, there is typically no reasonable expectation of privacy with regard to external views of one's automobile when it is operating in public. As the Supreme Court stated in *Katz v. United States*, "What a person knowingly exposes to the public ... is not a subject of Fourth Amendment protection."

Red light cameras and speed detection cameras have been attacked on due process grounds. But in 2010, the U.S. Circuit Court of Appeals for the Sixth Circuit upheld Akron, Ohio's speed detection cameras against a due process challenge, noting that "the ordinance provides for notice of the citation, an opportunity for a hearing, provision for a record of

RED-LIGHT CAMERAS: Cameras placed adjacent to public roadways for the purpose of assessing whether a car has passed through a red light and typically providing a private company with justification to send a citation to the registered owner of a vehicle.

SPEED-DETECTION CAMERAS: Cameras placed in public locations for the purpose of assessing whether a car is traveling over the speed limit; correlated citations can be sent to the vehicle's registered owner.

the hearing decision, and the right to appeal an adverse decision."[41] One year earlier, the Seventh Circuit had upheld Chicago's use of red light cameras.[42]

Some state courts also have authorized the use of red light cameras, including Florida's Supreme Court in 2018.[43] But in 2019, after the Texas Supreme Court refused to stop the use of red light cameras, Governor Greg Abbott signed a bill that banned the use of these cameras in the state.[44] In Missouri, an appellate court found red-light cameras to be unconstitutional in 2015.[45] Elsewhere, in a nuanced approached to this topic, in 2011, Tennessee enacted a law that banned all camera tickets for a driver who makes a right turn at a red light without stopping. This followed a ruling from a state appeals court that denoted a due process violation related to inconsistent standards regarding how long a driver was supposed to stop at a red light before turning. Nevertheless, other tickets can be given from activity seen on cameras in that state, with local officials having a choice of whether to use cameras.[46]

However, in other places, depending on a state's constitution, there could be separation of powers or delegation of powers issues related to police contracting the red-light camera penalty process to private companies. In Louisiana, for instance, many tickets have been overturned because courts have determined that parish charters do not allow any party outside of the police to give out tickets.

Moreover, as we will discuss in chapter 12, the Sixth Amendment protects a person's right to confront their accuser in a criminal case. That could become an issue when the *accuser* is a camera; even so, the actual accuser in these cases is probably an employee of a company or a police department—the person who watches the video of a car running a red light in order to justify issuance of the ticket.[47]

Finally, *Kansas v. Glover* (2020),[48] which is discussed in the previous chapter, confronts an ancillary aspect of red light cameras. Recall that in the *Glover* case, police following behind a car used a computer check to determine that the car's registered owner had a suspended license, and a traffic stop ensued. In upholding this stop, the Court ruled that the officer used a "commonsense inference" that a vehicle will be driven by its registered owner. Accordingly, for the purposes of red-light cameras, that same assumption could be used to justify mailing a ticket to the owner of a car that runs a red light, even without a direct indication of who was driving at the time of the infraction.

THE CONSTITUTION IN ACTION
Are Traffic Cameras Used Equitably?

While some might suggest that traffic cameras could provide a so-called *race neutral* approach to policing traffic violations, when considering the use of red light cameras and speed cameras, it is important to recognize where—as in, which neighborhoods—a city chooses to deploy such cameras. After all, the financial impacts of these cameras on a particular community can become significant as private companies attempt to collect fines and potential late fees on tickets.

Along these lines, a study from *The Washington Post* examined traffic camera and police-given tickets in the District of Columbia from 2016 through 2020, finding that: "62 percent of all the fines from automated systems and D.C. police—$467 million—were issued in neighborhoods where Black residents make up at least 70 percent of the population and where the average median household income is below $50,000. In overwhelmingly White and financially well-off census tracts, where average median household income levels are above $100,000, the city issued about $95.9 million in infractions."[49]

In research specific to red light camera and speed camera tickets, a study released by *ProPublica* in 2022 examined millions citations given in Chicago between 2015 and 2019. Data indicated that more than double the number

(continued)

of tickets were sent to zip codes with majority Black and Hispanic populations than were sent to majority-White zip codes.[50]

Similar findings from Chicago were apparent in a study released by researchers from the Department of Urban Policy and Planning at the University of Illinois-Chicago in 2022. Their report analyzed nearly 5 million traffic camera tickets given in Chicago from 2016–2019, finding that "majority Black census tracts have the highest rates of tickets per household, followed by majority Latino census tracts as compared to majority White or other tracts."[51] They also found that low-income residents faced late fees on 46% of tickets as opposed to upper-income residents, who dealt with such fees on 17% of tickets; in some areas of the city, 1% of annual household income was spent on tickets.

Defending the use of cameras in Chicago, a spokesperson for Mayor Lori Lightfoot noted that traffic-related deaths were "at epidemic levels," adding, "We feel strongly that cameras are a tool in the toolkit to help alleviate that."[52] And in that regard, the UIC study did indicate a statistically significant relationship between cameras and enhanced safety.[53]

In attempt to explain the data demonstrating that minority neighborhoods in Chicago were bearing an excessive burden of the City's overall camera fines, both of the aforementioned studies examined the matter of camera placement. For example, the UIC study noted that cameras within 350 feet of a freeway were more likely to result in a citation citywide and also observed that such cameras were more likely to be placed in majority-Black neighborhoods (21% of all cameras in such neighborhoods fit this criteria compared to 13% citywide).[54] Additionally, that study found that Latino neighborhoods were more likely to have cameras in school safety zones (comprising 71% of all cameras in those neighborhoods, compared to 41% city-wide).[55] This study also pointed to "road density" as a contributing factor to the proportion of camera tickets distributed in lower income neighborhoods. In this regard, the *ProPublica* report said the following: "The irony is that some of the factors that contribute to ticketing disparities, such as wider streets and lack of sidewalks in low-income communities of color, also make those neighborhoods more dangerous for pedestrians, cyclists and even motorists."[56]

Facial Recognition Technology

FACIAL RECOGNITION TECHNOLOGY: Computer-based systems that can link a photo or surveillance image with a known image of an individual that is housed in a database.

An emerging tool employed by law enforcement officials at all levels of government is facial recognition technology. In simple terms, this makes use of computer algorithms to match a photo of a person with examples of other photos found in some database of known individuals. This technology has its roots in software developed through the 1990s,[57] and recent advances in machine learning have helped computers become more adept at using facial characteristics, such as the distance between key features, to match images together.[58]

The first widespread use of the such technology is believed to be at the 2001 Super Bowl in Tampa where the faces of the 70,000 fans in the crowd were scanned—19 of whom were matched to outstanding warrants held by police, with one ACLU analyst saying of this event (which predated the 9/11 terrorist attacks): "Facial recognition was a very new, untested technology and it was still kind of science-fiction."[59]

Certainly, this technology has become more and more widespread in law enforcement contexts since that Super Bowl. For instance, a 2016 study from the Georgetown Law Center on Privacy & Technology indicated that "at least one in four state or local police departments possesses the ability to run facial recognition searches either directly or via a partnering agency."[60] A 2022 study from the same Georgetown Law Center also revealed that U.S. Immigration and Customs Enforcement officials have scanned one in three driver's licenses of all adults in the United States to build a facial recognition database.[61] Public records even indicate that the FBI ran over 52,000 facial recognition searches in fiscal year 2018.[62]

There are numerous law enforcement uses for this technology. For example, an officer might use a mug shot to verify the identity of an arrested suspect, or a suspect being investigated or interrogated in the field could have their image—whether taken from a surveillance camera or perhaps even a body camera or an officer's cell phone—matched against photos in a database with known identities. Usually, two types of photo matching are used. First, there is *one-to-one matching*, where a photo of a known person is matched against an image thought to be of that person, such as in verifying a passport. Second, there is *one-to-many matching*, where a surveillance image might be compared to an entire database of photos in the hope that a computer will locate a match.

A key to the quality and usefulness of facial recognition software is the database of photos against which an individual image is compared. Jack Laperruque, in an article entitled "Facing the Future of Surveillance," written for The Constitution Project's Task Force on Facial Recognition Surveillance, finds that the "FBI maintains the largest network of photo databases that are accessed for facial recognition surveillance in the United States."[63] The FBI actually has a special unit to handle facial recognition tasks, called the Facial Analysis, Comparison, and Evaluation (FACE) Services Unit. The FBI database of photos is drawn from an amalgam of sources, including mug shots from arrests and photos from passports and drivers' licenses. States can permit the FBI to use license photos, and currently more than 60 million such images are searchable by the FBI. Many states, in turn, are permitted to access and use the FBI's photo database. Yet some states have chosen to build their own databases, with Pennsylvania having one with more than 30 million photos and Florida having one with over 45 million. Such state-level databases are likely to be stocked with driver's license and mug shots photos, but also could include images that people publicly post on social media websites.

Beyond the FBI and local police, other government agencies make use of facial recognition technology. Immigration officials have facial recognition capability at airports, seaports, and other border crossings.[64] For example, a new pilot program started by U.S. Customs and Border Protection (CBP) in September 2021 uses facial recognition at the Anzalduas International Bridge in McAllen, Texas, near the Mexico border; people attempting to cross that bridge could have their picture taken and checked against a government database.[65] Federal agents at airports, such as TSA and CBP agents, could even use facial recognition software to assess watch lists to check if passengers boarding flights are banned from doing so.[66] TSA also makes use of facial recognition as a part of its SPOT Program, which stands for screening of passengers by observation techniques. Using nearly 100 different indicators, agents will select persons for additional pat-down searches or screens based on suggested indicators of nervousness or deception; critics have suggested that this program, for which nearly 3,000 agents are trained to take part, results in profiling that is ineffective in locating actual national security threats.[67]

For those who would like to voluntarily provide a photograph to the government, in 2021, the Transportation Security Administration began a pilot program, wherein individual travelers can choose to submit pictures to a facial recognition software system. This would allow those passengers to board airplanes without having to show an identification card; instead, when the person approaches TSA agents at the entrance to the boarding area, a picture of their face would be taken and compared to the database. The program is voluntary and currently in use, as of March 2021, at Detroit Metropolitan Wayne County Airport. The following disclaimer is posted on the TSA website about this program (the posting is required by a federal law, known as the Privacy Act):

> Providing this information is voluntary. If you do not provide it, you will proceed through the standard screening process at the checkpoint. TSA may share information that you provide with CBP, DHS S&T, law enforcement, intelligence agencies, or others under the published System of Records Notice—DHS/TSA-001 Transportation Security Enforcement Record System.

That disclaimer seems to indicate the possibility that government agencies might share photographic information about individual persons.

THE CONSTITUTION AND SOCIAL JUSTICE
Is Facial Recognition Software Racially Discriminatory?

Although facial recognition may seem like a powerful law enforcement tool for identifying suspected criminals, scholars have raised concerns over whether certain groups are treated unfairly by the commonly used facial recognition computer algorithms. This can be particularly problematic because of the number of Americans who—perhaps unbeknownst to them—have pictures in law enforcement databases. In an article entitled "Racial Discrimination in Face Recognition Technology," Alex Najibi from Harvard University points out that more than half of Americans have photographs on file with government agencies that could in turn use the photos for facial recognition analysis, but he also notes, "Of the dominant biometrics in use (fingerprint, iris, palm, voice, and face), face recognition is the least accurate and is rife with privacy concerns."[68] As Steve Nouri said in an article for *Forbes*, "AI systems learn to make decisions based on training data, which may contain skewed human decisions or represent historical or social inequities."[69] In the end, false identification matches could result in an improper detention, arrest, or even incarceration.

The first prominent study on this topic came from Joy Buolamwini and Timnit Gebru, who found that three facial analysis algorithms commonly used by law enforcement agencies, including ones created by Microsoft and IBM, misidentified Black women at error rates of up to 34.7%; the same algorithms only misidentified White men at error rates of up to 0.8%.[70] Furthermore, according to an article from the ACLU, "[a] subsequent study by [Joy] Buolamwini and [Deb] Raji at the Massachusetts Institute of Technology confirmed these problems persisted with Amazon's software."[71]

The federal government has conducted its own analysis as well, with a study from the U.S. Department of Commerce's National Institute of Standards and Technology examining 189 different algorithms from 99 developers, including many used by law enforcement agencies. The databases of photos included the following: mugshots collected by law enforcement in the United States; application photos of people who had applied for immigration benefits; photos submitted on visa applications for entry into the United States; and photos taken by immigration officials at border crossings. More than 18 million images from almost 8.5 million people were used in study.[72]

Ultimately, one source summarized the findings of this study by saying it "found that face recognition algorithms perform more poorly when examining the faces of women, people of color, the elderly, and children, raising serious concerns about police use of the technology across the United States and the world."[73] Another source, the *MIT Technology Review*, offered these four takeaways from the federal study: First, "[f]or one-to-one matching, most systems had a higher rate of false positive matches for Asian and African-American faces over Caucasian faces, sometimes by a factor of 10 or even 100"; this meant that a match was found when none should have been found in these cases. Second, however, the study found that algorithms created in Asian countries were more accurate in correctly matching Asian faces and also performed well on Caucasian faces. Third, the MIT review also said, "Algorithms developed in the US were all consistently bad at matching Asian, African-American, and Native American faces. Native

Americans suffered the highest false positive rates." Finally, the MIT review noted that "[o]ne-to-many matching … systems had the worst false positive rates for African-American women. …"[74] One potential explanation scholars have given for these discrepancies is that the resolution quality of photos of darker skinned individuals might be lacking. The lack of appropriate samples of such photos for *educating* computer algorithms also has been posited.

Najibi's work confronted another aspect of this discussion by evaluating where surveillance cameras tend to be placed. He noted that high-resolution cameras have been placed in parts of major cities like Detroit to essentially scan people's faces and potentially identify known criminals. In Detroit, in fact, images from these cameras are transmitted directly to the Detroit Police Department. Najibi offered a graphic depiction of the cameras' locations in that city, showing that their placement was aimed primarily at Black communities.[75] It is also noteworthy that, after the 9/11 attacks, the NYPD deployed cameras on public streets near mosques and also made use of automated license plate readers to scan the vehicles parked outside of mosques.[76]

Portland, Oregon and Boston, Massachusetts are among the cities that have already banned the use of facial recognition software. At the federal level, a bill called the Facial Recognition and Biometric Technology Moratorium Act has been proposed in Congress, and it would limit the use of such technology to situations in which a legislative body has authorized it; the bill also proposes some federal funds to be withheld from police departments that improperly use facial recognition technology. The bill was first introduced in 2020 and then reintroduced in June 2021 by a group of legislators from the House and Senate, but no action has been taken in Congress. It remains to be seen if specific legislation, or even court decisions related to facial recognition software—which could have ramifications for the Fourteenth Amendment—will be forthcoming.

Thermal Imagers

A **thermal imager** is an infrared camera; it essentially takes pictures of heat. This technology has numerous military and law enforcement applications. In the 1990s, police began to use thermal imagers to detect indoor marijuana grows. Growers would often use high-intensity lamps, which gave off considerable heat. The thermal imager could be used to detect the unusual level of heat given off by these lamps. These unusual heat signatures could then become the basis for establishing probable cause to obtain a search warrant.

In *Kyllo v. United States* (2001),[77] the Supreme Court invalidated the use of thermal imagers for searches of the home, unless a search warrant was obtained prior to use of the imager. Speaking for a sharply divided 5–4 bench, Justice Scalia said that "when the Government uses a device that is not in general public use, to explore details of the home that would previously have been unknowable without physical intrusion, the surveillance is a 'search' and is presumptively unreasonable without a warrant." In dissent, Justice Stevens argued that the case was controlled by the principle stated in *Katz v. United States*, to wit: "What a person knowingly exposes to the public, even in his own home or office, is not a subject of Fourth Amendment protection." In Justice Stevens's view, "the notion that heat emissions from the outside of a dwelling are

THERMAL IMAGER: A device that detects heat (infrared light).

a private matter implicating the protections of the Fourth Amendment ... is not only unprecedented but also quite difficult to take seriously."

JURISPRUDENCE

Thermal Imager Used in Search of Home
Kyllo v. United States, 533 U.S. 27 (2001)

In *Kyllo v. United States*, government officials from the U.S. Department of Interior received information that Danny Kyllo was growing marijuana inside his home. Agents sat inside a vehicle on a public street, across the road from Kyllo's home, and used a thermal imaging device known as the Agema Thermovision 210 to scan that home. The scan discerned an abnormal heat source inside, near the roof. Officers inferred that the heat source was derived from special lights used in growing marijuana and used this information, along with utility bills and informant statements, in a request to obtain a search warrant. The warrant was granted, and a subsequent search yielded approximately 100 marijuana plants, leading Kyllo to enter a conditional guilty plea.

On review, the Supreme Court found that Kyllo's Fourth Amendment rights had been violated. In ruling the initial observation—and, thus, the subsequent grant of a warrant—to be unconstitutional, the Court conceded that "visual intrusion" of the home could in some cases be acceptable under the plain view doctrine, noting that case law indicated that "the eye cannot ... be guilty of trespass." However, the Court found that the plain view doctrine did not apply here because the officers "did more than naked-eye surveillance of a home." Justice Scalia's majority opinion observed that when "the Government uses a device that is not in general public use, to explore details of the home that would previously have been unknowable without physical intrusion, the surveillance is a 'search' and is presumptively unreasonable without a warrant." Scalia specifically noted that the infrared beam conducted a "through-the-wall" search that could reveal "intimate" details of the home.

The majority opinion suggested the device in question was quite "crude" in terms of the image quality it revealed, but Justice Scalia deemed this fact irrelevant to analysis of the privacy invasion, saying, "To begin with, there is no necessary connection between the sophistication of the surveillance equipment and the 'intimacy' of the details that it observes—which means that one cannot say (and the police cannot be assured) that use of the relatively crude equipment at issue here will always be lawful." Explaining what the technology in question could reveal, in theory, Scalia hypothesized, "The Agema Thermovision 210 might disclose, for example, at what hour each night the lady of the house takes her daily sauna and bath—a detail that many would consider 'intimate'; and a much more sophisticated system might detect nothing more intimate than the fact that someone left a closet light on." The challenge for formulating case precedent to address this matter, then, was described as follows: "We could not, in other words, develop a rule approving only that through-the-wall surveillance which identifies objects no smaller than 36 by 36 inches, but would have to develop a jurisprudence specifying which home activities are 'intimate' and which are not. Scalia went on to say: "And even when (if ever) that jurisprudence were fully developed, no police officer would be able to know *in advance* whether his through-the-wall surveillance picks up 'intimate' details and thus would be unable to know in advance whether it is constitutional."

This discussion over the meaning of *intimate details*, and whether police could somehow conduct a warrantless search of the home if that search did not reveal intimate details, was extinguished when the Court said, "In *Silverman*, for example, we made clear that any physical invasion of the structure of the home, 'by even a fraction of an inch,' was too much ... and there is certainly no exception to the warrant requirement for the officer who barely cracks open the front door and sees nothing but the nonintimate rug on the vestibule floor. In the home, our cases show, all details are intimate details, because the entire area is held safe from prying government eyes."

Drone Searches

One unique issue that has become germane to Fourth Amendment dialogue connects to the use of **drones** in visual surveillance from above. According to a March 2020 study by Bard College and the Brookings Institute, there are "at least 1,578 state and local public safety agencies in the U.S. [that have] acquired drones."[78] Perhaps in response, more than a dozen states have passed laws requiring search warrants to be used in conjunction with drone searches of private property. But in other states, a warrantless drone search could, in theory, occur.

Not surprisingly, given the emerging nature of this technology, judicial review of warrantless drone searches is scant. However, two previously discussed Supreme Court cases (*California v. Ciraolo* and *Dow Chemical v. United States*) are relevant in that government officials in those cases were making observations and taking pictures from an overhead vantage point—and the actions were upheld by the high Court. Moreover, the Court's ruling in *Florida v. Riley* (1989)[79] approved police observations made from a helicopter at an altitude of 400 feet. From that altitude, police could see, with the naked eye, marijuana plants in a backyard. Of course, when attempting to extract parallels from these cases, it is worth noting that drone searches could take place at a significantly lower altitude and would, of course, require use of a sophisticated camera.

Additionally, there is also the precedent of *Kyllo v. United States* (2001) to consider in regard to whether drones might constitute some type of *unusual technology*. One could argue that drones have reached a point at which they are in *general public use*, as more than 17 million of them have been registered with the U.S. Department of Transportation.[80] Accordingly, the constitutionality of a drone search might—under *Kyllo* and the aerial surveillance cases—turn on whether it revealed information inside the home or whether the drone was flown at an especially low altitude.

In a 2021 case that is one the few nationwide court decisions on this topic, the Court of Appeals of the State of Michigan relied on the *Kyllo* precedent in finding that a Fourth Amendment violation had occurred when government officials used a drone—without a warrant—to take aerial pictures of a homeowner's backyard.[81] The legal issue at stake was less nefarious than drug cultivation, as the matter concerned an alleged violation of a town's zoning ordinances, which was a non-criminal matter.

Here, the opinion wrestled with whether to use the trespass doctrine or the reasonable expectation of privacy test, opting for the latter in light of the fact that a drone observation could occur partly from a vantage

DRONE: A compact flying machine that can be remotely controlled and flown at low altitudes, allowing for photographs or videos to be taken from above.

point that is not technically on a person's property. In this regard, the court said, "[W]e think there is little meaningful distinction for present purposes between 'just inside the property line' and 'just outside the property line.'" Applying the reasonable expectation of privacy test to this matter, the court said, "We decide this matter based upon defendants' reasonable expectation of privacy—critical to which is that any reasonable person would have *expected* a low-altitude drone overflight to be trespassory and exceptional, whether the drone flew as high as a football-field length or flew directly up to an open bathroom window." In conclusion, the court offered advice for government agents seeking to use a drone for surveillance of private property: "Our holding today is highly unlikely to preclude any legitimate governmental inspection or enforcement action short of outright 'fishing expeditions.' If a governmental entity has any kind of nontrivial and objective reason to believe there would be value in flying a drone over a person's property, as did plaintiff here, then we trust the entity will probably be able to persuade a court to grant a warrant or equivalent permission to conduct a search."

A key for this opinion, in terms of differentiating a drone from an observation made by an officer in a helicopter or a plane, seems to be the low-flying capabilities of a drone—a factor that carries unique privacy concerns. It should be noted that, as of summer 2022, litigation in this case was still ongoing. In May 2022, the Michigan Supreme Court remanded the case[82] to the intermediate appellate court for reconsideration in light of the U.S. Supreme Court's decision in *Pennsylvania Board of Probation and Parole v. Scott* (1998),[83] which had refused to extend the exclusionary rule beyond the criminal context.

Metal Detectors and Body Scanners

Metal detectors are commonly employed at schools, airports, jails, courthouses, and other public buildings. Typically, these involve a low level of intrusion upon privacy rights. For several decades, metal detectors called magnetometers were used to scan passengers at U.S. airports, without any significant privacy-related concerns. However, since 2007, those have been gradually replaced with Advanced Imaging Technology (AIT) body scanners. The movement toward widespread use of these scanners was advanced by the Obama administration in 2010, after a failed *underwear bombing* occurred on a flight from Amsterdam to Detroit on Christmas Day 2009. Two specific types of AIT scanners have been used in airports in the past decade—one based on electromagnetic waves and one based

METAL DETECTORS: Devices that can detect if a person walking through is carrying an object with metal.

ADVANCED IMAGING TECHNOLOGY (AIT) BODY SCANNERS: Body imaging devices used in U.S. airports to provide a detailed image of the human body prior to passengers boarding airline flights.

on X-ray technology. The latter, known as the *backscatter* technology scanners, were created by a government contractor named Rapiscan and raised particular concerns because of how much detail the machines revealed in their images of the nude human body; these were essentially full-body scans conducted with X-ray technology, and correlated concerns arose in regard to whether travelers even might be exposed to low doses of radiation.[84]

With passage of the FAA Reauthorization Act of 2012, Congress indicated that all scanners in U.S. airports were required to have certain privacy protections. Specifically, a type of software known as Automated Target Recognition software was to be used because it would distort the naked human body into a less-revealing image, while still allowing government officials to detect contraband. In response to passage of this law, the TSA announced that all backscatter scanners would be removed from U.S. airports by June 1, 2013 because Rapiscan could not guarantee implementation of this specialized software. All 250 of their scanners were, in fact, gone from U.S. airports by that deadline—although some were transferred for use in government buildings.

Since 2013, airports have been utilizing the full-body scanners in which electromagnetic waves are used to produce images that can reveal suspicious objects. An article in *Scientific American* explains the following:

> These [devices] use electromagnetic waves to generate high-resolution images of unusual objects that might be concealed by passenger clothing; these anomalies are then superimposed on the image of a mannequin to protect privacy. The frequencies of the waves used by these scanners are measured in tens of gigahertz (GHz), and at these frequencies the radiation is considered high-frequency non-ionizing radiation—the kind of that heats up molecules. Millimeter wave body scanners avoided many of the controversial issues that took down the backscatter x-ray machines. ...[85]

Obviously, there are powerful security interests behind the use of such devices. While metal detectors pose no serious threats to privacy and have been upheld universally by the courts, full-body scanners can reveal intimate details of the human anatomy and, thus, are questionable on Fourth Amendment grounds. However, in 2011, the U.S. Court of Appeals for the D.C. Circuit brushed aside such concerns in light of the ability of the scanners to detect nonmetallic substances that represent a threat to airline safety. The court also noted that the Transportation Security Administration had taken steps to protect personal privacy by blurring the images that security personnel view on their screens.[86]

Looking toward the future, the Department of Homeland Security's website includes discussion of technology that is being tested, including a whole-body scanner that could take an image of a person as they walked by, without them stopping,[87] as well as a special scanner that could take an image of shoes so as to allow passengers to keep those on while walking through security checkpoints—something that has been a concern since an attempting *shoe bombing* on a flight from Paris to Miami in December 2001.[88]

THE CONSTITUTION IN ACTION
Government Watch Lists

In furtherance of protecting national security, government agencies have some specified lists of names that could prevent certain individuals from taking part in airline travel within the United States. These lists could be used in conjunction with facial recognition software to identify people who are, for example, not permitted to fly on U.S. commercial airlines.

(continued)

More specifically, the FBI has a Terrorist Screening Division that maintains three separate lists. First, there is a No Fly List. If a person's name is on this list, they are banned from boarding a commercial airplane that is entering, leaving, or traveling within the United States. The list has more than 80,000 names on it,[89] and reasons for being on that list—though not entirely known to the public—apparently could range from suspected terrorist ties, to unruly behavior on flights (such as fighting or not complying with mask mandates).

There also is a Secondary Security Screening Selection list (often known as the *Selectee List*). People on this list are subjected to some type of enhanced security measures at airports. Then, there is a Terrorist Watchlist, which is believed to include the names of approximately 2,000,000 people who are thought to be linked to terrorist activity. This list does not automatically preclude travel in the United States, but it is used to inform the compilation of names on the No Fly List or the Secondary Screening list. The CDC even operates a Do Not Board List, in conjunction with TSA, which prevents would-be passengers whom the CDC believes to be carrying communicable diseases from boarding commercial airline flights.

In 2006, the ACLU brought forth a lawsuit, *Gordon v. FBI*, which dealt with a request under the Freedom of Information Act regarding how names are added to the No Fly List.[90] The U.S. government settled the lawsuit for $200,000 and also relented to making the names on the No Fly List public. Moreover, the TSA now has a Passenger Identity Verification Form, which allows a person who might share a name in common with someone on the No Fly List to demonstrate that the name on the list does not represent them. Additionally, there is a "Traveler Redress Inquiry Program" that permits an individual to request a review of whether it is accurate for their name to be on any of these lists.

In 2014, a woman named Rahinah Ibrahim won a lawsuit against the federal government when it was revealed that her name was added to the No Fly List as a result of *FBI error*. An FBI agent admitted at trial that he had filled in a form incorrectly, mistakenly putting Ibrahim's name on the list when she was a college student in the United States. In 2019, the U.S. Court of Appeals for the Ninth Circuit said that the Justice Department had shown "bad faith" in carrying on with appeals for this case.[91]

Tracking Devices

Prior to the advent of cell phones, people often used pagers and beepers that utilized radio waves. In *United States v. Knotts* (1983),[92] the Supreme Court confronted a case in which police placed a beeper inside a container of chloroform that was sold to a man suspected of making meth. Officers monitored the radio signal from the beeper to track the suspect to a secluded cabin. After several days of surveillance, police obtained a warrant, searched the cabin, and discovered a meth lab. In reviewing this matter, the Court held that monitoring the beeper signals was not a violation of the Fourth Amendment, as the suspect had no reasonable expectation of privacy with respect to the radio signals emanating from the beeper. Writing for the Court, Chief Justice Rehnquist observed, "Nothing in the Fourth Amendment prohibited the police from augmenting the sensory faculties bestowed upon them at birth with such enhancement as science and technology afforded them in this case." A key here was that the beeper was installed before the item came into the possession of Mr. Knotts, perhaps indicating that he accepted the item as is; beyond that, the majority opinion took note of the fact that the beeper tracked movements of the container on public roads and to an open field—things that also could have been observed via standard visual surveillance.

One year later, in *United States v. Karo* (1984),[93] the Court confronted a case in which a tracking device was placed into a container of ether. The ether was purchased by James Karo and his associates for the purposes of using it to extract cocaine embedded in clothing that had been imported to the United States. The seller of the ether turned out to be a government informant, and that informant placed a tracker (beeper) into the container before giving it to Karo. Once again, Karo, like Knotts, accepted the container with the tracker within it. The container of ether was then transported in a pickup truck to multiple homes and commercial storage facilities. Eventually, when police tracked the container from a storage facility to one of the suspect's homes, a warrant for that home was acquired—and the ether was seized from that location.

On review, the Supreme Court upheld the validity of the warrant, which was issued based on information derived from the tracker—but not without some caveats. As a starting point, just as in the *Knotts* case, the Court found that because the tracker was installed before the container was given to Karo, there was no violation of the Fourth Amendment connected to the installation of the tracker or to the transfer of the container to Karo. On this point, Justice White's majority opinion said, "Although the can may have contained an unknown and unwanted foreign object, it cannot be said that anyone's possessory interest was interfered with in a meaningful way."

A key difference from the *Knotts* case is that the *Karo* matter dealt with a beeper that was not only revealing transport of the container across public spaces but also into a private home and lockers in private storage facilities. In this regard, Justice White's majority opinion offered some protection for individuals against government use of trackers looking into the home, saying that:

> This case thus presents the question whether the monitoring of a beeper in a private residence, a location not open to visual surveillance, violates the Fourth Amendment rights of those who have a justifiable interest in the privacy of the residence. ... At the risk of belaboring the obvious, private residences are places in which the individual normally expects privacy free of governmental intrusion not authorized by a warrant, and that expectation is plainly one that society is prepared to recognize as justifiable. Our cases have not deviated from this basic Fourth Amendment principle."

Justice White's declaration about privacy in the home was not enough to render the search warrant in the *Karo* case void under the Fourth Amendment. He drew an important distinction, noting that police learned the location of the ether container by tracking it along *public roads* to the final destination of a home. In essence, White concluded that, although the information gleaned from the tracker while it was inside the home was not appropriate for use by law enforcement, officials could properly infer where the container's ultimate location was simply based on its travel along public streets. Therefore, although this decision represented a loss for Karo and his associates, the majority opinion provided some limits regarding the information government officials can glean from trackers that make their way inside a private home.

GPS Trackers

The advent of GPS (Global Positioning System) technology has offered law enforcement a much more sophisticated means of tracking persons. With origins in Cold War-era military research, these GPS trackers can be attached to an item, with satellites used to identify the item's location in real time.[94] In *United States v. Jones* (2012),[95] the Supreme Court invalidated police use of GPS tracking devices without prior judicial authorization, finding a Fourth Amendment violation in the warrantless attachment of a GPS locator to a car; the car's movements were tracked for twenty-eight days, and that information was used to link the vehicle's owner to drug activity. Although the Court's decision to overturn the conviction was unanimous, the justices split on the underlying rationale for the ruling, with five justices focusing on the physical intrusion of placing the GPS locator on the car (deemed improper under the trespass doctrine) and four justices focusing instead on

GPS TRACKER: A Global Positioning Systems device that can be attached to an item and used to track that item's movements in real-time.

the violation of a reasonable expectation of privacy associated with the lengthy electronic surveillance. This subtle but important distinction holds relevance for suggesting two different perspectives the Court might have when handling electronic surveillance cases in the future. Hence, although we discussed this case in chapter 7, we focus here upon the key differences between Scalia's majority opinion and Alito's concurring opinion. Scalia distilled the debate at hand by saying the following:

> The concurrence begins by accusing us of applying '18th-century tort law.' ... That is a distortion. What we apply is an 18th-century guarantee against unreasonable searches, which we believe must provide at a minimum the degree of protection it afforded when it was adopted. The concurrence does not share that belief. It would apply exclusively *Katz's* reasonable-expectation-of-privacy test, even when that eliminates rights that previously existed.

Thus, Scalia's opinion focused upon the common-law notion of a physical intrusion, applying that to the attachment of the GPS locator and deeming that the Fourth Amendment violation.

On the other hand, Justice Alito (joined by three others) found that placing a tracker on a vehicle in a public parking lot, one that is exposed to the public, was not in and of itself a violation of the Fourth Amendment. For Alito, the key was that the warrantless surveillance—in the form of consistent tracking of movements over a prolonged period of time—generated a violation of an expectation of privacy. Alito's primary concern seemed to be setting a precedent to prevent such warrantless surveillance in situations when government officials do not physically affix a tracker to personal property—but, perhaps, use an electronic "hack" to conduct surveillance. In this regard, Alito said the majority was "present[ing] particularly vexing problems" for those searches in which there is no physical contact.

Scalia's response to this concern was blunt; he declared, "We entirely fail to understand that point. For unlike the concurrence, which would make *Katz* the exclusive test, we do not make trespass the exclusive test. Situations involving merely the transmission of electronic signals without trespass would remain subject to *Katz* analysis." In other words, Scalia indicated that either the trespass doctrine or the *Katz* test could apply, but he preferred the former for this case because there was a physical intrusion. In deriding the concurrence's "exclusive use" of the *Katz* test, Scalia noted that an expectation of privacy approach to a person's movements along public streets could prove too narrow for effectively protecting privacy rights. On this point, Scalia said:

> In fact, it is the concurrence's insistence on the exclusivity of the *Katz* test that needlessly leads us into 'particularly vexing problems' in the present case. This Court has to date not deviated from the understanding that mere visual observation does not constitute a search. ... It may be that achieving the same result through electronic means, without an accompanying trespass, is an unconstitutional invasion of privacy, but the present case does not require us to answer that question.

The key for the concurring opinion appeared to be that twenty-eight days of monitoring was too long—almost as if to say that a normal person would at some point recognize a team of agents physically following them around for twenty-eight days and, thus, take countermeasures to preserve an expectation of privacy. But Scalia's retort to this point was that if twenty-eight days is deemed too long, we are left to wonder what the acceptable cutoff point would be. Scalia suggested that the concurrence's reliance on the expectation of privacy test in answering this question is what leads the matter "needlessly into additional thorny problems." Along these lines, he said the following of Alito's opinion:

> The concurrence posits that 'relatively short-term monitoring of a person's movements on public streets' is okay, but that 'the use of longer-term GPS monitoring in investigations of most offenses' is no good. ... That introduces yet another novelty into our jurisprudence. There is no precedent for the proposition that whether a search has occurred depends on the nature of the crime being investigated. And even accepting that novelty, it remains unexplained why a 4-week investigation is 'surely' too long. ... What of a 2-day monitoring of a suspected purveyor of stolen electronics? Or of a 6-month monitoring of a suspected terrorist? We may have to grapple with these 'vexing problems' in some future case where a classic trespassory search is not involved. ...

The dispute between the opinions, therefore, seemed to revolve around how to handle a future case where electronic surveillance is not connected to physical intrusion or a short-term tracking. For the matter at hand, Scalia was inclined to use the trespass doctrine—but it is important to recognize that, in speaking for the Court, his opinion leaves open the possibility of using either test to address government surveillance. We are left to wonder if a future Court might one day embrace the notion of an *electronic trespass*.

Searches of Cell Phones and Other Electronic Devices

As we pointed out in the previous chapter, police making a lawful arrest may search the person being arrested as well as the area under that person's "immediate control."[96] Often, a search incident to arrest will yield weapons, contraband, or incriminating evidence. In *Riley v. California* (2014),[97] the Supreme Court reviewed a case in which a police officer retrieved a smart phone from the pocket of David Riley, who was being arrested on weapons charges. The officer was able to access the contents of the phone, which contained images linking the man to a previous shooting. At trial, Riley unsuccessfully argued that the search of the contents of the phone did not fall within the scope of a warrantless search incident to arrest. In turn, that evidence was instrumental in Riley's conviction for attempted murder. In a unanimous decision, though, the Supreme Court reversed Riley's conviction.

Chief Justice John Roberts, writing for the Court, recognized the unique privacy implications of cell phone searches:

> Modern cell phones are not just another technological convenience. With all they contain and all they may reveal, they hold for many Americans 'the privacies of life'. ... The fact that technology now allows an individual to carry such information in his hand does not make the information any less worthy of the protection for which the Founders fought. Our answer to the question of what police must do before searching a cell phone seized incident to an arrest is accordingly simple—get a warrant.

As noted in chapter 8, the Court's decision in *Riley* recognized that exigent circumstances might well justify a warrantless search of a cell phone in certain situations. That chapter also discussed the fact that federal circuit courts have split on the question of whether searches of the content on electronic devices at a border crossing fall under the exigent circumstance doctrine; thus, certain surveillance tactics connected to accessing a phone might be permitted at some border crossings. In other contexts, according to Chief Justice Roberts's opinion in *Riley*, "Such exigencies could include the need to prevent the imminent destruction of evidence in individual cases, to pursue a fleeing suspect, and to assist persons who are seriously injured or are threatened with imminent injury."

Faraday Bags and the Imminent Destruction of Evidence

The majority opinion in *Riley v. California* indicated that the notion of imminent destruction of evidence could potentially provide government officials with a reason to conduct a warrantless cell phone search if there were legitimate fears that an accused criminal or their associates might facilitate the remote *wiping* of a device. More specifically, though, the Court observed that government officials could alleviate fears about remote wiping in two ways: (1) turning the phone off and removing its battery or—if concerns about encryption or passwords preclude doing so—(2) placing the phone in a Faraday bag while awaiting

FARADAY BAG: A metallic foil bag that can be placed over a device, such as a cell phone, to block any wireless communication with that device.

acquisition of a search warrant. A Faraday bag is named after scientist Michael Faraday and is described by Justice Roberts in the *Riley* opinion as "essentially sandwich bags made of aluminum foil." These "cheap, lightweight, and easy to use" items, he said, would allow police to leave a phone powered on and "place it in an enclosure that isolates the phone from radio waves." He noted that "a number of government agencies around the country already encourage the use of Faraday bags," citing a Department of Justice guide, entitled "Electronic Crime Scene Investigation: A Guide for First Respondents" (which was discussed in an amicus brief for the *Riley* case).

Beyond Cell Phones: Justice Alito's Concerns in *Riley v. California*

In a concurring opinion in *Riley v. California*, Justice Alito spoke of the importance of legislative bodies taking the lead in passing laws that offered enhanced protections from searches of electronic devices. He offered a prescient assessment of emerging technology in declaring that:

> Many forms of modern technology are making it easier and easier for both government and private entities to amass a wealth of information about the lives of ordinary Americans, and at the same time, many ordinary Americans are choosing to make public much information that was seldom revealed to outsiders just a few decades ago. In light of these developments, it would be very unfortunate if privacy protection in the 21st century were left primarily to the federal courts using the blunt instrument of the Fourth Amendment. Legislatures, elected by the people, are in a better position than we are to assess and respond to the changes that have already occurred and those that almost certainly will take place in the future.

Does *Plain View* Apply to the Contents of Electronic Devices?

It is not uncommon for police to seize computers and conduct forensic analysis of their hard drives. What if police have obtained a warrant to search a computer for evidence of securities fraud and inadvertently discover child pornography on the hard drive? An interesting decision from the Tenth Circuit raised questions about how (or if) the plain view doctrine should apply to the search of a computer. In United States v, Carey,[98] police obtained a warrant to arrest a man for selling drugs. Carey consented to a search of his apartment, and officers seized two computers and took them back to the police station. The officers then acquired a search warrant that authorized checking the computers for information connected to the "sale and distribution of controlled substances." When searching the computers, a detective did a keyword search of all documents for words like *money*, *accounts*, and *people*, but he found nothing to indicate files that discussed drug activity. He then opened a JPG file with a "sexually suggestive name," knowing the file contained a picture. The file turned out to be an image of child pornography. He went on to open more than 240 JPG files, finding similar evidence of child pornography—but not drug activity.

Ultimately, the Tenth Circuit ruled that the pictures were inadmissible because the opening of these files exceeded the scope of the search warrant. The government attempted to apply a plain view approach, saying that "a computer search such as the one undertaken in this case is tantamount to looking for documents in a file cabinet, pursuant to a valid search warrant, and instead finding child pornography." The court's majority opinion responded by saying that the pictures "were in closed files and thus not in plain view," adding, "Even if we employ the file cabinet theory, the testimony of Detective Lewis makes the analogy inapposite because he stated he knew ... each drawer was properly labeled and its contents were clearly described in the label." In language that foreshadowed the Supreme Court's decision in *Riley v. California* some fifteen years later, the Tenth Circuit then quoted from an article by Raphael Winick in the *Harvard Journal of Law and Technology*, saying: "Since electronic storage is likely to contain a greater quantity and variety of information than any previous storage method, computers make tempting targets in searches for incriminating information."[99] Thus far, the Supreme Court has left this issue to the circuit courts, which generally have followed the reasoning of the Tenth Circuit.[100]

THE CONSTITUTION IN ACTION
Apple and the FBI Clash over San Bernardino Terror Investigation

On December 2, 2015, a terrorist attack occurred in San Bernardino, California. The attack, which included a mass shooting and an attempted detonation of three bombs, targeted an annual training event and holiday party held by the San Bernardino County Department of Health in a banquet hall called the Inland Regional Center. Approximately 80 people were in attendance, and 14 were killed with 22 others injured.

The attack was perpetuated by a married couple. The husband, who was a U.S.-born citizen, was an employee of the County Department of Health, and his wife was born in Pakistan but held a valid *green card* for lawful permanent resident status in the United States. The couple fired more than 100 rounds of bullets in the banquet hall and left behind backpacks containing three pipe bombs that failed to detonate. Survivors were able to identify the husband, even though the pair wore masks and tactical vests. Approximately four hours after the attack, police engaged in pursuit of their vehicle. Shots were exchanged on public roadways, and the couple's vehicle came to a stop on San Bernardino Ave., in a suburban neighborhood.

Twenty-three officers, representing seven different law enforcement agencies, engaged in a shootout with the couple, with more than 400 bullets fired by police and more than 80 fired by the terrorists. The husband was killed by police after he exited the vehicle and continued shooting at police, and his wife was killed while continuing to fire at police from inside the car. Police would later discover 2,500 rounds of ammunition remaining in the vehicle. A third person would be arrested and charged with the federal crime of providing material support for terrorism, and in 2020, he was sentenced to 20 years in federal prison.[101]

In the aftermath of the terrorist attack, FBI agents sought access to husband's cell phone to see if any information about the attack could be found. While warrants were acquired, the Bureau was an unable to unlock the phone, which was an iPhone 5c with password protection. With previous versions of the iPhone, the FBI could use a *brute force* method, in which software would employ every possible four-digit number combination until the correct password was located—a process that typically took 25 minutes. But starting with Apple's iOS 9 operating system, which iPhone 5c was using, Apple instituted a safety feature that would cause the phone to lock if ten incorrect password attempts were entered.

The FBI requested assistance from Apple in hacking into the phone, but Apple declined, suggesting that such information would create broader security concerns for its product and set a precedent that Apple CEO Tim Cook called "dangerous" and "chilling."[102] Then-FBI Director James Comey testified in front of Congress twice (on February 9 and March 1) to convey the importance of Apple's assistance in opening this phone—saying there was no other way to open it—and the FBI sought a court order to compel Apple to provide assistance.

With a hearing set for March 22, 2016 in the U.S. District Court for the Central District of California, both sides prepared arguments as a novel court case seemed destined to address a controversy that juxtaposed national security against digital privacy rights. The stakes were higher than opening just one phone, as it was later revealed that the FBI had previously been unable to open 7,000 phones connected to various investigations.[103] However, one day before the scheduled hearing, the FBI made a request for a one-week delay, which the judge granted. Then, on March 28, 2016, the FBI surprised observers by announcing it would no longer need Apple's assistance in the matter.

Several years later, in 2021, an exclusive report from *The Washington Post* revealed that a hacking unit within FBI had enlisted the assistance of a small Australian company: Azimuth Security. That company's founder, Mark Dowd, who also enlisted the efforts of a Portland, Oregon-based computer expert, David Wang, had been able to exploit security weaknesses in iPhone applications. Working together, the pair were able open the San Bernardino phone for the FBI in March 2016.[104] Nevertheless, a report from *The Los Angeles Times* revealed that the phone contained only work-related information, and no information about the terrorist attack was found.[105]

Cell Phone Location Tracking

In 2012, the U.S. Court of Appeals for the Sixth Circuit held that government agents *pinging* a suspect's cell phone to get GPS location data—also known as cell site location information (CSLI)—was not a search within the meaning of the Fourth Amendment.[106] Upholding a conviction for drug trafficking and money laundering—where key evidence connected the suspect's past movements, as revealed by CSLI, to specific nearby crime scenes—the Sixth Circuit said, "There is no Fourth Amendment violation because [the defendant] did not have a reasonable expectation of privacy in the data given off by his voluntarily procured pay-as-you-go cell phone." That court also observed that "[w]hen criminals use modern technological devices to carry out criminal acts and to reduce the possibility of detection, they can hardly complain when the police take advantage of the inherent characteristics of those very devices to catch them." One of the judges on the panel disagreed on the Fourth Amendment issue, saying the following:

> I do not agree that [the defendant] lacked a reasonable expectation of privacy in the GPS data emitted from his cellular phone. In my view, acquisition of this information constitutes a search within the meaning of the Fourth Amendment, and, consequently, the officers were required to either obtain a warrant supported by probable cause or establish the applicability of an exception to the warrant requirement.

That dissenting voice presaged the Supreme Court's majority opinion in a different matter, *Carpenter v. United States* (2018).[107] In a 5–4 ruling for this case, the Court overturned a conviction in which cell phone location data obtained from service providers constituted key evidence in the case. Chief Justice Roberts wrote the opinion of the Court, which concluded that police normally must obtain a search warrant before

CELL PHONE LOCATION DATA: Refers to the signal given by an individual cell phone as it links to a nearby cell phone tower; an individual *ping* to a tower or a series of pings can reveal a person's location or movement over time.

acquiring cell phone location data from providers. Reaching that conclusion, Roberts refused to apply the third-party doctrine, saying instead:

> Given the unique nature of cell phone location records, the fact that the information is held by a third party does not by itself overcome the user's claim to Fourth Amendment protection. Whether the Government employs its own surveillance technology ... or leverages the technology of a wireless carrier, we hold that an individual maintains a legitimate expectation of privacy in the record of his physical movements. ...

Roberts also spoke to an expectation of privacy at stake in this case by saying, "A person does not surrender all Fourth Amendment protection by venturing into the public sphere." He observed how law enforcement techniques have changed over time by recognizing that:

> Prior to the digital age, law enforcement might have pursued a suspect for a brief stretch, but doing so 'for any extended period of time was difficult and costly and therefore rarely undertaken.' ... For that reason, 'society's expectation has been that law enforcement agents and others would not—and indeed, in the main, simply could not—secretly monitor and catalogue every single movement of an individual's car for a very long period.' Allowing government access to cell-site records contravenes that expectation.

Also of note, Roberts took umbrage with the scope of cell phone location data searches, noting, "With just the click of a button, the Government can access each carrier's deep repository of historical location information at practically no expense. ... A cell phone faithfully follows its owner beyond public thoroughfares and into private residences, doctor's offices, political headquarters, and other potentially revealing locales." On that point, he quoted to the *Riley v. California* opinion to demonstrate that "nearly three-quarters of smart phone users report being within five feet of their phones most of the time, with 12% admitting that they even use their phones in the shower." Highlighting the pervasiveness of the search in question in the *Carpenter* case, Roberts went so far as to say the following:

> [W]hen the Government tracks the location of a cell phone it achieves near perfect surveillance, as if it had attached an ankle monitor to the phone's user. ... In the past, attempts to reconstruct a person's movements were limited by a dearth of records and the frailties of recollection. With access to CSLI, the Government can now travel back in time to retrace a person's whereabouts. ...

In dissent, Justice Samuel Alito accused the majority of muddling Fourth Amendment law, saying: "The Court's reasoning fractures two fundamental pillars of Fourth Amendment law, and in doing so, it guarantees a blizzard of litigation while threatening many legitimate and valuable investigative practices upon which law enforcement has rightfully come to rely." Justice Thomas also wrote a dissenting opinion but went much further, calling for the repudiation of the landmark *Katz* decision:

> The more fundamental problem with the Court's opinion, however, is its use of the 'reasonable expectation of privacy' test, which was first articulated by Justice Harlan in *Katz v. United States* ... The *Katz* test has no basis in the text or history of the Fourth Amendment.

And, it invites courts to make judgments about policy, not law. Until we confront the problems with this test, *Katz* will continue to distort Fourth Amendment jurisprudence.

Despite the ruling in *Carpenter*, agents for U.S. Immigration and Customs Enforcement (ICE) have continued to make use of a device known as a "cell site simulator" (or a "Stingray"), which emits a signal similar to that of a cell tower—essentially tricking a cell phone into revealing its location. According to an ACLU report that relied upon Freedom of Information Act requests, there were more than 2,000 uses of this technique by ICE agents between 2013 and 2019.[108] Reports also have indicated that, since 2018, ICE has made use of an app known as SmartLINK to track the locations of immigrants who were in the United States awaiting adjudication of cases, including those awaiting decisions on asylum requests. These individuals were told to download the app onto a phone and were required to "check in" using voice messages and pictures that were matched against facial recognition software.[109]

Mass Electronic Surveillance

In the aftermath of the Church Committee report, which is discussed earlier in this chapter, Congress enacted the Foreign Intelligence Surveillance Act of 1978 (FISA).[110] This was designed to create a separate legal regime with respect to surveillance conducted by federal agents as a part of the gathering of foreign intelligence. More specifically, this act applied to communications between "foreign powers and agents of foreign powers" in regard to "foreign intelligence information." In these situations, the 1978 Act placed restrictions on government officials who attempted to engage in electronic surveillance where no warrant existed. FISA also created a specialized court—known as the FISA Court— to review requests for wiretaps, trap and trace devices, pen registers, and so on (pursuant to foreign intelligence gathering operations). This specialized court is staffed by a rotating group of federal district court judges who meet in Washington, D.C. to rule on applications from federal officials who seek search warrants related to FISA. Besides the particular categories defined in this law, other requests for search warrants dealing with surveillance are to be handled by the appropriate federal district courts.

FISA COURT: A court that was specifically created by the Foreign Intelligence Surveillance Act to evaluate government requests for warrants connected to surveillance of foreign actors.

Although the 1978 version of FISA originally applied exclusively to surveillance of foreign nationals operating inside the United States on behalf of foreign governments, in 2004, FISA was amended by Section 6001 of the Intelligence Reform and Terrorism Prevention Act.[111] That amendment enabled FISA to be applicable to so-called *lone wolf agents*, defined as those engaged in terrorist activity (or planning thereof) who were not connected to any foreign government.

FISA was amended again in 2008 to cover foreign nationals and U.S. citizens outside the country, as well. The FISA Amendments Act of 2008[112] also granted a seven-day warrantless search grace period for government officials, who could begin a FISA search as long as they subsequently filed a related search warrant request with the FISA court during that seven-day time frame. An older version of the grace period under the 1978 law lasted only 48 hours. The 2008 amendments also limited civil liability for businesses—perhaps, cell phone providers—that turned over telecommunications records to government officials, with the law going so far as to authorize the government's ability to destroy any record of those searches.

Reportedly, the FISA court rejected only 0.031% of warrant requests over a thirty-three-year time span, with a total of 12 rejections and 38,365 approvals from 1979 through 2015.[113] Reforms would arrive with the passage of a 2015 law discussed below, and data for 2020 indicate that 579 FISA applications were considered with the following outcomes: "404 orders were granted, 138 orders were modified, 24 orders were denied in part, and 13 applications were denied in full."[114]

The USA PATRIOT Act

After the 9/11 terrorist attacks, Congress enacted a law entitled Uniting and Strengthening America by Providing Appropriate Tools Required to Intercept and Obstruct Terrorism, known commonly by its acronym: the USA PATRIOT Act.[115] The law contained numerous provisions affecting criminal justice, most of which were relatively uncontroversial. However, Title II of the Act, entitled Enhanced Surveillance Procedures, proved to be extremely controversial.

One of the hotly debated provisions was Section 215.[116] This authorized the FISA Court to release an order demanding that any third-parties—including cell phone companies, rental car agencies, storage facilities, hotels, and more—give law enforcement access to "any tangible item" related to foreign intelligence germane to preventing terrorism or espionage; this was supposed to be based upon a demonstration of *reasonable grounds* to indicate espionage or terrorism-related activity. Beyond that, Section 206 of the Patriot Act allowed for the use of so-called *roving wiretaps*. This meant a wiretap warrant could be authorized not just for a specific phone number but, instead, to any devices that might belong to or might be accessed by a particular individual; in short, this section was known for allowing government officials to "follow the target."[117] Also controversially, Section 213 of PATRIOT ACT authorized the government to use *sneak and peek* warrants for electronic surveillance. As discussed in chapter 8, these are warrants that can be executed without immediately informing the person who is impacted by the search or seizure. Under the PATRIOT ACT, that lack of notification could connect to an indefinite period of time, based on the low standard of reasonableness.[118]

The National Security Agency's Mass Surveillance Programs

The National Security Agency (NSA) was created to further the secretive collection of intelligence. Whereas the CIA does this sort of thing through human interaction, the NSA exclusively goes about its objective through electronic means. The NSA had its origins in a U.S. Army agency known as the Cipher Bureau. That agency was created in 1917 to acquire intelligence related to World War I. Through the 1920s and 1930s, some other names were applied to the agency, including the Black Chamber, the Military Intelligence Branch, Section 8 (or MI8), the Cable and Telegraph Section, and the Code Compilation Company. During World War II, it was called the Signal Security Agency, and shortly thereafter, in 1949, the United States crafted the Army Security Agency as a means of centralizing intelligence collection across different branches of government. That would be transformed into the NSA, as it is known today, most likely in 1952 via a classified series of executive memos from President Harry Truman—although given the secrecy of this agency, its exact origin is somewhat unknown. Subsequently, in 1972, President Nixon issued an order that created a Central Security Service (CSS) within the NSA "to promote full partnership between NSA and the Service Cryptologic Components of the U.S. Armed Forces."[119]

NATIONAL SECURITY AGENCY: A federal U.S. government agency created to facilitate the electronic collection of intelligence.

Bulk Telephone Metadata Collection

Beginning in 2006, the National Security Agency (NSA) invoked authority supposedly granted by Section 215 of the USA PATRIOT Act to engage in bulk metadata collection, essentially creating a massive database containing the metadata associated with telephonic communications throughout the country. These metadata included the inbound and outbound telephone numbers dialed from all phones in the country as well as dates, times, and duration of calls. In essence, the bulk data collection program operated like a pen register, except it was not focused on one particular phone line—but instead on all phone lines in the country.

The PRISM Program

Under the Protect America Act of 2007,[120] the NSA established a highly classified program known as PRISM, which collected metadata gleaned from emails and internet calls with the cooperation of major companies, such as Facebook, Google, Apple, and Skype. The program came to light in 2013, when whistleblower Edward Snowden leaked classified NSA documents to the press. Not surprisingly, Snowden's revelations regarding PRISM and the bulk telephone metadata collection program led to litigation in the federal courts and, eventually, legislation enacted by Congress, as we discuss in the following section.

PRISM: A clandestine NSA program that involved widespread collection of metadata from the electronic activities of millions of Americans.

Litigation over NSA Mass Surveillance

Some courts have regularly dismissed privacy lawsuits filed against the NSA for a lack of standing—since it might be hard to know if the NSA is actually spying on a person.[121] Yet in December 2013, a federal district court ruled that bulk collection of American telephone metadata and internet communications was unconstitutional.[122] In his opinion in the case, Judge Richard J. Leon wrote, "I cannot imagine a more 'indiscriminate' and 'arbitrary' invasion than this systematic and high-tech collection and retention of personal data on virtually every single citizen for purposes of querying and analyzing it without prior judicial approval." And in 2015, the U.S. Court of Appeals for the Second Circuit held "the telephone metadata program exceeds the scope of what Congress has authorized and therefore violates §215."[123] More recently, the Ninth Circuit concluded "the government may have violated the Fourth Amendment and did violate the Foreign Intelligence Surveillance Act (FISA) when it collected the telephone metadata of millions of Americans."[124] Ultimately, in light of the secrecy under which the NSA operates, even with court rulings like these in place, it can be challenging to discern if the agency's ongoing activities are compatible with the U.S. Constitution.

FOCUS ON LAW ENFORCEMENT

Did the NSA Intercept of an Email Help Foil a Terrorist Plot?

On September 6, 2009, a counter-terrorist agent at the NSA, operating pursuant to a FISA warrant, intercepted an email from a naturalized U.S. citizen named Najibullah Zazi, who had sent emails to Al-Qaeda terrorist operatives in Pakistan. The emails involved requests for information on how to make bombs—in coded language seeking information about *flour* and *oil*. The bombs were allegedly intended to be detonated by suicide bombers in the New York City subway system in 2009, on the eighth anniversary of the 9/11 attacks. Details about why the government had been looking into those emails pursuant to a FISA warrant were not publicly released, but once the information of an impending attack was ascertained by NSA agents, it was immediately forwarded to the FBI.

The FBI's Joint Terrorism Task Force, in conjunction with the New York City Police Department, rapidly established surveillance on Zazi as he traveled by car from Denver into New York City. Federal agents scoured stores in the Denver area and located video of Zazi purchasing materials needed to manufacture bombs—heightening the urgency of the situation. As Zazi's car approached New York City, federal and local officials instituted a roadblock on the George Washington Bridge, which links New Jersey with New York City. All traffic was brought to a halt on the bridge, and explosive sniffing dogs were walked around many vehicles, but that was merely a ruse for officers to specifically target Zazi's vehicle. However, because Zazi had components for a bomb in the car but not an established device, search dogs did not alert to the vehicle. Thus, since officers had

no probable cause for a vehicle search, Zazi was allowed to enter New York City. Officials also believed Zazi was working with other people, and they hoped that by following him they could determine whom those individuals were. As it turned out, an NSA metadata search of Zazi's phone and email records helped reveal the identity of two coconspirators who had traveled with him to an Al-Qaeda training camp in Pakistan in 2008. All three individuals were in New York City and came under immediate surveillance.

A federal search warrant was issued for Zazi's vehicle, and late at night, without Zazi's knowledge, the car was towed from where he parked it on a New York City street and taken to a secure location. Once there, FBI evidence technicians undertook a thorough search of the vehicle, which included removing its tires and inspecting the undercarriage and gas tank. Inside the vehicle, they found Zazi's laptop computer, and FBI specialists were able to create a copy of the contents stored on the laptop's hard drive. The car was reassembled, and the computer and the vehicle were returned to their original locations—all within a few hours and without Zazi's knowledge. Subsequent searches of data taken from the computer revealed details of the bombing plot targeting New York City's subway system and also indicated Zazi and his associates had specific instructions for how to construct a bomb. The FBI continued to surveil all three individuals.

By September 10, 2009, Zazi had apparently become aware that FBI agents were looking into him. Agents had previously asked an Imam at a New York City mosque what information he could provide about Zazi, and it is believed the Imam relayed the FBI's interest to Zazi. (Zazi's lawyer, though, later suggested the fake roadblock on the George Washington Bridge had alerted his client to law enforcement's interest in him). Zazi and his coconspirators abandoned their plot, destroying their bomb-making materials before they fled New York City. Zazi would return to Denver, followed closely by FBI agents who later took him into custody for questioning. When faced with electronic evidence of his planning activities, Zazi admitted to his role in the plot. Seven people, including his two coconspirators, his father, and the Imam who alerted him to the FBI's inquiry, would later be convicted on federal charges. Zazi was found guilty of conspiracy to use weapons of mass destruction, material support for terrorism, and conspiracy to commit murder in a foreign country. Although he could have received a life sentence, because he helped the government in approximately 100 different terror-related investigations, he served just under ten years in the U.S. Penitentiary, Administrative Maximum Facility in Florence, Colorado—and was released in 2019.

Don Borelli, the assistant special agent in charge of the FBI's Joint Terrorism Task Force in New York City at the time of this investigation, lauded the role of the NSA in helping to foil the terrorists' plot, but in a documentary about this case, he did say: "Are we 100% safe? No, because we live in a free society. We don't want to be in a police state where we're constantly, 24/7 under surveillance and government listening to every phone call. I would never want that, myself, even as an FBI agent."[125]

The USA FREEDOM Act

Reacting to widespread criticism of the NSA's electronic surveillance programs, in 2015, Congress enacted the Uniting and Strengthening America by Fulfilling Rights and Ensuring Effective Discipline Over Monitoring Act, known as the USA FREEDOM Act.[126] The law explicitly banned the NSA from mass data collection of phone activity. The 2015 law also addressed Section 215, which was a temporary provision when the original PATRIOT Act was passed and was set to expire at the end of 2015. Congress extended it for four more years with passage of the USA FREEDOM Act (a subsequent one-year extension would follow).

Reforms to FISA that were embedded in the USA FREEDOM Act included enhanced transparency of FISA warrant decisions in the form of yearly disclosure to Congress of requests, approvals, and denials. Additionally, for any warrants that request a *novel* or *significant* interpretation of law, the FISA Court is supposed to appoint five individuals (usually lawyers) to act as amicus curiae in providing assistance to the court in making its determination. Finally, federal courts, including the Supreme Court, can review decisions of the FISA Court.

Parts of the USA FREEDOM Act expired in 2020, including the Section 215 extensions. Congress debated a USA FREEDOM Act Reauthorization bill into 2021 with no new legislation passed. Overall, it does seem as though legislative actors have joined judicial actors in attempting to create some parameters for shaping the contours of electronic surveillance in the United States today—as suggested in Justice Alito's concurring opinion in *Riley v. California*.

THE CONSTITUTION IN ACTION
FBI Obtains a Warrant to Seize Bitcoin Paid in Ransomware Attack

On June 7, 2021, the Department of Justice announced that the FBI had effectuated the seizure of $2.3 million in cryptocurrency that had been paid to an extortionist group called Darkside, who had perpetuated a ransomware attack against one of the United States' leading providers of gasoline. A ransomware attack occurs when some type of malware or computer virus is used to infect a computer or network, at which point an outside group can take control

(continued)

of the computer systems of a company or, perhaps, even a local government's operations. Demands for a ransom to be paid to restore service typically will follow—often coupled with threats of destroying (or, perhaps, revealing to the public) sensitive information if demands are not followed. This activity represents the crime of extortion, but in situations where the perpetrators operate in foreign countries while targeting U.S. businesses, bringing those criminals to justice can prove to be a challenge.

In this particular incident, the Darkside hacking operation targeted U.S.-based Colonial Pipeline, which has a base of operations in Houston, Texas and uses a series of pipelines that transport gasoline and jet fuel throughout the U.S., primarily in the Southeast. On May 6, 2021, the Colonial Pipeline computer systems were taken over by Darkside via a ransomware attack. The attack forced Colonial to shut down its pipeline operations in full.

Just hours after the attack, officials at Colonial Pipeline agreed to pay the requested ransom of 75 Bitcoins, which had a value at the time of more than $4 million. Darkside responded by providing a software program to enable Colonial to reboot its operations, although that process took about five days before everything was fully functional again. This was the most significant cyberattack on a U.S. critical infrastructure site in the nation's history.

Although Darkside is believed to be based somewhere in Eastern Europe, the FBI managed to recover, though an electronic seizure, a large portion of the ransom paid in this case. According to a press release issued by the Department of Justice, specific subdivisions of the DOJ that played a role in the investigation included the following: the Criminal Division's Money Laundering and Asset Recovery Section, the Criminal Division's Computer Crime and Intellectual Property Section, the National Security Division's Counterintelligence and Export Control Section, and the Ransomware and Digital Extortion Task Force. The DOJ's press released indicated that:

> … by reviewing the Bitcoin public ledger, law enforcement was able to track multiple transfers of Bitcoin and identify that approximately 63.7 bitcoins, representing the proceeds of the victim's ransom payment, had been transferred to a specific address, for which the FBI has the 'private key,' or the rough equivalent of a password needed to access assets accessible from the specific Bitcoin address. This Bitcoin represents proceeds traceable to a computer intrusion and property involved in money laundering and may be seized pursuant to criminal and civil forfeiture statutes. [127]

No information about how the FBI acquired the private key password was given, but a seizure warrant for this Bitcoin was authorized earlier on the day of the FBI's seizure, with the Honorable Laurel Beeler, U.S. Magistrate Judge for the Northern District of California, signing the warrant. In the end, the FBI recovered 63.7 Bitcoins of the original 75 that had been paid.

Social Media and Other Internet Activity

It goes without saying that the internet has become an inextricable part of most people's lives. Clearly, much of the loss of privacy in society today stems from voluntary posts by social media users. Simply put, there is no expectation of privacy in the online realm. Social media companies and internet service providers are not the government; therefore, the Fourth Amendment does restrict them. They can (and do) share information with law enforcement. When social media companies or ISPs balk at police requests for information (e.g., private chats or recently deleted posts), prosecutors can obtain subpoenas or search warrants to acquire the information. Moreover, law enforcement agencies at all levels of government now routinely monitor social media for evidence of criminal activity or leads in ongoing investigations.[128]

Ultimately, what people post on the internet can be used as evidence against them. While a person might have privacy settings to limit who can view certain social media posts, items made available to the public—whether in the form of pictures of text—are likely to be evaluated as being in plain view. Along these lines, as in noted chapter 4, Section 230 of the federal Communications Decency Act provides social media sites and internet service providers with immunity from civil or criminal liability related to what users choose to post online. The one exception added to federal law in 2018 relates to websites that allow their platforms to be used in furtherance of human trafficking; in such cases, the social media site could face civil or criminal liability.[129]

THE CONSTITUTION IN ACTION
Ill-Advised Facebook Posts Assist the Police

In some cases, criminals make the work of law enforcement quite easy. One important lesson for aspiring criminals to keep in mind, it seems, is that whatever one posts on social media—particularly without any concern for privacy settings—could be construed as being an item in plain view.

An example arose in 2016 from Stuart, Florida, where police were called to a house to investigate a potential battery. The suspect was gone by the time police arrived, but the alleged victim provided the suspect's name. Hoping to find some information about the suspect's whereabouts, police located his profile page on Facebook. The picture used for that page was a mug shot and wanted poster from a neighboring county. With further investigation, officials learned that he had two outstanding arrest warrants, and he was arrested the next day.[130] The Stuart Police Department then used its own official Facebook page to declare: "Facebook is a great way to communicate and connect with old friends and family. If you are wanted by the police, it's probably not a good idea to use the 'Wanted of the Week' poster of yourself as your profile pic."[131]

Elsewhere, in 2021, the Stoney County Sherriff's Office in Missouri was the beneficiary of a photo posted online. In this case, a man attempted to sell a catalytic converter on Facebook Marketplace, posting a picture of that item online for everyone to see. The problem, for him, was that the middle of the photo included the image of a clear plastic bag of methamphetamine and a syringe. After being tipped off to this photo within hours of its posting, police officers obtained a search warrant, and the following day, a search of the man's home yielded forty-eight grams of meth and an illegal gun.

The official Facebook page of the Stone County Sheriff's Office made it clear that officers reveled in this arrest, with a post saying: "Last night one of our Stone County residents posted a catalytic converter for sale on Marketplace. Apparently he must have been under the influence because in the background of his picture he posted, he left his large bag of meth and syringe on the coffee table. Take note, if you are selling items on social media, make sure your drugs are not in the background!"[132]

Criminals also should be aware that things they write on social media websites can be used against them in court. In one bizarre case from Tampa, Florida, a woman posted on Facebook that she was the "QUEEN OF IRS TAX FRAUD" (emphasis in original). That was among the posts a U.S. Attorney read in federal court before this woman was sentenced to twenty-one years in prison for allegedly defrauding the government of $3.1 million through a scheme to improperly acquire tax refunds. She also had posted a picture of herself holding large sums of cash and had boasted she would never be caught.[133] In situations like these, it seems, the notion of electronic surveillance is as simple as the click of a mouse and having a look at what criminals voluntarily post on the internet.

The IP Address: A Unique Identifier?

A key aspect of law enforcement investigations into computer activity revolves around the internet protocol (IP) address, which has been defined as an "online unique identifier."[134] Every computer has its own IP address, and a typical IP address will have four numbers, each between 0 and 255, with a decimal point in between each of the four. When

INTERNET PROTOCOL (IP) ADDRESS: A unique number that can be used to identify either an individual computer or a router that links a computer to the internet.

ROUTER: A device, often installed by an internet service provider, which enables a computer to connect to the internet.

someone connects an electronic device to the internet, the connection occurs through a **router** set up by an ISP. The router also has an IP address of its own, and when a person connects to a specific website, that router IP address links to the website.

Critically, for law enforcement purposes, a router IP address reveals information that can be publicly available—such as what websites are being visited through the router and a generalized location of computers connecting through the router. Nonetheless, a router IP address does not always reveal precisely what physical address or even what computer is using that router—especially in densely populated areas; for example, a router for an apartment building could be used by many computers, and beyond that, a private family's router in their home could be used by someone in a nearby home who knows (or hacks) a password. In some situations, police have raided the wrong homes based on incorrect IP address inferences.[135] But with experience, many law enforcement officials have learned to acquire added information beyond just the *geolocation* (geographical location) provided by a router. And in turn, circuit courts have begun evaluating law enforcement techniques in this realm.

In 2021, the Seventh Circuit's decision in *United States v. Soybel*[136] upheld the FBI's use of a pen register to obtain information about an alleged hacker. This case concerned a supply company called W.W. Grainger, which, in 2016, was victimized by a number of cyberattacks that resulted in millions of customers' records being deleted. The company's internal investigation revealed the attacks came from one router IP address. At that point, the FBI was notified. The FBI was able to determine that the router served all units within an apartment complex in Chicago—but further investigation was needed to link the hacking to an individual computer. In turn, the FBI obtained a court order under the Pen Register Act to examine, via use of a pen register and trap and trace device, web activity from the building, in general, and, more narrowly, from an apartment that belonged to a former Grainger IT employee named Soybel, who had been fired in 2014.

This particular court order required the building's ISP to attach the pen register to the building's master router. The pen register was capable of revealing what websites were being visited by computers in the building and when—but not specific content being accessed; as an example, the Seventh Circuit noted that, in this context, a pen register could tell authorities if a person visited a Google website but not if it was Gmail or YouTube. The pen register in this case enabled authorities to discern that 790 links were made between the router and a Grainger website—with all 790 coming from one individual computer; trap and trace of the master router could have played a role in revealing that the unique computer in question was Soybel's, since websites also communicate back with an individual computer (information that is then held in a router). Based on this information, Soybel was charged with violating the federal Computer Fraud and Abuse Act.[137]

In upholding this FBI's methods in this investigation, the majority opinion for the Seventh Circuit, after observing that the court had never been confronted with such a situation, drew a parallel to the Supreme Court's decision in *Smith v. Maryland*:

> IP pen registers are analogous in all material respects to the telephone pen registers that the Supreme Court upheld against a Fourth Amendment challenge in *Smith v. Maryland* ... (1979). The connection between Soybel's IP address and external IP addresses was routed through a third party—here, an Internet-service provider. Soybel has no expectation of privacy in the captured routing information, any more than the numbers he might dial from a landline telephone.

The Seventh Circuit also rejected Soybel's contention that *Carpenter v. United States* should render the FBI's actions a violation of the Fourth Amendment. On this point, the court said the following:

> *Carpenter* concerned historical cell-site location information ("CSLI"). The warrantless acquisition of that type of data implicates unique privacy interests that are absent here. Historical CSLI provides a detailed record of a person's past movements, which is made possible so long as he carries a cell phone. In contrast, the IP pen register had no ability to track Soybel's past movements. And *Carpenter* is also distinguishable based on the extent to which a person voluntarily conveys IP-address information to third parties.

One year prior to this decision from the Seventh Circuit, the Eleventh Circuit addressed a similar matter in *United States v. Trader* (2020).[138] In this case, a man named Trader sent pornographic images to a 9-year-old girl in North Carolina via an app called SayHi. The girl's parents informed local police, who, in turn, contacted the Department of Homeland Security (DHS). Federal agents from DHS observed that Trader's profile page on SayHi, a company based overseas, also revealed his username for an app called Kik, which was a U.S.-based company. DHS agents opted to reach out to Kik, since it was a domestic company, and without a court order, Kik officials willingly turned over Trader's email address and the IP address of a cell phone used to access his Kik account.

With that information, agents linked the IP address to a specific ISP, Comcast, which, upon request, (also without a court order) revealed the internet subscriber information of the IP address. The internet subscriber information contained the name of Mr. Trader's wife and their home's street address in Florida. At that point, agents acquired a search warrant for the home, which turned up electronic devices with evidence of Mr. Trader possessing child pornography as well as sexually abusing his daughters. He was charged with multiple federal crimes. Upholding this warrantless activity while distinguishing *Carpenter v. United States* as inapplicable (just as the Seventh Circuit had done), the Eleventh Circuit said, "Indisputably, email addresses and IP addresses were not at issue in *Carpenter*. The third-party doctrine applies, so the government did not need a warrant to obtain Trader's email address or internet protocol addresses from Kik."

INTERNET SUBSCRIBER INFORMATION: Personally identifiable information, such as a name, email address, or physical street address, connected to a router or computer's IP address.

Previously, with its 2014 decision in *United States v. Stanley*,[139] the Third Circuit evaluated unique methods employed by the head of a computer crimes unit of the Pennsylvania State Police. This officer entered a peer-to-peer network and used public information to detect an IP address that was sharing 77 files containing images of child pornography. By searching internet records that were available to the public, the officer found that the IP address was connected to a Comcast user in Pittsburgh, Pennsylvania. He then obtained a court order to compel Comcast to reveal internet subscriber information, and Comcast complied by providing a street address. At this point, police acquired a search warrant for that home and all computers within it. However, the subsequent search revealed no evidence of child pornography in the home, and it turned out the home had an internet router that was not password protected. The officer inferred that a nearby computer owner was making use of this router without permission—an act known as *mooching*. To locate this *moocher*, the officer attached a police computer to this router—with permission of the homeowner—and that police computer was used to reveal the IP address of a specific Mac computer linking up to the router—but still, no particular location for the Mac computer was apparent.

Next, the officer made use of software called MoocherHunter, in the hope of discerning where the outside computer linking to the router was located. This program was available to anyone as a free download from the creator's website, and all it required was a laptop and an antenna. The antenna was capable of giving off a signal to indicate how close it was to a mooching computer. By pointing the antenna in the air from within the house with the router, the officer received a strong signal coming from a nearby apartment complex, and then, from the sidewalk outside of that complex, he held the antenna up until it was able to home in on a single apartment. The officer used that information to obtain a search warrant—which could not have been acquired earlier because so many dwellings were in proximity to the original router; with the warrant in hand, officers entered this apartment and found images of child pornography on a Mac computer belonging to a man named Stanley.

The Third Circuit upheld this search by noting that the Moocher-Hunter software was different from the thermal imaging device pointed at a home, also from a sidewalk, in the *Kyllo v. United States* case. Specifically, the Third Circuit's majority opinion said, "Critical to *Kyllo's* holding ... was the fact that the defendant sought to confine his activities to the interior of his home. He justifiably relied on the privacy protections of the home to shield these activities from public observation."

In noting that Stanley's behavior was decidedly different, the court observed that "his conduct—sharing child pornography with other internet users via a stranger's internet connection—was deliberately projected outside of his home, ... beyond the threshold of his residence. In effect, Stanley opened his window and extended an invisible, virtual arm across the street to the Neighbor's router so that he could exploit his internet connection." The court went on to say, "In so doing, Stanley deliberately ventured beyond the privacy protections of the home, and thus, beyond the safe harbor provided by *Kyllo*." The Third Circuit also observed that in some states, including Pennsylvania, it is a crime to access a computer network without authorization, and in other states, theft of services provided by cable TV, telephone, or computers is a crime.[140] Such laws could further lessen an expectation of privacy when a person *mooches* off another's internet router.

Yet even though it upheld the search in question here, the Third Circuit refused to do so under the rationale of *Smith v. Maryland* and perhaps indicated a divergent set of rationales from more recent decisions in other circuits:

> Were we to hold that Stanley exposed his "signal" under *Smith* by transmitting it to a third-party router, we might open a veritable Pandora's Box of Internet-related privacy concerns. The Internet, by its very nature, requires all users to transmit their signals to third parties. ... This signal carries with it an abundance of detailed, private information about that user's Internet activity. A holding that an Internet user discloses her "signal" every time it is routed through third-party equipment could, without adequate qualification, unintentionally provide the government unfettered access to this mass of private information without requiring its agents to obtain a warrant. We doubt the wisdom of such a sweeping ruling, and in any event, find it unnecessary to embrace its reasoning.

Whether the Supreme Court takes up a case on this emerging issue of internet privacy remains to be seen, but in the end, these cases carry ramifications for all users of social media websites as well as the government agents tasked with investigating crimes committed through the internet.

THE CONSTITUTION IN ACTION
Privatizing Electronic Surveillance

In some situations, police departments might contract with private companies that can assist in the provision of electronic surveillance. One such company is called Desert Snow, which offers training for police departments that wish to make use of a system known as the Black Asphalt Electronic Networking and Notification System. This system is employed by some highway interdiction teams and allows police officers across the country to access and share information about drivers in the United States. Any officer can enter information into the database, which can then be accessed by other officers on the network. Information might include any of the following: drivers' license numbers, Social Security numbers, addresses, and even identifying features like hair color or tattoos—as well as subjective assessments of whether a motorist might be carrying large amounts of cash. In reviewing this partnership between police and the private sector, an article in *The Washington Post* observed, "A thriving subculture of road officers on the network now competes to see who can seize the most cash and contraband, describing their exploits in the network's chat rooms and sharing 'trophy shots' of money and drugs"; the article also indicated that "[s]ome police advocate highway interdiction as a way of raising revenue for cash-strapped municipalities."[141] We address this matter again in chapter 13, within our discussion of civil forfeiture.

Interception of Electronic Messages

Employees have a very low expectation of privacy with regard to emails sent via computers owned by their employers. Under the third-party doctrine, employers can turn over employees' emails to law enforcement agencies on request. To obtain emails or other data stored on private computers, though, government agents must obtain a search warrant. However, under the ECPA, email stored on a third party's computer (e.g., an ISP) for more than 180 days is considered to have been abandoned, and it, therefore, can be obtained by law enforcement officials without a court order.

As noted in the previous chapter, the Supreme Court's decision in *O'Connor v. Ortega* (1987)[142] found that government employers and supervisors are allowed to engage in warrantless searches of employees' offices and desks. There was no majority opinion in this case, but a plurality opinion said that these searches should be guided by a reasonableness standard, provided that any such search was connected to "noninvestigatory work-related reasons" and took into consideration the "operational realities of the workplace."

Application of these principles to electronic workplace communications would arrive with the Supreme Court's decision in *City of Ontario, California v. Quon* (2010).[143] As noted in chapter 8, this case involved a unanimous ruling that there was no Fourth Amendment violation when a police chief read transcripts of text messages that police officers under his command had written to each other through their work-issued pagers. Those messages revealed an improper romantic relationship that violated department policy, thereby leading to suspensions. Justice Kennedy's majority opinion observed the following:

> Under the approach of the *O'Connor* plurality, when conducted for a 'noninvestigatory, work-related purpos[e]' or for the 'investigatio[n] of work-related misconduct,' a government employer's warrantless search is reasonable if it is 'justified at its inception' and if 'the measures adopted are reasonably related to the objectives of the search and not excessively intrusive in light of' the circumstances giving rise to the search.

In the *Quon* case, the work-related purpose was said to be investigating the source of overage charges for excessive messaging, and the Supreme Court deemed this to be a reasonable justification for looking at the messages. Extrapolating a broader principle, then, it seems as though reasonable, work-related purposes could justify the warrantless viewing of many workplace electronic communications.

The concept of relevance here, as noted previously, is the Supreme Court's third-party doctrine, which was advanced in *Couch v. United States* (1973).[144] This doctrine posits that information a person voluntarily reveals or gives to a third party could forfeit any link to an expectation of privacy. A *third party* in this context refers to a person who is not acting as an agent of the government. This could apply, for example, if financial records are given to an accountant (which is what occurred in the *Couch* case) or if documents are given to a private package delivery company, like UPS or FedEx (but not the U.S. Postal Service, since that is a government agency). Finally, as discussed earlier in this chapter, the high Court's decision in *Carpenter v. United States* said the third-party doctrine should not apply to cell phone providers turning over to law enforcement any records of an individual cell phone user's GPS movement history.

JURISPRUDENCE

Pocket Dial Goes Wrong
Huff v. Spaw, 794 F.3d 543 (6th Cir. 2015)

A 2015 case from the U.S. Court of Appeals for the Sixth Circuit offered an assessment of an interesting work phone search. In *Huff v. Spaw* (2015), the Sixth Circuit addressed expectations of privacy connected with an accidental phone call, known commonly as a *pocket dial*. In this case, a man named Huff had his phone in a front-facing pocket on his shirt when he accidentally dialed a work colleague named Spaw on that phone. Spaw answered his own phone, receiving the mistaken call—but proceeded to listen for 91 minutes without saying a word. Spaw wrote down detailed notes on what Huff was saying to another work colleague and to Huff's wife. It turned out that this conversation included discussion of firing Spaw from his job. Spaw also recorded portions of the conversation.

Huff learned that the accidental call had been recorded and then sued Spaw for the tort of invasion of privacy, based on an alleged violation of the federal Omnibus Crime Control and Safe Streets Act of 1968. Huff lost his case at the district court level, and on review, Judge Danny Boggs of the Sixth Circuit wrote an opinion that also ruled against Huff, finding that, "[u]nder the plain-view doctrine, if a homeowner neglects to cover a window with drapes, he would lose his reasonable expectation of privacy with respect to a viewer looking into the window from outside of his property"; Judge Boggs went on to conclude that "the [plain view] doctrine applies to auditory as well as visual information." Ultimately, the court determined that a person who pocket dials another person loses any expectation of privacy in what they say while the call's recipient listens in to what is discussed.

Conclusion

A delicate balancing act is needed to preserve broad societal objectives like safeguarding national security and combatting terrorism, while simultaneously seeking to protect the individual liberties that are the hallmark of a free democratic society. At times, even a government *of the people* needs to engage in tactics that require surveillance of, and perhaps even tracking of, those very people. In the United States, where surveillance techniques have varied greatly over time and are constantly changing and emerging as technology evolves, it is often left to courts to untangle their compatibility with the Constitution and, more specifically, the Fourth Amendment.

Over the course of nearly a century, the Supreme Court has addressed a wide array of government surveillance techniques. The high Court has offered a significant body of case precedent focusing on government surveillance methods—with cases covering a variety of topics, including the following: rudimentary listening devices placed in public payphones; microphones extended from a stick to jut up against a wall; pen registers and trap and trace devices; surveillance conducted (and photographs taken) by officers in airplanes and helicopters; thermal imaging devices; GPS locators; and cell phone searches. Some cases have been examined with an assessment of physical intrusion into personal property—via the trespass doctrine—and other cases have applied a reasonable expectation of privacy approach. More recent developments that have yet to be confronted in detail by the courts include drone searches and facial recognition software.

Government agencies at all levels have made use of these various tools of surveillance, from state and local police to the FBI, DEA, TSA, and the U.S. Border Patrol. There also is the matter of evaluating methods used by the nation's bureaucratic agencies that are specifically tasked with gathering intelligence, such as the CIA and the NSA. In some cases, court review is insufficient for implementing safeguards that preserve individual rights in the face of government surveillance. Accordingly, legislative action may be needed to shape parameters that guide the actions of these government agencies, which have the mission of implementing advanced surveillance methods. Within the last decade, for instance, acts of Congress have attempted to halt the NSA's mass collection of metadata from cell phones belonging to millions of Americans and have even ordered the removal of revealing body scanners used by the TSA in U.S. airports.

Without question, as new technologies develop, courts and legislatures will collectively be confronted with new challenges that might have seemed unthinkable even a few years prior. What the future holds in this regard can be difficult to predict. Perhaps, police will one day carry lasers that reveal what people are carrying in their bags as they walk along public streets, or maybe cameras connected to computers will follow us constantly as we go about our daily lives, revealing our identity and precise location at the click of a button. In the end, courts and legislatures will play a role in determining what level of freedom individual citizens should expect to relinquish as the government uses innovative and evolving technologies to seek information that might help to control crime or to protect national security; hopefully, correlated consideration of Supreme Court precedents related to the Fourth Amendment will help to shape those policies that impact privacy rights in the twenty-first century and beyond.

Discussion Questions

1. In what situations would a hidden microphone violate a reasonable expectation of privacy? In what situations would it not? Are there any cases that preceded the Supreme Court's *Katz* ruling that might have served as a harbinger of the shift in Fourth Amendment jurisprudence that came from that case?

2. What changed between the Supreme Court's 1928 decision in *Olmstead v. United States* and the *Katz v. United States* decision of 1967? Distill the essence of that shift, and explain its importance for evaluating contemporary surveillance techniques.

3. How might the Supreme Court's decision-making regarding pen registers be used to evaluate the warrantless collection of metadata from the electronic communications of millions of Americans?

4. In what places would the use of camera recordings not violate a reasonable expectation of privacy? Where would the installation of a hidden camera without a warrant be likely to violate the Fourth Amendment?

5. What specific expectations of privacy are violated when government officials use a thermal imaging device to scan a home for abnormal heat emanations? Can you envision a scenario in which use of a thermal imaging device might implicate a violation of the trespass doctrine?

6. What Supreme Court case precedents are most relevant for evaluating the constitutionality of a police drone flying above someone's backyard, at an altitude of 50 feet, to take pictures of marijuana plants? What changes in the analysis if the drone allows police to look inside the home?

7. In what ways is the use of facial recognition software likely to lead to unjust outcomes within the criminal justice system? What types of facial recognition software usage would be compatible with a reasonable expectation of privacy?

8. By what standards would a court evaluate an airport body scanner that revealed detailed images of human anatomy? What would result in this type of scanner being banned in all circumstances? What legal standards and case precedent might permit its use?

9. Consider Justice Scalia's majority opinion and Justice Alito's concurring opinion in the GPS locator decision in *United States v. Jones* (2012). For what types of searches would each approach provide stronger protection for individual liberty under the Fourth Amendment?

10. What type of information that people typically store on a smartphone is likely to buttress the assertion that a phone should carry a heightened expectation of privacy? If an agent of law attempted to argue that going through the contents of a phone was no different than going through contents of file cabinet and its drawers, how would you counter that argument?

11. Regarding government attempts to track the GPS signal emanating from a cell phone, what situations would create a compelling reason to justify such a search? What case precedents speak to a heightened expectation of privacy in an individual's movements, even in public places?

12. How has Congress attempted to limit government power to conduct widespread surveillance in general and, more specifically, to collect cell phone metadata?

13. Jon Line, a student at Boca Grande State University, posted videos to one of his many social media accounts showing himself and numerous other young people consuming massive quantities of what were purported to be alcoholic beverages and appearing to be intoxicated. The videos were accompanied by comments from Line and others indicating that the "epic party" took place at a house near campus the previous evening. A day later, one of Jon's online friends shared the photos with the police. A subsequent investigation revealed that several of the individuals who appeared in the videos were underage. Line is now facing prosecution on several counts of contributing to the delinquency of a minor. He has filed a pretrial motion to suppress the video evidence, without which the case would have to be dismissed. If you were the trial judge, how would you rule on the motion?

14. Have the courts failed to adequately protect electronic communications in workplace settings? What limits, if any, should be placed upon application of the third-party doctrine, and in what case or cases has the Supreme Court suggested such limitations?

Endnotes

1   *Olmstead v. United States*, 277 U.S. 438 (1928).

2   *Katz v. United States*, 389 U.S. 347 (1967).

3   *Goldman v. United States*, 316 U.S. 129 (1942).

4   *Silverman v. United States*, 365 U.S. 505 (1961).

5   *Hoffa v. United States*, 385 U.S. 293 (1966).

6   *United States v. White*, 401 U.S. 745 (1971).

7   *Rathbun v. United States*, 355 U.S. 107 (1957).

8   Communications Act of 1934, Pub. L. 73–416, 48 Stat. 1064, 47 U.S.C. § 605.

9   *See Recording Phone Calls and Conversations*, JUSTIA (Oct. 2021) (for a discussion of state-by-state guidelines regarding "one-party" and "all-party" consent for recordings of conversations), https://www.justia.com/50-state-surveys/recording-phone-calls-and-conversations/.

10   18 U.S.C. § 2511

11   *Lane v. Allstate Insurance Company*, 114 Nev. 1176 (1998).

12   *Vermont v. Geraw*, 795 A.2d 1219 (Vt. 2002).

13   These state laws are often called *two-party consent* laws, but they require that all parties in a conversation give consent. Those states, as of 2021, are CA, CT (one party is required to avoid a violation of criminal law, and two parties must consent to avoid a civil suit), DE, FL, IL, MD, MA, MI, MT, OR (phone calls are one-party consent and in-person conversations are all-party consent), NH, PA, and WA. Although Michigan law requires all-party consent, one appellate court has said that one-party consent is acceptable in that state—*see Sullivan v. Gray*, 117 Mich. App. 476 (1982). For a discussion of state-by-state guidelines regarding one-party and two-party consent for recordings of conversations, *see* JUSTIA, *Recording Phone Calls and Conversations*, Oct. 2021, https://www.justia.com/50-state-surveys/recording-phone-calls-and-conversations/.

14   Title III of the Omnibus Crime Control and Safe Streets Act of 1968, Pub. L. 90-351, 82 Stat. 197, 18 U.S.C. §§ 2515-2520.

15   *Lee v. Florida*, 392 U.S. 378 (1968).

16   *United States v. United States District Court*, 407 U.S. 297 (1972).

17   *McGrain v. Daugherty*, 273 U.S. 135 (1927); *Watkins v. United States*, 354 U.S. 178 (1957).

18   U.S. Senate, *Senate Select Committee to Study Governmental Operations with Respect to Intelligence Activities*, https://www.senate.gov/about/powers-procedures/investigations/church-committee.htm.

19   See U.S. Senate Select Committee on Intelligence, *Intelligence Related Commissions, Other Select or Special Committees and Special Reports* (for the final report), https://www.intelligence.senate.gov/resources/intelligence-related-commissions.

20   *Smith v. Maryland*, 442 U.S. 735 (1979).

21   *See, e.g., People v. Blair*, 602 P.2d 738, 746 (Cal. 1979); *People v. Timmons*, 690 P.2d 213 (Colo. 1984); *State v. Rothman*, 779 P.2d 1 (Haw. 1989).

22   *Shaktman v. State*, 553 So. 2d 148 (Fla. 1989).

23   Electronic Communications Privacy Act (ECPA) of 1986, Pub. L. 99–508, 100 Stat. 1848.

24   Pen Register Act of 1986, 18 U.S.C. §§ 3121–3126.

25   See 18 U.S.C. § 3123 (issuance of an order for a pen register or a trap and trace device).

26   *Id.* at § 3127(3) (definitions for chapter).

27   Scott Shane & Colin Moynihan, *Drug Agents Use Vast Phone Trove, Eclipsing N.S.A.'s.*, N.Y. Times, Sept. 1, 2013.

28   Stored Communications Act of 1986, Pub. L. 99–508, 100 Stat. 1848, 18 U.S.C. §§ 2701–2712.

29   Clarifying Lawful Overseas Use of Data (CLOUD) Act, Pub L. 115–141 (2018).

30   *Microsoft Corp. v. United States*, 584 U.S. ___ (2018); see *Microsoft Corp. v. United States* (*In re a Warrant to Search a Certain E–Mail Account Controlled & Maintained by Microsoft Corp.*), 829 F.3d 197 (2nd Cir. 2016).

31   Lawrence Hurley, *Microsoft Calls for Dismissal of U.S. Supreme Court Privacy Fight*, Reuters, Apr. 3, 2018.

32   Adam Goldman & Matt Apuzzo, *With Cameras, Informants, NYPD Eyed Mosques*, Associated Press, Feb. 23, 2012.

33   *United States v. McIver and Eberle*, 186 F.3d 1119 (9th Cir. 1999).

34   *California v. Ciraolo*, 476 U.S. 207 (1986).

35   In this quote, Justice Powell cited *United States v. Karo*, 468 U.S. 705 (1984).

36 *Dow Chemical Co. v. United States*, 476 U.S. 227 (1986).

37 It should be noted that the Court has been more permissive with respect to *administrative* searches, especially those directed at closely regulated industries. *See, e.g., New York v. Burger*, 482 U.S. 691 (1987).

38 National Conference of State Legislatures, *Automated Enforcement Overview*, https://www.ncsl.org/research/transportation/automated-enforcement-overview.aspx.

39 Insurance Institute for Highway Safety, *Red Light Running* (updated May 2021), https://www.iihs.org/topics/red-light-running#communities-using-red-light-cameras.

40 Infrastructure Investment and Jobs Act of 2021, Pub. L. 117–58, 135 Stat. 429, 23 U.S.C. §§ 101–176.

41 *Mendenhall v. City of Akron*, 374 F. App'x 598 (6th Cir. 2010).

42 *Idris v. City of Chicago*, 552 F.3d 564, 565 (7th Cir. 2009).

43 *Jimenez v. State*, 246 So. 3d 219 (Fla. 2018)

44 Texas Transportation Code 707.021.

45 *Morgan Smith & Boyd v. City of St. Louis*, 409 S.W.3d 404, No. ED98263 (Mo. Ct. App. Jun. 11, 2013).

46 Associated Press, *Haslam to Sign Tennessee Traffic Bill into Effect*, TimesNews, May 27, 2011, https://www.timesnews.net/news/local-news/haslam-to-sign-tennessee-traffic-camera-bill-into-law/article_f01c2f63-13bc-5ef8-93f8-e07b9c8f8883.html.

47 Joe Gyan Jr., *This Court Ruling Might Put East Baton Rouge on Hook for Millions if it Loses Red-Light-Camera Lawsuit*, The Advocate, January 23, 2020, https://www.theadvocate.com/baton_rouge/news/courts/article_d97c7bb2-3df7-11ea-9dca-071f1cb9ad81.html.

48 *Kansas v. Glover*, 589 U.S. ____ (2020).

49 John Harden, *D.C. Parking, Traffic Tickets Snowball into Financial Hardships*, Wash. Post, Aug. 6, 2021, https://www.washingtonpost.com/dc-md-va/2021/08/06/dc-traffic-parking-tickets-black-neighborhoods/.

50 Emily Hopkins & Melissa Sanchez, *Chicago's 'Race-Neutral' Traffic Cameras Ticket Black and Latino Drivers the Most*, ProPublica, Jan. 11, 2022, https://www.propublica.org/article/chicagos-race-neutral-traffic-cameras-ticket-black-and-latino-drivers-the-most.

51 Stacey Sutton & Nebiyou Tilahun, Red Light and Speed Cameras: Analyzing the Equity and Efficacy of Chicago's Automated Camera Enforcement Program 6 (2022) (report to the City of Chicago Mayor's Office and Department of Transportation).

52 Hopkins & Sanchez, *supra* note 49.

53 Sutton & Nebiyou, *supra* note 50.

54 *Id.* at 6.

55 *Id.*

56 Hopkins & Sanchez, *supra* note 50 (They note, "According to a 2017 city report, Black Chicagoans are killed in traffic crashes at twice the rate of white residents.").

57 *See* Jennifer Tucker, How Facial Recognition Technology Came to Be, *The Boston Globe*, Nov. 23, 2018.

58 Tajha Chappellet-Lanier, *Facial Recognition Algorithms Are Getting a Lot Better, NIST Study Finds*, FedScoop, December 3, 2018, https://www.fedscoop.com/facial-recognition-algorithms-getting-lot-better-nist-study-finds/.

59 Kaleigh Rogers, *That Time the Super Bowl Secretly Used Facial Recognition Software on Fans*, Vice, Feb. 7, 2016, https://www.vice.com/en/article/kb78de/that-time-the-super-bowl-secretly-used-facial-recognition-software-on-fans.

60 *See* Clare Garvie et al., *The Perpetual Line-Up: Unregulated Police Face Recognition in America*, Center on Privacy & Technology at Georgetown Law, Oct. 18, 2016, at 10–12.

61   *See* Cindy Carcamo, *Immigration Officials Created Network That Can Spy on Majority of Americans, Report Says,* Los Angeles Times, May 10, 2022.

62   Federal Bureau of Investigation, November 2018 Next Generation Identification (NGI) System Fact Sheet (2018), https://www.fbi.gov/file-repository/ngi-monthly-fact-sheet/view; *see* Government Accountability Office, Face Recognition Technology: The FBI Should Ensure Better Privacy and Accuracy (GAO-16-267) 49 (2016), https://www.gao.gov/assets/gao-16-267.pdf.

63   The Constitution Project's Task Force on Facial Recognition Surveillance & Jake Laperruque, Facing the Future of Surveillance, POGO (March 4, 2019), https://www.pogo.org/report/2019/03/facing-the-future-of-surveillance/.

64   U.S Customs and Border Protection, *Biometrics,* https://biometrics.cbp.gov/; Calvin Biesecker, *CBP Set to Begin Face Recognition Evaluations of Pedestrians, Vehicle Occupants At Land Ports,* Defense Daily, June 28, 2018, https://www.defense-daily.com/cbp-set-begin-face-recognition-evaluations-pedestrians-vehicle-occupants-land-ports/; *see* Alex Perala, *IDEMIA Tech Aids CBP Trial of Biometric Screening at Sea Port,* Find Biometrics, Nov. 14, 2017, https://findbiometrics.com/idemia-cbp-biometric-screening-sea-port-411144/.

65   Editorial Staff, *US Border Patrol Introduces Facial Recognition at Texas Bridge,* Security Magazine, Sept. 21, 2021, https://www.securitymagazine.com/articles/96143-us-border-patrol-introduces-facial-recognition-at-texas-bridge.

66   Transportation Security Administration, *Biometrics Technology,* https://www.tsa.gov/biometrics-technology; Dami Lee, *TSA Lays out Plans to Use Facial Recognition for Domestic Flights,* The Verge, Oct. 15, 2018, https://www.theverge.com/2018/10/15/17979688/tsa-precheck-facial-recognition-airport-cbp-biometric-exit; *see* Frank Bajak & David Koenig, *Face Scans for US Citizens Flying Abroad Stirs Privacy Issues,* Associated Press, July 12, 2017, available at: https://apnews.com/article/acf6bab1f5ab4bc59284985a3babdca4.

67   Department of Homeland Security, *Screening of Passengers by Observation Techniques,* https://www.dhs.gov/publication/screening-passengers-observation-techniques-spot-program; Ashley Halsey III, *GAO Says There Is No Evidence That TSA Program to Spot Terrorists Is Effective,* Wash. Post, Nov. 13, 2013; Kelly Dickerson, *TSA SPOT Program is Scientifically Bogus,* Business Insider, May 16, 2015, https://www.businessinsider.com/tsa-spot-program-is-scientifically-bogus-2015-5; Staff Reports, *Report Questions Objectiveness, Cost-Efficiency Of TSA's Behavior Detection Program,* Security Infowatch, June 10, 2013, https://www.securityinfowatch.com/critical-infrastructure/news/10958287/tsas-spot-program-comes-under-fire-in-dhs-inspector-general-report.

68   Alex Najibi, *Racial Discrimination in Facial Recognition Technology,* Harvard University Science in the News, Blog, Science Policy: Special Edition: Science Policy and Social Justice, Oct. 24, 2020, https://sitn.hms.harvard.edu/flash/2020/racial-discrimination-in-face-recognition-technology/?web=1&wdLOR=cDA-B8038A-EDD3-CE46-9278-D10FD8FFBF98.

69   Steve Nouri, *Council Post: The Role of Bias in Artificial Intelligence,* Forbes, Feb. 3, 2021, https://www.forbes.com/sites/forbestechcouncil/2021/02/04/the-role-of-bias-in-artificial-intelligence/?sh=46b6b92d579d.

70   Joy Buolamwini & Timnit Gebru, *Gender Shades: Intersectional Accuracy Disparities in Commercial Gender Classification,* at 77–91 (2018) (Conf. Rep.), https://proceedings.mlr.press/v81/buolamwini18a.html.

71   Crockord Kade, *How is Face Recognition Surveillance Technology Racist?* American Civil Liberties Union, News & Commentary, June 16, 2020, https://www.aclu.org/news/privacy-technology/how-is-face-recognition-surveillance-technology-racist/ (citing Natasha Singer, *Amazon is Pushing Facial Technology That a Study Says Could be Biased,* N.Y. Times, Jan. 24, 2019).

72   Patrick Grother, Mei Ngan, & Kayee Hanaoka, *Face Recognition Vendor Test (FRVT), Part 3: Demographic Effects,* U.S. Dept. of Commerce (December 2019), https://nvlpubs.nist.gov/nistpubs/ir/2019/NIST.IR.8280.pdf.

73   Lauren Chambers, *Five Fast Facts From The Federal Study of Demographic Bias in Facial Recognition*, PrivacySOS, https://privacysos.org/blog/five-fast-facts-from-the-federal-study-of-demographic-bias-in-facial-recognition/.

74   Karen Hao, *A US government study confirms most face recognition systems are racist*, MIT Technology Review, Dec. 20, 2019, https://www.technologyreview.com/2019/12/20/79/ai-face-recognition-racist-us-government-nist-study/.

75   Najibi, *supra* note 67.

76   Adam Goldman & Matt Apuzzo, *With Cameras, Informants, NYPD Eyed Mosques*, Associated Press, Feb. 23, 2012, https://www.ap.org/ap-in-the-news/2012/with-cameras-informants-nypd-eyed-mosques.

77   *Kyllo v. United States*, 533 U.S. 27 (2001).

78   *Editorial: Do Police Need Search Warrants for Drones?* Pittsburgh Post-Gazette, Jan. 10, 2021, https://www.govtech.com/public-safety/editorial-do-authorities-need-search-warrants-for-drones.html.

79   *Florida v. Riley*, 488 U.S. 445 (1989).

80   *Editorial: Do Police Need Search Warrants for Drones?*, *supra* note 78.

81   *Long Lake Township v. Maxon*, 970 N.W. 2d 893 (Mich. Ct. App. 2021).

82   *Long Lake Township v. Maxon*, 973 N.W.2d 615 (Mich. 2022).

83   *Pennsylvania Board of Probation and Parole v. Scott*, 524 U.S. 357 (1998).

84   *See* Daniel S. Harawa, *The Post-TSA Airport: A Constitution Free Zone?* 41 Pepp. L. Rev. 1, 34 (2013); R. Gregory Israelsen, *Applying the Fourth Amendment's National-Security Exception to Airport Security and the TSA*, 78 J. Air L. & Com. 501, 537 (2013); Alexander A. Reinert, *Revisiting 'Special Needs' Theory via Airport Searches*, 106 NW. U. L. REV. Colloquy 207 (2012).

85   Farah Naz Khan, *Is That Airport Security Scanner Really Safe?* Sci. Am., Dec. 18, 2017, https://blogs.scientificamerican.com/observations/is-that-airport-security-scanner-really-safe/.

86   *Electronic Privacy Information Center v. Department of Homeland Security*, 653 F.3d 1 (D.C. Cir. 2011).

87   Department of Homeland Security, *Snapshot: Security at the Speed of Life*, (Jan. 17, 2018), https://www.dhs.gov/science-and-technology/news/2018/01/17/snapshot-security-speed-life.

88   Department of Homeland Security, *Snapshot: S&T Prototype Shoe Scanner May Improve Airport Security Experience*, June 18, 2019, https://www.dhs.gov/science-and-technology/news/2019/06/18/snapshot-prototype-shoe-scanner-may-improve-security.

89   This figure was revealed by U.S. Senator Dianne Feinstein, in the following memo her office made public in 2016: Memorandum (2016), https://www.feinstein.senate.gov/public/_cache/files/f/b/fb745343-1dbb-4802-a866-cfdfa300a5ad/BCD664419E5B375C638A0F250B37DCB2.nctc-tsc-numbers-to-congress-06172016-nctc-tsc-final.pdf.

90   *Gordon v. FBI*, 388 F. Supp. 2d 1028 (N.D. Cal. 2005).

91   *Ibrahim v. DHS*, No. 3:06-cv-545, slip op. at 63–75 (9th Cir. Jan. 2019).

92   *United States v. Knotts*, 460 U.S. 276 (1983).

93   *United States v. Karo*, *supra* note 34.

94   *See* GEOTAB, *History of GPS satellites and commercial GPS tracking*, June 23, 2020, https://www.geotab.com/blog/gps-satellites/.

95   *United States v. Jones*, 565 U.S. 400 (2012).

96   *Chimel v. California*, 395 U.S. 752 (1969).

97   *Riley v. California*, 573 U.S. 373 (2014).

98   *United States v. Carey*, 172 F.3d 1268 (10th Cir. 1999).

99   *Id.* (citing Raphael Winick, *Searches and Seizures of Computers and Computer Data*, 8 Harv. J. L. & Tech. 75 (1994)).

100 *See, e.g., United States v. Miranda*, 325 F. App'x 858 (11 Cir. 2009); *United States v. Turner*, 169 F.3d 84 (1st Cir. 1999); *United States v. Mann*, 592 F.3d 779 (7th Cir. 2010). *See* Scott D. Blake, *Let's Be Reasonable: Fourth Amendment Principles in the Digital Age*, 5 Seventh Circuit Rev. 491 (2010).

101 *See* Editorial Staff, *Everything We Know About the San Bernardino Terror Investigation So Far*, L.A. Times, Dec. 14, 2015, https://www.latimes.com/local/california/la-me-san-bernardino-shooting-terror-investigation-htmlstory.html; Joel Ruben, Richard Winton, Brittney Mejia, & Joseph Serna, *'All Hell Broke Loose' as Police Chased the San Bernardino Shooters*, L.A. Times, Dec. 13, 2015, https://graphics.latimes.com/san-bernardino-chase/.

102 Tim Cook's open letter to the public on this issue can be seen on Apple's website: Open letter from Tim Cook to the public (Feb. 16, 2016), https://www.apple.com/customer-letter/.

103 Joseph Tanfani, *Race to Unlock San Bernardino Shooter's iPhone Was Delayed By Poor FBI Communication, Report Finds*, L.A. Times, Mar. 27, 2018, https://www.latimes.com/politics/la-na-pol-fbi-iphone-san-bernardino-20180327-story.html.

104 *See* Ellen Nakashima & Reed Albergotti, *The FBI Wanted to Unlock the San Bernardino Shooter's iPhone. It Turned To A Little-Known Australian Firm*, Wash. Post, Apr. 14, 2021 (for further reading); *See* D. Hardawar, *An Australian Company Helped the FBI Unlock San Bernardino Shooter's iPhone*, Engadget, April 14, 2021, https://www.engadget.com/azimuth-apple-fbi-san-bernardino-iphone-unlock-141617737.html.

105 Joseph Tanfani, *Race to Unlock San Bernardino Shooter's iPhone Was Delayed by Poor FBI Communication, Report Finds*, L.A. Times, Mar. 27, 2018, https://www.latimes.com/politics/la-na-pol-fbi-iphone-san-bernardino-20180327-story.html.

106 *United States v. Skinner*, 690 F. 3d 772 (6th Cir. 2012).

107 *Carpenter v. United States*, 585 U.S. ___ (2018).

108 Alex Ramirez, *ICE Records Confirm that Immigration Enforcement Agencies are Using Invasive Cell Phone Surveillance Devices*, ACLU, May 27, 2020, https://www.aclu.org/news/immigrants-rights/ice-records-confirm-that-immigration-enforcement-agencies-are-using-invasive-cell-phone-surveillance-devices.

109 Davide Mamone, *ICE Gets Sued for Privacy Concerns Over Immigrant Tracking*, The Advocate, Apr. 20, 2022, https://www.govtech.com/public-safety/ice-gets-sued-for-privacy-concerns-over-immigrant-tracking.

110 Foreign Intelligence Surveillance Act of 1978, Pub. L. 95–511, 92 Stat. 1783, 50 U.S.C. §§ 1801–1813.

111 Intelligence Reform and Terrorism Prevention Act of 2004, Pub. L. 108–458, 118 Stat. 3638, 50 U.S.C. § 1801(b)(1).

112 FISA Amendments Act of 2008, Pub. L. 110–261, 122 Stat. 2436, 50 U.S.C. §§ 1801–1813.

113 Zack Whittaker, *Here's How Many U.S. Surveillance Requests Were Rejected in 2015*, ZDNet, Apr. 30, 2016, https://www.zdnet.com/article/us-spy-court-didnt-reject-a-single-secret-government-demand-for-data/.

114 *See* Roslynn R. Mauskopf, Report of the Director of the Administrative Office of the U.S. Courts on Activities of the Foreign Intelligence Surveillance Courts (year-by-year statistics on warrant requests to the FISA Court since 2015; the 2020 report is cited therein), https://www.uscourts.gov/statistics-reports/analysis-reports/directors-report-foreign-intelligence-surveillance-courts.

115 USA PATRIOT Act of 2001, Pub. L. 107–56, 115 Stat. 272.

116 50 U.S.C. § 1861.

117 50 U.S.C. § 1805(c)(2)(B).

118 18 U.S.C. § 3103a. *See* Brett Shumate, *From 'Sneak and Peek' to 'Sneak and Steal': Section 213 of the USA PATRIOT ACT*, 19 Reg. U. L. Rev. 203 (2006–2007) (for further reading on Section 213).

119 National Security Agency Central Security Services (CSS), www.nsa.gov.

120 Protect America Act of 2007, Pub. L. 110–55, 121 Stat. 552, 50 U.S.C. §§ 1801–1813.

121   *See, e.g., ACLU v. NSA*, 493 F.3d 644 (6th Cir. 2007) (cert. denied 2008); *Clapper v. Amnesty Int'l*, 568 U.S. 398 (where the Court found there was no standing to challenge FISA); *Wikimedia Found. v. NSA*, 143 F. Supp. 344 3d (D. Md. 2015) (dismissed again by the same court in 2019).

122   *Klayman v. Obama*, 957 F.Supp.2d 1 (2013).

123   *American Civil Liberties Union v. Clapper*, 785 F.3d 787 (2d Cir. 2015).

124   *United States v. Moalin*, 973 F. 3d 977 (9th Cir. 2020).

125   *See* Terrorism Close Calls: The New York City Subway Plot, (A NETFLIX Original Series 2018); Marshall Erwin, Connecting the Dots: Analysis of the Effectiveness of Bulk Phone Records Collection (2014), https://www.judiciary.senate.gov/imo/media/doc/011413RecordSub-Leahy.pdf.

126   USA FREEDOM Act of 2015, Pub. L. 114-23, 129 Stat. 268.

127   Department of Justice, Department of Justice Seizes $2.3 Million in Cryptocurrency Paid to Ransomware Extortionists Darkside (2021), https://www.justice.gov/opa/pr/department-justice-seizes-23-million-cryptocurrency-paid-ransomware-extortionists-darkside.

128   Justin P. Murphy & Adrian Fontecilla, *Social Media Evidence in Government Investigations and Criminal Proceedings: A Frontier of New Legal Issues*, 19 Rich. J. L. & Tech 11 (2013).

129   Fight Online Sex Trafficking Act-Stop Enabling Sex Traffickers Act of 2018, Pub. L. 155–164, 132 Stat. 1253.

130   Catherine Thorbecke, *Florida Suspect Uses His Own Wanted Poster as Facebook Profile Picture*, ABC NEWS, Sept. 2, 2016, https://abcnews.go.com/US/florida-suspect-wanted-poster-facebook-profile-picture/story?id=41822973

131   Chris Matyszczyk, *Fugitive used wanted poster as his Facebook profile pic, say police*, CNET, Sept. 4, 2016, https://www.cnet.com/culture/fugitives-had-wanted-poster-as-facebook-profile-pic-say-police/

132   Sanya Jain, *Man Arrested After He Forgot to Hide Bag of Meth in Facebook Pic*, NDTV.com, Oct. 5, 2021), https://www.ndtv.com/offbeat/man-arrested-after-he-forgot-to-hide-bag-of-meth-in-facebook-pic-2564377.

133   Patty Ryan, *Tampa 'First Lady' of Tax Refund Fraud Gets 21 Years in Prison*, Tampa Bay Times, Jul. 16, 2013, available at: https://www.tampabay.com/news/courts/criminal/tampa-first-lady-of-tax-refund-fraud-gets-21-years-in-prison/2131700/.

134   Cale Guthrie Weissman, *What Is an IP Address And What Can It Reveal About You?* Business Insider, May 18, 2015, https://www.businessinsider.com/ip-address-what-they-can-reveal-about-you-2015-5.

135   See, e.g., Erin Lawson. *Tracking Criminals with Internet Protocol Addresses: Is Law Enforcement Correctly Identifying Perpetrators?* 18 N.C. J.L. & Tech. 316 (2017).

136   *United States v. Soybel*, No 19-1936 (7th Cir. Sept. 8, 2021).

137   Computer Fraud and Abuse Act of 1986, Pub. L. 99-474, 100 Stat. 1213, 18 U.S.C. § 1030

138   *United States v. Trader*, 981 F.3d 961 (11th Cir. 2020).

139   *United States v. Stanley*, 753 F.3d 114 (3d Cir. 2014).

140   Among the states to make it a crime to access a computer network without permission are California, Colorado, Delaware, Indiana, Louisiana, Missouri, New Hampshire, New Jersey, Oklahoma, South Carolina, Pennsylvania, Texas, Vermont, and Washington; those with *theft-of-services* statutes related to internet activity are Alabama, Arizona, Delaware, Kentucky, Montana, New Hampshire, New Jersey, Pennsylvania, Utah, and Vermont.

141   Michael Sallah, Robert O'Harrow Jr., Steven Rich, & Gabe Silverman, *Stop and Seize: Aggressive Police Take Hundreds of Millions of Dollars from Motorists Not Charged with Crimes*, Wash. Post, Sept. 6, 2014, https://www.washingtonpost.com/sf/investigative/2014/09/06/stop-and-seize/?itid=lk_inline_manual_32.

142   *O'Connor v. Ortega*, 480 U.S. 709 (1987).

143 *City of Ontario, California v. Quon,* 560 U.S. 746 (2010).

144 *Couch v. United States,* 409 U.S. 322 (1973).

Credit

IMG 9.1: Copyright © 2014 Depositphotos/thomaslenne.

CHAPTER 10

The Fourth Amendment

Arrest, Detention, and Use of Force

"A democratic society ... naturally guards against the misuse of the law enforcement process. Zeal in tracking down crime is not in itself an assurance of soberness of judgment. Disinterestedness in law enforcement does not alone prevent disregard of cherished liberties. Experience has therefore counseled that safeguards must be provided against the dangers of the overzealous as well as the despotic."

—Justice Felix Frankfurter, writing for the Supreme Court
in *McNabb v. United States*, 318 U.S. 332 (1943)

Learning Objectives

After reading this chapter, you should understand how constitutional law governs the following:

1. Arrests pursuant to warrants
2. Warrantless arrests
3. Citizen's arrests
4. Use of force by police
5. Investigatory detentions and pat-down searches
6. Identification checks
7. Roadblocks and checkpoints
8. Immunity from arrest

Key Cases

Terry v. Ohio, 392 U.S. 1 (1968)
Delaware v. Prouse, 440 U.S. 648 (1979)
Tennessee v. Garner, 471 U.S. 1 (1985)
Graham v. Connor, 490 U.S. 386 (1989)
Florida v. J.L., 529 U.S. 266 (2000)
Atwater v. Lago Vista, 532 U. S. 318 (2001)
Hiibel v. Sixth Judicial District Court of Nevada, 542 U.S. 177 (2004)

Introduction

ARREST: The seizure of a person based on legal authority to do so.

An **arrest** occurs when police take an individual into custody for the alleged commission of a crime. Because an arrest is a *seizure* of a person, it is subject to the requirements of the Fourth Amendment.[1] As with the seizure of property, the Fourth Amendment calls for police to obtain a warrant to make an arrest. However, the courts have held that warrantless arrests are permissible when officers possess probable cause to make an arrest.[2] In effecting an arrest, police may use reasonable force and, under extreme circumstances, deadly force. The use of deadly force by police has become a major social and political issue, not merely a legal one.

INVESTIGATORY DETENTION: A brief detention of a suspect based on reasonable suspicion that crime is afoot.

An **investigatory detention** occurs when police temporarily detain a person based on reasonable suspicion that criminal activity is afoot. Often, an investigatory detention will lead to an arrest, as police may discover illegal weapons, drugs, or other contraband during the detention. Alternatively, police may determine that an arrest warrant has been issued for the person being detained. During an investigatory detention, otherwise known as a **stop and frisk**, police may pat down the outer garments of the person being detained to make sure the person is not carrying a concealed weapon.

STOP AND FRISK: A brief detention based on reasonable suspicion, including a pat-down search of the detainee's outer garments.

Both arrest and investigatory detention are fraught with constitutional issues, and courts are constantly reviewing the reasonableness of police conduct during such encounters with citizens. These issues arise not only when people are arrested and prosecuted but also in cases when individuals sue the police for violating their Fourth Amendment rights. (For discussion of lawsuits against the police and the related topic of qualified immunity, see chapter 7.)

Arrest Pursuant to a Warrant

As we know, the Fourth Amendment provides that "no Warrant shall issue but upon probable cause, supported by Oath or affirmation." To obtain an arrest warrant, an officer must appear before a judge or magistrate and make out an affidavit giving rise to probable cause. In making the probable cause determination, the judge or magistrate must consider the "totality of circumstances" described in the affidavit.[3]

An arrest warrant will be issued as a matter of course pursuant to an indictment by a grand jury, as the indictment requires a probable cause determination by the grand jury (see chapter 11). A specific type of arrest warrant, known as a capias or bench warrant, also may be issued by a judge in a case in which a defendant has failed to make a required appearance in court.

Unlike a search warrant, which must describe with particularity the place to be searched and the things to be seized, an arrest warrant need only specify the name of the person to be arrested, the crime the person is alleged to have committed, and the name of the judge or magistrate issuing the warrant. Moreover, unlike search warrants, arrest warrants are not time-limited, and it is not uncommon for police to make an arrest based on a warrant that has been outstanding for years.

ARREST WARRANT: A document signed by a judge or magistrate authorizing the arrest of a certain person.

CAPIAS: See bench warrant.

BENCH WARRANT: An arrest warrant issued by a judge authorizing the arrest of a person who has already been indicted or is in contempt of court.

THE CONSTITUTION IN ACTION

Florida Man Arrested When Police Mistake Krispy Kreme Donut Flakes for Meth: Isolated Incident or Systemic Issue with Field Testing Kits?

In December 2015, a 64-year-old man named Daniel Rushing was pulled over in Orlando, Florida for driving 42 mph in a 30-mph zone. At the officer's request, Rushing consented to a search of the vehicle. Additional officers arrived on the scene, and Rushing was notified that crystal-like, white flakes were found on the floorboard of his car. Officers used a field testing kit to conduct a cursory analysis of the flakes, and that testing apparently revealed the flakes to be methamphetamine. Rushing was immediately arrested based on the officer's assertion that the field testing kit yielded probable cause of criminal activity.

Rushing was in jail for approximately ten hours before he was released on bail. The evidence was later sent to the Florida Department of Law Enforcement for enhanced screening, and there it was revealed that the substances found in Rushing's car were not illegal drugs. What were those white flakes? Rushing had immediately given the officers an explanation while at roadside, saying, "That's glaze from a Krispy Kreme doughnut! I get one every other Wednesday."[4] Charges against Rushing were dropped, and after he filed a lawsuit for a violation of his Fourth Amendment rights, the city of Orlando agreed to settle the case by giving him $37,500.

One source indicates that, around the time of Rushing's arrest, Orlando police officers were using something called NIK—a brand of field testing kits used to assess whether substances are drugs or not; these kits were available at a cost of $18 for a box of ten.[5] A 2016 investigation published jointly by *ProPublica* and *The New York Times Magazine* declared, "Tens of thousands of people every year are sent to jail based on the results of a $2 roadside drug test. Widespread evidence shows that these tests routinely produce false positives."[6]

(continued)

This issue becomes especially problematic when the entire basis for an arrest is rooted in results from a field testing kit. In this regard, by evaluating data about false drug arrests from the state of Texas, the *ProPublica–New York Times* study observed, "The kits, or the officers interpreting them, got it wrong most often when dealing with small amounts of suspected drugs. Sixty-three percent of the [non-controlled substances] cases involved less than a gram of evidence." The significance of that figure for the arrest process is crucial because, as the authors noted, "The smallest possession cases are the ones in which a field test can be of greatest consequence; if officers find larger quantities of white powder in dozens of baggies or packaged in bricks, they have sufficient probable cause to make an arrest regardless of what a color test shows."[7] For those individuals who are accused of possessing small quantities of substances that are alleged to be contraband, then, police reliance on field testing kits as a part of plain-view observations can be especially unjust.

Warrantless Arrests

WARRANTLESS ARREST:
An arrest made by police without prior judicial authorization.

A warrantless arrest is generally permissible when police have probable cause to believe a person has committed a crime. The existence of exigent circumstances is not necessarily required.[8] Probable cause to make a warrantless arrest exists when the observable facts are "sufficient to warrant a prudent man in believing that the [suspect] had committed or was committing an offense."[9] Certainly, a warrantless arrest is allowable when a crime is committed in an officer's presence. However, warrantless arrests in felony cases can be made based on statements by victims, witnesses, or informants. Again, the existence of probable cause depends on the totality of circumstances.[10] In most jurisdictions, a warrantless arrest for a misdemeanor can be made only when the offense is committed in the presence of the arresting officer.

In an early case that attempted to provide context for the meaning of the term *probable cause, Brinegar v. United States* (1949),[11] the Supreme Court stated, "In dealing with probable cause, however, as the very name implies, we deal with probabilities. These are not technical; they are the factual and practical considerations of everyday life on which reasonable and prudent men, not legal technicians, act." Decades later, in its decision in *Adams v. Williams* (1972), the Court observed the following:

> Probable cause does not require the same type of specific evidence of each element of the offense as would be needed to support a conviction. ... Rather, the court will evaluate generally the circumstances at the time of the arrest to decide if the officer had probable cause for his action.

That quote included a reference to *Draper v. United States* (1959),[12] which illustrated this principle in action. In this case, an officer with twenty-nine years of experience waited at a train station in Denver, Colorado based solely on an informant's tip that a drug dealer carrying heroin and a tan zipper bag would be arriving on a specific train coming from Chicago. The officer, who had received reliable tips from this particular informant before, did, in fact, notice a suspect who matched the informant's description—which included details of physical traits and clothing—as the suspect exited a train that arrived from Chicago; moreover, the officer observed the man walking in hasty fashion toward the exit, at which point the officer effectuated an arrest. A search incident to arrest ensued, revealing a syringe inside the zippered bag and heroin inside an envelope in the man's raincoat pocket. Upholding this warrantless arrest based on probable cause, the majority opinion by Justice Charles E. Whittaker stated, "Probable cause exists where the 'facts and circumstances within their [the arresting officers'] knowledge and of which they had reasonably trustworthy information [are] sufficient in themselves to warrant a man of reasonable caution in the belief that' an offense has been or is being committed."[13] However, in dissent, Justice William O. Douglas invoked a quotation from two Georgetown University law professors in writing that:

> The finger of suspicion is a long one. In an individual case, it may point to all of a certain race, age group or locale. Commonly it extends to any who have committed similar crimes in the past. Arrest on mere suspicion collides violently with the basic human right of liberty. It can be tolerated only in a society which is willing to concede to its government powers which history and experience teach are the inevitable accoutrements of tyranny.[14]

Warrantless Arrests for Minor Misdemeanors

In the case of minor misdemeanors, such as traffic violations, the usual practice is for the officer to issue a citation, which requires the cited party to appear in court to litigate the charge or pay a predetermined fine in order to avoid the court appearance. Nonetheless, the Supreme Court has upheld warrantless arrests for minor misdemeanors. In *Atwater v. City of Lago Vista* (2001),[15] a woman was arrested for driving without a license, not having proof of insurance, not wearing a seatbelt, and failing to have her children wear seatbelts. Upholding the arrest, a sharply divided Supreme Court held that "[t]he arrest and booking were inconvenient and embarrassing to Atwater, but not so extraordinary as to violate the Fourth Amendment." The rule announced in the *Atwater* case is this: "If an officer has probable cause to believe that an individual has committed even a very minor criminal offense in his presence, he may, without violating the Fourth Amendment, arrest the offender." Writing for four dissenters, Justice Sandra Day O'Connor averred that "[g]iving police officers constitutional carte blanche to effect an arrest whenever there is probable cause to believe a fine-only misdemeanor has been committed is irreconcilable with the Fourth Amendment's command that seizures be reasonable."

Warrantless Arrests in the Home

Warrantless arrests involving the entry of the suspect's home are subject to more stringent requirements. In *Payton v. New York* (1980),[16] the Supreme Court ruled that, in the absence of exigent circumstances, a warrantless, nonconsensual entry into a suspect's home to make a felony arrest violates the Fourth Amendment. In that case, the Court struck down a New York law that permitted police to enter a home without a warrant, and with force, to make a routine felony arrest. However, in the case of a serious felony, if there is good reason to believe that the suspect is armed and dangerous, or that the failure to make an immediate arrest will likely result in the destruction of evidence, officers may enter the home to effectuate a warrantless arrest—in keeping with principles of hot pursuit (as discussed in chapter 8).[17]

Prompt Appearance Before a Magistrate

In cases when police have made a warrantless arrest, the arrestee must be brought before a judge or magistrate to confirm the legality of the arrest. As the Supreme Court recognized in *Gerstein v. Pugh* (1975),[18] "the detached judgment of a neutral magistrate is essential if the Fourth Amendment is to furnish meaningful protection from unfounded interference with liberty." Accordingly, in *Gerstein* the Court held that "the Fourth Amendment requires a judicial determination of probable cause as a prerequisite to extended restraint of liberty following arrest." Subsequently, in *County of Riverside v. McLaughlin* (1991),[19] the Court said that a person arrested without a warrant must be afforded a probable cause hearing within forty-eight hours of arrest. In chapter 11, we will revisit this issue as we discuss the *McNabb–Mallory* rule, derived from two Supreme Court cases that indicate a confession should be deemed inadmissible if an unreasonable delay occurs between the time of arrest and presentment in court.[20]

It is important to note that Section 412 of the USA PATRIOT Act permits "indefinite detention" of immigrants and noncitizens,[21] although this likely conflicts with the Supreme Court's decision in *Zadvydas v. Davis* (2001).[22] Additionally, Section 1021 of the National Defense Authorization Act of 2012,[23] signed by President Obama, allows the military to utilize indefinite detention "without trial until the end of hostilities" for persons who were "part of or substantially supported [Al Qaeda, the Taliban] or associated forces that are engaged in hostilities against the U.S. and its coalition partners"; it is possible that application of this law could run afoul of the principles articulated in the Supreme Court's decision in *Boumediene v. Bush* (2008), which will be discussed in chapter 14.[24]

JURISPRUDENCE

The Functional Equivalent of Arrest
Dunaway v. New York, 442 U.S. 200 (1979)

After a restaurant owner was killed during an attempted armed robbery, police took Irving Dunaway into custody and transported him to the police station. Dunaway was not told he was under arrest, but after interrogation, he confessed to the crime. Appealing his conviction for attempted robbery and felony murder, Dunaway argued that police officers violated his Fourth Amendment rights when they seized him and transported him to the police station for interrogation. The state of New York admitted that the police lacked probable cause to make an arrest but claimed the detention and interrogation of Mr. Dunaway was justified on the lesser standard of reasonable suspicion. The Supreme Court reversed Dunaway's conviction, holding police must have probable cause before conducting station-house detention and interrogation, irrespective of whether it is termed an *arrest*. Writing for the Court, Justice William Brennan concluded that "detention for custodial interrogation—regardless of its label—intrudes so severely on interests protected by the Fourth Amendment as necessarily to trigger the traditional safeguards against illegal arrest."

Citizen's Arrest

Under English common law, a person could make a warrantless citizen's arrest when a felony or breach of the peace was committed in that individual's presence. In 1885, the Supreme Court acknowledged the right of citizen's arrest but held it did not apply to the capture of military deserters.[25] Today, the common-law rule still prevails in some states, but in others, it has been revised or abolished by legislation.

Whereas some states—such as Washington, West Virginia, and Wisconsin—do not have any laws that explicitly authorize a citizen's arrest, more than 41 states do have such laws in place, but specific parameters within those statutes may vary. For instance, some states allow a citizen's arrest only in the case of a felony (e.g., Arkansas, Kentucky, Louisiana, Michigan, New Hampshire, Ohio, and Rhode Island), but others like Virginia and Missouri allow it in the case of a misdemeanor breach of peace. Wyoming allows for a citizen's arrest in the case of a felony, theft, or breach of peace. South Carolina law is unique in that it explicitly permits the use of deadly force in the course of a citizen's arrest.[26]

Elsewhere, North Carolina does not authorize a citizen's arrest but does permit a person to "detain" another who is suspected of "a felony, a breach of peace, a crime involving physical injury to another person, or a crime involving destruction of property."[27] The distinction between a citizen's arrest and the "detention" allowed in North Carolina can, of course, amount to a subjective one. North Carolina also is unique in that it permits a private party to request a warrant for another person's arrest.

Some states require that a crime be committed in the presence of the citizen making the arrest, whereas other states, including Alabama and Mississippi, allow for a citizen's arrest even when the crime is not directly witnessed. Maryland permits a citizen's arrest for a felony that is witnessed or when there is probable cause of a felony having been committed. In Tennessee, any misdemeanor can be the subject of a citizen's arrest, but it must be witnessed—yet a felony does not need to be witnessed by the person making a citizen's arrest as long as there is reasonable cause that the crime occurred. Most states require prompt presentment to law enforcement after a citizen's arrest has been made.[28] It is important to note that an arrest by an off-duty police officer is not considered a citizen's arrest; sworn officers can make a police arrest even when they are off-duty.

Even in states that do not have a statute specifically allowing for a citizen's arrest, it is possible that such an arrest could be justified via

CITIZEN'S ARREST: An arrest made by a private individual, rather than a law enforcement officer.

case precedent and the application of common law principles. For example, appellate courts in the state of Washington have authorized citizen's arrests for misdemeanors[29] and felonies.[30] In Massachusetts, judicial decisions have made it clear that a citizen's arrest is permitted in situations in which there is probable cause that a felony has occurred (even if the crime is not directly witnessed);[31] however, a citizen's arrest for a misdemeanor is explicitly prohibited by case law in that state. The latter was articulated in a case where the Supreme Judicial Court of Massachusetts refused to authorize a citizen's arrest by an off-duty police officer who was outside of their jurisdiction and, thus, acting as a private citizen when he arrested a person on misdemeanor charges.[32] Some states have laws in place that allow a police officer who is from the state to make an arrest outside of their jurisdiction; this might apply, for instance, to a county sheriff who is in a different county at the time of making an arrest.[33] Additionally, in the case of hot pursuit of a criminal across county lines, most states authorize an officer to effectuate an arrest.[34]

Georgia recently passed House Bill 479 to repeal and replace its prior Civil War-era law that permitted a citizen's arrest. The new bill, which was signed into law by Governor Brian Kemp in 2021, replaced a statute that had allowed any person to make a citizen's arrest. More narrow parameters in the new law allow for a citizen's arrest to apply in limited circumstances, such as when an employee of a business attempts to detain a person who is accused of stealing or when an employee of a restaurant detains a customer who attempts to leave without paying. The new law also specifically requires a crime to be witnessed, and it prohibits the use of deadly force pursuant to a citizen's arrest, unless applicable state laws regarding self-defense are relevant (e.g., if a person faces imminent danger of death or great bodily injury[35]). Georgia's old citizen's arrest law was passed in 1863 and likely was modeled after the federal Fugitive Slave Act of 1850, which permitted citizens to capture escaped slaves and return them to their owners. The changes in the Georgia law were enacted following the murder of Ahmaud Arbery, who was pursued, shot, and killed after three men mistook him for a burglar as he was jogging through their neighborhood. We discuss this case in the following box.

THE CONSTITUTION IN ACTION
The Murder of Ahmaud Arbery

In February 2020, a 25-year-old man named Ahmaud Arbery was shot and killed as he was jogging in the town of Satilla Shores, Georgia. Arbery was pursued by three men who mistakenly believed that he had committed a burglary at a nearby construction site on which a home was being renovated. Two of the men were inside one vehicle and armed with guns, while the other man followed in a separate vehicle and recorded the pursuit on his cell phone. The chase continued for more than five minutes, and Arbery was eventually pinned in by the vehicles, with one of the two armed men exiting their vehicle and shooting Arbery three times. In the immediate aftermath of the incident, local authorities did not make any arrests, and a local district attorney allegedly directed that arrests should not be made. The owner of the home on the construction site where Arbery had been spotted reported that nothing had been taken from that location.

More than two months after the incident, the Georgia Bureau of Investigation arrested the three men who pursued Arbery, and in June 2002, a grand jury issued an indictment for each of them on charges of murder and false imprisonment, plus additional offenses. After a trial in November 2021, the shooter was found guilty of murder and eight other felonies, including assault and false imprisonment. The other two men were found guilty of felony murder, false imprisonment, aggravated assault, and criminal attempt to commit a felony. In January 2022, a judge sentenced each of the men to a life sentence in prison, with only the man who took the video being given a chance at parole (although he must serve at least thirty years before having a parole hearing).

The FBI, at the request of Georgia's Attorney General, also began its own investigation into the incident in May 2020. By April 2021, a federal grand jury handed down indictments for federal charges related to commission of a hate crime, kidnapping, and using a firearm during a crime of violence. In January 2022, Arbery's family rejected a potential plea deal on these federal charges, and the case was scheduled for trial. In February 2022, a federal jury found all three men involved in Arbery's murder guilty of all charges. Ultimately, Arbery's death spurred legislators in the state of Georgia to repeal the state's existing law regarding citizen's arrest and replace it with a new statute that requires anyone making a citizen's arrest to actually witness a crime.

Use of Force in Making Arrests

Police are entitled to use reasonable force in making an arrest. Many high-profile use-of-force cases have made headlines around the country in recent years, with some cases polarizing Americans and leading to violent protests. Ultimately, each individual case must be examined in light of relevant statutes, constitutional principles, and applicable case precedent. In the end, the Supreme Court has noted that excessive use of force constitutes an unreasonable seizure in violation of the Fourth Amendment—but the key lies in discerning what is *excessive*.

> **EXCESSIVE USE OF FORCE:** The use of force by police beyond that which is reasonably necessary to effect an arrest.

What Constitutes Excessive Force?

In *Graham v. Connor* (1989),[36] the Supreme Court provided guidance to lower courts beset with claims of excessive force by police. In this matter, Dethorne Graham, who was a diabetic, requested that one of his friends, a man named Berry, drive him to a convenience store, so he could buy orange juice to quickly elevate his blood sugar. When Graham walked inside the store, he saw a long line of people and immediately walked back outside to request that Berry drive him to a friend's nearby house. Officer Connor of the Charlotte Police Department witnessed Graham's rapid entry and exit from the store and, suspicious of that behavior, the officer followed Berry's vehicle and initiated a traffic stop. Berry explained to the officer that Graham was having a "sugar reaction," but the officer ordered the men to wait in the car as he investigated if anything had been stolen from the store. Graham reacted by exiting the vehicle, running around it two times, and then sitting down on the curb, at which point he lost consciousness.

More Charlotte police officers arrived at the scene, and one officer rolled Graham onto the sidewalk before using handcuffs to secure his hands behind his back. All of the officers ignored Berry's pleas to provide Graham with sugar, with one reportedly saying: "I've seen a lot of people with sugar diabetes that never acted like this. Ain't nothing wrong with the M.F. but drunk. Lock the S.B. up." Officers picked Graham up and placed him face down on the front of Berry's car. Graham requested that the officers look in his wallet, where he had a diabetic decal. Refusing to do so, an officer told him to shut up and then pushed his face into the car's hood. Four officers then took Graham and tossed him headfirst into a police car, refusing him access to orange juice that a friend had brought to the scene. Eventually, a report came in that Graham had not done anything wrong while at the convenience store, and the officers released him. By that point, Graham has suffered a broken foot, cuts on his wrist, an injury to his shoulder, a bruise on his forehead, and, subsequent to the incident, he claimed to have a persistent ringing sound in his right ear.

Graham filed suit against the officers for a violation of his constitutional rights, but a federal district court dismissed the case, and the Fourth Circuit upheld the dismissal, with both courts relying upon a standard that required Graham to demonstrate police had used force *maliciously and sadistically*. On review, however, the Supreme Court articulated a new standard for viewing police use-of-force cases and remanded the case to the lower courts for further consideration with this newly-established principle—which continue to configure the contours by which these type of cases are analyzed in the present day.

At the outset, Chief Justice Rehnquist's majority opinion made it clear that the Fourth Amendment offers the appropriate framework for examining police use of force cases. He then noted, "Determining whether the force used to effect a particular seizure is 'reasonable' under the Fourth Amendment requires a careful balancing of *'the nature and quality of the intrusion on the individual's Fourth Amendment interests' against the countervailing governmental interests at stake*" [emphasis in original, quoting *United States v. Place* (1983)[37]]. Rehnquist's opinion recognized that police officers have difficult jobs and that they must make potentially life-altering decisions in an instant, as illustrated when he said:

> The "reasonableness" of a particular use of force must be judged from the perspective of a reasonable officer on the scene, rather than with the 20/20 vision of hindsight. ... The calculus of reasonableness must embody allowance for the fact that police officers are often forced to make split-second judgments—in circumstances that are tense, uncertain, and rapidly evolving—about the amount of force that is necessary in a particular situation.

The Chief Justice also indicated that the definition of *reasonableness* is based on an objectiveness standard—which is not dependent on the officer's state of mind. The question is whether an ordinary person would believe that such force was reasonable in the moment when it was used. He extrapolated on this point by saying:

> As in other Fourth Amendment contexts, however, the "reasonableness" inquiry in an excessive force case is an objective one: the question is whether the officers' actions are "objectively reasonable" in light of the facts and circumstances confronting them, without regard to their underlying intent or motivation. ... An officer's evil intentions will not make a Fourth Amendment violation out of an objectively reasonable use of force; nor will an officer's good intentions make an objectively unreasonable use of force constitutional.

This holding overturned the lower court's reliance on a standard that required a showing of *malicious and sadistic* intent to cause harm. Offering more detail to guide lower courts in applying the objective reasonableness standard to the facts of a particular case, Rehnquist cited the Court's 1985 decision in *Tennessee v. Garner* to state, "[I]ts proper application requires careful attention to the facts and circumstances of each particular case, including the severity of the crime at issue, whether the suspect poses an immediate threat to the safety of the officers or others, and whether he is actively resisting arrest or attempting to evade arrest by flight" [emphasis removed].[38]

Less than a decade after Chief Justice Rehnquist established these crucial standards of review, the Ninth Circuit took an interesting approach to applying the *Graham v. Connor* precedent. In *Scott v. Henrich* (1994),[39] the Ninth Circuit's majority found police officers had acted reasonably in shooting at a man, Scott, who had pointed a long gun at them when the officers approached his front door. One of the two officers fired his weapon at Scott but missed, and the other officer, mistakenly thinking Scott was shooting at them, fired four shots at Scott—killing him in the process. Finding that these officers had not violated Scott's Fourth Amendment rights, the Ninth Circuit observed that determinations of reasonable use of force need not take into account whether some alternative course of action would have been more ideal in retrospect. The majority made the following declaration about the difficult nature of policing in high-pressure situations:

> Requiring officers to find and choose the least intrusive alternative would require them to exercise superhuman judgment. In the heat of battle with lives potentially in the balance, an officer would not be able to rely on training and common sense to decide what would best accomplish his mission. Instead, he would need to ascertain the *least* intrusive alternative (an inherently subjective determination) and choose that option and that option only. Imposing such a requirement would inevitably induce tentativeness by officers, and thus deter police from protecting the public and themselves. It would also entangle the courts in endless second-guessing of police decisions made under stress and subject to the exigencies of the moment. Officers thus need not avail themselves of the least intrusive means of responding to an exigent situation; they need only act within that range of conduct we identify as reasonable.

In recent years, some states have passed laws to specifically codify police use-of-force principles into law. For example, in 2021, in the state of Washington, the state legislature passed a bill that said, "Except as

OBJECTIVE REASONABLENESS STANDARD: An approach to judging an officer's use of force that looks solely at the officer's actions, without regard to intentions or motivations. The test is whether an ordinary person would feel such force was reasonable in the moment it was used.

otherwise provided under this section, a peace officer may use physical force against a person when necessary to: Protect against criminal conduct where there is probable cause to make an arrest; effect an arrest; prevent an escape ...; or protect against an imminent threat of bodily injury to the peace officer, another person, or the person against whom force is being used."[40] Critics contended this law might make it difficult for police to restrain someone who is in the midst of a mental health crisis—although the state attorney general released an opinion encouraging officers to continue responding in such situations.[41] Rafael Padilla, the Police Chief of Kent, Washington, responded to the new law by saying, "We still want to be able to intervene even if it's not dangerous. If we don't have the resources to intervene in lower level situations, now this unresolved matter may have the opportunity to escalate."[42]

Other states have passed laws that seem to place limitations on police use of force. Several states have passed laws to restrict the use of so-called *less lethal* weapons, such as bean bags, rubber bullets, and tear gas—which may be used to disperse crowds.[43] Colorado has banned police from using deadly force against a person who commits a "minor or nonviolent offense," adding that "peace officers, in carrying out their duties, shall apply nonviolent means, when possible, before resorting to the use of physical force"; Colorado law does attest that physical force is permitted "if nonviolent means would be ineffective in effecting an arrest, preventing an escape, or preventing an imminent threat of serious bodily injury or death to the peace officer or another person."[44]

In California, a 2019 law shifted the justification for police use of force to a new standard that permits lethal force only when "necessary in defense of human life," although California law retains a subsection that allows the use of deadly force as follows: "To defend against an imminent threat of death or serious bodily injury to the officer or to another person."[45] The President of the California Police Chiefs Association, Ron Lawrence, responded to the passage of the law by saying, "We certainly have concerns about officers hesitating because they may be worried about the hyper-scrutiny they often receive after a use of force incident."[46]

Use of Force Against Fleeing Suspects

Four years prior to the *Graham v. Connor* decision, the high Court addressed the specific matter of deadly force being used against a suspect that was fleeing from police. In *Tennessee v. Garner* (1985),[47] the Court said, "We conclude that such force may not be used unless necessary to prevent the escape and the officer has probable cause to believe that the suspect poses a significant threat of death or serious physical injury to the officer or others." Later in the opinion, the Court added an additional caveat in saying, "... and if, where feasible, some warning has been given." A key consideration in these cases is the possibility of a threat posed to others in the community—something an officer might have to discern quickly in the case where, for instance, an armed suspect runs from police.

JURISPRUDENCE

The Supreme Court Restricts the Use of Deadly Force
Tennessee v. Garner, 471 U.S. 1 (1985)

Memphis police received a call indicating that someone was attempting to break into a neighboring home. Arriving on the scene, an officer went to the backyard, where he observed someone running from the house. After the suspect briefly stopped at a chain-link fence, the officer was able to observe that the suspect was a young man.

There was no indication the suspect was armed. When the officer yelled, "Police. Halt!" the suspect attempted to climb over the fence. The officer then discharged his weapon. The fatal bullet struck Edward Garner in the back of his head.

Tennessee law at the time provided that "if, after a police officer has given notice of an intent to arrest a criminal suspect, and the suspect flees or forcibly resists, 'the officer may use all the necessary means to effect the arrest'." The Supreme Court, speaking through Justice Byron White, held the Tennessee statute unconstitutional "insofar as it authorizes the use of deadly force against ... an apparently unarmed, nondangerous fleeing suspect." White added that, under these circumstances, "force may not be used unless necessary to prevent the escape and the officer has probable cause to believe that the suspect poses a significant threat of death or serious physical injury to the officer or others."

In the years since the *Garner* decision, the Supreme Court has evaluated multiple cases in which a suspect fled from police inside a vehicle. In *Scott v. Harris* (2007),[48] a police officer pursued a fleeing suspect in a high-speed automobile chase that took place at night and mostly on a narrow, two-lane road. After approximately ten miles and six minutes of pursuit, which included the suspect traveling at speeds of 85 mph, running through red lights, and passing cars by crossing the double yellow line in the road, the officer utilized a precision intervention technique, a maneuver that involved using the front bumper of the officer's car to force the suspect's vehicle off the road. The suspect's car flipped into an embankment, resulting in serious injuries that left him paralyzed from the neck down. The suspect sued the police, contending that his Fourth Amendment rights had been violated.

Writing for the Court, Justice Scalia found that the use of a police car's bumper to force a vehicle off the road was indeed a "seizure" under the Fourth Amendment, but he called it an "objectively reasonable" seizure. Citing the Court's prior decision about fleeing suspects, Scalia noted, "*Garner* did not establish a magical on/off switch that triggers rigid preconditions whenever an officer's actions constitute 'deadly force.'" Beyond that, Scalia rejected the contention that a judicial rule should be created to mandate that police discontinue high-speed pursuits at a certain point, with the majority opinion instead establishing a more police-friendly standard:

> [W]e are loath to lay down a rule requiring the police to allow fleeing suspects to get away whenever they drive so recklessly that they put other people's lives in danger. It is obvious the perverse incentives such a rule would create: Every fleeing motorist would know that escape is within his grasp, if only he accelerates to 90 miles per hour, crosses the double-yellow line a few times, and runs a few red lights. The Constitution assuredly does not impose this invitation to impunity-earned-by-recklessness. Instead, we lay down a more sensible rule: A police officer's attempt to terminate a dangerous high-speed car chase that threatens the lives of innocent bystanders does not violate the Fourth Amendment, even when it places the fleeing motorist at risk of serious injury or death.

Less than ten years later, in *Plumhoff v. Rickard* (2014),[49] the Court addressed yet another high-speed chase. In this case, a man sped away after a police officer pulled him over and asked him to step out of the car for a sobriety assessment. This chase involved multiple police cars and lasted more than five minutes at speeds that exceeded 100 mph. The suspect's vehicle eventually entered a parking lot, but he continued to drive erratically there, with his car even bumping into a police vehicle. Two officers exited their vehicles and witnessed the suspect's car rock back and forth as the driver deployed the accelerator, with his bumper continuing to make contact with a police car. At this point, one officer fired three shots into the suspect's car, which then reversed and began to flee from the scene. As the vehicle was fleeing, two other officers fired a combined twelve shots, striking the driver and passenger and causing the car to crash. Both the driver and passenger would die from injuries suffered by the gun shots and the crash.

The driver's daughter filed a lawsuit, and both a federal district court and the Sixth Circuit determined that a Fourth Amendment violation had occurred. However, on review, the Supreme Court reversed, recognizing that "[t]he inquiry requires analyzing the totality of the circumstances." Justice Alito's majority opinion pointed back to the *Scott* decision in saying, "... it is beyond serious dispute that Rickard's flight posed a grave public safety risk, and here, as in *Scott*, the police acted reasonably in using deadly force to end that risk." The opinion went on to confront the number of bullets that were fired at the suspects, arriving at the conclusion that the sheer volume of shots fired did not implicitly render the officer's actions unreasonable. "It stands to reason," wrote Alito, "that if police officers are justified in firing at a suspect in order to end a severe threat to public safety, the officers need not stop shooting until the threat has ended."

Ultimately, both the *Scott* and *Plumhoff* decisions resulted in the officers being granted qualified immunity, which meant a lawsuit against them could not be sustained. We discussed this concept in detail in chapter 7, in which we noted that the Supreme Court has ostensibly offered two pathways for officers to invoke qualified immunity: (1) if no constitutional violation has occurred and (2) even if a violation is found, the officer retains qualified immunity if no *clearly established precedent* indicated that the specific conduct at hand was a violation of some constitutional or statutory right. Moreover, pursuant to a 2009 decision of the high Court, the analysis of these factors can proceed in any order; therefore, the lack of a clearly established precedent can result in an officer being given qualified immunity, even without a court examining if a constitutional violation has occurred.[50]

These principles would feature prominently in *Brosseau v. Haugen* (2004),[51] which involved another shooting of a suspect who was fleeing from police in a vehicle. Here, a man named Haugen had been accused of theft, and police in Puyallup, Washington also learned that there was a warrant for his arrest related to drug offenses. When a report came in that Haugen was involved in a physical altercation near his mother's home, police responded. Haugen initially fled on foot, and officers spent 30–45 minutes looking for him with the assistance of search dogs.

When eventually spotted by police, Haugen jumped into a Jeep Cherokee. An officer approached the vehicle and smashed the driver's side window, subsequently hitting Haugen in the head with the butt of her gun. But Haugen was undeterred and started the Jeep, attempting to speed away—at which point the officer, after ordering him to stop, fired one shot through the driver's side rear window, striking him in the back. Haugen's car came to a stop less than a block away, and despite having a collapsed lung, he survived. He later pled guilty to various criminal charges but also filed a civil lawsuit claiming excessive use of force by the police officer who shot him. In her defense, the officer utilized criteria from the *Garner* decision, saying she was "fearful for the other officers on foot who [she] believed were in the immediate area, [and] for the occupied vehicles in [Haugen's] path and for any other citizens who might be in the area."[52]

On review, the Supreme Court's per curiam opinion relented that this case falls into the "hazy border between excessive and acceptable force." Nonetheless, without actually ruling as to whether a Fourth Amendment violation had occurred, the Court granted qualified immunity to the officer because no clearly established case precedent was said to specifically indicate that the conduct in question was unconstitutional. Along these lines, the Court quoted from *Saucier v. Katz* (2001), observing that:

> [T]here is no doubt that *Graham v. Connor* ... clearly establishes the general proposition that use of force is contrary to the Fourth Amendment if it is excessive under objective standards of reasonableness. Yet that is not enough. ... The relevant, dispositive inquiry in determining whether a right is clearly established is whether it would be clear to a reasonable officer that his conduct was unlawful in the situation he confronted.[53]

Juxtaposing key precedents with the case at hand, the *Brosseau* Court stated, "*Graham* and *Garner*, following the lead of the Fourth Amendment's text, are cast at a high level of generality." Accordingly, the Court asserted that "[i]t is important to emphasize that this inquiry 'must be undertaken in light of the specific context of the case, not as a broad general proposition.'" Ultimately, the specific context of this situation was interpreted in favor of the officer.

Despite the aforementioned court decisions, there are police departments with internal policies that place specific limitations on officers who are engaged in high-speed pursuits, with parameters ranging from requirements that lights and sirens are engaged to orders for pursuits to be ceased at certain thresholds of speed (perhaps, taking into account the danger posed by the offense that initiated the pursuit). Such policies can vary widely across jurisdictions, with some offering no restrictions at all.[54] A number of states even have laws that prevent officers from shooting at suspects who are fleeing in vehicles.[55]

A 2019 report from the International Association of Chiefs of Police offered data derived from a sample of 4,865 pursuits across 116 law enforcement agencies in the United States between the years of 2016 and 2018; analysis of this sample indicated the following:

> [M]ost pursuits were short in duration (57 percent were three minutes or less) and length (55 percent were 2 miles or less), but reached relatively high speeds (30 percent exceeded 91 miles per hour). Most pursuits reported (66 percent) began with a traffic violation, while only 6 percent were for a violent felony. Pursuits were most frequently terminated by the officer and/or supervisor (33 percent), followed by the driver stopping (26 percent). In the timeframe reported, no injuries were sustained to law enforcement or uninvolved persons 98 percent of the time and to the suspect 91 percent of the time. A total of 26 fatalities were reported—22 deaths involved the suspect and 4 deaths were of another, uninvolved person.[56]

Tasers and Stun Guns

It is now common for police officers across the country to carry a Taser, which is a device that shoots small cables that can attach to clothing or a person's body and then transmit an electrical charge capable of temporarily disabling most people. A similar device known as a *stun gun* also can emit an electrical charge—but it must be physically pressed into another person in order to deliver the electric impulse. Most states or local police departments require officers who carry Tasers or stun guns to undergo extensive training.[57]

Although most states place no restrictions on the general possession of these items, there are exceptions. Some states require a permit for ownership (Illinois and Michigan) or a permit to carry outside the home

TASER: An electric shock device used to temporarily incapacitate a person.

(Wisconsin). Indiana does not require a permit to own a stun gun, but it does for a Taser. Three states (Illinois, Maryland, and Minnesota) require a background check before the purchase of a stun gun or Taser. Arizona[58] and California[59] are among the states that have laws explicitly making it a crime to point any such device at an officer of the law. In all states that allow possession of a stun gun or Taser, the minimum age requirement is 18 years old.[60] Additionally, as one might expect, the TSA prohibits Tasers and stun guns in carry-on luggage, but it is permissible to have such items in checked baggage.[61]

Decades after the seminal decisions in *Graham* and *Garner*, the Supreme Court's ruling in *Kingsley v. Hendrickson* (2015)[62] confronted an excessive force claim involving a Taser. This case was brought by a man, Michael Kingsley, who was being held in a correctional facility while he was awaiting a trial. He filed a lawsuit claiming that his constitutional rights had been violated at the Monroe County Jail in Sparta, Wisconsin as a result of being handcuffed, having an officer's knee placed on his back, and, subsequently, being shocked with a Taser for approximately five seconds. A trial jury ruled in favor of the officers, and the Seventh Circuit rejected Kingsley's assertion that the jury should have been instructed to employ an *objective reasonableness* standard, with the Circuit Court's majority instead suggesting that a *subjective inquiry* into an officer's state of mind in that moment should control the analysis.[63]

Writing for a 5–4 majority that found in Kingsley's favor, Justice Breyer observed that "a pretrial detainee must show only that the force purposely or knowingly used against him was objectively unreasonable." Breyer cited to *Graham v. Connor*, observing that "... objective reasonableness turns on the 'facts and circumstances of each particular case.'" He added, "A court must make this determination from the perspective of a reasonable officer on the scene, including what the officer knew at the time, not with the 20/20 vision of hindsight." Bringing these *Graham* principles into the context of a pretrial detainee held at a correctional facility, Breyer cited *Bell v. Wolfish* (1979)[64] in declaring, "A court must also account for the 'legitimate interests that stem from [the government's] need to manage the facility in which the individual is detained,' appropriately deferring to 'policies and practices that in th[e] judgment' of jail officials 'are needed to preserve internal order and discipline and to maintain institutional security.'" A key set of rationales arrived when Breyer cited *Graham* in providing a list of criteria that can be used to evaluate the reasonableness of police use of force in correctional contexts (as seen in the box below). Applying these factors, the Court ruled the case should be remanded for reconsideration consistent with the principles articulated in Justice Breyer's opinion.

A 2005 decision from the U.S. Court of Appeals for the Fifth Circuit addressed a unique—and as the court decided, an improper—use of a Taser. In *Autin v. City of Baytown* (2005),[65] a police officer used a Taser on Naomia Autin, a 59-year-old woman who was using a brick to bang on her unresponsive brother's front door. The woman called police for assistance, but the officer who came to the scene said there was nothing he could do. At that point, the woman turned her back on the officer and picked up the brick to resume banging on the door. The officer responded by attempting to use his Taser to subdue her from behind, but the prongs malfunctioned—so he instead utilized a technique known as a *contact tase*, where the Taser is pressed into the body and an electric charge is emitted. He continued to repeat the contact tasing until Autin fell to the ground, with one Taser prong penetrating her skin. While falling, Autin hit her head on a pole, which resulted in a laceration. Holding this use of the Taser to be unreasonable, the Fifth Circuit said "it should not be forgotten that Autin was fifty-nine years old and five feet two inches tall," adding that "Autin was objectively unthreatening, she was not resisting arrest in any way, and her crime was minor"—with the caveat given that she was "at most committing the minor crime of criminal mischief."

In 2012, two Fifth Circuit decisions found the use of Tasers to be impermissible. In *Newman v. Guedry*,[66] a police officer used a Taser on a passenger who had exited a vehicle during a traffic stop. During a pat-down search, this person made an off-color joke after the officer's hand remained near his groin area. The officer responded by tasing the man, which the circuit court found unreasonable. Similarly, in *Massey v. Wharton*,[67] an officer confronted a man who was riding an ATV and complying with the officer's request to drive the ATV to a nearby location. Nevertheless, the officer deployed his Taser twice and used pepper spray to force the man off the ATV. The Fifth Circuit found that the man was "attempting to comply with the officer's commands, he was not a threat to the officers or others, and he was not attempting to flee. ..." As a result, the use of force was deemed unreasonable under the Fourth Amendment.

Obiter Dicta

"Considerations such as the following may bear on the reasonableness or unreasonableness of the force used: the relationship between the need for the use of force and the amount of force used; the extent of the plaintiff's injury; any effort made by the officer to temper or to limit the amount of force; the severity of the security problem at issue; the threat reasonably perceived by the officer; and whether the plaintiff was actively resisting. ... We do not consider this list to be exclusive. We mention these factors only to illustrate the types of objective circumstances potentially relevant to a determination of excessive force."

—*Justice Stephen Breyer, writing for the Supreme Court in* Kingsley v. Hendrickson, *576 U.S. 389 (2015)*

THE CONSTITUTION IN ACTION
Officer Mistakes Taser for Gun

In a tragic case from Minneapolis, Minnesota a 20-year-old man named Daunte Wright was shot and killed by a police officer after being pulled over for a traffic violation on April 11, 2021. Two officers were involved in the initial traffic stop—one was a 26-year veteran, and the other was a new officer who was being trained that day. The reasons given

(continued)

by the officers for the traffic stop were that Wright had improperly used a blinker, his vehicle had an expired license plate, and there was an air freshener hanging from the rearview mirror (which was illegal under Minnesota law at that time).

The officers learned that Wright had an outstanding arrest warrant for failing to appear in court on a prior weapons charge, and after Wright had been ordered out of the vehicle, the new officer attempted to place him in handcuffs. However, Wright stepped away from that officer and snuck back into his car. A third officer arrived on the scene and attempted to assist in extracting Wright from the car, with that officer reaching his arms through the window and appearing to struggle with Wright for control of the gearshift. At that point, the 26-year veteran officer said to Wright, "I'm going to tase you." She then yelled "Taser, Taser, Taser," but she mistakenly had her hand on a 9 mm Glock, and that gun was used to fire a bullet into Wright's side. He died on the scene. Body camera footage revealed the veteran officer's instantaneous shock at her mistake, as she immediately exclaimed, "I grabbed the wrong fucking gun" and then fell back onto the curb, placing her head downward into her hands. Soon thereafter, she would resign from the police force.

In December 2021, a jury found this officer guilty on the state criminal charge of manslaughter. On the witness stand, she indicated she had mistakenly grabbed her gun instead of her Taser, saying, "I'm sorry it happened. I didn't want to hurt anybody." The case was prosecuted by the state's assistant attorney general, Erin Eldridge, who in her closing argument said, "This was no little oopsie. This was not putting the wrong date on a check. This was not entering the wrong password somewhere. This was a colossal screw-up, a blunder of epic proportions. It was precisely the thing she had been warned about for years, and she had been trained to prevent it."[68] Ultimately, the officer was sentenced to two years imprisonment.

Pepper Spray

PEPPER SPRAY: A solution made from peppers that disables a person by causing extreme irritation to the eyes.

Most people are familiar with pepper spray, which is widely available, typically as a handheld cylindrical container that a person can carry and discharge to expel a chemical irritant (usually oleoresin capsicum), perhaps into the face of an individual who poses a threat. Most states have no restrictions on the possession of pepper spray, and it is legal to possess in some form in all 50 states—but some states do have subtle restrictions. Florida, for example, limits a person to carrying a maximum of two ounces, and Michigan is among the states to restrict the active oleoresin capsicum content, capping it at 18%, while Wisconsin sets that standard at 10%. New York restricts a person to "pocket-sized" pepper spray and limits sales to two units at a time. Some states have age limits for possession (16 years old in Michigan and Minnesota; 18 in more than a dozen states), and two states allow for possession at age 14 with parental permission (Virginia and Washington).[69]

Although the Supreme Court has yet to address the use of pepper spray, the issue has come up in the circuit courts. For example, a 2002 decision from the Eighth Circuit evaluated the pepper spraying of an inmate for refusing to take possession of a copy of a prison form, finding that "evidence [did] not show an objective need for the force ... because [the inmate] had not jeopardized any person's safety or threatened prison security."[70] In a 2010 case, the Fifth Circuit ruled it was unreasonable when officers "emptied two cans of chemical irritant into [the plaintiff's] cell and shot [the plaintiff] twenty-nine times with a pepper bell launcher"—even after the inmate had complied with demands.[71]

A more recent example is the Fifth Circuit's 2020 decision in *McCoy v. Alamu*,[72] which involved a Texas prison guard's use of pepper spray on an inmate. Although the inmate's injuries were minor, the court ruled that the guard acted improperly. In this regard, the court cited a 2010 Supreme Court decision in saying:

> Injury and force ... are only imperfectly correlated, and it is the latter that ultimately counts. An inmate who is gratuitously beaten by guards does not lose his ability to pursue an excessive force claim merely because he has the good fortune to escape without serious injury.[73]

In his defense, the officer claimed the deployment of pepper spray, which consumed 3.7 ounces of a 5-ounce can, was an "involuntary reaction" to the inmate throwing a "weapon"—which was said to be a roll of toilet paper. An internal prison report concluded that the use of pepper spray was "unnecessary and inconsistent with prison rules," and the officer was placed on probation for three months. Even though the Fifth Circuit found the use of pepper spray to be unwarranted, it concluded that the officer was cloaked with qualified immunity because no precedent had clearly established a showing that "isolated, single use of pepper spray" amounted to an unconstitutional act. In conclusion, the court said, "Above, we held that the spraying crossed that line. But it was not beyond debate that it did, so the law wasn't clearly established."

Use of Dogs in Making Arrests

Elsewhere in this textbook, we have discussed the efforts of drug-sniffing and bomb-sniffing dogs. But there are other types of canines that contribute to law enforcement efforts. Some dogs, for example, are trained to pursue suspects by tracking their scents, and these animals can play a vital role in securing a suspect for arrest. Within this category of canines, some might be trained to *bark and hold* (meaning they will bark at a person but not bite them unless they attack or flee), and some could be trained to be a fugitive track dog, which would entail pursuing and potentially biting a fleeing suspect, with the default being that the dog will bite unless commanded by a handler not to bite or commanded to release; tracking activity often occurs on a lengthy leash—usually

FUGITIVE TRACK DOG: A police dog trained to track persons who have evaded arrest.

around 20-feet long. Some dogs could be trained to perform both of these functions, depending on specific commands provided by a handler.

In 2013, the U.S. Court of Appeals for the Sixth Circuit considered an excessive force claim brought against the Springboro, Ohio Police Department as a result of the actions of a police dog named Spike. Spike went through a 300-hour training course with his primary handler to attain the state certification required for being a fugitive tracking dog in law enforcement settings. However, he was not given appropriate maintenance training and was involved in more than a dozen unwarranted biting incidents over the span of three years. The officer who was Spike's primary handler indicated that his supervisors failed to provide him with the time off needed to continue Spike's state-mandated maintenance training, despite repeated requests for that time off. In *Campbell v. City of Springboro* (2013),[74] the Sixth Circuit reviewed two of Spike's biting incidents—one of which involved a teenage girl hiding in an outdoor playhouse after fleeing a late night party and the other involving a man lying face down in a friend's backyard after he was locked out following a night of drinking.

Applying the criteria normally used to assess the objective reasonableness of a search, the court found there was no evidence either suspect had committed a serious crime, posed a threat to the officer or others, or was attempting to flee. Both, in fact, were lying down at the time they were bitten. The court went on to suggest "a possible causal link between injur[ies] and Spike's inadequate training."[75] Of significant note for supervisory officers, the court also indicated that liability could attach not only to the officer who served as the dog's primary handler but also to the police chief who served in an oversight role; on this point, the Sixth Circuit said:

> Although [the Chief] was not actively involved in the incidents involving Spike, a causal connection between his acts and omissions and the alleged constitutional injuries is suggested by the record. [The] Chief allowed Spike in the field even after his training had lapsed. He never required appropriate supervision of the canine unit and essentially allowed it to run itself. He failed to establish and publish an official K–9 unit policy, and he was seemingly oblivious to the increasing frequency of dog-bite incidents involving Spike.[76]

The Sixth Circuit did take note of two cases in which it had previously ruled in favor of police in lawsuits connected to dog bites, but the court indicated that these older decisions were factually different from the 2013 matters. In a 1988 case,[77] the court addressed an incident in which a suspect was killed by a police dog's bite—finding the officers had acted reasonably because the pursuit involved a suspected felon (a burglary suspect), who was hiding in a dark, enclosed building at night and posing a threat to the safety of officers; additionally, a verbal warning was provided before the dog was released. In a 1994 case,[78] the Sixth Circuit ruled in favor of officers who had allowed a dog to pursue a man who ran from a traffic stop after he was pulled over for speeding and reckless driving; that man took refuge in a dark, wooded area and refused to show police his hands when the dog approached, ignored a warning not to move, and had been given notice that the dog would be deployed if he failed to cooperate.

Summing up these past cases in its 2013 decision, the Sixth Circuit provided a template for the appropriate use of tracking canines by saying, "In both [of the past cases], the court determined that the suspects were potentially dangerous based upon the crimes they committed and their irrational behavior. Further, the spaces in which the suspects were located—an unlit building and a dark heavily wooded area—made police vulnerable to ambush." The court also added the important caveat that "the police dogs in these cases were properly trained and that the officers gave the suspects several warnings prior to allowing the dogs to engage the suspect."[79]

The Sixth Circuit again ruled in favor of police in *Baxter v. Bracey and Harris* (2018),[80] when the court considered the actions of Iwo, a canine working for police in Nashville, Tennessee. Mr. Baxter was spotted in the act of burglarizing a home and fled as police sirens and a police helicopter closed in; he hid within the basement of a nearby home, wedging himself between a chimney and a water heater. Iwo detected Baxter's presence from the top steps of the basement, and after multiple warnings from officers and an unheeded request for surrender, the officers released Iwo into the basement—where the canine corralled Baxter with a single bite to his arm (just as Iwo was trained to do). Baxter filed a suit claiming excessive use of force, with the crux of his claim revolving around the assertion that his hands were raised at the time of the dog bite. However, the Sixth Circuit took note of four key factors favoring the police: (1) an accusation of a serious crime; (2) a suspect hiding in an enclosed, unfamiliar location and posing an unknown threat; (3) a dog with proper training and no history of improper biting; and (4) repeated warnings from the officers (that were ignored by the suspect). The court concluded that "[a]ll of these facts would lead a reasonable officer to believe that the use of a canine to apprehend Baxter did not violate the Fourth Amendment."

Regarding Baxter's hands being raised, the court did recognize that this posed a confounding, potentially "mitigating" variable but added, "Baxter does not point us to any case law suggesting that raising his hands, on its own, is enough to put [the officers] on notice that a canine apprehension was unlawful in these circumstances." Recall, of course, that the suspects in the 2013 dog bite cases were both lying down. In the end, numerous details can become relevant to framing the contours of reasonable canine apprehension techniques.

Chokeholds

The death of George Floyd in May 2020 brought renewed concern for the use of chokeholds in law enforcement contexts. In the aftermath of Floyd's death, President Trump issued an executive order on June 16, 2020, entitled "Safe Policing for Safe Communities."[81] We discussed this executive order in chapter 2, where we noted that the order called for the use of "independent credentialing bodies" to "accelerate" self-assessment and improvement in the "practices and policies" of law enforcement agencies at the state, local, and university levels. On October 28, 2020, pursuant to this executive order, Attorney General William Barr outlined two

CHOKEHOLD: A method of restraining a person in which pressure is applied around the neck, restricting the flow of blood to the brain.

specific requirements that all police departments would need to meet to be properly credentialed—with that credentialing acting as a prerequisite for the receipt of any discretionary grant funding from the Department of Justice. Attorney General Barr's press release noted, "The President's Order requires agencies to meet two standards in order to be successfully credentialed: 1) that the agency's use of force policies prohibit chokeholds, except in situations where the use of deadly force is allowed by law; and 2) that the agency's use of force policies adhere to all applicable federal, state, and local laws."[82] Nearly a year later, in September 2021, the Department of Justice, under new Attorney General Merrick Garland, also announced a policy that limited federal officers to using chokeholds or "carotid restraints" only in situations when deadly force would be authorized (e.g., in a situation when imminent danger or serious bodily injury might exist).[83]

In the two years following George Floyd's death, state legislatures also were aggressive in addressing chokeholds. A number of states passed laws limiting the use of chokeholds to situations in which lethal force is permitted; others banned chokeholds completely. In New York, statewide regulations placed on chokeholds differed from those imposed on police in the state's largest city. The state assembly's 2020 law on this subject, the Eric Garner Anti-Chokehold Act, was named for a man who died in 2014 after a police officer—who suspected Garner of illegally selling untaxed cigarettes—placed him in a chokehold for approximately fifteen seconds and then pinned him to the ground. Garner, who uttered the phrase, "I can't breathe" at least eleven times, died of a heart attack in the minutes after being restrained. The Eric Garner Anti-Chokehold Act created criminal penalties for anyone "using a chokehold or similar restraint, applies pressure to the throat or windpipe of a person, hindering breathing or the intake of air, and causes serious physical injury or death."[84]

The New York City Police Department already had banned chokeholds as a part of department policy established back in 1993. Yet in 2020, the New York City Council went a step further by passing an ordinance that prohibited an officer from engaging in conduct that "compressed a suspect's diaphragm." This legislation was challenged by a coalition of eighteen police unions, led by New York City's Police Benevolent Association. In June 2021, the ordinance was struck down by the State Supreme Court in Manhattan, with Judge Laurence Love declaring the ordinance was "unconstitutionally vague" and specifically observing that "[t]he phrase 'compresses the diaphragm' cannot be adequately defined as written."[85] A year later, a New York appellate court reversed that decision and reinstated the ordinance.[86] The appellate court said that the lower court "should not have found the diaphragm compression ban to be unconstitutionally vague." Rather, it noted that the law "is sufficiently definite to give notice of the prohibited conduct and does not lack objective standards or create the potential for arbitrary or discriminatory enforcement.

In 1983, in City of *Los Angeles v. Lyons*,[87] the Supreme Court reviewed a request for a permanent injunction against the LAPD's use of chokeholds. This case stemmed from a traffic stop in which Adolph Lyons was pulled over because one of the taillights on his car was not functioning. In the altercation that ensued, officers applied a chokehold that caused Lyons to lose consciousness. Since he was not arrested, Lyons elected to initiate judicial review by seeking an injunction that would ban the use of chokeholds. While the case was pending, LA Police Chief Daryl Gates announced a new policy banning chokeholds. Lyons continued to pursue the injunction anyway—to make this ban a permanent one that could not be undone by a change in department policy at a later date. In a 5–4 decision, the Supreme Court refused to grant Lyons' request. Justice White's majority opinion settled on a jurisdictional issue, finding there was no "case or controversy"—as required for the high Court to hear a matter under Article III of the U.S. Constitution—and thus, the Court lacked jurisdiction to rule. The key was that the request for an injunction presumed some future harm would befall Mr. Lyons, as opposed to centering on an existing controversy causing harm in the present. In dissent, Justice Thurgood Marshall discussed the nature of chokeholds as follows:

> It is undisputed that chokeholds pose a high and unpredictable risk of serious injury or death. Chokeholds are intended to bring a subject under control by causing pain and rendering him unconscious. Depending on the position of the officer's arm and the force applied, the victim's voluntary or involuntary reaction, and his state of health, an officer may inadvertently crush the victim's larynx, trachea, or hyoid. The result may be death caused by either cardiac arrest or asphyxiation.

Nearly four decades after the *Lyons* decision, it seems as though many state and federal officials have begun to heed concerns related to use of this controversial tactic, with federal policies and state laws—as well as individual department policies—creating limitations on the use of chokeholds, even in places where there is no outright ban on the technique.

Use of Flash-Bang Grenades

When law enforcement officials execute raids on homes, whether pursuant to a search warrant or an arrest warrant, the assistance of a special weapons and tactics (SWAT) team typically is enlisted. One common tactic utilized in such raids involves throwing a flash-bang grenade into a premises as officers attempt to make entry. Designed originally for use by military forces in hostage rescue situations, flash-bangs produce an extremely bright burst of light and a very loud noise, which usually renders anyone within a few feet temporarily unable to see or hear. A 2015 report indicated that "at least 50 Americans have been seriously injured, maimed or killed by flashbangs since 2000," a figure that includes police officers injured in training activities.[88] In one major city, 84% of raids over a three-year period involved the use of flash-bangs, which a spokesperson for that department defended by saying, "You may see a large number of flashbang deployments, but what we see is a large service of warrants without gunfire."[89]

FLASH-BANG GRENADE: An explosive device that creates an extremely loud report and a flash of bright light, so as to disable a person exposed to it.

Although the Supreme Court has not yet addressed the use of flash-bangs, there are numerous federal circuit court decisions on this issue. Some of these decisions have upheld the use of flash-bangs, and some have not, with the decisions being largely dependent on specific factual circumstances.[90]

One of the most infamous incidents involving a flash-bang arose from a raid conducted by a SWAT team in Cornelia, Georgia in May 2014. As officers commenced a raid by entering a family's home at 2 a.m., a flash-bang grenade was thrown into the dwelling and landed in the crib of a 19-month-old child. That child suffered severe burns on his face and chest—injuries that would require lengthy hospitalization, multiple surgeries, and continual care. The warrant authorizing this raid was based on testimony given to a sheriff's deputy by the roommate of a confidential informant the deputy had previously known. The roommate claimed to have purchased $50 in meth from this home, but after the raid, no drugs were found there. Prior to the raid, no surveillance was conducted of the home to determine who might live there, and officers were unaware of the child's presence. The Department of Justice brought federal charges against the sheriff's deputy who requested the search warrant, claiming she had provided false information to a magistrate to procure the warrant; she was ultimately found not guilty by a jury, and no other criminal charges stemmed from the incident. The family received $3.6 million as a result of settlements reached in multiple civil suits.[91]

In a similar case in 2019, the U.S. Court of Appeals for the Eighth Circuit issued a decision that found a SWAT team in Kansas City had used unreasonable force during a raid in which they deployed a flash-bang grenade in close proximity to a two-year old.[92] The court recognized that "[t]he reasonableness of the use of flash-bang grenades depends upon the circumstances," indicating that these devices can play an important law enforcement purpose when the element of surprise is needed, but the opinion also took care to weigh potential dangers:

> [T]hese weapons also carry serious risks. The record evidence shows the flash-bang grenade used here is four times louder than a 12-gauge shotgun blast and emits a light 107 times brighter than the brightest high-beam vehicle headlight. It has a powerful enough concussive effect to break windows and put holes in walls. The flash-bang burns at around 5,000 degrees Fahrenheit, creating an obvious and serious risk of burning individuals, damaging property, and starting fires (as occurred here). In some cases, they can even be lethal.

Establishing parameters to guide the use of flash-bangs, the Eighth Circuit articulated what seems to be the most crucial factor justifying their use: "While the reasonableness of the use of flash-bang grenades while executing a warrant is not reducible to a simple and categorical rule, several considerations guide our analysis. Most importantly, we consider whether officers had reason to believe they would encounter a dangerous, violent suspect." The court clarified this point by saying that "[t]heir use is more likely to be reasonable if the officers expect to encounter an individual who is known to be armed and dangerous or who has a history of violence." For a second factor, the court stated that "[t]heir use is also more likely to be reasonable if the situation presents a need for the element of surprise in order to protect the safety of officers or others." However, the court also highlighted an important principle counseling against the use of a flash-bang in certain situations: "their use is less likely to be reasonable if officers unreasonably fail to ascertain whether innocent bystanders will be present in the area the flash-bang grenade is deployed."

We conclude this section by highlighting a 2014 decision from the Second Circuit that presents an important principle for those law enforcement officials who engage in the planning of SWAT raids. In *Terebesi v. Torreso*,[93] the Second Circuit said that a raid involving flash-bang grenades was unreasonable in light of the suspect only having "personal-use quantities" of drugs and not posing a threat to officers. More notably, perhaps, is that the Second Circuit found those law enforcement officials who played a role in planning the raid—and not just those who executed it—"may be liable under section 1983 to the extent that a plan for a search or seizure, as formulated and approved by those defendants, provides for and results in an unconstitutionally excessive use of force."

Duty to Intervene

A particularly vexing aspect of the George Floyd case was the lack of intervention from any other officers who were on the scene—but it is worth noting that it can be difficult for younger officers to step in and confront a senior officer in the midst of a tense situation. Along these lines, twelve states have passed laws that impose some type of a legal duty for other officers to intervene in certain situations; the specific reasons that require intervention can vary depending on the individual law. For example, intervention is required upon witnessing the use of "excessive or illegal force" in Colorado, Connecticut, and Illinois; slightly different language is used in Kentucky and Massachusetts laws, which employ the phrase "prohibited or unreasonable force" to guide mandatory intervention; elsewhere, "excessive force or prohibited restraint" creates the duty to intervene in Vermont, Washington, and the District of Columbia.[94]

Some states also build upon a *duty to intervene* with a *duty to report* any excessive force incidents to superior officers; and some states now have laws that create a *duty to render medical aid* when a suspect in custody suffers an injury. The punishments for violating such laws vary widely and can include the following: civil liability, disciplinary action, decertification, or even criminal liability.[95]

Misconduct Reporting and Decertification

The FBI created a National Use-of-Force Data Collection program in 2015, with collection of data beginning in 2019.[96] In 2021, there were 7,559 of 18,514 federal, state, local, and tribal law enforcement agencies providing use-of-force data to the FBI, which amounts to 54% of all those agencies.[97] According to the FBI's website, the objective of the data collection program is to compile "national-level statistics on law enforcement use-of-force incidents" and "basic information on the circumstances, subjects, and officers involved." Eleven states also retain publicly available databases that house details about officer misconduct, although most states require police departments to make misconduct information available through public records requests.[98]

A private group called the International Association of Directors of Law Enforcement Standards and Training (IADLEST) operates a different national database, called the National Decertification Index. According to the Council on Criminal Justice (CCJ), this Index has "information about nearly 30,000 officers across 45 states who have been decertified since decertification began in the 1960s." Yet the CCJ states, "[N]on-reporting by local agencies to the [review boards] that contribute to th[is] national index is widespread, and individually identifiable information is only available to state [review boards] and the roughly 4,000 law enforcement background investigators who presently have access."[99] Indiana, Massachusetts, and Washington are states that recently passed laws requiring notification to this specific database.

Beyond reporting of misconduct, there is decertification, which is the process through which officers who have engaged in serious misconduct or criminal offenses might be deemed ineligible to serve in a law enforcement capacity. In forty-seven states, the process will entail an evaluation and vote by a review board or panel. (California, New Jersey, and Rhode Island are the three states without such a board.)[100] According to the Council on Criminal Justice (CCJ), virtually all of these boards allow decertification of an officer who has been convicted of a felony, and a majority of state boards allow decertification for misdemeanor offenses, for failing to meet certain training requirements, or for official misconduct;[101] of course, there is a difference

DECERTIFICATION:
Revocation of a police officer's certificate or license based on misconduct.

between permitting decertification for these reasons and actually decertifying an officer.

The Brennan Center indicates that since the death of George Floyd, twelve states have passed laws that define additional reasons for either suspending or revoking a law enforcement official's certification. In Massachusetts, for instance, automatic revocation can occur for "making false arrests, creating or using falsified evidence, destroying evidence, perpetrating a hate crime, using excessive force that results in death or serious bodily injury, and more."[102] More than a dozen states also require law enforcement agencies to report police misconduct to state review panels.[103] There is variation between states in how a decertification review commences, with some states allowing any person to initiate the process with a complaint, and other states requiring notification from a law enforcement agency to the state panel.[104]

The composition of the decertification boards and panels themselves also varies across the country, with the CCJ observing that the New York State Police and Peace Officer Licensing Review Board has seven members—three appointed by the Governor, two picked by the state's attorney general, one appointed by the state senate's president pro tempore, and one appointed by the state assembly's speaker. Illinois has a Law Enforcement Certification Review Panel with eleven members—three are appointed by the Governor, eight chosen by the state's attorney general, and two picked from "communities with high rates of gun violence, incarceration, and metrics of social disadvantage."[105]

The CCJ study also gathered data regarding actual instances of decertification, finding that "[c]onsiderable variation is ... evident in the rate of decertification among states." Collating data from a variety of sources, the CCJ report observed the following:

> Some states decertify thousands of officers annually, while others decertify officers at a far lower rate.[106] One analysis found that Georgia (population 10.7 million) decertified 316 law enforcement officers in 2016, but similarly sized North Carolina (population 10.6 million) decertified just ten.[107] However, even states with comparatively robust decertification rates often fail to decertify officers who have been dismissed from multiple police departments within that state.[108]

There also is variation across states in terms of key decertification protocols, such as these: standards of proof used in misconduct hearings;

the process for allowing an officer to reacquire their certification; and the way in which a panel would assess an officer who resigned before an investigation could lead to decertification. Generally, when an officer faces some type of misconduct hearing (or, perhaps, even a criminal case related to their official actions), legal representation fees can be paid for by a police union fund. For example, Derek Chauvin received approximately $1 million in legal defense aid to support the twelve attorneys who assisted his case in the George Floyd murder trial.[109]

BODY CAMERAS: Cameras worn by police officers to record encounters with citizens.

FOCUS ON LAW ENFORCEMENT

Do Body Cameras Reduce Police Use of Force?

In the aftermath of cases that allegedly involve police misconduct, it is common for advocates of **body cameras** to suggest that requiring police to wear devices that record video and audio will serve as a deterrent to misconduct and will further accountability. Typically, such video is uploaded to a server where members of the public can request access to the video—but myriad state laws and local policies on that issue might restrict access to video in certain cases, particularly when investigations or trials are ongoing. According to the Council on Criminal Justice, as of 2016, more than 80% of "large" police departments across the country were making some use of body cameras, and approximately 50% of all departments were doing so.[110]

Regarding whether body cameras actually deter police misconduct, the ACLU, citing an article in *Criminology and Public Policy*, noted, "A comprehensive review of 70 empirical studies of body-worn cameras found that body cameras have not had statistically significant or consistent effects in decreasing police use of force."[111] Regarding the type of evidence a body camera might yield for use in a later trial, the ACLU discussed a report from George Mason University by saying, "One 2016 study found that 92.6 percent of prosecutors' offices in jurisdictions with body cameras have used that footage as evidence to prosecute civilians, while just 8.3 percent have used it to prosecute police officers."[112]

Moreover, it is important to consider that body cameras could be worn as officers travel into a number of different places, including inside private homes. When that possibility is coupled with the specter of an open records request that makes body camera footage available to the public, privacy trepidations become germane. Such concerns could be further heightened where police departments link body camera footage with facial recognition software.[113]

Overall, the companies that implement body camera footage were part of a $1.2 billion industry in 2020, with one company, Axon, serving as the largest single provider of body cameras in the United States and posting $680 million dollars in revenue that year alone. Minneapolis Police Officer Derek Chauvin was wearing an Axon camera when he knelt on the neck of George Floyd in May 2020—but that camera apparently fell off at some point, leaving a bystander's cell phone video as the primary record of the incident. Axon's closest competitor is Motorola, which claims to produce body cameras that fit tighter to an officer than Axon's cameras. Both companies have lobbied members of Congress to include the use of camera technology in bills that seek to reform policing practices.[114]

It also is important to consider that the costs of using body cameras in a major city's police department could amount to millions of dollars. A public records request made by a news outlet in Seattle, Washington, for instance, found that the initial cost of outfitting approximately 850 officers with body cameras was greater than one million dollars in 2018, with hundreds of thousands of dollars expected in annual software costs in subsequent years.[115] However, there is research indicating a potential decrease in citizen complaints against officers could be connected to the use of body cameras, and that could tilt the cost–benefit analysis in favor of acquiring cameras—although more research of this nature is needed.[116]

Investigatory Detention and Pat-Down Searches

PAT-DOWN SEARCH: A *frisk* of a suspect's outer garments in attempt to locate concealed weapons.

TERRY STOP: Another term for a stop and frisk, as allowed by the Supreme Court's landmark *Terry v. Ohio* (1968) decision.

An investigatory detention is a temporary seizure of a suspect based on reasonable suspicion that criminal activity is afoot. As the Supreme Court has recognized, "The Fourth Amendment does not require a policeman who lacks the precise level of information necessary for probable cause to arrest to simply shrug his shoulders and allow a crime to occur or a criminal to escape. On the contrary, ... it may be the essence of good police work to adopt an intermediate response."[117] An investigatory detention might be referred to as a **stop and frisk** or a pat-down search because, with reasonable suspicion, officers are permitted to conduct a search of a suspect's outer garments to make sure there is no concealed weapon that might be used against the officer or others nearby. This procedure also is termed a *Terry stop*, in reference to *Terry v. Ohio* (1968),[118] the landmark decision in which the Supreme Court recognized this particular exception to the probable cause requirement.

JURISPRUDENCE

The Seminal Case on Stop and Frisk
Terry v. Ohio, 392 U.S. 1 (1968)

Police Detective Martin McFadden was on patrol in downtown Cleveland, Ohio when he observed three men acting suspiciously as they repeatedly walked back and forth in front of a jewelry store. Concluding the men were preparing to rob the store, McFadden approached the men, identified himself as a police officer, and asked their names. When the men mumbled in response to his queries, McFadden seized one of the men and patted down his overcoat. The pat down revealed a concealed handgun. McFadden then instructed all three men to face a wall with their hands up, while he patted down the other two. This resulted in the seizure of another gun from one of the other men. All three men were transported to the police station, and charges were filed against the two from whom the concealed weapons had been seized.

Appealing their convictions for illegal possession of concealed weapons, the key question was whether the warrantless seizure of the guns in the absence of probable cause to detain the men was a violation of the Fourth Amendment. Ultimately, given the police officer's reasonable suspicion that criminal activity was in progress, the Supreme Court held that the detention and pat-down searches were reasonable. Writing for the Court, Chief Justice Earl Warren stressed the limited scope of the detention and searches at hand: "Officer McFadden confined his search strictly to what was minimally necessary to learn whether the men were armed and to disarm them once he discovered the weapons. He did not conduct a general exploratory search for whatever evidence of criminal activity he might find." Warren also emphasized the need to protect police officers and others nearby from concealed weapons, saying, "At the time he seized petitioner and searched him for weapons, Officer McFadden had reasonable grounds to believe that petitioner was armed and dangerous, and it was necessary for the protection of himself and others to take swift measures to discover the true facts and neutralize the threat of harm if it materialized."

What Constitutes Reasonable Suspicion?

Reasonable suspicion that would justify a *Terry* stop entails more than a mere hunch that someone is engaged in criminal activity. The majority opinion for *Terry* made this clear by citing *Brinegar v. United States* (1949).[119] In that case, the Supreme Court said an officer's familiarity with a previously-arrested suspect had led to a reasonable inference that the suspect's car, which appeared to be weighted down, was filled with illegally transported liquor; upholding the traffic stop in this case, the majority opinion from Justice Wiley B. Rutledge said that "... in determining whether the officer acted reasonably in such circumstances, due weight must be given not to his inchoate and unparticularized suspicion or 'hunch,' but to the specific reasonable inferences which he is entitled to draw from the facts in light of his experience." That notion of *something more than a hunch* would feature prominently in the *Terry* decision.

After *Terry*, the Supreme Court's opinion in *Brown v. Texas* (1979)[120] said that to justify a stop and frisk there must be "specific, objective facts indicating that society's legitimate interests require the seizure of the particular individual. ..." In the *Brown* case, officers stopped a man simply because he was seen walking in an area known for illegal drug activity. Writing for the Court, Chief Justice Warren E. Burger noted, "In the absence of any basis for suspecting appellant of misconduct, the balance between the public interest and appellant's right to personal security and privacy tilts in favor of freedom from police interference."

Another important post-*Terry* decision is *Adams v. Williams* (1972).[121] In this case, an officer was sitting in his patrol car in a gas station parking lot at 2:15 a.m. in Bridgeport, Connecticut. An informant, who was known to the officer and who had provided useful information in the past, walked up to the car and alerted the officer to a man who was said to be sitting in a nearby vehicle in possession of narcotics and holstering a gun on his waistband. The officer approached that vehicle and requested that the man, Robert Williams, open the driver's side door, but Williams instead lowered the window. The officer reached his arm into the car and felt at Williams' waist, detecting the presence of a loaded gun in the location indicated by the informant. An arrest was effectuated for illegal possession of a loaded firearm. After other officers arrived on the scene, a search incident to arrest revealed Williams had significant quantities of heroin in his clothing, and a machete and second gun were found inside the vehicle.

On review, Justice Rehnquist's majority opinion upheld the search, finding that the informant's tip "carried enough indicia of reliability" to justify the officer's approach and pat-down of the suspect's waist; subsequently, the officer's touching of the gun provided probable cause to seize the weapon and make an arrest for violation of state firearms laws in place at that time.

A primary concern permeating Rehnquist's opinion in *Adams v. Williams* is the protection of officer safety—so that leeway is provided for officers to address threats posed by armed individuals. To support this consideration, Rehnquist included a footnote citing FBI data indicating that, in 1971, 125 police officers were murdered—nearly all with guns.

Rehnquist's opinion also provided ample support for the use of informants in discerning reasonable suspicion. In this regard, Rehnquist observed that the "in-person" nature of the tip provided added credibility, which was an idea he articulated as follows: "This is a stronger case than obtains in the case of an anonymous telephone tip. The informant here came forward personally to give information that was immediately verifiable at the scene." The Chief Justice also emphasized that Connecticut law could have resulted in consequences related to a false police report if the informant had been lying—implying that this could be a deterrent to making a false report, and an added reason to trust the information.

Racial Profiling

Decades later, an important stop-and-frisk principle emanated from the high Court's decision in *Florida v. J.L.* (2000).[122] In this case, the Miami-Dade Police Department received a telephone tip suggesting a Black man wearing a plaid shirt was in possession of a gun at a bus stop. Police officers arrived at that location and saw three Black men standing at the bus stop, one of whom was wearing a plaid shirt. Officers conducted a pat-down search on that man, and the search revealed the presence of a concealed handgun. Reviewing this matter, a unanimous Court found that the search violated the Fourth Amendment, even through the lens of the lesser reasonable suspicion standard. Justice Ginsburg's majority opinion declared that "an anonymous tip lacking indicia of reliability ... does not justify a stop and frisk whenever and however it alleges the illegal possession of a firearm." She went on to note that the tip provided in this case "lacked sufficient indicia of reliability to provide reasonable suspicion to make a *Terry* stop: It provided no predictive information and therefore left the police without means to test the informant's knowledge or credibility." As noted in the discussion of racial profiling in chapter 3, the Supreme Court previously had indicated that race cannot be the sole factor used in the reasonable suspicion calculus.[123] Whether a suspect's race can be used as one of several factors in determining reasonable suspicion is a controversial question that remains unresolved.[124]

The High Crime Neighborhood and Running from Police

In another relevant case decided the same year as *Florida v. J.L.*, the Supreme Court confronted the notion of a "high-crime neighborhood" in *Illinois v. Wardlow* (2000).[125] In this case, a man named William Wardlow was in an area of Chicago that was known to police for being a neighborhood where drug trafficking was common. Additionally, Wardlow was standing in front of a building that was known to police as a place where illegal narcotics were sold. Around noon, four police cars drove past this building as Wardlow stood in front, and upon seeing the patrol cars, Wardlow ran quickly into a nearby alleyway. An officer pursued on foot, caught up with Wardlow, and then performed a pat-down search—which revealed an illegal gun and resulted in Wardlow's arrest. Although the Illinois Supreme Court found that Wardlow's Fourth Amendment rights had been violated, the Supreme Court of the United States reversed, upholding this pat-down search.

Addressing the concept of a high-crime neighborhood, Chief Justice Rehnquist's majority opinion made the observation that "[a]n individual's presence in an area of expected criminal activity, standing alone, is not enough to support a reasonable, particularized suspicion that the person is committing a crime." However, he added the following declaration: "[O]fficers are not required to ignore the relevant characteristics of a location in determining whether the circumstances are sufficiently suspicious to warrant further investigation." He went on to suggest "the fact that the stop occurred in a 'high crime area' [can be] among the relevant contextual considerations in a *Terry* analysis."

Beyond that, Rehnquist addressed Wardlow's "unprovoked flight" in running toward the alleyway by saying, "Our cases have also recognized that nervous, evasive behavior is a pertinent factor in determining reasonable suspicion. ... Headlong flight—wherever it occurs—is the consummate act of evasion: it is not necessarily indicative of wrongdoing, but it is certainly suggestive of such." Therefore, the conjunction of Wardlow's presence in a high-crime area and the running from police collectively provided the necessary reasonable suspicion for a pat-down, according to the Supreme Court. Justifying the use of these two criteria in establishing the reasonable suspicion threshold, Rehnquist highlighted the imperfections inherent in police work by opining, "[W]e cannot reasonably demand scientific certainty from judges or law enforcement officers where none exists. Thus, the determination of reasonable suspicion must be based on commonsense judgments and inferences about human behavior."

Rehnquist noted there could be "innocent reasons" inferred from a person running away as police cars arrived, and he relented that "flight is not necessarily indicative of ongoing criminal activity." But he added that in *Terry v. Ohio*, "[T]he conduct justifying the stop was ambiguous and susceptible of an innocent explanation." By permitting a pat-down search in that situation, Rehnquist suggested, "*Terry* recognized that the officers could detain the individuals to resolve ... ambiguity. In allowing such detentions, *Terry* accepts the risk that officers may stop innocent people," a risk weighted against the idea the "*Terry* stop is a ... minimal intrusion, simply allowing the officer to briefly investigate further. If the officer does not learn facts rising to the level of probable cause, the individual must be allowed to go on his way."

Drug Courier Profiles

An approach that allows police to rely upon the concept of *commonsense inferences* in articulating reasonable suspicion does seem likely to further the notion of *profiling*; of course, profiling based exclusively on race will violate the Fourteenth Amendment—but the Supreme Court has permitted other types of profiling by law enforcement. As noted in chapter 3, the Supreme Court's decision in *United States v. Sokolow* (1989)[126] authorized use of the so-called drug courier profile. In this case, DEA agents effectuated an investigatory detention of a man named Andrew Sokolow at the Honolulu International Airport after he had completed a round trip to Miami. Several factors led the agents to believe there was reasonable suspicion to surmise that Sokolow was trafficking drugs. He paid $2,100 cash (taken from a roll of $20 bills) to buy airline tickets; he was traveling to a city known as a hub for the drug trade; he used a name that did not match the name listed for the phone number he gave when buying his plane ticket; he spent only forty-eight hours in Miami, despite the fact that a round-trip flight between Hawaii and Miami takes about 20 hours; he checked no luggage at all; and he was described as acting nervous by a ticket agent in Honolulu and a DEA agent who observed him during a layover at the Los Angeles airport.

When he returned to Hawaii, DEA agents approached him as he exited the airport and was about to hail a taxi. Sokolow was escorted to a DEA office at the airport, where a drug detection dog named Donker offered a positive narcotics alert when sniffing Sokolow's luggage. Agents then

DRUG COURIER PROFILE: A set of characteristics developed by law enforcement to identify likely couriers of illegal drugs.

requested a search warrant to open the luggage, and after that was approved, they found 1,063 grams of cocaine. Sokolow was then arrested.

Upholding the investigatory detention and subsequent search in this case, the Supreme Court found that, although each of these factors could be linked to an innocent explanation when viewed in isolation, the "totality of circumstances" approach justified the investigatory detention. To this point, Chief Justice Rehnquist's majority opinion said, "Any one of these factors is not by itself proof of any illegal conduct and is quite consistent with innocent travel. But we think taken together they amount to reasonable suspicion." Debunking the notion that a "profile" of some sort would automatically amount to a violation of the Fourth Amendment, Rehnquist lauded the training of the agents involved by observing, "A court sitting to determine the existence of reasonable suspicion must require the agent to articulate the factors leading to that conclusion, but the fact that these factors may be set forth in a 'profile' does not somehow detract from their evidentiary significance as seen by a trained agent." In dissent, Justice Thurgood Marshall offered this stinging rebuke of DEA profiling tactics:

> It is highly significant that the DEA agents stopped Sokolow because he matched one of the DEA's "profiles" of a paradigmatic drug courier. In my view, a law enforcement officer's mechanistic application of a formula of personal and behavioral traits in deciding whom to detain can only dull the officer's ability and determination to make sensitive and fact-specific inferences "in light of his experience," ... particularly in ambiguous or borderline cases. Reflexive reliance on a profile of drug courier characteristics runs a far greater risk than does ordinary, case-by-case police work of subjecting innocent individuals to unwarranted police harassment and detention.

In the end, however, the majority opinion suggests that as long as a law enforcement agent can point to specific, articulable factors that, when taken together, offer reasonable suspicion of illegal activity, those factors—whether part of a pre-determined profile or not—can indeed justify an investigatory detention and a pat-down search.

Law Enforcement Intuition and Detective Work

In *United States v. Cortez* (1981),[127] the Supreme Court upheld the use of law enforcement "detective work" that created the "profile" of a specific criminal endeavor. In this case, Border Patrol agents observed sets of footprints that were repeatedly left in a particular section of the Arizona desert. Following the trail of prints, officers surmised that groups of eight to twenty people were regularly led from Mexico, through the desert, to what appeared to be a specific location on Highway 86 in Arizona. By observing the tracks over an approximately two-month period, the agents deduced the same person was leading different groups of people into the United States on clear weekend nights between 2 a.m. and 6 a.m. After three consecutive rainy nights leading into a weekend, officers set up surveillance near the spot on the highway where they expected a large vehicle to pick up illegal immigrants. When they noticed that a truck with a camper shell big enough to hold a group of people had made a round trip to that area, they initiated a traffic stop—discovering six illegal immigrants hiding in the back.

Ruling that the agents' hard work had in fact produced the reasonable suspicion needed to justify stopping this vehicle, Chief Justice Burger's majority opinion offered support for the deductions made by experienced law enforcement personnel. He paid particular homage to these agents' efforts to secure the border in his opinion, saying:

> This case portrays at once both the enormous difficulties of patrolling a 2,000-mile open border and the patient skills needed by those charged with halting illegal entry into this country. ... [W]hen used by trained law enforcement officers, objective facts, meaningless to the untrained, can be combined with permissible deductions from such facts to form a legitimate basis for suspicion of a particular person and for action on that suspicion. We see here the kind of police work often suggested by judges and scholars as examples of appropriate and reasonable means of law enforcement.

How Long May Police Detain Suspicious Persons?

The Supreme Court has refused to place an arbitrary time limit on investigatory detentions. Rather, the Court has considered the purpose of the stop and the time required for police to obtain any additional required information. In *Florida v. Royer* (1983),[128] for example, the Court held that a fifteen-minute detention of a suspect in a locked room at an airport was unreasonable—because even though federal agents said the suspect fit the description of a "drug courier profile," they lacked probable cause of illegal activity. Yet two years later, in *United States v. Sharpe* (1985),[129] the Court upheld a twenty-minute detention of a truck driver suspected of transporting marijuana. In both cases, the Court indicated that the length of an investigatory detention depends on the "totality of circumstances" involved. In essence, reasonable suspicion permits a brief period of detention, but as the Fifth Circuit once said, "A prolonged investigative detention may be tantamount to a *de facto* arrest"—and that, of course, would need to be justified by probable cause.[130]

The notion of a brief detention was applied not only to persons but also to luggage with the Supreme Court's decision in *United States v. Place* (1983).[131] In this matter, DEA agents in Miami believed a New York-bound passenger named Raymond Place fit the profile of a drug courier. But because Place was about to board his flight and refused to consent to a search, agents there could do nothing—instead, choosing to notify agents in New York of Place's impending arrival at LaGuardia Airport. Once he landed there, Place was approached by more DEA agents and again refused to consent to a search. Agents then seized his luggage to take it to a trained drug-sniffing dog. However, that dog was at a different airport altogether, and it took agents ninety minutes to take the bags there, initiating the dog sniff at New York's JFK Airport. The dog alerted to one of the man's two bags, and agents hoped to use that information to secure a search warrant. But because it was late on a Friday afternoon, no judge was readily available to issue a warrant. As a result, the agents kept the luggage over the weekend, acquired a warrant that Monday, and then found cocaine in Place's luggage. Not surprisingly, the Supreme Court ruled the extended detention of the luggage, as evaluated by the standard of reasonable suspicion, amounted to a violation of the Fourth Amendment. Justice O'Connor's majority opinion drew an important nexus between a passenger and their luggage by saying, "Particularly in the case of detention of luggage within the traveler's immediate possession, the police conduct intrudes on both the suspect's possessory interest in his luggage as well as his liberty interest in proceeding with his itinerary." The ability to travel with one's luggage—and without an extended delay incurred only on the basis of reasonable suspicion—yielded a Fourth Amendment violation in this case.

What if Other Incriminating Evidence Is Revealed by a Pat-Down Search?

Recall that in *Terry v. Ohio*, the Supreme Court justified the limited pat-down of a suspect's outer garments by the need to protect the officer and others from a concealed weapon. But what if an officer feels something that might be a weapon but turns out to be contraband? In *Minnesota v. Dickerson* (1993),[132] the Court held that "police may seize nonthreatening contraband detected through the sense of touch during a protective pat-down search of the sort permitted by *Terry*, so long as the search stays within the bounds marked by *Terry*." Those boundaries, of course, require a limited pat down of exterior clothing—and, essentially, mandate an officer to discern, by touch alone, that the item being felt is either contraband or something that poses a risk to officer safety; only one of those two things would permit a more invasive search, such as reaching into a pocket or, perhaps, searching an underlying layer of clothing.

Applying these principles in *Dickerson*, the Court disallowed the seizure of cocaine from a suspect's pocket because the officer suspected the lump he felt was cocaine "only after 'squeezing, sliding and otherwise manipulating the contents of the defendant's pocket'—a pocket which the officer already knew contained no weapon." In essence, the officer could not have had probable cause that what he felt was contraband simply by touching it. The Court did note that the officer had reasonable suspicion to conduct a pat-down search, but Justice White's majority opinion suggested the following:

> Although the officer was lawfully in a position to feel the lump in respondent's pocket, because *Terry* entitled him to place his hands upon respondent's jacket, the court below determined that the incriminating character of the object was not immediately apparent to him. Rather, the officer determined that the item was contraband only after conducting a further search, one not authorized by *Terry* or by any other exception to the warrant requirement.

Interestingly, though, Justice White's opinion rejected the Minnesota Supreme Court's attempt to create a categorical rule indicating that the sense of touch could *never* provide an officer with probable cause. Specifically, the state court said it would not "extend the plain view doctrine to the sense of touch [because] the sense of touch is inherently less immediate and less reliable than the sense of sight," adding that "the sense of touch is far more intrusive into the personal privacy that is at the core of the [F]ourth [A]mendment."[133] Therefore, even though Justice White's opinion found in Dickerson's favor, it provided something of a win for police in allotting for the possibility of *plain feel* seizures in future cases.

THE CONSTITUTION AND SOCIAL JUSTICE
Federal Court Limits NYPD's Use of Stop and Frisk

In August 2013, a federal district court judge issued a ruling that required the New York City Police Department (NYPD) to revamp its procedures for pat-down searches. In her written opinion in *Floyd v. City of New York*,[134] Judge Shira A. Scheindlin of the U.S. District Court for the Southern District of New York stated that the NYPD's prior use of pat downs amounted to "indirect racial profiling," through which officers were stopping Blacks and Hispanics without adequate grounds to denote the requisite reasonable suspicion. The judge's opinion cited statistics showing that approximately 90% of pat-downs in the city were conducted upon minorities.

Reported stop-and-frisk encounters peaked in New York City at over 685,000 stops in 2011, but following this lawsuit, those figures dropped precipitously. More recent data indicate that in 2019, there were 13,459 stop-and-frisk encounters involving NYPD officers. Of that sample, 8,867 people were found to be doing nothing illegal (66%); 7,981 of those stopped were Black (59%); 3,869 were Hispanic (29%); and 1,215 were White (9%).[135]

In response to the 2013 District Court ruling, long-time New York City Police Commissioner Bill Bratton defended his department's efforts to select certain neighborhoods to prioritize for methods like "stop and frisk," even if some of those areas might have higher minority populations. In 2014, he said, "So the idea is, from a policing standpoint, to put police resources into those areas to try and bring to them at least a level of security to raise their families. And by making it more secure, do what we've done in the rest of the city—where you'll come in and invest, where you will commit to areas of the city that years ago people thought you would've been crazy."[136] The underlying concept expressed by Bratton is often known as a *broken windows* approach to policing, which is meant to indicate that a focus upon lesser crimes can help to prevent larger ones; data supporting that concept is scant, however.

In the aftermath of the 2013 District Court decision, the NYPD created new internal guidelines for stop-and-frisk encounters. These included prohibitions on invoking reasonable suspicion for the following reasons: (1) on the basis of race, (2) for so-called *furtive movements* (which might involve a person fidgeting or acting nervously), (3) because a person is in a so-called "high crime" area, or (4) because an individual fit the *generalized profile* of a suspected criminal, such as *young Black male*.[137] Additionally, officers were instructed they should "be able to articulate facts establishing a minimal level of objective justification for making the stop," which is consistent with the Supreme Court standards set forth in *Terry v. Ohio*. The new policies also were to be read by commanding officers of all precincts at ten consecutive roll calls and to be posted in visible spaces within precincts.

Investigatory Detention of Automobiles

In the wake of *Terry v. Ohio*, state and federal courts upheld the practice of stopping automobiles based on reasonable suspicion. However, in *Delaware v. Prouse* (1979),[138] the Supreme Court disallowed an automobile stop merely to check a driver's license and registration. The Court said that "except in those situations in which there is at least articulable and reasonable suspicion that a motorist is unlicensed or that an automobile is not registered, or that either the vehicle or an occupant is otherwise subject to seizure for violation of law, stopping an automobile and detaining the driver in order to check his driver's license and the registration of the automobile are unreasonable under the Fourth Amendment." On the other hand, in *Alabama v. White* (1990),[139] the Court upheld an investigatory stop of a vehicle based on an anonymous tip that it was transporting cocaine. The Court noted that, in and of itself, the tip did not establish reasonable suspicion. Even so, because officers corroborated certain aspects of the tip before making the vehicle stop, the totality of circumstances did provide a reasonable basis for detaining the vehicle.

In *Michigan v. Long* (1983),[140] the Court upheld the limited search of a vehicle stopped under reasonable suspicion but indicated that the sole purpose of such a search is the need to locate a weapon that might be used against the police. Justice Sandra Day O'Connor, speaking for the Court, said that "the search of the passenger compartment of an automobile, limited to those areas in which a weapon may be placed or hidden, is permissible if the police officer possesses a reasonable belief based on 'specific and articulable facts which, taken together with the rational inferences from those facts, reasonably warrant' the officers in believing that the suspect is dangerous and the suspect may gain immediate control of weapons." We discussed auto stops in greater detail in chapter 8, but for this chapter, it is important to note that the same reasonable suspicion standard that justifies an auto stop also justifies a pat down; thus, the Supreme Court has said that, during a traffic stop, an officer can order a driver and passengers out of a vehicle for a pat down—the objective of protecting officer safety.[141]

Identification Checks

It is standard operating procedure during a *Terry* stop for police to request identification. Indeed, more than twenty states[142] have laws requiring a person to identify themselves during a valid police detention—although states vary in terms of what the punishment for failing to do so will be, with some states imposing a misdemeanor criminal penalty and even permitting arrest.[143] In *Hiibel v. Sixth Judicial District Court of Nevada* (2004),[144] the Supreme Court upheld an identification check law, saying, "The request for identity has an immediate relation to the purpose, rationale, and practical demands of a *Terry* stop." Of course, under *Delaware v. Prouse*, stopping someone only for the purpose of checking their identity is impermissible. Absent reasonable suspicion that someone is involved in criminal activity, police have no basis for demanding that person to identify themself. States also vary in terms of what constitutes valid identification in these situations; in Nevada, a person only needs to provide a name, but in Indiana and Ohio, for example, an officer can request proof of date of birth (which likely would come from showing a driver's license or other identification card).[145]

The Supreme Court also has noted that if a state's stop and identify law contains vague terms, then it can be struck down. In *Kolender v. Lawson* (1983),[146] for instance, the Court struck down a California law that required those individuals suspected of loitering to provide "credible and reliable" identification. The Court found the words credible and reliable to be vague and, therefore, said the law violated basic principles of due process protected by the Fourteenth Amendment.

Finally, an interesting aspect of the *Hiibel* decision is that it leaves open the possibility for a Fifth Amendment challenge if a similar case were to arise in the future. As we will discuss in chapter 11, that amendment offers a protection against self-incrimination. In the *Hiibel* case, the majority opinion observed there could be a situation in which a person answering an officer's request to provide a name actually results in the revelation of information that proves to be incriminating. The final paragraph of Justice Kennedy's majority opinion recognized this when he said, "Still, a case may arise where there is a substantial allegation that furnishing identity at the time of a stop would have given the police a link in the chain of evidence needed to convict the individual of a separate offense. In that case, the court can then consider whether the privilege applies, and, if the Fifth Amendment has been violated, what remedy must follow." Of course, since the facts of the *Hiibel* matter did

IDENTIFICATION CHECK: A temporary detention by a police officer for the purpose of ascertaining a person's identity.

not present such a scenario, Kennedy concluded with this declaration: "We need not resolve those questions here." We address this matter in greater detail in chapter 11.

Roadblocks and Checkpoints

Police use roadblocks not only to facilitate the apprehension of fleeing suspects but also to identify impaired drivers. Recall that in *Delaware v. Prouse*, the Supreme Court disallowed the random stoppage of particular vehicles to conduct license and registration checks. However, that decision offered a specific disclaimer that it did not "preclude the State of Delaware or other States from developing methods for spot checks that involve less intrusion or that do not involve the unconstrained exercise of discretion," adding that "[q]uestioning of all oncoming traffic at roadblock-type stops is one possible alternative."[147] Of course, because roadblocks and checkpoints do involve a restraint on the liberties of drivers, they must be *reasonable* under the Fourth Amendment.

In *Michigan Department of State Police v. Sitz* (1990),[148] the Supreme Court upheld a checkpoint established to identify drunk drivers. In his opinion for the Court, Chief Justice Rehnquist described how the checkpoint operated:

> All vehicles passing through a checkpoint would be stopped and their drivers briefly examined for signs of intoxication. In cases where a checkpoint officer detected signs of intoxication, the motorist would be directed to a location out of the traffic flow where an officer would check the motorist's driver's license and car registration and, if warranted, conduct further sobriety tests. Should the field tests and the officer's observations suggest that the driver was intoxicated, an arrest would be made. All other drivers would be permitted to resume their journey immediately.

Rehnquist concluded that "the balance of the State's interest in preventing drunken driving, the extent to which this system can reasonably be said to advance that interest, and the degree of intrusion upon individual motorists who are briefly stopped, weighs in favor of the state program."

On the other hand, in *Indianapolis v. Edmond* (2000),[149] the Court struck down a checkpoint designed to interdict illegal drugs. Justice O'Connor's majority opinion distinguished the Indianapolis checkpoint from the one upheld in *Michigan v. Sitz*, noting that the purpose of the former was detection of "ordinary criminal wrongdoing," while the function of the latter was the protection of motorists' safety. O'Connor stated emphatically that generalized law enforcement cannot be the justification for establishing a checkpoint; instead, she highlighted the need for individualized assessment in saying that:

> We decline to suspend the usual requirement of individualized suspicion where the police seek to employ a checkpoint primarily for the ordinary enterprise of investigating crimes. We cannot sanction stops justified only by the generalized and ever-present possibility that interrogation and inspection may reveal that any given motorist has committed some crime.

In a different context, in *Illinois v. Lidster* (2004),[150] the Court upheld a checkpoint designed to locate information about a fatal hit and run in which a vehicle had struck and killed a man on a bicycle. The checkpoint was set up one week after the incident, at the same time of night and in the same area, with police distributing flyers about the hit and run to all approaching vehicles. One man was arrested for DUI at the checkpoint, although he had nothing to do with the hit and run. The Supreme Court upheld this checkpoint and the correlated DUI arrest, observing that the checkpoint encompassed a low intrusion balanced against a "grave public concern." Justice Breyer's majority opinion stated that what the officers had done here could be characterized as "information-seeking" in regard to a specific event, and thus, this matter could be distinguished from the more generalized "crime control" roadblock that was struck down in City of *Indianapolis v. Edmond*. In chapter 8, we discussed roadblocks related to immigration checkpoints, which can have elements relevant to both the *Edmonds* and *Lidster* decisions—and thus could be upheld based on the specific parameters in place.

Previously, in *Brower v. County of Inyo* (1989),[151] the Supreme Court considered a *roadblock* of a different sort—one set to halt the progress of a suspect who was fleeing from police in a stolen vehicle traveling at a high rate of speed. In such situations, police might use metal spikes in the road in the hopes of puncturing a car's tires. But in this instance, police used an eighteen-wheel truck to block the road, set up behind a curve, and with the truck's headlights pointing in the direction of oncoming traffic. The suspect's vehicle ended up crashing into the truck, with the suspect dying on the scene. His estate filed a lawsuit claiming a Fourth Amendment violation had lead to wrongful death. Justice Scalia's majority opinion noted the character of this roadblock in determining that a "seizure" had occurred under the Fourth Amendment, but he left it for lower courts to assess, on remand, whether that seizure was unreasonable:

> Petitioners can claim the right to recover for Brower's death only because the unreasonableness they allege consists precisely of setting up the roadblock in such manner as to be likely to kill him. ... [I]f Brower had had the opportunity to stop voluntarily at the roadblock, but had negligently or intentionally driven into it, then, because of lack of proximate causality, respondents, though responsible for depriving him of his freedom of movement, would not be liable for his death.

Immunity from Arrest

Beyond the Fourth Amendment, other provisions of the Constitution are germane to the law of arrest. Under the Speech and Debate Clause (Article I, Section 6 of the U.S. Constitution), members of Congress enjoy absolute immunity from arrest for any speech or action within the sphere of legislative activity. Over the course of U.S. history, several members of Congress have invoked the Speech and Debate Clause in an effort to shield themselves from criminal prosecution. These attempts generally have been fruitless. In *United States v. Brewster* (1972),[152] the Supreme Court held that "a Member of Congress may be prosecuted under a criminal statute provided that the Government's case does not rely on legislative acts or the motivation for legislative acts."

The question of whether a sitting president can face criminal charges while in office is not answered in the Constitution and remains an unresolved one in case law, as well. However, a Justice Department policy established by its Office of Legal Counsel in 1973 (and reaffirmed 27 years later) states that a sitting president cannot be indicted for a criminal offense.[153] Nevertheless, in *Trump v. Vance* (2020),[154] the Supreme Court indicated that a sitting president did not have absolute immunity that precluded a response to subpoenas connected with a state grand jury probe into criminal wrongdoing. Writing for the Court's 7–2 majority in this case, Chief Justice Roberts said the following:

> Two hundred years ago, a great jurist of our Court established that no citizen, not even the President, is categorically above the common duty to produce evidence when called upon in a criminal proceeding. We reaffirm that principle today and hold that the President is neither absolutely immune from state criminal subpoenas seeking his private papers nor entitled to a heightened standard of need. The 'guard[ ] furnished to this high officer' lies where it always has—in 'the conduct of a court' applying established legal and constitutional principles to individual subpoenas in a manner that preserves both the independence of the Executive and the integrity of the criminal justice system.

We covered the topic of immunity for government officials in greater detail in Chapter 2.

Diplomatic Immunity

Under the Vienna Convention on Diplomatic Relations,[155] a treaty signed by the United States, foreign diplomats and their administrative staffs are immune from arrest and prosecution pursuant to the doctrine of diplomatic immunity. Accordingly, Section 5 of the Diplomatic Relations Act of 1978[156] states, "Any action or proceeding brought against an individual who is entitled to immunity with respect to such action or proceeding under the Vienna Convention on Diplomatic Relations, under section 3(b) or 4 of this Act, or under any other laws extending diplomatic privileges and immunities, shall be dismissed."

Yet according to a State Department document entitled "Diplomatic and Consular Immunity: Guidance for Law Enforcement and Judicial Authorities," police are not required to remain inert in all situations that might involve diplomatic immunity—as the document indicates that "in circumstances where public safety is in imminent danger or it is apparent that a grave crime may otherwise be committed, police authorities may intervene to the extent necessary to halt such activity."[157] With more than 100,000 representatives of foreign governments working in the United States, honoring the tenets of diplomatic immunity,

ABSOLUTE IMMUNITY: A type of immunity that confers complete protection against arrest and prosecution.

DIPLOMATIC IMMUNITY: A principle of international law under which foreign diplomats are immune from arrest and prosecution.

which this guidance document refers to as "one of the oldest elements of foreign relations"[158] (even dating back to the Ancient Greeks), is critical—especially in light of the principle known as "reciprocity,"[159] which in this context connotes a link between the treatment of foreigners in this country and how U.S. diplomats will be treated abroad.

An important aspect of diplomatic immunity is that high-level diplomats, such as ambassadors, are likely to have heightened levels of immunity, whereas lower-level staff may derive lesser protections. Two general types of immunity are relevant: (1) immunity for *official acts* connected to duties as a government representative and (2) *personal inviolability*, which is a generalized protection related to any accusation of criminal conduct, even that which is unconnected to official job duties. The State Department's guidance document indicates diplomatic agents and direct family members are entitled to "complete personal inviolability," which means they cannot be prosecuted in court "no matter how serious the offense"—and beyond that, "they may not be handcuffed ... arrested, or detained; and neither their property (including vehicles) nor residences may be entered of searched."[160] However, these protections for diplomatic immunity are not available to a U.S. citizen—which could, in some cases, be relevant for an American spouse of a foreign diplomat.[161] Lower-level diplomatic staff tend to have immunity from criminal prosecution for official acts, but have no civil immunity and no immunity related to acts that are not deemed *official*.

As previously noted, even if a person accused of a crime has diplomatic immunity, there is value in police officers conducting a thorough investigation. Evidence of a serious crime might motivate U.S. officials to request a waiver of immunity from the individual's home country—and that country could, in fact, choose to waive an individual person's immunity, even though the individual themselves could not do so. In this regard, the State Department's guidance document observes, "Frequently (and erroneously), immunity is understood to mean a pardon, total exoneration or total release from the responsibility to comply with the law"; the document goes on to say, "In actuality, [diplomatic] immunity is simply a legal barrier which precludes U.S. courts from exercising jurisdiction over cases against persons who enjoy it and in no way releases such person from the duty ... to respect the laws and regulations of the United States."[162] Using this statement to potentially offer specific guidance to law enforcement personnel, the document also says the following:

> Police authorities should never address the alleged commission of a crime by a person enjoying full criminal immunity with the belief that there is no possibility that a prosecution could result. The U.S. Department of State requests waivers of immunity in every case where the prosecutor advises that, but for the immunity, charges would be pursued. In serious cases, if a wavier is refused, the offender will be expelled from the United States and the U.S. Department of State will request that a warrant be issued. ...[163]

In theory, if an expelled person returned to the United States one day without immunity, they could then be prosecuted—or an existing arrest warrant could be used as the basis for prohibiting entry into the country. The State Department document does note, however, that a "residual immunity" could exist for "official acts," meaning a criminal prosecution at a later date would be unlikely for those. In simple terms, the State Department's advice to law enforcement is succinctly summarized as follows: "While police officers are obliged, under international law, to recognize the immunity of the envoy, they must not ignore or condone the commission of crimes."[164]

A 2020 article from Anna Raphael in the *Duke University Law Review* addresses the perception that diplomats might be inclined to behave badly, saying, "In light of this immunity, one might think that diplomats exploit their positions and threaten the safety of American citizens. ... But such abuse is not particularly widespread, and diplomats rarely commit violent crimes."[165] The author also finds that "abuse of immunity is usually confined to traffic violations."

Even so, this article highlights a potential loophole that federal circuit courts have permitted when it comes to diplomatic immunity, stating that "[t]he current U.S. legal regime permits a seldom-discussed retroactive application of diplomatic immunity, meaning that an individual can commit a crime, obtain diplomatic status, and then have that immunity 'shield' the individual from liability for those wrongful actions taken before the individual obtained such status."[166] In effect, a retroactive application of newly-acquired diplomatic immunity could occur.

In a 1984 case of this ilk, the Eleventh Circuit ruled in favor of a Saudi Arabian prince, who was accused of holding an Egyptian woman against her will in a condominium in Dade County, Florida. The prince was not a diplomat at the time of his conduct, and he only sought (and was granted) diplomatic status after legal action was commenced against him. The Circuit Court's majority opinion found that the prince should still be granted immunity:

> We hold that once the United States Department of State has regularly certified a visitor to this country as having diplomatic status, the courts are bound to accept that determination, and that the diplomatic immunity flowing from that status serves as a defense to suits already commenced. We therefore affirm the dismissal of the claims made against the Saudi Arabian diplomats in this case.[167]

Decades later, in 2014, a similar approach was taken by the U.S. District Court for the Southern District of New York. This court dismissed a criminal case against a consular officer from India, who had been charged with visa fraud and making false statements to the government. Once again, the diplomatic status was conferred after legal action began, and the District Court applied the protections of diplomatic immunity by saying, "The State Department has explained that 'criminal immunity precludes the exercise of jurisdiction by the courts over an individual whether the incident occurred prior to or during the period in which such immunity exists.'"[168] Ultimately, although the Supreme Court has never addressed this topic, the acquiescence of lower courts to the post-conduct application of diplomatic immunity allows that possibility to remain viable. See chapter 11 for more discussion on types of immunity that are provided to cooperating witnesses through deals made in exchange for testimony given in court.

Conclusion

In effectuating arrests, law enforcement officers must strike a balance between protecting the best interests of society at large—perhaps, in thwarting criminal activity or protecting national security—and simultaneously preserving the fundamental provisions embedded in the Bill of Rights, protections crafted by the Founders to thwart unwarranted government infringements upon personal liberty.

Certainly, at its most basic level, an arrest is a constraint upon liberty. Accordingly, courts have allowed for examinations of whether an arrest is to be considered reasonable under the Fourth Amendment. In this chapter, we observed that arrests must be based on the legal standard of probable cause, and we have seen that arrests can occur with or without a warrant, so long as they meet that baseline threshold. Some states permit a citizen's arrest, but in recent years, reform has been suggested after high-profile cases in which individuals have taken the law into their own hands.

The investigative process that culminates in an arrest often begins in more innocuous fashion—such as with an investigatory detention or a stop-and-frisk encounter. In these situations, police acting on the lesser standard of reasonable suspicion—which requires articulable facts that amount to something more than a hunch—are permitted to detain individuals, to conduct a limited pat down of outer clothing, and to ask for identification, but this limited detention must not occur for an unreasonable length of time. If the pat down yields probable cause of a threat to officer safety or illegal activity, though, then an extended detention, or even an arrest, could be feasible.

Controversy can ensue when any aspect of this process requires law enforcement officials to use force in carrying out their duties. In these situations, the Supreme Court has recognized that police officers have difficult jobs to do. They put their safety in peril on a minute-by-minute basis and must make split-second choices that can have life or death consequences. There is no occupation like it. But the Court also has made it clear that the Fourth Amendment governs police use of force—and unreasonable use of force can amount to an unconstitutional seizure. To guide the analysis of individual cases, the Court has crafted the objective reasonableness standard. Three key factors seem to impact the application of that standard in real-world contexts: the severity of an alleged crime, whether the suspect poses an immediate threat to the safety of the officers or to other people, and whether the suspect is resisting or attempting to flee from an arrest.

Moreover, through the years, law enforcement officials have created various tools and techniques for helping them effectively handle precarious situations, including flash-bang grenades, pepper spray, chokeholds, tracking dogs, roadblocks, and Tasers, to name a few. In situations where any of these are applied, case precedent can prove to be a valuable guide for what specific activity is permissible and what amounts to objectively unreasonable—and, thus, unconstitutional—conduct.

In subsequent chapters, we consider what comes after investigatory detentions, searches and seizures, and arrests. Our examination of interrogations, trials, and punishment in these later chapters will illustrate how the criminal justice process maneuvers beyond the incipient stages that lead up to formal custody. But it is in these early moments when the lives of suspects, officers, and even bystanders can change in an instant—and where savvy police instincts can prevent a tragedy that adversely impacts large segments of society; with those critical factors in mind, the objective reasonableness of different policing techniques must be evaluated for compatibility with the Fourth Amendment—with precise attention to the unique details of specific interactions between individual persons and officers of the law.

Questions for Thought and Discussion

1. How has the Supreme Court attempted to define the contours of *probable cause*? Is this standard too low or too high in terms of justifying an arrest—or is it appropriate? What types of situations would create the *functional equivalent* of an arrest?

2. Under what circumstances is a warrantless arrest permissible? Consider if the answer to that question varies across states. What would be the drawback to requiring a warrant for every arrest? Should certain

misdemeanor crimes be exempt from an arrest? If so, which crimes? What social justice issues arise from warrantless arrests for lesser offenses?

3.   What problems can arise when a state allows for a citizen's arrest? Are there any positives to allowing a citizen's arrest? Can you find real-world example to justify your answers to each of these questions?

4.   In what ways have states attempted to change the standards used for adjudicating police use-of-force cases, and why have such changes come about in recent years? Considering the tactics and devices police use in subduing suspected criminals who resist, which techniques or methods have been shown to comport with the Fourth Amendment, and which have not? In answering that question, you may wish to consider individualized instances of use and specific contexts that can show, for example, when use of a Taser is appropriate and when it is not. Overall, is the objective reasonableness standard a fair one for police officers? For suspected criminals? Could it be improved in any way?

5.   What factors can police use in attempting to create a either a generalized *profile* of a criminal, such as a drug courier profile, or a specific profile germane to evidence in a particular case? What can police not take into account when creating a profile? What are some factors that might appear innocent in isolation but which could, when taken with other criteria, provide reasonable suspicion for an investigatory detention? What types of situations are most likely to transition from investigatory detention or a pat-down search to an arrest?

6.   Assess the variation across states when it comes to *stop and identify* laws. What are the key differences in how states ask for a person to be identified and the punishment for not identifying oneself? Imagine that authorities have reasonable suspicion to detain a person but find no probable cause for an arrest. If that person were unable to produce any identification, though, what would be a reasonable amount of time to hold them?

7.   What types of roadblocks have been deemed constitutional by the Supreme Court? What is not permitted? If police establish a roadblock for the purpose of locating a nearby bank robbery suspect, and a car approaches with illegal drugs in plain view on the passenger seat, what factors might influence a court's decision as to the reasonableness of seizing those drugs?

8.   In what ways is the concept of diplomatic immunity controversial? What benefits does the United States derive from this concept? Suppose an ambassador from a foreign country commits a murder on U.S. soil. What steps could be taken to bring that person to justice?

Endnotes

[1]   *Payton v. New York*, 445 U. S. 573 (1980).

[2]   *United States v. Watson*, 423 U.S. 411 (1976).

[3]   *Illinois v. Gates*, 462 U.S. 213 (1983).

[4]   Laurel Wamsley, *Florida Man Awarded $37,500 After Cops Mistake Glazed Doughnut Crumb for Meth*, NPR, Oct. 16, 2017, https://www.npr.org/sections/thetwo-way/2017/10/16/558147669/florida-man-awarded-37-500-after-cops-mistake-glazed-doughnut-crumbs-for-meth.

[5]   *Id.*

6   Ryan Gabrielson & Topher Sanders, *Busted*, ProPublica, N.Y. Times Magazine, July 7, 2016, https://www.propublica.org/article/common-roadside-drug-test-routinely-produces-false-positives.

7   *Id.*

8   *United States v. Watson, supra* note 2.

9   *Beck v. Ohio*, 379 U. S. 89 (1964).

10 *Illinois v. Gates, supra* note 3.

11 *Brinegar v. United States*, 338 U.S. 160, 175 (1949).

12 *Draper v. United States*, 358 U.S. 307 (1958).

13 *Id.*, citing *Carroll v. United States*, 267 U.S. 132, 162 (1925).

14 *Draper v. United States*, 358 U.S. 307 (1958) (Douglas, J., dissenting, quoting Hogan and Snee, *The McNabb-Mallory Rule: Its Rise, Rationale, and Rescue*, 47 Geo. L.J. 1, 22 (1958)).

15 *Atwater v. Lago Vista*, 532 U.S. 318 (2001).

16 *Payton v. New York, supra* note 1.

17 *See, e.g.*, *Warden v. Hayden*, 387 U.S. 294 (1967).

18 *Gerstein v. Pugh*, 420 U.S. 103 (1975).

19 *County of Riverside v. McLaughlin*, 500 U.S. 44 (1991).

20 *McNabb v. United States*, 318 U.S. 332 (1943); *Mallory v. United States*, 354 U.S. 449 (1957).

21 USA PATRIOT Act, Pub. L. 107–56.

22 *Zadvydas v. Davis*, 533 U.S. 678 (2001).

23 National Defense Authorization Act of 2012, Pub. L. 112–81.

24 *Boumediene v. Bush*, 553 U.S. 723 (2008); see Cora Currier, *Cutting through the Controversy About Indefinite Detention and the NDAA*, ProPublica, Dec. 7, 2012 (for further reading on the NDAA), https://www.propublica.org/article/cutting-through-the-controversy-about-indefinite-detention-and-the-ndaa.

25 *Kurtz v. Moffitt*, 115 U.S. 487 (1885).

26 *See* SolutionsInstitute, *Citizen's Arrests Laws by State* (for thorough state-by-state discussion), https://solutions-institute.org/tools/citizens-arrest-laws-by-state/.

27 NC Leg. SUBCHAPTER IV. ARREST.

28 *See* SolutionsInstitute, *Citizen's Arrests Laws by State*, https://solutions-institute.org/tools/citizens-arrest-laws-by-state/.

29 *State v. Gonzales*, 24 Wn. App. 437, 604 P.2d 168 (1979); *Guijosa v. Wal-Mart Stores*, 101 Wash. App. 777, 6 P.3d 583 (2000).

30 *State v. Malone*, 106 Wn.2d 607, 724 P.2d 364 (1986); *State v. Miller*, 103 Wn.2d 792, 698 P.2d 554 (1985); *State v. Gonzales*, 24 Wn. App. 437, 604 P.2d 168 (1979). *See* Washington State Department of Licensing, *Summary of Citizen Arrest*, Oct. 11, 2005, https://www.dol.wa.gov/business/securityguards/docs/citizenarrest1.pdf.

31 *Commonwealth v. Harris*, 11 Mass. App. Ct. 165, 415 N.E.2d 216 (1981) (authorized a citizen's arrest by off-duty police officers acting outside of their jurisdictions; those officers had probable cause that the felony crime of child rape had occurred; this opinion contains an extensive list of similar cases from other states).

32 *Commonwealth v. Grise*, 398 Mass. 247, 496 N.E.2d 162 (1986) (prohibited the use of citizen's arrest by an off-duty police officer who witnesses a misdemeanor act of intoxicated driving outside of his jurisdiction).

33 *See, e.g.*, Sid Hemsley, *Extraterritorial Arrest*, Municipal Technical Advisory Services, Institute for Public Service (Tennessee law on this topic), https://www.mtas.tennessee.edu/knowledgebase/extraterritorial-arrests.

34 *See, e.g.*, Ashley Moody, *Advisory Legal Opinion - AGO 81-90*, MyFloridaLegal (a 1981 interpretation from the Florida Attorney General outlining parameters for pursuit across jurisdictions within the state), https://www.myfloridalegal.com/ago.nsf/Opinions/ACE1C0E81C92C233852565860068DF97.

35 Georgia's self-defense law is found at GA CODE § 16-3-21, *Use of Force in Defense of Self or Others; Evidence of Belief That Force Was Necessary in Murder or Manslaughter Prosecution*, https://law.justia.com/codes/georgia/2010/title-16/chapter-3/article-2/16-3-21.

36 *Graham v. Connor*, 490 U.S. 386 (1989).

37 *Id.* (quoting from *United States v. Place*, 462 U.S. 696 (1983)).

38 *Id.* (quoting from *Tennessee v. Garner*, 471 U.S. 1 (1985)).

39 *Scott v. Henrich*, 39 F.3d 912 (9th Cir. 1994).

40 RCW 10.120.020 (2021).

41 Associated Press, *AG's Office: New Use-Of-Force Law Doesn't Prevent Police Response*, Kitsap Sun, Aug. 18, 2021, https://www.kitsapsun.com/story/news/2021/08/06/new-use-force-law-doesnt-prevent-washington-police-response/5512624001/.

42 Angeli Kakade, *Police Feel 'at Risk' Under New Washington Law Limiting Use of Deadly Force*, King5 Local News, July 27, 2021, https://www.king5.com/article/news/local/police-risk-new-washington-law-limiting-use-deadly-force/281-3749ccd8-5323-4d33-8f64-fbd664532cd1.

43 Ram Subrmanian & Leily Arzy, *State Policing Reforms Since George Floyd's Murder*, Brennan Center, May 21, 2021, https://www.brennancenter.org/our-work/research-reports/state-policing-reforms-george-floyds-murder.

44 CO Revised Statutes, 18-1-707.

45 CAL. PEN. CODE 833-851.93.

46 Jorge L. Ortiz, *California's New Police Use-Of-Force Law Marks a 'Significant' Change In Law Enforcement. Here's Why*, USA Today (Aug. 20, 2019), https://www.usatoday.com/story/news/nation/2019/08/20/california-new-police-use-force-law-significant-change/2068263001/.

47 *Tennessee v. Garner, supra* note 38.

48 *Scott v. Harris*, 560 U.S. 372 (2007).

49 *Plumhoff v. Rickard*, 572 U.S. 765 (2014).

50 *See, e.g., Saucier v. Katz*, 533 U.S. 194 (2001); *Pearson v. Callahan*, 555 U.S. 223 (2009) (indicated that the two factors defining qualified immunity could be considered in any order, such that the lack of a clearly defined precedent could automatically result in a grant of qualified immunity and preclude the need for an assessment of whether a constitutional violation occurred); *D.C. v. Wesby*, 583 U.S. ___ (2017) (speaks to a need for *settled law* for qualified immunity to not apply).

51 *Brosseau v. Haugen*, 543 U.S. 194 (2004).

52 This quote is provided in the Supreme Court's opinion (*id.*), with a citation to the Circuit Court decision in *Haugen v. Brosseau*, 339 F.3d 857, at 895 (9th Cir. 2003).

53 *Id.* (quoting *Saucier v. Katz*, 533 U.S. 194 (2001)).

54 *See* Justin Thompson, *Police Pursuits: Are No-Pursuit Policies the Answer?* Criminal Justice Institute, School of Law Enforcement Supervision Session XXVI, Oct. 21, 2005, https://www.scotusblog.com/2021/07/high-speed-pursuit-liability-and-other-questions-surrounding-police-activities/; David P. Schultz, Ed Hudak, & Geoffrey P. Alpert, *Evidence-Based Decisions on Police Pursuits: The Officer's Perspective*, FBI's Law Enforcement Bulletin, Mar. 1, 2010, https://leb.fbi.gov/articles/featured-articles/evidence-based-decisions-on-police-pursuits-the-officers-perspective.

55   Subramanian & Arzy, *supra* note 43.

56   International Association of Chiefs of Police, *Vehicular Pursuits*, Law Enforcement Policy Center, Dec. 2019 (the document's internal footnote for this information is as follows: "Pursuit database (1/1/2016 - 12/31/2018 data). Note that participation in the data collection efforts associated with this database is voluntary and have not been subjected to rigorous analysis. The data represent 116 agencies and 4,865 pursuits." The report also offers the following source regarding a different sample of pursuit data: Brian A. Reaves, *Police Vehicle Pursuits, 2012–2013*, NCJ 250545 Department of Justice, Office of Justice Programs, Bureau of Justice Statistics (2017), https://bjs.ojp.gov/content/pub/pdf/pvp1213.pdf), https://www.theiacp.org/sites/default/files/2019-12/Vehicular%20Pursuits%20-%202019.pdf.

57   *See, e.g.*, Georgia's HB 1019 (signed into law in 2020).

58   AZ Code § 13-1213.

59   CA Code Chapter 9. Assault and Battery § 244.5.

60   *See* Megan Thompson, *Stun Gun Law by State: The Legal Guide for 2022*, Lawrina Legal Blog (August 31, 2021), https://lawrina.com/blog/stun-guns-laws-by-state/.

61   *See* Transportation Security Administration, *Stun Guns/Shocking Devices*, https://www.tsa.gov/travel/security-screening/whatcanibring/items/stun-gunsshocking-devices.

62   *Kingsley v. Hendrickson*, 576 U.S. 389 (2015).

63   *Kingsley v. Hendrickson*, 744 F.3d 443 (7th Cir. 2014).

64   *Bell v. Wolfish*, 441 U.S. 520 (1979).

65   *Autin v. City of Baytown, Tex.*, 174F. App'x 183 (5th Cir. 2005).

66   *Newman v. Guedry*, 703 F.3d 757, 762 (5th Cir. 2012).

67   *Massey v. Wharton*, 477 F. App'x 256 (5th Cir.2012).

68   *See* Vanessa Romo, Becky Sullivan, & Joe Hernandez, *Kim Potter is found guilty in the death of Daunte Wright*, NPR, Dec. 23, 2021, https://www.npr.org/2021/12/23/1066012247/kim-potter-trial-daunte-wright; Becky Sullivan, *Kim Potter Describes Officers' Struggle with Daunte Wright Before She Shot Him*, NPR, Dec. 17, 2021, https://www.npr.org/2021/12/17/1065071626/potter-expected-on-stand-as-trial-in-wright-death-nears-end.

69   World Population Review, *Pepper Spray Laws by State, 2021*, https://worldpopulationreview.com/state-rankings/pepper-spray-laws-by-state.

70   *Treats v. Morgan*, 308 F.3d 868, 870 (8th Cir. 2002).

71   *Chambers v. Johnson*, 372 F. App'x 471, 472 (5th Cir. 2010).

72   *McCoy v. Alamu*, No. 18-40856 (5th Cir. 2020).

73   *Id.* (citing *Wilkins v. Gaddy*, 559 U.S. 34 (2010)).

74   *Campbell v. City of Springboro*, 700 F.3d 779 (6th Cir. 2013).

75   The same court had issued a similar ruling in one of its 1995 cases, a matter in which a "little-trained" dog with only "bark and hold" capabilities—and with a history of biting—was allowed to bite a suspect who was already in handcuffs. *White v. Harmon*, 65 F.3d 169 (6th Cir. 1995).

76   *Campbell v. City of Springboro, supra* note 74.

77   *Robinette v. Barnes*, 854 F.2d 209 (6th Cir. 1988).

78   *Matthews v. Jones*, 35 F.3d 1046 (6th Cir. 1994).

79   *Campbell v. City of Springboro, supra* note 74.

80   *Baxter v. Bracey and Harris*, Case No. 18-5102 (6th Cir. Nov. 8, 2018).

81   Exec. Order No. 13929 (2020).

82   Department of Justice, The Department of Justice Announces Standards for Certifying Safe Policing Practices by Law Enforcement Agencies, Oct. 28, 2020, https://www.justice.gov/opa/pr/department-justice-announces-standards-certifying-safe-policing-practices-law-enforcement; *see* PoliceGrantsHelp Staff, *How the Executive Order on Safe Policing for Safe Communities Impacts Grant Funding*, police1.com, Jan. 12, 2021, https://www.police1.com/police-grants/articles/how-the-executive-order-on-safe-policing-for-safe-communities-impacts-grant-funding-c3JGCzJKeSLybM8t/.

83   Department of Justice, Department of Justice Announces Department-Wide Policy on Chokeholds and 'No-Knock' Entries, (2021), https://www.justice.gov/opa/pr/department-justice-announces-department-wide-policy-chokeholds-and-no-knock-entries.

84   Eric Garner Anti-Chokehold Act, NY Penal Law § 121.13.

85   Ali Watkins & Ashley Southhall, *N.Y.C.'s Police Chokehold Ban is Struck Down by Court*, N.Y. Times, June 23, 2021, https://www.nytimes.com/2021/06/23/nyregion/police-chokehold-ban-supreme-court.html.

86   *Police Benevolent Assn. of the City of N.Y v. City of New York*, 205 A.D.3d 552 (NY App. Div. 2022).

87   *City of Los Angeles v. Lyons*, 461 U.S. 95 (1983).

88   Julia Angwin & Abbie Nehring, *Hotter Than Lava*, ProPublica, Jan. 12, 2015, https://www.propublica.org/article/flashbangs

89   *Id.* (Little Rock (AR) Police Department Spokesperson Sidney gave the quote. The 84% figure is derived from raids conducted between 2011 and 2013 and includes 112 instances in which flash-bangs were recorded as being used.).

90   For cases ruling against police of flash-bangs, *see Milan v. Bolin*, 795 F.3d 726, 729–30 (7th Cir. 2015); *Boyd v. Benton Cty.*, 374 F.3d 773, 779 (9th Cir. 2004); *Estate of Escobedo v. Bender*, 600 F.3d 770, 784–86 (7th Cir. 2010); *Estate of Smith v. Marasco*, 318 F.3d 497 (3d Cir. 2003). For cases upholding the use of these devices, *see United States v. Boulanger*, 444 F.3d 76, 85 (1st Cir.2006); *Estate of Bing ex rel. Bing v. City of Whitehall*, 456 F.3d 555 (6th Cir. 2006); *United States v. Boulanger*, 444 F.3d 76, 85 (1st Cir. 2006); *Molina ex rel. Molina v. Cooper*, 325 F.3d 963, 973 (7th Cir. 2003); *United States v. Baker*, 16 F.3d 854 (8th Cir. 1994).

91   Department of Justice, Former Habersham County Deputy Sheriff Charged for her Role in Flash Bang Grenade Incident, July 22, 2015, https://www.justice.gov/usao-ndga/pr/former-habersham-county-deputy-sheriff-charged-her-role-flash-bang-grenade-incident; Christian Boone, *Relief and Rage as Jury Acquits Deputy in Raid That Maimed Baby*, Atl. J. Const., Dec. 11, 2015, https://www.ajc.com/news/crime--law/relief-and-rage-jury-acquits-deputy-raid-that-maimed-baby/udtZ8h6ljIn7DjB9IVKGMM/; Editorial Staff, *Federal Judge Awards $3.6 Million to Family of Toddler Injured in Raid*, WSB-TV 2, Feb. 26, 2016, https://www.wsbtv.com/news/local/federal-judge-awards-36-million-family-toddler-inj/152661850/.

92   *Z.J. v. Kansas City Board of Police Commissioners*, No. 17-3365 (8th Cir. 2019).

93   *Terebesi v. Torreso*, 764 F.3d 217, 239 (2d Cir. 2014).

94   *See* Subramanian & Arzy, *supra* note 43.

95   *Id.*

96   *See* Federal Bureau of Investigation, National Use-of-Force Data Collection (the database page on the FBI website) https://www.fbi.gov/services/cjis/ucr/use-of-force.

97   Federal Bureau of Investigation, *Crime Data Explorer*, https://crime-data-explorer.fr.cloud.gov/pages/le/uof.

98   John Kelly & Mark Nichols, *We Found 85,000 Cops Who've Been Investigated for Misconduct. Now You Can Read Their Records*, USA Today, Apr. 24, 2019, updated June 11, 2020, https://www.usatoday.com/in-depth/news/investigations/2019/04/24/usa-today-revealing-misconduct-records-police-cops/3223984002/.

99 Council on Criminal Justice, *Decertification*, Task Force of Policing, Apr. 14, 2021 (citing e-mail from Michael Becar, Exec. Dir., International Association of Directors of Law Enforcement Standards Training (Apr. 6, 2021)), https://counciloncj.foleon.com/policing/assessing-the-evidence/ix-decertification/.

100 Subramanian & Arzy, *supra* note 43.

101 Council on Criminal Justice, *supra* note 99.

102 Subrmanian and Leily, *supra* note 100

103 *Id.*

104 Council on Criminal Justice, *supra* note 99.

105 *Id.*

106 *Id.* (citing Matt Wynn, *Our Database of Troubled Cops, and How You Can Help*, USA Today, May 7, 2019).

107 Council on Criminal Justice, *supra* note 99 (citing Kelly and Nichols, *supra* note 98).

108 Council on Criminal Justice, *supra* note 99 (citing Devan Patel, *Florida Gave Thousands of Tarnished Officers a Second Chance. Hundreds Blew it Again*, Naples Daily News, Dec. 29, 2020, https://www.naplesnews.com/in-depth/news/crime/2020/12/29/hundreds-florida-officers-given-second-chance-blew-again/3764571001/.

109 Danielle Wallace, *Derek Chauvin's Defense Backed by $1M Minneapolis Police Union Fund, 12-Lawyer Team*, Fox News, Apr. 1, 2021, https://www.foxnews.com/us/derek-chauvin-defense-1-million-minneapolis-police-union-12-lawyer-team-george-floyd.

110 Council on Criminal Justice, *Body Cameras*, Task Force on Policing, Apr. 2021, https://counciloncj.foleon.com/policing/assessing-the-evidence/x-body-worn-cameras/.

111 Jennifer Lee, *Will Body Cameras Help End Police Violence?* ACLU, June 7, 2021, https://www.aclu-wa.org/story/%C2%A0will-body-cameras-help-end-police-violence%C2%A0 (citing Cynthia Lum, Megan Stoltz, Christopher Koper, & J. Amber Scherer, *Research on Body-Worn Cameras: What We Know, What We Need to Know* 18 Criminology & Public Policy, 93–118 (2019).

112 *Id.* (citing Linda Merola, Cynthia Lum, Christopher Koper, & Amber Scherer, *Body Worn Cameras and the Courts: A National Survey of State Prosecutors* (2016), https://bwctta.com/sites/default/files/Files/Resources/BWCProsecutors.pdf).

113 *Id.*

114 Akela Lacy, *Two Companies Fight to Corner the Police Body Camera Market*, The Intercept, Dec. 8, 2021, https://theintercept.com/2021/12/08/police-reform-body-cameras-axon-motorola/.

115 Linzi Sheldon, *Millions of Dollars, Privacy Concerns Surround Seattle Police Department Body Camera Program*, KIRO 7, Seattle, Feb. 7, 2018, https://www.kiro7.com/news/local/millions-of-dollars-privacy-concerns-surround-seattle-police-department-body-camera-program/692859188/.

116 Council on Criminal Justice, *Body Cameras*, Task Force on Policing, Apr. 2021, https://counciloncj.foleon.com/policing/assessing-the-evidence/x-body-worn-cameras/.

117 *Adams v. Williams*, 407 U.S. 143 (1972).

118 *Terry v. Ohio*, 392 U.S. 1 (1968).

119 *Brinegar v. United States*, 338 U.S. 160 (1949).

120 *Brown v. Texas*, 443 U.S. 47 (1979).

121 *Adams v. Williams*, 407 U.S. 143 (1972).

122 *Florida v. J.L.*, 529 U.S. 266 (2000).

123 *United States v. Brignoni-Ponce*, 422 U.S. 873 (1975).

124 Ric Simmons, *Race and Reasonable Suspicion*, 73 Fla. L. Rev. 413 (2021).

125 *Illinois v. Wardlow*, 528 U.S. 119 (2000).

126 *United States v. Sokolow*, 490 U.S. 1 (1989).

127 *United States v. Cortez*, 449 U.S. 411 (1981).

128 *Florida v. Royer*, 460 U.S. 491 (1983).

129 *United States v. Sharpe*, 470 U.S. 675 (1985).

130 *United States v. Shabazz*, 993 F.2d 431, 437 (5th Cir. 1993).

131 *United States v. Place, supra* note 37.

132 *Minnesota v. Dickerson*, 508 U.S. 366 (1993).

133 *Id.*, referencing *State v. Dickerson*, 481 N. W. 2d 840, 845 (1992).

134 *Floyd v. City of New York*, 959 F.Supp.2d 540 (S.D.N.Y. 2013).

135 NYACLU, *Stop and Frisk Data*, ACLU of New York, https://www.nyclu.org/en/stop-and-frisk-data.

136 Christopher Mathias, *NYPD Commissioner Defends 'Broken Windows' at Breakfast Costing $1,250 a Table*, HuffPost, Sept. 10, 2014, https://www.huffpost.com/entry/broken-windows-william-bratton-nypd_n_5799540.

137 Reuven Blau, Rocco Parascandola, & Thomas Tracy, *NYPD Issues New Stop-And-Frisk Rules That Ban Stops Based On Race*, New York Daily News, Mar. 3, 2015, https://www.nydailynews.com/new-york/nypd-issues-new-stop-and-frisk-rules-article-1.2136122.

138 *Delaware v. Prouse*, 440 U.S. 648 (1979).

139 *Alabama v. White*, 496 U.S. 325 (1990).

140 *Michigan v. Long*, 463 U.S. 1032 (1983).

141 *Pennsylvania v. Mimms*, 434 U.S. 106 (1977); *Maryland v. Wilson*, 519 U.S. 408 (1997).

142 *See* World Population Review, *Stop and Identify States 2022* (For a map of those states; Kansas City, Missouri has a stop-and-identify ordinance, even though the rest of the state does not. Texas and Oregon apply such a statute only to motorists), https://worldpopulationreview.com/state-rankings/stop-and-id-states.

143 Arrest is permitted in Arkansas, Florida, Georgia, and Rhode Island. In the following states, criminal penalties can attach to a failure to identify: Arizona, Florida, Indiana, Louisiana, New Mexico, Ohio, and Vermont. *See* Immigrant Legal Resource Center, *Stop and Identify Laws* (citing the assistance of the Kirkland & Ellis Law Firm), https://www.ilrc.org/sites/default/files/resources/stop_identify_statutes_in_us-lg-20180201v3.pdf.

144 *Hiibel v. Sixth Judicial District Court of Nevada*, 542 U.S. 177 (2004).

145 In Indiana and Ohio, officers can request a person's date of birth. Nevada simply requires a name to be provided.

146 *Kolender v. Lawson*, 461 U.S. 352 (1983).

147 *Delaware v. Prouse, supra* note 138.

148 *Michigan Department of State Police v. Sitz*, 496 U.S. 444 (1990).

149 *City of Indianapolis v. Edmond*, 531 U.S. 32 (2000).

150 *Illinois v. Lidster*, 540 U.S. 419 (2004).

151 *Brower v. County of Inyo*, 489 U.S. 593 (1989).

152 *United States v. Brewster*, 408 U.S. 501 (1972).

153 Department of Justice, *A Sitting President's Amenability to Indictment and Criminal Prosecution*, Oct. 16, 2000, https://www.justice.gov/olc/opinion/sitting-president%E2%80%99s-amenability-indictment-and-criminal-prosecution.

154 *Trump v. Vance*, 591 U.S. ____ (2020).

155 Vienna Convention on Diplomatic Relations, Apr. 18, 1961, 23 U.S.T. 3227, 500 U.N.T.S. 95.

156 Diplomatic Relations Act of 1978, Pub. L. 95–393, 92 Stat. 808, 22 U.S.C. § 254a-254b.

157 U.S. Department of State, *Diplomatic and Consular Immunity: Guidance for Law Enforcement and Judicial Authorities*, at 21, Aug. 2018, https://www.state.gov/wp-content/uploads/2019/07/2018-DipConImm_v5_Web.pdf.

158 *Id.* at 3.

159 *Id.* at 5.

160 *Id.* at 7.

161 *Id.* at 9.

162 *Id.* at 20.

163 *Id.* at 10.

164 *Id.* at 5.

165 Anna Raphael, *Retroactive Diplomatic Immunity*, 69 Duke L.J. 1425, 1426 (2020).

166 *Id.*

167 *Abdulaziz v. Metropolitan Dade County*, 741 F.2d 1328 (11th Cir. 1984).

168 *United States v. Khobragade*, 15 F. Supp. 3d 383 (S.D.N.Y. 2014).

Credit

CHAPTER 11

The Fifth Amendment

Rights of the Accused

"No person shall be held to answer for a capital, or otherwise infamous crime, unless on a presentment or indictment of a grand jury …; nor shall any person be subject for the same offense to be twice put in jeopardy of life or limb; nor shall be compelled in any criminal case to be a witness against himself, nor be deprived of life, liberty, or property, without due process of law. …"

—U.S. Constitution, Fifth Amendment

Learning Objectives

After reading this chapter, you should understand the importance of each of the following in the administration of criminal justice:

1. The foundational principle of due process of law
2. The role and function of the grand jury
3. The prohibition of double jeopardy
4. The protection against compulsory self-incrimination and the defendant's right not to testify
5. Self-incrimination and confessions of guilt during police interrogation
6. Self-incrimination in the context of identification procedures and physical evidence obtained from the accused

Key Cases

Hurtado v. California, 110 U.S. 516 (1884)
United States v. Calandra, 414 U.S. 338 (1974)
Blockburger v. United States, 284 U.S. 299 (1932)
Gamble v. United States, 587 U.S. ___ (2019)
Miranda v. Arizona, 384 U.S. 436 (1966)
Berghuis v. Thompkins, 560 U.S. 370 (2010)
New York v. Quarles, 467 U.S. 649 (1984)
Arizona v. Fulminante, 499 U.S. 279 (1991)
Schmerber v. California, 384 U.S. 757 (1966)

Introduction

The Fifth Amendment is concerned primarily, but not exclusively, with the rights of criminal defendants.[1] The amendment contains three specific protections for persons accused of crimes: (1) no one can be tried for a serious offense without first being indicted by a grand jury, (2) no one should be subjected to double jeopardy (i.e., being tried twice for the same offense), and (3) no one should be subjected to compulsory self-incrimination. In this chapter, we will examine each of these protections. We begin, however, with the Due Process Clause of the Fifth Amendment, which, according to the Supreme Court, subsumes many of the substantive and procedural rights articulated in the Constitution (as well as a number of unenumerated rights).

PROCEDURAL DUE PROCESS: The constitutional requirement that a person is entitled to fair notice and a fair hearing before government can take one's life, liberty, or property.

SUBSTANTIVE DUE PROCESS: The judicial doctrine holding that government actions that impinge upon a person's life, liberty, or property must be fair, reasonable, and just.

The Foundational Importance of Due Process

Declaring that no person "shall be deprived of life, liberty, or property without due process of law," the Due Process Clause of the Fifth Amendment is among the most impactful provisions within the Bill of Rights. Along with its counterpart in the Fourteenth Amendment, the Due Process Clause protects a broad range of procedural and substantive rights.

Procedural due process requires the government to treat persons fairly when it takes action that impinges on liberty and property interests, while substantive due process protects liberty in ways that go beyond the rights enumerated in the Constitution. For example, in 1954 the

Supreme Court relied on the Due Process Clause of the Fifth Amendment in striking down segregated schools in the District of Columbia. In *Bolling v. Sharpe* (1954),[2] the Court held that the Clause imposes an obligation on the federal government to provide equal protection of the laws, just as the Fourteenth Amendment imposes that duty on the states. More recently, the Court invoked the Clause to strike down a federal statute that denied benefits to married same-sex couples. Writing for the Court in *United States v. Windsor* (2013),[3] Justice Anthony Kennedy observed that "though Congress has great authority to design laws to fit its own conception of sound national policy, it cannot deny the liberty protected by the Due Process Clause of the Fifth Amendment."

In terms of criminal justice, due process requires that people accused of crimes have been given fair notice of what constitutes a crime as well as a fair opportunity to defend themselves in court.[4] Speaking for the Supreme Court in 1873, Justice Stephen J. Field observed that due process "is a rule as old as the law, and never more to be respected than now, that no one shall be personally bound until he has had his day in court, by which is meant until he has been duly cited to appear, and has been afforded an opportunity to be heard."[5]

As we have discussed throughout this text, the amendments to the U.S. Constitution include several specific safeguards for those accused of crimes, including numerous protections ensconced in the Fourth, Fifth, and Sixth Amendments. However, the Due Process Clauses prevent those provisions from being read as an exhaustive list—since notions of fair process could apply to a variety of contexts. For instance, later in this chapter, we will see that the Due Process Clause of the Fourteenth Amendment has been used by the Supreme Court to address coerced confessions and even police use of an unfairly suggestive lineup. While none of the amendments speak explicitly to these situations (in the way that amendments address, for example, unreasonable searches or the right to counsel), the broad coverage of due process acts an enhanced layer of protection against government infringement upon the liberties of accused criminals.

Additional due process considerations are addressed in other chapters, such as the requirement for prosecution to disclose evidence favorable to the accused (see chapter 12) and the right of inmates to have a hearing before being punished for violating prison rules (see chapter 13). We begin this chapter, though, by addressing two bedrock aspects of due process in criminal cases: the government's burden of proving a criminal case beyond a reasonable doubt and the prohibition of excessively vague laws.

The Reasonable Doubt Standard

According to numerous Supreme Court decisions dating back to 1880, in criminal trials, due process requires the government to carry the burden of proving the defendant's guilt beyond a reasonable doubt.[6] In an 1895 case, for example, the Court overturned a criminal conviction because a trial judge had instructed the jury it could find a defendant guilty "when the evidence was equally balanced regarding [an element of the crime]."[7]

As the Supreme Court recognized in *Holland v. United States* (1954), "[t]he Government must prove every element of the offense beyond a reasonable doubt, though not to a mathematical certainty."[8] A decade and a half later, in *In re Winship* (1970),[9] the Court expounded on the importance of the reasonable doubt standard, striking down a New York law that allowed juvenile offenders to be found guilty of a crime under the lesser standard of preponderance of the evidence. Justice William Brennan, writing for the Court, observed the following:

> It is critical that the moral force of the criminal law not be diluted by a standard of proof that leaves people in doubt whether innocent men are being condemned. It is also important

REASONABLE DOUBT STANDARD: The standard of proof in a criminal trial. The prosecution must prove the defendant's guilt beyond a reasonable doubt.

PREPONDERANCE OF THE EVIDENCE: The standard of proof in a civil trial. The plaintiff must prove the case by evidence that has greater weight than the countervailing evidence submitted by the defense.

in our free society that every individual going about his ordinary affairs have confidence that his government cannot adjudge him guilty of a criminal offense without convincing a proper factfinder of his guilt with utmost certainty.

Subsequently, in *Cage v. Louisiana* (1990),[10] the Court held that a trial judge violated due process by telling a jury that doubts regarding guilt needed to be "grave" or "substantial" to cross the threshold into reasonable doubt. Specifically, the trial judge had instructed the jury as follows:

> It must be such doubt as would give rise to a grave uncertainty. ... A reasonable doubt is not a mere possible doubt. It is an actual substantial doubt. It is a doubt that a reasonable man can seriously entertain. What is required is not an absolute or mathematical certainty, but a moral certainty.

Finding that this instruction created an unfair standard for the defendant, the Supreme Court said, "When [the trial judge's] statements are ... considered with the reference to 'moral certainty,' rather than evidentiary certainty, it becomes clear that a reasonable juror could have interpreted the instruction to allow a finding of guilt based on a degree of proof below that required by the Due Process Clause."

Despite rulings like these, the Court has long afforded leeway to trial judges in how they choose to convey or explain the reasonable doubt standard to a jury. In 1896, for example, the Court said, "The refusal to charge that where there is a probability of innocence, there is a reasonable doubt of guilt is not error when the court has already charged that the jury could not find the defendant guilty unless they were satisfied from the testimony that the crime was established beyond a reasonable doubt."[11] Nearly a century later, Justice Sandra Day O'Connor connected this idea to the concept of due process when she said the following in a 1994 opinion:

> The beyond a reasonable doubt standard is a requirement of due process, but the Constitution neither prohibits trial courts from defining reasonable doubt nor requires them to do so as a matter of course. Indeed, so long as the court instructs the jury on the necessity that the defendant's guilt be proven beyond a reasonable doubt, the Constitution does not require

that any particular form of words be used in advising the jury of the government's burden of proof.[12]

One area in which the reasonable doubt standard retains some pliability is with the use of affirmative defenses, in which the defendant admits to a particular act but denies criminal responsibility for it. In such cases, the burden of proof might shift to the defendant to demonstrate facts that negate culpability. For instance, the defense of entrapment requires defendants to prove they were induced to commit a crime by the police.[13] Likewise, defendants who claim duress must prove that illegal confinement or threats of harm coerced them to do something they would not do otherwise.[14]

The insanity defense provides another example of burden shifting. Under federal law established in the aftermath of John Hinckley's attempted assassination of President Reagan, a defendant "has the burden of proving the defense of insanity by clear and convincing evidence."[15] Moreover, in 2006, the Supreme Court indicated there is no due process violation if a state chooses to place a burden of proof upon a defendant in regard to using an insanity plea—nor is there a due process violation if a state eliminates consideration of an insanity plea altogether.[16] In 2020, the Court upheld insanity standards used in Kansas courts, where it was difficult to raise this defense. Justice Elena Kagan wrote the opinion for a 6–3 majority (with Justices Breyer, Sotomayor, and Ginsburg in dissent). Kagan found there was no due process violation associated with the Kansas standards, saying that would only be a concern when government action "offends some principle of justice so rooted in the traditions and conscience our people as to be ranked as fundamental."[17] In determining the insanity defense did not meet this threshold, Kagan went on to say that "[t]he question is whether a rule of criminal responsibility is so old and venerable—so entrenched in the central values of our legal system—as to prevent a State from ever choosing another." As a parallel, she observed that a 1968 decision of the high Court had allowed Texas to ban the use of chronic alcoholism as an attempted defense for the charge of public drunkenness.[18] Yet if a state tried to deviate from the reasonable doubt standard for guilty verdict, that would certainly run afoul of the rule posited by Kagan.

The Vagueness Doctrine

The Supreme Court has long held that due process requires people to have fair notice regarding what the criminal law prohibits.[19] A vague law violates this requirement and allows for arbitrary, capricious, and

AFFIRMATIVE DEFENSES: Defenses to criminal charges in which the defendant admits to the charged conduct but denies criminal intent.

ENTRAPMENT: An affirmative defense in which the defendant claims to have been induced by law enforcement to commit a crime that the person was not predisposed to commit.

discriminatory law enforcement.[20] Accordingly, the Court continuously has found that an excessively vague law violates due process.[21] Moreover, the vagueness doctrine applies not only to criminal prohibitions but to laws fixing sentences for crimes.[22]

In *Johnson v. United States* (2015),[23] the Supreme Court held that a provision of the federal Armed Career Criminal Act[24] was unconstitutionally vague. The Act mandated a fifteen-year prison sentence for convicted felons in possession of a firearm if they had three prior convictions for violent felonies. The law defined *violent felonies* as, among other things, "conduct that presents a serious potential risk of physical injury to another." Writing for the Court, Justice Antonin Scalia observed that the "indeterminacy" of this clause "denies fair notice to defendants and invites arbitrary enforcement by judges." Similarly, in *Sessions v. Dimaya* (2018),[25] the Court struck down a federal provision authorizing deportation of immigrants who commit "crimes of violence." That law defined a crime of violence as "any other offense that is a felony and that, by its nature, involves a substantial risk that physical force against the person or property of another may be used in the course of committing the offense." [26] Justice Kagan's opinion for the Court concluded that the law "could not be applied with the predictability the Constitution demands." And Justice Gorsuch penned a concurring opinion that opened with the following declaration: "Vague laws invite arbitrary power."

It must be noted that the Supreme Court has, on many occasions, invoked the Due Process Clause of the Fourteenth Amendment to apply the vagueness doctrine to state and local legislation. A couple examples will suffice for this text. An old Cincinnati, Ohio ordinance made it a crime for "three or more persons to assemble ... on any of the sidewalks ... and there conduct themselves in a manner annoying to persons passing by." In *Coates v. City of Cincinnati* (1971),[27] the Court struck down this ordinance, finding that due process was lacking because a person of "common intelligence must necessarily guess at its meaning."[28] The majority opinion written by Justice Potter Stewart declared the following:

> The city is free to prevent people from blocking sidewalks, obstructing traffic, littering streets, committing assaults, or engaging in countless other forms of antisocial conduct. It can do so through the enactment and enforcement of ordinances directed with reasonable specificity toward the conduct to be prohibited. ... It cannot constitutionally do so through the enactment and enforcement of an ordinance whose violation may entirely depend upon whether or not a policeman is annoyed.

In chapter 3, we discussed a Chicago "Gang Congregation Ordinance" that prohibited persons from congregating with a known gang members in public "without an apparent purpose." This was struck down by the Supreme Court in *Chicago v. Morales* (1999),[29] with Justice John Paul Stevens's majority opinion declaring "the freedom to loiter for innocent purposes is part of the 'liberty' protected by the Due Process Clause of the Fourteenth Amendment."[30] Stevens went on to note two reasons vagueness is problematic, first quoting a 1966 Court decision in saying, "It is established that a law fails to meet the requirements of the Due Process Clause if it is so vague and standardless that it leaves the public uncertain as to the conduct it prohibits. ..."[31] Next, he quoted a 1983 Supreme Court ruling in saying, "The broad sweep of the ordinance also violates 'the requirement that a legislature establish minimal guidelines to govern law enforcement.'"[32] In summary, fair notice of what constitutes a crime and safeguards against selective enforcement are paramount in the creation of any statute that defines criminal conduct.

Recusal

The term recusal is used when judges step aside from deciding cases in which they may have a conflict of interest. In 2009, the Supreme Court clarified standards for recusal by saying a judge should step aside if there is a "risk of actual bias," even if there is no tangible evidence of bias.[33] This matter involved a West Virginia judge who ruled on a case concerning a coal company executive from whom the judge had accepted a $3 million campaign donation. The judge's failure to recuse was thus deemed a violation of due process. It is worth noting, however, that there is no rule governing recusal of Supreme Court justices. And in recent years, certain justices have been criticized for their failure to recuse themselves in particular cases.[34]

RECUSAL: A judge's decision not to participate in a particular case based on an actual or perceived conflict of interest.

The Grand Jury

A grand jury is a group of citizens convened for the purpose of deciding whether the government has sufficient evidence to try someone for a criminal offense. Its roots lie deep in the soil of the English common law.[35] The purpose of the grand jury is to provide a check against unwarranted prosecution. Thus, the Fifth Amendment specifies, "No person shall be held to answer for a capital, or otherwise infamous crime, unless on a presentment or indictment of a grand jury. ..."

In *Hurtado v. California* (1884),[36] the Supreme Court held that a grand jury indictment was not essential to due process of law; therefore, the Fifth Amendment grand jury requirement was not made applicable to the states under the Fourteenth Amendment. That decision remains good law today—not because the grand jury is unimportant but because in many jurisdictions it has been supplanted by an alternative charging mechanism that arguably is more protective of the rights of the accused. Under the alternative model, the prosecutor files a charging document called an information. A preliminary hearing is then held to determine whether the information is supported by probable cause.

In federal courts, an indictment by a grand jury is required in felony cases; misdemeanors can be prosecuted by information. A federal grand jury consists of sixteen to twenty-three citizens selected at random from the population of the federal judicial district in which the grand jury is constituted. The maximum term a grand juror may serve is eighteen months. To hand down an indictment, at least twelve jurors must concur that the evidence presented to them provides probable cause to believe a particular person is guilty of a crime. Once indicted, a defendant is

GRAND JURY: A group of citizens convened either to conduct an investigation or determine whether there is sufficient evidence to warrant an indictment against a particular party.

INDICTMENT: A formal criminal charge issued by a grand jury.

INFORMATION: A charging document filed by a prosecutor.

PRELIMINARY HEARING: A hearing to determine whether there is probable cause to hold a defendant for trial.

ARRAIGNMENT:
A defendant's appearance before a trial court for the purpose of pleading to a criminal charge.

subject to immediate arrest (if they are not already in pretrial custody). The next step of the process is the **arraignment**, in which the defendant appears in federal district court to enter a plea with respect to the indictment. Federal law requires an indictment to be filed within thirty days of arrest.[37] The Supreme Court has ruled that an unreasonable delay in the filing of an indictment when a person is already in custody is a violation of due process.[38]

Roughly speaking, about half the states still use a grand jury for felony prosecutions (though the exact number of grand jurors can vary); the other half follow the information/preliminary hearing model. The preliminary hearing is held in open court. The prosecution is obligated to introduce sufficient evidence to convince the presiding judge that the defendant should be bound over for trial. The defense is not required to introduce evidence, but it may cross-examine the government's witnesses.

Grand Jury Secrecy

In stark contrast to preliminary hearings, grand jury sessions are held in secret. In his opinion for the Court in *United States v. Johnson* (1943),[39] Justice Felix Frankfurter spoke of the "indispensable secrecy of grand jury proceedings—as important for the protection of the innocent as for the pursuit of the guilty. ..." However, grand jury proceedings are recorded by a stenographer, and a defendant may be able to gain access to the minutes of the grand jury through a pretrial motion. Pursuant to a 1959 Supreme Court decision, to prevail on such a motion, the defense must "show that 'a particularized need' exists for the minutes which outweighs the policy of secrecy."[40]

Exclusion of Grand Jurors Based on Race

The Supreme Court has long recognized that "it is a denial of the equal protection of the laws to try a defendant of a particular race or color under an indictment issued by a grand jury ... from which all persons of his race or color have, solely because of that race or color, been excluded by the State. ..."[41] To successfully challenge an indictment on this basis, a minority defendant "must show that the procedure employed [in selecting the grand jury] resulted in substantial underrepresentation of his race or of the identifiable group to which he belongs."[42]

Evidence in Grand Jury Proceedings

The rules of evidence that apply to criminal trials do not apply to grand jury proceedings. For example, hearsay evidence is admissible before a grand jury, whereas it normally would not be at trial. In *Costello v. United States* (1956),[43] while upholding the use of hearsay in a grand jury proceedings, the Court adopted a deferential posture with respect to the evidence considered by grand juries. Justice Hugo Black wrote the following:

> If indictments were to be held open to challenge on the ground that there was inadequate or incompetent evidence before the grand jury, the resulting delay would be great indeed. The result of such a rule would be that, before trial on the merits, a defendant could always insist on a kind of preliminary trial to determine the competency and adequacy of the evidence before the grand jury.

This deferential posture was clearly manifest nearly two decades later, when in *United States v. Calandra* (1974),[44] the Court allowed grand juries to consider evidence obtained illegally in violation of the Fourth Amendment. Speaking for the Court, Justice Lewis Powell observed the following:

> Because the grand jury does not finally adjudicate guilt or innocence, it has traditionally been allowed to pursue its investigative and accusatorial functions unimpeded by the evidentiary and procedural restrictions applicable to a criminal trial. Permitting witnesses to invoke the exclusionary rule before a grand jury would precipitate adjudication of issues hitherto reserved for the trial on the merits, and would delay and disrupt grand jury proceedings.

Grand Jury Powers

Grand juries have the power to subpoena witnesses and documents, and a person who fails to honor a grand jury subpoena is subject to being held in contempt. To compel testimony, grand juries can issue use immunity, which means the testimony given by the witness cannot be used against that witness in a criminal prosecution. According to the Supreme Court's decision in *Kastigar v. United States* (1972),[45] the grant of use immunity also means other evidence derived from the immunized testimony cannot be used against the witness; beyond that, *Kastigar* stated that if the government tries to use any evidence against an immunized witness, it carries "the heavy burden of proving that all

USE IMMUNITY: A form of immunity that prohibits the prosecution from using immunized testimony as evidence against the witness.

of the evidence it proposes to use was derived from legitimate independent sources." Another form of immunity, known as **transactional immunity**, immunizes the witness completely with respect to the crime under investigation (and is rarely conferred because it precludes charges related to that crime).

A witness who refuses to cooperate after being granted immunity may be held in contempt. Typically, that would be a civil contempt, in which the witness is jailed until they agree to testify. As the D.C. Circuit has noted, "Under the rule of *Kastigar v. United States*, ... a grant of use immunity under 18 U.S.C. § 6002 enables the government to compel a witness's self-incriminating testimony. This is so because the statute prohibits the government both from using the immunized testimony itself and also from using any evidence derived directly or indirectly therefrom."[46]

> **CIVIL CONTEMPT:**
> A form of contempt in which a person is confined until they agree to comply with the order of a court.

Rights of Witnesses Appearing Before Grand Juries

Witnesses before grand juries can assert their privilege against compulsory self-incrimination and refuse to answer questions that might tend to incriminate them.[47] Even so, as noted above, the assertion of the Fifth Amendment privilege can be overcome by a grant of use immunity. Additionally, witnesses called to appear before grand juries have no right to be represented by counsel.[48] While witnesses before grand juries can invoke established privileges not to testify, including the attorney–client, doctor–patient, and spousal privileges,[49] there is no First Amendment privilege that shields a journalist from answering questions that would require divulging confidential sources.[50] We discuss these privileges in greater detail in chapter 12.

THE CONSTITUTION IN ACTION
Oliver North Wins Immunity-Based Appeal in Iran-Contra Case

In December 1986, Attorney General Edwin Meese appointed an independent counsel (or special prosecutor), named Lawrence Walsh, to investigate an apparent executive branch scandal known as the Iran-Contra affair. The scandal arose during Ronald Reagan's second term as president and allegedly involved high-ranking government officials attempting to fund anti-communist rebels in Nicaragua. The scheme was a convoluted one that allegedly included some or all of the following elements: the United States providing weapons to Israel with the knowledge that the weapons would be sold to Iran; in exchange for the weapons, Iran was to help facilitate the release of U.S. hostages held in Lebanon; the money derived from the weapon sales would be sent by U.S. officials to support the Contras, a Nicaraguan group of militants fighting against the country's pro-communist ruling regime (the Sandinistas). On November 3, 1986, the entire arrangement was revealed by a Beirut, Lebanon newspaper called *Al-Shiraa*.

In the ensuing weeks, Oliver North, a member of the U.S. government's National Security Council, allegedly destroyed documents associated with this Iran-Contra episode. Even after he was fired by President Reagan on

November 25, North apparently acquired government documents through his secretary, Fawn Hall, who allegedly smuggled them to North by hiding them in her clothing. In addition, North allegedly received money from a Swiss bank account in which profits from the weapons sales were kept, with some of those funds diverted to cover the costs of a security system for his home.

To acquire additional information about the scandal, a joint congressional committee investigating the matter granted use immunity to some high-ranking government officials, including North. After North provided his testimony, which was viewed by a nationwide television audience, the special prosecutor in the case brought criminal charges against him. At trial in the U.S. District Court for the District of Columbia, no mention was made of the statements given by North in front of Congress, and a jury found him guilty of three offenses: obstructing an investigation of Congress, destroying government documents, and accepting an illegal gratuity.

However, on appeal, North's attorneys claimed his Fifth Amendment right against self-incrimination had been violated during his criminal trial. Notably, his attorneys suggested North's statements given before Congress—which attained widespread publicity—could have influenced witnesses against him, and possibly even jurors in his case. On July 20, 1990, with the release of its decision in *United States v. Oliver L. North*,[51] the D.C. Circuit found in North's favor, setting aside his convictions. The court's opinion acknowledged, "The Fifth Amendment requires that the government establish priorities before making the immunization decision," adding that "[t]he government must occasionally decide which it values more: immunization … or prosecution. If the government chooses immunization, then it must understand … that it is taking a great chance that the witness cannot constitutionally be indicted or prosecuted."

In May 1991, the Supreme Court refused to hear the government's appeal of the D.C. Circuit's decision in this case, allowing the ruling to stand; in turn, in September of that year, a federal district court judge announced that all charges against North had been dropped at the request of the independent counsel. Ultimately, the Walsh investigation found no wrongdoing on the part of President Reagan, but more than a dozen government officials besides Oliver North were indicted on criminal charges, including Secretary of Defense Casper Weinberger, who faced charges of perjury and obstruction of justice. George H.W. Bush would issue a pardon to Weinberger in 1992 even before a trial commenced. In the end, all other indictments or convictions related to the Iran-Contra affair were vacated by presidential pardons or appellate court rulings.[52]

Double Jeopardy

The Fifth Amendment's Double Jeopardy Clause states "nor shall any person be subject for the same offense to be twice put in jeopardy of life or limb. …" In *Benton v. Maryland* (1969),[53] the Supreme Court said the protection against double jeopardy is "fundamental to the American scheme of justice" and is, therefore, applicable to both federal and state courts. Writing for the Supreme Court in *Green v. United States* (1957),[54] Justice Hugo Black explained the idea underlying the Double Jeopardy Clause, which "is that the State with all its resources and power should not be allowed to make repeated attempts to convict an individual for an alleged offense, thereby subjecting him to embarrassment, expense and ordeal and compelling him to live in a continuing state of anxiety and insecurity, as well as enhancing the possibility that even though innocent he may be found guilty." But what does it mean to be put in jeopardy twice?

It has long been settled that the government may not appeal an acquittal in a criminal case.[55] Similarly, if an appellate court overturns a conviction on the basis of insufficient evidence of guilt, the prosecution is barred from retrying the defendant.[56] However, the government may appeal an adverse ruling on a pretrial motion because the double jeopardy rule does not apply prior to the commencement of a trial.[57] Likewise, in the case of a mistrial (even one resulting from a jury being unable to reach a unanimous verdict), the Double Jeopardy Clause does not prevent a new trial from taking place.[58] Additionally, if the trial judge or an appellate

DOUBLE JEOPARDY: Being tried twice for the same offense.

MISTRIAL: A declaration from a trial judge putting an end to a trial due to a fatal error in procedure or a jury being unable to reach a verdict.

court overturns a guilty verdict as the result of a posttrial motion filed by the defendant, the prosecution may seek to retry the case (possibly without evidence that has been deemed inadmissible).[59]

Multiple Charges for the Same Offense

It is common for prosecutors to charge as many offenses as the facts of a case will support, as this gives the prosecution greater leverage in plea bargaining. But a prosecutor must take care not to charge a defendant with redundant crimes, as this is a form of double jeopardy. In *Blockburger v. United States* (1932),[60] the Court said, "The applicable rule is that, where the same act or transaction constitutes a violation of two distinct statutory provisions, the test to be applied to determine whether there are two offenses or only one is whether each provision requires proof of an additional fact which the other does not." In other words, the *Blockburger* test allows a defendant to be tried for two offenses if each offense includes a unique element. Prosecuting someone for false imprisonment and kidnapping stemming from the same incident would be double jeopardy, as the offense of kidnapping subsumes the crime of false imprisonment. On the other hand, consider a case in which an offender breaks into a home and steals jewelry from a bedroom drawer. In such a case, a prosecution for both burglary and theft would be permissible, as burglary and theft contain distinct elements.

An odd—and tragic—example of this concept arose in 2013 when a man in Dallas, Texas punched his girlfriend, who died seven days later. At first, the Dallas County Medical Examiner was unsure if she had died as a result of the punch or from complications related to her battle with cancer. Police detectives were immediately made aware of the woman's death but did not relay that information in a timely fashion to the local district attorney's office. Thus, prosecutors were initially under the impression that the case involved an assault, and the man was charged with that crime. He quickly pled guilty to a misdemeanor assault charge and received a sentence of 60 days in jail; he was set free after serving 20 days. It was not until six days after his guilty plea that the Dallas County Medical Examiner ruled the death a homicide. By this point, because a guilty plea for assault had been entered, the principle of double jeopardy prevented prosecutors from charging a homicide offense—since the same essential elements of the assault would apply to a correlated homicide case.[61] Had prosecutors waited until the extent of injuries was known, a more serious charge could have applied.

Prosecutions in State and Federal Court for the Same Offense

In our federal system, both the states and the national government are considered to be sovereign. As such, both have the power to enact and enforce criminal laws. In *Abbate v. United States* (1959),[62] the Supreme Court upheld the *separate sovereign* idea by authorizing separate state and federal charges concerning a plot to bomb buildings of the Southern Bell Telephone Company—with some of those buildings bearing a connection to federal agencies and the U.S. military. That same year, in *Bartkus v. Illinois*,[63] the Court upheld dual prosecutions by the state of Illinois and the federal government for the crime of bank robbery.

This idea was reiterated decades later in *Gamble v. United States* (2019),[64] in which the Supreme Court again held that "a crime under one sovereign's laws is not 'the same offence' as a crime under the laws of another sovereign"—with the words "same offence" harkening back to Fifth Amendment's guarantee that "nor shall any person be subject for the same offence to be twice put in jeopardy of life or limb." Therefore, the federal government and a state can prosecute a defendant successively for the same offense because each offense is considered to fall under *separate sovereigns*. This practice is relatively rare, though, because many state-level offenses do not have a counterpart in federal law. For example, there is no federal traffic code; enforcement of the rules of the road is left to state and local authorities. However, with the recent proliferation of federal crimes, the opportunities for state and federal prosecutions for the same offense have grown considerably. In the *Gamble* case, for example, the state of Alabama prosecuted the defendant for possessing a firearm as a convicted felon. The Supreme Court allowed a successive federal prosecution under a similar federal prohibition.

JURISPRUDENCE

Double Jeopardy Controversy Reaches the High Court
Gamble v. United States, 587 U.S. ___ (2019)

In November 2015, a man named Terance Martez Gamble was pulled over in Mobile, Alabama for driving with a damaged headlight. The officer who initiated the stop claimed to smell marijuana, using that as probable cause to search the vehicle; inside, he found drugs and a loaded 9-mm handgun. Gamble had a prior conviction for second-degree robbery in Alabama, and because this previous conviction was for a crime of violence, he was charged under state law for being a felon in possession of a firearm. He pled guilty and was given a ten-year prison sentence—but the judge said that nine years would be "suspended," effectively resulting in a punishment of one year's incarceration.

Federal prosecutors, perhaps feeling that this sentence was too lenient, also brought a similar case under a federal law that bans felons from possessing a firearm. Gamble's lawyers filed a motion to dismiss that federal indictment based on the principle of double jeopardy. The U.S. District Court for the Southern District of Alabama denied this motion, based upon the dual sovereignty doctrine, noting that the state of Alabama and the United States qualify as being separate sovereigns. On appeal, the U.S. Court of Appeals for the Eleventh Circuit upheld the District Court's denial of the motion to dismiss, and the Supreme Court granted certiorari. Distilling the importance of this case in anticipation of the high Court's decision, an article in *The Atlantic* posed a headline that read, "A Supreme Court Case Could Liberate Trump to Pardon His Associates."[65] In essence, the article contended that if the Supreme Court overturned the lower courts in this case, such a ruling would topple the basic principles of federalism upon which the country was founded.

But in a 7–2 decision, the Supreme Court affirmed the lower courts and said the principle of double jeopardy was not violated by dual criminal prosecutions for being a felon in possession of a firearm. In his majority opinion for a 7–2 Court, Justice Samuel Alito stated

(continued)

that the dual sovereignty doctrine emerges from the U.S. Constitution's structure and rests upon long-standing case precedent. Alito observed that "while our system of federalism is fundamental to the protection of liberty, it does not always maximize individual liberty at the expense of other interests." He added, "Gamble asks us to overrule the dual-sovereignty doctrine. He contends that it departs from the founding-era understanding of the right enshrined by the Double Jeopardy Clause. But the historical evidence assembled by Gamble is feeble; pointing the other way are the Clause's text, other historical evidence, and 170 years of precedent."

In dissent, Justice Ruth Bader Ginsburg declared, "The separate-sovereigns doctrine ... has been subject to relentless criticism by members of the bench, bar, and academy. Nevertheless, the Court reaffirms the doctrine, thereby diminishing the individual rights shielded by the Double Jeopardy Clause." Writing a separate dissent, Justice Neil Gorsuch stated, "A free society does not allow its government to try the same individual for the same crime until it's happy with the result." Implicit in both of these dissents was the idea that a proliferation of federal criminal statutes makes dual prosecutions more likely than in past eras, where case precedent supporting dual sovereignty was carved. Yet in response to this concern, Justice Alito's majority opinion argued, "Eliminating the dual-sovereignty rule would do little to trim the reach of federal criminal law, and it would not even prevent many successive state and federal prosecutions for the same criminal conduct unless we also overruled the long-settled rule that an 'offence' for double jeopardy purposes is defined by statutory elements, not by what might be described in a looser sense as a unit of criminal conduct."

Finally, there have been some unique contexts in which the notion of dual sovereignty has come under review. In 2020, for instance, the U.S. Court of Appeals for the Armed Forces addressed the case of Tim Hennis, who had been found not guilty of murder in a North Carolina court—only to later be found guilty of the same murder in a military court-martial.[66] In this instance, the military appeals court said there was no violation of the Double Jeopardy Clause, ostensibly because the military exists as an extension of the federal government, and thus amounts to a separate sovereign distinct from the states.

However, in a 2016 decision, the Supreme Court noted that Puerto Rico (as a territory, distinct from a state) and the United States do not represent separate sovereigns.[67] In this case, the majority opinion by Justice Kagan cited a 1937 Court decision, saying that because "the territorial and federal laws [were] creations emanating from the same sovereignty ... federal and territorial prosecutors 'd[o] not derive their powers to prosecute from independent sources of authority.'"[68]

In 2022, the Supreme Court also ruled that the Double Jeopardy Clause does not prohibit prosecutions in both a Tribal court and a federal district court for the same criminal act. This principle applies even if the Tribal court is one created through the Code of Federal Regulations (see chapter 2 for further discussion of Tribal courts.) Justice Amy Coney Barrett's majority opinion relied upon the idea that Tribal courts and federal courts are "separate sovereigns," and beyond that, she observed that a Tribal court and a federal district court address distinctly different offenses, even if those offenses arise from a singular action or omission.[69]

Compulsory Self-Incrimination

The protection against compulsory self-incrimination is among the most important rights of persons accused of crimes. We tend to associate the Fifth Amendment privilege with a criminal trial in which the defendant refuses to take the witness stand or, if they do, refuses to answer certain questions on the ground that the answers would tend to be incriminating. If the defendant *takes the Fifth*, as the expression goes, neither the judge nor the prosecutor is permitted to tell the jury that the defendant's silence may be construed as an admission of guilt.[70] Of course, jurors may draw this conclusion anyway.

The privilege not to testify extends beyond this classic scenario. In a criminal trial, it is not only the defendant who enjoys the right not to answer self-incriminating questions; any witness may exercise the privilege. After all, it is common that witnesses in criminal trials have some degree of criminal involvement themselves—if not in the specific case bring prosecuted, then in other criminal activities.

The privilege not to make incriminating statements also extends beyond the criminal trial. It applies to grand jury proceedings, pretrial hearings, agency investigations, legislative investigations, and even civil trials. Moreover, the freedom from self-incrimination applies not only "to answers that would in themselves support a conviction ... but likewise embraces those which would furnish a link in the chain of evidence needed to prosecute the claimant."[71] In 1892, the Supreme Court commented on the broad scope of the privilege:

> The meaning of the constitutional provision is not merely that a person shall not be compelled to be a witness against himself in a criminal prosecution against himself, but its object is to insure that a person shall not be compelled, when acting as a witness in any investigation, to give testimony which may tend to show that he himself has committed a crime.[72]

Four years later, in *Brown v. Walker* (1896),[73] the Supreme Court confronted the case of a man who was held in contempt of court after refusing to answer questions in front of a federal grand jury—questions that might have incriminated him in a federal crime. Ordering this man released from custody, the Court relied upon the Fifth Amendment's Self-Incrimination Clause to say, "So deeply did the iniquities of the ancient system impress themselves upon the minds of the American colonists that the States, with one accord, made a denial of the right to question an accused person a part of their fundamental law, so that a maxim which in England was a mere rule of evidence became clothed in this country with the impregnability of a constitutional enactment."

Incorporation of the Self-Incrimination Clause

In *Malloy v. Hogan* (1964),[74] a man was kept in jail for contempt of court because he refused to answer questions posed by a court-appointed *referee*, who was conducting an inquiry into illegal gambling in a particular county. Prior to this case, the constitutional protection against compulsory self-incrimination had not been applied to the state courts. Recognizing the fundamental character of this protection, the Supreme Court held that the Self-Incrimination Clause is applicable to the state courts. Justice William Brennan's opinion for the Court asserted that "[t]he Fourteenth Amendment secures against state invasion the same privilege that the Fifth Amendment guarantees against federal infringement—the right of a person to remain silent unless he chooses to speak in the unfettered exercise of his own will, and to suffer no penalty ... for such silence." Justice Brennan also stated, "Governments, state and federal, are thus constitutionally compelled to establish guilt by evidence independently and freely secured, and may not, by coercion, prove a charge against an accused out of his own mouth."

Laws Requiring People to Incriminate Themselves

The Supreme Court has held that the Self-Incrimination Clause prohibits the enactment of laws that require persons to report information that places them in jeopardy of prosecution. In *Marchetti v. United States* (1968),[75] the Court struck down a federal statute that required gamblers to register and pay a tax on what was then illegal income, saying compliance with the law would have the "direct and unmistakable consequence of incriminating" persons. Likewise, in *Haynes v. United States*, decided that same year,[76] the Court held that Congress could not make it a crime to fail to register an illegal firearm. And a year later, in *Leary v. United States* (1969),[77] the Court invalidated a provision of the Marihuana Tax Act of 1937 that required payment of a tax when a person purchased marijuana illegally. Speaking for the Court in *Leary*, Justice John M. Harlan (the younger) concluded that compliance with the law would identify a person as a member of a "selective group inherently suspect of criminal activities."

Police Interrogations and Incriminating Statements

In *Bram v. United States* (1897),[78] the Supreme Court first held that an involuntary confession violates the Self-Incrimination Clause. The case involved a sailor who was placed in irons, strip searched, and interrogated after being accused of several murders aboard a ship. Justice Edward White, speaking for the Court, determined "an influence was exerted, and, as any doubt as to whether the confession was voluntary must be determined in favor of the accused, we cannot escape the conclusion that error was committed by the trial court in admitting the confession under the circumstances disclosed by the record." Justice White concluded that "in the courts of the United States, wherever a question arises whether a confession is incompetent because not voluntary, the issue is controlled by that portion of the Fifth Amendment to the Constitution of the United States commanding that no person 'shall be compelled in any criminal case to be a witness against himself.'"

Bram was a federal case, and as noted above, it was not until *Malloy v. Hogan* (1964) that the Court extended the Self-Incrimination Clause to the state courts. In the interim, the Court adopted a broad due process approach that accorded substantial deference to state and local police with respect to the interrogation of suspects.[79] Nonetheless, in extreme cases involving beatings of suspects[80] or protracted interrogation,[81] the Court disallowed confessions that were deemed involuntary and, hence, unreliable. We provide details on several of these cases in the following section.

Prompt Presentment

As we discussed in chapter 10, the Supreme Court has said, in the aftermath of a warrantless arrest, there must be "prompt presentment" of the accused in front of a judge or magistrate, typically within 48 hours.[82] Federal Rules of Criminal Procedure actually stipulate any arrestee to be brought before a magistrate judge or state or local judicial officer "without unnecessary delay."[83] Moreover, the confluence of two Supreme Court cases from the 1940s and 1950s[84] has yielded the *McNabb–Mallory* rule, which indicates that if an unreasonable delay occurs, a confession given while a suspect awaits their first appearance in court is inadmissible. A 2009 decision from the Court found that this rule applies even if a confession is given voluntarily.[85] However, federal law does permit a jury to decide that a confession made within six hours of an arrest should be admissible.[86]

Early Approaches to Confessions and Due Process

A line of Supreme Court decisions traversing the late 1800s through the early 1960s made use of the Due Process Clause—from the Fourteenth Amendment, since these cases all concerned state action—in placing limits upon coercive tactics used by government officials when extracting confessions from suspected criminals. This line of cases began with *Hopt v. Utah* (1884),[87] where Justice John M. Harlan (the elder) extolled the importance of common law principles that called for the exclusion of confessions derived via threats of harm. In this case, Harlan's majority opinion granted that "[a] confession, if freely and voluntarily made, is evidence of the most satisfactory character," before adding the following caveat:

> But the presumption upon which weight is given to such evidence, namely, that one who is innocent will not imperil his safety or prejudice his interests by an untrue statement, ceases when the confession appears to have been made either in consequence of inducements of a temporal nature, ... or because of a threat or promise by or in the presence of such person, which, operating upon the fears or hopes of the accused, in reference to the charge, deprive him of that freedom of will or self-control essential to make his confession voluntary within the meaning of the law.

More than three decades would pass before the next major confession-related decision from the high Court, with a 1936 case addressing some of the most abhorrent practices ever used in the acquisition of a confession in the United States. In *Brown v. Mississippi* (1936),[88] a Black suspect was taken to the home of an alleged murder victim by sheriff's deputies and then was subjected to physical torture at the hands of a mob, which included the man being tied to a tree and whipped, then repeatedly hanged. In fact, at the trial, rope marks around this man's neck were still visible. Two other suspects in the case were taken to a police station, where they were stripped and laid upon chairs, at which point they were beaten across their backs with a leather strap that had buckles on it. Describing the "solemn farce of ... the free and voluntary confessions" that were acquired by sheriffs in this case, the majority opinion from Chief Justice Charles Evans Hughes derided the police use of "compulsion by torture to extort a confession." Hughes even pejoratively referred to "so-called confessions" and a "so-called trial" as he declared that the convictions were to be overturned.

Four years later, in *Chambers v. Florida* (1940),[89] the Court addressed confessions derived not from physical torture but, rather, from extended periods of interrogation—or, perhaps, from "psychological pressure." In this case, a murder investigation led authorities to take nearly forty Black men into custody, with four of them subjected to five consecutive days of interrogation—with no contact allowed from any outsiders or attorneys—leading up to an all-night questioning at the end of the fifth day. The questioning took place in a small room, with a suspect surrounded by four to ten officers. Even without physical coercion, this was deemed to be a violation of due process principles, with Justice Black offering some of the most compelling reasons the Court has ever provided for suppressing coerced confessions:

> The testimony of centuries, in governments of varying kinds over populations of different races and beliefs, stood as proof that physical and mental torture and coercion had brought about the tragically unjust sacrifices of some who were the noblest and most useful of their generations. The rack, the thumbscrew, the wheel, solitary confinement, protracted questioning and cross questioning, and other ingenious forms of entrapment of the helpless or unpopular had left their wake of mutilated bodies and shattered minds along the way to the cross, the guillotine, the stake and the hangman's noose. And they who have suffered most from secret and dictatorial proceedings have almost always been the poor, the ignorant, the numerically weak, the friendless, and the powerless.

Later, in Ashcraft v Tennessee (1944),[90] Justice Black would again address psychological forms of coercion. In this case, the suspected criminal was subjected to thirty-six hours of constant questioning with no rest, and he also had a blinding light directed toward his face during the interrogation. Determining that the inquisitory techniques at hand were a violation of the Due Process Clause of the Fourteenth Amendment, Justice Black presented an eloquent argument in saying:

> We think a situation such as that here shown by uncontradicted evidence is so inherently coercive that its very existence is irreconcilable with the possession of mental freedom by a lone suspect against whom its full coercive force is brought to bear. It is inconceivable that any court of justice in the land, conducted as our courts are, open to the public, would permit prosecutors serving in relays to keep a defendant witness under continuous cross-examination for thirty-six hours without rest or sleep in an effort to extract a 'voluntary' confession. Nor can we, consistently with Constitutional due process of law, hold voluntary a confession where prosecutors do the same thing away from the restraining influences of a public trial in an open courtroom.

Justice Black went on to declare that "[t]he Constitution of the United States stands as a bar against the conviction of any individual in an American court by means of a coerced confession."

Two similar cases arose five years later, with Justice Frankfurter writing the majority opinions for both—each time using the concept of due process to negate a confession acquired by a lengthy interrogation. A key factor in these cases was that the suspects were not brought before a judge in a timely fashion after their arrests. In *Turner v. Pennsylvania* (1949),[91] the Court ruled in favor of a suspect who was "interrogated by relays of police officers, sometimes during both the day and the night" over a period of five consecutive days in which he was denied an appearance in court and denied visitation by friends or attorneys. And in *Watts v. Indiana* (1949),[92] the Court found in favor of a man who was held for six days without an arraignment in court; he was kept in solitary confinement for the first two days and then spent part of the next three days being driven around for hours in a car with police officers. Justice Frankfurter's opinion declared that when a confession "is the product of sustained pressure by the police, it does not issue from a free choice." He went on to describe the impact of an unrelenting interrogation that occurs in the absence of a court appearance as follows:

> When a suspect speaks because he is overborne, it is immaterial whether he has been subjected to a physical or a mental ordeal. ... We would have to shut our minds to the plain significance of what here transpired to deny that this was a calculated endeavor to secure a confession through the pressure of unrelenting interrogation. The very relentlessness of such interrogation implies that it is better for the prisoner to answer than to persist in the refusal of disclosure, which is his constitutional right. ... This ... violates the underlying principle in our enforcement of the criminal law. Ours is the accusatorial, as opposed to the inquisitorial, system.

This decision helped cement a line of cases invalidating psychological pressure, or what Justice Frankfurter called a "mental ordeal," as a means of extracting confessions.

This line of cases also included a decision that employed due process to protect the rights of juveniles who find themselves subject to police interrogation. In *Haley v. Ohio* (1948),[93] a 15-year-old boy accused of murder was questioned from midnight to 5 a.m. following his arrest, without being given access to any friends, family, or legal counsel. Officers did hand him a piece of paper that said, "We want to inform you of your constitutional rights, the law gives you the right to make this statement or not as you see fit. It is made with the understanding that it may be used at a trial in court. ..." The boy eventually confessed to the crime, and at trial, a judge instructed the jurors to disregard the confession if they felt it was not voluntary. Justice William O. Douglas wrote for the Supreme Court in overturning the boy's conviction, finding that even though a written disclaimer and jury instruction were implemented, those safeguards were insufficient. Justice Douglas summarized the matter by saying:

> [W]e are told that this boy was advised of his constitutional rights before he signed the confession and that, knowing them, he nevertheless confessed. That assumes, however, that a boy of fifteen, without aid of counsel, would have a full appreciation of that advice, and that, on the facts of this record, he had a freedom of choice. We cannot indulge those assumptions. ... Formulas of respect for constitutional safeguards cannot prevail over the facts of life which contradict them. They may not become a cloak for inquisitorial practices and make an empty form of the due process of law for which free men fought and died to obtain.

The Warren Court's Approach to Police Interrogation

In 1957, the Supreme Court, under new Chief Justice Earl Warren, signaled an even higher level of judicial scrutiny for confessions extracted by state and local police. Specifically, the Warren Court produced a line of cases that addressed interrogations of individuals with mental deficiencies. In *Fikes v. Alabama* (1957),[94] for instance, the Court examined the case of a high school dropout named William Fikes, described in the majority opinion as "certainly of low mentality, if not mentally ill." Fikes, who was suspected in a series of burglaries and sexual assaults, was kept largely in isolation over the course of ten days in confinement, following a citizen's arrest, and he was subjected to periods of questioning that resulted in two confessions elicited five days apart—both given prior to any court appearance. Reviewing this matter, the Court noted that, even without *physical brutality*, due process principles were vitiated. Interestingly, Chief Justice Warren's majority opinion invoked the *totality of circumstances* approach commonly used in Fourth Amendment cases, saying, "The totality of the circumstances that preceded the confessions in this case goes beyond the allowable limits. The use of the confessions secured in this setting was a denial of due process."

One year after the *Fikes* decision, in *Payne v. Arkansas* (1958),[95] the Court invalidated a confession given by a man with a fifth-grade grade education, who had been held for three days without any counsel, was deprived of food and water, and was told by a police chief that thirty or forty people who "wanted to get him" would be at the station "in a few minutes." Justice Whittaker's majority opinion was clear in noting that the due process clause indicated the following: "The use in a state criminal trial of a defendant's confession obtained by coercion—whether physical or mental—is forbidden by the Fourteenth Amendment." A critical rationale arose when Whittaker foreclosed the state's argument that appellate courts should not be examining the validity of confessions, with Whittaker stating that "where the claim is that the prisoner's confession is the product of coercion, we are bound to make our own examination of the record to determine whether the claim is meritorious."[96] He also cited *Watts v. Indiana*, noting that due process protected against "torture of the mind as well as body" because "the will is as much affected by fear as by force."[97] An important aspect of the *Payne* decision was that even if other evidence exists to suggest a defendant is guilty, the presence of a coerced confession taints an entire trial. Justice Whittaker spoke to this point by saying, "[W]here, as here, a coerced confession constitutes a part of the evidence before the jury and a general verdict is returned, no one can say what credit and weight the jury gave to the confession."

One year later, the Court's analysis shifted to an individual with a junior high education who had a history of emotional problems. He was subjected to eight hours of continuous questioning by police, without the presence of counsel—despite his repeated requests for such assistance. In *Spano v. New York* (1959),[98] Chief Justice Warren wrote for the Court, which suppressed the confession, and offered the following declaration:

> The abhorrence of society to the use of involuntary confessions does not turn alone on their inherent untrustworthiness. It also turns on the deep-rooted feeling that the police must obey the law while enforcing the law; that, in the end, life and liberty can be as much endangered from illegal methods used to convict those thought to be criminals as from the actual criminals themselves.

Subsequently, in *Blackburn v. Alabama* (1960),[99] a man with a "permanent mental disability" (believed to be schizophrenia) was subjected to an interrogation lasting up to nine hours in a "small room which was at times filled with police officers"; he ultimately signed a confession that was written for him by a deputy sheriff. Once again, a majority opinion from Chief Justice Warren found an "egregious" due process violation, with Warren using the word "remote" to describe "the chances of the confession's having been the product of a rational intellect and a free will." The Chief Justice rejected the state's contention that the voluntariness of a confession could only be challenged in pretrial motions, stating, "Where the involuntariness of a confession is conclusively demonstrated at any stage of a trial, the defendant is deprived of due process by entry of judgment of conviction without exclusion of the confession."

The end of the high Court's early line of confession-related due process cases arrived with *Haynes v. Washington* (1963),[100] where a man was interrogated for sixteen hours as police repeatedly denied his requests to call his wife; officers even indicated he would not be allowed to speak with her until he signed a confession. Justice Arthur Goldberg's majority opinion found a "denial of due process of law" in this situation, stating,

Obiter Dicta

"Of course, detection and solution of crime is at best, a difficult and arduous task requiring determination and persistence on the part of all responsible officers charged with the duty of law enforcement. And certainly we do not mean to suggest that all interrogation of witnesses and suspects is impermissible. Such questioning is undoubtedly an essential tool in effective law enforcement. The line between proper and permissible police conduct and techniques and methods offensive to due process is, at best, a difficult one to draw, particularly in cases such as this, where it is necessary to make fine judgments as to the effect of psychologically coercive pressures and inducements on the mind and will of an accused. But we cannot escape the demands of judging or of making the difficult appraisals inherent in determining whether constitutional rights have been violated. We are here impelled to the conclusion, from all of the facts presented, that the bounds of due process have been exceeded."

—Justice Arthur Goldberg, writing for the Supreme Court in Haynes v. Washington, *373 U.S. 503 (1963)*

"We cannot blind ourselves to what experience unmistakably teaches: that, even apart from the express threat, the basic techniques present here—the secret and incommunicado detention and interrogation—are devices adapted and used to extort confessions from suspects." Yet Justice Goldberg would go on to offer advice for police regarding the value of confessions in general (see the box on previous page).

In the years that followed, the Court would adopt a dramatically different approach to confessions, especially after the incorporation of the Self-Incrimination Clause. The Warren Court indicated that custodial interrogation is inherently coercive and adopted prophylactic measures to protect suspects against coerced self-incrimination. In *Escobedo v. Illinois* (1964),[101] the Court recognized the right to have counsel present during interrogation. Justice Arthur Goldberg's opinion for the Court clearly manifested the Warren Court's greater solicitude for the rights of the accused. According to Justice Goldberg:

> [N]o system of criminal justice can, or should, survive if it comes to depend for its continued effectiveness on the citizens' abdication through unawareness of their constitutional rights. No system worth preserving should have to fear that, if an accused is permitted to consult with a lawyer, he will become aware of, and exercise, these rights. If the exercise of constitutional rights will thwart the effectiveness of a system of law enforcement, then there is something very wrong with that system.

The Landmark *Miranda* Decision

Protections for the rights of an accused criminal reached their zenith in the best-known criminal justice decision of the Warren era: *Miranda v. Arizona* (1966).[102] As everyone who has watched a TV crime drama knows, the *Miranda* decision requires police to advise suspects who have been taken into custody of their right to remain silent and their right to have counsel present during questioning. Failure to provide the *Miranda warnings* will (normally) result in the suppression of a confession from evidence at trial. The typical form of the *Miranda* warnings is as follows:

> You have the right to remain silent. Anything you say can and will be used against you in a court of law. You have the right to an attorney. If you cannot afford an attorney, one will be provided for you.

CUSTODIAL INTERROGATION: A situation in which police ask questions of a suspect who is not free to leave; generally, this condition of being in custody serves as a prerequisite for the reading of *Miranda* rights.

MIRANDA WARNINGS: Stemming from the Supreme Court's decision in *Miranda v. Arizona* (1966), these warnings are given by police to individuals who are taken into custody before they are interrogated. Persons being taken into custody are advised they have the right to remain silent, to have a lawyer present during questioning, and anything they say can and will be used against them in a court of law.

For the *Miranda* decision, the Supreme Court actually combined the case of Ernesto Miranda with three other similar cases from different parts of the country.[103] (Miranda's name was listed on the case because his name came first alphabetically.) Although the facts connected to Miranda's questioning receive the bulk of attention from legal scholars, Chief Justice Warren's opinion for a 5–4 majority made an observation about all four cases that were consolidated, noting they shared the following trait: "incommunicado interrogation of individuals in a police-dominated atmosphere."

Miranda's crimes were serious; he kidnapped and sexually assaulted an 18-year-old woman, grabbing her from a street in Phoenix, Arizona and forcing her into his car. There are conflicting reports about how he was identified as a suspect, but all versions indicate the car used in the attack was spotted by some member of the victim's family—a brother, cousin, or brother-in-law—who was acting upon the description and license plate provided by the victim. The car was traced to a woman who shared an apartment with her boyfriend, Ernesto Miranda. Police then asked Miranda to come to the station for voluntary questioning, and he complied. He was placed in a lineup with three men of similar height (but he was the only one wearing glasses), and the victim said that Miranda most resembled her attacker, but she could not make a definitive identification. Even so, police then told Miranda he had been positively identified, and he was placed under arrest.

Next, for a period of approximately two hours, he was subjected to questioning. At one point, the victim was brought into the room, and Miranda was asked if she was the person he attacked; he admitted she was the victim. After verbally revealing details of the crime that matched the victim's account, Miranda agreed to write a confession. Police provided the form upon which the confession was to be written, which included a disclaimer that the department had placed atop the first page, reading: "I ... do hereby swear that I make this statement voluntarily and of my own free will, with no threats, coercion, or promises of immunity, and with full knowledge of my legal rights, understanding any statement I make may be used against me." Below this warning, Miranda wrote a full confession in cursive script on one page of lined paper, beginning his admission by saying, "Seen a girl walking up the street. Overall, no physical coercion was used to elicit the confession, and the Maricopa County Superior Court admitted the statements into evidence. A jury found him guilty. Miranda's trial lawyer, Alvin Moore, appealed to the Arizona Supreme Court, which, in April 1965, upheld the conviction, finding no constitutional violation.

At this point, an ACLU lawyer named Robert Corcoran sought to assist in Miranda's appeal, and he solicited the assistance of noted Arizona trial attorney John Flynn. Flynn enlisted the help of John Frank, a well-known constitutional lawyer, and together, they appealed to the U.S. Supreme Court, asking the justices to clarify the scope of the ruling in *Escobedo v. Illinois*. Under that decision, police were permitted to question a suspect as a part of a "general inquiry into an unsolved crime," but when an investigation began to "focus on a particular suspect," the calculus shifted if a suspect had "been taken into police custody, [and] the police carr[ied] out a process of interrogations [aimed at] eliciting incriminating statements." In particular, the Court indicated that a constitutional violation occurs when "the suspect has requested and been denied an opportunity to consult with his lawyer, and the police have not effectively warned him of his absolute constitutional right to remain silent."[104]

Ultimately, in response to arguments put forth by attorneys Flynn and Frank using the *Escobedo* precedent, the Supreme Court ruled in Miranda's favor, finding that even with the disclaimer printed on his confession form, his Fifth and Sixth Amendment rights had been violated because he had not been specifically informed of his right to remain silent and his right to have a lawyer present during questioning. The majority opinion for the *Miranda* decision said, "Unless adequate protective devices are employed to dispel the compulsion inherent in custodial surroundings, no statement obtained from the defendant can truly be the product of his free choice." Chief Justice Warren went on to observe the following:

> [W]ithout proper safeguards the process of in-custody interrogation of persons suspected or accused of crime contains inherently compelling pressures which work to undermine the individual's will to resist and to compel him to speak where he would not otherwise do so freely. In order to combat these pressures and to permit a full opportunity to exercise the privilege against self-incrimination, the accused must be adequately and effectively apprised of his rights and the exercise of those rights must be fully honored.

This was a controversial ruling at the time, and some felt it would place an unnecessary burden on police officers around the country. In fact, a 1966 *New York Times* headline captured this sentiment by saying: "Miranda Decision Said to End the Effective Use of Confessions."[105] In spite of this dire pronouncement, though, people in contemporary American society have come to view *Miranda* rights as a commonplace component of police practices—and confessions do in fact remain a widely-used part of the criminal justice process. Of course, so do false confessions; just one year after the *Miranda* decision, for instance, the Supreme Court vacated a murder conviction based on a confession extracted after a police officer held a gun to a suspect's head and threatened to shoot him if he did not admit to the crime.[106]

In regard to what occurs when a confession is deemed inadmissible (whether by a trial judge or an appellate court), it is important to recognize that an accused criminal will not necessarily have the charges against them dismissed. Of course, any incriminating statements the defendant made while confessing are likely to be deemed inadmissible in court if a person is not read *Miranda* rights, but the prosecution can still proceed with other evidence. As an example, after the Supreme Court ruled in Ernesto Miranda's favor on June 13, 1966, he was still subjected to a second criminal trial in Phoenix. For the second trial, his confession was not admissible; nevertheless, in October 1967, a jury found him guilty based on other evidence, and the trial judge sentenced him to 20–30 years in prison. He was granted parole in 1972, only to be reincarcerated on a parole violation and then released again in December 1975. Just over a month later, on January 31, 1976, he was stabbed and killed when a fight broke out during a card game inside a bar in Phoenix called The Deuce. Police officers who arrived on the scene of Ernesto Miranda's murder actually would read *Miranda* warnings to two men who were there, and both men were freed after questioning. Nobody was ever convicted in this murder. Lying near Miranda's body when he died were *Miranda* cards, items he created with his picture on one side and the *Miranda* rights typed on the other side.

The *Miranda* decision brought about intense criticism of the Court for *coddling criminals*, especially from within the law enforcement community. However, as police training evolved, *Mirandizing* suspects soon became standard operating procedure. Today, the law enforcement community by and large supports the *Miranda* decision. In reaffirming the *Miranda* decision in *Dickerson v. United States* (2000),[107] the Supreme Court noted that "*Miranda* has become embedded in routine police practice to the point where the warnings have become part of our national culture."

Of course, like so many Supreme Court decisions, *Miranda* raised a host of new questions for the courts. We turn now to some of the most important of those questions.

How Does a Suspect Invoke the Right to Remain Silent?

In his majority opinion in *Miranda*, Chief Justice Warren stated, "If the individual indicates in any manner, at any time prior to or during questioning, that he wishes to remain silent, the interrogation must cease." But a key question remained salient for nearly five decades: exactly how does a suspected criminal properly indicate to police that desire to remain silent?

In *Berghuis v. Thompkins* (2010),[108] the Supreme Court clarified how a suspect should invoke the desire to remain silent. In this case, lawyers for the accused claimed he had remained "mostly silent" during the course of a three-hour murder interrogation, and thus, they argued, the interrogation should have been halted due to his reticence. The Supreme Court disagreed. Justice Kennedy's majority opinion quoted the *Miranda* decision in observing, "Thompkins did not say that he wanted to remain silent or that he did not want to talk with the police. Had he made either of these simple, unambiguous statements, he would have invoked his 'right to cut off questioning.'" The key word in this quote is *unambiguous*, as Justice Kennedy stated that any attempt at invoking the right to remain silent should meet that baseline threshold.

JURISPRUDENCE

Must a Person Speak to Invoke the Right to Remain Silent?
Berghuis v. Thompkins, 560 U.S. 370 (2010)

In this case, a man named Van Chester Thompkins was suspected of taking part in a drive-by shooting at a mall in Southfield, Michigan. One man died in the shooting, and another man was injured. Police located Mr. Thompkins in Ohio more than a year after the shooting, and he was brought to a police station for questioning in an 8 × 10-foot room, where he was seated at a desk similar to those found in schools.

After being advised of his *Miranda* rights, Thompkins was interrogated by detectives for a period of approximately three hours. The Supreme Court's opinion indicated he was "largely silent" but did give "a few limited verbal responses," which were described as primarily being "yeah," "no," or "I don't know." He also nodded his head at times in response to questions, and he gave a verbal declaration to indicate he did not "want a peppermint" presented by an officer as well as saying the chair he was "sitting in was hard."

At two hours and forty-five minutes into the interrogation, a detective asked, "Do you believe in God?" Thompkins responded by saying, "Yes," as tears began to fill his eyes. He was then asked, "Do you pray to God?" to which he again responded "Yes." Next, the detective asked, "Do you pray to God to forgive you for shooting that boy down?" Once again, Thompkins said, "Yes." The interrogation concluded soon after, and Thompkins was charged with first-degree murder. At trial, his responses to these questions were conveyed to jurors, and he ultimately was found guilty.

On appeal, his lawyers contended that Thompkins's relative silence in response to most questions posed by detectives should have been interpreted as evincing a desire to remain silent and, thus, ended the interrogation. The Supreme Court disagreed, finding that Thompkins had not *unambiguously* invoked his right to remain silent. Explaining why any attempt to invoke this right must be unambiguous, Justice Kennedy said, "There is good reason to require an accused who wants to invoke his or her right to remain silent to do so unambiguously. A requirement of an unambiguous invocation of *Miranda* rights results in an objective inquiry that 'avoid[s] difficulties of proof and ... provide[s] guidance to officers' on how to proceed in the face of ambiguity." That passage cited *Davis v. United States* (1994),[109] which we will discuss in the next chapter, as it pertains to the request for a lawyer.

Furthermore, considering an alternative to this standard and the burden it would place on police, Justice Kennedy said, "If an ambiguous act, omission, or statement could require police to end the interrogation, police would be required to make difficult decisions about an accused's unclear intent and face the consequence of suppression 'if they guess wrong.' Suppression of a voluntary confession in these circumstances would place a significant burden on society's interest in prosecuting criminal activity."

Some observers wondered if this decision meant a suspect would have to verbally declare they wished to remain silent—an ironic requirement. Even so, alternative means for clearly expressing that choice could be envisioned, such as communication through written word or sign language. Literally remaining silent, though, is not considered a clear enough method for doing so in unambiguous fashion.

A controversy related to literal silence arose in *Salinas v. Texas* (2013),[110] in which a suspect in two homicides voluntarily agreed to accompany officers to a police station for questioning. He was not read *Miranda* rights prior to questioning and was free to go at any time. Police asked him a number of questions over the course of a one-hour interrogation, most of which he answered. However, when officers asked whether shotgun shells found at a crime scene would match a gun recovered from his home, he did not answer and was said to have "[l]ooked down at the floor, shuffled his feet, bit his bottom lip, clenched his hands in his lap, [and] began to tighten up"; after "a few moments of silence," an officer asked other questions, which Salinas answered.

At trial, the jury heard testimony about how Salinas had gone silent in response to the key question about his gun. He did not testify during the trial and was found guilty—with the judge sentencing him to twenty years in prison. The Supreme Court granted cert. in this case, with the majority opinion observing that lower courts had previously offered conflicting perspectives on the question of whether silence in a noncustodial interrogation could be used against a defendant in a criminal trial.[111]

In a 5–4 decision, the high Court found there was no constitutional violation in this case. Justice Alito wrote for the Court, saying, "To prevent the privilege from shielding information not properly within its scope, we have long held that a witness who 'desires the protection of the privilege ... must claim it' at the time he relies on it." Alito reiterated this idea, saying, "Petitioner's Fifth Amendment claim fails because he did not expressly invoke the privilege against self-incrimination in response to the officer's question. It has long been settled that the privilege 'generally is not self-executing' and that a witness who desires its protection 'must claim it.'"

This *Salinas* decision applied only to noncustodial interrogation and did not disturb a prior Supreme Court decision in *Doyle v. Ohio* (1976),[112] which said that post-arrest silence could not be used against a suspect. Additionally, the Supreme Court long ago held that a defendant's decision not to testify in a trial cannot be used against them, which might happen if a prosecutor's closing argument suggested that an inference of guilt should be drawn from the decision not to testify. In fact, in *Griffin v. California* (1965),[113] the prosecutor said to the jury: "Essie Mae is dead; she can't tell you her side of the story. The defendant won't." To make matters worse, the judge in that case instructed the jury that "if he does not testify or if, though he does testify, he fails to deny or explain such evidence, the jury may take that failure into consideration as tending to indicate the truth of such evidence. ..." The Supreme Court found that any "comment on the refusal to testify is a remnant of the 'inquisitorial system of criminal justice,' ... which the Fifth Amendment outlaws. It is a penalty imposed by courts for exercising a constitutional privilege. It cuts down on the privilege by making its assertion costly."[114] Through that analysis, Griffin's conviction was overturned.

When Can Police Reinitiate an Interrogation?

In *Michigan v. Mosley* (1975),[115] the Court restated the core *Miranda* principle that when a suspect invokes the right to remain silent, an interrogation must stop immediately—but the *Mosley* case left open the possibility for police to reengage with a suspect at a later moment. Six years later, in *Edwards v. Arizona*,[116] the Court added a potential limitation to this concept by saying that a "presumption of involuntariness" surrounds any police effort to reinitiate an interrogation after a suspect has invoked their right to remain silent.

In 2010, a unanimous Supreme Court would offer long-awaited clarity on this issue with its decision in *Maryland v. Shatzer*.[117] In this case, Blaine Shatzer was incarcerated for an offense against a child when police detectives interrogated him about a separate matter—allegations of abuse against his own son. Shatzer invoked his right to remain silent, and police closed the case, only to reopen it more than two years later, when a different detective showed up at the prison to interrogate Shatzer. This interrogation occurred in a maintenance room, with Shatzer sitting at a desk as three detectives asked him questions. He was read *Miranda* rights, and after becoming emotional in response to a question, he made comments incriminating himself in the abuse of his child.

Prior to a trial, Shatzer's attorneys moved to have the incriminating statements excluded, and the Maryland Court of Appeals agreed that a Fifth Amendment violation had occurred. However, the Supreme Court of the United States reversed, finding no such violation and declaring that Shatzer's incriminating statements could be used in a trial. Furthermore, Justice Scalia's majority opinion set a specific standard for when police can reinitiate an interrogation after a suspect invokes *Miranda* rights. Two key elements apply in this analysis. First, the Court spoke of the need for "a break in custody that is of sufficient duration to dissipate its coercive effects." Second, in an effort to quantify an ideal minimum length for this "break," Justice Scalia observed, "It seems to us that period is 14 days. That provides plenty of time for the suspect to get reacclimated to his normal life, to consult with friends and counsel, and to shake off any residual coercive effects of his prior custody." Of course, when police attempt to reinitiate contact, the suspect could simply invoke the right to remain silent once again, and this fourteen-day *clock* would begin anew—something Shatzer opted not to do the second time he was questioned.

An additional element to untangle in this matter, though, was how precisely to construe the meaning of a *break in custody*. Certainly, a suspect who is free to leave a law enforcement or correctional setting and go home has been given a break in custody. But in this case, Shatzer was continuously incarcerated in a state prison. Nonetheless, Justice Scalia found that Shatzer's return to the "general prison population" after the first interrogation amounted to a "break in custody," with Scalia indicating that incarceration itself is not to be construed as "custody" in the sense of a continued interrogation. In this regard, Scalia said the following:

> Without minimizing the harsh realities of incarceration, we think lawful imprisonment imposed upon conviction of a crime does not create the coercive pressures identified in *Miranda*. Interrogated suspects who have previously been convicted of crime live in prison. When they are released back into the general prison population, they return to their accustomed surroundings and daily routine—they regain the degree of control they had over their lives prior to the interrogation. Sentenced prisoners, in contrast to the *Miranda* paradigm, are not isolated with their accusers. They live among other inmates, guards, and workers, and often can receive visitors and communicate with people on the outside by mail or telephone.

Overall, the *Shatzer* decision notwithstanding, it is important to note that without a break in custody, a suspect who has previously invoked their right to counsel is still entitled to have a lawyer present when police reinitiate interrogation, per the high Court's decision *Edwards v. Arizona* (1981). We will discuss this case in greater detail in the next chapter.

In addition, if a suspect invokes the right to terminate an interrogation and there is no break in custody, Supreme Court precedent prohibits officials of a different law enforcement agency from attempting to initiate questioning—such as county police taking over after federal officials were told that a suspect wished to remain silent.[118] Moreover, the high Court also has stated that it is a violation of the Fifth Amendment if the same officers who initially asked questions (only to have a suspect invoke their right to terminate the interrogation) attempt to reinitiate contact by asking the suspect questions about a separate, unrelated offense when there is no break in custody;[119] but with a break in custody and a 14-day wait, that could be permitted. We conclude this section by noting that the Supreme Court has never spoken to whether a person on parole is entitled to *Miranda* warnings before questioning by an agent of the government (perhaps, even a parole officer), and state supreme courts have split on this issue.[120]

What Constitutes Custodial Interrogation?

When someone is arrested and taken to the police station, they are in custody for *Miranda* purposes. That custody begins when the suspect is handcuffed or otherwise restrained. In that situation, the *Miranda* decision applies, and failure of police to provide the *Miranda* warnings is likely to result in the suppression of incriminating statements. On the other hand, questioning a driver during a routine traffic stop does not constitute custodial interrogation. In *Berkemer v. McCarty* (1984),[121] the Supreme Court addressed this issue and said that "[a]lthough an ordinary traffic stop curtails the 'freedom of action' of the detained motorist and imposes some pressures on the detainee to answer questions, such pressures do not sufficiently impair the detainee's exercise of his privilege against self-incrimination to require that he be warned of his constitutional rights." Along the same lines, the *Shatzer* decision observed that "temporary and relatively nonthreatening detention involved in a traffic stop or *Terry* stop does not constitute *Miranda* custody." [122]

Moreover, being detained by a private security guard is not considered custody for *Miranda* purposes. If a *mall cop* detains a suspect for shoplifting, any statements made by the suspect are not subject to *Miranda* requirements, as that decision applies only to custodial interrogation by law enforcement agents.[123] Of course, when police arrive at the mall to take the suspect into custody, *Miranda* rights would apply. Additionally, in a case that predated the *Miranda* decision, the Supreme Court found that general on-scene questioning of people at the scene of a crime can be permitted without informing people of their constitutional rights, as long as such questioning is not focused upon an individual who is taken into police custody.[124]

What about police questioning of persons who already are incarcerated for another offense? As noted in the discussion of the *Shatzer* case, it is not uncommon for prison inmates to be suspects in other unsolved crimes. An inmate clearly is in custody, but is it custody for *Miranda* purposes? In *Howes v. Fields* (2012),[125] the Supreme Court answered this question in the negative and indicated that *Miranda* rights need not be read in this context. This case involved an inmate named Randall Lee Fields, who was taken to a private conference room in the prison where he was questioned about, and ultimately confessed to, the sexual abuse of an adolescent male. This matter was different from the *Shatzer* case in that Fields was not given the *Miranda* warnings prior to this questioning, but he was told he was free to terminate the interview and be escorted back to his cell at any time. Writing for the Court, Justice Alito distinguished the interrogation of prison inmates from the type of custodial interrogation addressed in the *Miranda* case. In Alito's view, "service of a term of imprisonment, without more, is not enough to constitute *Miranda* custody." This is because, according to Alito, "standard conditions of confinement and associated restrictions on freedom will not necessarily implicate the same interests that the Court sought to protect when it afforded special safeguards to persons subjected to custodial interrogation." In simple terms, Alito declared the inmate was always "free" to return to his cell, adding that "[n]ot all restraints on freedom of movement amount to custody for purposes of *Miranda*." In dissent, Justice Ruth Ginsburg disagreed, arguing "the 'incommunicado interrogation [of Fields] in a police-dominated atmosphere,' without informing him of his rights, dishonored the Fifth Amendment privilege *Miranda* was designed to safeguard."

What Is Interrogation? Offhand Remarks

In *Rhode Island v. Innis* (1980),[126] the Supreme Court offered some clarity regarding when *Miranda* rights must be honored relative to the type of interrogation involved. In this case, five days after the 1975 murder of a taxi driver in Providence, Rhode Island another taxi driver reported being robbed by a man with a gun. Soon thereafter, police spotted a person matching the robber's description on the street, taking him into custody; no gun was located on his person. This man, named Thomas Innis, was then read *Miranda* rights by two different officers, and he indicated a desire to speak with an attorney. He was placed into a *police wagon*, with his seat residing behind a wire-mesh *cage* and three officers seated in front. As the wagon was driven toward a police station, one officer made it a point to say to another officer that there were "a lot of handicapped children running around in this area. ... God forbid one of them might find a weapon with shells and they might hurt themselves."

Innis then interjected, saying he "wanted to get the gun out of the way because of the kids in the area in the school." This occurred after approximately one mile of travel and no more than a few minutes in the car. Innis was brought back to the crime scene and read *Miranda* rights again, afterwards leading police to where his shotgun was located. At trial, his lawyers sought to suppress his statements and the gun from being used as evidence, but the trial judge denied the motion, saying there had been an "intelligent waiver" of *Miranda* rights. The Rhode Island Supreme Court reversed the trial court, finding a Fifth Amendment violation. However, on review, the U.S. Supreme Court decided the evidence had been properly admitted. Justice Stewart's opinion for a 6–3 majority announced a rule for when *Miranda* rights were applicable:

> We conclude that the *Miranda* safeguards come into play whenever a person in custody is subjected to either express questioning or its functional equivalent. That is to say, the term "interrogation" under *Miranda* refers not only to express questioning, but also to any words or actions on the part of the police (other than those normally attendant to arrest and custody) that the police should know are reasonably likely to elicit an incriminating response from the suspect. The latter portion of this definition focuses primarily upon the perceptions of the suspect, rather than the intent of the police. ... A practice that the police should know is reasonably likely to evoke an incriminating response from a suspect thus amounts to interrogation.

Therefore, *Miranda* rights can apply to the police questioning that typically occurs during a standard interrogation—or to its *functional equivalent*. Yet after articulating that rigorous standard for the application of *Miranda*, one that might have been construed as applying to the officer's statements inside the police wagon, the Court proffered a police-friendly standard for defining *functional equivalent*, noting that "since the police surely cannot be held accountable for the unforeseeable results of their words or actions, the definition of interrogation can extend only to words or actions on the part of police officers that they should have known were reasonably likely to elicit an incriminating response."

Ultimately, in applying this standard to the case at hand, Justice Stewart distilled the essence of his opinion as follows: "The case thus boils down to whether, in the context of a brief conversation, the officers should have known that the respondent would suddenly be moved to make a self-incriminating response." With that standard as a baseline, Stewart referred to the police comments in question as "offhand remarks," adding, "[W]e cannot say that the officers should have known that it was reasonably likely that Innis would so respond. This is not a case where the police carried on a lengthy harangue in the presence of the suspect."

Routine Booking Questions and Physical Evidence Exceptions

In *Pennsylvania v. Muniz* (1990), the Supreme Court further limited *Miranda* rights to situations that involved "evidence of a testimonial or communicative nature."[127] In this case, a man was driving on a Pennsylvania highway, when he was pulled over on suspicion of driving under the influence. He was taken to a booking center, where he was asked questions by officers, with his answers recorded on video. Those questions asked him to reveal the following information: name, address, height, weight, eye color, date of birth, and age. Additionally, he was asked, "What was the date of your sixth birthday?" His slurred speech in giving some answers was evident in the recording, and that video was played for a jury in his trial, where he was found guilty of DUI. He challenged the introduction of the video as evidence because he had not been read *Miranda* rights prior to answering the questions asked in this video.

In something of a mixed opinion, the Supreme Court found that parts of the video were admissible, but the question about the sixth birthday was not. A critical point in Justice Brennan's majority opinion indicated that, even when a person is in custody at a police station, routine booking questions (e.g., "What is your name?" or "What is your address?") do not need to be preceded by a reading of *Miranda* rights.[128] Brennan also said that physical evidence, meaning evidence that did not derive its value from the content of testimony, fell outside the scope a *Miranda* warning. Accordingly, Brennan found that prosecutors could indeed play a video for jurors to see Muniz slurring his speech in response to police questions—because the evidentiary value was tied to how he was speaking, as opposed to the content of what he was saying.

ROUTINE BOOKING QUESTIONS: A line of questioning that concerns basic personally identifying information, such as name, age, and address; this type of questioning generally does not require a *Miranda* warning even if a person is in police custody.

PHYSICAL EVIDENCE: Evidence that derives its value not from the content of any specific testimony but rather from what it reveals about some aspect of a person's physical state, such as blood evidence or if they are slurring words as they speak.

Nonetheless, regarding the officer asking, "Do you remember the date of your sixth birthday?" the Supreme Court ruled the jury should not have been allowed to see this portion of the video. That important distinction was drawn because, in terms of this question only, the content of Muniz's testimony was relevant—and not just the physical act of slurring his words. In essence, the dichotomy between these competing principles is tied into what the suspect said versus how the suspect said it.

The *Muniz* decision provides a rule for when *Miranda* warnings must be given. Two elements are essential: a person is in police custody *and* law enforcement officials attempt to elicit *testimonial evidence* (meaning, statements that would incriminate the person who is being interrogated of committing a crime). Unless both of these criteria are applicable, *Miranda* warnings do not have to be conveyed.

Interestingly, in a book called *Crafting Law on the Supreme Court: The Collegial Game*, the authors revealed that during the composition of the majority opinion for this case, Justice Brennan sent a letter to Justice Thurgood Marshall suggesting that Brennan (a decidedly liberal member of the Warren Court) only joined the majority in this case to strategically position himself as the author of the majority opinion, which was his choice as the senior member of the majority; his fear was that if he had not done so, "nothing would be left of *Miranda*."[129]

Exceptions to *Miranda*

If a statement is inadmissible under *Miranda*, does that mean it can never be used against the defendant? Beginning in 1971, a more conservative Supreme Court under Chief Justice Warren E. Burger carved out a series of important exceptions to the automatic suppression rule the Warren Court had adopted beginning with the *Miranda* decision. Some of these are straightforward. For example, "spontaneous declarations" or "spontaneous statements" made by an individual before police can reasonably read *Miranda* rights can be used in Court.[130] Not surprisingly, the Court also has found that statements made to undercover agents can be used at trial without a *Miranda* requirement being applicable.[131] And in *Florida v. Powell* (2010), the Court indicated there can be some flexibility shown regarding the exact phrasing used by an officer when they convey *Miranda* rights to a suspect. Thus, there is no set template that must be followed verbatim, provided the basic essence of *Miranda* rights is relayed to a suspect in a way that can be understood—which should include, it follows, translating into a foreign language when necessary. More complex categories of exceptions are considered in the following sections.

Impeachment of the Defendant's Testimony

In *Harris v. New York* (1971),[132] the Burger Court said that confessions suppressed under *Miranda* can nevertheless be used to impeach the credibility of a defendant who takes the stand and contradicts statements made during police interrogation. The Court observed that the privilege against compulsory self-incrimination "cannot be construed to include the right to commit perjury." In *Michigan v. Harvey* (1990),[133] the Court reiterated this proposition by allowing the use, at trial, of statements taken by police when an inmate was questioned without counsel present, even though he had requested a public defender at his arraignment. As we will discuss in chapter 12, case precedent indicated this questioning without appointed counsel amounted to a violation of the Sixth Amendment—but that violation did not render use of a statement impossible in court as it pertained to the impeachment of the defendant's own testimony that conflicted with statements given earlier to police, per the decision in *Harris v. New York*.

The Public Safety Exception

In *New York v. Quarles* (1984),[134] the Supreme Court carved out a **public safety exception** to *Miranda*. This case involved the arrest of a rape suspect in a grocery store. Upon frisking the suspect, police discovered an empty holster. Before *Mirandizing* the suspect, police asked, "Where's the gun?" The suspect nodded in the direction of empty boxes and said, "The gun is over there." Under a strict application of the *Miranda* rule, the defendant's statement would have been excluded from evidence, and under the **fruit of the poisonous tree doctrine**, the gun would have been suppressed as well. However, the Supreme Court upheld the admission of both the statement and the weapon and, in so doing, indicated that when police encounter an imminent threat to the public safety, they may ask questions aimed at defusing the threat prior to issuing the *Miranda* warnings. Justice William Rehnquist (before he was elevated to Chief Justice) wrote the Opinion of the Court, saying:

> We decline to place officers … in the untenable position of having to consider, often in a matter of seconds, whether it best serves society for them to ask the necessary questions without the *Miranda* warnings and render whatever probative evidence they uncover inadmissible, or for them to give the warnings in order to preserve the admissibility of evidence they might uncover but possibly damage or destroy their ability to obtain that evidence and neutralize the volatile situation confronting them.

In the wake of the *Quarles* decision, the public safety exception to *Miranda* has expanded. Today, before giving the familiar *Miranda* warnings, police routinely ask suspects being taken into custody about nearby weapons or other items that might pose a threat. Although the Supreme Court has not specifically addressed this topic, several federal circuit courts have upheld this practice.[135]

PUBLIC SAFETY EXCEPTION: An exception to the *Miranda* decision allowing police officers to ask questions of a suspect before providing the *Miranda* warnings to address an imminent threat to public safety.

FRUIT OF THE POISONOUS TREE DOCTRINE: Doctrine holding that evidence is inadmissible if it is derived from or obtained as the result of inadmissible evidence.

THE CONSTITUTION IN ACTION
Boston Marathon Bombing Suspect Interrogated Without *Miranda* Warnings

In the case of the Boston Marathon bombing of April 15, 2013, the lone surviving suspect, Dzhokhar Tsarnaev, was taken into custody by law enforcement around 6 p.m. on Friday, April 19, 2013. He was immediately transported to a hospital for treatment on injuries sustained during his flight from authorities, including injuries stemming from a gunshot wound to the face. Without reading *Miranda* rights, officials questioned Tsarnaev for more than 15 hours over

(continued)

the course of that weekend as he remained in the hospital. In response to questions, he gave mostly *yes* or *no* answers by nodding or shaking his head and also wrote responses in a notebook—but he was unable to speak clearly due to his facial injuries. He was not read *Miranda* rights until the evening of Monday, April 22, when he was formally charged with terrorist-related federal crimes and read his rights by a judge who appeared at his hospital bed. Federal officials indicated this delay in reading those rights was pursuant to the public safety exception articulated by the Supreme Court in *New York v. Quarles* (1984). Tsarnaev later was convicted of thirty federal offenses after a jury trial in 2015, and he would be sentenced to death. (In 2020, the U.S. Court of Appeals for the First Circuit ruled that the death sentence should be overturned—but that had nothing to do with the delay in reading *Miranda* rights.)[136]

Moreover, a 2010 Justice Department *guidance memo* suggested that the meaning of *public safety*, as discussed by the Supreme Court in *Quarles*, should be evaluated "in light of the magnitude and complexity of the threat often posed by terrorist organizations … and the nature of their attacks, the circumstances surrounding an arrest of an operational terrorist may warrant significantly more extensive public safety interrogation than would be permissible in an ordinary criminal case." The memo also declared that "FBI guidance instructs that, after any and all applicable public safety questions have been exhausted, agents should advise the arrestee of his *Miranda* rights." But the memo included a caveat, saying that "there may be exceptional situations in which continued unwarned interrogation is necessary to collect valuable and timely intelligence, and the government's interest in obtaining this intelligence—lawfully but without *Miranda* warnings—outweighs the disadvantages of proceeding in this fashion." A footnote in the memo did indicate that no opinion was being offered in regard to suspects who were already known to be represented by counsel or those who were already under indictment.[137]

In the end, the confluence of the Supreme Court's public safety exception and the Justice Department's expansive interpretation thereof resulted in an approximately seventy-two-hour delay between Tsarnaev's arrest and the reading of *Miranda* rights. As previously noted, Tsarnaev would file a successful appeal at the First Circuit regarding the sentencing phase of his capital case (which will discuss in chapter 14), but at no point did any appellate court take umbrage with the delay in the provision of *Miranda* warnings in this matter.

DERIVATIVE EVIDENCE: Evidence derived from or obtained via other evidence.

INDEPENDENT SOURCE DOCTRINE: Doctrine permitting evidence to be admitted against a criminal defendant as long as it was obtained independently from illegally obtained evidence.

The Inevitable Discovery Exception

The *Miranda* exclusionary rule applies not only to incriminating statements made by the accused but also to derivative evidence. Thus, if a confession led police to the location of a body or a weapon, for instance, that evidence derived from the confession should be excluded as the fruit of a poisonous tree (as discussed in chapter 7). However, under the independent source doctrine, evidence attacked by the defense as fruit of the poisonous tree may be admitted into evidence if it was obtained via an independent source. Even so, the prosecution has "the affirmative duty to prove that the evidence it proposes to use is derived from a legitimate source wholly independent of the compelled testimony."[138]

In *Nix v. Williams* (1984),[139] the Supreme Court rendered a decision in a macabre murder case, in which a young girl was kidnapped and her body disposed of in the woods. The case actually had been to the high Court seven years earlier. In that matter, *Brewer v. Williams* (1977),[140] the Court ordered the suppression of the defendant's incriminating statements to police, finding that the defendant, Williams, had invoked his right to have counsel present during questioning and the police violated that right by engaging him in a conversation about the need for a *Christian burial* of the victim.

But in 1984 the Supreme Court revisited the issue, this time focusing on a new variant of the independent source doctrine. The Court accepted Iowa's argument that the victim's remains would have been discovered inevitably by a search party that was combing the area where the remains were located. Writing for the Court's 7–2 majority, Chief Justice Burger opined, "[T]he search parties were approaching the actual location of the body, and we are satisfied, along with three courts earlier, that the volunteer search teams would have resumed the search had Williams not earlier led the police to the body, and the body inevitably would have been found." Thus, the **inevitable discovery exception** was born.

In clarifying this doctrine, Chief Justice Burger embedded an important definition in the following statement: "If the prosecution can establish by a preponderance of the evidence that the information ultimately or inevitably would have been discovered by lawful means—here, the volunteers' search—then the deterrence rationale has so little basis that the evidence should be received. Anything less would reject logic, experience, and common sense." The deterrence rationale discussed in that quote speaks to the idea that excluding illegally obtained evidence from a trial is meant to deter police from engaging in unconstitutional conduct. However, the Court mitigated such concerns in *inevitable discovery* situations by saying, "Significant disincentives to obtaining evidence illegally—including the possibility of departmental discipline and civil liability—also lessen the likelihood that the ultimate or inevitable discovery exception will promote police misconduct." In the end, the Court seemed to balance the interests of society against the rights of the accused before concluding that the "[e]xclusion of physical evidence that would inevitably have been discovered adds nothing to either the integrity or fairness of a criminal trial."

Finally, it is important to note the inevitable discovery exception is somewhat different from the independent source doctrine. The Supreme Court clarified this distinction in *Nix v. Williams* by saying, "The independent source doctrine allows admission of evidence that has been discovered by means wholly independent of any constitutional violation. That doctrine, although closely related to the inevitable discovery doctrine, does not apply here."

INEVITABLE DISCOVERY EXCEPTION: Doctrine permitting evidence to be admitted against a defendant as long as it was obtained independent of inadmissible evidence.

JURISPRUDENCE

The Inevitable Discovery Exception Helps Prosecutors Convict a Child Killer
Nix v. Williams, 467 U.S. 431 (1984)

In this horrific case, a 10-year-old girl was abducted from a YMCA in Des Moines, Iowa. A man named Robert Williams, who had a history of mental illness, was seen leaving the YMCA carrying a large, bundled blanket—with a witness reporting two legs appeared to be hanging out from the blanket. Williams thus became the prime subject of the police investigation, and his car was found the next day about 160 miles away from Des Moines in the city of Davenport, Iowa. Some of the child's clothing, and the blanket in question, were found at an interstate rest stop in between Des Moines and Davenport. Police surmised Williams had left the child somewhere near the rest stop, and a large search party of over 200 people was assembled to investigate the area, with searches covering all roads, structures, and ditches.

As the search was taking place, Williams surrendered to police in Davenport. Two detectives from Des Moines picked him up in Davenport and proceeded to drive him back to Des Moines. On the trip, one detective began to converse with Williams, and without relaying *Miranda* rights, the detective said the following: "I want to give you something to think about while we're traveling down the road. ... They are predicting several inches of snow for tonight, and I feel that you yourself are the only person that knows where this little girl's body is." The detective then indicated his belief that the child's body was in a nearby town, saying to Williams, "And since we will be going right past the area [where the body is] on the way into Des Moines, I feel that we could stop and locate the body, that the parents of this little girl should be entitled to a Christian burial for the little girl who was snatched away from them on Christmas [E]ve and murdered. After a snow storm, [we may not be] able to find it at all." Williams responded by asking questions about whether police had found certain items belonging to the child, and as the car approached the town of Mitchellville, Williams said he would lead the detectives to the body. He revealed the body had been left in a ditch two miles from the interstate, in an area where one search team was 2.5 miles away and heading in that direction; although the search had been temporarily halted at the moment Williams showed detectives where the body was located, it was scheduled to resume soon thereafter.

Williams was brought to trial on charges of first-degree murder. A pretrial motion to suppress evidence was denied, and Williams's statements made to officers while in the car were used against him, as was evidence derived from the body, including photographs of its condition when discovered. Williams was found guilty of murder, and his conviction was affirmed by the Iowa Supreme Court. Eventually, Williams was able to get his case before the U.S. Supreme Court, using a petition for habeas corpus.[141] The high Court ruled that the confession should be suppressed, but also said evidence of the body's location and condition could be used as evidence in a second trial. At that second trial in Des Moines, no mention was made of Williams's statements to police or the fact that he had led police to the body. Yet "evidence of the condition of her body as it was found, articles and photographs of her clothing, and the results of post-mortem medical and chemical tests on the body were admitted."[142] Williams was found guilty by a jury for a second time, and once again, the case made its way back to the U.S. Supreme Court.

Williams's lawyers invoked the fruit of the poisonous tree doctrine in suggesting that because he had not been read *Miranda* rights, not only should the confession have been excluded, but evidence derived from the body should be deemed inadmissible as well. Reviewing this matter in *Nix v. Williams* (1984), the Supreme Court said the evidence used at the second trial was acceptable under the so-called *inevitable discovery* doctrine. More specifically, Chief Justice Burger highlighted the importance of this doctrine by saying, "The purpose of the inevitable discovery rule is to block setting aside convictions that would have been obtained without police misconduct." Burger also made it clear that the exclusion of such evidence "adds nothing to either the integrity or fairness of a criminal trial"; moreover, he placed emphasis on "the enormous societal cost of excluding truth in the search for truth in the administration of justice," and he rejected any thoughts of suppressing the evidence in this case by observing that "[n]othing in this Court's prior holdings supports any such formalistic, pointless, and punitive approach."

Other Fruit of the Poisonous Tree Confession Cases

Other cases from the Supreme Court have clarified application of the fruit of the poisonous tree doctrine to confessions. In *Oregon v. Elstad* (1985),[143] the Court found that if an initial confession is found to be inadmissible for a failure to read *Miranda* rights, a second confession given after *Miranda* rights are read can be used as evidence as long as the first confession is not deemed to have been coerced. However, in *Missouri v. Seibert* (2004),[144] the Court held that when a first confession is found to be coerced, a subsequent Mirandized confession is inadmissible in court as well. Moreover, regarding confession-derived evidence, the Court's decision in *United States v. Patante* (2004)[145] indicated that if a confession was acquired without the recitation of *Miranda* rights but not found to be a coerced confession, a gun located as a result of the suspect's statements could be used as evidence at trial. In this case, the suspect interrupted an ATF agent before the agent could finish reading *Miranda* rights; specifically, after the agent had conveyed the right to remain silent (and nothing else), the suspect interjected and said he knew his rights, before giving statements that implicated himself in the illegal possession of a firearm. The Court's decision in this case is limited as precedent, however, because the justices were not able to find agreement on a majority opinion, instead producing a plurality opinion with multiple concurrences.

THE CONSTITUTION IN ACTION
Summary of *Miranda* Rights Considerations

When is the Miranda *Warning Required?*

- Custodial interrogation
- Questions seeking testimonial evidence
- "Functional equivalent" of questions seeking testimony

When is Miranda *Warning Not Required?*

- Not in police custody
- General on-scene questioning
- Routine booking questions
- Procurement of physical evidence
- Spontaneous statements by the accused
- Questioning by an undercover agent
- Public safety exceptions

Factors Affecting Admissibility of Confessions

The two principal factors judges will consider in responding to pretrial motions to suppress incriminating statements by the defendant are (1) whether the statement was made in violation of *Miranda* and (2) whether the statement was voluntary. While giving the *Miranda* warnings in a timely way creates a presumption of admissibility, it does not relieve officers of the duty to avoid a coerced confession. In determining whether a confession was voluntary, judges must consider the method of the interrogation, the conditions of custody, the defendant's physical and psychological state, the attitude of the police toward the suspect, and any delay between arrest and appearance before a magistrate. It should be noted that judges tend to be cautious in admitting confessions by juveniles, as they are more prone to manipulation by the police.[146]

Police Deception

Can the police deceive a suspect to elicit a confession? In *Frazier v. Cupp* (1969),[147] the Supreme Court reviewed a murder case in which police falsely informed the defendant his codefendant had confessed. Nevertheless, the trial judge held that the defendant's subsequent confession was voluntary. Considering the "totality of circumstances," the Court concluded, "The fact that the police misrepresented the statements that [the codefendant] had made is, while relevant, insufficient, in our view, to make this otherwise voluntary confession inadmissible." Similarly, in *Oregon v. Mathiason* (1977),[148] the Supreme Court upheld a conviction for burglary, where the police obtained a confession after falsely telling the defendant his fingerprints were found at the crime scene.

We should note that in 1986, the Supreme Court would say that the "totality of circumstances" approach should only apply if a confession is deemed to be coerced—not, for example, if *Miranda* rights are lacking through some other form of less-nefarious police conduct, such as merely forgetting to read those warnings.[149] Thus, the *totality* standard seems most germane to cases involving some type of coercion or deception.

Some states have passed laws to address deceptive interrogation tactics. In 2021, Illinois became the first state to enact a law that prohibits police from lying to minors during an interrogation, and other states, including Oregon, would follow with similar laws. State courts also have been asked to address specific forms of deceptive police practices. For instance, in Florida, a 1989 appellate court decision found that police showing a suspect a fake lab report, typed on official department stationery, amounted to a violation of constitutional rights.[150] In its opinion, the court noted the following:

> Unlike oral misrepresentations, manufactured documents have the potential of indefinite life and the facial appearance of authenticity. A report falsified for interrogation purposes might well be retained and filed in police paperwork. Such reports have the potential of finding their way into the courtroom.

Elsewhere, a 1999 decision from the Utah Supreme Court addressed a particularly egregious example of evidence fabrication, as officers falsely claimed to have all of the following (when, in fact, none of these existed): eyewitness testimony implicating the suspect, fingerprints at the crime scene, a ballistic test match, blood samples tying the suspect to the crime scene, a bloody shoeprint, blood spatter evidence, and phone records linking the suspect to the crime. Officers even said they had more evidence than prosecutors did in the O.J. Simpson murder case. Striking down use of a confession extracted after all of these falsehoods were presented, the Utah court said that "in certain cases, police misrepresentations may be sufficiently egregious to overcome a defendant's will so as to render a confession involuntary."[151] In 2003, a New Jersey appeals court reached a similar conclusion, striking down use of a confession derived after police played a fabricated audio tape involving a made-up statement from a fake eyewitness.[152]

More recently, in 2019, the Hawaii Supreme Court overturned a man's conviction because police had falsely claimed he failed a lie detector test.[153] The Hawaii court said the "deliberate deception" in relaying an "objective falsehood" rendered the confession inadmissible. One year later, the same court found police officers had violated constitutional rights by lying about the presence of DNA evidence when none existed.[154] In this case, the court cited to scholarly research in saying, "When confronted with false evidence such as DNA, which is uniquely identifying and therefore appears to be truly incontrovertible, the accused can come to believe that there is no alternative but to confess."[155] The court also said, "This is especially true when the false evidence is characterized as scientific because people generally expect scientific tests to be accurate and trustworthy."[156] In turn, the court concluded, "What ultimately makes deception about incontrovertible evidence insidious is the implied threat that it carries: independent incriminating evidence exists, so the accused should confess in order to enter a mitigating statement into the record."

In terms of scholarly research into this topic, Saul Kassin and others conducted a survey of 631 police detectives in the U.S. and Canada, finding that 92% admitted to using some type of *false-evidence tactic* during interrogations.[157] Moreover, a 2018 report from Brandon Bang and others, published in the *International Journal of Police Science and Management*, distills the scholarly literature as follows: "Presentation of false evidence ... has been shown to lead to false confession."[158] Yet most states allow police use of deception during interrogations, and in some cases, such as the one discussed in the following box, it can prove to be effective in eliciting a confession from a criminal who might be on the verge of getting away with a crime.

THE CONSTITUTION IN ACTION
A Woman Confesses to Drowning Her Children

In 1994, a woman named Susan Smith drowned her two sons—a three year old and one year old—by driving her car to a boat ramp and letting it roll into a lake in South Carolina as the children were strapped inside by their seatbelts. She falsely claimed to police she had been carjacked by an African American man while stopped at red light. She also made numerous TV appearances pleading for the safe return of her children. Police were skeptical of her story because the alleged red light only would have activated if another car was present at the intersection, and Smith herself claimed no other cars were nearby. No witnesses to the alleged carjacking, or to the drowning itself, were found.

Nine days after the incident, an officer told Smith surveillance video of the intersection existed and that this video served as proof she had not been telling the truth. Smith then confessed to the crime. She was later found guilty of two counts of murder and was sentenced to life in prison in 1995. The officer, though, was lying about the presence of surveillance footage; none existed.

In 2010, Smith submitted a hand-written appeal to a South Carolina court, suggesting her "Amanda rights" had been violated. Her contention might have been that the officer's deceptive question, which was not preceded by a reading of her rights, violated constitutional protections. A South Carolina judge rejected this appeal, though, and she continues to serve her prison sentence.[159]

Finally, it is important to note that the commonplace practice of plea bargaining, in which a prosecutor might offer a lesser sentence in exchange for an accused criminal's guilty plea, usually is not considered to be deceptive. Unless such promises are revoked after a confession or a guilty plea has been made, the Supreme Court has upheld the use of plea bargaining on multiple occasions, as we will discuss in greater detail in chapter 12.

Does Admission of an Improper Confession Automatically Require Reversal of a Conviction?

Prior to 1991, the prevailing rule was that a confession improperly admitted into evidence required an appellate court to overturn the conviction and remand the case for a new trial. But in *Arizona v. Fulminante* (1991),[160] the

HARMLESS ERROR DOCTRINE: Doctrine under which an appellate court should reverse a conviction only if an error allowed by the trial court was prejudicial to the defendant.

Supreme Court ruled the erroneous admission of an involuntary confession is subject to the harmless error doctrine. The doctrine stems from *Chapman v. California* (1967),[161] where the Court held that not all constitutional violations require automatic reversal on appeal. In *Chapman*, the Court said, "We conclude that there may be some constitutional errors which, in the setting of a particular case, are so unimportant and insignificant that they may, consistent with the Federal Constitution, be deemed harmless, not requiring the automatic reversal of the conviction." The key question is whether the trial court would have reached the same judgment in the absence of the error. However, in *Chapman*, the Court held that, to be considered harmless, an error must be found to be harmless beyond a reasonable doubt. In *Arizona v. Fulminante* (1991), detailed in the Jurisprudence box below, the Court applied this doctrine to incriminating statements that should have been excluded at trial—observing that if an appellate court finds, beyond a reasonable doubt, the evidence used at trial (other than the improper confession) was sufficient to support a conviction, then the conviction should not be overturned.

JURISPRUDENCE

Police Use Prison Informant to Secure a Confession
Arizona v. Fulminante, 499 U.S. 279 (1991)

This decision addressed the law enforcement tactic of using a police informant who is inside a prison, perhaps posing as an inmate, to collect information. In this case, Oreste Fulminante was a suspect in the killing of his daughter in Arizona. He was not immediately charged, though, and moved to New Jersey. There, he was convicted on a federal charge of being a felon in possession of a firearm. While incarcerated in federal prison, he met Anthony Sarivola, who was serving a sixty-day sentence for extortion. Unbeknownst to any inmates at the prison, Sarivola was working for the FBI as a paid informant, tasked with acquiring information about other crimes committed by fellow inmates. To further his rouse, Sarivola pretended to be an organized crime figure serving a lengthy sentence.

FBI agents were particularly interested in information about the murder of Fulminante's daughter, and Sarivola was instructed by agents to delve into this matter. Sarivola repeatedly asked Fulminante about the killing, but those queries were met with denials. In one conversation, Sarivola mentioned Fulminante was "starting to get some tough treatment and whatnot" and offered to protect him from other inmates in exchange for the truth about what happened to the girl, with Sarivola saying, "You have to tell me about it, you know. I mean, in other words, for me to give you any help." Fulminante then admitted to Sarivola he had shot his daughter twice in the head and left her body in the Arizona desert. After being released from federal prison, Fulminante confessed again—this time to Sarivola's wife. Both of those confessions were used against Fulminante during a murder trial in Arizona, where he was found guilty.

On review, Justice Byron White wrote for a 5–4 majority on the U.S. Supreme Court, saying, "Although the question is a close one, we agree with the Arizona Supreme Court's conclusion that Fulminante's confession was coerced. The Arizona Supreme Court found a credible threat of physical violence unless Fulminante confessed." White went on to observe that prior cases "have made clear that a finding of coercion need not depend upon actual violence by a government agent;

a credible threat is sufficient." He even cited to a 1960 decision in saying that "'coercion can be mental as well as physical, and ... the blood of the accused is not the only hallmark of an unconstitutional inquisition.'"[162]

Hence, although use of a prison informant remains a viable police tactic, such an informant cannot utilize statements that are deemed to be coercive.

The Problem of False Confessions

Although constitutional parameters are in place to protect against *false confessions*, there is ample evidence to indicate such confessions still do occur. Semantically, the Northwestern Center on Wrongful Convictions has defined the concept of a *false confession* with reference to three possible iterations: "The exoneree falsely confessed if (1) he or she made a false statement to authorities which was treated as a confession, (2) the authorities claimed that the exoneree made such a statement but the exoneree denied it, or (3) the exoneree made a statement that was not an admission of guilt, but was misinterpreted as such by the authorities."[163] Data from the Innocence Project indicate that approximately 25% "of the nation's more than 300 wrongful convictions overturned by DNA evidence involved some form of a false confession."[164] Beyond that, an article from the *Washington Post* observes, "According to the National Registry of Exonerations, 27 percent of people in the registry who were accused of homicide gave false confessions."[165] Additionally, scholars Steven Drizen and Richard Leo report that more than 80% of false confessions occur in homicide cases, which are likely to carry the most severe sentences of any crime.[166]

Among the factors listed by the Innocence Project as reasons given in research about the phenomenon of false confessions are these: "real or perceived intimidation"; "use of force ... or perceived threat of force"; "compromised reasoning ability of the suspect, due to exhaustion, stress, hunger, substance abuse, ... mental limitations, or limited education"; "devious interrogation techniques, such as untrue statements about the presence of incriminating evidence"; and "fear... that a failure to confess will lead to a harsher punishment."[167] Research also suggests that both police and everyday people (who might end up being jurors) tend to overestimate their ability to determine if someone is lying.[168] Moreover, after reviewing prior studies, Bang et al. conclude that "people with certain psychological disorders were more likely to confess, as were people who scored high on a self-report measure of compliance scale." They also noted that "juveniles and persons with a low intelligence quotient (IQ) have been found to be especially vulnerable to coercive and deceptive techniques."[169]

THE CONSTITUTION AND SOCIAL JUSTICE
An Impermissible Interrogation Tactic: The Threat of the All-White Jury
Bond v. State of Indiana, 9 N.E.3d 134 (Ind. 2014)

The Marshall Project has highlighted a specific interrogation tactic that some suggest is used too often in the questioning of Black suspects and which carries the potential for leading to a false confession. With this particular tactic, an interrogator will suggest the accused is likely to face an all-White jury that will be unsympathetic to their case. In 2014, evaluating an interrogation that made use of this suggestion, the Indiana Supreme Court ruled a suspect's confessions was invalid. This case, *Bond v. Indiana*, originated in Gary, Indiana, where a police detective said the following to a suspect named McLynnerd Bond approximately two hours into an interrogation: "Don't let twelve people who are from Schererville, Crown Point—white people, Hispanic people, other people that aren't from Gary,

(continued)

from your part of the hood—judge you. Because they're not gonna put people on there who are from your neck of the woods. You know that. They're not gonna be the ones to decide what happens to you. You know that. I know that. Everybody knows that."

Indiana's highest court issued an opinion declaring this tactic to be "an intentional misrepresentation of rights ensconced in the very fabric of our nation's justice system—the right to a fair trial and impartial jury, and the right not to be judged by or for the color of your skin—carried out as leverage to convince a suspect in a criminal case that his only recourse was to forego his claim of innocence and confess." The court went on to say that the detective had "intentionally played on the fear that Bond could not receive a fair trial because of his race. And in doing so, it gave truth to the fear." The opinion also offered the following conclusion: "We have long held that law enforcement officers conducting interrogations may use a range of tactics and techniques to persuade suspects to provide incriminating statements. And we understand that simple question-and-answer methods will not always be successful. But the flexibility afforded to law enforcement is still bound by state and federal constitutional protections."

Interestingly, the opinion began with this quote from Dr. Martin Luther King, Jr.'s, "Letter from Birmingham Jail" (April 16, 1963): "Let us all hope that the dark clouds of racial prejudice will soon pass away and the deep fog of mis-understanding will be lifted from our fear drenched communities. ..."

The Use of Recorded Confessions

One proposed solution for the issue of false confessions is mandating that law-enforcement interrogations be recorded. The federal government has done so since 2014, when a policy issued by the U.S. Department of Justice required all federal law enforcement agencies to record custodial interrogations of individuals accused of committing federal crimes. As of 2022, the number of states requiring such a recording had risen to 27—although the ways in which such requirements originated, and the crimes to which they applied, varied from state to state.

Some states have established their recording mandates through state supreme court rulings,[170] some through legislative acts,[171] and some through informal policies that are followed voluntarily by police departments.[172] Of those states that have such a mandate, only four—Alaska, Arkansas, Minnesota, and Montana—require recordings for interrogations pertaining to *all* criminal offenses; in Indiana, New Mexico, Utah, and Wisconsin, a recording is mandated only for felony interrogations; and other states mandate it for specific felonies, such as murder and rape.[173] In California, it is only required for situations in which a juvenile is charged with murder. In Oregon, a recording of an interrogation is needed in three situations: aggravated murder cases, any crime that could yield a mandatory minimum sentence, and for juveniles who would face a trial in adult criminal court.[174]

Yet although a recording might seem like panacea for false confessions, research psychologists have denoted potential pitfalls associated with prosecutors showing videotaped confessions to jurors. Bang et al., for example, suggest that a video focused exclusively on the suspect could fail to provide the appropriate context for depicting any influence exerted by the interrogator. More specifically, these researchers say the "commonplace practice of using suspect-only oriented cameras (i.e., single focus) results in observers and jurors perceiving confession statements as more voluntary than when the video focus is upon both the defendant and investigator." [175] G. Daniel Lassiter calls this a "camera perspective bias."[176] Research even has suggested that trials with a single-focus video of a suspect are more likely to result in a guilty verdict and a harsher sentence than a video that includes the interrogator.[177] Bang et al. go so far as to illustrate issues with so-called *recap videos* shown by prosecutors to distill certain portions of a videotaped confession; these montages, they suggest, can be prone to selective editing that results in *recap bias*, or could even portray the suspect as lacking in emotion because clips from a lengthy interrogation might depict a person who is tired without offering appropriate context regarding how long they have been interrogated.[178]

Another aspect of this dialogue ties into what repercussions follow if police fail to create a recording when required to do so. Maryland and New Mexico, although they require recordings, specify no remedy in law for a failure to do so, while in Kansas, cross-examination of an interrogator is said to be the only remedy. Only three states use a standard in which a confession is automatically excluded if it is not recorded (California, Connecticut, and Illinois, along with the District of Columbia). In Maine and Missouri, a fine can be issued to a law enforcement agency that fails to record a confession. Seven states use "court determination," in which a judge or jury makes a decision as to the admissibility of an unrecorded confession.[179] Five states (Colorado, Nebraska, Oregon, Vermont, and Wisconsin) use jury instruction as the primary remedy, meaning a judge tells jurors the law was not followed properly regarding the recording of a confession and thus, jurors should view a confession with some type of caution (although exact wording can vary from state to state); in Massachusetts, this idea has been codified into case precedent even though there is no law that requires recordings.[180] Nevertheless, Bang et al. suggest "the effectiveness and use of jury instruction should be questioned as most jurors likely presume that a person would never falsely implicate themselves in a crime that they did not commit."[181] Most states also allow for a *good faith exception* that allows an unrecorded confession to be admissible when no working camera is available. Finally, states vary in terms of how long a recording is stored.

In the end, there are scholars who question whether video recordings actually provide benefits for defendants.[182] Alternative solutions that tend to appear in literature include the following: limiting the duration of interrogations; limiting deception; limiting the use of polygraph or voice-stress analysis; limiting promises of leniency; limiting officers from suggesting blackout scenarios; utilizing pretrial *reliability hearings* for confessions; and using audio recordings instead of video recordings to eliminate the potential for viewer bias.[183]

An International *Miranda* Right?

The Supreme Court's decision in *Medellin v. Texas* (2008)[184] seems to speak to an international version of *Miranda* rights. This case involved an appeal brought on behalf of an undocumented immigrant from Mexico who had been convicted of murder in the state of Texas. His attorney initially brought an appeal to the International Court of Justice (ICJ) in the Netherlands, basing that appeal on a treaty called the Vienna Convention on Consular Relations, which was ratified by the U.S. Senate in 1969. Article 36 of that treaty says that when a foreign visitor is arrested in one of the more than 180 countries that are parties to the treaty, officials in the country of arrest must provide notification of the person's arrest to the embassy of their home country.

The appeal in Medellin's case was based on the fact that Texas authorities had not notified the Mexican embassy at any point following his arrest. In 2004, the ICJ issued a ruling that said Medellin's rights (and those of fifty other Mexican nationals) under the Vienna Convention had been violated by the U.S., and thus, a new trial should be afforded to Medellin in Texas.[185] In turn, President George W. Bush issued a presidential memorandum suggesting that the state of Texas provide a second trial.[186]

However, the Supreme Court presented a contrary perspective. In its 6–3 decision, the Court found that the ICJ's decision was not binding upon Texas courts—nor was the president's memorandum. Specifically, Chief Justice Roberts's majority opinion concluded "that neither [the ICJ decision] nor the President's Memorandum constitutes directly enforceable federal law. ..." Roberts went on to declare that treaties "do not by themselves function as binding federal law," adding that "while treaties 'may comprise international commitments ... they are not domestic law unless Congress has either enacted implementing statutes or the treaty itself conveys an intention that it be 'self-executing' and is ratified on these terms.'"[187] As a result, Medellin was executed in the state of Texas in August 2008.

Just months after the Supreme Court's *Medellin* decision, the Fourth Circuit released an opinion in a case where a 21-year-old U.S. citizen living in Saudi Arabia was interrogated by Saudi authorities about his alleged role in terrorist activity linked to Al-Qaeda. The man was questioned by agents of the Mabahith, the Saudi secret police, but American FBI agents were permitted to supply Saudi officials with a list of questions to ask him. Saudi officials rejected the majority of the questions submitted by the FBI but did ask six of them—including queries about the use of fake passports, plots to attack the United States, and plans to assassinate the president of the United States. No U.S. officials were in the interrogation room as the questions were asked, but FBI and Secret Service agents were permitted to view the questioning through a one-way mirror. The man confessed to taking part in planning activity in plots to hijack U.S. planes and to assassinate the U.S. president, among other terrorist-related offenses. Saudi officials then ceded custody of this man to the FBI, and he was flown to the United States in February 2005. He was found guilty of nine terrorist-related offenses in the U.S. District Court for the Eastern District of Virginia, with the judge sentencing him to thirty years in prison.

On appeal, his attorneys claimed the FBI's role in providing questions to Saudi officials amounted to a violation of *Miranda* rights. The Fourth Circuit's majority opinion in *United States v. Abu Ali* (2008)[188] rejected that claim. The Fourth Circuit offered the concession that "United States law enforcement officials may not intentionally evade the requirements of *Miranda* by purposefully delegating interrogation duties to foreign law enforcement officers and then having the fruits of the interrogation admitted at trial in the United States." Despite that declaration, the majority opinion added that "two exceptions have developed to the general rule that voluntary statements obtained by foreign officials during a custodial interrogation without benefit of *Miranda* warnings are admissible. Namely, such statements will not be admissible if obtained by foreign officials (1) engaged in a joint venture with, or (2) acting as agents of, United States law enforcement officers." In this case, the court found there was no joint venture between U.S. and Saudi officials because there was no *active* or *substantial* participation on the part of U.S. law enforcement agents.

THE CONSTITUTION IN ACTION

Evaluating the Reliability of Lie Detector Tests

A lie detector test, also known as a polygraph, is a largely discredited method of determining if someone is telling the truth. A typical polygraph examination will involve a person being asked questions while attached to electrodes through which several physiological measurements are taken, such as their pulse, blood pressure, perspiration, breathing rate, skin conductivity, and pupil dilation, among other things. An observer, allegedly a trained expert, will then make a determination regarding whether the person is revealing signs of deception in response to the questions. Some baseline questions for which answers are clearly known are often used in the full set of questions that are asked. Fewer than 20 states allow for the use of polygraph evidence in court,[189] and in some of those states, both parties in a case must agree to its use.[190]

In *United States v. Scheffer* (1998),[191] the Supreme Court addressed the case of Edward Scheffer, who was an airman in the Air Force. Per his job duties, he was subjected to regular polygraph examinations and drug testing, with one drug test revealing the presence of methamphetamine in his system. He was then brought to a court-martial on charges of using a controlled substance. His lawyer attempted to introduce evidence of a polygraph test that indicated *no deception* when he was asked about using drugs. Under the Military Rules of Evidence (Rule 707), though, the use polygraphs in a court-martial was prohibited. Scheffer appealed to the Supreme Court of the United States, which ruled against him 8–1.

Justice Thomas wrote the majority opinion, which said, "[T]here is simply no consensus that polygraph evidence is reliable. To this day, the scientific community remains extremely polarized about the reliability of polygraph techniques." Quoting a 1973 circuit court opinion,[192] Thomas went on to say, "A fundamental premise of our criminal trial system is that 'the *jury* is the lie detector'" (italics in original). Then, referring to those who are tasked with reading polygraph data, Thomas stated, "Unlike other expert witnesses who testify about factual matters outside the jurors' knowledge, such as the analysis of fingerprints, ballistics, or DNA found at a crime scene, a polygraph expert can supply the jury only with another opinion, in addition to its own, about whether the witness was telling the truth." Ultimately, with the following declaration, his opinion left it to individual jurisdictions to determine their own policies for the use of polygraphs (including the military, which was permitted to ban their use): "Jurisdictions, in promulgating rules of evidence, may legitimately be concerned about the risk that juries will give excessive weight to the opinions of a polygrapher, clothed as they are in scientific expertise and at times offering, as in respondent's case, a conclusion about the ultimate issue in the trial." He went on to conclude that: "Such jurisdictions may legitimately determine that the aura of infallibility attending polygraph evidence can lead jurors to abandon their duty to assess credibility and guilt."

Identification Procedures and Physical Evidence Obtained from the Accused

The Supreme Court has had held that the Self-Incrimination Clause applies only to testimonial evidence.[193] It does not apply to methods the police use to identify suspects. Thus, police fingerprinting and taking photographs of an arrested person do not fall within the Fifth Amendment prohibition. Nor does compelling a suspect to provide a handwriting sample[194] or a voice exemplar.[195] Suspects can be required to stand in a lineup, although it cannot be structured so as to bias a witness's identification of the accused, and a defense lawyer is permitted to be present during the lineup.[196] A crime victim also may be taken to where the suspect is being held to make an identification, but such procedures carry a risk of being unduly suggestive.[197] Alternatively, a victim or witness may be asked to identify a perpetrator from a set of mug shots, but this procedure also carries the risk of being overly suggestive. When evaluating identification procedures, courts must consider whether, under the totality of circumstances, the procedure gave rise to a substantial likelihood of misidentification.

TESTIMONIAL EVIDENCE: Oral evidence, as distinct from physical evidence.

LINEUP: A police procedure in which a suspect is included in a group with other persons and a victim or witness is asked to identify the perpetrator.

JURISPRUDENCE

A Lineup is Deemed to Be Unfair
Foster v. California, 394 U.S. 440 (1969)

In this case, Foster was alleged to have committed a robbery at a Western Union office. The manager of the office was taken to a police station and shown a lineup of three potential suspects, including Foster, who was 6-feet tall and wearing jacket similar to what the robber had worn, and two men who were much shorter. The manger was unable to definitively choose the robber from this lineup. Foster was then placed in an office, with the manager seated across from him at a table. The manager said he was still unsure. Several days later, another lineup was created with Foster and four men, and this time the office manager said he was "convinced" Foster was the robber. That statement was used at trial, and Foster was found guilty of robbery.

On review, in striking down the use of this identification at trial, the Supreme Court said, "The suggestive elements in this identification procedure made it all but inevitable that David would identify petitioner whether or not he was, in fact, 'the man.' In effect, the police repeatedly said to the witness, 'This is the man.' ... This procedure so undermined the reliability of the eyewitness identification as to violate due process." In the end, it was the breadth of the Due Process Clause of the Fourteenth Amendment that created a constitutional defect in this lineup.

Bodily Intrusions

In *Rochin v. California* (1952),[198] police officers illegally entered Rochin's home based merely on a tip that he was selling narcotics. In Rochin's bedroom, police spotted two capsules on the nightstand, whereupon Rochin swallowed the capsules to prevent their recovery by the police. After failing to induce Rochin to vomit by restraining him, forcing his mouth open, and pushing on his stomach, police took him to the hospital, where a doctor forcibly *pumped* his stomach, using an emetic tube. The police were able to recover the capsules, which turned out to contain morphine. Rochin was subsequently convicted of drug possession. Reviewing this case, the Supreme Court held that the actions of the police violated Rochin's due process rights. Justice Frankfurter wrote the opinion for the Court:

> [W]e are compelled to conclude that the proceedings by which this conviction was obtained do more than offend some fastidious squeamishness or private sentimentalism about combatting crime too energetically. This is conduct that shocks the conscience. Illegally breaking into the privacy of the petitioner, the struggle to open his mouth and remove what was there, the forcible extraction of his stomach's contents—this course of proceeding by agents of government to obtain evidence is bound to offend even hardened sensibilities. They are methods too close to the rack and the screw to permit of constitutional differentiation.

The *shocks the conscience* standard has been employed by the courts ever since to invalidate extreme actions by government agents—even ones that do not directly violate precedents related to the Fourth Amendment or the Self-Incrimination Clause. The Supreme Court has made clear that this standard is applicable only to the most extreme actions by police. Writing for the Court in *County of Sacramento v. Lewis* (1998),[199] Justice David Souter observed that "in a due process challenge to executive action, the threshold question is whether the behavior of the governmental officer is so egregious, so outrageous, that it may fairly be said to shock the contemporary conscience." Justice Souter went on to say that "conduct intended to injure in some way unjustifiable by any government interest is the sort of official action most likely to rise to the conscience-shocking level."

Blood and Breath Testing of Impaired Drivers

In *Schmerber v. California* (1966),[200] the Supreme Court upheld the use of blood-alcohol evidence obtained from a suspect through a blood draw while the suspect was unconscious. Schmerber was involved in an automobile accident, and police had probable cause to believe he was intoxicated. He was taken to a hospital where a doctor drew blood from his arm. Speaking through Justice Brennan, the Court said the following: (1) the Self-Incrimination Clause did not apply, as the case did not involve compelled testimony; 2) there was no Fourth Amendment violation, as police had probable cause to believe Schmerber was intoxicated and there was not sufficient time to obtain a warrant because blood-alcohol content is *evanescent evidence* that dissipates quickly over time; and (3) the nonconsensual blood draw did not violate substantive due process rights, as it did not *shock the conscience*. A subsequent decision from the Fifth Circuit found police cannot use deception to acquire consent for a blood draw; that decision also said a test taken for blood type did not fall under the *Schmerber evanescent evidence* exception because the "blood type would remain no matter how long it took to secure a warrant."[201]

Today, most states have implied consent statutes under which motorists agree to blood, urine, or breath testing for alcohol or drugs as a condition of receiving a driver's license. One who refuses such a test is subject to being fined, jailed, or having their license suspended. But in *Birchfield v. North Dakota* (2016),[202] the Supreme Court ruled that a state cannot fine someone for refusing to consent to a warrantless blood test. Following *Schmerber*, the Court's analysis in *Birchfield* focused on the Fourth Amendment—not the Self-Incrimination Clause. The blood draw was unconstitutional, in the Court's view, because there was no consent, no warrant was obtained, and there were not exigent circumstances to justify a warrantless search. It is important to note, though, that the Court did not find the same problems with respect to breath testing, which it deemed much less intrusive. Based on the *Birchfield* opinion, police are not required to obtain a warrant before administering a breath test, and a state may criminally sanction a motorist who refuses a breath test. This is discussed in greater detail in chapter 8, where we also note that a 2019 high Court decision indicates a warrant is not needed for a blood draw if the suspect is unconscious.[203]

DNA Testing

As noted in chapters 7 and 8, the Supreme Court's decision in *Maryland v. King*[204] allows police to use a cheek swab to acquire a DNA sample from a person who has been arrested. This can be done without a person's consent and without a warrant—although that decision only addressed arrests for *serious* offenses. Currently, about half of the states have laws permitting police to take DNA upon arrest for certain crimes, and the exact crimes vary across states.[205] Although Justice Kennedy's opinion in *Maryland v. King* was based on the Fourth Amendment, when it is viewed in conjunction with *Pennsylvania v. Muniz* and its approach for physical evidence (as previously noted in this chapter), one can infer that a *Miranda* warning is not required for a DNA cheek swab.

FOCUS ON LAW ENFORCEMENT

The Right to Remain Silent in Administrative Hearings

A police officer accused of misconduct is likely to face some type of disciplinary proceeding, which might include a department-led hearing or, in some places, a hearing before a state licensing board. Regardless of the exact mechanism, there are some constitutional safeguards that apply in these noncriminal contexts—since statements given in those contexts could, in theory, be used against an officer in a subsequent criminal case.

In 1967, less than seven months after its decision in *Miranda v. Arizona* (1966), the Supreme Court's opinion in *Garrity v. New Jersey*[206] created what some call *Garrity* rights for public employees who face questioning by their employers. The majority opinion from Justice Douglas indicated that when a public employee is questioned by an employer, the employee essentially is being questioned by an agent of the government; therefore, the Fifth Amendment protection against self-incrimination is applicable. Accordingly, termination (or any other adverse employment action) as a result of an employee's refusal to answer questions is impermissible. In particular, the majority opinion said that "the protection of the individual under the Fourteenth Amendment against coerced statements prohibits use in subsequent criminal proceedings of statements obtained under threat of removal from office, and that it extends to all, whether they are policemen or other members of our body politic."

In follow-up cases, the Supreme Court provided additional context for the application of *Garrity* rights. One of these decisions, *Gardner v. Broderick* (1968),[207] pitted a New York City police officer, Gardner, against the City's Police Commissioner, Broderick. Officer Gardner was given a subpoena to testify in front of a grand jury investigating an unlawful gambling operation allegedly tied to police officers. Gardner was advised of his right to remain silent but also was told that if he did not sign a waiver of those rights, he would be fired from his job. He refused to sign, and a department-led administrative hearing was convened, with the result being his termination from the NYPD. He sued for reinstatement, claiming a violation of the Fifth Amendment. On review, the Supreme Court found in favor of Officer Gardner. Justice Abe Fortas delivered the opinion of the Court, which declared, "The choice given petitioners was either to forfeit their jobs or to incriminate themselves. The option to lose their means of livelihood or to pay the penalty of self-incrimination is the antithesis of free choice to speak out or to remain silent."

Finally, it is important to understand that if an employee's statements that are worthy of protection under the *Garrity* decision are excluded from a criminal trial, that employee could still be convicted of criminal charges based on other evidence; *Garrity* does not provide an absolute immunity to a criminal charge.[208]

Conclusion

For the founders of the United States, declaring independence from Great Britain was based in large part on the desire to abolish oppressive police tactics that deprived colonists of basic procedural safeguards in the domain of criminal justice. Thus, it is not surprising that some constitutional amendments are directed at placing limits on government abuses of power in this area.

Notably, the Fifth Amendment contains a reference to "due process of law," which offers a broad guarantee of fairness in the criminal justice process—one that can be applied to myriad contexts, ranging from lineups to proof beyond a reasonable doubt being required for a guilty verdict at trial. Due process has even been used by the Supreme Court to protect against confessions being coerced by threats that are either physical, or even mental, in nature.

The Fifth Amendment also strives to protect against unwarranted prosecutions by invoking the notion of a grand jury, which can determine if enough evidence exists to hold a criminal trial. Equally important is the concept of double jeopardy, which places limitations on repeated trials for charges that encompass the same *essential elements*. Of course, we have noted in this chapter that state and federal charges for the same offense are permitted under the *separate sovereigns* doctrine.

Perhaps most important among the protections discussed in this chapter are the *Miranda* rights, which require police to inform those accused of crimes that they possess constitutional rights to remain silent and to have the assistance of legal counsel. These rights serve as safeguards in what some might call the inherently coercive environs of criminal interrogations.

However, *Miranda* rights are not required as a precursor for all police questioning—in keeping with the objectives of preserving police powers to properly investigate criminal activity and keeping society at large safe from illicit activity. The Supreme Court has noted that *Miranda* warnings are necessary when a person is in police custody (i.e., not free to go) and when an interrogation attempts to elicit testimonial evidence through express questioning or its functional equivalent—with the latter perhaps involving statements designed to indirectly elicit a confession, such as, "Do you believe in God?" Exceptions to the requirement for *Miranda* warnings include the protection of public safety, the work of undercover agents, spontaneous statements by a criminal, routine booking questions, and the procurement of physical evidence—like DNA, blood samples, or even videos of slurred speech.

It also is crucial to note that the Supreme Court requires accused criminals to *unambiguously* invoke the right to remain silent for it to become applicable, and if such an invocation of this right is made, police must halt an interrogation immediately. When a person fails to invoke their rights clearly, though, or when they voluntarily choose to speak to police, even their silence in response to a question could be used against them at trial. Moreover, if a confession is unconstitutionally acquired, the concept of inevitable discovery could allow for evidence derived from a confession to be used at trial, even if the confession itself is suppressed.

Overall, courts have used the Fifth Amendment to protect the rights of those accused of crimes as they move through pretrial processes that range from post-arrest lineups and interrogations to indictments for criminal offenses. Certainly, problems related to false confessions still pervade contemporary society, but at the very least, constitutional safeguards that were not available to this country's founders during the colonial period can provide avenues for successful appeals of criminal convictions today. Moreover, those safeguards—and attendant case precedents—have provided police with guidelines for ensuring the difficult task of bringing criminals to justice for their actions can be completed with appropriate attention to individual liberties.

In the ensuing chapters, we confront amendments relevant to the next phases in this process: the criminal trial and the imposition of punishment.

Discussion Questions

1.   Suppose a state legislature passed a law replacing the reasonable doubt standard with a less demanding standard of proof, preponderance of the evidence, for misdemeanor cases only. Would this law be constitutional? What constitutional principle would come into play here?

2. Does your state use the grand jury as the charging mechanism for routine felony cases? If so, would you favor abolishing the grand jury and replacing it with the information/preliminary hearing model?

3. Suppose a police officer accused of using excessive force in making an arrest is acquitted by a jury in a state criminal trial. Would the Double Jeopardy Clause prohibit a U.S. attorney from seeking an indictment of the police officer on federal civil rights charges?

4. Why did the founders provide for a protection against being compelled to give testimony against oneself? In what ways do different forms of immunity further the objectives of the Self-Incrimination Clause, and in what ways can immunity fail to further these objectives? Can you find real world examples?

5. The Supreme Court has crafted specific criteria for indicating when *Miranda* warnings must be read and when there are exceptions to the use of those warnings. Outline these key parameters for discerning when such warnings are needed and when they are not. Point to real-world examples when possible. How do cases like *Berghuis v. Thompkins* and *Salinas v. Texas* generate confusion over a so-called right to remain silent? In what ways has the Supreme Court attempted to give power back to police in the decades since the *Miranda* ruling?

6. What concerns related to "false confessions" persist in contemporary society—even with the widespread acceptance and use of *Miranda* warnings? How can those concerns be addressed?

7. In what ways can the collection of physical evidence create concerns related to self-incrimination? What other constitutional protections are relevant in the analysis of such situations? If a man is placed in a lineup with four other individuals who look nothing like him, what constitutional considerations apply to a motion to suppress evidence derived from that lineup? What might enable police to use evidence derived from a tainted procedure such as this?

Endnotes

1 The Fifth Amendment's Takings Clause, which we addressed briefly in chapter 3, limits the power of government to take private property for public use. *See, e.g., Nollan v. California Coastal Commission*, 483 U.S. 825 (1987).

2 *Bolling v. Sharpe*, 347 U.S. 497 (1954).

3 *United States v. Windsor*, 570 U.S. 744 (2013).

4 *See, e.g., Wisconsin v. Constantineau*, 400 U.S. 433 (1971); *Meacham v. Fano*, 427 U.S. 215 (1976); *Hamdi v. Rumsfeld*, 542 U.S. 507 (2004).

5 *Galpin v. Page*, 85 U.S. 350 (1873).

6 *Miles v. United States*, 103 U.S. 304 (1880); *see Davis v. United States*, 160 U.S. 469 (1895); *Holt v. United States*, 218 U.S. 245 (1910); *Wilson v. United States*, 232 U.S. 563 (1914); *Brinegar v. United States*, 338 U.S. 160 (1949); *Leland v. Oregon*, 343 U.S. 790 (1952); *Holland v. United States*, 348 U.S. 121 (1954); *Speiser v. Randall*, 357 U.S. 513 (1958).

7 *Davis v. United States, supra* note 6 (as described in *In re Winship*, 397, U.S. 358 (1970)).

8 *Holland v. United States*, 348 U.S. 121 (1954).

9 *In re Winship*, 397 U.S. 358 (1970).

10 *Cage v. Louisiana*, 498 U.S. 39 (1990).

11 *Allen v. United States*, 164 U.S. 492 (1896).

12   *Victor v. Nebraska*, 511 U.S. 1 (1994) (citing *Hopt v. Utah*, 110 U.S. 574 (1884)); *Taylor v. Kentucky*, 436 U.S. 478 (1978); *Jackson v. Virginia*, 443 U.S. 307 (1979).

13   *Jacobson v. United States*, 503 U.S. 540 (1992).

14   *United States v. Logan*, 49 F.3d 352 (8th Cir. 1995).

15   Insanity Defense Reform Act of 1984, 18 U.S.C. § 17(b).

16   *Clark v. Arizona*, 548 U.S. 735 (2006) (Kansas, Idaho, Montana, and Utah are states that do not allow such a defense to be raised in court.).

17   *Kahler v. Kansas*, 589 U.S. ___ (2020) Under Kansas law, a person can be found guilty of a crime even if it is determined that they cannot distinguish right from wrong; the only way to successfully employ an insanity claim is to use it in showing that the defendant lacked the level of mens rea required by a statute.

18   *Powell v. Texas*, 392 U.S. 514 (1968).

19   *McBoyle v. United States*, 283 U.S. 25 (1931).

20   *Papachristou v. City of Jacksonville*, 405 U.S. 156 (1972).

21   *See, e.g.*, *Connally v. General Construction Co.*, 269 U. S. 385 (1926); *Kolender v. Lawson*, 461 U. S. 352 (1983).

22   *United States v. Batchelder*, 442 U. S. 114, 123 (1979).

23   *Johnson v. United States*, 576 U.S. 591 (2015).

24   Armed Career Criminal Act of 1984, Pub. L. No. 98-473, 98 Stat. 2185, 18 U.S.C. § 924(e).

25   *Sessions v. Dimaya*, 84 U.S. ___ (2018).

26   Immigration and Nationality Act of 1952, Pub. L. 82-414, 66 Stat. 163, 18 U.S.C. § 16.

27   *Coates v. Cincinnati*, 402 U. S. 611 (1971).

28   *Id.* (citing *Connally v. General Construction Co.*, 269 U. S. 385 (1926)).

29   *City of Chicago v. Morales*, 527 U.S. 41 (1999).

30   *Id.* (citing *Kent v. Dulles*, 357 U.S. 116 (1958)); *Papachristou v. City of Jacksonville*, 405 U.S. 156 (1972).

31   *City of Chicago v. Morales*, *supra* note 29 (quoting *Giaccio v. Pennsylvania*, 382 U. S. 399 (1966)).

32   *City of Chicago v. Morales*, *supra* note 29.

33   *Caperton v. A.T. Massey Coal Co.*, 556 U.S. 868 (2009).

34   *See, e.g.*, Aaron Blake, *How Clarence Thomas's Recusal Controversy Compares to Others.* Wash. Post, Mar. 28, 2022, https://www.washingtonpost.com/politics/2022/03/28/thomas-ginsburg-past-recusals/.

35   The grand jury originated in the mid-twelfth century as an investigative agent of the Crown. By the thirteenth century, it began to function as a check against arbitrary and unwarranted prosecution. The common-law grand jury consisted of twenty-three persons, at least twelve of whom had to agree in order to hand down an indictment.

36   *Hurtado v. California*, 110 U.S. 516 (1884).

37   18 U.S.C. § 3161.

38   *United States v. Lovasco*, 431 U.S. 783 (1977).

39   *United States v. Johnson*, 319 U.S. 503 (1943).

40   *Pittsburgh Plate Glass Co. v. United States*, 360 U.S. 395 (1959).

41   *Hernandez v. Texas*, 347 U.S. 475 (1954).

42   *Castaneda v. Partida*, 430 U.S. 482 (1977).

43   *Costello v. United States*, 350 U.S. 359 (1956).

44   *United States v. Calandra*, 414 U.S. 338 (1974).

45   *Kastigar v. United States*, 406 U.S. 441 (1972).

46 *United States v. North*, 910 F.2d 843 (D.C. Cir. 1990).

47 *Lefkowitz v. Turley*, 414 U.S. 70 (1973).

48 *In re Groban*, 352 U.S. 330 (1957).

49 It is well established in American law that a doctor cannot be forced to disclose a communication with a patient that occurred within the professional relationship. The clergy–penitent privilege shields communications between a member of the clergy and a person who confesses to a crime during a spiritual counseling session. The spousal privilege shields communications within a marriage.

50 *Branzburg v. Hayes*, 408 U.S. 665 (1972).

51 *United States v. North*, 910 F.2d 843 (D.C. Cir. 1990).

52 *See* Greg Henderson, *Supreme Court Lets Stand Ruling on Oliver North*, United Press International, May 28, 1991, https://www.upi.com/Archives/1991/05/28/Supreme-Court-lets-stand-ruling-on-Oliver-North/9442675403200/; David Johnston, *Poindexter Wins Iran-Contra Case in Appeals Court*, N.Y. Times, Nov. 16, 1991, https://www.nytimes.com/1991/11/16/us/poindexter-wins-iran-contra-case-in-appeals-court.html.

53 *Benton v. Maryland*, 395 U.S. 784 (1969).

54 *Green v. United States*, 355 U.S. 184 (1957).

55 *United States v. Sanges*, 144 U.S. 310 (1892); *United States v. Ball*, 163 U.S. 662 (1896).

56 *Burks v. United States*, 437 U.S. 1 (1978).

57 *Crist v. Bretz*, 437 U.S. 28 (1978); *Serfass v. United States*, 420 U.S. 377 (1975).

58 *Oregon v. Kennedy*, 456 U.S. 667 (1982).

59 *United States v. Wilson*, 420 U.S. 332 (1975).

60 *Blockburger v. United States*, 284 U.S. 299 (1932).

61 DallasNews Administrator, *Dallas Man Arrested in Murder Case Goes Free Because Of Double Jeopardy*, Dallas Morning News, May 26, 2013, https://www.dallasnews.com/news/crime/2013/05/27/dallas-man-arrested-in-murder-case-goes-free-because-of-double-jeopardy/; *see* WFAA Staff and WFAA.com (WFAA), *Dallas DA's Office Cites Double Jeopardy in Declining to Prosecute Murder*, WFAA Dallas, March 10, 2014), https://www.wfaa.com/amp/article/news/crime/dallas-das-office-cites-double-jeopardy-in-declining-to-prosecute-murder/287-304696793.

62 *Abbate v. United States*, 359 U.S. 187 (1959).

63 *Bartkus v. Illinois*, 359 U.S. 121 (1959).

64 *Gamble v. United States*, 587 U.S. ___ (2019).

65 Natasha Bertrand, *A Supreme Court Case Could Liberate Trump to Pardon His Associates*, The Atlantic, Sept. 25, 2018, https://www.theatlantic.com/politics/archive/2018/09/trump-pardon-orrin-hatch-supreme-court/571285/.

66 *See United States v. Hennis*, No. 17-0263-AR, Crim. App. No. 20100304, (C.A.A.F. Feb. 28, 2020), https://www.armfor.uscourts.gov/newcaaf/opinions/2019OctTerm/170263.pdf; Death Penalty Information Center, New Brief—Recent Death-Penalty Decisions Through March 6, March 6, 2020, https://deathpenaltyinfo.org/stories/news-developments-recent-death-penalty-decisions-through-march-6; Thom Patterson, *Triple Murder Suspect Goes from Guilty to Innocent and Back to Guilty*, CNN, July 18, 2014, https://www.cnn.com/2014/07/18/us/death-row-stories-hennis/index.html.

67 *Commonwealth of Puerto Rico v. Sanchez Valle et al.*, 579 U.S. (2016).

68 *Id.* (citing *Puerto Rico v. Shell Co.*, 302 U.S. 253 (1937)).

69 *Denezpi v. United States*, 596 U.S. ___ (2022). Federal courts, for instance, hold jurisdiction over offenses listed in the Major Crimes Act (and federal domestic violence laws), whereas Tribal courts would have specified Tribal laws to enforce. See Chapter 2 for further discussion

70 *Griffin v. California*, 380 U.S. 609 (1965).

71 *Hoffman v. United States*, 341 U. S. 479, 486 (1951).

72 *Counselman v. Hitchcock*, 142 U.S. 547 (1892).

73 *Brown v. Walker*, 161 U.S. 591 (1896).

74 *Malloy v. Hogan*, 378 U.S. 1 (1964).

75 *Marchetti v. United States*, 390 U.S. 39 (1968).

76 *Haynes v. United States*, 390 U.S. 85 (1968).

77 *Leary v. United States*, 395 U.S. 6 (1969).

78 *Bram v. United States*, 168 U.S. 532 (1897).

79 *See, e.g., Lyons v. Oklahoma*, 322 U.S. 596 (1944).

80 *See Brown v. Mississippi*, 297 U.S. 278 (1936).

81 *See Ashcraft v. Tennessee*, 322 U. S. 143 (1944).

82 *County of Riverside v. McLaughlin*, 500 U.S. 44 (1991).

83 Federal Rules of Criminal Procedure, Rule 5(a); Initial Appearance.

84 *McNabb v. United States*, 318 U.S. 332 (1943); *Mallory v. United States*, 354 U.S. 449 (1957).

85 *Corley v. United States*, 556 U.S. 303 (2009).

86 18 U.S.C. § 3501(c) (Admissibility of confessions; the confession must be deemed voluntary by a judge and a jury must be allowed to decide what *weight* should be given to the confession.).

87 *Hopt v. Utah, supra* note 12.

88 *Brown v. Mississippi*, 297 U.S. 278 (1936).

89 *Chambers v. Florida*, 309 U.S. 227 (1940).

90 *Ashcraft v. Tennessee*, 322 U.S. 143 (1944).

91 *Turner v. Pennsylvania*, 338 U.S. 62 (1949).

92 *Watts v. Indiana*, 338 U.S. 49 (1949).

93 *Haley v. Ohio*, 332 U.S. 596 (1948).

94 *Fikes v. Alabama*, 352 U.S. 191 (1957).

95 *Payne v. Arkansas*, 356 U.S. 560 (1958).

96 *Id.* (citing *Lisenba v. California*, 314 U.S. 219 (1941) and, among other cases, *Brown v. Mississippi, supra* note 88); *Chambers v. Florida, supra* note 89.

97 *Watts v. Indiana*, 338 U.S. 49 (1949).

98 *Spano v. New York*, 360 U.S. 315 (1959).

99 *Blackburn v. Alabama*, 361 U.S. 190 (1960).

100 *Haynes v. Washington*, 373 U.S. 503 (1963).

101 *Escobedo v. Illinois*, 378 U.S. 478 (1964).

102 *Miranda v. Arizona*, 384 U.S. 436 (1966).

103 The other cases were *California v. Stewart, Vignera v. New York*, and *Westover v. United States*.

104 *Escobedo v. Illinois*, 378 U.S. 478 (1964).

105 *Miranda Decision Said to End Effective Use of Confessions*, N.Y. Times, August 21, 1966.

106 *Beecher v. Alabama*, 398 U.S. 35 (1967) (The accused criminal in this case was also in a hospital receiving morphine treatment for a police-inflicted gunshot wound to his leg at the time he confessed.).

107   *Dickerson v. United States*, 530 U.S. 428 (2000).

108   *Berghuis v. Thompkins*, 560 U.S. 370 (2010).

109   *Davis v. United States*, 512 U.S. 452 (1994).

110   *Salinas v. Texas*, 570 U.S. 178 (2013).

111   *See* Evelyn A. French, *When Silence Ought to Be Golden: Why the Supreme Court Should Uphold the Selective Silence Doctrine in the Wake of Salinas v. Texas*, 48 GA. L. Rev. 623 (2014).

112   *Doyle v. Ohio*, 426 U.S. 610 (1976).

113   *Griffin v. California*, 380 U.S. 609 (1965).

114   *Id.* (citing *Murphy v. Waterfront Comm.*, 378 U.S. 52, 55 (1964)).

115   *Michigan v. Mosley*, 423 U.S. 96 (1975).

116   *Edwards v. Arizona*, 451 U.S. 477 (1981).

117   *Maryland v. Shatzer*, 559 U.S. 98 (2010).

118   *Minnick v. Mississippi*, 498 U.S. 146 (1990).

119   *Arizona v. Roberson*, 486 U.S. 675 (1988).

120   *See, e.g., People v. Elliott*, 833 NW.2d 284 (Mich. 2013) (where the Michigan Supreme Court said *Miranda* rights are not required in situations where a parolee confesses to a parole officer); *Commonwealth v. Cooley*, 118 A.3d 370 (Penn. 2015) (where the Pennsylvania Supreme Court reached a different conclusion).

121   *Berkemer v. McCarty*, 468 U.S. 420 (1984).

122   *Maryland v. Shatzer, supra* note 117.

123   *United States v. Antonelli*, 434 F.2d 335 (2d Cir. 1970).

124   *Escobedo v. Illinois*, 378 U.S. 478 (1964).

125   *Howes v. Fields*, 565 U.S. 499 (2012).

126   *Rhode Island v. Innis*, 446 U.S. 291 (1980).

127   *Pennsylvania v. Muniz*, 496 U.S. 582 (1990) (citing *Schmerber v. California*, 384 U.S. 757 (1966)).

128   In chapter 10, we noted that in *Hiibel v. Nevada* (2004), the Supreme Court did indicate that this question, "What is your name?" could become problematic from a *Miranda* perspective if revealing one's name might indicate the existence of a warrant for their arrest. Even so, the opinion in *Hiibel* did not directly address this issue because such a scenario was not relevant in that case; this remains a potential conundrum for future cases to examine.

129   Forrest Maltzman, James Spriggs, & Paul Wahlbeck, Crafting Law on the Supreme Court: The Collegial Game 3–4 (2000).

130   *Rhode Island v. Innis* (1980), *supra* note 126.

131   *Illinois v. Perkins*, 496 U.S. 292 (1990).

132   *Harris v. New York*, 401 U.S. 222 (1971).

133   *Michigan v. Harvey*, 494 U.S. 344 (1990) (In this case, the Court found that even though *Michigan v. Jackson*, 475 U.S. 625 (1986) created a rule that required police to wait until an attorney arrived before interrogating a suspect who had requested a public defender at an arraignment, a violation of that rule did not preclude use of a statement introduced to impeach defense testimony at a trial.).

134   *New York v. Quarles*, 467 U.S. 649 (1984).

135   *See, e.g., United States v. Edwards*, 885 F.2d 377 (7th Cir. 1989); *Stauffer v. Zavaris*, 37 F.3d 1495 (10th Cir. 1994); *United States v. Brutzman*, 45 F.3d 437 (9th Cir.1994).

136   *United States v. Tsarnaev*, 968 F.3d 24 (1st Cir. 2020).

137   Office of the Attorney General, Memorandum for all United States Attorneys: Guidance for Conducting Interviews without Providing *Miranda* Warnings in Arrests of Terrorism Suspects, Oct. 19, 2010, https://www.justice.gov/sites/default/files/oip/legacy/2014/07/23/ag-memo-miranda-rights.pdf.

138   *Kastigar v. United States, supra* note 45.

139   *Nix v. Williams*, 467 U.S. 431 (1984).

140   *Brewer v. Williams*, 430 U.S. 387 (1977).

141   *Id.*

142   This description is provided by the Supreme Court's majority opinion in *Nix v. Williams, supra* note 139.

143   *Oregon v. Elstad*, 470 U.S. 298 (1985).

144   *Missouri v. Seibert*, 542 U.S. 600 (2004).

145   *United States v. Patante*, 542 U.S. 630 (2004).

146   *See Haley v. Ohio, supra* note 93.

147   *Frazier v. Cupp*, 394 U.S. 731 (1969).

148   *Oregon v. Mathiason*, 429 U.S. 492 (1977).

149   *Colorado v. Connelly*, 479 U.S. 157 (1986).

150   *State v. Cayward*, 520 So. 2d 971 (Fla. Dist. Ct. App. 1989).

151   *State v. Rettenberger*, 984 P.2d 1009 (Utah 1999).

152   *State v. Patton*, 826 A.2d 783 (N.J. Super. Ct. App. Div. 2003).

153   *State of Hawaii v. Keith Matusmoto*, SCWC-14-0000933 (HI Oct. 29, 2019).

154   *State v. Baker*, 465 P.3d 860 (Hawaii 2020).

155   *Id.* (citing Richard J. Ofshe & Richard A. Leo, *The Social Psychology of Police Interrogation: The Theory and Classification of True and False Confessions*, 16 Studies in Law, Politics, and Society 189–251 (1997).

156   *Id.* (citing Miriam S. Gohara, *A Lie for a Lie: False Confessions and the Case for Reconsidering the Legality of Deceptive Interrogation Techniques*, 33 Fordham Urb. L.J. 791–822 (2006)).

157   Saul. M. Kassin, Richard A. Leo, Christian A. Meissner, Kimberly D. Richman, Lori H. Colwell, & Amy-May Leach, *Police Interviewing and Interrogation: A Self-Report Survey of Police Practices and Beliefs*, 31 Law and Human Behavior 381–400 (2007); *see* Krista D. Forrest & William D. Woody, *Police Interrogation and Its Surprising Influence on Jurors' Perception of Confession Evidence*, 22 The Jury Expert 9–22 (2010).

158   Brandon Bang, Duane Stanton, Craig Hemmens, & Mary Stohr, *Police recording of custodial interrogations: A state-by-state legal inquiry*, 20 International Journal of Police Science & Management, 3–18, at 10 (2018) (citing Saul M. Kassin & Katherine L. Kiechel, *The Social Psychology of False Confessions: Compliance Internalization, and Confabulation*, 7 Psychological Science, 125–128 (1996)); Jessica K. Swanner, Denise R. Beike, & Alexander T. Cole, *Snitching, Lies, and Computer Crashes: An Experimental Investigation of Secondary Confessions*, 34 Law and Human Behavior 53–65 (2010).

159   Leigh Egan, *A Look Back At Susan Smith—The South Carolina Mom Who Killer Her 2 Young Sons*, ID Crimefeed, Oct. 25, 2017, https://www.investigationdiscovery.com/crimefeed/crime-history/a-look-back-at-the-susan-smith-case-23-years-after-the-south-carolina-mom-killed-her-2-young-sons

160   *Arizona v. Fulminante*, 499 U.S. 279 (1991).

161   *Chapman v. California*, 386 U. S. 18 (1967).

162   *Arizona v. Fulminante, supra* note 160 (citing *Blackburn v. Alabama*, 361 U.S. 199 (1960)).

163 Northwestern's Bluhm Legal Clinic, Center on Wrongful Convictions, *False and Coerced Confessions*, https://www.law.northwestern.edu/legalclinic/wrongfulconvictions/issues/falseconfessions/

164 Innocence Project, *False Confessions Happen More Than We Think*, March 14, 2011, https://innocenceproject.org/false-confessions-happen-more-than-we-think/.

165 Erin Blakemore, *Examining Why False Confessions Occur in the U.S. Criminal Justice System*, Wash. Post, June 23, 2019, https://www.washingtonpost.com/health/examining-why-false-confessions-occur-in-the-us-criminal-justice-system/2019/06/20/10128bb4-9207-11e9-aadb-74e6b2b46f6a_story.html.

166 Bang et al., *supra* note 158, at 10 (citing Steven A. Drizin & Richard A. Leo, *The Problem of False Confessions in the Post-DNA World*, 82 N.C. L. Rev. 891–1007 (2004)).

167 Innocence Project, *False Confessions & Recordings of Custodial Interrogations*, https://innocenceproject.org/false-confessions-recording-interrogations/.

168 *See, e.g.*, Saul M. Kassin, Christian A. Meissner, & Rebecca J. Norwick, *I'd Know a False Confession if I Saw One: A Comparative Study of College Students and Police Investigators*, 29 Law and Human Behavior 221–227 (2005); Saul M. Kassin, Richard A. Leo, Christian A. Meissner, Kimberly D. Richman, Lori H. Colwell, & Amy-May Leach, *Police Interviewing and Interrogation: A Self-Report Survey of Police Practices and Beliefs*, 31 Law and Human Behavior 381–400 (2007); Meijer Glynis Boggard, Ewout, Aldert Vrij, & Harald Merckelbach, *Strong, but Wrong: Lay People's and Police Officers' Beliefs about Verbal and Nonverbal Cues to Deception*, 11 PLOS ONE e015615 (2016).

169 Bang et al., *supra* note 158, at 10 (citing Drizin and Leo, *supra* note 166; Gisli Gudjonsson, The Psychology of Interrogations and Confessions: A Handbook (2003)).

170 States establishing mandatory recording policies through court decisions include Alaska, Arkansas, Indiana, Minnesota, New Jersey, and Utah.

171 States establishing recording polices via statute include California, Colorado, Connecticut, Illinois, Kansas, Maine, Maryland, Michigan, Missouri, Montana, Nebraska, New Mexico, New York, North Carolina, Oregon, Texas, Vermont, and Wisconsin.

172 In Rhode Island, the Rhode Island Police Accreditation Commission has asked all police departments in the state to record interrogations in capital cases. In Hawaii, all four of the state's major police department's (Kauai County, Hawaii County, Honolulu, and Maui County) voluntarily use recordings for interrogations of most serious offenses.

173 These states are Colorado, Connecticut, Illinois, Kansas, Maine, Maryland, Michigan, Mississippi, Nebraska, New Jersey, New York, North Carolina, Texas, and Vermont, as well as the District of Columbia.

174 *See* Bang et al., *supra* note 158, at 11–12.

175 *Id.*, at 6.

176 G. Daniel Lassiter, *Psychological Science and Sound Public Policy: Video Recording of Custodial Interrogation*, 65 American Psychologist, 768–779, (2010).

177 *Id.*, at 6 (citing Yael Granot, Emily Balcetis, Kristin E. Schneider, & Tom R. Tyler, *Justice is Not Blind: Visual Attention Exaggerates the Effects of Group Identification on Legal Punishment*, 143 Journal of Experimental Psychology 2196–2208, Dec. 2014; Todd C. Warner & Kerri. L. Pickel, *Camera Perspective and Trivial Details Interact to Influence Jurors' Evaluation of a Retracted Confession*, 16 Psychology, Crime & Law 493–506 (2010).

178 *Id.*, at 7 (citing G. Daniel Lassiter & Matthew Lindberg, *Video Recording Custodial Interrogations: Implications of Psychological Science for Policy and Practice*, 38 Journal of Psychiatry & Law 177–192 (2010); Celeste J. Snyder, G. Daniel Lassiter, Matthew J. Lindberg, & Shannon K. Pinegar, *Videotaped Interrogations and Confessions: Does a Dual-Camera Approach Yield Unbiased and Accurate Evaluations?* 27 Behavioral Sciences and the Law 451–466 (2009).

179 These states are Arizona, Michigan, Montana, New Jersey, New York, North Carolina, and Utah; among these states, all but Arkansas require that a jury is instructed that nonrecorded statements must be viewed with caution.

180 *Commonwealth v. DiGiambattista*, 442 Mass. 423, 813 N.E.2d 516 (Mass. 2004) (In this case, the Massachusetts Supreme Court said "where the utilization of recording is left to the unfettered discretion of law enforcement [as it is at present], and an officer has chosen not to record a particular interrogation, we think that it is only fair to point out to the jury that the party with the burden of proof has, for whatever reason, decided not to preserve evidence of that interrogation in a more reliable form, and to tell them that they may consider that fact as part of their assessment of the less reliable form of evidence that the Commonwealth has opted to present.")

181 Bang et al., *supra* note 158, at 14; *see* Saul. M. Kassin & Lawrence S. Wrightsman, *Prior Confessions and Mock Juror Verdicts*, 10 Journal of Applied Social Psychology 133–146 (1980); Krista D. Forrest & William D. Woody, *Police Interrogation and Its Surprising Influence on Jurors' Perception of Confession Evidence*, 22 Jury Expert 9–22 (2010); Saul M. Kassin, Christian A. Meissner, & Rebecca J. Norwick, *I'd Know a False Confession if I Saw One: A Comparative Study of College Students and Police Investigators*, 29 Law and Human Behavior, 221–227 (2005).

182 *See, e.g.*, Michael K. Kaiser, *Wrongful Convictions: If Mandatory Recording is the Antidote, Are the Side Effects Worth It?* 67 Ark. L. Rev. 167 (2014).

183 *See, e.g.*, Bang et al., *supra* note 158; Innocence Project, *supra* note 167.

184 *Medellin v. Texas*, 552 U.S. 491 (2008).

185 *Case Concerning Avena and Other Mexican Nationals (Mexico v. U.S.)*, 2004 I.C.J. 12.

186 Julian Ku, *The Medellin 'Memorandum' from the President*, OpinioJuris, Feb. 3, 2005, http://opiniojuris.org/2005/03/02/the-medellin-memorandum-from-the-president/.

187 *Medellin v. Texas*, *supra* note 184 (citing *Igartua–De La Rosa v. United States*, 417 F.3d 145, 150 (1st Cir. 2005) (en banc)).

188 *United States v. Abu Ali*, 528 F.3d 210 (4th Cir. 2008).

189 These states are Alaska, Arizona, Delaware, Georgia, Idaho, Indiana, Iowa, Kansas, Nevada, New Jersey, New Mexico, North Dakota, Ohio, Utah, Washington, and Wyoming.

190 These states are Arizona, California, Nevada, and Georgia.

191 *United States v. Scheffer*, 523 U.S. 303 (1998).

192 *United States v. Barnard*, 490 F.2d 907 (9th Cir. 1973).

193 *Schmerber v. California*, 384 U.S. 757 (1966).

194 *Gilbert v. California*, 388 U.S. 263 (1967).

195 *United States v. Dionisio*, 410 U.S. 1 (1973).

196 *United States v. Wade*, 388 U.S. 218 (1967).

197 *Stovall v. Denno*, 308 U.S. 293 (1967).

198 *Rochin v. California*, 342 U.S. 165 (1952).

199 *County of Sacramento v. Lewis*, 523 U.S. 833 (1998).

200 *Schmerber v. California*, *supra* note 193.

201 *Graves v. Beto*, 424 F.2d 524 (2nd Cir. 1970).

202 *Birchfield v. North Dakota*, 579 U.S. ___ (2016).

203 *Mitchell v. Wisconsin*, 588 U.S. ___ (2019).

204 *Maryland v. King*, 569 U.S. 435 (2013).

205 Charlotte Spencer, *What Is the Arrestee DNA Collection Law in Your State?* Biometrica, May 27, 2021, https://www.biometrica.com/what-is-the-arrestee-dna-collection-law-in-your-state/.

206 *Garrity v. New Jersey*, 385 U.S. 493, 500 (1967).

207 *Gardner v. Broderick*, 392 U.S. 273 (1968).

208 *Kastigar v. United States*, 406 U.S. 441 (1972).

Credit

CHAPTER 12

The Sixth Amendment

Rights Essential to a Fair Trial

"In all criminal prosecutions, the accused shall enjoy the right to a speedy and public trial, by an impartial jury of the State and district wherein the crime shall have been committed, which district shall have been previously ascertained by law, and to be informed of the nature and cause of the accusation; to be confronted with the witnesses against him; to have compulsory process for obtaining witnesses in his favor, and to have the Assistance of Counsel for his defence."

—U.S. Constitution, Sixth Amendment

Learning Objectives

After reading this chapter, you should understand the following:

1. The fundamental importance of the right to counsel
2. The scope of the right to trial by jury
3. Why trial judges are required to scrutinize negotiated guilty pleas
4. How Congress and the Supreme Court have sought to promote speedy trials
5. The right to a public trial and the free press/fair trial problem
6. How the Constitution affects evidence in criminal adjudication
7. The constitutional issues associated with trial juries

Key Cases

Gideon v. Wainwright, 372 U.S. 335 (1963)
Strickland v. Washington, 466 U.S. 688 (1984)
Duncan v. Louisiana, 391 U.S. 145 (1968)
In re Gault, 387 U.S. 1 (1967)
Bordenkircher v. Hayes, 434 U.S. 357 (1978)
Brady v. Maryland, 373 U.S. 83 (1963)
Batson v. Kentucky, 476 U.S. 79 (1986)
Ramos v. Louisiana, 590 U.S. ___ (2020)

Introduction

For the founders of the United States, a multitude of grievances festered during the colonial era, providing them with strong reasons for breaking away from the mother country. Prevalent among these grievances were concerns related to the administration of justice in criminal cases. The Declaration of Independence, in fact, specifically criticized King George III by saying, "He has obstructed the Administration of Justice, by refusing his Assent to Laws for establishing Judiciary powers." Thomas Jefferson's writing in the Declaration even offered a pejorative reference to a *mock Trial* in describing the nature of British-led judicial proceedings in the colonies, saying of the King, "He has made Judges dependent on his Will alone ... depriving us in many cases, of the benefits of Trial by Jury." Given such remonstrations in a Founding-era document, it should come as no surprise that an amendment in the Bill of Rights is devoted to ensuring fairness in criminal court proceedings.

The Sixth Amendment is concerned entirely with the fair adjudication of criminal charges. Thus, it guarantees "speedy and public" trials by impartial juries. It also ensures the defendant's right to use "compulsory process" (i.e., the subpoena) to compel testimony by favorable witnesses and to confront (i.e., cross-examine) witnesses for the prosecution. And critically, it guarantees the right to counsel in criminal cases. Buttressed by the Due Process Clause of the Fifth Amendment as well as the Due Process and Equal Protection Clauses of the Fourteenth Amendment, the rights enshrined in the Sixth Amendment are essential to the fair adjudication of criminal charges.

The Fundamental Nature of the Right to Counsel

Our examination of the Sixth Amendment begins with the right to counsel—in other words, the right to an attorney. Historically, the right to counsel meant the right to hire a lawyer if one could afford to do so. From the beginning, the Sixth Amendment has been interpreted to allow defendants to hire a lawyer in all federal criminal cases. Likewise, the right to employ counsel is recognized by the state constitutions. Accordingly, defendants have the right to retain counsel to represent them in all criminal prosecutions, including those in state courts, in federal courts, and in military tribunals. Of course, the right to hire a lawyer means little to a defendant who lacks the means to do so. And unfortunately, the majority of people charged with crimes, both in state and federal courts, cannot afford adequate legal representation.[1]

Counsel at Public Expense for Indigent Defendants

In chapter 1, we highlighted the landmark case of *Powell v. Alabama* (1932),[2] in which the Supreme Court vacated the death sentences of nine Black teenagers who (as was revealed years later) were wrongfully convicted of rape on the false testimony of two young white women. At issue before the Court in 1932 was whether the young men were denied due process of law by a trial in which they had only token legal representation that arrived the morning of the trial's beginning, giving counsel only a few moments with their clients before the commencement of courtroom proceedings. The Supreme Court took umbrage with this arrangement, observing that "during perhaps the most critical period of the proceedings against these defendants, that is to say, from the time of their arraignment until the beginning of their trial, when consultation, thoroughgoing investigation and preparation were vitally important, the defendants did not have the aid of counsel in any real sense, although they were as much entitled to such aid during that period as at the trial itself." Succinctly, in an oft-quoted passage, Justice George Sutherland stated the holding of the Court:

> In a capital case, where the defendant is unable to employ counsel and is incapable adequately of making his own defense because of ignorance, feeble mindedness, illiteracy, or the like, it is the duty of the court, whether requested or not, to assign counsel for him as a necessary requisite of due process of law, and that duty is not discharged by an assignment at such a time or under such circumstances as to preclude the giving of effective aid in the preparation and trial of the case.

Sutherland also noted that the legal profession encompasses specialized training that even the wealthy and educated may lack, with the Court's opinion stating, "Even the intelligent and educated layman has small and sometimes no skill in the science of law. If charged with crime, he is incapable, generally, of determining for himself whether the indictment is good or bad. He is unfamiliar with the rules of evidence. Left without the aid of counsel, he may be put on trial without a proper charge, and convicted upon incompetent evidence, or evidence irrelevant to the issue or otherwise inadmissible."

Powell v. Alabama illustrates the fundamental importance of counsel in the effectuation of the rights of the accused. Without competent legal representation, defendants are hard-pressed to assert their rights. Subsequent to the *Powell* decision, which conferred a right to counsel in death penalty cases only, the high Court's decision in *Johnson v. Zerbst* (1938)[3] mandated provision of counsel for defendants facing felony charges in federal cases. In this case, Justice Hugo Black's majority opinion declared that the right to counsel is "one of the safeguards of the Sixth Amendment deemed necessary to insure fundamental human rights of life and liberty."

In *Betts v. Brady* (1942),[4] the Supreme Court refused to extend the right to appointed counsel to indigent defendants in state court proceedings, ruling instead that this was a matter for the state courts and state legislatures to confront. Therefore, at this point in U.S. history, there was no federal constitutional right to appointed counsel beyond the conditions stated in *Powell v. Alabama* regarding capital cases. But two decades

Obiter Dicta

"The Sixth Amendment stands as a constant admonition that, if the constitutional safeguards it provides be lost, justice will not 'still be done.' It embodies a realistic recognition of the obvious truth that the average defendant does not have the professional legal skill to protect himself when brought before a tribunal with power to take his life or liberty, wherein the prosecution is presented by experienced and learned counsel. That which is simple, orderly and necessary to the lawyer, to the untrained layman may appear intricate, complex and mysterious."

—Justice Hugo Black, writing for the Supreme Court in Johnson v. Zerbst, *304 U.S. 458 (1938)*

later, the Court made a dramatic turnabout. In *Gideon v. Wainwright* (1963),[5] the Court held that indigent persons charged with felonies must be provided counsel at public expense. Writing for the Court, Justice Black declared that "in our adversary system of criminal justice, any person haled into court, who is too poor to hire a lawyer, cannot be assured a fair trial unless counsel is provided for him." He went on to distill the broader importance of counsel in a criminal proceeding by analyzing the power imbalance between the state and the accused in such a case:

> Governments, both state and federal, quite properly spend vast sums of money to establish machinery to try defendants accused of crime. ... Similarly, there are few defendants charged with crime, few indeed, who fail to hire the best lawyers they can get to prepare and present their defenses. That government hires lawyers to prosecute and defendants who have the money hire lawyers to defend are the strongest indications of the widespread belief that lawyers in criminal courts are necessities, not luxuries.

JURISPRUDENCE

An Inmate's Handwritten Appeal Changes the Legal System
Gideon v. Wainwright, 372 U.S. 335 (1963)

Clarence Earl Gideon was a 51-year-old man with a lengthy criminal record that included robbery and burglary. In 1961, he was accused of breaking into the Bay Harbor Pool Room, a bar near Panama City, Florida. At approximately 5:30 AM on June 3, 1961, someone smashed a window on the backside of the bar and went inside through the window frame, using a garbage can as a stepping stool to facilitate entry. The intruder consumed beers while inside and reportedly absconded with bottles of beer, soda, and wine, as well as approximately $50 worth of coins taken from a jukebox and a cigarette machine. A witness claimed that Gideon, who lived across the street from the bar and occasionally worked there, was responsible for the break-in. Gideon was taken into police custody later that day after being located at a nearby bar—where he had purchased beers by exclusively using coins; upon his arrest, he was found to be in possession of $25.28, all in change. He was

charged with breaking and entering with intent to commit petit larceny. He requested a lawyer to assist in his case, but that request was denied by the judge, who cited Florida law that only required appointment of counsel in death penalty cases (pursuant to Supreme Court precedent). In turn, Gideon was found guilty and sentenced to five years in state prison.

While in prison, Gideon—who had an eighth-grade education—conducted research and wrote letters to the FBI and the Florida Supreme Court, arguing that his Sixth Amendment right to counsel had been violated, but those pleas were not fruitful. Then, in January 1962, he composed a handwritten five-page letter on prison stationery and sent it to the Supreme Court of the United States, seeking a writ of certiorari to review his case. The letter opened by saying, "To the Honorable Earl Warren, Chief Justice of the United States, Comes now the petitioner, Clarence Earl Gideon, a citizen of the United

States of America, in proper person, and appearing as his own counsel." Gideon invoked due process in his letter, writing, "[A]t the time of his conviction and sentence, petitioner was without aid of counsel ... he was incapable adequately of making his own defense. ... <u>Counsel must be assigned to the accused if he is unable to employ one and is incapable adequately of making his own defense.</u> ... Petitioner was deprived of due process of law in the court below" (emphasis in original).

After receiving Gideon's petition, the Supreme Court of the United States granted review, and future Supreme Court Justice Abe Fortas would be appointed as Gideon's counsel in the case. With its unanimous ruling in *Gideon v. Wainwright*, released on January 15, 1963, the Supreme Court granted Gideon a new trial. Writing for the Court, Justice Black opined that Gideon's Sixth Amendment rights had been violated, declaring that:

> The right of one charged with crime to counsel may not be deemed fundamental and essential

to fair trials in some countries, but it is in ours. From the very beginning, our state and national constitutions and laws have laid great emphasis on procedural and substantive safeguards designed to assure fair trials before impartial tribunals in which every defendant stands equal before the law. This noble ideal cannot be realized if the poor man charged with crime has to face his accusers without a lawyer to assist him.

At Gideon's second trial in a Florida court, W. Fred Turner was appointed to represent him. Turner raised questions about the observations of the key eyewitness in the case and also took statements from a taxi driver who had picked up Gideon on the morning of the break-in but did not recall Gideon being in possession of soda, beer, or wine. The jury deliberated for about an hour before issuing its verdict: not guilty.

As a result of the *Gideon* decision, thousands of prisoners nationwide were set free or given new trials, and a new public defender system was installed in all Florida counties. Attorney General Robert F. Kennedy would offer a poignant comment on this case in a 1963 speech when he declared, "If an obscure Florida convict named Clarence Earl Gideon had not sat down in prison with a pencil and paper to write a letter to the Supreme Court; and if the Supreme Court had not taken the trouble to look at the merits in that one crude petition among all the bundles of mail it must receive every day, the vast machinery of American law would have gone on functioning undisturbed." Kennedy then captured the importance of this case by saying, "But Gideon did write that letter; ... And the whole course of legal history has been changed."[6]

The same day it decided *Gideon*, the Court held in *Douglas v. California*[7] that indigent felony defendants must be provided counsel for one appeal. Justice William O. Douglas spoke for the Court, declaring that "where the merits of the one and only appeal an indigent has as of right are decided without benefit of counsel, we think an unconstitutional line has been drawn between rich and poor."

Appointed Counsel in Misdemeanor Cases

The *Gideon* decision applied only to felony defendants. In *Argersinger v. Hamlin* (1972),[8] the Court extended *Gideon* to misdemeanors where defendants face possible jail sentences. Seven years later, in *Scott v. Illinois* (1979),[9] where a bench trial resulted in a $50 fine for the offense of shoplifting, a more conservative Court narrowed the right to appointed counsel by holding that "no indigent criminal defendant [can] be sentenced to a term of imprisonment unless the State has afforded him the right to assistance of appointed counsel in his defense." In other words, the right to appointed counsel does not apply in a misdemeanor case in which the defendant is not *actually* sent to jail (as distinct from a case in which the accused faces *possible* jail time). In dissent, Justice William Brennan argued that the position articulated in *Argersinger* "more faithfully implements the principles of the Sixth Amendment identified in *Gideon*." Also dissenting, Justice Harry Blackmun contended that the Court should follow the same standard it had previously embraced with respect to the right to a jury trial, under which "an indigent defendant in a state criminal case must be afforded appointed counsel whenever the defendant is prosecuted for a nonpetty criminal offense, that is, one punishable by more than six months' imprisonment."

The Public Defender System

Today, every state—and the federal government—has some type of public defender system through which a lawyer can be appointed for those who cannot afford one. The appointment request is usually addressed at an arraignment, when a judge can decide if a defendant is indigent or, depending on state procedures, counsel is automatically appointed upon request of the defendant or at the behest of the judge.

Data regarding nationwide public defender usage is scant, but according to the most recent information available from the Bureau of Justice Statistics (which dates to 2009), there were approximately 15,000 public defenders in the country, who handled over 5.6 million cases per year at the state and federal levels.[10]

Following the Supreme Court's *Gideon* decision, Congress, in 1964, passed the Criminal Justice Act,[11] which established a federal system for offering legal counsel to indigent defendants in federal cases; a 1970 amendment allows states the ability to create public defender services that correspond to their individual federal district courts. Two options exist from which states can choose. One is to establish a federal defender services office that covers a district court and possibly an adjacent one. For example, the Federal Defender Services of Eastern Tennessee provides representation for indigent defendants in cases before the U.S. District Court for Eastern Tennessee. Defender services offices are funded by the federal government and led by a Chief Public Defender selected to a four-year term by the federal circuit court for their jurisdiction. The Administrative Office of the U.S. Courts oversees defender services offices. The other option is to establish a federal community defender organization, which is actually funded through federal grants but incorporated under state law and operated as a nonprofit with a board of directors chosen by state officials. Taking both methods into account, there are currently eighty-one public defender systems that represent individuals in ninety-one of the ninety-four federal district courts.[12]

At the state level, different methods of providing counsel to the indigent exist. There are twenty-eight states that use a state-run (and state-funded) public defender system, whereas other states rely upon county or city-run systems that could be funded by local governments with state assistance. In some situations, state or local governments might make contracts with private attorneys or nonprofit groups. For example, Legal Aid Society of New York contracts with New York City and handles more than 300,000 cases a year; it is the nation's largest nonprofit organization providing legal assistance. In capital cases, assistance is often provided for appeals, such as through the nonprofit California Appellate Project. Moreover, the concept of *panel lists* exist in some states, through which private lawyers can be appointed at public expense when needed.[13]

The head of a public defender's office can be appointed (perhaps, by a governor) or elected, and names of state and local public defender offices can vary. Kentucky, for instance, has a state-run Department of Public Advocacy; some local areas around the country have community law offices. Some groups, such as Holistic Bronx Defenders in New York or the Louisiana Center for Children's Rights, take a "holistic" approach in terms of creating or linking with rehabilitation, educational, or even recreational programs.[14]

Generally, public defender offices are overworked and underfunded. Eight states require an application fee for an indigent defendant to pursue counsel from a public defender, and some pursue recovery of fees for legal services. Investigators can be employed to assist a public defender's office, but given the costs involved, six states had fewer than ten full-time investigators, according to a 2013 survey reported by the Bureau of Justice Statistics (BJS).[15] Tina Peng, of the Orleans Public Defenders Office in New Orleans, has spoken of the challenges of public defense work by saying, "Our office represents 85 percent of the people charged with crimes in Orleans Parish but has an annual budget about a third the size of the district attorney's. The American Bar Association recommends that public defenders not work on more than 150 felony cases a year. In 2014, I handled double that."[16] Elsewhere, Michael Berrett, head of the Missouri public defender system, described the nature of public defender work as follows:

> Here's what happens. Someone goes to local jail, and we go to them after two weeks. We say, 'Good news is we're going to work hard on your case; bad news it's going to be a while until we get to your case.' Most end up making plea deals just to get out of jail, not knowing that a conviction could follow them for the rest of their lives. In the meantime, these individuals lose their jobs, they lose their apartment, and a lot of them plead to crimes they don't commit. It happens every day. People take it because they want to get out.[17]

Ultimately, the disconnect between the ideal of providing counsel to the indigent and the reality of making that legal representation effective from a practical standpoint remains an ongoing challenge for public defenders across the country.

FOCUS ON LAW ENFORCEMENT

An Officer's Right to Representation in a Police Disciplinary Hearing

Because the Sixth Amendment begins with the phrase, "In all criminal prosecutions," there is no right to appointed counsel in an administrative hearing, such as a police disciplinary hearing. Even so, in keeping with principles of due process, the Supreme Court has allowed a person to retain their own counsel, at their own cost, for a hearing in which a deprivation of liberty or property interests is at stake.[18] For police disciplinary hearings, a local police union or police benevolent association (PBA) is likely to provide counsel—though membership in such an organization might require the payment of annual or monthly dues.

The Florida Police Benevolent Association provides an instructive example, as its website says "one of the primary benefits of membership is legal assistance." This organization retains two full-time in-house attorneys and other attorneys who can provide services to law enforcement officers at no cost. The Florida PBA website observes that such representation can be provided in any of the following: (1) a disciplinary case that involves suspension, demotion, or dismissal by an officer's agency; (2) a case brought in front of the state's Criminal Justice Standards and Training Commission (CJSTC), which can move to decertify an officer—with counsel offered in all phases of that process, including a probable cause hearing and a final hearing before the full CJSTC; (3) all parts of a criminal investigation, from on-scene questioning, through a grand jury investigation to a criminal trial; and (4) a civil suit arising out of law enforcement duties.[19]

Elsewhere, in the criminal trial of Minneapolis Police Officer Derek Chauvin, he received legal assistance paid for by Minnesota's largest union of police officers: the Minneapolis Police and Peace Officers Association (MPPOA).[20] That organization maintained a legal defense fund that offered up to $1 million for Chauvin's defense team, which consisted of as many as twelve attorneys working on his case.[21] Those attorneys were chosen from a rotating panel of lawyers, who are on retainer for the MPPOA and are experienced in officer-related cases. The benefits of such legal representation were still available to Chauvin, who had paid dues over the course of his nineteen-year career, even though he was fired less than a week after Floyd's death.

The Right to Counsel during Interrogation

In the previous chapter, we discussed the landmark case of *Miranda v. Arizona* (1966)[22] as it relates to the Fifth Amendment protection against compulsory self-incrimination. An equally important aspect of that decision, of course, involves the right to counsel. As Chief Justice Warren said in the majority opinion in *Miranda*:

> The circumstances surrounding in-custody interrogation can operate very quickly to overbear the will of one merely made aware of his privilege by his interrogators. Therefore, the right to have counsel present at the interrogation is indispensable to the protection of the Fifth Amendment privilege under the system we delineate today. Our aim is to assure that the individual's right to choose between silence and speech remains unfettered throughout the interrogation process. A once-stated warning, delivered by those who will conduct the interrogation, cannot itself suffice to that end among those who most require knowledge of their rights.

Chief Justice Warren went on to observe, "With a lawyer present, the likelihood that the police will practice coercion is reduced, and, if coercion is nevertheless exercised, the lawyer can testify to it in court." For many reasons, then, the *Miranda* warning informs a suspect of not only the right to remain silent but also the right to counsel.

Even prior to the *Miranda* ruling, the Supreme Court's decision in *Escobedo v. Illinois* (1964)[23] held that the Sixth Amendment right to counsel should apply as soon as a person is taken into police custody, with the Court recognizing that interrogation must cease immediately upon a suspect's request for counsel. Other Supreme Court cases have indicated that a right to counsel applies at all *critical stages* in criminal proceedings; the exact meaning of *critical stage* could vary based on specific nature of court procedures in a particular state, but such key moments typically include these two events: the arraignment, which involves a formal reading of criminal charges and the entering of a plea, and the preliminary hearing, when a judge decides if there is enough evidence to conduct a trial.

In 1961, the Supreme Court ruled that defendants were entitled to have counsel present at arraignments in the state of Alabama because that was the only time an insanity plea could be raised.[24] Additionally, a 1963 high Court decision indicated that the right to counsel applied at a preliminary hearing in Maryland, which was deemed a "critical stage" in that case because a guilty plea was entered without benefit of counsel.[25] Multiple cases also have reiterated that the right to have counsel present applies at any lineups that occur after an arrest has been made.[26] Overall, just as with the right to remain silent, when a person is in police custody, the right to counsel becomes essential.

Invoking the Right to Counsel

In chapter 11, we observed the Supreme Court has held that suspects who are being interrogated must invoke their right to remain silent in an *unambiguous* way to terminate questioning. The same logic underlying that principle is equally valid when it comes to invoking the right to counsel. Thus, if a person asks for a lawyer, the interrogation should stop immediately—but the request for a lawyer must be *unambiguous*. In 1994, the Supreme Court considered the case of a man named Robert Davis, who was accused of committing a murder at the Charleston Naval Base. Davis had been seen arguing with another man over a wager on a game of pool, and when that other man was found dead (beaten with a pool cue), Davis became the prime suspect.

Agents from Naval Criminal Investigative Service (NCIS) then conducted an interrogation. Davis was read his *Miranda* rights, and after about 90 minutes of questioning, he said, "Maybe I should talk to a lawyer." However, the interrogation continued after that statement, lasting for roughly another hour, and Davis eventually made statements incriminating himself in the killing. Those statements were used against him at trial, where he was found guilty of murder.

Reviewing this matter, the U.S. Court of Appeals for the Armed Forces found no violation of the Sixth Amendment, a conclusion with which the U.S. Supreme Court agreed in *Davis v. United States* (1994).[27] Justice Sandra Day O'Connor's majority opinion found Davis had failed to make an "unambiguous or unequivocal request for counsel." The Court hypothesized an alternative outcome that would require law enforcement to guess if a person actually wanted to invoke the right counsel or not, with Justice O'Connor saying, "Police officers would be forced to make difficult judgment calls about whether the suspect in fact wants a lawyer even though he has not said so, with the threat of suppression if they guess wrong." Despite this statement, and the ruling in this case, Justice O'Connor offered nonbinding advice for "police practice," observing the following:

> Of course, when a suspect makes an ambiguous or equivocal statement it will often be good police practice for the interviewing officers to clarify whether or not he actually wants an attorney. ... Clarifying questions help protect the rights of the suspect by ensuring that he gets an attorney if he wants one, and will minimize the chance of a confession being suppressed due to subsequent judicial second guessing as to the meaning of the suspect's statement regarding counsel. But we decline to adopt a rule requiring officers to ask clarifying questions.

It is also important to note that a defendant can change their mind about invoking counsel, right up to the point of pleading guilty. In *Chandler v. Fretag* (1954),[28] for instance, a defendant appeared in a Tennessee state court, without an attorney, with the intention of pleading guilty to charges of housebreaking and larceny, which carried a sentencing range of three to ten years. Upon his appearance, the judge informed the defendant that he faced life imprisonment under a habitual offender law. The defendant requested a continuance to speak with a lawyer, but that request was denied. He was found guilty and sentenced to life in prison. On review, the Supreme Court reversed the conviction, finding that the denial of a continuance to consult with counsel violated the defendant's constitutional rights.

JURISPRUDENCE

Louisiana Supreme Court Rejects "Lawyer, Dawg" Appeal
State v. Demesme, 228 So. 3d 1206 (La. 2017)

After two girls under the age of 18 accused him of sexual assault, Warren Demesme voluntarily agreed to sit for questioning with detectives from the New Orleans Police Department. Transcripts of the interrogation revealed that Demesme said, "I know that I didn't do it, so why don't you just give me a lawyer dog, 'cause this is not what's up." However, questioning continued after he said this, and his subsequent statements were used to incriminate Demesme at trial, where he was found guilty. In a 6–1 decision, the Louisiana Supreme Court refused to overturn the conviction, with Justice Scott J. Crichton citing the U.S. Supreme Court's decision in *Davis v. United States* (1994)[29] as the basis for proclaiming, "In my view, the defendant's ambiguous

(continued)

and equivocal reference to a 'lawyer dog' does not constitute an invocation of counsel that warrants termination of the interview."[30]

An article about this case from Erik De La Garza presented a counterargument by saying, "The justices' interpretation of Demesme's statement does not address the possibility that a comma between the words 'lawyer' and 'dog' would have cleared up the request, or that slang may have been involved. Merriam-Webster's dictionary offers two uses of the word 'dawg'—one of which is slang to mean 'man, buddy or dude.'"[31]

In the end, the official transcript of the interrogation reflected a different spelling than *dawg*, speaking instead of a *lawyer dog*—apparently a canine capable of practicing law. Of course, Demesme's use of a prefatory clause leading up to his request for counsel could be a confounding factor for his case, as he did open by saying, "Why don't you just give me"—before adding, "a lawyer, dawg." But overall, the Louisiana Supreme Court's decision reflects a strict reading of the *Davis v. United States* decision.

Further-Questioning Decisions

In chapter 11, we observed that once a request to remain silent is made, police cannot reinitiate questioning until there is a *break in custody* and a fourteen-day waiting period has passed, based on the Supreme Court's 2010 decision in *Maryland v. Shatzer*.[32] Previously, the Court's *Edwards v. Arizona* (1981)[33] decision also indicated that when a person requests counsel, future attempts at interrogation require the presence of counsel. In the *Edwards* case, police questioned a man, and despite the fact that he invoked counsel, officers returned the next day to interrogate him again; the Court's opinion on this matter created a *prophylactic rule*, indicating that if an interrogation does not cease immediately upon a suspect's request of counsel, and if subsequent attempts at interrogation occur without counsel, statements shall be inadmissible at trial. Presumably, the fourteen-day rule from *Shatzer* provides a time limitation on the application of that rule today.

Beyond that, the Supreme Court has made it clear that the request for counsel carries over to impact any other investigations by agents of law enforcement who were not involved with initial attempts at questioning. For example, in *Arizona v. Roberson* (1988),[34] a suspect was arrested on the scene of a burglary and taken into police custody. He invoked his right to counsel when asked questions about the alleged crime, and three days later, with no break in custody, a different officer interrogated him about a separate offense, a robbery. The Court found that the second interrogation was constitutionally defective because the initial request for counsel should have resulted in an attorney being present, even at the subsequent questioning about the robbery. Later, in *Minnick v. Mississippi* (1990),[35] the Court ruled that separate interrogations by federal agents and, subsequently, a local sheriff—all about the same alleged crimes—implicated a similar constitutional violation.[36]

A unique aspect of the re-interrogation issue came before the Supreme Court in *Massiah v. United States* (1964).[37] Winston Massiah, who was charged with federal drug offenses, invoked the right to counsel, pled not guilty, and was out on bail for three days when the FBI used his codefendant in a ruse designed to elicit incriminating statements. The codefendant was outfitted with a wire that allowed authorities to listen in on his conversation with Massiah, who did, in fact, make incriminating statements that were later used against him at trial. On review, the Court's majority found a violation of the Sixth Amendment right to counsel, saying, "We hold that the petitioner was denied the basic protections of that guarantee when there was used against him at his trial evidence of his own incriminating words, which federal agents had deliberately elicited from him after he had been indicted and in the absence of his counsel." The Court added that this right exists even outside of a police station, and Justice Stewart's majority said that Sixth Amendment protections "must apply to indirect and surreptitious interrogations as well as those conducted in the jailhouse."[38]

Ineffective Assistance of Counsel

Overall, the right to counsel is worthless if one's lawyer is incompetent. The Supreme Court has held that ineffective assistance of counsel can be the basis for overturning a conviction.[39] The issue often arises in cases involving indigent defendants who were represented at trial by public defenders or other court-appointed counsel. As Justice Thurgood Marshall wrote in 1984, "a person of means, by selecting a lawyer and paying him enough to ensure he prepares thoroughly, usually can obtain better representation than that available to an indigent defendant, who must rely on appointed counsel, who, in turn, has limited time and resources to devote to a given case."[40] In *Strickland v. Washington* (1984),[41] the Court said that a petitioner claiming ineffective assistance of counsel must make two showings:

> First, the defendant must show that counsel's performance was deficient. This requires showing that counsel made errors so serious that counsel was not functioning as the "counsel" guaranteed the defendant by the Sixth Amendment. Second, the defendant must show that the deficient performance prejudiced the defense. This requires showing that counsel's errors were so serious as to deprive the defendant of a fair trial, a trial whose result is reliable. Unless a defendant makes both showings, it cannot be said that the conviction or death sentence resulted from a breakdown in the adversary process that renders the result unreliable.

In *Williams v. Taylor* (2000),[42] the Court applied the standards articulated in *Strickland v. Washington* in overturning a death sentence because the defendant's lawyer failed to introduce any mitigating evidence during the sentencing phase of the trial. Three years later, in another capital murder case, *Wiggins v. Smith* (2003),[43] the Court overturned the defendant's death sentence for the same reason. Writing for the Court, Justice O'Connor concluded that "the available mitigating evidence, taken as a whole, 'might well have influenced the jury's appraisal' of Wiggins' moral culpability" and, thus, could have resulted in a lesser sentence than death.

As noted above, the Supreme Court has found that the right to effective assistance of counsel applies at all "critical stages" of the criminal process, and a 2017 decision applied to this concept to the entry of a plea.[44] In *Jae Lee v. United States* (2017),[45] the Court overturned a drug conviction of a defendant who had pled guilty on the advice of counsel. Jae Lee's lawyer erroneously informed him that his conviction would not result in his deportation from the country, even though he was a foreign national. Chief Justice John Roberts, speaking for the Court, found that "Lee has adequately demonstrated a reasonable probability that he would have rejected the plea had he known that it would lead to mandatory deportation."

Five years later, the Supreme Court's 6-3 decision in *Shinn v. Martinez Ramirez* (2022)[46] placed some limits on the use of ineffective counsel appeals. This ruling indicated that a federal court addressing a habeas corpus petition based on an ineffective counsel claim could only consider evidence raised in the state courts to assess if counsel was in fact ineffective. Speaking for the Court, Justice Thomas stressed the limited role that federal courts should play in reviewing state court determinations: "To respect our system of dual sovereignty, … the availability of habeas relief is narrowly circumscribed. … Among other restrictions, only rarely may a federal habeas court hear a claim or consider evidence that a prisoner did not previously present to the state courts in compliance with state procedural rules."

JURISPRUDENCE

Sleeping Lawyer Results in Sixth Amendment Violation
Burdine v. Johnson, 262 F.3d 336 (5th Cir. 2001)

In this case, a Texas man named Calvin Burdine was found guilty of capital murder and came within hours of being executed in 1987. A stay of execution was granted, though, and an appeal based on a Sixth Amendment ineffective counsel claim would reach the Fifth Circuit. This claim was based on a showing that Burdine's lawyer had repeatedly fallen asleep during the guilty—not guilty phase of his trial, with the jury foreman recalling he had seen the defense attorney fall asleep between two and five times as a prosecutor questioned witnesses. Another juror said the lawyer "would nod his head down on his chest" with his eyes closed; and another juror said he remembered the lawyer sleeping as many as ten times, with one instance being "a good probably at least ten minutes" during the prosecution's questioning of a witness.

On review, the Fifth Circuit, sitting en banc, found that the defendant's Sixth Amendment rights had been violated and ordered a new trial. The majority opinion provided an important, if obvious, realization by noting, "Unconscious counsel equates to no counsel at all. Unconscious counsel does not analyze, object, listen or in any way exercise judgment on behalf of a client."

In finding that the lawyer's dozing off had indeed resulted in *prejudice* in this case—as opposed to being a *harmless error*—the majority added, "An unconscious attorney does not, indeed cannot, perform at all. This fact distinguishes the sleeping lawyer from the drunk or drugged one. Even the intoxicated attorney exercises judgment, though perhaps impaired, on behalf of his client at all times during a trial. Yet, the attorney that is unconscious during critical stages of a trial is simply not capable of exercising judgment. The unconscious attorney is in fact no different from an attorney that is physically absent from trial. ..."

This would lead the court to a conclusion that, based on the Constitution, a new trial should be granted because: "When a state court finds on the basis of credible evidence that defense counsel repeatedly slept as evidence was being introduced against a defendant, that defendant has been denied counsel at a critical stage of his trial. In such circumstances, the Supreme Court's Sixth Amendment jurisprudence compels the presumption that counsel's unconsciousness prejudiced the defendant."

Self-Representation

PRO SE REPRESENTATION:
A term referring to a defendant who chooses to represent themselves in court.

In *Faretta v. California* (1975),[47] the Supreme Court held that the right to counsel is personal to the defendant. Therefore, defendants may elect to *knowingly* and *willingly* represent themselves at trial, which is known as pro se representation. Justice Potter Stewart's opinion for the Court in *Faretta* indicated that "forcing a lawyer upon an unwilling defendant is contrary to his basic right to defend himself if he truly wants to do so." Additionally, in a separate case, the high Court found that a defendant may not force an unwilling attorney to represent them.[48]

Of course, a judge has the discretion to determine if a defendant is not competent to represent themself. Moreover, a defendant who insists on representing themself at trial cannot later claim they received ineffective assistance of counsel.[49] In 1984, the Supreme Court even said there is no right to for a *pro se* defendant to get instructions from the judge as to court procedures;[50] in fact, a trial judge can terminate self-representation if a defendant engages in obstructive tactics.[51]

The Right to Trial by Jury

The right to trial by jury can be traced back to Magna Carta (1215), and in the Anglo-American legal tradition, this right has always been considered essential to the fair administration of justice. Speaking for the Supreme Court in *Duncan v. Louisiana* (1968),[52] Justice Byron White noted:

> [T]he jury trial provisions in the Federal and State Constitutions reflect a fundamental decision about the exercise of official power—a reluctance to entrust plenary powers over the life and liberty of the citizen to one judge or to a group of judges. Fear of unchecked power, so typical of our State and Federal Governments in other respects, found expression in the criminal law in this insistence upon community participation in the determination of guilt or innocence.

In *Duncan*, the Supreme Court held that the Sixth Amendment jury trial provision is applicable to the state courts. Justice White concluded that "the right of jury trial in serious criminal cases as a defense against arbitrary law enforcement qualifies for protection under the Due Process Clause of the Fourteenth Amendment, and must therefore be respected by the States." Notice the use of the qualifier, *serious*, in Justice White's statement. This implies jury trials are not constitutionally mandatory in cases involving certain minor offenses. More specifically, within a few years after the *Duncan* case was decided, the Court said the right to trial by jury only applies to offenses carrying a penalty of more than six months' imprisonment.[53]

Do Petty Offenses Merit Jury Trials?

Despite the language of Sixth Amendment, which states, "In all criminal prosecutions, the accused shall enjoy the right to a speedy and public trial, by an impartial jury…," the Court has consistently refused to extend the right to trial by jury to defendants charged with petty offenses. According to Justice White's opinion in *Duncan*, petty offenses "have always been held to be exempt from the otherwise comprehensive language of the Sixth Amendment's jury trial provisions."[54] But what are petty offenses? The law divides crimes into felonies (more serious) and misdemeanors (less serious). Petty crimes are the less serious misdemeanors, although there is no precise demarcation, and states vary regarding which misdemeanors are considered petty offenses. Generally speaking, violations of local ordinances and motor vehicle offenses are considered petty offenses. So too are nonviolent minor property crimes, such as shoplifting or pickpocketing. In California, petty offenses have been decriminalized and are considered to be *infractions* for which the penalty is the payment of a fine.[55] Under our federal system, though, states do not have to use standardized classifications of offenses or even standard terminology.

PETTY OFFENSES:
Criminal offenses that carry lesser punishment, typically six months or less of incarceration or a fine.

In *Blanton v. City of North Las Vegas* (1989),[56] the Supreme Court declared there is no right to jury trial in DUI cases. Justice Marshall's opinion for a unanimous bench observed "the statutory penalties are not so severe that DUI must be deemed a 'serious' offense for purposes of the Sixth Amendment." Even so, in most states today, defendants charged with DUI have a right to a jury trial, whether under state constitutional provisions or legislation. While states may not fall short of what is required by the federal Constitution, they may go beyond its protection of rights and liberties. Again, that is the nature of our federal system.

Typically, in cases involving petty crimes, courts of limited jurisdiction (such as a *general sessions court*) conduct summary trials that are completed in a matter of minutes. To extend the right of trial by jury to such cases would be an impediment to the efficient administration of justice and would require an enormous infusion of funds. Thus, the decision of the Supreme Court to exempt petty offenses would appear to represent a triumph of pragmatism over textualism.

Juvenile Justice

In 1967, in a landmark case called *In re Gault*,[57] the Supreme Court found that courts must observe the rudiments of due process when adjudicating cases of juvenile delinquency. However, in *McKeiver v. Pennsylvania* (1971),[58] the Court refused to extend the right to trial by jury to juvenile delinquency cases. Justice Harry Blackmun's plurality opinion observed, "If the jury trial were to be injected into the juvenile court system as a matter of right, it would bring with it into that system the traditional delay, the formality, and the clamor of the adversary system and, possibly, the public trial." Again, pragmatism won out.

JUVENILE COURT SYSTEM: A court that exclusively handles matters related to juvenile offenders, as defined under applicable state law.

Today, states decide for themselves when to move a case from juvenile courts into adult courts. In some places, a prosecutor makes that decision, whereas in others it may be up to a judge. Generally, certain serious offenses, like murder, automatically—by legislative decree—are transferred into adult court. Some states even use a *once an adult, always an adult* rule, whereby a juvenile who has been brought into adult court for one offense will be considered an adult for any future offenses. In 47 states, the oldest age at which a person can be brought into juvenile court is 17 years old; Vermont sets the age limit at 18, and three states (Georgia, Texas, and Wisconsin) use a maximum age of 16 years.[59]

In 2018, the National Conference of State Legislatures published a fifty-eight-page document, entitled "Principles of Effective Juvenile Justice Policy," which offered suggestions for improving the juvenile justice system nationwide, including the following: finding alterna-tives to incarceration for juveniles, improving conditions in juvenile detention facilities, ensuring juveniles of different demographics are given due process and are treated equally, and fostering research regarding youth development to inform decision-making about juvenile offenders.[60] States, of course, are free to choose their own pathways in implementing reforms.

Plea Bargaining

The criminal trial has long been regarded as the centerpiece of the crim-inal justice system. These days, however, criminal trials are few and far between. The overwhelming majority of criminal cases, both at the state and federal level, are resolved through plea bargaining. Prosecu-tors routinely induce defendants to plead guilty by reducing the level or number of charges or agreeing not to seek maximum sentences. It is important to recognize the Supreme Court has explicitly, and repeatedly, found no issue with the process of plea bargaining—where a prosecutor offers a potentially lesser punishment in exchange for a confession or guilty plea.[61] This is, of course, predicated on the notion that a plea is entered voluntarily, since a guilty plea, particularly one given without benefit of counsel, can be deemed the result of coercion—even at the hands of counsel—and, thus, overturned by an appellate court.[62] Further-more, a 2018 Supreme Court decision indicated that, in order to litigate a constitutional claim, a defendant can enter a conditional guilty plea and retain the right to file an appeal.[63]

In *Brady v. United States* (1970),[64] the Supreme Court upheld plea bar-gaining in clear terms, recognizing the "mutuality of advantage" that leads to most guilty pleas:

> For a defendant who sees slight possibility of acquit-tal, the advantages of pleading guilty and limiting the probable penalty are obvious—his exposure is reduced, the correctional processes can begin immediately, and the practical burdens of a trial are eliminated. For the State, there are also advantages—the more promptly imposed punishment after an admission of guilt may more effectively attain the objectives of punishment, and, with the avoidance of trial, scarce judicial and prosecutorial resources

PLEA BARGAINING:
The process through which a prosecutor and defender reach an agreement by which the defendant will plead guilty to a crime, typically in exchange for a lesser sentence than the maximum allowed by statute.

are conserved for those cases in which there is a substantial issue of the defendant's guilt or in which there is substantial doubt that the State can sustain its burden of proof.

A year later, in *Santobello v. New York* (1971),[65] the Court reaffirmed its acceptance of plea bargaining but took issue with a prosecutor offering a deal in which the accused would plead guilty to gambling offenses in exchange for the prosecutor making no sentencing recommendation to the judge. Yet after the defendant had pled guilty, a different prosecutor from the same prosecutor's office appeared at the sentencing hearing and asked the judge to impose the maximum sentence of one year; the judge honored that request and issued the one-year sentence. Although prosecutors attempted to defend the action as a mistake, the Supreme Court determined that "[t]he heavy workload may well explain these episodes, but it does not excuse them." The majority opinion from Chief Justice Burger went on to discuss the value of plea bargaining:

> The disposition of criminal charges by agreement between the prosecutor and the accused, sometimes loosely called "plea bargaining," is an essential component of the administration of justice. Properly administered, it is to be encouraged. If every criminal charge were subjected to a full-scale trial, the States and the Federal Government would need to multiply by many times the number of judges and court facilities.

Nonetheless, the opinion also went on to observe that a plea bargain must "presuppose fairness in securing agreement between an accused and a prosecutor," adding the following information:

> The plea must, of course, be voluntary and knowing and if it was induced by promises, the essence of those promises must in some way be made known. ... Those circumstances will vary, but a constant factor is that, when a plea rests in any significant degree on a promise or agreement of the prosecutor, so that it can be said to be part of the inducement or consideration, such promise must be fulfilled.

In a different case, the Supreme Court also has noted that a court can reject a guilty plea "in exercise of sound judicial discretion."[66]

Later, in *Bordernkircher v. Hayes* (1978),[67] the Court went so far as to allow a prosecutor to return to the grand jury to obtain an indictment under a habitual offender law because the defendant refused to plead guilty to the original charge. The defendant, who had two prior felony convictions, was informed that if he did not plead guilty and accept a five-year prison sentence on a forgery charge that carried a two-to-ten-year sentencing range, his case would be returned to the grand jury, with the government seeking an enhanced habitual offender penalty that could carry life imprisonment; the suspect refused the deal and was later convicted of the crime of uttering a forged instrument. With that being his third felony conviction, he was, in fact, sentenced to life in prison. The Supreme Court's majority opinion said there was no due process violation, noting "this case would be no different if the grand jury had indicted Hayes as a recidivist from the outset, and the prosecutor had offered to drop that charge as part of the plea bargain."

The Supreme Court has said that before accepting a defendant's guilty plea, the trial judge must ascertain that the prosecution has not made improper inducements to secure the plea and the defendant has made a "knowing an intelligent waiver" of their right to a trial.[68] Moreover, a trial judge can reject a plea deal because it does not serve the ends of justice. But rarely do trial judges reject plea bargains. One such instance occurred in late January 2022, when U.S. District Judge Lisa Godbey Wood refused to accept a plea deal in a civil rights prosecution. Travis McMichael was one of three men sentenced to life in prison without parole by a Georgia court for the murder of Ahmaud Arbery (see Chapter 10). In a subsequent federal civil rights prosecution, McMichael agreed to plead guilty on the condition he would spend thirty years in federal prison before being returned to the state of Georgia for the duration of his life sentence. Arbery's mother strongly protested the plea deal, as she believed it granted McMichael "preferred conditions of confinement." The judge gave McMichael the option of maintaining the guilty plea with the risk of a harsher sentence or going to trial.[69] McMichael chose to change his guilty plea to not guilty and exercise his right to a jury trial. In February 2022, a jury found McMichael and two codefendants (including his son) guilty of violating Arbery's civil rights. The judge doled out federal sentences of life in prison to Travis McMichael and his son, and thirty-five years for their codefendant—with the condition that they all serve their time in state prison.

> **HABITUAL OFFENDER LAW:** A statute that prescribes an enhanced punishment for repeated criminal offenses (typically three or more) regardless of what punishment is permissible under the law for the most recent offense.

JURISPRUDENCE

Bill Cosby's Guilty Verdict Overturned by Pennsylvania Supreme Court
Commonwealth v. Cosby, 252 A.3d 1092 (Pa. 2021)

In December 2015, Bill Cosby faced criminal charges related to allegations he drugged and sexually assaulted a woman in 2004. Other women had made similar accusations against Cosby, but the statute of limitations for such offenses meant that he would only face charges in this one case, which was itself filed just two weeks before the statutory deadline for doing so. Due to Cosby's celebrity status, the case attracted national media attention. After a 2017 trial resulted in a deadlocked jury and a mistrial, a second trial was held in 2018. This time, a jury found Cosby guilty on three counts of aggravated indecent assault. Cosby was incarcerated for three years until, in 2021, the Pennsylvania Supreme Court issued a 4–3 ruling that vacated his conviction.

The crux of Cosby's appeal to Pennsylvania's highest court was that a former district attorney, Bruce Castor Jr., had, in 2005, given Cosby a public assurance there would be no criminal charges in this matter. The majority opinion that set Cosby free included quotes from this D.A. indicating that he made these public declarations because that would permit a civil suit to go forward, since Cosby's ability to invoke his Fifth Amendment right to remain silent would be "for all time removed" because there was no threat of criminal prosecution.

In fact, when a civil suit was filed against Cosby in 2005, a judge told him he had to answer all questions in a deposition, and under questioning, Cosby admitted to purchasing Quaaludes to give to women. The civil case was settled for $3 million in 2006, with the documents from the case sealed from public view. But in 2015, after a judge ruled Cosby had violated a nondisclosure agreement, records related to the lawsuit—including transcripts of Cosby's answers in the deposition—were opened to the public. Ultimately, statements made by Cosby in the deposition in 2005 were used against him in the 2018 criminal trial.[70]

The prosecutor who made the 2005 assurances to Cosby was defeated in a 2015 election by a new prosecutor, Kevin Steele, who brought the criminal case against Cosby. Cosby's lawyers said the new prosecution violated a publicly declared non-prosecution agreement, even though nothing was put in writing.

In June 2021, the Pennsylvania Supreme Court overturned Cosby's conviction.[71] The court's lengthy

(continued)

opinion cited the U.S. Supreme Court's decision in *Santobello v. New York* (1971), in which the high Court ruled a promise made by one prosecutor in securing a plea deal must be honored by a new, replacement prosecutor, who attempted to deviate from the prior agreement. The Pennsylvania Supreme Court found Cosby was denied due process, saying, "When an unconditional charging decision is made publicly and with the intent to induce action and reliance by the defendant, and when the defendant does so to his detriment ... denying the benefit of that decision is an affront to fundamental fairness, particularly when it results in a criminal prosecution that was foregone for more than a decade." Following this decision, Bill Cosby was released from prison. Prosecutors asked the U.S. Supreme Court to review the decision, but in March 2022, the Court denied certiorari, thereby ending the case.[72]

The Right to a Speedy Trial

In *Klopfer v. North Carolina* (1967),[73] the Supreme Court applied the Speedy Trial Clause of the Sixth Amendment to the state courts. Chief Justice Earl Warren spoke for the Court, saying, "The history of the right to a speedy trial and its reception in this country clearly establish that it is one of the most basic rights preserved by our Constitution." Five years later, in *Barker v. Wingo* (1972),[74] the Court reiterated the importance of the right to a speedy trial but refused to set forth time limits. Rather, the Court articulated a four-part test to determine whether a defendant's right to a speedy trial had been violated. Under this test, courts must consider the following factors: length of the delay in the commencement of trial; the reason for the delay; whether the defendant had asserted the right to a speedy trial; and whether the delay was prejudicial to the defense.

Application of this test was apparent in *Doggett v. United States* (1992),[75] in which the Supreme Court found a Sixth Amendment violation connected to a delay of more than eight years between indictment and trial. The defendant, Doggett, was indicted on drug charges in Florida in 1980. However, four days before the indictment, he had left for Panama, where he lived until 1982. DEA agents in the United States were aware of Doggett being arrested in Panama on drug charges filed by local officials there, but no formal extradition request was made, and U.S. agents did little to follow up on the matter, only finding that Doggett had left Panama for Columbia at some point. Doggett actually reentered the United States in 1982, passing through U.S. Customs in New York City without any issues. He moved to Virginia and lived openly, under his real name, working with computers. In 1988, a U.S. Marshals credit check of individuals who had outstanding warrants brought Doggett back into the purview of law enforcement, leading to his arrest.

Applying the four factors from *Barker v. Wingo*, Justice Souter's majority opinion observed the following: (1) the 8.5-year delay was *extraordinary*; (2) the Government bore blame for this delay through its negligence in pursuing Doggett in lax fashion; (3) Doggett was unaware of the indictment until 1988 and asserted his right to a speedy trial promptly upon learning of it; and (4) the delay prejudiced his ability to put forth a defense. Justice Souter summarized the balancing of concerns at play in this case as follows:

> Our speedy trial standards recognize that pretrial delay is often both inevitable and wholly justifiable. The government may need time to collect witnesses against the accused, oppose his pretrial motions, or, if he goes into hiding, track him down. We attach great weight to such considerations when balancing them against the costs of going forward with a trial whose probative accuracy the passage of time has begun by degrees to throw into question.[76]

The Speedy Trial Act of 1974

In 1974, Congress enacted the Speedy Trial Act,[77] which established time limits for the commencement of trials and the completion of pretrial stages of criminal prosecutions in federal courts. Under the Act, formal charges (whether by information or indictment) must be filed within thirty days after arrest or service of the summons. A trial must commence within seventy days after formal charges are filed, but the Act allows for delays associated with the litigation of pretrial motions and the unavailability of defendants due their involvement in other judicial proceedings. In 1979, Congress amended the statute to ensure defendants have adequate time to prepare for trial. Unless the defendant waives this provision, the trial cannot start for thirty days after the defendant's first appearance in court.[78]

THE CONSTITUTION IN ACTION
Speedy Trial Violation in Case of Capitol Riot Defendant

In March 2022, federal prosecutors took the unusual step of admitting, in a court filing, they had violated the Speedy Trial Act in the case against Lucas Denney, a Texas man who was arrested on December 13, 2021, on charges related to the U.S. Capitol riots of January 6, 2021. He appeared in front of a magistrate judge in a federal district court in Texas on December 14, 2021, with this judge ordering Denney to be transferred to D.C. to face charges. He was then held in a Texas jail awaiting transfer and eventually was moved to a Virginia detention center on January 31, 2021. After multiple Zoom meetings between attorneys who were attempting to schedule a court date in D.C., a February 25th meeting resulted in a court date given for two weeks later, to be held on March 7, 2022. But on March 2, 2022, Denney's lawyer filed a motion for his release because an indictment was not obtained within thirty days of arrest and because a preliminary hearing had not been offered within fourteen days, both in violation of the Speedy Trial Act. To complicate matters, on March 7th, the date of Denney's scheduled court arraignment, a federal grand jury did, in fact, issue an indictment for one count of assault related to Denney allegedly striking an officer with a PVC pipe during the Capitol riot.

On March 14, 2022, a video hearing was held in this matter, overseen by a federal magistrate judge serving on the U.S. District Court for the District of Columbia. Denney's attorney sought dismissal of the charge. Surprisingly, prosecutors submitted a brief for this case in which they admitted to violating the Speedy Trial Act—yet sought the ability to dismiss the single charge and then refile new charges, claiming, "dismissal should be without prejudice because the offense is serious, the error was unintentional, and the delay has not prejudiced Denney." The brief admitted to an error in saying, "To be sure, the government failed to comply with the Speedy Trial Act in this case," before going on to suggest, "But there is no evidence of bad faith, a pattern of neglect, or something more than an isolated incident that resulted from a number of unfortunate factors." The written brief added, "There was nothing intentional or nefarious about the delay. It was an isolated incident, unlikely to happen again, and the time frame—while undoubtedly regrettable—is nevertheless not significantly egregious to warrant dismissal with prejudice."[79]

Ultimately, the magistrate judge overseeing this matter acknowledged Denney's rights had been violated—but declined to release him from custody immediately, stating a further hearing would be needed regarding the matter of prejudice. The judge spoke to the sheer volume of Capitol riot prosecutions, saying, "It feels like the government has bitten off more than it can chew here." The judge then said of Denney's situation, "You have been lost for months. There's no excuse to treat a human being like that. ... There is no circumstance under which any person should be forgotten."

On March 17, 2022, rather than wait for a subsequent hearing regarding whether the government's violation of the Speedy Trial Act should result in a dismissal of the charge against him, Denney opted to plead guilty to that offense—in the hope of avoiding more serious charges that could have potentially arisen at a later date; the guilty plea establishes the possibility of a double jeopardy challenge if further charges are brought against him stemming from the January 6th Capitol riot.[80]

Investigative Delay

What about a situation in which the defendant was not arrested until after they were indicted for crimes committed several years before? Speaking for the Supreme Court in *United States v. Marion* (1971),[81] Justice Byron White noted, "Inordinate delay between arrest, indictment, and trial may impair a defendant's ability to present an effective defense." Yet in this case, the Court found there was no violation of the right to a speedy trial when federal officials took more than three years to investigate the owners of a home alarm installation business for fraudulent practices. The Federal Trade Commission—responding to consumer complaints about service paid for but not provided—issued a cease-and-desist order against this company in February 1967, at which point the business closed permanently. A U.S. Attorney began an investigation into criminal charges soon thereafter, but a nineteen-count criminal indictment was not released until April 1970. The two defendants claimed the lengthy investigation period had violated their rights—but Justice White's opinion for a unanimous Supreme Court disagreed, offering the following limits on the use of speedy trial objections raised by defendants:

> Invocation of the speedy trial provision ... need not await indictment, information, or other formal charge. But we decline to extend the reach of the amendment to the period prior to arrest. Until this event occurs, a citizen suffers no restraints on his liberty and is not the subject of public accusation: his situation does not compare with that of a defendant who has been arrested and held to answer.

The Supreme Court addressed this topic again in *United States v. Lovasco* (1977),[82] when, in the words of Justice Thurgood Marshall, it held "that to prosecute a defendant following investigative delay does not deprive him of due process, even if his defense might have been somewhat prejudiced by the lapse of time." In this case, federal officials were aware for approximately eighteen months of the defendant's role in the illegal trafficking of stolen firearms. The defense claimed two key witnesses who could have helped its case died during that time frame and, thus, alleged the defense case was prejudiced by their unavailability for trial. However, Justice Marshall found that "prosecutors are under no duty to file charges as soon as probable cause exists, but before they are satisfied they will be able to establish the suspect's guilt beyond a reasonable doubt." In considering the alternative, Marshall added, "To impose such a duty 'would have a deleterious effect both upon the rights of the accused and upon the ability of society to protect itself.'" He then addressed the potential for correlated harm to defendants if charges were rushed, opining that: "From the perspective of potential defendants, requiring prosecutions to commence when probable cause is established is undesirable because it would increase the likelihood of unwarranted charges being filed, and would add to the time during which defendants stand accused but untried."

Delays Due to Dropped Charges

In *United States v. MacDonald* (1982),[83] the Supreme Court stated that if a person is charged with a crime, but the charges are dropped, those charges can be refiled at a later date without violating the right to a speedy trial. This case involved an army captain, living at Fort Bragg, North Carolina, who was charged in May 1970 with the murders of his wife and two children. But those charges were dropped soon thereafter, and he was discharged from the military. Nevertheless, the case was reopened and presented to a grand jury four years later, with an indictment on three counts of murder handed down in January 1975. MacDonald was subsequently found guilty of the three murders.

On appeal, MacDonald claimed a violation of the right to a speedy trial, but the Supreme Court's 6–3 majority ruled otherwise, with Chief Justice Burger's majority opinion saying, "Once charges are dismissed, the speedy trial guarantee is no longer applicable." Burger expounded upon this holding with the following declaration: "At that point, the formerly accused is, at most, in the same position as any other subject of a criminal investigation. Certainly, the knowledge of an ongoing criminal investigation will cause stress, discomfort, and perhaps a certain disruption in normal life. This is true whether or not charges have been filed and then dismissed. But with no charges outstanding, personal liberty is certainly not impaired to the same degree as it is after arrest while charges are pending."

Delays Due to Incarceration in Another Jurisdiction

In *Fex v. Michigan* (1993),[84] the U.S. Supreme Court offered a ruling regarding a *detainer*, which is when one jurisdiction holds a person wanted in another, pending extradition to the place that wishes to bring criminal charges. In this case, the defendant was formally charged with armed robbery in Michigan, while he was incarcerated, on a different charge, in Fort Wayne, Indiana. Under procedures in place at that time in Michigan, via an interstate agreement on detainers,[85] there was a 180-day time frame for the start of a trial involving a detainer in another state. But in this case, after Michigan officials notified Indiana officials of a desire to bring the defendant to Michigan, the Indiana officials took a lengthy 22 days to forward the prisoner's requested *disposition* (a notice of whether the prisoner would contest extradition). Michigan officials wanted those 22 days to be excluded from the 180-day *clock*, and the Supreme Court's majority agreed. Justice Scalia's opinion stated that the 180-day count "does not commence until the prisoner's request for final disposition of the charges against him has actually been delivered to the court and prosecuting officer of the jurisdiction that lodged the detainer against him."

JURISPRUDENCE

Bad Counterfeiter Represents Self, Cites Speedy Trial Violation
Zedner v. United States, 547 U.S. 489 (2006)

Jacob Zedner tried to open accounts at seven different banks with fake bond certificates purporting to be worth $10 million. In the words of Justice Samuel Alito, "The quality of the counterfeiting was, to put it mildly, not expert." One bond was labeled as issued by the nonexistent "Ministry of Finance of U.S.A" and others included misspelled words like "Thunted States," "Onited States," "Dhtladelphia," "Cgicago," and "forevev." He was indicted on counterfeiting charges on April 4, 1996, in the U.S. District Court for the Eastern District of New York.

A conference in front of the trial judge was held on November 8, 1996, at which time the defendant's lawyer asked for the case to be held over until January 1997, so further gathering of evidence and psychiatric testing could occur. The judge agreed but with a condition.

Since January was a busy month at that court, the judge said, "I think if I'm going to give you that long an adjournment, I will have to take a waiver for all time." The defense was then presented with a preprinted form, created by the court on its own, entitled "Waiver of Speedy Trial Rights." The defendant and his counsel lawyer signed the form. Ultimately, the trial did not begin until April 2003.

The gap included the following: a lawyer quitting over the fact the defendant tried to claim the bonds were real and needed to be authenticated; the need for multiple psychiatric evaluations to determine if the defendant was competent for trial; the defendant taking over as his own lawyer; the defendant then trying (unsuccessfully) to subpoena the president of the United States, the Chairman of the Federal Reserve

(*continued*)

Board, the Attorney General, the Secretary of State, the late Chinese leader Chiang Kai-shek, and "The Treasury Department of Treasury International Corporation." Eventually, Zedner was found guilty.

In 2006, the Supreme Court addressed this case and said a defendant could not waive their speedy trial rights for all time; thus, the district court's presentation of a form with such a waiver was unconstitutional. Justice Alito also noted that a claim for a violation of speedy trial rights could be raised even after a trial has ended—it need not be raised before a trial begins. Additionally, even if the defense requests a continuance, there still could be a speedy trial violation regarding how long it takes to bring a case to trial subsequent to the continuance. To that point, Alito observed that the Speedy Trial Act "has no provision excluding periods of delay during which a defendant waives the application of the Act." He also spoke to broader reasons for a speedy trial beyond those implicating the defendant's own interests by saying "the Act was designed with the public interest firmly in mind," adding, "That public interest cannot be served ... if defendants may opt out of the Act entirely." A lengthy continuance, therefore, must be based on a "finding that the ends of justice served by the granting of such continuance outweigh the best interests of the public and the defendant in a speedy trial."

The Right to a Public Trial

Writing for the Supreme Court in *In re Oliver* (1948),[86] Justice Black observed, "It is 'the law of the land' that no man's life, liberty or property be forfeited as a punishment until there has been a charge fairly made and fairly tried in a public tribunal." With that pronouncement, the Court incorporated the right to a public trial into the Fourteenth Amendment, making it applicable in state and local courts as well as federal tribunals. Justice Black's *law of the land* phrase harkened back to Magna Carta, in which trial by one's peers was first recognized in English law. His opinion added the observation that "[w]hatever other benefits the guarantee to an accused that [their] trial be conducted in public may confer upon our society, the guarantee has always been recognized as a safeguard against any attempt to employ our courts as instruments of persecution."

But what if the defendant asks to have the trial closed to the public? In *Richmond Newspapers v. Virginia* (1980),[87] the Supreme Court held that trials must remain open irrespective of the defendant's wishes. Announcing the judgment of the Court, Chief Justice Burger invoked the First Amendment, saying "the right to attend criminal trials is implicit in the guarantees of the First Amendment; without the freedom to attend such trials, which people have exercised for centuries, important aspects of freedom of speech and 'of the press could be eviscerated.'"

In 1984, the Supreme Court ruled the public trial requirement extends beyond the trial per se and also applies to jury selection.[88] But in another case decided that same year, *Waller v. Georgia* (1984),[89] the Court said that, under certain circumstances, pretrial hearings may be closed. Justice Powell's majority opinion for this case articulated a test to determine whether closures of pretrial hearings are warranted. Under this test, "the party seeking to close the hearing must advance an overriding interest that is likely to be prejudiced, the closure must be no broader than necessary to protect that interest, the trial court must consider reasonable alternatives to closing the proceeding, and it must make findings adequate to support the closure." This is a difficult standard to meet, as evidenced by the Court's 2010 decision in *Presley v. Georgia*.[90] In that case, the Court overruled a trial judge who ordered jury selection to be closed to the public, noting that this judge failed "to consider all reasonable alternatives to closure."

In 2017, the Court addressed another case in which jury selection was closed to the public, reiterating the concept that "the right to an open courtroom protects the rights of the public at large, and the press, as well, as the rights of the accused."[91] However, in this case the majority refused to overturn the conviction simply based on the failure to provide jury selection that was open to the public. The Court said that because the claim was not raised at trial but, rather, later as a part of an ineffective counsel claim, there had to be some showing of prejudice or "fundamental unfairness," with the majority instead interpreting the matter as a "harmless error."

More recently, in *Boumediene v. Bush* (2008),[92] the Supreme Court decided that basic Fifth Amendment protections should apply at Guantanamo Bay and other U.S.-controlled territories outside of the geographical boundaries of the United States. The writ of habeas corpus could be used in these instances to impact military commissions or tribunals that might be prone to hosting trials held outside the public eye.

The Free Press/Fair Trial Problem

In *Sheppard v. Maxwell* (1966),[93] the Supreme Court held that a defendant in a sensational murder case had been denied the right to a fair trial because the trial judge failed to insulate the trial from "massive, pervasive and prejudicial publicity." The case concerned Dr. Samuel Sheppard, who was accused of murdering his wife in Bay Village, Ohio, in 1954. Sheppard was found guilty after a nine-week trial in Cuyahoga County Court, where a pervasive media presence was apparent each day of the proceedings. In overturning the conviction in this case, Justice Tom Clark's majority opinion said, "[W]e believe that the arrangements made by the judge with the news media caused Sheppard to be deprived of that 'judicial serenity and calm to which [he] was entitled.'" In describing the chaos that pervaded this trial, Clark said the following:

> The fact is that bedlam reigned at the courthouse during the trial, and newsmen took over practically the entire courtroom, hounding most of the participants in the trial, especially Sheppard. At a temporary table within a few feet of the jury box and counsel table sat some 20 reporters, staring at Sheppard and taking notes. The erection of a press table for reporters inside the bar is unprecedented. The bar of the court is reserved for counsel, providing them a safe place in which to keep papers and exhibits and to confer privately with client and co-counsel. It is designed to protect the witness and the jury from any distractions, intrusions or influences, and to permit bench discussions of the judge's rulings away from the hearing of the public and the jury. Having assigned almost all of the available seats in the courtroom to the news media, the judge lost his ability to supervise that environment.

Moreover, Justice Clark spoke to the impact of the press on the jury, observing, "The total lack of consideration for the privacy of the jury was demonstrated by the assignment to a broadcasting station of space next to the jury room on the floor above the courtroom, as well as the fact that jurors were allowed to make telephone calls during their five-day deliberation." This realization linked the media coverage to the possibility of undue influence upon the juror's decisions. Concluding the majority opinion, Clark offered guidelines for future matters of this ilk when he said, "The carnival atmosphere at trial could easily have been avoided, since the courtroom and courthouse premises are subject to the control of the court." Among the suggestions offered by Clark included limiting the number of media members in the courtroom and preventing them from handling trial exhibits as well as limiting witnesses from hearing the testimony of other witnesses—testimony that was often relayed verbatim in newspaper accounts in this case.

It is interesting to note, though, that Justice Clark's majority opinion was sensitive to the importance of open trials that can be covered by the press; to this point, he said, "A responsible press has always been regarded as the handmaiden of effective judicial administration, especially in the criminal field. Its function in this regard is documented by an impressive record of service over several centuries. The press does not simply publish information about trials, but guards against the miscarriage of justice by subjecting the police, prosecutors, and judicial processes to extensive public scrutiny and criticism." Even so, Clark quoted from *Bridges v. California* (1941)[94] in saying, "Legal trials are not like elections, to be won through the use of the meeting-hall, the radio, and the newspaper," and he also quoted to *Chambers v. Florida* (1940)[95] in declaring that "the Court has insisted that no one be punished for a crime without 'a charge fairly made and fairly tried in a public tribunal free of prejudice, passion, excitement, and tyrannical power.'" In the end, Justice Clark summarized the matter by declaring that "the presence of the press at judicial proceedings must be limited when it is apparent that the accused might otherwise be prejudiced or disadvantaged."

Change of Venue

To reduce the potentially prejudicial impact of pretrial publicity, judges can take several steps. Closure of a pretrial hearing is an extreme option, and it is likely to be closely scrutinized on appeal. Another option is to change the **venue** of the trial. Rule 21(a) of the Federal Rules of Criminal Procedure provides, "Upon the defendant's motion, the court must transfer the proceeding as to that defendant to another district ... if the court is satisfied that there exists in the district where the prosecution is pending so great a prejudice against the defendant that the defendant cannot obtain a fair and impartial trial at any place fixed for holding court in that district." State court systems have similar rules; however, the burden is on the defendant to show the necessity of a change of venue and trial judges hold wide discretion in deciding whether to grant such a request.

In *Skilling v. United States* (2010),[96] the Supreme Court ruled that a federal district judge acted properly in denying the defendant's motion for a change of venue. Jeffrey Skilling, an executive of the Houston-based Enron Corporation, was on trial for several federal crimes, including insider trading, securities fraud, wire fraud, and making false statements to auditors. The trial took place in Houston, before the U.S. District Court for the Southern District of Texas. Skilling claimed that

VENUE: The specific geographic location of a criminal trial.

widespread hostility to him in Houston, where Enron was based, along with extensive pretrial publicity, made it impossible to select an impartial jury. Speaking for the Supreme Court, Justice Ruth Bader Ginsburg observed that "news stories about Enron did not present the kind of vivid, unforgettable information we have recognized as particularly likely to produce prejudice, and Houston's size and diversity diluted the media's impact." Further working against Skilling was the fact that the jury even found him not guilty on some of the charges against him, indicating prejudice did not pervade all deliberations. A judge's instruction also asked jurors to refrain from viewing any online, print, or television media during the trial.

Voir Dire

Something else trial judges can do to shield defendants from prejudicial pretrial publicity is extend the process of jury selection in an effort to maximize the impartiality of the panel that ultimately judges the accused. During voir dire, both the prosecution and defense lawyers question prospective jurors to eliminate those who might favor the other side. A judge concerned about pretrial publicity can be more liberal in granting challenges for cause based on a lawyer's suspicion of bias. The judge also can increase the number of peremptory challenges available to both sides; these allow lawyers for each side to excuse jurors that they deem unacceptable for any reason other than race or sex (as we will discuss below). Ultimately, extending voir dire delays the onset of the trial, but it is considered the best means of securing an impartial jury.[97]

VOIR DIRE: The process of jury selection in which attorneys (prosecutors and defense counsel) ask questions of prospective jurors.

Gag Orders

A trial judge can issue a gag order, prohibiting the attorneys and witnesses from talking to the press about the case while the trial is underway.[98] But such an order imposed on the press is unlikely to survive a First Amendment challenge. Absent extreme circumstances, courts cannot prohibit the media from reporting information regarding a criminal prosecution.[99]

GAG ORDER: A command from a judge barring discussion of a specific matter, typically issued to jurors in a high-profile case.

Restrictions Imposed on Juries

Judges also have the authority to impose restrictions on jurors during a trial, such as prohibiting them from discussing the case with others outside the jury and even sequestering the jury in a hotel until the completion of the trial. These maneuvers are designed to limit the influence of outside sources, such as media coverage or even conversations with friends and family. The O.J. Simpson murder trial of 1994 involved the longest sequestration of a jury, lasting 245 days. In the George Zimmerman trial of 2013, the judge permitted the sequestered jury to have some time outside the hotel, allowing for them go to bowling, attend movies, and even go shopping. Concerns can arise over the psychological impact of sequestration on jurors as well as the possibility that jurors will be susceptible to groupthink while they spend so much time together. Accordingly, sequestration generally is reserved for high-profile cases with extensive media coverage.[100]

Cameras in the Courtroom

In *Estes v. Texas* (1965),[101] the Supreme Court held that the defendant was denied a fair trial because the proceedings were televised against the defendant's objection. Writing for a closely divided bench, Justice Clark speculated about the adverse effects of television coverage on defendants, attorneys, witnesses, judges, and jurors. According to Clark, "They are effects that may, and in some combination almost certainly will, exist in any case in which television is injected into the trial process."

When the *Estes* case was decided, only two states allowed cameras in the courtroom. That changed during the 1970s, as numerous state courts began to allow live radio and TV coverage of court proceedings. In 1978, the American Bar Association proposed a new standard, allowing for live TV and radio coverage if it was carried out unobtrusively. Three years later, in *Chandler v. Florida* (1981),[102] the Supreme Court modified its position on cameras in the courtroom. Chief Justice Burger spoke for a unanimous Court in expressing a preference for state courts to police themselves on this issue:

> Dangers lurk in this, as in most experiments, but unless we were to conclude that television coverage under all conditions is prohibited by the Constitution, the states must be free to experiment. We are not empowered by the Constitution to oversee or harness state procedural experimentation; only when the state action infringes fundamental guarantees are we authorized to intervene. We must assume state courts will be alert to any factors that impair the fundamental rights of the accused.

By the 1980s, televised criminal trials had become standard fare in most states. Today, all fifty states permit live television coverage under certain conditions. However, TV cameras (and even still cameras) are still prohibited by rule in federal courtrooms.[103] This is why TV news stories about federal trials and hearings rely on artists' sketches. Among federal judges, there is still widespread sentiment that live TV coverage detracts from the dignity of judicial proceedings. Yet since 1955, the Supreme Court has made audio recordings of oral arguments, and these recordings can be accessed via the Court's website (although cameras are not permitted inside the Court during oral argument).[104]

Evidence in Criminal Trials

The Sixth Amendment guarantees a defendant the right "to be confronted with the witnesses against him" as well as the right "to have compulsory process for obtaining witnesses in his favor." These two provisions affect the nature of the evidence that will come into play in a trial, as do the Due Process Clauses of the Fifth and Fourteenth Amendments.

THE CONSTITUTION IN ACTION
Video Testimony During the COVID-19 Pandemic

During the COVID-19 pandemic, many people became accustomed to the idea of meeting with others via Zoom or other online meeting platforms like Google Meet, Skype, or WebEx. On May 4, 2020, in fact, the Supreme Court of the United States held an oral argument over Zoom for the first time ever. Other courts began to make use of such procedures throughout 2020, and by 2021, appeals related to the use of video testimony—particularly regarding the notion of public trials and the right to confront witnesses—began to filter into appellate courts.

In August 2021, a decision from the Court of Appeals of Kentucky directly confronted a matter in which a witness did not appear in court, strictly for COVID-related reasons. This witness was an inmate in a federal prison, and he testified against a defendant accused of insurance fraud. On review, the Kentucky court found that a violation of the Confrontation Clause had occurred, stating as follows: "Over the past year, numerous federal district courts have held that, absent a specific showing that an individual witness was particularly vulnerable to COVID-19, and that other precautionary measures would not adequately protect the witness, general concerns about the spread of the virus do not justify abridging a defendant's right to in-person confrontation."[105]

Thinking about the prospect of widespread use of online court proceedings, it is important to recognize that use of videoconferencing can be an issue for some who lack internet access. Judge Clemens Landau from Salt Lake City Judicial Court in Utah, speaking at the National Center for State Courts' Court Technology Conference in 2021, stated that unique measures were taken to address this issue in his area. Notably, he said that judges and the public brought laptops to parking lots near homeless encampments to offer internet access. He also noted that laptops and internet hotspots were taken by kayak and canoe to homeless populations living along riverbanks. Landau even said his court had begun experimenting with online scheduling tools that allowed participants to indicate their need for counsel or other accommodations, such as an interpreter. Moreover, differences in quality of access—perhaps, related to whether someone uses a cell phone or a laptop to connect—can also be an issue; in that regard, it seems that being able to see a person's entire face is essential in these settings.[106]

The Right of Confrontation

The Confrontation Clause was included in the Sixth Amendment to prevent people from being convicted of crimes based on written statements by witnesses. Rather, a witness for the prosecution must appear in open court, give testimony, and be subject to cross-examination by the defense. In *Pointer v. Texas* (1965),[107] the Supreme Court held that the Confrontation Clause is an essential part of due process and is, therefore, incumbent upon the state courts through the Fourteenth Amendment. Speaking for the Court, Justice Black averred that "no one, certainly no one experienced in the trial of lawsuits, would deny the value of cross-examination in exposing falsehood and bringing out the truth in the trial of a criminal case"; therefore, the right of confrontation is a "fundamental right essential to a fair trial in a criminal prosecution." In a prior case from 1959, Chief Justice Warren indicated this right could be especially important "where the evidence consists of the testimony of individuals whose memory might be faulty or who, in fact, might be perjurers or persons motivated by malice, vindictiveness, or intolerance, prejudice, or jealousy."[108]

CROSS EXAMINATION: A term for the questioning of a witness who was not called to the stand by the attorney who is doing the questioning; this questioning follows direct examination.

Subsequently, in 1968, the high Court found a violation of the Confrontation Clause in a case in which the prosecution refused to reveal a witness's name and address.[109] Justice Stewart's majority opinion for this matter declared the following:

> In the present case, there was not, to be sure, a complete denial of all right of cross-examination. But the petitioner was denied the right to ask the principal prosecution witness either his name or where he lived, although the witness admitted that the name he had first given was false. Yet, when the credibility of a witness is in issue, the very starting point in 'exposing falsehood and bringing out the truth' through cross-examination must necessarily be to ask the witness who he is and where he lives. The witness' name and address open countless avenues of in-court examination and out-of-court investigation. To forbid this most rudimentary inquiry at the threshold is effectively to emasculate the right of cross-examination itself.

HEARSAY EVIDENCE:
A term that refers to out-of-court statements relayed by a witness who is not the speaker.

Were it an absolute requirement, though, the right of confrontation would exclude from criminal trials all hearsay evidence, a term that refers to out-of-court statements that are relayed by a witness who is not the speaker. But courts have long recognized several exceptions to the prohibition of hearsay evidence. Notably, declarations made by a person who is dying are admissible in a homicide case focusing on that person's death. Justice Henry B. Brown, writing for the Court in 1897, observed that "[d]ying declarations are an exception to the general rule that only sworn testimony can be received, the fear of impending death being assumed to be as powerful an incentive to truth as the obligation of an oath."[110]

Even so, in *Giles v. California* (2008),[111] the Supreme Court held that the dying declaration exception was reserved for statements made "by a speaker who was both on the brink of death and aware that he was dying." In applying this concept to a man who had killed his girlfriend, the Court ruled that statements she had made to police officers about fearing harm from her boyfriend could not be used at trial because they were uttered prior to the day she died. Justice Scalia's majority opinion said, "We decline to approve an exception to the Confrontation Clause unheard of at the time of the founding or for 200 years thereafter." Scalia did allow for the possibility of the victim's statements being admissible if the murder was shown to be motivated by a desire to prevent testimony—in keeping with a common law principle known as *forfeiture by wrongdoing*, which refers to a wrongful act that renders another person unable to testify; the case was remanded to lower courts to examine the motive for the murder and its compatibility with this principle.

More recently, in *Hemphill v. New York* (2022),[112] the Supreme Court refused to allow a hearsay exception that would have permitted a jury to hear the written confession of a coperpetrator (who was not available to testify because he was out of the country). In the view of the Court, attempts by the prosecutor to portray the confession as necessary in order to impeach the defendant's attempt to place blame solely on the coperpetrator were unpersuasive. Justice Sotomayor's majority opinion cited *Giles v. California* and *Crawford v. Washington* (2004),[113] in again focusing upon "exceptions established at the time of the founding" as the only viable reasons for allowing unconfronted testimony in a criminal trial.

It is important to point out that courts can take reasonable measures to shield a witness from retaliation, particularly if a witness is in some type of protective police custody, such as the U.S. Federal Witness Protection Program, also known as the Witness Security Program (WITSEC). This program, which is administered by the U.S. Marshals Service, was created pursuant to the Organized Crime Control Act of 1970 and amended by the Comprehensive Crime Control Act of 1984.[114]

Eyewitness Testimony

The right of confrontation is particularly important in cases in which eyewitness testimony is essential to the prosecution's case. In 2012, the Supreme Court addressed the topic of eyewitness testimony, holding "that the Due Process Clause does not require a preliminary judicial inquiry into the reliability of an eyewitness identification when the identification was not procured under unnecessarily suggestive circumstances arranged by law enforcement."[115]

Despite that ruling, almost half of the states have taken steps to mitigate problems related to eyewitness misidentification, which we address in the following box. Some states have taken these steps through legislation, some through court cases, some through agency actions, and some through task force recommendations.[116] For example, several states require all lineups to be conducted in *double blind* fashion, in which neither the administrator nor the victim knows whom the perpetrator is.[117] The body of research on this topic also suggests a *sequential lineup*, one in which suspects (or photos) are shown one by one in sequence—as opposed to lined up next to on another—is less likely to result in incorrect identifications; the sequential lineup, however, also appears less likely to result in an actual suspect being identified—although the extent of that effect varies based on which study one consults.[118] Sequential lineups are required by law in Connecticut, North Carolina, West Virginia, and Wisconsin; blind administration is used in Connecticut, Ohio, North Carolina, Texas, West Virginia, Wisconsin, and Vermont; specific instructions given to witnesses to ensure that they are not pressured into picking a suspect are required in Illinois, North Carolina, West Virginia, and Ohio.

In New Jersey, a state supreme court ruling requires double-blind and sequential lineups as well as jury instructions regarding issues in eyewitness identification, including a warning to jurors about flaws related to reliance on cross-racial identifications.[119] The Oregon Supreme Court has called for double-blind administration of lineups as well as for instructions indicating it is acceptable for a victim not to make an identification and that a lineup might not even include a suspected criminal. Oregon law also requires a witness to have "personal knowledge" regarding a matter in order to testify about it at trial.[120]

In 2017, the U.S. Department of Justice released a memo to the heads of federal law enforcement agencies regarding eyewitness testimony. The memo does not require the use of double-blind or sequential lineups, noting instead there may be instances in which the former is impractical. The memo does offer suggested instructions that an administrator should relay to a witness prior to a lineup (whether in person or by use of photographs), including these directives:

> 6.3.1 In a moment, you will be shown a group of photographs. The group of photographs may or may not contain a photograph of the person who committed the crime of which you are the victim [*or witness*].

> 6.3.4 You may not recognize anyone. That is okay. Just say so. Whether or not you select someone, we will continue to investigate the case.

> 6.3.5. Do not assume that I know who committed this crime.[121]

THE CONSTITUTION AND SOCIAL JUSTICE
Is Eyewitness Testimony Racially Biased?

Data from the Innocence Project indicate, "Mistaken eyewitness identifications contributed to approximately 69% of the more than 375 wrongful convictions in the United States overturned by post-conviction DNA evidence."[122] Hal Arkowitz and Scott O. Lilienfeld address this topic in a *Scientific American* article, entitled "Why Science Tells Us Not to Rely on Eyewitness Accounts," in which they say, "Eyewitness testimony is fickle and, all too often, shockingly inaccurate."[123] Their analysis of Innocence Project data on wrongful convictions connected to improper witness identification reveals, "33 percent of the wrongful convictions were based on the testimony of two or more eyewitnesses."[124]

A separate study of Innocence Project data conducted by Stephen Chew of Samford University shows that 41% of the wrongful convictions based on faulty eyewitness testimony "involved cross-racial misidentifications."[125] On this important topic, Christian Meissner and John Brigham conducted an analysis of 39 studies into "own-race bias," covering more than 5,000 total participants over 30 years, and found that "results indicated a 'mirror effect' pattern in which own-race faces yielded a higher proportion of hits and a lower proportion of false alarms compared with other-race faces."[126] Attempting to explain the unreliability of eyewitness testimony, Thomas Albright has observed, "Broadly speaking, eyewitness misidentifications can be characterized as failures of visual perception or memory, the former being seeing things inaccurately, the latter being loss of accuracy or precision in the storage, maintenance, and recall of what was seen."[127] More specifically, research has noted that high-stress situations, such as living through a crime, can adversely impact memory.[128] Additionally, the presence of a weapon—upon which an eyewitness is likely to focus their attention—has been shown to have a negative impact on the ability to recall what a suspect's face looked like.[129]

Scientific studies also have illustrated that witnesses to crimes do not recall information about suspects as well as they think they do. This body of literature dates back to 1954, when an article called "They Saw a Game" highlighted how poorly students who witnessed a fight at a football game between Princeton University and Dartmouth College remembered the identities of those involved.[130] More recent studies have demonstrated the fallibility of human identification and recall through experiments in which people see events and attempt to recall information, and some of those studies use imaging of the brain to buttress their findings;[131] other studies have found that jurors and judges tend to overestimate the veracity of an eyewitness identification.[132]

Despite all the shortcomings found with eyewitness testimony, its usage remains a commonplace part of criminal trials throughout the United States. As previously noted, though, states are beginning to implement reforms related to the use of double-blind and sequential lineups; whether additional reforms are forthcoming remains to be seen.

Recorded Testimony of Witnesses Who Do Not Appear at Trial

The Supreme Court has upheld the admission of recorded testimony from a witness who is not available at trial as long as it bears sufficient "indicia of reliability." In *Ohio v. Roberts* (1980),[133] the Court allowed the prosecution to use recorded testimony of a witness who testified at the preliminary hearing but could not be located for the trial. Under the test articulated in this case, trial judges were given the discretion to determine whether the testimony of an unavailable witness bears sufficient indicia of reliability. This test would be refined twenty-four years later.

In *Crawford v. Washington* (2004),[134] a man was prosecuted for attempted murder after he allegedly stabbed another man who tried to rape his wife. The wife witnessed the stabbing and made a recorded statement to the police. At trial, though, the wife exercised the **marital privilege** under Washington law and did not testify against her husband. The trial judge still allowed the recorded statement obtained by the police to be admitted into evidence, and the defendant was convicted. The Supreme Court overturned the conviction because the wife had not actually testified in court. Justice Scalia spoke for the Court, writing that "the Sixth Amendment demands what the common law required: unavailability *and* a prior opportunity for cross-examination" (emphasis added). Prior to the *Crawford* decision, testimony of an unavailable witness could have been used at trial based on a showing of "reliability."[135] Justice Scalia's majority opinion dismissed this "reliability" standard by saying, "Dispensing with confrontation because testimony is obviously reliable is akin to dispensing with jury trial because a defendant is obviously guilty. This is not what the Sixth Amendment prescribes." He went on to say that the Sixth Amendment "is most naturally read as a reference to the right of confrontation at common law, admitting only those exceptions established at the time of the founding." With that in mind, Scalia offered a new standard for evaluating this issue; according to his opinion, "[w]here testimonial statements are at issue, the only indicium of reliability sufficient to satisfy constitutional demands is the one the Constitution actually prescribes: confrontation." Even so, he did say, "We leave for another day any effort to spell out a comprehensive definition of 'testimonial.'"

"Another day" would arrive two years later when, in *Davis v. Washington* (2006),[136] the Court held that recorded 911 calls were not "testimonial" in nature and, therefore, could be admitted into evidence. Such evidence can be particularly important in domestic violence cases.

MARITAL PRIVILEGE: A concept that prevents one spouse from testifying against another in a criminal case, with exceptions for domestic abuse.

In *Davis*, the Court evaluated a case where a woman told a 911 operator she was being attacked by her ex-boyfriend, whom she said was "using his fists" to hit her. The man, Adrian Davis, fled as the 911 call was taking place, but police caught up to him and arrested him. At his trial, the woman did not testify, invoking marital privilege (which was permissible, since she had married the man she accused of attacking her). Nonetheless, prosecutors played a recording of the 911 call for the jury to hear, and Davis was convicted of a felony for violating a no-contact order. He appealed, stating that his Sixth Amendment right to confront witnesses had been violated by the playing of the 911 tape. However, Justice Scalia's majority opinion for the Court said that recording was admissible, finding that it was not "testimonial evidence" because the call's "primary purpose was to enable police assistance to meet an ongoing emergency." He also said of the witness: "She simply was not acting as a *witness;* she was not *testifying*" (emphasis in original). But Scalia was careful to note, "This is not to say a conversation which begins as an interrogation to determine the need for emergency assistance cannot, as the Indiana Supreme Court put it, 'evolve into testimonial statements,' ... once that purpose has been achieved."

Types of Privilege

The topic of confronting witnesses becomes especially important in cases when certain *privileges* preclude a person from testifying in court. For example, as noted, all fifty states allow for marital privilege, which could prevent a person from testifying against a spouse. Even so, there are exceptions to this privilege under most state laws, including for instances of domestic violence and child abuse. There also are privileges against testifying that relate to other relationships, such as doctor–patient privilege, which exists in all 50 states in some form—although whether this applies to all medical professionals can vary. The federal government's Federal Rules of Evidence 501 mentions a privilege connected to the testimony of a psychotherapist, but there is no general federal privilege for all doctor–patient interaction. All states also have some form of clergy–penitent privilege, although certain states may limit this privilege to confessions, and beyond that, definitions of *clergy* can vary; additionally, exceptions typically exist for child abuse cases.[137] All privileges can usually be waived when imminent harm is probable.

Child Witnesses

A witness must be competent to testify in a criminal case, and a young child may not be competent to do so. There is no precise minimum age required for children to testify. Trial judges must make this determination in individual cases. In doing so, judges must consider not only the child's age, but also their maturity and, above all, the child's understanding of the need to tell the truth.[138]

An important issue with respect to juvenile witnesses involves the defendant's right of confrontation. Historically, confrontation meant the defendant could look the witness in the eye during testimony and cross-examination. But should a child who is the victim of abuse be required to testify in open court and be subjected to cross-examination? In *Maryland v. Craig* (1990),[139] a closely divided Supreme Court upheld a procedure in which the cross-examination of a six-year-old witness was done remotely by video and, thus, did not allow for a face-to-face confrontation. Writing for the majority in addressing this "one-way" video transmission, Justice O'Connor concluded "that a State's interest in the physical and psychological well-being of child abuse victims may be sufficiently important to outweigh, at least in some cases, a defendant's right to face his or her accusers in court." Justice Scalia and three other justices dissented, saying, "Seldom has this Court failed so conspicuously to sustain a categorical guarantee of the Constitution against the tide of prevailing current opinion."

Although *Maryland v. Craig* dealt with confrontation via a one-way transmission of video, a 2002 Order of the Supreme Court includes the following quote from Justice Scalia, which seems to extend, implicitly, the *Craig* decision to a two-way transmission:

> I cannot comprehend how one-way transmission ... becomes transformed into full-fledged confrontation when reciprocal transmission is added. As we made clear in *Craig*, ... a purpose of the Confrontation Clause is ordinarily to compel accusers to make their accusations in the defendant's presence—which is not equivalent to making them in a room that contains a television set beaming electrons that portray the defendant's image. Virtual confrontation might be sufficient to protect virtual constitutional rights; I doubt whether it is sufficient to protect real ones.[140]

Some statements made by children can be admitted into evidence without the need for the child to appear in court. Out-of-court statements that are not *testimonial* in nature are not subject to the Confrontation Clause. Yet these statements may have tremendous probative value. In *Ohio v. Clark* (2015),[141] the Supreme Court allowed statements made by a three-year-old boy to a preschool teacher to be used against the defendant in a child abuse case. Noting that "[s]tatements by very young children will rarely, if ever, implicate the Confrontation Clause," the Court ruled that the child's statements, made in response to queries from the teacher, were nontestimonial in nature and therefore not subject to confrontation in court.

However, in *Coy v. Iowa* (1988) the Supreme Court struck down a trial court's decision to place a large screen between a child witness and a defendant.[142] In this case, Justice Scalia's majority opinion said, "The screen at issue was specifically designed to enable the complaining witnesses to avoid viewing appellant as they gave their testimony, and the record indicates that it was successful in this objective. ... It is difficult to imagine a more obvious or damaging violation of the defendant's right to a face-to-face encounter." Scalia went on to observe the following:

> It is always more difficult to tell a lie about a person 'to his face' than 'behind his back.' In the former context, even if the lie is told, it will often be told less convincingly. The Confrontation Clause does not, of course, compel the witness to fix his eyes upon the defendant; he may studiously look elsewhere, but the trier of fact will draw its own conclusions. Thus the right to face-to-face confrontation serves much the same purpose as a less explicit component of the Confrontation Clause that we have had more frequent occasion to discuss — the right to cross-examine the accuser; both 'ensur[e] the integrity of the factfinding process.'

Lower Court Rulings on Video Testimony

The federal circuit courts have offered varying interpretations of Supreme Court video testimony decisions. In 1999, the Second Circuit allowed two-way video testimony from an adult witness who had a fatal illness and was in the Witness Protection Program.[143] Decisions from the Eleventh Circuit and the Fifth Circuit also have allowed for remote testimony of a witness with a serious illness.[144] Nevertheless, in 2018, the Ninth Circuit refused to extend the *Maryland v. Craig* decision to an adult sex trafficking victim who was a minor at the time the offense was committed against her, but an adult by the time of trial.[145]

In 2008, the Fourth Circuit found no Confrontation Clause violation in the use of a videotaped deposition in which two officials in Saudi Arabia who had interrogated a suspected terrorist there provided testimony about what that suspect had said; the court observed that concerns related to travel and visa issues for entry into the United States were germane in this instance.[146] Yet in 2006, the Eleventh Circuit found a constitutional violation related to video testimony given by two witnesses to a crime who were in Australia. The majority opinion for that case said, "The simple truth is that confrontation through a video monitor is not the same as physical face-to-face confrontation."[147]

In at least seven states (Arkansas, Idaho, Kansas, Louisiana, Michigan, New Hampshire, and Virginia), laws have been passed to allow crime lab analysts to testify remotely instead of being physically present in a courthouse. The rationale underlying these laws is that in-person testimony would result in missed time working at the lab. State court analysis of such laws is emerging. In 2016, the New Mexico Supreme Court found video testimony from a forensic analyst violated the Confrontation Clause. The analyst in this case had moved out of the state by the time the trial began, but the court said, "Inconvenience to the witness is not sufficient reason to dispense with this constitutional right."[148] Elsewhere, the Michigan Supreme Court reviewed a case in which a trial court in that state accepted two-way video testimony from a crime lab worker in Utah, where a sample had been sent for analysis because Michigan labs were overworked. Finding a violation of the Confrontation Clause, the Michigan Supreme Court said that "expense is not a justification for a constitutional shortcut."[149]

More recently, in January 2022, the Supreme Court of Missouri ruled witness testimony via Zoom in a criminal case violated the Confrontation Clause of the Sixth Amendment.[150] In this case, the testifying witness worked for a crime lab, and he gave testimony about a link between the defendant and a DNA sample found on a victim's clothing. Zoom testimony was used because the lab employee was on paternity leave and, thus, said he could not appear in person for the trial. The Missouri Supreme Court's opinion observed that "[m]ost federal and state courts … hold a defendant's rights under the Confrontation Clause are violated by the use of two-way video procedure unless such procedure is necessary to further an important public policy and the reliability of the testimony is otherwise assured." In this case, the court said that "the witness in this case was neither a victim nor a child," adding that the trial court "made no finding that [the witness] was unavailable." Thus, the court refused to accept the proposition that "two-way video procedures categorically satisfy the safeguards of the Confrontation Clause."

Witnesses are not the only courtroom participants who have occasion to appear via video; sometimes, a judge must do so. In 2003, the Sixth Circuit allowed for an evidence suppression hearing in the U.S. District Court for the Western District of Tennessee to be overseen remotely by a judge from a federal district court in Michigan—a scenario necessitated by a shortage of judges on the Memphis-based district court in Tennessee.[151] The Sixth Circuit's majority found no violation of the Confrontation Clause because the defendant could still confront witnesses, as only the judge was appearing on video. Still, multiple circuit court decisions have held that the use of videoconferencing during a sentencing hearing violates a defendant's rights, whether it is the judge who appears by video[152] or the defendant.[153]

Compulsory Process

The term compulsory process is synonymous with the power of subpoena. A person who receives a subpoena is compelled to appear in court to give testimony. Failure to appear constitutes contempt of court.

The right of the defendant to subpoena favorable witnesses is essential to a fair trial. In *Washington v. Texas* (1967),[154] Chief Justice Earl Warren observed the following:

> The right to offer the testimony of witnesses, and to compel their attendance, if necessary, is in plain terms the right to present a defense, the right to present the defendant's version of the facts as well as the prosecution's to the jury, so it may decide where the truth lies. Just as an accused has the right to confront the prosecution's witnesses for the purpose of challenging their testimony, he has the right to present his own witnesses to establish a defense. This right is a fundamental element of due process of law.

The right to subpoena witnesses in one's defense is not absolute. In *Taylor v. Illinois* (1988),[155] the Supreme Court allowed a trial judge to preclude a defense witness from testifying due to the willful misconduct by defense counsel in failing to include the witness on the list provided to the prosecution under the rules of **discovery**. Discovery is a concept that can require each side in a criminal case to provide certain information about witnesses and evidence to the other side, although exceptions can apply. Justice Stevens spoke for the Court in this matter, saying the following:

> The accused does not have an unfettered right to offer testimony that is incompetent, privileged, or otherwise inadmissible under standard rules of evidence. The Compulsory Process Clause provides him with an effective weapon, but it is a weapon that cannot be used irresponsibly.

States vary regarding exactly what types of material must be turned over as a part of discovery. In Texas, for example, each side in a case must reveal, ahead of the trial, a list of witness's names, contact information, criminal history, written and recorded statements, and cooperation agreements—but records of oral statements need not be turned over; in Pennsylvania, though, a witness's oral statements must be turned over but not their criminal history (although it seems as though the latter could be located through public records). States also vary regarding requirements for producing documents and depositions; generally, grand jury transcripts are not a part of discovery.[156] As of

COMPULSORY PROCESS: The idea that certain witnesses in a criminal case can be compelled to testify pursuant to a subpoena that requires them to appear in court.

DISCOVERY: A term describing the requirement for each side in a criminal case to share certain information with the other side, such as the names of witnesses.

2022, more than two-thirds of the states had specific rules—through statute or case precedent—regarding government *e-discovery*, a term referencing electronically stored information, such as emails.[157] The Department of Justice issued a set of "recommendations" for "electronically stored information (ESI) discovery production in federal criminal cases" in 2012.[158]

Disclosure of Exculpatory Evidence

In *Brady v. Maryland* (1963),[159] the Supreme Court held it is a violation of due process for the prosecution to withhold exculpatory evidence from the defense, regardless of whether the prosecution was acting in bad faith. To withhold such evidence, said Justice William O. Douglas for the Court, "casts the prosecutor in the role of an architect of a proceeding that does not comport with standards of justice. ..." In Douglas's view, "Society wins not only when the guilty are convicted, but when criminal trials are fair; our system of the administration of justice suffers when any accused is treated unfairly."

In *United States v. Agurs* (1976),[160] the Court held that the prosecutor's duty to disclose evidence favorable to the accused is not limited to situations in which the defense requests disclosure of such evidence. However, it also held there is a constitutional violation only "if the omitted evidence creates a reasonable doubt that did not otherwise exist." Therefore, the prosecutor's failure to disclose evidence does not automatically require reversal of the defendant's conviction.

States vary regarding whether evidence not considered exculpatory (also known as non-*Brady* material) needs to be revealed to the defense in a criminal case—and in some situations, whether evidence is, indeed, exculpatory can become a matter for debate.[161]

EXCULPATORY EVIDENCE: A term describing the requirement for the prosecution to share with the defense any evidence in a criminal case that tends to show the defendant is not guilty.

THE CONSTITUTION IN ACTION
Boston Crime Lab Malfeasance Leads to Discovery Issues

Although their work should adhere to principles of scientific neutrality, employees in state-run crime labs usually work in conjunction with police departments—and, in some sense, prosecutors' offices—to process evidence and produce reports that could indicate, for example, if a substance seized by officers is, in fact, some type of contraband, such as illegal drugs. Even so, when those people tasked with testing these seized items fail to respect basic principles of due process in carrying out their duties, repercussions will resonate throughout the criminal justice system. Two recent scandals from crime labs in Massachusetts are instructive.

In November 2020, the Suffolk District Attorney in Massachusetts vacated 108 prior convictions for drug offenses in response to tampering charges levied against a chemist who worked at the Hinton State Laboratory Institute in Boston. Back in 2013, that chemist, Annie Dookhan, was found guilty on charges of obstruction of justice, perjury, and tampering with evidence. The charges stemmed from false test results she produced at this lab. Instead of testing every sample that came in, she would sign paperwork indicating substances were drugs without actually conducting any tests.[162] According to one report, "She eventually told investigators she tripled the productivity rates of her colleagues by not actually testing all the drugs that came before her."[163]

A separate lab in Amherst, Massachusetts faced a scandal of its own when a lab chemist named Sonja Farak pled guilty to tampering with evidence and possession of illegal drugs. Farak admitted to using drugs sent to the lab for identification, in some cases taking the drugs out of the lab. Her habits included using cocaine, methamphetamine, and LSD. She was sentenced to eighteen months in prison, and evidence indicated she used drugs in the lab nearly every day for a period of eight years, from 2005 until she was caught in 2013, when a supervisor noticed missing samples.[164]

Between the two Boston lab scandals, more than 35,000 criminal cases would be dismissed. Sanctions also were brought against prosecutors who, thinking the scope of the malfeasance in the Farak case was limited to a span of mere months, allegedly failed to disclose to defense attorneys evidence of tainted samples going back longer in time. Mental health worksheets filled out by Farak revealed her drug use had extended back for years, but those sheets were not turned over to defense attorneys, instead remaining in boxes at the prosecutor's office.

Reviewing the actions of these attorneys, a special hearing officer for the state's Board of Bar Overseers issued a ninety-eight-page report that recommended a two-year law license suspension for one attorney and formal reprimands for two others; the three had worked as assistant attorneys in the state's attorney general office, which led the Farak investigation. The hearing officer determined these three attorneys had failed to turn over exculpatory evidence to defense counsel in drug cases connected to the scandal, finding that "emails and conduct during the Farak investigation demonstrated a disturbing attitude toward defense counsel, who were simply trying to do their job in defending their clients' rights." The report also concluded defense counsel who sought documents that might help show the extent of Farak's drug use "were appropriately following up when the evidence they had seen (2011 newspaper articles, for example) that suggested to them that Farak's misconduct had begun years earlier than the Commonwealth was acknowledging."[165] In the end, this case serves as a stark reminder that a failure to disclose exculpatory evidence can result in a dismissal of criminal charges as well as disciplinary action against attorneys.

Admissibility of Scientific Evidence and Expert Testimony

Today, criminal trials often involve scientific evidence and expert testimony. Although the admissibility of such evidence is not a constitutional question per se, it is definitely a factor in determining whether a defendant receives a fair trial. Prior to 1993, the federal courts employed what was known as the *Frye* test, as it stemmed from a 1923 federal circuit court decision in *Frye v. United States*.[166] Under that test, which is still employed in some states, the results of scientific tests or procedures are admissible only if they have gained general acceptance. But in *Daubert v. Merrell Dow Pharmaceuticals* (1993),[167] the Court held that the admissibility of scientific evidence must consider whether the evidence can be empirically tested, is falsifiable, has a known error rate, and can be subjected to peer review. The *Daubert* standard, as it has come to be known, also relies on a judge to serve as the *gatekeeper* of what evidence to permit a jury to hear. Six years later, in a case involving a blown tire that led to a motorcycle crash, the Court ruled that testimony by engineers and other experts who are not scientists is also subject to the *Daubert* criteria.[168] Because *Daubert* was not based on constitutional law, but rather on the Federal Rules of Evidence, state courts are not required to follow it. Currently, most states use the *Daubert* standard (perhaps, with modifications), whereas the following states adhere to the Frye standard: California, Illinois, Maryland, Minnesota, New Jersey, New York, Pennsylvania, and Washington.[169]

Most criminal justice students are familiar with the commonly employed forms of forensic evidence. These include fingerprint analysis, generally conducted through the Automated Fingerprint

Identification System (AFIS), which has been maintained by the FBI since 1999. Such a database can facilitate searches for points of commonality between samples from crime scenes and known samples of fingerprints; courts typically admit fingerprint evidence that has eight to twelve points in common. The FBI also maintains the Combined DNA Index System (CODIS), which can be used to match DNA samples from crime scenes against exemplars from known offenders. The National DNA Index System also catalogs DNA from all states. The federal DNA Identification Act[170] requires this type of evidence to be kept private, and bans on familial DNA searches—those designed to find a relative connected to a DNA sample—exist in Maryland and the District of Columbia.

Recently, controversy arose in San Francisco following the revelation that police there had allegedly attempted to match the DNA of crime victims to unsolved cases, to see if those victims actually were perpetrators of other offenses. One such case resulted in charges being dropped by the district attorney after public backlash over a rape victim being charged with a property crime after police entered her DNA into a database.[171]

Fingerprint and DNA evidence have become well regarded in courts, even though such evidence could be considered *circumstantial* from the standpoint that it still needs to be linked, by inference, to a criminal act; unfortunately, though, not all forms of forensic science have turned out to be reliable. In April 2015, a report from *The Washington Post* revealed that the Department of Justice and the FBI found extensive flaws in testimony given from 1972 to 1999 by technicians in an FBI forensic unit devoted to microscopic hair comparisons. The report stated, "Of 28 examiners with the FBI Laboratory's microscopic hair comparison unit, 26 overstated forensic matches in ways that favored prosecutors in more than 95 percent of the 268 trials reviewed ... according to the National Association of Criminal Defense Lawyers (NACDL) and the Innocence Project, which are assisting the government with the country's largest post-conviction review of questioned forensic evidence." The report went on to note, "The cases include those of 32 defendants sentenced to death. Of those, 14 have been executed or died in prison."[172]

According to *The Washington Post*, "subjective, pattern-based forensic techniques—like hair and bite-mark comparisons ... have contributed to wrongful convictions in more than one-quarter of 329 DNA-exoneration cases since 1989."[173] Bite mark analysis—which involves attempts at trying to match teeth marks found at a crime scene (possibly on a victim's body) with some type of dental impression created of suspect's teeth—has proven to be especially unreliable. In fact, according to the California Innocence Project, "[a]lthough bite mark evidence has been used across the country in many criminal prosecutions, there is no real scientific support or research into the accuracy or reliability of bite mark evidence."[174]

Also found to be unreliable is polygraph evidence, which the Supreme Court said should be excluded from criminal trials with its decision in *United States v. Scheffer* (1998),[175] although the Court's decision in *James v. Illinois* (1990)[176] leaves open the possibility for evidence that is initially deemed inadmissible to later be admitted as "rebuttal testimony," which can be used to impeach a statement made by opposing counsel.

Beyond the nature of the evidence itself, it is important to recognize that all states have standards for how evidence is handled and transported from a crime scene to other environments, such as crime labs or evidence storage facilities. These regulations usually address the concept of *chain of custody*, but specific requirements can vary. For example, Tennessee Rule of Evidence 901(a) discusses parameters for "chain of custody" and allows for more relaxed standards for items that are "resistant to change," as opposed to items that are "susceptible to alteration."[177]

THE CONSTITUTION IN ACTION
The *Body Farm* at the University of Tennessee

In Knoxville, Tennessee, a place known as the *Body Farm* is used for research into the decomposition of dead bodies. The site's official name is the University of Tennessee Anthropological Research Facility, and it sits on 2.5 acres of land behind the University of Tennessee Medical Center. It was founded in the 1980s by forensic anthropologist Dr. William Bass.

His motivation for starting this facility arose in 1977 after he was asked to consult with police about identifying a dead body. Bass's estimates in that case missed the age of the body by more than 113 years. His suggestion that the deceased had been dead for a few months seemed comical after the remains turned out to be those of a Civil War-era soldier named Colonel William Shy,[178] who had been embalmed and entombed in an iron casket that preserved his remains remarkably well. Bass then created the *Body Farm* so that scientists could examine dead bodies left in varying contexts and learn more about establishing time of death—a factor that can be very important as law enforcement officials attempt to solve crimes. Typically, around 100 bodies are donated to the *Body Farm* every year. Once decomposition is complete (generally after one to two years), skeletons are housed in a nearby facility for teaching purposes. The *Body Farm* also houses a database of more than one million photographs of bodies in various states of decay.

The unique research that has occurred at the *Body Farm* includes the work of Dr. Arpad Vas, who testified in a Florida courtroom at the trial of Casey Anthony in 2011, telling the jury about the "odor of death" in the trunk of Anthony's car. More specifically, he detailed how the chemical composition of the air in that trunk was consistent with air that normally surrounds a decaying body.[179] More recent research from the *Body Farm* has indicated that when a body is buried, nearby soil and plants are impacted in noticeable ways. This line of research specifically aims, in the words of plant scientist Dr. Neal Stewart, to observe "how trees and shrubs may change their chemistry, biology and physical appearance in response to cadavers"; that includes an assessment of how the color of leaves can change based on the nearby presence of a dead body—information that could be valuable to law enforcement in search of missing persons.[180]

Additionally, Dr. Steven Symes has conducted *saw-tooth analysis* on dead bodies, cataloging how different tools leave unique markings in bone when used to cut a body apart; law enforcement officials can match his database to marks found on bones at crime scenes and even use him as an expert witness.[181] Forensic entomology also takes place at the *Body Farm*, and that can indicate what types of insects are attracted to a body at various stages of decomposition, even helping to establish time of death.[182] Overall, it is left to individual judges to determine what types of research will be suitable for a courtroom, but the rigorous empirical methods in place at the *Body Farm* assist in making a strong case for the inclusion of innovative methods in forensic science at criminal trials.

Constitutional Issues Associated with Trial Juries

A jury trial implicates another set of constitutional considerations. Above all, the Sixth Amendment requires an impartial jury. The Supreme Court has considered numerous issues involving trial juries, including how large they must be, the qualifications to serve on a jury, the jury selection process, the instructions that trial judges give to juries before they deliberate, and whether jury verdicts must be unanimous.

Jury Size

Under the common law, a trial jury consisted of twelve men. The tradition of the twelve-member jury continues in the federal courts and most states. However, some states employ smaller juries in noncapital cases. In *Williams v. Florida* (1970),[183] the Supreme Court upheld the use of six-person juries in the trial of felony offenses. Yet in *Ballew v. Georgia* (1978),[184] the Court said that a five-person jury was not acceptable under the

Sixth Amendment. Justice Harry Blackmun wrote for the Court in *Ballew*, stressing "the fundamental importance of the jury trial to the American system of criminal justice" and noting "that the State has offered little or no justification for its reduction to five members." Blackmun expressed concern that further reducing the size of juries might lead to "inaccurate and possibly biased decision making" and prevent juries from "truly representing their communities."

Qualifications to Serve on a Jury

Historically, as previously noted, jury service was limited to men, and African Americans and other people of ethnic minorities were systematically excluded as well. But in *Smith v. Texas* (1940),[185] a unanimous Supreme Court said, "It is part of the established tradition in the use of juries as instruments of public justice that the jury be a body truly representative of the community." Eventually, the Court would abolish (at least officially) sex and race discrimination with respect to jury service. Exclusion of African Americans from jury service was invalidated in 1965;[186] exclusion of women was struck down a decade later.[187] The Ninth Circuit also has applied these principles to preclude the use of a peremptory challenge based on a prospective juror's sexual orientation.[188]

In all state and federal jurisdictions, jurors must be at least eighteen years of age. Jurors also must be residents of the state or district in which the trial is to be held, and convicted felons whose civil rights have not been restored are commonly excluded from jury service.

THE CONSTITUTION AND SOCIAL JUSTICE
Should Convicted Felons Be Allowed to Serve on Juries?

As of 2022, only the following states permit those individuals with prior felony convictions to serve on juries: California, Colorado, Illinois, Iowa, and Maine; furthermore, none of these states allow an individual to serve on a jury until completion of a criminal sentence.[189] On the other hand, more than thirty states ban jury service by those with any prior felony conviction.[190] Alabama has a ban based on those felonies that involve "moral turpitude"; and some states even ban jury service by persons with misdemeanor convictions.[191] The federal government bans jury service pursuant to all felony convictions and in any case in which charges are pending. Pending criminal charges can be a barrier to jury service in some states, as well.[192] In more than half the states, a ban on jury service related to criminal activity is considered permanent, whereas other states allow an application to reinstate rights related to voting or gun ownership, with correlate restoration of jury-service rights.[193] Regardless of specific policies regarding jury service by those with criminal records, if a particular jurisdiction draws its prospective juror list from voting records, those with felony convictions could be excluded through that mechanism.

As a result of these types of bans, approximately 20 million people nationwide are prohibited from serving on juries by virtue of a prior felony conviction.[194] Moreover, as of the 2010 Census, greater than 36% of Americans with felony convictions are Black, while 13% of the total population is Black.[195] Data also indicate 33% of Black men in New York are banned from jury service as well as approximately 30% of Black men in California (prior to a 2019 change in jury selection laws there).[196]

Eric Binnall, a convicted felon who authored a book entitled *Twenty Million Angry Men: The Case for Including Convicted Felons in Our Jury System*, has said, "Courts and lawmakers allege that those with a felony conviction would jeopardize the jury process because they purportedly lack the requisite character to serve, and/or harbor an inherent bias, making each adversarial to the state," but he points out shortcomings in that argument through the use of mock trial experiments showing that former felons "demonstrated a normal distribution of pretrial biases."[197] Empirical studies in other contexts buttress that contention. Samuel Sommers of Tufts University has conducted research with mock juries and found that "heterogeneous groups deliberated longer and considered a wider range of information than did homogenous groups." He also determined that "these differences did not simply result from Black participants adding unique perspectives to the discussion," noting that White participants "… raised more case facts … and were more amenable to discussion of race-related issues when they were members of a diverse group."[198] Another scholar contends that, according to relevant research, "with a racially mixed jury, jurors are more likely to respect different racial perspective and to confront their own prejudice and stereotypes when such beliefs are recognized and addressed during deliberations."[199] Overall, scientific literature has offered important data to consider when evaluating what it means to have a *jury of one's peers*.

Jury Selection Procedures

As previously mentioned above, jury selection (voir dire) consists of questioning prospective jurors by counsel for both sides. Both the prosecution and the defense can challenge prospective jurors they feel might be biased against their side. These challenges take two forms: challenges for cause require a ruling from the judge, while peremptory challenges do not. Challenges for cause are unlimited, and could apply, for example, if a juror has a prior history with a party to a case; peremptory challenges typically are capped at three per side, and could be based on any number of factors other than race or sex, as we discuss in the examples provided below.

In *Batson v. Kentucky* (1986),[200] the Supreme Court ruled that peremptory challenges must not to be used as means of racial exclusion. Under *Batson*, a peremptory challenge that is ostensibly racial is subject to scrutiny by the trial judge via a *Batson* hearing. In the context of such a hearing, the lawyer making the peremptory challenge must articulate a valid nonracial reason for excluding that particular citizen from the jury. Reflecting on its holding in *Batson*, the Court's majority opinion from Justice Powell said the following:

> By requiring trial courts to be sensitive to the racially discriminatory use of peremptory challenges, our decision enforces the mandate of equal protection and furthers the ends of justice. In view of the heterogeneous population of our Nation, public respect for our criminal justice system and the rule of law will be strengthened if we ensure that no citizen is disqualified from jury service because of his race.

Eight years after *Batson*, in *J.E.B. v. Alabama ex rel. T.B.* (1994),[201] the Court struck down sex-based peremptory challenges. Writing for the Court in that case, Justice Harry Blackmun observed, "Failing to provide jurors the same protection against gender discrimination as race discrimination could frustrate the purpose of *Batson* itself."

CHALLENGE FOR CAUSE: An attempt by an attorney in a criminal case to dismiss a prospective juror for a reason that would preclude the juror's ability to reach an impartial decision in the case, such as prejudice or conflict of interest.

PEREMPTORY CHALLENGE: Refers to an attempt by an attorney to dismiss a prospective juror based on a factor that does not explicitly require an explanation but which cannot be based on race or sex; each side in a criminal case is typically given a limited number of these challenges.

Later, in *Miller-El v. Cockrell* (2003),[202] the Court ruled in favor of a death row inmate who had been convicted of murder in Dallas County, Texas. The prisoner had appealed because the prosecutor used peremptory challenges to remove ten out of eleven prospective Black jurors. Justice Kennedy's majority opinion pointed to the number of strikes and noted that some of the prosecutor's so-called *race-neutral* reasons, which included jurors' feelings about the death penalty and jurors' family history of criminal convictions, also applied to White jurors who were not challenged.

Subsequently, in *Davis v. Ayala* (2015),[203] a defendant facing three murder charges in California sought a *Batson* hearing after the prosecutor used seven peremptory challenges on Black or Hispanic jurors. The trial judge held a hearing but only for the prosecutor to provide alternative explanations for the challenges; the judge did not permit defense counsel to even attend. On review, the Supreme Court found this to be a "harmless error." One year later, though, in *Foster v. Chatman* (2016),[204] the Court overturned a conviction in a case in which the prosecutor had written a *B* next to names of all Black jurors listed on a form that later became public. Four Black jurors were removed by that prosecutor using peremptory challenges, leaving an all-White jury. On review, the Supreme Court found a *Batson* violation. The majority opinion extensively cited to *Snyder v. Louisiana* (2008),[205] saying that when reasons are given for striking prospective jurors of one race, but similar reasons could have applied to prospective jurors of another race, there is a *Batson* issue. In the *Snyder* case, in fact, the prosecutor made references to the O.J. Simpson trial during jury selection and struck five Black prospective jurors, leaving an all-White jury in place for the trial. In the sentencing phase, that prosecutor also mentioned that he believed O.J. *got away with it*, and all of these factors played a role in the high Court's decision to reverse the conviction.

More recently, in 2019, the Supreme Court's decision in *Flowers v. Mississippi*[206] found a *Batson* violation in a case where five prospective Black jurors were excused, and the jury was ultimately comprised of eleven White members and only one Black member. Justice Brett Kavanagh, writing for the Court's 7–2 majority, took note of the fact that the prosecutor asked an average of twenty-nine questions of Black jurors and only eleven of White jurors. Flowers had been subjected to six different trials for the same offense, including multiple trials overturned on appeal by state courts that found *Batson* violations, but following the Supreme Court's 2019 decision, the prosecutor indicated the charges would be dropped.

Prior to this line of cases regarding jury selection for trials, the Supreme Court's 1972 decision in *Peters v. Kiff*[207] found a violation of due process and equal protection under the Fourteenth Amendment based on the racial composition of a grand jury in Muscogee County, Georgia. Writing for the Court in that case, Justice Thurgood Marshall opined the following:

> When any large and identifiable segment of the community is excluded from jury service, the effect is to remove from the jury room qualities of human nature and varieties of human experience the range of which is unknown, and perhaps unknowable. It is not necessary to assume that the excluded group will consistently vote as a class in order to conclude, as we do, that its exclusion deprives the jury of a perspective on human events that may have unsuspected importance in any case that may be presented.

The Court later confronted a unique version of a *Batson* challenge in *Powers v. Ohio* (1991).[208] In this case, a White defendant claimed his constitutional rights were violated when six of the nine Black jurors in the jury pool were dismissed by peremptory challenges. Relying on the Fourteenth Amendment's Equal Protection

Clause, Justice Kennedy's majority opinion found that "a criminal defendant may object to race-based exclusions of jurors effected through peremptory challenges whether or not the defendant and the excluded juror share the same race." Kennedy also analyzed this matter from a jury-service perspective, saying, "Although an individual juror does not have the right to sit on any particular petit jury, he or she does possess the right not to be excluded from one on account of race." He added that "white jurors are subject to the same risk of peremptory challenges based on race as are all other jurors."

Death Qualification of Jurors

Another way individuals can be excluded from jury service relates to what is known as *death qualification*, whereby those who indicate during voir dire that they have an objection to the use of capital punishment—in a state where the death penalty is permitted by statute—can be excluded from jury service on the premise that they are refusing to uphold the law. We discuss this topic in greater detail in chapter 14, where we observe that the Supreme Court has permitted this type of exclusion.

Jury Instructions

As noted out in the previous chapter, the Supreme Court has held that due process requires courts to employ the reasonable doubt standard in trying criminal cases. Indeed, the prosecution must prove every element of the alleged offense beyond a reasonable doubt.[209] In a jury trial, the judge must instruct the jury on the application of the reasonable doubt standard. The Supreme Court has never adopted a particular form that such an instruction must take; as long as the instruction correctly conveys the principle to the jury, due process is satisfied.[210] In *Victor v. Nebraska* (1994),[211] the Court rejected a challenge to a jury instruction that defined the reasonable doubt standard as "an actual and substantial doubt reasonably arising from the evidence." Victor, who had been sentenced to death for murder, argued that the use of the term *substantial* overstated the degree of doubt a jury must have to convict. Justice O'Connor's opinion for the Court agreed that the language was "somewhat problematic" but concluded it was unlikely "that the jury would have interpreted this instruction to indicate that the doubt must be anything other than a reasonable one." The trial judge's instruction also defined the absence of reasonable doubt in terms of *moral certainty*. Again, Justice O'Connor expressed reservations about the language but concluded that, taken as a whole, the jury instruction accurately conveyed the reasonable doubt standard; to this point, she said, "Though we reiterate that we do not countenance its use, the inclusion of the 'moral certainty' phrase did not render the instruction given in Victor's case unconstitutional."

The Unanimity Requirement

Throughout U.S. history, the federal courts and nearly all state courts have required juries to reach unanimous agreement to render a verdict in a criminal trial. However, in two controversial decisions in 1972, the Supreme Court upheld rules allowing nonunanimous verdicts in Louisiana (which permitted 10–2 guilty verdicts in noncapital cases) and Oregon (which allowed 11–1 guilty verdicts in noncapital cases).[212] In so doing, the Court held that due process does not require verdicts in criminal cases to be unanimous. Justice William O. Douglas, dissenting in the Louisiana case, said the following:

> When verdicts must be unanimous, no member of the jury may be ignored by the others.
> When less than unanimity is sufficient, consideration of minority views may become

nothing more than a matter of majority grace. In my opinion, the right of all groups in this Nation to participate in the criminal process means the right to have their voices heard. A unanimous verdict vindicates that right. Majority verdicts could destroy it.

Justice Thurgood Marshall also dissented, arguing that the abandonment of the unanimity rule undermined the reasonable doubt standard; along these lines, he declared, "The doubts of a single juror are, in my view, evidence that the government has failed to carry its burden of proving guilt beyond a reasonable doubt."

It has been said that in constitutional law, today's dissent can become tomorrow's majority opinion. That aphorism certainly rings true with respect to the jury unanimity rule, for in *Ramos v. Louisiana* (2020),[213] the Supreme Court overturned its 1972 precedents. Justice Neil Gorsuch wrote the Court's opinion, which asserted the unanimity rule was part of the original understanding of the Sixth Amendment:

Wherever we might look to determine what the term "trial by an impartial jury trial" meant at the time of the Sixth Amendment's adoption—whether it's the common law, state practices in the founding era, or opinions and treatises written soon afterward—the answer is unmistakable. A jury must reach a unanimous verdict in order to convict.

Justice Gorsuch proceeded to explain that, under the doctrine of incorporation, the Sixth Amendment must mean the same thing in state courts as it means in federal court:

This Court has long explained that the Sixth Amendment right to a jury trial is "fundamental to the American scheme of justice" and incorporated against the States under the Fourteenth Amendment. This Court has long explained, too, that incorporated provisions of the Bill of Rights bear the same content when asserted against States as they do when asserted against the federal government. So if the Sixth Amendment's right to a jury trial requires a unanimous verdict to support a conviction in federal court, it requires no less in state court.

Some scholars referred to 10–2 guilty verdicts in Louisiana as "Jim Crow's last stand,"[214] a reference to the post-Civil War origins of nonunanimous criminal court verdicts in the state—a movement some say was spurred by fears over one or two holdout Black jurors preventing a conviction. In 2018, 65% of Louisiana voters approved a ballot measure (Amendment 2) that requires unanimous jury verdicts in felony cases (though the ballot measure did not retroactively overturn prior convictions). The Supreme Court's *Ramos* decision cemented that need for unanimity in all criminal cases in the state. Highlighting the value of these changes, the New Orleans-based newspaper *The Advocate* conducted a study of nearly 1,000 cases over a six-year period (prior to 2018) and found that "40 percent of trial convictions ... came over the objections of one or two holdouts. When the defendant was black, the proportion went up to 43 percent, versus 33 percent for white defendants. In three-quarters of the 993 cases in the newspaper's database, the defendant was black."[215]

Notably, in *Edwards v. Vannoy* (2021),[216] the Supreme Court refused to apply the *Ramos* decision retroactively to cases arising under federal habeas corpus review of state court convictions. The Court's newest member, Justice Brett Kavanaugh, wrote the opinion for the Court, insisting that while new rules of criminal procedure do apply retroactively to cases on direct review, they do not apply to cases brought into federal court by prisoners who already have exhausted their appellate remedies in the state courts. In a strongly worded dissent,

Justice Elena Kagan castigated the majority for allowing an injustice to continue, saying that:

> The result of today's ruling is easily stated. *Ramos* will not apply retroactively, meaning that a prisoner whose appeals ran out before the decision can receive no aid from the change in law it made. So Thedrick Edwards, unlike Evangelisto Ramos, will serve the rest of his life in prison based on a 10-to-2 jury verdict. Only the reasoning of today's holding resists explanation.

FEDERAL HABEAS CORPUS REVIEW: Federal judicial review of a state prisoner's case pursuant to a writ of habeas corpus.

The Deadlocked Jury

One of the consequences of the unanimity rule is that juries are more likely to be deadlocked. All it takes is one juror who stubbornly refuses to see the case in the same way as do the other eleven. Of course, as dramatized in the classic film *Twelve Angry Men*,[217] the one stubborn holdout may be right! In the case of a deadlocked jury, the trial judge will first call the jury back into the courtroom and issue what is known as an *Allen* charge. The charge, as stated in *Allen v. United States* (1896),[218] is as follows:

> [I]f much the larger number were for conviction, a dissenting juror should consider whether his doubt was a reasonable one. ... If, upon the other hand, the majority were for acquittal, the minority ought to ask themselves whether they might not reasonably doubt the correctness of a judgment that was not concurred in by the majority.

DEADLOCKED JURY: A jury that is unable to reach a unanimous verdict.

***ALLEN* CHARGE:** A judge's instruction to a deadlocked jury exhorting jurors to listen to one another's arguments and reconsider their own positions in order to arrive at a verdict.

Should this exhortation prove fruitless in terms of precipitating a unanimous decision, the judge has no choice but to declare a mistrial. It will then be up to the prosecution to decide whether to retry the case before a different jury or to offer the defendant a greater inducement to enter a guilty plea and forego a new trial. Recall that the Double Jeopardy Clause offers little protection against a new trial following a mistrial. Legally, it is as if the first trial never took place unless the mistrial is the result of prosecutorial misconduct.

Jury Nullification

A trial jury has the prerogative to exercise its judgment and return a verdict of not guilty or guilty of a lesser offense. Sometimes, trial juries ignore the evidence or the law and acquit a defendant because they object to the law under which the defendant was prosecuted or believe the prosecution was otherwise unjust. This controversial practice is known as jury nullification, and there is nothing a trial judge can do about it. On the other hand, a judge can set aside a guilty verdict returned by a jury. In this regard, it is often said that a trial judge acts as a *thirteenth juror*.

The Jury's Role in Sentencing

As you shall see in chapter 14, juries play an important role in death penalty cases. For the most part, sentences in criminal cases are determined by trial judges. In felony cases, there usually is a separate sentencing hearing weeks after the verdict has been rendered and the jury dismissed.

Sentencing Enhancements

In *Apprendi v. New Jersey* (2000),[219] the Court held that any fact relied upon by a court to enhance a sentence must be submitted to the jury and proven beyond a reasonable doubt. In this case, a judge issued an enhanced sentence based on a finding that a hate crime had occurred. Reversing this sentence and stating that the Sixth Amendment requires the jury—not a judge—to find the existence of a hate crime, Justice Scalia's majority opinion offered the following exhortation:

> What ultimately demolishes the case for the dissenters is that they are unable to say what the right to trial by jury *does* guarantee if, as they assert, it does not guarantee-what it has been assumed to guarantee throughout our history-the right to have a jury determine those facts that determine the maximum sentence the law allows. They provide no coherent alternative.

We discuss the concept of hate-crime sentencing enhancements in greater detail in chapter 13.

The Federal Sentencing Guidelines

In an attempt to reduce sentencing disparities, Congress in 1984 established the United States Sentencing Commission and gave it the authority to create sentencing guidelines for the federal courts. The guidelines were designed to structure the discretion of federal district judges. In *United States v. Booker* (2005),[220] the Supreme Court held that any facts not already in evidence that judges rely upon in making determinations under the Guidelines must be, in light of *Apprendi v. New Jersey*, submitted to the jury and proven beyond a reasonable doubt. The effect of this decision was making the U.S. Sentencing Guidelines advisory, rather than mandatory. We discuss the federal sentencing enhancements in chapter 13.

Mandatory Minimum Sentences

In *Alleyne v. United States* (2013),[221] the Supreme Court held that any fact that increases the mandatory minimum in a criminal case is an "element" that must be submitted to the jury. In this case, federal law called for a five-year minimum sentence for "carrying" a firearm during the commission of a "crime of violence," but that escalated to seven years if the firearm were "brandished" or ten years if the firearm were "discharged." The trial judge unilaterally decided to impose the seven-year sentence, but on review, the high Court set it aside, finding that the Sixth Amendment right to a trial by jury had been violated because, as Justice Thomas stated in the majority opinion:

> [T]he essential Sixth Amendment inquiry is whether a fact is an element of the crime. When a finding of fact alters the legally prescribed punishment so as to aggravate it, the fact necessarily forms a constituent part of a new offense and must be submitted to the jury. ... One reason is that each crime has different elements and a defendant can be convicted only if the jury has found each element of the crime of conviction.

In summary, based on case precedent, any factor besides prior criminal history that enhances the punishment for a crime must be submitted to a jury, which must indicate, typically on a separate verdict form, whether the existence of that factor has been found. We will discuss the correlated topics of mandatory minimum sentences and sentencing enhancements in greater detail in chapter 13.

JURISPRUDENCE

Memorabilia inside Courthouse Results in a New Trial
State of Tennessee v. Gilbert
Tennessee Court of Criminal Appeals at Nashville
No. M2020-01241-CCA-R3-CD (Tenn. Crim. App. 2021)

In December 2021, an appeals court in Tennessee ruled that a defendant's Sixth Amendment rights were violated because a jury deliberated his assault case while sitting in a courthouse room where Confederate memorabilia was on display. Among the items in the jury room were a painting of Confederate President Jefferson Davis, a painting of a Confederate army officer, and a Confederate battle flag.

The defense attorney argued that these items had created an "inherently prejudicial room" in violation of the Black defendant's right to a fair trial and an impartial jury. Reviewing this matter, the Tennessee Court of Criminal Appeals said that "although the government may choose to convey any message that it wants to the general public, it may not convey *any* message at all to the jurors in a criminal case." The opinion went on to declare, "Because Giles County may not convey any message to the jury, we conclude that permitting the jury to deliberate in a room filled with Confederate memorabilia exposed the jury to extraneous information or improper outside influence." The court then cited to a prior Tennessee Supreme Court decision, observing, "The validity of a verdict returned by a jury that 'has been subjected to either extraneous prejudicial information or an improper outside influence ... is questionable.'"[222] As a result, based on the appellate court finding a *presumption of prejudice*, a new trial was ordered.

Conclusion

In keeping with the founders' concerns regarding unjust criminal prosecutions at the hands of the British during the colonial period, the Sixth Amendment offers robust protections for those accused of crimes in the United States. Chief among these is the right to be represented by legal counsel. As noted in the previous chapter, this right is inextricably intertwined with the Fifth Amendment right to refrain from self-incrimination, and thus, *Miranda* warnings address both crucial elements.

As we have discussed, though, an accused criminal who is in police custody must unambiguously invoke these rights for them to apply. If indigent defendants request appointed counsel, a lawyer will be provided for them, generally through a public defender's office—although the amount of time that an overworked assistant public defender might devote to an individual case might well affect the quality of representation. Beyond that, ineffective counsel remains a viable reason to raise a Sixth Amendment appeal as well.

Overall, the right to counsel is essential in all critical phases of the criminal justice process—most notably, prior to and during a criminal trial. The Sixth Amendment guarantees a right to a trial by jury, and case precedent indicates that a prospective juror cannot be removed from consideration for jury service based on race or sex. Moreover, the Supreme Court recently indicated that a unanimous jury verdict—typically, among 12 jurors—is required for a criminal conviction; ultimately, the unanimity requirement creates a high threshold that is capable of guarding against an unjust conviction, particularly when coupled with the presumption of innocence and the necessity of proof beyond a reasonable doubt.

Constitutional safeguards also protect the speed with which one is brought to trial after being formally charged—to prevent lengthy delays that leave a person dangling in a form of legal uncertainty for prolonged periods. Also protected is the notion of a trial that is open to the public, which the founders valued so as to preclude the possibility of a closed-door hearing in which rights were likely to be trampled. A public trial also connects to the idea of confronting witnesses in open court—in turn enabling a jury to best assess the veracity of witness statements. Exceptions to the Confrontation Clause exist for so-called *nontestimonial* evidence, such as a 911 call that might be played for a jury. All these concepts have been illuminated recently during the COVID-19 pandemic—from the speed with which cases are brought to the possibility of trials taking place over the internet and what that means for phrases like *public trial* and *right to confront*. While Supreme Court case precedent has previously allowed for video testimony in child abuse cases, future appellate review of the manner in which courts adapted to life in a pandemic likely will be forthcoming in the next few years.

This chapter also has considered different types of scientific evidence as well as eyewitness testimony. Scholars have pointed out instances in which the reliability of such evidence can be viewed as suspect. How a judge functions in the role of the *gatekeeper* regarding the admissibility of both evidence and witness testimony—processes likely to be impacted by case precedent and applicable statutes—can play a significant role in the administration of justice.

Finally, we have examined the use of sentence enhancements to demonstrate that the right to a jury trial also includes the right to have every element of a crime—even those that enhance punishment—proven to a jury. In the next chapter, we focus more on aspects of punishment in the criminal justice process, but we will retain the theme of viewing key constitutional amendments as a means for preventing arbitrary and unilateral infringements upon individual liberty in the criminal justice context. After all, in a criminal trial, the government operates a vast machinery and can marshal extensive resources that are not likely to be available to an individual person. The protections inscribed in the Sixth Amendment are of paramount importance for evening out this power imbalance.

Discussion Questions

1. Even though counsel is supposed to be appointed for an indigent defendant, what societal obstacles remain when it comes to the attainment of viable legal counsel for those who are poor? What advantages exist for those who have resources when it comes to the criminal justice system?

2. Are there situations in which a defendant might find it more advantageous to waive their right to trial by jury and, instead, opt for a trial by judge? What matters can confound the notion of a *jury of one's peers*?

3. What are the pros and cons of plea bargaining from the perspective of a defendant? What about from the perspective of a prosecutor? And what about the point of view of the victim? What elements of plea bargaining can become coercive? Consider the intersection of plea bargaining and the lack of effective counsel; for indigent defendants, why might it be more likely that a plea deal is accepted?

4. Under what circumstances is it acceptable for there to be a delay in the start of a trial? How would delays caused by a pandemic impact the application of this Sixth Amendment protection?

5. Under what circumstances is it acceptable for a judge to close a courtroom to the media? What are the reasons courts typically attempt to remain open to the public and the media?

6. Choose any form of forensic evidence discussed in this chapter. Explain how a judge would determine if that evidence should be admissible in court under either the *Frye* standard or the *Daubert* standard.

7. Why has the Supreme Court overturned precedent and insisted on unanimous verdicts in all criminal cases?

Endnotes

1   Caroline Wolf Harlow, Defense Counsel in Criminal Cases, NCJ 179023 (2000).

2   *Powell v. Alabama*, 287 U.S. 45 (1932).

3   *Johnson v. Zerbst*, 304 U.S. 458 (1938).

4   *Betts v. Brady*, 316 U.S. 455 (1942).

5   *Gideon v. Wainwright*, 372 U.S. 353 (1963).

6   Attorney General Robert F. Kennedy, Speech Before the New England Conference on the Defense of Indigent Persons Accused of Crime (Nov. 1, 1963).

7   *Douglas v. California*, 372 U.S. 353 (1963).

8   *Argersinger v. Hamlin*, 407 U.S. 25 (1972).

9   *Scott v. Illinois*, 440 U.S. 367 (1979).

10 Lynn Langton & Donald Farole Jr., *Census of Public Defender Offices*, State Public Defender Programs, September 2009, https://bjs.ojp.gov/library/publications/public-defender-offices-2007-statistical-tables-revised.

11 18 U.S.C. § 3006(a).

12 United States Courts, Defender Services, https://www.uscourts.gov/services-forms/defender-services. Any federal district, or combination of adjacent districts where 200 or more individuals require public counsel in a year can be served by a federally funded public defender system. Approximately 4,000 lawyers, investigators, paralegals, and others work in the federal system. Three federal districts do not use a public defender system, instead relying on private counsel selected from a list of *panel attorneys* approved by the federal government; those districts are the Southern District of Georgia, the Eastern District of Kentucky, and the District of the Northern Mariana Islands. Nationwide, there are more than 10,000 panel attorneys, who can assist when needed, perhaps in cases involving attorney shortages or conflicts of interest; *see* Charles Bethea, *Is This the Worst Place to Be Poor and Charged with a Federal Crime?* The New Yorker, Nov. 5, 2021.

13 Yale Law School, Career Development Office, *Criminal Defense*, https://law.yale.edu/sites/default/files/area/department/cdo/document/cdo_criminal_defense_public.pdf.

14 The Bronx Defenders, *Holistic Defense, Defined*, https://www.bronxdefenders.org/holistic-defense/; Louisiana Center for Children's Rights, Children's Defense Team, https://www.laccr.org/what-we-do/defending-children/childrens-defense-team/.

15 Bureau of Justice Statistics, *State-Administered Indigent Defense Systems* (2013), https://bjs.ojp.gov/library/publications/state-administered-indigent-defense-systems-2013.

16 Tina Peng, *I'm a Public Defender, It's Impossible for Me to Do a Good Job Representing My Clients*, Wash. Post, Sept. 3, 2015, https://www.washingtonpost.com/opinions/our-public-defender-system-isnt-just-broken--its-unconstitutional/2015/09/03/aadf2b6c-519b-11e5-9812-92d5948a40f8_story.html.

17 Phil McCausland, *Public Defenders Nationwide Say They're Overworked and Underfunded*, NBC News, Dec. 11, 2017, available at: https://www.nbcnews.com/news/us-news/public-defenders-nationwide-say-they-re-overworked-underfunded-n828111.

18 *Goldberg v. Kelly*, 397 U.S. 254 (1970).

19 Florida Police Benevolent Association, *Legal Services*, https://www.flpba.org/legal-services/.

20 Minnesota Police and Peace Officers Association, *About Us*, https://www.mppoa.com/index.php/about/about-us.

21 Eric Ferkenhof, *Eric Nelson Isn't Working Alone to Defend Derek Chauvin: A Police Legal Fund Is Backing Him up with a Dozen Lawyers and $1 Million*, USA Today, March 30, 2021, https://www.usatoday.com/story/news/nation/2021/03/30/derek-chauvin-trial-eric-nelson-defense-george-floyd/6969253002/.

22 *Miranda v. Arizona*, 384 U.S. 436 (1966).

23 *Escobedo v. Illinois*, 378 U.S. 478 (1964).

24 *Hamilton v. Alabama*, 368 U.S. 52 (1961).

25 *White v. Maryland*, 373 U.S. 59 (1963).

26 *United States v. Wade*, 388 U.S. 218 (1967); *Moore v. Illinois*, 434 U.S. 220 (1977); *Kirby v. Illinois*, 406 U.S. 682 (1972) (finding that a lineup prior to arrest does not require counsel).

27 *Davis v. United States*, 512 U.S. 452 (1994).

28 *Chandler v. Fretag*, 348 U.S. 3 (1954).

29 *Davis v. United States*, *supra* note 27.

30 *State v. Demesme*, 228 So. 3d 1206 (La. 2017).

31 Erik De La Garza, *Louisiana Court Finds Suspect's 'Lawyer Dog' Request Falls Short*, Courthouse News Service, Nov. 1, 2017, https://www.courthousenews.com/louisiana-court-finds-suspects-lawyer-dog-request-falls-short/.

32 *Maryland v. Shatzer*, 559 U.S. 98 (2010).

33 *Edwards v. Arizona*, 451 U.S. 477 (1981).

34 *Arizona v. Roberson*, 486 U.S. 675 (1988).

35 *Minnick v. Mississippi*, 498 U.S. 146 (1990).

36 A nuanced rule correlated with these cases arose in *Michigan v. Jackson*, 475 U.S. 625 (1986), which said that a defendant's request for counsel made at an arraignment prohibits any police interrogation until counsel physically arrives. However, that decision was overturned by *Montejo v. Louisiana*, 556 U.S. 778 (2009), when the Court raised concerns about applying this standard in the more than 25 states that automatically appoint counsel at an arraignment even if it is not requested by the defendant. In this case, Jesse Jay Montejo was arraigned for first-degree murder following a preliminary hearing in Louisiana, where a lawyer is automatically appointed for an indigent defendant at their arraignment. But later, on the day of his arraignment, before counsel could arrive to speak with Montejo, he took a trip with police to locate the murder weapon. During this trip, police suggested Montejo write an apology letter to the victim's widow, and he did so; at his trial, that letter was admitted as evidence, and he was found guilty. On appeal, his lawyer suggested the letter should have been deemed inadmissible because it was written without the presence of counsel. The Supreme Court disagreed, calling the *Jackson* standard for waiting on a lawyer's arrival to be "unworkable." Moreover, the Court said there were other, sufficient protections already in place for criminal defendants. Justice Scalia made this point clear in summarizing a prior line of cases as follows: "Under *Edwards'* prophylactic protection of the *Miranda* right, once such a defendant 'has invoked his right to have counsel present,' interrogation must stop. ... And under *Minnick's* prophylactic protection of the *Edwards* right, no subsequent interrogation may take place until counsel is present, 'whether or not the accused has consulted with his attorney.' ... These three layers of prophylaxis are sufficient. Under the *Miranda-Edwards-Minnick* line of cases (which is not in doubt), a defendant who does not want to speak to the police without counsel present need only say as much when he is first approached and given the *Miranda* warnings. ... *Jackson* is simply superfluous." Next, Justice Scalia addressed the societal costs of having such a superfluous rule in place: "The principal cost of applying any exclusionary rule 'is, of course, letting guilty and possibly dangerous criminals go free. ...'" He added, "*Jackson* not only 'operates to invalidate a confession given by the free choice of suspects who have received proper advice of their *Miranda* rights but waived them nonetheless,' ... but also deters law enforcement officers from even trying to obtain voluntary confessions. ... Without these confessions, crimes go unsolved and criminals unpunished. These are not negligible costs, and in our view the *Jackson* Court gave them too short shrift."

37 *Massiah v. United States*, 377 U.S. 201 (1964).

38 In making this assertion, Stewart cited Judge Hays of the U.S. Court of Appeals for the Second Circuit, who had dissented in Massiah's 1962 case at that court; *Massiah v. United States*, 307 F.2d 62 (2d Cir. 1962).

39 *McMann v. Richardson*, 397 U. S. 759 (1970).

40 *Strickland v. Washington*, 466 U.S. 668 (1984) (Marshall, J., dissenting).

41 *Id.*

42 *Williams v. Taylor*, 529 U.S. 362 (2000).

43 *Wiggins v. Smith*, 539 U.S. 510 (2003).

44 *Lafler v. Cooper*, 566 U. S. 156 (2012).

45 *Jae Lee v. United States*, 582 U.S. ___ (2017).

46 *Shinn v. Ramirez Martinez*, 596 U.S. ___ (2022).

47 *Faretta v. California*, 422 U.S. 806 (1975).

48 *Wheat v. United States*, 486 U.S. 153 (1988).

49 See *Bundy v. Dugger*, 850 F.2d 1402 (11th Cir. 1988).

50 *McKaskle v. Wiggins*, 465 U.S. 168 (1984).

51 *Illinois v. Allen*, 397 U.S. 337 (1970).

52 *Duncan v. Louisiana*, 391 U.S. 145 (1968).

53 *Baldwin v. New York*, 399 U.S. 66 (1970); *Codispoti v. Pennsylvania*, 418 U.S. 506 (1974).

54 *Duncan v. Louisiana*, *supra* note 52.

55 Terrence Fraser, *Proposition 47 Did Not End Prosecution of Thefts Under $950 In California*, Associated Press, July 23, 2021, https://apnews.com/article/fact-checking-160551360299.

56 *Blanton v. City of No. Las Vegas*, 489 U.S. 538 (1989).

57 *In re Gault*, 387 U.S. 1 (1967).

58 *McKeiver v. Pennsylvania*, 403 U.S. 528 (1971).

59 Anne Teigen, *Juvenile Age of Jurisdiction and Transfer to Adult Court Laws*, National Conference of State Legislatures, Apr. 8, 2021, https://www.ncsl.org/research/civil-and-criminal-justice/juvenile-age-of-jurisdiction-and-transfer-to-adult-court-laws.aspx.

60 National Conference of State Legislatures, Principles of Effective Juvenile Justice Policy (2018), https://www.ncsl.org/Portals/1/Documents/cj/JJ_Principles_122017_31901.pdf.

61 *See, e.g., North Carolina v. Pearce*, 395 U.S. 711 (1969); *Blackledge v. Allison*, 431 U.S. 63 (1977); *Jae Lee v. United States*, 582 U.S. ___ (2017); *Class v. United States*, 583 U.S. ___ (2018).

62 *See Kercehval v. United States*, 274 U.S. 220 (1927); *Moore v. Michigan*, 355 U.S. 155 (1957).

63 *Class v. United States*, *supra* note 61.

64 *Brady v. United States*, 397 U.S. 742 (1970).

65 *Santobello v. New York*, 404 U.S. 257 (1971).

66 *Lynch v. Overholser*, 369 U.S. 705 (1962).

67 *Bordenkircher v. Hayes*, 434 U.S. 357 (1978).

68 *Boykin v. Alabama*, 395 U.S. 238 (1969).

69 Bill Hutchinson, *Judge Rejects Plea Deal for Father and Son in Federal Case over Ahmaud Arbery's Murder*, ABC News, Jan. 31, 2022, https://abcnews.go.com/US/ahmaud-arberys-family-slams-federal-prosecutors-deal-men/story?id=82577871.

70 Chris Francescani & Luchina Fisher, *Bill Cosby: Timeline of His Fall From 'America's Dad' to His Release from Prison*, ABC News, June 30, 2021, https://abcnews.go.com/Entertainment/bill-cosby-trial-complete-timeline-happened-2004/story?id=47799458.

71 Editorial Staff, *Bill Cosby's Conviction Is Overturned. Read the Court's Opinion*, N.Y. Times, June 30, 2021, https://www.nytimes.com/interactive/2021/06/30/arts/television/bill-cosby-court-opinion.html.

72 *Pennsylvania v. Cosby*, 595 U.S. ___ (2022); *see* Graham Bowley, *Supreme Court Will Not Review Decision to Overturn Bill Cosby's Conviction*, N.Y. Times, Mar. 7, 2022, https://www.nytimes.com/2022/03/07/arts/television/bill-cosby-conviction-supreme-court.html.

73 *Klopfer v. North Carolina*, 386 U.S. 213 (1967).

74 *Barker v. Wingo*, 407 U.S. 514 (1972).

75 *Doggett v. United States*, 505 U.S. 647 (1992).

76 *Id.* (Souter also offered the following observation of where this case sat on a continuum: "Between diligent prosecution and bad-faith delay, official negligence in bringing an accused to trial occupies the middle ground. While not compelling relief in every case where bad-faith delay would make relief virtually automatic, neither is negligence automatically tolerable simply because the accused cannot demonstrate exactly how it has prejudiced him.")

77 Speedy Trial Act of 1974, Pub. L. 93-619, 88 Stat. 2080, as amended in 1979, Pub. L. 96-43, 93 Stat. 327, 18 U.S.C. §§ 3161-3174.

78 18 U.S.C. § 3161(c)(2). *See also: United States v. Rojas-Contreras*, 474 U.S. 231 (1985).

79 United States' Response to Defendant Lucas Denney's Emergency Motion for Release from Custody and Emergency Motion to Dismiss Case, *United States v. Denney*, Case No. 22-0070 (RDM), March 14, 2022, https://www.documentcloud.org/documents/21416740-denneygovtflg031422.

80 Josh Gerstein, *Judge Takes Unusual Guilty Plea from Capitol Riot Suspect*, Politico, Mar. 17, 2022, https://www.politico.com/news/2022/03/17/judge-takes-guilty-plea-capitol-riot-suspect-00018309; Josh Gerstein, *Judge: Massive Scope of Jan. 6 Probe Led to Rights Being 'Trampled*,' Politico, Mar. 7, 2022, https://www.politico.com/news/2022/03/07/judge-jan-6-probe-rights-trampled-00014808; Josh Gerstein, *Feds Admit Breaking Law with Delay in Case Against Alleged Jan. 6 Rioter*, Politico, Mar. 14, 2022, https://www.politico.com/news/2022/03/14/feds-admit-breaking-law-with-delay-in-case-against-alleged-jan-6-rioter-00017003

81 *United States v. Marion*, 404 U.S. 307 (1971).

82 *United States v. Lovasco*, 431 U.S. 783 (1977).

83 *United States v. MacDonald*, 456 U.S. 1 (1982).

84 *Fex v. Michigan*, 507 U.S. 43 (1993).

85 *See* U.S. Department of Justice Archives, *Interstate Agreement on Detainers*, https://www.justice.gov/archives/jm/criminal-resource-manual-534-interstate-agreement-detainers.

86 *In re Oliver*, 333 U.S. 257 (1948).

87 *Richmond Newspapers, Inc. v. Virginia*, 448 U.S. 555 (1980).

88 *Press-Enterprise Co. v. Superior Court of California*, 464 U.S. 501 (1984).

89 *Waller v. Georgia*, 467 U.S. 39 (1984).

90 *Presley v. Georgia*, 558 U.S. 209 (2010).

91 *Weaver v. Massachusetts*, 582 U.S. ___ (2017).

92 *Boumediene v. Bush*, 553 U.S. 723 (2008).

93 *Sheppard v. Maxwell*, 384 U.S. 333 (1966).

94 *Bridges v. California*, 314 U.S. 252 (1941).

95 *Chambers v. Florida*, 309 U.S. 227 (1940).

96 *Skilling v. United States*, 561 U.S. 358 (2010).

97 J. M. Salerno, J. C. Campbell, H. J. Phalen, S. R. Bean, V. Hans, D. Spivack, & L. Ross, *The Impact of Minimal Versus Extended Voir Dire and Judicial Rehabilitation on Mock Jurors' Decisions in Civil Cases*, 45 Law and Human Behavior, 336–355.

98 *Sheppard v. Maxwell, supra* note 93.

99 *Nebraska Press Association v. Stuart*, 427 U.S. 539 (1976).

100 *See* Thomas MacMillan, *How the Psychological Toll of Isolation Might Be Affecting Bill Cosby Jurors*, The Cut, June 15, 2017, https://www.thecut.com/2017/06/sequestered-jury-psychological-toll-cosby-trial.html.

101 *Estes v. Texas*, 381 U.S. 532 (1965).

102 *Chandler v. Florida*, 449 U.S. 560 (1981).

103 Federal Rule of Criminal Procedure 53 states: "Except as otherwise provided by a statute or these rules, the court must not permit the taking of photographs in the courtroom during judicial proceedings or the broadcasting of judicial proceedings from the courtroom."

104 United States Supreme Court, *Argument Audio*, https://www.supremecourt.gov/oral_arguments/argument_audio/2021.

105 *Commonwealth v. Gardner*, No. 2020-CA-1383-MR (Ky. Ct. App. Aug. 13, 2021).

106 Jule Pattison-Gordon, *Will Remote Tech for Court Services Improve Digital Equity?* Government Technology, Jan./Feb. 2022), https://www.govtech.com/janfeb2022-will-remote-tech-for-court-services-improve-digital-equity.

107 *Pointer v. Texas*, 380 U.S. 400 (1965). Yet, in *Illinois v. Allen*, 397 U.S. 337 (1970), the Court said an unruly defendant can be removed from court if, after a judge's warning, disruptive behavior continues.

108 *Green v. McElroy*, 360 U.S. 474 (1959).

109 *Smith v. Illinois*, 390 U.S. 129 (1968).

110 *Carver v. United States*, 164 U.S. 694 (1897).

111 *Giles v. California*, 554 U.S. 353 (2008) (The hearsay exception discussed in this case is known as "forfeiture by wrong-doing," which signifies that a person's wrongful act that prevents another person from testifying could result in hearsay statements being admitted at trial—but only if the wrongful act is motivated by a desire to prevent testimony.).

112 *Hemphill v. New York*, 595 U.S. ___ (2022).

113 *Crawford v. Washington*, 541 U.S. 36 (2004).

114 Organized Crime Control Act of 1970, 84 Stat. 922–923; Comprehensive Crime Control Act of 1984, 98 Stat. 1976.

115 *Perry v. New Hampshire*, 565 U.S. 228 (2012).

116 *See* National Conference of State Legislatures, *Practices in Eyewitness Identification* (for state-by-state procedures), https://www.ncsl.org/Documents/cj/PracticesInEyewitnessIdentification.pdf.

117 Michael Ollove, *Police Are Changing Lineups to Avoid False IDS*, Pew, July 13, 2018, https://www.pewtrusts.org/en/research-and-analysis/blogs/stateline/2018/07/13/police-are-changing-lineups-to-avoid-false-ids.

118 Nancy Steblay, Jennifer E. Dysart, Solomon Fulero, & R.C.L. Lindsay, *Eyewitness Accuracy Rates in Sequential and Simultaneous Lineup Presentations: A Meta-Analytic Comparison*, 25 Law and Human Behavior, 459–473 (2001); Christian A. Meissner, Colin G. Tredoux, Janat F. Parker, & Otto H. Maclin, *Eyewitness decisions in simultaneous sequential lineups: A dual-process detection theory analysis*, 33 Memory & Cognition 783–792 (2005); Curt A. Carlson, Scott D. Gronlund, & Steven E. Clark, *Lineup Composition, Suspect Position, and the Sequential Lineup Advantage*, 14 Journal of Experimental Psychology: Applied 118–128 (2008); Scott D. Gronlund, Curt A. Carlson, Sarah B. Dailey, & Charles A. Godosell, *Robustness of the Sequential Lineup Advantage*, 15 Journal of Experimental Psychology: Applied 140–152 (2009); Nancy K. Steblay, Jennifer E. Dysart, & Gary L. Wells, *Seventy-Two Tests of the Sequential Lineup Superiority Effect: A Meta-Analysis and Policy Discussion*, 17 Psychology, Public Policy, and Law, 99–139 (2011); Laura Mickes, Heather D. Flowe, & John T. Wixted, *Receiver Operating Characteristic Analysis of Eyewitness Memory: Comparing the Diagnostic Accuracy of Simultaneous Versus Sequential Lineups*, 18 Journal of Experiment Psychology: Applied 361–376 (2012).

119 *State v. Henderson*, 208 N.J. 208, 27 A.3d 872 (N.J. 2011).

120 *State v. Lawson*, 352 Or. 724, 291 P.3d 673 (Or. 2012).

121 Memorandum from Sally Yates, Deputy Attorney General for heads of department law enforcement components all department prosecutors, Eyewitness Identification: Procedures for Conducting Photo Arrays (Jan. 6, 2017), https://www.justice.gov/file/923201/download.

122 *Eyewitness Identification Reform*, Innocence Project, https://innocenceproject.org/eyewitness-identification-reform/.

123 Hal Arkowtiz & Scott O. Lilienfeld, *Why Science Tells Us Not to Rely on Eyewitness Accounts*, Scientific American, Jan. 1, 2010, https://www.scientificamerican.com/article/do-the-eyes-have-it/.

124 *Id.*

125 Stephen L. Chew, *Myth: Eyewitness Testimony Is the Best Kind of Evidence*, Association for Psychological Science, Aug. 20, 2018, https://www.psychologicalscience.org/teaching/myth-eyewitness-testimony-is-the-best-kind-of-evidence.html.

126 Christian A. Meissner & John C. Brigham, *Thirty Years of Investigating the Two-Race Bias in Memory for Faces: A Meta-Analytic Review*, 7 Psychology, Public Policy, and Law 3–35 (2001).

127 Thomas Albright, *Why Eyewitnesses Fail*, 114 Proceedings of the National Academy of Sciences of the United States of America 7758–7764 (2017).

128 Kenneth A. Deffenbacher, Brian H. Bornstein, Steven D. Penrod, & E. Kiernan McGorty, *A Meta-Analytic Review of the Effects of High Stress on Eyewitness Memory*, 28 Law and Human Behavior, 687–706 (2004).

129 Jonathan M. Fawcett, Emily J. Russell, Kristine A. Peace, and John Christie, *Of Guns and Geese: A Meta-Analytic Review of the 'Weapon Focus' Literature*, 19 Psychology, Crime & Law, 35–66 (2013).

130 Albert Hastorf & Hadley Cantril, *They Saw a Game: A Case Study*, 49 Journal of Abnormal and Social Psychology 129–134 (1954).

131 Elizabeth Loftus, *Planting Misinformation in the Human Mind: A 30-Year Investigation of the Malleability of Memory*, 12 Learning and Memory 361–366 (2005); Maria S. Zaragoza, Robert F. Belli, & Kristie E. Payment, *Misinformation Effects and the Suggestibility of Eyewitness Memory*, in Do Justice and Let the Sky Fall: Elizabeth Loftus and Her Contributions to Science, Law, and Academic Freedom 35–63 (Maryanne Garry & Harlene Hayne eds., 2007); Maria S. Zaragoza & Sean M. Lane, *Source Misattributions and the Suggestibility of Eyewitness Memory*, 20 Journal of Experimental Psychology: Learning, Memory, and Cognition 934–945 (1994).

132 Tanja R. Benton, David F. Ross, Emily Bradshaw, W. Neil Thomas, & Gregory S. Bradshaw (2006), *Eyewitness Memory is Still not Common Sense: Comparing Jurors, Judges and Law Enforcement to Eyewitness Experts*, 20 Applied Cognitive Psychology, 115–129 (2006).

133 *Ohio v. Roberts*, 448 U.S. 56 (1980).

134 *Crawford v. Washington*, 541 U.S. 36 (2004).

135 *See, e.g., Ohio v. Roberts, supra* note 133.

136 *Davis v. Washington*, 547 U.S. 813 (2006).

137 *See* F. Robert Radel II and Andrew Labbe, *The Clergy–Penitent Privilege: An Overview*, GSPALAW, https://www.gspalaw.com/wp-content/uploads/2015/12/Clergy-Penitent-Privilege.pdf.

138 *Wheeler v. United States*, 159 U.S. 523 (1895).

139 *Maryland v. Craig*, 497 U.S. 836 (1990).

140 *See* Order of the Supreme Court, 207 F.R.D. 89 (2002).

141 *Ohio v. Clark*, 576 U.S. 237 (2015).

142 *Coy v. Iowa*, 487 U.S. 1012 (1988).

143 *United States v. Gigante*, 166 F.3d 75 (2d Cir. 1999).

144 *Harrell v. Butterworth*, 251 F.3d 926 (11th Cir. 2001); *Horn v. Quarterman*, 508 F.3d 306 (5th Cir. 2007) (dealt with a witness who had a terminal illness).

145 *United States v. Carter*, 907 F.3d 1199 (9th Cir. 2018).

146 *United States v. Abu Ali*, 528 F.3d 210 (4th Cir. 2008).

147 *United States v. Yates*, 438 F.3d 1307 (11th Cir. 2006).

148 *State v. Thomas*, 376 P.3d 184 (N.M. 2016).

149 *People v. Jemison*, No. 157812, 2020 WL 3421925 (Mich. June 22, 2020).

150 *State of Missouri v. Rodney Smith*, No. SC99086, Jan. 11, 2022.

151 *United States v. Burke*, 345 F.3d 416 (6th Cir. 2003).

152 *United States v. Navarro*, 169 F.3d 228, 235-39 (5th Cir. 1999) (when the judge appeared via video from a different location than where the attorneys and defendants were); *United States v. Torres-Palma*, 290 F.3d 1244, 1248 (10th Cir. 2002)

(when a judge was brought in from another district for the trial but had returned to his home and could only appear for sentencing via video).

153 *United States v. Lawrence*, 248 F.3d 300, 303-04 (4th Cir. 2001) (when a defendant appeared via video from prison).

154 *Washington v. Texas*, 388 U.S. 14 (1967).

155 *Taylor v. Illinois*, 484 U.S. 400 (1988).

156 *See* Strengthening the Sixth, *Discovery in the States* (for state-by-state rules regarding discovery procedures), https://www.strengthenthesixth.org/Discovery/States/States.

157 Tom O'Connor, Digital War Room, *Electronic Discovery for the Rest of Us—The Rules*, Oct. 20, 2021, https://www.digitalwarroom.com/blog/electronic-discovery-for-the-rest-of-us-the-rules-1.

158 Department of Justice (DOJ) and Administrative Office of the U.S. Courts (AO) Joint Working Group on Electronic Technology in the Criminal Justice System, Recommendations for Electronically Stored Information (ESI) Discovery Production in Federal Criminal Cases (2012), https://www.fd.org/sites/default/files/Litigation%20Support/final-esi-protocol.pdf.

159 *Brady v. Maryland*, 373 U.S. 83 (1963).

160 *United States v. Agurs*, 427 U.S. 97 (1976).

161 Marc Allen, *Non-Brady Legal and Ethical Obligations on Prosecutors to Disclose Exculpatory Evidence: Prepared for the National Registry of Exonerations* (2018), https://www.law.umich.edu/special/exoneration/Documents/NRE_Exculpatory_Evidence_Obligations_for_Prosecutors.pdf.

162 Jackson Cote, *Massachusetts Drug Lab Scandal: Suffolk DA Vacates 100-Plus Convictions Tied to Former Chemist Annie Dookhan*, MassLive (updated Nov. 17, 2020), https://www.masslive.com/boston/2020/11/massachusetts-drug-lab-scandal-suffolk-da-vacates-100-plus-convictions-tied-to-former-state-chemist-annie-dookhan.html.

163 Katie Mettler, *How a Lab Chemist Went from 'Superwoman' to Disgraced Saboteur of More Than 20,000 Drug Cases*, Wash. Post, Apr. 21, 2017, https://www.washingtonpost.com/news/morning-mix/wp/2017/04/21/how-a-lab-chemist-went-from-superwoman-to-disgraced-saboteur-of-more-than-20000-drug-cases/.

164 Laura Wagner, *Ex-Chemist in Massachusetts Was High on Drugs at Work for 8 Years*, Reuters, May 4, 206, https://www.npr.org/sections/thetwo-way/2016/05/04/476755684/ex-chemist-in-massachusetts-was-high-on-drugs-at-work-for-8-years.

165 Deborah Becker, *Suspensions and a Reprimand Proposed for Prosecutors Admonished in Drug Lab Scandal*, WBUR, Oct. 12, 2021, https://www.wbur.org/news/2021/10/12/farak-bbo-disciplinary-recommendations.

166 *Frye v. United States*, 293 F. 1013 (D.C. Cir. 1923).

167 *Daubert v. Merrell Dow Pharmaceuticals, Inc.*, 509 U.S. 579 (1993).

168 *Kumho Tire Co. v. Carmichael*, 526 U.S. 137 (1999).

169 *See* Wickert Matthiesen & S.C. Lehrer, Admissibility of Expert Testimony in All 50 States (2022), https://www.mwl-law.com/wp-content/uploads/2018/02/ADMISSIBILITY-OF-EXPERT-TESTIMONY.pdf.

170 42 U.S.C. § 14132.

171 Vanessa Romo, *San Francisco DA Drops Charges Against Woman Linked to Crime Through Rape Victim DNA*, NPR, Feb. 17, 2022, https://www.npr.org/2022/02/17/1081634509/san-francisco-da-drops-charges-against-woman-linked-to-crime-through-rape-victim.

172 Spencer Hsu, *FBI Admits Flaws in Hair Analysis over Decades*, Wash. Post, Apr. 18, 2015, https://www.washingtonpost.com/local/crime/fbi-overstated-forensic-hair-matches-in-nearly-all-criminal-trials-for-decades/2015/04/18/39c-8d8c6-e515-11e4-b510-962fcfabc310_story.html; *see* FBI, *FBI Testimony on Microscopic Hair Analysis Contained Errors in at Least 90 Percent of Cases in Ongoing Review*, FBI.gov, Apr. 20, 2015, https://www.fbi.gov/news/pressrel/press-releases/fbi-testimony-on-microscopic-hair-analysis-contained-errors-in-at-least-90-percent-of-cases-in-ongoing-review.

173 *Id.*

174 California Innocence Project, *Bite Mark Evidence*, https://californiainnocenceproject.org/issues-we-face/bite-mark-evidence/.

175 *United States v. Scheffer*, 523 U.S. 303 (1998).

176 *James v. Illinois*, 493 U.S. 307 (1990).

177 *See State v. Cannon*, No. E2005-01237-SC-R11-CD (Tenn. Crim. App. April 29, 2008; *State v. Cannon*, No. E2011-02624-CCA-R3-CD (Tenn. Crim. App. Dec. 5, 2012) (for Tennessee Supreme Court cases on this subject).

178 The Office of Communications and Marketing, *Advancing the Evidence*, Volunteer Stories, Nov. 13, 2017, updated May 1, 2019, https://www.utk.edu/volunteer_stories/advancing-evidence.

179 John North & Leslie Ackerson, *The Body Farm: Research Never Stops at UT Forensic Center*, WBIR, July 23, 2021, https://www.wbir.com/article/news/local/the-body-farm-research-never-stops-at-ut-forensic-center/51-9d6796e4-b899-4a18-b5fe-7022563b0c26.

180 The Conversation, *Plants Might Be Able to Tell Us About the Location Of Dead Bodies*, *Helping Families Find Missing People*, Sept. 3, 2020, https://theconversation.com/plants-might-be-able-to-tell-us-about-the-location-of-dead-bodies-helping-families-find-missing-people-145420; *see* Holly Brabazon, Jennifer DeBruyn, Scott Lenaghan, Fei Li, Amy Z. Mundorf,, Dawnie W. Steadman, & C. Neal Jr. Stewart, *Plants to Remotely Detect Human Decomposition*, *Trends in Plant Science*, 25 Science & Society 947–949, Oct. 1, 2020, https://www.cell.com/trends/plant-science/fulltext/S1360-1385(20)30243-0.

181 Steven A. Symes, Morphology of Saw Marks in Human Bone: Identification of Class Characteristics (1992) (Ph.D. dissertation, University of Tennessee), https://trace.tennessee.edu/utk_graddiss/1253.

182 Charity Owings, *Files and Death: My Career in Forensic Entomology and Current Entomological Research at the 'Body Farm*,' University of Tennessee, Feb. 12, 2021, https://epp.tennessee.edu/event/flies-and-death-my-career-in-forensic-entomology-and-current-entomological-research-at-the-body-farm/.

183 *Williams v. Florida*, 399 U.S. 78 (1970).

184 *Ballew v. Georgia*, 435 U.S. 223 (1978).

185 *Smith v. Texas*, 311 U.S. 128 (1940).

186 *Swain v. Alabama*, 380 U.S. 202 (1965).

187 *Taylor v. Louisiana*, 419 U.S. 522 (1975).

188 *Smithkline Beecham Corp. v. Abbott Labs.*, 740 F.3d 471 (9th Cir. 2014) (This case involved a civil lawsuit.).

189 Ginger Jackson-Gleich, *Rigging the Jury: How Each State Reduces Jury Diversity by Excluding People with Criminal Records*, Prison Policy Initiative, Feb. 18, 2021, https://www.prisonpolicy.org/reports/juryexclusion.html.

190 As of 2022, the following states had a ban on jury service by those with any prior felony conviction: Alaska, Arizona, Arkansas, Connecticut, Delaware, Georgia, Hawaii, Idaho, Indiana, Kansas, Kentucky, Louisiana, Massachusetts, Michigan, Minnesota, Mississippi, Missouri, Montana, Nebraska, Nevada, New Hampshire, New Mexico, New York, North Carolina, North Dakota, Ohio, Oklahoma, Rhode Island, South Dakota, Utah, Vermont, Virginia, Washington, West Virginia, Wisconsin, and Wyoming.

191 Florida, Maryland, and D.C. ban jury service for those with any misdemeanor or any felony conviction; in the following states, the standard is any felony and some misdemeanors: New Jersey, Oregon (crime involving violence or dishonesty), Pennsylvania (any crime punishable by more than one year), South Carolina (any crime punishable by more than one year), Tennessee (perjury), and Texas (theft).

192 Connecticut, Kentucky, Louisiana, and Massachusetts exclude jury service by any person who is currently facing felony charges. Florida, Maryland, Texas, and D.C. have exclusions for misdemeanor offenses.

193   Those states where a ban is temporary include the following: California, Connecticut, Colorado, Idaho, Illinois, Indiana, Iowa, Kansas, Maine, Massachusetts, Montana, New Mexico, Nevada, North Carolina, North Dakota, Ohio, Rhode Island, South Dakota, Washington, and Wisconsin.

194   Juliet Isselbacher, *Should Convicted Felons Serve on Juries?* Harvard Magazine, June 3, 2021, https://www.harvardmagazine.com/2021/06/felons-and-juries.

195   Jackson-Gleich, *supra* note 189.

196   *Id.*

197   Isselbacher, *supra* note 194.

198   Samuel R. Sommers, *On Racial Diversity and Group Decision Making: Identifying Multiple Effects of Racial Composition on Jury Deliberations*, 90 Journal of Personality and Social Psychology 597–612 (2006).

199   Deborah Ramirez, *Affirmative Jury Selection: A Proposal to Advance Both the Deliberative Ideal and Jury Diversity*, University of Chicago Legal Forum 161–177 (1998).

200   *Batson v. Kentucky*, 476 U.S. 79 (1986).

201   *J.E.B. v. Alabama ex rel. T.B.*, 511 U.S. 127 (1994).

202   *Miller-El v. Cockrell*, 537 U.S. 322 (2003) (The decision was reaffirmed two years later in *Miller-El v. Dretke*, 545 U.S. 231 (2005).).

203   *Davis v. Ayala*, 576 U.S. 257 (2015).

204   *Foster v. Chatman*, 578 U.S. ___ (2016).

205   *Snyder v. Louisiana*, 578 U.S. 488 (2008).

206   *Flowers v. Mississippi*, 588 U.S. ___ (2019).

207   *Peters v. Kiff*, 407 U.S. 493 (1972).

208   *Powers v. Ohio*, 499 U.S. 400 (1991).

209   *In re Winship*, 397 U. S. 358 (1970).

210   *Holland v. United States*, 348 U. S. 121, 140 (1954).

211   *Victor v. Nebraska*, 511 U.S. 1 (1994).

212   *Johnson v. Louisiana*, 406 U.S. 356 (1972); *Apodaca v. Oregon*, 406 U.S. 404 (1972).

213   *Ramos v. Louisiana*, 590 U.S. ___ (2020).

214   Thomas Aiello, Jim Crow's Last Stand: Nonunanimous Criminal Jury Verdicts in Louisiana, LSU Press (2019).

215   Jeff Adelson, Gordon Russell, & John Simerman, *How an Abnormal Louisiana Law Deprives, Discriminates and Drives Incarceration: Tilting the Scales*, The Advocate, Apr. 1, 2018, https://www.nola.com/news/courts/article_8e284de1-9c5c-5d77-bcc5-6e22a3053aa0.html.

216   *Edwards v. Vannoy*, 593 U.S. ___ (2021).

217   Twelve Angry Men (MGM 1957).

218   *Allen v. United States*, 164 U.S. 492 (1896).

219   *Apprendi v. New Jersey*, 530 U.S. 466 (2000).

220   *United States v. Booker*, 543 U.S. 220 (2005).

221   *Alleyne v. United States*, 570 U.S. 99 (2013).

222   *State v. Blackwell*, 664 S.W.2d 686 (Tenn. 1984).

Credit

CHAPTER 13

The Eighth Amendment

Prohibition of Excessive Bail, Excessive Fines, and Cruel and Unusual Punishments

"Excessive bail shall not be required, nor excessive fines imposed, nor cruel and unusual punishments inflicted."

—U.S. Constitution, Eighth Amendment

Learning Objectives

After reading this chapter, you should understand the following:

1. The controversy over pretrial detention and bail reform
2. How civil forfeitures can be treated as excessive fines
3. The evolution of judicial interpretation of the Cruel and Unusual Punishments Clause
4. Mandatory sentencing and other elements of mass incarceration

Key Cases

United States v. Salerno, 481 U.S. 739 (1987)
Timbs v. Indiana, 586 U.S. ___ (2019)
Robinson v. California, 370 U.S. 660 (1962)
Bearden v. Georgia, 461 U.S. 660 (1983)
Johnson v. United States, 576 U.S. 591 (2015)

Ewing v. California, 538 U.S. 11 (2003)
Miller v. Alabama, 567 U.S. 460 (2012)
Jones v. Mississippi, 593 U.S. ___ (2021)

Introduction

The text of the Eighth Amendment was taken nearly verbatim from the English Bill of Rights (1689), which provided "[t]hat excessive bail ought not to be required, nor excessive fines imposed, nor cruel and unusual punishments inflicted. ... " This brief language contains three protections that are extremely important to people accused of crimes. For those awaiting trial on criminal charges, the possibility of being released on bail—as opposed to remaining inside a jail cell while awaiting trial—can be crucial for maintaining a job or pursuing an education. Moreover, previous chapters have addressed criminal procedures that essentially culminate in the forms of punishment subject to analysis under the Eighth Amendment. Goals of punishment can vary from case to case and might include rehabilitation, retribution, and deterrence. But overall, whether a punishment takes the form of probation, fine, forfeiture of property, incarceration, commitment in a mental institution, or even death, the principles of the Eighth Amendment must be honored.

Bail and Pretrial Detention

Obiter Dicta

"The statutes of the United States have been framed upon the theory that a person accused of crime shall not, until he has been finally adjudged guilty in the court of last resort, be absolutely compelled to undergo imprisonment or punishment, but may be admitted to bail not only after arrest and before trial, but after conviction and pending a writ of error."

Justice Horace Gray, writing for the Supreme Court in Hudson v. Parker, *156 U.S. 277 (1895)*

The term **bail** refers to the pretrial release of persons accused of crimes on the condition that they post a cash bond that will be forfeited should they fail to appear in court at the appointed time. The practice is deeply rooted in the English common law and has been recognized by Parliament as far back as the late-thirteenth century.[1] As previously noted, the English Bill of Rights (1689) asserted the right to be free from excessive bail, and this concept was adopted by the framers of our Bill of Rights. Notice, however, that the Eight Amendment does not say there is a right to bail but only that bail shall not be excessive. In passing the Judiciary Act of 1789,[2] Congress recognized a right to bail "except where the punishment may be death, in which case it shall not be admitted but by the supreme or a circuit court, or by a justice of the supreme court, or a judge of a district court, who shall exercise their discretion herein. ..." And in 1895, the Supreme Court held that the statutory right to bail applies not only prior to trial but also after conviction as defendants seek to appeal to higher courts.[3] Today, a judge will set a bail amount, often at an initial appearance or an arraignment and generally after holding a hearing in which lawyers for the state and defense make arguments regarding an appropriate amount.

The Prohibition of Excessive Bail

In 1926, a federal appeals court said the purpose of the Excessive Bail Clause "is to prevent the practical denial of bail by fixing the amount so unreasonably high that it cannot be given."[4] Twenty-five years later, in *Stack v. Boyle* (1951),[5] the Supreme Court held that excessive bail is that which is "higher than an amount reasonably calculated to fulfill the purpose of assuring the presence of the defendant" in court. And in *Schilb v. Kuebel* (1971),[6] the Court recognized the application of the Excessive Bail Clause to the state courts. Writing for the Court, Justice Harry Blackmun observed, "Bail, of course, is basic to our system of law, … and the Eighth Amendment's proscription of excessive bail has been assumed to have application to the States through the Fourteenth Amendment."

> **EXCESSIVE BAIL:**
> An unconstitutionally high payment amount that is set as a condition for pretrial release as an accused awaits trial; a violation of the Eighth Amendment.

The Supreme Court has refused to quantify *excessive bail* and has left the matter to the discretion of lower court judges and magistrates. In recent years, there has been widespread criticism of the cash bail system used in many states, in which the amount of bail is determined according to a preset schedule based on the offense charged. This system often results in poor defendants awaiting trial in jail, while wealthier defendants can *bond out*. Accordingly, some states have changed their laws to require judges setting bonds to make a more individualized assessment, one that includes an examination of a defendant's ability to pay. In the federal courts, judges are required to make an individualized assessment and "may not impose a financial condition that results in the pretrial detention of the person."[7]

Bounty Hunters

Because most defendants cannot afford to post the full amount of bail on their own, they may depend on the services of a bonding company, which will post bond in exchange for the payment of a nonrefundable premium—usually 10% to 15% of the amount of total bail amount. (Unfortunately, many defendants cannot afford to even pay the 10% premium to the bonding company.) If the defendant pays a bonding company but fails to appear in court, that company is responsible for 100% of the bail amount, and thus, many bonding companies in such a

BOUNTY HUNTER:
An individual who, generally working on behalf of a bonding company, attempts to recapture an accused criminal who has failed to appear for trial in violation of terms of bail.

situation will hire a bounty hunter to track down the missing person and bring them back, with the bounty hunter typically paid 10 to 20% of the overall bond.

Not all bounty hunters achieve the fame of reality-TV star Duane Lee Chapman, better known as Dog the Bounty Hunter, but data show that most are successful in finding their fugitives. A 2019 article in *The Seattle Times* quotes Brian Johnson, a professor of criminology at Grand Valley State University, who has said that 20% of people out on bail will fail to appear in court (roughly 30,000 people every year)—with bounty hunters generally locating about 90% of them.[8]

States vary in how they regulate bounty hunters. Four states—Illinois, Kentucky, Oregon, and Wisconsin—ban bounty hunters altogether. Four other states—Arkansas, Florida, Ohio, and Texas—ban private bounty hunters but allow employees of a bail bonding company to pursue a suspect who skips bail. Seventeen states have no licensing or regulation of bounty hunters, while the rest have some form of regulations or licensing. Regulations might include requirements to notify local police of any pursuits in their jurisdiction or caveats related to when entry onto private property is permitted (normally allowed only if the wanted person owns the property).

Among the states with licensing or certification requirements, there is significant variation, particularly regarding the need for training courses and the impact of a criminal record on the licensing process. More than a dozen states will not license a bounty hunter who has a felony conviction. New York requires a bounty hunter to have three years of previous law-enforcement experience (and New Jersey requires five). New York also has approved a curriculum for training bounty hunters and has regulations regarding who can train them.

Other states offer fewer parameters for licensing. It has been reported that the state of Washington's Department of Licensing rejected just two out of more than 400 bounty hunter applications over the course of a decade. Further, out of 187 bounty hunters licensed in that state as of June 2018, 75 had been charged with a felony or misdemeanor and 54 had been convicted of one. The licensing process in Washington requires 32 hours of training, which can include *self-study*, and there is no statewide curriculum. In contrast, a license to style hair and give manicures in that state requires 1,600 hours of training from a state-approved instructor.[9]

The 1872 Supreme Court decision in *Taylor v. Taintor*[10] made it clear that those who post bond for a suspect that flees are responsible to the court for the full amount of bail, even if that suspect misses their court date because they end up arrested elsewhere or extradited to face charges in another jurisdiction. The majority opinion from Justice Noah Haynes Swayne authorized broad powers for bounty hunters, whom he referred to as "sureties" in this declaration:

> When bail is given, the principal is regarded as delivered to the custody of his sureties. Their dominion is a continuance of the original imprisonment ... They may pursue him into another state; may arrest him on the Sabbath, and, if necessary, may break and enter his house for that purpose. The seizure is not made by virtue of new process. None is needed. It is likened to the rearrest by the sheriff of an escaping prisoner.

To reiterate, though state law can place restrictions on bounty hunters that move beyond the language of this 1872 high Court decision, the opinion indicated constitutional protections are not implicated when a bounty hunter is working independently of law enforcement.

THE CONSTITUTION IN ACTION
The Sordid Saga of Robert Durst Includes Bail Jumping

Born in the 1940s, Robert Durst, heir to a multi-billion-dollar New York City real estate fortune, came to be a suspect in multiple crimes over the course of his life, including the following: the 1982 disappearance of his first wife Kathleen McCormack, for which he was officially charged on October 22, 2021; the 2000 death of his friend Susan Berman, for which he was found guilty on a first-degree murder charge in September 2021; and the 2001 killing of a neighbor, a man named Morris Black, for which Durst was found not guilty in 2003.

Durst's first homicide arrest occurred in October 2001 after police located Morris Black's body parts floating in Galveston Bay off the coast of Texas. Durst posted $250,000 bail but missed a court appearance one week after his arrest. He was recaptured over a month later when, on November 30, 2001, he was arrested for trying to steal a sandwich, a newspaper, and Band-Aids from a Wegman's supermarket in Bethlehem, Pennsylvania. Two guns and Morris Black's driver's license were found in Durst's rental car at the time of his arrest.

Durst stood trial for Black's murder in 2003, claiming self-defense while admitting to dismembering the body and throwing its remains in the bay (although Black's head was never recovered). A Galveston jury, apparently accepting claims of self-defense put forth by Durst's lawyers, found him not guilty of first-degree murder in November 2003. But upon Durst's acquittal, he was quickly charged with two counts of bail jumping (for not appearing in court following his arrest) and one count of evidence tampering (for cutting up Black's body). The trial judge set bail on these three counts at $1 billion each, with the $3 billion total believed to be the highest ever given, at that time, in a U.S. case.

Durst's lawyers appealed the bail as excessive, and in June 2004, a Texas appeals court agreed, with the majority opinion saying, "These amounts were so excessive, no one could meet them, not Durst and not any of the bail companies. ... This is an example of bail being used as an instrument of oppression."[11] The appellate court suggested a bail in the range of $450,000 to $600,000.

In September 2004, Durst pleaded guilty to the bail jumping and evidence tampering charges, and three months later, he pleaded guilty to a federal gun charge stemming from his escape to Pennsylvania. For these crimes, he served time in prison until July 2005, when he was released and placed on parole in Texas. In December 2005, he was caught violating the terms of that parole—which required permission before he could travel—when he went to a shopping mall and was spotted by the Galveston judge who had presided over his murder trial. Durst was returned to prison and then released again in March 2006.

Durst would face other criminal charges over the next decade, including a trespass charge in New York City and a charge for urinating on a candy rack at a CVS store in Houston, but he would not face another homicide offense until 2015, when, against the advice of counsel, he gave interviews to the filmmakers of an HBO documentary series called *The Jinx: The Life and Deaths of Robert Durst*. This series addressed evidence that connected Durst to the killing of Susan Berman, implying Berman had knowledge of how Durst's first wife had been killed. The series ends with footage of Durst in a bathroom, perhaps unaware that his microphone is still on, saying to himself, among other things,

(continued)

"There it is. You're caught," and "What did I do? Killed them all, of course." He later claimed to have been using meth during the taping.

In March 2015, a few days before the airing of the final episode in this HBO series, a Los Angeles judge signed an arrest warrant for Durst on charges of first-degree murder in the death of Susan Berman. He was arrested several days later by FBI agents in New Orleans, where he had checked into a hotel using a fake identification card. A passport, a map of Cuba, five ounces of marijuana, and a loaded firearm were found in his room. He was initially held in Louisiana on a state charge of being a felon in possession of a gun, with bail on that charge denied because the judge deemed him a flight risk. A federal charge of being a felon in possession of a gun also was filed. Durst pleaded guilty to the federal gun charge in February 2016 and was given an 85-month prison sentence. The state gun charge was dropped, and he was extradited to California to await trial for murder in the Berman case.

Pretrial motions in the Los Angeles murder case began in 2018, but delays related to Durst's health and the COVID-19 pandemic pushed the trial into 2021. The trial included jurors seeing parts of the HBO episodes on the case, and in September 2021, the jury found Durst guilty of first-degree murder. One month later, he was sentenced to life in prison. He died in prison in January 2022.[12]

Pretrial Detention

A defendant who cannot afford bail, or even the premium to a bonding company, is likely to be detained in jail awaiting the disposition of the case. On its face, pretrial detention would appear to contradict the presumption of innocence. Nevertheless, in *United States v. Salerno* (1987),[13] the Supreme Court upheld provisions of the Bail Reform Act of 1984,[14] which authorized pretrial detention not only to prevent flight to avoid prosecution but also to protect the community against a dangerous offender. Speaking for the Court, Chief Justice William Rehnquist wrote:

PRETRIAL DETENTION: Reference to an accused criminal being held in custody after arrest and before a criminal trial begins.

> In our society, liberty is the norm, and detention prior to trial or without trial is the carefully limited exception. We hold that the provisions for pretrial detention in the Bail Reform Act of 1984 fall within that carefully limited exception. The Act authorizes the detention prior to trial of arrestees charged with serious felonies who are found after an adversary hearing to pose a threat to the safety of individuals or to the community which no condition of release can dispel. ... We are unwilling to say that this congressional determination, based as it is upon that primary concern of every government—a concern for the safety and indeed the lives of its citizens—on its face violates either the Due Process Clause of the Fifth Amendment or the Excessive Bail Clause of the Eighth Amendment.

Justice Thurgood Marshall, joined by Justice William Brennan, dissented, averring that the Court's decision "disregards basic principles of justice established centuries ago and enshrined beyond the reach of governmental interference in the Bill of Rights." Justice John Paul Stevens also wrote a dissent in which he agreed that "allowing pretrial detention on the basis of future dangerousness is unconstitutional."

The Bail Reform Act applies only to the federal courts, and within the past decade, as state prisons have witnessed extensive overcrowding, movements for bail reform at the state level have gained traction.

The Scope of Pretrial Detention in the United States

Statistics highlight the magnitude of pretrial detention issues across the United States. Notably, a 2019 report from the Vera Institute of Justice says, "Approximately two-thirds of the more than 740,000 people held in locally run jails across the United States have not been convicted of a crime—they are presumed innocent and simply waiting for their day in court."[15]

More specifically, Cynthia Jones, who is executive director of the Pretrial Racial Justice Initiative, has observed that, "Nationally, approximately 62% of all people placed in jail are pretrial detainees charged with nonviolent offenses." She also stated, "Most pretrial defendants are not in jail because there is some reason to believe that, if released, they will re-offend or fail to return for future court dates. Rather, they are simply too poor to pay the money bond imposed by the court as a condition of their release." Jones even recognized that those waiting for a trial might suffer a loss of employment or educational prospects, creating "a strong incentive for pretrial detainees to plead guilty—regardless of their guilt or innocence—which starts a cycle of imprisonment that is a major driver of mass incarceration." In this regard, research from Arnold Foundation "shows that those held in pretrial detention are three times more likely to be sentenced to prison and receive longer prison sentences than defendants on pretrial release."[16]

Beyond those observations, Jones cited the Bureau of Justice Statistics, saying, "While blacks and Latinos together comprise approximately 30% of the general population in the United States, they represent 50% of all pretrial detainees."[17] Moreover, data collected by the Prison Policy Initiative indicated that "[i]n large urban areas, Black felony defendants are over 25% more likely than white defendants to be held pretrial."[18]

In a different context, in *Johnson v. Arteaga-Martinez* (2022), an 8-1 majority of the Supreme Court ruled that federal law does not require bail hearings to be provided for noncitizens who are detained while immigration courts process their cases, regardless of the length of the detention; the Court's decision, however, did not address the constitutionality of such detention.[19]

State-Level Bail Reforms

In the past decade, many states have taken steps toward reforming their procedures for pretrial release. Generally speaking, bail reform movements have emphasized either reductions in, or the complete elimination of, the use of cash bail. Some states have started to make use of a computerized **risk assessment algorithm** that takes into account factors related to the defendant's likelihood of appearing in court and the possibility of them committing another crime; some of the factors in a typical algorithm might include criminal history (including violent and nonviolent offenses), education, age of first offense, occupation, prior failures to appear in court, and family ties in the community.[20] The exact items are often unknown, since the algorithms are proprietary created by for-profit companies. But when in use, an algorithm-based *risk score* is intended to guide a judge in making decisions about a release on **cashless bail**.

RISK-ASSESSMENT ALGORITHM: A computerized analysis used in some jurisdictions to either assist a judge in setting cash bail amounts or replace the use of cash bail; the algorithm uses multiple factors to predict an accused criminal's likelihood of appearing in court for trial and their likelihood of re-offending.

CASHLESS BAIL: A method for providing release for an accused criminal prior to trial without requiring any monetary payment as a condition of release; often used in conjunction with risk-assessment algorithms.

Not surprisingly, bail reform efforts have varied dramatically across states. For example, Vermont does not make use of any algorithms but has instituted a maximum bail of $200 for some misdemeanors and requires a judge to take the defendant's financial situation into account when setting bail. In California, a 2018 law did away with cash bail and replaced it with an algorithmic analysis; however, it was repealed after being put to a vote of the people in a 2020 referendum, with some proponents of repeal speaking to flaws in the algorithms—not to mention the business and tax revenue lost within the state's $2-billion-dollar-a-year bail bonding industry. The California Supreme Court then issued a 2021 ruling that required judges to consider a defendant's ability to pay when making a bail decision.[21] Elsewhere, Illinois passed the Pretrial Fairness Act, which will take effect in 2023, preventing judges from setting any kind of monetary bail that results in an accused criminal either being held or not being held based on a comprehensive risk assessment.[22]

In Alaska, a law that took effect in 2018 requires judges to release individuals charged with nonviolent misdemeanors when they have low risk scores generated by an algorithm. A newly established Pretrial Enforcement Division in that state has been tasked with creating risk assessment reports for judges and ensuring that drug and alcohol testing, as well as electronic monitoring, is utilized in conjunction with pretrial release. The first head of that division, Geri Fox, told the *Anchorage Daily News* that pretrial detainees cost the state $150 a day to house.[23] With the new law in effect, Alaska expected a 13% drop in the number of detainees and a $380 million savings by 2024.[24] Other states have had positive results with similar measures. Since 2017, New Jersey has used an algorithm to guide bail decisions for misdemeanor offenses, noting a subsequent 44% reduction in the number of pretrial detainees housed in correctional facilities there.[25] Washington, D.C. removed cash bail in 1992; by 2018, 94% of defendants were released without posting cash bail, and 88% showed up for court hearings. Over the period of 2013 to 2017, 88% of those released pretrial committed no follow-up crimes, and 98% committed no subsequent violent crime.[26]

Not all states have seen success with such efforts, though. In 2016, voters in New Mexico passed a state constitutional amendment that eliminated cash bail for most crimes, with an exception for cases in which prosecutors could show the defendant posed a danger to the community, but the new procedures also gave judges discretion in defining which offenders were too dangerous to go free—apparently leading to an increase in pretrial detainees. An *NBC News* report found, "From 2015 to 2016—prior to the elimination of cash bail—only eight defendants were held in jail without bond across four New Mexico counties, including

Santa Fe County, according to a University of New Mexico study." Yet the report showed that from January to October in 2020, "at least 30 defendants in Santa Fe County alone were held without bond."[27]

In New York state, bail was eliminated for nonviolent offenses in 2019, but after a rise in crime rates in New York City, this was repealed. Similarly, officials in Atlanta ended cash bail in 2018 but then saw the rate of failures to appear in court double.[28] Even so, an *NBC News* report found that in Chicago, bail reform has been shown to have "no impact on new criminal activity or new violent criminal activity by those defendants released pretrial," with reforms said to have "saved defendants and their families more than $31.4 million in the six months after bail reform was implemented."[29] Houston saw reform come about through the ruling of a federal court,[30] and one study showed no risk of reoffending related to those who received cashless release on misdemeanor charges in that city.[31]

Notably, there are some charitable groups, such as The Bail Project, that are willing to pay the bail money for accused criminals across the country.[32] In 2022, legislators in Kentucky debated restrictions on the use of such charitable groups, including a ban on charitable bail payments over $5,000 or in any amount for domestic violence offenses. Legislative action was spurred after a woman was hit and killed by a driver released from jail the day before via a $5,000 payment made by The Bail Project; further controversy ensued when The Bail Project posted a $100,000 bail for a man accused of shooting at a mayoral candidate in Louisville.[33]

Where Does Bail Money Go?

An ancillary aspect of this discussion is the topic of where bail money goes once it is collected. In 2019, the Fifth Circuit addressed this issue in *Caliste v. Cantrell*,[34] which was brought on behalf of several indigent defendants who were required to pay bail in New Orleans, Louisiana. The Fifth Circuit found a conflict of interest in the application of a Louisiana law that permitted 1.8% of bail money to be deposited in the New Orleans court's Judicial Expense Fund, which could cover anything from employee salaries to coffee costs. The majority opinion for this case opened with the declaration, "No man can be judge in his own case," before adding, "That centuries-old maxim comes from Lord Coke's ruling that a judge could not be paid with the fines he imposed." The Supreme Court also announced this concept in *Tumey v. Ohio* (1927),[35] which we discuss later in this chapter.

Although the money from bail decisions in Louisiana was not going directly to the judges in specific cases, the Fifth Circuit observed that the court "receives something almost as important: funding for various judicial expenses, most notably money to help pay for court reporters, judicial secretaries, and law clerks." This inherent conflict of interest, which the Fifth Circuit deemed a violation of due process principles, was summed up as follows: "So the more often the magistrate requires a secured money bond as a condition of release, the more money the court has to cover expenses. And the magistrate is a member of the committee that allocates those funds."

THE CONSTITUTION AND SOCIAL JUSTICE
Are Bail-Setting Algorithms Compatible with Notions of Fairness?

For proponents of algorithms and cashless bail, the goal of using a computerized risk assessment is reducing or eliminating bias in decisions on pretrial detention. However, critics of the algorithms suggest there are flaws inherent in them as well. One of the studies that has been most critical of pretrial-release algorithms comes from authors at *ProPublica*. Their research involved an assessment of more than 10,000 pretrial-detainee decisions in Broward

(continued)

County, Florida. In that county, an oft-used algorithm known as COMPAS, as distributed by a company called North-pointe, incorporated more than 130 factors in ranking arrestees on a scale from 1 to 10.[36]

The *ProPublica* study claimed that the "score proved remarkably unreliable in forecasting violent crime," with the authors saying, "Only 20 percent of the people predicted to commit violent crimes actually went on to do so." But the authors added that when all crimes were considered, including misdemeanors, such as driving without a license, "Of those deemed likely to re-offend, 61 percent were arrested for any subsequent crime within two years." Most alarmingly, perhaps, the authors observed, "The formula was particularly likely to falsely flag Black defendants as future criminals, wrongly labeling them this way at almost twice the rate as White defendants. White defendants were mislabeled as low risk more often than Black defendants." Even when the authors "ran a statistical test that isolated the effect of race from criminal history and recidivisms, as well as from defendant's age and gender," it turned out that "Black defendants were still 77 percent more likely to be pegged as higher risk of committing a future violent crime and as 45 percent more likely to be predicted to commit a future crime of any kind."[37]

Perhaps not surprisingly, the company that sells the algorithm released a statement saying, "Northpointe does not agree that the results of [the *ProPublica*] analysis, or the claims being made upon that analysis, are correct or that they accurately reflect the outcomes from the application of the model."[38] Stanford researchers also examined the Broward County data from the *ProPublica* study and released a rebuttal through *The Washington Post*, indicating that the COMPAS algorithm was, in fact, effective in predicting which individuals given pretrial release were likely to recommit crimes. Specifically, that study said, "Defendants assigned the highest risk score reoffended at almost four times the rate as those assigned the lowest score (81 percent vs. 22 percent)." *The Washington Post* article also noted that recidivism rates at each level of the 1–10 scale were consistent across race. The authors addressed this point by saying, "For example, among defendants who scored a seven on the COMPAS scale, 60 percent of white defendants reoffended, which is nearly identical to the 61 percent of black defendants who reoffended." They even found "approximate equality between white and black defendants holds for every one of Northpointe's 10 risk levels."[39]

Nevertheless, *The Washington Post* study did not dispute a key *ProPublica* finding, conceding that "among defendants *who ultimately did not reoffend*, blacks were more than twice as likely as whites to be classified as medium or high risk (42 percent vs. 22 percent). Even though these defendants did not go on to commit a crime, they are nonetheless subjected to harsher treatment by the courts."[40] Moreover, this study also indicated "Black defendants are more likely to be classified as medium or high risk (58 percent vs. 33 percent)." *ProPublica* issued a response that did not challenge the analysis offered in the story in *The Washington Post*—but *ProPublica* suggested that interpretation of the data and its meaning for notions of *fairness* could turn on whether one wishes to attain a predictive value of who will reoffend or who will not reoffend, as it is difficult for one algorithm to succeed in meeting both objectives; in simple terms, both studies could, in theory, be offering correct interpretations of the Broward County data.[41]

In other research, the Pretrial Justice Institute—which advocated previously for use of something called a nine-point PSA algorithm in bail decisions—reversed course in February 2020, posting a statement on their website asking for added safeguards in judges' bail decisions that revolved around algorithms. A key concern was described by Tenille Patterson, who was an executive partner at the Pretrial Justice Institute: "We saw in jurisdictions that use the tools and saw jail populations decrease that they were not able to see disparities decrease, and in some cases they saw disparities increase." For a specific example, she pointed to New Jersey, where "jail populations fell nearly by half after the changes, which took effect in 2017, eliminating cash bail and introducing the PSA algorithm. But the demographics of defendants stuck in jail stayed largely the same: about 50 percent black and 30 percent white."[42] The implication in these statements is that the underlying racial discrepancies the algorithms were supposed to remedy still remained in place.

However, a study from Alex Albright of Harvard University focused on the state of Kentucky and offered differing results. That state makes use of an algorithm for bail decisions but, like many other states, allows judges to overrule risk-factor scores created by computers. Albright's research revealed that the algorithm was not introducing bias into the pretrial detention process but, rather, it was the judges' decisions of when to override the algorithm that was allowing bias to permeate the process.[43] Other data from Kentucky showed that releasing more individuals prior to trial has not led to issues with public safety in that state.[44]

In the end, whether an algorithm is somehow introducing bias into the process of determining bail remains an unsolved question. Perhaps as more states make use of such procedures and more data become available to analyze, added statistical clarity will emerge. For now, though, there seems to be no clear-cut answer regarding whether using risk assessment algorithms, on their own, represents a preferred method of ensuring fairness in decisions concerning pretrial release.

Pretrial Detention of Juveniles

In *Schall v. Martin* (1984),[45] the Supreme Court upheld a New York law that allowed judges to order the pretrial detention of juveniles if there is a serious risk that they "may before the return date commit an act which if committed by an adult would constitute a crime." Noting the unique character of the juvenile justice system, the Court said that pretrial detention serves to protect both the juvenile and society, and need not be considered punishment. Chief Justice Rehnquist wrote for the Court, stressing the "legitimate interest in protecting a juvenile from the consequences of his criminal activity—both from potential physical injury which may be suffered when a victim fights back or a policeman attempts to make an arrest and from the downward spiral of criminal activity into which peer pressure may lead the child." Rehnquist suggested that the deprivation of liberty is less significant in the case of a juvenile who is merely transferred from parental control to supervision by the state. As in the *Salerno* case, Justices Marshall, Brennan, and Stevens dissented. Justice Marshall spoke for all three, noting "there is a qualitative difference between imprisonment and the condition of being subject to the supervision and control of an adult who has one's best interests at heart." Concluding that the effects of pretrial detention on juveniles is "overwhelmingly detrimental," Marshall could perceive "no public purpose advanced by the statute sufficient to justify the harm it works."

Pretrial Detention in Domestic Assault Cases

Today, most states have laws restricting or placing conditions on pretrial release in domestic violence cases. Some states even have brief mandatory detention periods before a defendant can be released on bail for these charges. In 2012, the U.S. Court of Appeals upheld a policy under which persons arrested for domestic assault would be held for twelve hours before being released on bail.[46] Understandably, conditions of pretrial release in domestic violence cases typically include avoiding contact with the victim and staying away from the victim's home, school, or workplace.

Use of Force in Pretrial Detention

In *Kingsley v. Hendrickson* (2015),[47] the Supreme Court's 5–4 decision held that due process protects pretrial detainees from the excessive use of force by officers. Kingsley was arrested on drug charges in Wisconsin and while detained pretrial in a county jail cell, he covered the light in his cell with a piece of paper (because the light could not be turned off by an inmate). Guards repeatedly demanded that the paper be removed, and after Kingsley failed to comply, he was handcuffed and moved to a different cell by four officers; in that cell, he was forced onto a concrete bunk bed, with one officer driving his knee into Kingsley's back and forcing his head into the bunk and another officer shocking Kingsley with a TASER for approximately five seconds. Kingsley filed an excessive force claim, but a jury in federal district court ruled against him. He appealed, citing an improper jury instruction, and the Supreme Court agreed with him, ordering a new trial. The Court said a jury in any use-of-force case involving a pretrial detainee should be instructed to use a standard of *objective* reasonableness, not *subjective* reasonableness. In an article for Georgetown University's *American Criminal Law Review*, Kate Lambroza summed up the difference between these standards by saying, "Whereas the objective standard requires that the official *should* have known of the risk ..., the subjective standard requires that the official was *actually aware* that [the prisoner] suffered a substantial risk ... and did nothing to abate the risk" (emphasis in original).

In chapter 10, we discussed the Supreme Court's ruling in *Graham v. Connor* (1989),[48] which held that use-of-force cases outside of correctional facilities are governed by an objective reasonableness standard, which the *Graham* Court described as speaking to the "perspective of a reasonable officer on the scene," while protecting an officer who "acted in good faith." In essence, the *Kingsley* case simply applies this standard inside correctional facilities—pertaining to treatment of pretrial detainees but not to the treatment of those who have been convicted of crimes. Justice Breyer's majority opinion for *Kingsley* offered added clarity for the application of objective reasonableness in a corrections setting, saying the following:

> Considerations such as the following may bear on the reasonableness or unreasonableness of the force used: the relationship between the need for the use of force and the amount of force used; the extent of the plaintiff's injury; any effort made by the officer to temper or to limit the amount of force; the severity of the security problem at issue; the threat reasonably perceived by the officer; and whether the plaintiff was actively resisting. ... We do not consider this list to be exclusive. We mention these factors only to illustrate the types of objective circumstances potentially relevant to a determination of excessive force.

Other Claims by Pretrial Detainees

Even though the *Kingsley* case requires that the objective reasonableness standard apply to use-of-force cases involving pretrial detainees, circuit courts have split regarding what standard to apply in other claims raised by pretrial detainees, such as those involving conditions of confinement,[49] inadequate medical care,[50] and "failure-to-protect."[51] Arguably, the Supreme Court's decision in *Bell v. Wolfish* (1979)[52] suggests that an objective reasonableness standard should apply in all of these situations. Whereas a subjective approach could require, for example, an inmate to tell an officer they are sick, a gang is trying to harm them, or their toilet is overflowing, an objective standard might require an officer to draw an inference of harm from, for instance, any of the following: the sight of an inmate lying on the ground in a fetal position, an inmate being surrounded by a group of other inmates, or a toilet making an odd noise.

In the *Bell* decision, the Court's majority indicated that pretrial detainees should not be subjected to *punishment* (since they have not been convicted of crimes), and more specifically, the Court said pretrial detainees can succeed in challenging facility policies that are not "rationally related to a legitimate nonpunitive governmental purposes" or which "appear excessive in relation to that purpose." The *Bell* case, which we addressed briefly in chapter 9 regarding its search and seizure elements, examined complaints raised by pretrial detainees housed in the Metropolitan Correctional Center in New York City. The specific complaints pertained to these situations: the use of cavity searches for inmates following all interaction with visitors; *double bunking* in cells originally designed for one person; limits on receiving shipments of books not sent directly from a publisher, bookstore, or book club; and a ban on food packages shipped from outside the facility. The majority opinion in *Bell* rejected all these complaints, noting that "the problems that arise in the day-to-day operation of a corrections facility are not susceptible of easy solutions." Accordingly, Chief Justice Rehnquist's majority opinion declared, "Prison administrators therefore should be accorded wide-ranging deference in the adoption and execution of policies and practices that in their judgment are needed to preserve internal order and discipline and to maintain institutional security." Overall, this case appeared to take an objective reasonableness approach to evaluating this correctional facility's policies.

Pretrial Confinement in a Mental Institution

In *Greenwood v. United States* (1956),[53] the Supreme Court upheld the pretrial commitment of an accused felon who had been determined to be incompetent to stand trial. Federal law has long allowed for the civil commitment of a person who, after a hearing, is deemed to be incompetent.[54] In the *Greenwood* case, the Court ruled the federal statute allowing temporary commitment of an incompetent defendant is a valid exercise of Congress's implied powers. Justice Felix Frankfurter, writing for the Court, observed the following:

> This commitment, and therefore the legislation authorizing commitment in the context of this case, involve an assertion of authority, duly guarded, auxiliary to incontestable national power. As such, it is plainly within congressional power under the Necessary and Proper Clause.

CIVIL COMMITMENT: A period of confinement, generally in a mental health facility and, perhaps, for an undetermined period of time because a court determines an individual represents a danger to themselves or others.

Excessive Fines

Constitutional protection against excessive fines can be traced back to Magna Carta (1215), which stated, "A Free-man shall not be amerced [fined] for a small fault, but after the manner of the fault and for a great fault after the greatness thereof. ..." Writing in the late-eighteenth century, William Blackstone observed that under the common law, "no man shall have a larger amercement imposed upon him, than his circumstances or personal estate will bear. ..."[55] Of course, throughout much of English history, this principle was honored more in the breach than in the observance, which is why the framers of the Bill of Rights found it necessary to include the prohibition of excessive fines in the Eighth Amendment.

In *Timbs v. Indiana* (2019),[56] the Supreme Court held that the prohibition of excessive fines, being fundamental to liberty, is enforceable against the states under the Due Process Clause of the Fourteenth Amendment. Writing for the Court, Justice Ruth Bader Ginsburg declared that "the historical and logical case for concluding that the

EXCESSIVE FINES: A monetary penalty a court deems to be disproportionate and, thus, a violation of the Eighth Amendment.

Fourteenth Amendment incorporates the Excessive Fines Clause is overwhelming."

Civil Asset Forfeiture

The *Timbs* case did not involve a fine in the conventional sense but rather the forfeiture of valuable property. Tyson Timbs was charged with dealing heroin, and upon arrest, police seized his Land Rover SUV. He pleaded guilty in Indiana state court and was sentenced to one year of home detention, five years of probation, a court-ordered drug treatment program, and $1,203 in fees. Beyond that sentence from the trial court, though, the state also sought forfeiture of the Land Rover on the grounds that it had been used to transport heroin. The forfeiture was brought as a civil case against the property itself—distinct from the criminal charges levied against Timbs. Examining this matter, the Indiana Supreme Court ruled in favor of the state, observing that the Excessive Fines Clause only impacted federal action, since the clause had never been incorporated.

On review, the U.S. Supreme Court reversed Indiana's highest court and incorporated the Excessive Fines Clause. Noting that the maximum fine for Timbs's offense was $10,000, the Court held that the seizure of an SUV worth more than $40,000 amounted to an excessive fine. In a majority opinion that cited historic documents that had previously put limits on excessive government fines—including the Charter of Liberties of Henry I (from 1101); the Magna Carta (from 1215); and the English Bill of Rights (from 1689)—Justice Ginsburg's majority opinion in *Timbs* declared, "For good reason, the protection against excessive fines has been a constant shield throughout Anglo-American history: Exorbitant tolls undermine other constitutional liberties."

This was not the first time the Supreme Court brought civil asset forfeiture under the ambit of the Excessive Fines Clause. In *Austin v. United States* (1993),[57] the Court held that a forfeiture proceeding commenced by the federal government against a mobile home and an auto body shop amounted to an excessive fine visited upon a man convicted of possession of cocaine with intent to distribute. Two key points emerged from this opinion. First, the Court said that forfeiture "constitutes 'payment to a sovereign as punishment for some offense,' and, as such, is subject to the limitations of the Eighth Amendment's Excessive Fines Clause."[58] Second, the Court noted that, while "some provisions of the Bill of Rights are expressly limited to criminal cases"—such as the Self-Incrimination Clause of the Fifth Amendment and all protections offered in criminal prosecutions by

CIVIL ASSET FORFEITURE:
A mechanism through which government agents can seize an individual person's private property even without a crime being charged, provided there is an applicable level of proof under relevant state or federal law (usually proof by preponderance of the evidence) to connect the property to an illegal act; generally, an individual can attempt to recover the item through court proceedings; rightly-seized items become property of the government.

the text of the Sixth Amendment—"the text of the Eighth Amendment includes no similar limitation." Thus, the Excessive Fines Clause could be applied to a punishment in a civil forfeiture case. Ultimately, what made the *Timbs* case significant was that the Court extended the doctrines underlying *Austin* to state-level forfeitures.

How Does Civil Asset Forfeiture Work?

Civil asset forfeiture is rooted in seventeenth-century English maritime law and has been used by federal and state law enforcement officials throughout U.S. history.[59] In 1970, Congress passed the Organized Crime Control Act, which specifically authorized seizures of aircrafts, boats, and vehicles used in drug trafficking.[60] Under current federal law, law enforcement can seize property, including cash, if they can show—by a preponderance of evidence—there is a connection between the property and criminal activity.[61] This low standard of proof can be applied even without making an arrest, much less bringing criminal charges or acquiring a criminal conviction with proof beyond a reasonable doubt. Hence, this process is called *civil asset forfeiture.*

To contest a federal civil asset forfeiture, the property owner can bring a case to court in an attempt to get the property back. But under federal law, the burden falls on the property's owner to demonstrate they are an "innocent owner"; they must do so by showing—also by preponderance of the evidence—that the property is not connected to illegal activity.[62] If a person cannot afford counsel to wage this defense in court, federal law allows for the possibility of appointed representation in such a case.[63]

States exhibit significant variation in civil forfeiture procedures. Four states have banned civil forfeiture, replacing it with *criminal forfeiture*, whereby a person must be found guilty of a crime before property can be seized. Those states, and the years the bans were enacted, are as follows: Maine (2021), Nebraska (2016), New Mexico (2015), and North Carolina (1985). More than fifteen states now require a criminal conviction before a civil forfeiture can occur, but those states have stopped short of banning civil forfeiture altogether.

States that permit civil forfeiture without criminal convictions typically use similar standards as the federal government, often requiring law enforcement to meet a low threshold like preponderance of evidence or probable cause to effectuate a civil asset forfeiture. In turn, individual property owners can seek to recover their property by going to court and demonstrating the property was legally acquired, usually through a preponderance of evidence standard. But fifteen states now place the burden of proof on the government when the property owner comes forward to contest a forfeiture, and Arizona, Iowa, and Virginia have shifted to a *clear and convincing evidence* standard for police to justify a forfeiture action—a slightly higher burden to meet than preponderance of evidence. The Institute for Justice maintains an updated catalog of state-level reform efforts on its website and has noted that variation exists regarding what different states require law enforcement to do with seized items.[64]

Where Does Civil Forfeiture Money Go?

Historically, little oversight has existed regarding how federal and state law enforcement agencies use forfeiture funds. When property is seized, it can be sold at auction or used by law enforcement. Any cash from such sales, or even cash that is seized directly, potentially becomes property of a law enforcement agency that could then use it in any way. At the federal level, the Department of Justice manages an Asset Forfeiture Fund for property and cash seized by DOJ agencies like the FBI; there also is a Treasury Forfeiture Fund for revenue seized by agencies in the Department of Treasury or the Department of Homeland Security. Other federal agencies may be able retain property and cash seized for their own benefit.

At the state level, many police departments can keep up to 100% of forfeiture funds, and in some jurisdictions, a District Attorney's office can share in the proceeds.[65] But reform movements are building momentum on this issue. Missouri and Indiana are among a handful of states that now require a percentage of forfeiture funds to be given to educational programs. Seven states have directed funds to be used for other government purposes besides law enforcement. Georgia has enacted percentage limits on how much can go to police departments and a D.A.'s office, also allocating some money for indigent defense services, drug rehabilitation programs, and victim assistance funds. Additionally, more than half the states also have reporting requirements that mandate disclosure of how forfeiture funds are used and how much is taken each year. In some states, if a person wins a forfeiture hearing, attorney's fees can be paid to them.[66]

In cases in which money rightfully belongs to a crime victim, restitution may be facilitated with seized funds, but a 2020 Supreme Court decision[67] gave law enforcement some leeway in not returning all proceeds. The FBI's website proclaims the following:

> We've had a lot of success with forfeiture actions in terms of going after criminal enterprises, but our emphasis on compensating victims has paid off as well. In the past two fiscal years, FBI forfeitures—criminal and civil—have allowed the government to return more than $100 million to victims of crime following criminal restitution orders. And since fiscal year 2000, the Department of Justice as a whole has returned more than $4 billion in forfeited funds to crime victims.[68]

Even so, the latest *Policing for Profit* report from the Institute for Justice indicates that "forfeiture proceeds mostly support law enforcement budgets, not crime victims or community programs."[69] Moreover, Dan Alban, the codirector of the Institute for Justice's National Initiative to End Forfeiture Abuse, stated that "in recent years, we have published multiple studies based on federal government data that found that civil forfeiture is ineffective at fighting crime but is used to generate more revenue when there are budget shortfalls."[70]

The Equitable Sharing Program

Regardless of state limitations on civil forfeiture emerging around the United States, a federal program known as *equitable sharing* or *federal adoption* allows state and local police to partner with federal law enforcement on a forfeiture, and the state and local departments can get up to 80% of the money raised, even if their state law bans forfeitures. This program is made possible by a provision in the Comprehensive Crime Control Act of 1984. In 2015, Attorney General Eric Holder announced that use of equitable sharing would be limited to situations in which there is a need to "protect public safety,"[71] but that restriction was reversed in 2016 under Attorney General Loretta Lynch.[72] In 2017, Attorney General Jeff Sessions issued a policy and guidelines statement that said, "[L]aw enforcement agencies who wish to participate in the Department's Equitable Sharing Program now must now provide their officers with enhanced training on asset forfeiture laws." Sessions also noted that the program would be used to "prioritize assets that will most effectively advance our overall goal of reducing violent crime."[73]

According to the latest *Policing for Profit* report, between 2000 and 2019, $8.8 billion was paid by the federal government to state and local law enforcement as a part of "equitable sharing" forfeitures.[74] In a separate study,

The Washington Post examined a Department of Justice database of forfeitures, which the authors acquired through a Freedom of Information Act request. This study revealed there had been 61,998 cash seizures made through the Equitable Sharing Program since 9/11/2001, totaling more than $2.5 billion; of those, state and local authorities kept more than $1.7 billion, and the Department of Justice, Department of Homeland Security, and other federal agencies kept approximately $800 million. Roughly 50% of the seizures were for less than $8,800. The study also found that "only a sixth of the seizures were legally challenged, in part because of the costs of legal action against the government." Nevertheless, looking at the subset of those cases in which there was a challenge, in 41% of cases, the government agreed to return money—and in those cases in which money was returned, the appeals process took more than a year "and often required owners of the cash to sign agreements not to sue police over the seizures."[75]

How Prevalent is Civil Forfeiture?

Statistics in the *Policing for Profit* report indicated that states and the federal government seized $68.8 billion under civil asset forfeiture programs between 2000 and 2018—but not all states retain data on this topic (only 21 are believed to do so), so the figure is likely much higher.[76] In defense of civil forfeiture, the authors of a *Washington Post* article stated, "There is no question that state and federal forfeiture programs have crippled powerful drug-trafficking organizations, thwarted an assortment of criminals and brought millions of dollars to financially stressed police departments." The authors also said, "As the drug trade ramped up throughout the 1980s, money deposited into Justice's federal forfeitures fund increased from $27 million in 1985 to $556 million in 1993. (It reached $2.6 billion in 2007.) Some of that increase was driven by Operation Pipeline, a nationwide DEA program launched in 1986 to promote highway interdiction training for state and local police."[77]

However, while proponents of civil asset forfeiture might point to the need to stop largescale drug trafficking rings or other criminal enterprises, research regarding the twenty-one states that release civil forfeiture data indicate the median forfeiture since 2000 has been $1,276.[78] Such a low number indicates that many forfeitures are not targeting largescale criminal enterprises but, rather, ordinary people.

Furthermore, some studies have suggested that minorities are more likely to be subjected to civil forfeiture. For instance, the *Orlando Sentinel* won a Pulitzer Prize in 1993 for observing that the Volusia County Sheriff's Office in Florida had used state seizure laws to take $8 million from drivers, with nine out of ten of those drivers being minorities.[79] More recently, a 2021 article published in the *International Public Management Journal* analyzed seizures at more than 2,000 police departments between 1993 and 2007, finding a relationship between forfeiture revenue and minority population share.[80] Additionally, an article in *USA Today* spoke of that 2021 study by observing, "Other studies and several media investigations, including a 2019 series by St. Louis Public Radio and a 2014 series in *The Washington Post*, reached the same conclusion."[81] *The Washington Post* analysis referenced in that quote was entitled "Stop and Seize," and it found that in 400 federal court cases in which people challenged forfeiture seizures and were successful in getting some money back, the majority were Black, Hispanic, or another minority.[82] Supreme Court Justice Clarence Thomas actually cited work from *The Washington Post* in his statement dissenting to a denial of cert. in *Leonard v. Texas* (2017), with Thomas writing, "These forfeiture operations frequently target the poor and other groups least able to defend their interests in forfeiture proceedings."[83]

FOCUS ON LAW ENFORCEMENT

Handheld Device Allows Police to Seize Funds from Prepaid Cards

Civil asset forfeiture can apply to any type of property. It could involve seizures of contraband, such as illegal drugs or weapons. It also could apply to things like money, cars, airplanes, boats, and homes that are not inherently illegal to possess. The *Policing for Profit* report indicated, that in terms of raw dollar value, cash was most likely to be the subject of civil forfeiture across the country. Data from Florida for 2017–18 was representative of this fact, showing a 47% cash and 47% automobile breakdown when it came to total seizures, but in terms of overall value, cash represented 8% of total revenue from forfeitures in the state.[84]

More recently, technology believed to have originated with research conducted by the Department of Homeland Security can enable police to take funds directly from a prepaid card. Known as ERAD, which stands for Electronic Recovery and Access to Data, this handheld device looks similar to a credit card terminal that might be seen in a store. But it can be used by law enforcement officials, whether roadside, in a police station, or elsewhere, to freeze or seize the funds that have been loaded onto prepaid credit cards or gift cards. (The device cannot be used to take money from a nonprepaid card.) A 2015 press release from the Department of Homeland Security indicated that, since field testing of ERAD began, approximately $1 million had been seized by state and local police using such devices.[85]

The head of the company that makes the devices, ERAD Group, Inc., has said the devices are in use in hundreds of police departments around the country, in about half the states. That company is paid a percentage of money seized, generally between 5 and 8%, in addition to equipment and service fees.[86] One of the first states to see use of these devices was Oklahoma, where a news report from *Oklahoma Watch* indicated that "law enforcement officials say the devices are essentially part of the arms race between police and drug traffickers, who in recent years have been loading pre-paid cards with millions of dollars for transport as part of the drug trade, thus decreasing the likelihood of seizure by law enforcement." The article quoted the public information officer for Oklahoma Highway Patrol, who said of drug dealers, "They're basically using pre-paid cards instead of carrying large amounts of cash."[87]

Yet a report from NPR's Mark Kim observed the potential pitfalls of such seizures for low-income individuals who might rely upon prepaid cards. Kim cited a Pew research report that said, "28 percent of [prepaid] cardholders have income directly deposited and 41 percent [do not have a checking account], compared with just 8 percent of the American public overall." Moreover, he cited Pew in noting that "42 percent of prepaid cardholders have no emergency savings and 21 percent have used a payday loan, approximately four times the rate as those in the general population."[88]

In 2016, the Eighth Circuit ruled there was no Fourth Amendment violation connected to warrantless police searches of the magnetic strips on the back of credit, debit, or gift cards, presumably paving the way for warrantless seizures of money from such cards.[89] In this case, after a man was pulled over for following a semitruck too closely, a canine alert led to a search of the vehicle, and approximately sixty gift or debit cards were found, including those issued by American Express, Visa, Mastercard, and Subway. A search of magnetic strips revealed many of the cards had been *recoded* with stolen account information. Upholding this search, the Eighth Circuit said there was no reasonable expectation of privacy in the magnetic strips because, "In the normal course, all of the information found in the magnetic strips on American Express credit cards is identical to the information in plain view on the front of the cards."

Civil Forfeiture and the Right to Counsel

An interesting aspect of civil forfeiture relates to the possibility that money seized from a person—before they are brough to trial in a criminal case—could impact their ability to afford legal counsel. In 1989, the Supreme

Court issued two opinions regarding this subject on the same day. In *United States v. Monsanto* (1989),[90] the Court addressed the government's pretrial seizure of the assets belonging to a man who was accused of leading a largescale heroin distribution organization. Reviewing this matter, the high Court said that "neither the Fifth nor the Sixth Amendment to the Constitution requires Congress to permit a defendant to use assets adjudged to be forfeitable to pay that defendant's legal fees."

In the other case decided that same day, *Caplin & Drysdale, Chartered v. United States* (1989),[91] the Court reached a similar conclusion—this time in an appeal brought by a law firm that represented an alleged drug dealer. The firm sought access to $25,000 the defendant had placed in an escrow account for payment of legal fees prior to his indictment as well as $170,000 for unpaid legal services provided to the defendant after his indictment. Access to the money was blocked when the government initiated forfeiture proceedings against the defendant's assets and prevented any transfer of funds. Federal law does allow seizure of property a criminal has transferred to a third party—unless that third party can demonstrate they were "reasonably without cause to believe that the property was subject to forfeiture."[92] Ruling against the law firm, the majority opinion, again from Justice White, said the following:

> A defendant has no Sixth Amendment right to spend another person's money for services rendered by an attorney, even if those funds are the only way that that defendant will be able to retain the attorney of his choice. A robbery suspect, for example, has no Sixth Amendment right to use funds he has stolen from a bank to retain an attorney to defend him if he is apprehended. The money, though in his possession, is not rightfully his; the Government does not violate the Sixth Amendment if it seizes the robbery proceeds and refuses to permit the defendant to use them to pay for his defense.

However, in dissent, Justice Blackmun expressed concerns that this decision might make it more difficult for some defendants to secure counsel, noting, "Had it been Congress' express aim to undermine the adversary system as we know it, it could hardly have found a better engine of destruction than attorney's-fee forfeiture." He added the following:

> If the Government restrains the defendant's assets before trial, private counsel will be unwilling to continue, or to take on, the defense. Even if no restraining order is entered, the possibility of forfeiture after conviction will itself substantially diminish the likelihood that private counsel will agree to take the case. The 'message [to private counsel] is 'Do not represent this defendant or you will lose your fee.' That being the kind of message lawyers are likely to take seriously, the defendant will find it difficult or impossible to secure representation.'[93]

More recently, in *Luis v. United States* (2016),[94] the Supreme Court said the government could not prevent a defendant from accessing money needed to retain counsel when the money had not been linked directly to criminal activity. In this case, a woman was accused of acquiring approximately $45 million from health care fraud crimes, but she had only $2 million in her possession as her trial approached. The government sought to seize that remaining money but could not prove it was directly connected to her crimes. As a result, the Court found that seizure of that money would violate the Sixth Amendment, with Justice Thomas offering a concurring opinion indicating that:

> The common law … offers an administrable line: A criminal defendant's untainted assets are protected from Government interference before trial and judgment. His tainted assets, by contrast may be seized before trial as contraband or through a separate in rem proceeding. Reading the Sixth Amendment to track the historical line between tainted and untainted assets makes good sense."

Subsequently, the Supreme Court's 8–1 decision in *Liu v. Securities and Exchange Commission* (2020)[95] spoke to another situation in which separating ill-gotten gains from other money was at issue. In this decision, the Court upheld the SEC's authority to seek a disgorgement, which is synonymous with a forfeiture in civil court. But the decision also placed some limits on how much could be seized.[140] In this case, Liu had raised approximately $27 million in investments for a so-called *cancer-treatment center*, but he put some of the money into personal accounts and used some money for business purposes that were not revealed to investors. Liu's attorneys argued the government's seizure of funds should not include *legitimate business expenses*, but the SEC wanted the forfeiture of all money Liu had acquired from his investors. Justice Sonia Sotomayor's majority opinion stated that "courts must deduct legitimate business expenses before ordering disgorgement," adding, "The Court holds today that a disgorgement award that does not exceed a wrongdoer's net profits and is awarded for victims is equitable relief permissible under § 78u(d)(5)." Sotomayor pointed out that "when the 'entire profit of a business or undertaking' results from … wrongful activity," all proceeds can be disgorged.

In addition, Sotomayor's opinion recognized that federal law required giving compensation from "net profits" back to the victims of this fraud.[96] Even so, Sotomayor did not indicate all proceeds from a forfeiture must be returned to the victims in a fraud case; rather, she said, "The equitable nature of the profits remedy generally requires the SEC to return a defendant's gains to wronged investors for their benefit." In dissent, Justice Thomas took umbrage with Justice Sotomayor's use of the word "generally" in that sentence, with Thomas exhorting, "Requiring the SEC to only 'generally' compensate victims is inconsistent with traditional equitable principles." He even went so far as to declare that "the award should be used to compensate victims, not to enrich the Government."

DISGORGEMENT:
A penalty applied, usually as the result of a criminal conviction, that allows the government to seize illegally-acquired money or property from an offender, perhaps to return some or all of it to the rightful owner.

THE CONSTITUTION IN ACTION
Department of Justice Seizes Movie Revenue from *The Wolf of Wall Street*

In July 2016, the Department of Justice filed a forfeiture action unlike any ever taken by the federal government, with a complaint filed in the U.S. District Court for the Central District of California[97] seeking seizure of "the rights to profits, royalties, and distribution proceeds" from *The Wolf of Wall Street*, an Oscar-nominated movie. Released in 2013, the movie generated nearly $400 million in gross revenue, making it the highest-earning film in the career of legendary Hollywood director Martin Scorsese. The movie was based on the memoir of a man named Jordan Belfort, whose character is portrayed by Leonardo DiCaprio. The movie depicted Belfort's actions after cofounding an investment firm in New York in 1989, with his tactics allegedly including high-pressure sales pitches and fraudulent claims designed to artificially inflate stock prices. Belfort was accused of causing more than $200 million of losses for investors, and in 1999, he pleaded guilty to federal charges of fraud and money laundering. He was sentenced to four years in prison and served twenty-two months behind bars.[98]

Interestingly, though, the government's attempt to seize the proceeds of *The Wolf of Wall Street* film had nothing to do with Belfort's crimes—rather, they were primarily connected to the illegal actions of those who funded the film's creation. The movie's production was partially bankrolled by a company called Red Granite Pictures, which provided more than $60 million. All that money was improperly diverted to Red Granite from a sovereign wealth fund designed to assist the Malaysian government with improvements in that country. The fund, known as 1MDB, was partially controlled by a Malaysian businessman named Low Taek Jho, better known as Jho Low. Low, who received a degree from the Wharton School of Business at the University of Pennsylvania, is believed to have diverted more than $4.5 billion from the 1MDB fund into his personal bank accounts to fuel an extravagant way of living that including purchases of cars; jewelry; high-end artwork, including a Van Gogh and a Monet; a Bombardier Global 5000 jet plane; a $250 million *superyacht*; and luxury properties in New York City and Beverly Hills—among other items. Jho Low also diverted money to Red Granite, which was cofounded by the stepson of a former Malaysian Prime Minister.[99]

Movie revenue became one part of the federal government's attempt to seize improperly used money from the 1MDB fund, with the total forfeiture action involving more than $1 billion, making it the largest-ever in U.S. history at that time. Eventually, rather than seizing the movie rights to *The Wolf of Wall Street*, the Department of Justice agreed to a $60 million settlement with Red Granite, with $57 million sent back to the Malaysian government and $3 million given to the Department of Justice to recoup the costs of the investigation into this matter.[100] Items seized by the government also included items given by Jho Low to DiCaprio, including the trophy for an Academy Award for Best Actor in a Leading Role that had been won by Marlon Brando in 1955 for his role in the movie *On the Waterfront*; Low had apparently purchased this item and presented it as a birthday gift to DiCaprio—potentially as a form of consolation after DiCaprio did not win an Oscar for his leading role in *The Wolf of Wall Street*.[101]

Jho Low still faces criminal charges from the U.S. Department of Justice but has, thus far, evaded prosecution by fleeing to China and leading a clandestine lifestyle there. Meanwhile, in 2022, Jordan Belfort brought a lawsuit against Red Granite, alleging in a Los Angeles court filing that the company had defrauded him into releasing the rights to his book without revealing that ill-gotten proceeds were funding the film. The Jho Low saga has been featured in a book called *Billion Dollar Whale: The Man Who Fooled Wall Street, Hollywood, and the World*,[102] with a TV series based on that book forthcoming.

Other Interesting Civil Forfeiture Cases

With civil asset forfeiture, a case is brought against a piece of property, not against a person. This could include cash, cars, boats, houses, and, as illustrated in the previous box, even a motion picture can be named as the defendant in a forfeiture case.

According to an NPR article that cited *Policing for Profit*, 88% of federal civil forfeiture cases are processed "administratively," rather than judicially.[103] This means those cases do not get into court—often because law enforcement officials convince the property owner to sign a document relinquishing their right to challenge the seizure, possibly in exchange for law enforcement agreeing not to bring criminal charges; alternatively, a negotiation might occur in which the owner of cash agrees to give up some of the money to the government in exchange for keeping the rest—which might make sense given the potential lawyer's fees related to challenging a civil asset forfeiture in court. Along these lines, the *Policing for Profit* stated only 22% of civil asset forfeiture cases went to trial in a sample derived from four states that keep such records.[104]

Cases that do make it into court generally have interesting names because the case is brought against property itself. For example, in *United States v. $1,074,900.00 in U.S. Currency*,[105] a federal district court judge in Nebraska ruled in favor of a woman named Tara Mishra, who had more than a million dollars of her personal cash seized from the trunk of a car. She had earned this money through her career as an exotic dancer in California and kept the cash primarily in safe deposit boxes. Upon brokering a deal to purchase (in cash) a bar in New Jersey called the 46 Lounge, Mishra trusted two friends, Mr. and Mrs. Dheri, to drive the money from California to New Jersey, while Mishra flew ahead to get business plans in place. Unfortunately for her, those friends were pulled over in their Hertz rental car on an interstate highway in Lincoln, Nebraska after being clocked at 93 mph by an officer of the Nebraska State Patrol. The driver consented to a search of the vehicle, and the officer opened the trunk, finding two duffle bags and one backpack containing the cash. Suggesting the money was connected to drug trafficking—essentially because dryer sheets and clear plastic baggies were present—the officer seized it all, but no criminal charges were brought. Once the money was taken to the police station, officers claimed a K-9 named Debo alerted to the presence of drugs on the bills. The money was then converted into a cashier's check, which was standard practice for that department when dealing with seizures over $300.

On review, Judge Joseph Bataillon of the U.S. District Court for the District of Nebraska wrote that "the government failed to show a substantial connection between drugs and the money." He added, "'Lots of money' is not sufficient basis in and of itself generally for forfeiture." Regarding the government's claim that trace signs of drugs were found on the currency, Judge Bataillon said that "nearly all money is tainted with the odor of drugs,"[106] even citing Supreme Court Justice John Paul Stevens, whose dissent in *Bennis v. Michigan* (1996) spoke of forfeitures based on drug evidence being on dollar bills by saying, "Without some form of an exception for innocent owners, the potential breadth of forfeiture actions for illegal proceeds would be breathtaking indeed. It has been estimated that nearly every United States bill in circulation—some $230 billion worth—carries trace amounts of cocaine, so great is the drug trade's appetite for cash."[107] In the end, the district court judge concluded the following:

> Ms. Mishra has proven by a preponderance of the evidence that she is the owner of the defendant currency. Pursuant to 21 U.S.C. § 881 and 18 U.S.C. § 983(d)(1)-(6), the court finds Ms. Mishra did have control over the money and directed the Dheris to deliver the money to New Jersey for the purchase of the business. For the foregoing reasons the claimant Tara Mishra is entitled to judgment directing the United States government to return to her $1,074,900 in United States currency or the equivalent in a check, plus legal interest measured since March 3, 2012.

Not all forfeiture cases involve sums of cash; some address objects or property, and these can carry odd-sounding names as well. For instance, in *United States v. Approximately 64,695 Pounds of Shark Fins* (2008),[108] the Ninth Circuit evaluated a seizure of shark fins effectuated by Coast Guard officers who searched a U.S. vessel that was in international waters near Guatemala. The officers found shark fins on this vessel and seized them for an alleged violation of the federal Shark Finning Prohibition Act of 2000.[109] On review, however, the Ninth Circuit said the seizure amounted to a violation of due process rights. The court said the federal law in question did not prohibit shark fin transfers or possession at sea (unlike delivery at a U.S. port). The case also turned on the definition of *fishing vessel*, with the court saying the ship in question was not to be defined as such and, therefore, was not covered by the shark finning law. Ultimately, the Ninth Circuit concluded, with no connection between the shark fins and an illegal act, the property should not have been confiscated.

Another unusually named case resulted in a win for federal officials after members of the U.S. Marshals Service seized a shipment of boxes that arrived at a dock in Mequon, Wisconsin on the shores of Lake Michigan. The boxes contained items known as *clacker balls*, which are toys made up of two acrylic balls that have been tied together by string. When the shipper of these boxes, a toy manufacturer named Ace Novelty Company, challenged the government's forfeiture action, a federal district court in Wisconsin upheld the seizure with its ruling in *United States v. Article Consisting of 50,000 Carboard Boxes More or Less, Each Containing One Pair of Clacker Balls* (1976).[110] The court concluded the seizure was a justified one, based on these toys being considered hazardous to children under the Federal Hazardous Substances Act[111] as well as regulations of the Consumer Product Safety Commission.[112] Satisfied the preponderance of the evidence pointed to the items being illegal, the court upheld the forfeiture.

Some forfeiture cases begin in state courts before appeals carry them into federal courts. An example comes from the Supreme Court's 1965 decision in *One 1958 Plymouth Sedan v. Pennsylvania*,[113] which said a civil forfeiture will be deemed invalid when the item seized has been taken in violation of the Fourth Amendment. In this case, officers of the Pennsylvania Liquor Control Board pulled a car over as it entered the city of Philadelphia from New Jersey by crossing the Benjamin Franklin Bridge. According to the officers' statements, the car was stopped because it was allegedly "low in the rear, quite low," which they inferred to mean there was contraband in the trunk. With the vehicle stopped, and without consent, the officers opened the trunk and found thirty-one cases of liquor that lacked the required Pennsylvania tax seals. Officers seized the liquor and the car. Lower courts found there was no probable cause to justify this search, ending any criminal prosecution. But the state continued with a forfeiture action and took the vehicle.

On review, the Supreme Court of the United States ruled the car should be returned to its owner. Justice Goldberg's majority opinion cited the high Court's 1886 decision in *Boyd v. United States*,[114] which said that when papers seized in violation of the Fourth Amendment were used to make the case for civil forfeiture, the forfeiture itself was invalid. Specifically, Justice Goldberg applied that prior case to the *Plymouth Sedan* matter by saying, "Th[e] authoritative statement and the holding by the Court in *Boyd* that the Government could not seize evidence in violation of the Fourth Amendment for use in a forfeiture proceeding would seem to be dispositive of this case." He went on to add that "the Commonwealth could not establish an illegal use without using the evidence resulting from the search which is challenged as having been in violation of the Constitution." Making the case for a return of the property, Justice Goldberg observed an important dichotomy between what gets returned by police and what doesn't, noting that "the return of the automobile to the owner would not subject him to any possible criminal penalties for possession or frustrate any public policy concerning automobiles, as automobiles. This distinction between what has been described as contraband per se and only derivative contraband has indeed been recognized by Pennsylvania itself in its requirement of mandatory forfeiture of illegal liquor, and stills, and only discretionary forfeiture of such things as automobiles illegally used." That statement indicated, of course, that if the government seizes an inherently illegal item like, say, cocaine, the illegal item need not be returned—an important caveat.

JURISPRUDENCE

Supreme Court of South Dakota Upholds Seizure of Pets
South Dakota v. Fifteen Impounded Cats, 785 N.W.2d 272 (S.D. 2010)

One of the most bizarre civil forfeiture cases is *South Dakota v. Fifteen Impounded Cats*, heard by the Supreme Court of South Dakota in 2010. In this instance, a woman named Patricia Edwards had fifteen cats in her car as she traveled from Texas to Montana. She was stopped by a police officer in Pierre, South Dakota—after she backed her vehicle out of a parking spot at a convenience store and nearly hit the officer's police car. The officer detained Ms. Edwards and looked inside her vehicle—which was cluttered with boxes, coolers, clothing, and a dirty litter box, along with fifteen living cats roaming freely. He ordered the seizure of the cats pursuant to civil asset forfeiture, which was permitted under South Dakota law upon a showing of "exigent circumstances." The basis of the forfeiture action was that the cats were climbing in the back seat and onto the rear dashboard, blocking the driver's visibility through the rear windshield, allegedly in violation of South Dakota traffic laws. The cats were taken to a local branch of the Humane Society to be put up for adoption, but the woman sued seeking the return of her animals. On review, South Dakota's highest court upheld the forfeiture by a 3–2 vote.[115]

The state's Justice Gilbertson wrote the majority opinion for this case, and he agreed with a lower court, finding "impoundment" of the cats could be justified through the "health and safety hazards created by Edwards's traveling on a public roadway and through a crowded parking lot with fifteen small animals wandering around loose in her jam-packed vehicle to distract her and interfere with her ability to see where she was going." He spoke of a "significant safety risk to the public," noting this was a "busy convenience store in Pierre on an August night." He even observed, "Because of the cats in the back window, Edwards failed to see the patrol car behind her and nearly backed into it. What if, instead of the officer's patrol car, a less visible child on a skateboard or bicycle had passed by at that same moment?" He also spoke to the burden of proof needed, recognizing that "[t]his was not a criminal case ... where the elements of an offense had to be proven beyond a reasonable doubt"; thus, he said lower court acted appropriately "in determining that exigent circumstances justified the impoundment of Edwards's cats."

In dissent, South Dakota's Justice Severson proclaimed, "Despite the State's avowed concerns regarding Ms. Edwards's ability to operate her vehicle amid her fifteen cats, the State did not cite her with a traffic violation." He also took note of the care she had provided the cats, and the lack of evidence regarding animal cruelty, by saying, "Ms. Edwards provided her cats with food, water, protection from the elements, adequate sanitation, and affection. Her cats had been spayed or neutered and had received their immunizations. Indeed, Dr. Joseph Engelhart, a veterinarian in Huron, South Dakota, examined Ms. Edwards's cats one month prior to their seizure and found them in 'good health' with 'no evidence of neglect.'" In contrast, once the cats were seized, they were taken to a shelter and kept in cages, only allowed out for short periods of time. The dissent concluded, "The claims of 'exigent circumstances' and inhumane treatment are a pretext. If safe operation of the vehicle was the concern, the police should have addressed that issue and not exposed the taxpayers to the cost of caring for animals wrongfully seized from Ms. Edwards. Ms. Edwards's cats should be returned to her care."

Cruel and Unusual Punishments

As previously noted, the Cruel and Unusual Punishments Clause is rooted in the English Bill of Rights. English monarchs had often demanded grisly punishments of those convicted of treason or sedition. The framers of our Bill of Rights wanted to make sure such punishments would not be imposed by the newly created national government. Even so, there is no evidence they intended to outlaw the death penalty or corporal punishment, neither of which came under much scrutiny prior to the twentieth century.

It was not until 1878 that the Supreme Court had occasion to interpret the Cruel and Unusual Punishments Clause. In *Wilkerson v. Utah* (1878),[116] the Court upheld a death sentence imposed on a man convicted of murder in what was then the Utah Territory. The Court distinguished capital punishment by hanging or firing squad from the grislier forms of execution, such as being drawn and quartered, burned at the stake, or publicly dissected. In the Court's view, ordinary forms of capital punishment did not raise constitutional problems as long as they were lawfully prescribed and imposed.

In *Weems v. United States* (1910),[117] the Supreme Court considered a punishment imposed on an American citizen by a court in the Philippines, which was an American colony at the time. Weems's fifteen-year prison sentence for attempting to defraud the government required *hard and painful labor* while shackled. The Court addressed the notion of disproportionate sentencing and found the punishment was excessive relative to the crime, declaring that "it is a precept of justice that punishment for crime should be graduated and proportioned to offense." The Court, per Justice Joseph McKenna, also noted, "The Eighth Amendment is progressive, and does not prohibit merely the cruel and unusual punishments known in 1689 and 1787, but may acquire wider meaning as public opinion becomes enlightened by humane justice."

Evolving Standards of Decency

The idea that the meaning of the Cruel and Unusual Punishment Clause must evolve to reflect changing attitudes about justice resurfaced in *Trop v. Dulles* (1958),[118] when Chief Justice Earl Warren said that Clause "must draw its meaning from the evolving standards of decency that mark the progress of a maturing society." In this case, the Court ruled that stripping a natural-born U.S. citizen of their citizenship as punishment for a crime amounted to cruel and unusual punishment. Although Chief Justice Warren's opinion spoke only for a plurality of justices, the concept of evolving standards of decency would figure prominently in the Warren Court's Eighth Amendment jurisprudence in the years to come.

Status Offenses

One of the most important Warren Court decisions under the Eighth Amendment was *Robinson v. California* (1962).[119] The significance of the case is twofold. First, the Court, for the first time, held that the Cruel and Unusual Punishments Clause applies to the states via the Fourteenth Amendment. Second, the Court said it is unconstitutional to punish someone for their status, as distinct from a prohibited act. Robinson was prosecuted for being addicted to narcotics—not for possession, but merely for being an addict. Speaking for the Court, Justice Potter Stewart concluded "that a state law which imprisons a person thus afflicted as a criminal, even though he has never touched any narcotic drug within the State or been guilty of any irregular behavior there, inflicts a cruel and unusual punishment in violation of the Fourteenth Amendment." It is important to

STATUS OFFENSES:
A criminal charge against an individual simply on the basis of that person being a member of a group or having a certain condition, like being a drug addict; the Supreme Court has found these to be a violation of the Eighth Amendment's Cruel and Unusual Punishment Clause.

PROBATION: An alternative to incarceration that allows a person accused of a crime to remain free from a jail or prison setting, provided certain conditions are met, such as not using drugs, not traveling out of state, and not committing further crimes.

RESTITUTION: A payment, often required by a court, made by a criminal to the victim of the crime to compensate for a loss suffered by the victim.

DEBTORS' PRISON:
A term applied to situations in which an individual is sentenced to incarceration solely for an inability to pay some type of court-ordered fine or fee.

note, however, that the Court has never held that juveniles cannot be found delinquent for status offenses, such as incorrigibility or ungovernability. This is because juvenile offenses are not considered crimes, and juvenile courts are not bound by the same standards of due process as are the criminal courts.

Revocation of Probation for Failure to Pay Fines or Make Restitution

In many cases, especially those involving nonviolent offenses and first-time offenders, sentencing judges will impose probation in lieu of a jail sentence. Judges are permitted to impose reasonable conditions on probationers, such as avoiding places alcohol is served or submitting to monthly drug tests. Another common condition of probation is the requirement for the probationer to make restitution to the victim. Failure to make restitution or abide by any conditions of probation often results in the revocation of probation, which means the defendant is incarcerated for the duration of the probationary period. According to the Supreme Court, an indigent defendant is entitled to counsel at a revocation hearing.[120] Unfortunately, indigent defendants are often unable to make restitution payments or pay fines and could face revocation for that reason alone.

Therefore, a confounding issue with completion of probation, for some offenders, lies in the concept of debtors' prison, which refers to the incarceration of a person solely because they cannot pay a debt. The notion of incarcerating someone for a debt dates back at least to the Roman Empire and was a common practice in the United States until just before the mid-1800s, when many state constitutions were amended with bans on debtors' prisons and federal laws, including bankruptcy laws, addressed the topic.[121] Yet this type of incarceration seems to have become commonplace once again over the course of the past two decades, as judges in the United States have imprisoned individuals who cannot pay court fees or fines.

From a semantic standpoint, a fine is a punishment for an illegal act and will be defined by law (typically as a range of values like $500 to $1,000), with a specific amount imposed by a judge. Court fees, on the other hand, can be established by individual jurisdictions or defined by state law. Today, what might be called *criminal procedure fees* or *criminal justice fees* can quickly add up and become a burden for those accused of crimes—even before a person is found guilty of charged offenses. Across the fifty states, such fees could include any or all of the following: public defender fees, bail investigation fees, DNA testing fees, crime lab fees, prison stays (or *room and board* fees), meal fees, electronic monitoring fees, drug testing fees, jury fees, probation and supervision fees, court fees, and restitution to a victim. Some courts—or the for-profit companies that administer payments—also tack on payment plan fees and processing fees.[122] Moreover, a court-ordered fine or restitution could accrue late fees or interest when not paid. In some places, even alternatives to incarceration like community service can come with a fee for taking part.[123]

A failure to pay fines or fees can lead to a prison sentence, a revocation of probation, or, in some cases, a defendant in a criminal case simply choosing incarceration as an alternative to fines or fees. All of this can happen in spite of the fact that Congress has banned debtors' prisons and three Supreme Court cases have found constitutional issues with imprisoning a person for failure to pay a debt.

The Supreme Court's first assessment of this topic arrived in *Williams v. Illinois* (1970),[124] where a man was sentenced to the maximum penalty under Illinois law for the crime of petty theft: one year imprisonment and a fine of $500 plus court costs of $5. When his one year of incarceration was completed, he could not pay the fine, and according to Illinois law at the time, he was to be kept in prison for additional time to *work off* the $500 at a rate of $5 per day. On review, the Court found this to be a violation of the Fourteenth Amendment's Equal Protection Clause, with Chief Justice Burger's majority opinion saying a state "may not ... subject a certain class of convicted defendants to a period of imprisonment beyond the statutory maximum solely by reason of their indigency."

One year later, in *Tate v. Short* (1971),[125] the Supreme Court reached a similar conclusion in the matter of a Texas man who was fined $425 for traffic offenses. Pursuant to state law, when he could not pay, he was sentenced to prison time to pay down the fine at a rate of $5 per day. The Court once again took umbrage with incarceration for a failure to pay, with the majority opinion from Justice Brennan raising issues with the ultimate objectives of such an arrangement:

> Since Texas has legislated a "fines only" policy for traffic offenses, that statutory ceiling cannot, consistently with the Equal Protection Clause, limit the punishment to payment of the fine if one is able to pay it, yet convert the fine into a prison term for an indigent defendant without the means to pay his fine. Imprisonment in such a case is not imposed to further any penal objective of the State. It is imposed to augment the State's revenues, but obviously does not serve that purpose; the defendant cannot pay, because he is indigent, and his imprisonment, rather than aiding collection of the revenue, saddles the State with the cost of feeding and housing him for the period of his imprisonment.

The Supreme Court Limits, but Does Not Prohibit, Incarceration for Failure to Pay

In *Bearden v. Georgia* (1983),[126] the Supreme Court held that a court must not automatically revoke probation solely based on the probationer's failure to pay fines or make restitution. Rather, the court should make an individualized assessment of the probationer's situation and modify the order of probation accordingly. In this case, a man pleaded guilty to burglary and a charge of theft by receiving stolen property. As a first-time offender, he was given probation on the condition that he pay a $500 fine and $250 in restitution. The court required a payment of $100 on the day of sentencing, then $100 the next day, and $550 within four months. The first $200 were paid immediately with money the man borrowed from friends, but after losing his job, he notified his probation officer he would not be able to remit the remaining funds before the four-month deadline expired. His probation was then revoked by a judge, and he was sentenced to prison time. On review, the Supreme Court's majority opinion from Justice Sandra Day O'Connor expounded upon the two earlier cases on this subject:

> Only if alternative measures are not adequate to meet the State's interests in punishment and deterrence may the court imprison a probationer who has made sufficient bona fide efforts to pay. To do otherwise would deprive the probationer of his conditional freedom simply because, through no fault of his own, he cannot pay the fine. Such a deprivation would be contrary to the fundamental fairness required by the Fourteenth Amendment.

Justice O'Connor also bluntly declared that "if the State determines a fine or restitution to be the appropriate and adequate penalty for the crime, it may not thereafter imprison a person solely because he lacked the resources to pay it." She even said that "... if the probationer has made all reasonable efforts to pay the fine or restitution, and yet cannot do so through no fault of his own, it is fundamentally unfair to revoke probation automatically without considering whether adequate alternative methods of punishing the defendant are available."

However, this language from *Bearden v. Georgia* was tempered by other parts of the opinion, such as when Justice O'Connor quoted to the *Tate* decision in saying, "[O]ur holding today does not suggest any constitutional infirmity in imprisonment of a defendant with the means to pay a fine who refuses or neglects to do so." A key point arose when she clarified the notion of refusing to pay by injecting the word "willfully" into the discussion, stating, "If the probationer has willfully refused to pay the fine or restitution when he has the means to pay, the State is perfectly justified in using imprisonment as a sanction to enforce collection." She went on to add to this standard by speaking of a lack of *bona fide efforts* to pay fines or fees as grounds for imprisonment:

> Similarly, a probationer's failure to make sufficient bona fide efforts to seek employment or borrow money in order to pay the fine or restitution may reflect an insufficient concern for paying the debt he owes to society for his crime. In such a situation, the State is likewise justified in revoking probation and using imprisonment as an appropriate penalty for the offense.

Reform Efforts in the Wake of Bearden v. Georgia

Ultimately, *Bearden v. Georgia* leaves trial judges with substantial discretion in determining which defendants are *willfully* refusing to make *bona fide efforts* to pay fines or fees. One year after that decision, in fact, Michigan became the first state to charge inmates for the costs of imprisonment, and others would quickly follow with similar measures; today, more than forty states bill defendants for public defender usage, room and board for prison stays, electronic monitoring, and probation services.[127] In the end, language in this crucial decision has laid the groundwork for people to be imprisoned for lesser offenses, such as in the following recent cases: a Michigan man sentenced to jail for not paying a fine for fishing out of season, a Georgia man sentenced to twelve months for not paying a fine related to stealing a can of beer worth less than $2, and a homeless veteran who was incarcerated for twenty-two days for entering an abandoned building while intoxicated.[128]

Although some might suggest fees are necessary to keep up with maintenance costs related to operating a courtroom, such salaries of employees, electric and heating bills, phones, and copy machines,[129] there is data to suggest the costs to taxpayers of incarcerating a person can be greater than the debt collected (unless, of course, added fees for the incarceration are tacked on).[130] A study of Texas and New Mexico counties conducted by the Brennan Center for Justice found that 41 cents of every dollar of revenue raised goes to court operations and prison costs, making "fees and fines ... an inefficient source of government revenue."[131] A separate report from the Brennan Center also observed, "Across the board, we found that states are introducing new user fees, raising the dollar amounts of existing fees, and intensifying the collection of fees and other forms of criminal justice debt such as fines and restitution. But in the rush to collect, made all the more intense by the fiscal crises in many states, no one is considering the ways in which the resulting debt can undermine reentry prospects, pave the way back to prison or jail, and result in yet more costs to the public."[132] Indeed, a cycle of poverty and incarceration can ensue when courts imprison those who cannot afford to pay fines or fees. Some states even permit judges to suspended driver's licenses of those who cannot pay court fees or fines—perhaps, exacerbating issues related to finding work; in 2020, the Sixth Circuit found that such suspensions under state laws in Michigan and Tennessee were valid.[133]

Colorado, Georgia, and Missouri are among states to seek reform in this area; legislation in those states requires judges to make individualized determinations of a defendant's ability to pay before seeking incarceration as an option to resolve a debt.[134] Elsewhere, in 2019, the Fifth Circuit precipitated reform in Orleans Parish Criminal Court in New Orleans, Louisiana by finding in favor of six defendants in criminal cases who claimed their Fourteenth Amendment due process and equal protection rights were violated because fines and fees imposed in the Orleans Parish court (in amounts ranging from $148 to $901.50) were deposited in a Judicial Expense Fund from which the very judges imposing the fines could later allocate money for paying their staffs.[135] In this case, the Fifth Circuit cited the Supreme Court's *Tumey v. Ohio* (1927)[136] ruling, which said, "Every procedure which would offer a possible temptation to the average man as a judge to forget the burden of proof required to convict the defendant, or which might lead him not to hold the balance nice, clear, and true between the State and the accused denies the latter due process of law."

Applying this principle to the matter at hand, the Fifth Circuit said, "In sum, when everything involved in this case is put together, the 'temptation' is too great." The Fifth Circuit also cited other Supreme Court decisions that spoke to the possibility of judicial conflicts of interest, including *Massey v. A.T. Caperton Coal Co.* (2009),[137] which ruled judges should recuse themselves from matters that carry a "probability of bias," even if there is no showing of actual bias. In practical terms, these standards were used by the Fifth Circuit to mandate an overhaul of how court fees and fines are spent.

THE CONSTITUTION AND SOCIAL JUSTICE
Man Sent to Prison for a Speeding Ticket

A 2015 story in *The Atlantic*, entitled "Locked Up for Being Poor," relayed the plight of a 19-year-old man named Kevin Thompson, who was sent to jail in DeKalb County, Georgia after getting pulled over for a routine speeding infraction.[138] When the officer stopped him, it was determined that his driver's license had not been renewed. A judge in traffic court imposed an $810 fine, but because Thompson could not afford to pay, the judge called for a thirty-day probation period during which the ticket needed to be paid in full.

In Georgia at this time, 80% of probation cases were overseen by private, for-profit companies, and this matter was referred to one called Judicial Correction Services, Inc. Thompson met with a *parole officer* from JCS every week and made payments totaling $85. The JCS company kept $30 of that $85 as a fee, which meant the $30 did not

(continued)

count towards his total owed. When Thompson told the *parole officer* he could not complete his payment during the required time frame, she ordered him to appear before a judge. The judge then sentenced him to time in jail for failure to pay.

The ACLU, which has said that these types of for-profit probation operations disproportionately impact minorities,[139] filed a lawsuit against DeKalb County on behalf of Thompson, noting that "nearly all probationers jailed by the DeKalb County Recorder's Court for failure to pay are black." Less than two months later, a settlement was reached in the suit. Thompson was given a monetary payment of $70,000 for him and his attorney, and the Chief Judge for this court, Nelly Withers, agreed to a set of *affirmative policy changes* that all judges would abide by when hearing cases.

Those changes included an agreement to have all judges retain a bench card, which essentially amounted to a list of instructions. These instructions included the following guiding principles: judges would inform indigent defendants of the right to counsel and waive the $50 fee normally charged for public defenders if the defendant cannot pay it. Further, the court agreed to indigency hearings before a person is sent to jail for a failure to pay; in the context of these hearings, a defendant's ability to pay a fine (or to acquire resources to do so) is to be formally addressed, along with the "adequacy of alternatives to incarceration," before a person is sent to jail.[140]

Corporal Punishment

At the time the Eighth Amendment was framed, corporal punishment (mainly flogging) was commonly imposed for a range of crimes, including many misdemeanors. By the twentieth century, corporal punishment had been replaced by fines and incarceration. However, paddling was still being practiced in public schools across the country. By the 1970s, a growing movement sought to ban paddling in public schools, and in the mid-1970s, the Supreme Court was asked to declare paddling a form of cruel and unusual punishment. By a single vote, the Court declined to do so. In *Ingraham v. Wright* (1977),[141] the Supreme Court held that the Cruel and Unusual Punishments Clause does not apply to the administration of corporal punishment in public schools. Indeed, finding that school officials use of *paddling* to hit students did not amount to an Eighth Amendment violation, the Court held that the Clause applies only within the criminal justice context, saying, "The prisoner and the school child stand in wholly different circumstances," adding, "The school child has little need for the protection of the Eighth Amendment." Since that decision was released, though, a majority of states have enacted laws outlawing corporal punishment in schools.

CORPORAL PUNISHMENT: A physical penalty meted out in response to a crime or, perhaps, bad behavior in a school setting; an example would be a person being beaten with a paddle.

Mandatory Sentences and Mass Incarceration

Based on data from 2015, the most-recent global prison census indicated that more than 25% of the world's prison population was in the United States. The United States led all countries in terms of total number of prisoners, with over 2.2 million, coming in second in number of prisoners per 100,000 people, with 698—trailing only the Seychelles, an archipelago nation off the eastern coast of Africa.[142] According to the Prison Policy Initiative, "The American criminal justice system holds almost 2.3 million people in 1,833 state prisons, 110 federal prisons, 1,772 juvenile correctional facilities, 3,134 local jails, 218 immigration detention facilities, and 80 Indian Country jails as well as in military prisons, civil commitment centers, state psychiatric hospitals, and prisons in the U.S. territories."[143]

In an article for the Prison Policy Initiative, Emily Widra found that in December 2020, despite some releases related to COVID, states were, on average, at 75% or higher in prison occupancy—and the federal prisons were operating at more than 100% capacity. Maine was the only state under 50% capacity.[144] (We discuss overcrowding and COVID-19 next chapter.)

The dollar cost of mass incarceration is staggering. According to the U.S. Bureau of Prisons, operating the nation's prison system costs taxpayers at least $80 billion per year. Of course, there are additional costs borne by the families of incarcerated persons, most notably the loss of income prisoners might otherwise generate. Other burdens include travel costs associated with visitation, exorbitant fees for phone calls and emails to and from prisoners, and funds provided to inmates to cover personal care items and foods beyond those provided by the prison.[145]

THE CONSTITUTION IN ACTION
Do Private Prisons Contribute to Mass Incarceration?

Privately-run prisons—those that are not overseen by the government with the use of taxpayer revenue—housed approximately 116,000 inmates in the U.S. in 2019.[146] That figure represents only about 8% of the total U.S. prison population, so little evidence suggests that such prisons are driving mass incarceration; in fact, the use of private prisons has declined nationwide by 16% since 2012.[147]

In 2019, privately-run, for-profit facilities were in use in thirty-one states. Montana had the highest percentage of any state in terms of prisoners housed in private facilities, at 47%. Texas, which has been using private prisons longer than any state (since 1985), had the largest number of prisoners in private facilities, at more than 12,000.[148]

Federal use of private facilities and companies include prisons, halfway houses, and home confinement monitoring services, all of which had more than 27,000 individuals under their watch in 2019.[149] But in 2021, President Biden issued an executive order[150] indicating that all existing contracts between the federal government and private prison companies would not be renewed after they expire; an exception was made for immigration detention facilities.[151] Notably, as of 2022, more than 81% of undocumented immigrants detained by the federal government are in private facilities.[152]

Although a traditional narrative suggests that private prisons drive up incarceration rates because profit is tied to having inmates inside the facilities, in a 2020 article for the *Arizona State Law Journal*, author John Pfaff disputes these claims by pointing out that government-run prisons do a fine job of keeping incarceration rates high on their own; specifically, he said, "Public prisons, like private prisons, have strong incentives to keep prison populations high. And public prisons, like private prisons, do not have strong incentives to focus on programming and treatment. The two institutions are not identical, and in some situations, the specific differences—per diem payments, say, versus annualized wage bills—will make a difference. But by and large, the distinctions are much more of form than function."[153]

Thus, an overarching point from Pfaff suggested that although many private prisons charge government entities for *empty beds* that fall below *occupancy minimums*, this type of issue stems from poorly written contracts government bodies create with private prisons. He implied that wording those contracts to create different incentives, such as reducing recidivism, could lead to better outcomes.[154] Beyond that, improving services like inmate educational programs, work training, provision of government-issued identification cards, and more could also prove to be beneficial.

(continued)

A 2018 report in *The New York Times* discussing drivers of the use of private prisons cited the lobbying of politicians, with the authors speaking of two major companies that provide private prison services: "Much of the industry's power, critics say, is linked to campaign donations. GEO Group and CoreCivic have given nearly $9 million over the past fifteen years to state candidates and parties across the United States, ... according to the National Institute on Money in State Politics."[155]

Regarding the overall effectiveness of private prisons, the Brennan Center invoked a 2014 report from *The Public Interest* to suggest private prisons "fail to save states money."[156] A 2016 study from Brookings also declared, "Private prisons do not currently offer a clear advantage of their public-sector counterparts in terms of cost or quality" but that study noted the difficulty of drawing comparisons across different correctional institutions that house different types of offenders (violent, nonviolent, healthy, unhealthy, etc.).[157] More specifically, a 2016 report from the Office of the Inspector General in the Department of Justice indicated that disciplinary issues and assaults (involving both inmates on inmates and officials on inmates) were more likely to occur in private prisons than in government-run prisons.[158] However, Pfaff pointed out that this DOJ research does not represent the only study to address these topics, adding that an assessment of other literature indicates "studies fail to paint any sort of clear picture," calling results "muddy" and saying they "seem to suggest, more than anything else, that there's little clear difference between the two types of prisons."[159]

MANDATORY MINIMUM SENTENCES: A criminal punishment, or enhancement to a punishment, defined through an act of the state legislature and which provides no discretion for judges to deviate from the prescribed penalties that appear in the law; classic examples relate to punishments established based on the weight of contraband involved in a drug crime or punishments tied to using a gun in the commission of a crime.

MASS INCARCERATION: A term used to describe a society that imprisons an inordinately high number of individuals—often nonviolent offenders—perhaps, from certain socioeconomic demographics.

Mandatory Minimum Sentences

During the 1980s, Congress enacted a series of laws requiring mandatory minimum prison sentences for defendants convicted of various federal crimes, including drug and firearms offenses. Many states did likewise. Mandatory minimum sentences have been controversial ever since, especially as they have been linked to overcrowding of prisons and mass incarceration, which can be defined as a high percentage of incarceration within a population—this may be especially noticeable among certain racial, age, or socioeconomic demographics.

Notably, according to a spring 2021 report, more than half a million of the people in the U.S. prison population are incarcerated for a drug-related offense, which are the types of crimes most likely to be subject to mandatory minimums.[160] At the federal level, mandatory minimums for drug offenses were created by the Anti-Drug Abuse Act of 1986 and the Anti-Drug Abuse Act of 1988.[161] These laws limited the discretion of judges in doling out sentences for crimes, instead tying minimum sentences to the weight of drugs involved in possession or distribution offenses. For instance, under federal law, a ten-year mandatory minimum (with a maximum sentence of life in prison) applies to the following: 50 grams or more of meth, 1 kilogram of more of heroin, 5 kilograms or more of cocaine, 280 grams or more of crack cocaine, 100 kilograms or more of marijuana (or 1,000 or more plants), or 10 grams or more of LSD. There are also twenty-year mandatory minimums for operating a premises for drug manufacturing or distribution (put into law by a bill known as the *crack house statute*) and a twenty-year mandatory minimum for being a "drug kingpin," which is defined as the leader of an organization of five more individuals who "engage in a continuing series of drug violations [producing] substantial income."[162]

At the state level, New York was the first to create mandatory minimum drug laws, doing so in 1973 with passage of so-called *Rockefeller laws*, named after the governor at the time, Nelson Rockefeller. Michigan and Florida followed with their own versions in the 1970s. Although the Florida laws remain in effect, New York and Michigan repealed these minimum sentencing laws in the early 2000s. In 2008, Robert Perry, the New York state senator who was the original sponsor of the nation's first mandatory minimum drug law, observed the following:

> The Rockefeller Drug Laws have failed to achieve their goals. Instead they have handcuffed our judges, filled our prisons to dangerously overcrowded conditions, and denied sufficient drug treatment alternatives to nonviolent addicted offenders who need help.[163]

Along these lines, Greg Newburn and Sal Nuzzo offered a 2019 study for the James Madison Institute, finding mandatory minimums have failed to curtail drug trafficking as well as noting that the repeal of such laws where they once existed had not led to an increase in violent crimes; overall, they suggested that what such laws succeed in doing is driving up prison populations.[164]

In assessing this issue from a social justice perspective, a 2014 study published in the *Journal of Political Economy*[165] examined over 35,000 federal criminal cases between FY 2006 and FY 2008.[166] The study found that when prosecutors decide to charge mandatory minimums, "*ceteris paribus*, black men have 1.75 times the odds of facing such charges, which is equivalent to a 5 percentage point (or 65%) increase in the probability for the average defendant." The authors also stated, "The initial mandatory minimum charging decision alone is capable of explaining more than half of the black–white sentence disparities not otherwise explained by precharge characteristics."[167] The authors did observe the overall conviction rate to be the same for Black and White defendants but when isolated to mandatory minimum cases, the conviction rate was 4.5% for White defendants versus 7.5% for Black defendants.[168] Approximately 11.4% of all cases resulted in a mandatory minimum charge.[169]

The Crack Cocaine Discrepancy

One area in which mandatory minimums have appeared to be particularly unjust is sentences given for possession of crack cocaine, which is a crystallized version of cocaine that can be created by mixing powdered cocaine with baking soda and then heating the resultant mixture. Under the Anti-Drug Abuse Act of 1986, possession of 50 grams of crack cocaine (the typical weight of a candy bar) would yield a mandatory ten-year prison sentence; conversely, to receive the same ten-year sentence for possessing cocaine in a pure, powdered form, a person would need to be found with 5,000 grams (which would be enough to fill a typical suitcase). Additionally, possession of 5 grams of crack cocaine connected to five-year minimum, whereas 500 grams of pure cocaine were needed for a similar sentence. This became known as the 100-to-1 rule. Federal mandatory minimums even considered the entire weight of confiscated material, which would include any baking soda.[170] The Fair Sentencing Act of 2010 addressed the **crack cocaine discrepancy** and shifted the weight parameters such that the ratio difference from crack cocaine to powdered cocaine became approximately eighteen-to-one. However, that shift was not made retroactive to previous cases until 2018, when the First Step Act of 2018 required retroactive application to pre-2010 crack cocaine sentences.[171] In 2019, based on the First Step Act, the

Justice Department decided to release more than 3,000 inmates who had been serving time for pre-2010 crack cocaine convictions.[172]

A 2021 majority opinion in *Terry v. United States*,[173] written by Justice Thomas, explained the legislative history underpinning the sentencing disparity for crack cocaine as follows:

> In the mid-1980s, the United States witnessed a steep surge in the use of crack cocaine, and news of high-profile, cocaine-related deaths permeated the media. Witnesses before Congress, and Members of Congress themselves, believed that a "crack epidemic" was also fueling a crime wave. Crack, they said, was far more addictive and dangerous that powder cocaine; it was cheaper and thus easier to obtain; and these and other factors spurred violent crime.

In the *Terry* decision, though, a unanimous Supreme Court ruled against a man who was serving a lengthy prison sentence of 188 months after a 2008 conviction for possessing four grams of crack cocaine. He had pleaded guilty to this offense in exchange for two gun charges being dropped, and his sentence was not tied into a mandatory minimum. His lawyers claimed he should be entitled to resentencing under the First Step Act, but the Court disagreed, with the majority opinion stating that the Fair Sentencing Act of 2010 and the First Step Act of 2018 both addressed mandatory minimum sentences only.

The ACLU argued, on behalf of Terry, that "only those convicted of possessing large amounts of crack cocaine would get the benefit of retroactive resentencing, while those convicted of small amounts would not. That perverse result rests on a misreading of the text of the statute [the Fair Sentencing Act] and frustrates its ameliorative purpose."[174] In the majority opinion, however, Justice Thomas said that applying these laws to situations not addressed in their text would require the Court to "convert nouns to adjectives and vice versa," adding, "In light of the clear text, we hold that ... the Fair Sentencing Act modified the statutory penalties only for ... offenses that triggered mandatory-minimum penalties."

Other Mandatory Minimum Reforms

As a result of the Violent Crime Control and Law Enforcement Act of 1994,[175] judges have some discretion regarding when to apply a mandatory minimum sentence. Under this law, a defendant can be eligible for a *safety valve*, which gives a judge the ability to offer a sentence below a mandatory minimum, if each of five specified criteria are demonstrated by the defense by a preponderance of the evidence (as addressed during a sentencing hearing). These five factors are as follows: a limited criminal history, which is defined as being below a certain threshold of criminal history *points* assigned to prior offenses;[176] not having used violence in their drug crime; not having committed a crime resulting in death; being a *limited actor*, as opposed to a leader; and providing information and assistance to law enforcement, as possible. The First Step Act of 2018 expanded *safety valves to* maritime cases and raised the number of criminal history *points* someone could have while still remaining eligible for relief under the first factor.

In *Harmelin v. Michigan* (1991),[177] the Supreme Court confronted a case in which a man convicted of possessing 672 grams of cocaine was sentenced to life in prison without the possibility of parole under Michigan's mandatory sentencing scheme. Upholding the sentence, the Court could not reach a majority on the question of whether the Cruel and Unusual Punishments Clause requires proportionality in sentencing—a departure from prior cases on this topic. Speaking for a plurality on this question, Justice Antonin Scalia objected to judges being allowed to second-guess legislative judgments with respect to criminal penalties:

> The real function of a constitutional proportionality principle, if it exists, is to enable judges to evaluate a penalty that *some* assemblage of men and women *has* considered proportionate—and to say that it is not. For that real-world enterprise, the standards seem so inadequate that the proportionality principle becomes an invitation to imposition of subjective values.

We will revisit additional Supreme Court decisions on the concept of *proportionality* in sentencing later in this chapter, particularly regarding *three strikes* laws for repeat offenders.

THE CONSTITUTION IN ACTION

Florida Man in *Cocaine Island* Venture Avoids Mandatory Minimum Sentence

In 2012, in the U.S. District Court for the Middle District of Florida, a man named Rodney Hyden was found guilty of "attempting to possess with the intent to distribute 5 kilograms or more of cocaine." This crime carried a mandatory minimum sentence of ten years in federal prison, but the judge in this case opted to invoke a *safety valve* and, instead, issued a sentence carrying a mere sixty days of incarceration. That decision was tied into Rodney, a father of two who owned his own construction company in Gainesville, not having any previous criminal record—as well as the unique circumstances of his first foray into becoming a drug trafficker.

Rodney's saga was featured in a 2018 Netflix documentary called *The Legend of Cocaine Island* as well as in a *GQ Magazine* story called "The Great Cocaine Treasure Hunt." Although some details remain unverified, Rodney's pathway toward drug trafficking seemed to begin when he overheard a man named Julian Harris tell a campfire story about a bale of cocaine, wrapped in plastic, that unexpectedly washed up near a beach in Puerto Rico over a decade earlier. Julian claimed he had pulled the bale off the shoreline and buried it in the sand on a piece of property he and his wife shared in Puerto Rico. But even though Julian estimated the street value of the cocaine to be around $2 million, he left it behind when he separated from his wife and moved to Florida, meaning the drugs had been entombed in the sand for more than fifteen years. Rodney, whose construction business had suffered during the recession of 2008, sought out more information, and after speaking to Julian further, he felt he had isolated the location of this "buried treasure."

Next, with the help of some other people, Rodney made two unsuccessful trips to Puerto Rico—with the treasure hunt scuttled by the lack of an appropriate shovel (and strength) to break through calcified sand as well as the presence of a U.S. Army building that was near the dig site. Moreover, unknown to Rodney, one member of his team

(continued)

had previously been arrested for possession of 130 oxycodone pills after getting pulled over in Alachua County, Florida. That man faced a mandatory minimum sentence of fifteen years in prison. To curry favor with law enforcement officials in the hope of making a deal for a lesser charge, this man agreed to provide information about other crimes; it was he who initially prodded Rodney to pursue the recovery of the cocaine, and this informant even introduced Rodney to a federal undercover agent named Ryan McEnany, who was employed by Homeland Security Investigations (a division of U.S. Immigration and Customs Enforcement). Agent McEnany worked with a Florida deputy sheriff named Joe Rawley on bringing other undercover agents into the operation, and the group convinced Rodney that if the map of the location were to be turned over to them, their crew could retrieve the cocaine and give it to Rodney, minus a fee for their efforts. Rodney's lawyer would later describe one of these undercover agents, who posed as a drug trafficking kingpin, as "Hollywood good."

Ultimately, Rodney agreed to this plan and revealed the location of the drugs. Local law enforcement agents in Puerto Rico apparently dug up the cocaine where it was marked on the *treasure map*, but it turned out to be degraded from being buried, and only 2.2 kilos tested positive as cocaine. Still, the undercover agents in the United States put together a duffel bag of 18 kilos material, some of it cocaine, in keeping with the amount Rodney expected. Agents then sent pictures of those bags to Rodney, implying they had successfully retrieved the drugs from Puerto Rico. Rodney was told he could pick up the cocaine from the trunk of a vehicle in the parking lot of a Gander Mountain store in St. Augustine, Florida. Rodney did, in fact, appear at that location, and in an otherwise empty parking lot, he took possession of the duffel bag containing cocaine. He was arrested by federal agents seconds later.

The formal charge against him was one of *attempt*, since Rodney had not actually distributed any cocaine, but a mandatory minimum sentence still could have been applicable. His defense attorney claimed he had been the victim of police entrapment, but he was found guilty by a jury. As previously noted, the judge used a safety valve to give him a sixty-day sentence, which Rodney served in a medium-security prison in Georgia. The sentence also included 20 hours per week of community service for five years, which he completed by building houses for Habitat for Humanity, putting his construction skills to use—while avoiding a mandatory minimum of ten-years' incarceration.[178]

Mandatory Minimums in Gun Crime Cases

The federal Armed Career Criminal Act of 1984 (ACCA)[179] requires a minimum sentence of fifteen years in prison for persons convicted of being a convicted felon in possession of a firearm if that defendant has three or more prior convictions for "violent felony" offenses or "serious drug offenses." In *Johnson v. United States* (2015),[180] the Supreme Court struck down this provision of the ACCA on vagueness grounds (but the Court has never found the statute void under the Cruel and Unusual Punishment Clause). In the majority opinion in this case, Justice Scalia found that the phrase "crime of violence" was unconstitutionally vague in violation of due process principles.

Further analysis of this law arrived in *Wooden v. United States* (2022),[181] where the Court unanimously overturned a mandatory minimum sentence under the ACCA. In this matter, the defendant was found guilty of being a felon in possession of a firearm. Seventeen years earlier, he had burglarized ten storage units in the same facility. In seeking punishment for the firearms conviction, prosecutors treated these offenses as ten prior *occasions*, which resulted in a fifteen-year minimum sentence under the ACCA based on the presence of multiple prior offenses. However, Justice Elena Kagan's opinion for the Court concluded that Wooden's "one-after-another-after-another burglary of ten units in a single storage facility occurred on one 'occasion,' under a natural construction of that term and consistent with the reason it became part of ACCA." Accordingly, application of the mandatory minimum was deemed inconsistent with the statute's construction.

Part of the ACCA also defines mandatory minimum sentences for possession or use of a firearm in drug trafficking.[182] The penalties for having a gun during the commission of a drug crime are as follows: five years for carrying, seven years for brandishing, and ten years for discharging. The type of weapon possessed is also relevant, with mandatory minimums applicable as follows: ten years for a short-barreled rifle or shotgun and a semi-automatic weapon and 30 years for a machine gun, destructive device (e.g., a bomb), or silencer. In *Smith v. United States* (1993),[183] the Supreme Court upheld application of the machine-gun mandatory minimum to a man who traded a machine gun for briefcase full of cocaine, with the majority opinion from Justice O'Connor applying a *Webster's Dictionary* definition of the word *use* to indicate the accused had *used* a machine gun in the commission of a drug crime.

This law also has a twenty-five-year mandatory minimum for a repeat violation of the statute, but the First Step Act of 2018 curtailed application of that provision, so two violations of the law occurring at the same time will not trigger a mandatory minimum; one conviction must precede the other, thereby eliminating a tactic known as *stacking*.[184] Nonetheless, a mandatory minimum gun charge is likely to be added onto any other crimes committed at the same time, such that an underlying drug offense and a gun offense would result in separate charges.

In 2018, the U.S. Sentencing Commission issued a report about mandatory gun sentencing. It showed that federal prosecutors charged at least two offenses (e.g., a gun crime and a drug crime) in more than 85% of convictions related to these laws; plea bargains made up the 15% of cases in which a single charge of only the gun enhancement was applied.[185] This report also indicated that approximately 16.8% of all mandatory minimum sentences in 2016 were for gun crimes, and roughly 30.8% of all firearms offenses included a mandatory minimum sentence. The average sentence for a case involving a mandatory minimum gun crime was 136 months for a single violation of the law and 327 months for multiple violations (e.g., for brandishing and using a semi-automatic, which could trigger two statutory clauses).[186] The report also stated, "In Fiscal Year 2016, Black offenders were convicted of a firearms offense carrying a mandatory minimum and subject to that penalty more often than any other racial group [approximately 53%]. Hispanic offenders comprised the next largest group [approximately 29%]."[187]

Three Strikes *Laws*

Another form of mandatory minimum sentencing can be found in laws that require long prison terms, including life imprisonment, for persons with prior felony convictions. In *Ewing v. California* (2003),[188] the Supreme Court upheld California's *Three Strikes and You're Out* law, which mandated an **indeterminate sentence** of twenty-five years to

INDETERMINATE SENTENCE: A criminal punishment that carries no specified ending.

life for persons convicted of a felony after two prior convictions for "serious" or "violent" felonies. The case involved a repeat offender who was sentenced to twenty-five years to life after he was convicted of stealing a set of expensive golf clubs. Upholding Ewing's sentence, the Court split 5–4 but was unable to produce a majority opinion. Justice O'Connor's plurality opinion said the law "reflects a rational legislative judgment, entitled to deference, that offenders who have committed serious or violent felonies and who continue to commit felonies must be incapacitated." O'Connor recognized an Eighth Amendment prohibition against *grossly disproportionate* sentences but found that Ewing's sentence did not qualify as such. Justice Scalia concurred in the judgment but continued to insist there is no proportionality requirement with respect to noncapital offenses. The dissenters disagreed on both counts. Noting that "Ewing's sentence is, at a minimum, 2 to 3 times the length of sentences that other jurisdictions would impose in similar circumstances," Justice Breyer concluded it was grossly disproportionate to his offense and, therefore, invalid under the Eighth Amendment.

However, previously, in *Solem v. Helm* (1984),[189] the Supreme Court found a habitual offender law inapplicable to a South Dakota man who was found guilty of writing a $100 check from a fictitious account; the maximum penalty for the offense was five years in prison, but because this was the defendant's seventh felony conviction, the state applied a habitual offender statute and sentenced him to life in prison without the possibility of parole. Mr. Helm's prior offenses were all nonviolent charges related to theft, burglary, and DUI. Overturning this sentence, the Court observed, "The final clause [of the Eighth Amendment] prohibits not only barbaric punishments, but also sentences that are disproportionate to the crime committed."

Justice Powell's majority opinion in *Solem* provided factors for courts to consider when assessing proportionality, with Powell also noting this list was not meant to be read as "exhaustive": "In sum, a court's proportionality analysis under the Eighth Amendment should be guided by objective criteria, including (i) the gravity of the offense and the harshness of the penalty; (ii) the sentences imposed on other criminals in the same jurisdiction; and (iii) the sentences imposed for commission of the same crime in other jurisdictions."

Earlier in this chapter, though, we mentioned that *Harmelin v. Michigan* (1991) seemed to call into question if proportionality could rightfully be addressed under the Eighth Amendment. Some clarity on this topic was achieved with the Court's ruling *Lockyer v. Andrade* (2003).[190] Decided the same day as *Ewing v. California*, this case involved a man named

HABITUAL OFFENDER LAW: A criminal punishment through which a repeat offender, generally a person with three or more convictions for violent felonies, is given an enhanced penalty that goes beyond the maximum penalty for the most recently-charged offense; life in prison is a possibility under some laws of the type.

Leandro Andrade, who was given a three strikes penalty for stealing fewer than ten children's movie video-tapes from two K-Mart stores. The Supreme Court upheld this sentence, differentiating the matter from *Solem v. Helm* by saying Mr. Andrade had a chance at parole through this twenty-five-to-life sentence, whereas Mr. Helm did not have that opportunity, given his life-without-parole sentence. The Court in *Lockyer v. Andrade* seemed to acknowledge the lack of clarity in precedent on this topic by saying the "gross disproportionality principle, the precise contours of which are unclear, [is] applicable only in the 'exceedingly rare' and 'extreme' case." Hence, the rule emanating from this case is that a proportionality analysis could, in theory, occur under the Eighth Amendment, but such analysis is to be used sparingly, in extreme cases—like in the life-with-out-parole sentence for a $100 bad check in *Solem* but apparently not for the twenty-five-to-life sentence for stealing videotapes.

Mandatory Punishments for Sex Offenders

Federal law also provides for mandatory minimum sentencing for certain sex abuse offenses, and an example appears in the following box. Punishment for sex offenders also includes a requirement to place their names in a searchable sex offender registry. The federal Sex Offender Notification and Registration Act of 2006 (SORNA)[191] defines a "sex offender" as a person who was convicted of an offense "that has an element involving a sexual act or sexual contact with another"; there are other ways to be classified as a sex offender, including for violations of laws that deal with sex trafficking and prostitution offenses involving minors.[192] An offender meeting any criterion under this law has three days after their sentencing to register in any state in which they reside, work, or attend school; moving to a new state necessitates an updated registration entry as well. Registration includes the offender providing their name, address, and other identifying information.

In *Gundy v. United States* (2019),[193] the Supreme Court upheld a directive of Attorney General Alberto Gonzales, released as an interim rule in February 2007, requiring registration for offenses committed prior to passage of SORNA in 2006. The Supreme Court sustained this directive, as discussed in chapter 3.

In another case that involved the sentencing of sex offenders, *Packingham v. North Carolina* (2017),[194] the Supreme Court addressed a North Carolina law that barred sex offenders from visiting social media sites that allow minors to have accounts. A unanimous Court found that this law violated the First Amendment. Even so, it is not uncommon for sex offenders to have limited internet access while incarcerated. We discuss this topic more in chapter 4, which covers freedom of speech.

JURISPRUDENCE

How a Comma Changed the Application of a Mandatory Minimum
Lockhart v. United States, 577 U.S. 347 (2016)

Punctuation marks in laws can be crucial, as evident in the Supreme Court's decision in *Lockhart v. United States* (2016). In this case, Lockhart was found guilty in federal district court on charges related to posses-sion of child pornography. According to federal law, for such an offense, a mandatory minimum sentence of ten years would apply if he had a prior conviction for the following: "aggravated sexual abuse, sexual abuse, or abusive sexual conduct involving a minor or ward."[195] The word "or" in this statute indicates that a previous conviction for any one of the three listed offenses would yield a mandatory ten-year prison sentence.

In Lockhart's case, he did in fact have a prior con-viction for sexual abuse, but it involved his 53-year-old

(*continued*)

girlfriend. Potential application of the mandatory minimum, thus, turned on whether the phrase "involving a minor or ward" applied to all three offenses in the list—or just to the last one in the list. Congress devised these sentencing parameters for cases involving possession of child pornography, so one might infer that "minor or ward" should apply to all three listed crimes. But at the trial court, Lockhart was given the ten-year mandatory minimum sentence, despite his prior offense being against a 53-year-old woman. He appealed this punishment to the Supreme Court.

In a 7–2 ruling, the Court upheld the ten-year sentence, rejecting Lockhart's argument that the phrase "involving a minor or ward" should apply to all three offenses listed in the statute. Justice Sotomayor's majority opinion instead found that Lockhart's conviction involving his girlfriend triggered the mandatory minimum, even though she was 53 years old and, therefore, not a minor or ward.

The majority opinion determined that the "involving a minor or ward" clause only modified the third crime listed—"abusive sexual conduct"—but not the other two crimes: aggravated sexual abuse and sexual abuse. Accordingly, Lockhart's conviction for a crime against a 53-year-old woman qualified as sexual abuse, meaning there did not need to be any consideration of whether the woman was a minor or a ward. Yet if his crime had been abusive sexual conduct, that would have had to be against a minor or ward to invoke the ten-year sentence.

Look once again at the statute, which spoke of these three crimes in a list: "aggravated sexual abuse, sexual abuse, or abusive sexual conduct involving a minor or ward." The Court's conclusion was based on the presence of a comma before the word "or," with the comma acting almost like a barrier that isolated "involving a minor or ward" from the first two crimes in the list. This type of comma is typically called an *Oxford*, or *serial*, comma, which is a term referring to a comma that comes before the last item in a list. If the Oxford comma were not included, the law would say the following: "aggravated sexual abuse, sexual abuse or abusive sexual conduct involving a minor or ward." If that were the case, then the phrase "involving a minor or ward" likely would have applied to the second crime in the list, "sexual abuse," since the barrier would no longer be present—and as a result, Lockhart's prior conviction for sexual abuse against a 53-year-old woman would not have required the mandatory minimum because she was not a minor or ward.

In a dissenting opinion, Justice Kagan expressed her disagreement with the majority by focusing on the intent of the law (stopping offenses involving child pornography) as well as the general meaning of a sentence that carries an Oxford comma. For context, she offered the following example: "Imagine a friend told you that she hoped to meet 'an actor, director, or producer involved with the new *Star Wars* movie.' You would know immediately that she wanted to meet an actor from the *Star Wars* cast—not an actor in, for example, the latest *Zoolander*."

Civil Commitment of Dangerous Offenders Who Have Completed Their Prison Terms

In *United States v. Comstock* (2010),[196] the Supreme Court upheld a federal statute that allows federal district courts to order the civil commitment of mentally ill, sexually dangerous prisoners beyond the date they are due to be released from prison. Speaking through Justice Breyer, the Court upheld the statute as an expression of Congress's implied powers. In previous cases, the Court upheld similar laws at the state level.[197]

Hate Crimes Enhancements

As of 2021, forty-seven states and the District of Columbia have hate-crime enhancement laws in place—while Arkansas, South Carolina, and Wyoming do not. These types of laws normally apply to crimes of violence and serve to increase the punishment if a victim

HATE-CRIME ENHANCEMENT:
An additional penalty added to a crime, such as assault, because the offense was motivated by bias against an individual belonging to a specific demographic group.

is attacked on the basis of specified characteristics, such as race, sex, gender, or sexual orientation (as listed in the law). In 1993, the Supreme Court upheld a Wisconsin hate crime law by rejecting a First Amendment freedom of speech challenge brought by a man convicted of a hate crime for making comments about the victim's race during an assault.[198] Additionally, it is important to reiterate that, as noted in chapter 12, the Supreme Court has found that any factor used to enhance a sentence, besides criminal history, must be proven to a jury; this includes a hate-crime enhancement.[199]

At the federal level, Congress has defined a hate crime as an offense motivated by "actual or perceived race, color, religion, or national origin of any person." This definition is provided in the Violent Crime Control and Law Enforcement Act of 1994.[200] Moreover, the Matthew Sheppard and James Byrd Jr. Hate Crimes Prevention Act of 2009 added "gender, gender identity, sexual orientation, or disability" to the list of "protected classes"; it also eliminated any need for a crime victim to be taking part in a federally-protected activity for a federal hate crime to be applicable.[201] The men for whom this law is named were murder victims attacked for reasons of bias. Matthew Sheppard was a homosexual man who was beaten to death after being tied to a fence in Wyoming, and James Byrd was a Black man in Texas who was chained to a pickup truck and dragged to his death.

Consecutive and Concurrent Sentencing

When multiple charges lead to convictions at the same time, a trial judge typically has discretion when determining whether to add the sentencing for all offenses together—a process known as consecutive sentencing. The opposite of this is known as concurrent sentencing, whereby sentences for different crimes are essentially served at the same time. For instance, if a person were to be found guilty of burglary and arson, with each crime resulting in a ten-year prison sentence, a judge could use consecutive sentencing to create a twenty-year prison term or could instead determine that both sentences run concurrently, meaning there would be an actual sentence of ten years in prison. States may provide parameters regarding when consecutive sentencing is appropriate, such as for repeat offenders. But with overcrowding a paramount concern in many prisons, concurrent sentencing has become something of a norm, possibly even in situations when state and federal charges are brought at the same time.[202]

The Supreme Court has never addressed the applicability of the Eighth Amendment to the imposition of consecutive sentences, but

CONSECUTIVE SENTENCING: Refers to the decision to add together the number of years of incarceration in two or more criminal convictions, requiring an offender to serve the combined total; for example, two consecutive sentences of five years would require ten years of service in prison.

CONCURRENT SENTENCING: Refers to the decision to have the number of years of incarceration related to two or more criminal convictions served simultaneously; for example, two concurrent sentences of five years would both be completed after five years in prison.

in 2013, the Sixth Circuit's decision in *United States v. Nikolovski*[203] remanded a case for resentencing after a federal district court judge in Michigan sentenced a defendant to 120 months for bank fraud and 96 months for money laundering. The sentences were ordered to run consecutively for a total of 216 months of incarceration. Yet the per curiam opinion from the Sixth Circuit questioned if this might have been a mistake—a sign of how rare consecutive sentencing can be. The Sixth Circuit ordered a remand and resentence, offering an odd hypothesis regarding no explanation for a consecutive sentence being given by the trial court:

> The only phrase that communicates the intent to vary upward yet more with a consecutive sentence is the single word "consecutively." This gives us pause. Common sense and experience tells us that the words "concurrently" and "consecutively," which are used in the same context, start with the same three letters, and have the same number of syllables, could easily be confused. A slip of the tongue or a mistake in reporting could have distorted the district court's intent, and there are no other clues in the transcript that would lead us to conclude with more confidence that the district court actually intended to impose consecutive sentences. The consequences of a potential mistake are large in this case, as the word "consecutively" increased Nikolovski's sentence to fully twice the top of the Guidelines range.

Again, the appellate court's concern for the lack of any explanation for why consecutive sentences were chosen seems to speak to sentencing norms that embrace concurrent sentencing in most jurisdictions today.

100% Service and Parole

At the federal level, parole was abolished in 1987. However, the First Step Act of 2018 allows federal inmates to accrue up to fifty-four days of good-time credit per year, which can be used to end a prison term early. Beyond that, under this law, *earned-time credit* is made available for certain federal inmates who take part in education or work training programs.[204] At the state level, judges often have discretion, at sentencing, to require 100% service of a prison term—but that is generally reserved for repeat offenders. If 100% service is not mandated by statute or by a judge, a defendant likely will become eligible for parole at some point

GOOD-TIME CREDIT: A reduction in a convicted criminal's period of incarceration based on good behavior while in prison.

100% SERVICE: A requirement for a convicted criminal to serve the entirety of their prison sentence, without any chance of early release through parole.

PAROLE: Early release from prison, typically based on a decision made by majority vote of a group of people known as a parole board, who oversee a hearing regarding a convict's suitability for being released.

before serving the complete duration of a sentence. A parole board votes at scheduled intervals in a prisoner's sentence to determine whether early release in the form of parole should be granted as well as to outline what conditions should be attached to parole (e.g., not traveling outside of the state, drug testing, or avoiding certain individuals with criminal ties). In some areas of the country where prison overcrowding is a significant concern, parole might be granted as soon as 30% of a sentence is complete, particularly for first-time or nonviolent offenders. Conversely, some states, such as Tennessee, recently have passed *Truth-in-Sentencing* bills that require 100% service for certain violent offenses.[205]

Life Sentences for Juvenile Offenders

In *Roper v. Simmons* (2005),[206] a case we will discuss next chapter, the Supreme Court halted application of the death penalty to those who were under the age of 18 at the time they committed their crimes. Since that decision, a line of four cases has applied the Eighth Amendment to other sentences for juvenile offenders.

In *Graham v. Florida* (2010),[207] the high Court ruled that giving a minor a sentence of life without parole for a nonhomicide offense amounted to a violation of the Cruel and Unusual Punishment Clause. The majority opinion in this case spoke of "a global consensus against the sentencing practice in question," observing that only the United States allowed for this type of punishment for nonhomicidal offenses. At the time of this decision, thirty-seven states allowed for such a sentence, with 123 individuals incarcerated under these parameters, seventy-seven of which were in Florida with the other forty-six spread across ten states. Requiring the overturn of such sentences, Justice Kennedy's majority opinion spoke of "special difficulties encountered by counsel in juvenile representation," including that juveniles "mistrust adults and have limited understandings of the criminal justice system and the roles of the institutional actors within it ... [and] are less likely than adults to work effectively with their lawyers to aid in their defense." The majority also pointed to juveniles having "[d]ifficulty in weighing long-term consequences; a corresponding impulsiveness; and reluctance to trust defense counsel." The conclusion from Justice Kennedy was that these factors "all can lead to poor decisions by one charged with a juvenile offense."

Two years later, in *Miller v. Alabama* (2012),[208] the Supreme Court extended the *Graham* decision by applying it to juvenile homicide offenders, finding that a mandatory sentence of life without parole for these offenders violated the Eighth Amendment. In this case, Justice Kagan's majority opinion said that "children are constitutionally different from adults for purposes of sentencing," adding a citation to *Graham* in concluding that "[b]ecause juveniles have diminished culpability and greater prospects for reform ... 'they are less deserving of the most severe punishments.'" Citing to *Roper v. Simmons*, Justice Kagan highlighted three issues juveniles often must overcome: 1) a "'lack of maturity and an underdeveloped sense of responsibility,' lead[ing] to recklessness, impulsivity, and heedless risk-taking"; 2) they "'are more vulnerable ... to negative influences and outside pressures,' including from their family and peers," partly because "they have limited 'contro[l] over their own environment' and lack the ability to extricate themselves from horrific, crime-producing settings"; and 3) a juvenile's "character is not as 'well formed' as an adult's; [his] traits are 'less fixed' and his actions less likely to be 'evidence of irretrievabl[e] deprav[ity].'" With these factors considered together, the Court suggested that "youth matters" when assessing the proportionality of a sentence. This case did not, however, eliminate all chances of a life sentence without parole for a juvenile. That sentence can still be given, but the key is that it cannot be a mandatory sentence defined by a legislative body; rather, it must come from a judge's assessment of relevant sentencing criteria.

Subsequently, in *Montgomery v. Louisiana* (2016),[209] the Supreme Court considered whether *Miller v. Alabama* should be made retroactive to all prior juvenile offenders who were given mandatory life-without-parole sentences. In the *Montgomery* case, the petitioner, Henry Montgomery, was 17 years old when he killed a sheriff's deputy sheriff named Charles Hurt in Baton Rouge, Louisiana, in 1963. Montgomery was given a mandatory life-without-parole sentence—but the potential for a reprieve arrived with the Supreme Court's *Miller* decision in 2012. Writing for the Court four years later in *Montgomery v. Louisiana*, Justice Kennedy made it clear that the *Miller* decision should in fact apply retroactively, observing the following:

> In light of what this Court has said in *Roper, Graham*, and *Miller* about how children are constitutionally different from adults in their level of culpability, ... prisoners like Montgomery must be given the opportunity to show their crime did not reflect irreparable corruption; and, if it did not, their hope for some years of life outside prison walls must be restored.

This decision did not automatically set such individuals free but, rather, required those inmates previously given a mandatory life-without-parole sentence to be afforded a resentencing hearing—where a judge still could consider the possibility of life without parole, but at least such a sentence would not have been applied in mandatory fashion, automatically given after conviction. In the matter at hand, Montgomery was resentenced to life with the possibility of parole. The Louisiana Board of Pardons and Committee on Parole then denied parole in 2018 and 2019, but a unanimous vote in November 2021 led to Montgomery's release after having served fifty-seven years in state prison.[210]

More recently, in *Jones v. Mississippi* (2021),[211] the Supreme Court made it clear that during a sentencing hearing for a juvenile homicide offender, a judge still has discretion to give a sentence of life without parole, even without a factual showing of "permanent incorrigibility." In this case, Brett Jones killed his grandfather after an argument in Shannon, Mississippi in 2004, stabbing him to death with a kitchen knife. Jones was given a mandatory life sentence with no chance of parole. After the *Miller* decision, his lawyers requested a resentencing hearing, which was granted—but at that hearing, the judge determined that life without parole was still the appropriate punishment. On appeal, Jones's lawyers contended there needed to be a showing of "permanent incorrigibility" in that sentencing hearing to justify this sentence for a juvenile offender. However, by a 5–4 vote, the Supreme Court disagreed, with Justice Kavanaugh's majority opinion citing the *Miller* decision, observing the judge simply needed to "follow a certain process—considering an offender's youth and attendant characteristics—before imposing a life without parole sentence." No rigid rule for demonstrating permanent incorrigibility needed to apply. In sum, the Court upheld the notion of a "discretionary sentencing system," in which a judge could apply factors they deemed relevant. Justice Kavanaugh said this approach was both "necessary" and "sufficient" for preserving constitutional safeguards.

Nevertheless, the majority opinion also observed, "Time and again, the Court has recognized that children are constitutionally different from adults for purposes of sentencing. ... Juvenile offenders 'cannot with reliability be classified among the worst offenders....'" That quote cited the Court's 2005 decision in *Roper v. Simmons*, which we will discuss in the next chapter as we confront the most severe punishment of them all: the death penalty—a punishment courts have attempted to limit to society's most culpable offenders.

Conclusion

In this chapter, we have examined important criminal procedure protections related to the Eighth Amendment—provisions that can be especially important for defendants hailing from lower socioeconomic strata. For example, an inability to pay bail could lead to an innocent person spending time in jail as they await trial. Along these lines, we noted that many states are moving toward some form of bail reform, with computer algorithms being used to perform risk assessments regarding a defendant's likelihood of appearing in court or likelihood of reoffending. It remains to be seen if these methods will provide equitable outcomes.

This chapter also included discussion of civil asset forfeiture, a process through which law enforcement officials can seize private property simply by forging a connection between that property and illegal action—even if the property's owner is not charged with a crime. Some states have taken steps to abolish or limit this practice, but in much of the country, property can be seized based on the low legal standard of preponderance of the evidence, with the property's owner then bearing the burden of demonstrating their items (or money) were legally acquired. Through a program known as equitable sharing, the federal government and state governments can even share in the proceeds of civil forfeiture seizures. Once again, those who lack the resources to defend their property in court may be at a disadvantage in these cases, although the Supreme Court's incorporation of the Excessive Fines Clause, in a 2019 case involving civil forfeiture, provides some hope for a constitutional remedy in such matters.

Additionally, we have spent time in this chapter addressing the Eighth Amendment protection against cruel and unusual punishment. We have discussed the modern Supreme Court's interpretation of the Clause in light of evolving standards of decency. In this regard, we noted that the Court has prohibited the imposition of punishment merely for one's status, holding instead that punishment can only be applied when there is a specific criminal act.

We also assessed the concept of debtors' prisons, which is a term applied to situations in which people are incarcerated (or have their probation revoked) because they cannot afford to make restitution or to pay court fees or fines. Although the Supreme Court has found the general notion of debtors' prisons incompatible with the Eighth Amendment, an exception lies in the possibility for a judge to incarcerate a person for willfully refusing to make required payments.

With prison overcrowding continuing to plague the United States, which houses approximately 25% of the world's prison population, judicial assessments of mandatory minimum sentences have taken on paramount importance. Mandatory minimums—which proliferated during the 1980s and are most commonly tied to drug and gun offenses—restrict a judge's discretion in doling out a sentence to a guilty party, forcing deference to legislative decrees of which sentence should apply. One area in which mandatory minimums have seemed particularly unjust is sentences for crack cocaine possession, which between 1986 and 2010 were linked to mandatory prison terms that would only apply to powdered cocaine quantities that were 100 times greater. Equally controversial are habitual offender laws, which can ascribe lengthy sentences to crimes that individually would not carry such steep penalties. Even so, reforms in the use of mandatory minimum sentences have gradually become available, such as through passage of the First Step Act of 2018. For those defendants with limited criminal histories, a safety valve can preclude the application of harsh sentences.

Yet for those with prior criminal histories, lengthier terms of incarceration can stem not only from mandatory minimums but also through concepts such as consecutive sentencing, 100% (no-parole) service, and even the specter of civil commitment (which is most often used for repeat sex offenders). A key lies in linking harsh penalties with the most culpable and most dangerous of criminals—which, as noted in this chapter, helps to explain why the Supreme Court has placed limits on mandatory life sentences for juvenile offenders.

Ultimately, recidivism remains a problem for many criminal offenders—and protecting society from the ill effects of repeated criminal activity is certainly a compelling objective; balancing that pursuit against principles of proportionality and applying harsh sentences to the most culpable offenders lies at the core of Eighth Amendment jurisprudence. In the next chapter, we turn to the application of Eighth Amendment protections to the most serious of all punishments: the death penalty—as well as to the conditions in which prisoners are confined.

Discussion Questions

1. What problems are inherent in the process of asking accused criminals to post cash as a prerequisite for release prior to trial? In what ways can this be a positive thing? Are there certain individuals in society who are more likely to be treated unjustly under such a system? Since some states have turned to computer algorithms to play a part in this process, what would be the appropriate role (if any) for the use of such algorithms? Should algorithms supplement the work of judges in setting cash bail amounts, replace the work of judges, or be used a part of a hybrid approach? What does the preferred method look like in practice?

2. Consider that civil asset forfeiture generally proceeds through two phases: the seizure, often based on a preponderance of evidence that an item is connected to illegal activity, and a property owner's attempt to get the property back, often through a court hearing in which the burden rests on the property owner. What changes can be made to make this process more equitable? You may wish to look to states where reform has already been enacted when formulating your response. In what ways does civil asset forfeiture help society at large? What evidence is there to support the notion that this procedure is not serving law enforcement officials' needs in civil asset forfeiture? What evidence shows it is still effective in achieving some law enforcement objectives?

3. Besides capital punishment, what are some types of punishments that have been deemed cruel and unusual by the Supreme Court? Is there any evidence to suggest such punishments are more likely to befall those who lack financial resources? Is there anything odd about the Supreme Court using evolving standards of decency as the guiding test for evaluating the meaning of this clause in the Eighth Amendment? What has the Court said is definitely not cruel and unusual punishment?

4. In what ways have mandatory minimum sentences contributed to the U.S. prison population being what it is today? Besides those sentences, what other factors have led to this burgeoning population? How did the COVID-19 pandemic impact prison populations? What can be done to reduce prison populations while maintaining the overall safety of society at large? What negative consequences might ensue following proposed reforms discussed in this chapter?

Endnotes

1   Statute of Westminster the First of 1275, 3 Edw. 1, ch. 12.

2   Judiciary Act of 1789, 1 Stat. 91 § 33 (1789).

3   *Hudson v. Parker*, 156 U.S. 277 (1895).

4   *United States v. Motlow*, 10 F.2d 657 (7th Cir. 1926).

5   *Stack v. Boyle*, 342 U.S. 1 (1951).

6   *Schilb v. Kuebel*, 404 U.S. 357 (1971).

7   18 U.S.C. § 3142(c)(2).

8   Daphne Congcong Zhang, *Lax Washington Oversight of Bounty Hunters Sets Stage For Mayhem, Tragedy*, The Seattle Times, Jan. 11, 2019, https://www.seattletimes.com/seattle-news/times-watchdog/high-adrenaline-bounty-hunter-industry-operates-with-little-oversight-despite-concerns-over-training-tactics/.

9   *Id.*

10 *Taylor v. Taintor*, 83 U.S. 366 (1872).

11 *Ex parte Robert Durst*, Petitioner, Nos. 14-03-01421-CR, 14-03-01423-CR, 14-04-00194-CR (Tex. App. Jun. 1, 2004).

12 *See* Robert McFadden, *Robert Durst, Real Estate Scion Convicted as a Killer, Dies at 78*, N.Y. Times, Jan. 10, 2022, https://www.nytimes.com/2022/01/10/obituaries/robert-durst-dead.html; Paul Valentine, *Robert Durst, Heir to New York Real Estate Fortune and Convicted Murderer, Dies at 78*, Wash. Post, Jan. 10, 2022, https://www.washingtonpost.com/local/obituaries/robert-durst-dead/2022/01/10/1b432e52-dfdd-11e9-be96-6adb81821e90_story.html; Lianne Hart, *Durst's $3 Billion Bail Ruled Excessive*, L.A. Times, June 3, 2004, https://www.latimes.com/archives/la-xpm-2004-jun-03-na-durst3-story.html.

13 *United States v. Salerno*, 481 U.S. 739 (1987).

14 Bail Reform Act of 1984, Pub. L. 98-473, 98 Stat. 1837, 18 U.S.C. §§ 3141-3150, 3156.

15 Leon Digard, *Justice Denied: The Harmful and Lasting Effects of Pretrial Detention*, Vera Institute of Justice, Vera Evidence Brief, Apr. 2019, https://www.vera.org/downloads/publications/Justice-Denied-Evidence-Brief.pdf.

16 Cynthia Jones, *Decision Points: Disproportionate Pretrial Detention of Blacks and Latinos Drives Mass Incarceration*, HuffPost, Nov. 11, 2015, https://www.huffpost.com/entry/pretrial-detention-blacks-and-latinos_b_8537602.

17 *Id.* (citing Todd Minton & Zhen Zeng, *Jail Inmates at Midyear, 2014*, Bureau of Justice Statistics, June 2015, https://bjs.ojp.gov/library/publications/jail-inmates-midyear-2014); *see* Equal Justice Initiative, *Disproportionate Pretrial Detention of People of Color Drives Mass Incarceration*, Dec. 17, 2015, https://eji.org/news/people-of-color-disproportionately-detained-pretrial/.

18 Wendy Sawyer, *How Race Impacts Who is Detained Pretrial*, Prison Policy Initiative, Oct. 9, 2019, https://www.prison-policy.org/blog/2019/10/09/pretrial_race/.

19 *Johnson v. Arteaga-Martinez*, 596 U.S. ___ (2022), found that bail hearings were not required under the Immigration and Nationality Act, as codified at 9 U.S.C. § 1231(a); an earlier decision in *Jennings v. Rodriguez*, 596 U.S. ___ (2018) indicated that this law did not require bail hearings in immigration cases of illegal entry to the United States or cases involving deportation for criminal offenses. The 2022 decision expanded this idea to all detention of noncitizens, even in situations where detention exceeds six months. A separate decision in *Johnson v. Guzman Chavez*, 594 U.S. ___ (2021) had found bail hearings inapplicable to those who had been deported and then returned to the U.S. to seek asylum based on a fear of persecution or torture in their country of origin.

20   *See* Advancing Pretrial Policy & Research, *How the PSA Works* (Northpointe, which is a company that produced a widely-used algorithm called COMPAS, had 137 data points involved in its assessment.) https://advancingpretrial.org/psa/factors/.

21   *In re Humphrey*, 11 Cal.5th 135 (Cal. 2021).

22   Maria Cramer, *Illinois Becomes First State to Eliminate Cash Bail*, N.Y. Times, Feb. 23, 2021, https://www.nytimes.com/2021/02/23/us/illinois-cash-bail-pritzker.html.

23   Devin Kelly, *Alaska Courts Are Now Using a Computer Algorithm in Bail Decisions*, Anchorage Daily News, Jan. 7, 2018, https://www.adn.com/alaska-news/crime-courts/2018/01/07/alaska-courts-are-now-using-a-computer-algorithm-in-bail-decisions/.

24   Terry Schuster, *Alaska's Criminal Justice Reforms: A Brief from the Pew Charitable Trusts*, Pew, Dec. 2016, https://www.pewtrusts.org/~/media/assets/2016/12/alaskas_criminal_justice_reforms.pdf.

25   Beatrix Lockwood & Annaliese Griffin, *The System: The State of Bail Reform*, The Marshall Project (updated Oct. 30, 2020), https://www.themarshallproject.org/2020/10/30/the-state-of-bail-reform.

26   Pretrial Services Agency of the District of Columbia, *Outcomes for Last Four Years*, https://www.psa.gov/?q=node/558; *see* Beatrix Lockwood & Annaliese Griffin, *The System: The State of Bail Reform*, The Marshall Project (updated Oct. 30, 2020), https://www.themarshallproject.org/2020/10/30/the-state-of-bail-reform.

27   Anita Hassan, *New Mexico Eliminated Cash Bail—But Now One County Locks up More People Without Bond Before Trial*, NBC News, Dec. 8, 2020 (citing Jenna Dole, Kristine Denman, Joel Robinson, Graham White, & Ashleigh Maus, *Bail Reform: Baseline Measures*, New Mexico Statistical Analysis Center, Oct. 2019, http://isr.unm.edu/reports/2019/bail-reform-baseline-measures.pdf), https://www.nbcnews.com/news/us-news/new-mexico-eliminated-cash-bail-now-one-county-locks-more-n1250257.

28   Wilborn P. Nobles III, *Atlanta City Council Votes to Form Group to Review Bail Laws*, Atl. J. Const., Apr. 22, 2021, https://www.ajc.com/news/atlanta-news/atlanta-city-council-votes-to-form-group-to-review-bail-laws/54L75BFIYBANDAUCCE7BDI2DAY/.

29   Safia Samee Ali, *Did Illinois Get Bail Reform Right? Criminal Justice Advocates Are Optimistic*, NBC News, Feb. 15, 2021, https://www.nbcnews.com/news/us-news/did-illinois-get-bail-reform-right-criminal-justice-advocates-are-n1257431.

30   Andrew Schneider & Paul Debenedetto, *The Bail Bond Industry Hopes a Recent Court Ruling Kills Harris County's Reforms. Supporters Don't See That Happening*, Houston Public Media, Jan. 17, 2022, https://www.houstonpublicmedia.org/articles/news/criminal-justice/2022/01/17/417173/a-federal-appeals-court-ruling-may-endanger-harris-countys-misdemeanor-bail-reform-settlement/.

31   Andrew Schneider, *Harris County Democrats Block Proposal to Void Recent Bail Reforms*, Houston Public Media, Jan 24, 2022 (citing Duke University, *Monitoring Pretrial Reform in Harris County: Second Report of the Court-Appointed Monitor* (2021), https://sites.law.duke.edu/odonnellmonitor/wp-content/uploads/sites/26/2021/03/ODonnell-Monitor-Second-Report-v.-31.pdf), https://www.houstonpublicmedia.org/articles/news/criminal-justice/2022/01/24/417612/harris-county-commissioners-weigh-proposal-to-void-recent-bail-reforms/.

32   The Bail Project, https://bailproject.org.

33   Ryan Van Velzer, *Ky. Bill Would Limit When Groups Can Bail People out of Jail*, 89.3 WFPL, Feb. 23, 2022, https://wfpl.org/ky-bill-would-limit-when-groups-can-bail-people-out-of-jail/.

34   *Caliste v. Cantrell*, 937 F.3d 525 (5th Cir. 2019).

35   *Tumey v. Ohio*, 273 U.S. 510 (1927).

36   Julia Angwin, Jeff Larson, Surya Mattu, & Lauren Kirchner, *Machine Bias*, ProPublica, May 23, 2016, https://www.propublica.org/article/machine-bias-risk-assessments-in-criminal-sentencing.

37   Jeff Larson, Surya Mattu, Lauren Kirchner, & Julid Angwin, *How We Analyzed the COMPAS Recidivism Algorithm*, ProPublica, May 23, 2016, https://www.propublica.org/article/how-we-analyzed-the-compas-recidivism-algorithm.

38   Angwin, et al., *supra* note 36.

39   Sam Corbett-Davies, Emma Pierson, Avi Feller, & Sharad Goel, *A Computer Program Used for Bail and Sentencing Decisions Was Labeled Biased Against Blacks. It's Actually Not That Clear*, Wash. Post, Oct. 17, 2016, https://www.washingtonpost.com/news/monkey-cage/wp/2016/10/17/can-an-algorithm-be-racist-our-analysis-is-more-cautious-than-propublicas/.

40   *Id.*

41   Julia Angwin & Jeff Larson, *Bias in Criminal Risk Scores is Mathematically Inevitable, Researchers Say*, ProPublica Dec. 30, 2016, https://www.propublica.org/article/bias-in-criminal-risk-scores-is-mathematically-inevitable-researchers-say.

42   Tom Simonite, *Algorithms Were Supposed to Fix the Bail System. They Haven't*, Wired, Feb. 19, 2020, https://www.wired.com/story/algorithms-supposed-fix-bail-system-they-havent/.

43   Alex Albright, *If You Give a Judge a Risk Score: Evidence from Kentucky Bail Decisions*, Sept. 3, 2019, The Little Dataset, https://thelittledataset.com/about_files/albright_judge_score.pdf.

44   Ashley Spalding, *New Data Helps Pave the Way for Bail Reform in Kentucky*, Kentucky Center for Economic Policy, Jan. 21, 2021, https://kypolicy.org/new-data-helps-pave-way-for-bail-reform-in-kentucky/.

45   *Schall v. Martin*, 467 U.S. 253 (1984).

46   *Fields v. Henry County*, 701 F.3d 180 (6th Cir. 2012).

47   *Kingsley v. Hendrickson*, 576 U.S. 389 (2015).

48   *Graham v. Connor*, 490 U.S. 386 (1989).

49   For cases challenging conditions of confinement for pretrial detainees, the Second Circuit has used the objective reasonableness standard; *see Darnell v. Pineiro*, 849 F.3d 17, 32-35 (2d Cir. 2017). But the Eleventh Circuit has used a subjective standard for such cases; *see De Veloz v. Miami-Dade County*, 756 F. App'x 869, 877 (11th Cir. 2018).

50   For cases challenging inadequate medical care for pretrial detainees, the Seventh Circuit has used the objective reasonableness standard; *see Miranda v. County of Lake*, 900 F.3d 335, 352 (7th Cir. 2018). But the Eighth Circuit has used a subjective standard for such cases; *see Whitney v. County of St. Louis*, 887 F.3d 857, 860 (8th Cir. 2018).

51   For cases raising a claim prison officials failed to protect a pretrial detainee from harm, the Ninth Circuit has used the objective reasonableness standard; *see Castro v. County of Los Angeles*, 833 F. 3d 1060, 1069-71 (9th Cir. 2016). But the Fifth Circuit has used a subjective standard for such cases; *see Leal v. Wiles*, 734 F. App'x 905, 910-912 (5th Cir. 2018).

52   *Bell v. Wolfish*, 441 U.S. 520, 561 (1979).

53   *Greenwood v. United States*, 350 U.S. 366 (1956).

54   18 U.S.C. § 4246.

55   W. Blackstone, Commentaries on the Laws of England 372 (1769).

56   *Timbs v. Indiana*, 586 U.S. ___ (2019).

57   *Austin v. United States*, 509 U.S. 602 (1993).

58   *Id.* (citing *Browning-Ferris Industries v. Kelco Disposal*, 492 U.S. 257, 265 (1989)).

59   *See* Navigation Act of 1660; Act of July 31, 1789, ch. 5, § 12, 1 Stat. 39 (from the first Congress); *see Boyd v. United States*, 116 U.S. 616 (1886) (for further discussion of these origins); *Austin v. United States*, 509 U.S. 602 (1993).

60   Organized Crime Control Act of 1970, Pub. L. 91-452, 84 Stat. 922–3.

61   18 U.S.C. § 983(c).

62   18 U.S.C. § 983 (d)(1).

63   18 U.S.C. § 983(b).

64   Institute for Justice, *Civil Forfeiture Reforms on the State Level*, https://ij.org/legislative-advocacy/civil-forfeiture-legislative-highlights; *see* Anne Teigen, & Lucia Bragg, *Evolving Civil Asset Forfeiture Laws*, 26 NCSL, Feb. 2018, https://www.ncsl.org/research/civil-and-criminal-justice/evolving-civil-asset-forfeiture-laws.aspx.

65   Lisa Knepper, Jennifer McDonald, Kathy Sanchez, & Elyse Pohl, *Policing for Profit: The Abuse of Civil Asset Forfeiture* (3rd ed.), Institute for Justice, Dec. 14, 2020, 35–36, https://ij.org/report/policing-for-profit-3/; *see* J. Justin Wilson, *New Report Find Civil Forfeiture Rakes in Billions Each Year, Does Not Fight Crime*, Institute for Justice, Dec. 15, 2020, https://ij.org/press-release/new-report-finds-civil-forfeiture-rakes-in-billions-each-year-does-not-fight-crime-2/.

66   Anne Teigen & Lucia Bragg, *Evolving Civil Asset Forfeiture Laws*, 26 NCSL, Feb. 2018, https://www.ncsl.org/research/civil-and-criminal-justice/evolving-civil-asset-forfeiture-laws.aspx.

67   *Liu v. Securities and Exchange Commission*, 591 U.S. ___ (2020).

68   FBI, *Seizing Crime Proceeds and Compensating Victims: Forfeiture as an Effective Law Enforcement Tool*, FBI.gov, Jan. 17, 2017, https://www.fbi.gov/news/stories/forfeiture-as-an-effective-law-enforcement-tool.

69   Policing for Profit, *supra* note 65 ("In 2018, agencies in 13 states with expenditure data spent almost no proceeds on victims and just 9% on community programs on average.").

70   Joe Davidson, *Police Seize Property Without Charges and Pocket the Proceeds. There's a Bipartisan Move to Crack Down*, Wash. Post, Dec. 10, 2021, https://www.washingtonpost.com/politics/2021/12/10/civil-asset-forfeiture-police-raskin-mace-congress/.

71   U.S. Department of Justice, *Attorney General Prohibits Federal Agency Adoptions of Assets Seized by State and Local Law Enforcement Agencies Except Where Needed to Protect Public Safety*, Jan. 16, 2015, https://www.justice.gov/opa/pr/attorney-general-prohibits-federal-agency-adoptions-assets-seized-state-and-local-law.

72   Christopher Ingraham, *The Feds Have Resumed a Controversial Program That Lets Cops Take Stuff and Keep It*, Wash. Post, Mar. 26, 2016, https://www.washingtonpost.com/news/wonk/wp/2016/03/28/the-feds-have-resumed-a-controversial-program-that-lets-cops-take-stuff-and-keep-it/.

73   U.S. Department of Justice, *Attorney General Sessions Issues Policy and Guidelines on Federal Adoptions of Assets Seized by State or Local Law Enforcement*, July 19, 2017, https://www.justice.gov/opa/pr/attorney-general-sessions-issues-policy-and-guidelines-federal-adoptions-assets-seized-state.

74   Policing for Profit, *supra* note 65.

75   Michael Sallah, Robert O'Harrow, Jr., Steven Rich, & Gabe Silverman, *Stop and Seize: Aggressive Police Take Hundreds of Millions of Dollars from Motorists Not Charged with Crimes*, Wash. Post, Sept. 6, 2014, https://www.washingtonpost.com/sf/investigative/2014/09/06/stop-and-seize/?itid=lk_inline_manual_32.

76   Lisa Knepper, Jennifer McDonald, Kathy Sanchez, & Elyse Pohl, *Policing for Profit: The Abuse of Civil Asset Forfeiture* 5 (3rd ed. 2020), https://ij.org/report/policing-for-profit-3/; *see* J. Justin Wilson, *New Report Find Civil Forfeiture Rakes in Billions Each Year, Does Not Fight Crime*, Institute for Justice, Dec. 15, 2020, https://ij.org/press-release/new-report-finds-civil-forfeiture-rakes-in-billions-each-year-does-not-fight-crime-2/.

77   Sallah, et al., *supra* note 75.

78   Policing for Profit, *supra* note 65.

79   Sallah, et al., *supra* note 75.

80   Sean Nicholson-Crotty, Jill Nicholson-Crotty, Danyao Li, & Sian Mughan, *Race, Representation, and Assets Forfeiture*, 24 International Public Management Journal 47–66 (2021).

81 Aallyah Wright, *Federal Loophole Thwarts State Efforts to Curb Civil Asset Forfeiture by Police*, USA Today, Aug. 19, 2021, https://www.usatoday.com/story/news/nation/2021/08/19/states-work-scale-back-civil-forfeiture-laws-amid-federal-loophole/8181774002/.

82 Sallah et al., *supra* note 75.

83 *Leonard v. Texas*, 580 U.S. ___ (2017) (Thomas, J., dissenting).

84 Policing for Profit, *supra* note 65.

85 U.S. Dept. of Homeland Security, S&T's Prepaid Card Reader Aids Law Enforcement in Seizing Fraudulent Cards, Aug. 31, 2015, https://www.dhs.gov/science-and-technology/prepaid-card-reader-aids-seizing-fraudulent-cards

86 Mark H. Kim, *Device Lets Police Seize Digital Cash, Raises Civil Liberties Concerns*, NPR, July 2, 2016, https://www.npr.org/sections/alltechconsidered/2016/07/02/483394735/device-lets-police-seize-digital-cash-raises-civil-liberties-concerns.

87 Clifton Adcock, *New Front in Civil Forfeiture: Authorities Get Devices to Seize Funds Loaded to Prepaid Cards*, Oklahoma Watch, June 7, 2016, updated Oct. 28, 2019, https://oklahomawatch.org/2016/06/07/new-front-in-civil-forfeiture-okla-authorities-get-devices-to-seize-funds-loaded-onto-prepaid-cards/.

88 Kim, *supra* note 86.

89 *United States v. De L'Isle*, 825 F.3d 426 (8th Cir. 2016).

90 *United States v. Monsanto*, 491 U.S. 600 (1989).

91 *Caplin & Drysdale, Chartered v. United States*, 491 U.S. 617 (1989).

92 21 U.S.C. § 853.

93 *Caplin & Drysdale*, *supra* note 91 (citing *United States v. Badalamenti*, 614 F. Supp. 194, 196 (S.D.N.Y. 1985)).

94 *Luis v. United States*, 578 U.S. ___ (2018).

95 *Liu v. Securities and Exchange Commission*, 591 U.S. ___ (2020).

96 15 U.S.C. § 78u(d)(5).

97 The case name is *United States v. "The Wolf of Wall Street" Motion Picture, Including Any Rights to Profits, Royalties, and Distribution Proceeds*. No. CV 16-16-5362 (C.D. Cal. 2016).

98 Jordan Belfort, *The Wolf of Wall Street* (2006) (Belfort's memoir).

99 *See* Christian Barker, *New Charge for Jho Low, As 1MDB Scandal Becomes TV Series*, Forbes, June 17, 2021, https://www.forbes.com/sites/christianbarker/2021/06/17/new-charge-for-jho-low-as-1mdb-scandal-becomes-tv-series/?sh=792138f35744.

100 Alex Ritman, *U.S. Returns Seized 'Wolf of Wall Street' Millions to Malaysia*, The Hollywood Reporter, May 7, 2019, https://www.hollywoodreporter.com/business/business-news/us-returns-seized-wolf-wall-street-millions-malaysia-1208292/.

101 Travis Clark, *Leonardo Dicaprio Had to Return Marlon Brando's Oscar, and the Financier Who Gave it to Him as a Birthday Present Is Now Reportedly a Fugitive on the Run*, Business Insider, Dec. 12, 2018, https://www.businessinsider.com/why-leonardo-dicaprio-returned-oscar-given-to-him-by-jho-low-2018-12.

102 Tom Wright & Bradley Hope, Billion Dollar Whale (2018).

103 Kim, *supra* note 86.

104 Policing for Profit, *supra* note 65.

105 *United States v. $1,074,900.00 in U.S. Currency*, 932 F.Supp.2d 1053 (D. Neb. 2013); *see* Louis Hochman, *Judge: Give Stripper Back $1 Million Cash Seized After Traffic Stop*, NJ.com, July 24, 2013, updated Jan. 17, 2019, https://www.nj.com/morris/2013/07/judge_returns_1_million_to_stripper_says_theres_no_proof_its_connected_to_drugs.html.

106 *Id.* (citing *Muhammed v. Drug Enforcement Agency*, 92 F.3d 648 (8th Cir. 1996)).

107 *Bennis v. Michigan*, 516 U.S. 442, 460 n.1 (1996) (Stevens, J., dissenting).

108 *United States v. Approximately 64,695 Pounds of Shark Fins*, 520 F.3d 976 (9th Cir. 2008).

109 Shark Finning Prohibition Act of 2000, Pub. L. 106–557, 114 Stat. 2772, 16 U.S.C. § 1857.

110 *United States v. Article Consisting of 50,000 Carboard Boxes More or Less, Each Containing One Pair of Clacker Balls*, 413 F. Supp. 1281 (D. Wisc. 1976).

111 15 U.S.C. § 1261.

112 16 C.F.R. § 1500.18(a).

113 *One 1958 Plymouth Sedan v. Pennsylvania*, 380 U.S. 693 (1965).

114 *Boyd v. United States*, 116 U.S. 616 (1886).

115 *South Dakota v. Fifteen Impounded Cats*, 785 N.W.2d 272 (S.D. 2010).

116 *Wilkerson v. Utah*, 99 U.S. 130 (1878).

117 *Weems v. United States*, 217 U.S. 349 (1910).

118 *Trop v. Dulles*, 356 U.S. 86 (1958).

119 *Robinson v. California*, 370 U.S 660 (1962).

120 *Gagnon v. Scarpelli*, 411 U.S. 778 (1973).

121 *See* Christopher D. Hampson, *The New American Debtors' Prisons*, 44 American Journal of Criminal Law 1–48 (2016) (for further reading about this era; a key federal law discussed therein was passed in 1839 as 5 Stat. 321, and it made it clear individuals should not be imprisoned for debt in states where such practice was banned. The author also offers a discussion of 1800s federal laws relevant to the Bankruptcy Clause of Article I, Section 8 (Clause 4) in the U.S. Constitution; such laws often included protections related to debtors' prisons.).

122 Editorial Staff, *Guilty and Charged: State-by-State Court Fees*, NPR, May 19, 2014, https://www.npr.org/2014/05/19/312455680/state-by-state-court-fees; *see* Joseph Shapiro, *As Court Fees Rise, The Poor Are Paying the Price*, NPR, May 19, 2014, https://www.npr.org/2014/05/19/312158516/increasing-court-fees-punish-the-poor.

123 Shapiro, *supra* note 122.

124 *Williams v. Illinois*, 399 U.S. 235 (1970).

125 *Tate v. Short*, 401 U.S. 395 (1971).

126 *Bearden v. Georgia*, 461 U.S. 660 (1983).

127 Joseph Shapiro, *Supreme Court Ruling Not Enough to Prevent Debtors Prisons*, NPR, May 21, 2014, https://www.npr.org/2014/05/21/313118629/supreme-court-ruling-not-enough-to-prevent-debtors-prisons.

128 *Id.*

129 *See* Shapiro, *supra* note 122 (This article quotes one court administrator in Michigan as saying, "The only reason that the court is in operation and doing business at that point in time is because that defendant has come in and is a user of those services. They don't necessarily see themselves as a customer because, obviously, they're not choosing to be there. But in reality they are."), https://www.npr.org/2014/05/19/312158516/increasing-court-fees-punish-the-poor.

130 Alan Sherter, *As Economy Flails, Debtors' Prisons Thrive*, CBS News, Apr. 5, 2013, https://www.cbsnews.com/news/as-economy-flails-debtors-prisons-thrive/.

131 Matthew Menendez, Lauren-Brooke Eisen, Noah Atchison, & Michael Crowley, *The Steep Cost of Criminal Justice Fees and Fines*, Brennan Center for Justice, Brennan Center, Nov. 21, 2019, https://www.brennancenter.org/our-work/research-reports/steep-costs-criminal-justice-fees-and-fines.

132 Alicia Bannon, Rebekah Diller, & Mitali Nagrecha, *Criminal Justice Debt: A Barrier to Reentry*, Brennan Center for Justice, Oct. 4, 2010, https://www.brennancenter.org/our-work/research-reports/criminal-justice-debt-barrier-reentry.

133 *Robinson v. Long*, No. 18-6121 (6th Cir. May. 20, 2020).

134 Harvard Law Review, *State Bans on Debtors' Prisons and Criminal Justice Debt*, 129 Harv. L. Rev. (2016).

135 *Cain v. White*, 937 F.3d 446 (5th Cir. 2019).

136 *Tumey v. Ohio*, 273 U.S. 510, 532-534.

137 *Caperton v. A.T. Massey Coal Co.*, 556 U.S. 868 (2009) (The Fifth Circuit also cited to the following cases related to judicial conflicts of interest: *In re Murchison*, 349 U.S. 133 (1955); *Ward v. Village of Monroeville, Ohio*, 409 U.S. 57 (1972); *Aetna Life Ins. Co. v. Lavoie*, 475 U.S. 813, 821 (1986)).

138 Jessica Pishko, *Locked Up for Being Poor: How Private Debt Collectors Contribute to a Cycle of Jail, Unemployment, and Poverty*, The Atlantic, Feb. 25, 2015, https://www.theatlantic.com/national/archive/2015/02/locked-up-for-being-poor/386069/.

139 American Civil Liberties Union, *In for a Penny: The Rise of America's New Debtors' Prisons*, Oct. 2010, https://www.aclu.org/files/assets/InForAPenny_web.pdf.

140 ACLU, *Settlement Agreement and Release of Claims* (the settlement Agreement for *Thompson v. Dekalb County*, negotiated through the United States District Court of the Northern District of Georgia, Atlanta Division), https://www.aclu.org/files/assets/thompson_v_dekalb_county_settlement_agreement_03182015.pdf.

141 *Ingraham v. Wright*, 430 U.S. 651 (1977).

142 Roy Walmsley, *World Prison Population List* (11th ed.), International Center for Prison Studies (2015), https://www.prisonstudies.org/sites/default/files/resources/downloads/world_prison_population_list_11th_edition_0.pdf.

143 Wendy Sawyer & Peter Wagner, *Mass Incarceration: The Whole Pie 2020*, Prison Policy Initiative, Mar. 24, 2020, https://www.prisonpolicy.org/reports/pie2020.html.

144 Emily Widra, *Since You Asked: Just How Overcrowded Were Prisons Before the Pandemic, and in This Time of Social Distancing, How Overcrowded Are They Now?* Prison Policy Initiative, Dec. 21, 2020, https://www.prisonpolicy.org/blog/2020/12/21/overcrowding/.

145 Beatrix Lockwood & Nicole Lewis, *The Hidden Cost of Incarceration*, The Marshall Project, Dec. 17, 2019, https://www.themarshallproject.org/2019/12/17/the-hidden-cost-of-incarceration.

146 Kevin Muhitch & Ghandnoosh Nazgol, *Private Prisons in the United States*, The Sentencing Project, Mar. 3, 2021 (citing E. Ann Carson, *Bureau of Justice Statistics, Prisoner's Series, 2000–2019*, National Prisoner Statistics (NPS) Program, Bureau of Justice Statistics, U.S. Department of Justice, https://bjs.ojp.gov/data-collection/national-prisoner-statistics-nps-program) https://www.sentencingproject.org/publications/private-prisons-united-states/.

147 *Id.*

148 *Id.*

149 *Id.*

150 Exec. Order 14006 (2021).

151 Lauren-Brooke Eisen, *Biden's Order to Eliminate DOJ Private Prison Contracts*, The Brennan Center, Aug. 27, 2021, https://www.brennancenter.org/our-work/research-reports/breaking-down-bidens-order-eliminate-doj-private-prison-contracts.

152 Muhitch and Nazgol, *supra* note 146.

153 John F. Pfaff, *The Incentives of Private Prisons*, 52 Ariz. St. L.J. 991 (2020).

154 *Id.* at 992–996.

155 Timothy Williams & Richard A. Oppel, Jr., *Escapes, Riots and Beatings. But States Can't Seem to Ditch Private Prisons*, N.Y. Times, Apr. 10, 2018, https://www.nytimes.com/2018/04/10/us/private-prisons-escapes-riots.html.

156 Julia Bowling, *Are Private Prisons Good Investments for States?* The Brennan Center, Apr. 15, 2014, https://www.brennan-center.org/our-work/analysis-opinion/are-private-prisons-good-investments-states.

157 Megan Mumford, Diane Whitmore Schanzenbach, & Ryan Nunn, *The Economics of Private Prisons*, 7 Brookings, Oct. 20, 2016, https://www.brookings.edu/research/the-economics-of-private-prisons/.

158 U.S. Department of Justice Office of Inspector General, *Review of the Federal Bureau of Prisons' Monitoring of Contract Prisons*, Aug. 2016, (The eight categories of conduct analyzed in this report were (1) contraband; (2) reports of incidents; (3) lockdowns; (4) inmate discipline; (5) telephone monitoring; (6) selected grievances; (7) urine drug testing; (8) sexual misconduct; in all but positive drug tests and sexual misconduct, private prisons had more of each category and also had higher rates of assault (both inmate and official to inmate).), https://oig.justice.gov/reports/2016/e1606.pdf.

159 Pfaff, *supra* note 153, at p. 1000.

160 Jacob Kang-Brown, Chase Montagnet, & Jasmine Heiss, *People in Jail and Prison in Spring 2021*, Vera Institute, June 2021, https://www.vera.org/downloads/publications/people-in-jail-and-prison-in-spring-2021.pdf.

161 Anti-Drug Abuse Act of 1986, Pub. L. 99-570, 100 Stat. 3207; Anti-Drug Abuse Act of 1988, Pub. L. 100-690, 102 Stat. 4181.

162 *See* Department of Justice, *Frequently Used Federal Drug Statutes* (For a list of mandatory minimum sentence parameters for drug offenses), https://www.justice.gov/usao-nh/frequently-used-federal-drug-statutes.

163 Greg Newburn & Sal Nuzzo, *Mandatory Minimums, Crime, and Drug Abuse: Lessons Learned and Paths Ahead*, Feb. 2019, (citing Testimony of Robert A. Perry, on behalf of The New York Civil Liberties Union, before the New York State Assembly Committees on Codes, Judiciary, Correction, Health, Alcoholism and Drug Abuse, and Social Services regarding The Rockefeller Drug Laws (May 8, 2008), https://www.nyclu.org/en/publications/rockefeller-drug-laws-cause-racial-disparities-huge-taxpayer-burden.) (New York started the process of repealing some mandatory minimums in 2004, with all repealed by 2009. Michigan repealed mandatory life sentences for trafficking more than 650 grams of heroin or cocaine in 1998 and all mandatory minimums in 2003.), https://www.jamesmadison.org/wp-content/uploads/2019/02/PolicyBrief_MandatoryMinimums_Feb2019_v04.pdf.

164 Newburn and Nuzzo, *supra* note 163.

165 M. Marit Rehavi & Sonja B. Starr, *Racial Disparities in Federal Criminal Sentences*, 122 Journal of Political Economy 1320–54 (2014), https://repository.law.umich.edu/articles/1414/.

166 Records were drawn from records of the U.S. Marshals Service, U.S. Sentencing Commission, federal prosecutors offices, and federal courts.

167 Rehavi and Starr, *supra* note 165, at 1323, 1327, 1336.

168 *Id.* at 1336.

169 *Id.* at 1345.

170 *See* Deborah Vagins & Jeselyn McCurdy, *Cracks in the System: 20 Years of the Unjust Federal Crack Cocaine Law*, ACLU (2006), https://www.aclu.org/other/cracks-system-20-years-unjust-federal-crack-cocaine-law.

171 First Step Act of 2018, Pub. L. 115–391, 132 Stat. 5194.

172 U.S. Department of Justice, Department of Justice Announces the Release of 3,100 Inmates Under First Step Act, Publishes Risk and Needs Assessment System, July 19, 2019, https://www.justice.gov/opa/pr/department-justice-announces-release-3100-inmates-under-first-step-act-publishes-risk-and.

173 *Terry v. United States*, 593 U.S. ___ (2021).

174 *Id.*

175 Violent Crime Control and Law Enforcement Act of 1994, Pub. L. 103–322, 108 Stat. 1796.

176 Under the federal *point system*, one point is given for a prior conviction with a sentence of less than sixty days; two points are given for prior convictions with a sentence between sixty days and thirteen months; three points are given for prior convictions resulting in a sentence greater than thirteen months. For a safety valve to apply under the

current standards, a defendant must have a point total of four or less, excluding one-point offenses. The defendant also must not have any single three-point offense or a *violent* two-point offense, and any offense resulting in death is disqualifying. A number of prior convictions do not count toward the safety valve point totals, including fifteen-year-old three-point convictions, ten-year old one- or two-point convictions; or five-year old one- or two-point convictions; juvenile adjudications; court-martial convictions; tribal convictions; expunged convictions; petty offenses or minor misdemeanors like hunting and fishing violations; juvenile truancy; gambling and prostitution offenses with less than thirty days imprisonment or probation of less than a year. The 1994 law set these standards, but the First Step Act of 2018 changed the first criteria from one point or less to four points or less and added a protection for maritime crimes.

177 *Harmelin v. Michigan*, 501 U.S. 957 (1991).

178 Daniel Riley, *The Great Cocaine Treasure Hunt*, GQ Magazine, Oct. 2, 2017, https://www.gq.com/story/the-great-co-caine-treasure-hunt?MBID=social_twitter; Jim Schoettler, *Federal sting involving treasure maps, buried cocaine leads to arrest in St. Augustine*, Jacksonville.com, Aug. 13, 2012, https://www.jacksonville.com/story/news/crime/2012/08/13/federal-sting-involving-treasure-maps-buried-cocaine-leads-arrest-st/15857706007/; U.S. Immigration and Customs Enforcement, Newsroom, *GQ Article Highlights ICE Involvement in Florida Cocaine Sting*, Apr. 7, 2015, https://www.ice.gov/news/releases/gq-article-highlights-ice-involvement-florida-cocaine-sting; *United States v. Hyden*, Case No. 3:12-cr-148-J-99TJC-JBT (M.D. Fla. Dec. 11, 2013).

179 18 U.S.C. § 924.

180 *Johnson v. United States*, 576 U.S. 591 (2015).

181 *Wooden v. United States*, 595 U.S. ____ (2022).

182 18 U.S.C. § 924(c).

183 *Smith v. United States*, 508 U.S. 223 (1993) (Although this case turned on what it meant to "use" a firearm "during and in relation to" a drug crime, the current law speaks only to possession of such a weapon during such a crime.).

184 The First Step Act eliminated *stacking* of sentences, which refers to a situation in which two violations of the law are charged at the same time to make a first-time offender become a repeat offender and, thus, subject to the twenty-five-year mandatory minimum.

185 United States Sentencing Commission, Federal Gun Mandatory Minimum Penalties, Report-at-a-Glance (2018), https://www.ussc.gov/sites/default/files/pdf/research-and-publications/backgrounders/RG-gun-mm.PDF; *see* Mandatory Minimum Penalties for Firearms Offenses in the Federal Criminal Justice System, (2018), https://www.ussc.gov/sites/default/files/pdf/research-and-publications/research-publications/2018/20180315_Firearms-Mand-Min.pdf.

186 United States Sentencing Commission, Federal Gun Mandatory Minimum Penalties, Report-at-a-Glance (2018), https://www.ussc.gov/sites/default/files/pdf/research-and-publications/backgrounders/RG-gun-mm.PDF; *see* United States Sentencing Commission, Mandatory Minimum Penalties for Firearms Offenses in the Federal Criminal Justice System (2018), https://www.ussc.gov/sites/default/files/pdf/research-and-publications/research-publications/2018/20180315_Firearms-Mand-Min.pdf.

187 United States Sentencing Commission, Federal Gun Mandatory Minimum Penalties, *supra* note 181.

188 *Ewing v. California*, 538 U.S. 11 (2003).

189 *Solem v. Helm*, 463 U.S. 277 (1983).

190 *Lockyer v. Andrade*, 538 U.S. 63 (2003) (An important aspect of this case was that it was a habeas corpus petition, which meant there needed to be an "unreasonable application of clearly established federal law." But the majority opinion did not find clearly established precedent in regard to sentencing proportionality.).

191 Adam Walsh Child Protection and Safety Act of 2006, Title 1, 18 U.S.C. § 2250

192 34 U.S.C. § 20911 —Relevant definitions, including Amie Zyla expansion of sex offender definition and expanded inclusion of child predators

193 *Gundy v. United States*, 588 U.S. ____ (2019).

194 *Packingham v. North Carolina*, 582 U.S. ____ (2017).

195 18 U.S.C. § 2252(b)(2).

196 *United States v. Comstock*, 560 U.S. 126 (2010).

197 *Kansas v. Hendricks*, 521 U. S. 346 (1997); *Kansas v. Crane*, 534 U. S. 407 (2002).

198 *Wisconsin v. Mitchell*, 508 U.S. 47 (1993).

199 *Apprendi v. New Jersey*, 530 U.S. 466 (2000); *Alleyne v. United States*, 570 U.S. 99 (2013).

200 Violent Crime Control and Law Enforcement Act of 1994, 108 Stat. 1796.

201 Matthew Sheppard and James Byrd Jr. Hate Crimes Prevention Act of 2009, 18 U.S.C. § 249, enacted as Division E of the National Defense Authorization Act of 2010; *see* Barack Obama, Remarks by the President at Reception Commemorating the Enactment of the Hate Crimes Prevention Act, U.S. Dept. of Justice: https://www.justice.gov/crt/matthew-shepard-and-james-byrd-jr-hate-crimes-prevention-act-2009-0.

202 *See* Erin Goffette, *Sovereignty in Sentencing: Concurrent and Consecutive Sentencing of a Defendant Subject to Simultaneous State and Federal Jurisdiction*, 37 Val. U. L. REV. 1035 (2003).

203 *United States v. Nikolovski*, 565 F. App'x 397 (6th Cir. 2014).

204 The First Step Act of 2018 provides $250 million in funding for such programs and even allows for nonprofit groups and faith-based organizations to conduct them. The law also enables *low-risk* offenders to receive early release into halfway houses, and it broadens the application of *compassionate release* for terminally ill or elderly inmates. Certain violent offenders and sex traffickers are not permitted to acquire credits related to early release.

205 Tennessee Public Chapter 988, https://wapp.capitol.tn.gov/apps/BillInfo/Default.aspx?BillNumber=HB2656

206 *Roper v. Simmons*, 543 U.S. 551 (2005).

207 *Graham v. Florida*, 560 U.S. 48 (2010).

208 *Miller v. Alabama*, 567 U.S. 460 (2012).

209 *Montgomery v. Louisiana*, 577 U.S. 190 (2016).

210 Equal Justice Initiative, *Henry Montgomery Released After 57 Years in Prison for Crime at 17*, Nov. 17, 2021, https://eji.org/news/henry-montgomery-released-after-57-years-in-prison-for-crime-at-17/.

211 *Jones v. Mississippi*, 593 U.S. ____ (2021).

Credit

CHAPTER 14

The Eighth Amendment
The Death Penalty and Prisoners' Rights

"The [Eighth] Amendment embodies 'broad and idealistic concepts of dignity, civilized standards, humanity, and decency ...,' against which we must evaluate penal measures. Thus, we have held repugnant to the Eighth Amendment punishments which are incompatible with 'the evolving standards of decency that mark the progress of a maturing society.'"

—Justice Thurgood Marshall, writing for the Supreme Court
in *Estelle v. Gamble*, 429 U.S. 97 (1976), citing *Trop v. Dulles*, 356 U.S. 56 (1958)

Learning Objectives

After reading this chapter, you should understand the following:

1. The evolving constitutional law on the death penalty
2. The Supreme Court's approach to cases involving methods of execution
3. The Supreme Court's approach to cases involving a death row inmate's mental state
4. Other issues related to equity and the death penalty, including the impact of juvenile status and race on executions
5. The scope of prisoners' constitutional rights

Key Cases

Furman v. Georgia, 408 U.S. 238 (1972)
Gregg v. Georgia, 428 U.S. 153 (1976)
Kennedy v. Louisiana, 554 U.S. 407 (2008)
Baze v. Rees, 553 U.S. 35 (2008)
Glossip v. Gross, 576 U.S. 863 (2015)
Bucklew v. Precythe, 587 U.S. ___ (2019)
Atkins v. Virginia, 536 U.S. 304 (2002)
Roper v. Simmons, 543 U.S. 551 (2005)
Estelle v. Gamble, 429 U.S. 97 (1976)
Hutto v. Finney, 437 U.S. 678 (1978)

Introduction

BIFURCATED TRIAL:
A method upheld by the Supreme Court for trying cases involving a potential death sentence; it encompasses a two-stage criminal proceeding, in which the first phase revolves around whether the offender is guilty or not guilty and the second phase involves an assessment of what the appropriate punishment should be.

In this chapter, we focus more narrowly on two of the most controversial applications of the Eighth Amendment's protection against cruel and unusual punishment: the death penalty and prisoners' rights. We begin with capital punishment, the most serious sanction that can be imposed for the commission of a crime. In the early 1970s, the Supreme Court temporarily halted capital punishment nationwide, only authorizing its return after a new method for its imposition had been crafted: the so-called bifurcated trial. The high Court hoped this novel framework would help offer some consistency in the application of death sentences—by limiting them to the most heinous of murders. A litany of decisions over the ensuing decades have seen the Court further limit the imposition of the ultimate sanction. These decisions have addressed issues as varied as the execution of minors, the execution of those with intellectual disabilities or mental illnesses, what crimes should be eligible for the death penalty, and even methods of execution.

The other broad topic for this chapter is the relevance of the Eighth Amendment to prison conditions. Not surprisingly, the Supreme Court has carved out specific standards for addressing narrow categories of prison-related issues, and in the second half of this chapter, we provide an examination of the key precedents determining prisoners' rights under the Cruel and Unusual Punishment Clause. Specific attention will be paid to matters like medical care, use of force by corrections officials, protection from harm by other inmates, overcrowding, conditions of incarceration, and even the controversial practice of solitary confinement.

Capital Punishment: The Background

The process of bringing a capital case begins with a prosecutor making the decision to seek the death penalty. In the following sections, we will trace this process from that initial choice made on behalf of the state to the actual execution—a journey that can take decades to complete, in light of the numerous appeals that typically ensue following a guilty verdict and capital sentence.

As of 2022, twenty-seven states permitted the death penalty. Of those twenty-seven, three had governor-imposed moratoria, which meant no actual executions were taking place (California, Oregon, and Pennsylvania). This remains a contentious topic in many places, with some states having halted capital punishment via state supreme court decisions or legislative acts, with others having retained it through votes of the people in statewide ballot measures.[1]

Nationwide, in 2019, there were twenty-two prisoners executed across eight different states. Texas led all states with nine executions, and Alabama, Georgia, and Tennessee were next on the list with three executions each. By 2022 there were approximately 2,500 convicted inmates on death row in U.S. prisons, including forty-four on federal death row.[2] Since 1976, only five states have averaged two or more executions per year. Those are Texas, which has nearly 600 total executions over that time frame, followed by four states with approximately 100 each: Virginia, Oklahoma, Florida, and Missouri. Overall, the number of total executions in the United States has trended downward since 1976.[3]

In addition to state governments, the federal government is also able to implement capital punishment—generally, for federal murder charges. After not holding an execution since 2003, the Department of Justice resumed executions in 2020, with three in July of that year and then ten more before President Trump left office in January 2021. The U.S. Armed Forces are also permitted to impose a death sentence upon military personnel, but a military execution has not occurred in over six decades.

From an appellate standpoint, prior to the 1960s, courts showed very little interest in the constitutionality of the death penalty. We have already noted how, in *Wilkerson v. Utah* (1878),[4] the Supreme Court opined that conventional forms of execution did not raise constitutional problems if they were lawfully prescribed and imposed. Twelve years later, in the case of *In re Kemler* (1890),[5] the Court upheld the use of the electric chair as a means of capital punishment. Chief Justice Melville Fuller spoke for a unanimous bench:

> Punishments are cruel when they involve torture or a lingering death; but the punishment of death is not cruel within the meaning of that word as used in the Constitution. It implies there something inhuman and barbarous—something more than the mere extinguishment of life.

In fact, following this case, it would take nearly a century for the high Court to discern any constitutional defects in the imposition of capital punishment.

The Willie Francis Case and Botched Executions

In 1947, the Supreme Court went so far as to allow a young African American man to be electrocuted twice—the first time having failed to result in his death due to the electric chair being set up improperly. In a plurality opinion announcing the judgment of the Court in the Willie Francis case, Justice Stanley Reed called the first attempt an "unforeseeable accident" and also observed that "the fact that petitioner has already been subjected to a current of electricity does not make his subsequent execution any more cruel in the constitutional sense than any other execution."[6] In dissent, Justice Harold Burton (joined by three of his colleagues) wrote that the state's intent to subject Willie Francis to another trip to the electric chair "shocks the most fundamental instincts of civilized man." Justice Felix Frankfurter's decisive concurring opinion found no constitutional infirmity in Louisiana's procedure, despite his "personal feeling of revulsion against a State's insistence on its pound of flesh." He referred to the first attempt as "an innocent misadventure" and declared that the second attempt would not be "repugnant to the conscience of mankind," quoting the Double Jeopardy case of *Palko v. Connecticut* (1937).[7]

An additional layer to this case involved the fact that Willie Francis was seventeen when he first went to the electric chair. He was eighteen when he was finally put to death after the Supreme Court allowed the execution to go forward. As we will see in the following sections, such an execution of a person who was under 18 at the time of their offense would not be permitted today—a sign that views on capital punishment, both from the general public and appellate courts, have evolved over time.

Furman v. Georgia: The Supreme Court Strikes Down the Death Penalty

In *Furman v. Georgia* (1972),[8] the Court struck down Georgia's death penalty law and effectively halted the administration of capital punishment across the country. The Court's holding was set forth in a brief per curiam opinion, which said simply that "that the imposition and carrying out of the death penalty in these cases constitute cruel and unusual punishment in violation of the Eighth and Fourteenth Amendments." The decision was 5–4, with each of the nine justices offering their own view of the death penalty in a concurring or dissenting opinion.

Two of the justices, William Brennan and Thurgood Marshall, asserted that the death penalty was inherently unconstitutional. Justice Marshall, stressing the "evolving standards of decency that mark the progress of a maturing society," concluded that the death penalty is "morally unacceptable to the people of the United States at this time in their history." Similarly, Justice Brennan insisted that the death penalty is "fatally offensive to human dignity."

The three other justices in the majority stated various reasons why, in their judgment, Georgia's death penalty law was defective. Their reasons centered on the fact that Georgia left the question of death wholly to the discretion of the jury. For Justice William O. Douglas, the system was "pregnant with discrimination, and discrimination is an ingredient not compatible with the idea of equal protection of the laws that is implicit in the ban on 'cruel and unusual' punishments." In Justice Byron White's view, the death penalty was so rarely imposed that it had lost any deterrent value, with his opinion observing: "I cannot avoid the conclusion that, as the statutes before us are now administered, the penalty is so infrequently imposed that the threat of execution is too attenuated to be of substantial service to criminal justice." But the opinion that turned out to be most influential was that of Justice Potter Stewart, who declared "the Eighth and Fourteenth Amendments cannot tolerate the infliction of a sentence of death under legal systems that permit this unique penalty to be so wantonly and so freakishly imposed."

In a dissenting opinion joined by the other three dissenters, Chief Justice Warren Burger called for judicial restraint, saying, "There are no obvious indications that capital punishment offends the conscience of society to such a degree that our traditional deference to the legislative judgment must be abandoned." Justice Harry

Blackmun, also dissenting, admitted to "distaste, antipathy, and, indeed, abhorrence" for the death penalty and indicated that, were he a legislator, he would vote to abolish capital punishment. Furthermore, as a jurist, Blackmun said he found the Court's decision "difficult to accept or to justify as a matter of history, of law, or of constitutional pronouncement."

Gregg v. Georgia: The Court Reinstates Capital Punishment

In the wake of *Furman v. Georgia*, thirty-five states modified their death penalty statutes. While these laws varied in their particulars, they all adopted procedures designed to channel the discretion of juries with an eye toward making the imposition of capital punishment fairer and more predictable. Under these revised laws, death penalty cases require a bifurcated trial, which involves two stages. In the first stage of the capital trial, guilt is determined according to the usual procedures, rules of evidence, and standard of proof. If the jury finds the defendant guilty, a second phase of the trial takes place, in which the same jury considers whether the death penalty should be imposed. To return a death sentence, the jury must find that at least one of several aggravating factors specified by statute was present in the defendant's crime. Moreover, the jury must find that any mitigating factors introduced by the defense are outweighed by the aggravating factor or factors.

Four years after the *Furman* decision, the Supreme Court revisited this issue by evaluating Georgia's newly-created procedure for capital cases. In *Gregg v. Georgia* (1976),[9] a 7–2 majority of the Supreme Court upheld the use of the death penalty as applied through a bifurcated trial. Justices Brennan and Marshall dissented, renewing their objections to the use of capital punishment in any circumstance. Conversely, the majority in *Gregg* stated that "concerns expressed in *Furman* that the penalty of death not be imposed in an arbitrary or capricious manner can be best met by a system that provides for a bifurcated proceeding." The addition of the sentencing phase, coupled with application of aggravating factors, it was believed, would offer the possibility of consistent application of capital punishment across different crimes and defendants. But would it work out that way in practice?

It is worth noting that on the same day *Gregg v. Georgia* was decided, the high Court struck down a North Carolina law that made the death penalty mandatory in cases of first-degree murder. Justice Potter Stewart's opinion announcing the judgment of the Court in *Woodson v. North Carolina* (1976)[10] found that one of the principal defects of the law was "its failure to allow the particularized consideration of relevant aspects

AGGRAVATING FACTORS: Criteria that indicate one crime is somehow more egregious than other similar crimes and, thus, worthy of a harsher punishment; they are often referenced in the sentencing phase of a death penalty case, when such factors cannot be outweighed by mitigating factors for a capital sentence to be levied.

of the character and record of each convicted defendant before the imposition upon him of a sentence of death." Thus, under *Furman*, *Gregg*, and *Woodson*, the jury cannot be given complete discretion in capital sentencing, but neither can it be denied the opportunity to engage in a particularized review of the various factors that would inform a just decision regarding who deserves to die for their criminal offense.

Understanding the Sentencing Phase in a Capital Case

The sentencing phase of a capital case focuses on aggravating and mitigating factors. A prosecutor will present evidence of the former, and the defense will present evidence of the latter. Aggravating factors can be thought of as criteria that make the homicide in question especially egregious—or, although this might sound odd, somehow *worse* than other homicides. Aggravating factors are normally listed in an act of a state legislature. Common aggravating factors include the killing of a police officer, the killing of an elected official, the killing of a young child, the killing of an elderly person, or the commission of another felony along with the murder. A list of the aggravating factors defined by the Texas Legislature for use in capital cases in that state is provided in the box on the next page.

Presenting evidence of aggravating factors, a prosecutor will likely be permitted to offer evidence that was deemed inadmissible during the first phase of the trial. This could include crime scene photos that portray an image of a dead body, something a judge might have found prejudicial in the first phase, but which becomes acceptable under the looser standards many courts employ in the sentencing phase. Another example is victim impact testimony; this could include relatives of a murder victim speaking about their loss—testimony that can resonate powerfully with jurors. Although this type of testimony is not typically permitted in the first phase of a capital case, the Supreme Court's decision in *Payne v. Tennessee* (1991) allowed its use in the sentencing phase.[11] In the *Payne* case, the murder victim's mother testified about the impact of the killing on the victim's three-year-old son. The majority opinion said the following:

> We hold that, if the State chooses to permit the admission of victim impact evidence and prosecutorial argument on that subject, the Eighth Amendment

MITIGATING FACTORS: Criteria that indicate excuses for the commission of a crime, which might lessen the offender's level of culpability in the eyes of those considering punishment; in a death penalty case, if these outweigh aggravating factors, a capital sentence cannot be given, according to Supreme Court precedent.

VICTIM IMPACT TESTIMONY: Information often relayed by the prosecution in the sentencing phase of a death penalty case, usually speaking to the manner in which the victim's injuries or death have affected those around them, such as children or other dependents.

erects no *per se* bar. A State may legitimately conclude that evidence about the victim and about the impact of the murder on the victim's family is relevant to the jury's decision as to whether or not the death penalty should be imposed.

The *Payne* decision leaves open the possibility for a trial judge, appellate court, or even a state legislature to carve some limits on what a jury is allowed consider in the sentencing phase. For example, in 2005, the Colorado Supreme Court overturned a death sentence because jurors had consulted a copy of the Bible.[12] In 2008, however, the Supreme Court of the United States refused to hear an appeal of a California Supreme Court ruling that upheld a prosecutor's decision to show jurors a twenty-minute photo montage of the victim's life; hence, no constitutional violation was discerned in that situation.[13]

THE CONSTITUTION IN ACTION
Aggravating Factors for Capital Punishment Cases in Texas
Tex. Penal Code § 19.03

1)   the person murders a peace officer or fireman who is acting in the lawful discharge of an official duty and who the person knows is a peace officer or fireman;
2)   the person intentionally commits the murder in the course of committing or attempting to commit kidnapping, burglary, robbery, aggravated sexual assault, arson, obstruction or retaliation, or terroristic threat ...;
3)   the person commits the murder for remuneration or the promise of remuneration or employs another to commit the murder for remuneration or the promise of remuneration;
4)   the person commits the murder while escaping or attempting to escape from a penal institution;
5)   the person, while incarcerated in a penal institution, murders another:
    A.   who is employed in the operation of the penal institution; or
    B.   with the intent to establish, maintain, or participate in a combination or in the profits of a combination;
6)   the person:
    A.   while incarcerated for an offense..., murders another; or
    B.   while serving a sentence of life imprisonment or a term of 99 years ..., murders another;
7)   the person murders more than one person:
    A.   during the same criminal transaction; or
    B.   during different criminal transactions but the murders are committed pursuant to the same scheme or course of conduct;
8)   the person murders an individual under 10 years of age; or
9)   the person murders another person in retaliation for or on account of the service or status of the other person as a judge or justice of the supreme court, the court of criminal appeals, a court of appeals, a district court, a criminal district court, a constitutional county court, a statutory county court, a justice court, or a municipal court.

Mitigating factors in a capital case can be thought of as reasons for jurors to feel the defendant, although guilty of the crime in question, is not culpable to the point of deserving a death sentence. Most testimony about mitigating factors would not be admissible during the first phase of a capital case, but during the sentencing phase, witnesses can be used to relay information that might provide an *excuse* or engender sympathy with jurors. These could include, for instance, discussion of alcohol or drug problems, the defendant's history of mental illness, the lack of a prior criminal record, the possibility that a victim incited an incident leading to death, the defendant acting under some kind of duress, or the defendant having a lesser role in the crime than other perpetrators who had leadership roles.

A series of cases from the Supreme Court has addressed the role of mitigating factors in a death penalty case. In 1978, the Court struck down an Ohio law that mandated the death penalty for cases of aggravated murder and precluded consideration of mitigating factors; the Court found that a jury must be permitted to consider mitigating factors.[14] Later, in *Hitchcock v. Dugger* (1987),[15] the Court struck down a Florida law, finding that jurors should not be limited to considering only a list of mitigating factors delineated by a state legislature. As a result, it is up to individual jurors to consider anything they deem to be a mitigating factor when examining the defendant's level of culpability. One year later, in *Mills v. Maryland* (1988),[16] the Court struck down a Maryland law that required jurors to unanimously agree on the existence of a mitigating factor for it to be considered in the balancing of aggravating and mitigating circumstances. The net result of these cases is that individual jurors can decide for themselves if aggravating factors outweigh *any* mitigating factors.

In later cases, though, the Court provided decisions that tend to favor prosecutors as they pursue imposition of the death penalty. In *Kansas v. Marsh* (2006),[17] the Court upheld a Kansas law that allowed a jury to impose the death penalty when all jurors were in unanimous agreement that aggravating factors were *not outweighed* by mitigating factors. In this case, the controversy revolved around the fact that a death sentence could, in theory, be given when jurors felt aggravating and mitigating factors were in *equipoise*; thus, jurors in this state were never instructed that aggravating factors must outweigh mitigating factors, since the two groups of factors being in balance could be used to justify a death sentence. Ten years later, in *Kansas v. Carr* (2016),[18] the Court ruled that a judge's refusal to instruct a jury that mitigating factors do not need to be proven "beyond a reasonable doubt" creates no constitutional violation—because no such instruction is required by the Eighth Amendment.[19]

Judge or Jury?

In the aftermath of the Supreme Court's *Gregg v. Georgia* decision, there were four states—Arizona, Idaho, Montana, and Nebraska—that left judges, not juries, to untangle the assessment of aggravating and mitigating circumstances in the second phase of bifurcated trials. While a jury would handle the guilty phase in these states, a judge took over for sentencing. The Supreme Court halted this system with its decision in *Ring v. Arizona* (2002),[20] which held that the Sixth Amendment requires a death sentence to be imposed by a jury, not a judge, unless the defendant has waived their right to a trial by jury. However, in *Schriro v. Summerlin* (2004),[21] the Court declared that the *Ring* decision was not a "retroactive" one, which meant those prisoners who had been sentenced to death by a judge before the *Ring* case would not be granted a new sentencing hearing. The key rationale in this case focused upon the fact that the *Ring* decision was a procedural one, as opposed to a substantive assessment of a law.

Subsequently, in *Hurst v. Florida* (2016),[22] the Supreme Court struck down Florida's version of a bifurcated trial because it gave a judge the ability to override a jury's decision by having "final say" over a jury's "recommendation" of whether to impose a death sentence. In this case, the jury had recommended a death sentence by a 7–5 vote; the judge then had discretion in enforcing that decision and did, in fact, opt for the death penalty. A similar procedure also was in use in Alabama, Delaware, and Montana at that time. The Court said a jury must be given the responsibility of imposing a death sentence (unless the defendant waives their right to a trial by jury).

Jury Unanimity

The majority opinion in *Hurst v. Florida* left unresolved the question of whether unanimity among jurors was required in the sentencing phase of capital cases. At the time of that case, Delaware, Alabama, and Florida were the three states that did not require a unanimous vote of jurors during the sentencing phase for a capital sentence to be given—even though, as noted in the previous chapter, a unanimous vote of jurors is needed to find the defendant guilty of a crime in the first stage of a bifurcated trial.

Following the high Court's *Hurst* decision, the Delaware Supreme Court ruled that unanimous jury votes in the sentencing phase would be required for capital cases in that state.[23] In Florida, on May 7, 2016, Governor Rick Scott signed a law in 2016 that mandated a minimum jury vote of 10–2 during the sentencing phase for a death sentence to be imposed—the same standard used in Alabama. But later in 2016, the Florida Supreme Court, hearing the *Hurst* case on remand, announced a requirement for unanimous jury verdicts in the sentencing phase.[24] Nonetheless, in an unusual twist, with new members on that court in 2020, this decision was reversed, with the Florida high court opting to allow 11–1 verdicts in the sentencing phase.[25] As of 2022, only Florida and Alabama allowed for the possibility of nonunanimous capital sentences.

THE CONSTITUTION IN ACTION
Death Qualification of a Jury

Critics of capital punishment contend that a process called *death qualification of juries* represents an inherent source of bias. As discussed in chapter 13, a jury is chosen from a *venire*, or pool, of potential candidates; each side in the case can dismiss prospective jurors for reasons other than race or sex. Death qualification, though, refers to the dismissal of prospective jurors who indicate an objection to the death penalty, as a general matter, during voir dire.

According to the Supreme Court, a prospective juror can be excused for this reason alone: that person has demonstrated the inability to consider all options allowed by law. In fact, in four cases—*Witherspoon v. Illinois* (1968),[26] *Adams v. Texas* (1980),[27] *Lockhart v. McCree* (1986),[28] and *Uttecht v. Brown* (2007)[29]—the Supreme Court has said death-qualified juries are not a violation of the Constitution. Moreover, in *White v. Wheeler* (2015),[30] the Court's per curiam opinion even upheld a Kentucky trial judge's decision to allow a peremptory challenge removing a prospective juror who "could not give sufficient assurance of neutrality or impartiality in considering whether the death penalty should be imposed"—even though the juror did not specifically say they would never be able to impose the death penalty.

Some have hypothesized that death-qualified juries are more likely to exclude women and minorities—and, beyond that, are more likely to return a death sentence.[31] Chief Justice Rehnquist's majority opinion in *Lockhart v. McCree*, however, said, "Death qualification, unlike the wholesale exclusion of blacks, women or Mexican-Americans from jury service, is carefully designed to serve the state's concededly legitimate interest in obtaining a single jury that can properly and impartially apply the law to the facts of the case at both the guilt and sentencing phases of a capital trial." In contrast, Justice Thurgood Marshall's dissent averred that the removal of prospective jurors who are opposed to the death penalty "allows the state a special advantage in those prosecutions where the charges are most serious and the possible punishments the most severe."

Ineffective Counsel in the Sentencing Phase

It is possible for an ineffective counsel claim under the Sixth Amendment, as discussed in chapter 13, to apply to the sentencing phase of a bifurcated trial. For instance, in *Williams v. Taylor* (2000),[32] the Supreme Court ruled that the defendant's counsel was ineffective for a failure to present evidence of possible mitigating factors during the sentencing phase. The majority opinion from Justice Stevens applied the *Strickland* test and found there was a reasonable probability of a different sentence if the lawyer had introduced such evidence.

Subsequently, in *Wiggins v. Smith* (2003),[33] the defendant's lawyer did not bring forth mitigating evidence of Wiggins's challenging upbringing, which included alleged physical and sexual abuse by his foster parents. Justice O'Connor's majority opinion for the Court deemed this failure to be a violation of the right to counsel, bluntly observing that "any reasonably competent attorney would have pursued such leads," and thus, "[counsel] fell short of professional standards."

Death-Eligible Offenses

As a result of a series of cases that followed *Gregg v. Georgia*, the Supreme Court has, in effect, limited states to giving capital sentences only in cases of murder. For example, in *Coker v. Georgia* (1977),[34] the Court held that the death penalty cannot be imposed for the crime of rape. Speaking for the Court, Justice Byron White concluded "that a sentence of death is grossly disproportionate and excessive punishment for the crime of rape, and is therefore forbidden by the Eighth Amendment as cruel and unusual punishment." Nearly three decades later, the Court reaffirmed and amplified this holding in a case that involved a man convicting of raping his 8-year-old stepdaughter. In *Kennedy v. Louisiana* (2008),[35] Justice Anthony Kennedy, writing for a sharply divided bench, prevented the state of Louisiana from executing this man, saying the Eighth Amendment "bars the death penalty for the rape of a child where the crime did not result, and was not intended to result, in death of the victim." Thus, by applying a type of proportionality assessment, the Court has effectively limited capital punishment to cases of aggravated murder, typically first-degree murder (that which involves an element of premeditation).

Death Penalty for Felony Murder

In many states, the crime of felony murder is applied when perpetrators take part in an *inherently dangerous* felony and then someone dies during the commission of that felony. Some states treat felony murder as equivalent to first-degree murder; accordingly, such an offense could be listed as a death-eligible homicide—even for a criminal who was taking part in a felony but did not intend for the death to occur and did not do the killing.[36] In certain jurisdictions, this possibility could even apply if someone other than the perpetrators to the crime—such as a security guard—killed a person, whether it was an accidental shooting of a bystander or, perhaps, a justifiable shooting of one of the criminals (see the following box for discussion of the latter).

But should this doctrine of felony murder be used to give the getaway driver in a robbery a death sentence if one of the getaway driver's fellow perpetrators killed a person during the robbery? In *Enmund v. Florida* (1982),[37] the Supreme Court answered that question in the negative. Justice White's majority opinion said, "The question before us is not the disproportionality of death as a penalty for murder, but rather the validity of capital punishment for Enmund's own conduct. The focus must be on his culpability, not on that of those who committed the robbery and shot the victims, for we insist on 'individualized consideration as a constitutional requirement in imposing the death sentence. ...'"[38] The Court took umbrage with the fact that fifteen states, at that time, allowed for a death sentence in situations when the defendant neither intended for the killing to happen nor committed the killing. This scenario was said to be a violation of the Eighth Amendment.

Even so, life in prison can still be given for felony murder. While some suggest this can lead to unjust outcomes regarding the match between criminal intent and punishment—not to mention holding one person accountable for another's actions—it remains a viable possibility in many states, and is meant to serve as a deterrent to participation in dangerous felonies.[39]

JURISPRUDENCE

Indiana's Supreme Court Overturns Felony Murder Convictions of the *Elkhart Four*
Sharp v. State, 42 N.E.3d 512 (Ind. 2015)

In October 2012, five teenagers in Elkhart, Indiana broke into a home they thought was unoccupied, looking to commit a burglary. However, the homeowner was asleep in an upstairs room, and after being awoken by the break-in, he grabbed his gun and fired at the teenagers, killing one of them in an act of self-defense. In a surprising move, the local prosecutor charged the four surviving teenagers with felony murder—for the death of their friend. Indiana law allows a charge of felony murder to apply when a death occurs while perpetrators are committing or attempting to commit any of a specified list of felonies, including burglary.[40]

Three of the teenagers in this case were found guilty of felony murder by a jury, and the other pleaded guilty to felony murder. Sentences for the four ranged from forty-five to fifty-five years in prison. On appeal, the Indiana Supreme Court overturned the felony murder convictions, noting the teenagers had not engaged in "dangerously violent and threatening conduct" and that their actions were not "clearly the mediate or immediate cause" of their friend's death.[41] The court ordered the teenagers to be resentenced on burglary charges, and all four were given burglary sentences of nine or ten years.[42]

The felony murder statute remains in place in Indiana, with the state's Supreme Court noting the objective of deterring criminals from taking part in such dangerous crimes in the first place. Scenarios such as the one that occurred here, when someone other than the felon does the killing, invoke a discussion of *agency theory*, a legal concept under which a criminal is responsible only for the actions of their co-perpetrators (known as their *agents*), versus an opposing idea, called *proximate cause theory*, under which a criminal is responsible for whatever is foreseeably *set in motion* by their criminal conduct; different jurisdictions take different approaches to applying these frameworks.[43]

In its ruling, the Indiana Supreme Court continued to support the notion that members of a criminal group could, in fact, be charged for felony murder if someone in their group dies during commission of the felony. For example, the court pointed to a prior case in which a felon shot at police, who then returned fire and killed the felon's co-perpetrator; in another case that was cited, a felon held a man at gunpoint, and then a struggle ensued over the gun, which discharged and killed a co-felon. The Indiana Supreme Court observed that these were valid examples of felony murder charges because "the common thread uniting [these cases] was that an armed defendant engaged in violent and threatening conduct, either as a principle or an accessory, that resulted in the 'mediate or immediate cause' of a co-perpetrator's death." The court differentiated those cases from that of the Elkhart Four, noting, "By contrast the record here shows that when the group broke and entered the residence of the homeowner intending to commit a theft—a burglary—not only were they unarmed, but also neither the Appellants nor their cohorts engaged in any dangerously violent and threatening conduct."

Federal Crimes That Are Death Eligible

The federal government retains the ability to issue a death sentence. Pursuant to the Federal Death Penalty Act, which is Title VI of the Violent Crime Control and Law Enforcement Act of 1994, a number of crimes could result in such a sentence, including the following: "bringing in and harboring certain aliens resulting in death," "murder committed during a drug-related drive-by shooting," "civil rights offenses resulting in death," "murder committed in a Federal Government facility," "murder of a Federal judge or Federal law enforcement official," "murder by a federal prisoner," and "murder committed at an airport serving international civil aviation."[44]

Beyond those offenses, the federal government retains the ability to execute for certain nonhomicide offenses, such as treason or espionage. However, only one person has ever been executed for treason against the federal government; William Bruce Mumford was hanged for treason in 1862, during the Civil War. The most recent executions for espionage were of Julius and Ethel Rosenberg, a married couple electrocuted in 1953 after they were found guilty of spying for the Soviet Union, offering that country U.S. military intelligence that included plans for the design of nuclear weapons.

There are two other nonhomicide charges in federal law that could, by statute, result in a death sentence: one is related to trafficking in quantities of drugs that exceed the amounts in five-year minimum sentencing parameters by at least 600 times,[45] and the other speaks to an attempt to kill an officer, juror, or witness in a case involving a continuing criminal enterprise.[46] Yet it remains to be seen if the Supreme Court would permit an execution for any of these nonhomicide charges in light of the *Kennedy v. Louisiana* decision, since neither crime involves a death.

The U.S. Armed Forces allows a death sentence for fourteen different offenses under the Uniform Code of Military Justice (UCMJ); these include murder, rape, espionage sedition, espionage, and mutiny—although some offenses are only subject to the death penalty if committed during wartime, including: desertion, assaulting or willfully disobeying a superior commanding officer, acting as a spy, and misbehavior as a sentinel or lookout (which could include being drunk while on duty).[47] The most recent execution by the U.S. military was in 1961.[48]

Today, the constitutionality of a capital sentence for some military offenses remains in question—something the Supreme Court noted in its majority opinion for *United States v. Briggs* (2020),[49] which said, "We have never considered a direct Eighth Amendment challenge to a sentence of death for rape under the UCMJ." Yet in this case, a unanimous Court allowed the military to prosecute three rape cases by evading a five-year statute of limitations that typically applies to noncapital crimes under the UCMJ. To enable this result, Justice Alito's majority opinion treated rape as if it were still a capital offense within the military, and because there is no statute of limitations on a capital offense under the UCMJ, the prosecutions could move forward.

Methods of Execution

From the founding of this country through the nineteenth century, hanging was the preferred mode of capital punishment for civilians convicted of capital crimes. The gallows were employed not only for murderers but for those convicted of horse theft, train robbery, rape, and various other serious felonies. Hangings were public spectacles designed to impress the many onlookers with the consequences of crime. The introduction of the electric chair in the late-nineteenth century and the gas chamber shortly thereafter immediately reduced the number of hangings but moved executions inside the walls of prisons. Although the law would allow for a small number of witnesses, executions would no longer be public spectacles. Hangings inside prisons occurred as recently as the 1990s, but they became increasingly rare as the twentieth century progressed. It is unlikely we will ever see another execution by hanging in this country, with the last one having occurred in Delaware in 1996—but three states still allow for it by law (Delaware, New Hampshire, and Washington).

The Firing Squad

Historically, the armed forces employed **firing squads** to execute deserters and military members convicted of capital crimes by courts martial. Utah, first as a territory and later as a state, also employed firing squads to execute civilians convicted of capital offenses. In *Wilkerson v. Utah* (1878),[50] a case we discussed previously, the Supreme Court upheld a law first passed by Utah's territorial legislature in 1862, under which judges could sentence offenders to death by shooting, hanging, or beheading. Wallace Wilkerson, who had been convicted of premeditated murder, opted for the firing squad; his death took twenty-seven minutes, after shooters missed his heart. Writing for a unanimous Court, Justice Nathan Clifford differentiated shooting and hanging from the grislier forms of execution that had been practiced in England. While the former were, in Clifford's view, well within acceptable parameters, the latter might well be banned as cruel and unusual punishments. He specifically noted that "public dissection," "burning alive," and "punishments of torture" were "forbidden" under the Eighth Amendment—in what marks the only time the Supreme Court has ever offered clear limits regarding which methods of execution are *not* permitted.

As of 2022, the state of Utah continues to employ the firing squad as a backup method if lethal injection drugs become unavailable or, potentially, if requested by a death row inmate, with its most recent use coming in 2010. In a 2017 dissenting opinion, Justice Sonia Sotomayor observed, "In addition to being near instant, death by shooting may also be comparatively painless." She also noted that, "historically, the firing squad has yielded significantly fewer botched executions."[51]

Deborah Denno, a Fordham Law School professor who researches executions, has said that Utah's executions by firing squad have resulted in "quick deaths" when used in the past four decades.[52] Mississippi and Oklahoma also have long-standing statutes that authorize use of the firing squad, generally when other methods become unavailable; and in 2021 South Carolina passed a law calling for use of the firing squad or the state's 109-year old electric chair when lethal injection drugs are unavailable.[53]

FIRING SQUADS:
A method of execution that involves multiple shooters firing a gun at the death row inmate.

THE CONSTITUTION IN ACTION
Utah Convict Gary Gilmore Requests an Expedited Death by Firing Squad

Following reinstatement of the death penalty after the Supreme Court's 1976 *Gregg v. Georgia* decision, the first execution in the country in more than ten years took place in Utah in 1977. The death row inmate in this case, Gary Gilmore, had been convicted of two murders that occurred in July 1976. Gilmore killed a gas station attendant named Max Jensen in Orem, Utah, and the next day, he killed a motel manager named Benny Bushnell in Provo, Utah. Both victims had complied with Gilmore's demands for money but were still ordered to lie on the ground and then shot in the head. Gilmore accidentally shot himself in the hand while trying to get rid of the gun, and a witness who spotted him hiding the gun in some trees reported his license plate number to police. Soon thereafter, Utah State Police pulled that vehicle over and took Gilmore into custody. In Provo City Court, an FBI ballistics expert testified that the gun Gilmore attempted to hide matched the gun used in the murder of Bushnell, and Gilmore was found guilty of that crime after a two-day trial in October 1976. In the sentencing phase of the bifurcated trial, the jury unanimously voted to impose the death penalty.

(*continued*)

In a maneuver that would be unusual to witness today, Gilmore waived all of his appeals and asked for his death to be expedited. There were appeals brought on his behalf by his mother as well as the ACLU, with the latter resulting in some temporary stays of execution. Gilmore responded to these efforts by saying, at a Board of Pardons hearing in November 1976, "I would like them all—including the group of reverends and rabbis from Salt Lake City—to butt out. This is my life and this is my death. It's been sanctioned by the courts that I die and I accept that."[54] Utah offered a choice of hanging or firing squad, and Gilmore reportedly said, "I'd prefer to be shot."[55]

After a stay of execution was overturned by the Tenth Circuit on the morning of January 17, 1977 (and with no relief offered by the Supreme Court), preparations were made to get a firing squad in place at Point of the Mountain state prison, just outside of Salt Lake City. In Utah, procedures for a firing squad execution call for five shooters to be drawn from volunteer law enforcement personnel who have requested to take part; usually, those are individuals from the county where the crime occurred. Each shooter is given a .30 caliber Winchester rifle and stands 25 feet away from the inmate, who is restrained in a chair with a target placed over their chest. The rifles are placed into holes in a wooden wall that is between the shooters and the inmate, and sandbags and mattresses surround the inmate to prevent the ricochet of bullets. Shooters' names are to remain anonymous, and one of the guns is loaded with a blank round or nonlethal wax bullets, so it will be harder to know which officers killed the inmate.

Prior to the shooting, the condemned prisoner is given two minutes to speak, and Gilmore used that time to say, "Let's do this."[56] A black hood was placed over his head, and all shooters with live rounds hit their target with steel-jacketed ammunition. Gilmore died swiftly at 8:07 a.m., seconds after being shot and a little more than three months after he was found guilty at trial. Gilmore had requested for his organs to be donated, and his corneas, liver, and pituitary glands were passed on to others—but his kidneys could not be used due to bullet wounds. His remains were cremated, and his ashes were dumped over Utah from an airplane.

The Electric Chair

ELECTRIC CHAIR:
A method of execution that involves a death row inmate being strapped to a chair and exposed to a high-voltage electric current until death occurs.

The electric chair was invented in the early 1880s, and by the 20th century it had become the dominant means of capital punishment in the United States. We have seen how, in 1890, the Supreme Court upheld the use of the electric chair as a means of execution in the case of *In re Kemler*[57] and how, in 1947, the Court even allowed a young man to be sent to the chair a second time after the first attempt failed to extinguish his life.[58] Despite this judicial authorization, with the advent of lethal injection in the late 1970s, states began to move away from the use of the electric chair. By 2010, most states had abolished the electric chair, although a few continued to authorize it as an alternative to lethal injection, should the latter procedure become unavailable. Tennessee is the only state that has continued to use the electric chair as a primary method of execution, with five executions via electrocution taking place between 2018 and 2020, plus one in 2007. A 2014 law passed in that state and signed by Governor Bill Haslam actually required use of the electric chair if lethal injection drugs become unavailable.[59] Other states to authorize use of an electric chair, generally when other methods are not available, include the following: Alabama, Arkansas, Florida, Kentucky, Mississippi, Oklahoma, and South Carolina.

The Gas Chamber

The **gas chamber** came into use as a means of execution in the 1920s and was adopted by a small number of states as an alternative to the electric chair. In 1996, the U.S. Court of Appeals for the Ninth Circuit declared California's gas chamber to be cruel and unusual punishment.[60] Following that decision, the California legislature amended its death penalty law to give condemned prisoners the option of dying by lethal injection. In light of that development, the Supreme Court vacated and remanded the Ninth Circuit's decision.[61] Because the high Court has never found this method to be unconstitutional, using a gas chamber remains a possibility under laws in Arizona, Maryland, Mississippi, Missouri, and Wyoming.

Arizona was the last state to execute a prisoner by this method, doing so in 1999, when an inmate who chose to die in this way was strapped to a chair inside the state's lone gas chamber, a green-painted metal box built in 1949 of roughly six feet in width and eight feet in height. Cyanide pellets were then dropped into a vat of acid inside the chamber, creating a toxic cloud of smoke that took approximately eighteen minutes to kill the inmate. A report from *The Guardian* in 2021 indicated that preparations were being made to revive use of the gas chamber in Arizona. Executions had been halted in that state since a 2014 lethal-injection execution lasted more than two hours before the inmate died. But public records revealed by *The Guardian* showed that the Arizona Department of Corrections had spent close to $2,000 on materials needed to make hydrogen cyanide gas—including a $1,533 purchase of solid potassium cyanide as well as purchases of sulfuric acid and sodium hydroxide pellets; other documents indicated that inspections of the gas chamber's *air tightness* had been conducted using a candle.[62] In the following section, we consider a Supreme Court case involving a Missouri prisoner's request to be executed via a gas chamber as an alternative to the state's preferred method of lethal injection.

Lethal Injection

By the first decade of the twentieth century, lethal injection had become the dominant means of carrying out capital punishment across the United States. Although lethal injection is widely seen as a humane alternative to the electric chair and the gas chamber, it has not been without controversy, and the Supreme Court has addressed this method of execution in a series of cases. In *Baze v. Rees* (2008),[63] the Court, splitting 7–2, upheld Kentucky's lethal injection protocol after a group of Kentucky death row inmates brought suit, seeking to replace the state's existing combination of lethal injection drugs.

LETHAL INJECTION: A method of execution that generally involves a death row inmate being injected with a combination of drugs that subsequently produce death; this is the most common method of execution in the United States.

At the time, Kentucky employed the same three-drug cocktail that was in use for executions in thirty states and by the federal government. Under this protocol in Kentucky, a medical professional with more than one year of experience in providing anesthesia would insert an IV line into the prisoner's arm; the first substance that entered the body was sodium thiopental, which rendered the inmate unconscious; second, a drug called pancuronium bromide was used to instill paralysis; and finally, potassium chloride was used to stop the heart. The Kentucky inmates wanted this three-drug progression replaced with a one-drug method that would rely solely upon a barbiturate, which is typically used by veterinarians to euthanize animals. No state had ever used that method of execution for humans, but the prisoners claimed this would prove to be more humane by eliminating the possibility of a malfunction with the first drug in Kentucky's protocol; concerns abounded as to whether such a malfunction could lead to a conscious suffocation when the other drugs were administered, but no evidence of the likelihood of this type of adverse outcome was demonstrated by the inmates.

In a plurality opinion announcing the judgment of the Court in *Baze v. Rees*, Chief Justice John Roberts wrote that the Eighth Amendment prohibits "the wanton infliction of pain"—not simply the possibility thereof. Roberts specifically noted, "In order to meet their 'heavy burden' of showing that Kentucky's procedure is 'cruelly inhumane,' ... petitioners point to numerous aspects of the protocol that they contend create opportunities for error." He went on to diminish the prisoners' claims by saying, "We agree with the state trial court and State Supreme Court, however, that petitioners have not shown that the risk of an inadequate dose of the first drug is substantial." He also declared, "And we reject the argument that the Eighth Amendment requires Kentucky to adopt the untested alternative procedures petitioners have identified." Roberts then stated that the inmates' request "overlooks the States' legitimate interest in providing for a quick, certain death." Accordingly, by balancing the state interest against individual liberty, the Court opted to uphold the use of lethal injection.

Although the Kentucky case dealt with a hypothetical malfunction involving a lethal injection protocol, on April 29, 2014, the execution of an Oklahoma death row inmate lasted for an especially-long forty-three minutes from the time of injection to the time of death, with some reports indicating the inmate sat up fourteen minutes into the execution.[64] A 2015 dissenting opinion from Justice Sotomayor included a reference to this execution, saying, "Various witnesses reported that Lockett began to writhe against his restraints, saying, '[t]his s*** is f***ing with my mind,' 'something is wrong,' and '[t]he drugs aren't working.'"[65]

A root cause of the problems with this execution stemmed from the fact that drugs used in the typical lethal injection protocols had become more difficult for states to acquire, often because manufacturers were being pressured by groups that objected to capital punishment, and in turn, the manufacturers (especially those based in Europe) were refusing to provide the drugs to states. To replace the first drug normally used in its three-drug combination (because of shortages), Oklahoma officials initially substituted a drug called pentobarbital, but when a Danish manufacturer refused to provide more—in response to pressure from anti-death penalty groups—the state substituted in a sedative drug called midazolam. Additionally, in place of the typical second drug, Oklahoma officials substituted vecuronium bromide. Beyond that, at the time of the execution, the amounts of the drugs were not revealed, nor were the origins of the drugs, in keeping with an Oklahoma law that mirrors laws in other states; in fact, reports indicated the drugs were purchased in cash and the dosage of the first drug was five times less than it should have been.[66] Yet in 2016, the Tenth Circuit addressed a lawsuit from this prisoner's estate and ruled the forty-three-minute execution did not amount to cruel and unusual punishment—instead, calling it an "innocent misadventure" and "isolated mishap."[67]

Subsequent to that botched execution, four Oklahoma death row inmates, all convicted of murders, brought suit to challenge the use of untested lethal injection protocols. However, in *Glossip v. Gross* (2015),[68] the Supreme Court upheld Oklahoma's lethal injection procedures, even if there were new and secret combinations of drugs in use. Although the Court split 5–4, it produced a majority opinion authored by Justice Samuel Alito, which observed the following:

> Our decisions in this area have been animated in part by the recognition that because it is settled that capital punishment is constitutional, "[i]t necessarily follows that there must be a [constitutional] means of carrying it out." ... And because some risk of pain is inherent in any method of execution, we have held that the Constitution does not require the avoidance of all risk of pain. ... After all, while most humans wish to die a painless death, many do not have that good fortune. Holding that the Eighth Amendment demands the elimination of essentially all risk of pain would effectively outlaw the death penalty altogether.

Justice Alito's opinion also established a test for method-of-execution lawsuits, noting, "To succeed on an Eighth Amendment method-of-execution claim, a prisoner must establish that the method creates a demonstrated risk of severe pain and that the risk is substantial when compared to the known and available alternatives." Thus, the burden of proof falls to the petitioner to demonstrate a likelihood of harm *and* another method of execution that carries a lesser risk of pain. Applying this framework, Alito ruled that the petitioners had failed to meet their burden on both parts of the test.

In a lengthy dissenting opinion, Justice Stephen Breyer called for a wholesale examination of the death penalty in light of its "lack of reliability, the arbitrary application of a serious and irreversible punishment, individual suffering caused by long delays, and lack of penological purpose. ..." Justice Sonia Sotomayor's dissent, on the other hand, focused on the lethal injection protocol employed by Oklahoma and the likelihood that the drugs used acted to mask the severe pain experienced by the condemned inmate. She suggested the firing squad might well be preferable to lethal injection, noting that "such visible yet relatively painless violence may be vastly preferable to an excruciatingly painful death hidden behind a veneer of medication."

After the Supreme Court's ruling in *Glossip v. Gross*, the State of Oklahoma scheduled Richard Glossip for execution on September 30, 2015, at 3 p.m. However, just minutes before the lethal injection was to be administered, Oklahoma's governor granted an indefinite stay of execution. The stay reportedly was linked to questions regarding the drugs in the lethal injection protocol, with the state mistakenly receiving a shipment of potassium acetate instead of potassium chloride (the typical third drug in the protocol). No revised execution date has been set since then.[69]

More recently, in *Bucklew v. Precythe* (2019),[70] the Supreme Court addressed a case in which a Missouri prisoner formally requested to be executed by the gas chamber instead of the state's preferred method: lethal injection. He claimed lethal injection would cause him excessive pain because he suffered from vascular tumors, with lethal injection creating a risk of those tumors rupturing. Nevertheless, the Court refused his request in a 5–4 decision, with the majority opinion from Justice Neil Gorsuch citing *Glossip v. Gross* in declaring that "the Eight Amendment does not guarantee a prisoner a painless death—something that, of course, isn't guaranteed to many people, including most victims of capital crimes."

The majority opinion for *Bucklew* also noted the existence of a "*Baze-Glossip* test," which was used by the Eighth Circuit in analyzing this matter before it reached the high Court. Regarding this test, Justice Gorsuch offered the ensuing observation:

> Having (re)confirmed that anyone bringing a method of execution claim alleging the infliction of unconstitutionally cruel pain must meet the *Baze-Glossip* test, we can now turn to the question whether Mr. Bucklew is able to satisfy that test. Has he identified a feasible and readily implemented alternative method of execution the State refused to adopt without a legitimate reason, even though it would significantly reduce a substantial risk of severe pain?

Adding more clarity to the nuances of this *Baze-Glossip* test, Gorsuch again cited *Glossip* and identified two burdens on any inmate seeking a new method of execution, saying, "*First*, an inmate must show that his proposed alternative method is not just theoretically 'feasible' but also 'readily implemented.' ... This means the inmate's proposal must be sufficiently detailed to permit a finding that the State could carry it out 'relatively easily and reasonably quickly.'" Next, Gorsuch went on to reference *Baze*, saying, "*Second*, and relatedly, the State had a 'legitimate' reason for declining to switch from its current method of execution as a matter of law. ... Rather than point to a proven alternative method, Mr. Bucklew sought the adoption of an entirely new method—one that had 'never been used to carry out an execution' [in Missouri] and had 'no track record of successful use.'" Gorsuch then buttressed the state interest at hand when he said that "choosing not to be the first to experiment with a new method of execution is a legitimate reason [for the state] to reject it."

Overall, Gorsuch concluded that the petitioner was unable to show that there was an alternative tried and tested method of execution that would substantially reduce the risk of severe pain. Again, Justice Sotomayor dissented, saying "there is no sound basis in the Constitution for requiring condemned inmates to identify an available means for their own executions." In a separate dissent, Justice Breyer reiterated his general reservations about the death penalty:

> It may be that there is no way to execute a prisoner quickly while affording him the protections that our Constitution guarantees to those who have been singled out for our law's most severe sanction. And it may be that, as our Nation comes to place ever greater importance upon ensuring that we accurately identify, through procedurally fair methods, those who may lawfully be put to death, there simply is no constitutional way to implement the death penalty.

With this line of cases from *Baze* to *Glossip* to *Bucklew*, lethal injection continues to be a preferred method of execution in most states that offer capital punishment—when such drugs are available. Because of potential shortages, states will occasionally *trade* for drugs with other states, and most now retain one or more backup methods as well. Discussing his book, *Gruesome Spectacle: Botched Executions and America's Death Penalty*, Professor Austin Sarat of Amherst College observed, "If you look over the course of the 20th Century, about 3% of all American executions were botched," a conclusion he reached after examining nearly all of the 9,000 U.S. executions from 1890 to 2010. His findings revealed, though, that the rate of botched executions involving lethal injections was significantly higher than the overall rate, coming in at 7.1%.[71]

JURISPRUDENCE

Justice Alito Provides a Brief History of Executions
Glossip v. Gross, 576 U.S. 863 (2015)

Following a botched execution in which an Oklahoma death row inmate took forty-three minutes to die from a lethal injection protocol and even sat up more than ten minutes after the anesthetic drug was administered, four other death row inmates filed suit seeking to block their impending executions as cruel and unusual punishment. Ruling against these inmates, Justice Alito's majority opinion offered three paragraphs that provide an in-depth history of Supreme Court jurisprudence on methods of execution.

First, he began with discussion of the Founding era through the late 1800s, summarizing this era as follows:

> The death penalty was an accepted punishment at the time of the adoption of the Constitution and the Bill of Rights. In that era, death sentences were usually carried out by hanging. ... Hanging remained the standard method of execution through much of the 19th century, but that began to change in the century's later years. ... In the 1880's, the Legislature of the State of New York appointed a commission to find 'the most humane and practical method known to modern science of carrying into effect the sentence of death in capital cases.' ... The commission recommended electrocution, and in 1888, the Legislature enacted a law providing for this method of execution. ... In subsequent years, other States followed New York's lead in the 'belief that electrocution is less painful and more humane than hanging.'

Next, Justice Alito moved into the 1900s, when different methods of execution made their way into the American criminal justice system:

> In 1921, the Nevada Legislature adopted another new method of execution, lethal gas, after concluding that this was 'the most humane manner known to modern science.' ... The Nevada Supreme Court rejected the argument that the use of lethal gas was unconstitutional, and other States followed Nevada's lead. Nevertheless, hanging and the firing squad were retained in some States, and electrocution remained the predominant method of execution until the 9-year hiatus in executions that ended with our judgment in *Gregg v. Georgia*.

Finally, Justice Alito indicated why the Court would be ruling against the Oklahoma death row inmates in this case, just as the Court had in every previous method-of-execution case in its history:

> After *Gregg* reaffirmed that the death penalty does not violate the Constitution, some States once again sought a more humane way to carry out death sentences. They eventually adopted lethal injection, which today is 'by far the most prevalent method of execution in the United States.'" Alito then added: "While methods of execution have changed over the years, "[t]his Court has never invalidated a State's chosen procedure for carrying out a sentence of death as the infliction of cruel and unusual punishment.

The Death Penalty and the Offender's Mental State

In *Ford v. Wainwright* (1986),[72] the Supreme Court held that the Eighth Amendment bars the execution of a person who is insane. Writing for a plurality of justices, Justice Thurgood Marshall declared, "It is no less abhorrent today than it has been for centuries to exact in penance the life of one whose mental illness prevents him from comprehending the reasons for the penalty or its implications." Of course, it must be noted that Justice Marshall was a steadfast opponent of the death penalty under all circumstances.

Two decades later, in *Panetti v. Quarterman* (2007),[73] the Court reiterated the position taken by Justice Marshall in *Ford v. Wainwright*. Justice Anthony Kennedy spoke for the Court:

> [I]t might be said that capital punishment is imposed because it has the potential to make the offender recognize at last the gravity of his crime and to allow the community as a whole, including the surviving family and friends of the victim, to affirm its own judgment that the culpability of the prisoner is so serious that the ultimate penalty must be sought and imposed. The potential for a prisoner's recognition of the severity of the offense and the objective of community vindication are called in question, however, if the prisoner's mental state is so distorted by a mental illness that his awareness of the crime and punishment has little or no relation to the understanding of those concepts shared by the community as a whole.

In 2019, the Supreme Court cited both the *Ford* and *Panetti* holdings in its opinion for *Madison v. Alabama*.[74] With the *Madison* decision, the Court—which had previously issued multiple rulings involving this petitioner[75]—temporarily halted the execution of an Alabama inmate named Vernon Madison, who was suffering from dementia. The majority opinion from Justice Elena Kagan, which remanded the case for further consideration, established some baseline principles for such cases by saying the following:

> [U]nder *Ford* and *Panetti*, the Eighth Amendment may permit executing Madison even if he cannot remember committing his crime. Second, under those same decisions, the Eighth Amendment may prohibit executing Madison even though he suffers from dementia, rather than delusions. The sole question on which Madison's competency depends is whether he can reach a "rational understanding" of why the State wants to execute him.

Providing added clarity, Justice Kagan also observed that the *Panetti* case "asks about understanding, not memory—more specifically, about a person's understanding of why the State seeks capital punishment for a crime, not his memory of the crime itself. And the one may exist without the other." Although the *Madison* case was remanded for reconsideration in light of the principles Kagan articulated, before additional legal action could conclude, Madison died in prison of natural causes at the age of 69.[76]

Intellectual Disability and the Death Penalty

In a line of cases beginning in 2002, the Supreme Court has applied the *evolving standards of decency* standard to place limits on the execution of individuals with certain intellectual disabilities. However, the precise definition of what exactly constitutes an intellectual disability has largely been left to the states to untangle, with high Court decisions providing broad parameters that offer a modicum of guidance.

First, in *Atkins v. Virginia* (2002),[77] the idea of "evolving standards" was said to prohibit the execution of those with "mental retardation." The *Atkins* decision heavily cited a case it was essentially overturning, *Penry v. Lynaugh* (1989),[78] where Justice O'Connor's majority opinion had noted, "Mental retardation is a factor that may well lessen a defendant's culpability for a capital offense." Although O'Connor's opinion in *Penry* granted that a jury should have been permitted to consider this factor, she stopped short of saying the Eighth Amendment always bars the execution of the mentally disabled. Even so, the majority opinion for *Atkins*, written by Justice Stevens, observed that many state legislatures had already taken steps to prevent such executions by 2002, perhaps offering an indication of evolving standards in this area. Along these lines, Justice Stevens opined, "It is not so much the number of these states that is significant, but the consistency of the direction of change. ... [There is] powerful evidence that today our society views mentally retarded offenders as categorically less culpable than the average criminal." With that, a ban on such executions emerged in case precedent.

However, the *Atkins* decision left tremendous leeway for states when it comes to determining the meaning of the phrase *mentally retarded.* The majority opinion presented three considerations for guiding this type of assessment: (1) "[s]ubaverage intellectual functioning," potentially evaluated via an intelligence quotient (IQ) test with a score below 70; (2) "[l]imitations in adaptive skills such as communication, self-care, and self-direction"; and (3) "a manifestation of factors 1 and 2 before an individual reaches the age of 18."

More than a decade later, as society's use of the term *retarded* became more limited, the Supreme Court's decision in *Hall v. Florida* (2014)[79] indicated a correlated shift in nomenclature, with Justice Kennedy's majority opinion molding the *Atkins* standard to apply as a prohibition on the execution of individuals who were defined as "intellectually disabled." Specifically, Kennedy cited the *Atkins* decision in saying, "This Court has held that the Eighth and Fourteenth Amendments to the Constitution forbid the execution of persons with intellectual disability." Kennedy then took umbrage with the way officials in Florida had applied the *Atkins* framework, primarily because those officials defined intellectual disability exclusively through a score below 70 on an IQ test. Justice Kennedy addressed this approach by observing, "If, from test scores, a prisoner is deemed to have an IQ above 70, all further exploration of intellectual disability is foreclosed. This rigid rule, the Court now holds, creates an unacceptable risk that persons with intellectual disability will be executed, and thus is unconstitutional."

Kennedy went on to note, "Florida's rule disregards established medical practice in two interrelated ways. It takes an IQ score as final and conclusive evidence of a defendant's intellectual capacity when experts in the field would consider other evidence. It also relies on a purportedly scientific measurement of the defendant's abilities, his IQ score, while refusing to recognize that the score is, on its own terms, imprecise." In the end, rather than the formulaic approach used in Florida, the Court recommended a more generalized assessment that involved consideration of "deficits in adaptive functioning" and "established medical practice" in the realm of cognitive functioning.

One year later, the Supreme Court reaffirmed elements of the *Hall* decision with its ruling in *Brumfield v. Cain* (2016).[80] In this case, a Louisiana trial court refused to provide a defendant in a capital case, Kevan Brumfield, with an evidentiary hearing in which his intellectual capacity could be evaluated for an *Atkins* claim. The Court found the trial court's refusal to be a violation of the Eighth Amendment. Justice Sotomayor's majority opinion chastised the lower court for focusing too much on Brumfield's IQ score (which was 75) without adequate examination of adaptive impairment. In Louisiana, a person could be defined as having *adaptive impairment* if there was evidence of deficiencies in three of six *areas of major life activity.* In applying this standard to *Brumfield*, Sotomayor said the following:

> An individual, like Brumfield, who was placed in special education classes at an early age, was suspected of having a learning disability, and can barely read at a fourth-grade level, certainly would seem to be deficient in both "[u]nderstanding and use of language" and "[l]earning"—two of the six "areas of major life activity". ... And the evidence of his low birth weight, of his commitment to mental health facilities at a young age, and of officials'

administration of antipsychotic and sedative drugs to him at that time, all indicate that Brumfield may well have had significant deficits in at least one of the remaining four areas.

Therefore, Justice Sotomayor determined that an evidentiary hearing should have been granted. She concluded her opinion by noting the severity of Brumfield's crime, which was the murder of a police officer in Baton Rouge—a fact upon which Justice Thomas focused in his dissent. Sotomayor responded directly to the dissent, acknowledging the heinous act but also focusing on the constitutional questions at stake:

> We do not deny that Brumfield's crimes were terrible, causing untold pain for the victims and their families. But we are called upon today to resolve a different issue. There has already been one death that society rightly condemns. The question here is whether Brumfield cleared [the Antiterrorism and Effective Death Penalty Act of 1996's] procedural hurdles, and was thus entitled to a hearing to show that he so lacked the capacity for self-determination that it would violate the Eighth Amendment to permit the State to impose the "law's most severe sentence," … and take his life as well. That question, and that question alone, we answer in the affirmative.

The Supreme Court further refined the *Atkins* holding with its decision in *Moore v. Texas* (2017),[81] when a 5–3 majority ruled that the state of Texas had relied too heavily upon IQ tests in rejecting a death row inmate's claim of intellectual disability. The Court added an interesting element to the *Atkins* calculus by saying Texas officials had erred in failing to consider *current medical diagnostic standards* as a factor in defining intellectual disability. Justice Ginsburg's majority opinion cited to the *Atkins* and *Hall* decisions to reiterate, "States have some flexibility, but not 'unfettered discretion,' in enforcing the *Atkins* holding." She then expressed concern for the fact that "'[i]f the States were to have complete autonomy to define intellectual disability as they wished,' we have observed, '*Atkins* could become a nullity, and the Eighth Amendment›s protection of human dignity would not become a reality.' The medical community's current standards supply one constraint on States' leeway in this area."

The recognition of how evolving medical standards and *improved understanding over time* can play a role in updating the *Atkins* holding ultimately stands as a critical component of the *Moore v. Texas* decision. Beyond that, according to the Court's ruling in *McWilliams v. Dunn* (2017),[82] released just three months later, an indigent defendant in a capital case is entitled to a state-funded mental health assessment by a trained medical professional—a caveat that could ensure that the core principles of *Atkins* are respected when a defendant lacks financial resources.

THE CONSTITUTION IN ACTION
Exonerations, Deterrence, and Costs: Evaluation of the Death Penalty

Competing arguments related to the death penalty often involve juxtapositions related to, on one hand, the use of capital punishment as a deterrent to crime and, on the other hand, risks related to the executions of innocent persons. Costs of implementing the death penalty are also relevant to such dialogue, particularly in light of the length of time that typically spans the interval between the commission of a capital offense and an execution for that crime.

One of the few widespread statistical analyses that addresses exonerations of those sentenced to death comes from Death Penalty Information Center (DPIC).[83] Their data indicate that for every 8.3 people given a death sentence, one person is wrongfully sentenced to die. Wrongful convictions of this type were observed in twenty-nine states. The DPIC study also found that 70% of death penalty exonerations included "misconduct by police, prosecutors, or other government officials" and 80% of those cases involved perjury or other types of false accusations. False confessions and mistaken eyewitness identification, topics we have covered elsewhere in this text, were also contributing factors discussed in the study. Additionally, data demonstrate that misconduct played a role in 78.8% of exonerations involving Black defendants and 58.2% of exonerations involving White defendants. The length of time it took to reveal these improper convictions was also staggering in some cases, eight of which took more than thirty years to be corrected. A key in most exonerations was testing DNA evidence, but the reality is that many cases, particularly older ones, lack any such evidence for testing.

Moreover, other factors to consider include the fact that some states had in the past allowed judges to overrule juries and some have allowed for nonunanimous juries to recommend a death sentence; these mechanisms seem to contribute to death sentences for the innocent. For example, fifteen percent of exonerations involved a judge overruling a jury that had recommended life in prison, including twenty-three in Florida, five in Alabama, and one in Delaware—the three states that do not currently require unanimous juries for doling out a death sentence.[84]

In terms of the costs of housing a death row inmate, the Equal Justice Initiative says, "The death penalty is far more expensive than a system in which life imprisonment without parole is the maximum sentence. Sophisticated studies at the state level show that the death penalty costs taxpayers more than life without parole."[85]

From a broader perspective, costs and exonerations, of course, are balanced against discussions of whether the death penalty deters crime. In this regard, according to the Equal Justice Initiative, "After more than three decades of research examining whether the threat of a death sentence deters people from committing aggravated murders, there is no reliable evidence that the death penalty deters murder or that it protects police." That quote was followed by a reference to research from the National Research Council of the National Academies of Sciences, which the Equal Justice Initiative used to say that "studies claiming the death penalty has a deterrent effect are fundamentally flawed."[86] The Equal Justice Initiative also cited to the Death Penalty Information Center in saying, "Studies also have shown that murder rates … are consistently higher in states that have the death penalty."[87] Of course, numerous variables can play a role in explaining a particular state's murder rate, but a sizable body of literature has found little statistical evidence to support the notion of a deterrent effect emanating from the death penalty.

Equity Considerations in Capital Punishment

"Evolving standards of decency" were again relevant for the Supreme Court in *Roper v. Simmons* (2005),[88] which found that the Eighth Amendment barred application of the death penalty to an offender who was under the age of 18 at the time they committed their capital crime. Based on this ruling, those individuals can never be executed for any crimes committed while they were minors. This decision overruled a precedent from 1989 that had permitted such executions,[89] a shift that Justice Kennedy's majority opinion for *Roper* addressed by saying, "Because the Eighth Amendment 'draw[s] its meaning from … evolving standards of decency,' … significant changes in societal mores over time may require us to reevaluate a prior decision. Nevertheless, it remains 'this Court's prerogative alone to overrule one of its precedents.'"

More narrowly, in assessing *societal mores*, perhaps as a beacon of evolving standards of decency, the Supreme Court remarked that a majority of state legislatures had enacted prohibitions on executing those who were minors at the time of their offenses. The Court also looked to international norms, finding the following:

> It is proper that we acknowledge the overwhelming weight of international opinion against the juvenile death penalty, resting in large part on the understanding that the instability and emotional imbalance of young people may often be a factor in the crime. … The opinion

of the world community, while not controlling our outcome, does provide respected and significant confirmation for our own conclusions.

As noted in our discussion of life sentences in the previous chapter, the *Roper* case also spoke to a lessened sense of culpability related to the crimes of juveniles, for three primary reasons: 1) a "lack of maturity and an underdeveloped sense of responsibility", 2) the fact that juveniles are "more vulnerable or susceptible to negative influences and outside pressures", and 3) the supposition that "the character of a juvenile is not as well formed as that of an adult." Coalescing these factors, Justice Kennedy concluded, "The susceptibility of juveniles to immature and irresponsible behavior means 'their irresponsible conduct is not as morally reprehensible as that of an adult.'"

Justice Kennedy also considered two of the primary justifications for the death penalty, discussing their applicability to juvenile offenders in this fashion:

> Whether viewed as an attempt to express the community's moral outrage or as an attempt to right the balance for the wrong to the victim, the case for retribution is not as strong with a minor as with an adult. Retribution is not proportional if the law's most severe penalty is imposed on one whose culpability or blameworthiness is diminished, to a substantial degree, by reason of youth and immaturity. As for deterrence, it is unclear whether the death penalty has a significant or even measurable deterrent effect on juveniles, as counsel for the petitioner acknowledged at oral argument.

Race and the Death Penalty

The current death row population demographics, considering all state and federal death row inmates, indicates that 42% are White (1,032), 41% are Black (998), 14% are Latino (335), and 3% are classified as "other."[90] Yet studies that incorporate control variables are capable of revealing more meaningful context for these raw numbers. Along these lines, there is a sizable body of scholarly research examining the impact of race on the imposition of capital punishment.

Early studies from the 1940s and 1950s found significant disparities in administration of the death penalty based on the race of defendants.[91] Specifically, according to one summary, "these studies determined that Blacks were indicted, charged, convicted, and sentenced to death in disproportionate numbers. ..."[92] Even so, these early works were criticized for failing to implement adequate statistical controls.[93]

In 1983, David Baldus, Charles Pulaski, and George Woodworth published what is still the most prominent of the modern, controlled studies regarding race and the death penalty.[94] Using data from more than 2,000 death penalty cases in Georgia from 1973 to 1979, the Baldus Study found that the race of the defendant was *not* a significant predictor of death penalty decisions. The study did, however, determine that offenders who killed White victims were more likely to receive the death penalty, even after controlling for many other relevant variables, including the nature of the crime, the location of the crime, and the characteristics of offender and victim.

The findings of the Baldus Study have been buttressed by a substantial body of subsequent research. In 2004, Baldus and Woodworth noted that "empirical evidence generally suggests that the United States death penalty system is no longer characterized by the systemic discrimination against Black defendants. ..."[95] In other work, Gross and Mauro looked at eight southern states and found the presence of a White victim was a significant predictor of a death sentence.[96] Radelet and Pierce examined death-eligible cases in Florida from 1976–1987, noting defendants were 3.4 times more likely to receive a death sentence for killing a White victim.[97] Likewise, Paternoster found that, in South Carolina from 1977–1981, capital charges were 9.6 times more likely when the victim was White.[98]

Other studies have arrived at similar conclusions regarding the race of a victim.[99] Notably, in 1990, the U.S. General Accounting Office (GAO) observed that, of twenty-eight previous studies of race and the death penalty, 82% found evidence that the victim's race influenced the defendant's likelihood of either being charged with capital murder by a prosecutor or being sentenced to death by a jury.[100] Baldus and Woodworth also reviewed eighteen studies from 1990 to 2003 and again noted that while the race of the defendant did not have a significant impact on likelihood of receiving a death sentence, the race of the victim did.[101] Moreover, in their review of extant research, Radelet and Borg concluded in 2000 that "the death penalty is between three and four times more likely to be imposed in cases in which the victim is White rather than Black."[102]

More recent studies have also found that the race of the victim is a significant predictor of a death sentence in Maryland,[103] Illinois,[104] California,[105] Colorado,[106] and North Carolina.[107] However, in Nebraska, the Baldus and Woodworth study uncovered no evidence of a race-of-victim effect, which might be attributed to the fact that cases that were more likely to advance to the death penalty phase arose in urban geographic regions that were more populated with minorities.[108]

Yet despite this body of scholarship, courts have been reluctant to apply society-wide data to an individual defendant's case. In *McCleskey v. Kemp* (1987),[109] the Supreme Court addressed the case of a Georgia death row inmate who relied on the Baldus Study in raising an argument about discrimination in application of the death penalty. Rejecting this appeal, the Court noted that a specific defendant needed to provide evidence of individualized discrimination. Justice Lewis Powell's majority opinion for a 5–4 Court indicated that "the Baldus study does not demonstrate a constitutionally significant risk of racial bias affecting the Georgia capital sentencing process." More specifically, the opinion stated that "to prevail under the Equal Protection Clause, McCleskey must prove that the decisionmakers in *his* case acted with discriminatory purpose" (emphasis in original). Dissenting, Justice Stevens observed the following:

> [T]here exist certain categories of extremely serious crimes for which prosecutors consis-
> tently seek, and juries consistently impose, the death penalty without regard to the race of
> the victim or the race of the offender. If [the State] were to narrow the class of death-eligible
> defendants to those categories, the danger of arbitrary and discriminatory imposition of
> the death penalty would be significantly decreased, if not eradicated.[110]

The key, then, might be determining how to account for "extremely serious crimes" because as Cheatwood said, so-called "lesser" homicides—"where the crime is not as brutal or as heinous"—provide more of an opportunity for "racism to come into play."[111] In the following box, we offer some nonracial indicators of what literature has found to explain death sentence decisions.

THE CONSTITUTION IN ACTION

Besides Race, What Factors Influence Who Gets the Death Penalty?

1. Having multiple murder victims stands as a key explanatory variable. As Baldus et al. said, "Additional deaths amplify culpability ... [and] are so egregious that they should have comparably harsh procedural outcomes."[112] Previous literature has controlled for the number of victims and determined the likelihood of a death sentence increases with that number, including the work of Pierce and Radelet,[113] Radelet and Pierce,[114] Baldus et al.,[115] Unah,[116] Phillips,[117] and Weiss et al.[118]

2. A defendant who has committed another felony along with a murder seems to face an increased likelihood of a death sentence; Pierce and Radelet,[119] Kremling et al.,[120] Songer and Unah,[121] Unah,[122] Phillips,[123] and Williams et al.[124] all observed that a sexual assault committed with a murder increases the odds of receiving a death sentence.

3. Williams et al. also noted that "several studies find that cases with female victims are more likely to receive a death sentence than cases with male victims." Further, Williams et al.'s own research indicated that the victim's sex is more relevant to juries than to prosecutors.[125]

4. Cheatwood's research found that cases involving the killing of law enforcement officers are highly likely to lead to a death sentence.[126]

5. Phillips said that a prior felony conviction can impact likelihood of a death sentence,[127] as did Weiss et al.[128] and Baldus et al.[129] Pierce and Radelet also stated that "the defendant's prior criminal history [is] generally considered to be an important factor in the imposition of the death penalty," with such a history increasing the likelihood of a death sentence.[130]

6. Streib examined cases from 1900 to 2005 and found that female defendants were less likely to be given the death penalty than male defendants, even when controlling for similar crimes.[131] Discussing Streib's work, Songer and Unah said, "Empirical evidence suggests widespread reluctance on the part of prosecutors, judges and juries to sentence female offenders to death."[132] Hindson et al. also determined that prosecutors seek the death penalty more often against males.[133]

Prisoners' Rights

Prior to the 1970s, Supreme Court case precedent regarding the rights of prisoners was scant regarding topics like prison conditions, medical treatment, and overcrowding. Through that decade, some standards would begin to emerge from the high Court, as society itself begin to grapple more seriously with issues concerning the rehabilitation of offenders. Initial examinations of prisoners' rights from the Court did not focus upon the Eighth Amendment, though, and instead involved the Fourteenth Amendment's Due Process Clause.

To begin, in *Wolf v. McDonnell* (1974),[134] the Court found that the Due Process Clause required a state to offer procedural protections, such as hearings, to prisoners "when [they are] deprived of good time credits because of serious misconduct"—in places where those good time credits are permitted under state law. Two years later, in *Meachum v. Fano* (1976),[135] the Court held that a prisoner is not entitled to a voice in whether they are transferred to a different prison.

From those modest beginnings, over the course of the next two decades, the concept of prisoners' rights would evolve to address—and, in many instances, protect—the rights of those who are incarcerated. In the remainder of this section, we focus upon Eighth Amendment concepts, but in chapters 4 and 5, we address the speech and religious rights of the incarcerated.

The Right to Medical Treatment

Just five months after the *Meachum v. Fano* opinion was released, the Supreme Court's first major decision applying the Eighth Amendment to the medical treatment of prisoners arrived with the ruling in *Estelle v. Gamble* (1976).[136] In this case, J.W. Gamble suffered a back injury when a bale of cotton fell on him as he was unloading it from a truck during a prison work detail. He received limited medical treatment, and a doctor proclaimed him to be in *first class* medical condition by January of 1977, when Gamble was put into solitary confinement for telling prison officials he was unable to work because of back pain. He filed a lawsuit, suggesting his treatment at the hands of prison officials violated the Eighth Amendment.

On review, the Supreme Court declared that inadequate medical treatment for prisoners could, in fact, constitute cruel and unusual punishment. Justice Marshall's majority opinion created a specific framework for evaluating such cases: the deliberate indifference standard. This was evident when he said, "We therefore conclude that deliberate indifference to serious medical needs of prisoners constitutes the 'unnecessary and wanton infliction of pain,' [citing *Gregg v. Georgia*] ... proscribed by the Eighth Amendment." A key phrase in that quote is *serious medical needs*, which does not include minor medical issues, like cuts, scrapes, or minor bruises. Justice Marshall also linked this standard to both prison doctors and prison guards, saying, "This is true whether the indifference is manifested by prison doctors in their response to the prisoner's needs or by prison guards in intentionally denying or delaying access to medical care or intentionally interfering with the treatment once prescribed."

Yet Justice Marshall's majority opinion was careful to add a volitional component to the analysis, which he did by saying, "This conclusion does not mean, however, that every claim by a prisoner that he has not received adequate medical treatment states a violation of the Eighth Amendment. An accident, although it may produce added anguish, is not on that basis alone to be characterized as wanton infliction of unnecessary pain." The need for *wanton infliction*—which could come in the form of intentionally denying medical care or providing inadequate medical care—is an essential component of showing the deliberate indifference requisite for an Eighth Amendment violation related to prisoner medical care. Finally, it is worth noting that this opinion, in quoting an Eighth Circuit decision, said that the Eighth Amendment is meant to embody "'broad and idealistic concepts of dignity, civilized standards, humanity, and decency.'"[137]

DELIBERATE INDIFFERENCE STANDARD: A legal requirement that must be demonstrated for a prison official to be held liable in civil court for a lawsuit related to the treatment of prisoners in a correctional facility, including lawsuit related to inadequate medical care.

More than a decade after *Estelle v. Gamble*, a 1988 decision[138] from the high Court expanded its holding with the declaration that any physician who has a contract with a state to perform medical services for a prison—even private practice physicians—are considered state actors, and thus, their conduct in treating (or failing to treat) prisoners could give rise to a claim for cruel and unusual punishment.

THE CONSTITUTION IN ACTION
COVID-19 Lawsuits Address Prisoner Health Care

According to the Prison Policy Initiative, which cited data from the *Journal of the American Medical Association*, the death rate from COVID-19 in prisons was more than double that of the U.S. population at large.[139] Another report from the Prison Policy Initiative found, "Deaths in prison increased by 46% nationwide. More than 6,100 people died in prison in 2020, which was 1,930 more deaths than in 2019."[140]

In the midst of the pandemic, particularly in the spring and summer of 2020, there seemed to be a concerted effort in some jurisdictions of the country to release nonviolent prisoners as a means of easing overcrowding—although many such efforts were short-lived. Pathways to release varied across branches of government. In some states, executive orders were used by governors to commute sentences or to order early release. For example, Oklahoma's governor commuted sentences of more than 450 prisoners; Washington's governor commuted nearly 300 sentences; and Kentucky's governor released more than 800 offenders with less than six months left on their sentences, with a focus on those with medical vulnerabilities.[141] Legislative acts also played a role. For instance, in New Jersey, which had the highest prison death rate for COVID-19, Governor Phil Murphy signed legislation calling for early release of those with less than a year left on sentences (up to eight months early), cutting the prison population in the state by 40% over 11 months. The program was paused in October 2021 and then restarted in February 2022.[142]

Moreover, lawsuits related to Eighth Amendment challenges stemming from the spread of COVID-19 in prisons abounded, with settlements reached in many of these cases. In February 2021, for example, North Carolina agreed to release 3,500 prisoners through a settlement crafted in response to a lawsuit brought by the ACLU and NAACP.[143] Elsewhere, in March 2021, a settlement in an eleven-month-old federal lawsuit in Illinois led to early release for approximately 1,000 state prisoners there.[144] Multiple California courts ordered early releases, including an October 2020 state appeals court ruling for San Quentin Prison to cut its population by half[145] and a December 2020 directive that Orange County reduce its jail population by half to facilitate social distancing.[146] In May 2020, a federal court order also led to the Federal Bureau of Prisons releasing 837 prisoners of a "medically vulnerable subclass" at a prison in Elkton, Ohio; all of those prisoners were over the age of 65 with some type of health issue.[147] In April 2020, the Hawaii Supreme Court appointed a special master to oversee inmate releases through coordination with public defenders, leading to more than 600 releases, but the program ended by June 2020.[148] Even ICE reduced a holding facility population by close to 90%, following an ACLU lawsuit filed in May 2020.[149]

Other lawsuits have been aimed at effectuating changes in COVID-19 protocols within prisons. Notably, a unique lawsuit was filed on behalf of Arkansas prisoners in January 2022, alleging prison physicians gave inmates pills that were said to be "vitamins, antibiotics, or steroids"—when, in fact, the inmates were given the anti-parasitic drug Ivermectin (which some sources claimed could be a treatment for COVID-19); the ACLU official who filed the lawsuit, Gary Sullivan, said, "No one—including incarcerated individuals—should be deceived and subject to medical experimentation."[150] In April 2021, a lawsuit led an Oregon prison, the Snake River Correctional Institution, to implement stronger safeguards related to mask policies and testing.[151] Across the country, in the summer of 2021, the City of Philadelphia agreed to $125,000 settlement over a federal class-action lawsuit that claimed, among other things, that prisoners held in city-run facilities were not given their required time outside of cells, were not provided access to soap or hand sanitizer, and were exposed to surfaces in the prison that had not been disinfected.[152] In February 2022, Washington, D.C. also settled a COVID-related lawsuit, by agreeing to regular inspections of jails as well as to ensuring provision of hygiene products and timely medical care.[153]

Despite the wide array of lawsuits and early release examples delineated above, a January 2022 article from Wendy Sawyer of the Prison Policy Initiative observed that "[p]rison, jail, and probation populations dropped dramatically from 2019-2020, but these drops were due to mainly to emergency responses to COVID-19, and correctional populations have already started rebounding toward pre-pandemic levels."[154] In a separate piece for the Prison Policy Initiative, Emily Widra observed, "Data from 2020, recently released by the Bureau of Justice Statistics, shows that prisons nationwide released 10% fewer people in 2020 than in 2019. Instead, data suggest most of the population drops we've seen over the past 20 months are due to reduced prison admissions, not increasing releases."[155] To this point, Sawyer specifically found that, "The decrease in the incarcerated population was not related to releases, but rather the 40% drop in prison admissions and 16% drop in jail admissions."[156] Data also indicated that parole boards granted fewer instances of parole during 2020 than 2019,[157] and Sawyer said that "many so-called 'exits' from probation and parole were actually deaths," adding that "in eight states, at least 2% of 'releases' were, in fact, deaths."[158]

Use of Force in Prison Settings

In chapter 10 we discussed the use of force by police officers, noting that the Supreme Court has applied an objective reasonableness standard under the Fourth Amendment when evaluating claims that an officer used has used excessive force.[159] While the use of force by correctional officers is actionable under the Eighth Amendment, the standard by which courts evaluate such claims is rather different. In *Estelle v. Gamble* (1976) the Supreme Court said that, with respect to prisoners, "only the *'unnecessary and wanton infliction of pain'* ... *constitutes cruel and unusual punishment forbidden by the Eighth Amendment*" (emphasis in original). That phrase laid a foundation for prison officials to have greater leeway in using force inside correctional facilities.

The Supreme Court's ruling in *Whitley v. Albers* (1986)[160] cemented the notion of enhanced flexibility for corrections officials when it comes to maintaining (or restoring) order and discipline in the prison context. In this case, a corrections official was taken hostage by inmates as a riot broke out inside an Oregon state prison. To secure the safe release of the hostage, other officials fired shotgun blasts at a low height into an area where a group of inmates could have been blocking access to the cell block where the hostage was kept. One prisoner, who was shot in the leg, filed suit, claiming the gunshot amounted to cruel and unusual punishment. However, the high Court disagreed, finding no constitutional violation.

Justice O'Connor's majority opinion referenced past cases, observing "the deliberate indifference standard articulated in *Estelle* was appropriate in the context presented in that case because the State's responsibility to attend to the medical needs of prisoners does not ordinarily clash with other equally important governmental responsibilities." In illuminating how courts might review the provision of such medical care (or the lack thereof), she went on to suggest that "... 'deliberate indifference to a prisoner's serious illness or injury,' ... can typically be established or disproved without the necessity of balancing competing institutional concerns for the safety of prison staff or other inmates."

Next, O'Connor spoke more directly to these "competing interests" in a use-of-force context by saying the following:

> [I]n making and carrying out decisions involving the use of force to restore order in the face of a prison disturbance, prison officials undoubtedly must take into account the very real threats the unrest presents to inmates and prison officials alike, in addition to the possible harms to inmates against whom force might be used. ... In this setting, a deliberate indifference standard does not adequately capture the importance of such competing obligations, or convey the appropriate hesitancy to critique in hindsight decisions necessarily made

Obiter Dicta

"After incarceration, only the unnecessary and wanton infliction of pain ... constitutes cruel and unusual punishment forbidden by the Eighth Amendment. To be cruel and unusual punishment, conduct that does not purport to be punishment at all must involve more than ordinary lack of due care for the prisoner's interests or safety. ... It is *obduracy and wantonness, not inadvertence or error in good faith*, that characterize the conduct prohibited by the Cruel and Unusual Punishments Clause, whether that conduct occurs in connection with establishing conditions of confinement, supplying medical needs, or restoring official control over a tumultuous cellblock."

—Justice Sandra Day O'Connor, writing for the Supreme Court in Whitley v. Albers, *475 U.S. 312 (1986)*

in haste, under pressure, and frequently without the luxury of a second chance.

The majority opinion then quoted the Second Circuit, in the process distilling a more refined test for evaluating use-of-force situations in prison settings:

> Where a prison security measure is undertaken to resolve a disturbance, such as occurred in this case, that indisputably poses significant risks to the safety of inmates and prison staff, we think the question whether the measure taken inflicted unnecessary and wanton pain and suffering ultimately turns on 'whether force was applied in a good faith effort to maintain or restore discipline or maliciously and sadistically for the very purpose of causing harm.'[161]

The viability of the *Whitley* opinion was apparent six years later in *Hudson v. McMillian* (1992),[162] when a 6-3 majority, again speaking through an opinion from Justice O'Connor, said, "[W]e hold that whenever prison officials stand accused of using excessive physical force in violation of the Cruel and Unusual Punishments Clause, the core judicial inquiry is that set out in *Whitley*: whether force was applied in a good-faith effort to maintain or restore discipline, or maliciously and sadistically to cause harm." In this 1992 decision, the Court confronted a case in which corrections officers beat an inmate in a Louisiana prison while he was handcuffed and shackled, leaving him with bruises, facial swelling, and teeth that were loosened, along with a cracked dental plate. Prior to the beating, a supervisor had told the officers "not to have too much fun." In this case, the Court reached the important conclusion that physical force can amount to cruel and unusual punishment, even when there is no serious bodily injury.

Subsequently, in *Hope v. Pelzer* (2002),[163] the Supreme Court addressed the claims of an Alabama prison inmate who was handcuffed and tied to a hitching post on two occasions, with the latter lasting for seven hours and including the denial of any bathroom access. Although prison officials claimed they were subduing a disruptive inmate, the majority opinion from Justice Stevens declared that "the Eighth Amendment violation is obvious." In Stevens's view, "This punitive treatment amounts to gratuitous infliction of 'wanton and unnecessary' pain that our precedent clearly prohibits." Therefore, although prison use-of-force cases are governed by standards that provide significant deference to corrections officials—so that they might maintain order in challenging, chaotic situations—the high Court has still found there are constitutional limits to that deference.

Protection from Harm

Certainly, situations arise in the context of a prison setting in which harm befalls an inmate not at the hands of prison officials but, rather, at the hands of other inmates. But at what point must corrections officials provide an inmate with protection from such harm? The Supreme Court provided an answer in *Farmer v. Brennan* (1994),[164] when the majority opinion from Justice Souter said that claims of prison officials failing to protect a prisoner from harm required a showing of "deliberate indifference" on the part of those officials, which would imply that officials were aware of a threat of harm and did nothing to prevent it. In this case, a prisoner named Farmer had undergone a sex change operation—shifting from male to female genitalia—but prison officials still placed Farmer into the male general population, where Farmer was then beaten and raped by a cell mate. Farmer filed suit, claiming a violation of the Eighth Amendment, but a federal district court judge dismissed his case, and the Seventh Circuit agreed with that outcome. But on review, the Supreme Court remanded the case for reconsideration in the lower courts, with a directive for use of the deliberate indifference standard.

Justice Souter also provided a more specific depiction of deliberate indifference, observing that it "entails more than mere negligence," instead equating it with something he called subjective recklessness— where the word *subjective* connoted an assessment of what the official knew at the moment that gave rise to a claim (not what an outsider ascribes to that moment in hindsight). Justice Souter defined this idea of subjective recklessness as follows:

> We hold ... that a prison official cannot be found liable under the Eighth Amendment for denying an inmate humane conditions of confinement unless the official knows of and disregards an excessive risk to inmate health or safety; the official must both be aware of facts from which the inference could be drawn that a substantial risk of serious harm exists, and he must also draw the inference. This approach comports best with the text of the Amendment as our cases have interpreted it. The Eighth Amendment does not outlaw cruel and unusual "conditions"; it outlaws cruel and unusual "punishments."

SUBJECTIVE RECKLESSNESS: A legal standard often connected to lawsuit related to a failure of prison officials to protect an inmate from harm; this standard requires a prison official to have been aware of and consciously disregarded the risk of harm to an inmate.

THE CONSTITUTION AND SOCIAL JUSTICE
The Case of *Farmer v. Brennan* Leads to Passage of a New Federal Law

Dee Farmer, who was born a biological male and later transitioned to a transgender woman, was sentenced to federal prison after being found guilty of credit card fraud in 1986. Prior to incarceration, Farmer had received breast implants, taken estrogen therapy, and undergone what the Supreme Court's majority opinion for this case called "unsuccessful 'black market' testicle-removal surgery." Farmer continued to receive hormone therapy in prison via drugs that were smuggled in, and also wore clothing in a feminine manner, such as with a shirt "off one shoulder" (according to the Supreme Court's discussion of legal briefs filed in this case).

In a sign of how differently society looked upon issues of gender identity in this era, the Supreme Court's opinion said that Farmer was "diagnosed by medical personnel of the Bureau of Prisons as a transsexual," suggesting this was looked upon as a psychiatric disorder according to 1980s American Medical Association and American Psychiatric Association standards.[165] Under federal prison rules, upon incarceration at the Federal Correctional Institute in Oxford, Wisconsin in 1986, Farmer was placed into the male general population based on biological sex at birth. Three years later, Farmer was transferred to the U.S. Penitentiary in Terre Haute, Indiana, apparently for disciplinary reasons, according to court records. A federal penitentiary facility is, in the Supreme Court's words, for "more troublesome prisoners." Upon arrival there, Farmer was originally placed in administrative segregation but soon thereafter was sent to the male general population, where Farmer was beaten and raped by a cell mate.

Farmer, acting as the attorney of record, filed a lawsuit against prison officials claiming a violation of the Eighth Amendment. After unsuccessful cases in federal district court and at the Seventh Circuit, Farmer found some success at the Supreme Court, which remanded the case for reconsideration in light of new guiding principles. However, on remand, a federal district court jury that was instructed to follow the Supreme Court's preferred standards for a subjective recklessness approach to deliberate indifference ruled against Farmer.

Yet the publicity of Farmer's case brought national attention to the problem of prison rape. That attention, in turn, led to Congress passing the Prison Rape Elimination Act of 2003,[166] which, according to the National Institute of Justice, "requires that federal, state and local correctional facilities maintain and enforce a zero-tolerance policy toward sexual assault for both inmate-on-inmate and staff-on-inmate misconduct."[167] Moreover, every year since the passage of this law, the Bureau of Justice has been required to catalog a statistical review of prison rape claims. The 2012 report, for example, indicated approximately 4% of state and federal inmates and 3.2% of local jail inmates claimed to have been the victim of sexual assault by an inmate or by a corrections facility employee at some point during their incarceration.[168] Ultimately, although Farmer's lawsuit itself was not successful, its legacy has impacted protection-from-harm cases through the present day—both via an applicable federal law and through the standards of review emanating from the Supreme Court decision that carries Farmer's name.[169]

Prison Conditions

In *Rhodes v. Chapman* (1981),[170] two inmates who shared a cell in an Ohio state prison brought a lawsuit challenging the practice of *double celling*, which referred to two inmates being housed in the same prison cell. The Supreme Court found no violation of the Eighth Amendment in this matter, with Justice Powell's majority opinion bluntly stating, "The Constitution does not mandate comfortable prisons." Powell offered guidance derived from case precedent by observing, "Conditions [in prison] must not involve the wanton and unnecessary infliction of pain, nor may they be grossly disproportionate to the severity of the crime warranting imprisonment." Applying that standard, he found nothing wrong with the practice of double celling, which, in this case, involved bunk beds and a toilet in each cell. Powell brusquely noted that "prisons, which house persons convicted of serious crimes, cannot be free of discomfort. Thus, these considerations properly are weighed by the legislature and prison administration, rather than a court."

Beyond that, Powell provided a broad declaration related to Eighth Amendment jurisprudence, generally, by quoting *Gregg v. Georgia* in saying, "This Court must proceed cautiously in making an Eighth Amendment judgment, because, unless we reverse it, '[a] decision that a given punishment is impermissible under the Eighth Amendment cannot be reversed short of a constitutional amendment. …'" Extensive deference to prison officials and legislative actors, then, is a key principle that emerges from this case.

Later, in *Wilson v. Seiter* (1991),[171] a prisoner in an Ohio state prison brought forth a lawsuit that, according to the Supreme Court's majority opinion, made claims of "overcrowding, excessive noise, insufficient locker storage space, inadequate heating and cooling, improper ventilation, unclean and inadequate restrooms, unsanitary dining facilities and food preparation, and housing with mentally and physically ill inmates." Justice Scalia's opinion of the Court made it clear that the evolving standards of decency test from *Trop v. Dulles* was still relevant in a case such as this, noting, "No static 'test' can exist by which courts determine whether conditions of confinement are cruel and unusual, for the Eighth Amendment 'must draw its meaning from the evolving standards of decency that mark the progress of a maturing society.'"

Justice Scalia's opinion in this case is particularly noteworthy for distilling the appropriate standards to analyze a prisoner's challenge to conditions of confinement. Scalia began by noting that the Eighth Amendment can apply to "challenges to conditions of confinement" because the Court has "made it clear that the conditions are themselves *part of the punishment*, even though not specifically 'meted out' by a statute or judge" (emphasis in original). He specifically applied this standard to health services by noting, "Indeed, the medical care a prisoner receives is just as much a 'condition' of his confinement as the food he is fed, the clothes he is issued, the temperature he is subjected to in his cell, and the protection he is afforded against other inmates."

But Scalia also observed the need for showing some type of ill intent on the part of prison officials for any claim of cruel and unusual punishment to be successful. While past cases might have reserved such an intent requirement only for cases involving physical harm, on this point, Scalia said the following:

> These cases mandate inquiry into a prison official's state of mind when it is claimed that the official has inflicted cruel and unusual punishment. … if a prison boiler malfunctions accidentally during a cold winter, an inmate would have no basis for an Eighth Amendment claim, even if he suffers objectively significant harm. … The source of the intent requirement is not the predilections of this Court, but the Eighth Amendment itself, which bans only cruel and unusual *punishment*. If the pain inflicted is not formally meted out as *punishment* by the statute or the sentencing judge, some mental element must be attributed to the inflicting officer before it can qualify." (emphasis in original)

The next key was determining "what state of mind applies in cases challenging prison conditions." In this regard, Justice Scalia stated that "our cases say that the offending conduct must be wanton," but he then articulated a potential dichotomy in how this standard could be applied across different contexts, observing the following:

> *Whitley* makes clear, however, that, in this context, wantonness does not have a fixed meaning, but must be determined with "due regard for differences in the kind of conduct against which an Eighth Amendment objection is lodged." … Where (as in *Whitley*) officials act in

response to a prison disturbance, their actions are necessarily taken "in haste, under pressure," and balanced against "competing institutional concerns for the safety of prison staff or other inmates." ... In such an emergency situation, we found that wantonness consisted of acting "*maliciously and sadistically for the very purpose of causing harm.*"

Despite adhering to that approach for situations in which prison safety could be compromised, Justice Scalia suggested an altogether different standard should be applied when addressing prisoner medical issues; regarding the latter, he quoted to *Whitley* and said that "the State's responsibility to attend to the medical needs of prisoners does not ordinarily clash with other equally important governmental responsibilities,' ... so that, in that context, as *Estelle* held, 'deliberate indifference' would constitute wantonness."

In summary, the *Whitley* standard could apply to use of force in a prison riot, but a deliberate indifference standard (which would be easier for a prisoner to demonstrate) is applicable to lawsuits about prison conditions impacting medical care. Ultimately, the *Wilson v. Seiter* case was remanded to lower courts for further consideration in light of the principles articulated by Justice Scalia.

Beyond these case precedents, the First Step Act of 2018[172] includes provisions to guide federal prison conditions. The law prohibits shackling pregnant inmates and also states that feminine hygiene products will be provided to inmates at no cost. It even calls for prisoners to be incarcerated within 500 miles of their homes when possible.

THE CONSTITUTION IN ACTION

Private Prison Closes in Mississippi After Federal Judge Highlights Deplorable Conditions

In 2015, U.S. District Court Judge Carlton Reeves issued a ruling that called the privately-run Walnut Grove prison in Mississippi "a picture of such horror as should be unrealized anywhere in the civilized world." Accordingly, even though this was a privately-run facility, the judge found that the Mississippi Department of Corrections was in violation of the Eighth Amendment because it had contracted to provide services that resulted in a failure to protect prisoners from violence at the hands of "gangs run amok."[173] That facility was permanently closed in September 2016.[174]

The contract between the state of Mississippi and the company operating the Walnut Grove facility was negotiated in 2012 by the former Commissioner of the Mississippi Department of Corrections, Christopher Epps. Epps resigned two years later and was charged with nearly forty federal crimes related to bribery, money laundering, and tax evasion. These charges arose after an FBI investigation nicknamed Operation Mississippi Hustle revealed Epps had taken approximately $1.4 million in bribes from private companies looking to acquire contracts for running prisons in that state; in 2017, Epps was sentenced to serve nearly twenty years in prison.[175]

The company that ran the Walnut Grove facility, Management and Training Corporation (MTC), had previously been stripped of a contract for running a prison facility in Arizona; a report from the Arizona Department of Corrections (ADC) blamed the company for a 2010 escape in which three prisoners from an MTC-run prison in Kingman, Arizona committed two murders, a kidnapping, and other crimes. Staff cutbacks and a lack of timely notification of the escape were cited in the report.[176] Overall, even though amendments typically apply only to government actors, when the government contracts with a private company for services, constitutional violations can, in fact, stem from private action.

Prison Overcrowding

In *Brown v. Plata* (2011),[177] the Supreme Court took the drastic step of upholding a lower court directive requiring the release of as many as 46,000 prisoners from the California state prison system, which was holding nearly double the number of inmates it was designed to keep. This 2011 decision was the culmination of two class action suits filed in federal district courts in 1990 and 2001 on behalf of state prisoners who were contesting the lack of adequate medical treatment in prisons that were overcrowded.[178] These cases led to the lower court appointing a special master and a receiver, respectively, to help oversee efforts at solving these issues. However, as years passed, those overseeing these efforts had noticed little progress.

Describing the ramifications of the population overload that persisted in these prisons, the opinion of the Court in *Brown v. Plata*, penned by Justice Kennedy said, "Overcrowding has overtaken the limited resources of prison staff; imposed demands well beyond the capacity of medical and mental health facilities; and created unsanitary and unsafe conditions that make progress in the provision of care difficult or impossible to achieve." The majority opinion also observed that California prisons were understaffed when it came to medical professionals, with vacancy rates "as high as 20% for surgeons, 25% for physicians, 39% for nurse practitioners, and 54.1% for psychiatrists." The key was how to go about solving these problems.

Prior to the case reaching the Supreme Court, the matter was referred to a three-judge panel of federal district court judges, which addressed this issue by ordering the release of enough prisoners to lower the overall population to 137.5% of capacity.[179] Under a federal law called the Prison Litigation Reform Act of 1995 (PLRA),[180] the judicial power to release prisoners as a means of addressing an Eighth Amendment violation does exist, but resides only in this kind of three-judge panel (as opposed to a single-judge district court). Nevertheless, according the *Brown v. Plata* majority opinion, the PLRA requires that "no prospective relief shall issue with respect to prison conditions unless it is narrowly drawn, extends no further than necessary to correct the violation of a federal right, and is the least intrusive means necessary to correct the violation." The *Plata* decision also cited that statute in stating, "When determining whether these requirements are met, courts must 'give substantial weight to any adverse impact on public safety or the operation of a criminal justice system.'" Part of Justice Kennedy's task in *Brown v. Plata* was evaluating whether the release of 46,000 prisoners—as a means of rectifying an overcrowding issue that implicated cruel and unusual punishment—was compatible with the PLRA.

Justice Kennedy offered some reservations in noting that "[t]he release of prisoners in large numbers—assuming the State finds no other way to comply with the order—is a matter of undoubted, grave concern." Nonetheless, upholding the three-judge panel's release order, his majority opinion observed the following:

> In reaching its decision, the three-judge court gave "substantial weight" to any potential adverse impact on public safety from its order. The court devoted nearly 10 days of trial to the issue of public safety, and it gave the question extensive attention in its opinion. Ultimately, the court concluded that it would be possible to reduce the prison population "in a manner that preserves public safety and the operation of the criminal justice system." ... The three-judge court credited substantial evidence that prison populations can be reduced in a manner that does not increase crime to a significant degree.

In dissent, Justice Scalia excoriated his colleagues in the majority:

> One would think that, before allowing the decree of a federal district court to release 46,000 convicted felons, this Court would bend every effort to read the law in such a way as to avoid that outrageous result. Today, quite to the contrary, the Court disregards stringently drawn provisions of the governing statute, and traditional constitutional limitations upon the power of a federal judge, in order to uphold the absurd. The proceedings that led to this result were a judicial travesty.

Justice Kennedy's majority opinion acknowledged that finding an appropriate remedy for a prison overcrowding issue is a difficult task. However, he declared that "[w]hen necessary to ensure compliance with a constitutional mandate, courts may enter orders placing limits on a prison's population." But Kennedy looked at the release order as a last resort after all other options had been exhausted. He suggested the state might address the overcrowding problem "by raising the design capacity of its prisons or by transferring prisoners to county facilities or facilities in other States." Of course, the prospect of building new prisons quickly enough to resolve the overcrowding issue would certainly seem unrealistic in terms of satisfying the judicial decrees emerging from *Brown v. Plata* and its precursor cases. Even so, given that the initial complaint in this matter was filed two decades before the high Court's 2011 decision, other options might have been available for the state to consider along the way.

FOCUS ON LAW ENFORCEMENT

Former Police Officer Incarcerated in Isolation Unit of Federal Prison

After Derek Chauvin was found guilty in the death of George Floyd, Eighth Amendment considerations became germane, as one of his attorneys argued, in a sentencing memo, for leniency in punishment—based on the supposition that "convictions for officer-involved offenses significantly increase the likelihood of him becoming a target in prison."[181] The trial judge sentenced Chauvin to twenty-two and a half years in prison, and he initially was incarcerated in the state's only maximum security prison: the Minnesota Correctional Facility at Oak Park Heights. According to reports from *ABC News* and *The New York Times*, a spokesperson for the Minnesota Department of Corrections indicated that, when housed in this facility, Chauvin was placed into an "administrative segregation wing" and isolated for twenty-three hours a day in a cell, out of concerns for his safety.[182] The website for the Minnesota Department of Corrections indicates that the "Administrative Control Unit" is appropriate "when continued presence in the general population could pose a particular safety concern."[183]

In December 2021, Chauvin pleaded guilty to federal charges in connection to George Floyd's death, paving the way for a move to federal prison—even though the federal charges led to a sentence of twenty to twenty-five years (whereas he could have been given parole on the state charges in as little as fifteen years). Neama Rahmani, a former federal prosecutor, who now leads a group called West Coast Trial Lawyers, said this of Chauvin's transfer: "The general reason is federal prison just tends to be safer and nicer than state prison and local jails. There are many reasons for that. They're just managed better by the Bureau of Prisons, where state and local jails just are not. There is overcrowding issues in state prisons and local jails that you just don't have in federal prison."[184] She also noted the practical concerns related to Chauvin's former occupation, saying, "He's been a police officer for quite some time and he's arrested a lot of folks and probably put them in Minnesota state prison. It's much less likely that he's going to run into people that he's had interactions with in federal prison. So, it's going to be a lot safer for him."[185] In the end, considerations such as these can speak to whether incarceration conditions amount to cruel and unusual punishment in violation of the Eighth Amendment.

Solitary Confinement

Solitary confinement, the practice of isolating an inmate (or a group of inmates) from the general prison population for an extended period of time, often in cramped spaces, has long been a source of controversy. Although the Supreme Court has never offered a ruling that specifically addresses whether solitary confinement is compatible with the Eighth Amendment, in *Hutto v. Finney* (1978),[186] the Court reviewed the use of something called *punitive isolation* in the Arkansas prison system. The majority opinion for this case described the practice as incarceration for "an indeterminate period of time" in a confined space with other inmates, with specific details including the following:

> An average of 4, and sometimes as many as 10 or 11, prisoners were crowded into windowless 8' × 10' cells containing no furniture other than a source of water and a toilet that could only be flushed from outside the cell. ... At night, the prisoners were given mattresses to spread on the floor. Although some prisoners suffered from infectious diseases such as hepatitis and venereal disease, mattresses were removed and jumbled together each morning, then returned to the cells at random in the evening. ... Prisoners in isolation received fewer than 1,000 calories a day; their meals consisted primarily of 4-inch squares of "grue," a substance created by mashing meat, potatoes, oleo, syrup, vegetables, eggs, and seasoning into a paste and baking the mixture in a pan.

In its opinion for this case, the Court upheld a district court order limiting punitive isolation to thirty days per inmate, with Justice Stevens' majority opinion observing, "Confinement in a prison or in an isolation cell is a form of punishment subject to scrutiny under Eighth Amendment standards." He also quoted the district court ruling in this matter, which referred to punitive confinement conditions in Arkansas state prisons as "a dark and evil world completely alien to the free world."[187]

Yet the practical reality of the *Hutto* decision is that it allowed the practice of punitive isolation to continue—albeit with time limits. Since that decision, no majority opinion from the high Court has revisited this topic, but other opinions have raised concerns related to solitary confinement, even in cases about other subjects.

For example, in *Davis v. Ayala* (2015),[188] Justice Kennedy penned a concurring opinion in which he discussed the topic of solitary confinement. Kennedy addressed Ayala's decades in solitary confinement, noting

SOLITARY CONFINEMENT: A controversial action taken against inmates in a correctional facility, often as a result of disciplinary misconduct, which results in the inmate being confined in isolation within the correctional facility and given limited access, if any, to other people.

Ayala was housed in a windowless cell "no larger than a typical parking spot," with only one hour outside of the cell per day and limited contact with other people. Kennedy used that imagery to highlight the negative repercussions that such conditions can have on a prisoner's physical and mental health. Kennedy specifically referenced the "human toll wrought by extended terms of isolation" and dubbed solitary confinement to be the "edge of madness ... perhaps madness itself." Further, he lamented that this topic "has not been a matter of sufficient public inquiry or interest." Expressing the need for continuing judicial oversight of this issue, Justice Kennedy observed the following:

> Years on end of near-total isolation exact a terrible price. ... In a case that presented the issue, the judiciary may be required, within its proper jurisdiction and authority, to determine whether workable alternative systems for long-term confinement exist, and, if so, whether a correctional system should be required to adopt them. Over 150 years ago, Dostoyevsky wrote, 'The degree of civilization in a society can be judged by entering its prisons.' ... There is truth to this in our own time.

Justice Kennedy's concurring opinion would impact the writing of at least one other Supreme Court Justice. In 2017, Justice Stephen Breyer issued a dissent in a cert denial;[189] therein, he quoted some of Justice Kennedy's words in the *Davis v. Ayala* concurrence, with Justice Breyer echoing the following concerns:

> Members of this Court have recognized that "[y]ears on end of near-total isolation exact a terrible price." ... Long ago we observed that solitary confinement was "considered as an additional punishment of such a severe kind that it is spoken of ... as "a further terror and peculiar mark of infamy." ... And as I have previously pointed out, we have written that the uncertainty a person experiences during just four weeks of confinement under threat of execution is "one of the most horrible feelings to which [a person] can be subjected." ... What legitimate purpose does it serve to hold any human being in solitary confinement for 40 years awaiting execution? What does this tell us about a capital punishment system that, in my view, works in random, virtually arbitrary, ways?

Justice Breyer's words were penned two years after one of the most well-chronicled and horrific juvenile solitary confinement matters in U.S. history: the case of Kalief Browder (see the following box).

THE CONSTITUTION AND SOCIAL JUSTICE
The Tragic Case of Kalief Browder: The Horrors of Juvenile Solitary Confinement

Movements seeking an end to solitary confinement, particularly for juvenile offenders, often cite the case of Kalief Browder, who committed suicide in 2015 after being incarcerated for three years as he awaited trial in New York City. Prior to his death, Browder's story was chronicled in an article written by Jennifer Gonnerman for *The New Yorker*.[190] His ordeal began on May 15, 2010, when police cars approached him and a friend as they walked home from a party. Officers said a witness claimed to have had a backpack stolen by Browder and some of his friends—although the witness offered conflicting stories about when the crime allegedly occurred (varying by more than a week) and about what exactly was taken. Browder was ordered held on $3,000 bail but could not afford to pay; later, after his indictment, bail was revoked altogether.

Browder was incarcerated in New York City's Rikers Island, a prison located on an island in the East River, between the New York City boroughs of Queens and the Bronx. Notorious for its harsh conditions, Rikers was described in a report by a U.S. Attorney's Office as having a "deep-seated culture of violence."[191] This is where the teenage Browder was kept for more than 1,000 days, with more than of those 700 spent in solitary confinement. In terms of the nature of his confinement, surveillance video released in 2015 showed a handcuffed Browder being beaten by a guard, and a second video showed him being beaten by a group of ten or more inmates.[192]

How could this lengthy incarceration without a trial be compatible with the right to a speedy trial? Browder was indicted by a grand jury on July 28, 2010. Soon after, the assistant district attorney handling the case filed a *notice of readiness* for trial, and the case was docketed on the court calendar—but not until December 10, 2010. The Bronx D.A.'s office had more than 5,000 felony cases that year, and the Bronx County Criminal Court was understaffed with judges; thus, lengthy delays were the norm there. Keeping with the Sixth Amendment right to a speedy trial, under New York state law, felony cases were to be ready for trial within six months of a defendant being arraigned. However, that standard could be met with the filing of a notice of readiness, after which the six-month time frame might be paused for a variety of reasons. In 2011, in fact, 74% of felony cases in the Bronx had extended beyond six months without going to trial.[193]

In Browder's case, the prosecutor repeatedly filed requests for one-week or two-week delays, often claiming to be busy with other cases. A typical request took the form of the following statement: *The People are not ready. We are requesting one week.* Given court backlogs for scheduling, though, a one-week request often led to a six-week delay before another court appearance for Browder. Similar requests to delay were made by the prosecutor—and granted by the judge—in June, August, November, and December of 2011 as well as in June, September, November, and December of 2012. Again, because a notice of readiness had been filed, and because the delays were blamed on court backlogs, these tactics did not necessarily amount to a violation of speedy trial rights. Beyond that, in Browder's case, there was no record of his public defender ever filing a request to dismiss the matter over a speedy trial claim.

Browder rejected multiple plea deals from prosecutors and even one from a judge that would have seen him released almost immediately if he would have plead guilty to a misdemeanor charges; instead, he was steadfast in proclaiming his innocence. On May 29, 2013, in his thirty-first appearance in court for this case, Browder was notified that the D.A.'s office would be dismissing the case because the key witness had moved to Mexico and was not available to testify. It is not clear how the long the D.A. was aware of the inability to bring the case to trial, but plea negotiations geared toward extracting a guilty plea could have continued even after the D.A. understood the case would not be brought to trial.

Following Browder's release, a lawsuit was filed against New York City and corrections officials over his treatment. In the *New Yorker* article, Browder was quoted as saying, "People tell me because I have this case against the city I'm all right. But I'm not all right. I'm messed up. I know that I might see some money from this case, but that's not going to help me mentally. I'm mentally scarred right now. That's how I feel. Because there are certain things that changed about me and they might not go back."[194] That quote was harbinger of tragedy to follow.

On June 6th, 2015, Kalief Browder committed suicide at the age of 22, hanging himself in his parent's home. Browder's family continued to pursue the lawsuit against the city, which was amended to a wrongful death claim. In 2019, New York City agreed to settle the case for $3.3 million.[195]

Publicity over Kalief Browder's case, spurred in part by publication of the *New Yorker* article and his subsequent death, would precipitate reforms around the country. In December 2014, New York City Mayor Bill de Blasio announced that solitary confinement would no longer be used for those aged 16 and 17 in New York City's correctional facilities, with that ban later extended to anyone under the age of 21. Additionally, after Browder's incarceration, more than a dozen states curtailed the practice of juvenile solitary confinement.[196] The First Step Act of 2018 also eliminated the use of solitary confinement for juvenile offenders kept in federal prisons.

Efforts to ban solitary confinement altogether in New York City were announced toward the end of Mayor de Blasio's final term in 2020, but incoming mayor Eric Adams resisted that plan. When more than two dozen city council members penned a letter asking Mayor Adams to honor the ban, Adams responded thusly:

> What I'm going to do, I'm going to ignore them. If they like it or not, I'm the mayor. Those who are romanticizing this issue, I'm asking them, go do a week on Rikers Island. Spend time there. Then you come out and tell me that dangerous [inmates] should walk up and down and not be held accountable."[197]

New York City has plans to close Rikers Island by 2026, but the end of solitary confinement before then—even in other city correctional facilities—remains in doubt.

At the federal level, in 2016 President Obama announced a ban on solitary confinement for juvenile offenders in federal prisons, citing the Browder case in an op-ed article he wrote for *The Washington Post*.[198] In the article, Obama asked, "How can we subject prisoners to unnecessary solitary confinement, knowing its effects, and then expect them to return to our communities as whole people?" Obama concluded that solitary confinement "doesn't make us safer. It's an affront to our common humanity."

Conclusion

In this chapter, we have examined the most severe criminal punishment that can be levied in the United States: the death penalty. The Supreme Court repeatedly has discussed two key justifications for the application of capital punishment: retribution and deterrence. Evidence of states deterring crime by applying capital punishment—ostensibly by *sending a message* to would-be criminals—is lacking; further, the paucity of executions nationwide in recent years as well as the lengthy delays between crimes and executions, which can involve decades of appeals, make it harder to advance a case for deterrence as a viable justification.

In terms of retribution, which can be a subjective standard based on one's individual views, the high Court has taken the approach of linking it with concepts of culpability—as if to indicate that the most culpable offenders, such as those who commit the most heinous murders, deserve the most severe form of retribution. A part of evaluating this culpability has been tied, in case precedent, to evaluating criminal punishments through the "evolving standards of decency" standard. This is a unique approach from the standpoint that courts typically do not look to public opinion in making decisions, but when it comes to assessments of what forms of punishment are cruel and unusual, this type of analysis has, in fact, become the norm.

Applying this standard, the Court temporarily halted the death penalty in 1972, but then in 1976 reinstated it with the apparent safeguards of a bifurcated trial, which was designed to funnel death sentences toward the most heinous offenses, such as those murders in which aggravating factors were not outweighed by mitigating factors. In subsequent cases, the court has further narrowed the scope of the death penalty.

For example, capital punishment essentially has been limited to the crime of first-degree murder. Moreover, the Court has halted capital punishment for those who were under the age of 18 at the time of committing their crimes—notably, by looking to state legislatures and even international norms as barometers of "evolving standards of decency" on this subject. The Court also has attempted to limit executions of those with intellectual disabilities, but in the process has given states tremendous leeway in terms of defining that phrase, within the malleable contours provided by case precedent; this remains an evolving area of Eighth Amendment jurisprudence. Underlying all of these limitations on the death penalty is the notion of ensuring that high levels of culpability correlate with the imposition of the harshest penalty this country offers.

When it comes to methods of execution, however, nearly 150 years of precedent from the Supreme Court have essentially allowed states unfettered freedom to experiment with different ways of executing death row inmates, with all of the following having been upheld under Eighth Amendment analysis: firing squad, electric chair, and even lethal injection with untested combinations of drugs.

For those prisoners who are not facing the possibility of execution, but rather find themselves incarcerated in challenging conditions, notions of cruel and unusual punishment can be brought to bear on a variety of contexts. In this chapter, we have noted that, with overcrowding being an issue in many of these settings, prison conditions related to things like medical care, inmate-on-inmate abuse, and even use of force by corrections officials who are tasked with maintaining order in often chaotic settings, can all provide fodder for constitutional appraisals.

As a baseline, the Court has required prisoners to demonstrate the officials have shown deliberate indifference toward prisoners' rights; without such a showing, prisoners have little chance of succeeding on an Eighth Amendment cruel and unusual punishment claim. Even so, whereas that standard has become the norm for cases involving medical care, a situation involving use of force to maintain order is likely to be evaluated through legal standards that are more friendly for corrections officers.

Some issues also remain for future cases to address, such as assessments of equity in the death penalty and even examinations of solitary confinement's place—if any—in prison settings. In the end, courts bear the difficult chore of protecting society from the most culpable offenders as well as ensuring law enforcement officials have the leeway needed to maintain order and discipline inside correctional facilities; nonetheless, humane treatment that allots for some possibility of rehabilitation and, for those who can safely do so, reassimilation into society at large, can be essential for breaking *cycles* of incarceration.

Difficult balancing acts lie at the heart of the Supreme Court's Eighth Amendment jurisprudence, which, for decades, has grappled with how punishments for crimes should comport with the "evolving standards of decency" that can help a society to *progress* and *mature* as it strives to distill justice within the realm of crime and punishment. Ultimately, discerning how to defend the overall welfare and safety of an organized society, while simultaneously safeguarding individual liberties—even for those accused of heinous crimes—remains the core conundrum that confronts all those who bravely accept the challenges inherent to toiling within the American criminal justice system.

Discussion Questions

1. Has the bifurcated trial met its intended objective of reserving capital sentences for the most egregious offenders? What Supreme Court cases have furthered this objective? What Supreme Court cases have hindered this objective? What data can you find that speak to this question?
2. In what ways has the Court placed limits on when capital punishment can be applied, besides cases involving mental health or juvenile offenders? In what ways has the "evolving standards" approach played a role in the cases you identified?

3. In what ways has the Supreme Court addressed the mental health of condemned prisoners, and more specifically, when can mental state or mental illness serve as a reason for halting an execution? How do states vary in their approach to these issues? What can states not do when evaluating these issues, according to case precedent? What is a state allowed to consider when attempting to define intellectual disability in the context of capital punishment?

4. For more than one hundred years, the Supreme Court has ruled against prisoners in every case involving a challenge to methods of execution. Why do you think this has occurred? Why has the evolving standards of decency test been replaced by the *Baze-Glossip* test on this issue, and how does the latter favor the government? Can you envision a situation in which an inmate could use the *Baze-Glossip* test and be successful in an appeal regarding method of execution? Would use of a guillotine be permitted under existing Supreme Court case precedent?

5. Consider the topic of executing offenders who were juveniles at the time they committed their capital crimes. What rationales have driven the Supreme Court to halt such executions? Why did the Court feel the need to apply a *bright-line* rule at the age of 18? Could this issue have been left to individual judges to decipher in the moment, or would that have been inadequate? How does the ban on these types of executions connect to the analysis put forth in cases addressing life sentences for juveniles, as discussed in the previous chapter? Besides age, what other demographic factors can spark controversial discussions regarding who gets the death penalty? Can you find data that support a specific position regarding what factors are predictive of which offenders are given capital sentences by jurors or when prosecutors are more likely to seek a capital sentence?

6. Which issues are likely to reoccur in litigation brought by prisoners against the faculties in which they are incarcerated? What legal tests has the Supreme Court carved to examine the key issues you identified? In what ways do these tests establish a *balancing act* in which certain government interests must be juxtaposed against the Eighth Amendment right to be free from cruel and unusual punishment? Does that balancing act shift based on what type of claim is made? How did COVID-19 alter the dynamic of this analysis? Are there any people who are particularly vulnerable to abuse in prison settings, and if so, what can be done to protect those individuals?

Endnotes

1. States to retain capital punishment through ballot measure votes include California (2016); Nebraska (2016); and Oklahoma (2016); states to halt with supreme court decisions include Delaware (2016); Washington (2018); states to halt with legislative acts include New Hampshire (2019); Colorado (2020); Virginia (2021).

2. Death Penalty Information Center, *Death Row* (2022), https://deathpenaltyinfo.org/death-row/overview; Death Penalty Information Center, *List of Federal Death Row Prisoners* (2022), https://deathpenaltyinfo.org/state-and-federal-info/federal-death-penalty/list-of-federal-death-row-prisoners.

3. *See also* Death Penalty Information Center, *Executions by State and Year*, (for state-by-state data), https://deathpenaltyinfo.org/executions/executions-overview/executions-by-state-and-year.

4. *Wilkerson v. Utah*, 99 U.S. 130 (1878).

5. *In re Kemmler*, 136 U.S. 436 (1890).

6. *Louisiana ex rel. Francis v. Resweber*, 329 U.S. 459 (1947).

7   *Palko v. Connecticut*, 302 U.S. 319 (1937).

8   *Furman v. Georgia*, 408 U.S. 238 (1972).

9   *Gregg v. Georgia*, 428 U.S. 153 (1976).

10 *Woodson v. North Carolina*, 428 U.S. 280 (1976).

11 *Payne v. Tennessee*, 501 U.S. 808 (1991).

12 *People v. Harlan*, 109 P.3d 616 (Colo. 2005).

13 *Kelly v. California and Zamudio v. California, cert denied*, 555 U.S. 1020 (2008).

14 *Lockett v. Ohio*, 435 U.S. 586 (1978).

15 *Hitchcock v. Dugger*, 481 U.S. 393 (1987).

16 *Mills v. Maryland*, 486 U.S. 367 (1988).

17 *Kansas v. Marsh*, 548 U.S. 163 (2004).

18 *Kansas v. Carr*, 577 U.S. 108 (2016).

19 Prior to abolishing the death penalty in 2020, the state of Colorado used an interesting three-step method in the sentencing phase. In the first part of the sentencing phase, the prosecutor presented evidence of aggravating factors, and jurors would deliberate about this; if jurors unanimously found the presence of at least one aggravating factor, the sentencing phase continued; if the jurors did not, a life sentence was imposed. In the second sentencing phase, the defense led the proceedings, presenting evidence of mitigating factors. The jury then deliberated and, absent a finding that mitigating factors outweigh aggravating factors, could vote unanimously to proceed on to the final phase; if there was not a unanimous vote to do so, a life sentence was given. In the third sentencing phase, *victim impact testimony* was offered. Subsequently, the jury could impose a capital sentence through a unanimous vote; otherwise, a life sentence was given.

20 *Ring v. Arizona*, 536 U.S. 584 (2002).

21 *Schiro v. Summerlin*, 542 U.S. 348 (2004).

22 *Hurst v. Florida*, 577 U.S. 92 (2016).

23 *Rauf v. Delaware*, 145 A.3d 430 (Del. 2016) (This decision was then made to apply retroactively in *Powell v. State*, 153 A.3d 69 (Del. 2016).).

24 *Hurst v. State*, 202 So. 3d 40 (Fla. 2016).

25 *State v. Poole*, 297 So. 3d 487, 292 So. 3d 694 (Fla. 2020).

26 *Witherspoon v. Illinois*, 391 U.S. 510 (1968).

27 *Adams v. Texas*, 448 U.S. 38 (1980).

28 *Lockhart v. McCree*, 476 U.S. 162 (1986).

29 *Uttecht v. Brown*, 551 U.S. 1 (2007).

30 *White v. Wheeler* 577 U.S. 73 (2015).

31 Mona Lynch & Craig Haney, *Death Qualification in Black and White: Racialized Decision Making and Death-Qualified Juries*, 40 Law & Policy 1–24 (2018); Richard Salgado, *Tribunals Organized to Convict: Searching for a Lesser Evil in the Capital Juror Death-Qualification Process in United States v. Green*, BYU L. Rev. 519 (2005); Claudia L. Cowan, William C. Thompson, & Phoebe C. Ellsworth, *The Effects of Death Qualification on Jurors' Predisposition to Convict and on the Quality of Deliberation*, 8 Law and Human Behavior 53–79 (1984).

32 *Williams v. Taylor*, 529 U.S. 362 (2000).

33 *Wiggins v. Smith*, 539 U.S. 510 (2003).

34 *Coker v. Georgia*, 433 U.S. 584 (1977).

35 *Kennedy v. Louisiana*, 554 U.S. 407 (2008).

36 *See, e.g.*, Tennessee Code Annotated § 39-13-202(a)(2) (lists the following felonies [only] as capable of yielding a felony murder charge: act of terrorism, arson, rape, robbery, burglary, theft, kidnapping, aggravated child abuse, aggravated child neglect, rape of a child, aggravated rape of a child or aircraft piracy).

37 *Enmund v. Florida*, 458 U.S. 782 (1982).

38 *Id.* (citing *Lockett v. Ohio*, 435 U.S. 586 (1978)).

39 *See* Shobha L. Mahadev & Steven Drizin, *Felony Murder, Explained*, The Appeal, March 4, 2021, https://theappeal.org/the-lab/explainers/felony-murder-explained/.

40 Indiana Code § 35-42-1-1 (The crimes that qualify for felony murder in Indiana are arson, burglary, child molesting, consumer product tampering, kidnapping, rape, robbery, human trafficking, promotion of human labor trafficking, promotion of human sexual trafficking, promotion of child sexual trafficking, promotion of sexual trafficking of a younger child, child sexual trafficking, and carjacking.).

41 *Sharp v. State*, 42 N.E.3d 512 (Ind. 2015).

42 Kristine Guerra, *Elkhart Four Felony Murder Convictions Overturned by Indiana Supreme Court*, IndyStar, Sept. 18, 2015; Jasmine Brown, LaurenEffron, & Sally Hawkins, *Indiana Man, 21, Who Was Sentenced to 50 Years in Prison in 'Elkhart 4' Controversial Felony Murder Case, Enjoys Freedom*, ABC News (Feb. 17, 2016), https://abcnews.go.com/US/indiana-man-21-sentenced-50-years-prison-elkhart/story?id=33919381.

43 *See State v. Sophophone*, 270 Kan. 703, 19 P.3d 70 (Kan. 2001).

44 Death Penalty Info, *Federal Laws Providing for the Death Penalty*, https://deathpenaltyinfo.org/stories/federal-laws-providing-death-penalty.

45 18 U.S.C. § 3591 (b).

46 18 U.S.C. § 3591(b)(2).

47 10 U.S.C. §§ 886-934.

48 Ashley Fantz, *A Look at the Last U.S. Soldier Executed by the Military*, CNN (July 28, 2013), https://www.cnn.com/2013/07/28/justice/military-execution-soldier-profile/index.html.

49 *United States v. Briggs*, 592 U.S. ___ (2020).

50 *Wilkerson v. Utah*, *supra* note 4.

51 *Arthur v. Dunn*, 580 U.S. ___ (2017) (Sotomayor, J., dissenting).

52 Brady McCombs, *Utah's Firing Squad: How Does it Work?* Associated Press, Mar. 24, 2015.

53 Victoria Hansen, *Death Row Inmates Sue After They're Asked to Pick Firing Squad or Electric Chair*, NPR (May 20, 2021), https://www.npr.org/2021/05/20/998600135/south-carolina-reinstates-firing-squad-but-not-without-legal-challenges.

54 Andrea Lyon, *The Death Penalty: What's Keeping It Alive?* (2015), at 2.

55 C.M. Frankie, *Why Did Gary Gilmore Choose to be Executed by Firing Squad?*, A&E: True Crime Blog, Dec. 9, 2021, https://www.aetv.com/real-crime/gary-gilmore-execution

56 *Id.*; *see* Marcos Ortiz, *The Justice Files: The Execution of Gary Gilmore*, ABC4 Utah, Nov. 17, 2019, https://www.abc4.com/news/justice-files/the-justice-files-the-execution-of-gary-gilmore-2/; Lily Rothman, *The Strange Story of the Man Who Chose Execution by Firing Squad*, Time (Mar. 12, 2015).

57 *In re Kemler*, *supra* note 5.

58 *Louisiana ex rel. Francis v. Resweber*, *supra* note 6.

59 Erik Schelzig, *Gov. Haslam Signs Bill to Allow Electric Chair In Tennessee*, Associated Press/Tennessean, May 22, 2014.

60 *Fierro v. Gomez*, 77 F.3d 301 (9th Cir. 1996).

61   *Gomez v. Fierro*, 519 U.S. 918 (1996).

62   Ed Pilkington, *Arizona 'Refurbishes' its Gas Chamber to Prepare for Executions, Documents Say*, The Guardian, May 28, 2021, https://www.theguardian.com/us-news/2021/may/28/arizona-gas-chamber-executions-documents.

63   *Baze v. Rees*, 553 U.S. 35 (2008).

64   Samantha Schmidt, *Botched Okla. Execution That Took 43 Minutes Not Cruel and Inhumane, Court Rules*, Wash. Post, Nov. 17, 2016.

65   *Glossip v. Gross*, 576 U.S. 863 (2015) (Sotomayor, J., dissenting).

66   Paige Williams, *Witness to a Botched Execution*, The New Yorker, April 30, 2014; *see* Rachel Weiner, *Virginia Detail Protocol for Controversial Execution Drug*, Wash. Post, Apr. 30, 2014.

67   *Estate of Lockett v. Fallin*, 841 F.3d 1098 (10th Cir. 2016).

68   *Glossip v. Gross*, *supra* note 65.

69   Erin McCann, *Oklahoma Governor Stays Execution of Richard Glossip amid Drug Concerns*, The Guardian (Sep. 30, 2015), https://www.theguardian.com/us-news/2015/sep/30/richard-glossip-oklahoma-execution; David Kroll, *Oklahoma Governor Halts Glossip's Execution, Potassium Drug Mix-Up*, Forbes, Sep. 30, 2015, https://www.forbes.com/sites/davidkroll/2015/09/30/oklahoma-governor-halts-glossips-execution-bought-the-wrong-i-v-potassium/?sh=-1238ba114716.

70   *Bucklew v. Precythe*, 587 U.S. ___ (2019).

71   Debbie Siegelbaum, *America's 'Inexorably' Botched Executions*, BBC News, Aug. 1, 2014, https://www.bbc.com/news/magazine-28555978; Austin Sarat, *Gruesome Spectacles: Botched Executions and America's Death Penalty* (2014).

72   *Ford v. Wainwright*, 477 U.S. 399 (1986).

73   *Panetti v. Quarterman*, 551 U.S. 930 (2007).

74   *Madison v. Alabama*, 586 U.S. ___ (2019).

75   In 2016, a 4–4 tie from the Supreme Court (owing to Justice Scalia's death) left in place an Eleventh Circuit stay of execution. In 2017, though, the Court lifted a lower court stay of execution in *Dunn v. Madison*, 583 U.S. ___ (2017). After new evidence became available, the Court issued a stay of execution in 2018, agreeing to hear the matter as *Madison v. Alabama*.

76   Ivana Hrynkiw, *Vernon Madison, One Of The Longest-Serving Alabama Death Row Inmates, Dies*, Mobile Real-Time News, Feb. 24, 2020, https://www.al.com/news/mobile/2020/02/vernon-madison-one-of-the-longest-serving-alabama-death-row-inmate-dies.html.

77   *Atkins v. Virginia*, 536 U.S. 304 (2002).

78   *Penry v. Lynaugh*, 492 U.S. 302 (1989).

79   *Hall v. Florida*, 572 U.S. 701 (2014).

80   *Brumfield v. Cain*, 576 U.S. 305 (2015).

81   *Moore v. Texas*, 581 U.S. ___ (2017).

82   *McWilliams v. Dunn*, 582 U.S. ___ (2017) (This decision cited *Ake v. Oklahoma*, 470 U.S. 68 (1985), which indicated that when an indigent defendant can convince a trial judge that "mental condition" is a "significant factor" relevant to "criminal culpability" and "punishment," then an independent mental health assessment [usually through a psychiatrist] must be provided.).

83   *DPIC Adds Eleven Cases to Innocence List, Bringing National Death-Row Exoneration Total to 185*. Death Penalty Information Center, Feb. 18, 2021, https://deathpenaltyinfo.org/news/dpic-adds-eleven-cases-to-innocence-list-bringing-national-death-row-exoneration-total-to-185

84   *Id.*

85   Equal Justice Initiative, *Death Penalty* (citing Death Penalty Information Center, *State Studies on Monetary Costs* (2017)), https://deathpenaltyinfo.org/policy-issues/costs/summary-of-states-death-penalty; Reid Wilson, *Red States Move to End Death Penalty*, The Hill, Feb. 4, 2019, https://thehill.com/homenews/state-watch/428361-red-states-move-to-end-death-penalty), https://eji.org/issues/death-penalty/.

86   Daniel Nagin & John V. Pepper, eds., *Deterrence and the Death Penalty* (2012), https://www.nap.edu/catalog/13363/deterrence-and-the-death-penalty.

87   Equal Justice Initiative, *Death Penalty* (citing Death Penalty Information Center, *Capital Punishment and Police Safety*, https://deathpenaltyinfo.org/policy-issues/deterrence/capital-punishment-and-police-safety), https://eji.org/issues/death-penalty/.

88   *Roper v. Simmons*, 543 U.S. 551 (2005).

89   *Stanford v. Kentucky*, 492 U.S. 361 (1989).

90   Death Penalty Info, *Current U.S. Death Row Population by Race*, (figures drawn from NACCP-LDF Death Row USA, as of January 1, 2022), https://deathpenaltyinfo.org/death-row/overview/demographics; *see* Deborah Fins, *A Quarterly Report by the NACCP Legal Defense and Educational Fund, Inc.*, Death Row USA, Jan. 1, 2022, https://www.naacpldf.org/wp-content/uploads/DRUSAWinter2022.pdf.

91   *See, e.g.*, Harold Garfinkel, *Research Note on Inter- and Intra-Racial Homicides*, 27 Soc. Forces 369 (1949); Elmer Johnson, *Selective Factors in Capital Punishment*, 36 Social Forces 165–169 (1957); Charles Mangum, The Legal Status of the Negro (1940).

92   William J. Bowers, Glenn L. Pierce, & John F. McDevitt, *Legal Homicide: Death as Punishment in America, 1864–1982* 69–70 (1984).

93   Gary Kleck, *Racial Discrimination in Criminal Sentencing: A Critical Evaluation of the Evidence with Additional Evidence on the Death Penalty*, 46 American Sociological Review 783–805 (1981).

94   David Baldus, Charles Pulaski, & George Woodworth, *Comparative Review of Death Sentences: An Empirical Study of the Georgia Experience* 74 J. Crim. L. & Criminology 661 (1983).

95   David Baldus & George Woodworth, *Race Discrimination and the Legitimacy of Capital Punishment: Reflections on the Interaction of Fact and Perception*, 53 DePaul L. Rev. 1411, 1412 (2004).

96   Samuel R. Gross & Robert Mauro, *Death and Discrimination: Racial Disparities in Capital Sentencing* 35 (1989).

97   Michael Radelet & Glenn Pierce, *Choosing Who Will Die: Race and the Death Penalty in Florida*, 43 Fla. L. Rev. (1991).

98   Raymond Paternoster, *Race of the Victim and Location of Crime: The Decision to Seek the Death Penalty in South Carolina*, 74 Journal of Crime and Criminology 754–785 (1983).

99   Richard Lempert, *Capital Punishment in the '80s: Reflections on the Symposium*, 74 Journal of Crime and Criminology 1101–1114 (1983); Sheldon Ekland-Olson, *Structured Discretion, Racial Bias, and the Death Penalty: The First Decade after Furman in Texas*, 69 Social Science Quarterly 853–873 (1988); Michael Radelet & Glenn Pierce, *Race and Prosecutorial Discretion in Homicide Cases*, 19 Law and Society Review, 587–622 (1985); Dwayne Smith, *Patterns of Discrimination in Assessments of the Death Penalty: The Case of Louisiana*, 15 Journal of Criminal Justice 279–286 (1987).

100   U.S. Gen. Accounting Office, GAO/GGD-90-57, *Death Penalty Sentencing: Research Indicates Pattern of Racial Disparities*, 1–2 (1990).

101   David Baldus & George Woodworth, *Race Discrimination and the Death Penalty: An Empirical and Legal Overview, in* America's Experiment with Capital Punishment 501, 517–19 (2003).

102   Michael Radelet & Marian Borg, *The Changing Nature of Death Penalty Debates*, 26 Annual Review of Sociology 43–61 (2000).

103   Raymond Pasternoster, Robert Brame, Sarah Bacon, & Andrew Ditchfield, *Justice by Geography and Race: The Administration of the Death Penalty in Maryland, 1978–1999*, 4 U. MD. L.J. Race Relig. Gender & Class (2004).

104   Glenn Pierce & Michael Radelet, Race, *Region and Death Sentencing in Illinois, 1988–1997*, 81 Ore. L. Rev. (2002).

105   Glenn Pierce & Michael Radelet, *The Impact of Legally Inappropriate Factors on Death Sentencing for California Homicides*, 46 Santa Clara L. Rev. 1 (2005).

106   Stephanie Hindson, Hillary Potter, & Michael Radelet, *Race, Gender, Region and Death Sentencing in Colorado, 1980–1999*, 77 U. Colo. L. Rev. 549 (2006); *see* Meg Beardsley, Sam Kamin, Justice Marceau, & Scott Phillips, *Disquieting Discretion: Race, Geography & The Colorado Death Penalty in the First Decade of the Twenty-First Century*, 92 Den. U. L. Rev. 431 (2015) (a follow-up study).

107   Michael Radelet & Glenn Pierce, *Race and the Death Penalty in North Carolina, 1980–2007*, 89 N. Car. L. 2119 (2011).

108   David Baldus, George Woodworth, Catherine Grosso, & Aaron Christ, *Arbitrariness and Discrimination in the Administration of the Death Penalty: A Legal and Empirical Analysis of the Nebraska Experience (1973–1999)*, 81 Neb. L. Rev. 486 (2002).

109   *McCleskey v. Kemp*, 481 U.S. 279 (1987).

110   *Id.*, at 367 (Stevens, J., dissenting). For articulation of similar ideas later in Stevens's career, including from a 2005 speech to the American Bar Association, *see* James Liebman & Lawrence C. Marshall, *Less Is Better: Justice Stevens and the Narrowed Death Penalty*, 74 Fordham L. Rev. 1607, 1646 (2006); Elisabeth Semel, *Reflections on Justice John Paul Stevens' Concurring Opinion in* Baze v. Rees: *A Fifth Gregg Justice Renounces Capital Punishment*, 43 U.C. Davis L. Rev. 783 (Feb. 2010).

111   Deral Cheatwood, *Capital Punishment for the Crime of Homicide in Chicago, 1870–1930*, 92 Journal of Criminal Law and Criminology 843–866 (2002).

112   David Baldus, Julie Brin, Neil Weiner, & George Woodworth, *Evidence of Racial Discrimination in the Use of the Death Penalty: A Story from Southwest Arkansas with Special Reference to the Case of Death Row Inmate Frank Williams, Jr.*, 76 Tenn L. Rev. 555, 578 (2009).

113   Glenn Pierce & Michael Radelet, *Death Sentencing in East Baton Rouge Parish, 1990–2008*, 71 LA. L. Rev. 647, 668 (2011).

114   Radelet & Pierce, *supra* note 107, at 2139.

115   Baldus et al., *supra* note 112, at 578.

116   Isaac Unah, *Choosing Those Who Will Die: The Effect of Race, Gender, and Law in Prosecutorial Decisions to Seek the Death Penalty in Durham County, North Carolina*, 15 Mich. J. Race & L. 135, 143 (2009).

117   Scott Phillips, *Racial Disparities in the Capital of Capital Punishment*, 45 Hous. L. Rev. 807, 820 (2008).

118   Robert Weiss, Richard Berk, & Catherine Lee, *Assessing the Capriciousness of Death Penalty Charging*, 30 Law and Society Review 607–626, 623 (1996).

119   Pierce & Radelet, *supra* note 113, at 664.

120   Janine Kremling, M. Dwayne Smith, John K. Cochran, Beth Bjerregaard, & Sondra Fogel, *The Role of Mitigating Factors in Capital Sentencing Before and After McKoy v. North Carolina*, 24 Justice Quarterly 357–381 (2007).

121   Michael Songer & Isaac Unah, *The Effect of Race, Gender, and Location on Prosecutorial Decisions to Seek the Death Penalty in South Carolina*, 58 S. Car. L. Rev. 161, 192 (2006).

122   Unah, *supra* note 116, at 160–61.

123 Phillips, *supra* note 117, at 820.

124 Marian Williams, Stephen Demuth, & Jefferson Holcomb, *Understanding the Influence of Victim Gender in Death Penalty Cases: The Importance of Victim Race, Sex-Related Victimization, and Jury Decision-Making*, 45 Criminology 865–892 (2007).

125 *Id.*

126 Cheatwood, *supra* note 111, at 863.

127 Phillips, *supra* note 117, at 820.

128 Weiss et al., *supra* note 118, at 623.

129 Baldus et al., *supra* note 112, at 584.

130 Pierce & Radelet, *supra* note 113, at 78.

131 Victor Streib, *Death Penalty for Female Offenders*, 58 U. Cin. L. Rev. 845 (1990).

132 Songer & Unah, *supra* note 121, at 183.

133 Hindson et al., *supra* note 106, at 572.

134 *Wolf v. McDonnell*, 418 U.S. 539 (1974).

135 *Meachum v. Fano*, 427 U.S. 215 (1976).

136 *Estelle v. Gamble*, 429 U.S. 97 (1976).

137 *Id.* (citing *Jackson v. Bishop*, 404 F.2d 571, 579 (8th Cir. 1968)).

138 *West v. Atkins*, 487 U.S. 42 (1988).

139 Widra Emily, *State Prisons and Local Jails Appear Indifferent to COVID Outbreaks, Refuse to Depopulate Dangerous Facilities*, Prison Policy Initiative, Feb. 10, 2022 (citing Neal Marquez, Julie Ward, Kalind Parish, Brendan Saloner, & Sharon Dolovich, *COVID-19 Incidence and Mortality with the US Population, April 5, 2020 to April 3, 2021, Research Letter*, 326 Journal of the American Medical Association 1865–1867 (2021)), https://www.prisonpolicy.org/blog/2022/02/10/february2022_population/.

140 Wendy Sawyer, *New Data: The Changes in Prisons, Jails, Probation, and Parole in The First Year of the Pandemic*, Prison Policy Initiative (Jan. 11, 2022) https://www.prisonpolicy.org/blog/2022/01/11/bjs_update/.

141 *See also* Prison Policy Initiative, *The Most Significant Criminal Justice Policy Changes from the COVID-19 Pandemic* (Mar. 3, 2022) (for discussion of these and other examples), https://www.prisonpolicy.org/virus/virusresponse.html.

142 Karen Yi, *NJ's COVID-19 Prison Release Program Restarts Thursday with 260 Freed Early*, Gothamist, Feb. 9, 2022, https://gothamist.com/news/njs-covid-19-prison-release-program-restarts-thursday-with-260-freed-early.

143 Disability Rights North Carolina, *Civil Rights Organizations Announce Settlement Agreement Securing at Least 3,500 Early Releases from State Prisons in COVID-19 Lawsuit*, Feb. 25, 2021, (the case name is *NAACP et al. v. Cooper et al.* (Wake County Superior Court 20-CVS-500110)), https://disabilityrightsnc.org/news/press-release/covid-19-lawsuit-settlement-guarantees-3500-early-releases.

144 Jason Mesiner & Annie Sweeney, *About 1,000 Illinois Prisoners to Be Released Under COVID-19 Lawsuit Settlement*, Chicago Trib., Mar. 23, 2021.

145 Bob Egelko, *San Quentin Must Release or Transfer Half Its Prisoners Because of Lack Of COVID Care, Court Rules*, S.F. Chron., Oct. 20, 2020.

146 Leila Miller, *Court Orders Orange County Sheriff to Cut Jail Population in Half to Prevent Spread Of Virus*, L.A. Times, Dec. 12, 2020; *see also* Prison Policy Initiative, *The Most Significant Criminal Justice Policy Changes from the COVID-19 Pandemic*, Mar. 3, 2022, https://www.prisonpolicy.org/virus/virusresponse.html.

147   ACLU Ohio, *A Federal Judge Issues Order to Enforce Compliance, Requiring Elkton Prison Officials to Expedite Transfer & Release of Medically Vulnerable Subclass Through Home Confinement and Compassionate Release*, May 19, 2020, https://www.acluohio.org/en/press-releases/federal-judge-issues-order-enforce-compliance-requiring-elkton-prison-officials; *see Wilson et al. v. Williams et al.*, Case: 4:20-cv-00794-JG (Order of James S. Gwin, U.S. District Judge, Northern District of Ohio), https://www.acluohio.org/sites/default/files/Order-on-motion-to-enforce.pdf.

148   HNN Staff, *COVID-19 risk decreased, state Supreme Court ends inmate early release program*, Hawaii News Now, June 5, 2020, https://www.hawaiinewsnow.com/2020/06/05/state-supreme-court-ends-release-prisoners-covid-precaution/.

149   ACLU Massachusetts, *Ice Reduces Plymouth County Correctional Facility Population Due to COVID-19*, ACLU Lawsuit (April 2, 2021), https://www.aclum.org/en/news/ice-reduces-plymouth-county-correctional-facility-population-due-covid-19-aclu-lawsuit; *see* ACLU Massachusetts, *Augusto v. Muniz* May 21, 2020, https://www.aclum.org/en/cases/augusto-v-moniz.

150   Joe Hernandez, *Arkansas Inmates Are Suing After Being Given Ivermectin to Treat COVID-19*, NPR, Jan. 18, 2022, https://www.npr.org/2022/01/18/1073846967/arkansas-inmates-ivermectin-lawsuit-covid-19.

151   Liliana Frankel, *Oregon Prison COVID-19 Lawsuit Ruling Hailed as a Landmark for Prisoner's Rights*, Oregon Live, Apr. 19, 2021, https://www.oregonlive.com/politics/2021/04/oregon-prison-covid-19-lawsuit-ruling-hailed-as-a-landmark-for-prisoners-rights.html.

152   Michael Tanenbaum, *Philly Agrees to $125,000 Settlement for Failure to Give Prisoners Required out-of-Cell Time During COVID-19 Pandemic*, Philly Voice, June 23, 2021, https://www.phillyvoice.com/philly-prisoners-covid-19-lawsuit-settlement-inmates-out-of-cell-time-bail-jails/.

153   Spencer Hsu, *D.C. Jail Settles Lawsuit over Inmate Covid Conditions by ACLU, Public Defender Service*, The Wash. Post, Feb. 15, 2022, https://www.washingtonpost.com/dc-md-va/2022/02/15/dc-jail-covid-settlement/.

154   Wendy Sawyer, *New data: The changes in prisons, jails, probation, and parole in the first year of the pandemic*, Prison Policy Initiative, Jan. 11, 2022, https://www.prisonpolicy.org/blog/2022/01/11/bjs_update/.

155   Emily Widra, *State Prisons and Local Jails Appear Indifferent to COVID Outbreaks, Refuse to Depopulate Dangerous Facilities*, Prison Policy Initiative, Feb. 10, 2022, https://www.prisonpolicy.org/blog/2022/02/10/february2022_population/.

156   Saywer, *supra* note 154.

157   Prison Policy Initiative, *The Most Significant Criminal Justice Policy Changes from the COVID-19 Pandemic*, March 3, 2022, https://www.prisonpolicy.org/virus/virusresponse.html.

158   Widra, *supra* note 155.

159   *Graham v. Connor*, 490 U.S. 386 (1989).

160   *Whitley v. Albers*, 475 U.S. 312 (1986).

161   *Id.* (citing *Johnson v. Glick*, 481 F.2d 1028, 1033 (2nd Cir. 1973)).

162   *Hudson v. McMillian*, 503 U.S. 1 (1992).

163   *Hope v. Pelzer*, 536 U.S. 730 (2002).

164   *Farmer v. Brennan*, 511 U.S. 825, 833 (1994).

165   Justice Souter's opinion cited the following: American Medical Association, Encyclopedia of Medicine 1006 (1989); American Psychiatric Association, Diagnostic and Statistical Manual of Mental Disorders 74–75 (3rd rev. ed. 1987). It is unclear whether Souter was conveying these ideas on his own or he was observing that prison officials classified Farmer as suffering from a psychiatric disorder. Either way, such ideas were generally representative of the era.

166   Prison Rape Elimination Act of 2003, 108 Pub. L. 79, 117 Stat 972, 42 U.S.C. §§ 15601–15609.

167   National Institute of Justice, *Prison Rape Elimination Act*, March 7, 2014, https://nij.ojp.gov/topics/articles/prison-rape-elimination-act.

168   *Id.* (citing Allen Beck & Marcus Berzofsky, *Sexual Victimization in Prisons and Jails Reported by Inmates, 2011–12*, U.S. Dept. of Justice, Bureau of Justice Statistics, May 2013, https://bjs.ojp.gov/content/pub/pdf/svpjri1112.pdf).

169   *Farmer v. Brennan, supra* note 164.

170   *Rhodes v. Chapman*, 452 U.S. 337 (1981).

171   *Wilson v. Seiter*, 501 U.S. 294 (1991).

172   First Step Act of 2018, Pub. L. 115–391, 132 Stat. 5194.

173   Southern Poverty Law Center, *Walnut Grove*, https://www.splcenter.org/seeking-justice/case-docket/cb-et-al-v-walnut-grove-correctional-authority-et-al; *Charlton DePriest et al. v. Walnut Grove Correctional Authority et al.*, Order, Civil Action No. 3:10-cv-663-CWR-FKB (2015).

174   ACLU, *Notorious Private Prison Closes Today in Walnut Grove, Mississippi*, Sept. 25, 2016, https://www.aclu.org/press-releases/notorious-private-prison-closes-today-walnut-grove-mississippi.

175   Jerry Mitchell & Jimmie E. Gates, *Chris Epps, Cecil McCrory Plead Guilty to Corruption*, The Clarion Ledger, Feb. 25, 2015, https://www.clarionledger.com/story/news/2015/02/25/epps-pleads-guilty/23990739/; Jimmie E. Gates, *Chris Epps Sentenced to Almost 20 Years*, The Clarion Ledger, May 24, 2017; https://www.clarionledger.com/story/news/2017/05/24/chris-epps-sentencing/341916001/.

176   Matt Clarke, *Report Faults Private Prison Company for Deadly Arizona Prison Break*, Prison Legal News, March 15, 2011, https://www.prisonlegalnews.org/news/2011/mar/15/report-faults-private-prison-company-for-deadly-arizona-prison-break/.

177   *Brown v. Plata*, 563 U.S. 493 (2011).

178   *Coleman v. Wilson*, No. 90-cv-00520 (E.D. Cal. Dec. 4, 1989) (filed on behalf of prisoners with serious mental illnesses); *Plata v. Davis*, No. 01-cv-01351 (N.D. Cal. Apr. 5, 2001) (filed on behalf of prisoners with medical conditions who claimed to be receiving inadequate care).

179   Judges from the Eastern and Northern Districts of California comprised the panel, since the underlying cases came from these districts. The ruling was issued as: Opinion and Order at 183, *Coleman v. Schwarzenegger*, No. 90-cv-00529, No. 01-cv-01341 (E.D. Cal, N.D. Cal, Aug. 4, 2009). For further reading on the procedural history of this matter, *see* Margo Schlanger, *Plata v. Brown and Realignment: Jails, Prisons, Courts, and Politics*. 48 Harv. C. R. -C.L.L. Rev. 165 (2013).

180   Prison Litigation Reform Act of 1995, Pub. 104–134, 110 Stat. 1321, codified at 18 U.S.C. § 3626(a) and 42 U.S.C. § 1997e.

181   Chao Xiong, *Chauvin's Prison Time to Involve Continued Isolation*, Star Tribune, June 25, 2021 (This article links to the June 2, 2021 sentencing memorandum filed by Chauvin's attorneys.).

182   Nicholas Bogel-Burroughs & Tim Arango, *Derek Chauvin Is Being Held in Solitary Confinement for 23 Hours a Day*, N.Y. Times, April 21, 2021; Bill Hutchinson, *Derek Chauvin Wants To Go To Federal Prison, Even Though It Means He'll Do More Time*, ABC News, December 21, 2021, https://abcnews.go.com/US/derek-chauvin-federal-prison-means-hell-time/story?id=81845835.

183   Minnesota Department of Corrections, *Administrative Control Unit*, https://mn.gov/doc/facilities/oak-park-heights/administrative-control-unit/.

184   Hutchinson, *supra* note 182.

185   *Id.*

186   *Hutto v. Finney*, 437 U.S. 678 (1978).

187   *Id.* (citing *Holt v. Sarver*, 309 F. Supp. 362, 381 (E.D. Ark. 1970)).

188   *Davis v. Ayala*, 576 U.S. 257 (2015).

189   *Smith v. Ryan*, Director, Dept. of Corrections, 581 U.S. ___ (2017).

190   Jennifer Gonnerman, *Before the Law: A Boy Was Accused of Taking a Backpack. The Courts Took the Next Three Years of His Life*, The New Yorker, Sept. 29, 2014, https://www.newyorker.com/magazine/2014/10/06/before-the-law.

191   *Id.* The report was produced by the U.S. Attorney's Office for the Southern District of New York in 2015.

192   Avianne Tan, *New Video Shows Teen Slammed by Guard, Beaten by Inmates in Rikers Island Jail*, ABC News, Apr. 24, 2015, https://abcnews.go.com/US/video-shows-teen-slammed-guard-beaten-inmates-rikers/story?id=30558028.

193   Gonnerman, *supra* note 190.

194   *Id.*

195   Benjamin Weiser, *Kalief Browder's Suicide Brought Changes to Rikers. Now It Has Led to a $3 Million Settlement*, N.Y. Times, Jan. 24, 2019, https://www.nytimes.com/2019/01/24/nyregion/kalief-browder-settlement-lawsuit.html.

196   Clare Sestanovich, *NYC Declares an End to Solitary for Inmates Under 21*, The Marshall Project, Jan. 14, 2015, https://www.themarshallproject.org/2015/01/14/nyc-declares-an-end-to-solitary-for-inmates-under-21; Eli Hager, *Ending Solitary for Juveniles: A Goal Grows Closer*, The Marshall Project, Aug. 1, 2017, https://www.themarshallproject.org/2017/08/01/ending-solitary-for-juveniles-a-goal-grows-closer.

197   NBC New York, *Adams 'to Ignore' Council Members' Request to End Solitary Confinement*, Dec. 22, 2021, https://www.nbcnewyork.com/news/politics/im-going-to-ignore-them-adams-on-council-members-letter-about-solitary-confinement/3463395/.

198   Barack Obama, *Why We Must Rethink Solitary Confinement*, Wash. Post, Jan. 25, 2016, https://www.washingtonpost.com/opinions/barack-obama-why-we-must-rethink-solitary-confinement/2016/01/25/29a361f2-c384-11e5-8965-0607e0e265ce_story.html.

Credit

Appendix A: The Constitution of The United States of America

We the People of the United States, in Order to form a more perfect Union, establish Justice, insure domestic Tranquility, provide for the common defense, promote the general Welfare, and secure the Blessings of Liberty to ourselves and our Posterity, do ordain and establish this Constitution for the United States of America.

Article I

Section 1

All legislative Powers herein granted shall be vested in a Congress of the United States, which shall consist of a Senate and House of Representatives.

Section 2

(1) The House of Representatives shall be composed of Members chosen every second Year by the People of the several States, and the Electors in each State shall have the Qualifications requisite for Electors of the most numerous Branch of the State Legislature.

(2) No Person shall be a Representative who shall not have attained to the age of twenty-five Years, and been seven Years a Citizen of the United States, and who shall not, when elected, be an Inhabitant of that State in which he shall be chosen.

(3) Representatives and direct Taxes shall be apportioned among the several States which may be included within this Union, according to their respective Numbers, which shall be determined by adding to the whole Number of free Persons, including those bound to Service for a Term of Years, and excluding Indians not taxed, three fifths of all other Persons. The actual Enumeration shall be made within three Years after the first Meeting of the Congress of the United States, and within every subsequent Term of ten Years, in such Manner as they shall by Law direct. The Number of Representatives shall not exceed one for every thirty Thousand, but each State shall have at Least one Representative; and until such enumeration shall be made, the State of New Hampshire shall be entitled to chuse three, Massachusetts eight, Rhode Island and Providence Plantations one, Connecticut five, New York six, New Jersey four, Pennsylvania eight, Delaware one, Maryland six, Virginia ten, North Carolina five, South Carolina five, and Georgia three.

(4) When vacancies happen in the Representation from any State, the Executive Authority thereof shall issue Writs of Election to fill such Vacancies.

(5) The House of Representatives shall chuse their Speaker and other Officers; and shall have the sole Power of Impeachment.

"The Constitution of The United States of America," 1787.

Section 3

(1) The Senate of the United States shall be composed of two Senators from each State, chosen by the Legislature thereof, for six Years; and each Senator shall have one Vote.

(2) Immediately after they shall be assembled in Consequence of the first Election, they shall be divided as equally as may be into three Classes. The Seats of the Senators of the first Class shall be vacated at the Expiration of the second Year, of the second Class at the Expiration of the fourth Year, and of the third Class at the Expiration of the sixth Year, so that one third may be chosen every second Year; and if Vacancies happen by Resignation, or otherwise, during the Recess of the Legislature of any State, the Executive thereof may make temporary Appointments until the next Meeting of the Legislature, which shall then fill such Vacancies.

(3) No Person shall be a Senator who shall not have attained, to the Age of thirty Years, and been nine Years a Citizen of the United States, and who shall not, when elected, be an Inhabitant of that State for which he shall be chosen.

(4) The Vice President of the United States shall be President of the Senate, but shall have no Vote, unless they be equally divided.

(5) The Senate shall chuse their other Officers, and also a President pro tempore, in the Absence of the Vice President, or when he shall exercise the Office of the President of the United States.

(6) The Senate shall have the sole Power to try all Impeachments. When sitting for that Purpose, they shall be on Oath or Affirmation. When the President of the United States is tried, the Chief Justice shall preside: And no Person shall be convicted without the Concurrence of two thirds of the Members present.

(7) Judgment in Cases of Impeachment shall not extend further than to removal from Office, and disqualification to hold and enjoy any Office of honor, Trust or Profit under the United States: but the Party convicted shall nevertheless be liable and subject to Indictment, Trial, Judgment and Punishment, according to Law.

Section 4

(1) The Times, Places and Manner of holding Elections for Senators and Representatives, shall be prescribed in each State by the Legislature thereof; but the Congress may at any time by Law make or alter such Regulations, except as to the Places of chusing Senators.

(2) The Congress shall assemble at least once in every Year, and such Meeting shall be on the first Monday in December, unless they shall by Law appoint a different Day.

Section 5

(1) Each House shall be the Judge of the Elections, Returns and Qualifications of its own Members, and a Majority of each shall constitute a Quorum to do Business; but a smaller Number may adjourn from day to day, and may be authorized to compel the Attendance of absent Members, in such Manner, and under such Penalties as each House may provide.

(2) Each House may determine the Rules of its Proceedings, punish its Members for disorderly Behaviour, and, with the Concurrence of two thirds, expel a Member.

(3) Each House shall keep a Journal of its Proceedings, and from time to time publish the same, excepting such Parts as may in their Judgment require Secrecy; and the Yeas and Nays of the Members of either House on any question shall, at the Desire of one fifth of those Present, be entered on the Journal.

(4) Neither House, during the Session of Congress, shall, without the Consent of the other, adjourn for more than three days, nor to any other Place than that in which the two Houses shall be sitting.

Section 6

(1) The Senators and Representatives shall receive a Compensation for their Services, to be ascertained by Law, and paid out of the Treasury of the United States. They shall in all Cases, except Treason, Felony and Breach of the Peace, be privileged from Arrest during their Attendance at the Session of their respective Houses, and in going to and returning from the same; and for any Speech or Debate in either House, they shall not be questioned in any other Place.

(2) No Senator or Representative shall, during the Time for which he was elected, be appointed to any civil Office under the Authority of the United States, which shall have been created, or the Emoluments whereof shall have been increased during such time; and no Person holding any Office under the United States, shall be a Member of either House during his Continuance in Office.

Section 7

(1) All Bills for raising Revenue shall originate in the House of Representatives; but the Senate may propose or concur with Amendments as on other Bills.

(2) Every Bill which shall have passed the House of Representatives and the Senate, shall, before it become a Law, be presented to the President of the United States; If he approve he shall sign it, but if not he shall return it, with his Objections to that House in which it shall have originated, who shall enter the Objections at large on their Journal, and proceed to reconsider it. If after such Reconsideration two thirds of that House shall agree to pass the Bill, it shall be sent, together with the Objections, to the other House, by which it shall likewise be reconsidered, and if approved by two thirds of that House, it shall become a Law. But in all such Cases the Votes of both Houses shall be determined by Yeas and Nays, and the Names of the Persons voting for and against the Bill shall be entered on the Journal of each House respectively. If any Bill shall not be returned by the President within ten Days (Sunday excepted) after it shall have been presented to him, the Same shall be a Law, in like Manner as if he had signed it, unless the Congress by their Adjournment prevent its Return, in which Case it shall not be a Law.

(3) Every Order, Resolution, or Vote to which the Concurrence of the Senate and House of Representatives may be necessary (except on a question of Adjournment) shall be presented to the President of the United States; and before the Same shall take Effect, shall be approved by him, or being disapproved by him, shall be repassed by two thirds of the Senate and House of Representatives, according to the Rules and Limitations prescribed in the Case of a Bill.

Section 8

(1) The Congress shall have Power To lay and collect Taxes, Duties, Imposts and Excises, to pay the Debts and provide for the common Defence and general Welfare of the United States; but all Duties, Imposts and Excises shall be uniform throughout the United States;

(2) To borrow Money on the credit of the United States;

(3) To regulate Commerce with foreign Nations, and among the several States, and with the Indian Tribes;

(4) To establish an uniform Rule of Naturalization, and uniform Laws on the subject of Bankruptcies throughout the United States;

(5) To coin Money, regulate the Value thereof, and of foreign Coin, and to fix the Standard of Weights and Measures;

(6) To provide for the Punishment of counterfeiting the Securities and current Coin of the United States;

(7) To establish Post Offices and post Roads;

(8) To promote the Progress of Science and useful Arts, by securing for limited Times to Authors and Inventors the exclusive Right to their respective Writings and Discoveries;

(9) To constitute Tribunals inferior to the supreme Court;

(10) To define and punish Piracies and Felonies committed on the high Seas, and Offenses against the Law of Nations;

(11) To declare War, grant Letters of Marque and Reprisal, and make Rules concerning Captures on Land and Water;

(12) To raise and support Armies, but no Appropriation of Money to that Use shall be for a longer Term than two Years;

(13) To provide and maintain a Navy;

(14) To make Rules for the Government and Regulation of the land and naval Forces;

(15) To provide for calling forth the Militia to execute the Laws of the Union, suppress Insurrections and repel Invasions;

(16) To provide for organizing, arming, and disciplining, the Militia, and for governing such Part of them as may be employed in the Service of the United States, reserving to the States respectively, the Appointment of the Officers, and the Authority of training the Militia according to the discipline prescribed by Congress;

(17) To exercise exclusive Legislation in all Cases whatsoever, over such District (not exceeding ten Miles square) as may, by Cession of particular States, and the Acceptance of Congress, become the Seat of the Government of the United States, and to exercise like Authority over all Places purchased by the Consent of the Legislature of the State in which the Same shall be, for the Erection of Forts, Magazines, Arsenals, dock-Yards, and other needful Buildings;—And

(18) To make all Laws which shall be necessary and proper for carrying into Execution the foregoing Powers, and all other Powers vested by this Constitution in the Government of the United States, or in any Department or Officer thereof.

Section 9

(1) The Migration or Importation of such Persons as any of the States now existing shall think proper to admit, shall not be prohibited by the Congress prior to the Year one thousand eight hundred and eight, but a Tax or Duty may be imposed on such Importation, not exceeding ten dollars for each Person.

(2) The Privilege of the Writ of Habeas Corpus shall not be suspended unless when in Cases of Rebellion or Invasion the public Safety may require it.

(3) No Bill of Attainder or ex post facto Law shall be passed.

(4) No Capitation, or other direct, Tax shall be laid, unless in Proportion to the Census or Enumeration herein before directed to be taken.

(5) No Tax or Duty shall be laid on Articles exported from any State.

(6) No Preference shall be given by any Regulation of Commerce or Revenue to the Ports of one State over those of another; nor shall Vessels bound to, or from, one State, be obliged to enter, clear or pay Duties in another.

(7) No Money shall be drawn from the Treasury, but in Consequence of Appropriations made by Law; and a regular Statement and Account of the Receipts and Expenditures of all public Money shall be published from time to time.

(8) No Title of Nobility shall be granted by the United States: And no Person holding any Office of Profit or Trust under them, shall, without the Consent of the Congress, accept of any present, Emolument, Office, or Title, of any kind whatever, from any King, Prince or foreign State.

Section 10

(1) No State shall enter into any Treaty, Alliance, or Confederation; grant Letters of Marque and Reprisal; coin Money; emit Bills of Credit; make any Thing but gold and silver Coin a Tender in Payment of Debts; pass any Bill of Attainder, ex post facto Law, or Law impairing the Obligation of Contracts, or grant any Title of Nobility.

(2) No State shall, without the Consent of Congress, lay any Imposts or Duties on Imports or Exports, except what may be absolutely necessary for executing its inspection Laws: and the net Produce of all Duties and Imposts, laid by any State on Imports or Exports, shall be for the Use of the Treasury of the United States; and all such Laws shall be subject to the Revision and Control of the Congress.

(3) No State shall, without the Consent of Congress, lay any Duty of Tonnage, keep Troops, or Ships of War in time of Peace, enter into any Agreement or Compact with another State, or with a foreign Power, or engage in War, unless actually invaded, or in such imminent Danger as will not admit of Delay.

Article II

Section 1

(1) The executive Power shall be vested in a President of the United States of America. He shall hold his Office during the Term of four Years, and, together with the Vice President, chosen for the same Term, be elected, as follows:

(2) Each State shall appoint, in such Manner as the Legislature thereof may direct, a Number of Electors, equal to the whole Number of Senators and Representatives to which the State may be entitled in the Congress: but no Senator or Representative, or Person holding an Office of Trust or Profit under the United States, shall be appointed an Elector.

The Electors shall meet in their respective States, and vote by Ballot for two Persons, of whom one at least shall not be an Inhabitant of the same State with themselves. And they shall make a List of all the Persons voted for, and of the Number of Votes for each; which List they shall sign and certify, and transmit sealed to the Seat of the Government of the United States, directed to the President of the Senate. The President of the Senate shall, in the presence of the Senate and House of Representatives, open all the Certificates, and the Votes shall then be counted. The Person having the greatest Number of Votes shall be the President, if such Number be a Majority of the whole Number of Electors appointed; and if there be more than one who have such Majority, and have an equal Number of Votes, then the House of Representatives shall immediately chuse by Ballot one of them for President; and if no Person have a Majority, then from the five highest on the List the said House shall in like Manner chuse the President. But in chusing the President, the Votes shall be taken by States, the Representation from each State having one Vote; a quorum for this Purpose shall consist of a Member or Members from two thirds of the States, and a Majority of all the States shall be necessary to a Choice. In every Case, after the Choice of the President, the Person having the greatest Number of Votes of the Electors shall be the Vice President. But if there should remain two or more who have equal Votes, the Senate shall chuse from them by Ballot the Vice President.

(3) The Congress may determine the Time of chusing the Electors, and the Day on which they shall give their Votes; which Day shall be the same throughout the United States.

(4) No Person except a natural born Citizen, or a Citizen of the United States, at the time of the Adoption of this Constitution, shall be eligible to the Office of President; neither shall any Person be eligible to that Office who shall not have attained to the Age of thirty five Years, and been fourteen Years a Resident within the United States.

(5) In Case of the Removal of the President from Office, or of his Death, Resignation, or Inability to discharge the Powers and Duties of the said Office, the Same shall devolve on the Vice President, and the Congress may by Law provide for the Case of Removal, Death, Resignation or Inability, both of the President and Vice President, declaring what Officer shall then act as President, and such Officer shall act accordingly, until the Disability be removed, or a President shall be elected.

(6) The President shall, at stated Times, receive for his Services, a Compensation, which shall neither be increased nor diminished during the Period for which he shall have been elected, and he shall not receive within that Period any other Emolument from the United States, or any of them.

(7) Before he enter on the Execution of his Office, he shall take the following Oath or Affirmation:—"I do solemnly swear (or affirm) that I will faithfully execute the Office of President of the United States, and will to the best of my Ability, preserve, protect and defend the Constitution of the United States."

Section 2

(1) The President shall be Commander in Chief of the Army and Navy of the United States, and of the Militia of the several States, when called into the actual Service of the United States; he may require the Opinion,

in writing, of the principal Officer in each of the executive Departments, upon any Subject relating to the Duties of their respective Offices, and he shall have Power to grant Reprieves and Pardons for Offenses against the United States, except in Cases of Impeachment.

(2) He shall have Power, by and with the Advice and Consent of the Senate, to make Treaties, provided two thirds of the Senators present concur; and he shall nominate, and by and with the Advice and Consent of the Senate, shall appoint Ambassadors, other public Ministers and Consuls, Judges of the supreme Court, and all other Officers of the United States, whose Appointments are not herein otherwise provided for, and which shall be established by Law: but the Congress may by Law vest the Appointment of such inferior Officers, as they think proper, in the President alone, in the Courts of Law, or in the Heads of Departments.

(3) The President shall have Power to fill up all Vacancies that may happen during the Recess of the Senate, by granting Commissions which shall expire at the End of their next Session.

Section 3

He shall from time to time give to the Congress Information of the State of the Union, and recommend to their Consideration such Measures as he shall judge necessary and expedient; he may, on extraordinary Occasions, convene both Houses, or either of them, and in Case of Disagreement between them, with Respect to the Time of Adjournment, he may adjourn them to such Time as he shall think proper; he shall receive Ambassadors and other public Ministers; he shall take Care that the Laws be faithfully executed, and shall Commission all the Officers of the United States.

Section 4

The President, Vice President and all Civil Officers of the United States, shall be removed from Office on Impeachment for, and Conviction of, Treason, Bribery, or other high Crimes and Misdemeanors.

Article III

Section 1

The judicial Power of the United States, shall be vested in one supreme Court, and in such inferior Courts as the Congress may from time to time ordain and establish. The Judges, both of the supreme and inferior Courts, shall hold their Offices during good Behaviour, and shall, at stated Times, receive for their Services, a Compensation, which shall not be diminished during their Continuance in Office.

Section 2

(1) The judicial Power shall extend to all Cases, in Law and Equity, arising under this Constitution, the Laws of the United States, and Treaties made, or which shall be made, under their Authority;—to all Cases affecting Ambassadors, other public Ministers and Consuls;—to all Cases of admiralty and maritime Jurisdiction;—to Controversies to which the United States shall be a party;—to Controversies between two

or more States;—between a State and Citizens of another State;—between Citizens of different States;—between Citizens of the same State claiming Lands under Grants of different States, and between a State, or the Citizens thereof, and foreign States, Citizens or Subjects.

(2) In all Cases affecting Ambassadors, other public Ministers and Consuls, and those in which a State shall be Party, the supreme Court shall have original Jurisdiction. In all the other Cases before mentioned, the supreme Court shall have appellate Jurisdiction, both as to Law and Fact, with such Exceptions, and under such Regulations as the Congress shall make.

(3) The Trial of all Crimes, except in Cases of Impeachment, shall be by Jury; and such Trial shall be held in the State where the said Crimes shall have been committed; but when not committed within any State, the Trial shall be at such Place or Places as the Congress may by Law have directed.

Section 3

(1) Treason against the United States, shall consist only in levying War against them, or in adhering to their Enemies, giving them Aid and Comfort. No Person shall be convicted of Treason unless on the Testimony of two Witnesses to the same overt Act, or on Confession in open Court.

(2) The Congress shall have Power to declare the Punishment of Treason, but no Attainder of Treason shall work Corruption of Blood, or Forfeiture except during the Life of the Person attainted.

Article IV

Section 1

Full Faith and Credit shall be given in each State to the public Acts, Records, and judicial Proceedings of every other State. And the Congress may by general Laws prescribe the Manner in which such Acts, Records and Proceedings shall be proved, and the Effect thereof.

Section 2

(1) The Citizens of each State shall be entitled to all privileges and Immunities of Citizens in the several States.

(2) A Person charged in any State with Treason, Felony, or other Crime, who shall flee from Justice, and be found in another State, shall on Demand of the executive Authority of the State from which he fled, be delivered up, to be removed to the State having Jurisdiction of the Crime.

(3) No Person held to Service of Labour in one State, under the Laws thereof, escaping into another, shall, in Consequence of any Law or Regulation therein, be discharged from such Service or Labour, but shall be delivered up on Claim of the Party to whom such Service or Labour may be due.

Section 3

(1) New States may be admitted by the Congress into this Union; but no new State shall be formed or erected within the Jurisdiction of any other State; nor any State be formed by the Junction of two or more States, or Parts of States, without the Consent of the Legislatures of the States concerned as well as of the Congress.

(2) The Congress shall have power to dispose of and make all needful Rules and Regulations respecting the Territory or other Property belonging to the United States; and nothing in this Constitution shall be so construed as to Prejudice any Claims of the United States, or of any particular State.

Section 4

The United States shall guarantee to every State in this Union a Republican Form of Government, and shall protect each of them against Invasion; and on Application of the Legislature, or of the Executive (when the Legislature cannot be convened) against domestic Violence.

Article V

The Congress, whenever two thirds of both Houses shall deem it necessary, shall propose Amendments to this Constitution, or, on the Application of the Legislatures of two thirds of the several States, shall call a Convention for proposing Amendments, which, in either Case, shall be valid to all Intents and Purposes, as Part of this Constitution, when ratified by the Legislatures of three fourths of the several States, or by Conventions in three fourths thereof, as the one or the other Mode of Ratification may be proposed by the Congress; Provided that no Amendment which may be made prior to the Year One thousand eight hundred and eight shall in any Manner affect the first and fourth Clauses in the Ninth Section of the first Article; and that no State, without its Consent, shall be deprived of its equal Suffrage in the Senate.

Article VI

(1) All Debts contracted and Engagements entered into, before the Adoption of this Constitution, shall be as valid against the United States under this Constitution, as under the Confederation.

(2) This Constitution, and the Laws of the United States which shall be made in Pursuance thereof; and all Treaties made, or which shall be made, under the Authority of the United States, shall be the supreme Law of the Land; and the Judges in every State shall be bound thereby, any Thing in the Constitution or Laws of any State to the Contrary notwithstanding.

(3) The Senators and Representatives before mentioned, and the Members of the several State Legislatures, and all executive and judicial Officers, both of the United States and of the several States, shall be bound by Oath or Affirmation, to support this Constitution; but no religious Test shall ever be required as a Qualification to any Office or public Trust under the United States.

Article VII

The Ratification of the Conventions of nine States, shall be sufficient for the Establishment of this Constitution between the States so ratifying the Same.

Amendment I (1791)

Congress shall make no law respecting an establishment of religion, or prohibiting the free exercise thereof; or abridging the freedom of speech, or of the press; or the right of the people peaceably to assemble, and to petition the Government for a redress of grievances.

Amendment II (1791)

A well regulated Militia, being necessary to the security of a free state, the right of the people to keep and bear Arms, shall not be infringed.

Amendment III (1791)

No Soldier shall, in time of peace be quartered in any house, without the consent of the Owner, nor in time of war, but in a manner to be prescribed by law.

Amendment IV (1791)

The right of the people to be secure in their persons, houses, papers, and effects, against unreasonable searches and seizures, shall not be violated, and no Warrants shall issue, but upon probable cause, supported by Oath or affirmation, and particularly describing the place to be searched, and the persons or things to be seized.

Amendment V (1791)

No person shall be held to answer for a capital, or otherwise infamous crime, unless on a presentment or indictment of a Grand Jury, except in cases arising in the land or naval forces, or in the Militia, when in actual service in time of War or public danger; nor shall any person be subject for the same offence to be twice put in jeopardy of life or limb; nor shall be compelled in any criminal case to be a witness against himself, nor be deprived of life, liberty, or property, without due process of law; nor shall private property be taken for public use, without just compensation.

Amendment VI (1791)

In all criminal prosecutions, the accused shall enjoy the right to a speedy and public trial, by an impartial jury of the State and district wherein the crime shall have been committed, which district shall have been previously ascertained by law, and to be informed of the nature and cause of the accusation; to be confronted with the witnesses against him; to have compulsory process for obtaining witnesses in his favor, and to have the Assistance of Counsel for his defence.

Amendment VII (1791)

In Suits at common law, where the value in controversy shall exceed twenty dollars, the right of trial by jury shall be preserved, and no fact tried by a jury, shall be otherwise re-examined in any Court of the United States, than according to the rules of the common law.

Amendment VIII (1791)

Excessive bail shall not be required, nor excessive fines imposed, nor cruel and unusual punishments inflicted.

Amendment IX (1791)

The enumeration in the Constitution, of certain rights, shall not be construed to deny or disparage others retained by the people.

Amendment X (1791)

The powers not delegated to the United States by the Constitution, nor prohibited by it to the States, are reserved to the States respectively, or to the people.

Amendment XI (1798)

The Judicial power of the United States shall not be construed to extend to any suit in law or equity, commenced or prosecuted against one of the United States by Citizens of another State, or by Citizens or Subjects of any Foreign State.

Amendment XII (1804)

The Electors shall meet in their respective states and vote by ballot for President and Vice-President, one of whom, at least, shall not be an inhabitant of the same state with themselves; they shall name in their ballots the person voted for as President, and in distinct ballots the person voted for as Vice-President, and they shall make distinct lists of all persons voted for as President, and of all persons voted for as Vice-President, and of the number of votes for each, which lists they shall sign and certify, and transmit sealed to the seat of the government of the United States, directed to the President of the Senate;—The President of the Senate shall, in the presence of the Senate and House of Representatives, open all the certificates and the votes shall then be counted;—The person having the greatest number of votes for President, shall be the President, if such number be a majority of the whole number of Electors appointed; and if no person have such majority, then from the persons having the highest numbers not exceeding three on the list of those voted for as President, the House of Representatives shall choose immediately, by ballot, the President. But in choosing the President, the votes shall be taken by states, the representation from each state having one vote; a quorum for this purpose shall consist of a member or members from two-thirds of the states, and a majority of all the states shall be necessary to a choice. And if the House of Representatives shall not choose a President whenever the right of choice shall devolve upon them, before the fourth day of March next following, then the Vice-President shall act as President, as in the case of the death or other constitutional disability of the President—The person having the greatest number of votes as Vice-President, shall be the Vice-President, if such number be a majority of the whole number of Electors appointed, and if no person have a majority, then from the two highest numbers on the list, the Senate shall choose the Vice-President; A quorum for the purpose shall consist of two-thirds of the whole number of Senators, and a majority of the whole number shall be necessary to a choice. But no person constitutionally ineligible to the office of President shall be eligible to that of Vice-President of the United States.

Amendment XIII (1865)

Section 1

Neither slavery nor involuntary servitude, except as a punishment for crime whereof the party shall have been duly convicted, shall exist within the United States, or any place subject to their jurisdiction.

Section 2

Congress shall have power to enforce this article by appropriate legislation.

Amendment XIV (1868)

Section 1

All persons born or naturalized in the United States and subject to the jurisdiction thereof, are citizens of the United States and of the State wherein they reside. No State shall make or enforce any law which shall abridge the privileges or immunities of citizens of the United States; nor shall any State deprive any person of life, liberty, or property, without due process of law; nor deny to any person within its jurisdiction the equal protection of the laws.

Section 2

Representatives shall be apportioned among the several States according to their respective numbers, counting the whole number of persons in each State, excluding Indians not taxed. But when the right to vote at any election for the choice of electors for President and Vice-President of the United States, Representatives in Congress, the Executive and Judicial officers of a State, or the members of the Legislature thereof, is denied to any of the male inhabitants of such State, being twenty-one years of age, and citizens of the United States, or in any way abridged, except for participation in rebellion, or other crime, the basis of representation therein shall be reduced in the proportion which the number of such male citizens shall bear to the whole number of male citizens twenty-one years of age in such State.

Section 3

No person shall be a Senator or Representative in Congress, or elector of President and Vice-President, or hold any office, civil or military, under the United States, or under any State, who, having previously taken an oath, as a member of Congress, or as an officer of the United States, or as a member of any State legislature, or as an executive or judicial officer of any State, to support the Constitution of the United States, shall have engaged in insurrection or rebellion against the same, or given aid or comfort to the enemies thereof. But Congress may by a vote of two-thirds of each House, remove such disability.

Section 4

The validity of the public debt of the United States, authorized by law, including debts incurred for payment of pensions and bounties for services in suppressing insurrection or rebellion, shall not be questioned. But neither the United States nor any State shall assume or pay any debt or obligation incurred in aid of insurrection or rebellion against the United States, or any claim for the loss or emancipation of any slave; but all such debts, obligations and claims shall be held illegal and void.

Section 5

The Congress shall have power to enforce, by appropriate legislation, the provisions of this article.

Amendment XV (1870)

Section 1

The right of citizens of the United States to vote shall not be denied or abridged by the United States or by any State on account of race, color, or previous condition of servitude.

Section 2

The Congress shall have power to enforce this article by appropriate legislation.

Amendment XVI (1913)

The Congress shall have power to lay and collect taxes on incomes, from whatever source derived, without apportionment among the several States, and without regard to any census or enumeration.

Amendment XVII (1913)

The Senate of the United States shall be composed of two Senators from each State, elected by the people thereof, for six years; and each Senator shall have one vote. The electors in each State shall have the qualifications requisite for electors of the most numerous branch of the State legislatures.

When vacancies happen in the representation of any State in the Senate, the executive authority of such State shall issue writs of election to fill such vacancies: Provided, That the legislature of any State may empower the executive thereof to make temporary appointments until the people fill the vacancies by election as the legislature may direct.

This amendment shall not be so construed as to affect the election or term of any Senator chosen before it becomes valid as part of the Constitution.

Amendment XVIII (1919)

Section 1

After one year from the ratification of this article the manufacture, sale, or transportation of intoxicating liquors within, the importation thereof into, or the exportation thereof from the United States and all territory subject to the jurisdiction thereof for beverage purposes is hereby prohibited.

Section 2

The Congress and the several States shall have concurrent power to enforce this article by appropriate legislation.

Section 3

This article shall be inoperative unless it shall have been ratified as an amendment to the Constitution by the legislatures of the several States, as provided in the Constitution, within seven years from the date of the submission hereof to the States by the Congress.

Amendment XIX (1920)

The right of citizens of the United States to vote shall not be denied or abridged by the United States or by any State on account of sex.

Congress shall have power to enforce this article by appropriate legislation.

Amendment XX (1933)

Section 1

The terms of the President and Vice President shall end at noon on the 20th day of January, and the terms of Senators and Representatives at noon on the 3d day of January, of the years in which such terms would have ended if this article had not been ratified; and the terms of their successors shall then begin.

Section 2

The Congress shall assemble at least once in every year, and such meeting shall begin at noon on the 3d day of January, unless they shall by law appoint a different day.

Section 3

If, at the time fixed for the beginning of the term of the President, the President elect shall have died, the Vice President elect shall become President. If a President shall not have been chosen before the time fixed for the beginning of his term, or if the President elect shall have failed to qualify, then the Vice President elect shall act as President until a President shall have qualified; and the Congress may by law provide for the case wherein neither a President elect nor a Vice President elect shall have qualified, declaring who shall then act as President, or the manner in which one who is to act shall be selected, and such person shall act accordingly until a President or Vice President shall have qualified.

Section 4

The Congress may by law provide for the case of the death of any of the persons from whom the House of Representatives may choose a President whenever the right of choice shall have devolved upon them, and for the case of the death of any of the persons from whom the Senate may choose a Vice President whenever the right of choice shall have devolved upon them.

Section 5

Sections 1 and 2 shall take effect on the 15th day of October following the ratification of this article.

Section 6

This article shall be inoperative unless it shall have been ratified as an amendment to the Constitution by the legislatures of three-fourths of the several States within seven years from the date of its submission.

Amendment XXI (1933)

Section 1

The eighteenth article of amendment to the Constitution of the United States is hereby repealed.

Section 2

The transportation or importation into any State, Territory or possession of the United States for delivery or use therein of intoxicating liquors, in violation of the laws thereof, is hereby prohibited.

Section 3

This article shall be inoperative unless it shall have been ratified as an amendment to the Constitution by conventions in the several States, as provided in the Constitution, within seven years from the date of the submission hereof to the States by the Congress.

Amendment XXII (1951)

Section 1

No person shall be elected to the office of the President more than twice, and no person who has held the office of President, or acted as President, for more than two years of a term to which some other person was elected President shall be elected to the office of the President more than once. But this Article shall not apply to any person holding the office of President when this Article was proposed by the Congress, and shall not prevent any person who may be holding the office of President, or acting as President, during the term within which this Article becomes operative from holding the office of President or acting as President during the remainder of such term.

Section 2

This Article shall be inoperative unless it shall have been ratified as an amendment to the Constitution by the legislatures of three-fourths of the several States within seven years from the date of its submission to the States by the Congress.

Amendment XXIII (1961)

Section 1

The District constituting the seat of Government of the United States shall appoint in such manner as the Congress may direct:

> A number of electors of President and Vice President equal to the whole number of Senators and Representatives in Congress to which the District would be entitled if it were a State, but in no event more than the least populous State; they shall be in addition to those appointed by the States, but they shall be considered, for the purposes of the election of President and

Vice President, to be electors appointed by a State; and they shall meet in the District and perform such duties as provided by the twelfth article of amendment.

Section 2
The Congress shall have power to enforce this article by appropriate legislation.

Amendment XXIV (1964)
Section 1
The right of citizens of the United States to vote in any primary or other election for President or Vice President, for electors for President or Vice President, or for Senator or Representative in Congress, shall not be denied or abridged by the United States or any State by reason of failure to pay any poll tax or other tax.

Section 2
The Congress shall have power to enforce this article by appropriate legislation.

Amendment XXV (1967)
Section 1
In case of the removal of the President from office or of his death or resignation, the Vice President shall become President.

Section 2
Whenever there is a vacancy in the office of the Vice President, the President shall nominate a Vice President who shall take office upon confirmation by a majority vote of both Houses of Congress.

Section 3
Whenever the President transmits to the President pro tempore of the Senate and the Speaker of the House of Representatives his written declaration that he is unable to discharge the powers and duties of his office, and until he transmits to them a written declaration to the contrary, such powers and duties shall be discharged by the Vice President as Acting President.

Section 4
Whenever the Vice President and a majority of either the principal officers of the executive departments or of such other body as Congress may by law provide, transmit to the President pro tempore of the Senate and the Speaker of the House of Representatives their written declaration that the President is unable to discharge the powers and duties of his office, the Vice President shall immediately assume the powers and duties of the office as Acting President.

Thereafter, when the President transmits to the President pro tempore of the Senate and the Speaker of the House of Representatives his written declaration that no inability exists, he shall resume the powers and duties of his office unless the Vice President and a majority of either the principal officers of the executive department or of such other body as Congress may by law provide, transmit within four days to the President pro tempore of the Senate and the Speaker of the House of Representatives their written declaration that the

President is unable to discharge the powers and duties of his office. Thereupon Congress shall decide the issue, assembling within forty-eight hours for that purpose if not in session. If the Congress, within twenty-one days after receipt of the latter written declaration, or, if Congress is not in session, within twenty-one days after Congress is required to assemble, determines by two-thirds vote of both Houses that the President is unable to discharge the powers and duties of his office, the Vice President shall continue to discharge the same as Acting President; otherwise, the President shall resume the powers and duties of his office.

Amendment XXVI (1971)

Section 1

The right of citizens of the United States, who are eighteen years of age or older, to vote shall not be denied or abridged by the United States or by any State on account of age.

Section 2

The Congress shall have power to enforce this article by appropriate legislation.

Amendment XXVII (1992)

No law, varying the compensation for the services of the Senators and Representatives, shall take effect, until an election of Representatives shall have intervened.

Appendix B: Glossary of Key Terms

100% service: A requirement for a convicted criminal to serve the entirety of their prison sentence, without any chance of early release through parole.

absolute immunity: Doctrine under which judges, prosecutors, legislators, and certain other officials are completely immunized against civil liability for their official actions.

actual malice: Judicial standard that requires "public figures" to demonstrate intentional falsehood or reckless disregard of the truth to prevail on a defamation claim.

administrative search exception: Doctrine exempting searches by administrative agencies from normal Fourth Amendment requirements.

administrative search warrants: Search warrants issued by judges or magistrates on the application of administrative personnel.

administrative state: A government characterized by a high level of bureaucracy.

Advanced Imaging Technology (AIT) body scanners: Body imaging devices used in U.S. airports to provide a detailed image of the human body prior to passengers boarding airline flights.

affidavit: A sworn declaration attesting to a set of facts.

affirmative action: Policies and programs that provide preferential treatment based on race, ethnicity, gender, or other characteristics.

affirmative defenses: Defenses to criminal charges in which the defendant admits to the charged conduct but denies criminal intent.

aggravating factors: Criteria that indicate one crime is somehow more egregious than other similar crimes and, thus, worthy of a harsher punishment; they are often referenced in the sentencing phase of a death penalty case, when such factors cannot be outweighed by mitigating factors for a capital sentence to be levied.

***Allen* charge:** A judge's instruction to a deadlocked jury exhorting jurors to listen to one another's arguments and reconsider their own positions in order to arrive at a verdict.

anticipatory search warrant: A warrant issued based on probable cause to believe that at a future time evidence of a crime will be found at a specific place.

appellate courts: Higher courts that review the decisions of trial courts.

appellate jurisdiction: The authority of a court to review the decisions of lower courts.

arraignment: A defendant's appearance before a trial court for the purpose of pleading to a criminal charge.

arrest: The seizure of a person based on legal authority to do so.

arrest warrant: A document signed by a judge or magistrate authorizing the arrest of a certain person.

Articles of Confederation: The first constitution for the United States, adopted in 1777 and ratified in 1781.

assault weapons: Military-style semiautomatic rifles and pistols containing detachable magazines capable of holding large numbers of rounds.

asylum: Protection granted persons who have fled their home countries because they fear persecution; those granted asylum are eligible for permanent residency in the United States.

automobile exception: The doctrine under which police with probable cause may stop and search an automobile without a warrant.

ballot initiative: A process through which a requisite number of voters can petition a state legislature to hold a statewide referendum on an issue of public policy.

bench warrant: An arrest warrant issued by a judge authorizing the arrest of a person who has already been indicted or is in contempt of court.

bifurcated trial: A method upheld by the Supreme Court for trying cases involving a potential death sentence; it encompasses a two-stage criminal proceeding, in which the first phase revolves around whether the offender is guilty or not guilty and the second phase involves an assessment of what the appropriate punishment should be.

bill of attainder: A legislative act declaring a party guilty of a crime without use of judicial trial.

Bill of Rights: The first ten amendments to the Constitution.

***Bivens* remedy:** A lawsuit filed against a federal official for an alleged violation of a constitutional right, as permitted under certain circumstances by the Supreme Court in *Bivens v. Six Unknown Named Agents* (1971).

body cameras: Cameras worn by police officers to record encounters with citizens.

border search: A routine search of persons crossing the border into the United States.

bounty hunter: An individual who, generally working on behalf of a bonding company, attempts to recapture an accused criminal who has failed to appear for trial in violation of terms of bail.

Brady Bill: A commonly employed moniker for the nation's federal law that requires background checks to be performed by federally licensed firearms dealers before they can sell firearms to prospective buyers.

canine search: A search performed by a dog trained to detect certain items by smell.

capias: See **bench warrant**.

case law: The law as enunciated by courts in deciding cases.

cashless bail: A method for providing release for an accused criminal prior to trial without requiring any monetary payment as a condition of release; often used in conjunction with risk-assessment algorithms.

cell phone location data: Refers to the signal given by an individual cell phone as it links to a nearby cell phone tower; an individual *ping* to a tower or a series of pings can reveal a person's location or movement over time.

certiorari: The mechanism by which an appellate court exercises its discretion in deciding to review a lower court decision.

challenge for cause: An attempt by an attorney in a criminal case to dismiss a prospective juror for a reason that would preclude the juror's ability to reach an impartial decision in the case, such as prejudice or conflict of interest.

checks and balances: Mechanisms built into a constitution to prevent one branch from exerting authority without influence from the other branches.

chokehold: A method of restraining a person in which pressure is applied around the neck, restricting the flow of blood to the brain.

citizen's arrest: An arrest made by a private individual, rather than a law enforcement officer.

civil asset forfeiture: A mechanism through which government agents can seize an individual person's private property even without a crime being charged, provided there is an applicable level of proof under relevant state or federal law (usually proof by preponderance of the evidence) to connect the property to an illegal act; generally, an individual can attempt to recover the item through court proceedings; rightly-seized items become property of the government.

civil commitment: A period of confinement, generally in a mental health facility and, perhaps, for an undetermined period of time because a court determines an individual represents a danger to themselves or others.

civil contempt: A form of contempt in which a person is confined until they agree to comply with the order of a court.

clear and present danger doctrine: The doctrine under which the First Amendment does not protect speech that constitutes a clear and present danger of accomplishing something the government has a right to prohibit.

closely regulated industries: Businesses subjected to long-standing and pervasive government regulation.

commercial speech: Speech that relates to the economic interests of the speaker and which is often protected by the Supreme Court at a lower level than other types of speech, such as political speech.

community caretaker exception: An exception to the warrant requirement that allows officers to seize evidence discovered during activities that are unrelated to criminal enforcement, such as providing assistance to people in distress.

compelling interest: A justification strong enough to support limits placed on the fundamental rights of individuals who are impacted by laws, actions, or other government policies.

compulsory process: The idea that certain witnesses in a criminal case can be compelled to testify pursuant to subpoena that requires them to appear in court.

concurrent sentencing: Refers to the decision to have the number of years of incarceration related to two or more criminal convictions served simultaneously; for example, two concurrent sentences of five years would both be completed after five years in prison.

confidential informant: An informant whose identity is known to the police but held in confidence.

consecutive sentencing: Refers to the decision to add together the number of years of incarceration in two or more criminal convictions, requiring an offender to serve the combined total; for example, two consecutive sentences of five years would require ten years of service in prison.

consent searches: Searches performed with the consent of the person whose person or property is being searched.

constitutional democracy: A constitutional republic in which rights, especially the right to vote, are guaranteed to all citizens.

constitutional law: The body of judicial decisions interpreting provisions of the Constitution.

constitutional republic: A state in which representatives are elected and the rules of government are set forth in a constitution.

constitutional supremacy: The idea that a constitution is superior to ordinary legislation.

content neutrality: A government restriction on speech that does not discriminate based on viewpoint but, rather, applies equally to all expression, regardless of content.

contraband: Items which are illegal to possess.

cooperative federalism: The modern notion of federalism, stressing cooperation between the national and the state and local governments.

corporal punishment: a physical penalty meted out in response to a crime or, perhaps, bad behavior in a school setting; an example would be a person being beaten with a paddle.

crack cocaine discrepancy: Reference to the fact that possession of crack cocaine, a form of the drug that involves mixing pure powdered cocaine with baking soda; carries harsher mandatory minimum sentences than possession of the same weight in pure powdered cocaine.

crime scene exception: An exception to the warrant requirement under which police arriving promptly at a crime scene may conduct a brief search to secure the scene and locate evidence and suspects.

critical race theory: An academic perspective that stresses the foundational nature of slavery in the creation of the United States and the idea that the nation's laws and institutions are inherently racist and, therefore, unjust.

cross-examination: A term for the questioning of a witness who was not called to the stand by the attorney who is doing the questioning; this questioning follows direct examination.

curtilage: Under common law, the enclosed space surrounding a dwelling house.

custodial interrogation: A situation in which police ask questions of a suspect who is not free to leave; generally, this condition of being in custody serves as a prerequisite for the reading of *Miranda* rights.

deadlocked jury: A jury that is unable to reach a unanimous verdict.

debtors' prison: A term applied to situations in which an individual is sentenced to incarceration solely for an inability to pay some type of court-ordered fine or fee.

decertification: Revocation of a police officer's certificate or license based on misconduct.

defamation: A false public statement that causes damage to the reputation of a person or business.

deliberate indifference standard: A legal requirement that must be demonstrated for a prison official to be held liable in civil court for a lawsuit related to the treatment of prisoners in a correctional facility, including lawsuit related to inadequate medical care.

derivative evidence: Evidence derived from or obtained via other evidence.

designated public forum: A government-controlled facility that has been made available to the public for certain uses, such as for meeting or performances; these often include meeting rooms, auditoriums, gymnasiums, and amphitheaters that might otherwise be closed to the public.

diplomatic immunity: A principle of international law under which foreign diplomats are immune from arrest and prosecution.

direct democracy: A government by the people directly, whereby the people vote directly on policy making rather than electing representatives who craft policy on behalf of society.

discovery: A term describing the requirement for each side in a criminal case to share certain information with the other side, such as the names of witnesses.

disgorgement: A penalty applied, usually as the result of a criminal conviction, that allows the government to seize illegally-acquired money or property from an offender, perhaps, to return some or all of it to the rightful owner.

disparate impact: Facially neutral policies that have unequal effects on different groups.

double jeopardy: Being tried twice for the same offense.

drone: A compact flying machine that can be remotely controlled and flown at low altitudes, allowing for photographs or videos to be taken from above.

drug courier profile: A set of characteristics developed by law enforcement to identify likely couriers of illegal drugs.

due process of law: The requirement that government follow the law and treat people fairly when taking actions that affect their lives, liberties, or property.

eavesdropping: Refers to the tactic of listening in on a conversation without permission to do so.

electric chair: A method of execution that involves a death row inmate being strapped to a chair and exposed to a high-voltage electric current until death occurs.

emergency searches: Warrantless searches conducted by police responding to emergencies, such as active shooters, fires, and bomb threats.

eminent domain: The power of government to take private property for public use.

entrapment: An affirmative defense in which the defendant claims to have been induced by law enforcement to commit a crime that the person was not predisposed to commit.

enumerated powers: Legislative powers explicitly stated in a constitution.

equal protection of the laws: Equal justice under the law for all persons; the right to be free from official discrimination based on race, ethnicity, religion, gender, sexual orientation, and other characteristics.

Establishment Clause: The first clause of the First Amendment, which prohibits government from establishing religion.

evanescent evidence: Evidence that is likely to disappear if not seized immediately.

ex post facto law: A law that criminalizes an act theretofore noncriminal and allows for retroactive prosecution of that act. Also, any law that retroactively increases punishments or changes evidentiary rules to facilitate a conviction.

excessive bail: An unconstitutionally high payment amount that is set as a condition for pretrial release as an accused awaits trial; a violation of the Eighth Amendment.

excessive fines: A monetary penalty a court deems to be disproportionate and, thus, a violation of the Eighth Amendment.

excessive use of force: The use of force by police beyond that which is reasonably necessary to effect an arrest.

exclusionary rule: A judicial rule holding that evidence obtained in violation of the Fourth Amendment is generally not admissible in a criminal prosecution of the person whose rights were violated.

exculpatory evidence: A term describing the requirement for the prosecution to share with the defense any evidence in a criminal case that tends to show the defendant is not guilty.

executive order: An official written directive issued by the president based on statutory or constitutional authority and published in the *Federal Register*.

executive privilege: The power of a chief executive to withhold certain information from disclosure to the public or to other governmental actors.

exigent circumstances: Situations in which an emergency or imminent threat can be used to justify a warrantless search.

facial recognition technology: Computer-based systems that can link a photo or surveillance image with a known image of an individual that is housed in a database.

Faraday bag: A metallic foil bag that can be placed over a device, such as a cell phone, to block any wireless communication with that device.

federal habeas corpus review: Federal judicial review of a state prisoner's case pursuant to a writ of habeas corpus.

federalism: The constitutional division of sovereignty between a central government and a set of regional governments.

felonies: More serious crimes that carry prison sentences usually greater than one year.

fighting words: Speech inherently likely to provoke a violent reaction from an ordinary person and, therefore, not deserving of protection under the First Amendment.

firing squads: A method of execution that involves multiple shooters firing a gun at the death row inmate.

FISA Court: A court that was specifically created by the Foreign Intelligence Surveillance Act to evaluate government requests for warrants connected to surveillance of foreign actors.

flash-bang grenade: An explosive device that creates an extremely loud report and a flash of bright light, so as to disable a person exposed to it.

Free Exercise Clause: The second clause of the First Amendment, which protects an individual's right to exercise religious beliefs.

freedom of association: A liberty that the Supreme Court has recognized as a correlate to the First Amendment rights to freedom of speech and assembly to protect the ability of individuals to gather with other like-minded individuals, often to form political alliances.

fruit of the poisonous tree doctrine: Doctrine holding that evidence is inadmissible if it is derived from or obtained as the result of inadmissible evidence.

fugitive track dog: A police dog trained to track persons who have evaded arrest.

fundamental right: A right requiring a high level of judicial protection. Fundamental rights include those enumerated in the Bill of Rights as well as other implicit constitutional rights, such as the right of privacy.

fundamental rights doctrine: A reference to those individual rights and liberties that are deemed most essential within an ordered society and which are protected rigorously by courts.

gag order: A command from a judge barring discussion of a specific matter, typically issued to jurors in a high-profile case.

general warrant: A warrant that is not particular regarding the place to be searched or the things to be seized.

good faith exception: An exception to the exclusionary rule under which evidence need not be suppressed as long as officers were acting in good faith reliance on a search warrant that was later determined to be unsupported by probable cause.

good-time credit: A reduction in a convicted criminal's period of incarceration based on good behavior while in prison.

government speech doctrine: The doctrine under which governmental entities can take positions on issues without facing First Amendment challenges for viewpoint discrimination.

GPS tracker: A Global Positioning Systems device that can be attached to an item and used to track that item's movements in real-time.

grand jury: A group of citizens convened either to conduct an investigation or determine whether there is sufficient evidence to warrant an indictment.

habeas corpus: A court order requiring a person in custody to be brought before a court to determine the legality of that custody.

habitual offender law: A statute that prescribes an enhanced punishment for repeated criminal offenses (typically three or more) regardless of what punishment is permissible under the law for the most recent offense.

harmless error doctrine: Doctrine under which an appellate court should reverse a conviction only if an error allowed by the trial court was prejudicial to the defendant.

hate speech: A category of speech that discriminates against or denigrates individuals based on demographic characteristics but which the Supreme Court has, nonetheless, protected under the First Amendment.

hate-crime enhancement: An additional penalty added to a crime, such as assault, because the offense was motivated by bias against an individual belonging to a specific demographic group.

hearsay evidence: A term that refers to out-of-court statements relayed by a witness who is not the speaker.

heightened scrutiny (or intermediate scrutiny): A judicial approach to judging gender-based discrimination as well as time, place, and manner regulations of the exercise of First Amendment rights. Under heightened scrutiny, government carries the burden of providing an exceedingly persuasive justification for its policies.

hot pursuit: The close and avid pursuit of a fleeing suspect.

identification check: A temporary detention by a police officer for the purpose of ascertaining a person's identity.

imminent destruction of evidence: The situation in which police may conduct a warrantless search and seizure to prevent the immediate destruction of evidence.

imminent lawless action: The doctrine established by the Supreme Court holding that speech advocating illegal action, which has a likelihood of quickly producing such action, does not merit First Amendment protection.

impeachment: The constitutional mechanism for removing officials from office, usually through a vote taken by members of a legislative body.

implied powers: Legislative powers implied by constitutional language.

independent source doctrine: Doctrine under which improperly seized evidence can be admitted into evidence if police can demonstrate some other method by which the same evidence was lawfully acquired.

indeterminate sentence: A criminal punishment that carries no specified ending.

indictment: A formal criminal charge issued by a grand jury.

inevitable discovery exception: An exception to the fruit of the poisonous tree doctrine that allows the admission of evidence derived from inadmissible evidence if it inevitably would have been discovered independently by lawful means.

information: A formal criminal charge filed by a prosecutor.

injunction: A court order requiring a party to do or cease doing something.

intermediate scrutiny: A legal doctrine through which courts evaluate time, place, and manner restrictions as well as sex discrimination cases; requires restrictions to be justified by a narrowly tailored significant (or substantial) government interest and the provision of ample alternatives for people to exercise their rights.

internet protocol (IP) address: A unique number that can be used to identify either an individual computer or a router that links a computer to the internet.

internet subscriber information: Personally identifiable information, such as a name, email address, or physical street address, connected to a router or computer's IP address.

inventory search: A search of a person being arrested or a vehicle being impounded to make an inventory of personal property found on that person or within that automobile.

investigatory detention: A brief detention of a suspect based on reasonable suspicion that crime is afoot.

judicial review: The power of courts to strike down laws and other actions of government that violate constitutional principles.

jury nullification: A jury's decision to ignore the law and/or the evidence in acquitting a defendant or convicting the defendant of a lesser crime than charged.

justice: The condition in which people are treated fairly and receive what they deserve.

juvenile court system: A court that exclusively handles matters related to juvenile offenders, as defined under applicable state law.

knock-and-announce requirement: The requirement that police knock and announce their presence when executing a search warrant.

large-capacity magazines: A term typically applied to a weapon capable of holding an amount of ammunition that is deemed illegal under state law.

least restrictive means: A component of the *Sherbert* test, which is used by courts to evaluate free exercise of religion claims; this component requires a compelling interest advanced by the government to justify infringement upon religious exercise to be examined closely to determine if another policy could also advance the compelling interest but with a more limited intrusion upon religious liberty.

legitimate interest: A permissible goal—something government clearly is empowered to pursue.

***Lemon* test:** A legal framework evolving from the Supreme Court's 1963 decision in *Lemon v. Kurtzman* and used by courts to examine laws or government action implicating the Establishment Clause of the First Amendment; it requires the government to justify a policy by demonstrating a secular purpose, showing that religion is neither advanced nor inhibited, and establishing religion and government are not excessively entangled.

lethal injection: A method of execution that generally involves a death row inmate being injected with a combination of drugs that subsequently produce death; this is the most common method of execution in the United States.

libel: Defamation of character through written word or electronic media.

limited public forum: A subcategory of the *designated public forum*; a facility made available for use by a specific group but to which other groups must be allowed access in an effort to accommodate expression of different viewpoints; an example would be a classroom on a public university campus that has been opened for use by an outside group.

lineup: A police procedure in which a suspect is included in a group with other persons and a victim or witness is asked to identify the perpetrator.

living Constitution: The notion that the meaning of the Constitution evolves over time through changing judicial interpretation.

mandatory minimum sentences: A criminal punishment, or enhancement to a punishment, defined through an act of the state legislature and which provides no discretion for judges to deviate from the prescribed penalties that appear in the law; classic examples relate to punishments established based on the weight of contraband involved in a drug crime or punishments tied to using a gun in the commission of a crime.

marital privilege: A concept that prevents one spouse from testifying against another in a criminal case, with exceptions for domestic abuse.

martial law: A condition in which the military temporarily assumes control of law enforcement in a particular area.

mass incarceration: The condition in which an unusually large proportion of the population is imprisoned.

mens rea: The mental element of a crime; criminal intent.

metadata: Data associated with a phone call or other form of electronic communication, including the phone numbers or email addresses, date and time of the call, and duration of the call.

metal detectors: Devices that can detect if a person walking through is carrying an object with metal.

minimal scrutiny: A judicial approach to judging laws that infringe on liberty generally or discriminate on the basis of characteristics not subject to strict or heightened scrutiny.

ministerial exception: An idea created by the Supreme Court to suggest religious organizations, like churches and religious schools, can make employment decisions regarding certain important positions without consideration of potential violations of existing employment discrimination laws.

***Miranda* warnings:** Stemming from the Supreme Court's decision in *Miranda v. Arizona* (1966), these warnings are given by police to individuals who are taken into custody before they are interrogated. Persons being taken into custody are advised they have the right to remain silent, to have a lawyer present during questioning, and anything they say can and will be used against them in a court of law.

misdemeanors: Less serious crimes for which the maximum penalty is a fine or a term of incarceration of less than one year.

mistrial: A declaration from a trial judge putting an end to a trial due to a fatal error in procedure or a jury being unable to reach a verdict.

mitigating factors: Criteria that indicate excuses for the commission of a crime, which might lessen the offender's level of culpability in the eyes of those considering punishment; in a death penalty case, if these outweigh aggravating factors, a capital sentence cannot be given, according to Supreme Court precedent.

narrow tailoring: The requirement for a policy that impinges on constitutional rights to be constructed in such a way as to limit the extent to which it curtails those rights.

National Instant Criminal Background Check System: A national computerized database that contains information that can be used to quickly assess whether a specific person seeking to purchase a weapon falls into the category of a *prohibited possessor*—perhaps, for having a felony conviction or for having been institutionalized as mentally ill.

742 | Constitutional Law Today: Foundations for Criminal Justice

National Security Agency: A federal U.S. government agency created to facilitate the electronic collection of intelligence.

national supremacy: The doctrine holding that when federal and state powers collide, the federal government prevails, assuming the federal government's action is constitutional.

no-knock entry: A situation in which law enforcement agents, perhaps pursuant to a no-knock warrant, execute entry without knocking or announcing their presence.

no-knock warrant: A search warrant that grants police officers the authority to enter a specified area without the need to knock and announce themselves prior to entering.

nonpublic forum: A government-controlled area also designated for a specific purposes and to which access can be restricted, such as an airport; speech and assembly rights in such places may be protected by courts at lesser levels than in traditional open spaces like public forums.

objective reasonableness standard: An approach to judging an officer's use of force that looks solely at the officer's actions, without regard to intentions or motivations. The test is whether an ordinary person would feel such force was reasonable in the moment it was used.

obscenity: Extreme pornography not protected under the First Amendment and incompatible with contemporary community standards.

open fields: A person's real property lying beyond the curtilage.

ordinances: Laws enacted by local governing bodies.

original jurisdiction: The authority of a court of law to adjudicate a case for the first time.

originalism: The idea that a constitutional provision must be interpreted according to its accepted meaning at the time it was adopted.

overbreadth doctrine: A legal standard indicating that a government restriction, often on expression, burdens more conduct than is necessary to further a government objective, indicating the individual conduct in question should remain protected.

parens patriae: A theory suggesting government holds the responsibility for caring for individuals who are not capable of caring for themselves; this could apply to government officials acting in place of parents who are not serving the best interests of a child.

parole: Early release from prison, typically based on a decision made by majority vote of a group of people known as a parole board, who oversee a hearing regarding a convict's suitability for being released.

pat-down search: A *frisk* of a suspect's outer garments in attempt to locate concealed weapons.

pen register: A device that records the numbers dialed from a particular phone line (outgoing calls).

pepper spray: A solution made from peppers that disables a person by causing extreme irritation to the eyes.

***per se* rule:** A generalized rule that does not take into account special circumstances.

peremptory challenge: Refers to an attempt by an attorney to dismiss a prospective juror based on a factor that does not explicitly require an explanation but which cannot be based on race or sex; each side in a criminal case is typically given a limited number of these challenges.

permanent injunction: A court order permanently enjoining the defendant with respect to some unlawful action; issued only after notice to the defendant and a hearing.

petty offenses: Criminal offenses that carry lesser punishment, typically six months or less of incarceration or a fine.

physical evidence: Evidence that derives its value not from the content of any specific testimony but rather from what it reveals about some aspect of a person's physical state, such as blood evidence or if they are slurring words as they speak.

plain view doctrine: The doctrine under which agents may make a warrantless seizure of evidence that comes into their plain view, as long as they have the right to be where they are when that evidence is discovered.

plea bargaining: The process through which a prosecutor and defender reach an agreement by which the defendant will plead guilty to a crime, typically in exchange for a lesser sentence than the maximum allowed by statute.

police power: The authority of state legislatures to make laws to promote public health, safety, order, welfare, and decency.

preemption: The doctrine that federal law supersedes state law, either expressly or by implication; can also apply to state law superseding local law.

preliminary hearing: A hearing to determine whether there is probable cause to hold a defendant for trial.

preliminary injunction: An injunction issued without a hearing but only after the judge has determined the plaintiff is likely to succeed on the merits and will suffer irreparable harm without immediate relief.

preponderance of evidence: Evidentiary standard under which a proposition is deemed to be true if there is more evidence for it than against it.

presidential directive: A broad term that includes executive orders, presidential memoranda, and presidential proclamations.

presidential memorandum: An official written directive by the president similar to an executive order but without the requirement that it be published in the *Federal Register*.

presumption of innocence: The rule whereby a defendant in a criminal trial is presumed innocent and the prosecution must prove the defendant's guilt.

pretrial detention: Reference to an accused criminal being held in custody after arrest and before a criminal trial begins.

pretrial motions: Requests by either party to a case seeking a ruling or an order prior to the commencement of a trial.

prior restraint: Commonly known as censorship, this term describes an attempt by the government to prevent the public release of information—perhaps, by censoring the publication of a newspaper article or book; an act that will be closely scrutinized by courts.

PRISM: A clandestine NSA program that involved widespread collection of metadata from the electronic activities of millions of Americans.

private forum: A building, facility, or outdoor space owned by a private entity, such as a shopping mall; constitutional protections do not confer assembly or speech rights in such settings.

***pro se* representation:** A term referring to a defendant who chooses to represent themselves in court.

probable cause: Knowledge of specific facts giving one reasonable grounds for believing that criminal activity is afoot.

probation: An alternative to incarceration that allows a person accused of a crime to remain free from a jail or prison setting, provided certain conditions are met, such as not using drugs, not traveling out of state, and not committing further crimes.

procedural criminal law: The branch of the law that sets forth the procedures to be followed in law enforcement and the prosecution and adjudication of criminal cases.

procedural due process: The requirement that government provide fair notice and a fair hearing before depriving a person of life, liberty, or property.

profanity: A term typically used to describe curse words and other language that might offend some members of society.

prosecutorial discretion: The authority of prosecutors to decide whether to file criminal charges and, if so, which charges to bring.

public figure: A person who has, by virtue of their choice in occupation or by voluntarily making public statements about political issues, achieved a level of notoriety or fame in society, such as a politician or person running for office; if such a person brings a defamation lawsuit, proof of actual malice—or reckless disregard for the truth—is required.

public forum: Open areas of land that are maintained by government, such as public parks, sidewalks, and town squares, which courts have traditionally protected for public gatherings and open displays of expression.

public safety exception: An exception to the *Miranda* decision allowing police officers to ask questions of a suspect before providing the *Miranda* warnings to address an imminent threat to public safety.

qualified immunity: Immunity from civil liability that protects public officials for their actions, unless they violate clearly established statutory or constitutional rights that a reasonable person should have known about.

racial profiling: The impermissible practice in which law enforcement authorities target people based on race.

rational basis test: A deferential test through which courts evaluate the constitutionality of government action impinging on individual rights and liberties by determining if it is rationally related to a legitimate government interest; the most lenient form of judicial scrutiny, this test merely requires a challenged law or policy to be rationally related to a legitimate governmental interest.

rational relationship: A reasonable connection between ends and means.

reasonable doubt standard: The standard of proof in a criminal case: the government must prove all the elements of a crime beyond a reasonable doubt.

reasonable expectation of privacy: An expectation that one's activities in a certain place are private. One must have exhibited a subjective expectation of privacy, and that expectation must be one that society is prepared to recognize as reasonable.

reasonable suspicion: Suspicion based on specific and articulable facts that criminal activity is afoot.

recusal: A judge's decision not to participate in a particular case based on an actual or perceived conflict of interest.

red flag laws: State laws allowing judges to issue risk protection orders authorizing the temporary seizure of firearms from persons believed to be a threat to themselves or others.

red-light cameras: Cameras placed adjacent to public roadways for the purpose of assessing whether a car has passed through a red light and typically providing a private company with justification to send a citation to the registered owner of a vehicle.

referendum: An election in which the voters decide a question of policy, typically regarding the passage or repeal of a state statute or constitutional provision.

regulatory state: A government characterized by numerous regulations promulgated by bureaucratic agencies.

Religious Freedom Restoration Act (RFRA): A 1993 federal law, passed in response to the Supreme Court's decision in *Employment Decision v. Smith*, requiring courts to evaluate free exercise of religion cases according to the *Sherbert* test. Based on case precedent and a congressional amendment, it applies only to the actions of federal officials.

representative democracy: A system in which voters elect representatives to make decisions on their behalf.

restitution: A payment, often required by a court, made by a criminal to the victim of the crime to compensate for a loss suffered by the victim.

right of privacy: The unenumerated constitutional right shielding certain intimate personal decisions from governmental interference.

risk protection order: An order issued by a judge authorizing the temporary seizure of firearms from a person believed to be a threat to themself or others.

risk-assessment algorithm: A computerized analysis used in some jurisdictions to either assist a judge in setting cash bail amounts or replace the use of cash bail; the algorithm uses multiple factors to predict an accused criminal's likelihood of appearing in court for trial and their likelihood of re-offending.

router: A device, often installed by an internet service provider, which enables a computer to connect to the internet.

routine booking questions: A line of questioning that concerns basic personally identifying information, such as name, age, and address; this type of questioning generally does not require a *Miranda* warning even if a person is in police custody.

search incident to arrest: A warrantless search of a person being placed under arrest as well as the area within that person's immediate grasp and control.

search warrant: An order issued by a judge or magistrate authorizing officials to search a particular place and seize particular things.

secular purpose: A nonreligious justification for a law or government policy; a key component of *Lemon* test analysis pursuant to the Establishment Clause.

seditious libel: A term derived from English law to indicate that speech criticizing the government or advocating the overthrow of government could be punished.

selective incorporation: The judicial doctrine under which specific provisions of the Bill of Rights deemed essential to a scheme of ordered liberty are applied to state action via the Due Process Clause of the Fourteenth Amendment.

separate but equal doctrine: The discredited doctrine that held segregation of the races was not a denial of equal protection of the law.

separation of church and state: A principle that courts have found implicit in the Establishment Clause of the First Amendment, which indicates a bifurcation between government and religion.

separation of powers: Constitutional principle by which the legislative, executive, and judicial powers are located in different branches of government.

***Sherbert* test:** A judicial framework created by the Supreme Court to evaluate cases involving First Amendment free exercise of religion claims; it requires the government to justify an undue burden upon the exercise of a sincere religious belief by demonstrating a compelling interest that is implemented in the least restrictive means for religious exercise.

shield law: A law enacted to protect reporters from being required to provide testimony in a criminal proceeding when doing so might force a reporter to reveal the identity of confidential informants.

silver platter doctrine: Antiquated doctrine under which federal and state authorities could share illegally obtained evidence before the exclusionary rule was made applicable to all jurisdictions.

sincere religious belief: A religious belief deemed to be authentic enough, based on long-standing practices and regular meetings of participants, to justify the assertion of a free exercise claim.

slander: Defamation of character through spoken word.

sneak and peek search: An illegal warrantless search that is later rectified by a warrant authorizing a more extensive search of the same premises.

social justice: Equal rights under the law and fairness in the division of wealth, privilege, and opportunity in society.

solitary confinement: A controversial action taken against inmates in a correctional facility, often as a result of disciplinary misconduct, which results in the inmate being confined in isolation within the correctional facility and given limited access, if any, to other people.

special needs search: A search performed in the absence of particularized suspicion, for the purpose of preventing or minimizing the risk of harm.

speed-detection cameras: Cameras placed in public locations for the purpose of assessing whether a car is traveling over the speed limit; correlated citations can be sent to the vehicle's registered owner.

standing: The right to challenge an action in court because one has suffered or is likely to suffer a real and substantial injury or deprivation of rights.

stare decisis: The common-law doctrine that holds that courts should follow precedent.

state action doctrine: The judicial doctrine under which the Fourteenth Amendment's due process and equal protection clauses apply only to governmental policies and actions, as opposed to private party actions.

states' rights: The rights reserved for the states by the Tenth Amendment.

status offenses: A criminal charge against an individual simply on the basis of that person being a member of a group or having a certain condition, like being a drug addict; the Supreme Court has found these to be a violation of the Eighth Amendment's Cruel and Unusual Punishment Clause.

statutes: Generally applicable laws enacted by legislatures.

stop and frisk: A brief detention based on reasonable suspicion, including a pat-down search of the detainee's outer garments.

strict scrutiny: The most rigorous legal framework through which courts evaluate fundamental rights and liberties, by requiring government to justify restrictions with a narrowly tailored policy in furtherance of a compelling governmental interest; also used by courts to analyze claims of racial discrimination under the Fourteenth Amendment; an approach to judging official discrimination based on race, religion, or national origin in which that discrimination is presumed to be unconstitutional.

subjective recklessness: A legal standard often connected to lawsuit related to a failure of prison officials to protect an inmate from harm; this standard requires a prison official to have been aware of and consciously disregarded the risk of harm to an inmate.

substantive criminal law: The branch of the law that defines crimes and punishments.

substantive due process: The doctrine that due process requires laws to be fair, reasonable, and just and not unreasonably intrusive on a person's liberty.

suspect classification doctrine: The judicial doctrine under which official discrimination based on race, religion, or national origin is considered to be inherently suspect and, therefore, subjected to strict scrutiny.

suspicionless search: A search that is not based reasonable suspicion or probable cause.

Taser: An electric shock device used to temporarily incapacitate a person.

***Terry* stop:** Another term for a stop and frisk, as allowed by the Supreme Court's landmark *Terry v. Ohio* (1968) decision.

testimonial evidence: Oral evidence, as distinct from physical evidence.

thermal imager: A device that detects heat (infrared light).

third-party doctrine: The doctrine under which a person has no reasonable expectation of privacy with regard to information voluntarily given to a third party.

time, place, and manner regulations: Restrictions on assembly or expression that are content-neutral and do not completely ban activity but, rather, place limitations regarding how or when assembly or speech can occur; such restrictions are usually evaluated by courts with the legal test of intermediate scrutiny.

torts: Non-criminal wrongs done intentionally or through negligence, the remedy for which is a civil suit for damages.

totality of circumstances test: A test for determining probable cause based on the entire collection of relevant facts in a particular case.

trap and trace device: A device that records phone numbers from which a particular number is dialed (incoming calls).

treason: The crime of giving "aid and comfort" to the enemies of one's own country or levying war against one's own country.

trespass doctrine: The doctrine that to commit a Fourth Amendment violation, law enforcement agents must physically intrude on someone's property.

trial courts: Tribunals that make findings of fact and apply laws in determining which side should prevail in a civil or criminal case.

true threats: Credible communications calling for violence against other persons.

undue burden: A governmental restriction upon religious exercise deemed to be sufficient enough to require justification, under the *Sherbert* test, via an assessment of a compelling interest and least restrictive means of implementation.

unfunded mandate: A federal legislative act that places a burden upon state and local officials without providing appropriate funding for enforcement of the act.

unitary executive: The theory that the executive branch should be completely under the control of the chief executive.

use immunity: A form of immunity that prohibits the prosecution from using immunized testimony as evidence against the witness.

venue: The specific geographic location of a criminal trial.

victim impact testimony: Information often relayed by the prosecution in the sentencing phase of a death penalty case, usually speaking to the manner in which the victim's injuries or death have affected those around them, such as children or other dependents.

victims' rights: Refers to the various rights possessed by victims of crimes.

void-for-vagueness doctrine: The doctrine, derived from due process, which holds that excessively vague criminal laws are invalid because they fail to provide adequate notice of what is permissible and what is prohibited.

voir dire: The process of jury selection in which attorneys (prosecutors and defense counsel) ask questions of prospective jurors.

voter suppression: A term applied to a variety of policies and practices designed to discourage voting by minorities.

warrantless arrest: An arrest made by police without prior judicial authorization.

wiretap: An electronic connection to a phone line that permits those conducting surveillance to listen to both sides of a conversation.

writ of habeas corpus: A court order requiring an official holding a person in custody to appear in court, so the legality of that custody can be determined.

Table of Cases

A

Abbate v. United States, 359 U.S. 187 (1959), 501

Abington School District v. Schempp, 374 U.S. 203 (1963), 202, 204

ACLU v. Alvarez, 679 F. 3d 583 (7th Cir. 2012), 146

Adamson v. California, 332 U.S. 46 (1947), 104

Adams v. Texas, 448 U.S. 38 (1980), 667

Adams v. Williams, 407 U.S. 143 (1972), 297, 442, 467

Adderley v. Florida, 385 U.S. 39 (1966), 178

Aguilar v. Texas, 378 U.S. 108 (1964), 296

A.L.A. Schechter Poultry Corp. v. United States, 295 U.S. 495 (1935), 34

Alabama v. White, 496 U.S. 325 (1990), 352

Allen v. United States, 164 U.S. 492 (1896), 589

Alleyne v. United States, 570 U.S. 99 (2013), 591

Almeida-Sanchez v. United States, 413 U.S. 266 (1973), 363

American Legion et al. v. American Humanist Association, 588 U.S. (2019), 208

Apprendi v. New Jersey, 530 U.S. 466 (2000), 590–591

Argersinger v. Hamlin, 407 U.S. 25 (1972), 549

Arizona v. Fulminante, 499 U.S. 279 (1991), 525–527

Arizona v. Gant, 556 U.S. 332 (2009), 334

Arizona v. Hicks, 480 U.S. 321 (1987), 328

Arizona v. Roberson, 486 U.S. 675 (1988), 554

Arizona v. United States, 567 U.S. 387 (2012), 35–36, 129

Arver v. United States, 245 U.S. 366 (1918), 93–94

Ashcraft v. Tennessee, 322 U. S. 143 (1944), 506

Ashcroft v. Free Speech Coalition, 535 U.S. 234 (2002), 160

Atkins v. Virginia, 536 U.S. 304 (2002), 678–679, 680

Atwater v. City of Lago Vista (2001), 443

Austin v. United States, 509 U.S. 602 (1993), 616–617

Autin v. City of Baytown, Tex., 174F. App'x 183 (5th Cir. 2005), 455

B

Bailey v. Alabama, 219 U.S. 219 (1911), 93

Bailey v. United States, 568 U.S. 186 (2013), 293

Ballew v. Georgia, 435 U.S. 223 (1978), 583–584

Bantam Books, Inc. v. Sullivan, 372 U.S. 58 (1963), 158

Barker v. Wingo, 407 U.S. 514 (1972), 562

Barnes v. Glen Theatre, Inc., 501 U.S. 560 (1991), 161

Barron v. Baltimore, 32 U.S. 243 (1833), 92

Barr v. Lafon, 538 F. 3d 554 (6th Cir. 2008), 188

Bartkus v. Illinois, 359 U.S. 121 (1959), 501

Batson v. Kentucky, 476 U.S. 79 (1986), 128, 585, 586

Baxter v. Bracey and Harris, Case No. 18-5102 (6th Cir. Nov. 8, 2018), 459

Baze v. Rees, 553 U.S. 35 (2008), 673, 674, 676

Bearden v. Georgia, 461 U.S. 660 (1983), 629–631

Bell v. Hood, 327 U.S. 678 (1946), 71

Bell v. Wolfish, 441 U.S. 520, 561 (1979), 313, 365, 454, 614

Bennis v. Michigan, 516 U.S. 442, 460 n.1 (1996), 624

Benton v. Maryland, 395 U.S. 784 (1969), 109, 111, 499

Berghuis v. Thompkins, 560 U.S. 370 (2010), 512–513

Berkemer v. McCarty, 468 U.S. 420 (1984), 515

Bethel School District No. 403 v. Fraser, 478 U.S. 675 (1986), 188

Betts v. Brady, 316 U.S. 455 (1942), 107, 109, 547

Biden v. Missouri, 595 U.S. (2022), 117

Birchfield v. North Dakota, 579 U.S. (2016), 361, 533

Bivens v. Six Unknown Named Agents of the Federal Bureau of Narcotics, 403 U.S. 388 (1971), 71, 305–307

Blackburn v. Alabama, 361 U.S. 190 (1960), 508

Blanton v. City of No. Las Vegas, 489 U.S. 538 (1989), 558

Blockburger v. United States, 284 U.S. 299 (1932), 500

Board of County Commissioners of Bryan City v. Brown, 520 U.S. 397 (1997), 305

Board of Education v. Allen, 392 U.S. 236 (1968), 205

Board of Education v. Earls, 536 U.S. 822 (2002), 369

Bob Jones University v. United States, 461 U.S. 574 (1983), 228

Bolling v. Sharpe, 347 U.S. 497 (1954), 491

Bond v. State of Indiana, 9 N.E.3d 134 (Ind. 2014), 527–528

Bond v. United States, 572 U.S. 844 (2014), 22, 279–280

Boos v. Barry, 485 U.S. 312 (1988), 183

Bordenkircher v. Hayes, 434 U.S. 357 (1978), 46, 560

Bostock v. Clayton County, 590 U.S. (2020), 124, 230–231

Boumediene v. Bush, 553 U.S. 723 (2008), 89, 444, 567

Bowers v. Hardwick, 478 U.S. 186 (1986), 68, 114

Boyd v. United States, 116 U.S. 616 (1886), 625

Brady v. Maryland, 373 U.S. 83 (1963), 580

Brady v. United States, 397 U.S. 742 (1970), 559–560

Bram v. United States, 168 U.S. 532 (1897), 504

Brandenburg v. Ohio, 395 U.S. 444 (1969), 148–149

Branzburg v. Hayes, 408 U.S. 665 (1972), 168–169

Brewer v. Williams, 430 U.S. 387 (1977), 303, 520–521

Bridges v. California, 314 U.S. 252 (1941), 568

Brigham City v. Stuart, 547 U. S. 398, 403 (2006), 335

Brinegar v. United States, 338 U.S. 160 (1949), 442, 467

Brosseau v. Haugen, 543 U.S. 194 (2004), 311

Brower v. County of Inyo, 489 U.S. 593 (1989), 476

Brown v. Board of Education, 347 U.S. 483 (1954), 34, 67–68, 94, 118–119

Brown v. Illinois, 422 U.S. 590 (1975), 302

Brown v. Mississippi, 297 U.S. 278 (1936), 505

Brown v. Plata, 563 U.S. 493 (2011), 693–694

Brown v. Texas, 443 U.S. 47 (1979), 467

Brown v. Walker, 161 U.S. 591 (1896), 503

Brumfield v. Cain, 576 U.S. 305 (2015), 679–680

Bucklew v. Precythe, 587 U.S. (2019), 675–676

Bumper v. North Carolina, 391 U.S. 543 (1968), 323–324

Burdine v. Johnson, 262 F.3d 336 (5th Cir. 2001), 556

Burwell v. Hobby Lobby Stores, Inc., 573 U.S. 682 (2014), 228

Byrd v. United States, 584 U.S. (2018), 355–356

C

Cady v. Dombrowski, 413 U.S. 433 (1973), 345–346, 348

Caetano v. Massachusetts, 577 U.S. (2016), 247–248

Cage v. Louisiana, 498 U.S. 39 (1990), 492

Calder v. Bull, 3 U.S. 386 (1798), 88

California v. Carney, 471 U.S. 386 (1985), 355

California v. Ciraolo, 476 U.S. 207 (1986), 280, 328, 355, 397, 405

Caliste v. Cantrell, 937 F.3d 525 (5th Cir. 2019), 611

Calvary Chapel Dayton Valley v. Sisolak, 591 U.S. (2020), 216–217

Campbell v. City of Springboro, 700 F.3d 779 (6th Cir. 2013), 458

Caniglia v. Strom, 593 U.S. (2021), 265, 347–348

Cantwell v. Connecticut, 310 U.S. 296 (1940), 107, 111, 211, 218

Caperton v. A.T. Massey Coal Co., 556 U.S. 868 (2009), 631

Carmell v. Texas, 529 U.S. 513 (2000), 89

Carpenter v. United States, 585 U.S. (2018), 285, 415–416, 425, 428

Carroll v. United States, 267 U. S. 132 (1925), 353, 363

Carson v. Makin, 596 U.S. (2022), 209

Chambers v. Florida, 309 U.S. 227 (1940), 505, 568

Chandler v. Florida, 449 U.S. 560 (1981), 553, 570

Chaplinsky v. New Hampshire, 315 U.S. 568 (1942), 144, 162

Chapman v. California, 386 U. S. 18 (1967), 526

Chartered v. United States, 491 U.S. 617 (1989), 621

Chicago, Burlington & Quincy Railroad Co. v. City of Chicago, 166 U.S. 226 (1897), 105, 111

Chimel v. California, 395 U.S. 752 (1969), 332–334, 341

Chisholm v. Georgia, 2 U.S. 419 (1793), 68

Church of the Lukumi Babalu Aye v. City of Hialeah, 508 U.S. 520 (1993), 225

Citizens United v. Federal Election Commission, 558 U.S. 310 (2010), 184

City of Boerne v. Flores, 521 U.S. 507 (1997), 215–216, 223

City of Chicago v. Morales, 527 U.S. 41 (1999), 102–103, 494

City of Indianapolis v. Edmond, 531 U.S. 32 (2000), 372, 475–476

City of Ontario, California v. Quon, 560 U.S. 746 (2010), 373, 428

City Tahlequah, Oklahoma v. Bond, 595 U.S. (2022), 311–312

Coates v. Cincinnati, 402 U. S. 611 (1971), 494

Coffin v. United States, 156 U.S. 432 (1895), 101

Cohen v. California, 403 U.S. 15 (1971), 162

Coker v. Georgia, 433 U.S. 584 (1977), 668

Collins v. Virginia, 584 U.S. (2018), 284, 354

Collins v. Yellin, 594 U.S. (2021), 50

Colonnade Catering Corporation v. United States, 392 U.S. 72 (1970), 369, 370

Commonwealth v. Cosby, 252 A.3d 1092 (Pa. 2021), 561–562

Connick v. Myers, 461 U.S. (1983), 186

Coolidge v. New Hampshire, 403 U.S. 443 (1971), 287, 328

Costello v. United States, 350 U.S. 359 (1956), 497

Couch v. United States, 409 U.S. 322 (1973), 285, 428

County of Allegheny v. American Civil Liberties Union, 492 U.S. 573 (1989), 207, 210

County of Riverside v. McLaughlin, 500 U.S. 44 (1991), 444

County of Sacramento v. Lewis, 523 U.S. 833 (1998), 532–533

Coy v. Iowa, 487 U.S. 1012 (1988), 577

Craig v. Boren, 429 U.S. 190 (1976), 120

Crawford v. Washington, 541 U.S. 36 (2004), 573, 575

Cruzan v. Missouri Health Department, 497 U.S. 261 (1990), 115

Cruze-Gulyas v. Minard, 918 F.3d 494 (6th Cir. 2019), 151

Cupp v. Murphy, 412 U.S. 291 (1973), 341

Cutting v. City of Portland, Maine, 802 F. 3d 79 (1st Cir. 2015), 184

D

Daniels v. Williams, 474 U.S. 327 (1986), 304–305

Daubert v. Merrell Dow Pharmaceuticals, Inc., 509 U.S. 579 (1993), 581

Davis v. Ayala, 576 U.S. 257 (2015), 586, 695–696

Davis v. Beason, 133 U.S. 333 (1890), 220

Davis v. United States, 564 U.S. 229 (2011), 301, 512, 553–554

Davis v. Washington, 547 U.S. 813 (2006), 575–576

DeJonge v. Oregon, 299 U.S. 353 (1937), 107, 111

Delaware v. Prouse, 440 U.S. 648 (1979), 348–349, 473–475

Dennis v. United States, 341 U.S. 494 (1951), 148

Dickerson v. United States, 530 U.S. 428 (2000), 511

District of Columbia v. Heller, 554 U.S. 570 (2008), 16, 239, 242–245, 247–248, 267–269

District of Columbia v. Wesby, 583 U.S. (2018), 310

Dobbs v. Jackson Women's Health, 597 U.S. (2022), 113

Doggett v. United States, 505 U.S. 647 (1992), 562

Douglas v. California, 372 U.S. 353 (1963), 549

Dow Chemical Co. v. United States, 476 U.S. 227 (1986), 397

Doyle v. Ohio, 426 U.S. 610 (1976), 513

Draper v. United States, 358 U.S. 307 (1958), 442–443

Dred Scott v. Sandford, 60 U.S. 393 (1857), 68

Dunaway v. New York, 442 U.S. 200 (1979), 444

Duncan v. Kahanamoku, 327 U.S. 304 (1946), 55

Duncan v. Louisiana, 391 U.S. 145 (1968), 109, 111, 557

E

Edwards v. Aguillard, 482 U.S. 578 (1987), 205, 210

Edwards v. Arizona, 451 U.S. 477 (1981), 513–515, 554

Edwards v. Vannoy, 593 U.S. (2021), 588

Egbert v. Boule, 596 U.S. (2022), 306

Eisenstadt v. Baird, 405 U.S. 438 (1972), 112

Elkins v. United States, 364 U.S. 206 (1960), 298

Elonis v. United States, 575 U.S. (2015), 152

Employment Division v. Smith, 494 U.S. 872 (1990), 211, 213–215, 221, 223, 225, 227, 229, 234

Engel v. Vitale, 370 U.S. 421 (1962), 204, 210

Enmund v. Florida, 458 U.S. 782 (1982), 668

Epperson v. Arkansas, 393 U.S. 97 (1968), 205

Equal Employment Opportunity Commission v. Abercrombie & Fitch Stores, 575 U.S. (2015), 231

Erie v. Pap's A. M., 529 U.S. 277 (2000), 161

Escobedo v. Illinois, 378 U.S. 478 (1964), 509, 510–511, 552

Espinoza v. Montana Dept. of Revenue, 591 U.S. (2020), 209–210

Estate of Redd v. Love, 848 F.3d 899 (10th Cir. 2017), 293–294

Estelle v. Gamble, 429 U.S. 97 (1976), 659, 685–687, 692

Estes v. Texas, 381 U.S. 532 (1965), 570

Everson v. Board of Education, 330 U.S. 1 (1947), 107, 111, 203–205

Ewing v. California, 538 U.S. 11 (2003), 639–641

Ex parte Bollman, 8 U.S. 75 (1807), 87

Ex parte Garland, 71 U.S. 333 (1866), 88

Ex parte Milligan, 71 U.S. 2 (1866), 54–55

Ex parte Wall, 107 U.S. 265 (1883), 98

F

Faretta v. California, 422 U.S. 806 (1975), 556

Farmer v. Brennan, 511 U.S. 825, 833 (1994), 689–690

Federal Communications Commission v. Pacifica Foundation, 438 U.S. 726 (1978), 171

Fernandez v. California, 571 U.S. 292 (2014), 325

Fex v. Michigan, 507 U.S. 43 (1993), 565

Fields v. City of Philadelphia, 862 F.3d 353 (3d Cir. 2017), 146

Fikes v. Alabama, 352 U.S. 191 (1957), 507

First Church of Cannabis v. Marion County, (Marion Co. Cir. Ct., July 6, 2018), 224

Fiske v. Kansas, 274 U.S. 380 (1927), 106, 111

Flippo v. West Virginia, 528 U.S. 11 (1999), 330–331

Florida v. Harris, 568 U.S. 237 (2013), 358–359

Florida v. J. L., 529 U.S. 266 (2000), 129, 295–296, 468

Florida v. Jardines, 569 U.S. 1 (2013), 283, 348, 357–358

Florida v. Jimeno, 500 U.S. 248 (1991), 324

Florida v. Powell (2010), 518

Florida v. Riley, 488 U.S. 445 (1989), 405

Florida v. Royer, 460 U.S. 491 (1983), 471

Florida v. Wells, 495 U.S. 1 (1990), 347

Flowers v. Mississippi, 588 U.S. (2019), 586

Floyd v. City of New York, 959 F.Supp.2d 540 (S.D.N.Y. 2013), 472

Ford v. Wainwright, 477 U.S. 399 (1986), 677–678

Foster v. California, 394 U.S. 440 (1969), 532

Foster v. Chatman, 578 U.S. (2016), 586

Fowler v. Rhode Island, 345 U.S. 67 (1953), 216

Fox v. Washington, 236 U.S. 273 (1915), 149

Franks v. Delaware, 438 U.S. 154 (1978), 294, 295

Frazier v. Cupp, 394 U.S. 731 (1969), 324, 524

Frisby v. Schultz, 487 U.S. 474 (1988), 183

Frontiero v. Richardson, 411 U.S. 677 (1973), 120

Frye v. United States, 293 F. 1013 (D.C. Cir. 1923), 581

Fulton v. Philadelphia, 593 U.S. (2021), 214–215, 229

Furman v. Georgia, 408 U.S. 238 (1972), 662–664

G

Gamble v. United States, 587 U.S. (2019), 256, 501–502

Garcetti v. Ceballos, 547 U.S. 410 (2006), 186

Gardner v. Broderick, 392 U.S. 273 (1968), 534

Georgia v. Randolph, 547 U.S. 103 (2006), 325–326

Gerstein v. Pugh, 420 U.S. 103 (1975), 444

Gertz v. Robert Welch, Inc., 418 U.S. 323 (1974), 167

Giboney v. Empire Storage & Ice Co., 336 U. S. 490 (1949), 149

Gideon v. Wainwright, 372 U.S. 335 (1963), 109, 111, 548–550

Gilbert v. Homar, 520 U.S. 924 (1997), 99

Giles v. California, 554 U.S. 353 (2008), 572–573

Gilk v. Cunniffee, 655 F. 3d 78 (1st Cir. 2011), 146

Glossip v. Gross, 576 U.S. 863 (2015), 675–677

Goldman v. United States, 316 U.S. 129 (1942), 387–388

Goldman v. Weinberger, 475 U.S. 503 (1986), 219

Gonzales v. O Centro Espírita Beneficente União do Vegetal, 546 U.S. 418 (2006), 223–224

Gonzales v. Raich, 545 U.S. 1 (2005), 42

Gooding v. Wilson, 405 U.S. 518 (1972), 150–151

Good News Club v. Milford Central School, 533 U.S. 98 (2001), 177

Graham v. Connor, 490 U.S. 386 (1989), 293, 294, 447–450, 453–454, 614

Graham v. Florida, 560 U.S. 48 (2010), 645

Grayned v. City of Rockford, 408 U.S. 104 (1972), 102, 176

Green v. United States, 355 U.S. 184 (1957), 499

Greenwood v. United States, 350 U.S. 366 (1956), 615

Gregg v. Georgia, 428 U.S. 153 (1976), 663–664, 666, 668, 671, 677, 685, 691

Gregory v. Ashcroft, 501 U.S. 452 (1991), 123

Griffin v. California, 380 U.S. 609 (1965), 513

Griffin v. Wisconsin, 483 U.S. 868 (1987), 362, 366–367, 369

Griswold v. Connecticut, 381 U.S. 479 (1965), 112

Guinn & Beal v. United States, 238 U.S. 347 (1915), 94

Gundy v. United States, 588 U.S. (2019), 641

H

Hague v. Committee for Industrial Organization, 307 U.S. 496 (1939), 175

Haig v. Agee, 453 U.S. 280 (1981), 169

Haley v. Ohio, 332 U.S. 596 (1948), 506–507

Hall v. Florida, 572 U.S. 701 (2014), 679, 680

Hanlon v. Berger, 526 U.S. 808 (1999), 309

Harmelin v. Michigan, 501 U.S. 957 (1991), 637, 640

Harris v. New York, 401 U.S. 222 (1971), 518

Harris v. United States, 422 F.3d 222 (2005), 321, 326–327, 345

Haupt v. United States, 330 U.S. 631 (1947), 87

Haynes v. United States, 390 U.S. 85 (1968), 298, 504, 508–509

Hazelwood v. Kuhlmeier, 484 U.S. 260 (1988), 188

Healy v. James, 408 U.S. 169 (1972), 189

Heien v. North Carolina, 574 U.S. 54 (2014), 302

Hein v. Freedom from Religion Foundation, 551 U.S. 587 (2007), 210

Hemphill v. New York, 595 U.S. (2022), 573

Hererra v. Collins, 506 U.S. 390 (1993), 90

Hernandez v. Mesa, 589 U.S. (2020), 306

Herndon v. Lowry, 301 U.S. 242 (1937), 147

Herring v. United States, 555 U.S. 135 (2009), 301

Hester v. United States, 265 U.S. 57 (1924), 282

Hiibel v. Sixth Judicial District Court of Nevada, 542 U.S. 177 (2004), 474–475

Hill v. Colorado, 530 U.S. 703 (2000), 183

Hitchcock v. Dugger, 481 U.S. 393 (1987), 666

Hoffa v. United States, 385 U.S. 293 (1966), 388

Holland v. United States, 348 U.S. 121 (1954), 491

Holt v. Hobbs, 574 U.S. 352 (2015), 232

Hope v. Pelzer, 536 U.S. 730 (2002), 688

Hopt v. Utah, 110 U.S. 574 (1884), 505

House v. Bell, 547 U.S. 518 (2006), 90

Houston v. Lack, 487 U.S. 266 (1988), 62

Howes v. Fields, 565 U.S. 499 (2012), 515

Hudson v. McMillian, 503 U.S. 1 (1992), 688

Hudson v. Michigan, 547 U.S. 586 (2006), 291

Hudson v. Palmer, 468 U.S. 517 (1984), 366

Hudson v. Parker, 156 U.S. 277 (1895), 604

Huff v. Spaw, 794 F.3d 543 (6th Cir. 2015), 429

Humphrey's Executor v. United States, 295 U.S. 602 (1935), 50

Hurley v. Irish American Gay, Lesbian, and Bisexual Group of Boston, 515 U.S. 557 (1995), 184

Hurst v. Florida, 577 U.S. (2016), 666, 667

Hurtado v. California, 110 U.S. 516 (1884), 105, 110, 495–496

Hustler Magazine v. Falwell, 485 U.S. 46 (1988), 167

Hutto v. Finney, 437 U.S. 678 (1978), 695

Iancu v. Brunetti, 588 U.S. (2018), 154

Illinois v. Caballes, 543 U.S. 405 (2005), 356, 358–360, 372

Illinois v. Gates, 462 U.S. 213 (1983), 295–296

Illinois v. Lafayette, 462 U.S. 640 (1983), 347

Illinois v. Lidster, 540 U.S. 419 (2004), 475–476

Illinois v. McArthur, 531 U.S. 326 (2001), 339–340

Illinois v. Rodriguez, 497 U. S. 177 (1990), 324–325

Illinois v. Wardlow, 528 U.S. 119 (2000), 468

Imbler v. Pachtman, 424 U.S. 409 (1976), 72

Ingraham v. Wright, 430 U.S. 651 (1977), 632

In re Gault, 387 U.S. 1 (1967), 558

In re Kemmler, 136 U.S. 436 (1890), 661, 672

In re Neagle, 135 U.S. 1 (1890), 51, 53

In re Oliver, 333 U.S. 257 (1948), 108, 111, 566

In re Quinlan, 355 A.2d 647 (NJ 1976), 115

In re Winship, 397 U.S. 358 (1970), 101, 491

International Society for Krishna Consciousness, Inc. v. Lee, 505 U.S. 830 (1992), 175, 184, 218

J

Jacobson v. Massachusetts, 197 U.S. 11 (1905), 116, 158

James v. Illinois, 493 U.S. 307 (1990), 582

J.E.B. v. Alabama ex rel. T.B., 511 U.S. 127 (1994), 585

Jenkins v. Georgia, 418 U.S. 153 (1974), 159

Johnson v. Arteaga-Martinez, 596 U.S. (2022), 609

Johnson v. United States, 576 U.S. 591 (2015), 102, 494, 638

Johnson v. Zerbst, 304 U.S. 458 (1938), 547, 548

Jones v. Mississippi, 593 U.S. (2021), 646

K

Kahler v. Kansas, 589 U.S. (2020), 101–102

Kansas v. Carr, 577 U.S. 108 (2016), 666

Kansas v. Glover, 589 U.S. (2020), 350, 399

Kansas v. Marsh, 548 U.S. 163 (2004), 666

Kastigar v. United States, 406 U.S. 441 (1972), 497–498

Katz v. United States, 389 U.S. 347 (1967), 278, 313, 386–387, 398, 403, 416–417

Kawakita v. United States, 343 U.S. 717 (1952), 87

Kee v. City of Rowlett, 247 F.3d 206 (5th Cir. 2001), 389

Kennedy v. Bremerton School District, 597 U.S. (2022), 232

Kennedy v. Louisiana, 554 U.S. 407 (2008), 668, 670

Kentucky v. King, 563 U.S. 452 (2011), 323, 340

Kent v. Dulles, 357 U.S. 116 (1958), 92

Keyishian v. Board of Regents, 385 U.S. 589 (1967), 190

Kingsley v. Hendrickson, 576 U.S. 389 (2015), 454–455, 613–614

Klopfer v. North Carolina, 386 U.S. 213 (1967), 111, 562

Korematsu v. United States, 323 U.S. 214 (1944), 51, 53

Kyllo v. United States, 533 U.S. 27 (2001), 280, 403–405, 427

L

LaLonde v. County of Riverside, 204 F.3d 947 (9th Cir. 2000), 311

Lange v. California, 594 U.S. (2021), 338

Lawrence v. Texas, 539 U.S. 558 (2003), 34, 68, 114–115

Leary v. United States, 395 U.S. 6 (1969), 504

Lee v. Florida, 392 U.S. 378 (1968), 391

Lee v. Weisman, 505 U.S. 577 (1992), 204, 210

Lemon v. Kurtzman, 403 U.S. 602 (1971), 205–206, 210

Leonard v. Texas, 580 U.S. (2017), 619

Lewis v. City of New Orleans, 415 U.S. 130 (1974), 151

Liu v. Securities and Exchange Commission, 591 U.S. (2020), 622

Lloyd Corp., Ltd. v. Tanner, 407 U.S. 551 (1972), 177

Lochner v. New York, 198 U.S. 45 (1905), 103, 104

Lockhart v. McCree, 476 U.S. 162 (1986), 667

Lockhart v. United States, 577 U.S. (2016), 641–642

Lockyer v. Andrade, 538 U.S. 63 (2003), 640–641

Los Angeles v. Lyons 461 U.S. 95 (1983), 460–461

Loving v. Virginia, 388 U.S. 1 (1967), 118

Luis v. United States, 578 U.S. (2018), 621–622

Lustig v. United States, 338 U.S. 74 (1949), 298

Lynch v. Donnelly, 465 U.S. 668 (1984), 207, 210

M

Madison v. Alabama, 586 U.S. (2019), 678

Madsen v. Women's Health Center, Inc., 512 U.S. 753 (1994), 182–183

Mahanoy Area School District v. B.L., 594 U.S. (2021), 188

Malley v. Briggs, 475 U.S. 335 (1986), 74

Malloy v. Hogan, 378 U.S. 1 (1964), 109, 111, 503–504

Mapp v. Ohio, 367 U.S. 643 (1961), 108, 298–299, 343

Marbury v. Madison, 5 U.S. 137 (1803), 5–6, 9–10, 12, 15–16, 164

Marchetti v. United States, 390 U.S. 39 (1968), 503–504

Marshall v. Barlow's, Inc., 436 U.S. 307 (1978), 370

Marsh v. Chambers, 463 U.S. 783 (1983), 206, 210

Martin v. Rollins, No. 19–1586 (1st Cir. 2020), 146

Maryland v. Craig, 497 U.S. 836 (1990), 576–577

Maryland v. King, 569 U.S. 435 (2013), 280, 533

Maryland v. Shatzer, 559 U.S. 98 (2010), 514–515, 554

Maryland v. Wilson, 519 U.S. 408 (1997), 351

Massachusetts Board of Retirement v. Murgia, 427 U.S. 307 (1975), 122

Massachusetts v. Upton, 466 U.S. 727 (1984), 296–297

Massey v. Wharton, 477 F. App'x 256 (5th Cir.2012), 455

Massiah v. United States, 377 U.S. 201 (1964), 554

Masterpiece Cakeshop v. Colorado Civil Rights Commission, 584 U.S. (2018), 229

Matal v. Tam, 582 U.S. (2017), 153

Mathews v. Eldridge, 424 U.S. 319 (1976), 99

Maxwell v. Dow, 176 U.S. 581 (1900), 105, 109

McCleskey v. Kemp, 481 U.S. 279 (1987), 683

McCoy v. Alamu, No. 18-40856 (5th Cir. 2020), 457

McCreary County v. ACLU, 545 U.S. 844 (2005), 208, 210

McCullen v. Coakley, 573 U.S. 464 (2014), 183

McCulloch v. Maryland, 17 U.S. 316 (1819), 35, 40

McDonald v. City of Chicago, 561 U.S. 742 (2010), 110–111, 245–246, 245–249, 261, 268–269

McGirt v. Oklahoma, 591 U.S. (2020), 67

McGowan v. Maryland, 366 U.S. 420 (1961), 204

McKeiver v. Pennsylvania, 403 U.S. 528 (1971), 558

McWilliams v. Dunn, 582 U.S. (2017), 680

Meachum v. Fano, 427 U.S. 215 (1976), 684–685

Medellin v. Texas, 552 U.S. 491 (2008), 529–530

Meritor Savings Bank v. Vinson, 477 U.S. 57 (1986), 121

Michigan Department of State Police v. Sitz, 496 U.S. 444 (1990), 475

Michigan v. DeFillippo, 443 U.S. 31 (1979), 301

Michigan v. Fisher, 558 U.S. 45 (2009), 336

Michigan v. Harvey, 494 U.S. 344 (1990), 518

Michigan v. Long, 463 U.S. 1032 (1983), 473

Michigan v. Mosley, 423 U.S. 96 (1975), 513

Michigan v. Summers, 452 U.S. 692 (1981), 293

Michigan v. Tyler, 436 U.S. 499 (1978), 330, 335

Microsoft Corp. v. United States, 584 U.S. (2018), 396

Miller-El v. Cockrell, 537 U.S. 322 (2003), 90, 586

Miller v. Alabama, 567 U.S. 460 (2012), 645–646

Miller v. California, 413 U.S. 15 (1973), 159

Miller v. Florida, 482 U.S. 423 (1987), 89

Mills v. Maryland, 486 U.S. 367 (1988), 666

Mincey v. Arizona, 437 U.S. 385 (1978), 330–331, 335

Minersville School District v. Gobitis, 310 U.S. 586 (1940), 219

Minnesota v. Carter, 525 U.S. 83 (1998), 300

Minnesota v. Dickerson, 508 U.S. 366 (1993), 328–329, 472

Minnesota v. Olson, 495 U.S. 91 (1990), 300

Minnick v. Mississippi, 498 U.S. 146 (1990), 554

Miranda v. Arizona, 384 U.S. 436 (1966), 94, 109, 303, 509–520, 522–523, 530, 533–535, 552–553

Mississippi University for Women v. Hogan, 458 U.S. 718 (1982), 120

Missouri v. Holland (1920), 17

Missouri v. McNeely, 569 U.S. 141 (2013), 342, 361

Missouri v. Seibert, 542 U.S. 600 (2004), 523

Mistretta v. United States, 488 U.S. 361 (1989), 34

Mitchell v. Wisconsin, 588 U.S. (2019), 361–362

Monell v. Department of Social Services of the City of New York, 436 U.S. 658 (1978), 305

Montgomery v. Louisiana, 577 U.S. (2016), 646

Moore v. Texas, 581 U.S. (2017), 680

Morse v. Frederick, 551 U.S. 393 (2007), 188

Muehler v. Mena, 544 U.S. 93 (2005), 293

Mullenix v. Luna, 577 U.S. 7 (2015), 310

Murray v. United States, 487 U.S. 533 (1988), 343–344

Myers v. United States, 272 U.S. 52 (1926), 50

N

NAACP v. Alabama ex rel Patterson, 357 U.S. 449 (1958), 92

NAACP v. Claiborne Hardware Co., 485 U.S. 886 (1982), 185

Nardone v. United States, 308 U.S. 338 (1939), 303

National Federation of Independent Business v. Department of Labor (combined with *Ohio et al. v. Department of Labor*), 595 U.S. (2022), 117

National Treasury Employees Union v. Von Raab, 489 U.S. 656 (1989), 373

Navarette v. California, 572 U.S. 393 (2014), 297, 351

Near v. Minnesota, 283 U.S. 697 (1931), 106, 111, 164–165

New Jersey v. T.L.O., 469 U.S. 325 (1985), 367, 368–369

Newman v. Guedry, 703 F.3d 757, 762 (5th Cir. 2012), 455

New York State Pistol and Rifle Association v. Bruen, 597 U.S. (2022), 248, 262–263, 267, 269

New York Times Co. v. United States, 403 U.S. 713 (1971), 165

New York Times v. Sullivan, 376 U.S. 254 (1964), 166–167

New York v. Belton, 453 U.S. 454 (1981), 334

New York v. Burger, 482 U.S. 691 (1987), 370

New York v. Class, 475 U.S. 106 (1986), 354

New York v. Ferber, 458 U.S. 747 (1982), 159

New York v. Quarles, 467 U.S. 649 (1984), 519–520

Nix v. Williams, 467 U.S. 431 (1984), 303, 520–522

Norris v. Alabama, 294 U.S. 587 (1935), 24

O

Obergefell v. Hodges, 576 U.S. (2015), 124

O'Connor v. Ortega, 480 U.S. 709 (1987), 373, 428

Ogletree v. Cleveland State University, No. 1:21-cv-00500-jpc (N.D. Ohio 2022), 397–398

Ohio v. Clark, 576 U.S. 237 (2015), 577

Ohio v. Roberts, 448 U.S. 56 (1980), 575

Olmstead v. United States, 277 U.S. 438 (1928), 277–278, 281, 385, 387, 390

One 1958 Plymouth Sedan v. Pennsylvania, 380 U.S. 693 (1965), 625

Oregon v. Elstad, 470 U.S. 298 (1985), 523

Oregon v. Mathiason, 429 U.S. 492 (1977), 524

Oregon v. Mitchell, 400 U.S. 112 (1970), 68

Osborne v. Ohio, 495 U.S. 103 (1990), 68, 160

Oyler v. Boles, 368 U.S. 448 (1962), 46

P

Packingham v. North Carolina, 582 U.S. (2017), 641

Palko v. Connecticut, 302 U.S. 319 (1937), 107, 109, 192

Panetti v. Quarterman, 551 U.S. 930 (2007), 678

Papish v. University of Missouri, 410 U.S. 667 (1973), 189

Payne v. Arkansas, 356 U.S. 560 (1958), 507, 508

Payne v. Tennessee, 501 U.S. 808 (1991), 664–665

Payton v. New York, 445 U.S. 573 (1980), 327, 333, 338, 443–444

Pearson v. Callahan, 555 U.S. 223 (2009), 309–310

Pennsylvania v. Mimms, 434 U.S. 106 (1977), 351

Pennsylvania v. Muniz, 496 U.S. 582 (1990), 517, 533

Penry v. Lynaugh, 492 U.S. 302 (1989), 678

People v. Boomer, 655 N.W.2d 255 (M.I. 2002), 162

People v. Rodriguez, 267–268

People v. Woody, 61 Cal.2d 716 (Cal. 1964), 222–223

Perez v. United States, 402 U.S. 146 (1971), 42

Pickering v. Board of Education, 391 U.S. 563 (1968), 185

Pierce v. Dist. of Columbia, 146 F. Supp. 3d 197 (D.D.C. 2015), 64

Pierson v. Ray, 386 U.S 547 (1967), 308

Planned Parenthood of Southeastern Pennsylvania v. Casey, 505 U.S. 833 (1992), 113

Plessy v. Ferguson, 163 U.S. 537 (1896), 117

Plumhoff v. Rickard, 572 U.S. 765 (2014), 451–452

Pointer v. Texas, 380 U.S. 400 (1965), 111, 571

Powell v. Alabama, 287 U.S. 45 (1932), 24, 547

Powers v. Ohio, 499 U.S. 400 (1991), 586–587

Presley v. Georgia, 558 U.S. 209 (2010), 566

Press-Enterprise Co. v. Superior Court of California, 464 U.S. 501 (1984), 170

Prince v. Massachusetts, 321 U.S. 158 (1944), 226–227

Printz v. United States, 521 U.S. 898 (1997), 92

R

Rakas v. Illinois, 439 U.S. 128 (1978), 300

Ramirez v. Collier, 595 U.S. (2022), 232–233

Ramos v. Louisiana, 590 U.S. (2020), 588–589

Rankin v. McPherson, 483 U.S. 378 (1987), 186

Rasul v. Bush, 542 U.S. 466 (2004), 89

Rathbun v. United States, 355 U.S. 107 (1957), 389, 391

R.A.V. v. City of St. Paul, 505 U.S. 377 (1992), 153

Rawlings v. Kentucky, 448 U.S. 98 (1980), 300

Red Lion Broadcasting Co. v. FCC, 395 U.S. 367 (1969), 171

Reed v. Reed, 404 U.S. 71 (1971), 120

Reed v. Town of Gilbert, 576 U.S. 155 (2015), 183

Reno v. American Civil Liberties Union, 521 U.S. 844 (1997), 71, 159

Renton v. Playtime Theatres, Inc., 475 U.S. 41 (1986), 161

Reynolds v. United States, 98 U.S. 145 (1878), 210–211–214, 220–221, 223

Rhodes v. Chapman, 452 U.S. 337 (1981), 690

Ricci v. DeStefano, 557 U.S. 557 (2009), 127

Richards v. Wisconsin, 520 U.S. 385 (1997), 290

Richmond Newspapers v. Virginia, 448 U.S. 555 (1980), 169–170, 566

Riley v. California, 573 U.S. 373 (2014), 334, 365, 411–414, 416, 421

Ring v. Arizona, 536 U.S. 584 (2002), 666

Rivas-Villegas v. Coresluna, 595 U.S. (2022), 311

Roberts v. United States Jaycees, 468 U.S. 609 (1984), 184

Robinson v. California, 370 U.S. 660 (1962), 108–109, 111, 627–628

Rochin v. California, 342 U.S. 165 (1952), 342–343, 532

Rodriguez v. United States, 575 U.S. 348 (2015), 322, 359–360

Roe v. Wade, 410 U.S. 113 (1973), 18, 111–113

Roman Catholic Diocese of Brooklyn v. Cuomo, 592 U.S. (2020), 217

Romer v. Evans, 517 U.S. 620 (1996), 123

Roper v. Simmons, 543 U.S. 551 (2005), 645–646, 681–682

Rosenberger v. Rectors and Visitors of the University of Virginia, 515 U.S. 819 (1995), 189

Rosen v. United States, 161 U.S. 29 (1896), 158

Roth v. United States, 354 U.S. 476 (1957), 158

S

Safford Unified Sch. Dist. v. Redding, 557 U.S. 364 (2009), 368

Salinas v. Texas, 570 U.S. 178 (2013), 513

Santa Fe Independent School Dist. v. Doe, 530 U.S. 290 (2000), 204–205, 210

Santobello v. New York, 404 U.S. 257 (1971), 560, 562

Saucier v. Katz, 533 U.S. 194 (2001), 309, 453

Scales v. United States, 367 U.S. 203 (1961), 148

Schall v. Martin, 467 U.S. 253 (1984), 613

Schenck v. United States, 249 U.S. 47 (1919), 144, 147

Schick v. Reed, 419 U.S. 256 (1974), 56

Schilb v. Kuebel, 404 U.S. 357 (1971), 111, 605

Schiro v. Summerlin, 542 U.S. 348 (2004), 666

Schlup v. Delo, 513 U.S. 298 (1995), 90

Schmerber v. California, 384 U.S. 757 (1966), 339, 341–342, 533

Schneckloth v. Bustamonte, 412 U.S. 218 (1973), 324

Scott v. Harris, 560 U.S. 372 (2007), 451–452

Scott v. Henrich, 39 F.3d 912 (9th Cir. 1994), 449

Scott v. Illinois, 440 U.S. 367 (1979), 549

Scott v. Sandford, 60 U.S. 393 (1857), 11–12

Segura v. United States, 468 U.S. 796 (1984), 303

Seila Law v. Consumer Financial Protection Bureau, 591 U.S. (2020), 50

Sessions v. Dimaya, 84 U.S. (2018), 494

Shapiro v. McManus, 577 U.S. (2015), 60

Sharp v. State, 42 N.E.3d 512 (Ind. 2015), 669

Sheppard v. Maxwell, 384 U.S. 333 (1966), 567

Sherbert v. Verner, 374 U.S. 398 (1963), 212–213, 221–224, 227–229, 234

Shinn v. Ramirez Martinez, 596 U.S. (2022), 555

Shipley v. California, 395 U.S. 818 (1969), 333

Silverman v. United States, 365 U.S. 505 (1961), 333, 388, 404

Silverthorne Lumber Co. v. United States, 251 U.S. 385 (1920), 302–303

Skilling v. United States, 561 U.S. 358 (2010), 568–569

Smith v. Maryland, 442 U.S. 735 (1979), 393–394, 425, 427

Smith v. Texas, 311 U.S. 128 (1940), 584

Smith v. United States, 508 U.S. 223 (1993), 639

Snyder v. Louisiana, 552 U.S. 472 (2008), 586

Snyder v. Phelps, 562 U.S. 443 (2011), 154

Soldal v. Cook County, 506 U.S. 56 (1992), 281, 355

Solem v. Helm, 463 U.S. 277 (1983), 640, 641

Solorio v. United States, 483 U.S. 435 (1987), 49

South Bay United Pentecostal Church v. Newsom, 590 U.S. (2020), 54, 216

South Carolina v. Katzenbach, 383 U.S. 301 (1966), 95

South Dakota v. Dole, 483 U.S. 203 (1987), 20

South Dakota v. Fifteen Impounded Cats, 785 N.W.2d 272 (S.D. 2010), 626

South Dakota v. Neville, 459 U.S. 553 (1983), 362

South Dakota v. Opperman, 428 U.S. 364 (1976), 346–348

Spano v. New York, 360 U.S. 315 (1959), 508

Spence v. State of Washington, 418 U.S. 405 (1974), 156

Spinelli v. United States, 393 U.S. 410 (1969), 296

Stack v. Boyle, 342 U.S. 1 (1951), 605

Standing Akimbo v. United States, 594 U.S. (2021), 42

Stanford v. Texas, 379 U.S. 476 (1965), 289

State of Tennessee v. Gilbert (2021), 591

State University of New York v. Fox, 492 U.S. 469 (1989), 189

State v. Demesme, 228 So. 3d 1206 (La. 2017), 553–554

Stoner v. California, 376 U.S. 483 (1969), 326, 333

Stone v. Graham, 449 U.S. 39 (1980), 207–208

Strickland v. Washington, 466 U.S. 688 (1984), 555, 668

Stromberg v. California, 283 U.S. 359 (1931), 155

T

Tate v. Short, 401 U.S. 395 (1971), 629

Taylor v. Illinois, 484 U.S. 400 (1988), 579

Taylor v. Riojas, 592 U.S. (2020), 311

Taylor v. Taintor, 83 U.S. 366 (1872), 606–607

Tennessee v. Garner, 471 U.S. 1 (1985), 448–451

Terebesi v. Torreso, 764 F.3d 217, 239 (2d Cir. 2014), 462

Terminiello v. City of Chicago, 337 U.S. 1 (1949), 150

Terry v. Ohio, 392 U.S. 1 (1968), 349, 466–469, 472–474

Terry v. United States, 593 U.S. (2021), 131–132, 636

Texas v. Johnson, 491 U.S. 397 (1989), 156–157

Tharpe v. Sellers, 583 U.S. (2018), 90–91

Thompson v. Louisiana 469 U.S. 17 (1984), 331

Thornhill v. Alabama, 310 U.S. 88 (1940), 147

Timbs v. Indiana, 586 U.S. (2019), 110, 111, 615–616

Tinker v. Des Moines Independent Community School District, 393 U.S. 503 (1969), 155, 188

Torcaso v. Watkins, 367 U.S. 488 (1961), 212

Town of Greece v. Galloway, 572 U.S. 565 (2014), 206

Trinity Lutheran Church of Columbia v. Comer, 582 U.S. (2017), 209

Trop v. Dulles, 356 U S 56 (1958), 627, 659, 691

Trump v. Hawaii, 585 U.S. (2018), 57

Trump v. Vance, 591 U.S. (2020), 57, 476–477

Tumey v. Ohio, 273 U.S. 510 (1927), 611, 631

Turner v. Pennsylvania, 338 U.S. 62 (1949), 506

Turner v. Safley, 482 U.S. 78 (1987), 232

Twining v. New Jersey, 211 U.S. 78 (1908), 105, 109

U

United States v. Abu Ali, 528 F.3d 210 (4th Cir. 2008), 530

United States v. Agurs, 427 U.S. 97 (1976), 580

United States v. Approximately 64,695 Pounds of Shark Fins, 520 F.3d 976 (9th Cir. 2008), 625

United States v. Armstrong, 517 U.S. 456 (1996), 128

United States v. Arredondo, 996 F.3d 903 (8th Cir. 2021), 329

United States v. Article Consisting of 50,000 Carboard Boxes More or Less, Each Containing One Pair of Clacker Balls, 413 F. Supp. 1281 (D. Wisc. 1976), 625

United States v. Arvizu, 534 U.S. 266 (2002), 349

United States v. Banks, 540 U.S. 31 (2003), 290

United States v. Bean, 537 U.S. 71 (2002), 256

United States v. Biswell, 406 U.S. 311, 316 (1972), 369–370

United States v. Booker, 543 U.S. 220 (2005), 590

United States v. Brewster, 408 U.S. 501 (1972), 476

United States v. Briggs, 592 U.S. (2020), 670

United States v. Brignoni-Ponce, 422 U.S. 873 (1975), 129, 364

United States v. Brown, 381 U.S. 437 (1965), 88

United States v. Bryant, 579 U.S. (2016), 66

United States v. Byrd, No. 19-2986 (3rd Cir. 2020), 356

United States v. Calandra, 414 U.S. 338 (1974), 497

United States v. Castleman, 572 U.S. 157 (2014), 255

United States v. Comstock, 560 U.S. 126 (2010), 642

United States v. Cortez, 449 U.S. 411 (1981), 130, 350, 470

United States v. Cruikshank, 92 U.S. 542 (1876), 105, 241

United States v. Davis, 482 F.2d 893 (9th Cir. 1973), 372

United States v. Drayton, 536 U.S. 194 (2002), 323

United States v. Eichman, 496 U.S. 310 (1990), 156

United States v. Freed, 401 U.S. 601 (1971), 258

United States v. Grubbs, 547 U.S. 90 (2006), 288–289

United States v. $1,074,900.00 in U.S. Currency, 932 F.Supp.2d 1053 (D. Neb. 2013), 624

United States v. Jacobsen, 466 U.S. 109 (1984), 285

United States v. Johnson, 319 U.S. 503 (1943), 496

United States v. Jones, 565 U.S. 400 (2012), 358, 281–282, 409

United States v. Karo, 468 U.S. 705 (1984), 408–409

United States v. Knotts, 460 U.S. 276 (1983), 408–409

United States v. Lanier, 520 U.S. 259 (1997), 97

United States v. Lee, 274 U.S. 559 (1927), 334

United States v. Leon, 468 U S 897 (1984), 85, 301

United States v. Lovasco, 431 U.S. 783 (1977), 564

United States v. MacDonald, 456 U.S. 1 (1982), 564–565

United States v. Marion, 404 U.S. 307 (1971), 564

United States v. Martinez-Fuerte, 428 U.S. 543 (1976), 364

United States v. Matlock, 415 U.S. 164 (1974), 325

United States v. McIver and Eberle, 186 F.3d 1119 (9th Cir. 1999), 396

United States v. Meza-Rodriguez, 798 F.3d 664 (7th Cir. 2015), 252

United States v. Miller, 307 U.S. 174 (1939), 241–243, 250, 269

United States v. Monsanto, 491 U.S. 600 (1989), 621

United States v. Montoya de Hernandez, 473 U.S. 53 (1985), 365

United States v. National Treasury Employees Union, 513 U.S. 454 (1995), 187

United States v. Nikolovski, 565 F. App'x 397 (6th Cir. 2014), 644

United States v. Nixon, 418 U.S. 683 (1974), 56–57

United States v. O'Brien, 391 U.S. 367 (1968), 155, 158

United States v. Oliver L. North, 910 F.2d 843 (D.C. Circ. 1990), 499

United States v. Ortiz, 422 U.S. 891 (1975), 363

United States v. Paradise, 480 U.S. 149 (1987), 126–127

United States v. Patante, 542 U.S. 630 (2004), 523

United States v. Place, 462 U.S. 696, 707 (1983), 360, 448, 471

United States v. Richards, 755 F.3d 269 (5th Cir. 2014), 161

United States v. Robinson, 414 U.S. 218 (1973), 333

United States v. Ross, 456 U.S. 798 (1982), 292

United States v. Salerno, 481 U.S. 739 (1987), 608–609, 613

United States v. Salvucci, 448 U.S. 83 (1980), 300

United States v. Santana, 427 U.S. 38 (1976), 338–339

United States v. Scheffer, 523 U.S. 303 (1998), 531, 582

United States v. Seeger, 380 U.S. 163 (1965), 219

United States v. Sharpe, 470 U.S. 675 (1985), 360, 471

United States v. Sokolow, 490 U.S. 1 (1989), 129, 469

United States v. Soybel, No 19-1936 (7th Cir. Sept. 8, 2021), 424

United States v. Stanley, 753 F.3d 114 (3d Cir. 2014), 426

United States v. Steiger, 318 F.3d 1039 (11th Cir. 2003), 285

United States v. Stevens, 559 U.S. 460 (2010), 160–161

United States v. Stewart, 348 F. 3d 1132 (9th Cir. 2003), 250–251

United States v. The Progressive, 476 F. Supp. 990 (W.D. Wis. 1979), 165

United States v. Trader, 981 F.3d 961 (11th Cir. 2020), 425

United States v. Turner, 169 F.3d 84 (1st Cir. 1999), 425

United States v. United States District Court, 407 U.S. 297 (1972), 391

United States v. Virginia, 518 U.S. 515 (1996), 120–121

United States v. White, 401 U.S. 745 (1971), 386, 388–389

United States v. Williams, 553 U.S. 285 (2008), 149

United States v. Windsor, 570 U.S. 744 (2013), 491

Utah v. Strieff, 579 U.S. (2016), 302

Uttecht v. Brown, 551 U.S. 1 (2007), 667

Uzuegbunam v. Preczewski, 592 U.S. (2021), 190

V

Vale v. Louisiana, 399 U.S. 30 (1970), 333

Van Buren v. United States, 593 U.S. (2021), 69

Vance v. Bradley, 440 U.S. 93 (1979), 123

Van Orden v. Perry, 545 U.S. 677 (2005), 208, 210

Vernonia School District v. Acton, 515 U.S. 646 (1995), 369

Victor v. Nebraska, 511 U.S. 1 (1994), 587

Village of Schaumburg v. Citizens for a Better Environment, 444 U.S. 620 (1980), 184

Virginia v. Black, 538 U.S. 343 (2003), 152, 157

W

Wallace v. Jaffree, 472 U.S. 38 (1985), 204

Waller v. Georgia, 467 U.S. 39 (1984), 566

Walz v. Tax Commission of the City of New York, 397 U.S. 664 (1970), 209–210

Warden v. Hayden, 387 U.S. 294 (1967), 337–338

Ward v. Rock Against Racism, 491 U.S. 781 (1989), 182

Washington v. Glucksberg, 521 U.S. 702 (1997), 115

Washington v. Texas, 388 U.S. 14 (1967), 111, 579

Watchtower Bible & Tract Society v. Village of Stratton, 536 U.S. 150 (2002), 218

Watts v. Indiana, 338 U.S. 49 (1949), 506–508

Watts v. United States, 394 U.S. 705 (1969), 152

Wayte v. United States, 470 U.S. 598 (1985), 46

Weeks v. United States, 232 U.S. 383 (1914), 297–299

Weems v. United States, 217 U.S. 349 (1910), 16, 627

Welsh v. Wisconsin, 466 U.S. 470 (1984), 338

West Virginia State Board of Education v. Barnette, 319 U.S. 624 (1943), 187, 212, 219, 230

White v. Wheeler 577 U.S. 73 (2015), 667

Whitley v. Albers, 475 U.S. 312 (1986), 687–688, 691–692

Wiener v. United States, 357 U.S. 349 (1958), 50

Wiggins v. Smith, 539 U.S. 510 (2003), 555, 668

Wilkerson v. Utah, 99 U.S. 130 (1878), 627, 661, 670–671

Williams v. Florida, 399 U.S. 78 (1970), 583

Williams v. Illinois, 399 U.S. 235 (1970), 629

Williams v. Taylor, 529 U.S. 362 (2000), 555, 667–668

Wilson v. Arkansas, 514 U.S. 927 (1995), 289–390

Wilson v. Layne, 526 U.S. 603 (1999), 308–309

Wilson v. Seiter, 501 U.S. 294 (1991), 691–692

Winston v. Lee, 470 U.S. 753 (1985), 279

Wisconsin v. Yoder, 406 U.S. 205 (1972), 227

Witherspoon v. Illinois, 391 U.S. 510 (1968), 667

Wolf v. Colorado, 338 U.S. 25 (1949), 108, 111, 277, 298–299

Wolf v. McDonnell, 418 U.S. 539 (1974), 684

Wong Sun v. United States, 371 U.S. 471 (1963), 303

Wooden v. United States, 595 U.S. (2022), 638

Wood v. Eubanks, No. 20-3599 (6th Cir. 2022), 163

Y

Yates v. United States, 354 U.S. 298 (1957), 46–47, 148

Ybarra v. Illinois, 444 U.S. 85 (1979), 289

Youngstown Sheet & Tube Co. v. Sawyer, 343 U.S. 579 (1952), 51–53

Z

Zadvydas v. Davis, 533 U.S. 678 (2001), 444

Zedner v. United States, 547 U.S. 489 (2006), 565–566

Zelman v. Simmons-Harris, 536 U.S. 639 (2002), 210

Zemel v. Rusk, 381 U.S. 1 (1965), 168

Index

100% service, 644–645

A

abortion decisions, 112–114
absolute immunity, 72, 476–477
access to government information, 168
actual malice, 166
administrative hearings, 534
administrative searches, 369–371
administrative state, 21
admiralty and maritime jurisdiction, 60
admissibility of confessions, 523–529
admissibility of scientific evidence, 581–582
adult-oriented businesses, 161–162
Advanced Imaging Technology (AIT) body scanners, 406
advocacy of unlawful conduct, 147–149
affidavit, 287
affirmative action, 125–128
affirmative defenses, 493
age discrimination, 122–123
Age Discrimination in Employment Act (ADEA), 123
aggravating factors, 663–664
Aguilar-Spinelli *Test*, 296
airport searches, 371–372
Alabama Department of Public Safety, 126
Alban, Dan, 618
Albright, Alex, 612
Albright, Thomas, 574
Alito, Samuel, 323, 326, 340, 361, 416, 675
Allen charge, 589
American flag, 156
Americans with Disabilities Act (ADA), 125
amicus curiae, 63
Amos, Scott, 360
animal cruelty, 160–161
animal sacrifice, 225
anticipatory search warrant, 288–289
Anti-Drug Abuse Act of 1986, 634–635
Anti-Drug Abuse Act of 1988, 634

Antiterrorism and Effective Death Penalty Act of 1996 (AEDPA), 90
appeals from criminal convictions, 70
appellate courts, 3
appellate jurisdiction, 58
appointed counsel in misdemeanor cases, 549–550
Arbery, Ahmaud, 446–447, 561
Arkowitz, Hal, 574
Armed Career Criminal Act of 1984 (ACCA), 638
arraignment, 496
arrest, 440
    searches incident to, 331–334
    warrant, 441
Article I Courts, 62
Articles of Confederation, 6–7
assault weapons, 257
asylum, 65
Autin, Naomia, 455
automobile exception, 353
automobile searches at roadside, 353–356

B

bail, 604–615
bail money, 611
Bail Reform Act of 1984, 608
bail-setting algorithms, 611–612
Baldus, David, 682–683
ballot initiatives, 38–39
Barrett, Amy Coney, 113, 217
Barr, William, 459–460
Bass, William, 583
Belfort, Jordan, 623
bench warrant, 441
Berrett, Michael, 551
Biden, Joe, 52–53, 63, 633
bifurcated trial, 660
bill of attainder, 88–89
Bill of Rights, 12–14, 91–93.
    See also specific Amendment
    importance of, 92
    incorporation of, 104–110
    Ninth Amendment, 92
    original inapplicability of, 92–93
    supreme court, 111
    Tenth Amendments, 92
Binnall, Eric, 584

Bipartisan Safer Communities Act, 260
Bivens doctrine, 24
Bivens remedy, 305
Black, Hugo, 16, 55, 104, 108–109, 112, 506, 547, 566
Black, Morris, 607
Blackmun, Harry, 34, 584–585, 621, 662–663
Blackstone, William, 6, 17, 615
Blasio, Bill de, 697
blood and breath testing of impaired drivers, 533
bodily intrusions, 532–533
body cameras, 465
Body Farm, 583
body scanners, 406–408
Bond, McLynnerd, 527
border search, 363–365
Borelli, Don, 421
botched executions, 661–664
bounty hunters, 605–606
Brady Bill, 253
Brady Handgun Violence Prevention Act, 253–256
Brando, Marlon, 623
Bratton, Bill, 473
Brennan, William, 109, 151, 346, 491, 503, 517, 549, 609, 613, 629, 662–663
Breyer, Stephen, 340, 454–455, 614, 696
Brigham, John, 574
Browder, Kalief, 696–697
Brown, Henry B., 572
buffer zones, 182–184
bulk telephone metadata collection, 419
bump stocks, 21, 260
Burdine, Calvin, 556
Bureau of Alcohol, Tobacco, Firearms and Explosives, 258–259
Bureau of Justice Statistics (BJS), 551
Burger, Warren E., 56–57, 120, 328, 347, 397, 467, 470, 518, 521, 560, 565–566, 662
Burton, Harold, 662
Bush, G., 55, 89, 209, 499, 529
Byrd, James, 643

C

Caballes, Roy, 357
Calabrese, J. Philip, 398
cameras in the courtroom, 570
canine searches at roadside, 356–360
  limits on, 359–360
  police dogs, 357–359
capias, 441
capital punishment, 661
  equity considerations in, 681–684
carceral state, 48
Cardozo, Benjamin, 142
Carta, Magna, 5
case law, 2
case study, 36
cashless bail, 609
cell phone, 411–415
  location data, 415–417
  location tracking, 415–417
  searches incident to arrest, 334
cell site location information (CSLI),
  415, 425
certiorari, 63
CFR court, 66
chain of custody, 582
challenge for cause, 585
Chapman, Lee, 606
Chauvin, Derek, 465, 551, 694
checkpoints, 475–476
checks and balances, 33–34
Chew, Stephen, 574
Chiang Kai-shek, 566
chief executive roles, 49–57
  appointment and removal
    powers, 49–51
  directives, 51–52
  emergency powers, 53–54
  executive clemency, 56
  executive orders, 51–52
  martial law, 54–55
  memorandum, 51–52
  writ of habeas corpus, 54–55
child pornography, 159–160
child witnesses, 576–577
chokeholds, 459–461
Ciraolo, Dante, 397
citizen's arrest, 445–446
civic duties, 219
civil asset forfeiture, 616–619
civil commitment, 615, 642–643
civil contempt, 498
civil forfeiture, 619, 620–622,
  624–626
civil liability, 72–73
civil rights and liberties, expansion
  of, 23
civil rights laws, 227–229

Civil War Amendments, 93–97
  Fifteenth Amendment, 94–95
  Thirteenth Amendment, 93
claims of discrimination, 122–125
Clark, Tom, 108, 567–568, 570
clear and present danger doctrine,
  144
clear and probable danger, 148
Clifford, Nathan, 671
Clinton, Bill, 72
closely regulated industries, 370
CLOUD Act, 396
Coke, Edward, 5
Colby, William, 392
Comey, James, 50
Commentaries on the Laws of England
  (Blackstone), 6
commercial speech, 173–174
commonsense inferences, 469
Communications Decency Act, 423
community caretaker exception,
  346
compelling governmental interest,
  145
compelling interest, 119, 212–213,
  246
compensation, 91
Comprehensive Crime Control Act of
  1984, 573
compulsory process, 578–580
compulsory school attendance, 227
compulsory self-incrimination,
  502–504
compulsory vaccination, 116–117
Computer Fraud and Abuse Act, 425
concealed microphones, 386–390
concurrent sentencing, 643–644
confessions, 504–507
  admissibility of, 523–529
  cases, 523
confidential informant, 295–297
confrontations between citizens and
  police officers, 151
conscientious objection to military
  service, 219
consecutive sentencing, 643–644
consent searches, 322–326
  reason behind, 323–324
  scope of a search, 324
  third-party consent, 324–326
constitution
  address prisoner health care, 686
  aggravating factors for capital
    punishment, 665
  and social justice, 292
  arrest of man in Florida, 441–442
  bail-setting algorithms, 611–612

Bill of Rights, 12–14
Body Farm, 583
Boston Marathon Bombing,
  519–520
Bureau of Alcohol, Tobacco, Firearms and Explosives, 258–259
Capitol Riot defendant, 563
clash of Apple and FBI, 414–415
death penalty, 680–681, 684
death qualification of a jury, 667
discovery, 580–581
eyewitness testimony, 574
Facebook posts to assist police, 423
FBI's warrant to seize Bitcoin paid
  in ransomware attack, 421–422
federal courts review, 157–158
federal legalization, 43–44
firing squad, 671–672
First Amendment, 184
First Amendment issue, 149
First Amendment rights, 143–144,
  146
freedom of religion and cultural
  diversity, 230
government surveillance, 392–393
government watch lists, 407–408
immunity-based appeal, 498–499
in action, 15, 19–20, 36–37
IRS rules, 220
January 6h Capitol Riot, 176
lie detector tests, 530–531
living, 17–19
mandatory minimum sentence,
  637–638
mass incarceration, 633–634
mass shooting, 254–255
murder of Ahmaud Arbery,
  446–447
new, 7–11
new federal law, 690
officer mistakes taser for gun,
  455–456
panhandling, 184
private prison, 692
privatizing electronic surveillance, 427
profanity, 163
ratification of, 12
representation in Congress, 8
Satanic Temple, 222
seizure of movie revenue by
  Department of Justice, 623
slavery and, 10–11
snake handling, 225
social justice and, 24, 52–53, 130,
  181, 402–403, 472–473, 527–528,
  584–585

solitary confinement, 696–697
speeding ticket, 631–632
Stolen Valor Act, 174
suicide case, 115–116
supremacy clause, 43–44
Supreme Court, 64
traffic cameras, 399–400
unprecedented search of an
  ex-president's home, 288
U.S. Department of Justice (DOJ),
  45
U.S. Marijuana Policies, 36–37
video testimony during the
  COVID-19 pandemic, 571
Vitter Amendment, 265–266
woman confession to drowning
  her children, 525
constitutional democracy, 20–21
constitutional development, 20–25
constitutional interpretation, 15–20,
  67–68
constitutionalism, 4–6
constitutional issues, 23
constitutional issues in trial
  juries, 583–591
constitutional law
  defined, 2
  importance for criminal
    justice, 2–3
  overview, 2
  role of courts in, 3–4
  U.S. Constitution, 6–15
constitutional policing, 25
constitutional republic, 20–21
constitutional rights, 71–74
constitutional rights of privacy,
  111–117. *See also* right of privacy
constitutional sources of rights,
  85–132
  Bill of Rights, 91–93, 104–110
  Civil War Amendments, 93–97
  constitutional right of privacy,
    111–117
  due process of law, 97–104
  equal protection of laws, 117–132
  overview, 86
  rights protection, 86–91
constitutional supremacy, 5–6
constitutional system, 31–75
  access to judicial review, 69–74
  executive branch of government,
    44–57
  exercise of judicial review, 67–68
  federalism, 32, 35–36
  judiciary, 58–67
  legislative branch of government,
    37–43

overview, 31
  separation of powers, 32–35
  structural features of, 32–36
constitutional violation, 24–25
contact tase, 455
content neutral, 180
contraband, 327
conviction, 525–526
convict lease system, 11
cooperative federalism, 35
Corcoran, Robert, 510
corporal punishment, 632
Cosby, Bill, 561–562
courts
  appellate, 3
  role of, 3–4
  trial, 3
crack cocaine discrepancy, 635–636
creationism v. evolution, 205
Crichton, Scott J., 553
crime scene exception, 331
crime scenes, searches of, 329–331
criminal convictions, appeals
  from, 70
criminal investigation, 56–57
criminal justice, 2–3
  equal protection of laws and,
    128–132
  First Amendment, 143
Criminal Justice Act, 550
criminal referrals, 47–48
criminal trials
  evidence in, 570–583
critical infrastructure trespass bills,
  177–179
critical race theory (CRT), 130
cross burning, 157
cross-examination, 571
cruel punishments, 627–632
curfews, 182
curtilage, 282–283
custodial interrogation, 509

D

Davis, Adrian, 576
Davis, Robert, 552–553
deadlocked jury, 589
death-eligible offenses, 668–670
death penalty, 659–698
  botched executions, 661–664
  capital punishment, 661
  equity considerations in capital
    punishment, 681–684
  for felony murder, 668–669
  methods of execution, 670–677
  offender's mental state, 677–681
  prisoners' rights, 684–698

sentencing phase in capital case,
  664–670
  Willie Francis case, 661–664
death qualification of jurors, 587, 667
Death with Dignity Act, 115
debtors' prison, 628
decertification, 463–465
defamation, 166–168
Deferred Action for Childhood
  Arrivals (DACA) controversy, 52
delays due to dropped charges,
  564–565
delegation of legislative power, 34–35
deliberate indifference standard, 685
Demesme, Warren, 553–554
Denney, Lucas, 563
Dennis, Eugene, 148
Denno, Deborah, 671
derivative evidence, 302–303, 520
designated public forums, 176–177
detectaphone, 388
detective work, 470–471
detention of persons on premises
  during a search, 293
DiCaprio, Leonardo, 623
diplomatic immunity, 477–479
direct democracy, 39
disability discrimination, 124–125
discovery, 579–581
discrimination
  age, 122–123
  claims of, 122–125
  disability, 124–125
  gender identity, 123–124
  prohibitions of, 119–120
  race, 126–127
  reverse, 127–128
  sex, 119–121
disfavored judicial activity, 24
disgorgement, 622
disparate impact of criminal laws,
  130–131
displays of Ten Commandments,
  207–208
DNA testing, 533
dogs use in making arrests, 457–459
Dookhan, Annie, 580
double jeopardy, 499–502
Douglas, William O., 144, 209, 507,
  549, 580, 662
draft card, 155–156
dress codes and grooming
  requirements, 231
drone searches, 405–406
dropped charges
  delays due to, 564–565
drug courier profile, 469–470

due process, 14, 86, 97–104, 490–495,
    504–507
  police disciplinary hearing, 99
  procedural, 98–99
  rights of accused, 101–103
  substantive, 103–104
DUI-related searches, 361–362
Dunaway, Irving, 444
Durst, Robert, 607–608
duty to intervene, 463

E

eavesdropping, 387
Edwards, Thedrick, 589
Eighth Amendment. *See* cruel
    punishments; death penalty;
    excessive fines; prisoners' rights;
    unusual punishments
electric chair, 672
Electronic Communications Privacy
    Act (ECPA), 394–395
electronic devices, 413–414
electronic devices searches at border,
    385–430
  body scanners, 406–408
  cell phone location data, 415–417
  cell phones and, 411–415
  concealed microphones, 386–390
  drone searches, 405–406
  facial recognition technology,
    400–403
  interception of electronic
    messages, 428–429
  internet activity, 422–427
  mass electronic surveillance,
    417–422
  metal detectors, 406–408
  pen registers, 393–396
  remote camera, 396–400
  social media, 422–427
  thermal imagers, 403–404
  tracking devices, 408–411
  trap and trace devices, 393–396
  video surveillance, 396–400
  wiretaps, 390–393
electronic media regulation,
    170–171
electronic messages
  interception of, 428–429
emergency powers, 53–54
emergency searches, 335
eminent domain, 98
employee prayer in public school
    setting, 232
Engelhart, Joseph, 626
English Bill of Rights, 5, 604
entrapment, 493

enumerated powers, 39
Epps, Christopher, 692
Equal Pay Act (EPA), 121
equal pay considerations, 121–122
equal protection of laws, 86,
    117–132
  affirmative action, 125–128
  claims of discrimination, 122–125
  criminal justice and, 128–132
  expanding prohibitions of
    discrimination, 119–120
  modern civil rights law, 118–119
  sex discrimination, 119–121
  suspect classification doctrine, 118
equal protection of the laws, 14
equitable sharing program, 618–619
equity considerations in capital
    punishment, 681–684
Establishment Clause, 202
evanescent evidence, 341–342
evidence
  imminent destruction of,
    412–413
  in criminal trials, 570–583
exception
  inevitable discovery, 520–521
  to *Miranda*, 518–523
excessive bail, 605
excessive fines, 615–626
exclusionary rule, 108, 297–303
  alternative to, 304–312
exculpatory evidence, 580
execution
  methods of, 670–677
executive branch of government,
    44–57
  jails and prisons, 48
  law enforcement agencies, 44
  military justice system, 49
  prosecutorial agencies, 44–46
  regulatory agencies, 47–48
  role of chief executive, 49–57
executive clemency, 56
executive order, 51–52
executive privilege, 56
exemption from policies and work
    assignments, 231–232
exigent circumstances, 286–287,
    335–343, 374
expansion of civil rights and
    liberties, 23
expectations of privacy, 388
expert testimony, 581–582
Ex Post Facto, 294
ex post facto law, 88–89
expressive conduct, 155–158
eyewitness testimony, 573–574

F

FAA Reauthorization Act of 2012, 407
facial recognition technology,
    400–403
Fair Sentencing Act of 2010, 635–636
false confessions, 527
Faraday bag, 412–413
Faraday, Michael, 413
Farak, Sonja, 581
Farmer, Dee, 690
fatal police shooting of homeowner,
    336–337
Federal Communications Act, 391
federal court system, 59–67
  Article I Courts, 62
  Immigration Courts, 65–66
  Tribal Court System, 66–67
  United States Supreme Court,
    63–64
  U.S. Courts of Appeals, 61–62
  U.S. District Court, 60
federal crimes, 669–670
federal criminal charges, 312
federal criminal law
  power of congress to enact, 41–43
  proliferation of, 21–22
Federal Death Penalty Act, 669
federal habeas corpus, 89–90
federal habeas corpus review,
    588–589
federalism, 7, 32, 35–36
  case study, 36
  cooperative, 35
The Federalist Papers, 12
Federal Kidnapping Act, 41
federal prohibition of *bump stocks* via
    rulemaking, 260
federal sentencing guidelines,
    590–591
felonies, 39
felony murder, 668–669
Fields, Randall Lee, 515
Field, Stephen J., 491
Fifteenth Amendment, 14
Fifth Amendment, 97–104
fighting words, 150–151
Fight Online Sex Trafficking Act
    (FOSTA), 171–173
Fikes, William, 507
Firearm Owners' Protection Act,
    252–253
firing squads, 670–672
First Amendment, 141–191
  adult-oriented businesses, 161–162
  advocacy of unlawful conduct,
    147–149
  child pornography, 159–160

commercial speech, 173–174
criminal justice, 143
expressive conduct, 155–158
fighting words, 150–151
freedom of association, 184–185
freedom of press, 163–173
hate speech, 153–154
incorporation of, 106–107
jurisprudence, 144–146
obscenity, 158–159
offensive speech, 153–154
overview, 142
pornography on internet, 159
profanity, 162
protections for religious freedom,
    201–234
public forum, 174–184
rights, 143
rights of public employees, 185–187
rights of students, 187–190
rights on college campuses,
    189–190
symbolic speech, 155–158
true threats, 152–153
First Step Act, 635–637, 639, 692, 697
FISA Court, 417–418
flash-bang grenade, 461–463
Flippo, James, 330
Floyd, George, 54, 459–460, 464, 694
Flynn, John, 510
Food and Drug Administration
    (FDA), 48
Foreign Assistance Act of 1974, 393
Foreign Intelligence Surveillance Act
    of 1978 (FISA), 417
Fourteenth Amendment, 14–15,
    97–104
Fourth Amendment. *See also* arrest;
    electronic devices searches
    at border; freedom from
    unreasonable searches
    and seizures; investigatory
    detention; rights of the accused;
    use of force in making arrests;
    warrantless searches
    adoption and extension of, 276–277
    apply of, 284–285
    incorporation of, 277
Fox, Geri, 610
Francis, Willie, 662
Frankfurter, Felix, 506, 615, 662
freedom from unreasonable searches
    and seizures, 275–313
    exclusionary rule, 297–303
    overview, 276
    probable cause, 294–297
    process for obtaining a warrant,
        287–289

reasonable expectations of privacy,
    278–281
    trespass doctrine redux, 281–284
    warrant requirement, 286–294
freedom of association, 184–185
Freedom of Information Act, 619
freedom of press, 163–173
freedom of religion *versus* lgbtq
    rights, 229
Free Exercise Clause, 202, 211–216
free exercise of religion, 210–211
free press/fair trial problem, 169–170,
    567–570
fruit of the poisonous tree doctrine,
    303, 519
fugitive track dog, 457–459
Fuller, Melville, 661
functional equivalent of arrest, 444
fundamental right, 246
fundamental rights doctrine, 145
further-questioning decisions,
    554–555

G
gag order, 569
Gamble, J. W., 685
Gamble, Terance Martez, 501
Garland, Merrick, 460
Garner, Edward, 451
gas chamber, 673
Gates, Daryl, 460
gender identity discrimination,
    123–124
general warrant, 276
George, Floyd, 465
George III (King), 546
Gideon, Clarence Earl, 548–549
Gilmore, Gary, 671–672
Ginsburg, Ruth Bader, 357, 359, 502,
    569, 615, 680
Glorious Revolution, 5
Glover, Charles Jr., 350
Goldberg, Arthur, 112, 509, 625
Gonnerman, Jennifer, 696
Gonzales, Alberto, 641
good faith exception, 301–302
good-time credit, 644
Gorsuch, Neil, 124, 494, 502, 588
government
    assistance to religious schools,
        205–206
    legislative branch of, 37–43
    speech doctrine, 179–180
    surveillance, 392–393
Government Accountability Office
    (GAO), 172
GPS trackers, 409–411

graffiti, 179–180
Graham, Dethorne, 447–448
Grainger, W.W., 424
grand juries, 105, 495–499
    powers, 497–498
    proceedings, 496–497
    rights of witnesses appearing
        before, 498
    secrecy, 496
grand jurors based on race, 496
Gross, Samuel R., 683
*Gruesome Spectacle: Botched Executions
    and America's Death Penalty*
    (Sarat), 676
Gun Control Act, 251–252
gun crime cases, 638–639
gun-free zones, 263–264
gun rights for law enforcement
    personnel, 267–268

H
habeas corpus, 89–91
    federal, 89–90
    petitions for, 70
habitual offender law, 560–561, 640
Hall, Fawn, 499
Hamilton, Alexander, 9–10, 86
Harlan, John M., 112, 117, 387,
    504–505
harmless error doctrine, 526
Harris, Clayton, 358
Haslam, Bill, 672
hate-crime enhancement,
    642–643
Hate Crimes Prevention Act of 2009,
    643
hate speech, 153–154
Health and Human Services (HHS),
    53
hearsay, 296
hearsay evidence, 572
heightened scrutiny (or intermediate
    scrutiny), 120–121
Heller decision, 242–243
Hennis, Tim, 502
high crime neighborhood,
    468–469
Hinckley, John, 493
Hobby Lobby Case, 228–229
Holmes, Oliver Wendell, 17, 103, 144,
    147
home, warrantless arrests in,
    443–444
hot pursuit, 335, 337–339
House Bill 479, 446
Hughes, Charles Evans, 93, 505
Hyden, Rodney, 637

I

identification checks, 474–475
identification procedures, 531–534
illegal drugs use, 222–224
Immigration Courts, 65–66
imminent destruction of evidence, 335, 339–343, 412–413
imminent lawless action, 148–149
immunity-based appeal, 498–499
immunity from arrest, 476–479
immunity from civil liability, 72–73
impaired drivers, blood and breath testing of, 533
impeachment, 49–50
impeachment of defendant's testimony, 518
implied consent laws, 362
implied powers, 39
incarceration for failure to pay, 629–630
incorporation
    importance of, 246–247
    initial resistance to, 105
    of bill of rights, 104–110
    of First Amendment freedoms, 106–107
    of Fourth Amendment, 277
    of free exercise clause, 211–216
    of rights essential to criminal justice, 107–110
    of Second Amendment, 245–247
    process of, 105–106
    status of, 110
    theory of, 104–105
incriminating statements, 504–531
independent source doctrine, 344, 520
indeterminate sentence, 639–641
indictment, 105, 495
indigent defendants, 547–550
ineffective assistance of counsel, 555–556
ineffective counsel, 667–668
inevitable discovery exception, 303, 520–521
information, 105, 495
information stored, 395–396
injunctions, 70–71
inmate's handwritten appeal, 548–549
intellectual disability, 678–680
interception of electronic messages, 428–429
interlocutory appeal, 70
intermediate scrutiny, 180
International Emergency Economic Powers Act (IEEPA), 53

internet, 171–173
internet activity, 422–427
internet protocol (IP) address, 423–427
internet subscriber information, 425
interrogation, 516–517
inventory searches, 345–348
investigatory detention, 440, 466–473
Investment and Jobs Act, 398
Israelsen, R. Gregory, 372

J

Jackson, Robert, 53
jails and prisons, 48
jail searches, 365–366
Jefferson, Thomas, 546
Jensen, Max, 671
Jho, Low Taek, 623
Johnson, Brian, 606
Jones, Alex, 168
Jones, Brett, 646
Jones, Cynthia, 609
judge, 666
judicial review, 5–6
    access to, 69–74
    exercise of, 67–68
judiciary, 58–67
    federal court system, 59–67
    state court systems, 58–59
Judiciary Act of 1789, 604
jurisprudence
    animal cruelty, 160–161
    bad counterfeiter, 565–566
    Bill Cosby's guilty verdict, 561–562
    constitutional interpretation, 69
    double jeopardy, 501–502
    executions, 677
    federal civil rights law, 97
    federal criminal law, 22
    felony murder convictions, 669
    forced vomiting, 342–343
    Fourteenth Amendment, 94
    free exercise cases, 213
    functional equivalent of arrest, 444
    gang ordinance, 102–103
    habeas corpus, 90–91
    importance of meeting deadlines for appeals, 62
    incorporation, 110
    inevitable discovery exception, 522
    inmate's handwritten appeal, 548–549
    lineup, 532
    loansharking, 42
    magazine reviews, 167

mandatory miknimum, 641–642
memorabilia inside courthouse, 591
murder scene exception, 330
Native American religious rituals, 214
plain view seizure, 329
pocket dial, 429
police checking your license plate, 350
police hiding microphone at grave site, 389
police usage of prison informant to secure confession, 526–527
prosecutorial discretion, 46–47
religious exercise, 232–233
Religious Freedom Restoration Act, 224
remaining silent, 512
rights of protestors, 178
right to discriminate, 228
Robert Durst bail jumping, 607–608
SCOTUS, 57
searches incident to arrest, 332–333
Second Amendment, 241–242
seizure of pets, 626
self-defense, 244–245
seminal case on stop and frisk, 466
shock the conscience standard, 342–343
Sixth Amendment violation, 556
slavery, 11–12
speech, 151
supreme court, 9–10
Terrence Byrd case remand, 356
thermal imager used in search of home, 404
Thirteenth Amendment, 93–94
use of deadly force, 450–451
video scanning of a student's room during an online exam, 397–398
Westboro Baptist Church (WBC), 154
jury, 666
    instructions, 587
    nullification, 589–590
    role in sentencing, 590–591
    selection, 128
    selection procedures, 585–587
    size, 583–584
    unanimity, 667
justice, 3
juvenile court system, 558–559
juvenile justice, 558–559
juvenile offenders, 645–646

K

Kagan, Elena, 339, 358–359, 493–494, 589, 638, 642, 645, 678
Karo, James, 408–409
Kassin, Saul, 525
Kavanaugh, Brett, 124, 586, 588, 646
Kee, Darlie, 389
Kemp, Brian, 446
Kennedy, Anthony, 36, 114, 123–124, 127, 215, 356, 366, 373, 428, 474–475, 491, 512, 533, 586–587, 646, 668, 678, 681–682, 693–696
Kennedy, John F., 87
Kennedy, Robert F., 549
Kim, Kim, 620
Kingsley, Michael, 454
Klan, Ku Klux, 148, 157
knock and announce requirement, 289–290

L

Lambroza, Kate, 613
Landau, Clemens, 571
large-capacity magazines, 262
law enforcement, 25, 360, 420–421
    9/11 first responders, 40–41
    agencies, 44
    body cameras, 465
    federal prison, 694
    gun rights, 268
    intuition, 470–471
    military in, 55
    personnel, 186–187
    police disciplinary hearing, 551
    right to remain silent in adminis-
        trative hearings, 534
    vaccine exemptions, 218
Law Enforcement Officers Killed
    and Assaulted Data Collection
    (LEOKA), 25
Lawrence, Ron, 450
least restrictive means, 213
legalization of marijuana, 36
legislative authority of congress,
    39–40
legislative branch of government,
    37–43
legislative courts, 62
legislative power
    delegation of, 34–35
    of local governments, 39
legitimate interest, 246–247
Lemon test, 205, 208–209
lethal injection, 673–677
Letters of the Federal Farmer, 12
libel, 166
lie detector tests, 530–531

life sentences, 645–646
Lilienfeld, Scott O., 574
limited public forum, 176–177
lineup, 531–532
living Constitution, 17–19
lone wolf agents, 418
lower court rulings on video
    testimony, 577–578
Lyons, Adolph, 460

M

Madison, James, 2, 4, 8, 12, 33, 166
magazine capacity limits, 262–263
Magna Carta, 557, 566
mandatory minimums, 638–639,
    641–642
    reforms, 636–637
    sentences, 591, 634–642
mandatory punishments for sex
    offenders, 641
mandatory sentences, 632–646
Marihuana Tax Act of 1937, 504
marijuana legalization, 360
marital privilege, 575
Marshall, John, 5, 15, 87, 93
Marshall, Thurgood, 109, 461, 470,
    555, 558, 564, 586, 588, 609, 613,
    662–663, 667, 677–678
martial law, 54–55
Martin, Casey, 125
mass electronic surveillance,
    417–422
mass incarceration, 4, 632–646
Mauro, Robert, 683
McCormack, Kathleen, 607
McEnany, Ryan, 638
McFadden, Martin, 466
McLean, John, 38
McMichael, Travis, 561
medical treatment, 685–686
Meese, Edwin, 498
Meissner, Christian, 574
mens rea, 101
mental institution, 615
mentally retarded, 679
metadata, 393
metal detectors, 406–408
methods of execution, 670–677
military in law enforcement, 55
military justice system, 49
minimal scrutiny, 122
ministerial exception, 227
minor misdemeanors, 443
Miranda, Ernesto, 510–511
Miranda Right, 529–530
Miranda warnings, 509–511
misconduct reporting, 463–465

misdemeanors, 39
Mishra, Tara, 624
mistrial, 499–500
Mitchell, Gerald, 361
mitigating factors, 664
modern civil rights law, 118–119
modern First Amendment
    jurisprudence, 145–146
Montesquieu, 33
Moore, Alvin, 510
motor homes and rental cars,
    warrantless searches of,
    355–356
Moynihan, Colin, 395
multiple charges for same offense,
    500
Mumford, William Bruce, 87, 669
Murphy, Phil, 686

N

Najibi, Alex, 402–403
narrowly tailored, 119, 126
narrow tailoring, 246
National Defense Authorization Act
    of 2012, 444
National Firearms Act, 250–251
National Industrial Recovery Act
    (NIRA), 34
National Instant Criminal
    Background Check System, 253
National Security Agency
    Mass Surveillance Programs,
    418–420
national supremacy, 35
nativity scenes and other holiday
    displays, 207
Naval Criminal Investigative Service
    (NCIS), 44
Newburn, Greg, 635
The New York Times, 67
Nineteenth Amendment, 14
Nixon Administration, 391–392
noise ordinances, 182
no-knock warrants, 290–291
nonpublic forums, 175
nonroutine border searches, 364–365
Nuzz, Sal, 635

O

Obama, Barack, 52, 444
objective reasonableness, 448–449,
    454
O'Brien, David Paul, 155
obscenity, 158–159
O'Connor, Sandra Day, 355, 473, 475,
    492, 553, 576, 587, 630, 640, 668,
    678, 687

offender's mental state, 677–681
offensive speech, 153–154
official prayers, 206–207
Omnibus Crime Control and Safe
    Streets Act of 1968, 390, 429
open fields, 282–283
ordinances, 39
Organized Crime Control Act, 573,
    617
originalism, 16–17
original jurisdiction, 58
overbreadth doctrine, 145–146

P

Pachtman, Richard, 72
Padilla, Rafael, 450
panhandling, 184
paradise decision, 126–127
parens patriae, 226
parole, 644–645
parolees searches, 366–367
pat-down search, 466–473
patriotic rituals and civic duties, 219
Patterson, Tenille, 612
peek and sneak searches, 343–345
pen registers, 393–396
Pentagon Papers Case, 165
pepper spray, 456–457
peremptory challenges, 585
permanent injunction, 71
per se rule, 342
petitions for habeas corpus, 70
petty offenses, 557–558
Pfaff, John, 633
physical evidence, 517–518, 531–534
physical intrusion (or trespass), 388
Pierce, Glenn, 683–684
Place, Raymond, 471
plain view doctrine, 326–329
plea bargaining, 559–562
pocket dial, 429
police deception, 524–525
police detain suspicious persons, 471
police dogs, 357–359
police interrogations, 504–531
police officers, 373–374
police power, 38, 103
police raids, 290–291
police reinitiating interrogation,
    513–515
polygamy, 221–222
pornography
    child, 159–160
    on internet, 159
Posse Comitatus Act, 55
post-Heller/McDonald Supreme Court
    decisions, 247–249

Powell, Lewis, 167, 327, 392, 397, 497,
    683, 690
preemption, 35
preliminary hearing, 495
preliminary injunction, 71
preponderance of evidence, 58
preponderance of the evidence,
    491–492
presidency, 8–9
presidential directive, 51–52
presidential memorandum, 51–52
presumption of innocence, 101
pretextual stop, 349
pretrial confinement, 615
pretrial detainees
    other claims by, 614–615
pretrial detention, 604–615
    in domestic assault cases, 613
    United States, 609
    use of force in, 613
pretrial detention of juveniles, 613
pretrial motions, 69–70
prior restraint, 106–107, 164–165
PRISM program, 419
prison conditions, 690–692
prisoners' rights, 684–698
Prison Litigation Reform Act of 1995
    (PLRA), 693
prison overcrowding, 693–694
prison searches, 365–366
privacy rights of gun owners, 265
private communication, 388
private forums, 177
private prison, 692
privatizing electronic
    surveillance, 427
privileges, 576
probable cause, 286, 294–297
probation, 628–632
probationers searches, 366–367
procedural criminal law, 3
procedural due process, 98–99, 490
process for obtaining a
    warrant, 287–289
profanity, 162
profanity and indecency in
    media, 171
prohibition of excessive
    bail, 605–608
proliferation of federal criminal
    law, 21–22
prompt presentment, 504
prosecution, 128
prosecutorial agencies, 44–46
prosecutorial discretion, 46
pro se representation, 556
protection from harm, 689

protection of confidential sources,
    168–169
public defender system, 550–551
public expense, 547–550
public figures, 166
public forum, 174–184
public safety exception, 519
public schools searches, 367–369
public sector workplace, 230–232
Pulaski, Charles, 682

Q

qualifications to serve on a jury, 584
qualified immunity, 25, 73–74, 307

R

race discrimination in officer hiring,
    126–127
racial profiling, 129–130, 468
racial segregation, 68
Radelet, Michael, 683–684
Rahmani, Neama, 694
Ramos, Evangelisto, 589
random searches, 366
Raphael, Anna, 479
rational basis test, 122, 175–176, 246
rational relationship, 246–247
Reagan, Ronald, 493, 498
reasonable doubt, 58
reasonable doubt standard, 101,
    491–493
reasonable grounds, 367, 418
reasonable suspicion, 322, 467–471
reconstruction-era civil rights
    legislation, 95–97
recorded confessions, 528–529
recorded testimony of witnesses,
    575–576
recusal, 495
red flag laws, 264–265
red light cameras, 398–399
Reed, Stanley, 662
Reeves, Carlton, 692
referenda, 38–39
referendum, 38
reform efforts, 630–631
regulatory agencies, 47–48
regulatory state, 21
Rehnquist, William, 324, 333–334,
    346, 608
religion
    and public education, 204–206
    and welfare of children, 226–227
    free exercise of, 210–211
    in public sector workplace, 230–232
    official acknowledgements of,
        206–208

religious assembly and expression, 216
religious beliefs, 212
religious freedom, 201–234
    civic duties, 219
    civil rights laws, 227–229
    COVID-19 cases, 216–218
    free exercise of religion, 210–211
    incorporation, 211–216
    in military, 219
    interpretive foundations, 210–211
    overview, 202–203
    patriotic rituals, 219
    public sector workplace, 230–232
    religion and welfare of children, 226–227
    religious assembly and expression, 216
    religious rights of prisoners, 232
    separation of church and state, 203–210
    unconventional religious practices, 220–226
Religious Freedom Restoration Act (RFRA), 215–216
religiously motivated action, 212–213
religious rights of prisoners, 232
remaining silent, 512–513
remote camera, 396–400
representative democracy, 39
reproductive freedom, 112–114
restitution, 628
restoration of gun rights for felons, 256–257
restricting felons from possessing firearms, 256
restrictions imposed on juries, 569–570
reverse discrimination, 127–128
right of privacy, 111–117
    compulsory vaccination, 116–117
    on college campuses, 189–190
    reproductive freedom, 112–114
    right to die, 115
    sexual freedom, 114–115
    to a public trial, 567–570
rights, 143
    of confrontation, 571–578
    of police officers, 186–187
    of public employees, 185–187
    of students, 187–190
    of witnesses, 498
    to a speedy trial, 562–566
    to medical treatment, 685–686
    to proselytize and solicit funds, 218
    to trial by jury, 557–559

rights essential to a fair trial, 545–593
    constitutional issues in trial juries, 583–591
    evidence in criminal trials, 570–583
    plea bargaining, 559–562
    right to a public trial, 567–570
    right to a speedy trial, 562–566
    right to counsel, 546–557
    right to trial by jury, 557–559
rights of the accused, 489–535
    compulsory self-incrimination, 502–504
    double jeopardy, 499–502
    due process, 490–495
    grand jury, 495–499
    identification procedures, 531–534
    incriminating statements, 504–531
    physical evidence, 531–534
    police interrogations, 504–531
rights protection
    bill of attainder, 88–89
    ex post facto law, 88–89
    habeas corpus, 89–91
    limitation of treason, 87–88
right to counsel, 546–557, 620–622
    during interrogation, 552–555
    invoking of, 552–553
right to die, 115
right to keep and bear arms, 239–269
    Bipartisan Safer Communities Act, 260
    Brady Handgun Violence Prevention Act, 253–256
    federal prohibition of bump stocks via rulemaking, 260
    federal regulation of firearms and other weapons, 250–268
    Firearm Owners' Protection Act, 252–253
    Gun Control Act, 251–252
    gun-free zones, 263–264
    gun rights for law enforcement personnel, 267–268
    magazine capacity limits, 262–263
    National Firearms Act, 250–251
    open and concealed carry, 263
    overview, 240
    privacy rights of gun owners, 265
    red flag laws, 264–265
    regulating undetectable firearms and "ghost guns,", 259–260
    restoration of gun rights for felons, 256–257
    restricting felons from possessing firearms, 256

short-lived federal assault weapons ban, 257–258
    state age restrictions on gun purchases, 266
    State and Local Gun Laws, 261
    state assault weapon bans, 261–262
    weapons on college campuses, 263
right to remain silent
    in administrative hearings, 534
Riley, David, 411
risk assessment algorithm, 609–610
risk protection order (RPO), 264
roadblocks, 475–476
roadside
    automobile searches at, 353–356
    canine searches at, 356–360
Roberts, John, 325, 335–336, 352, 412–413, 416, 477, 529, 555, 674
Roberts, Owen, 107, 147
Rockefeller, Nelson, 635
Rodriguez, Denny, 359
Roosevelt, Franklin, 63, 392
Rosenberg, Ethel, 670
Rosenberg, Julius, 670
router, 424
Routier, Darin, 389
routine and special needs searches, 362–374
routine booking questions, 517–518
routine border searches, 364–365
roving wiretaps, 418
running from police, 468–469
Rushing, Daniel, 441–442
Rutledge, Wiley B., 467

S
sacramental sex, 226
same offense
    multiple charges for, 500
    prosecutions in state and federal court, 501
Santana, Dominga, 338
Sarat, Austin, 676
Sarivola, Anthony, 526
saving construction, 68
Scalia, Antonin, 149, 242–244, 344, 367, 369, 404, 410–411, 451, 476, 514, 565, 572, 575, 577, 590, 691, 694
Scheindlin, Shira A., 472
school prayer cases, 204–205
scientific evidence, 581–582
Scorsese, Martin, 623
searches and seizures, 277–284
    by nongovernmental actors, 285
searches incident to arrest, 331–334
search pursuant to warrant, 292

search warrant, 286
Second Amendment. *See also* right to keep and bear arms
    early jurisprudence, 241–242
    incorporation of, 245–247
    meaning of, 240–249
    right to keep and bear arms, 239–269
secondary offenses, 352–353
Section, 171–173
secular purpose, 205–206
seditious libel, 164
seizure, 277–284
seizure of pets, 626
selective enforcement and prosecution, 128
selective incorporation, 105
selective referral, 364
self-incrimination, 503–504
self-incrimination clause, 503
self-representation, 556–557
semi-automatic weapons, 257
sentencing enhancements, 590
sentencing phase, 667–668
sentencing phase in capital case, 664–670
separate but equal doctrine, 117–118
separation of church and state, 203–210
    Lemon test, 208–209
    official acknowledgements of religion, 206–208
    religion and public education, 204–206
    sunday closing laws and liquor sales, 204
    tax exemptions and subsidies, 209–210
separation of powers, 8, 32–35
sex discrimination, 119–121
Sex Offender Notification and Registration Act of 2006 (SORNA), 641
sex offenders, 641
sexual freedom, 114–115
sexual harassment in workplace, 121
sexual orientation, 123–124
Shane, Scott, 395
Shark Finning Prohibition Act of 2000, 625
Shatzer, Blaine, 514
Sheppard, Matthew, 643
Sheppard, Samuel, 567
Sherbert test, 212, 213–215
shield law, 169
short-lived federal assault weapons ban, 257–258

significant statistical disparity, 127
silver platter doctrine, 298
Simpson, O. J., 524, 570
sincere religious belief, 212
Sixth Amendment. *See* rights essential to a fair trial
slander, 166
slavery, 10–11
Small Business Administration (SBA), 47
Smith, Susan, 525
snake handling, 225
sneak and peek searches, 343–345
social justice, 21
    and constitution, 527–528
    constitution and, 20–130, 24, 52–53, 402–403, 472–473, 584–585
    eyewitness testimony, 574
    new federal law, 690
    solitary confinement, 696–697
    speeding ticket, 631–632
social media, 171–173, 422–427
solitary confinement, 695–697
Sotomayor, Sonia, 354, 622, 671, 674, 680
Souter, David, 325, 532
special needs searches, 362–374
speech integral to criminal conduct, 149
speech-related considerations, 187
speed detection cameras, 398–399
speeding ticket, 631–632
Speedy Trial Act, 563, 566
standards of decency, 627
standing, 300–301
stare decisis, 3–4
state action doctrine, 96
state age restrictions on gun purchases, 266
State and Local Gun Laws, 261
state assault weapon bans, 261–262
state court systems, 58–59
state legislative powers, 37–39
state-level bail reforms, 609–611
states' rights, 12–13
status offenses, 627–628
statutes, 37
Steele, Kevin, 561
Stevens, John Paul, 327, 358, 403, 494, 609, 613, 624, 668, 679, 683
Stewart, Potter, 46, 109, 112, 324, 330, 333, 341, 388–389, 394, 627, 662–663
Stolen Valor Act, 174
stop and frisk, 440
Stop Enabling Sex Traffickers Act (SESTA), 171–173

Stored Communications Act of 198, 395
street art, 179–180
strict judicial scrutiny, 145
strict scrutiny, 118–119, 145, 246
stun guns, 453–455
subjective recklessness, 689
subsequent amendments, 14–15
substantive criminal law, 3
substantive due process, 103–104, 490
suppressor, 251
supreme court, 9–10
    Bill of Rights, 111
supreme court limits, 629–630
Supreme Court of the United States (SCOTUS), 57
suspect classification doctrine, 118–119
suspicionless searches, 362–363
Sutherland, George, 547
Swayne, Noah Haynes, 607
symbolic speech, 155–158
Symes, Steven, 583

T
Taney, Roger, 93
tasers, 453–455
tax exemptions and subsidies, 209–210
Terry stop, 466, 468
testimonial evidence, 531
thermal imagers, 403–404
third-party consent, 324–326
third-party doctrine, 394
Thirteenth Amendment, 14, 93
Thomas, Clarence, 42, 351, 531, 591, 619, 622, 636
Thompkins, Van Chester, 512
Three Strikes and You're Out law, 639–641
time, place, and manner regulations, 180–184
torts, 66
totality of circumstances, 296–297
tracking devices, 408–411
traffic stops, 348–353
    anonymous tips leading to, 351–352
    requests to exit vehicle during, 350–351
    secondary offenses, 352–353
transactional immunity, 498
trap and trace devices, 393–396
treason, 87–88
trespass doctrine, 277–278
trespass doctrine redux, 281–284
trespassory test, 387

trial courts, 3
Tribal Court System, 66–67
true threats, 152–153
Trump, Donald, 49, 459
Tsarnaev, Dzhokhar, 519
Twenty Million Angry Men: The Case for Including Convicted Felons in Our Jury System (Binnall), 584
Twenty-Sixth Amendment, 14

U

unanimity requirement, 587–589
unconventional religious practices, 220–226
underwear bombing, 406
undetectable firearms and "ghost guns,", 259–260
undue burden, 212
unfunded mandate, 253
Uniform Code of Military Justice (UCMJ), 49
unitary executive, 50
United States Supreme Court, 63–64
unusual punishments, 627–632
unusual technology, 328
USA FREEDOM Act, 421
USA PATRIOT Act, 418, 444
U.S. Constitution, 6–15
    articles in, 8
    presidency, 8–9
    representation in Congress, 8
    supreme court, 9–10
U.S. Courts of Appeals, 61–62
U.S. District Court, 60
use immunity, 497
use of force
    against fleeing suspects, 450–453
    chokeholds, 459–461
    deadly, 450–451
    decertification, 463–465
    duty to intervene, 463
    excessive use of force, 447
    flash-bang grenade, 461–463
    fugitive track dog, 457–459

in making arrests, 447–465
    misconduct reporting, 463–465
    pepper spray, 456–457
    tasers and stun guns, 453–455
use of force in prison settings, 687–689

V

vagueness doctrine, 102, 493–495
Vas, Arpad, 583
venue, 568–569
victim impact testimony, 664
victims' rights, 38
video surveillance, 396–400
Vinson, Fred, 148
Violent Crime Control and Law Enforcement Act of 1994, 643, 669
void for-vagueness doctrine, 102
voir dire, 569
voter suppression, 95

W

Wardlow, William, 468
warrant
    arrest pursuant to, 441
warrantless arrests, 442–443
    for minor misdemeanors, 443
    in home, 443–444
warrantless searches, 321–375. *See also specific types*
    automobile searches at roadside, 353–356
    canine searches at roadside, 356–360
    consent searches, 322–326
    crime scenes, searches of, 329–331
    DUI-related searches, 361–362
    exigent circumstances, 335–343
    inventory searches, 345–348
    plain view doctrine, 326–329
    routine and special needs searches, 362–374

searches incident to arrest, 331–334
sneak and peek searches, 343–345
traffic stops, 348–353
workplace rights of government employees, 373–374
warrant requirement, 286–294
    detention of persons on premises during a search, 293
    execution of search warrants, 289–290
    Ex Post Facto, 294
    no-knock warrants, 290–291
    particularity requirement, 289
    process for obtaining a warrant, 287–289
    search pursuant to warrant, 292
    use of force in execution of a warrant, 293
Warren Court, 108–110, 212–213
Warren, Earl, 90, 118, 390, 466, 507–509, 510, 552, 562, 571, 579, 627
weapons on college campuses, 263
Weiden, David, 67
White, Byron, 109, 112, 325, 368, 451, 472, 526, 557, 564, 621, 662, 668
Whittaker, Charles E., 507
Widra, Emily, 633, 687
Williams, Michael, 149
Williams, Robert, 467, 522
Willie Francis case, 661–664
wiretaps, 390–393
    warrantless, 391–392
Withers, Nelly, 632
Wood, Lisa Godbey, 561
Woodworth, George, 682–683
writ of habeas corpus, 54–55

Z

Zazi, Najibullah, 420–421
Zedner, Jacob, 565–566
Zimmerman, George, 570

CPSIA information can be obtained
at www.ICGtesting.com
Printed in the USA
LVHW060748310323
743083LV00009B/52

9 781793 557629